fifth edition

Canadian
Organizational
Behaviour

Steven L. McShane
University of Western Australia

McGraw-Hill
Ryerson

Toronto Montreal Boston Burr Ridge, IL Dubuque, IA Madison, WI New York
San Francisco St. Louis Bangkok Bogotá Caracas Kuala Lumpur Lisbon London
Madrid Mexico City Milan New Delhi Santiago Seoul Singapore Sydney Taipei

The McGraw·Hill Companies

McGraw-Hill Ryerson

CANADIAN ORGANIZATIONAL BEHAVIOUR
Fifth Edition

Copyright © 2004 by McGraw-Hill Ryerson Limited, a Subsidiary of The McGraw-Hill Companies. Copyright © 2001, 1998 by McGraw-Hill Ryerson Limited. All rights reserved. Previous editions copyright © 1995 and 1992 by Richard D. Irwin, a Times Mirror Higher Education Group, Inc. company. No part of this publication may be reproduced or transmitted in any form or by any means, or stored in a data base or retrieval system, without the prior written permission of McGraw-Hill Ryerson Limited, or in the case of photocopying or other reprographic copying, a licence from The Canadian Copyright Licensing Agency (Access Copyright). For an Access Copyright licence, visit www.accesscopyright.ca or call toll free to 1-800-893-5777.

ISBN: 0-07-091232-7

4 5 6 7 8 9 10   TCP   0 9 8 7 6 5

Care has been taken to trace ownership of copyright material contained in this text; however, the publisher will welcome any information that enables them to rectify any reference or credit for subsequent editions.

Vice President, Editorial and Media Technology: Patrick Ferrier
Sponsoring Editor: Lenore Gray Spence
Managing Editor, Development: Kim Brewster
Marketing Manager: Kelly Smyth
Manager, Editorial Services: Kelly Dickson
Senior Supervising Editor: Margaret Henderson
Copy Editor: Gillian Scobie
Production Coordinator: Jennifer Wilkie
Photo Permissions: Alison Derry/Permissions Plus
Composition: Bookman Typesetting
Cover Design: Sharon Lucas
Cover Image: Zebras: Pal Hermansen/The Image Bank
Printer: Transcontinental Printing Group

Canadian Cataloguing in Publication Data
McShane, Steven Lattimore
    Canadian organizational behaviour / Steven L. McShane

Triennal.
[1st ed.]-
Vols. For 1998-   accompanied by: Instructor's manual, Test bank and computer disks (9 cm.).
Published in: Toronto, 1995-   ; published by: McGraw-Hill Ryerson, 1998-   .
ISBN 0-07-091232-7 (5th edition)

1. Organizational behavior.   2. Organizational behavior—Canada.   I. Title.

HD58.7.M33   658.3   C98-300627-X rev

Printed in Canada

ABOUT THE AUTHOR

Steven L. McShane

Steven L. McShane is Professor of Management in the Graduate School of Management at the University of Western Australia (UWA). Steve has also taught in the business faculties at Simon Fraser University and Queen's University in Canada. He is a past president of the Administrative Sciences Association of Canada.

Steve earned his PhD from Michigan State University, a Master of Industrial Relations from the University of Toronto, and an undergraduate degree from Queen's University in Kingston. He receives high teaching ratings from MBA and doctoral students both in Perth, Australia, and in Singapore, where he teaches senior officers in the Singapore Armed Forces.

Steve is also the co-author with Professor Mary Anne Von Glinow of *Organizational Behavior: Emerging Realities for the Workplace Revolution*, 2nd edition (2003), McGraw-Hill's highly successful American adaptation of this text. He is co-author with Professor Tony Travaglione of *Organisational Behaviour on the Pacific Rim* (2003), McGraw-Hill's most recent organizational behavior book published in that region. Steve has published several dozen articles and conference papers on the socialization of new employees, gender bias in job evaluation, wrongful dismissal, media bias in business magazines, and other diverse issues.

Along with teaching and writing, Steve enjoys spending his leisure time swimming, bodysurfing, canoeing, skiing, and travelling with his wife and two daughters.

BRIEF CONTENTS

CONTENTS

v

CHAPTER THREE
Perception and Learning in Organizations   70

CHAPTER SEVEN
Work-Related Stress and Stress Management   198

PART FOUR

Organizational Processes

CHAPTER FIFTEEN
Organizational Structure and Design   426

CHAPTER SIXTEEN
Organizational Culture   454

Welcome to a new era of organizational behaviour! Virtual teams are replacing committees. Values and self-leadership are replacing command-and-control supervision. Knowledge is replacing infrastructure. Companies are looking for employees with emotional intelligence, not just technical smarts. Globalization has become the mantra of corporate survival. Co-workers aren't down the hall; they're at the other end of an Internet connection located somewhere else on the planet.

Canadian Organizational Behaviour, Fifth Edition, is written in the context of these emerging workplace realities. This edition explains how emotions guide employee motivation, attitudes, and decisions; how values have become the new resource to shape workplace behaviour; how a person's social identity relates to team dynamics, stereotyping, and organizational culture; and how appreciative inquiry has become one of the most important strategies in organizational change. This book also presents the new reality that organizational behaviour is not just for managers; it is relevant and useful to anyone who works in and around organizations.

CANADIAN AND GLOBAL ORIENTATION

Canadian Organizational Behaviour, Fifth Edition, is written by a Canadian for Canadians. It includes several Canadian cases and makes solid use of Canadian scholarship in organizational behaviour. Along with its research foundation, the Canadian orientation is apparent in the Canadian examples scattered throughout the textbook. For example, you will read about the team dynamics of a Calgary crew that rescued an ailing doctor in Antarctica; about the negotiation style of Bombardier Inc. CEO Paul Tellier; about values and corporate social responsibility at Vancouver-based Mountain Equipment Co-op; about rewards, empowerment, and other applied performance practices at WestJet; and about the communication practices of CEO Ian Gourley at Hiram Walker & Sons in Walkerville, Ontario.

Love it or hate it, globalization is part of the emerging reality of organizations. So, along with its Canadian focus, *Canadian Organizational Behaviour*, Fifth Edition introduces globalization in the opening chapter and highlights global issues in every chapter. To further emphasize the emerging reality of globalization, every chapter in this edition has one or more *GLOBAL Connections*—highlighted features that link OB con-

GLOBAL CONNECTIONS 9.2

Extreme Teambuilding in Asia

Perched on a narrow beam eight metres above the ground, Wu Xi never stopped thinking about the possibility of falling. The 30-year-old engineer at Ericsson Cyberlab in Singapore was roped together with five colleagues as they scaled their way up a 25-metre pyramid. "I was so scared, but I couldn't give up," says Wu. "My team members held onto me very firmly and they kept encouraging me."

Throughout Asia, companies are discovering the benefits of unusual teambuilding activities outside the typical office environment. Wu Xi and her co-workers climbed over rock walls, inched across planks, scaled cargo nets, and performed other daunting tasks to improve team dynamics at the Swedish telecommunication firm's Asian research unit. "We all made it to the top with lots of difficulties," explains Ericsson Cyberlab director Andreas Fasbender. "But the best part was that you could really achieve more as a team."

Anker Bir took a different approach to team building. Employees at the Indonesian brewery spent a day in sophisticated gear stalking their rivals with laser guns at Laser Quest in Surabaya. Team members worked together to protect a box, a king or a queen, or to fight a super-powerful vampire with unlimited lives and ammunition.

Endro Hariyadi, an Anker Bir account representative, says that employees are more comfortable at work after they blast away at each other with laser guns. "We're all friends here, even if we don't get along well in the office," he jokes.

Sources: D. Goh, "Firms Strike Out for Adventure Learning," *Sunday Times (Singapore),* April 8, 2001, pp. 7, 29; F. Whaley, "Shooting for Success," *Asian Business,* February 2000, p. 48.

www.cyberlab.com.sg

Employees at Ericsson Cyberlab in Singapore scale great heights to build team spirit. © *H-Y How, Straits Times (Singapore)* cepts to organizational incidents in diverse countries. For example, *GLOBAL Connections* features describe how Japanese firms are taking employees to "smile school" to improve their emotional labour; how Infosys has created a "Silicon Valley culture" in Bangalore, India; how companies in the United Kingdom are improving communication by banning e-mail one day each week; how Ericsson employees in Singapore are building more effective teams through teambuilding; and how Australian travel agency, Flight Centre, has an organizational structure modelled after African tribes!

LINKING THEORY WITH REALITY

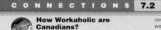

CONNECTIONS 7.2

How Workaholic are Canadians?

Staring out from the cover of *Confessions of a Street Addict*, James Cramer looks like a dangerous man. In fact, he admits that he was an addict. "I had many of the problems you see in addicts—they can't stay away, they need more and more, they love the adrenaline and then it takes control of their lives," says Cramer.

James Cramer's "street" is Wall Street and his addiction is to his work. The cofounder of TheStreet.com and Smart Money magazine is a repentant workaholic who had the symptoms that scholars have associated with this affliction. He was obsessed with market trades, became a tyrant in the office whenever a stock went south, and lost touch with his family. Even casual gatherings were evaluated by whether they added value to his work. "You might get together with me for a drink and I would be thinking 'Why am I wasting my time?'" Cramer recalls.

How many Canadians are as workaholic as James Cramer? The question is difficult to answer because of disagreement among scholars regarding definition and measurement of workaholism. According to a recent Statistics Canada study, 27 percent of adult Canadians say they are workaholics. Men and women about equally identify themselves as workaholics. Not surprisingly,

over half of employees working more than 60 hours per week consider themselves workaholics. Those who report being workaholics in the Statistics Canada study worry more, experience more stress, and are less happy with life (although they also say they enjoy their jobs).

The Statistics Canada study relies on a single item self-report, so probably overestimates the number of traditional workaholics in this country. A potentially better estimate comes from a study by Professor Ron Burke at York University of over 500 MBA alumni. Relying on academic conceptualization and measurement, Burke was able to group respondents into the three types of workaholism. The study found that 16 percent of the MBA alumni surveyed are traditional workaholics, 19 percent are enthusiastic workaholics, and 14 percent are work enthusiasts.

Sources: A. Kemeny, "Driven to Excel: A Portrait of Canada's Workaholics," *Canadian Social Trends*, Spring 2002, pp. 2–7; J. J. Cramer, *Confessions of a Street Addict* (New York: Simon & Schuster, 2002); J. Langton, "Wall Street Made me a Monster," *Evening Standard*, May 27, 2002; R. J. Burke, "Workaholism among Women Managers: Personal and Workplace Correlates," *Journal of Managerial Psychology*, 15 (2000), pp. 520–34; R. J. Burke, "Workaholism and Extra-work Satisfactions," *International Journal of Organizational Analysis*, 7 (1999), pp. 352–64.

www.statcan.ca

PART TWO VIDEO CASE STUDY   **Case 5**   **CBC**

BALANCING WORK AND LIFE

Work–life balance is the hottest topic among human resource executives these days, and for good reason. Most Canadians have a serious lack of balance, which is costing employers plenty. "We've seen an alarming increase in the amount of stress leave that people are on," says Nora Spinks, one of Canada's leading experts on work–life balance. "It's one of the fastest growing short-term disabilities that there is, that employers are now having to look at."

Companies have introduced several practices to minimize the damage to time-stressed staff, such as fitness programs, career breaks, daycare centres, flex-time, job sharing, telework, and so on. But a major Canadian study has reported that Canadians are still stressed.

"If we look at about a decade ago only about ten percent of the workforce was working a 50 hour plus week," explains Carleton University business professor Linda Duxbury. "We now see that about one in four people are working that many hours." The study also discovered that over one-third of professional and managerial men and women say that the way they're trying to cope is simply by not having kids.

University of Guelph professor Peter Hausdorf says that part of the problem is that employers don't want to deal with the main cause of poor work–life balance: workload. "[Employers] seem reluctant to deal with the fact that the issue is ... workload and what they would rather do is focus on other aspects. So [they'll] have fitness facilities to deal with stress. These are all good things but they're not dealing with the core issue, which is the volume of work."

Courtney Pratt, CEO of Toronto Hydro, admits his company is pushing staff too hard, but he

doesn't see much choice while Toronto hydro prepares for privatization. "But when you get into a crunch like we're in, there's not a whole lot you can do other than I think you have to empathize with people," Pratt admits. "You do whatever you can to try and give them the time off that they need but quite frankly, we need their intellectual horse-power right now and it's not an option."

Linda Duxbury sees the issue differently: "Excuse me, but how can you afford to continue to operate this way?" she warns. "Look at your absenteeism. Look at your turnover. Look at your prescription and benefit costs. Look at your succession planning." Nora Spinks notes that the need to keep good staff is another reason to encourage work–life balance: "If you're competing for the same people that somebody else is, and now offering flexibility and support of work environments and stress-free opportunities, people are going to be attracted to there before they're attracted to an organization where it's rigid, it's structured, it's high stress."

Discussion Questions

1. Explain how companies that encourage work–life balance might be more successful than those pushing more hours of work out of their staff.

2. What other topics in the first two parts of this book explain how work–life balance may improve organizational effectiveness?

Source: Dianne Buckner, "Balancing Work and Life," CBC *Venture*, April 7, 2002.

Every chapter of *Canadian Organizational Behaviour*, Fifth Edition, is filled with real-life examples to make OB concepts more meaningful and reflect the relevance and excitement of this field. For example, you will read how Vancouver City Savings Credit Union has become one of Canada's most successful financial institutions through its corporate culture; how New Zealand's The Warehouse has become one of the world's top-performing discount department store chains by supporting personal and ethical values; how the Silicon Valley design firm IDEO has become a global icon for innovation by fostering employee creativity; and how conflict continues between Air Canada and former Canadian Airlines pilots who now work at Canada's national airline.

These real-life stories appear in many forms. Every chapter of *Canadian Organizational Behaviour*, Fifth Edition, is filled with photo captions and in-text anecdotes about work life in this new millennium. Each chapter also includes *Connections*, a special feature that "connects" OB concepts with real organizational incidents. Case studies in each chapter and video case studies in each part also connect OB concepts to the emerging workplace realities. These stories provide representation across Canada and around the planet. Moreover, these examples cover a wide range of industries—from software to city government—and from small businesses to the *Financial Post 500*.

ORGANIZATIONAL BEHAVIOUR KNOWLEDGE FOR EVERYONE

Another distinctive feature of *Canadian Organizational Behaviour*, Fifth Edition, is that it is written for everyone in organizations, not just "managers." The philosophy of this book is that everyone who works in and around organizations needs to understand and make use of organizational behaviour knowledge. The new reality is that people throughout the organization—systems analysts, production employees, accounting professionals—are assuming more responsibilities as companies remove layers of bureaucracy and give non-management staff more autonomy over their work. This book helps everyone to make sense of organizational behaviour and provides the tools to work more effectively in the workplace.

CONTEMPORARY THEORY FOUNDATION

Canadian Organizational Behaviour, Fifth Edition, has a solid foundation of contemporary and classic scholarship. You can see this in the references. Each chapter is based on dozens of articles, books, and other sources. The most recent literature receives thorough coverage, resulting in what the publishers and I believe is the most up-to-date organizational behaviour textbook available. These references also reveal that we reach out to information systems, marketing, and other disciplines for new ideas. At the same time, this textbook is written for students, not the scholars whose work is cited. Consequently, you won't find details about the research methods of specific studies. Also, the names of researchers or their affiliations are rarely mentioned in the text. The philosophy of this textbook is to present OB scholarship in ways that students will remember long after the final examination.

Canadian Organizational Behaviour was the first textbook to discuss workplace emotions, social identity theory, appreciative inquiry, search conferences, the employee-customer-profit chain model, and several other groundbreaking topics. This edition is particularly innovative and contemporary with the latest knowledge on individualism–collectivism, innate drives theory, Schwartz's values model, counterproductive work behaviours, learning orientation, virtual teams, workaholism, executive coaching, and emotions in decision making.

CONTINUOUS DEVELOPMENT

Canadian Organizational Behaviour is *not* a "Canadianized" adaptation of an American book. Although I also co-author *Organizational Behaviour* in the United States (now in its successful second edition) and *Organisational Behaviour on the Pacific Rim* (first edition was published in 2002), all three books update each other in a virtuous cycle of continuous development. *Canadian Organizational Behaviour*, Fifth Edition, updates information from the Pacific Rim book, and the next American edition will update this book.

This is apparently the only business textbook anywhere that practices continuous development because it is the only book where the lead author actively writes in all three regions. This global approach to textbook development ensures that *Canadian Organizational Behaviour* offers Canadians the latest organizational behaviour concepts, issues, and examples at the time of publication. The next section highlights the results of this continuous development process.

CHANGES TO THE FIFTH EDITION

SELF-ASSESSMENT EXERCISE 10.6

MEASURING YOUR CREATIVE PERSONALITY

Purpose This self-assessment is designed to help you to measure the extent to which you have a creative personality.

Instructions Listed below is an adjective checklist with 30 words that may or may not describe you. Put a mark in the box beside the words that you think accurately describe you. Please DO NOT mark the boxes for words that do not describe you. When finished, you can score the test using the scoring key in Appendix B. This exercise is completed alone so students can assess themselves without concerns of social comparison. However, class discussion will focus on how this scale might be applied in organizations, and the limitations of measuring creativity in work settings.

Adjective Checklist		
Affected ☐	Honest ☐	Reflective ☐
Capable ☐	Humorous ☐	Resourceful ☐
Cautious ☐	Individualistic ☐	Self-confident ☐
Clever ☐	Informal ☐	Sexy ☐
Commonplace ☐	Insightful ☐	Sincere ☐
Confident ☐	Intelligent ☐	Snobbish ☐
Conservative ☐	Inventive ☐	Submissive ☐
Conventional ☐	Mannerly ☐	Suspicious ☐
Dissatisfied ☐	Narrow interests ☐	Unconventional ☐
Egotistical ☐	Original ☐	Wide interests ☐

Source: Adapted from and based on information in H. G. Gough and A. B. Heilbrun, Jr., *The Adjective Check List Manual* (Palo Alto, Calif." Consulting Psychologists Press, 1965); and H. G. Gough.

SELF-ASSESSMENT EXERCISE 10.7

TESTING YOUR CREATIVE BENCH STRENGTH

Go to the Student CD for the interactive version of this exercise.

Purpose This self-assessment is designed to help you determine how well you engage in divergent thinking to identify problems and their solutions creatively.

Instructions This self-assessment consists of 12 questions that require divergent thinking to identify the answers. Answer each question in the space provided. When finished, look at the correct answer for each question, along with an explanation.

ADDITIONAL CASES

CASE 1   Arctic Mining Consultants
CASE 2   A Window on Life
CASE 3   Big Screen's Big Failure
CASE 4   Intelligentsia
CASE 5   Perfect Pizzeria
CASE 6   TriVac Industries, Inc.
CASE 7   Westray

CASE 1   Arctic Mining Consultants

Tom Parker enjoyed working outdoors. At various times in the past, he had worked as a ranch hand, high steel rigger, headstone installer, prospector, and geological field technician. Now 43, Parker is a geological field technician and field coordinator with Arctic Mining Consultants. He has specialized knowledge and experience in all nontechnical aspects of mineral exploration, including claim staking, line cutting and grid installation, soil sampling, prospecting, and trenching. He is responsible for hiring, training, and supervising field assistants for all Arctic Mining Consultants' programs. Field assistants are paid a fairly low daily wage (no matter how long they work, which may be up to 12 hours or more) and are provided meals and accommodation. Many of the programs are operated by a project manager who reports to whom had previously worked with Parker, as the field assistants. To stake a claim, the project team marks a line with flagging tape and blazes along the perimeter of the claim, cutting a claim post every 500 metres (called a "length"). The 15 claims would require almost 100 kilometres of line in total. Parker had budgeted seven days (plus mobilization and demobilization) to complete the job. This meant that each of the four stakers (Parker, Talbot, Boyce, and Millar) would have to complete a little over seven "lengths" each day. The following is a chronology of the project.

Day 1

The Arctic Mining Consultants crew assembled in the morning and drove to Eagle Lake, where they

---

Canadian Organizational Behaviour, Fifth Edition, is the result of reviews over the past two years by more than 100 organizational behaviour scholars and teachers in several countries. This feedback, along with a continuous scan of relevant literature, has resulted in numerous improvements. First, you will notice significant changes to the textbook structure. Guided by extensive reviewer feedback, the chapters are more clearly organized around individual, team, and organizational levels of analysis. The early chapters focus on individual differences, with the more stable characteristics (values, personality) presented before the more fluid characteristics (emotions, attitudes). This edition also combines individual and team decision making into one chapter, splits and extends team dynamics concepts across two chapters, and moves stress management to the end of the individual part of the book. This edition also listened to reviewers by reducing the book's length.

Along with structural improvements, *Canadian Organizational Behaviour*, Fifth Edition, has a distinctly stronger global emphasis and more experiential learning support. In particular, this edition nearly doubles the number of self-assessments and includes a CD where students can complete these assessments more efficiently. *Canadian Organizational Behaviour* is one of the few books with comprehensive cases, and this edition further supports instructor requests for more of these lengthier cases. You will also find several new cases and team exercises in each chapter of the book.

Almost every chapter has been substantially updated with new conceptual and anecdotal material. Here are some of the most significant improvements within each chapter of this edition:

■   *Chapter 1: Introduction to the Field of Organizational Behaviour*—The section on trends in OB now includes a new subsection on values, ethics, and corporate social responsibility, as well as completely rewritten subsections on globalization, information technology, and OB. The systematic research anchor now recognizes grounded theory methodology, and the chapter adds new information on telework as well as OB and the bottom line.

Chapter 2: Individual Behaviour, Values, and Personality—This completely rewritten chapter places the most stable individual differences (values, personalty) near the beginning of the book. It also includes groundbreaking research on individualism and collectivism, new coverage of Schwartz's values model (which dominates the values literature), a new section on values congruence, and new information on counterproductive work behaviours. This chapter also includes a new section on Canadian, Francophone, and First Nations values as well as updated information on ethical principles and employee competencies.

Chapter 3: Perception and Learning in Organizations—This completely rewritten chapter logically combines perceptions and learning. Stereotyping, practicing self-fulfilling prophecy, diversity awareness, and empathy are revised and updated based on new literature. Social identity theory is also updated here due to the rapidly growing OB literature on this subject. This chapter also introduces Kolb's experiential learning model and the important concept of learning orientation.

Chapter 4: Workplace Emotions and Attitudes—*Canadian Organizational Behaviour* was the first OB textbook (in 1998) to fully discuss workplace emotions, and this significantly revised chapter continues this leadership with the most up-to-date definition and model of emotions and emotional intelligence. The chapter also introduces groundbreaking ideas from neurology and evolutionary psychology on the dual rational-emotional processes in attitudes and behaviour. This edition also includes the exit-voice-loyalty-neglect (EVLN) model of job satisfaction, important new research on the relationship between job satisfaction and job performance, new information on effects of surface versus deep acting emotional labour on emotional dissonance, a new model relating job satisfaction to customer service, and updated information on organizational commitment.

Chapter 5: Motivation in the Workplace—Innate drives theory, one of the most important conceptual developments in employee motivation, is introduced in this chapter. This edition also has a new section on organizational justice, including full discussion on procedural justice and motivation. Executive coaching, building a company of entrepreneurs, and a combination of goal setting with feedback are also new features of this chapter.

Chapter 6: Applied Performance Practices—This appropriately renamed chapter includes a new section on empowerment, updated information on self-leadership in practice, and discussion of the balanced scorecard.

Chapter 7: Work-Related Stress and Stress Management—This popular chapter includes new information on workaholism and workplace bullying, as well as updates on the job burnout model and Canadian work hours as a stressor. It also features highlights from the major Higgins/Duxbury study of work-life balance in Canada.

Chapter 8: Foundations of Team Dynamics—The topic of teams is now split into two chapters with new material, as requested by several reviewers. This chapter offers a revised discussion on types of teams and details about task interdependence.

- *Chapter 9: Developing High Performance Teams*—This new chapter integrates the topics of self-directed work teams, virtual teams, team trust, and team-building. It provides the latest knowledge on virtual teams, including why they exist and how to design them. The chapter also updates information on challenges to self-directed work teams.
- *Chapter 10: Decision Making and Creativity*—Based on the preferences of most instructors, this completely rewritten chapter integrates decision making, creativity, and team decision making. The chapter includes new information on the dual rational-emotional processes in decision making, both in problem identification and making choices. It also presents a new model of employee involvement in decision making, new information on implicit favourite and information processing distortion in decision making, new information on constructive conflict in decision making, and more explicit identification and critique of the "rational" and "bounded rationality" decision-making processes.
- *Chapter 11: Communicating in Teams and Organizations*—This chapter is moved later in the book for a more logical flow of topics. It includes new information on the effect of information technologies on the organizational grapevine and on the communication benefits of instant messaging in business. The chapter also updates the sections on media richness and communication issues in open office spaces.
- *Chapter 12: Power and Influence in the Workplace*—This chapter offers an entirely new presentation and orientation on the types of influence in the workplace. It also adds a new section on contingencies of influence and makes a better connection between influence and organizational politics.
- *Chapter 13: Conflict and Negotiation in the Workplace*—The main change in this chapter is the revised conflict management styles list that reflects new literature on this topic.
- *Chapter 14: Leadership in Organizational Settings*—This chapter introduces new research on cross-cultural issues in leadership, including findings from the GLOBE Project on cross-cultural leadership. It also adds new information on how women and men are evaluated as leaders.
- *Chapter 15: Organizational Structure and Design*—This chapter offers new information on divisional structures, including the general decline of geographic divisional structures. It also includes updated information on network structures as well as centralization-decentralization.
- *Chapter 16: Organizational Culture*—This chapter is similar to the previous edition, but it includes several updated references and examples.
- *Chapter 17: Organizational Change*—This chapter features several structural changes to streamline the information and improve flow of topics. In particular, it has a new section on three approaches to organizational change (action research, appreciative inquiry, parallel learning structures). The chapter updates information on creating an urgency to change, search conferences as a change process, the action research approach to organizational change, and the appreciative inquiry approach to organizational change.

SUPPORTING THE LEARNING PROCESS

The changes described above refer only to the text material. *Canadian Organizational Behaviour*, Fifth Edition, also has improved technology, supplements, cases, videos, team exercises, and self-assessments.

Student Learning CD   The Student CD-ROM, packaged free with each text, encourages students to think critically and to be active learners. The Student CD-ROM includes:

- Building Your Management Skills—interactive modules that encourage hands-on learning about OB topics, such as motivation and leadership
- Interactive Self-Assessment Exercises—tied directly to the end-of-chapter material in the text
- Chapter Outlines—complete summaries of each chapter
- Chapter Fill-In-the-Blank Quizzes—tied to chapter content
- Chapter True/False Quizzes—tied to chapter content
- Video Clips—examples of how real companies are applying organizational concepts and theory
- Video Notes—guiding students on "what to watch for" in the videos
- Video Quizzes tied to the video clips—multiple-choice and fill-in-the-blank questions
- Special link to OBOnline—(see details below)
- Special link to PowerWeb—(see details below)

Student Online Learning Centre   *Canadian Organizational Behaviour* first introduced Web-based support for students in 1995, and continues that tradition with a comprehensive and user-friendly Online Learning Centre. The site includes practice questions in a format similar to those found in the test bank, links to relevant external Web sites, and other valuable resources for students such as:

- Chapter outlines and objectives
- Chapter summaries
- Online quizzing
- Video streaming and full video listing and questions by part
- Links to relevant external Web sites
- Link to OB Online
- Link to PowerWeb
- Searchable glossary

OBOnline   is our new OB online experience. Through the wonders of the latest Web technology, students can:

- Choose exercises from a list of topics
- Run activities and self-assessments geared toward groups & teams, individual differences, international organizational behaviour, and motivation & empowerment
- Launch into "Business Around the World" to find an outstanding resource for researching and exploring Organizational Behaviour Online

PowerWeb   is dynamic and easy to use. It provides supplemental content that is course-based and saves time. PowerWeb is the first online supplement to offer students access to the following:

- Course-specific current articles refereed by content experts
- Course-specific, real-time news
- Weekly course updates
- Interactive exercises and assessment tools
- Student study tips

- Web research tips and exercises
- Refereed and updated research links
- Daily news
- Access to the Northernlight.com's Special Collection of journals and articles

Video Cases *Canadian Organizational Behaviour*, Fifth Edition, provides a full complement of video cases to liven up the classroom experience. Most segments are from the Canadian Broadcasting Corporation, and include topics such as workplace loyalty, scenario planning, executive coaching, and work–life balance. Other video programs illustrate stress management, corporate culture, organizational change, decision making, business ethics, and globalization. These segments can be viewed through video streaming on the Online Learning Centre or in class in a VHS format.

CASE STUDY 11.1

BRIDGING THE TWO WORLDS—THE ORGANIZATIONAL DILEMMA

By William Todorovic, University of Waterloo.

I had been hired by a Toronto based company, ABC Limited, and it was my first day of work. I was 26 years old, and I was now the manager of ABC's customer service group, which looked after customers, logistics, and some of the raw material purchasing. My superior, George, was the vice-president of the company. ABC manufactured most of its products from aluminum, a majority of which were destined for the construction industry.

As I walked around the shop floor, the employees appeared to be concentrating on their jobs, barely noticing me. Management held daily meetings in which various production issues were discussed. No one from the shop floor was invited to the meetings, unless there was a specific problem. Later I also learned that management had separate washrooms and separate lunchrooms as well as other perqs, which floor employees did not

TEAM EXERCISE 11.2

ANALYZING THE ELECTRONIC GRAPEVINE

Purpose This exercise is designed to help you understand the dynamics of grapevine communication.

Instructions This activity is usually conducted in between classes as a homework assignment. The instructor will divide the class into teams (although this activity can also be conducted by individuals). Each team will be assigned a large organization that has active posting on electronic grapevine Web sites such as Vault.com.

During the assignment, each team reads through recent postings of messages about the organiza-

tion. Based on these raw comments, the team should be prepared to answer the following questions in the next class (or whenever the exercise will be debriefed in class):

1. What are the main topics in recent postings about this organization? Are they mostly good or bad news? Why?
2. To what extent do these postings seem to present misinformation or conflicting information?
3. Should corporate leaders intervene in these rumours? If so, how?

TEAM EXERCISE 11.3

TINKER TOY COMMUNICATION

Purpose This exercise is designed to help you understand the importance of media richness and related issues that affect communicating effectively.

Materials This activity requires one student on each team to have a cellular telephone that he/she is willing to use for this exercise. Alternatively, in-house land-line telephones or walkie-talkies may be used. The instructor will provide each team with a set of pieces from Tinker Toy, Lego, Mega Blocks, straws, or other materials suitable for

building. Each pair of teams must have identical pieces in shape, size, and colour. This activity also requires either two large rooms or one large room and a few smaller rooms.

Instructions

- *Step 1:* The instructor will divide the class into an even number of teams, each with 4 to 5 students. Teams should have the same number of members where possible. Remaining students can serve as observers. Teams are paired (e.g.,

Chapter Cases and Additional Cases Every chapter includes at least one short case that challenges students to diagnose issues and apply ideas from that chapter. Several comprehensive cases also appear at the end of the book. Several cases are new to this book and are written by Canadian instructors from St. John to Vancouver. Others, such as Arctic Mining Consultants, are classics that have withstood the test of time.

Team Exercises and Self-Assessments Experiential exercises and self-assessments represent an important part of the active learning process. *Canadian Organizational Behaviour*, Fifth Edition, facilitates that process by offering one or two team exercises in every chapter. Many of these learning activities are not available in other organizational behaviour textbooks, such as Where in the World are We? (Chapter 10) and A Not-so-Trivial Cross-Cultural Communication Game (Chapter 11). This edition also has nearly three dozen self-assessments in the book or on the student CD. Self-assessments personalize the meaning of several organizational behaviour concepts, such as workaholism, personal values, self-leadership, empathy, stress, creative disposition, and tolerance of change.

Indexes, Margin Notes, and Glossary *Canadian Organizational Behaviour* tries to avoid unnecessary jargon, but the field of organizational behaviour (as with every other discipline) has its own language. To help you learn this language, key terms are highlighted in bold and brief definitions appear in the margin. These definitions are also presented in an alphabetical glossary at the end of the text. We have also developed comprehensive indexes of content, names, URLs and organizations described in this book.

INSTRUCTOR SUPPORT MATERIALS

Canadian Organizational Behaviour, Fifth Edition, includes a variety of supplemental materials to help instructors prepare and present the material in this textbook more effectively.

i-Learning Sales Specialist   Your *Integrated Learning Sales Specialist* is a McGraw-Hill Ryerson representative who has the experience, product knowledge, training, and support to help you assess and integrate any of the below-noted products, technology, and services into your course for optimum teaching and learning performance. Whether it's how to use our test bank software, helping your students improve their grades, or how to put your entire course online, your *i*-Learning Sales Specialist is there to help. Contact your local *i*-Learning Sales Specialist today to learn how to maximize all McGraw-Hill Ryerson resources!

Instructor Online Learning Centre   Along with the Student OLC (see above), *Canadian Organizational Behaviour* includes a password-protected Web site for instructors. The site offers:

- Downloadable supplements: Microsoft® PowerPoint® Presentations, Instructor's Manual, Transparency Masters
- Video streaming and full video listing and questions/answers by chapter
- Link to OB Online
- Link to PowerWeb
- Online updates to chapter topics
- PageOut
- Sample syllabi
- Links to OB news
- Updates and other resources

Instructor's Resource CD-ROM   The Instructor's Resource Manual, Brownstone Computerized Test Bank, Microsoft PowerPoint Presentations, and the Test Bank (MS Word files) are compiled in electronic format on a CD-ROM for your convenience in customizing multimedia lectures.

Microsoft® PowerPoint® Presentations   *Canadian Organizational Behaviour* was the first OB textbook (in 1995) to introduce a complete set of PowerPoint® Presentation files. This resource is now more sophisticated than ever. Each PowerPoint® file has more than 18 slides relating to the chapter, all of which display one or more photographs from the textbook.

Instructor's Resource Manual   Steve McShane co-wrote the *Instructor's Resource Manual* to ensure that it represents the textbook's content and supports instructor needs. Each chapter includes the learning objectives, glossary of key terms, a chapter synopsis, complete lecture outline with thumbnail images of corresponding PowerPoint® slides, solutions to the end-of-chapter discussion questions, and comments on photo caption critical thinking questions. It also includes teaching notes for the chapter case(s), additional cases, team exercises, and self-assessments. Many chapters include supplemental lecture notes and additional suggested videos. The *Instructor's Resource Manual* also includes notes for the end-of-text cases and blackline transparency masters.

Test Bank and Computerized Test Bank   The *Test Bank* includes more than 2,400 multiple choice, true/false, and essay questions. Steve McShane wrote all questions, the majority of which have been tested in class examinations. Each question identifies the relevant page reference and difficulty level. The entire *Test Bank* is also available in an updated version of Brownstone's computerized testing software. Instructors receive special software that lets them design their own examinations from the test bank questions. It also lets instructors edit test items and add their own questions to the test bank.

Video Package   Accompanying the text is a series of video segments drawn from CBC broadcasts, the McGraw-Hill Management library, ABC Australia, and various other sources. These videos have been chosen to visually aid students in tying real-world organizational behaviour issues to the text and to illuminate key ideas and concepts. The video segments are available in VHS format for use in class and through video streaming on the Online Learning Centre by both instructors and students. Instructor-related material for use with the video cases is available from the Instructor Centre of the OLC.

Create a custom course Website with **PageOut**, free with every McGraw-Hill Ryerson textbook.

To learn more, contact your McGraw-Hill Ryerson publisher's representative or visit www.mhhe.com/solutions

PageOut   This unique point-and-click course Web site tool enables you to create a high-quality course Web site without knowing HTML coding. With PageOut, you can post your syllabus online, assign McGraw-Hill Online Learning Centre content, add links to important off-site resources, and maintain student results in the online grade book.

WebCT/Blackboard   For faculty requiring online content, *Canadian Organizational Behaviour*, Fifth Edition, is available in two of the most popular delivery platforms: WebCT and Blackboard. These platforms are designed for instructors who want complete control over course content and how it is presented to students. They provide instructors with user-friendly and highly flexible teaching tools that enhance interaction between students and faculty.

i-Services   McGraw-Hill Ryerson offers you a unique *i*-Services package upon adoption of this textbook. This includes technical support, access to our educational technology conferences, and custom e-Courses, to name just a few. Please speak to your *i*-Learning Sales Specialist for details.

ACKNOWLEDGMENTS

Canadian Organizational Behaviour, Fifth Edition, symbolizes the power of teamwork. More correctly, it symbolizes the power of a *virtual team* because I wrote this book from Perth, Australia, and Singapore with editorial and production support from people located in several places throughout Canada. Superb virtual teams require equally superb team members, and we were fortunate to have this in our favour. Sponsoring Editor Lenore Gray Spence led the way with unwavering support, while solving the behind-the-scenes challenges that made everyone's lives much easier. Kim Brewster (Managing Editor, Development) demonstrated amazingly cool coordination skills as this author pushed the deadline limits so students could have the latest OB knowledge. The keen copy-editing skills of Gillian Scobie made *Canadian Organizational Behaviour*, Fifth Edition, incredibly error-free. Margaret Henderson, our Senior Supervising Editor, met the challenge of a tight production schedule. Thanks also to Kelly Dickson, Manager of Editorial Services, for her ongoing support. Sharon Lucas provided an excellent cover design. Alison Derry triumphed to deliver the many photos that I selected for this edition. Thanks to you all. This has been an exceptional team effort!

As was mentioned earlier, more than 100 instructors around the world reviewed parts or all of *Canadian Organizational Behaviour*, Fifth Edition, or its editions in other regions over the past two years. This represents one of the most comprehensive and global reviews of any OB textbook. The following people from Canadian colleges and universities provided the most recent feedback for improvements specifically for *Canadian Organizational Behaviour*. Their compliments were energizing, and their suggestions significantly improved the final product:

Gordon Barnard *Durham College*
Céleste Brotheridge *University of Regina*
James Buchkowsky *Saskatchewan Institute of Applied Science and Technology*
Ron Burke *York University*
Claude Dupuis *Athabasca University*
Regena Farnsworth *University of New Brunswick, Saint John*
B.J. Gdanski *Fanshawe College*
Jim Green *University of Toronto*
Bernard Gross *Red River College*
Anne Harper *Humber College*
Jean Helms-Mills *Acadia University*
Roy Kirby *Carleton University*
Raymond Lee *University of Manitoba*
Beverly Linnell *Southern Alberta Institute of Technology*
Richard Marleau *Canadore College*
Susan Meredith *Selkirk College*
Albert Mills *Saint Mary's University*
Penny Perrier *Sault College of Applied Arts & Technology*
Wilf Ratzberg *British Columbia Institute of Technology*
Shirley Richards *Humber College*
Sudhir Saha *Memorial University*
Don Schepens *Grant MacEwan College*
Andrea Soberg *Trinity Western University*
Barbara Thistle *George Brown College*
Bill Todorovic *University of Waterloo*
Alvin Turner
Xiaonyun Wang *University of Manitoba*
Gerrie Waugh *Capilano College*

I would also like to extend sincere thanks to the exceptional efforts of Sandra Steen, University of Regina, who updated and compiled new end-of-chapter Discussion Questions, as well as co-authored the Instructor's Resource Manual. Sandra's enthusiasm for the project is much admired and appreciated.

I am also very grateful to the many instructors in Canada and abroad who contributed cases and exercises to this edition of *Canadian Organizational Behaviour*:

Jeffrey Bagraim *University of Cape Town, South Africa*
Hazel Bothma *University of Cape Town, South Africa*
James Buchkowsky *Saskatchewan Institute of Applied Science & Technology*
Sharon Card *Saskatchewan Institute of Applied Science & Technology*
Beth Gilbert *University of New Brunswick, Saint John*

Cheryl Harvey *Wilfrid Laurier University*
Lisa Ho *Louis Vuitton, Singapore*
Roy Kirby *Carleton University*
Theresa Kline *University of Calgary*
David L. Luechauer *Butler University, U.S.A.*
Fiona McQuarrie *University College of the Fraser Valley*
Susan Meredith *Selkirk College*
Albert Mills *Saint Mary's University*
Kim Morouney *Wilfrid Laurier University*
Caroline O'Connell *Saint Mary's University*
Gary M. Shulman *Miami University, U.S.A.*
Bill Todorovic *University of Waterloo*
Alvin Turner

Along with the reviewers, contributors, and editorial team, I would to like to extend special thanks to my students for sharing their learning experiences and assisting with the development of the three organizational behaviour textbooks in Canada, the United States, and the Pacific Rim. These students include officers attending my MBA classes at SAFTI Military Institute's Command and Staff College in Singapore, and Master of Business Administration students at the University of Western Australia.

I am also very grateful to my colleagues at the Graduate School of Management who teach organizational behaviour, including (in alphabetical order): Gail Broady, Renu Burr, Stacy Chappell, Catherine Jordan, Sandra Kiffin-Petersen, Chris Perryer, David Plowman, and Chris Taylor. These wonderful people listen patiently to my ideas, diplomatically correct my wayward thoughts, and share their experiences using the American or Pacific Rim editions of this book in Perth (Australia), Jakarta (Indonesia), Manila (Philippines), Shanghai (People's Republic of China), and Singapore.

Finally, I am forever indebted to my wife Donna McClement and to our wonderful daughters, Bryton and Madison. Their love and support give special meaning to my life.

Introduction to the Field of Organizational Behaviour

Learning Objectives

- Define organizational behaviour and give three reasons for studying this field of inquiry.

- Discuss how globalization influences organizational behaviour.

- Summarize the apparent benefits and challenges of telework.

- Identify changes in Canada's work force in recent years.

- Describe employability and contingent work.

- Explain why values have gained importance in organizations.

- Define corporate social responsibility and argue for or against its application in organizations.

- Identify the five anchors on which organizational behaviour is based.

- Diagram an organization from an open systems view.

- Define knowledge management and intellectual capital.

- Identify specific ways that organizations acquire and share knowledge.

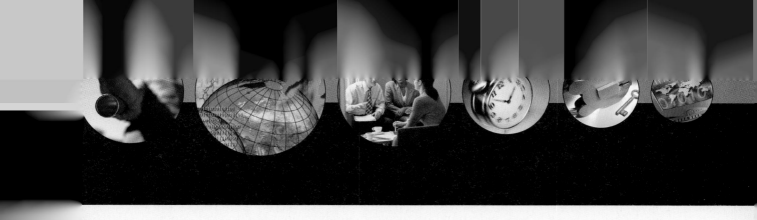

A traveller from the Middle East had an unusual request when he recently took his family to the Four Seasons hotel in Washington, D.C. "My kids haven't seen Santa Claus since we've arrived," he lamented to the Four Seasons staff. It didn't take long for assistant front-office manager Liliana Vidal-Quadras (shown in photo) to find an employee and costume to play Santa for a few hours.

This incident is just one of many that illustrates why Four Seasons Hotels and Resorts is recognized as one of the world's leading operators of luxury hotels. Responsible for over 53 properties in 24 countries, the Toronto-based company has racked up more awards than any other hotel chain, and is the only Canadian company on *Fortune* magazine's prestigious list of the 100 best companies to work for in America. Four Seasons is also an innovator, introducing the first mini-bars and hairdryers in bathrooms, 24-hour services, and free overnight shoe shines. Most of these creative ideas were suggested by employees.

Four Seasons goes to extraordinary lengths to hire people who value customer service and mutual respect. "Ultimately, how you treat one another in a company will lead to success," emphasizes Four Seasons CEO Isadore Sharp, who founded Four Seasons in 1960. Finding employees with the right values and attitudes includes sifting through more than 4,000 candidates to fill 250 positions at the company's newest hotel in Prague, Czech Republic. Once hired, front-line staff complete a rigorous five-step customer service training program.

Four Seasons keeps on top of morale by surveying staff every 18 months (satisfaction scores have remained above 90 percent for the past 15 years). No one with five or more years of service can be fired without senior management approval. The company even avoided laying off staff after the terrorist attacks on September 11, 2001. "We decided many years ago that our distinguishing edge would be exceptional service," explains founder Isadore Sharp. "As the standard bearers of that service, our employees are treated with the same care and thoughtfulness as our guests."[1] ■

Four Seasons Hotels and Resorts has leveraged the power of organizational behaviour to become one of the top luxury hotels in the world as well as one of the best places to work.
Mario Tama, National Post

www.fourseasons.com

Four Seasons Hotels and Resorts has become a leader in the hospitality industry mainly because it applies organizational behaviour theories and concepts. More than ever, organizations are relying on these ideas and practices to remain competitive. For example, Four Seasons pays close attention to employee competencies and attitudes. It relies on the creativity of its staff through a culture that supports employee involvement. The company is driven by a strong set of organizational values reinforced by the visionary leadership of founder Isadore Sharp.

This book is about people working in organizations. Its main objective is to help you understand behaviour in organizations and to work more effectively in organizational settings. Organizational behaviour knowledge is not only for managers and leaders. It is relevant and useful to anyone who works in and around organizations. In this chapter, we introduce you to the field of organizational behaviour, outline the main reasons why you should know more about it, highlight some of the organizational trends influencing the study of OB, describe the fundamental perspectives behind the study of organizations, and introduce the concept that organizations are knowledge and learning systems.

THE FIELD OF ORGANIZATIONAL BEHAVIOUR

organizational behaviour

The study of what people think, feel, and do in and around organizations.

Organizational behaviour (OB) is the study of what people think, feel, and do in and around organizations. OB scholars systematically study individual, team, and structural characteristics that influence behaviour within organizations. By saying that organizational behaviour is a field of study, we mean that scholars have been accumulating a distinct knowledge about behaviour within organizations— a knowledge base that is the foundation of this book.

By most estimates, OB emerged as a distinct field around the 1940s.[2] However, its origins can be traced much further back. Plato wrote about the essence of leadership. Aristotle addressed the topic of persuasive communication. The writings of 16th-century Italian political theorist Niccolo Machiavelli laid the foundation for contemporary work on organizational power and politics. In 1776, Adam Smith advocated a new form of organizational structure based on the division of labour. One hundred years later, German sociologist Max Weber wrote about rational organizations and initiated discussion of charismatic leadership. Soon after, Frederick Winslow Taylor introduced the systematic use of goal setting and rewards to motivate employees. In the 1920s, Elton Mayo and his colleagues conducted productivity studies at Western Electric's Hawthorne plant in the United States. They reported that an informal organization—employees casually interacting with others—operates alongside the formal organization. OB has been around for a long time; it just wasn't organized into a unified discipline until after World War II.

What are Organizations?

Organizations have existed as long as people have worked together. Archaeologists have discovered massive temples dating back to 3,500 BC that were constructed through the organized actions of many people.[3] We have equally impressive examples of contemporary organizations, ranging from Wal-Mart, the world's largest and most successful retailer, to the giant oil sands projects around Fort McMurray, Alberta. Equally impressive are temporary organizations, such as the Sydney

"Big" is too small a word to describe Syncrude Canada's organizational presence near Fort McMurray, Alberta. The world's largest producer of crude oil from oil sands employs nearly 4,000 people directly and at least that many people through contractors to produce over 80 million barrels of oil per year (which is expected to double by 2008). The oil sands facilities are almost impossible to comprehend, from the gargantuan 380-tonne trucks to the massive array of pipes as big as pick-up trucks and drag lines longer than football fields. Operating 24 hours every day, Syncrude has a fleet of 90 buses to ferry employees between Fort McMurray and the work sites.[4] In your opinion, what organizational behaviour concepts described in this book would have the greatest influence on the success of Syncrude and other mammoth projects? *Image Courtesy of Syncrude Canada Ltd.*
www.syncrude.com

Olympics and the special teams that coordinated thousands of passengers stranded in Halifax and other Canadian cities following the terrorist attacks on September 11, 2001.

"[A] company is one of humanity's most amazing inventions," says Steven Jobs, CEO of Apple Computer and Pixar Animation Studios. "It's totally abstract. Sure, you have to build something with bricks and mortar to put the people in, but basically a company is this abstract construct we've invented, and it's incredibly powerful."[5]

organizations
Groups of people who work inter-dependently toward some purpose.

So, what are these powerful constructs that we call **organizations**? They are groups of people who work interdependently toward some purpose.[6] Organizations are not buildings or other physical structures. Rather, they consist of people who interact with each other to achieve a set of goals. Employees have structured patterns of interaction, meaning that they expect each other to complete certain tasks in a coordinated way—in an *organized* way.

Organizations have a purpose, whether it's producing oil from oil sands or selling books on the Internet. Some organizational behaviour scholars are skeptical about the relevance of goals in a definition of organizations.[7] They argue that an organization's mission statement may be different from its true goals. They also question the assumption that all organizational members believe in the same goals. These points may be true, but imagine an organization without goals: it would consist of a mass of people wandering around aimlessly without any sense of direction. Overall, organizations likely have a collective sense of purpose, even though this purpose is not fully understood or agreed upon.

Why Study Organizational Behaviour?

Organizational behaviour seems to get more respect from people who have been in the workforce a while than from students who are just beginning their careers. Many of us specialize in accounting, marketing, information systems, and other fields with corresponding job titles, so it's understandable that students focus on these career paths. After all, who ever heard of a career path leading to a "Vice-president of OB" or a "Chief OB Officer"?

Even if organizational behaviour doesn't have its own job title, most people in the work force come to realize that this field is a potential gold mine of valuable knowledge. The fact is, everyone in the work force needs to understand, predict, and influence behaviour (both our own and of others) in organizational settings (see Exhibit 1.1). Marketing students learn marketing concepts and computer science students learn about circuitry and software code. But everyone benefits from organizational behaviour knowledge to address the people issues when trying to apply marketing, computer science, and other ideas.

Understanding, predicting, and influencing   Every one of us has an inherent need to understand and predict the world in which we live.[8] Much of our time is spent working in or around organizations, so the concepts offered in this and other OB textbooks will help you to partially satisfy that innate drive. The knowledge presented in this book also gives you the opportunity to question and rebuild

EXHIBIT 1.1

Reasons
for studying
organizational
behaviour

your personal theories that have developed through observation and experience. Look at the "It All Makes Sense" self-assessment at the end of this chapter. How many of these statements are true? Even if you correctly answer most of them, the information you read in this book can further develop and crystallize your personal beliefs so they more accurately model and predict organizational behaviour.

It's nice to understand and predict organizational events, but most of us want to influence the environment in which we live. Whether you are a marketing specialist or a computer engineer, OB knowledge will help you to influence organizational events by understanding and applying concepts in motivation, communication, conflict, team dynamics, and other topics. In fact, some scholars emphasize that the usefulness of OB research depends on more than just understanding and predicting behaviour, it also depends on the degree to which practitioners can interpret research results and apply them.[9]

This book takes the view that organizational behaviour knowledge is for everyone—not just managers. Indeed, as organizations reduce layers of management and delegate more responsibilities to the rest of us, the concepts described in this book will become increasingly important for anyone who works in and around organizations. We all need to understand organizational behaviour and to master the practices that influence organizational events. That's why you won't find very much emphasis here on "management." Yes, organizations will continue to have managers ("adult supervision," as young employees cynically call them), but their roles have changed. More important, the rest of us are now expected to manage ourselves. As one forward-thinking organizational behaviour scholar wrote many years ago: everyone is a manager.[10]

OB and the bottom line   So far, our answer to the question "Why study OB?" has focused on how OB knowledge benefits you as an individual. But it is increasingly clear that organizational behaviour knowledge is also important for the organization's financial health. A recent study of over 700 Canadian, American, and European firms calculated that companies applying performance-based rewards, employee communication, work-life balance, and other organizational behaviour ideas have three times the level of financial success as companies without these OB practices. Moreover, the study provides evidence that OB practices *cause* better financial performance, not the other way around. This finding is not new to Warren Buffett and other financial gurus who, for many years, have considered an organization's leadership and the quality of its employees as one of the top predictors of that firm's financial potential.[11]

ORGANIZATIONAL BEHAVIOUR TRENDS

There has never been a better time to learn about organizational behaviour. The pace of change is accelerating, and most of the transformation is occurring in the workplace. Let's take a brief tour through five trends in the workplace: globalization, information technology, the changing work force, emerging employment relationships, and workplace values and ethics.

Globalization

Betty Coulter is a typical 21-year-old North American college or university grad. She wears the latest jeans and is a faithful fan of the hottest American TV shows. At least, that's what Betty will say, if asked, when you call her about a broken appliance. In reality, Betty is Savitha Balasubramanyam, an employee at a call centre in Bangalore, India. "It doesn't matter if I'm really Betty or Savitha," says Balasubramanyam with a well-practised American accent. "What matters is that at the end of the day I've helped the customer."[12]

Welcome to the world of globalization! Whether they are software giants in Europe or call centres in India, competitors are just as likely to be located in a distant part of the world as within your own country. SAP, the German software giant, is the leader in enterprise software. Wipro Technologies, India's largest software company, routinely wins multimillion-dollar contracts from the likes of General Electric, Home Depot, and Nokia. CustomerAsset, where Savitha Balasubramanyam works, provides seamless customer service—complete with American accent!—from India's technology hub.

globalization
When an organization extends its activities to other parts of the world, actively participates in other markets, and competes against organizations located in other countries.

Globalization occurs when an organization extends its activities to other parts of the world, actively participates in other markets, and competes against organizations located in other countries.[13] Many firms have had "international" operations for many years, but these were usually import-export businesses or fairly independent subsidiaries that served local markets. Globalization, on the other hand, connects and coordinates these geographically-dispersed segments so they serve global customers and compete against other global businesses.[14]

Globalization isn't new to Canadians. William Cornelius Van Horne, the Canadian Pacific Railway CEO who built the legendary Banff Springs hotel in 1888, once said: "If we can't export the scenery, we'll import the tourists."[15] Today, it is Quebecor, Nortel Networks, JDS Uniphase, and other firms who push the limits of globalization. But globalization also applies to small companies such as SiGe Semiconductor. With fewer than 100 employees, the Ottawa-based high-tech firm already has sales offices in several countries and has hired experts from Britain, Ireland, Denmark, the U.S. and other countries, some of whom still live abroad and commute to Ottawa.[16]

Implications for organizational behaviour Globalization influences several aspects of organizational behaviour—some good, some not so good. Globalization is applauded for increasing organizational efficiency and providing a broader net to attract valuable knowledge and competencies (as SiGe has done). It potentially opens up new career opportunities and provides a greater appreciation of diverse needs and perspectives.

But globalization also presents new challenges.[17] The debate about whether globalization makes poor countries wealthier or poorer adds a new ethical dimension to corporate decisions.[18] Firms also need to adjust their organizational structures and forms of communication to assist their global reach. Globalization adds more diversity to the work force, which affects the organization's culture and introduces new forms of values-based conflict among employees.

Globalization is also identified as one of the main sources of increased competitive pressures, mergers, and market volatility. These environmental conditions, in turn, reduce job security, increase work intensification, and demand more work flexibility from employees. Thus, globalization might partly explain why Canadians now work longer hours, have heavier workloads, and experience more work-family conflict (due mainly to lack of time to fulfill both obligations) than at any time in recent decades (see Chapter 7).[19] "Any company, whether international or not, has to look at the way globalization has impacted the way we work," warns an executive at the global healthcare company GlaxoSmithKline.

"And even if you're not global, there's a competitor or customer somewhere who is."[20]

Last, globalization influences the study of organizational behaviour. Scholars are paying more attention to cross-cultural values (as we discuss later in this section) and are more sensitive to whether their theories are relevant in other societies. We cannot assume that work teams, empowerment, performance-based rewards, or other organizational behaviour practices that are effective in one country will be as effective in other parts of the world.[21] For instance, approximately 150 scholars have been collaborating in a consortium called Project GLOBE to study leadership and organizational practices across dozens of countries.[22] This level of global investigation has become increasingly necessary as we discover the complex effects of values and other differences across cultures.

Globalization has important implications for how we learn about organizational behaviour. The best performing companies may be in Finland, Brazil, or Singapore, not just in Calgary or Toronto. That's why this book presents numerous examples from around the planet. We want you to learn from the best, no matter where their headquarters are located.

Information Technology and OB

By day, Nana Frimpong is the official woodcarver for King Otumfuo Osei Tutu II in the royal Asante court of Ghana, West Africa. But when he isn't carving stools for the king, Frimpong sells his wares over the Internet. Demand from international buyers is so strong that he now employs a staff of 15 carvers. In this country of 19 million people and only 100,000 telephones, Frimpong is something of a celebrity and role model of the country's potential prosperity. "There are a lot of

"Can't talk now. I'm in a seminar about improving communication with technology."

Nana Frimpongs in the Asante nation," says King Tutu. "Many can be helped through the Internet."[23]

Whether we make fibre-optic routers in Ottawa or wooden stools in Ghana, the Internet and other forms of information technology are changing our lives. They are connecting people around the planet and allowing small businesses in developing countries to compete in the global marketplace. Within organizations, information technology blurs the temporal and spatial boundaries between individuals and the organizations that employ them. It redesigns jobs, reshapes the dynamics of organizational power and politics, and creates new standards for competitive advantage through knowledge management.[24] Information technology also generates new communication patterns unheard of a decade or two ago. While attending a meeting, some employees now carry on parallel conversations: they talk to the group while communicating wirelessly through Blackberry or other devices to specific people in the same room! Two other emerging work activities attributed to information technology are telework and virtual teams.

Telework   It's 9 a.m., the beginning of another busy day for Paolo Conconi, the Italian-born owner of Hong Kong electronic-parts maker MPS Electronics. But Conconi doesn't worry about fighting Hong Kong traffic to get to work. His office is at home, far away on the Indonesian island of Bali. Conconi's office is a table by the swimming pool, where he checks e-mail and calls staff and clients in Europe and Asia. "I've organized my work so that I can do it from anywhere," he says. "As long as I have electricity and one or two phone lines, that's all I need."[25]

Paolo Conconi is among the tens of millions of people who have altered their employment relationship through **telework** (also called *telecommuting*)—an alternative work arrangement where employees work at home or a remote site, usually with a computer connection to the office. Some teleworkers have highly structured, formal agreements with the employer; others engage in "guerrilla" telework, informal ad hoc arrangements with their immediate supervisor.

Some sources applaud the benefits of telework. Telecommunications giant AT&T estimates that by avoiding daily travel, teleworkers have better work-family balance and are about 10 percent more productive than before they started working from home. According to a recent Ipsos-Reid poll, most teleworkers in Canada also say that this arrangement improves their job satisfaction and work-family balance. "I enjoy this so much that I don't ever want to do anything else," says Mary Ellen Newell. After years working for the Royal Bank of Canada in an office setting, Newell now works for the bank out of her home in Mississauga, Ontario, selling credit-card services and debit machines to small and medium-sized businesses.[26]

Against these positive outcomes, telework poses a number of challenges for organizations and employees.[27] Along with some degree of technological savvy, teleworkers need to be self-motivated, organized, and have sufficient fulfilment of social needs elsewhere in their life. Employers need to shift from "face time" (the amount of physical presence at work) evaluation criteria to outcome-based measures of performance in the "no-see-um" world of telework. Telework also creates risks in office politics (see Chapter 12). Finally, a recent Quebec study suggests that companies expect about 10 percent more productivity from teleworkers, and that employees seem to be quite happy to provide these higher standards.

Virtual teams   Information technology also facilitates the development of virtual teams. **Virtual teams** are teams whose members operate across space, time,

telework
Also called telecommuting, it is working from home, usually with a computer connection to the office.

virtual teams
Teams whose members operate across space, time, and organizational boundaries and are linked through information technologies to achieve organizational taks.

and organizational boundaries and are linked through information technologies to achieve organizational tasks.[28] There is currently a flurry of research activity regarding the types of work best suited to virtual teams and the conditions that facilitate and hinder their effectiveness. Some conclusions are beginning to emerge from these preliminary studies.

One observation is that virtual teams are still teams, first and foremost, so their dynamics are similar to those of co-located teams (whose members are located in the same physical area). For example, team development and sub-group cliques are found in virtual teams in ways similar to co-located teams. However, virtual teams require different strategies to build trust and deal with members who are not pulling their weight. Virtual teamwork also calls for unique leadership skills, such as greater empathy and persuasive tactics. Information technology is a critical feature of virtual teams because it's a lifeline for them.[29] These and other virtual team issues will be discussed more fully in Chapter 9.

The Changing Work Force

Walk into almost any McDonald's in Toronto and you might think you have entered a United Nations building. The fast-food restaurant employs people from almost as many cultures as live in this multicultural city. "We want our staff to represent the community it serves, that is the way it has always been and always will be," says a McDonald's Canada executive. By any global standard, Canada is a multicultural society that embraces this diversity. Indeed, a recent survey indicates that 82 percent of Canadians believe that governments should preserve and enhance multiculturalism in Canada.[30]

Like McDonald's Canada, most organizations in this country have an increasingly diverse multicultural workforce because of the country's increasing demographic diversity. Exhibit 1.2 illustrates the primary and secondary dimensions of this diversity. The primary categories—gender, ethnicity, age, race, sexual orientation, and mental/physical qualities—represent personal characteristics that influence an individual's socialization and self-identity. The secondary dimensions are features that we learn or have some control over throughout our lives, such as education, marital status, religion, and work experience.

The Canadian work force has become more diverse along many of these primary and secondary dimensions. For instance, more than one-half of all immigrants to Canada now come from Asia, compared with only 3 percent a few decades ago. At the same time, the percentage of immigrants from Europe and the United States has fallen to 25 percent. The First Nations population is increasing faster than that of European Canadians, particularly in Manitoba and Saskatchewan. The result is an increasing population mosaic that is reflected in the Canadian workplace. Cultural diversity is particularly apparent in Metropolitan Toronto where ethnic minorities represent almost one-half of the population.[31]

However, scholars are increasingly troubled by attempts to distinguish people by their ethnicity. Some point out that interracial marriages make ethnic distinctions both difficult and inappropriate. Others warn that distinguishing people by their ethnicity merely reinforces stereotyping. In particular, there is a risk that non-white Canadians are viewed as "perpetual foreigners," even though their families may have moved to this country generations ago.[32]

Another form of diversity is the increasing representation of women in the workforce. Women now represent nearly 50 percent of the paid work force in

EXHIBIT 1.2

Primary and
secondary
dimensions of
workforce diversity

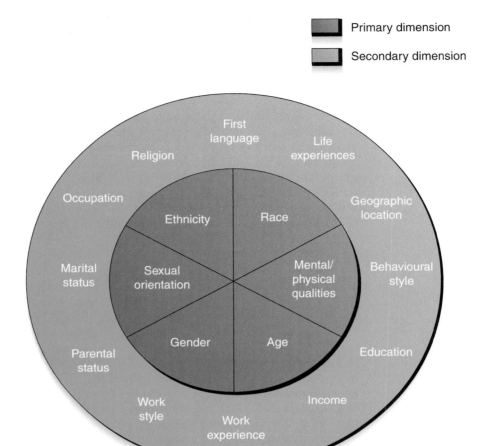

Canada, compared to just 20 percent a few decades ago. Gender-based shifts continue to occur within occupations. For example, Canadian medical schools now graduate more women than men each year, whereas in the 1960s 90 percent of medical school graduates were men.[33]

Age cohorts represent another primary dimension of workforce diversity.[34] Baby boomers—people born between 1946 and 1964—have somewhat different values and expectations in the workplace than Generation-X employees—those born between 1964 and 1977.[35] According to several writers, the typical baby boomer tends to expect and desire more job security (at least, at this stage in his or her career). In contrast, Gen-Xers are typically less loyal to one organization, and in return expect less job security. Gen-Xers tend to be motivated more by workplace flexibility and the opportunity to use new technology. Baby-boomers tend to be workaholics, so they can improve their economic and social status. Some writers describe how Generation-Y employees (those born in the decade or so after 1977) expect plenty of responsibility and involvement in their employment relationship. While these statements certainly don't apply to everyone in each cohort, they reflect the fact that different generations bring different values and expectations.[36]

Banana magazine, the cheeky Asian-Canadian lifestyle and cultural publication, reflects Canada's increasing cultural diversity. Started by entrepreneurs Karen Yong (right), Mark Simon (front), and Jory Levitt (with publicist Frances Wu at left) after attending university in Victoria, B.C., the magazine is aimed at young westernized Asians who want to explore and enjoy their ethnicity. *Banana* also highlights the fact that ethnicity is an increasingly complex idea, because increasingly Canadians have a multicultural heritage. For example, Mark Simon is half Vietnamese, a quarter Filipino, and a quarter French.[37] How do magazines such as *Banana* encourage multiculturalism in Canada? *Mark van Manen/Vancouver Sun.*
www.bananamag.com

Implications for organizational behaviour   Diversity presents both opportunities and challenges in organizations. It can become a competitive advantage by improving decision making and team performance on complex tasks.[38] For many businesses, a diverse work force is also necessary to provide better customer service in the global marketplace. "We go out of our way to recruit from a melting pot of nationalities," says an executive at Amadeus, a developer of worldwide airline reservation software near Nice, France. "We believe that our product is superior because of the different cultures of the people developing it."[39]

Along with its benefits, workforce diversity presents new challenges.[40] For instance, women have made up a large portion of the workforce for the past two decades, yet they are still underrepresented in senior positions. Racism still raises its ugly head from time to time in Canada. Various organizational behaviour topics, including stereotyping (Chapter 3) and influence tactics (Chapter 12) address these issues. Diversity also influences team development (Chapters 8 and 9) and the potential for conflict among employees (Chapter 13).

Emerging Employment Relationships

employability
An employment relationship in which people are expected to continually develop their skills to remain employed.

The changing work force, new information technology, and globalization have fuelled substantial changes in employment relationships. Employees face increasing turbulence in their work and employment relationship due to mergers, corporate restructuring, and privatization of government-managed organizations.[41] Out of this turbulence has emerged a "new deal" employment relationship, called **employability**, that replaces the implied guarantee of lifelong employment in return for loyalty.

Employability requires employees to perform a variety of work activities rather than hold specific jobs, and they are expected to continuously learn skills that will keep them employed. From this perspective, individuals must anticipate future organizational needs and develop new competencies that match those needs. Corporate leaders claim that employability is necessary so that organizations can adapt to the rapidly changing business environment. However, employability also has implications for job design, organizational loyalty, workplace stress, and other topics in this book.[42]

Contingent work   Another employment shift is the increasing percentage of the workforce in **contingent work**. Contingent work includes any job in which the individual does not have an explicit or implicit contract for long-term employment, or one in which the minimum hours of work can vary in a nonsystematic way.[43] Statistics Canada estimates that 12 percent of the work force has "nonpermanent" employment.[44]

Who are these contingent workers? A small, but highly publicized, cadre of professional contingent workers are known as "free agents." Free agents possess valued competencies, so they tend to get desired work in the marketplace. They are usually confident in their independence, and are less interested in permanent employment.[45] A much larger group of contingent workers called "temporary temporaries" accept temporary work because they are unable to find permanent employment. Some have outdated skills; others lack work experience. Temporary temporaries accept contingent work to meet basic economic needs, gain work experience, and find leads to more permanent employment.

Contingent workers are an increasing portion of the work force because they provide companies with greater flexibility in terms of the number of people or variety of skills required.[46] For example, skilled contractors (free agents) bring valuable knowledge to the organization that is immediately applied and shared with others. Information technology makes it easier for people in some professions to contract out their services without worrying about commuting or travel. Another reason for the increasing number of contingent workers is that many have fewer benefits and less job security, so they reduce payroll costs. However, some critics suggest that contingent workers have less training and work experience, which leads to lower quality products or services and higher accident rates.[47]

Workplace Values and Ethics

The opening story in this chapter mentioned that the success of Four Seasons Hotels and Resorts can be partly attributed to its values, and in hiring people with compatible values. **Values** represent stable, long-lasting beliefs about what is important in a variety of situations. They are evaluative standards that help us define what is right or wrong, or good or bad, in the world.[48] Values dictate our priorities, our preferences, and our desires. They influence our motivation, decisions, and actions. "Ninety-nine percent of what we say is about values," advises Anita Roddick, founder of The Body Shop.[49]

Cultural, personal, and organizational values have been studied by organizational behaviour scholars for several decades.[50] *Cultural values*, which we discuss in Chapter 2 (along with personal and ethical values) represent the dominant prescriptions of a society. They are usually influenced by religious, philosophical, and political ideologies. *Personal values* incorporate cultural values, as well as

contingent work
Any job in which the individual does not have an explicit or implicit contract for long-term employment, or one in which the minimum hours of work can vary in a nonsystematic way.

values
Stable, long-lasting beliefs about what is important in a variety of situations.

organizational culture

The basic pattern of shared assumptions, values, and beliefs governing the way employees within an organization think about and act on problems and opportunities.

other values socialized by parents, friends, and personal life events. *Organizational values*, which are discussed in Chapter 16 (on **organizational culture)**, are widely and deeply shared by people within the organization.[51]

Importance of Values in the Workplace

Values are not new to organizational behaviour, but this topic's popularity has increased noticeably in recent years.[52] One reason is that corporate leaders are looking for better ways to guide employee decisions and behaviour. Today's increasingly educated and independent workforce resents the traditional "command-and-control" supervision, and financial rewards are far from perfect. Values represent a potentially powerful way to keep employees' decisions and actions aligned with corporate goals. Values are the unseen magnet that pulls employees in the same direction. They foster a common bond and help to ensure that we all pull in the same direction—regardless of our individual tasks and ranks.[53] GLOBAL Connections 1.1 provides a clear example of the importance of values in organizational success. The Warehouse is rated as one of the world's best discount retailers, and one of the main reasons for the New Zealand company's success is its emphasis on values.

A second reason for the recent interest in values is that globalization has raised our awareness of and sensitivity to differences in values across cultures. Global organizations face the challenge of ensuring that employees make consistent decisions and actions around the world even though they may have diverse cultural values. Reinforcing a common organizational culture isn't an easy answer because some organizational values may conflict with some individual and societal values.[54]

The third reason why values have gained prominence is that organizations are under increasing pressure to engage in ethical practices and corporate social responsibility. **Ethics** refers to the study of moral principles or values that determine whether actions are right or wrong and outcomes are good or bad (see Chapter 2). We rely on our ethical values to determine "the right thing to do." Ethical behaviour is driven by the moral principles we use to make decisions. These moral principles represent fundamental values.

Unfortunately, a lot of people give executives low grades on their ethics report cards these days.[55] Enron Energy and WorldCom (founded by Canadian Bernie Ebbers) were two of the largest bankruptcies in American history. More important, they have become icons of unethical and possibly illegal conduct by corporate executives. Canadians also have examples of ethical misconduct: Bre-X (salting mine samples) and Montreal-based film company Cinar Corp. (misappropriated funds), to name a couple.[56] These corporate catastrophes emphasize the importance of business ethics and raise more interest in the role of values in the workplace.

ethics

The study of moral principles or values that determine whether actions are right or wrong and outcomes are good or bad.

Corporate social responsibility   Over 30 years ago, economist Milton Friedman pronounced that "there is one and only one social responsibility of business—to use its resources and engage in activities designed to increase its profits."[57] Friedman was a respected scholar, but this argument was not one of his more popular—or accurate—statements. Today, any business that follows Friedman's advice will face considerable trouble in the marketplace. Indeed, only 20 percent of 2,000 Canadians recently surveyed agreed with Friedman; in contrast, more than 70 percent believe that business executives have a responsibility to take into account the impact their decisions have on employees, local communities,

Cultivating Values at New Zealand's The Warehouse

Who is the most successful discount retailer in the world? Most people would probably say Wal-Mart or the French giant Carrefour. Yet the best of the breed may be The Warehouse, an Auckland, N.Z.-based company that sells lots of cheap stuff in 130 distinctive big red box stores throughout New Zealand and Australia. The Warehouse was recently praised by *Forbes* magazine as "easily one of the best retail operations in the entire world." The *Wall Street Journal* rated it as the second best performing small-cap company in the Asia-Pacific region.

What is so special about The Warehouse? Founder Stephen Tindall will gladly tell you that "people first" values is the main reason for the company's success. "We have discovered that our policies of putting team members first … makes them feel good about the business they work for," explains Tindall. "This feel-good attitude enables our team members to put the customers first and to provide exceptional service to them."

The Warehouse extends its "feel good" values to the community and environment. It has adopted Sweden's "Natural Step" sustainable development process to reduce dependence on non-renewable substances. Its timber procurement policy restricts purchases to sustainably-produce timber furniture products. It has commissioned an independent social audit, the results of which appear in annual reports.

Perhaps its strongest symbol of corporate social responsibility is The Warehouse's aim to eliminate landfill waste by 2020. To achieve this daunting "zero waste" objective, 29 stores have odourless worm farms to digest all organic refuse from the premises. Eight of

"People first" values and social responsibility have made The Warehouse in New Zealand one of the world's top-rated discount retailers. *Courtesy of The Warehouse*

The Warehouse stores have already achieved this zero waste goal.

Sources: J. Doebele, "Kiwi Category Killer," *Forbes*, August 20, 2001; S. Fea, "Tindall Pushes Zero Waste," *Southland Times (Chistchurch, NZ))*, May 11, 2001, p. 3; A. Miriyana, "A Southern Man," *Sunday Star-Times (Auckland, NZ)*, March 4, 2001, p. A3; "Warehouse Grasps the Bigger Picture," *New Zealand Herald*, January 4, 2001; M. Alexander, "Warehouse Boss just Loves Seeing Red," *Sunday Star-Times (Auckland, NZ)*, December 31, 2000; J. E. Hilsenrath, "Value Creators: In the Company of Asia's Superheroes," *Asian Wall Street Journal*, December 8, 2000, p. P3; S. Hendery, "Warehouse Plans to Give us All a Foot in the Store," *New Zealand Herald*, November 25, 2000; S. Hendery, "Expansion hits Warehouse sales," *New Zealand Herald*, November 8, 2000.
www.thewarehouse.co.nz

and the country. In other words, Canadians expect organizations in this country to engage in corporate social responsibility.[58]

Corporate social responsibility (CSR)
An organization's moral obligation towards its stakeholders.

Corporate social responsibility (CSR) refers to an organization's moral obligation toward its **stakeholders.** Stakeholders are the shareholders, customers, suppliers, governments, and any other groups with a vested interest in the organization.[59] As part of corporate social responsibility, many companies have adopted the *triple bottom line* philosophy. This means they try to support or "earn positive returns" in the economic, social, and environmental spheres of sustainability. Firms adopting the triple bottom line aim to survive and be profitable in the marketplace (economic), but they also intend to maintain or improve conditions for society (social) as well as the physical environment.[60]

More than ever, companies in Canada and elsewhere are coming under scrutiny for their CSR practices. For instance, discussion about the working conditions of

stakeholders

Shareholders, customers, suppliers, governments, and any other groups with a vested interest in the organiztion.

suppliers has been a topic of discussion at recent annual shareholder meetings of the Hudson's Bay Company. The Canadian retailer requires suppliers to abide by a social responsibility and ethics code, but shareholders want Hudson's Bay to conduct periodic blind checks on suppliers to ensure they abide by that code.[61]

Companies are discovering that not just shareholders want companies to practice CSR. Job applicants, current employees, and suppliers also decide whether to associate with an organization based on how well it applies virtuous values. "People increasingly prefer to work for or do business with what is deemed to be a socially responsible company," says Nick Wright, London-based head of corporate responsibility at investment bank UBS Warburg.[62]

While corporate leaders are quick to climb aboard the social responsibility rhetoric, it seems that few have the motivation or ability to translate their words into deeds. Accounting giant PricewaterhouseCoopers found that two-thirds of 1,000 chief executives surveyed around the world said corporate social responsibility was vital to the profitability of any company, yet only 24 percent of them publicly report on their social responsibility practices.[63]

A few years ago, Vancouver City Savings Credit Union made a commitment to the triple bottom line, and to a transparent and balanced process of assessing the company's social and environmental performance. VanCity retains an independent, external social auditor to report on the inclusivity, embeddedness, and continuous improvement of its social and environmental performance. Specifically, the auditor considers how well VanCity genuinely engages its stakeholders, integrates corporate social responsibility into all its operations and policy making, and applies what it learns to improve future performance on the triple bottom line. "If companies take a chance, and take their corporate strategy in a new direction—one that respects people, the environment, and the bottom line—they will profit in ways they never dreamed of," advises VanCity CEO Dave Mowat.[64] Why do organizations such as VanCity apply the triple bottom line, whereas most companies in Canada do not? *Tom Burley Photography.*
www.vancity.com

THE FIVE ANCHORS OF ORGANIZATIONAL BEHAVIOUR

Globalization, information technology, the changing work force, emerging employment relationships, and workplace values are just a few of the trends that we will explore in this textbook. To understand these and other topics, organizational behaviour scholars rely on a set of basic beliefs or knowledge structures (see Exhibit 1.3). These conceptual anchors represent the way that OB researchers think about organizations and how they should be studied. Let's look at each of the five beliefs that anchor the study of organizational behaviour.

The Multidisciplinary Anchor

Organizational behaviour is anchored around the idea that the field should develop from knowledge in other disciplines, not just from its own isolated research base.[65] In other words, OB should be multidisciplinary. The upper part of Exhibit 1.4 identifies the traditional disciplines from which organizational behaviour knowledge has developed. For instance, sociologists have contributed to our knowledge of team dynamics, organizational socialization, organizational power, and other aspects of the social system. The field of psychology has aided our understanding of most issues relating to individual and interpersonal behaviour. Recently, the subfield of evolutionary psychology has contributed new ideas about the origins of human drives and behaviour, including innate human drives, social orientations, and cognitive and affective (thinking and feeling) processes.[66]

The bottom part of Exhibit 1.4 identifies some of the emerging fields from which organizational behaviour knowledge is acquired. The communications field helps us to understand the dynamics of knowledge management, electronic mail, corporate culture, and employee socialization. Information systems scholars are exploring the effects of information technology on team dynamics, decision making, and knowledge management. Marketing scholars have enhanced our understanding of job satisfaction and customer service, knowledge management, and creativity. Women's studies scholars are studying perceptual biases and power relations between men and women in organizations.

Five conceptual anchors of organizational behaviour

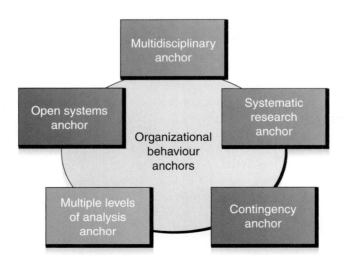

Multidisciplinary
anchor of
organizational
behaviour

Discipline	Relevant OB topics
Traditional	
Psychology	Drives, perception, attitudes, personality, job stress, emotions, leadership
Sociology	Team dynamics, roles, socialization, communication patterns, organizational power, organizational structure
Anthropology	Corporate culture, organizational rituals, cross-cultural dynamics, organizational adaptation
Political science	Intergroup conflict, coalition formation, organizational power and politics, decision making, organizational environments
Economics	Decision making, negotiation, organizational power
Industrial engineering	Job design, productivity, work measurement
Emerging	
Communications	Knowledge management, electronic mail, corporate culture, employee socialization
Information systems	Team dynamics, decision making, knowledge management
Marketing	Knowledge management, creativity, decision making
Women's studies	Organizational power, perceptions

The true test of OB's multidisciplinary anchor is how effectively OB scholars continue to transfer knowledge from traditional and emerging disciplines. History suggests that fields of inquiry tend to become more inwardly focused as they mature.[67] However, some OB scholars have recently argued that OB is hardly inwardly focused. Instead, it probably suffers from a "trade deficit"—importing far more knowledge from other disciplines than it exports to other disciplines. This occurs because many OB scholars are have been trained in other fields (e.g., psychology, sociology) and merely replicate research from those fields and put it in an organizational context. By borrowing heavily from other fields, OB runs the risk of perpetually lagging behind other disciplines and having little of its own knowledge to offer. Perhaps OB scholars need to focus more of their research on topics that are unique to organizational behaviour.[68]

The Systematic Research Anchor

scientific method
A set of principles and procedures that help researchers to systematically understand previously unexplained events and conditions.

A second anchor is the use of systematic research methods. . Traditionally, scholars have relied on the **scientific method** by forming research questions, systematically collecting data, and testing hypotheses against those data. Typically, this approach relies on quantitative data (numeric information) and statistical procedures to test hypotheses. The idea is to minimize personal biases and distortions about organizational events.

grounded theory
A process adopted in most qualitative research of developing knowledge through the constant interplay of data collection, analysis, and theory development.

More recently, OB scholars have also adopted a **grounded theory** approach to developing knowledge. Grounded theory is the process of developing a theory through the constant interplay between data gathering and developing theoretical concepts. This dynamic and cyclical view of the research process allows qualitative methods, including observation and participation, to be used in the data collection process, rather than just quantitative data collection (i.e. numeric data).[69] It also recognizes that it is not easy to remove personal biases from the research process. Appendix A at the end of this book provides an overview of research design and methods commonly found in organizational behaviour studies.

The Contingency Anchor

contingency approach
The idea that a particular action may have different consequences in different situations.

"It depends" is a phrase that OB scholars often use to answer a question about the best solution to an organizational problem. The statement may frustrate some people, yet it reflects an important way of understanding and predicting organizational events, called the **contingency approach**. This anchor states that a particular action may have different consequences in different situations. In other words, no single solution is best in all circumstances.[70]

Many early OB theorists have proposed universal rules to predict and explain organizational life, but there are usually too many exceptions to make these "one best way" theories useful. For example, in Chapter 14 we learn that leaders should use one style (e.g., participation) in some situations and another style (e.g., direction) in other situations. Thus, when faced with a particular problem or opportunity, we need to understand and diagnose the situation, and select the strategy most appropriate *under those conditions*.[71]

Although contingency-oriented theories are necessary in most areas of organizational behaviour, we should also be wary about carrying this anchor to an extreme. Some contingency models add more confusion than value compared to universal models. Consequently, we need to balance the sensitivity of contingency factors with the simplicity of universal theories.

The Multiple Levels of Analysis Anchor

This textbook divides organizational behaviour topics into three levels of analysis: individual, team, and organization (see Exhibit 1.5). The individual level includes the characteristics and behaviours of employees as well as the thought processes that are attributed to them, such as motivation, perceptions, personalities, attitudes, and values. The team level of analysis looks at the way people interact. This includes team dynamics, decisions, power, influence tactics, conflict, and leadership. At the organizational level, we focus on how people structure their working relationships and on how organizations interact with their environments.

EXHIBIT 1.5

Three levels of analysis in organizational behaviour

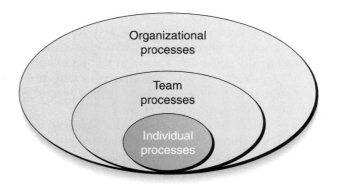

Although an OB topic is typically pegged into one level of analysis, it usually relates to all three levels.[72] For instance, communication is located in this book as a team process, but we also recognize that it includes individual and organizational processes. Therefore, you should try to think about each OB topic at the individual, team, and organizational levels, not just at one of these levels.

The Open Systems Anchor

Hewlett-Packard may have lots of buildings and equipment, but CEO Carly Fiorina says that her job is to nurture something that is alive. "I think that a company is a living system," says Fiorina. "It is an organism, it is operating in other living systems, and a leader has to think about the company as a living, breathing system."[73] Carly Fiorina is describing the fifth anchor of organizational behaviour— the view that organizations are **open systems**.

open systems

Organizations that take their sustenance from the environment and, in turn, affect that environment through their output.

Organizations are open systems because they take their sustenance from the environment and, in turn, affect that environment through their output. A company's survival and success depend on how well employees sense environmental changes and alter their patterns of behaviour to fit those emerging conditions.[74] In contrast, a closed system has all the resources needed to survive without dependence on the external environment. Organizations are never completely closed systems, but monopolies operating in very stable environments can ignore customers and others for a fairly long time without adverse consequences.

As Exhibit 1.6 illustrates, organizations acquire resources from the external environment, including raw materials, employees, financial resources, information, and equipment. Inside the organization are numerous subsystems, such as processes (communication and reward systems), task activities (production, marketing), and social dynamics (informal groups, power dynamics). With the aid of technology (such as equipment, work methods, and information), these subsystems transform inputs into various outputs. Some outputs (e.g., products and services) may be valued by the external environment, whereas other outputs (e.g., employee layoffs, pollution) have adverse effects. The organization receives feedback from the external environment regarding the value of its outputs and the availability of future inputs. This process is cyclical and, ideally, self-sustaining, so that the organization may continue to survive and prosper.

EXHIBIT 1.6

Open systems view of organizations

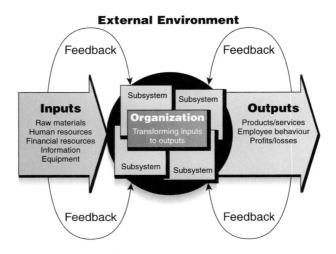

External environment and stakeholders   It is almost a cliché to say that most organizations today operate in more dynamic fast-paced environments than they did a few decades ago. To illustrate how fast organizations are changing, consider this: In the 1920s, companies stayed on the S&P 500 stock exchange list an average of 67 years. Today, the average company life cycle on the S&P 500 is about 12 years. In other words, your grandparents could work for the same organization all of their lives, whereas you will likely outlive two or three companies.[75] Similarly, the most valued companies in Canada today—such as Research in Motion, Sierra Wireless, and Creo Products—were either junior start-ups or nonexistent 20 years ago. And unless these firms anticipate and adapt to continual change, few of them will be around 20 years from now.

As open systems, successful organizations monitor their environments and take appropriate steps to maintain a compatible fit with the new external conditions. Recent studies reveal that successful organizations adapt quickly to those rapidly changing environments.[76] To maintain a close alignment with the external environment, they develop a dynamic capability—the ability to change their outputs and transformational process that produce those outputs. This does not mean that successful organizations change continuously and rapidly. On the contrary, Nortel, 360Networks, and a host of other firms changed so quickly that they depleted resources and overshot the needs of the environment. Rather, successful organizations have the capability to change quickly, while also recognizing the need for internal systems alignment.

Stakeholders represent a central part of the internal and external environment. As mentioned earlier, these include any person or entity with a vested interest in the organization. Stakeholders influence the firm's access to inputs and ability to discharge outputs. And unless they pay attention to the needs of stakeholders, organizational leaders may find their business in trouble. In other words, leaders may put their organization at risk if they pay attention only to shareholders and ignore their broader corporate social responsibility.[77] We see this stakeholder misalignment when job applicants avoid companies that lack corporate social responsibility and when organizations fail to treat their employees and suppliers with respect.

Systems as interdependent parts   The open systems anchor states that organizations consist of many internal subsystems that need to be continuously aligned with each other. As companies grow, they develop more and more complex subsystems that must coordinate with each other in the process of transforming inputs to outputs.[78] These interdependencies can easily become so complex that a minor event in one subsystem may amplify into serious unintended consequences elsewhere in the organization.

The open systems anchor is an important way of viewing organizations. However, it has traditionally focused on physical resources that enter the organization and are processed into physical goods (outputs). This was representative of the industrial economy, but not of the "new economy," where the most valued input is knowledge.

knowledge management
Any structured activity that improves an organization's capacity to acquire, share, and use knowledge in ways that improve its survival and success.

KNOWLEDGE MANAGEMENT

Organizational behaviour scholars have built on the open system anchor to create an entire sub-field of research dedicated to the dynamics of **knowledge management**. Knowledge management is any structured activity that improves an organization's capacity to acquire, share, and use knowledge in ways that improves its survival and success.[79] The knowledge that resides in an organization is called its **intellectual capital**. Intellectual capital is the sum of everything an organization knows that gives it a competitive advantage—including its human capital, structural capital, and relationship capital.[80]

intellectual capital

The sum of an organization's human capital, structural capital, and relationship capital.

- *Human capital*—This is the knowledge that employees possess and generate, including their skills, experience, and creativity.
- *Structural capital*—This is the knowledge captured and retained in an organization's systems and structures. It is the knowledge that remains after all the human capital has gone home.
- *Relationship capital*—This is the value derived from an organization's relationships with customers, suppliers, and other external stakeholders who provide added value for the organization. For example, this includes customer loyalty as well as mutual trust between the organization and its suppliers.[81]

Knowledge Management Processes

Intellectual capital represents the *stock* of knowledge held by an organization. This stock of knowledge is so important that some companies try to measure its value.[82] But knowledge management is much more than the organization's stock of knowledge. It is a *process* that develops an organization's capacity to acquire, share, and use knowledge more effectively. This process is often called **organizational learning** because companies must continuously learn about their environments in order to survive and succeed through adaptation.[83] The "capacity" to acquire, share, and use knowledge means that companies have established systems, structures, and organizational values that support the knowledge management process. Let's look more closely at some of the strategies companies use to acquire, share, and use knowledge.

organizational learning

The knowledge management process in which organizations acquire, share, and use knowledge to succeed.

Knowledge acquisition   Knowledge acquisition includes the organization's ability to extract information and ideas from its environment as well as through insight. One of the fastest and most powerful ways to acquire knowledge is through **grafting**—hiring individuals or acquiring entire companies. For instance, ATI Technologies, the Toronto-based graphics company, is picking up plenty of knowledge by hiring the most experienced Nortel staff laid off over the past year. "Nortel is the company with the skill sets that ATI is looking for," says an ATI executive.[84] Knowledge also enters the organization when employees learn about the external environment. Wal-Mart executives do this by systematically shopping at competitor stores every week. More commonly, employees acquire external knowledge by meeting with vendors, attending seminars and conferences, and learning directly from clients.[85] A third knowledge acquisition strategy is through experimentation. Companies receive knowledge through insight as a result of research and other creative processes (see Chapter 10).[86]

grafting

The process of acquiring knowledge by hiring individuals or buying entire companies.

Knowledge sharing   Many organizations are reasonably good at acquiring knowledge, but waste this resource by not effectively disseminating it. As several executives have lamented: "I wish we knew what we know." Studies report that knowledge sharing is usually the weakest link in knowledge management.[87] Valuable ideas sit idly—rather like unused inventory—or as hidden "silos of knowl-

communities of practice
Informal groups bound together by shared expertise and passion for a particular activity or interest.

edge" throughout the organization. One organizational unit might apply useful ideas to improve performance or customer service, whereas a nearby unit does not know about these better procedures.

Organizations need to improve communication to improve knowledge sharing (see Chapter 11). Some companies encourage knowledge sharing through **communities of practice**. These are informal groups bound together by shared expertise and passion for a particular activity or interest.[88] For example, as one of the top 20 knowledge management companies in the world, Waterloo, Ontario-based Clarica Life Insurance Company has created a community of practice among its 3,000 sales agents.

Knowledge use   Acquiring and sharing knowledge are wasted exercises unless knowledge is effectively put to use. To do this, employees must realize that the knowledge is available and that they have enough freedom to apply it. This requires a culture that supports experiential learning (see Chapter 3).

Clarica Life Insurance Company (now part of Sun Life of Canada) saw the need to supplement its knowledge management strategy with a virtual forum where its 3,000 independent agents across Canada could share knowledge. Through its company-wide intranet (called Clarica Connects), the Waterloo, Ontario-based firm established the Agent Network to help agents develop and share their expertise in ways that would generate innovative solutions. A group of 150 agents pilot-tested this confidential network while a steering committee helped them to see the opportunities of this community of practice. Ultimately, the company's goal is more than to have sales agents share knowledge throughout Canada. It is to teach them how to form their own communities with customers, thereby acquiring knowledge through a stronger customer relationship.[89] Along with independent sales agents, what other professional groups would benefit from an intranet-based community of practice? *Copyright © Masterfile*
www.clarica.com

Organizational Memory

Intellectual capital can be lost as quickly as it is acquired. Corporate leaders need to recognize that they are the keepers of an **organizational memory**. This unusual metaphor refers to the storage and preservation of intellectual capital. It includes information that employees possess as well as knowledge embedded in the organization's systems and structures. It includes documents, objects, and anything else that provides meaningful information about how the organization should operate.

How do organizations retain intellectual capital? One way is by keeping good employees. When many high-tech companies laid off an unprecedented number of people to cut costs during the recent "tech wreck," Apple Computer held on to its talent. "Our main asset is human talent, and we cannot afford to lose it," explains Apple's chief financial officer, Fred Anderson.[90] A second strategy is to systematically transfer knowledge before employees leave. This occurs when new recruits apprentice with skilled employees, thereby acquiring knowledge that is not documented.

A third organizational memory strategy is to transfer knowledge into structural capital.[91] This includes bringing out hidden knowledge, organizing it, and putting it in a form that can be available to others. This is what the organizing committee for the Sydney Olympics (SOCOG) did. SOCOG received mostly informal and anecdotal information from the Atlanta Olympics on how to run this type of event. To ensure

organizational memory
The storage and preservation of intellectual capital.

that future Olympics would have more knowledge, every division and functional area within SOCOG was asked to complete an extensive template of how they set up their operations. This resulted in 90 manuals that document everything from organizational structure and stakeholders to staffing and budgets.[92]

Before leaving the topic of organizational memory and knowledge management, you should know that successful companies also *unlearn*. Sometimes it is appropriate for organizations to selectively forget certain knowledge.[93] This means that they should cast off the routines and patterns of behaviour that are no longer appropriate. Employees need to rethink their perceptions, such as how they should interact with customers and which is the "best way" to perform a task. As we shall discover in Chapter 17, unlearning is essential for organizational change.

THE JOURNEY BEGINS

This chapter gives you some background about the field of organizational behaviour. But it's only the beginning of our journey. Throughout this book, we will challenge you to learn new ways of thinking about how people work in and around organizations. We begin this process in Chapter 2 by presenting a basic model of individual behaviour, then, over the next six chapters, introducing various stable and mercurial characteristics of individuals that relate to elements of the individual behaviour model. Next, this book moves to the team level of analysis. We begin by examining a basic model of team effectiveness and specific features of high performance teams, then consider decision making and creativity, communication, power and influence, conflict and negotiation, and leadership in team settings. Finally, we shift our focus to the organizational level of analysis, where we examine in detail the topics of organizational structure, organizational culture, and organizational change.

CHAPTER SUMMARY

Organizational behaviour is a relatively young field of inquiry that studies what people think, feel, and do in and around organizations. Organizations are groups of people who work interdependently toward some purpose. OB concepts help us to predict and understand organizational events, adopt more accurate theories of reality, and influence organizational events. This field of knowledge also improves the organization's financial health.

There are several trends in organizational behaviour. The first trend, globalization, requires corporate decision makers to be more sensitive to cultural differences, and seems to be associated with the recent rise in job insecurity, work intensification, and other sources of work-related stress. Information technology, the second trend, blurs the temporal and spatial boundaries between individuals and the organizations that employ them. It has contributed to the growth of telework—an alternative work arrangement where employees work at home or a remote site, usually with a computer connection to the office.

Information technology is also a vital ingredient in virtual teams—teams whose members operate across space, time, and organizational boundaries.

A third trend in organizations is the increasingly diverse workforce. Diversity potentially improves decision making, team performance, and customer service, but it also presents new challenges. A fourth trend is the employment relationships that have emerged from the changing work force, information technology, and globalization forces. Employment relationship trends include employability and contingent work. Values and ethics represent the fifth trend. In particular, companies are learning to apply values in a global environment, and are under pressure to abide by ethical values and higher standards of corporate social responsibility.

Organizational behaviour scholars rely on a set of basic beliefs to study organizations. These anchors include beliefs that OB knowledge should be multidisciplinary and based on systematic research, that organizational events usually have contingencies, that organizational behaviour can be viewed from three levels of analysis (individual, team, and organization), and that organizations are open systems.

The open systems anchor suggests that organizations have interdependent parts that work together to continually monitor and transact with the external environment. They acquire resources from the environment, transform them through technology, and return outputs to the environment. The external environment consists of the natural and social conditions outside the organization. External environments are generally much more turbulent today, so organizations must become adaptable and responsive.

Knowledge management develops an organization's capacity to acquire, share, and use knowledge in ways that improves its survival and success. Intellectual capital is knowledge that resides in an organization, including its human capital, structural capital, and relationship capital. It is a firm's main source of competitive advantage. Organizations acquire knowledge through grafting, individual learning, and experimentation. Knowledge sharing occurs mainly through various forms of communication. Knowledge sharing includes communities of practice, networks where people share their expertise and passion for a particular activity or interest. Knowledge use occurs when employees realize that the knowledge is available and that they have enough freedom to apply it. Organizational memory refers to the storage and preservation of intellectual capital.

KEY TERMS

Communities of practice, p. 24

Contingency approach, p. 20

Contingent work, p. 14

Corporate social responsibility (CSR), p. 16

Employability, p. 13

Ethics, p. 15

Globalization, p. 8

Grafting, p. 23

Grounded theory, p. 19

Intellectual capital, p. 23

Knowledge management, p. 22

Open systems, p. 21

Organizational behaviour (OB), p. 4

Organizational culture, p. 15

Organizational learning, p. 23

Organizational memory, p. 25

Organizations, p. 5

Scientific method, p. 19

Stakeholders, p. 17

Telework, p. 10

Values, p. 14

Virtual teams, p. 10

DISCUSSION QUESTIONS

1. "Organizational behaviour seems to get more respect from people who have been in the workplace a while than from students who are just beginning their careers." Why would the knowledge of OB be important to those of us who specialize in a field such as accounting, marketing, engineering, etc.?

2. Look through the list of chapters in this book and discuss how globalization could influence each organizational behaviour topic.

3. "Organizational theories should follow the contingency approach." Comment on the accuracy of this statement.

4. Employees in the City of Calgary's water distribution unit were put into teams and encouraged to find ways to improve efficiency. The teams boldly crossed departmental boundaries and areas of management discretion in search of problems. Employees working in other parts of the City of Calgary began to complain about these intrusions. Moreover, when some team ideas were implemented, the city managers discovered that a dollar saved in the water distribution unit may have cost the organization two dollars elsewhere. Use the open systems anchor to explain what happened here.

5. After hearing a seminar on knowledge management, an oil company executive argues that this perspective ignores the fact that oil companies could not rely on knowledge alone to stay in business. They also need physical capital (such as pumps and drill bits) and land (where oil is located). In fact, these two may be more important than what employees carry around in their heads. Discuss the merits of the oil executive's comments.

6. Fully describe intellectual capital, and explain how an organization can retain this capital.

7. What effect, if any, does the increasing diversity of the workforce have on managing and working in organizations?

8. Find two recent news items and explain how this information relates to corporate social responsibility.

THE GREAT IDEA THAT WASN'T

By Fiona McQuarrie, University College of the Fraser Valley.

Irina cradled her baby daughter in her arms and looked at the piles of unfinished work covering her desk. She wondered how such a great idea—telecommuting to her job while working at home—had gone so wrong in only three months.

Irina was a mortgage officer at a large Canadian bank. She had joined the bank twelve years ago, and had worked her way through successively more responsible jobs until she achieved her current position four years ago. She enjoyed the work, assisting clients in completing mortgage applications and then processing and approving or rejecting the applications. Irina found it very satisfying to help her clients achieve their dream of owning their own home or business. However, the real estate market in her city had become increasingly competitive, and her employer had responded to the greater demand for mortgages by promising better customer service than the other banks. This resulted in the mortgage officers working longer or different hours—sometimes as many as 80 hours a week—to be more available to potential clients.

When Irina and her husband discovered that their first child was on its way, they were delighted. But Irina saw there would be problems when the baby was born. Obtaining full-time day care for a new baby was nearly impossible, not to mention expensive. She certainly could not continue to work 80 hours a week, and her husband was not able to alter his work schedule to stay home and care for the baby.

So Irina went to her supervisor, David, and her department head, Ottavio, and made a proposal. She offered to continue working full-time once the baby was born, but she wanted to telecommute from home. "Much of my work is on the phone, which I can do from home as well as I can at work," she told them. "And if I have a computer at home, I can do most of the processing of the applications there as well. I can also work outside regular office hours, because I won't have to leave when the building closes." David agreed to the idea, as long as Irina would come into the office once a week for the regular mortgage officers' meeting. Ottavio was more reluctant, pointing out that a similar scheme had been tried several years ago and was unsuccessful, but eventually he also agreed, since Irina had an exceptional work record.

Irina took a month off work when Sarah was born, but eagerly returned to work as a telecom-muter. The company provided her with a computer, modem, and printer at home similar to what she had in her office, and arranged for a courier to deliver and pick up mortgage applications once a day. At first, the telecommuting arrangement worked well. Irina did not have to get dressed up for work, she did not have to fight traffic or find a parking space, and she was able to work while spending time with her new daughter.

The first major problem Irina encountered was in trying to find a useable place to work in her house. With Sarah's arrival, most of the free space in the house had been taken up with baby furniture and supplies. For the first few weeks, Irina tried working at the kitchen table, but she found that the computer was too bulky to move on and off the table every mealtime. She eventually purchased a second-hand desk and set it up in a corner of the living room, right next to the television set. While this arrangement allowed her to keep all her work in one place, it also meant that the work was always visible, even when she was trying to relax and watch TV.

Irina then discovered that caring for an infant was far more demanding than she had expected. Sarah was a good baby, but frequently she would cry when the phone rang and keep crying even after the phone was answered. Irina also found it difficult to arrange times to call clients back, since she had to fit those calls around Sarah's feeding schedule. And, since Irina often had to get up in the night to take care of Sarah, she frequently felt exhausted during the day. Although Irina had arranged to be available to clients outside of regular office hours, she often found that she was so tired, especially in the evening, that she was not very productive during those times.

Once a week, as agreed, Irina came in to the office for the regular mortgage officers' meeting. She enjoyed seeing her co-workers, but she was somewhat disturbed by the remarks they made about her new work arrangements. "So what's happening on all the soap operas on TV? I bet you can watch those whenever you want!" "It must be nice not to have to work as hard as we do here." Irina also found that while the meetings were informative, there was a lot at work that she was missing out on. Frequently discussion would focus on someone she didn't know, and only after she asked would she be told that the person had just been hired. People would also leave or be transferred to new positions, and Irina would not know about that either unless it came up in the discussion. Irina also found that the mortgage officers who worked in the office were getting many more clients than she was, simply because they were available to help new clients visiting the bank's offices.

After last week's meeting, David asked to see Irina privately in his office. He told her that he had received several phone calls from clients complaining about a baby crying in the background while they were talking to Irina. He also said that Ottavio had expressed concern about Irina's level of productivity since she had started telecommuting. Irina asked what the problem with her productivity was. David told her that since she did not have to spend time driving to and from work and dealing with distractions in the office, the bank expected her to be more productive than the other mortgage officers. In fact, David said, Ottavio had even wondered if Irina was working the hours she had promised, since her productivity did not seem to match the hours she claimed she was putting in.

"Well, David," Irina responded, "I am working as hard as I ever did, and I am doing what I agreed to do, including coming into the office once a week. The company is saving money by not having to provide an office for me here at work, and I am making myself available to clients outside regular office hours as I promised. I don't know what else I can do."

"All I can say," said David, "is that Ottavio is very concerned about your productivity and the image you are communicating to clients. In fact, Ottavio said that these were the same problems the company encountered before when they let people telecommute. If things don't improve within the next month or so, we will have to ask you to return to your regular hours at the office."

Discussion Questions

1. What are the major problems in this telework arrangement?

2. Is it Irina's or the bank's responsibility to solve these problems?

3. What solutions can you suggest to the problems that you have identified?

TEAM EXERCISE 1.2

HUMAN CHECKERS

Purpose This exercise is designed to help students understand the importance and application of organizational behaviour concepts.

Materials None, but the instructor has more information about the team's task.

Instructions

- *Step 1:* Form teams with six students. If possible, each team should have a private location where team members can plan and practice the required task without being observed or heard by other teams.

- *Step 2:* All teams will receive special instructions in class about the team's assigned task. All teams have the same task and will have the same amount of time to plan and practice the task. At the end of this planning and practice, each team will be timed while completing the task in class. The team that completes the task in the least time wins.

- *Step 3:* No special materials are required or allowed for this exercise. Although the task is not described here, students should learn the following rules for planning and implementing the task:

  Rule #1: You cannot use any written form of communication or any props other than chairs to assist in the planning or implementation of this task.

  Rule #2: You may speak to other students in your team at any time during the planning and implementation of this task.

  Rule #3: When performing the task, you must move only in the direction of your assigned destination. In other words, you can only move forward, not backward.

  Rule #4: When performing the task, you can move forward to the next space, but only if it is vacant (see Exhibit 1).

  Rule #5: When performing the task, you can move forward two spaces, if that space is vacant. In other words, you can move around a student who is one space in front of you to the next space if that space is vacant (see Exhibit 2).

Exhibit 1 **Exhibit 2**

- *Step 4:* When all teams have completed their task, the class will discuss the implications of this exercise for organizational behaviour.

Discussion Questions

1. Identify organizational behaviour concepts that the team applied to complete this task.

2. What personal theories of people and work teams were applied to complete this task.

3. What organizational behaviour problems occurred and what actions were (or should have been) taken to solve them.

TEAM EXERCISE 1.3

DEVELOPING KNOWLEDGE FROM MISTAKES

Purpose   The problem that people have with their mistakes isn't so much the mistake itself. Rather, it's that they do not take the time to learn from those mistakes. This exercise is designed to help you understand how to gain knowledge from past mistakes in a specific situation.

Instructions

- *Step 1:* The class will be divided into small teams (4–6 people). The instructor will identify a situation that students would have experienced and, therefore, probably have made mistakes. This could be the first day at work, the first day of a class you attended, or a social event, such as a first date.

- *Step 2:* After the topic has been identified, each team member writes down an incident in which something went wrong in that situation. For example, if the topic is the first day of classes, someone might note how they were late for class because they forgot to set their alarm clock.

- *Step 3:* Each student describes the mistake to other team members. As an incident is described, students should develop a causal map of the incident. They should ask why the problem happened, what the consequences of this incident were, did it happen again, and so on. The knowledge might not be as obvious as you think. For example, in the incident of being late, the learning might not be that we should ensure the alarm clock is set. It may be a matter of changing routines (going to bed earlier), rethinking our motivation to enroll in a program, and so on.

- *Step 4:* As other incidents are analyzed, the team should begin to document specific knowledge about the incident. Think of this knowledge as a road map for others to follow when they begin their first day of class, first day at work, first date, etc.

Source: This exercise was developed by Steven L. McShane, based on ideas in P. LaBarre, "Screw Up, and Get Smart," *Fast Company*, Issue 19 (November 1998), p. 58.

SELF-ASSESSMENT EXERCISE 1.4

IT ALL MAKES SENSE?

Purpose   This exercise is designed to help you understand how organizational behaviour knowledge can help you understand life in organizations.

Instructions   Read each of the statements below and circle whether each statement, in your opinion, is true or false. The class will consider the

answers to each question and discuss the implications for studying organizational behaviour. After reviewing these statements, the instructor will provide information about the most appropriate answer. (Note: This activity may be done as a self-assessment or as a team activity.)

1.	True	False	A happy worker is a productive worker.
2.	True	False	Decision makers tend to continue supporting a course of action even though information suggests that the decision is ineffective.
3.	True	False	Organizations are more effective when they prevent conflict among employees.
4.	True	False	It is better to negotiate alone than as a team.
5.	True	False	Companies are most effective when they have a strong corporate culture.
6.	True	False	Employees perform better without stress.
7.	True	False	Effective organizational change always begins by pinpointing the source of its current problems.
8.	True	False	Female leaders involve employees in decisions to a greater degree than do male leaders.
9.	True	False	People in Japan value group harmony and duty to the group (high collectivism) more than Canadians or Americans (low collectivism).
10.	True	False	Top-level executives tend to exhibit a Type A behaviour pattern (i.e. hard-driving, impatient, competitive, short-tempered, strong sense of time urgency, rapid talkers).
11.	True	False	Employees usually feel overreward inequity when they are paid more than co-workers performing the same work.

Copyright © 2003 Steven L. McShane.

S E L F · A S S E S S M E N T   E X E R C I S E   1.5

TELEWORK DISPOSITION ASSESSMENT

 (Go to the student CD for the interactive version of this exercise.)

Purpose This exercise is designed to help you assess the extent to which you possess the personal characteristics most suitable for telework.

Instructions This instrument asks you to indicate the degree to which you agree or disagree with each of the statements provided. You need to be honest with yourself for a reasonable estimate of your locus of control. The results provide a rough indication of how well you would adapt to telework. Please keep in mind that this scale only considers your personal characteristics. Other factors, such as organizational, family, and technological systems support must also be taken into account.

Copyright © 2003 Steven L. McShane.

 After studying the preceding material, be sure to check out our Online Learning Centre at
www.mcgrawhill.ca/college/mcshane
for more in-depth information and interactivities that correspond to this chapter.

A BORDER RUNS THROUGH IT

CBC journalist Joan Leishman takes us to Nogales, a city divided by the Mexican/U.S. border. This documentary describes what life is like for Mexicans who live in one culture but work each day in another. It looks at the effects of a U.S. economic recession; the September 11, 2001, terrorist attacks in the U.S.; and of cheaper labour in China on the employment of people in the *maquilla dora* factories of this border town. We also see how economic shifts in Nogales, Mexico, are taking their toll on the economy of Nogales, Arizona.

This video focuses on Nogales because it illustrates the stark contrasts of a first and third world nation, and their increasing interconnectedness. The high wall, erected years ago to divide the city that crosses two nations, is a symbol throughout the program. Some equate it with the Berlin Wall that once divided East and West Germany. The anxiety of terrorism and illegal immigration has turned this area into a militarized zone. The locals are stopped several times each day to justify their right to live in the United States. To some Americans with Mexican heritage, life in Nogales, Arizona, can be unsettling. To others, trying to enter the United States for work is a constant struggle.

Discussion Questions

1. Does this video case paint a positive or negative picture of globalization? Is this is fair portrayal of the globalization phenomenon?

2. What other organizational behaviour topics were apparent in this program?

Source: J. Leishman, "A Border Runs through It," CBC *The National*, June 12, 2002.

2

Individual Behaviour, Values, and Personality

Learning Objectives

AFTER READING THIS CHAPTER, YOU SHOULD BE ABLE TO:

- Diagram the MARS model.

- Describe three basic ways to match individual competencies to job requirements.

- Identify five types of individual behaviour in organizations.

- Define values and explain why values congruence is important.

- Define the six main values that vary across cultures.

- Summarize the key features of First Nations values.

- List four ethical principles.

- Explain how moral intensity, ethical sensitivity, and the situation influence ethical behaviour.

- Identify the "Big Five" personality dimensions.

- Summarize the personality concepts behind the Myers-Briggs Type Indicator.

- Explain how personality relates to Holland's model of vocational choice.

In 1971, a bunch of University of British Columbia students opened an outdoor gear store with a values-based business model that defied rational thinking at the time. They wanted to create an environmentally-friendly and democratic company where customers would pay a one-time $5 membership fee and have the right to vote for the company's board of directors.

Over 30 years later, these values have catapulted Mountain Equipment Co-op (MEC) into a successful retail chain with outlets across Canada and 1.8 million members worldwide. The Vancouver-based company designs over half of its products, then farms the manufacturing out to firms in Canada and overseas that satisfy MEC's standards for quality and social responsibility. MEC monitors each manufacturer's pay, employment standards, safety, and environmental practices because it wants to contract with suppliers who will "carry forward our principles and our values, both in building the product and in the way they run their business," explains Naomi Ozaki, head of MEC's production department.

MEC's "walk lightly upon the Earth" values are evident everywhere. Products use less harmful dyes and have minimal packaging. Catalogues are printed on recycled paper, and catalogue purchases to Eastern Canada are shipped by rail to minimize environmental impact. Even the company's stores have environmentalism in mind. For instance, MEC's new Toronto store (shown in the photo), consists of recycled wood beams and concrete floors, as well as a huge rooftop garden that adds both insulation and greenery to Toronto's downtown.

Mountain Equipment Co-op tries to align its organizational values with the personal values of its employees and client members. *Courtesy of Mountain Equipment Co-op*

"The continuous search for profit is not the fundamental point for the Co-op," says MEC chief executive Peter Robinson. "Our core purpose is to offer high-quality [outdoor gear] to our members at the lowest possible price, and we believe in trying to achieve the leading edge on issues that affect social and environmental responsibility."[1]

www.mec.ca

Values and social responsibility have become important trends in organizations, and this opening story about Mountain Equipment Co-op illustrates the importance of these concepts. After introducing the topic of individual behaviour, this chapter explores two of the most stable and deeply embedded influences on individual behaviour in the workplace: values and personality.

This chapter begins by presenting a basic model of individual behaviour and results (called the MARS model) and outlining the main types of behaviour in the workplace. The next section looks closely at values, including Schwartz's model of personal values, issues relating to values congruence, the dynamics of cross-cultural values, and the foundations of ethical values in the workplace. In the latter part of this chapter, we examine the relationship between personality and behaviour, the five-factor model of personality, the Myers-Briggs Type Indicator, and other personality characteristics that are often discussed in organizational behaviour research.

MARS MODEL OF INDIVIDUAL BEHAVIOUR AND RESULTS

What causes individual behaviour and performance in the workplace? This question has been the holy grail of much research in organizational behaviour, and is the focus of the next six chapters in this book. As you might imagine, OB scholars have looked at numerous variables drawn from several disciplines and theoretical perspective to understand the dynamics of individual behaviour. Over the next few pages, we begin the journey to understanding these dynamics by presenting a basic model of individual behaviour (called the MARS model) and outlining the main types of behaviour in organizational settings. Then we set out to examine the main individual difference topics underlying the MARS model, beginning with two of the most stable influences: values and personality.

The MARS model. illustrated in Exhibit 2.1, is a useful starting point to understanding the drivers of individual behaviour and results. The model highlights the

EXHIBIT 2.1   MARS model of individual behaviour and results

Individual characteristics

MARS model

Values

Personality

Perceptions

Emotions and attitudes

Stress

Motivation

Ability

Role perceptions

Situational factors

Behaviour and results

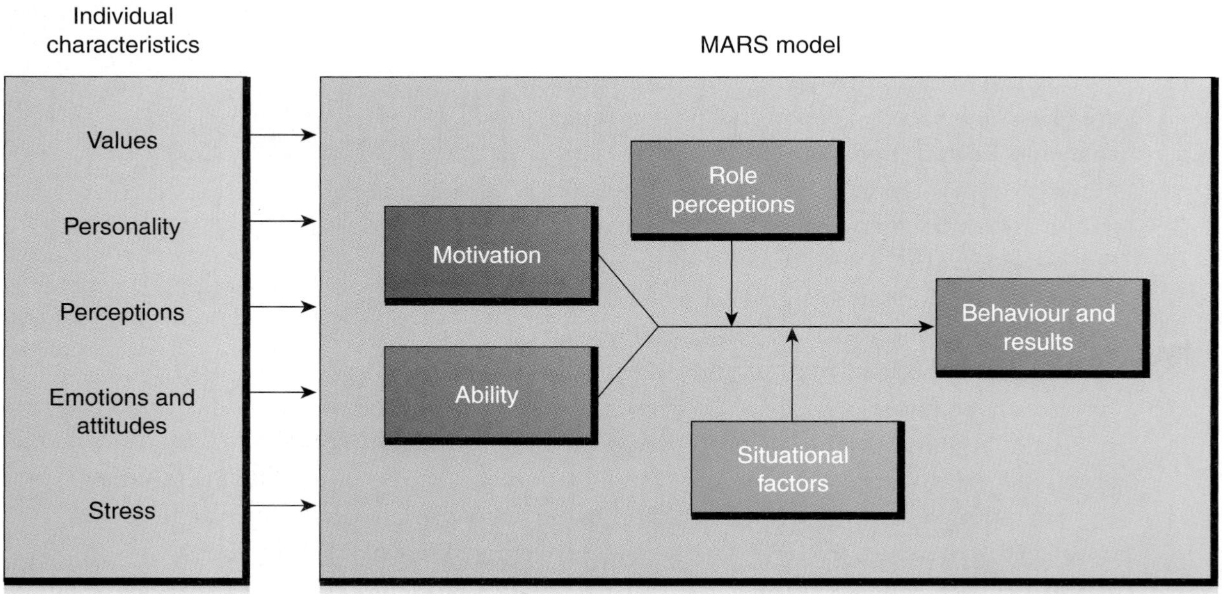

The MARS Model Helps Singapore Airlines Soar in Customer Service

Singapore Airlines (SIA) is obsessed with providing exceptional customer service. The island state's national airline has a limited domestic market, so it competes directly with other airlines for passengers. "Excellent service has been the foundation stone of our success," says a senior SIA executive.

SIA starts its customer service journey by carefully selecting job applicants. Flight attendants are specially screened for their customer-orientation values and other competencies. Prospective managers must pass a series of tests and two interviews. Overall, only one in 50 applicants receives a job offer. "Quality people are the company's most important resource, and the most rigorous quality control process we apply is for staff selection," says a former SIA chief executive.

Extensive training is another strategy SIA uses to achieve its high customer service standards. The airline spends 12 percent of payroll on training, compared with 2.3 percent in the average Singaporean firm. Cabin crew complete a five-month course where they learn every possible element of service, from social etiquette to emergency procedures. SIA's most recent training initiative, called Transforming Customer Service, encourages staff to go beyond the routine to serve customers uniquely. "The most important thing that you can do for customers is to make them feel cared for as individuals," explains an SIA executive.

Selection and training guide SIA skills and role perceptions, but the airline also pays attention to employee motivation through company-wide financial rewards and a customer-focused culture. As for support through situational factors, SIA has one of the world's most modern fleets, including being the premier

Singapore Airlines applies the MARS model of individual behaviour to provide exceptional customer service.
Courtesy of Singapore Airlines

customer for Boeing 777 jets. The result is an organization that consistently leads the global airline industry in customer service ratings and profitability.

Sources: R. Rosen, P. Digh, M. Singer, and C. Phillips, *Global Literacies* (New York: Simon & Schuster, 2000), pp. 247–248; L. McCauley, "How May I Help You?: Unit of One," *Fast Company*, March 2000, p. 93; J.B. Cunningham and P. Gerrard, "Characteristics of Well-Performing Organizations in Singapore," *Singapore Management Review*, 22 (January 2000), pp. 35–64; J. Pfeffer, "Seven Practices of Successful Organizations," *California Management Review*, 40 (1998) pp. 96–124; B. Davis, "Why Singapore Airlines is the World's Most Profitable Airline," *Asian Business Review*, December 1996, pp. 34–36.
www.singaporeair.com

four factors that directly influence an employee's voluntary behaviour and resulting performance motivation, ability, role perceptions, and situational factors. These four factors are represented by the acronym "MARS."

The MARS model shows that these four factors have a combined effect on individual performance. If any factor weakens, employee performance will decrease. For example, highly motivated salespeople (motivation) who understand their job duties (role perceptions) and have sufficient resources (situational factors) will not perform their jobs as well if they lack sufficient knowledge and other competencies (ability) to market the company's products or services. Companies that excel in customer service and other aspects of employee performance pay attention to all four factors. GLOBAL Connections 2.1 describes how paying attention to employee abilities, motivation, role perceptions, and situational factors has helped Singapore Airlines become one of the world's top-rated airlines.

Exhibit 2.1 also shows that the four factors in the MARS model are influenced by several other individual variables that we will discuss over the next few chapters. Personality and values are longer-lasting individual characteristics,[2] so we look at them later in this chapter. Emotions, attitudes, and stress are shorter-term characteristics, whereas individual perceptions and learning are usually somewhere in between. Each of these factors relate to the MARS model in various ways. For example, personal values affect an employee's motivation through emotions and tend to shape role perceptions through the perceptual process. Learning influences an employee's ability, role perceptions, and motivation, as we shall learn in Chapter 3. Before examining these individual characteristics, let's briefly introduce the four elements of the MARS model, followed by an overview of the different types of individual behaviour and results in the workplace.

Employee Motivation

motivation
The forces within a person that affect his or her direction, intensity, and persistence of voluntary behaviour.

Motivation represents the forces within a person that affect his or her direction, intensity, and persistence of voluntary behaviour.[3] *Direction* refers to the fact that motivation is goal-oriented, not random. People are motivated to arrive at work on time, finish a project a few hours early, or aim for many other targets. *Intensity* is the amount of effort allocated to the goal. For example, two employees might be motivated to finish their project a few hours early (direction), but only one of them puts forth enough effort (intensity) to achieve this goal. Finally, motivation involves varying levels of *persistence*, that is, continuing the effort for a certain amount of time. Employees sustain their effort until they reach their goal or give up beforehand. Chapter 5 looks more closely at the conceptual foundations of employee motivation, while Chapter 6 considers some applied performance practices.

Ability

When executives at Stream International chose London, Ontario for the site of its 900-person call centre, the decision criterion at the top of their list was workforce ability. "What we found in London, with the education system here, are strong skills in the technology field and customer-service skills to manage people over the phone," explained Kim McCann, Canadian vice-president of operations for the Boston-based company when the decision was announced.[4]

ability
Both the natural aptitudes and learned capabilities required to successfully complete a task.

Stream International and other organizations are keenly aware that employee abilities make a difference in behaviour and task performance. **Ability** includes both the natural aptitudes and learned capabilities required to successfully complete a task. *Aptitudes* are the natural talents that help employees learn specific tasks more quickly and perform them better. For example, you cannot learn finger dexterity; rather, some people have a more natural ability than others to manipulate small objects with their fingers. There are many different physical and mental aptitudes, and our ability to acquire skills is affected by these aptitudes. *Learned capabilities* refer to the skills and knowledge that you have actually acquired. This includes the physical and mental skills you possess as well as the knowledge you acquire and store for later use.

competencies
The abilities, values, personality traits, and other characteristics of people that lead to superior performance.

Employee competencies   Skills, knowledge, aptitudes, and other personal characteristics that lead to superior performance are typically bunched together into the concept of **competencies**.[5] Competencies are generic, meaning that they are relevant for a wide variety of jobs. For instance, the Royal Bank of Canada looks for people with a strong customer orientation, social skills, willingness to learn, and need for achievement. Competencies are often grouped into three categories—technical, analytic/conceptual, and interpersonal—and several jobs would require the same competencies within each of these three groups.[6]

Most large Canadian organizations spend a lot of money finding out the key competencies for superior work performance, but the competency perspective has a few problems.[7] One concern is disagreement whether other personal characteristics such as personal values and personality are also considered competencies. The definition of competencies also seems to vary considerably between North American and European scholars. Another concern is that some companies describe competencies so broadly that they are difficult to identify in reality. Last, most firms try to identify a single cluster of competencies, yet researchers increasingly believe that alternative combinations of competencies may be equally successful. In other words, companies hire people with one set of skills and abilities, when people with a different set of personal characteristics would be equally effective in the job.

Person-job matching There are three basic ways to match individuals and their competencies with job requirements.[8] One strategy is to select applicants whose existing competencies best fit the required tasks. This includes comparing each applicant's competencies with the requirements of the job or work unit. A second approach is to provide training so employees develop required skills and knowledge. This doesn't seem to be a popular strategy in Canadian firms, unfortunately. The Organization for Economic Co-operation and Development reports that only 31 percent of Canadian businesses invest in ongoing employee training, compared with 74 percent in Japan and 80 percent in Britain.[9]

The third person-job matching strategy is to redesign the job so employees are only given tasks within their capabilities. MediaOne did this after introducing e-mail as a form of customer communication at its call centres. Executives at the U.S. cable television systems company realized that call centre staff with strong verbal communication skills aren't necessarily good at written communication. "Many people who can carry on a good conversation on the phone could not put a cogent thought down in writing if they tried," says a MediaOne executive. The company identified employees with strong written

Joel McIsaac (shown in photo) and several other skilled tradespeople are dangling from ropes for a week to develop skills as remote access technicians (known as RATs) at Remote Access Technology Inc. in Dartmouth, Nova Scotia. Remote Access sends its RAT teams to oil rigs, refineries, power generating stations, pulp and paper plants, and other sites where people must gain access to extreme heights or depths. The company has plenty of business in Canada and the United States, but finding people with the right competencies is a challenge. In addition to being skilled electricians, painters, or blasters, RATs require exceptional strength, agility, and a comfort with heights to work in these demanding conditions.[10] Which of the three person-job matching strategies would be most effective for remote access technicians? *E. Wynne. Reprinted with permission from the Halifax Herald Limited*
www.rat.ca

communication skills and redesigned their tasks so they would be responsible for answering e-mail questions.[11]

Role Perceptions

Along with sufficient motivation and the right set of competencies, employees require accurate **role perceptions** to achieve desired behaviour and results.[12] Employees have accurate role perceptions when they understand the specific tasks assigned to them, the relative importance of those tasks, and the preferred behaviours to accomplish those tasks. Role perceptions clarify the preferred direction of effort. For example, an employee might not realize that it is part of his or her job to lock up at night. Another staff member might choose a method of closing accounts that is acceptable in other companies but not in his firm. In each case, employees have the necessary competencies but they lack clarity regarding their job duties or preferred behaviours for accomplishing those duties.

One Canadian survey reported that fewer than half of employees interviewed said their managers described their goals and assignments clearly. This is unfortunate because inaccurate role perceptions cause employees to exert effort toward the wrong goals, and ambiguous role perceptions lead to lower effort.[13] To improve role perceptions, companies need to ensure that employees understand their required responsibilities and to show how these goals relate to organizational goals. Employees also clarify their role perceptions as they work together over time and receive frequent and meaningful performance feedback.

Situational Factors

Job performance doesn't depend just on motivation, ability, and role perceptions; it is also affected by the situation in which the employee works. Situational factors include conditions beyond the employee's immediate control that constrain or facilitate his or her behaviour and performance.[14] Some situational characteristics—such as consumer preferences and economic conditions originate from the external environment and, consequently, are beyond the employee's and organization's control. However, other factors—such as time, people, budget, and physical work facilities—are controlled by others in the organization. Corporate leaders need to carefully arrange these conditions so employees can achieve their performance potential. Lockheed Martin's jet fighter production facility does this by asking employees to identify obstacles created by management that prevent them from performing effectively.[15]

Motivation, ability, role perceptions, and situational factors affect all conscious workplace behaviours and their performance outcomes. In the next section, we introduce the five categories of behaviour in organizational settings.

TYPES OF INDIVIDUAL BEHAVIOUR IN ORGANIZATIONS

People engage in many different types of behaviour in organizational settings. Exhibit 2.2 highlights the five types of behaviour discussed most often in the organizational behaviour literature: task performance, organizational citizenship, counterproductive work behaviours, joining and staying with the organization, and work attendance.

Task Performance

The most obvious category of individual behaviours in the workplace are those that support the organization's objectives. Goal-directed behaviours under the individual's control that support organizational objectives are known as **task performance**.[16] These include physical behaviours as well as mental processes leading to behaviours. For example, foreign exchange traders make decisions and take actions to exchange currencies. Employees in most jobs have more than one task performance dimension. Foreign exchange traders, for example, must be able to identify profitable trades, work cooperatively with clients and co-workers in a stressful environment, assist in training new staff, and work on special telecommunications equipment without error. Some are more important than others, but only by considering all performance dimensions can we fully evaluate an employee's contribution to the organization.

Exhibiting Organizational Citizenship

For the past 60 years, scholars have known that employees in successful organizations do more than perform their assigned tasks well. They also "walk the extra mile" by engaging in various organizational citizenship behaviours. **Organizational citizenship** refers to behaviours that extend beyond the employee's normal job duties.[17] Some of the most frequently mentioned organizational citizenship behaviours include helping others without selfish intent, gracefully tolerating occasional impositions, being involved in organizational activities, avoiding unnecessary conflicts, and performing tasks that extend beyond normal role requirements. Some scholars have tried to organize these behaviours, noting that some cause things to happen whereas others try to prevent bad things from happening. However, recent evidence suggests that organizational citizenship behaviours are highly related to each other and are influenced by the same characteristics.[18]

We will learn throughout this book about various reasons why some employees are good organizational citizens and others are not. Later in this chapter, for example, we learn that people with a conscientiousness personality trait have higher

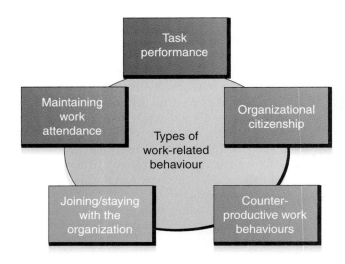

organizational citizenship. In Chapter 5, we learn that organizational citizenship is higher among employees who believe the company is treating them fairly.

Counterproductive Work Behaviours

counter-productive work behaviours (CWBs)

Potentially harmful voluntary behaviours enacted on an organization's property or employees.

According to a recent Canadian study, managers don't just rely on task performance and organizational citizenship behaviours to evaluate employees in performance reviews. Some also pay attention to the employee's **counterproductive work behaviours (CWBs)**.[19] CWBs are voluntary behaviours that potentially harm the organization by directly affecting its functioning or property, or by hurting employees in a way that will reduce their effectiveness.[20] Scholars have recently identified five categories of CWBs: abuse of others (e.g., insults and nasty comments), threats (threatening harm), work avoidance (e.g., tardiness), work sabotage (doing work incorrectly), overt acts (theft). Notice from this list that CWBs include both acts of commission (deliberately harming the organization and its employees), as well as acts of omission (ignoring or avoiding actions that would benefit colleagues and the organization).

We will learn about several influences on counterproductive behaviours throughout this book. For instance, stress is a known cause of workplace violence and aggression (Chapter 7). Perceptions of organizational injustice predict theft, sabotage, and failure to comply with rules and directives from management (Chapter 5). CWBs are also associated with personality traits such as Machiavellianism, which is described later in Chapter 12.

Joining and Staying with the Organization

Task performance, organizational citizenship and the lack of counterproductive work behaviours are obviously important for the organization's success. But what many corporate leaders are chanting about these days is the need to attract and keep talented employees. The simple fact is that if qualified people don't join and stay with the organization, none of the performance-related behaviours will occur. Little wonder, then, that attracting and retaining talented employees is one of the top five (from a list of 39) nonfinancial factors used by Wall Street's decision makers to pick stocks.[21]

The importance of hiring qualified people is obvious when we consider the consequences of staff shortages. From oil and gas workers to weather forecasters, Canada's corporate leaders face serious challenges finding enough qualified people to achieve the organization's goals.[22] An extreme example is the nursing shortage that is felt worldwide. For example, St. Paul's Hospital in Vancouver was recently forced to close the doors of its emergency room for the first time in a century because the hospital was full. The problem wasn't just too many patients; it was that the hospital has closed more than 60 beds over the previous year because it can't fill 135 vacancies for registered nurses. "We can't get the staff to cover the patient beds," explains Jeremy Etherington, vice-president of medical affairs for Providence Health Care, which includes St. Paul's, St. Vincent's, and Mount St. Joseph hospitals.[23]

Beyond avoiding staff shortages, effective organizations continuously search out the most qualified people. As consulting firm McKinsey & Co. highlighted in its report "The War for Talent," organizations need to acquire knowledge by hiring the best employees. A more recent McKinsey report concludes that successful

Karlene Coyne, Maja Morris, Brad Jones, Michelle Lalonde, and Belinda Marcos (from left to right in photo) have a lot to smile about. Hospitals across Canada are struggling to find enough nurses to keep beds open, which means that these University of Alberta nursing grads are in hot demand. "There's such an open market out there for nurses right now," says Belinda Marcos. "The job opportunities are endless." Some Canadian hospitals have closed their emergency rooms due to nurse shortages. Patients in The Pas are occasionally flown to larger centres because of nursing shortages in the northern town's hospital. These incidents drive home the fact that organizations need enough qualified staff to stay in business.[24] What actions would you recommend to a large hospital that faces this shortage of nurses? *Chris Schwarz, Edmonton Journal* **www.ualberta.ca**

companies win the talent war by applying many of the ideas in this book—building trust and loyalty, having visionary leaders, offering enriched jobs, and financially rewarding performance.[25]

Keeping talented employees   The war for talent includes keeping the best people, not just hiring them. As we learned in Chapter 1, much of an organization's intellectual capital is the knowledge employees carry around in their heads. Long-service employees, in particular, have valuable information about work processes, corporate values, and customer needs. Very little of this is documented anywhere. Thus, knowledge management involves keeping valuable employees with the organization. "At 5 p.m., 95% of our assets walk out the door," says an executive at SAS Institute, a leading statistics software firm. "We have to have an environment that makes them want to walk back in the door the next morning."[26]

The problem is that many employees don't return the next morning. Over half of the 500 executives recently surveyed worldwide identified retaining talented employees as the top people issue in the company. Even with recent layoffs in some industries, the emerging employability attitude toward work and continuing shortages in some industries (e.g., IT, nursing) will keep turnover rates near record levels.[27]

job satisfaction
A person's attitude regarding his or her job and work content.

Why do people quit their jobs? Traditionally, OB scholars have identified low job satisfaction as the main cause of turnover. **Job satisfaction** is a person's evaluation of his or her job and work context (see Chapter 4). Employees become dissatisfied with their employment relationship, which motivates them to search for and join another organization with better conditions. While this is still viewed as a useful perspective, scholars have recently suggested that specific "shock events" need to be considered.[28] These events, such as a boss's unfair decision or a conflict episode with a co-worker, create strong emotions that engage employees in the process of thinking about and searching for alternative employment.

Maintaining Work Attendance

Along with attracting and retaining employees, organizations needs everyone to show up for work at scheduled times. Statistics Canada reports that more than 700,000 employees—about 7 percent of the full-time workforce—are absent from work at some time during any given week due to illness or personal reasons. This rate is higher than most other OECD countries and is up from 5.5 percent less than a decade ago. Absenteeism costs around $10 billion each year to the Canadian economy, including work delays and shutdowns. For example, the Western Health Care Corporation, which operates hospitals in Cornerbrook and other Newfoundland communities, spends about 5 percent of its budget on sick leave. Absenteeism has been so high among Toronto firefighters that fire vehicles are pulled out of service up to 500 times per month due to staff shortages.[29]

What causes people to be absent from work? Situational factors—such as a snowstorm or car breakdown—certainly influence work attendance.[30] Ability is also a source of absenteeism, such as when employees are incapacitated by illness or injury. Motivation is a third factor. Employees who experience job dissatisfaction or work-related stress are more likely to be absent or late for work because taking time off is a way to temporarily withdraw from stressful or unsatisfying conditions. Absenteeism is also higher in organizations with generous sick leave because this benefit limits the negative financial impact of taking time away from work.[31]

Several individual factors shown earlier with the MARS model influence the direct causes of these five types of workplace behaviour. The remainder of this chapter looks closely at two of the most stable factors: values and personality.

VALUES IN THE WORKPLACE

values
Stable, long-lasting beliefs that guide a person's preferences for outcomes or courses of action in a variety of situations.

The opening story described how Mountain Equipment Co-op has adopted a values-based business model, in which organizational decisions and actions are consciously directed by a clear set of core values. **Values** are stable, evaluative beliefs that guide our preferences for outcomes or courses of action in a variety of situations.[32] They are perceptions about what is good or bad, right or wrong. Values don't just represent what we want; they state what we "ought" to do—socially desirable ways to achieve our needs. They influence our choice of goals and the means for achieving those goals. Indeed, without values to guide us, it would be difficult to make any decisions.

People arrange values into a hierarchy of preferences, called a **value system**. Some individuals value new challenges more than they value conformity. Others value generosity more than frugality. Each person's unique value system is developed and reinforced through socialization from parents, religious institutions,

value system
An individual's hierarchical arrangement of beliefs.

friends, personal experiences, and (as we shall learn later in this chapter) the society in which we live. As such, a person's hierarchy of values is stable and long lasting. For example, one study found that the value systems of a sample of adolescents were remarkably similar twenty years later when they were adults.[33]

In Chapter 1, we learned that values research is gaining prominence in organizational behaviour. Organizations are under increasing pressure to apply ethical values in their business practices. Values are also replacing direct supervision as a more acceptable way to guide employee behaviour. Third, globalization has raised our awareness of and sensitivity to differences in values across cultures. Beyond these current issues, values are important because they influence so much of what we experience in organizational settings, such as perceptions, decision making, leadership behaviour, and organizational citizenship.[34]

Types of Values

Values come in many shapes and forms, and scholars have devoted considerable attention to organizing them into coherent groups. The model in Exhibit 2.3, developed and tested by social psychologist Shalom Schwartz, has received considerable research support across more than 40 countries.[35] Schwartz reduced

EXHIBIT 2.3   Schwartz's values circumplex

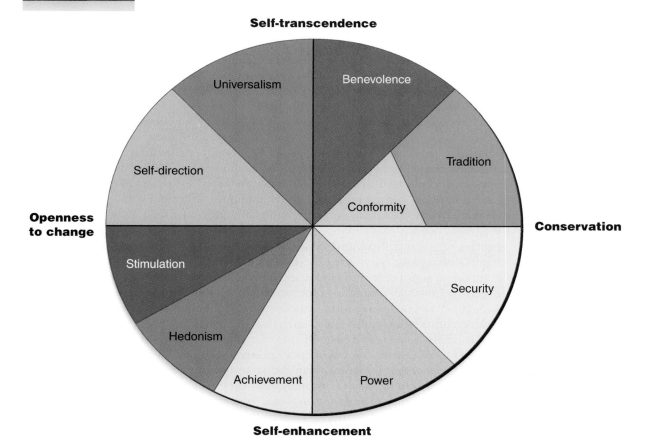

dozens of personal values into these 10 broader domains of values, and has further organized these domains into four clusters structured around two higher-order bipolar dimensions.

One dimension in Schwartz's model has openness to change at one extreme and conservation at the other extreme. Openness to change represents the extent to which a person is motivated to pursue innovative ways; it corresponds to the values of self-direction (independent thought and action) and stimulation (excitement and challenge). Conservation, the opposite end of this dimension, is the extent to which a person is motivated to preserve the status quo. Conservation is associated with the values of conformity (adherence to social norms and expectations), security (safety and stability), and tradition (moderation and preservation of the status quo).

The other bipolar dimension in Schwartz's model ranges from self-enhancement to self-transcendence. Self-enhancement, which refers to how much a person is motivated by self-interest, is related to the values of achievement (pursuit of personal success) and power (dominance over others). Self-transcendence, the other extreme of this dimension, refers to the motivation to promote the welfare of others and nature and relates to the values of benevolence (concern for others in one's life) and universalism (concern for the welfare of all people and nature).

The dimensions of values identified in Schwartz's model are primarily related to individual values, but values also apply to organizations, professions, societies, and other entities. Furthermore, we need to distinguish *espoused values* from *enacted values*. Espoused values are the values that we want others to believe we abide by. Individuals, organizations, professions, or even societies might say they value environmentalism, creativity, and politeness, whether or not they really do value these things in practice. Values are socially desirable, so people create a positive public image by claiming to believe in values that others expect them to embrace. Enacted values, on the other hand, are the values-in-use, the values we actually rely on to guide our decisions and actions.[36]

Values Congruence

A few years ago, Copenhagen Business School professor Peter Pruzan held a seminar on workplace values with executives at a large European-based multinational manufacturing company. Working in teams, the executives developed a list of their five most important personal values. The personal values list included honesty, love, beauty, peace of mind, and happiness (most of which fall under the categories of universalism and benevolence in Exhibit 2.3). In the afternoon, the teams developed a list of the enacted (not espoused) values of their company. The company values list included success, efficiency, power, competitiveness, and productivity (most of which are represented by achievement and power in Exhibit 2.3). In other words, the organization's values were almost completely opposite to the executives' personal values. After an embarrassing silence, the CEO briefly spoke, announcing that he would consider resigning. He said that he had actively constructed a monster, a corporate Frankenstein![37]

The CEO of the European firm didn't resign, but he and his executive team learned an important lesson, namely, that they needed to pay much more attention to the congruence of personal and organizational values. **Values congruence** refers to situations where two or more entities have similar value systems. In the example of the European manufacturer, the organization's value system was

values congruence
A situation wherein two or more entities have similar value systems.

Along with searching for oil and gas deposits, Woodside Petroleum has been searching its soul for a set of corporate values more congruent with the personal values of its employees. A few years ago a survey revealed that Woodside's employees were unhappy with some of the firm's apparent values (such as caution, bureaucracy, and control). To help instill a more compatible organizational value system, Woodside, Australia's largest energy producer, hired consultants McKinsey & Company to apply a performance culture model that emphasizes values congruence. According to McKinsey's own studies, companies that align the personal values of staff with those of the business grow up to 22% faster than comparable companies. "In the simplest terms, it is about enabling people to be themselves at work," says a consultant who worked with Woodside on the transformation.[39] What are the consequences of aligning organizational values with the personal values of employees?
Courtesy of Woodside Energy
www.woodside.com.au

incongruent with the value systems of its employees. Unfortunately, person-organization values incongruence seems to be common. One study reported that 76 percent of the managers surveyed believe that a conflict exists between their own ethical beliefs and their company's values. Another study found that managers saw significant differences between their personal values and organizational practices.[38]

Incongruence between the value systems of employees and their organization has a number of consequences. Values are guideposts, so employees whose values differ significantly from the organization's values might make decisions incompatible with the organization's goals. Incongruence also leads to lower job satisfaction and organizational commitment, as well as higher stress and turnover among employees.[40] "We've found that the higher the disconnect between one's values and those of the organization, the higher the potential for burnout," says Jayne Hayden, manager of the Career Resource Centre at the University of Waterloo.[41]

Does this mean that the most successful organizations perfectly align employee values with the organization's values? Not at all! While a comfortable degree of values congruence is necessary for the reasons noted above, organizations also benefit from some level of values *incongruence*. As we will learn in Chapter 10, employees with diverse values offer different perspectives to issues, which may lead to better decision making. The conflict resulting from values incongruence among employees can sharpen everyone's thinking about the definition of the problem and the rationale for preferred choices. Moreover, too much congruence can create a "corporate cult" that potentially undermines creativity, organizational flexibility, and business ethics (see Chapter 16).[42]

Values congruence applies to more than employees and companies within one country. It also relates to the compatibility of the organization's values with the prevailing values of the society in which it conducts business.[43] This fact is particularly important as information technology and globalization increase the frequency of cross-cultural interaction. For example, an organization from one society that tries to impose its value system on employees located in another culture may have difficulty keeping those employees and maintaining favourable relations with their communities. SC Johnson was aware of this need for values congruence for its Australian business. The American household products firm is "a family company with family values." But Australians generally like to separate their work from their personal lives, so SC Johnson tweaked its values somewhat. "You can't sell that family company idea in Australia, so we position it as family values with work/life balance," explains an SC Johnson executive.[44] Let's look more closely at cross-cultural values.

VALUES ACROSS CULTURES

Anyone who has worked long enough in other countries will know that values differ across cultures. Some cultures value group decisions, whereas others think a leader should take charge. Meetings in Germany usually start on time, whereas they might be half an hour late in Brazil without much concern. We need to understand differences in cultural values to avoid unnecessary conflicts and subtle tensions between people from different countries.

Individualism and Collectivism

individualism
The extent to which a person values independence and personal uniqueness.

No cross-cultural values have received more attention—or controversy and misunderstanding—than individualism and collectivism. **Individualism** is the extent to which we value independence and personal uniqueness. Highly individualist people value personal freedom, self-sufficiency, control over their own lives, and being appreciated for the unique qualities that distinguish them from others. This value relates most closely to the self-direction dimension in Exhibit 2.3. **Collectivism** is the extent to which we value our duty to groups to which we belong, and to group harmony. Highly collectivist people define themselves by their group membership and value harmonious relationships within those groups.[45] Collectivism is located within the conservation range of values (security, tradition, conformity) in Exhibit 2.3.

collectivism
The extent to which people value duty to groups to which they belong, and to group harmony.

You might think from these definitions that individualism and collectivism are opposites. Until recently, many scholars thought so, too, but the two concepts are actually unrelated, according to research studies.[46] Some people and cultures value both high individualism and high collectivism, for example.

How individualistic and collectivistic are Canadians? Exhibit 2.4 shows that Canadians with European heritage are relatively more individualistic than people in most other countries. Only people in some South American countries (such as Chile and Peru) are more individualistic. Exhibit 2.4 also shows that European Canadians are relatively low in collectivism, whereas people in Italy, Taiwan, Peru, Zimbabwe, and most other countries are higher in collectivism.

One notable observation in Exhibit 2.4 is that people in Japan are less collectivist than most cultures. This is in stark contrast to statements in many cross-cultural books that Japan is one of the most collectivist countries on the planet! The problem was that a major study over 20 years ago identified Japan as collectivist, but measured collectivism in a way that bears little resemblance to how the concept is usually defined.[47] Subsequent studies have reported that Japan is relatively low on the collectivist scale (as Exhibit 2.4 reveals), but this truth has been slow to take hold.

Other Cross-Cultural Values

power distance
The extent to which people accept unequal distribution of power in a society.

Organizational scholars have studied many other values in cross-cultural research, but four of them predominate: power distance, uncertainty avoidance, achievement–nurturing orientation, and long/short-term orientation.[48]

■   *Power distance*—**Power distance** is the extent to which people accept unequal distribution of power in a society. Those with high power distance accept and

EXHIBIT 2.4

Individualism and collectivism in selected countries

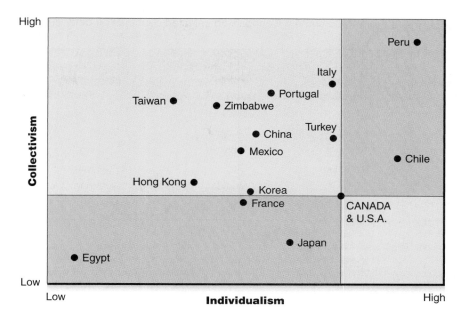

Source: Based on information in D. Oyserman, H. M. Coon, and M. Kemmelmeier, "Rethinking Individualism and Collectivism: Evaluation of Theoretical Assumptions and Meta-Analyses," *Psychological Bulletin*, 128 (2002), pp. 3–72. The countries shown here represent only a sample of those in Oyserman's meta-analysis.

NOTE: Canada and the United States were combined by Oyserman because other recent research has found the two countries are approximately the same in individualism and collectivism. The ratings for Canada and the United States refer only to people with European heritage in those countries.

value unequal power, whereas those with low power distance expect relatively equal power sharing. In high power distance cultures, employees are comfortable receiving commands from their superiors, and conflicts are resolved through formal rules and authority. In contrast, participative management is preferred in low power distance cultures, and conflicts are resolved more through personal networks and coalitions.[49]

- *Uncertainty avoidance*—**Uncertainty avoidance** is the degree to which people tolerate ambiguity (low uncertainty avoidance) or feel threatened by ambiguity and uncertainty (high uncertainty avoidance). Employees with high uncertainty avoidance value structured situations where rules of conduct and decision making are clearly documented. They usually prefer direct rather than indirect or ambiguous communications.

- *Achievement versus nurturing orientation*—Achievement-oriented cultures value assertiveness, competitiveness, and materialism.[50] They appreciate people who are tough and favour acquiring money and material goods. In contrast, people in nurturing-oriented cultures emphasize relationships and the well-being of others. They focus on human interaction and caring rather than competition and personal success.

- *Long- versus short-term orientation*—People in different cultures also differ in their long- or short-term orientation. Those with a long-term orientation anchor their thoughts more in the future than in the past and present. They value thrift, savings, and persistence, whereas those with a short-term orientation place more emphasis on the past and present, such as respect for tradition and fulfilling social obligations.

uncertainty avoidance

The degree to which people tolerate ambiguity or feel threatened by ambiguity and uncertainty.

EXHIBIT 2.5	Comparing Canada with selected countries on other cultural values

Country	Power distance	Uncertainty avoidance	Achievement vs. nurturing orientation	Long- vs. short-term orientation
Canada	Low	Low	Achievement	Short-term
China	High	Medium	Medium	Long-term
France	High	High	Medium	Short-term
Japan	Medium	High	Achievement	Long-term
Netherlands	Low	Medium	Nurturing	Medium
Russia	High	High	Nurturing	Short-term

Sources: Based on G. Hofstede, "Cultural Constraints in Management Theories," *Academy of Management Executive*, 7 (1993), pp. 81–94; G. Hofstede, "The Cultural Relativity of Organizational Practices and Theories," *Journal of International Business Studies*, 14 (Fall 1983), pp. 75–89. For the "Achievement vs. Nurturing Orientation" and "Long vs. Short Term Orientation" scales, "medium" indicates that the country is near the middle of the two poles of the dimension. Long-short term orientation for Canada is inferred from the United States data.

Exhibit 2.5 provides the best estimate of how Canadians compare to some other cultures on these four values. In general, Canadians have a low power distance and short-term orientation. They are moderately achievement-oriented and have somewhat low uncertainty avoidance (i.e. they can tolerate ambiguity). This information provides the best comparison available of these values across cultures, but it is far from ideal. The information for the first three scales was collected from IBM employees worldwide more than a quarter century ago, and the fourth scale is based on a student sample. However, it is possible that neither IBM employees nor students represent the general population.[51]

One concern with all cross-cultural values research is the assumption that everyone in a society has similar cultural values. This may be true in a few countries, but not in culturally diverse societies such as Canada. One recent social survey divided Canadians into 13 fairly distinct groups in terms of their social values. Other research has found a wide range of long/short-term orientation within the United States, Australia, and Chile. By attributing certain values to an entire society, we are engaging in a form of stereotyping that limits our ability to understand the more complex reality of that society.[52]

Canadian Values

Wal-Mart has become Canada's largest retailer since entering this country a decade ago, but the American company stumbled over Canada's cultural values along the way. The effusive American-style greeters seem a little too phoney to Canadians, and the Wal-Mart cheer that employees must repeat every morning is considered a bit too cult-like. Selling guns in department stores wasn't well received in Canada, either.[53] Wal-Mart has discovered that Canadian values are different from their American cousins in subtle, yet important ways. The patriotic "I am Canadian" beer commercials shout out some of these differences, but surveys have more precisely identified the distinctiveness of Canadian values.

One noticeable difference, according to Toronto social values pollster Environics Research, is that Canadians are less deferent than Americans to patriarchal and institutional authority. Consider the following observation: Twenty years ago, 42 percent of Canadians agreed or strongly agreed with the statement: "The father of the family must be the master in his own house." Agreement with this statement dropped to 26 percent by 1992 and to just 20 percent today. In contrast, 48 percent of Americans agree or strongly agree with this statement today, a slight *increase* from 42 percent a decade ago. In other words, while Canadians have distanced themselves from traditional patriarchal authority, Americans are embracing it more than in the recent past![54]

The Canadian preference for egalitarianism rather than patriarchal authority is consistent with other surveys that identify Canadians as more liberal than their American counterparts. These surveys also indicate that Canadians put a higher value on collective rights, the role of government in society, diversity, and tolerance.[55] We celebrate multiculturalism and proudly support a cultural mosaic rather than a homogeneous melting pot. In contrast, social values surveys indicate that Americans are more conservative and ideological. They are also somewhat more moralistic, individualistic, self-reliant, and materialistic.[56] Americans have supported cultural diversity in recent years, but probably not to the same extent as in Canada. For example, former Prime Minister Joe Clark recently served as marshal of Calgary's Gay Pride parade. It will probably be a while before a current or former American president accepts a similar role.

Francophone values   As was mentioned earlier, several subcultures operate in diverse countries such as Canada. One of the longest known sources of cultural diversity in this country has been the so-called "two solitudes" between English and French Canadians.[57] Historically, French Canadians (Francophones) have been identified as less materialistic and more collectivist, traditional, and respectful of authority (higher power distance) than English Canadians (Anglophones). Studies in the 1970s also indicated that Francophones were more achievement-oriented than Anglophones.[58]

The problem with these earlier observations is that they probably don't represent Francophone or Anglophone values today. Only a few studies have examined differences in cultural values between these two groups in recent years, but the limited evidence suggests that the two cultures may have converged on some key values. One study reported that Anglophones and Francophones are more similar to each other than to Americans on values relating to happiness. Another study discovered that Anglophone and Francophone Canadian public sector male managers had similar degrees of individualism and collectivism.[59]

French and English Canadians still differ on some values, however. Whereas Francophones were once more traditional, they are now more liberal and permissive than Anglophones. For example, the earlier-mentioned Environics survey found that Quebecois had the lowest scores among Canadians on respect for patriarchal authority (i.e. father as the master of the house). At least two studies recorded that support for gender equality is higher among Francophones than Anglophones. Francophones also hold less traditional values toward marriage, sexual activity, and nonmarried parenthood. As one respected Canadian scholar wrote several years ago, "Quebec, once the most conservative part of Canada, has become the most liberal on social issues."[60]

First Nations values in Canada   First Nations people in Canada also have a unique set of cultural values, making them just as distinct from European

Walk into the Legislative Assembly of Nunavut, Canada's newest territory, and you will soon realize that Inuit culture is quite different from the Western values embedded in Robert's Rules of Order. Politicians aren't grouped into political parties sitting across from each other. Indeed, there are no political parties, just 19 members seated in a circle. This lack of partisanship is representative of Inuit culture. "The one thing that reflects the Inuit culture the most is the consensus system of government," explains John Amagoalik, who chaired the Nunavut Implementation Commission. Low power distance and high collectivism are also found in many other First Nations cultures in Canada, as well as in organizations founded by people with First Nations heritage.[62] By adopting consensus values, how would Inuit organizations operate differently from other organizations in Canada? *CP/Kevin Frayer*
www.assembly.nu.ca

Canadians as Canadians are from Americans. Research suggests that organizations with First Nations founders and leaders tend to have a strong collectivist value, low power distance, low uncertainty avoidance, and a relatively nurturing value orientation.[61] The long-term orientation value has not yet been explored.

The strong collectivist orientation is based on traditional First Nations ideals regarding survival of the small group. Low power distance is apparent by the preference for consensus-oriented decision making and selection of people based on their expertise rather than status (except elders). People in First Nations organizations seem to have a lower uncertainty avoidance value than those in non-First Nations Canadian companies, as indicated by fewer rules and procedures in First Nations companies and the preference for internalized beliefs about respect, sharing, and wholeness to guide employee behaviour. Finally, First Nations firms adopt a relatively nurturing value orientation: they emphasize the well-being of co-workers, maintain positive relationships and place decidedly less emphasis on material gain and goal accomplishment compared with non-First Nations organizations.

The low power distance and high collectivist value orientation of First Nations organizations was apparent a few years ago when the people of the Meadow Lake

First Nations in Northwest Saskatchewan demanded that political and corporate leaders in the area more fully apply traditional values about the land and its use in forestry activities, and adopt a more consensus-based approach to decision-making. These values are now entrenched in the Meadow Lake Tribal Council's 20-year development plan. More recently, the Westbank First Nation band faced the possibility that its employees would join a labour union. Band leaders and elders have expressed concern that a labour union violates the band's ancient culture and emphasis on working in harmony.[63]

In summary, Canadians hold value systems that to some extent vary with each other and with people from other societies. These values guide our decisions and actions, and distinguish us from people in other cultures. Values are also the foundation of ethical behaviour. Chapter 1 described how business ethics has gained prominence as corporate wrongdoing has shaken the confidence of investors and customers alike in the marketplace. In the next section, we look more closely at ethical values and behaviour in the workplace.

ETHICAL VALUES AND BEHAVIOUR

ethics

The study of moral principles or values that determine whether actions are right or wrong and outcomes are good or bad.

Our discussion of values would be incomplete without examining the dynamics of ethics in the workplace. **Ethics** refers to the study of moral principles or values that determine whether actions are right or wrong and outcomes are good or bad. We rely on our ethical values to determine "the right thing to do." Employees and customers value companies and their leaders with ethical values. Indeed, surveys indicate that an employer's integrity is just as important to most employees as their income.[64]

Unfortunately, it isn't easy to determine the right thing to do. Consider the dilemma that Talisman Energy has faced over the past few years by investing in the Sudan. As Connections 2.2 describes, executives at the Calgary-based oil company argue that the right thing to do is to maintain their investment in the Sudan because they believe this action benefits both shareholders and the people of Sudan. Critics, on the other hand, argue that Talisman is supporting a regime that undermines human rights and shows a lack of care toward those who are vulnerable in these circumstances.

Four Ethical Principles

To better understand the ethical dilemmas facing Talisman and other organizations, we need to consider the various ethical principles that people rely on to make decisions. Philosophers and other scholars have identified several ethical principles incorporating different values and logical foundations, but most of these can be condensed to four basic groups—utilitarianism, individual rights, distributive justice, and care.[65] You might prefer one over the others based on your personal values. However, all four principles should be actively considered to put important ethical issues to the test.

utilitarianism

The moral principle stating that decision makers should seek the greatest good for the greatest number of people when choosing among alternatives.

■ *Utilitarianism*—**Utilitarianism** advises us to seek the greatest good for the greatest number of people. In other words, we should choose the option providing the highest degree of satisfaction to those affected. This is sometimes known as a consequential principle because it focuses on the consequences of our actions, not on how we achieve those consequences. Talisman executives

Talisman Energy Walks an Ethically-Fine Line

In the late 1990s, Talisman Energy Inc., Canada's second largest petroleum producer, was looking for new sources of oil investment as its reserves dwindled in western Canada. One appealing option was to purchase an oil company in the Sudan, an African country where production costs were low and reserves had solid long-term prospects. "From the perspective of reserves, operating costs and pricing, Sudan looked very attractive," says Brian Prokop, an investment analyst who worked at Talisman at the time. Sudan was in a civil war and there was global concern about serious human rights violations, but the economics of buying into Sudanese oil development was too good for Talisman to pass up.

Less than one week after Talisman invested in the Sudan, the U.S. government imposed sanctions against the Sudanese government, claiming that it sponsored terrorism, mostly from oil profits. This left Talisman's executives with a huge ethical dilemma: Should they pull out of Sudan, thereby losing a large investment and future earnings, or should they continue to invest in that country?

Talisman's decision makers chose the latter route, but also began working with people in that war-torn country to improve their way of life. For example, the company poured more than $10 million into the construction of Sudanese schools and clinics. Meanwhile, the Canadian government put pressure on Talisman to sign a code of ethical conduct developed by the Canadian oil industry. Criticism against Talisman continued to mount in spite of the Canadian firm's attempts to offset the moral damage with goodwill activities. Two American lawyers filed a civil lawsuit alleging that Talisman had participated in human rights abuses in Sudan.

Talisman defended its Sudanese investment for nearly four years, saying that it was aiding development in one of the world's poorest countries. Yet, when the company recently sold its stake in the venture, Talisman's CEO acknowledged that the ethical dilemma hurt the Calgary company's share price.

Sources: J. Wells, "Talisman Left Few Benefits, Report Says," *Toronto Star*, November 16, 2002, p. B10. D. Yedlin, "Bottom-Line Focus Doesn't Always Pay," *Calgary Herald*, June 14, 2002; M. Drohan, "Corporations Add Values," *Globe and Mail*, February 24, 2000; C. Harrington, "Talisman Says Peacemaking is the Business of Governments, Not Business," *Vancouver Sun*, February 18, 2000.
www.talisman-energy.com

---

seem to rely on utilitarianism because they mainly argue that the benefits of investing in Sudan outweigh the costs to shareholders, Sudanese citizens, and others. One problem with utilitarianism is that it is almost impossible to evaluate the benefits or costs of many decisions, particularly when many stakeholders have wide-ranging needs and values. Another problem is that utilitarianism judges morality by the results, not the means to attaining those results.

individual rights principle

The moral principle stating that every person is entitled to legal and human rights.

- *Individual rights*—The **individual rights principle** reflects the belief that everyone has entitlements that let them act in a certain way. Some of the most widely cited rights are freedom of movement, physical security, freedom of speech, fair trial, and freedom from torture.[66] The individual rights principle includes more than legal rights; it also includes human rights that everyone is granted as a moral norm of society. For example, the right to education and knowledge isn't a legal requirement everywhere, but most of us believe that it is a human right. One problem with individual rights is that certain individual rights may conflict with others. Shareholders' rights to be informed about corporate activities may ultimately conflict with an executive's right to privacy, for example.

distributive justice principle

The moral principle stating that people who are similar should be rewarded similarly, and those dissimilar should be rewarded differently.

- *Distributive justice*—The **distributive justice principle** suggests that people who are similar in relevant ways should receive similar benefits and burdens and those who are dissimilar should receive different benefits and burdens in proportion to their dissimilarity. For example, we expect two employees who contribute equally in their work should receive similar rewards, and that those who make a lesser contribution should receive less. A variation of this principle says that inequalities are acceptable where they benefit the least well off in society. Thus, employees in risky jobs should be paid more if this benefits others who are less well off. One problem with the distributive justice principle is that it is difficult to agree on who is "similar" and what factors are "relevant." Most of us agree that race and gender should not be relevant when distributing paycheques. But should rewards be determined purely by an employee's performance, or should effort, seniority, and other factors also be taken into account?

care principle
The moral principle stating that we should benefit those with whom we have special relationships.

■ *Care*—The **care principle** states that the morally correct action is one that expresses care in protecting the special relationships that individuals have with each other. Whereas distributive justice emphasizes impartiality, the ethic of care principle emphasizes partiality—favouring those with whom we have special relationships. The idea behind the ethic of care is that our self-perception is based on relationships with others. Consequently, our self-esteem and worth is influenced by how well we support and nurture those relationships.[67] The challenge of the care principle is that it can degenerate into unjust favouritism, such as the "old boys" network. This, in effect, conflicts with both distributive justice and utilitarianism.

Moral Intensity, Ethical Sensitivity, and Situational Influences

Along with ethical principles and their underlying values, we need to consider three other factors that influence ethical conduct in the workplace: the moral intensity of the issue, the individual's ethical sensitivity, and situational factors.

moral intensity
The degree to which an issue demands the application of ethical principles.

Moral intensity is the degree to which an issue demands the application of ethical principles. The higher the moral intensity, the more ethical principles should provide guidance to resolve the issue. Stealing from your employer is usually considered high on moral intensity, whereas using a company pen for personal use is much lower on the scale. Several factors influence the moral intensity of an issue, such as the extent that the issue clearly produces good or bad consequences, others in the society think it is good or evil, the issue quickly affects people, the decision maker feels close to the issue, and the person is able to influence the issue.[68]

ethical sensitivity
A personal characteristic that enables people to recognize the presence and determine the relative importance of an ethical issue.

Even if an issue has high moral intensity, some employees might not recognize its ethical importance because they have low ethical sensitivity. **Ethical sensitivity** is a personal characteristic that enables people to recognize the presence and determine the relative importance of an ethical issue.[69] Ethically sensitive people are not necessarily more ethical. Rather, they are more likely to recognize whether an issue requires ethical consideration, and can more accurately estimate the moral intensity of the issue. Ethically sensitive people tend to have higher empathy. They also have more information about the specific situation. For example, accountants would be more ethically sensitive regarding accounting procedures than someone who has not received training in this profession.

The third important factor explaining why good people do bad things is the situation in which the unethical conduct occurs. A few recent surveys have reported that employees regularly experience corporate pressure that leads to selling beyond customers' needs, lying to the client, or making unrealistic promises. Other surveys have found that most employees believe they experience so much pressure it compromises their ethical conduct. For instance, nearly two-thirds of the managers in one academic study stated that pressure from top management causes people further down the hierarchy to compromise their beliefs, whereas 90 percent of top management disagreed with this statement.[70] The point here is not to justify unethical conduct, but to recognize the situational factors that influence wrongdoing so that organizations can correct these problems in the future.

Supporting Ethical Behaviour

Most large and medium-size organizations in Canada apply one or more strategies to improve ethical conduct. According to one survey, 85 percent of Canadian firms have a written ethical code of conduct. The code of ethics at McNeil Consumer Healthcare in Guelph, Ontario, is 50 pages long. Each year, the document is circulated and managers must sign it. Job applicants at UPS Canada receive a copy of the UPS Business Code of Conduct before they decide to join. "We want our employees to know from day one that we are expecting them to preserve our legacy of honesty, integrity, and ethical behaviour," says a UPS Canada executive.[71]

Ethical codes establish the organization's ethical standards and signal to employees that the company takes ethical conduct seriously, but most scholars agree that companies need more active strategies to improve ethical conduct.[72] Unfortunately, surveys suggest that Canadian companies generally have implemented relatively few ethics strategies. Nortel Networks holds a two-hour business ethics awareness presentation and has a 1-800 number for employees to report suspected ethics abuses or to seek advice on ethics issues. Other firms have in-depth ethics training programs that use case studies where employees apply and, it is hoped, internalize ethical values. A few companies also have ethics advisors or committees to provide guidance on specific ethical issues, and audit their ethics initiatives to ensure they are working.[73]

Leaders have an equally strong influence on the moral fibre of an organization.[74] As we will learn in Chapter 14, effective leaders have integrity in the eyes of their followers. By the same token, leaders must demonstrate ethical integrity to be effective. They do this by focusing on the organization's shared vision in a culture of openness and dialogue. By acting with the highest standards of moral conduct, leaders not only gain support and trust from followers, they role-model the ethical standards that employees are more likely to follow.

PERSONALITY IN ORGANIZATIONS

Ethical, cross-cultural, and other values are relatively stable characteristics, so they are an important influence on individual behaviour. Another individual characteristic with long-term stability is personality. In fact, there is considerable evidence that values and personality traits are interrelated and influence each other.[75] The final section of this chapter examines how the key features of personality relate to workplace behaviour.

personality
The relatively stable pattern of behaviours and consistent internal states that explain a person's behavioural tendencies.

Personality refers to the relatively stable pattern of behaviours and consistent internal states that explain a person's behavioural tendencies.[76] Personality has both internal and external elements. External traits are the observable behaviours that we rely on to identify someone's personality. For example, we can see that a person is extroverted by the way he or she interacts with other people. The internal states reflect the thoughts, values, and genetic characteristics that we infer from the observable behaviours.

We say that personality explains behavioural tendencies because people do not behave completely consistently with their personality profile in every situation. In particular, personality traits are less evident in situations where social norms, reward systems, and other conditions constrain our behaviour.[77] For example, talkative people remain relatively quiet in a library where "no talking" rules are explicit and strictly enforced.

The Origins of Personality

Over the next few pages, we will look at personality traits and trait models that add to our knowledge of individual behaviour in organizations. However, behind these trait categories is a battle among psychologists regarding the origins of personality.[78] Some scholars staunchly believe that personality is based purely on genetic code and, consequently, does not change through socialization (upbringing) or traumatic events in our lives. They point to evidence that personality traits are connected to specific parts of the brain and chemical activities in the body. Evolutionary psychologists have taken this perspective a step further by explaining how personality has been shaped by generations of social evolution. Other psychologists, without denying some of the effects of genetics, argue that the environment in which we live influences our personality.[79]

Personality and Organizational Behaviour

At one time, scholars often explained employee behaviour in terms of personality traits, and companies regularly administered personality tests to job applicants. This changed in the 1960s when researchers reported that the relationship between personality and job performance is actually very weak.[80] They cited problems with measuring personality traits and explained that the connection between personality and performance exists only under very narrowly defined conditions. Companies stopped using personality tests due to concerns that these tests might unfairly discriminate against visible minorities and other identifiable groups.

Over the past decade, personality has regained some of its credibility in organizational settings.[81] Recent studies report that specific personality traits predict several work-related behaviours, stress reactions, and emotions fairly well under certain conditions. Scholars have reintroduced the idea that effective leaders have identifiable traits and that personality explains some of a person's positive attitudes and life happiness. Personality traits seem to help people find the jobs that best suit their needs.[82] Personality is still considered a relatively poor selection test, but this hasn't stopped many companies from using personality tests and assessments to hire executives. For instance, Carly Fiorini had to complete a two-hour, 900-question personality test as part of the process to select her as Hewlett-Packard's new chief executive.[83] With these caveats in mind, let's look at the main personality traits and dimensions currently studied in organizational settings.

"Big Five" Personality Dimensions

Since Plato, scholars have been trying to develop lists of personality traits. About 100 years ago, a few personality experts tried to catalogue and condense the many personality traits that had been described over the years. They found thousands of words in *Roget's Thesaurus* and *Webster's Dictionary* that described personality traits. They aggregated these words into 171 clusters, then further shrunk them down to five abstract personality dimensions. Using more sophisticated tech-

"Big Five" personality dimensions
The five abstract dimensions representing most personality traits: conscientiousness, agreeableness, neuroticism, openness to experience, and extroversion (CANOE)

niques, recent investigations have identified the same five dimensions—known as the **"Big Five" personality dimensions**.[84] These five dimensions, represented by the handy acronym "CANOE," are shown in Exhibit 2.6 and described below:

- *Conscientiousness*—**Conscientiousness** refers to people who are careful, dependable, and self-disciplined. Some scholars argue that this dimension also includes the will to achieve. People with low conscientiousness tend to be careless, less thorough, more disorganized, and irresponsible.
- *Agreeableness*—This includes the being courteous, good-natured, empathic, and caring. Some scholars prefer the label of "friendly compliance" for this dimension, with its opposite being "hostile noncompliance." People with low agreeableness tend to be uncooperative, short-tempered, and irritable.
- *Neuroticism*—Neuroticism characterizes people with high levels of anxiety, hostility, depression, and self-consciousness. In contrast, people with low neuroticism (high emotional stability) are poised, secure, and calm.
- *Openness to experience*—This dimension is the most complex and has the least agreement among scholars. It generally refers to the extent that people are sensitive, flexible, creative, and curious. Those who score low on this dimension tend to be more resistant to change, less open to new ideas, and more fixed in their ways.
- *Extroversion*—**Extroversion** characterizes people who are outgoing, talkative, sociable, and assertive. The opposite is **introversion**, which refers to those who are territorial and solitary. Introverts do not necessarily lack social skills. Rather, they are more inclined to direct their interests to ideas than to social events. Introverts feel quite comfortable being alone, whereas extroverts do not.

conscientiousness
A "Big Five" personality dimension that characterizes people who are careful, dependable, and self-disciplined.

extroversion
A "Big Five" personality dimension that characterizes people who are outgoing, talkative, sociable, and assertive.

Several studies have found that these personality dimensions affect work-related behaviour and job performance.[85] Champions of organizational change (people who effectively gain support for new organizational systems and practices) seem to be placed along the positive end of the five personality dimensions described above.[86] People with low neuroticism tend to work better than others in

EXHIBIT 2.6

"Big Five" personality dimensions

Dimension	People who score "high" on this dimension tend to be more:
Conscientiousness	Careful, dependable, self-disciplined
Agreeableness	Courteous, good-natured, empathic, caring
Neuroticism	Anxious, hostile, depressed
Openness to experience	Sensitive, flexible, creative, curious
Extroversion	Outgoing, talkative, sociable, assertive

high stressor situations. Those with high agreeableness tend to handle customer relations and conflict-based situations more effectively.

Conscientiousness has taken centre stage as the most valuable personality trait for predicting job performance in almost every job group. Conscientious employees set higher personal goals for themselves, are more motivated, and have higher performance expectations than do employees with low levels of conscientiousness. High-conscientiousness employees tend to have higher levels of organizational citizenship and work better in companies that give employees more freedom than in traditional "command and control" workplaces. Employees with high conscientiousness, as well as agreeableness and emotional stability, also tend to provide better customer service.[87]

Myers-Briggs Type Indicator

introversion
A "Big Five" personality dimension that characterizes people who are territorial and solitary.

Over half a century ago, the mother and daughter team of Katherine Briggs and Isabel Briggs-Myers developed the **Myers-Briggs Type Indicator (MBTI)**, a personality inventory designed to identify individuals' basic preferences for perceiving and processing information. The MBTI builds on the personality theory proposed in the 1920s by Swiss psychiatrist Carl Jung, which identifies the way people prefer to perceive their environment as well as obtain and process information. Jung suggested that everyone is either extroverted or introverted in orientation and has particular preferences for perceiving (sensing or intuition) and deciding on action (thinking or feeling). The MBTI is designed to measure these as well as a fourth dimension relating to how people orient themselves to the outer world (judging versus perceiving).[88] Extroversion and introversion were discussed earlier, so let's examine the other dimensions:

Myers-Brigg Type Indicator (MBTI)
A personality test that measures each of the traits in Jung's model.

Sensing/Intuition—Some people like collecting information through their five senses. Sensing types use an organized structure to acquire factual, preferably quantitative, details. Sensers are capable of synthesizing large amounts of seemingly random information to form quick conclusions. In contrast, intuitive people collect information nonsystematically. They rely more on subjective evidence as well as on their intuition and sheer inspiration.

Thinking/Feeling—Thinking types rely on rational cause-effect logic and the scientific method (see Chapter 1) to make decisions. They weigh the evidence objectively and unemotionally. Feeling types, on the other hand, consider how their choices affect others. They weigh the options against their personal values rather than by logic.

Judging/Perceiving—Some people prefer order and structure in their relationship with the outer world. These judging types enjoy the control of decision making and want to resolve problems quickly. In contrast, perceiving types are more flexible. They like to spontaneously adapt to events as they unfold and want to keep their options open.

The MBTI questionnaire combines the four pairs of traits into 16 distinct types. For example, corporate executives tend to be ESTJs, meaning they are extroverted, sensing, thinking, and judging types. Each of the 16 types has its strengths and weaknesses. ENTJs are considered natural leaders, ISFJs have a high sense of duty, and so on. These types indicate a person's preferences, not the way they necessarily behave all of the time.

At a recent semi-annual retreat in Maine, employees at GVA Thompson Doyle Hennessey & Stevens did more than run rapids. Everyone at the Boston real estate company completed the Myers-Briggs Type Indicator and learned how their personalities can help them to more effectively relate to each other. For example, the assessments revealed that salespeople don't mind working in a crazed atmosphere, whereas support staff prefer a calmer environment. Both groups now understand each other better.[91] How is the MBTI being used here? Is this an effective use of this instrument? *Courtesy of GVA Thompson Doyle Hennessey & Stevens*
www.graboston.com

Effectiveness of the MBTI   Is the MBTI useful in organizations? Many business leaders think so. The MBTI is one of the most widely used personality tests in work settings.[89] For example, City Bank & Trust in Oklahoma (now part of BancFirst) used the MBTI to help executives understand each other after the merger of several smaller banks. "[MBTI] really was a breakthrough as far as us being able to have empathy for one another," says Bill Johnstone, who was City Bank & Trust president at the time.[90] The MBTI is equally popular for career counselling and some executive coaching.

Yet, in spite of its popularity, evidence regarding the effectiveness of the MBTI and Jung's psychological types is mixed.[92] The MBTI does a reasonably good job of measuring Jung's psychological types, and predicts preferences for information processing in decision making and for particular occupations. However, other evidence is less supportive of the MBTI's ability to predict job performance. One possible exception is that some MBTI dimensions are associated with some dimensions of emotional intelligence (see Chapter 4).[93] Overall, the MBTI seems to improve self-awareness for career development and mutual understanding, but probably should not be used in selecting job applicants.

Other Personality Traits

The Big Five personality dimensions and the MBTI don't capture every personality trait. We will discuss a few others where they fit specific topics in later chapters, such as positive and negative affectivity (Chapter 4), Type A/Type B Behaviour Patterns (Chapter 7), and Machiavellianism (Chapter 12). Two other personality traits that you should know are locus of control and self-monitoring.

locus of control
A personality trait referring to the extent to which people believe events are within their control.

Locus of control   **Locus of control** refers to a generalized belief about the amount of control people have over their own lives. Individuals who feel that they are very much in charge of their own destiny have an *internal locus of control;* those who think that events in their life are due mainly to fate/luck or powerful others have an *external locus of control*. People with an external locus can feel in control in familiar situations (such as opening a door or serving a customer), but their underlying locus of control would be apparent in new situations in which control over events is uncertain.

People perform better in most employment situations when they have moderately strong internal locus of control. They tend to be more successful in their careers and earn more money than their external counterparts. Internals are particularly well suited to leadership positions and other jobs requiring initiative, independent action, complex thinking, and high motivation. Internals are also more satisfied with their jobs, cope better in stressful situations, and are more motivated by performance-based reward systems. This last point was supported in a recent study of Hong Kong bank tellers. Tellers with an internal locus of control had more positive work attitudes following a promotion than did tellers with a more external locus of control.[94]

self-monitoring

A personality trait referring to an individual's level of sensitivity and ability to adapt to situational cues.

Self-monitoring   **Self-monitoring** refers to an individual's level of sensitivity and ability to adapt to situational cues. High self-monitors can adjust their behaviour quite easily and therefore show little stability in other underlying personality traits. In contrast, low self-monitors are more likely to reveal their moods and personal characteristics, so it is relatively easy to predict their behaviour from one situation to the next.[95] The self-monitoring personality trait has been identified as a significant factor in many organizational activities. Employees who are high self-monitors tend to be better at social networking, interpersonal conversations, and leading people. They are also more likely than low self-monitors to be promoted within the organization and to receive better jobs elsewhere.[96]

Self-monitoring, locus of control, conscientiousness, and many other personality traits help us to understand individual behaviour in organizations. One fairly successful application of personality is in the area of vocational choice.

Personality and Vocational Choice

At one time, Miriam Goldberger produced sound effects for movies. She then ran a prenatal and postpartum women's fitness program, and later edited books for a publisher. She performed each job well, but was frustrated with the work environment (dark, cramped sound rooms), lack of job autonomy, or people. That's when Goldberger took stock of what she liked and didn't like. "I can't behave in meetings," Goldberger admits. "I can't use diplomatic doublespeak. I'm movement-oriented; I enjoy physical hard work, and I like to do something different every day."

With that self-assessment, Miriam Goldberger decided to turn her favourite hobby—gardening—into a full-time career. Today, she is president of Wildflower Farm in the rolling hills of Schomberg, Ontario, north of Toronto. Goldberger and her husband (a former advertising executive) landscape gardens, design meadows, and sell low-maintenance wildflowers. The couple gave up stable paycheques and scaled back their lifestyle, but now earn more than ever before.[97]

Miriam Goldberger and many other people have discovered that a career is not just about matching your skills with job requirements. It is a complex alignment of personality, values, and competencies with the requirements of work and characteristics of the work environment. Goldberger may have been talented in these other jobs, but her personality and values were more aligned with physical work that produces tangible results. John Holland, a career development scholar, was an early proponent of this notion that career success depends on the degree of *congruence* between the person and his or her work environment.[98] Congruence refers to the extent that someone has the same or similar personality type as the environment in which they are working. Some research has found that high congruence leads to better performance, satisfaction, and length of time in that career, but other studies are less supportive of the model.[99]

Holland's six types   Holland's theory classifies both individual personalities and work environments into six categories: realistic, investigative, artistic, social, enterprising, and conventional. Exhibit 2.7 defines these types of people and work environments, along with sample occupations representing those environments.

| EXHIBIT 2.7 | Holland's six types of personality and work environment |

Holland Type	Personality traits	Work environment characteristics	Sample occupations
Realistic	Practical, shy, materialistic, stable	Work with hands, machines, or tools; focus on tangible results.	Assembly worker; dry cleaner, mechanical engineer
Investigative	Analytic, introverted, reserved, curious, precise, independent	Work involves discovering, collecting, and analyzing; solving problems.	Biologist, dentist, systems analyst
Artistic	Creative, impulsive, idealistic, intuitive, emotional	Work involves creation of new products or ideas, typically in an unstructured setting	Journalist, architect, advertising executive
Social	Sociable, outgoing, conscientious, need for affiliation	Work involves serving or helping others; working in teams	Social worker, nurse, teacher, counsellor
Enterprising	Confident, assertive, energetic, need for power	Work involves leading others; achieving goals through others in a results-oriented setting.	Salesperson, stockbroker, politician
Conventional	Dependable, disciplined, orderly, practical, efficient	Work involves systematic manipulation of data or information	Accountant, banker, administrator

Sources: Based on information in D.H. Montross, Z.B. Leibowitz, and C.J. Shinkman, *Real People, Real Jobs* (Palo Alto, CA: Davies-Black, 1995); J.H. Greenhaus, *Career Management* (Chicago, Ill.: Dryden, 1987).

Few people fall squarely into only one of Holland's classifications. Instead, Holland refers to a person's degree of *differentiation*; that is, the extent to which the individual fits into one or several types. A highly differentiated person is aligned with a single category, whereas most people fit into two or more categories.

Since most people fit into more than one personality type, Holland developed a model shaped like a hexagon with each personality type around the points. *Consistency* refers to the extent that a person is aligned with similar types, (next to each other in the hexagon), whereas dissimilar types are opposite. For instance, the enterprising and social types are next to each other in Holland's model, so individuals with both enterprising and social personalities have high consistency.

Practical implications of Holland's theory   Does Holland's theory work? It is certainly the most popular vocational fit model in existence and is the basis of much career counselling. And while some of the research supports Holland's general premises, scholars are concerned with specific aspects of the model. One problem is that Holland's personality types represent only the Big Five personality dimensions of openness and extroversion even though other personality dimensions should be relevant to vocational fit.[100] Another limitation is that Holland's hexagon doesn't represent the true relationships among the six types because some opposing categories are less opposite than others. There are also doubts about whether Holland's model can be generalized to other cultures. Aside from these concerns, Holland's model does seem to explain individual attitudes and behaviour to some extent.[101]

Personality and values lay some of the foundation for our understanding of individual behaviour in organizations. However, people are also influenced by the environments in which they live and work. How we perceive that environment and how our interactions with our environment enable us to learn are the two topics presented in the next chapter.

CHAPTER SUMMARY

Individual behaviour is influenced by motivation, ability, role perceptions, and situational factors (MARS). Motivation consists of internal forces that affect the direction, intensity, and persistence of a person's voluntary choice of behaviour. Ability includes both the natural aptitudes and learned capabilities required to successfully complete a task. Role perceptions are a person's beliefs about what behaviours are appropriate or necessary in a particular situation. Situational factors are environmental conditions that constrain or facilitate employee behaviour and performance.

Five types of behaviour are discussed most often in organizational behaviour literature. Task performance represents physical behaviours as well as mental processes that support the organization's objectives. Organizational citizenship refers to behaviours that extend beyond the employee's normal job duties. Counterproductive work behaviours are voluntary and potentially harm the organization by directly affecting its functioning or property, or by hurting employees in a way that will reduce their effectiveness. Joining and staying with the organization is a fourth category of work-related behaviour. The fifth type of work-related behaviour is work attendance.

Values are stable, evaluative beliefs that guide our preferences for outcomes or courses of action in a variety of situations. They influence our decisions and interpretations of what is ethical. People arrange values into a hierarchy of preferences called a value system. Shalom Schwartz grouped the dozens of individual values described by scholars over the years into ten broader domains, which are further reduced to four quadrants of a circle. Organizations need to pay attention to values congruence—the similarity of values across systems (such as individuals with organizational values).

Six values that differ across cultures are individualism, collectivism, power distance, uncertainty avoidance, masculinity-femininity, and long/short-term orientation. Recent research has significantly

changed our earlier knowledge about individualism and collectivism. Canadians and Americans differ on some key values, whereas the values of Francophone and Anglophone Canadians have converged in recent years. First Nations people are distinct from other Canadians, having strong collectivist values, low power distance, low uncertainty avoidance, and a relatively nurturing value orientation.

Four values that guide ethical conduct are utilitarianism, individual rights, distributive justice, and care. Three other factors that influence ethical conduct are the extent that an issue demands ethical principles (moral intensity), the person's ethical sensitivity to the presence and importance of an ethical dilemma, and situational factors that cause people to deviate form their moral values. Companies improve ethical conduct through a code of ethics, ethics training, ethics advisors, and the conduct of corporate leaders.

Personality refers to the relatively stable pattern of behaviours and consistent internal states that explain a person's behavioural tendencies. Psychologists continue to debate the origins of personality, but most believe it is shaped by both heredity and environmental factors. Most personality traits are represented within the "Big Five" personality dimensions (CANOE): conscientiousness, agreeableness, neuroticism, and openness to experience, and extroversion. Conscientiousness is a relatively strong predictor of job performance.

The Myers-Briggs Type Indicator measures how people prefer to focus their attention, collect information, process and evaluate information, and orient themselves to the outer world. Another popular personality trait in organizational behaviour is locus of control, which is a generalized belief about the amount of control people have over their own lives. Another trait, called self-monitoring, refers to an individual's level of sensitivity and ability to adapt to situational cues. John Holland developed a model of vocational choice that defines six personalities and their corresponding work environments.

KEY TERMS

Ability, p. 36

"Big Five" personality dimensions, p. 56

Care principle, p. 53

Collectivism, p. 46

Competencies, p. 36

Conscientiousness, p. 56

Counterproductive work behaviours, p. 40

Distributive justice principle, p. 52

Ethical sensitivity, p. 53

Ethics, p. 51

Extroversion, p. 56

Individual rights principle, p. 52

Individualism, p. 46

Introversion, p. 57

Job satisfaction, p. 42

Locus of control, p. 58

Moral intensity, p. 53

Motivation, p. 36

Myers-Briggs type Indicator (MBTI), p. 57

Organizational citizenship, p. 39

Personality, p. 54

Power distance, p. 47

Role perceptions, p. 38

Self-monitoring, p. 59

Task performance, p. 39

Uncertainty avoidance, p. 47

Utilitarianism, p. 52

Value system, p. 42

Values congruence, p. 44

Values, p. 42

DISCUSSION QUESTIONS

1. An insurance company has high levels of absenteeism among the office staff. The head of office administration argues that employees are misusing the company's sick leave benefits. However, some of the mostly female staff members have explained that family responsibilities interfere with work. Using the MARS model, as well as your knowledge of absenteeism behaviour, discuss some of the possible reasons for absenteeism here and how it might be reduced.

2. You notice that sales representatives in eastern Ontario made 20 percent fewer sales to new clients over the past quarter than salespeople located elsewhere in Canada. Use the MARS model to explain why the eastern Ontario sales reps' performance may have been lower than elsewhere.

3. "Most large Canadian organizations spend a lot of money finding out the key competencies for superior work performance." What are the potential benefits and pitfalls associated with identifying competencies?

4. What is the difference, if any, between an "espoused" value and "enacted" value? What are the implications to individual behaviour in organizations?

5. Your company is beginning to expand operations in Japan and wants you to form working relationships with Japanese suppliers. Considering only the values of individualism and uncertainty avoidance, what should you be aware of or sensitive to in your dealings with these suppliers? You may assume that your contacts hold typical Japanese values along these dimensions.

6. How do First Nations values potentially differ from non-First Nations values?

7. Compare moral intensity and ethical sensitivity.

8. Look over the four pairs of psychological types in the Myers-Briggs Type Indicator and identify the personality type (i.e. four letters) that would be best for a student taking this course. Would this type be appropriate for students in other fields of study (e.g., biology, fine arts)?

C A S E   S T U D Y   2.1

HEADING FOR THE BIG APPLE

By Jeffrey Bagraim, University of Cape Town.

It has been three months since Julius Goodman sat back in his chair and reflected on his great career success. On his desk, fresh out of its envelope, was confirmation that he was being transferred to BigCo's head office in New York for five years. "Watch me take a bite out of the Big Apple," the South African executive remembered musing to himself.

Julius had been sure that this assignment, as vice-president of marketing for a new product division, would be the ticket to his promotion to the Executive Management Team. He had been sure his wife, Stella, and two children, Dave (aged 15) and Mark (aged 13), would be ecstatic. It was "a dream come true."

Julius had been selected because he seemed to have all the attributes to enable someone to work well abroad. He was well known in the Cape Town office for his global perspective on business issues and he always thought about the "big picture" when making decisions. Others enjoyed working with him and he displayed an uncommon sensitivity to the individual needs of the diverse team that reported to him. He had developed a reputation as a developer of people and as someone who thrived on change and uncertainty at work and in life. He particularly enjoyed participating in BigCo's global benchmarking exercise and embraced BigCo's objective of developing a world-class South African operation. His flexibility, people skills, and general management ability had flagged him for future promotion. Now he was being given the opportunity to prove himself, and he knew it.

He remembered how he had returned home at 7 p.m. to tell his wife and two teenage sons about his good fortune and he smiled when he remembered how excited they had been. It took several weeks for the reality of the impending transition to sink in.

At first, his family joked about the move and set agendas for what they would do when they arrived in New York, but as time wore on they began asking more practical questions. Stella began asking questions he could not answer: What would happen to their beloved pet, Goliath (a great Dane)? How would she break the news to her colleagues at the charity where she did voluntary work every morning? Would they have to sell their home and furniture?

The questioning process started a bit later for Dave and Mark. At first they only wanted to know one thing: when would they visit Disneyland? After a while, frustrated by the ambiguous answers Julius gave them, they turned their attention to more practical concerns: What would happen to their studies? Where would they go to school? What would become of their sports training? How would they cope in the winter? They were very excited but they did begin to express some regret about being uprooted from their school, their friends, and their brand new car, which they shared.

Anyway, the family was sure about one thing: that they would fit into the American way of life without any trouble. After all, American culture was very familiar to them. They even joked about how they were learning American English. But on reflection, Julius realized that his family had relied on television to ensure a successful transition. It would not be sufficient.

Julius refused to attend any of BigCo's training programs, which had been designed to prepare executives for cross-national transfers. He was usually eager to attend training courses but he was under tremendous time pressure and after looking over the course content he felt sure that learning about issues such as stress management, business etiquette in different countries, financial management, and self-awareness would be a waste of his time. He discouraged Stella from attending the spouse program. He was convinced that such training was a low priority given the massive task Stella was facing in preparing the family for the move. After all they were moving to America, not China. How different could America be?

Julius had read that General Motors spent over $500,000 a year on cross-cultural training for the approximately 150 employees and their families who are transferred abroad every year. He knew that several BigCo executives who had transferred had later applied to return home long before their assignments were completed. He was thankful that he had been selected for an American assignment. He could scarcely imagine the difficulties of those being transferred to places with a completely different language and culture. He was sure that his transition into American life would be smooth and painless.

The first few days in New York were exciting. The family felt like they were on holiday. Everything was as they had dreamed it would be, the streets were thronged with people, the variety of goods was amazing, and the people were friendly and open. Julius found his fellow workers at the New York office to be both friendly and brimming with useful advice. He took a few days off to sort himself out and dedicated this time to finding a permanent place to live. He could not believe what a complicated decision choosing a neighbourhood was and he was mystified by the seemingly archaic rental agreement he was asked to sign. Choosing a school for his children was equally difficult and he was concerned that they would need a long time to adjust to the American school system. Everything was so different.

Julius and his family soon began to miss all the things that they were used to at home in Cape Town. They missed cricket and rugby. They missed

Peppermint Crisps, fish paste, and Mrs Ball's chutney, but most of all they missed their family and friends. New York may have been the Big Apple but it was impossible to find a decent tasting chocolate bar or friends to replace those "back home." They missed home and he had not even begun work yet. The few days he had anticipated he would need to "sort himself out" kept on being extended.

Julian began work after a two week settling in period and soon realized that working life in the New York office was very different from that in the Cape Town office. He found his American colleagues to be very brash and aggressive. He was not used to their individualistic, independent approach to solving problems. He was not used to the bluntness they displayed in meetings and the urgency with which they approached their work. The consultative, time intensive decision-making approach he was used to was simply not going to be appropriate with his rather impatient and assertive colleagues. He also wondered about their short-term orientation and the rationalistic manner they approached issues. Julius was convinced that his consensus-building approach to decision-making would add value but he knew that he had to prove himself before trying to introduce new approaches. Overall, though he was impressed by his colleagues' drive, tenacity, and ability to work hard, he sometimes suspected that the long hours they put in were not as productive as they could have been. It seemed that they were trying very hard to impress the CEO. They may have called the CEO by his first name but they respected his position of authority and his power.

Since his first day at work, Julius enjoyed the casual manner in which people interacted and the casual dress code that the New York office promoted. Nevertheless, he knew that interpersonal competition was intense and that everyone had to watch his or her own back. Julius also soon realized that the labour laws that had protected him in South Africa did not exist in America. He saw his colleagues being fired without all the formalities and inquiries that he had taken for granted as part of his working life. Julius began to change; he became tense, more competitive, still friendly but on guard. This was proving to be a very stressful assignment. He had to make it work. This assignment could sink him. The pressure built up and he began to work longer and longer hours.

To add to his woes, his family seemed to be having an increasingly difficult time. Stella found it difficult to make friends and began to feel very isolated. She found that she had little in common with the American women who lived nearby and the South African New Yorkers she met were working extremely long hours and could rarely meet with her. She found it hard not to work (she was not allowed to work by the authorities). Though she did not have the same degree of fear that she had in South Africa, she actually began to miss some of the "real problems" in South Africa. Everything here seemed less important, less serious. And she missed her car. Before coming to New York, she had not used public transportation since her childhood; now she travelled on the underground trains every day. She also wondered that there were no seasons for fruit and vegetables . . . everything was available year round. These were not problems but they added to her sense of dislocation.

On a social level, both Julius and Stella had heard that America was very informal. They found that this greatly simplified the reality. Dining out was often a formal affair and going out to dinner in a suit seemed very strange to Julius. Both of them were startled by the meticulous punctuality of their friends but they soon adjusted. The widespread ignorance about South Africa of people they met was initially funny, then irritating. Some people were very knowledgeable about South Africa but many were extremely ignorant, "Do you know Joey Stewart, he's been in Algeria for six years, you must know him? Do you have lions roaming near Cape Town?"

Despite all their difficulties, Julius and his family remained convinced that the transfer to New York had been a positive experience. New York was an exciting place and they were going to go home in only a few years! Of course, the excitement of the first few days did wear off, and the reality was more of a culture shock than they had ever anticipated, but the worst was over and they could now begin to enjoy what the city had to offer. It was clear that the holiday was over and that it would take a very long time (if not forever) to feel like a "New Yorker." Perhaps he should have attended that training course after all.

Discussion Questions

1. In selecting someone for a foreign assignment, what criteria would you set in the selection process?

2. What factors should organizations consider when trying to facilitate the smooth cross-cultural transitions of their employees?

3. What are the cultural characteristics of American national culture that affect organizational behaviour in American organizations?

4. What are the benefits to a global organization of encouraging their employees to accept foreign assignments (cross-cultural exchanges)?

5. In which countries are employees *most like* employees in your country and in which countries are employees *least like* those in your country?

6. How would you describe your national culture and why is it often very difficult to identify it?

CASE STUDY 2.2

PUSHING PAPER CAN BE FUN

A large American city government was putting on a number of seminars for managers of various departments throughout the city. At one of these sessions, the topic discussed was motivation—how to motivate public servants to do a good job. The plight of a police captain became the central focus of the discussion:

> I've got a real problem with my officers. They come on the force as young, inexperienced rookies, and we send them out on the street, either in cars or on a beat. They seem to like the contact they have with the public, the action involved in crime prevention, and the apprehension of criminals. They also like helping people out at fires, accidents, and other emergencies.
>
> The problem occurs when they get back to the station. They hate to do the paperwork, and because they dislike it, the job is frequently put off or done inadequately. This lack of attention hurts us later on when we get to court. We need clear, factual reports. They must be highly detailed and unambiguous. As soon as one part of a report is shown to be inadequate or incorrect, the rest of the report is suspect. Poor reporting probably causes us to lose more cases than any other factor.
>
> I just don't know how to motivate them to do a better job. We're in a budget crunch and I have absolutely no financial rewards at my disposal. In fact, we'll probably have to lay some people off in the near future. It's hard for me to make the job interesting and challenging because it isn't—it's boring, routine paperwork, and there isn't much you can do about it.
>
> Finally, I can't say to them that their promotions will hinge on the excellence of their paperwork. First of all, they know it's not true. If their performance is adequate, most are more likely to get promoted just by staying on the force a certain number of years than for some specific outstanding act. Second, they were trained to do the job they do out in the streets, not to fill out forms. All through their career it's the arrests and interventions that get noticed.
>
> Some people have suggested a number of things, like using conviction records as a performance criterion. However, we know that's not fair— too many other things are involved. Bad paperwork increases the chance that you will lose in court, but good paperwork doesn't necessarily mean you'll win. We tried setting up team competitions based upon the excellence of the reports, but the officers caught on to that pretty quickly. No one was getting any type of reward for winning the competition, and they figured why should they bust a gut when there was no payoff?
>
> I just don't know what to do.

Discussion Questions

1. What performance problems is the captain trying to correct?

2. Use the MARS model of individual behaviour and performance to diagnose the possible causes of the unacceptable behaviour.

3. Has the captain considered all possible solutions to the problem? If not, what else might be done?

Source: T. R. Mitchell and J. R. Larson, Jr., *People in Organizations*, 3rd ed. (New York: McGraw-Hill, 1987), p. 184. Used with permission.

COMPARING CULTURAL VALUES

Purpose This exercise is designed to help you determine the extent that students hold similar assumptions about the values that dominate in other countries.

Instructions The names in the left column represent labels that a major consulting project identified with business people in a particular country, based on its national culture and values. These names appear in alphabetical order. In the right column are the names of countries, also in alphabetical order, corresponding to the labels in the left column.

■ *Step 1:* Working alone, students will connect the labels with the countries by relying on their perceptions of these countries. Each label is associated with only one country, so each label will be connected to only one country, and vice versa. Draw a line to connect the pairs, or put the label number beside the country name.

■ *Step 2*: The instructor will form teams of four or five students. Members of each team will compare their results and try to reach consensus on a common set of connecting pairs.

■ *Step 3*: Teams or the instructor will post the results for all to see the extent that students hold common opinions about business people

in other cultures. Class discussion can then consider the reasons why the results are so similar or different, as well as the implications of these results for working in a global work environment.

Values Labels and Country Names	
Country Label (alphabetical)	Country Name (alphabetical)
1. Affable Humanists	Australia
2. Ancient Modernizers	Brazil
3. Commercial Catalysts	Canada
4. Conceptual Strategists	China
5. Efficient Manufacturers	France
6. Ethical Statesmen	Germany
7. Informal Egalitarians	India
8. Modernizing Traditionalists	Netherlands
9. Optimistic Entrepreneurs	New Zealand
10. Quality Perfectionists	Singapore
11. Rugged Individualists	Taiwan
12. Serving Merchants	United Kingdom
13. Tolerant Traders	United States

Source: Based on R. Rosen, P. Digh, M. Singer, and C. Phillips, *Global Literacies* (New York: Simon & Schuster, 2000).

ETHICS CHECK

Purpose This exercise is designed to help you assess your ethical response to various business and nonbusiness situations.

Instructions Read each of the scenarios below and indicate the likelihood that you would respond in the way indicated in the question in each scenario. There is no scoring key for this

scale. Instead, the instructor will present the results of other students who have completed this instrument. This exercise is completed alone so students assess themselves honestly without being concerned about social comparison. However, class discussion will focus on business ethics and the issue of ethical sensitivity.

ETHICS CHECK SCALE					
Please indicate the probability that you would do each of the following:	**Yes** ▼	**Probably Yes** ▼	**Unsure** ▼	**Probably No** ▼	**No** ▼
1. At work you use many different software packages. Several weeks ago your supervisor ordered a new package for you that several of your colleagues are currently using. The software is now late in arriving. The package would aid you tremendously in completing your current project, but is not absolutely necessary Earlier today your supervisor brought her copy of the software over to you and suggested that you copy it onto your computer for use until your copy arrives. You know that the software is licensed to be installed onto only one computer. Do you copy the software?	☐	☐	☐	☐	☐
2. While at lunch with several of your colleagues last week you overheard a discussion about a client company's financial situation. An accountant working closely with the company noticed significant decreases in sales and receivables. He wasn't sure exactly how bad it was until he heard a rumour at the company about the possibility of filing for bankruptcy. You're now worried because you own a significant block of shares in the company. Do you sell the shares based on this inside information?	☐	☐	☐	☐	☐
3. Yesterday you drove to the store with your neighbour and her young son. When you got back out to the car, your neighbour noticed that her son had picked up a small item from the store worth about $5 that wasn't paid for. Your neighbour reprimanded the child and then turned to you and said she was ready to go. You asked her if she was going to go back into the store to pay for the item. She said it's not worth the hassle. Do you refuse to drive her home unless she goes back to the store and pays for the item?	☐	☐	☐	☐	☐
4. While on a trip out of town on business you had dinner with your sister. Your company has a policy of reimbursing dinner expenses up to $50 per meal. The total cost for this meal for both you and your sister was $35.70. The cost of your meal alone was $16.30. You know that others in your company routinely submit claims for dinner expenses for non-business parties. Do you claim the entire amount for reimbursement?	☐	☐	☐	☐	☐

Source: Adapted from R. R. Radtke, "The Effects of Gender and Setting on Accountants' Ethically Sensitive Decisions," *Journal of Business Ethics*, 24 (April 2000), pp. 299–312.

SELF-ASSESSMENT EXERCISE 2.5

IDENTIFYING YOUR SELF-MONITORING PERSONALITY

Purpose This self-assessment is designed to help you to estimate your level of self-monitoring personality.

Instructions The statements in this scale refer to personal characteristics that might or might not be characteristic of you. Mark the box indicating the extent that the statement is true or false as a characteristic of you. This exercise is completed alone so students assess themselves honestly without concerns of social comparison. However, class discussion will focus on the relevance of self-monitoring personality in organizations.

SELF-MONITORING SCALE

Indicate the degree to which you think the following statements are true or false.	Very False ▼	Somewhat False ▼	Slightly More False than True ▼	Slightly More True than False ▼	Somewhat True ▼	Very True ▼
1. In social situations, I have the ability to alter my behaviour if I feel that something else is called for.	☐	☐	☐	☐	☐	☐
2. I am often able to read people's true emotions correctly through their eyes.	☐	☐	☐	☐	☐	☐
3. I have the ability to control the way I come across to people, depending on the impression I wish to give them.	☐	☐	☐	☐	☐	☐
4. In conversations, I am sensitive to even the slightest change in the facial expression of the person I'm conversing with.	☐	☐	☐	☐	☐	☐
5. My powers of intuition are quite good when it comes to understanding others' emotions and motives.	☐	☐	☐	☐	☐	☐
6. I can usually tell when others consider a joke in bad taste, even though they may laugh convincingly.	☐	☐	☐	☐	☐	☐
7. When I feel that the image I am portraying isn't working, I can readily change it to something that does.	☐	☐	☐	☐	☐	☐
8. I can usually tell when I've said something inappropriate by reading the listener's eyes.	☐	☐	☐	☐	☐	☐
9. I have trouble changing my behaviour to suit different people and different situations.	☐	☐	☐	☐	☐	☐
10. I have found that I can adjust my behaviour to meet the requirements of any situation I find myself in.	☐	☐	☐	☐	☐	☐
11. If someone is lying to me, I usually know it at once from that person's manner of expression.	☐	☐	☐	☐	☐	☐
12. Even when it might be to my advantage, I have difficulty putting up a good front.	☐	☐	☐	☐	☐	☐
13. Once I know what the situation calls for, it's easy for me to regulate my actions accordingly.	☐	☐	☐	☐	☐	☐

Source: R. D. Lennox and R. N. Wolfe, "Revision of the Self-Monitoring Scale," *Journal of Personality and Social Psychology*, 46 (June 1984), pp. 1348–64. The response categories in this scale have been altered slightly due to limitations with the original scale responses.

SELF-ASSESSMENT EXERCISE | 2.6

IDENTIFYING YOUR DOMINANT VALUES

 Go to the Student CD for an interactive version of this exercise.

Purpose This self-assessment is designed to help you to identify your dominant values in Schwartz's values model.

Instructions This instrument consists of numerous words and phrases, and you are asked to indicate whether each word or phrase is highly opposed or highly similar to your personal values, or some point in between these two extremes. When you have finished answering all items, the results will indicate your values on Schwartz's 10 value groups described in this chapter.

INDIVIDUALISM–COLLECTIVISM SCALE

 Go to the Student CD for an interactive version of this exercise.

Purpose This self-assessment is designed to help you to identify your level of individualism and collectivism.

Instructions This scale consists of several statements, and you are asked to indicate how well each statement describes you. Read each statement in this self-assessment and select the response that best indicates how the statement describes you. You need to be honest with yourself to receive a reasonable estimate of your level of individualism and collectivism.

Copyright © 1995 by Sage Publications. Used by permission of Sage Publications, Inc.

IDENTIFYING YOUR LOCUS OF CONTROL

 Go to the Student CD for an interactive version of this exercise.

Purpose This self-assessment is designed to help you to estimate the extent to which you have an internal or external locus of control personality.

Instructions This instrument asks you to indicate the degree to which you agree or disagree with each of the statements provided. You need to be honest with yourself to obtain a reasonable estimate of your locus of control. The results show your relative position in the internal-external locus continuum and the general meaning of this score.

Copyright © Paul E. Spector. All rights reserved. Used with permission.

MATCHING HOLLAND'S CAREER TYPES

 Go to the Student CD for an interactive version of this exercise.

Purpose This self-assessment is designed to help you to understand Holland's career types.

Instructions Holland's theory identifies six different types of work environments and occupations. Few jobs fit purely in one category, but all have a dominant type. Your task is to state the Holland type that you believe best fits each of the occupations presented in the instrument. While completing this self-assessment, you can open your book to the exhibit describing Holland's six types.

Copyright © 2003 Steven L. McShane.

 After studying the preceding material, be sure to check out our Online Learning Centre at
www.mcgrawhill.ca/college/mcshane
for more in-depth information and interactivities that correspond to this chapter.

3

Perception and Learning in Organizations

Learning Objectives

- Outline the perceptual process.

- Explain how we perceive ourselves and others through social identity.

- Outline the reasons why stereotyping occurs and the perceptual problems it creates.

- Describe three ways to minimize the adverse effects of stereotyping.

- Describe the attribution process and two attribution errors.

- Summarize the self-fulfilling prophecy process.

- Explain how empathy and the Johari Window can help improve our perceptions.

- Define learning.

- Describe the A-B-C model of behaviour modification and the four contingencies of reinforcement.

- Describe the three features of social learning theory.

- Summarize the four components of Kolb's experiential learning model.

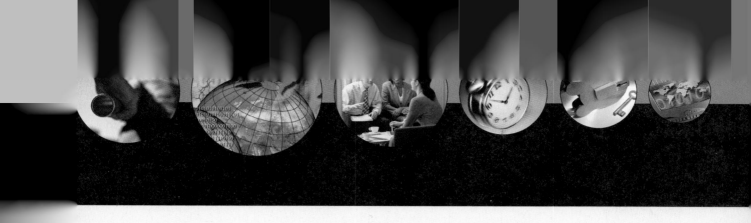

Women make up 59 percent of university graduates in Canada, but only about 20 percent of graduates in engineering programs. "Women are still in the minority here," says Azar Mouzari, a fourth year student of electrical engineering at the University of Ottawa. "You can feel it. When I went into a class of 40 or 50, there were only three or four women."

One of the problems, according to researchers and industry leaders, is that the stereotype of engineers doesn't fit the self-images most women want for themselves. "The whole hacker culture, the idea of living and breathing computer science at the exclusion of all else, is discouraging to women," explains York University sociologist Lorna Erwin. "This is very powerful and very negative stuff," adds Hiromi Matsui, a professor at Simon Fraser University and president of the Canadian Coalition of Women in Engineering, Science and Technology.

Another problem is that women tend to perceive themselves as less capable, even though men and women perform equally well in engineering. This may be partly a self-fulfilling prophecy caused by some instructors and peers. For example, Monique Frize, an engineering professor at both Carleton University and the University of Ottawa, notes that professors make eye contact more frequently with men than women, men are often referred to by first names, and men are called on to answer more difficult questions.

University of Ottawa student Azar Mouzari, shown here with Dean Tyseer Aboulnasr, and other women are underrepresented in engineering programs partly because the stereotype of engineers doesn't fit the self-images most women want for themselves. *Lynn Ball, The Ottawa Citizen*

Professor Erwin says this lack of self-confidence causes female engineers to blame themselves for any poor results in school. Even though they receive the same grades as male students, women are more likely to leave engineering programs. "Guys that aren't doing well will blame the prof, or the book, or the class that sucks," says University of Calgary engineering student Justyna Krzysiak. "Girls tend to blame themselves more. They'll say 'I'm just not smart enough to be an engineer,' or, 'this isn't really for me.'" The guys stay because they blame the situation, the female students leave because they blame themselves.[1] ▪

www.uottawa.ca

The opening story illustrates how various perceptual processes—including stereotyping, attributions, self-fulfilling prophecy, and social identity— explain why women represent only a small percentage of engineers in Canada and other countries. **Perception** is the process of receiving information about and making sense of the world around us. It involves deciding which information to notice, how to categorize this information, and how to interpret it within the framework of our existing knowledge. The opening story is just one example of how we need to be particularly aware of the perceptual process and its repercussions in this world of increasing diversity and globalization.

perception
The process of selecting, organizing, and interpreting information in order to make sense of the world around us.

This chapter begins by describing the perceptual process, that is, the dynamics of selecting, organizing, and interpreting external stimuli. Social identity theory, which has recently become a leading perceptual theory in organizational behaviour, is introduced. Next, we look at the dynamics of stereotyping, including ways of minimizing stereotype biases in the workplace. Attribution, self-fulfilling prophecy, and other perceptual issues are then discussed, followed by an overview of empathy and the Johari Window as general strategies to minimize perceptual problems. The latter part of this chapter looks at learning in organizations, including the elements of behaviour modification, social learning theory, and experiential learning.

THE PERCEPTUAL PROCESS

The Greek philosopher Plato wrote that we see reality only as shadows reflecting against the rough wall of a cave.[2] In other words, reality is filtered through an imperfect perceptual process. This imperfect process, illustrated in Exhibit 3.1, begins when environmental stimuli are received through our senses. Most stimuli are screened out; the rest are organized and interpreted based on various information processing activities. The resulting perceptions influence our emotions and behaviour toward those objects, people, and events.[3]

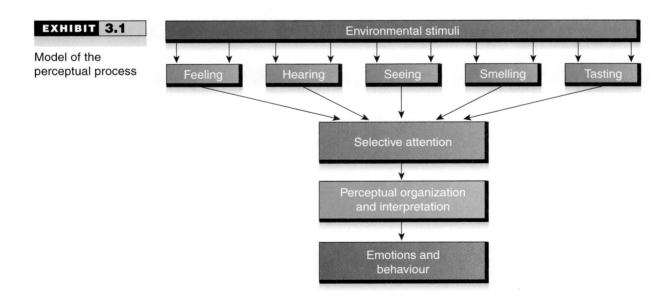

EXHIBIT 3.1

Model of the perceptual process

Selective Attention

Our five senses are constantly bombarded with stimuli. Some things get noticed, but most are screened out. A nurse working in post-operative care might ignore the smell of recently disinfected instruments or the sound of co-workers talking nearby. Yet that nurse would immediately notice a small flashing red light on the nursing station console because it signals that a patient's vital signs are failing. This process of filtering information received by our senses is called **selective attention.**

One influence on selective attention is the size, intensity, motion, repetition, and novelty of the target (including people). The red light on the nursing station console receives attention because it is bright (intensity), flashing (motion), and a rare event (novelty). As for people, we would notice two employees having a heated debate if co-workers normally don't raise their voices (novelty and intensity). Notice that selective attention is also influenced by the context in which the target is perceived. You might be aware that a client has a German accent if the meeting takes place in Toronto, but not if the conversation took place in Germany, particularly if you had been living there for some time. On the contrary, it would be your Canadian accent that others would notice!

Characteristics of the perceiver   Selective attention depends on more than the object and context. It is also affected by the characteristics of the perceiver. We tend to remember information that is consistent with our values and attitudes and ignore information that is inconsistent with them. For example, interviewers who develop positive feelings toward a job applicant early in the interview tend to subsequently screen out negative information about that candidate.[4] In extreme cases, our emotions screen out large blocks of information that threaten our beliefs and values. This phenomenon, called *perceptual defence*, protects our self-esteem and may be a coping mechanism to minimize stress in the short run.[5]

Selective attention is also affected by our expectations.[6] An African proverb says: "It is on the regular path we take that the wild beast attacks." In other words, through experience, we are conditioned to anticipate routine events. Unique events are excluded from our thoughts—until it is too late. In organizational settings, expectations prevent decision makers from seeing opportunities and competitive threats. For this reason, experts urge us to develop *splatter vision*—taking everything in as a whole while focusing on nothing. Truck drivers learn to expect the unexpected, such as a child darting out onto the road. Jet fighter pilots constantly check their peripheral vision, not just what's ahead of them. Police detectives try to avoid forming theories too early in criminal investigations with few leads or suspects. "When you get a theory, it can put blinders on what really happened," explains Ottawa-Carleton police detective Roch Lachance about a homicide where there were few leads or suspects.[7]

Perceptual Organization and Interpretation

After selecting stimuli, we usually simplify and "make sense" of it. This involves organizing the information into general categories and interpreting it. We rely on perceptual grouping principles to organize people and objects into recognizable and manageable patterns or categories. This *perceptual grouping* occurs in a number of ways. It occurs when we make assumptions about people based on their similarity or proximity to others. It also occurs when we think we see trends in

selective attention

The process of filtering information received by our senses.

otherwise ambiguous information. Another form of perceptual grouping is closure, such as filling in missing information about what happened at a meeting that you missed (e.g., who was there, where it was held).

Perceptual grouping helps us to make sense of the workplace, but it can also inhibit creativity and open-mindedness. It puts blinders on our ability to organize and interpret people and events differently. Perceptual grouping is influenced by our broader assumptions and beliefs, known as mental models.

Mental models   Communications guru Marshall McLuhan once wrote that people wear their own set of idiosyncratic goggles. In his colourful way, McLuhan was saying that each of us holds a unique view of what the world looks like and how it operates. These idiosyncratic goggles are known as **mental models**.[8] Mental models are the broad world views or "theories-in-use" that people rely on to guide their perceptions and behaviours. For example, most of us have a mental model about attending a college or university lecture or seminar. We have a set of assumptions and expectations about how people arrive, arrange themselves in the room, ask and answer questions, and so forth. We can create a mental image of what a class would look like in progress.

Mental models help us make sense of our environment, but they may blind us from seeing that world in different ways.[9] For example, accounting professionals tend to see corporate problems in terms of accounting solutions, whereas marketing professionals see the same problems from a marketing perspective. Mental models also block our recognition of new opportunities. How do we change mental models? It's a tough challenge. After all, we developed models from several years of experience and reinforcement. The first step is to constantly question our existing mental models and assumptions. Working with people from diverse backgrounds is another way to break out of existing mental models.

> **mental models**
> The broad world-views or "theories-in-use" that people rely on to guide their perceptions and behaviours.

SOCIAL IDENTITY THEORY

> **social identity theory**
> A model that explains self-perception and social perception in terms of the person's unique characteristics (personal identity) and membership in various social groups (social identity).

The perceptual process is an interactive dynamic between our self-perceptions and the perceptions of others. **Social identity theory** explains this process of self-perception and social perception.[10] According to social identity theory, people develop their self-perceptions through personal identity and social identity. *Personal identity* includes the individual's unique characteristics and experiences, such as physical appearance, personality traits, and special talents. An unusual achievement that distinguishes you from other people becomes a personal characteristic with which you partially identify yourself.

Social identity, on the other hand, refers to our self-perception as members in various social groups. For example, one person might have a self-identity as a Canadian, a graduate of the University of New Brunswick, and an employee at CIBC World Markets. This social categorization process helps us to locate ourselves within the social world (see Exhibit 3.2).

People adopt degrees of personal and social identity, depending on the situation.[11] If your organizational behaviour class is well represented by gender, race, and specialization (marketing, finance, etc.), then, in terms of your personal identity characteristics, you would tend to identify yourself (e.g., "I'm probably the only one in this class who has trekked through Malaysia's Cameron Highlands!"). On the other hand, if you are a computer science student in a class consisting mostly of business students, then your group membership—your *social identity*—

EXHIBIT 3.2

Self-perception and
social perception
through social
identity

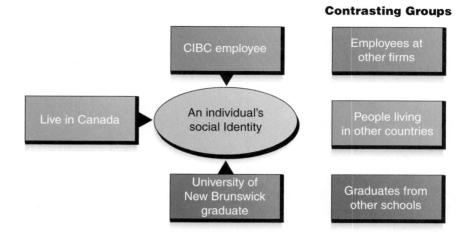

Contrasting Groups

would dominate your self-perception. In this situation, you would define yourself more by your field of specialization ("I'm from computer science") than by any personal identity characteristics. As your distinguishing social identity becomes known to others, they, too, would likely identify you by that feature.

We tend to perceive ourselves as members of several groups, not just one or two. In this respect, social identity is a complex combination of many memberships, which are determined by personal priorities. But which groups form our social identity? We tend to like to have a positive self-image, so we identify with groups that support this positive image. This explains why medical doctors usually define themselves in terms of their profession, whereas people in low status jobs are less likely to do so. It also explains why some people like to mention their employer and others never mention where they work.[12]

Perceiving Others through Social Identity

Social identity theory doesn't just explain how we develop self-perceptions. It also explains the dynamics of *social perception*—how we perceive others. In particular, it describes how and why we categorize others into homogeneous and often less favourable groups. Social identity is a *comparative* process, meaning that we define ourselves in terms of our differences with people who belong to other groups. To simplify this comparison process, we tend to *homogenize* people within social categories. We think that people within our group share certain traits, and people in comparison groups share a different set of traits. This may be partly true, but we further exaggerate these differences. For example, students from one university often describe students from a rival school (particularly before a sports competition) as though they come from a different planet!

Comparison and homogenization explain why we perceptually group other people and overgeneralize their traits. But we also tend to develop less positive (or sometimes downright negative) images of people outside our social identity groups. Why do we disparage people who are different from us? The answer is that our self-identity involves contrasting the groups we belong to with other groups. To maintain a positive self-image, we usually construct favourable images of our own social identity group and, as a result, less favourable images of people belonging to other social categories. This is particularly true when the other groups are in competition and conflict with our social identity groups. While that threat exists, the negative image of opponents preserves our self-image.[13]

To summarize, the social identity process explains how we perceive ourselves and others. This perceptual process makes our social world easier to understand. However, it also becomes the basis for stereotyping people in organizational settings, which we discuss next.

STEREOTYPING IN ORGANIZATIONAL SETTINGS

stereotyping
The process of assigning traits to people based on their membership in a social category.

Stereotyping is the process of assigning traits to people based on their membership in a social category.[14] It is an extension of social identity theory and a product of our natural process of organizing information. Stereotypes thus define people by the demographic or other observable groups to which they belong. The stereotyping process begins when we develop social categories and assign traits that are difficult to observe. For instance, students might form a stereotype that professors are both intelligent and absent-minded. Personal experiences shape stereotypes to some extent, but mostly we adopt the stereotypes provided to us within our culture (such as from socialization and movie characters).[15]

Next, people are assigned to one or more social categories based on easily observable information about them, such as their gender, appearance, or physical location. Observable features allow us to assign people to a social group quickly and without much investigation. Lastly, the cluster of traits linked to the social category is assigned to people identified as members of that group. For example, we assume that professors are absent-minded, at least until we know them better.

Why Stereotyping Occurs

Stereotyping occurs for three reasons.[16] First, trying to absorb the unique constellations of attributes about each person we meet is a huge cognitive challenge; there is too much information to remember. Instead, we rely on a natural process called *categorical thinking*—grouping people and objects into preconceived categories that are stored in our long-term memory. This categorization process is the basis of stereotyping. Second, we have a strong need to understand and anticipate how others will behave. We don't have much information when first meeting someone, so we rely heavily on stereotypes to fill in the missing pieces.

Last, stereotyping enhances our self-perception and social identity. Recall from social identity theory that we develop our self-perception by identifying with certain social groups and contrasting them with other groups. To define yourself as a Canadian female, for instance, you tend to rely on stereotypes of males and of people from other cultures. To enhance our self-concept, we sometimes tend to emphasize the positive aspects of the groups to which we belong and emphasize the negative aspects of contrasting groups. We do this by unconsciously assigning inaccurate traits to people in those different groups, thus creating less favourable images of other groups. Moreover, as Canadian researchers have recently discovered, we are particularly motivated to use negative stereotypes toward people who hurt our self-esteem.[17]

Problems with Stereotyping

Early writers warned that stereotypes were almost completely false or, at best, exaggerated the traits of people in those groups. Scholars now take a more mod-

Most people are surprised to learn that Charlotte St. Germain is an oil refinery process operator. Their stereotype is of men crawling around the refinery's massive network of pipes and equipment with heavy overalls, steel-tipped boots, and a hard hat. "People often say, 'You don't look like the sort of person to be doing that'," says the 50-something grandmother. St. Germain is one of three women among the 115 process operators at the Shell Scotford Refinery near Fort Saskatchewan, Alberta. Her retraining from an office job to process operator 20 years ago makes her a pioneer in this traditionally male job. "She has paved the way for women to take on such jobs," says another female process operator.[18] Why do we rely on stereotyping when forming perceptions of people? *The Edmonton Sun, Christine Vanzella*
www.shell.ca

erate view. They say that stereotypes generally have some inaccuracies, some overestimation or underestimation of real differences, and some degree of accuracy.[19] Still, we should remember that stereotypes do not accurately describe every person in that social category. For instance, research has found that people with physical disabilities are stereotyped as being quiet, gentle-hearted, shy, insecure, dependent, and submissive.[20] While this may be true of some people, it is certainly not characteristic of everyone who has a physical disability. Another concern with stereotypes is that they cause us to ignore or misinterpret information that is inconsistent with the stereotype.[21] If we meet a professor with a good short-term memory, we tend to initially ignore that observation.

A more serious problem with stereotyping is that it lays the foundation for prejudice and intentional or unintentional discrimination.[22] **Prejudice** refers to unfounded negative emotions and attitudes toward people belonging to a particular stereotyped group. Prejudice leads to intentional acts of discrimination. For instance, the owner of a Canadian Tire store in Kelowna, B.C. hired a relatively inexperienced young man for the job of automotive manager rather than offer the job to a woman who was employed as manager-in-training in the automotive section. The woman had 20 years of experience at Canadian Tire, including 10 years as automotive manager at another store, but the store owner didn't want to promote her to the management position. The B. C. Human Rights Tribunal concluded that the Canadian Tire store owner had discriminated against the woman.[23]

Even when corporate decision makers try to minimize prejudicial attitudes, they might engage in *unintentional discrimination* which limits the opportunities of qualified employees and job applicants. Unintentional discrimination occurs when people rely on stereotypes to establish notions of the "ideal" person in specific roles.[24] A person who doesn't fit the ideal is likely to receive a less favourable evaluation. This is increasingly apparent in recent age discrimination claims. Recruiters say they aren't biased against older job applicants, yet older workers have a much more difficult time gaining employment even though research indicates they are well qualified.

prejudice
The unfounded negative emotions toward people belonging to a particular stereotyped group.

Minimizing Stereotyping Bias

If stereotyping is such a problem, shouldn't we try to avoid this process altogether? Unfortunately, it's not that simple. Most scholars agree that categorizing information (including stereotyping people) is a natural process related to the mechanics

The National Hockey League has 600 players from 18 nationalities. It's also an aggressive game where players sometimes vent their emotions with racial slurs. "People are always picking on your heritage," says Philadelphia Flyers goalie John Vanbiesbrouck. "We're living in a stereotypical world, where nicknames come before names, and that sometimes leads to other things." To minimize these problems, the NHL requires every player to attend diversity awareness training each year. In these sessions, players learn to appreciate ethnic differences as well as the negative consequences for the NHL of racial slurs. "Obviously the problem has crept into our game and to pro sports in general," says an NHL player after a diversity awareness session. "There should be a professional respect."[29] Along with this training, how else could the NHL minimize ethnic stereotyping? © REUTERS/Andy Clark/TimePix
www.nhl.com

of brain functioning.[25] In other words, it's a hardwired activity that we can't avoid. Moreover, as previously mentioned, stereotyping minimizes mental effort, fills in missing information, and is part of the social identity process.[26] The good news is that while we might not be able to prevent the *activation* of stereotypes, we can minimize the *application* of stereotypic information in our decisions and actions. Three strategies for minimizing the application of stereotyping are diversity awareness training, meaningful interaction, and decision-making accountability.

Diversity awareness training   Organizations can minimize the adverse consequences of stereotyping through diversity awareness training. Most diversity programs educate employees about the organizational benefits of diversity and the problems with stereotyping. Many try to dispel myths about people from visible minority and other demographic groups. Some sessions rely on role playing and exercises to help employees discover the subtle, yet pervasive effects of stereotyping in their decision making and behaviour.[27] Diversity training does not correct deep-rooted prejudice; it probably doesn't even change stereotypes in tolerant people. What diversity training can do, however, is to increase our sensitivity to equality and motivate us to block inaccurate perceptions arising from ingrained stereotypes.[28]

Although diversity awareness training can reduce our reliance on stereotypes, some training sessions can reinforce rather than weaken stereotyping.[30] Specifically, by teaching employees about cross-cultural values, diversity training replaces popular stereotypes with "sophisticated stereotyping." The problem with this sophisticated stereotyping is that many societies are quite diverse, so the images of an entire culture may not apply to specific people within that culture (see Chapter 2). Unfortunately, employees do not learn this point in diversity sessions, so they develop overly simplistic beliefs about people from other cultures.

Meaningful interaction   Another potentially effective way to minimize the adverse effects of stereotyping is to have people interact with each other. This practice is based on the **contact hypothesis**, which says that the more we interact with someone, the less we rely on stereotypes to understand that person.[31] For instance, United Parcel Service (UPS) and Hoechst Celanese send their senior staff into communities markedly different from their own to educate them about diversity issues. By working with people and groups from different backgrounds than their own, these executives gain a deeper understanding of their different perspectives and experiences. "Joining these organizations has been more helpful to me than two weeks of diversity training," concludes a Hoechst Celanese executive.[32]

contact hypothesis
The theory that as individuals interact with one another they rely less on stereotypes about each other.

Although the contact hypothesis sounds simple, we need to be aware of two important points. The first is that increased contact tends to reduce reliance on stereotypes only when participants have equal status on a common, meaningful goal involving close and frequent interaction. People who are extroverted and have a high self-monitoring personality also tend to be more receptive when interacting with people of different backgrounds.[33] The Hoechst Celanese executives probably worked on meaningful tasks with visible minorities in a context where their status as corporate executives was less relevant. With similar status and a common, meaningful task, these executives would eventually rely less on their stereotypes of people in those communities. In contrast, if these executives spent an hour talking to lower level employees in their own organization, the benefits of direct contact would be minimal due to the status differences, limited interaction, and the lack of a common, engaging goal.

The second important point is that interacting with people on a meaningful task with equal status tends to minimize our *application* of our stereotypes to those specific people, but generally *does not* change our stereotype of the group to which those people belong. For instance, working closely with an accountant on an important project probably won't change your stereotype of accountants, but you would develop more accurate perceptions of that specific accountant. The explanation for this is that stereotypes are difficult to alter because they are heavily influenced by socialization and cultural images.

Decision-making accountability   A third way to minimize the biasing effects of stereotyping is to make decision makers accountable for the information they rely on and the criteria they use to make choices in organizational decisions.[34] Whether selecting job applicants or handing out preferred assignments, decisions tend to be swayed by discriminatory stereotypes unless decision makers are forced to actively search for and evaluate information. Accountability encourages this active information processing process and, consequently, motivates decision makers to set aside their stereotypic perceptions with more accurate information.

ATTRIBUTION THEORY

attribution process

The perceptual process of deciding whether an observed behaviour or event is largely caused by internal or external factors.

The opening story to this chapter noted that female engineering students tend to blame themselves for poor performance in school, whereas male students tend to blame external causes. This process of assigning credit or blame to yourself or the situation is called the **attribution process**. The attribution process involves deciding whether an observed behaviour or event is largely caused by internal or external factors.[35] Internal factors, such as an individual's ability or motivation, originate from within a person. We make an *internal attribution* when we believe that an employee performs the job poorly because he or she lacks the necessary competencies or motivation. External factors originate from the environment, such as lack of resources, other people, or just luck. An *external attribution* would occur if we believe that the employee performs the job poorly because he or she didn't receive sufficient resources to do the task.

How do people determine whether to make an internal or external attribution about a co-worker's excellent job performance or a supplier's late shipment? They rely on the three attribution rules shown in Exhibit 3.3. Internal attributions are made if the observed individual behaved this way in the past (high consistency), if he or she behaves like this toward other people or in different situations (low

EXHIBIT 3.3

Rules of attribution

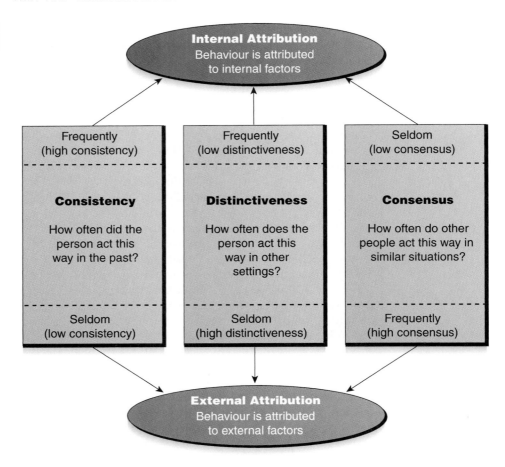

distinctiveness), and if other people do not behave this way in similar situations (low consensus). On the other hand, an external attribution is made when there is low consistency, high distinctiveness, and high consensus.

The following example will help to clarify the three attribution rules. Suppose an employee is making poor quality products one day on a particular machine. We would probably conclude that there is something wrong with the machine (an external attribution) if the employee has made good quality products on this machine in the past (low consistency), the employee makes good quality products on other machines (high distinctiveness), and other employees have recently had quality problems on this machine (high consensus). On the other hand, we would make an internal attribution if the employee usually makes poor quality products on this machine (high consistency), other employees produce good quality products on this machine (low consensus), and the employee also makes poor quality products on other machines (low distinctiveness).[36]

Attributions influence most behaviours and decisions in the workplace.[37] For instance, your co-workers and boss are more likely to get upset with you if they believe your absenteeism or lateness is due to your lack of motivation rather than to traffic, sick kids, or other conditions beyond your control. Research has found that employees receive larger bonuses or pay increases when decision makers attribute good performance to the employee's ability or motivation. Employees are also more self-confident and tend to have higher job satisfaction when they believe positive feedback relates to events within their control rather than to external causes.[38]

Attribution Errors

fundamental attribution error

The tendency to attribute the behaviour of other people more to internal than to external factors.

The attribution process is far from perfect. The most fundamental error we make in attribution is called (not surprisingly) **fundamental attribution error**. This refers to the tendency to attribute the behaviour of other people more to internal than to external factors. If an employee is late for work, observers are more likely to conclude that the person is lazy than to think that external factors may have caused this behaviour. Fundamental attribution error occurs where there is limited information about the situational factors affecting other people. The person performing the behaviour is naturally more sensitive to situational influences. This can lead to disagreement over the degree to which employees should be held responsible for their poor performance or absenteeism.[39] The observer blames the employee's lack of motivation or ability, whereas the employee does not feel responsible because the behaviour seems to be due to factors beyond his or her control.

self-serving bias

A perceptual error whereby people tend to attribute their favourable outcomes to internal factors and their failures to external factors.

Another attribution error, known as **self-serving bias**, is the tendency to attribute our favourable outcomes to internal factors and our failures to external factors. Simply put, we take credit for our successes and blame others or the situation for our mistakes. The existence of self-serving bias in corporate life has been well documented. One recent example is a study that monitored a small government organization as it introduced a performance management system. The study found that 90 percent of the employees who received lower-than-expected performance ratings blamed this on their supervisor, the organization, the appraisal system, or other external causes. Only a handful blamed themselves for the unexpected results.[40] Research has also reported this self-serving bias in corporate annual reports.[41] As we read in GLOBAL Connections 3.1, executives in Hong Kong and the United Kingdom have been very creative in identifying external causes for their poor performance.

Aside from these errors, attributions vary from one person to another based on personal values and experiences. For instance, female managers are less likely than male managers to make internal attributions about their job performance.[42] Overall, we need to be careful about personal and systematic biases in the attribution process within organizations.

SELF-FULFILLING PROPHECY

For the past few decades, Ottawa restaurant owner David Smith has known that employees achieve remarkable performance levels when their boss believes they can do it. "When you show people you believe in them, it's amazing what can happen," advises Smith. As owner of Nate's Deli, Smith has seen his high expectations make some employees confident enough to take on more challenging assignments in the organization. "I've put busboys into tuxedos," he says.[43]

David Smith has been practising **self-fulfilling prophecy**. Self-fulfilling prophecy occurs when our expectations about another person cause that person to act in a way that is consistent with those expectations.[44] In other words, our

Hong Kong and British Firms Produce Creative External Attributions

To distance themselves from accounting delays and poor profits, some Hong Kong and British executives have a knack for offering unusual external attributions for their performance shortcomings.

A-Max Holdings Ltd. (formerly Kessel International Holdings Ltd.), a Hong Kong manufacturer of battery-operated toys and gadgets, advised shareholders that it couldn't provide its annual figures on time because of "repeated electricity failure in the head office of the company that shut down the company's computer system on various occasions." The electrical failures occurred eight months earlier, but maybe shareholders wouldn't notice this gap.

Interform Ceramics Technologies Ltd. offered a more complex explanation for its late accounting reports. The large Hong Kong ceramics company put its accounting books in storage during a move to a new office. Then, according to a notice to its shareholders, most of its accounting staff left the company. The remaining staff apparently weren't able to retrieve the books, although Interform didn't explain why.

British executives seem to get their financial reports submitted on time, but they are equally adept at distancing themselves from the causes of poor sales or profits. One British IT firm tried to explain how a snowstorm on the east coast of the United States had somehow undermined its profits for the year. Executives at a brewery blamed their poor results a few years ago on mining pit closures in the North East and the launch of Britain's National Lottery.

A few years ago, several firms claimed that poor sales were caused by the "Diana effect." DFS, a British furniture chain, explained that customers were too grief-stricken by the death of Princess Diana to think about buying new furniture. DFS executives also suggested that the hot summer weather had led to falling sales.

Sources: J. Ashworth, "Warning: Yet another Excuse on the Line," *Times of London*, August 8, 2001, p. 20; G. Manuel, "Why Hong Kong Firms Are Late Filing Results," *Asian Wall Street Journal*, August 3, 2001, p. 1.

---

self-fulfilling prophecy

Occurs when our expectations about another person cause that person to act in a way that is consistent with those expectations.

perceptions can influence reality. Exhibit 3.4 illustrates the four steps in the self-fulfilling prophecy process using the example of a supervisor and subordinate.[45]

1. *Expectations formed*—The supervisor forms expectations about the employee's future behaviour and performance. These expectations are sometimes inaccurate, because first impressions are usually formed from limited information.

2. *Behaviour toward the employee*—The supervisor's expectations influence his or her treatment of employees.[46] Specifically, high-expectancy employees (those expected to do well) receive more emotional support through nonverbal cues (e.g., more smiling and eye contact), more frequent and valuable feedback and reinforcement, more challenging goals, better training, and more opportunities to demonstrate their performance.

3. *Effects on the employee*—The supervisor's behaviours have two effects on the employee. First, through better training and more practice opportunities, a high-expectancy employee learns more skills and knowledge than a low-expectancy employee. Second, the employee becomes more self-confident, thus more highly motivated and more willing to set more challenging goals.[47]

4. *Employee behaviour and performance*—With higher motivation and better skills, high-expectancy employees are more likely to demonstrate desired behaviours and better performance. The supervisor notices this, which supports his or her original perception.

Self-Fulfilling Prophecies in Practice

Employees are more likely to be victims of negative self-fulfilling prophecy than beneficiaries of positive self-fulfilling prophecy.[48] How can organizations harness

The self-fulfilling
prophecy cycle

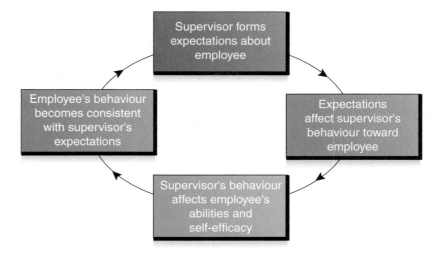

the power of positive self-fulfilling prophecy? Researchers initially recommended that leaders should become aware of the self-fulfilling prophecy effect and learn how to exhibit contagious enthusiasm. Unfortunately, these training programs have had limited success, partly because leaders have difficulty maintaining positive perceptions toward employees who, in their minds, aren't very good.[49]

More recently, experts have recommended a three-pronged approach in which leaders develop positive self-fulfilling prophecies by creating a learning orientation, applying appropriate leadership styles, and building self-efficacy in employees.[50] First, leaders need to develop a **learning orientation**, that is, they need to appreciate the value of the employee learning, not just accomplishing, tasks. They do this by accepting reasonable mistakes as a natural part of the learning process. Second, leaders need to apply appropriate leadership behaviours to all employees. In other words, they practise the contingency approach to leadership that we will learn about in Chapter 14. For employees who are new to a position or task, this would usually include providing frequent, objective feedback and creating a positive relationship by showing support.

Self-fulfilling prophecies are mainly due to the employee's self-efficacy, so the third strategy is to teach leaders how to increase **self-efficacy**. Self-efficacy refers to a person's belief that he or she has the ability, motivation, and resources to complete a task successfully.[51] People with high self-efficacy have a "can do" attitude toward a specific task and, more generally, toward other challenges in life. Leaders can increase employee self-efficacy by showing employees that they possess the necessary knowledge and skills, by displaying confidence in the employee's competencies, and by having employees observe others, similar to them, performing the tasks effectively.

learning orientation

The extent that an organization or individual supports knowledge management, particularly opportunities to acquire knowledge through experience and experimentation.

self-efficacy

A person's belief that he or she has the ability, motivation, and resources to complete a task successfully.

OTHER PERCEPTUAL ERRORS

Self-fulfilling prophecy, attribution, and stereotyping are processes that both assist and interfere with the perceptual process. Four other well-known perceptual errors in organizational settings are primacy effect, recency effect, halo effect, and projection.

Primacy Effect

primacy effect
A perceptual error in which we quickly form an opinion of people based on the first information we receive about them.

Primacy effect is the term used to describe the lasting effect of first impressions. We all tend to quickly form an opinion of people based on the first information we receive about them.[52] This rapid perceptual organization occurs because we need to make sense of the world around us. Moreover, we tend to categorize people fairly quickly because this is easier on our brain cells than remembering every detail about a person. For example, if we first meet someone who avoids eye contact and speaks softly, we quickly conclude that the person is bashful. It is easier to remember the person as bashful than to recall the specific behaviours exhibited during the first encounter.

Unfortunately, first impressions—particularly negative first impressions—are difficult to change. The problem is that after categorizing someone as bashful, we tend to select only the information that supports our first impression and screen out information that opposes it. Negative impressions tend to "stick" more than positive impressions because negative characteristics are more easily attributed to the person, whereas positive characteristics are often attributed to the situation.[53]

Recency Effect

recency effect
A perceptual error in which the most recent information dominates our perception of others.

The **recency effect** occurs when the most recent information available dominates our perception of others.[54] That information has a greater influence on our perception of someone than our first impression when the first impression has worn off with the passage of time.

The recency effect is found in performance appraisals, for which supervisors must recall every employee's performance over the previous year. Recent performance information dominates the evaluation because it is the most easily recalled. Some employees are well aware of the recency effect and use it to their advantage by getting their best work on the manager's desk just before the performance appraisal is conducted.

Halo Error

halo error
A perceptual error whereby our general impression of a person, usually based on one prominent characteristic, colours our perception of other characteristics of that person.

Halo error occurs when our general impression of a person, usually based on one prominent characteristic, colours our perception of other characteristics of that person.[55] If we meet a client who speaks in a friendly manner, we tend to infer a

DILBERT reprinted by permission of United Feature Syndicate, Inc.

host of other favourable qualities about that person. If a colleague doesn't complete tasks on time, we tend to view his or her other traits unfavourably. In each case, one trait important to the perceiver forms a general impression, and this impression becomes the basis for judgments about other traits. Halo error is most likely to occur when concrete information about the perceived target is missing or we are not sufficiently motivated to search for it.[56] Instead, we use our general impression of the person to fill in the missing information.

Halo error has received considerable attention in research on performance appraisal ratings.[57] Consider this situation: two employees have the same level of work quality, work quantity, and customer relations performance, but one tends to be late for work. Tardiness might not be an important factor in work performance, but the supervisor has a negative impression of employees who are late for work. Halo error would cause the supervisor to rate the tardy employee lower on *all* performance dimensions because the tardiness created a negative general impression of that employee. The punctual employee would tend to receive higher ratings on *all* performance dimensions even though his or her performance level is really the same as that of the tardy employee. Clearly, halo error distorts our judgments and can result in poor decision making.

Projection

projection bias
A perceptual error in which we believe that other people have the same beliefs and behaviours that we do.

Projection bias occurs when we believe other people have the same beliefs and behaviours as us.[58] If you're eager for a promotion, you might think that others in your position are similarly motivated. If you're thinking of quitting your job, you start to believe that other people are also thinking of quitting. Projection bias is also a defence mechanism to protect our self-esteem. If we break a work rule, projection bias justifies the infraction by claiming that "everyone does it." We feel more comfortable with the thought that our negative traits exist in others, so we believe others also have these traits.

IMPROVING PERCEPTIONS

We can't bypass the perceptual process, but we should make every attempt to minimize perceptual biases and distortions. Earlier, we learned about using diversity awareness and contact practices to minimize the adverse effects of biased stereotypes. Two other broad perceptual improvement practices are developing empathy and improving self-awareness.

Improving Perceptions through Empathy

empathy
A person's ability to understand and be sensitive to the feelings, thoughts, and situations of others.

Empathy refers to a person's understanding and sensitivity to the feelings, thoughts, and situation of others. Empathy has both a cognitive (thinking) and emotional component.[59] The cognitive component, sometimes called *perspective taking*, is the intellectual understanding of another person's situational and individual circumstances.[60] The emotional component refers to experiencing the feelings of the other person. You are empathic when you are actively visualizing the other person's situation (perspective taking), and feeling that person's emotions in that situation.

Empathizing with others is an important part of the perceptual process because it improves our sensitivity to the external causes of another person's performance and behaviour. This has the effect of minimizing fundamental attribu-

Increasing Empathy by Being There

Visualize this: You're in a local Safeway grocery store when a shoplifter runs out with stolen goods. Chasing in hot pursuit is the Safeway store manager. An unusual occurrence, perhaps, but this particular incident is even more unusual because the store manager is Simon Laffin, finance director of Safeway's British operations. Laffin spent four months as a store manager to get a better feel of the business he helps to lead. "Most retail bosses kid themselves that they really know their company," says Laffin. "But if they haven't worked on the shopfloor recently, then they don't really know about their business."

Simon Laffin and other executives are bringing their perceptions back into focus by working alongside frontline employees. Annette Verschuren, president of Home Depot Canada, keeps in touch with employees and customers by working in the retailer's stores and participating with employees in community events. Tom Andruskevich, president and CEO of Birks Jewellers, works on the floor of Birks' Montreal store three or four weekends every year during the Christmas rush.

The BBC television program "Back to the Floor" has encouraged more than 50 British chief executives to spend a week on the front lines while the cameras recorded the experience. Most received rude awakenings as they discovered that serving customers or making a product isn't quite as perfect or simple as it looks from the executive suite. "You can be briefed about an issue by your managers for years," complains Tom Riall, who spent a week collecting garbage when he was CEO of waste-disposal company Onyx UK. "But until you experience it for yourself, you don't really understand it."

Annette Verschuren, president of Home Depot Canada, keeps her perceptions in focus by working in the stores and participating in community service events. *CP/Ken Faught*

Sources: D. Penner, "Putting the Boss out Front," *Vancouver Sun*, June 7, 2002; "Lessons from the Line," *Fast Company*, Issue 56 (March 2002), p. 36; C. Hayward, "Back to the Floor," *Financial Management*, November 2001, pp. 22-23; F. Shalom, "Home Depot Attacks," *Montreal Gazette*, June 10, 1999, pp. C1, C2.
www.homedepot.com

tion error, described earlier in this chapter. A supervisor who imagines what it's like to be a single mother, for example, would become more sensitive to the external causes of lateness and other events among these employees.

Empathy comes naturally to some people. However, the rest of us can develop empathy skills by receiving feedback on how well we seem to empathize. For instance, Pratt & Whitney Canada CEO Alain Bellemare recalls his first job after graduating from engineering, when a supervisor gave him valuable feedback in the fine art of empathy. "He was phenomenal in coaching me in how to talk to people and how to be sensitive to their situation," Bellemare recalls.[61] Another way to increase empathy with employees and customers is by literally "walking in their shoes." Connections 3.2 describes how some corporate leaders are learning to empathize with their employees and the customers they serve by spending time in front-line jobs.

Know Yourself: Applying the Johari Window

Knowing yourself—becoming more aware of your values, beliefs, and prejudices—is a powerful way to improve your perceptions.[62] Let's say you had an unpleasant experience with lawyers and have developed negative emotions toward people in that profession. Being sensitive to these emotions should enable you to regulate your behaviour more effectively when working with legal professionals. Moreover, if co-workers are aware of your phobia about lawyers, they are more likely to understand your actions and help you to improve in the future.

The **Johari Window** is a popular model for understanding how co-workers can increase their mutual understanding.[63] Developed by Joseph Luft and Harry Ingram (hence the name *Johari*), this model divides information about yourself into four "windows"—open, blind, hidden, and unknown—based on whether your values, beliefs, and experiences are known to you and to others (see Exhibit 3.5). The *open area* includes information about you that is known both to you and others. For example, both you and your co-workers may be aware that you don't like to be near people who smoke cigarettes. The *blind area* refers to information that is known to others but not to you. For example, your colleagues might notice that you are embarrassed and awkward when meeting someone confined to a wheelchair, but you are unaware of this fact. Information known to you but unknown to others is found in the *hidden area*. We all have personal secrets about our likes, dislikes, and personal experiences. Finally, the *unknown area* includes your values, beliefs, and experiences that aren't known to you or others.

The main objective of the Johari Window is to increase the size of the open area so that both you and your colleagues are aware of your perceptual limitations. This is partly accomplished by reducing the hidden area through *disclosure*—informing others of your beliefs, feelings, and experiences that may influence the work relationship.[64] The open area also increases through *feedback* from others about your behaviours. This information helps you to reduce your blind area, because co-workers often see things in you that you don't. Finally, the

Johari Window
The model of personal and interpersonal understanding that encourages disclosure and feedback to increase the open area and reduce the blind, hidden, and unknown areas of oneself.

EXHIBIT 3.5

Johari Window

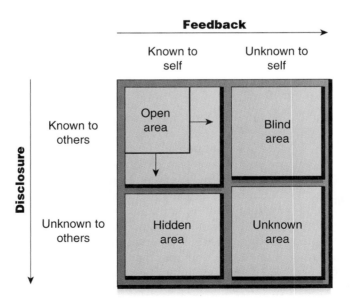

Source: Based on J. Luft, *Group Processes* (Palo Alto, CA: Mayfield, 1984).

combination of disclosure and feedback occasionally produces revelations about information in the unknown area.

The Johari Window applies to some diversity awareness and meaningful contact activities that we described earlier. By learning about cultural differences and communicating more with people from different backgrounds, we gain a better understanding of their behaviour. Engaging in open dialogue with co-workers also applies the Johari Window. As we communicate with others, we naturally tend to disclose more information about ourselves and eventually we feel comfortable providing candid feedback to them.

The perceptual process is the filter through which information passes from the external environment to our brain. As such, it is really the beginning of the learning process, which we discuss next.

LEARNING IN ORGANIZATIONS

learning
A relatively permanent change in behaviour that occurs as a result of a person's interaction with the environment.

Learning is a relatively permanent change in behaviour (or behaviour tendency) that occurs as a result of a person's interaction with the environment.[65] Learning occurs when the learner behaves differently. For example, we can see that you have "learned" computer skills when you operate a keyboard and windows more quickly than before. Learning occurs when behaviour change is due to interaction with the environment. This means that we learn through our senses, such as through study, observation, and experience.

Learning is essential for knowledge management—the organization's capacity to acquire, share, and use knowledge in ways that improves its survival and success (see Chapter 1).[66] Learning also influences individual behaviour and performance through three elements of the MARS model described in Chapter 2. First, people acquire skills and knowledge through learning opportunities, which gives them the competencies to perform tasks more effectively. Second, learning clarifies role perceptions. Employees develop a better understanding of their tasks and of the relative importance of their work activities. Third, learning motivates employees. Employees are more motivated to perform certain tasks when they learn that their effort will result in desired performance. Indeed, one major consulting firm recently reported that the ability to learn new skills was one of the top five factors motivating people to accept employment with an organization.[67]

Learning Explicit and Tacit Knowledge

When employees learn, they acquire both explicit and tacit knowledge. Explicit knowledge is organized and can be communicated from one person to another. The information you receive in a lecture is mainly explicit knowledge because the instructor packages and consciously transfers it to you. Explicit knowledge can be written down and given to others.

tacit knowledge
Knowledge embedded in our actions and ways of thinking, and transmitted only through observation and experience.

However, explicit knowledge is really only the tip of the knowledge iceberg. Most of what we know is **tacit knowledge**.[68] You have probably said to someone: "I can't tell you how to do this, but I can show you." Tacit knowledge is not documented; rather, it is action-oriented and known below the level of consciousness. Some writers suggest that tacit knowledge also includes an organization's culture and a team's implicit norms. People know these values and rules exist, but they are difficult to describe and document.[69] Tacit knowledge is acquired through observation and direct experience.[70] For example, airline pilots learn to operate commercial jets more by watching experts and practising on flight simulators than through lectures. They acquire tacit knowledge by directly experiencing the complex interaction of behaviour with the machine's response.

The rest of this chapter introduces three perspectives of learning tacit and explicit knowledge: reinforcement, social learning, and direct experience. Each perspective offers a different angle for understanding the dynamics of learning.

BEHAVIOUR MODIFICATION: LEARNING THROUGH REINFORCEMENT

behaviour modification
A theory that explains learning in terms of the antecedents and consequences of behaviour.

One of the oldest perspectives of learning, called **behaviour modification** (also known as *operant conditioning* and *reinforcement theory*), takes the rather extreme view that learning is completely dependent on the environment. Behaviour modification does not question the notion that thinking is part of the learning process, but views human thoughts as unimportant intermediate stages between behaviour and the environment.[71] Our experience with the environment teaches us to alter our behaviours so that we maximize positive consequences and minimize adverse consequences.[72]

A-B-Cs of Behaviour Modification

Behaviour modification recognizes that behaviour is influenced by two environmental contingencies: the antecedents that precede behaviour and the consequences that follow it. These principles are part of the A-B-C model of behaviour modification shown in Exhibit 3.6. The central objective of behaviour modification is to change behaviour (B) by managing its antecedents (A) and consequences (C).[73]

Antecedents are events that precede behaviour, informing employees that certain behaviours will have particular consequences. An antecedent may be a sound from your computer signalling that an e-mail has arrived, or a request from your supervisor to complete a specific task by tomorrow. These antecedents let employees know that a particular action will produce particular consequences. Notice that antecedents do not cause operant behaviours. The computer sound doesn't

EXHIBIT 3.6 A-B-C's of behaviour modification

Antecedents What happens before behaviour	Behaviour What person says or does	Consequences What happens after behaviour

Example

Warning light flashes on operator's console	Operator switches off the machine's power supply	Co-workers thank operator for stopping the machine

Sources: Adapted from T. K. Connellan, *How to Improve Human Performance*, (New York: Harper & Row, 1978), pg. 50; F. Luthans and R. Kreitner, *Organizational Behavior Modification and Beyond*, (Glenview, IL: Scott, Foresman, 1985), pp. 85–88.

cause us to open our e-mail. Rather, the sound is a cue telling us that certain consequences are likely to occur if we engage in certain behaviours.

Although antecedents are important, behaviour modification focuses mainly on the *consequences* of behaviour. Consequences are events that follow a particular behaviour and influence its future occurrence. Generally speaking, people tend to repeat behaviours that are followed by pleasant consequences, and less likely to repeat behaviours that are followed by unpleasant consequences or no consequences at all.

Contingencies of Reinforcement

Behaviour modification identifies four types of consequences, collectively known as the *contingencies of reinforcement*, which strengthen, maintain, or weaken behaviour. Exhibit 3.7 describes these contingencies: positive reinforcement, negative reinforcement, punishment, and extinction.[74]

- *Positive reinforcement*—**Positive reinforcement** occurs when the *introduction* of a consequence *increases or maintains* the frequency or future probability of a behaviour. Receiving a bonus after successfully completing an important project usually creates positive reinforcement because it typically increases the probability that you will use those behaviours in the future.
- *Negative reinforcement*—**Negative reinforcement** occurs when the *removal or avoidance* of a consequence *increases or maintains* the frequency or future probability of a behaviour. Supervisors apply negative reinforcement when they stop criticizing employees whose substandard performance has improved. By withholding the criticism, employees are more likely to repeat

positive reinforcement Occurs when the introduction of a consequence increases or maintains the frequency of future probability of a behaviour.

negative reinforcement Occurs when the removal or avoidance of a consequence increases or maintains the frequency of future probability of a behaviour.

EXHIBIT 3.7   Contingencies of reinforcement

	Consequence is introduced	**No consequence**	**Consequence is removed**
Behaviour increases or is maintained	**Positive reinforcement** Example: You receive a bonus after successfully completing an important project.		**Negative reinforcement** Example: Supervisor stops criticizing you when your job performance improves.
Behaviour decreases	**Punishment** Example: You are threatened with a demotion or discharge after treating a client badly.	**Extinction** Example: Co-workers no longer praise you when you engage in dangerous pranks.	**Punishment** Example: You give up your "employee of the month" parking spot to this month's winner.

behaviours that improve their performance.[75] Negative reinforcement is sometimes called avoidance learning because employees engage in the desired behaviours to avoid unpleasant consequences (such as being criticized by your supervisor or being fired from your job.)

punishment
Occurs when a consequence decreases the frequency or future probability of a behaviour.

■ *Punishment*—**Punishment** occurs when a consequence *decreases* the frequency or future probability of a behaviour. It may occur by introducing an unpleasant consequence or removing a pleasant consequence (see Exhibit 3.7). An example of the former would be an employee being threatened with a demotion or discharge after treating a client badly. The latter form of punishment would occur when a salesperson has to give a cherished parking spot to another employee who has a higher sales performance for the month.

extinction
Occurs when the target behaviour decreases because no consequence follows it.

■ *Extinction*—**Extinction** occurs when the target behaviour decreases because no consequence follows it. For example, if an employee plays practical jokes that are potentially dangerous or costly, this behaviour might be extinguished by discouraging others from praising the employee when he or she engages in these pranks. Behaviour that is no longer reinforced tends to disappear; it becomes extinct. In this respect, extinction is a do-nothing strategy.[76]

Which contingency of reinforcement should we use in the learning process? In most situations, positive reinforcement should follow desired behaviours and extinction (do nothing) should follow undesirable behaviours. This is because there are fewer adverse consequences when applying these contingencies compared with punishment and negative reinforcement. However, some form of punishment (dismissal, suspension, demotion, etc.) may be necessary for extreme behaviours, such as deliberately hurting co-workers or stealing inventory. Indeed, research suggests that, under certain conditions, punishment maintains a sense of equity.[77] However, punishment and negative reinforcement should be applied cautiously because they generate negative emotions and attitudes toward the punisher (e.g., supervisor) and organization.

Schedules of Reinforcement

Along with the types of consequences, behaviour modification identifies the schedule that should be followed to maximize the reinforcement effect. In fact, there is some evidence that scheduling the reinforcer affects learning more than the size of the reinforcer.[78] The most effective schedule of reinforcement for learning new tasks is *continuous reinforcement*—reinforcing every occurrence of the desired behaviour. Employees thus learn desired behaviours quickly. When the reinforcer is removed, extinction also occurs very quickly.

The other schedules of reinforcement are intermittent. Most people get paid on a *fixed interval schedule* because they receive their reinforcement (pay cheque) after a fixed period of time. A *variable interval schedule* is common for promotions. Employees are promoted after a variable amount of time. If you are given the rest of the day off after completing a fixed amount of work (e.g., stocking shelves in the store), then you would have experienced a *fixed ratio schedule*—reinforcement after a fixed number of behaviours or accomplishments. Lastly, companies often use a *variable ratio schedule* in which employee behaviour is reinforced after a variable number of times. Salespeople experience variable ratio reinforcement when they make a successful sale (the reinforcer) after a varying number of client calls. They might make four unsuccessful calls before receiving an order on the fifth one, then make 10 more calls before receiving the next order, and so on.

The variable ratio schedule is a low-cost way to reinforce behaviour because employees are rewarded infrequently. It is also highly resistant to extinction. Suppose your boss walks into your office at varying times of day. Chances are that you would work consistently better throughout the day than if your boss visits at exactly 11 a.m. every day. If your boss doesn't walk into your office at all on a particular day, you would still expect a visit right up to the end of the day if the previous visits were random.

Behaviour Modification in Practice

Everyone practises behaviour modification in one form or another. We thank people for a job well done, are silent when displeased, and sometimes try to punish those who go against our wishes. Behaviour modification also occurs in various formal programs to reduce absenteeism, minimize accidents, and improve task performance. When implemented correctly, the results are generally impressive[79] For instance, VJS Foods, a British food company, reduced absenteeism by giving employees with perfect attendance each month two chances to win C$800. Rhode Island shipyard Electric Boat recently awarded C$4,000 to each of 20 winners drawn from a pool of 955 employees who had not called in sick for at least two years. Student attendance improved (particularly in the last hour of classes) when some Los Angeles high schools introduced a lottery-based prize to students who were not absent over the previous week.[80]

In spite of these favourable results, behaviour modification has several limitations.[82] It is more difficult to apply to conceptual activities than to observable behaviours. For example, it's much easier to reward employees for good work attendance than for good problem solving. A second problem is "reward inflation," in which the reinforcer is eventually considered an entitlement. For this reason, most behaviour modification programs must run infrequently and for short durations. A third problem is that the variable ratio schedule often takes the form of a lottery, which conflicts with the ethical values of some employees. Finally, behaviour modification's radical "behaviourist" philosophy (that human thinking processes are unimportant) has few followers anymore because of fairly strong evidence that people *can learn* through mental processes, such as observing others and thinking logically about possible con-

Nova Chemicals introduced a million dollar "Recruitment and Retention Program" to reinforce good attendance and continued employment at its Joffre, Alberta construction site. Absenteeism reached 20 percent on some Fridays before long weekends, threatening the project's completion deadline. Nova Chemicals' solution was to reward employees who achieved perfect attendance with a chance to win one of ten $2,000 prizes each week. A final draw of four $100,000 grand prizes encouraged employees to stay until the end of their contract. Nova's behaviour modification program cut absenteeism rates by 25 percent and dramatically improved employment levels.[81] Would this type of reinforcement work as effectively for employees in long-term jobs, such as assembly line workers? *Courtesy of Nova Chemicals*
www.novachem.com

sequences.[83] Thus, without throwing away the principles of behaviour modification, most learning experts today also embrace the concepts of social learning theory.

SOCIAL LEARNING THEORY: LEARNING BY OBSERVING

social learning theory

A theory stating that much learning occurs by observing others and then modelling the behaviours that lead to favourable outcomes and avoiding behaviours that lead to punishing consequences.

Social learning theory states that much learning occurs by observing others and then modelling behaviours that lead to favourable outcomes and avoiding behaviours that lead to punishing consequences.[84] There are three related features of social learning theory: behavioural modelling, learning behaviour consequences, and self-reinforcement.

Behavioural Modelling

People learn by observing the behaviours of a role model on the critical task, remembering the important elements of the observed behaviours, and then practising those behaviours.[85] Behavioural modelling works best when the model is respected and the model's actions are followed by favourable consequences. For instance, recently-hired college graduates should learn by watching a previously-hired college graduate who successfully performs the task.

Behavioural modelling is a valuable form of learning because that is how tacit knowledge and skills are mainly acquired from others. Earlier in our discussion of learning, we learned that tacit knowledge is the subtle information about required behaviours, the correct sequence of those actions, and the environmental consequences (such as a machine response or customer reply) that should occur after each action. The adage that a picture is worth a thousand words applies here. It is difficult to document or verbally explain how a master baker kneads dough better than someone less qualified. Instead, we must observe these subtle actions that make that difference to develop a more precise mental model of the required behaviours and the expected responses. Behavioural modelling also guides role perceptions. Leaders model the behaviour they expect from others, for example.

Behaviour modelling and self-efficacy   Behavioural modelling increases self-efficacy because people gain more self-confidence after seeing someone else do something than if they are simply told what to do. This is particularly true when observers identify with the model, such as someone who is similar in age, experience, gender, and related features. You might experience this when working in a student support group. You form a "can-do" attitude when another student similar to you describes how he or she was able to perform well in a course that you are now taking. You learn not only what has to be done, but that others like you have been successful at this challenge.

Self-efficacy is also affected by initial experiences that occur when practising the previously modelled behaviour. Observers gain confidence when the environmental cues follow a predictable pattern and there are no unexpected surprises when they practise the behaviour.[86] For example, computer trainees develop stronger self-efficacy when they click the mouse and get the same computer response as the model did when performing the same behaviour. The expected response gives trainees a greater sense of control over the computer because they can predict what will happen following a particular behaviour.

Learning Behaviour Consequences

A second element of social learning theory says that we learn the consequences of behaviour in ways other than through direct experience. In particular, we learn by logically thinking through the consequences of our actions and by observing the consequences that other people experience following their behaviour. On the first point, we often anticipate desirable or adverse consequences through logic. We expect either positive reinforcement or negative reinforcement after completing an assigned task, and either punishment or extinction after performing the job poorly because that is a logical conclusion based on ethical values.

We also learn to anticipate consequences by observing the experiences of other people. Civilizations have relied on this principle for centuries, by punishing civil disobedience in public to deter other potential criminals.[87] Learning behaviour consequences occur in more subtle ways in contemporary organizations. Consider the employee who observes a co-worker receiving a stern warning for working in an unsafe manner. This event would reduce the observer's likelihood of engaging in unsafe behaviours because he or she has learned to anticipate a similar reprimand following those behaviours.[88]

Self-Reinforcement

The final element of social learning theory is *self-reinforcement*. Self-reinforcement occurs whenever an employee has control over a reinforcer but doesn't "take" the reinforcer until completing a self-set goal.[89] For example, you might be thinking about taking a work break after you finish reading the rest of this chapter—and not before! You could take a break right now, but you don't use this privilege until you have achieved your goal of reading the chapter. The work break is a form of positive reinforcement that is self-induced. You use the work break to reinforce completion of a task. Numerous consequences may be applied in self-reinforcement, ranging from raiding the refrigerator to congratulating yourself on completing the task.[90] Self-reinforcement has become increasingly important because employees are given more control over their working lives and are less dependent on supervisors to dole out positive reinforcement and punishment.

LEARNING THROUGH EXPERIENCE

Mandy Chooi is about to meet with a lower level manager who has botched a new assignment. She is also supposed to make a strategy presentation to her boss in three hours, but the telephone won't stop ringing and she is deluged with e-mail. It's a stressful situation. Fortunately, the Motorola human resources executive from Beijing is sitting in a simulation to develop and test her leadership skills. "It was hard. A lot harder than I had expected," says Chooi. "It's surprising how realistic and demanding it is."[91]

Many organizations are shifting their learning strategy away from the classroom toward a more experiential approach. Classrooms transfer explicit documented knowledge, but most tacit knowledge and skills are acquired through experience as well as observation.[92] Experiential learning has been conceptualized in many ways, but one of the most enduring perspectives is Kolb's experiential learning model, shown in Exhibit 3.8.[93] This model illustrates experiential learning as a cyclical four-stage process.

EXHIBIT 3.8

Kolb's experiential
learning model

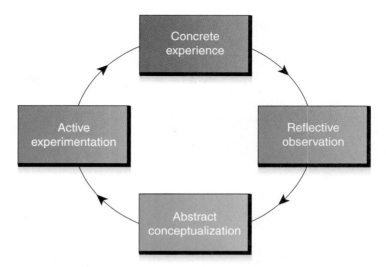

Sources: Based on information in J. E. Sharp, "Applying Kolb Learning Style Theory in the Communication Classroom," *Business Communication Quarterly* 60 (June 1997), pp. 129–34; D. A. Kolb, *Experiential Learning* (Englewood Cliffs, NJ: Prentice Hall, 1984).

Concrete experience involves sensory and emotional engagement in some activity. It is followed by reflective observation, which involves listening, watching, recording, and elaborating on the experience. The next stage in the learning cycle is abstract conceptualization. This is the stage in which we develop concepts and integrate our observations into logically sound theories. The fourth stage, active experimentation, occurs when we test our previous experience, reflection, and conceptualization of a particular context.

Notice from this model that experiential learning includes the polar opposite of concrete experience and abstract conceptualization. We need to experience concrete reality as well as form abstract concepts from that reality. Experiential learning also involves the polar opposites of active experimentation and passive reflection. People tend to prefer, and operate better in, some stages than others due to their particular competencies and personalities. Still, experiential learning requires all four stages in proper balance.

Experiential Learning in Practice

Learning through experience works best where there is a strong *learning orientation*.[94] Organizations with a strong learning orientation value knowledge management and, in particular, the generation of new knowledge as employees achieve their goals. If an employee initially fails to perform a task, then the experience might still be a valuable learning opportunity. In other words, organizations encourage employees to appreciate the process of individual and team learning, not just the performance results.

Organizations achieve a learning orientation culture by rewarding experimentation and recognizing mistakes as a natural part of the learning process. They encourage employees to take reasonable risks so they can ultimately discover new and better ways of doing things. Without a learning orientation, mistakes are hid-

Dozens of passengers were bleeding, unconscious, or dazed and confused after a GO train collided with a gas tanker truck in Newmarket, Ontario. "There was pandemonium on the train," says passenger Peggy Martin, sporting a large bleeding gash on her arm. "People were screaming and crying." Fortunately, the gory scene was a realistic mock disaster, named Exercise Timothy, complete with 50 volunteer casualties covered with fake blood who acted out their roles. The idea behind this activity is that emergency crews need to acquire tacit knowledge through experiential learning. "Exercise Timothy is the first test of mass casualty ever conducted by the Region, and is a major part of a program to educate our employees and evaluate our emergency plans," explains York Region chair Bill Fisch.[96] How does this emergency training exercise apply Kolb's experiential learning model? *D. Cameron, Toronto Star*
www.region.york.on.ca

action learning
A variety of experiential learning activities in which employees are involved in a "real, complex, and stressful problem," usually in teams, with immediate relevance to the company.

den and problems are more likely to escalate or re-emerge later. It's not surprising, then, that one of the most frequently mentioned lessons from the best performing manufacturers is to expect mistakes. "[Mistakes] are a source of learning and will improve operations in the long run," explains an executive at Lockheed Martin. "[They] foster the concept that no question is dumb, no idea too wild, and no task or activity is irrelevant."[95]

Action learning   The fastest growing form of experiential learning in the workplace is called **action learning**. Action learning refers to a variety of experiential learning activities in which employees are involved in a "real, complex, and stressful problem," usually in teams, with immediate relevance to the company.[97] In action learning, the task becomes the source of learning.

Kolb's experiential learning model presented earlier is usually identified as the main template for action learning.[98] Action learning requires concrete experience with a real organizational problem. The process includes "learning meetings" in which participants reflect on their observations regarding the problem or opportunity. The action learning team is responsible for conceptualizing or applying a model to solve the problem or opportunity. Then the team tests the model through experimentation in the real setting. For example, an action learning team at Carpenter Technology was given the challenge to investigate the steel manufacturer's strategy for entry into India. The team investigated the opportunity, wrote up its recommendation, and participated in its implementation.[99]

Action learning is considered one of the most important ways to develop executive competencies.[100] It involves both tacit and explicit learning, forces employees to diagnose new situations, and makes them rethink current work practices. At the same time, the results of action learning potentially add value to the organization by creating a better work process or service. For example, one of Motorola's action learning teams spent several months learning how to create and manage a software business.[101]

This chapter has introduced you to two fundamental activities of human behaviour in the workplace: perceptions and learning. These activities involve receiving information from the environment, organizing it, and acting on it as a learning process. Perceptions and learning are mainly cognitive (thinking) processes, but they are influenced by—and have an influence on—the emotional side of human behaviour. In the next chapter, we consider the dynamics of emotions and attitudes in the workplace.

CHAPTER SUMMARY

Perception involves selecting, organizing, and interpreting information to make sense of the world. Selective attention is influenced by characteristics of the target, the target's setting, and the perceiver. Perceptual grouping principles organize incoming information. This is also influenced by our emotions, expectations, and mental models.

According to social identity theory, people perceive themselves by their unique characteristics and membership in various groups. They also develop homogeneous, and usually positive, images of people in their own groups, and usually less positive homogeneous images of people in other groups. This leads to overgeneralizations and stereotypes.

Stereotyping is the process of assigning traits to people based on their membership in a social category. Stereotyping economizes mental effort, fills in missing information, and enhances our self-perception and social identity. However, stereotyping also lays the foundation for prejudice and intentional or unintentional discrimination. We can't prevent the activation of stereotyping, but we can minimize the stereotypic information we apply in our decisions and actions. Three strategies to minimize the influence of stereotypes are diversity awareness training, meaningful interaction, and decision-making accountability.

The attribution process involves deciding whether the behaviour or event is largely due to the situation (external attributions) or to personal characteristics (internal attributions). Two attribution errors are fundamental attribution error and self-serving bias. Self-fulfilling prophecy occurs when our expectations about another person cause that person to act in a way that is consistent with those expectations. Leaders can create positive self-fulfilling prophecies by supporting a learning orientation, applying contingency-oriented leadership styles, and increasing the employee's self-efficacy.

Four other perceptual errors commonly noted in organizations are primacy effect, recency effect, halo effect, and projection. We can minimize these and other perceptual problems through empathy and becoming more aware of our values, beliefs, and prejudices (Johari Window).

Learning is a relatively permanent change in behaviour (or behaviour tendency) that occurs as a result of a person's interaction with the environment. Learning is an important part of knowledge management and influences ability, role perceptions, and motivation in the MARS model of individual performance.

The behaviour modification perspective of learning states that behaviour change occurs by altering its antecedents and consequences. Antecedents are environmental stimuli that provoke (not necessarily cause) behaviour. Consequences are events following behaviour that influence its future occurrence. Consequences include positive reinforcement, negative reinforcement, punishment, and extinction. The schedules of reinforcement also influence behaviour.

Social learning theory states that much learning occurs by observing others and then modelling those behaviours that seem to lead to favourable outcomes and avoiding behaviours that lead to punishing consequences. It also recognizes that we often engage in self-reinforcement. Behavioural modelling is effective because it transfers tacit knowledge and enhances the observer's self-efficacy.

Many companies now use experiential learning because employees do not acquire tacit knowledge through formal classroom instruction. Kolb's experiential learning model is a cyclical four-stage process that includes concrete experience, reflective observation, abstract conceptualization, and active experimentation. Action learning refers to a variety of experiential learning activities in which employees solve problems or opportunities, usually in teams, with immediate relevance to the organization.

KEY TERMS

Action learning, p. 96

Attribution process, p. 79

Behaviour modification, p. 89

Contact hypothesis, p. 78

Empathy, p. 85

Extinction, p. 91

Fundamental attribution error, p. 81

Halo error, p. 84

Johari Window, p. 87

Learning orientation, p. 83

Learning, p. 88

Mental models, p. 74

Negative reinforcement, p. 90

Perception, p. 72

Positive reinforcement, p. 90

Prejudice, p. 77

Primacy effect, p. 84

Projection bias, p. 85

Punishment, p. 91

Recency effect, p. 84

Selective attention, p. 73

Self-efficacy, p. 83

Self-fulfilling prophecy, p. 82

DISCUSSION QUESTIONS

1. You are part of a task force to increase worker responsiveness to emergencies on the production floor. Identify four factors that should be considered when installing a device that will get every employee's attention when there is an emergency.

2. What mental models do you have about attending a college or university lecture? Are these mental models helpful? Could any of these mental models hold you back from achieving the full benefit of the lecture?

3. Contrast "personal" and "social" identity. Do you define yourself in terms of the university or college you attend? Why or why not? What implications does your response have for the future of your university or college?

4. During a diversity management session, a manager suggests that stereotypes are a necessary part of working with others. "I have to make assumptions about what's in the other person's head, and stereotypes help me do that," she explains. "It's better to rely on stereotypes than to enter a working relationship with someone from another culture without any idea of what they believe in!" Discuss the merits of and problems with the manager's statement.

5. At the end of an NHL hockey game the coach of the losing team was asked to explain his team's defeat. "I don't know," he begins, "we've done well in this rink over the past few years. Our busy schedule over the past two weeks has pushed the guys too hard, I guess. They're worn out. You probably noticed that we also got some bad breaks on penalties tonight. We should have done well here, but things just went against us." Use attribution theory to explain the coach's perceptions of the team's loss.

6. Describe how a manager or coach could use the process of self-fulfilling prophecy to enhance an individual's performance.

7. Describe a situation when you used behaviour modification to influence someone's behaviour. What specifically did you do? What was the result?

8. Why are organizations moving toward the use of experiential approaches to learning? What conditions are required for success?

CASE STUDY 3.1

NUPATH FOODS LTD.

James Ornath read the latest sales figures with a great deal of satisfaction. The vice-president of marketing at Nupath Foods Ltd. was pleased to see that the marketing campaign to improve sagging sales of Prowess cat food was working. Sales volume of the product had increased 20 percent in the past quarter compared with the previous year, and market share was up.

The improved sales of Prowess could be credited to Denise Roberge, the brand manager responsible for cat foods at Nupath. Roberge had joined Nupath less than two years ago as an assistant brand manager after leaving a similar job at a consumer products firm. She was one of the few women in marketing management at Nupath and had a promising career with the company. Ornath was pleased with Roberge's work and tried to let her know this in the annual performance reviews. He now had an excellent opportunity to reward her by offering the recently vacated position of market research coordinator. Although technically only a lateral transfer with a modest salary increase, the marketing research coordinator job would give Roberge broader experience in some high-profile work, which would enhance her career with Nupath. Few people were aware that Ornath's own career had been boosted by working as marketing research coordinator at Nupath several years before.

Denise Roberge had also seen the latest sales figures on Prowess cat food and was expecting Ornath's call to meet with her that morning. Ornath began the conversation by briefly mentioning the favourable sales figures, and then explained that he wanted Roberge to take the marketing research coordinator job. Roberge was shocked by the news. She enjoyed brand management and particularly the challenge involved with controlling a product that directly affected the company's profitability. Marketing research coordinator was a technical support position—a "backroom" job—far removed from the company's bottom-line activities. Marketing research was not the route to top management in most organizations, Roberge thought. She had been sidelined.

After a long silence, Roberge managed a weak "Thank you, Mr. Ornath." She was too bewildered to protest. She wanted to collect her thoughts and reflect on what she had done wrong. Also, she did not know her boss well enough to be openly critical. Ornath recognized Roberge's surprise, which he naturally assumed was her positive response to hearing of this wonderful career opportunity. He, too, had been delighted several years earlier about his temporary transfer to marketing research to round out his marketing experience. "This move will be good for both you and Nupath," said Ornath as he escorted Roberge from his office.

Roberge had several tasks to complete that afternoon, but was able to consider the day's events that evening. She was one of the top women in brand management at Nupath and feared that she was being sidelined because the company didn't want women in top management. Her previous employer had made it quite clear that women "couldn't take the heat" in marketing management and tended to place women in technical support positions after a brief term in lower brand management jobs. Obviously Nupath was following the same game plan. Ornath's comments that the coordinator job would be good for her was just a nice way of saying that Roberge couldn't go any further in brand management at Nupath. Roberge was now faced with the difficult decision of confronting Ornath and trying to change Nupath's sexist practices or submitting her resignation.

Discussion Questions

1. What symptom(s) exist in this case to suggest that something has gone wrong?

2. What root causes have led to these symptoms?

3. What actions should the organization take to correct these problems?

Copyright © Steven L. McShane.

TEAM EXERCISE 3.2

THE REINFORCEMENT EXERCISE

Purpose This exercise is designed to help you understand how the contingencies of reinforcement in behaviour modification affect learning.

Materials Any objects normally available in a classroom will be acceptable for this activity.

Instructions The instructor will ask for three volunteers, who are then briefed outside the classroom. The instructor will spend a few minutes briefing the remaining students in the class about their duties. Then, one of the three volunteers will enter the room to participate in the exercise. When completed, the second volunteer enters the room and participates in the exercise. When completed, the third volunteer enters the class and participates in the exercise.

Your instructor will have more details at the start of this activity.

ASSESSING YOUR GENERAL SELF-EFFICACY

Purpose This exercise is designed to help you understand the concept of self-efficacy and to estimate your general self-efficacy.

Overview Self-efficacy refers to a person's belief that he or she has the ability, motivation, and resources to complete a task successfully. Self-efficacy is usually conceptualized as a situation-specific belief. You may believe that you can perform a certain task in one situation, but are less confident with that task in another situation. However, there is also evidence that people develop a more general self-efficacy if they perform tasks in a variety of situations. This exercise helps you to estimate your general self-efficacy.

Instructions Read each of the statements below and circle the response that best fits your personal belief. Then use the scoring key in Appendix B of this book to calculate your results. This self-assessment is completed alone so that students can rate themselves honestly without being concerned about comparisons. However, class discussion will focus on the meaning of self-efficacy, how this scale might be applied in organizations, and the limitations of measuring self-efficacy in work settings.

New General Self-Efficacy Scale				
To what extent does each statement describe you? Indicate your level of agreement by marking the appropriate response on the right.	Strongly Agree ▼	Agree ▼	Neutral ▼	Disagree ▼	Strongly Disagree ▼
1. I will be able to achieve most of the goals that I have set for myself.	☐	☐	☐	☐	☐
2. When facing difficult tasks, I am certain that I will accomplish them.	☐	☐	☐	☐	☐
3. In general, I think that I can obtain outcomes that are important to me.	☐	☐	☐	☐	☐
4. I believe I can succeed at most any endeavour to which I set my mind.	☐	☐	☐	☐	☐
5. I will be able to successfully overcome many challenges.	☐	☐	☐	☐	☐
6. I am confident that I can perform effectively on many different tasks.	☐	☐	☐	☐	☐
7. Compared to other people, I can do most tasks very well.	☐	☐	☐	☐	☐
8. Even when things are tough, I can perform quite well.	☐	☐	☐	☐	☐

Source: G. Chen, S. M. Gully, and D. Eden, "Validation of a New General Self-Efficacy Scale," *Organizational Research Methods*, 4 (January 2001), pp. 62–83.

ASSESSING YOUR PERSPECTIVE-TAKING (COGNITIVE EMPATHY)

 Go to the Student CD for an interactive version of this exercise.

Purpose This exercise is designed to help you understand and estimate your propensity for perspective taking, which represents the cognitive (thinking) aspect of empathy.

Instructions This instrument asks you to indicate the degree to which each of the statements presented does or does not describe you very well. You need to be honest with yourself for a reasonable estimate of your level of perspective taking. The results show your level of perspective-taking as well as the general meaning of this score.

ASSESSING YOUR EMOTIONAL EMPATHY

 Go to the Student CD for an interactive version of this exercise.

Purpose This exercise is designed to help you understand and to estimate your propensity for emotional empathy.

Instructions This instrument asks you to indicate the degree to which each of the statements presented does or does not describe you very well. You need to be honest with yourself for a reasonable estimate of your level of perspective taking. The results show your level of emotional empathy as well as the general meaning of this score.

 **Online LearningCentre** with POWERWEB

After studying the preceding material, be sure to check out our Online Learning Centre at
www.mcgrawhill.ca/college/mcshane
for more in-depth information and interactivities that correspond to this chapter.

CHAPTER 4

Workplace Emotions and Attitudes

Learning Objectives

- Define emotions and identify the two dimensions around which emotions are organized.

- Diagram the model of emotions, attitudes, and behaviour.

- Identify the conditions that require and problems with emotional labour.

- Outline the four components of emotional intelligence.

- Summarize the effects of job dissatisfaction in terms of the exit-voice-loyalty-neglect model.

- Compare the effects of affective and continuance commitment on employee behaviour.

- Describe five strategies to increase organizational commitment.

- Contrast transactional and relational psychological contracts.

- Discuss the trend towards employability.

If history is any guide, SaskTel won't be laying off any employees for a long time. The Regina-based telecommunications company hasn't laid off anyone since it was founded in 1908. "[Layoffs] aren't going to happen as long as we can help it," says Byron Pointer, SaskTel's vice-president of human resources and industrial relations.

By avoiding layoffs, SaskTel is building a more loyal work force. "I have lots of friends who looked for greener grass and moved to Alberta, Toronto or Ottawa," explains John Hill, a SaskTel electrical engineer who plans and designs information technology systems. "Most have bounced from company to company. Loyalty just doesn't exist. Here [at SaskTel] you've got loyalty."

Along with job security, employees proudly identify with SaskTel because the company applies humanitarian values (fairness, courtesy, moral integrity), keeps staff informed of company developments, and is a model of corporate social responsibility. For instance, SaskTel works with First Nations communities to improve employment opportunities for First Nations youth, provides donations to over 1,500 community organizations, and demonstrates stewardship of the environment. "If you told your mother you'd turned down a job at SaskTel, she'd shoot you," jokes Jason Durant, who plans and researches new e-business initiatives at SaskTel.

SaskTel has built a loyal workforce by avoiding layoffs, keeping employees informed, providing exciting job opportunities, and demonstrating corporate social responsibility. *Courtesy SaskTel*

Another driver of employee loyalty is SaskTel's local and international achievements. SaskTel was the first in North America to introduce high-speed DSL Internet access. Its international subsidiary, SaskTel International, developed and installed the fibre-optic communications network in the underground channel connecting England and France. The company also provides unique work opportunities for SaskTel staff in Africa and Australia.

The result of pride and positive attitudes at SaskTel is a top-notch customer service reputation. "It all starts with the people who do the work," says Garry Simmons, president of SaskTel International. "Their adaptability and positive attitude allow us to succeed, and we've heard so many positive comments from our partners in Tanzania and elsewhere about the quality of our people."[1] ■

www.sasktel.com

SaskTel and numerous other Canadian firms are paying a lot more attention to employee emotions and attitudes these days. That's because the emotions people experience and their evaluative judgments about various aspects of work make a difference in the organization's performance, customer loyalty, and employee well-being. This chapter presents the most up-to-date information available on the topic of workplace emotions and attitudes. We begin by understanding the meaning and types of emotions. We follow this by a close look at how attitudes are formed, and new thinking about how emotions influence both attitudes and behaviour in the workplace.

Next, we consider the dynamics of emotional labour, including the conditions requiring and ways of supporting emotional labour. This leads into the popular topic of emotional intelligence, which presents the current perspective on the components of emotional intelligence and ways of improving this ability. Job satisfaction, the most widely studied work attitude, is then discussed. We look at job satisfaction among Canadians, the effects of job satisfaction on work behaviour, and new findings regarding the relationship between job satisfaction and employee performance and customer satisfaction. The next section provides an overview of organizational commitment, including the types of commitment, consequences of commitment, and ways to build affective commitment. Organizational commitment is strongly influenced by trust and the psychological contract, so the final section of this chapter looks at the meaning and elements of both concepts.

EMOTIONS IN THE WORKPLACE

The tragic events of September 11, 2001, in the United States are permanently etched in our minds. The four hijacked planes and the collapse of the World Trade Center towers evoked a variety of emotions in people, such as anger, sadness, and fear. Airline employees particularly identified with these shocking events. "We were torn apart," says Lucie Leduc, a flight attendant with Air Transat in Montreal. "We could totally imagine it. . . . There were flight attendants who couldn't fly for a while; some are still not flying."[2]

emotions
Psychological and physiological episodes experienced toward an object, person, or event that create a state of readiness.

Lucie Leduc and her co-workers at Air Transat experienced the strong emotions associated with the events of September 11, 2001. **Emotions** are psychological and physiological episodes experienced toward an object, person, or event that create a state of readiness.[3] There are a few key components to this definition. First, emotions are brief events or "episodes." Your anger toward a co-worker, for instance, would typically subside within a few minutes. Second, emotions are directed toward someone or something. We experience joy, fear, anger, and other emotional episodes toward tasks, customers, public speeches we present, a software program we are using, and so on. This contrasts with *moods*, which are less intense emotional states that are not directed toward anything in particular.[4]

A third feature of this definition is that we experience emotions both psychologically and physiologically. Your anger toward a co-worker would be triggered from the psychological processes of perceiving a particular situation (e.g., discovering that the co-worker may have erased several hours of your work from the computer system) and appraising that situation against your values and expectations. The physiological dimension of emotions might consist of higher blood pressure and increased adrenalin. It also consists of facial expressions, such as pursing your lips and furrowing your eyebrows when you discover that the computer work has been erased.

"Biosensors. The whole company knows instantly when I'm displeased."

Copyright © Ted Goff. 2001 www.tedgoff.com Used with permission.

Last, emotions create a state of readiness. Emotional episodes are communications to ourselves. They make us aware of events that may affect our survival and well-being. Some emotions (e.g., anger, surprise, fear) are particularly strong "triggers" that demand our attention, interrupt our train of thought, and generate the motivation to act on the environment.[5]

Types of Emotions

People experience numerous emotions in the workplace and other settings. Some scholars have clustered all emotions into six primary categories: anger, fear, joy, love, sadness, and surprise. For example, alarm and anxiety cluster together to form the primary emotional category called fear.[6] However, emotions are more commonly organized around two or three dimensions.[7] The most widely recognized dimensional view of emotions is the Affect Circumplex Model shown in Exhibit 4.1, which organizes emotions on the basis of their pleasantness and activation (the extent that the emotion produces alertness or engagement). Fear, for example, is an unpleasant experience (i.e. we try to avoid conditions that generate fear) and has high activation (i.e. it motivates us to act). Emotions on the opposite side of the circle have the opposite effect. As we see in Exhibit 4.1, calm is the opposite to fear; it is a pleasant experience that produces very little activation in us.

Emotions, Attitudes, and Behaviour

Emotions play an important role in workplace behaviour. To understand the influence of emotions on behaviour, we first need to understand the concept called attitudes. **Attitudes** represent the cluster of beliefs, assessed feelings, and behavioural intentions toward a person, object, or event (called an *attitude object*).[8] Attitudes are *judgments*, whereas emotions are *experiences*. Attitudes involve logical reasoning, whereas we sense emotions. We also experience most emotions briefly, whereas our attitude toward someone or something is more stable over time. Attitudes include three components: beliefs, feelings, and behavioural intentions.

attitudes
The cluster of beliefs, assessed feelings, and behavioural intentions toward an object.

- *Beliefs*—your established perceptions about the attitude object—what you believe to be true. For example, you might believe that mergers result in layoffs. Or you might believe that mergers ensure survival in an era of globalization. These beliefs develop from past experience and learning.[9]
- *Feelings*—your positive or negative evaluations of the attitude object. Some people think mergers are good; others think they are bad. Your like or dislike of mergers represents your assessed feelings toward the attitude object.
- *Behavioural intentions*—your motivation to engage in a particular behaviour with respect to the attitude object. You might plan to quit rather than stay with the company during the merger. Alternatively, you might intend to e-mail senior executives to tell them this merger was a good decision.

EXHIBIT 4.1

Affect circumplex
model

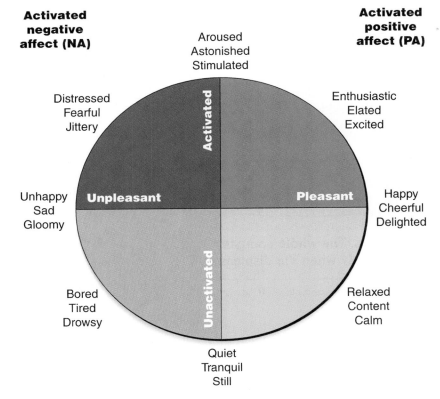

Source: J. Larson, E. Diener, and R. E. Lucas, "Emotion: Models, Measures, and Differences," In R. G. Lord, R. J. Klimoske, & R. Kanfer (Eds.) *Emotions in the Workplace* (San Francisco: Jossey-Bass, 2002), pp. 64–113.

Traditionally, scholars have taken the view that the three components of attitude influence behaviour through a purely rational process. This rational attitude–behaviour model is illustrated on the left side of Exhibit 4.2. The perceived environment influences our beliefs about an attitude object. We then calculate our feelings toward the attitude object based on these beliefs. The resulting evaluative judgments (feelings) lead to behavioural intentions, and behavioural intentions lead to behaviour under certain circumstances.

Let's look at each stage of this rational process more closely. First, we calculate our feelings from our beliefs. This process, known as the *expectancy-value model*, says that feelings are determined by the person's beliefs about the attitude object's expectancy of producing specific outcomes as well as by the value (good or bad) of those outcomes. Let's say that you believe (expectancy) the consequences of mergers are mostly negative (value), such as that they are disruptive, result in layoffs, and usually lose money for the company. Even if you recognize a couple of positive outcomes of mergers, you would likely develop negative feelings toward mergers (i.e. you dislike mergers).

Next, feelings influence your behavioural intentions. People with the same feelings may form different behavioural intentions based on their unique past experience. Suppose your company announced it would merge with a larger company. Employees who think mergers are bad (feelings) may intend to quit whereas others might want to complain about the decision. People choose the behavioural intention they think will work best for them.

Model of emotions, attitudes, and behaviour

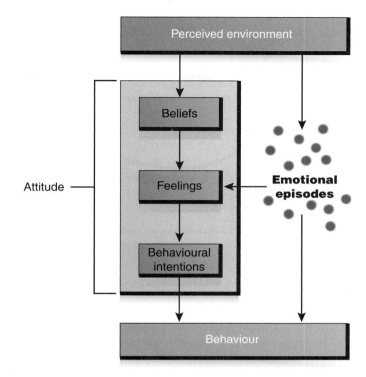

Finally, behavioural intentions are better than feelings or beliefs at predicting a person's behaviour.[10] Even so, scholars have reported for many years that behavioural intentions alone are relatively weak predictors of behaviour. The main reason for this weak relationship is that behavioural intentions represent the motivation to act, yet the other three factors in the MARS model—ability, role perceptions, and situational factors—also influence individual behaviour (see Chapter 2). You might intend to write a letter complaining about the announced merger, but a heavy workload and family obligations prevent you from completing this intended task.

Linking emotions to attitudes and behaviour Notice that the rational model —which has dominated attitude research for decades—does not mention emotions in either attitude formation or the prediction of behaviour. This neglect dates back to Plato, Descartes, and other philosophers who urged scholars to separate emotion from reasoning. Today, we know that the rational attitude model is incomplete because it ignores emotions. Indeed, evidence is mounting that emotions play an important role in understanding both attitudes and behaviour.[11]

So, where do emotions fit in? Neuroscience provides some guidance here. Neuroscientists report that our perceptions of the external world are routed to two parts of the brain—the emotional centre and the rational centre.[12] The expectancy-value attitude model represents the rational brain centre process. The emotional centre also receives the perceptual information, but processes it much faster and with less precision. The incoming information produces emotional episodes that are tagged to the information. Imagine hearing that the organization where you work will soon merge with a larger competitor. Upon hearing this announcement, you might immediately experience surprise, optimism, anger, excitement, or other emotions. The emotional centre tagged emotions to the announcement, indicating that the situation threatens or supports your survival and well-being.

The right side of Exhibit 4.2 offers a simplified presentation of how emotions get integrated with the rational process and influence behaviour. The emotional centre generates emotions regarding the attitude object based on a "quick and dirty" assessment of perceived environment information (e.g., you are surprised, excited, or angry on hearing the merger announcement). Those emotions are then transmitted to the rational centre, which is more slowly analyzing the information. The emotional markers influence your judgment about the announcement and shape your feelings toward the attitude object. If you experience anxiety and irritation when hearing the merger announcement, then you would likely develop negative feelings toward it.[13]

You can see how emotions affect our workplace attitudes. When performing our jobs or interacting with co-workers, we experience a variety of emotions that shape our longer-term feelings toward the company. The more positive emotions we have, the more we form positive attitudes toward the organization and various things within it. Not surprisingly, some employers try to create lots of positive emotions through various "fun" activities in the workplace, as Connections 4.1 describes. In each case, the idea is to create emotions that result in favourable judgments about the organization.

One last observation about the attitude model in Exhibit 4.2 is the arrow that goes directly from the emotional episodes to behaviour. This indicates that people react behaviourally to their emotions, not just to their judgments (attitudes). When upset, an employee might stomp out of a meeting, bang a fist on the desk, or burst into tears. When overjoyed, an employee might embrace a co-worker or break into a little dance. Even minor emotions cause us to change facial expressions and other subtle behaviours. These actions are not carefully thought out. They are fairly automatic emotional responses that serve as coping mechanisms in that situation.[14]

cognitive dissonance
Occurs when people perceive an inconsistency between their beliefs, feelings, and behaviour.

Cognitive dissonance   Emotions and attitudes usually lead to behaviour, but behaviour sometimes influences our attitudes through the process of **cognitive dissonance**.[15] Cognitive dissonance occurs when we perceive an inconsistency between our beliefs, feelings, and behaviour. This inconsistency creates an uncomfortable tension (dissonance) that we are motivated to reduce by changing one or more of these elements. Behaviour is usually the most difficult element to change, particularly when it is known to everyone, was done voluntarily, and can't be undone. Thus, we usually change our beliefs and feelings instead, to reduce the inconsistency.

positive affectivity (PA)
The tendency to experience positive emotional states.

Emotions and personality   Our coverage of the dynamics of workplace emotions wouldn't be complete until we mentioned that a person's emotions are also partly determined by their personality, not just their workplace experiences. **Positive affectivity** (PA) is the tendency to experience positive emotional states. It is very similar to extroversion, described in Chapter 3 as a characteristic of people who are outgoing, talkative, sociable, and assertive. In contrast, some people are high on **negative affectivity** (NA), which is the tendency to experience negative

negative affectivity (NA)
The tendency to experience negative emotions.

Creating Positive Emotions in the Workplace

At a recent "winter carnival," MDS Nordion employees were treated to hot apple cider and chili at the company's on-site ice rink. The Ottawa-based company, which is the world's largest supplier of medical isotopes, added to the levity with relay races, a mock sumo wrestling event, and sleigh rides. "There's always something fun like that going on," says an MDS Nordion executive.

Fun at work? It sounds like an oxymoron. But in order to attract and keep valuable talent, companies are finding creative ways to generate positive emotions in the workplace. When Vancouver City Hall employees got cranky a while ago, the municipality brought in an improv comedy team to put smiles back on their faces. Research in Motion employees in Waterloo, Ontario, enjoy barbeques, Popsicle days, and the occasional rock concert. At DY4 Systems Inc. in Ottawa, employees sit on plastic chairs that double as curling rocks for their human curling event.

At Kryptonite, CEO Gary Furst dresses up as a Scottish warrior in the movie *Braveheart*, complete with kilt, face-paint, and bagpiper, when he hands out the bonus cheques. Furst and other executives at the Boston-based bicycle lock maker have also dyed their hair green, held game shows, and hired musicians to entertain the troops. "You really need to find innovative, provocative and fun ways to motivate people," advises Furst. "Work can either be a drag or a lot of fun."

These fun and games may seem silly, but some corporate leaders are deadly serious about their value. "It's pretty simple," explains Nathan Rudyk, president of

MDS Nordion employees have some fun during their annual winter carnival. *Courtesy of MDS Nordion.*

DigIT Interactive Inc. (now part of Quebecor) in Montreal. "If you want to make the most money, you must attract the best people. To get the best people, you must be the most fun."

Sources: R. Yerema, *Canada's Top 100 Employers, 2002* (Toronto: MediaCorp Canada, 2002), pp. 172-75, 233-34; M. Shaw, "A Motivating Example," *Network World Fusion*, May 14, 2001; P. Chisholm, "Redesigning Work," *Maclean's*, March 5, 2001, pp. 34-38; J. Elliott, "All Work and No Play can Chase Workers Away," *Edmonton Journal*, February 28, 2000; A. Daniels, "Humour Specialists Bring Fun to Workplace," *Vancouver Sun*, January 29, 2000.
www.mds.nordion.com

emotions.[16] Employees with high NA tend to be more distressed and unhappy because they focus on the negative aspects of life.

To what extent do these personality traits influence emotions and behaviour? Some research reports that PA and NA employees differ in their attendance, turnover, and how they react to job satisfaction. NA is also associated with various stages of job burnout (see Chapter 7).[17] However, other evidence suggests that PA and NA have relatively weak effects on work-related attitudes.[18] Overall, it seems that PA and NA influence emotions and attitudes in the workplace, but their effects are not as strong as situational factors.

MANAGING EMOTIONS AT WORK

The Elbow Room Cafe is packed and noisy on this Saturday morning. A customer at the restaurant in Vancouver, B.C., half shouts across the room for more coffee. A passing waiter scoffs: "You want more coffee, get it yourself!" The customer only laughs. Another diner complains loudly that he and his party are running late and need their food. This time, restaurant manager Patrick Savoie speaks up: "If you're in a hurry, you should have gone to McDonald's." The diner and his companions chuckle.

To the uninitiated, the Elbow Room Café is an emotional basketcase, full of irate guests and the rudest staff west of the Canadian Rockies. But it's all a performance—a place where guests can enjoy good food and play out their emotions about dreadful customer service. "It's almost like coming to a theatre," says Savoie, who spends much of his time inventing new ways to insult the clientele.[19]

Whether giving the most insulting service at Elbow Room Café in Vancouver or the friendliest service at SaskTel in Saskatchewan, employees are usually expected to manage their emotions in the workplace. **Emotional labour** refers to the effort, planning, and control needed to express organizationally desired emotions during interpersonal transactions.[20] When interacting with co-workers, customers, suppliers, and others, employees are expected to abide by *display rules*. These rules are norms requiring employees to display certain emotions and to withhold others.

> **emotional labour**
> The effort, planning, and control needed to express organizationally desired emotions during interpersonal transactions.

Conditions Requiring Emotional Labour

Air Canada employees need to smile more often. That's the advice of Air Canada chief executive Robert Milton in a recent letter urging staff to win back the hearts of passengers. "In everyday life, you make your consumer decisions based on where you receive the best overall value and, in the case of a tie, we all do the same thing—we go to where the people are the nicest," says Milton. Over at The Beer Store's call centre in London, Ontario, staff are also encouraged to "smile" through their voices. "Our thing is, 'let them hear you smile,'" says Patricia Robertson, who is responsible for The Beer Store's call centre.[21]

At Air Canada, The Beer Store, and every other organization in Canada, employees are expected to engage in some level of emotional labour. People experience more emotional labour when their jobs require frequent and long durations of voice or face-to-face contact with clients and others.[22] For instance, caregivers at a nursing home must show courtesy, promote positive emotions, and control the emotions of residents while hiding their own fatigue, anger, and other true emotions. Emotional labour is also more challenging when the job requires employees to display a variety of emotions (e.g., anger as well as joy) and intense emotions (e.g., showing delight rather than a weak smile). Bill collectors face these challenges. They must learn to show warmth to anxious first-time debtors and irritation (but not anger) toward debtors who seem indifferent to their financial obligations.[23]

Jobs vary to the extent that employees must abide by the display rules. "Smile: we are on stage" is one of the most important rules that employees learn at the Ritz-Carlton in San Francisco.[24] The extent that someone must follow display rules also depends on the power and personal relationship of the person receiving the service. You would closely follow display rules when meeting the owner of a client's organization, whereas more latitude might be possible when serving a friend. There are also cross-cultural differences in emotional display norms and values. One survey reported that 83 percent of Japanese believe it is inappropriate to get emotional in a business context, compared with 40 percent of Americans, 34 percent of French, and 29 percent of Italians. In other words, Italians are more likely to accept or tolerate people who display their true emotions at work, whereas this would be considered rude or embarrassing in Japan.[25]

Emotional Dissonance

Comedian George Burns once said: "The secret to being a good actor is honesty. If you can fake *that*, you've got it made." Burns' humour highlights the fact that most of us have difficulty hiding our true emotions all the time. Instead, emotions "leak" out as voice intonations, posture, and in other subtle ways.[26] The problem is particularly true of anger, which is one of the most difficult emotions to control. This conflict between required and true emotions is called **emotional dissonance**, and it is a significant cause of stress and job burnout (see Chapter 7).[27] Emotional dissonance is most common where employees must display emotions that are quite different from their true feelings and where emotional display rules are highly regulated.

emotional dissonance
The conflict between required and true emotions.

Does emotional dissonance always create stress? Not necessarily. A recent Canadian study revealed that stress and burnout levels depend on whether employees manage the emotional labour requirements through surface acting or deep acting.[28] George Burns was referring to *surface acting*—thinking through and acting out behaviours that reflect the required emotions even though you hold quite different emotions. An example of surface acting would be smiling at a customer even though you feel irritated by that person. Surface acting is stressful because you have to act out behaviours while holding back your true emotions, which are incompatible with those behaviours.

Deep acting, on the other hand, involves changing your emotions to meet the job requirements. Rather than feeling irritated by a particular customer, you apply strategies that make you less irritated and generally happier to work with this person. For example, you might think that the customer is irritating due to their personal problems and that you might help make their life a little better through good service. Thus, deep acting involves shifting your true emotions so they are more compatible with the required emotions, rather than having a conflict between your required and true emotions. Not only does this reduce stress; it also gives you a sense of accomplishment if your performance is effective.

Supporting Emotional Labour

Many organizations support emotional labour by teaching employees the subtle behaviours that express appropriate emotions. This occurs at some airlines where flight attendants and check-in staff complete videotaped exercises and receive feedback on their emotional labour. The feedback helps them to learn the subtle art of expressing organizationally desired emotions. Earlier, we mentioned that people in Japan traditionally expect a narrow range of emotional displays. But this is changing as companies discover that employee smiles are good for business. GLOBAL Connections 4.2 describes how some Japanese companies are sending their employees to "smile school" where they learn the fine art of displaying pleasant emotions.

Along with training, some corporate leaders believe that the best way to support emotional labour is by hiring employees with competencies for displaying desired emotions. Isadore Sharp, founder and CEO of Toronto-based Four Seasons Hotels and Resorts Inc. says: "You can train [employees] to do any job," but employees must bring the right attitude with them. Famous Players also hires for attitude. The Canadian theatre chain holds casting calls where "outgoing and bubbly" job applicants are identified as they sing and dance in front of the other

Japanese Employees Learn Service with a Smile

Hiroshi Ieyoshi and three dozen other gas station attendants are gathered for some tough after-hours training. They're learning how to smile. "It's easy to say you should smile at the customers," says Ieyoshi, the earnest 33-year-old pump manager after the 90-minute seminar. "But to be honest, it all depends on how I feel at the moment."

Ieyoshi isn't the only one who has trouble smiling at customers. In Japanese culture, hiding your emotions is considered a virtue. The society values group harmony, and any expression of emotion violates that harmony by focusing on the individual's feelings. Now, companies are throwing out the straight-faced tradition and increasing sales with smiling employees.

Leading the smile revolution is Yoshihiko Kadokawa, president of the Smile Amenity Institute and author of *The Power of a Laughing Face*. The former retail executive discovered that even in this dour society, the friendliest clerks consistently have the highest sales. "I have found, through my surveys, that sales personnel could beef up sales by as much as 20 percent each day by just smiling more at their customers," says Kadokawa.

McDonald's Corp. puts such a premium on smiling faces in Japan that the company screens out those who are too poker-faced. While applicants describe a pleasant experience, interviewers evaluate whether their faces reflect the pleasure they're discussing. McDonald's wants all of its employees to provide the friendly service at the price stated on the menu: "Smiles, 0 yen."

In spite of the cultural barriers, some Japanese employees have acquired a natural ability to smile as much as Westerners. In the class with gas station attendants, Kutaro Matsunaga stands out. But he has been practising for a long time. "[M]y name means 'happy man,' and I always want to make my customers happy," explains Matsunaga, with a smile.

Sources: S. Kakuchi, "Put on a Happy Face," *Asian Business*, 36 (March 2000), p. 56; V. Reitman, "Learning To Grin—And Bear It," *Los Angeles Times*, February 22, 1999, p. A1.

Students at the Smile Amenity Institute practise smiling (right) with instructor Yoshihiko Kadokawa (left). *Copyright © Ohmori Satoru.*

candidates.[29] Another personal characteristic that is important for managing emotions is emotional intelligence, which we discuss next.

Emotional Intelligence (EI)

Each year, the U.S. Air Force hires about 400 recruiters, and each year up to 100 of them are fired for failing to sign up enough people for the service. Selecting and training 100 new recruiters costs $3 million, not to mention the hidden costs of their poor performance. So Rich Handley, head of Air Force recruiting, decided to give 1,200 recruiters a new test that measured how well they manage their emotions and the emotions of others. He discovered that the top recruiters were better at asserting their feelings and thoughts, empathizing with others, feeling happy in life, and being aware of their emotions in a particular situation. The next year, Handley selected new recruiters partly on their results of this emotions test. The result: only eight recruiters got fired or quit a year later.[30]

To select the best recruiters, the U.S. Air Force considers more than the cognitive intelligence of job applicants; it also looks at their **emotional intelligence (EI).** EI is the ability to perceive and express emotion, assimilate emotion in thought, understand and reason with emotion, and regulate emotion in oneself and others.[31] In other words, EI represents a set of competencies that allow us to perceive, understand, and regulate emotions in ourselves and in others.

Emotional intelligence has quickly become a popular topic among academics and practitioners. Unfortunately, it has also generated a considerable amount of hype, resulting in exaggerations and some confusion about the qualities and consequences of emotional intelligence. Therefore, let's begin by describing the components of EI as presented by psychologists Peter Salovey and John Mayer, who introduced the term over a decade ago. The most recent version of the Salovey–Mayer model, shown in Exhibit 4.3, identifies four components of EI and arranges them into a hierarchy:[32]

1. *Perceiving and Expressing Emotions*—This refers to the ability to recognize the meaning of emotions that you and others express, the ability to express emotions accurately, and the ability to detect false emotions. For example, this category would include the ability to tell when you have offended someone, to know when someone is sincerely happy to see you, and to be able to show spe-

emotional intelligence (EI)
The ability to perceive and express emotion, assimilate emotion in thought, understand and reason with emotion, and regulate emotion in oneself and others.

EXHIBIT 4.3

Salovey–Mayer model of emotional intelligence

Level 4 (highest)	Managing emotions	• Regulate emotions in yourself and others
Level 3	Understanding emotions	• Understand combinations of emotions • Understand how an emotion will change to another emotion
Level 2	Assimilating emotions	Use emotions to: • prioritize information • make judgments • perceive situations differently
Level 1 (lowest)	Perceiving and expressing emotions	• Recognize emotions • Express emotions • Detect false emotions

cific emotions to others. Perceiving and identifying emotions is the most basic level of EI because the other tiers depend on this fundamental ability.

2. *Assimilating Emotions*—This second level of EI involves bringing (assimilating) emotions into our perceptions and judgment. Emotions help us to prioritize information, make judgments more effectively, and perceive a situation differently. For example, by shifting your emotions from excited to relaxed, you can develop different perspectives of problems and opportunities.

3. *Understanding Emotions*—This third level includes the ability to understand combinations of emotions as well as how an emotion will likely make a transition to another emotion. For instance, people with high emotional intelligence would recognize the complex combination of hate and fear, and they would know that fear often changes to relief.

4. *Managing Emotions*—The fourth and highest level of EI refers to the ability to regulate emotions in yourself and others. People with high EI know how to keep calm in situations where others would get angry. They are also able to generate or control emotions in others, such as building excitement among employees at a meeting.

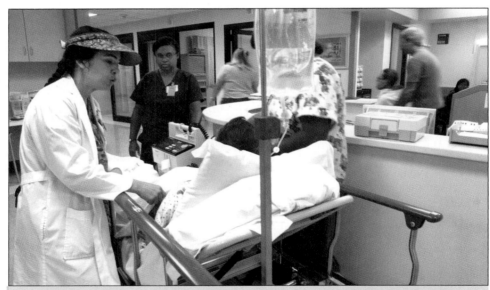

Physicians have above average IQs (about 120 in Canada and the United States), but their average emotional intelligence score hovers around 90—well below the population average of 100. "We're taught to look at things analytically, but our biggest difficulties are not analytic," admits Darryl Heustis, M.D., vice president for medical affairs at the Jerry L. Pettis Memorial VA Medical Center in Loma Linda, California. "Without understanding our emotions and others' emotions, we're not going to do as well." Fortunately, Heustis and others are attending special classes at the Veteran's Administration where they receive their personal emotional intelligence profile and learn to improve their emotional intelligence.[33] Looking at the four dimensions in the Salovey–Mayer model, why is it important for physicians to have a high emotional intelligence?
Copyright © Peter Phun/The Press-Enterprise
www.llu.edu

EI has its roots in social intelligence literature that was introduced over 80 years ago, but scholars spent most of the intervening years focused on cognitive intelligence (IQ).[34] Now, the U.S. Air Force and others are realizing that EI is an important set of competencies in the performance of most jobs. As we described in Chapter 2, people perform better when their aptitudes—including general intelligence—match the job requirements. Most jobs also involve social interaction, so employees also need emotional intelligence to work effectively in social settings. The evidence indicates fairly strongly that emotional intelligence makes a difference in organizations. Studies have reported that people with high EI scores are better at interpersonal relations, perform better in jobs requiring emotional labour, and are more successful in many aspects of job interviews. Teams whose members have high emotional intelligence initially perform better than teams with low EI.[35]

Improving emotional intelligence   Emotional intelligence is related to several personality traits described in Chapter 3, including extroversion, conscientiousness, agreeableness, and emotional stability, and low neuroticism.[36] Still, EI can be learned to some extent. Endpoint Research, a Canadian firm specializing in pharmaceutical and biotechnology clinical trials, has put all 65 of its employees through the EI assessment so they can develop their weak areas. Methodist Hospitals of Dallas has also introduced emotional intelligence training to its management group, with the CEO front-and-centre participating in the program.[37]

These training programs may help, but people don't develop emotional intelligence just by learning about its dimensions. They require personal coaching, plenty of practice, and frequent feedback. Emotional intelligence also increases with age; it is part of the process called maturity.[38] Overall, emotional intelligence offers considerable potential, but we also have a lot to learn about its measurement and effects on people in the workplace.

So far our discussion has laid the foundations of emotions and attitudes, but scholars are also interested in specific attitudes in the workplace. The next two sections of this chapter look at two of the most widely studied attitudes: job satisfaction and organizational commitment.

JOB SATISFACTION

job satisfaction
A person's attitude regarding his or her job and work content.

Job satisfaction describes a person's evaluation of his or her job and work context.[39] It is an *appraisal* of the perceived job characteristics, work environment, and emotional experiences at work. Satisfied employees have a favourable evaluation of their job, based on their observations and emotional experiences. Job satisfaction is really a collection of attitudes about specific facets of the job.[40] Employees can be satisfied with some elements of the job while simultaneously dissatisfied with others. You might like your co-workers, but are less satisfied with workload or other aspects of the job. For most of us, job satisfaction is an important part of life. One recent survey reported that over 80 percent of people working in southern Saskatchewan said that how satisfied they are with their job is a somewhat or very important determinant of their satisfaction with life.[41]

How Satisfied are Canadians at Work?

Surveys indicate that between 82 and 86 percent of Canadians are moderately or very satisfied overall with their jobs.[42] The results of one recent survey, shown in

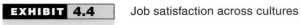

EXHIBIT 4.4   Job satisfaction across cultures

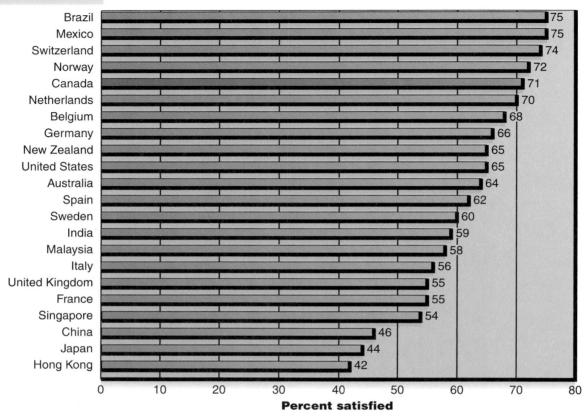

Source: Based on Ipsos-Reid survey of 9,300 employees in 39 countries in middle of Year 2000. See "Ipsos-Reid Global Poll Finds Major Differences in Employee Satisfaction Around the World," Ipsos-Reid News Release, January 8, 2001. A sample of 22 countries across the range are shown here, including all of the top scoring countries.

Exhibit 4.4, indicate that Canadian employees have the fifth highest job satisfaction ratings among 39 countries. Brazilians and Mexicans are the most satisfied, whereas employees in Japan and Hong Kong are the least satisfied. Another survey found that Canadians had the second highest job satisfaction, after Brazilians, among the 10 largest economies in the world.[43] Do these surveys mean that we have high job satisfaction? Well, maybe, but probably not as high as these statistics suggest. The problem is that surveys often use a single direct question, such as "How satisfied are you with your job?." Many dissatisfied employees are reluctant to reveal their feelings in a direct question because this is tantamount to admitting that they made a poor job choice and are not enjoying life.

How do we know that overall satisfaction ratings are inflated? One indication is that one-half of Canadians say they would leave if another organization offered a similar job with slightly higher pay! Also, fewer than half of Canadians would recommend their company as the best place to work in the community.[44] We also need to keep in mind that cultural values make it difficult to compare job satisfaction across countries.[45] People in China, South Korea, and Japan tend to subdue their emotions in public, so they probably avoid extreme survey ratings such as "very satisfied."

Job Satisfaction and Work Behaviour

Annette Verschuren, president of The Home Depot Canada, pays a lot of attention to job satisfaction. "I can tell you within two seconds of entering a store whether morale is good," says Verschuren. The main reason for her interest is that job satisfaction is a key driver to corporate success. "With an unhappy workforce you have nothing and you will never be great," Verschuren warns.[46]

Home Deport Canada, Fours Seasons Hotels and Resorts, Telus Corp, and a flock of other Canadian firms are paying a lot more attention to job satisfaction these days. In some firms, executive bonuses depend partly on employee satisfaction ratings. The reason for this attention is simple: job satisfaction affects many of the individual behaviours introduced in Chapter 2. A useful template to organize and understand the consequences of job dissatisfaction is the **exit-voice-loyalty-neglect (EVLN) model**. As the name suggests, the EVLN model identifies four ways employees respond to dissatisfaction:[47]

exit-voice-loyalty-neglect (EVNL) model
The four ways, as indicated in the name, employees respond to job dissatisfaction.

- *Exit*—Exit refers to leaving the situation, including searching for other employment, actually leaving the organization, or transferring to another work unit. Employee turnover is a well-established outcome of job dissatisfaction, particularly for employees with better job opportunities elsewhere. Recent evidence also suggests that exit is linked to specific "shock events," such as a conflict episode or an important violation of your expectations.[48] These shock events produce more than just dissatisfaction; they generate strong emotions that energize employees to think about and search for alternative employment.

- *Voice*—In the original EVLN model, voice is defined as any attempt to change, rather than escape from, the unsatisfying situation. Many researchers have subsequently viewed voice purely as a positive or constructive response, such as directly trying to solve the problem with management or actively helping to improve the situation. However, voice can also be more confrontational, for example, by filing formal grievances.[49] In extreme cases, some employees might engage in counterproductive behaviours to get attention and force changes in the organization. Thus, voice might be more correctly viewed as either constructive or destructive.

- *Loyalty*—Loyalty has been described in different ways.[50] The most widely held view is that "loyalists" are employees who respond to dissatisfaction by patiently waiting—some say "suffer in silence"—for the problem to work itself out or get resolved by others.[51]

- *Neglect*—Neglect includes reducing work effort, paying less attention to quality, and increasing absenteeism and lateness. It is generally considered a passive activity that has negative consequences for the organization. Research clearly establishes that dissatisfied employees tend to be absent more often;[52] the relationship between satisfaction and job performance is more complex, as we will discuss below.

Which of the four EVLN alternatives do employees use? It depends on the person and the situation. One factor is the availability of alternative employment. With poor job prospects, employees are less likely to use the exit option. Employees who identify with the organization (organizational commitment, which we discuss later) are also more likely to use voice rather than exit. Personality is another influence on the choice of action. People with high conscientiousness are less likely to engage in neglect and more likely to engage in voice (as are people high in extroversion and low in neuroticism). Finally, past experience influences our choice of action. Employees who were unsuccessful with voice in the past are more likely to engage in exit or neglect when experiencing job dissatisfaction in the future.[53]

Job Satisfaction and Performance

One of the oldest beliefs in the business world is that "a happy worker is a productive worker." Is this statement true? Organizational behaviour scholars have waffled on this question for the past century. In the 1980s, researchers strongly concluded that job satisfaction has a weak or negligible association with task performance.[54] Now the evidence suggests that the popular saying may be correct after all. Citing problems with the earlier studies, a groundbreaking analysis of previous research recently concluded that there is a *moderate* relationship between job satisfaction and job performance. In other words, happy workers are more productive workers *to some extent*.[55]

The moderate relationship between job satisfaction and performance begs the next question: Why isn't the relationship stronger? There are many reasons, but let's look at the three most common ones.[56] One argument is that general attitudes (such as job satisfaction) don't predict specific behaviours very well. As we learned with the EVLN model, job dissatisfaction doesn't always result in lower job effort (neglect). Instead, some employees continue to work productively while they complain (voice), look for another job (exit), or patiently wait for the problem to get fixed (loyalty).

A second explanation is that job performance leads to job satisfaction (rather than vice versa), but only when performance is linked to valued rewards. Higher performers receive more rewards and, consequently, are more satisfied than low-performing employees who receive fewer rewards. The connection between job satisfaction and performance isn't stronger because many organizations do not reward good performance. The third explanation is that job satisfaction might influence employee motivation, but this has little influence on performance in jobs where employees have little control over their job output (such as assembly line work). This point is consistent with recent evidence that the job satisfaction–performance relationship is strongest in complex jobs, where employees have more freedom to perform their work or to slack off.[57]

Roger Greene (wearing goggles in photo) isn't taking any chances on poor customer service. The CEO and founder of Ipswitch Inc. has taken all 130 employees —plus one guest each—on a four-day cruise in the Bahamas. The cruise is the Lexington, Virginia, software maker's way of thanking employees for steady financial performance. It's also consistent with Greene's larger objective to keep employees happy so they will continue to provide exceptional customer service. Ipswitch employees also get five weeks of paid time off, child and elder care, domestic partner benefits, and a concierge service. "If employees are treated well," Greene explains, "they will treat the customers well, and then the profits will come."[58] Along with job satisfaction, what other work attitude described in this chapter might explain why a trip to the Bahamas increases customer service? © *John Wilcox, Boston Herald*
www.ipswitch.com

Job Satisfaction and Customer Satisfaction

Along with the job satisfaction–performance relationship, corporate leaders are making strong statements that happy employees make happy customers. "We demand more of our employees, but we do our best to assure they are happy," says an executive at Toronto-based Four Seasons Hotels and Resorts. "Employees who are happy provide better service." Gordon Bethune, CEO of Continental Airlines, echoes this opinion: "We treat our people well, and in turn, they treat our customers well. Happy employees equal customer satisfaction."[59]

Fortunately, these views are supported by recent studies in marketing and organizational behaviour. Marketing experts, in particular, have developed a model that relates employee satisfaction to customer satisfaction and profitability. As shown in Exhibit 4.5, this "employee-customer-profit chain" model suggests that increasing employee satisfaction and loyalty results in higher customer perceptions of value, which improves the company's profitability.[60]

There are two main reasons why job satisfaction has a positive effect on customer service.[61] First, job satisfaction affects a person's general mood. Employees who are in a good mood are more likely to display friendliness and positive emotions, which puts customers in a better mood. Second, satisfied employees are less likely to quit their jobs, and longer-service employees have more experience and better skills to serve clients. Lower turnover also gives customers the same employees to serve them, so there is more consistent service. There is some evidence that customers build their loyalty to specific employees, not to the organization, so keeping employee turnover low tends to build customer loyalty.[62]

Before leaving this topic, it's worth mentioning that job satisfaction does more than improve work behaviours and customer satisfaction. Job satisfaction is also an ethical issue that influences the organization's reputation in the community. People spend a large portion of their time working in organizations, and many societies now expect companies to provide work environments that are safe and enjoyable. Indeed, Canadians and Americans closely monitor ratings of the

EXHIBIT 4.5

The employee-customer-profit chain model

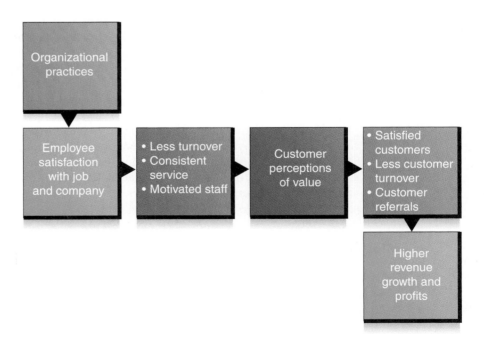

best companies to work for, an indication that employee satisfaction is a virtue worth considerable goodwill to employers. This virtue is apparent when an organization has low job satisfaction. The company tries to hide this fact and, when morale problems become public, corporate leaders are usually quick to improve the situation.

ORGANIZATIONAL COMMITMENT

organizational commitment

The employee's emotional attachment to, identification with, and involvement in a particular organization.

During the mid-1800s, Samuel Cunard founded Cunard Lines, the greatest steamship line ever to cover the Atlantic ocean. The energetic Nova Scotian was able to make ship transportation dependable and safe, long before it was thought possible, by having the best ships, officers, and crew. He insisted on safety before profits and, by listening to his technical experts, was able to introduce the latest innovations. Above all, Cunard had the quaint notion that if you picked people well, paid them well, and treated them well, they would return the favour with loyalty and pride.[63]

Nearly 150 years later, Samuel Cunard's assumptions about **organizational commitment** have found strong support in organizational behaviour research. Organizational commitment refers to the employee's emotional attachment to, identification with, and involvement in a particular organization.[64] Organizational behaviour scholars call this *affective commitment* because it refers to the individual's feelings toward the organization. Affective commitment is called organizational loyalty when the organization is the target of the individual's commitment. However, affective commitment can also refer to loyalty toward co-workers, customers, or a profession.[65] In this book, we will concentrate mainly on the employee's overall commitment to the organization.

continuance commitment

A bond felt by an employee that motivates him to stay only because leaving would be costly.

Along with affective commitment, employees have varying levels of **continuance commitment**.[66] Continuance commitment occurs when employees believe it is in their own personal interest to remain with the organization. In other words, this form of commitment is a calculative bond with the organization, rather than an emotional attachment. For example, you may have met people who do not particularly identify with the organization where they work but feel bound to remain there because it would be too costly to quit. Continuance commitment is this motivation to stay because of the high cost of leaving.[67]

Is organizational loyalty declining? According to some surveys, it is. One poll reported that a decade ago 62 percent of Canadians were loyal to their employers. This has fallen in the three subsequent surveys to the point where only 49 percent are loyal today. On a global comparison, one survey indicates that Canadians rank 16th out of 32 countries in employee loyalty, whereas another poll of 360,000 people in the 10 wealthiest countries placed Canada in fourth spot, behind Brazil, Spain, and Germany.[68]

Consequences of Organizational Commitment

If organizational loyalty is declining, then it would be bad news for employers. Research suggests that a loyal workforce can be a significant competitive advantage. Employees with high levels of affective commitment are less likely to quit their jobs and be absent from work. Organizational commitment also improves customer satisfaction because long-tenure employees have better knowledge of work practices, and clients like to do business with the same employees. Employees with high affective commitment also have higher work motivation and organizational citizenship, and somewhat higher job performance.[69]

However, employees can have too much affective commitment. One concern is that organizational loyalty results in low turnover, which limits the organization's opportunity to hire new employees with new knowledge and fresh ideas. Another concern is that loyalty results in conformity, which holds back creativity. There are also cases of dedicated employees who have violated laws to defend the organization.

Consequences of continuance commitment   A greater concern than having too much affective commitment is the tendency of some firms to support continuance commitment. Many firms tie employees financially to the organization through low-cost loans and stock options. For instance, when CIBC took over Merrill Lynch's Canadian retail brokerage business, Merrill's top financial advisors received retention bonuses worth up to one year's pay if they stayed long enough with the merged company. Anglo Irish Bank relies on equally large "loyalty bonuses" to reduce turnover of new staff. People who are hired at the Irish bank receive half their bonus after 12 months of employment and the other half six months later. "The hope," says an Anglo Irish Bank executive, "is to keep them a little longer."[70]

These "golden handcuffs" usually do reduce turnover, but they also increase continuance commitment, not affective commitment. Research (much of it in Canada) suggests that employees with high levels of continuance commitment have *lower* performance ratings and are *less* likely to engage in organizational citizenship behaviours! Furthermore, unionized employees with high continuance commitment are more likely to use formal grievances, whereas employees with high affective commitment engage in more constructive problem solving when employee–employer relations sour.[71] Although some level of financial connection may be necessary, employers should not confuse continuance commitment with employee loyalty. Employers still need to win employees' hearts (affective commitment) beyond tying them financially to the organization (continuance commitment).

Building Organizational Commitment

There are almost as many ways to building organizational loyalty as topics in this textbook, but the following list of activities is most prominent in the literature:[72]

- *Justice and support*—Affective commitment is higher in organizations that fulfil their obligations to employees and abide by humanitarian values, such as fairness, courtesy, forgiveness, and moral integrity.[73] These values relate to the concept of organizational justice that we discuss in the next chapter. Similarly, organizations that support employee well-being tend to cultivate higher levels of loyalty in return.[74]
- *Job security*—Layoff threats are one of the greatest blows to employee loyalty, even among those whose jobs are not immediately at risk.[75] Building commitment doesn't require lifetime employment guarantees, but firms should offer enough job security that employees feel some permanence and mutuality in the employment relationship. SaskTel (described at the beginning of this chapter), Alberta Energy Co., and Magna International have fiercely loyal employees partly because these companies have avoided layoffs throughout their entire history.[76]

When the British Columbia government announced that it would cut one-third of its work force over three years, the news sent shockwaves throughout the province. It also likely had a damaging effect on employee loyalty, even among those who kept their jobs. "People are really worried," explains B.C. government employee Terry Hughes (shown in photo). "I know no one is trying to be malicious, but it's just the uncertainty and apprehension." Government officials say they are trying to be fair about the process, but Russell Katzer would like more information. "People are hearing things through the media and that just creates a whole lot more uncertainty," says the Victoria court clerk.[80] What could the B.C. government do to minimize the amount of employee loyalty lost due to these layoffs? *Debra Brash, Victoria Times Colonist* **www.gov.bc.ca**

- *Organizational comprehension*—Affective commitment is a person's identification with the company, so it makes sense that this attitude is strengthened when employees are connected to organizational events and people. Specifically, employees become more loyal when communication processes keep them informed about what is happening in the company (see Chapter 11), and when they have opportunities to interact with co-workers across the organization.[77]

- *Employee involvement*—Employees feel that they are part of the organization when they make decisions that guide the organization's future.[78] Through participation, employees begin to see how the organization is a reflection of their decisions. In this way, involvement strengthens the company as part of the employee's social identity. Employee involvement also builds loyalty because giving this power is a demonstration of the company's trust in its employees.

- *Trusting employees*—**Trust** occurs when we have positive expectations about another party's intentions and actions toward us in risky situations.[79] Trust means putting faith in the other person or group. It is also a reciprocal activity. In order to receive trust, you must demonstrate trust. Trust is important for organizational commitment because it touches the heart of the employment relationship. Employees identify with and feel obliged to work for an organization only when they trust its leaders. We will discuss trust more fully in the context of high performance teams (Chapter 9).

Look closely at some of the recommendations above (job security, humanitarian values, trust) and you will see that one of the key influences on organizational commitment is the employment relationship. In particular, affective commitment is sensitive to fulfilment and violation of the psychological contract, which we look at in the last section of this chapter.

PSYCHOLOGICAL CONTRACTS

trust
Positive expectations about another party's intentions and actions toward us in risky situations.

Some employees at the Toyota Canada factory in Cambridge, Ontario, are upset that the company is forcing them to work overtime. The automaker's new models are selling well, so employees must perform up to two hours of overtime almost every day to keep up with demand. Employees may be disciplined if they refuse. The problem, say some workers, is that overtime used to be voluntary at Toyota. Now, government legislation allows more flexibility in the amount of overtime employers can require, so Toyota is relying on the contract that employees signed when they were hired. That contract gives the company the right to impose overtime, which employees claim was never applied, until now.[81]

Toyota Canada employees experienced the shock of having their psychological contract violated. This isn't unusual. According to one university study, 24 percent of employees are "chronically" angry at work, mostly because they felt their employer violated basic promises and didn't fulfill the psychological contract.[82] The **psychological contract** refers to the individual's beliefs about the terms and conditions of a reciprocal exchange agreement between that person and another party.[83] This is inherently perceptual, so one person's understanding of the psychological contract may differ from another's. In employment relationships, psychological contracts consist of beliefs about what the employee is entitled to receive from the employer and what he or she is obliged to offer the employer in return. For example, Toyota Canada employees believed that their psychological contract included the right to refuse overtime, whereas the employer says its employment forms include the right to impose overtime.[84]

Everyone has a unique psychological contract, but one British study has found some common elements. Specifically, employers expect employees to work contracted hours, perform quality work, deal honestly with clients, guard the organization's reputation, treat property carefully, dress and behave correctly, and engage in some organizational citizenship. The psychological contract for most British employees emphasizes fairness in decisions (e.g., selection, promotion, and layoffs), the application of rules, and allocation of pay and benefits. Employees also expect enough personal time off, consultation on matters affecting them, minimal interference in how they do their job, supportive leadership, reward for long service and good performance, a safe work environment, and as much job security as the organization can reasonably provide.[85]

Types of Psychological Contracts

Psychological contracts vary in many ways. One of the most fundamental differences is the extent to which they are transactional or relational.[86] As Exhibit 4.6 describes, *transactional contracts* are primarily short-term economic exchanges. Responsibilities are well defined around a fairly narrow set of obligations that do not change over the life of the contract. People hired in temporary positions and as consultants tend to have transactional contracts. To some extent, new employees also form transactional contracts until they develop a sense of continuity with the organization.

Relational contracts, on the other hand, are rather like marriages; they are long-term attachments that encompass a broad array of subjective mutual obligations. Employees with a relational psychological contract are more willing to contribute their time and effort without expecting the organization to pay back this debt in the short term. Relational contracts are also dynamic, meaning that the parties tolerate mutual obligations and expect that those obligations are not necessarily balanced in the short run. Not surprisingly, organizational citizenship behaviours are more likely to prevail under relational than transactional contracts. Permanent employees are more likely to believe they have a relational contract.

Employee attitudes have important effects on relational and transactional psychological contracts. According to a recent Canadian study, employees with high continuance commitment are significantly more likely to view their psychological contract as transactional, whether or not they have high affective commitment.[87] In contrast, employees with high affective commitment are significantly more likely to view their psychological contract as relational, but only when they have

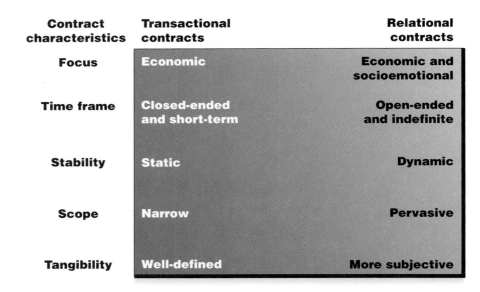

EXHIBIT 4.6

Types of
psychological
contracts in
employment

Contract characteristics	Transactional contracts	Relational contracts
Focus	Economic	Economic and socioemotional
Time frame	Closed-ended and short-term	Open-ended and indefinite
Stability	Static	Dynamic
Scope	Narrow	Pervasive
Tangibility	Well-defined	More subjective

Source: Based on information in D. M. Rousseau and J. M. Parks, "The Contracts of Individuals and Organizations," *Research in Organizational Behavior*, 15 (1993), pp. 1–43.

low continuance commitment. In other words, continuance commitment creates a more formal contractual relationship in the minds of employees, whereas affective commitment generates a more relational psychological contract.

From Security to Employability

Nearly half a century ago in his best selling book *Organization Man,* William H. Whyte painted a satirical picture of typical American white-collar employees. These dedicated employees worked in secure jobs with steady promotions through the hierarchy. They often devoted their entire lives to the same company, put in regular hours, and rarely thought about moving to another company.[88] The implicit contract was that if you were loyal to the company and performed your job reasonably well, the company would be loyal to you by providing job security and managing your career development.[89]

Mergers, corporate restructuring, privatization of government-managed organizations, and other forms of marketplace turbulence have replaced this psychological contract in many organizations.[90] The emerging contract is employability, whereby employees must take responsibility for their own careers by continually developing new competencies for future work opportunities within and beyond the organization. In this "new deal," jobs are temporary events and organizations are no longer perceived as paternalistic institutions that take care of their employees. Rather, organizations are customers, and employees keep their jobs by continuing to offer valuable skills and knowledge to their clients. From this perspective, individuals must anticipate future organizational needs and develop new competencies accordingly.[91]

Employability has been hyped in the media and management literature, but to what extent does it exist in reality? Quite a bit, according to one recent study that found that students and recruiters generally agreed on the meaning and relevance

Japan's New Psychological Contract

Ogura Junpei is looking for a job after graduating from Japan's Keio University. But he isn't interested in a career with one of the traditional job-for-life Japanese companies. Instead, Ogura has found more challenging work and better pay at a consulting firm and a foreign investment bank. "I'm not just looking for a job," explains Ogura, "but a place where I find it worthwhile to work."

Japan's well-known psychological contract—lifetime employment, steady advancement, and seniority-based pay increases—is starting to fall apart. One reason is that Japan's long recession has forced Honda, Sony, NEC, and other major corporations to introduce performance-based relationships that weaken job security guarantees. The other reason is that many younger Japanese employees want challenging work and better pay now, not after waiting a decade or more. "I'm suffocating from the rigid seniority system in my office," complains a young electronics engineer with a major Japanese company.

Not every young Japanese employee is abandoning the lifetime employment relationship. "Lifelong employ-ment is suitable to the Japanese character," explains Kentaro Takahashi, a 23-year-old engineering graduate. "From long ago, people donated their whole lives to the company. So we should give our full support to our new firm."

Still, Takahashi's psychological contract is becoming the exception. One recent survey revealed that 80 percent of Japanese employees in their twenties strongly intend to switch jobs within the next ten years. Further proof was the recent turnout of hundreds of job seekers at one of Japan's first international job fairs, where more than 50 foreign firms were recruiting. "The young urban Japan is already voting for change with their careers," says Kenneth Courtis, strategist and chief economist at Deutsche Bank Group in Tokyo.

Sources: J-I. Lee, "Recent Exodus of Core Human Resources Disturbing Trend for Domestic Companies," *Korea Herald*, May 14, 2001; "Trend of Caring for Employees Waning among Japan's Companies," *Japan Weekly Monitor*, May 7, 2001; M. Zielenziger, "The Fading Salary Man," *National Post*, April 5, 2000, p. C15; M. Mutsuko, "Who Needs Life Employment?" *AsiaWeek*, March 17, 2000; B. McKenna, "Restructuring Fever Sweeps Japan," *Globe and Mail*, May 29, 1999.

of employability in the workplace.[92] Business students, in particular, seem to hold higher expectations than other student groups about the employee's obligations to remain employable. These results are consistent with a recent poll reporting that 68 percent of Canadians believe job security is a thing of the past, and that only 41 percent think their employer is loyal to them. "The environment is switching from job security to skill security," advises an executive at TD Bank in Toronto.[93]

Permanence of employability Will the pendulum swing from employability back to job security during times of low unemployment when employees have enough power to push for more job guarantees? Perhaps to some extent, but two factors will likely preserve the psychological contract of employability for the foreseeable future. One factor, as we noted earlier, is increasing turbulence in the business environment. Global competition, deregulation, and information technologies have made it difficult for employers to provide the job security that was possible in more stable conditions. Organizations need employability to remain flexible and adaptive.

The other factor is changing employee expectations. Some scholars suggest that job security has less value to Generation-X and Generation-Y employees than to baby-boomers. Workforce newcomers have mainly experienced a psychological contract based on employability and are comfortable with minimal employment guarantees. "Employees are developing the view that their only job security in the future must be based on their ability and their competence," says Gary L. Howard, a Motorola vice president, "and not on keeping a job at some particular company."[94] This trend is also apparent in Japan, traditionally a stalwart of company loyalty and lifetime employment. GLOBAL Connections 4.3 describes how some recent Japanese university graduates prefer challenging work and performance-based pay to lifelong employment.

Psychological contracts are changing, as is the entire field of organizational behaviour, by embracing new knowledge about emotions in the workplace. Emotional brain centres, emotional labour, emotional intelligence, and other topics in this chapter were unheard of a decade ago. Now they are essential reading to improve our grasp of the complex dynamics of employee attitudes and behaviour. You will discover several references to emotion-related concepts throughout this book, including the next chapter on employee motivation.

CHAPTER SUMMARY

Emotions are psychological and physiological episodes experienced toward an object, person, or event which create a state of readiness. Emotions are typically organized into a bipolar circle (circumplex) based on their pleasantness and activation. Emotions differ from attitudes, which refer to the cluster of beliefs, feelings, and behavioural intentions toward a person, object, or event. Beliefs are a person's established perceptions about the attitude object. Feelings are positive or negative evaluations of the attitude object. Behavioural intentions describe the motivation to engage in a particular behaviour toward a target.

Attitudes have traditionally been studied as a rational process of analyzing the value and expectancy of outcomes of the attitude object. Thus, beliefs predict feelings, which predict behavioural intentions, which predict behaviour. But this traditional perspective overlooks the role of emotions, which have an important influence on attitudes and behaviour. Emotions typically form before we think through situations, so they influence this rational attitude formation process. Emotions also affect behaviour directly.

Behaviour sometimes influences our subsequent attitudes through cognitive dissonance. People also have the personality traits of positive or negative affectivity, which affect their emotions and attitudes.

Emotional labour refers to the effort, planning, and control needed to express organizationally desired emotions during interpersonal transactions. This is more common in jobs with frequent and lengthy customer interaction, where the job requires a variety of emotions displayed, and where employees must abide by the display rules. Emotional labour creates problems because true emotions tend to leak out, and conflict between expected and true emotions (emotional dissonance) causes stress and burnout. However, stress from emotional dissonance can be minimized through deep acting rather than surface acting.

Emotional intelligence is the ability to perceive and express emotion, assimilate emotion in thought, understand and reason with emotion, and regulate emotion in oneself and others. This concept includes four components arranged in a hierarchy: perceiving and expressing emotions, assimilating emotions, understanding emotions, and managing emotions. Emotional intelligence can be learned to some extent, particularly through personal coaching.

Job satisfaction describes a person's evaluation of his or her job and work context. Satisfaction depends on the level of discrepancy between what people expect to receive and what they experience. Although surveys indicate Canadians are highly satisfied with their jobs, these results may be somewhat inflated by the use of single-item questions and cultural differences. The exit-voice-loyalty-neglect model outlines four possible consequences of job dissatisfaction. Job satisfaction has a moderate relationship with job performance and with customer satisfaction. Job satisfaction is also a moral obligation in many societies.

Affective organizational commitment (loyalty) refers to the employee's emotional attachment to, identification with, and involvement in a particular organization. This contrasts with continuance commitment, which is a calculative bond with the organization. Affective commitment improves motivation and organizational citizenship, and somewhat higher job performance, whereas continuance commitment is associated with lower performance and organizational citizenship. Companies build loyalty through justice and support, some level of job security, organizational comprehension, employee involvement, and trust.

The psychological contract refers to the individual's beliefs about the terms and conditions of a reciprocal exchange agreement between that person and another party. Transactional psychological contracts are primarily short-term economic exchanges, whereas relational contracts are long-term attachments that encompass a broad array of subjective mutual obligations. Employees with high continuance commitment tend to have more transactional contracts, whereas employees with high affective commitment tend to have more of a relational psychological contract. Meanwhile, employees and employers in Canada and other countries have shifted from a psychological contract based on job security and loyalty to one of employability.

KEY TERMS

Attitudes, p. 106

Cognitive dissonance, p. 109

Continuance commitment, p. 120

Emotional dissonance, p. 111

Emotional intelligence, p. 113

Emotional labour, p. 110

Emotions, p. 104

Employability, p. 125

Exit-voice-loyalty-neglect (EVLN) model, p. 117

Job satisfaction, p. 115

Negative affectivity, p. 109

Organizational (affective) commitment, p. 120

Positive affectivity, p. 109

Psychological contract, p. 123

Trust, p. 122

DISCUSSION QUESTIONS

1. After a few months on the job, Susan has experienced several emotional episodes ranging from frustration to joy about the work she has been assigned. Use the attitude model to explain how these emotions affect Susan's level of job satisfaction with the work itself.

2. A recent study reported that college instructors are frequently required to engage in emotional labour. Identify the situations in which emotional labour is required for this job. In your opinion, is emotional labour more troublesome for college instructors or for telephone operators working at a 911 emergency service?

3. "Emotional intelligence is more important than cognitive intelligence in influencing an individual's success." Do you agree or disagree with this statement? Support your perspective.

4. Describe a time when you effectively managed someone's emotions. What happened? What was the result?

5. The latest employee satisfaction survey in your organization indicates that employees are unhappy with some aspects of the organization. However, management tends to pay attention to the single-item question asking employees to indicate their overall satisfaction with the job. The results of this item indicate that 86 percent of staff members are very or somewhat satisfied, so management concludes that the other results refer to issues that are probably not important to employees. Explain why management's interpretation of these results may be inaccurate.

6. "Happy employees create happy customers." Discuss.

7. What factors influence an employee's organizational loyalty?

8. "The emerging psychological contract is employability." What is the employee's responsibility in this "new deal"?

CASE STUDY 4.1

THE LANGUAGE INCIDENT

By Beth Gilbert, University of New Brunswick, Saint John.

While studying business administration at a university in Ontario, Susan was fortunate enough to be selected to participate in an exchange program between the Ontario and Quebec provincial governments. Susan had pursued several French courses at university and was grateful for the opportunity to live and work in a French environment. She looked forward to receiving career-related work experience in a different language and improving her French language skills.

Susan's co-workers in her department were very patient as she struggled to improve her French, and her interactions with her French-speaking colleagues were positive. Things were going well until Susan had to go to another department in a distant part of the building to get some information. When she approached the clerk in the other department and requested the needed information in French, he looked flustered, turned red in the face, and without saying a word, hurried off to find someone who could speak English.

Susan was annoyed and embarrassed that the clerk had decided to bring in someone who could speak English. Although her French was far from perfect, she had always been able to make herself understood, with some effort on both parts. Susan wondered why this had happened and what she could do differently in the future to avoid a similar situation occurring again.

Discussion Questions:

1. What happened? Specifically, what emotions might the clerk have been feeling? What emotions do you think Susan was feeling?

2. Why did this happen? Of what value is emotional intelligence in a situation such as this?

3. What could Susan and the clerk have done differently to improve the outcome?

CASE STUDY 4.2

STEVENS COMPUTING SYSTEMS

By James Buchkowsky, Saskatchewan Institute of Applied Science & Technology.

Stevens Computing Systems (SCS) is a software design and network solutions consulting firm. One of its key clients is a wholesale distributor that focuses on a call centre and online ordering business.

While SCS's founder and CEO, Shane Stevens, was on a much needed family vacation, a problem arose. Just as the Stevens family was boarding a tour bus for an afternoon of sightseeing, Shane got a page from head office. After hesitating for a moment, he sent the family on the tour and headed back to the hotel to call in.

Once on the phone, Shane was informed that a problem had occurred with the wholesaler ordering system when one of SCS's best programmers made a mistake while updating some software code. Apparently, recent orders worth several hundred thousand dollars were affected and now there was no way to sort out which ones had been processed. Naturally, the wholesaler's managers were livid and threatened everything from cancelling SCS's contract to legal action.

Shane resisted his initial reaction, which was to assign blame, and instead asked what had been done about the problem. He was told that his most senior manager had not gotten involved in solving the problem directly because he said he lacked the technical knowledge. However, the manager did suspend the programmer who had made the error and tried to distance SCS as a company from her.

After ending the phone conversation, Shane decided to cut his vacation short, and returned home determined to personally resolve this situation. His first act was to go to the employee's home to tell her he understood nobody's perfect and that she was no longer suspended. Next, Shane organized all the available software designers and programmers to generate solutions for the problem. He then not only met with the wholesaler's managers but also entertained the entire management team at his country club.

In the end, the wholesaler's managers were satisfied with Shane's offer of a full range of computing services at a very attractive rate. This not only retained the existing contract but actually increased the amount of business between the two companies. And yes, the same SCS programmer, who had made the initial error, was once again providing system services to the wholesaler.

Discussion Question

1. Describe how Shane Stevens used each of the four components of emotional intelligence to solve the problems in this case.

RANKING JOBS ON THEIR EMOTIONAL LABOUR

Purpose This exercise is designed to help you understand the jobs in which people tend to experience higher or lower degrees of emotional labour.

Instructions

■ *Step 1:* Individually rank the extent to which the jobs listed below require emotional labour. In other words, assign a "1" to the job you believe requires the most effort, planning, and control to express organizationally desired emotions during interpersonal transactions. Assign a "10" to the job you believe requires the least amount of emotional labour. Mark your rankings in column 1.

■ *Step 2:* The instructor will form teams of 4 or 5 members and each team will rank the items based on consensus (not simply averaging the individual rankings). These results are placed in column 2.

■ *Step 3:* The instructor will provide expert ranking information. This information should be written in column 3. Then, students calculate the differences in columns 4 and 5.

■ *Step 4:* The class will compare the results and discuss the features of jobs with high emotional labour.

Occupational Emotional Labour Scoring Sheet					
Occupation	**(1)** **Individual** **Ranking**	**(2)** **Team** **Ranking**	**(3)** **Expert** **Ranking**	**(4)** **Absolute** **Difference** **of 1 and 3**	**(5)** **Absolute** **Difference** **of 2 and 3**
Bartender					
Cashier					
Dental hygienist					
Insurance adjuster					
Lawyer					
Librarian					
Postal clerk					
Registered nurse					
Social worker					
Television announcer					
			TOTAL		
				Your score	Team score

(The lower the score, the better)

SCHOOL COMMITMENT SCALE

Purpose This exercise is designed to help you understand the concept of organizational commitment and to assess your commitment to the college or university you are attending.

Overview The concept of commitment is as relevant to students enrolled in college or university courses as it is to employees working in various organizations. This self-assessment adapts a popular organizational commitment instrument so it refers to your commitment as a student to the school where you are attending this program.

Instructions Read each of the statements below and circle the response that best fits your personal belief. Then use the scoring key in Appendix B of this book to calculate your results. This self-assessment is completed alone so that students can rate themselves honestly without concerns of social comparison. However, class discussion will focus on the meaning of the different types of organizational commitment and how well this scale applies to the commitment of students toward the college or university they are attending.

To what extent does each statement describe you? Indicate your level of agreement by marking the appropriate response on the right.	Strongly Agree ▼	Moderately Agree ▼	Slightly Agree ▼	Neutral ▼	Slightly Disagree ▼	Moderately Disagree ▼	Strongly Disagree ▼
1. I would be very happy to complete the rest of my education at this school.	☐	☐	☐	☐	☐	☐	☐
2. One of the difficulties of leaving this school is that there are few alternatives.	☐	☐	☐	☐	☐	☐	☐
3. I really feel as if this school's problems are my own.	☐	☐	☐	☐	☐	☐	☐
4. Right now, staying enrolled at this school is a matter of necessity as much as desire.	☐	☐	☐	☐	☐	☐	☐
5. I do not feel a strong sense of belonging to this school.	☐	☐	☐	☐	☐	☐	☐
6. It would be very hard for me to leave this school right now even if I wanted to.	☐	☐	☐	☐	☐	☐	☐
7. I do not feel emotionally attached to this school.	☐	☐	☐	☐	☐	☐	☐
8. Too much of my life would be disrupted if I decided to move to a different school now.	☐	☐	☐	☐	☐	☐	☐
9. I do not feel like part of the "family" at this school.	☐	☐	☐	☐	☐	☐	☐

Table header title: **School Commitment Scale**

School Commitment Scale (cont.)

To what extent does each statement describe you? Indicate your level of agreement by marking the appropriate response on the right.	Strongly Agree ▼	Moderately Agree ▼	Slightly Agree ▼	Neutral ▼	Slightly Disagree ▼	Moderately Disagree ▼	Strongly Disagree ▼
10. I feel that I have too few options to consider leaving this school.	☐	☐	☐	☐	☐	☐	☐
11. This school has a great deal of personal meaning for me.	☐	☐	☐	☐	☐	☐	☐
12. If I had not already put so much of myself into this school, I might consider completing my education elsewhere.	☐	☐	☐	☐	☐	☐	☐

Source: Adapted from: J. P. Meyer, N. J. Allen, and C. A. Smith, "Commitment to organizations and occupations: Extension and test of a three-component model," *Journal of Applied Psychology*, 78 (1993), pp. 538–551.

SELF-ASSESSMENT EXERCISE 4.5

THE DISPOSITIONAL MOOD SCALE

 Go to the Student CD for an interactive version of this exercise.

Purpose This exercise is designed to help you understand mood states or personality traits of emotions and to assess your own mood or emotion personality.

Instructions This self-assessment consists of several words representing various emotions that you might have experienced. For each word presented, indicate the extent to which you have felt this way generally across all situations **over the past six months**. You need to be honest with yourself to receive a reasonable estimate of your mood state or personality trait on these scales. The results provide an estimate of your level on two emotional personality scales. This instrument is widely used in research, but it is only an estimate. You should not assume that the results are accurate without a more complete assessment by a trained professional.

After studying the preceding material, be sure to check out our Online Learning Centre at
www.mcgrawhill.ca/college/mcshane
for more in-depth information and interactivities that correspond to this chapter.

Online **LearningCentre** with POWERWEB

Motivation in the Workplace

Learning Objectives

- Compare and contrast Maslow's needs hierarchy theory with Alderfer's ERG theory.

- Describe Lawrence and Nohria's four innate drives and explain how these drives influence motivation and behaviour.

- Summarize McClelland's learned needs theory, including the three needs he studied.

- Discuss the practical implications of needs-based motivation theories.

- Diagram the expectancy theory model and discuss its practical implications for motivating employees.

- Describe the characteristics of effective goal setting and feedback.

- Summarize the equity theory model, including how people try to reduce feelings of inequity.

- Identify the factors that influence procedural justice, as well as the consequences of procedural justice.

While attending college, Chris Emery and Larry Finnson discovered that the fudge-graham wafer-chopped cashew clusters Emery's grandmother sent them were a hit with friends. After informal product testing, they named the product Clodhoppers and formed Winnipeg-based Krave's Candy Co. Armed only with $20,000 from friends and family, Emery and Finnson rented a derelict 700-square-foot industrial space and transformed a couple of old kettle cookers and some packaging equipment into a makeshift production line.

Clodhoppers was not an instant national success. Emery and Finnson tirelessly handed out samples around Winnipeg and haunted local craft fairs and retailers. Still, their entrepreneurial drive kept them optimistic that the business would grow. "The fact that both our dads were entrepreneurs gave us the example and inspiration to try it ourselves," explains Larry.

The big break for Clodhoppers came when the founders talked their way into a local Wal-Mart outlet—a renegade act that caught the attention of Wal-Mart Canada's headquarters where all purchases are supposed to be cleared. When Wal-Mart Canada's chief buyer became one of Krave's biggest supporters, Clodhoppers spread to all Wal-Mart Canada stores. Other Canadian retailers soon followed, and Dairy Queen introduced a Clodhopper Blizzard at its Canadian outlets. "They saw the potential in the product and the passion Larry and I have," says Emery.

Chris Emery and Larry Finnson have an entrepreneurial drive that has helped the Winnipeg-based founders of Krave's Candy make Clodhoppers a national success. *Courtesy of Krave's Candy Co./ Peter Bregg/Maclean's*

Larry and Chris's entrepreneurial motivation also caught the attention of Lee Scott, president and chief executive of Wal-Mart Stores Inc. in the United States, when he passed by the Clodhopper booth at a Toronto trade show. Lee was so impressed by Chris, Larry, and their Clodhoppers that he fast-tracked the product onto the shelves of 3,000 Wal-Mart stores.

The key to entrepreneurial success, says Chris Emery, is to believe in yourself and have a strong partnership. "When we're together and we're on, we're unstoppable and unbeatable," says Emery. "We're also the best of friends, and have the same entrepreneurial spirit," adds Finnson.[1] ■

www.kraves.com

Chris Emery and Larry Finnson have become icons of the Canadian entrepreneurial spirit. They also illustrate the value of motivating yourself and others to perform beyond expectations. **Motivation** refers to the forces within a person that affect his or her direction, intensity, and persistence of voluntary behaviour.[2] Motivated employees are willing to exert a particular level of effort (intensity), for a certain amount of time (persistence), toward a particular goal (direction). Even when people have clear work objectives, the right skills, and a supportive work environment, they must have sufficient motivation to achieve work objectives.

Most employers—92 percent of them, according to one recent survey[3]—agree that motivating employees has become more challenging. One reason is that globalization has dramatically changed the jobs that people perform and has resulted in numerous forms of corporate restructuring and downsizing. These actions have significantly damaged the levels of trust and commitment necessary for employees to make any efforts beyond the minimum requirements.[4] Some organizations have completely given up on motivation from the heart and, instead, rely on pay-for-performance and layoff threats. These strategies may have some effect (both positive and negative), but they do not capitalize on the employee's motivational potential.

A second problem is that as companies flatten their hierarchies to reduce costs, they can no longer rely on supervisors to practice the old "command-and-control" methods of motivating employees. This is probably just as well, because direct supervision is incompatible with the values of today's educated work force. Still, many businesses have not discovered other ways to motivate employees.

Last, employee needs are changing. Younger generations of employees are bringing different expectations to the workplace than their baby-boomer counterparts.[5] Workforce diversity and globalization have added to this complexity because diverse employees typically have diverse values. Recall from Chapter 2 that values represent stable, long-lasting beliefs that guide a person's preferences for outcomes or courses of action in a variety of situations. These values influence what we want, what we need, and what organizations should and should not do to fulfill those needs.

In this chapter, we look at the prominent theories of motivation in organizational settings. We begin by looking at needs-based motivation theories, including Maslow's needs hierarchy, Alderfer's ERG theory, the innate drives theory, and McClelland's learned needs theory. Next, this chapter details expectancy theory, which applies a rational decision perspective to the topic of motivation. The third section of this chapter covers the key elements of goal setting and feedback, including the topics of multisource feedback and executive coaching. In the final section, we look at organizational justice, including the dimensions and dynamics of equity theory and procedural justice.

NEED-BASED THEORIES OF MOTIVATION

Most contemporary theories recognize that motivation begins with individual needs and their underlying drives. **Needs** are deficiencies that energize or trigger behaviours to satisfy those needs. For instance, you probably always have a strong need for food and shelter. At other times, your social needs may be unfulfilled. Unfulfilled needs create a tension that makes us want to find ways to reduce or satisfy those needs. The stronger your needs, the more motivated you are to satisfy them. Conversely, a satisfied need does not motivate.[6] In this section, we will look at two popular needs hierarchy theories, an emerging theory of innate drives, and a theory of learned needs.

Needs Hierarchy Theory

One of the earliest and best-known needs-based theories is **needs hierarchy theory.** Developed by psychologist Abraham Maslow, this theory condenses the numerous needs that scholars have identified into a hierarchy of five basic categories.[7] At the bottom are *physiological needs*, which include the need to satisfy biological requirements for food, air, water, and shelter. Next are *safety needs*—the need for a secure and stable environment and the absence of pain, threat, or illness. *Belongingness* includes the need for love, affection, and interaction with other people. *Esteem* includes self-esteem through personal achievement as well as social esteem through recognition and respect from others. At the top of the hierarchy is *self-actualization*, which describes the need for self-fulfillment—the sense that a person's potential has been realized.

Maslow recognized that we are motivated simultaneously by several needs, but that behaviour is mostly motivated by the lowest unsatisfied need at the time. As a person satisfies a lower level need, the next highest need in the hierarchy becomes the primary motivator. This is known as the **satisfaction-progression process**. Even if a person is unable to satisfy a higher need, he or she will be motivated by it until it is eventually satisfied. Physiological needs are initially the most important and people are motivated to satisfy them first. As those needs become gratified, safety needs emerge as the strongest motivator. As safety needs are satisfied, belongingness needs become most important, and so forth. The exception to the satisfaction-progression process is self-actualization; as people experience self-actualization, they desire more rather than less of this need.

Maslow's needs hierarchy is one of the best-known organizational behaviour theories and is still widely cited in professional publications.[8] However, scholars have mostly dismissed Maslow's theory because it is much too rigid to explain the dynamic and unstable characteristics of employee needs.[9] Researchers have found that individual needs do not cluster neatly around the five categories described in the model. Moreover, gratification of one need level does not necessarily lead to increased motivation to satisfy the next higher need level.

ERG Theory

ERG theory was developed by organizational behaviour scholar Clayton Alderfer to overcome the problems with Maslow's needs hierarchy theory.[10] ERG theory groups human needs into three broad categories: existence, relatedness, and growth. (Notice that the theory's name is based on the first letter of each need.) As Exhibit 5.1 illustrates, existence needs correspond to Maslow's physiological and safety needs. Relatedness needs refer mainly to Maslow's belongingness needs. Growth needs correspond to Maslow's esteem and self-actualization needs.

Existence needs include a person's physiological and physically related safety needs, such as the need for food, shelter, and safe working conditions. **Relatedness needs** include a person's need to interact with other people, receive public recognition, and feel secure around people (i.e. interpersonal safety). **Growth needs** consist of a person's self-esteem through personal achievement, as well as the concept of self-actualization presented in Maslow's model.

---

satisfaction-progression process

A process whereby people become increasingly motivated to fulfill a higher need as a lower need is gratified.

ERG theory

Alderfer's motivation theory of three instinctive needs arranged in a hierarchy, in which people progress to the next higher need when a lower one is fulfilled, and regress to a lower need if unable to fulfill a higher one.

existence needs

A person's physiological and physically related safety needs, such as the need for food, shelter, and safe working conditions.

relatedness needs

A person's need to interact with other people, receive public recognition, and feel secure around people.

growth needs

A person's self-esteem through personal achievement as well as the concept of self-actualization.

EXHIBIT 5.1

Comparing Maslow's
needs hierarchy and
Alderfer's ERG
theory

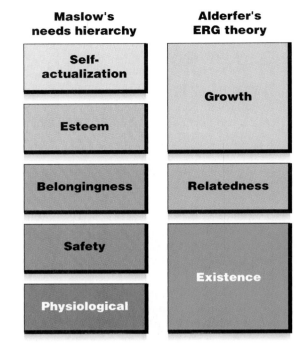

EXHIBIT 5.1

Comparing Maslow's
needs hierarchy and
Alderfer's ERG
theory

**frustration–
regression
process**

A process whereby a
person who is unable
to satisfy a higher
need becomes frus-
trated and regresses
back to the next
lower need level.

ERG theory states that an employee's behaviour is motivated simultaneously by more than one need level. Thus, you might try to satisfy your growth needs (such as by completing an assignment exceptionally well) even though your relatedness needs aren't completely satisfied. However, ERG theory applies the satisfaction-progression process described in Maslow's needs hierarchy model, so lower needs tend to dominate a person's motivation until they are satisfied. As existence needs are satisfied, for example, related needs become more important.

Unlike Maslow's model, however, ERG theory includes a **frustration–regression process** whereby those who are unable to satisfy a higher need become frustrated and regress to the next lower need level. For example, if existence and relatedness needs have been satisfied, but growth need fulfillment has been blocked, we become frustrated and relatedness needs will again emerge as the dominant source of motivation.

ERG theory has received better research support than Maslow's needs hierarchy, mainly because human needs cluster more neatly around the three categories proposed by Alderfer than the five categories in Maslow's hierarchy. The combined processes of satisfaction-progression and frustration-regression also provide a more complete explanation of why employee needs change over time.[11] However, scholars increasingly doubt that human beings have any inherent needs hierarchy.[12] Instead, some argue that people prioritize their needs around their personal values (see Chapter 2). Others suggest that people change their needs priority as they alter their personal and social identity. Specifically, employees tend to be driven by growth needs when they see themselves as unique (personal identity), and are driven by relatedness needs when they define themselves in terms of their group memberships (social identity). In summary, people might have a needs hierarchy, but it is probably not hard-wired in human nature as ERG theory and Maslow's needs hierarchy theory assume.

Innate Human Drives

Although many scholars now doubt that people have a predetermined needs hierarchy, they have not abandoned the notion that needs are part of human nature. On the contrary, a recent groundswell of interest in evolutionary psychology has led some scholars to investigate the extent to which needs are based on innate drives, that is, hard-wired into our genes and manifested as conscious emotions that influence rational calculations.[13] Various evolutionary theories have been used to explain the development of innate drives, including Darwin's "survival of the fittest" view that the human species adapted innate drives that improved future prospects of survival and regeneration. In other words, drives represent the human adaptive advantage.[14] They have evolved with the environment and with the development of human physical and social capabilities to ensure survival of the species.

Four fundamental drives   The search for innate human drives is still in its infancy, but Harvard Business School professors Paul Lawrence and Nitin Nohria have recently proposed four fundamental human drives that provide an initial foundation: the drive to acquire, to bond, to learn, and to defend.[15]

Although Veto Mariano is happy to find a new job, he still feels a profound loss of friendship from his recent layoff after 16 years of employment with Triangle Suspension Systems Ltd. The Cambridge, Ontario-based truck springs manufacturer shut down due to poor sales, putting all 120 staff out of work. "You lose a lot of friends," acknowledges Mariano, shown here with former Triangle co-workers. Leonard Lee feels a similar sense of loss. "It's sad," says Lee, who is president of the union local that represents Triangle's production workers. "I've worked with these guys for years." Evolutionary psychologists say that people have an innate drive to bond, so layoffs create negative emotions because friendship bonds are torn apart.[18] How would the other three innate human drives be affected by layoffs? *D. Bebee, © The Record, Waterloo Region, Ontario, Canada.*
www.trianglegroup.com

- *Drive to Acquire*—This is the drive to seek, take, control, and retain objects and personal experiences. The drive to acquire extends beyond basic food and water; it also includes the need for relative status and recognition in society. Thus, it is the foundation of competition and the basis of our need for esteem. Lawrence and Nohria suggest that the drive to acquire is insatiable because the purpose of human motivation is to achieve a higher position than others, not just to fulfill one's physiological needs.[16]

- *Drive to Bond*—This is the drive to form social relationships and develop mutual caring commitments with others. It also explains why people form social identities by aligning their self-image with various social groups (see Chapter 3). Research indicates that people invest considerable time and effort forming and maintaining relationships without any special circumstances or ulterior motives.[17] Moreover, people experience negative emotions fairly consistently when relationships are dissolved, such as when a business shuts down or co-workers are laid off. The drive to bond motivates people to cooperate and, consequently, is a fundamental ingredient in the success of organizations and the development of societies.

- *Drive to Learn*—This is the drive to satisfy one's curiosity, to know and understand ourselves and the environment around us. When observing something that is inconsistent with or beyond our current knowledge, we experience a tension that motivates us to close that information gap. The drive to learn fulfills our need for personal and social identity (see Chapter 3) and is related to the higher order needs of growth and self-actualization described earlier.

- *Drive to Defend*—This is the drive to protect ourselves physically and socially. Probably the first drive to develop, it creates a "fight or flight" response in the face of personal danger. The drive to defend goes beyond protecting our physical self. It includes defending our relationships, our acquisitions, and our belief systems. The drive to defend is always reactive—it is triggered by threat. In contrast, the other three drives are always proactive—we actively seek to improve our acquisitions, relationships, and knowledge.[19]

How do these innate drives translate into motivation and behaviour? Evolutionary psychologists believe that our perceptions of the external world are routed to two parts of the brain—the emotional centre and the rational centre.[20] The emotional centre, which operates faster than the rational centre, relies on innate drives to code the relevance and strength of the perceived information. Situations that violate or support these drives receive emotional markers (fear, excitement, anger, etc.). The emotionally coded information is transmitted to the rational centre of the brain where it is evaluated in the context of memory and competencies. The rational centre then makes a conscious choice that motivates behaviour.[21]

Innate drives speed up the decision-making process because the emotional markers created by these drives highlight the alternative actions to avoid and the alternatives to favour. Emotional markers also become the conscious sources of human motivation. For example, suppose your department has just received a new computer system that you are eager to try out (drive to learn), but your boss has restricted use of the new equipment. Your boss's interference sets off emotional markers (anger, frustration) that demand your attention and energize you to remove that barrier. Thus, to get rid of the anger or frustration, you boldly ask your boss to let you use the new equipment. You can see that emotional intelligence, which we discussed in Chapter 4, plays an important role in this process. Emotional intelligence competencies operate in the rational centre to temper the emotional impulses and direct our effort toward socially acceptable behaviour.

Research seems to support the notion that the brain processes information both emotionally and rationally. However, we are still a long way from knowing whether the four drives described by Lawrence and Nohria are truly hard-wired, and whether they exist more or less equally in everyone. We should also remember that there is considerable debate about various evolutionary psychology theories, including whether these theories can ever be adequately tested.[22] However, this emerging model of human motives provides a useful template for understanding the origins of human motivation and the relevance of emotions in the motivation process.

McClelland's Theory of Learned Needs

The needs-based models described so far look at the individual's primary or instinctive needs and their relative importance in life. However, people also have secondary needs or drives that are learned and reinforced through childhood learning, parental styles, and social norms. Several learned needs can motivate us at the same time. Psychologist David McClelland devoted his career to studying three secondary needs that he considered particularly important sources of motivation: need for achievement, need for affiliation, and need for power.

Need for achievement (nAch)   The opening story to this chapter described how the strong entrepreneurial drive of Chris Emery and Larry Finnson motivated them to turn Emery's grandmother's recipe into a popular Canadian treat. The founders of Krave's Candy have a drive to acquire, but they also seem to have developed, through their parents, a strong **need for achievement (nAch)**. People with a high nAch want to accomplish reasonably challenging goals through their own efforts. They prefer working alone rather than in teams and to choose tasks with a moderate degree of risk (i.e. neither too easy nor impossible to complete). High nAch people also desire unambiguous feedback and recognition for their success.

Successful entrepreneurs tend to have a high nAch, possibly because they establish challenging goals for themselves and thrive on competition.[23] A recent study of high-technology entrepreneurs in British Columbia supports earlier findings that money is a weak motivator among these achievement-oriented people, except when it provides feedback and recognition.[24] In contrast, employees with a low nAch perform their work better when money is used as a financial incentive. Corporate and team leaders should have a somewhat lower nAch because they must delegate work and build support through involvement (characteristics not usually found in high achievers). However, high nAch people may perform well in large companies where they are given considerable independence—as though they are running their own business.[25] GLOBAL Connections 5.1 reports on how corporate leaders in most countries want a company of entrepreneurs because of their high need for achievement, willingness to take risks, and ability to provide creative ideas.

Need for affiliation (nAff)   **Need for affiliation (nAff)** refers to a desire to seek approval from others, conform to their wishes and expectations, and avoid conflict and confrontation. People with a strong nAff want to form positive relationships with others. They try to project a favourable image of themselves and take other steps to be liked by others. Moreover, high nAff employees actively support others and try to smooth out conflicts that occur in meetings and other social settings. High nAff employees tend to be more effective than those with a low nAff in coordinating roles, such as helping diverse departments work on joint projects. They are also more effective in sales positions where the main task is cultivating long-term relations with prospective customers. More generally, employees with high nAff prefer working with others rather than alone, tend to have better attendance records, and tend to be better at mediating conflicts.

Although people with high nAff are more effective in many jobs requiring social interaction, they tend to be less effective at allocating scarce resources and making other decisions that potentially generate conflict. For example, research has found that executives with a high nAff tend to be indecisive and are perceived as less fair in the distribution of resources. Thus, people in these decision-making positions must have a relatively low need for affiliation so that their choices and actions are not biased by a personal need for approval.[26]

need for achievement (nAch)
A learned need in which people want to accomplish reasonably challenging goals through their own efforts, like to be successful in competitive situations, and desire unambiguous feedback regarding their success.

need for affiliation (nAff)
A learned need in which people seek approval from others, conform to their wishes and expectations, and avoid conflict and confrontation.

Creating a Company of Entrepreneurs

Matsushita Electric Industrial Co. is trying to create a company of entrepreneurs. The Japanese electronics manufacturer, which is best known for its Panasonic and National brand names, is setting up an internal venture capital fund that will provide financial support to employees with creative ideas. "We would be searching for entrepreneurs internally and will venture to create new business areas or develop new business models," says Matsushita president Kunio Nakamura.

Matsushita is not alone in its effort to encourage entrepreneurial spirit within the organization. Seventy percent of the 900 Board-level executives recently surveyed in 22 countries say that entrepreneurship is very important to the success of their organization. "Our entrepreneurship has fuelled our economic growth over the past years," says Jens Beier, co-CEO and co-founder of the German company IMPRESS.

Companies want more entrepreneurial employees because of their drive to succeed, willingness to take risks, and ability to generate creative ideas. "Entrepreneurship is having an urge towards improvement and having a drive to act within a limited time scale," says Cor Boonstra, CEO of the Dutch electronics company Philips. The problem, according to the survey, is that few executives think they have an entrepreneurial workforce. On the contrary, one executive in the study suggested that "many organizations and managers beat the entrepreneurial spirit out of employees."

Maintaining an entrepreneurial workforce is also a concern at Accenture, the Chicago-based consulting firm that conducted the survey. "This is a big issue for us," explains Vernon Ellis, Accenture's international chairman in London. "Accenture is founded on entrepreneurial spirit, but now that we have over 75,000 staff, there is a danger that our sheer size and complexity could stifle this."

According to the Accenture report, leaders can create a company of entrepreneurs by clarifying the firm's purpose and shared values, supporting and reinforcing entrepreneurial behaviour, and creating small businesses within the larger organization (as Matsushita is doing with its venture capital fund).

Sources: V. Ellis, "Now We All Need to be Entrepreneurs," *Times of London*, August 22, 2001; Accenture, *Liberating the Entrepreneurial Spirit* (London: Accenture, August 2001); "Matsushita Electric Sets up 86 Million Dollar Fund for Employees' Ideas," *Agence France Presse*, January 11, 2001. **www.matsushita.co.jp**

---

need for power (nPow)
A learned need in which people want to control their environment, including people and material resources, to benefit either themselves (personalized power) or others (socialized power).

Need for power (nPow) **Need for power (nPow)** refers to a desire to control one's environment, including people and material resources. People with a high nPow want to exercise control over others and are concerned about maintaining their leadership position. They frequently rely on persuasive communication (see Chapter 12), make more suggestions in meetings, and tend to publicly evaluate situations more frequently. Some people have a high need for *personalized power*. They enjoy their power for its own sake and use it to advance their career and other personal interests. It is a symbol of status and a tool to fulfill personal needs more than a delicate instrument to serve stakeholders. Others mainly have a high need for *socialized power*. They want power as a means to help others, such as improving society or increasing organizational effectiveness.[27]

Corporate and political leaders have a high nPow because this motivates them to influence others—an important part of the leadership process (see Chapter 14).[28] However, McClelland argues that effective leaders should have a high need for socialized rather than personalized power. They have a high degree of altruism and social responsibility and are concerned about the consequences of their own actions on others. In other words, leaders must exercise their power within the framework of moral standards. The ethical guidance of their need for power develops follower trust and respect for the leader, as well as commitment to the leader's vision.[29]

Learning needs McClelland argued that achievement, affiliation, and power needs are learned rather than instinctive. Accordingly, he developed training programs that strengthen these needs. In his achievement motivation program, trainees practise writing achievement-oriented stories after reading others and practising achievement-oriented behaviours in business games. They also complete a detailed achievement plan for the next two years and form a reference group with other trainees to maintain their newfound achievement motive style.[30]

These programs seem to work. For example, participants attending a need for achievement course in India subsequently started more new businesses, had greater community involvement, invested more in expanding their businesses, and employed twice as many people as nonparticipants. Research on similar achievement-motive courses for North American small business owners reported dramatic increases in the profitability of the participants' businesses.

Practical Implications of Needs-based Motivation Theories

Needs-based theories of motivation offer several recommendations. First, corporate leaders need to balance the drive to acquire (competition) with the drive to bond (cooperation). To achieve this balance, Lawrence and Nohria recommend financial and symbolic rewards that emphasize both individual achievement and teamwork.[31] Organizations also need to support the drive to learn by giving employees opportunities to experience novel situations and practise new skills. As for the drive to defend, corporate leaders need to minimize unnecessary threats to the personal safety, well-being, and social relationships that employees value.

Needs-based theories also suggest that different people have different needs at different times. Some employees are ready to fulfill growth needs, whereas others are still struggling to satisfy their minimum existence needs. Needs also change as people enter new stages of their life, so rewards that motivate people at one time may have less motivational value in later years. This suggests that employees are not equally motivated by the same thing. The solution is to offer employees a choice of rewards. Telus Corporation accomplishes this by awarding points to employees who deserve special recognition. "There is a catalogue you can select a gift from with those points," explains a Telus executive. "You can get a trip or camping gear or anything that would relate to your lifestyle." These gifts are valued more than standardized rewards because employees choose gifts they value the most.[32]

Lastly, needs-based theories warn us against relying too heavily on financial rewards as a source of employee motivation.[33] While money does motivate

Executives at EnCana Corporation know that money isn't the only way to motivate employees. But this point became vividly clear soon after the Calgary-based energy company launched its "High-Five" recognition program. The program gave employees and managers the right to recommend any deserving colleague for a high-five card, which is redeemable for $5.00. But rather than cashing in their cards for money, many employees displayed the cards in their offices. The visible symbol of recognition was apparently worth more to many people than the cash value of the card.[34] Under what conditions would money be a strong motivator? *CP/Adrian Wyld.*

www.encana.com

employees to some extent, there are potentially more powerful sources of motivation, such as challenging assignments, learning opportunities, and praise from colleagues and corporate leaders.

EXPECTANCY THEORY OF MOTIVATION

expectancy theory
The motivation theory based on the idea that work effort is directed toward behaviours that people believe will lead to desired outcomes.

Our earlier discussion of innate drives emphasized the role of emotions in human motivation, but we noted that people also engage in a rational process to direct their effort. This rational process is best represented by a popular perspective of motivation called expectancy theory. **Expectancy theory** is based on the idea that work effort is directed toward behaviours that people believe will lead to desired outcomes.[35] Through experience, we develop expectations about whether we can achieve various levels of job performance. We also develop expectations about whether job performance and work behaviours lead to particular outcomes. Finally, we naturally direct our effort toward outcomes that help us fulfill our needs.

Expectancy Theory Model

The expectancy theory model is presented in Exhibit 5.2. The key variable of interest in expectancy theory is *effort*—the individual's actual exertion of energy. An individual's effort level depends on three factors: effort-to-performance (E→P) expectancy, performance-to-outcome (P→O) expectancy, and outcome-valences (V). Employee motivation is influenced by all three components of the expectancy theory model. If any component weakens, motivation weakens.

effort-to-performance (E→P) expectancy
The individual's perceived probability that his or her effort will result in a particular level of performance.

E→P expectancy   The **effort-to-performance (E→P) expectancy** is the individual's perception that his or her effort will result in a particular level of performance. Expectancy is defined as a *probability*, and therefore ranges from 0.0 to 1.0. In some situations, employees may believe that they can unquestionably accomplish the task (a probability of 1.0). In other situations, they expect that even their highest level of effort will not result in the desired performance level (a probability

EXHIBIT 5.2

Expectancy theory of motivation

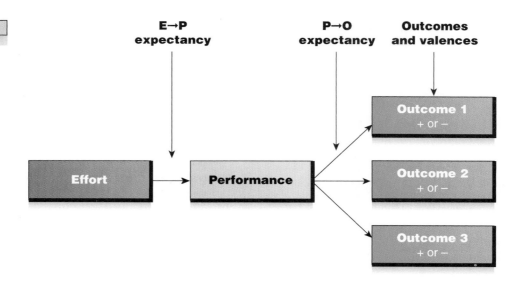

of 0.0). For instance, unless you are an expert skier, you probably aren't motivated to try some of the black diamond ski runs at Whistler. The reason is a very low E→P expectancy. Even your best effort won't get you down the hill feet first! In most cases, the E→P expectancy falls somewhere between these two extremes.

performance-to-outcome (P→O) expectancy
The perceived probability that a specific behaviour or performance level will lead to specific outcomes.

P→O expectancy   The **performance-to-outcome (P→O) expectancy** is the perceived probability that a specific behaviour or performance level will lead to specific outcomes. This probability is developed from previous learning. For example, students learn from experience that skipping class either ruins their chance of a good grade or has no effect at all. In extreme cases, employees may believe that accomplishing a particular task (performance) will *definitely* result in a particular outcome (a probability of 1.0), or they may believe that this outcome will have *no effect* on successful performance (a probability of 0.0). More often, the P→O expectancy falls somewhere between these two extremes.

One important issue in P→O expectancies is which outcomes we think about. We certainly don't evaluate the P→O expectancy for every possible outcome. There are too many of them. Instead, we only think about outcomes that are of interest to us at the time. One day, your motivation to complete a task may be fuelled mainly by the likelihood of getting off work early to meet friends. Other times, your motivation to complete the same task may be based more on the P→O expectancy of a promotion or pay increase. The main point is that your motivation depends on the probability that a behaviour or job performance level will result in outcomes that you think about beforehand.

valence
The anticipated satisfaction or dissatisfaction that an individual feels toward an outcome.

Outcome valences   The third element in expectancy theory is the **valence** of each outcome that you consider. Valence refers to the anticipated satisfaction or dissatisfaction that an individual feels toward an outcome. It ranges from negative to positive. (The actual range doesn't matter; it may be from −1 to +1, or from −100 to +100.) An outcome valence refers to a person's feelings toward the outcome and is determined by perceptions about how much the outcome will fulfill or interfere with the person's needs and drives. It is also influenced by our personal values (see Chapter 2). Outcomes have a positive valence when they are consistent with our values and directly or indirectly satisfy our needs; they have a negative valence when they oppose our values and inhibit need fulfilment. If you have a strong relatedness (social) need, for example, then you would value group activities and other events that help to fulfill that need. Outcomes that move you further away from fulfilling your social needs—such as working alone from home—will have a strong negative valence.

Expectancy Theory in Practice

One of the appealing characteristics of expectancy theory is that it provides clear guidelines for increasing employee motivation by altering the person's E→P expectancies, P→O expectancies, and/or outcome valences.[36] Several practical implications of expectancy theory are listed in Exhibit 5.3 and described below.

Increasing E→P expectancies   E→P expectancies are influenced by the individual's self-efficacy. Recall from Chapter 3 that self-efficacy refers to a person's belief that he or she has the ability, motivation, and situational contingencies to complete a task successfully. People with high self-efficacy have a "can do" atti-

EXHIBIT 5.3   Practical applications of expectancy theory

Expectancy theory component	Objective	Applications
E→P expectancies	To increase the belief that employees are capable of performing the job successfully	• Select people with the required skills and knowledge. • Provide required training and clarify job requirements. • Provide sufficient time and resources. • Assign simpler or fewer tasks until employees can master them. • Provide examples of similar employees who have successfully performed the task. • Provide coaching to employees who lack self-confidence.
P→O expectancies	To increase the belief that good performance will result in certain (valued) outcomes	• Measure job performance accurately. • Clearly explain the outcomes that will result from successful performance. • Describe how the employee's rewards were based on past performance. • Provide examples of other employees whose good performance has resulted in higher rewards.
Valences of outcomes	To increase the expected value of outcomes resulting from desired performance	• Distribute rewards that employees value. • Individualize rewards. • Minimize the presence of countervalent outcomes.

tude toward a specific task and, more generally, with other challenges in life. Some companies increase this "can do" attitude by assuring employees that they have the necessary competencies, clear role perceptions, and favourable situational conditions to reach the desired levels of performance. This involves properly matching employees to jobs based on their abilities, clearly communicating the tasks required for the job, and providing sufficient resources for them to accomplish those tasks. Coaching also improves self-efficacy and, consequently, the employee's E→P expectancies regarding specific tasks. Similarly, E→P expectancies are learned, so positive feedback typically strengthens employee self-efficacy.[37] Behaviour modification and behavioural modelling also tend to increase E→P expectancies in many situations.

Increasing P→O expectancies   The most obvious ways to improve P→O expectancies are to measure employee performance accurately and distribute more valued rewards to those with higher job performance. Many organizations have difficulty putting this straightforward idea into practice. Some executives are reluctant to withhold rewards for poor performance because they don't want to experience conflict with employees. Others don't measure employee performance very well. For instance, the Canadian government's Human Resources Development Department consistently paid its managers and executives performance bonuses even though a scathing audit revealed dismal record-keeping and mismanagement of $1 billion in job creation funds.[38] Chapter 6 looks at reasons why rewards aren't connected to job performance.

P→O expectancies are perceptions, so employees should *believe* that higher performance will result in higher rewards. Having a performance-based reward system is important, but this fact must be communicated. When rewards are distributed, employees should understand that their rewards have been based on past performance. More generally, companies need to regularly communicate the existence of a performance-based reward system through examples, anecdotes, and public ceremonies.

Increasing outcome valences   Performance outcomes influence work effort only when they are valued by employees.[39] This brings us back to what we learned from the needs-based theories of motivation, namely, that companies must pay attention to the needs and reward preferences of individual employees. They should develop more individualized reward systems so that employees who perform well are offered a choice of rewards.

Expectancy theory also emphasizes the need to discover and neutralize countervalent outcomes. These are performance outcomes that have negative valences, thereby reducing the effectiveness of existing reward systems. For example, peer pressure may cause some employees to perform their jobs at the minimum standard even though formal rewards and the job itself would otherwise motivate them to perform at higher levels.

Does Expectancy Theory Fit Reality?

Expectancy theory is one of the more difficult theories to test, and it has had problems with research methods.[40] In spite of these challenges, it is one of the better theories for predicting work effort and motivation. For example, studies have applied expectancy theory to predict a person's motivation to use a decision support system, leave the organization, work with less effort in a group setting, and engage in organizational citizenship behaviours.[41]

Some critics have suggested that expectancy theory is culture-bound, arguing that the theory makes Western-oriented assumptions that employees have strong feelings of personal control.[42] In reality, expectancy theory does not assume that people feel they have complete control over their lives; on the contrary, the E→P expectancy varies directly with the employee's perceived control over the work situation. Research indicates that expectancy theory predicts employee motivation in different cultures.[43]

Another challenge is that expectancy theory seems to ignore the central role of emotion in employee effort and behaviour. As we learned earlier in this and previous chapters, emotion serves an adaptive function that demands our attention and energizes us to take action. The valence element of expectancy theory captures some of this emotional process, but only peripherally. Thus, theorists probably need to redesign the expectancy theory model in light of new information about the importance of emotions in motivation and behaviour.[44]

GOAL SETTING AND FEEDBACK

Mitel Corp., the Ottawa-based maker of telephone network gear, has a secret weapon to keep project deadlines on time. It's an enormous digital clock—seven feet long and one foot tall—placed in the cafeteria that measures everything from 10ths of a second to days in a year. Beside the clock is a whiteboard that lists

goals
The immediate or ultimate objectives that employees are trying to accomplish from their work effort.

goal setting
The process of motivating employees and clarifying their role perceptions by establishing performance objectives.

interim deadlines for all major projects at the telecommunications development company. Whenever a team misses a deadline, Mitel executives put a red slash through the date for everyone to see. Employees initially complained, but the results have silenced the critics. Mitel's average length of product development time has dropped from 70 to 50 weeks.[45]

Mitel and other organizations have discovered that goal setting is one of the most effective theories of motivation in organizations.[46] **Goals** are the immediate or ultimate objectives that employees are trying to accomplish from their work effort. **Goal setting** is the process of motivating employees and clarifying their role perceptions by establishing performance objectives. Goal setting potentially improves employee performance in two ways: (1) by stretching the intensity and persistence of effort and (2) by giving employees clearer role perceptions so their effort is channelled toward behaviours that will improve work performance.

Some companies apply goal setting through a formal process known as **management-by-objectives (MBO).** There are a few variations of MBO programs, but they generally identify organizational objectives, then cascade them down to work units and individual employees. MBO also includes regular discussion of goal progress.[47] Although MBO has been criticized for creating too much paperwork, it can be an effective application of goal setting.

By setting specific, challenging goals for its employees, CDW Computer Centers Inc. has become a leading direct marketer of computers and peripherals. "We set BHAGS—which are big, hairy, aggressive goals," says CDW president and CEO John A. Edwardson (shown in photo). "The current BHAG is $11 million in bonuses shared with the employees of the company when we hit $7 billion in revenue." Edwardson explains that the previous stretch goal was called "5432," which referred to $5 million in bonuses for $3 billion in sales by 2000. CDW employees exceeded that goal, which nearly tripled the company's revenue from three years earlier.[48] To what extent is this goal-setting process compatible with the characteristics of effective goals? © Jim Robinson/Tribune
www.cdw.com

Characteristics of Effective Goals

Goal setting is more complex than simply telling someone to "to your best." Instead, organizational behaviour scholars have identified six conditions to maximize task effort and performance. These include specific goals, relevant goals, challenging goals, goal commitment, participation in goal formation (sometimes), and goal feedback.[49]

- *Specific goals*—Employees put more effort into a task when they work toward specific goals rather than "do your best" targets.[50] Specific goals have measurable levels of change over a specific and relatively short time frame, such as "reduce scrap rate by 7 percent over the next six months." Specific goals communicate more precise performance expectations, so employees can direct their effort more efficiently and reliably.
- *Relevant goals* —Goals must also be relevant to the individual's job and within his or her control. For example, a goal to reduce waste materials would have little value if employees don't have much control over waste in the production process.
- *Challenging goals*—Employees tend to process task knowledge more actively and engage in work effort more intensely and persistently when they have challenging rather than easy goals. Challenging goals also fulfill a person's need for

management by objectives (MBO)
A participative goal-setting process in which organizational objectives are cascaded down to work units and individual employees.

achievement or growth needs when the goal is achieved.[51] Cisco Systems and other organizations emphasize "stretch goals"—goals that are challenging enough to stretch the employee's abilities and motivation toward peak performance. Stretch goals are effective if employees receive the necessary resources and are not overstressed in the process.[52]

■ *Goal commitment*—Although goals should be challenging, employees also need to be committed to accomplishing goals. Thus, we need to find an optimal level of goal difficulty where the goals are challenging yet employees are still motivated to achieve them.[53] This is the same as the E→P expectancy that we learned about in the section on expectancy theory.[54] The lower the E→P expectancy that the goal can be accomplished, the less committed (motivated) the employee is to the goal.

■ *Goal participation (sometimes)*—Goal setting is usually (but not always) more effective when employees participate in setting goals.[55] Employees identify more with goals they are involved in setting than goals assigned by a supervisor. In fact, today's workforce increasingly expects to be involved in goal setting and other decisions that affect them. Participation may also improve goal quality, because employees have valuable information and knowledge that may not be known to those who initially formed the goal. Thus, participation ensures that employees buy into the goals and have the competencies and resources necessary to accomplish them.

■ *Goal Feedback*—Feedback is another necessary condition for effective goal setting.[56] **Feedback** is any information that people receive about the consequences of their behaviour. Feedback lets us know whether we have achieved the goal or are properly directing our effort toward it. Feedback is also an essential ingredient in motivation because our growth needs can't be satisfied unless we receive information on goal accomplishment. Feedback is so central to goal setting that we will look more closely at it next.

feedback
Any information that people receive about the consequences of their behaviour.

Characteristics of Effective Feedback

Feedback is a key ingredient in goal setting and employee performance.[57] It clarifies role perceptions by communicating what behaviours are appropriate or necessary in a particular situation. Feedback improves ability by frequently providing information to correct performance problems.[58] This is known as *corrective feedback*, because it makes people aware of their performance errors and helps them correct those errors quickly. Lastly, feedback is a source of motivation. It fulfills personal needs and makes people more confident that they are able to accomplish certain tasks.

Feedback is a necessary part of goal setting, so it shouldn't be surprising that many of the elements of effective goal setting also apply to effective feedback (see Exhibit 5.4). First, feedback should be *specific*. The information provided should be connected to the details of the goal, such as "you exceeded your sales quota by 5 percent last month" rather than subjective and general phrases such as "your sales are going well." Notice that specific feedback focuses on the task, not the person. This reduces the person's defensiveness when receiving negative feedback.

Second, feedback must be *relevant*, that is, it must relate to the individual's behaviour rather than to conditions beyond the individual's control. This ensures that the feedback is not distorted by situational factors.[59] Third, feedback should be *timely*—available as soon as possible after the behaviour or results. Timeliness helps employees see a clear association between their behaviour and its consequences.

EXHIBIT 5.4

Characteristics of
effective feedback

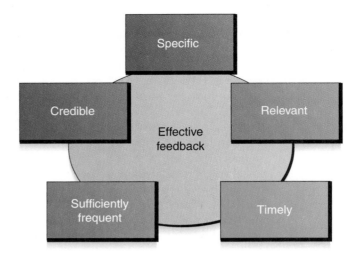

Fourth, feedback should be *sufficiently frequent*. How often is "sufficiently frequent"? The answer depends on at least two contingencies. One contingency is the employee's knowledge and experience with the task. Feedback is a form of reinforcement, so employees working on new tasks should receive more frequent feedback because they require more behaviour guidance and reinforcement (see Chapter 3). Employees who are repeating familiar tasks can receive less frequent feedback. The second contingency is the task cycle (how long it takes to complete each task). Feedback is necessarily less frequent in jobs with a long cycle time (e.g., executives and scientists) than in jobs with a short cycle time (e.g., grocery store cashiers).

Last, feedback should be *credible*. Employees are more likely to accept feedback (particularly corrective feedback) from trustworthy and credible sources.[60] One increasingly popular way to increase feedback credibility is through multisource feedback.

Multisource feedback   Telus Corporation, CREO, Radical Entertainment, and many other Canadian firms have tried to improve the credibility of feedback by introducing multisource feedback.[61] Multisource feedback is often called **360-degree feedback** because anonymous feedback is received from a full circle of people around the employee, including subordinates, peers, supervisors, and customers.[62] One recent study reported that 43 percent of Canada's largest firms use multisource feedback and that this process is most commonly applied to managers rather than to nonmanagement employees. Most plans (87 percent) also give employees complete freedom to choose who will rate them.[63]

Research suggests that multisource feedback provides more complete and accurate information than information from a supervisor alone.[64] It is particularly useful when the supervisor is unable to observe the employee's behaviour or performance throughout the year. Lower level employees also feel a greater sense of fairness and open communication when they are able to provide upward feedback about their boss's performance.

Multisource feedback also creates challenges.[65] Having several people review so many other people can be expensive and time consuming. With multiple opinions, the 360-degree process can also produce ambiguous and conflicting feedback, so

360-degree feedback
Performance feedback received from a full circle of people around an employee.

employees may require guidance to interpret the results. A third concern is that peers may provide inflated rather than accurate feedback to avoid conflicts over the forthcoming year. Last, critical feedback from many people can have emotional consequences. "Initially you do take it personally," admits Russell Huerta, a senior accounts manager at software maker Autodesk. "[360-degree feedback] is meant to be constructive, but you have to internally battle that." Huerta manages his emotional reaction to the feedback by pretending the advice is about someone else, then learning how to improve his own behaviour from that information. "It's almost an out-of-body experience, to take your mind and your emotions out of it," he recommends.[66]

Executive coaching   Another rapidly growing practice involving feedback and motivation is executive coaching. **Executive coaching** is defined as a helping relationship using a wide variety of behavioural methods to help clients identify and achieve goals for their professional performance and personal satisfaction.[67] Coaching is usually conducted by an external consultant and is essentially one-on-one "just-in-time" personal development using feedback and other techniques. Coaches do not provide answers to the employee's problems. Rather, they are "thought partners" who offer more accurate feedback, open dialogue, and constructive encouragement to improve the client's performance and personal well-being. They ask provocative questions, offer perspective, and help clients clarify choices.

Connections 5.2 describes how executive coaching has a number of vocal supporters among executives and professionals in Canada. They echo preliminary research suggesting that executive coaching is more effective than behavioural modelling at helping people change their behaviour and achieve their goals more quickly. Coaching is particularly useful for improving emotional intelligence, interpersonal skills, and related activities that require specific feedback and support in a real-time work environment.[68] However, some writers also urge caution because it seems that anyone can call him- or herself an executive coach, and many people in these positions treat the symptoms rather than the causes of executive problems.[69]

Choosing feedback sources   Executive coaches and multisource feedback represent two social sources of feedback, but employees can also receive feedback from non-social sources.[70] The job itself can be a non-social source of feedback. Many employees see the results of their work effort while they are making a product. Some professionals have "executive dashboards" on their computer screens that display the latest measures of sales, inventory, and other indicators of corporate success.[71] Other companies post critical performance information for employees to see. Walk into a typical call centre and you will likely notice electronic displays where employees can see how many callers are waiting, the average time they have been waiting, and the length of time for each call.[72]

The preferred feedback source depends on the purpose of the information. To learn about their progress toward goal accomplishment, employees usually prefer non-social feedback sources, such as computer printouts or feedback directly from the job. This is because information from non-social sources is considered more accurate than from social sources. Corrective feedback from non-social sources is also less damaging to self-esteem. This is probably just as well because social sources tend to delay negative information, leave some of it out, and distort the bad news in a positive way.[73]

executive coaching

A helping relationship using behavioural methods to assist clients in identifying and achieving goals for their professional performance and personal satisfaction.

A Coach for Executives

Greg Ball is a great thinker, but admits that his people skills need work. "Strategically, I'm good and logically I'm very good," says the director of communications in the Toronto offices of vaccine pharmaceutical firm Aventis Pasteur. "The people side for me is the area where I don't know the right answer." So, Aventis pays an executive coach to help Ball see his work situations from different perspectives and to entertain different approaches. Executive coaching makes a lot of sense, says Ball. "If you're a professional athlete, you have a coach. I want to be a professional businessperson and, therefore ... I should have a coach, too."

Aventis Pasteur, BC Hydro, the City of Richmond (B.C.), Ryzex, Nesbitt Burns, Providence Health Care, Great Pacific Management, and numerous other Canadian firms have made executive coaching their personal development tool of choice among professionals in the corporate world. Some evidence suggests that the one-on-one approach by a neutral consultant provides an effective way to clarify personal and work-related goals, and to receive ongoing feedback toward those goals. "[Clients] are looking for a silent partner to help them stay motivated, someone with whom to brainstorm and strategize," says Vancouver-based executive coach Teresia LaRocque. "Coaching is simply a relationship with someone who is paid to tell you the absolute truth," adds executive coach Nancy Gerber.

Michael Nott is another convert to executive coaching. "I was better at my job and more efficient instantly," says the manager at financial services company Great Pacific Management in Vancouver. "At the end of one year, I couldn't believe the improvement. If I had all the answers in my head, I wouldn't need a coaching program. But I need to think outside of my head. With

"Coaching is simply a relationship with someone who is paid to tell you the absolute truth," says executive coach Nancy Gerber, shown here with client Liz Sanford. *Copyright © Jean Shifrin, The Atlanta Journal-Constitution.*

coaching, one becomes more accomplished with less effort invested due to working smarter."

Coaching bridges the gap between your current status and your future goals, explains Toronto-based executive coach Angela Alpe. "Whether your ultimate goal is to create strong leadership, enhance management performance, break down communication barriers or create balance between your work and home life, an executive coach works with you to put to use the expertise you already possess, making your objectives reality."

Sources: C. Adams, "Coaches Offer More than Game Plan," *Globe and Mail*, July 8, 2002, p. C1; A. Ferris, "Business Coach Helps Companies Get Most Out of People," *Guelph Mercury*, November 22, 2001, p. A1; P. Withers, "Bigger and Better," *BC Business*, April 2001, p. 50; K. Kicklighter, "Put Me In, Coach," *The Atlanta Journal-Constitution*, January 12, 2001, p. E1. **www.coachingcircles.com**

When employees want to improve their self-image, they seek out positive feedback from social sources. It feels better to have co-workers say you are performing the job well than to discover this from a computer printout.[74] Positive feedback from co-workers and other social sources motivates mainly because it fulfills relatedness as well as growth needs.

Applications and Limitations of Goal Setting and Feedback

Goal setting and feedback have a few limitations. One problem is that when goals are tied to monetary incentives, many employees tend to select easy rather than difficult goals.[75] In some cases, employees have negotiated goals with their supervisor that they've already completed! Employees with high self-efficacy and need for achievement tend to set challenging goals whether or not they are financially rewarded for their results. However, employers should typically separate goal setting from the pay-setting process to minimize the politics of goal setting.[76]

Another limitation is that we can't apply goal setting to every performance dimension of every job. We can usually find some measurable goals, but many other dimensions of job performance complex and long-term performance outcomes that are difficult to measure. The result is that goal setting can focus employees on a narrow subset of short-term performance indicators. The saying "What gets measured, gets done" applies here. Thus, goal setting may cause more performance problems in the long term that it solves in the short term.

In spite of these concerns, goal setting and feedback are widely supported by both academic literature and practitioner experience.[77] The objective nature of goal setting is particularly appreciated. For example, Payless Shoe Source replaced its traditional performance appraisal system with a simple goal-setting process that evaluated employees for exceeding, meeting, or falling short of their goals. The changeover improved performance and minimized some of the organizational politics and feelings of injustice that often accompany employee performance activities.[78] Organizational justice, which we discuss next, is an important perspective on employee motivation.

ORGANIZATIONAL JUSTICE

distributive justice
The perceived fairness in outcomes we receive relative to our contributions and the outcomes and contributions of others.

Corporate leaders and OB scholars have long known that to maximize employee motivation, satisfaction, and organizational commitment, they need to treat people fairly. Although it seems simple enough, organizational justice covers several issues and has two distinct forks: distributive justice and procedural justice.[79] **Distributive justice** refers to perceived fairness in the outcomes we receive relative to our contributions and the outcomes and contributions of others. **Procedural justice,** on the other hand, refers to the fairness of the procedures used to decide the distribution of resources. For example, you might feel a sense of unfairness if someone else instead of you is promoted to a job (distributive injustice), but this feeling is reduced somewhat because you also believe the decision makers had no apparent bias and seemed to consider all of the relevant information to make the decision (procedural justice). Each of these dimensions of workplace justice includes a variety of issues, which we introduce over the next few pages.

procedural justice
The fairness of the procedures used to decide the distribution of resources.

Distributive Justice and Equity Theory

Barb Nuttall felt that she wasn't being paid fairly as a Canada Safeway cashier in Regina, Saskatchewan. Nuttall noticed that most of the food retailer's cashiers are women and that they get paid about 35 cents an hour less than the mostly-male food clerks. Both jobs have similar value and require a lot of lifting. In fact, cashiers handle money, so this higher responsibility should make their job worth more to Safeway. With these concerns in mind, Nuttall and other Safeway cashiers fought to have their pay increased to the same level as food clerks. The Saskatchewan Human Rights Commission became involved and Canada Safeway recently negotiated a collective agreement that would raise cashier salaries in line with food clerks.[80]

Canada Safeway's cashiers experienced the emotional tension created by feelings of distributive injustice, which motivated them to act on those emotions.

People apply different rules or standards to determine what is a "fair" distribution of pay and other outcomes. Some of us apply an *equality principle* in which everyone should receive the same outcomes. Others might apply a *need principle* in which those with the greatest need should receive more outcomes than others with less need. Barb Nuttall and other Safeway cashiers applied the most common distributive justice rule in organizational settings, known as the *equity principle*. According to this principle, outcomes should be proportional to the individual's (or group's or organization's) inputs. This reflects the distributive justice principle of ethics described in Chapter 2. Employees and organizations typically use a combination of these three principles, particularly for different situations.[81] For example, companies typically give all employees the same employee benefits (equality principle) and allow employees with heavy family demands more paid time off (need principle). However, by far the most common distributive justice principle is equity, which we discuss next.

equity theory

Theory that explains how people develop perceptions of fairness in the distribution and exchange of resources.

Elements of equity theory   Over several decades, scholars have elaborated the equity principle through **equity theory**, which says that employees determine whether allocations are fair by comparing their own outcome/input ratio to the outcome/input ratio of some other person.[82] The outcome/input ratio is the value of the outcomes you receive divided by the value of inputs you provide in the exchange relationship. Inputs include skills, effort, experience, amount of time worked, performance results, and other employee contributions to the organization. Employees see their inputs as investments into the exchange relationship. For Canada Safeway cashiers, these inputs included their level of responsibility, amount of lifting, and other factors. Outcomes are the things employees receive from the organization in exchange for the inputs, such as pay, promotions, recognition, or an office with a window. Employees receive many outcomes and they weight each outcome and input differently, so it isn't always easy to determine the overall values. In the case involving Safeway cashiers, the main outcome is the paycheque.

Equity theory states that we compare our outcome/input ratio with a comparison other.[83] In our earlier example, Canada Safeway cashiers in Saskatchewan compared themselves with food clerks, probably because it is easier to get information about co-workers than from people working elsewhere. However, the

EXHIBIT 5.5   Equity theory model

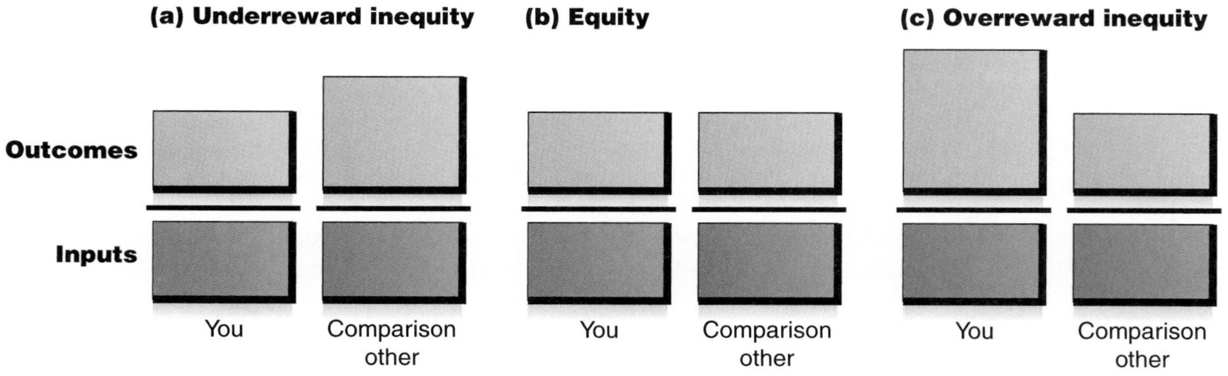

(a) Underreward inequity   **(b) Equity**   **(c) Overreward inequity**

Outcomes

Inputs

You   Comparison other   You   Comparison other   You   Comparison other comparison other may be another person, group of people, or even you in the past. It may be someone in the same job, another job, or another organization. Chief executives have no direct comparison within the firm, so they tend to compare themselves with their counterparts in other organizations. Some research suggests that employees frequently collect information on several referents to form a "generalized" comparison other.[84] For the most part, however, the comparison other varies from one person to the next and is not easily identifiable.

Equity evaluation We form an equity evaluation after determining our own outcome/input ratio and comparing this with the comparison other's ratio. Let's consider the Canada Safeway cashiers again. The cashiers feel *underreward inequity* because the food clerks receive higher outcomes (pay) for inputs that are, at best, comparable to what the cashiers contribute. This condition is illustrated in Exhibit 5.5 (a).

In the *equity condition*, the cashiers would believe that their outcome/input ratio is similar to the food clerks' ratio. If the cashiers feel they provide the same inputs as the clerks, then they would feel equity if both job groups received the same pay and other outcomes (see Exhibit 5.5 (b)). If the cashiers claim they make a greater contribution because they have more responsibility, then they would have feelings of equity only if they receive proportionally more pay than the food clerks receive. Lastly, it is possible that some Canada Safeway food clerks experienced *overreward inequity* (Exhibit 5.5 (c)). The food clerks would feel that their jobs have the same value as the cashiers, yet they earn more money. However, overreward inequity isn't as common as underreward inequity.

Correcting inequity feelings People feel an uncomfortable emotional tension when they perceive inequity. A strong enough tension motivates employees to reduce the inequity by applying one or more of the following strategies.[85] Employees who feel underpaid sometimes *reduce their inputs* by reducing their effort, performance, and organizational citizenship if these actions don't affect their paycheque.[86] Alternatively, they might try to *increase their outcomes*, such as personally asking for a pay increase or joining a labour union to demand changes.[87] Safeway cashiers increased their outcomes by having the Saskatchewan Human Rights Commission investigate their complaint. Some people who feel underrewarded also increase their outcomes by using company resources for personal gain.

Rather than changing their own inputs and outcomes, some people *act on the comparison other*. Employees who feel overrewarded might encourage the referent to work at a more leisurely pace. Those who feel underrewarded might subtly suggest that the overpaid co-worker should be doing a larger share of the workload. Equity evaluation is a subjective perceptual process, so a fourth way that employees reduce feelings of inequity is by *changing their perceptions*.[88] Overrewarded employees typically follow this strategy because it's easier to increase their perceived inputs (seniority, knowledge, etc.) than to

"O.K., if you can't see your way to giving me a pay raise, how about giving Parkerson a pay cut?"

ask for less pay! As author Pierre Berton once said: "I was underpaid for the first half of my life. I don't mind being overpaid for the second half."[89]

If the previous strategies are ineffective, then employees sometimes *change the comparison other* to someone having a more compatible outcome/input ratio. Lastly, some people try to reduce inequity feelings by getting away from the inequitable situation (called *leaving the field*). Thus, equity theory explains some instances of employee turnover and job transfer. This also explains why an under-rewarded employee might take more time off work even though he or she is not paid for this absence.

Individual differences through equity sensitivity   So far, we have described equity theory as though everyone has the same feelings of inequity in a particular situation. The reality, however, is that people vary in their **equity sensitivity**, that is, their outcome/input preferences and reaction to various outcome/input ratios.[90] At one end of the equity sensitivity continuum are the "Benevolents"—people who are tolerant of situations where they are underrewarded. They might still prefer equal outcome/input ratios, but don't mind if others receive more than they do for the same inputs. In the middle are people who fit the standard equity theory model. These "Equity Sensitives" want their outcome/input ratio to be equal to the outcome/input ratio of the comparison other. As the ratios become different, these people feel an uncomfortable tension. At the other end are the "Entitleds." These people feel more comfortable in situations where they receive proportionately more than others. They might accept having the same outcome/input ratio as others, but would prefer receiving more than others performing the same work.[91]

Why are some people Benevolents and others Entitleds? Personality is one factor. Research has found that Benevolents have more of an internal locus of control whereas Entitleds tend to have an external locus of control. Benevolents also have higher levels of conscientiousness and agreeableness.

Problems with equity theory   Equity theory is widely cited in OB literature, but it has a number of limitations.[92] One concern is that the theory isn't sufficiently specific to predict employee motivation and behaviour. It doesn't indicate which inputs or outcomes are most valuable, and doesn't identify the comparison other against which the outcome/input ratio is evaluated. These vague and highly flexible elements have led some scholars to suggest that equity theory offers little value. A second problem is that equity theory incorrectly assumes people are individualistic, rational, and selfish. In reality, people are social creatures who define themselves as members of various group memberships (see social identity theory in Chapter 3). They share goals with other members of these groups and commit themselves to the norms of their groups. A third limitation is that recent studies have found that equity theory accounts for only some of our feelings of fairness or justice in the workplace. Scholars now say that procedural justice, which we look at next, is at least as important as distributive justice.

Procedural Justice

For many years, OB scholars believed that distributive justice was more important than procedural justice in explaining employee motivation, attitudes, and behaviour. This belief was based on the assumption that people are driven mainly by self-interest, so they try to maximize their personal outcomes. Today, we know

equity sensitivity
One's outcome/input preferences and reaction to various outcome/input ratios.

that people seek justice for its own sake, not just as a means to improve their pay cheque. Thus, procedural justice seems to be as important as (some experts say more important than) distributive justice in explaining employee attitudes, motivation, and behaviour.[93]

Structural rules   Procedural justice is influenced by both structural rules and social rules (see Exhibit 5.6).[94] Structural rules represent the policies and practices that decision makers should follow. The most frequently identified structural rule in procedural justice research is that people believe they should have a "voice" in the decision process.[95] Voice allows employees to convey what they believe are relevant facts and perspectives to the decision maker, and it provides a "value expressive" function, that is, an opportunity to speak one's mind. Other structural rules are that the decision maker is unbiased, relies on complete and accurate information, applies existing policies consistently, has listened to all sides of the dispute, and allows the decision to be appealed to a higher authority.[96]

Social rules   Along with structural rules, procedural justice is influenced by social rules, that is, standards of interpersonal conduct between employees and decision makers. This set of rules is sometimes called *interactional justice* because it refers to how the decision maker treats employees during the process. Two social rules that stand out in the procedural justice literature are respect and accountability. Regarding respect, employees feel greater procedural justice when they are treated with respect. For instance, one recent Canadian study found that non-white nurses who experienced racism tended to file grievances only after

EXHIBIT 5.6   Components of organizational justice

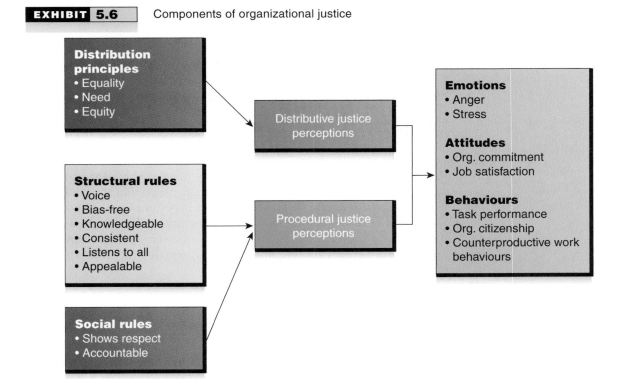

experiencing disrespectful treatment in their attempt to resolve the racist situation. Similarly, another study found that employees with repetitive strain injuries were more likely to file workers' compensation claims after experiencing disrespectful behaviour from management.[97] The other social rule is accountability. People believe that they are entitled to explanations about decisions, particularly when the results have potentially negative consequences for them.

Consequences of procedural injustice   Procedural justice has a strong influence on our emotions and attitudes, such as lower organizational commitment and trust. Employees tend to experience anger toward the source of the injustice, which makes them aware of the injustice and motivates them to act on this situation. This anger generates various response behaviours that scholars categorize as either withdrawal or aggression.[98] Notice how these response behaviours are similar to the fight or flight responses described earlier in the chapter regarding situations that activate our drive to defend.

With respect to withdrawal, those who experience procedural injustice are less willing to comply with the higher authorities who created the injustice. If employees believe their boss relies on an unfair decision process, then those employees tend to be less motivated to follow orders in the future. Withdrawal also includes lower motivation to attend work, engage in organizational citizenship (e.g., being less helpful and tolerant of others), and perform tasks at a high standard.

Aggressive responses to procedural injustice include a variety of counterproductive work behaviours, including sabotage, theft, conflict, and acts of violence.[99] However, most employees who experience injustice respond with milder forms of retaliation, such as showing indignation and denouncing the decision maker's competence. Research suggests that being treated unfairly undermines our self-esteem and social status, particularly when the injustice is known to others. Consequently, employees retaliate to restore their self-esteem and reinstate their status and power in the relationship with the perpetrator of the injustice. Employees also engage in these counterproductive behaviours to educate the decision maker, thereby minimizing the chance of future injustices.[100]

Organizational Justice in Practice

Throughout our discussion on organizational justice, it is apparent that feelings of distributive or procedural justice or injustice can have significantly positive or negative effects on employees and the organization. One of the clearest lessons from equity theory is that we need to continually treat people fairly in the distribution of organizational rewards. Unfortunately, this is perhaps one of life's greatest challenges because it seems that most of us have unique opinions about the value of inputs and outcomes. Decision makers need to carefully understand these dynamics along with the distribution rules—equity, equality, or need—that the organization wants to apply.

But corporate leaders need to consider more than fair distribution of rewards. They need to create a workplace where employees believe that the decision-making *process* is also fair. Research has shown that training programs can help people improve their procedural fairness. In one Canadian study, supervisors participated in role-play exercises to develop several procedural justice practices in the disciplinary process, such as maintaining the employee's privacy, giving employees some control over the process, avoiding arbitrariness, and exhibiting a supportive demeanour. Judges subsequently rated supervisors who received the procedural justice training as behaving more fairly than supervisors who did not receive the training. In another Canadian study, managers received procedural justice training through lectures, case studies, role playing, and discussion. Three months later, subordinates of the trained managers had significantly higher organizational citizenship behaviours than the subordinates of managers who did not receive procedural justice training.[101] Overall, it seems that justice can be improved in the workplace.

CHAPTER SUMMARY

Motivation refers to the forces within a person that affect his or her direction, intensity, and persistence of voluntary behaviour in the workplace. As a new generation of employees enters the workplace and as globalization creates a more diverse workforce, companies need to rethink their motivational practices.

Two motivation theories—Maslow's needs hierarchy and Alderfer's ERG theory—propose how employee needs change over time through a needs hierarchy. Maslow's theory groups needs into a hierarchy of five levels and states that the lowest needs are initially most important, but higher needs become more important as the lower ones are satisfied. Alderfer's ERG theory groups needs into a hierarchy of three levels: existence, relatedness, and growth. It also suggests that those who are unable to satisfy a higher need become frustrated and regress back to the next lower need level. Both Maslow's and Alderfer's theories are popular, but many scholars now doubt that people have an inherent hierarchy of needs.

Paul Lawrence and Nitkin Nohria proposed an evolutionary psychology theory involving four innate drives—the drive to acquire, bond, learn, and defend. These drives create emotional markers that indicate the relevance and strength of perceived information about our environments and thereby motivate us to act on those conditions. McClelland's learned needs theory argues that people have secondary needs or drives that are learned rather than instinctive, including the need for achievement, need for power, and need for affiliation.

The practical implications of needs-based motivation theories are that corporate leaders need to balance the demands and influences of the different innate drives. They must also recognize that different people have different needs at different times. These theories also warn us against relying too heavily on financial rewards as a source of employee motivation.

Expectancy theory states that work effort is determined by the perception that effort will result in a particular level of performance (E→P expectancy), the perception that a specific behaviour or performance level will lead to specific outcomes (P→O expectancy), and the valences that the person feels for those outcomes. The E→P expectancy increases by improving the employee's ability and confidence to perform the job. The P→O expectancy increases by measuring performance accurately, distributing higher rewards to better performers, and showing employees that rewards are performance based. Outcome valences increase by finding out what employees want and using these resources as rewards.

Goal setting is the process of motivating employees and clarifying their role perceptions by establishing performance objectives. Goals are more effective when they are specific, relevant, challenging, have employee commitment, and accompanied by meaningful feedback. Participative goal setting is important in some situations. Effective feedback is specific, relevant, timely, credible, and sufficient frequent (which depends on the employee's knowledge/experience with the task and the task cycle). Two increasingly popular forms of feedback are multisource (360-degree) assessment and executive coaching. Feedback from non-social sources is also beneficial.

Organizational justice consists of distributive justice (perceived fairness in the outcomes we receive relative to our contributions and the outcomes and contributions of others) and procedural justice (fairness of the procedures used to decide the distribution of resources). Equity theory, which considers the most common principle applied in distributive justice, has four elements: outcome/input ratio, comparison other, equity evaluation, and consequences of inequity. The theory also explains what people are motivated to do when they feel inequitably treated. Equity sensitivity is a personal characteristic that explains why people react differently to varying degrees of inequity.

Procedural justice is influenced by both structural rules and social rules. Structural rules represent the policies and practices that decision makers should follow. Giving employees "voice" in the decision process is the most commonly identified. Social rules refer to standards of interpersonal conduct between employees and decision makers and are exempli-fied by showing respect and providing accountability for decisions. Procedural justice is as important as distributive justice, and influences organizational commitment, trust, and various withdrawal and aggression behaviours.

KEY TERMS

Distributive justice, p. 151

Effort-to-performance (E→P) expectancy, p. 142

Equity sensitivity, p. 154

Equity theory, p. 152

ERG theory, p. 135

Executive coaching, p. 149

Existence needs, p. 135

Expectancy theory, p. 142

Feedback, p. 147

Frustration-regression process, p. 136

Goal setting, p. 146

Goals, p. 146

Growth needs, p. 135

Management-by-objectives (MBO), p. 147

Motivation, p. 134

Need for achievement (nAch), p. 139

Need for affiliation (nAff), p. 139

Need for power (nPow), p. 140

Needs, p. 134

Needs hierarchy theory, p. 134

Performance-to-outcome (P→O) expectancy, p. 143

Procedural justice, p. 151

Relatedness needs, p. 135

Satisfaction-progression process, p. 135

360-degree feedback, p. 148

Valence, p. 143

DISCUSSION QUESTIONS

1. Identify three reasons why motivating employees is become increasingly challenging.

2. Harvard Business School professors have recently proposed four fundamental human drives. Relate these innate drives to Maslow's needs hierarchy theory and Alderfer's ERG theory. How are they similar? How do they differ?

3. Use all three components of expectancy theory to explain why some employees are motivated to show up for work during a snowstorm whereas others don't make any effort to leave their homes.

4. What are the limitations of expectancy theory in predicting an individual's work effort and behaviour?

5. Several service representatives are upset that the newly hired representative with no previous experience will be paid $1,000 a year above the usual starting salary in the pay range. The department manager explained that the new hire would not accept the entry-level rate, so the company raised the offer by $1,000. All five reps currently earn salaries near the top of the scale ($10,000 higher), although they all started at the minimum starting salary a few years earlier. Use equity theory to explain why the five service representatives feel inequity in this situation.

6. Using your knowledge of the characteristics of effective goals, establish two meaningful goals related to your performance in this class.

7. When do employees prefer feedback from non-social rather than social sources? Explain why non-social sources are preferred under these conditions.

8. Inequity can occur in the classroom as well as in the workplace. Identify classroom situations in which you experienced feelings of inequity. What can instructors do to maintain an environment that fosters both distributive and procedural justice?

NO FAIR PAY IN *THIS* PLACE

By Susan Meredith, Selkirk College.

It was my degree in business administration that Mr. James admired when he hired me to manage his western satellite office in B.C. The focus of my work was planning and problem solving with occasional crisis intervention. I was also responsible for supervising several employees, including our public relations rep, Dan Donaldson. Dan's job was to write the press releases and schedule all the public appointments and appearances for Mr. James while he was in town. Dan had a double degree in journalism and political science. I often wondered if his education had prepared him for the office politics that would become so much a part of our lives while working for Mr. James at the other end of the country from Toronto where our head office was located.

I was never really sure why the head office was in Toronto as no product was produced and virtually no service rendered from Toronto. Yet it was the heart of the organization. On the other hand, the front lines of the job were here in B.C. where the client base was centred, yet our work was treated as insignificant. Was it because we didn't generate any revenue? We certainly felt that our customer base was obvious proof that our work was critical to the organization. So important in fact that without us to represent the firm regionally, there would be no customer contact at all, therefore no business—period.

One day during an unusual but welcome pause from the incessant demands of the telephone, fax, and walk-in traffic, Dan and I were complaining about our jobs. We started comparing them with Helen's, our one colleague at head office. What was it she did, anyway? We wondered what our days would be like without the heavy load of unhappy clients and their urgent demands and especially without the stress. While we both knew that without these complaining customers neither of us would have a job, there were some days when that really didn't seem like a bad thing.

It was just prior to one of Mr. James' hectic but brief cross-country check-ups that this unexpected lull happened. In the process of confirming the schedule with Dan we began to discuss our "comparison other"—the horrible head office honcho, Helen. Inevitably we found ourselves speculating in a not very complimentary way, about Helen's interpersonal skills, or rather, lack of them. Dan wanted to know if I knew how much Helen was making.

No, how could I? This had always been a forbidden topic of discussion. At the time of hiring Mr. James made a point of emphatically instructing each new person not to discuss their salary with any other employees. The justification had always been that we wouldn't want to upset them, would we?

While I was responsible for submitting everyone's time sheets, in the eight months I'd been with Mr. James I had never dared ask anyone anything about their salaries. Yet, to my surprise I didn't hesitate telling Dan that I was earning $30,000 a year, which was pretty disappointing since I had 20 years of customer relations and supervisory experience. Plus with my recent honours degree in business I had been hoping to make more than before I spent four hard years in university.

Dan couldn't believe I was only making $30,000. He had just assumed I was making the same as Horrible Helen who had virtually no customer contact, no one to supervise, no university education and no seniority. Dan swore he knew for certain Helen was making $40,000 in only ten months instead of my twelve. That worked out to an annual salary of $48,000. I was getting really upset—really fast!

Dan and I hashed this about until the boss came in. I had to decide if I believed Dan and if so what was I going to do. I chose to wait and seek proof one way or the other. Not an easy task in this secrecy shrouded environment. As it turned out Dan would be going to Toronto when the boss was returning next week. Feeling responsible for bringing up the whole upsetting subject, Dan promised to find and send me a copy of Helen's contract.

By the time I saw the contract for myself I had worked myself into quite a dither. I stewed and fretted and when I couldn't stand it anymore I scheduled a meeting with the boss during his next monthly check-up session. I was determined that I would convince him of my superior performance, academic achievements, work experience, and interpersonal skills.

When the day came, I was ready. I was so ready that I barely waited for Mr. James to get seated before I began. However, I'd barely gotten started when Mr. James quietly agreed. He agreed so readily that I didn't have to finish my arguments. I didn't have to persuade him of anything. Stunned, I stopped, searching for something nice to say, and that's when he said in his quiet air of dismissal – "Nobody said it was fair, but that's what staff earn in Toronto and that's what you are worth out here." All he was interested in was how I had found out about Helen's salary.

That was the end of the discussion. There was no validation. No explanation and no satisfaction. Mr. James apparently couldn't care less how I felt. He certainly ignored me and as far as I was concerned that meant he ignored his investment in me. I knew I'd never work as hard for him as I had in the past. For that matter I didn't want to work for him at all.

I'm embarrassed to say my attitude took a serious nosedive and my work habits did too. Within weeks my output matched my salary—about $18,000 a year less than what I had been doing

previously. I had a really hard time taking any calls from Helen. I wanted to scream at her and she didn't even know. It wasn't just the money, either. If Mr. James had said anything about my dedication, my hard work, the reputation building I had accomplished—anything at all, I might have been able to get over the injustice. Since none of that happened, I left before my next evaluation. Still he said nothing.

Discussion Questions

Author's note: This case is primarily intended to illustrate equity theory and job dissatisfaction as well as perceptions, stress, and cognitive dissonance.

1. What are some of the elements that contributed to this employee's feelings of inequality?

2. Why was the Toronto worker considered a "comparison other" but not the co-worker in B.C?

3. How was the inequity solved?

4. What other factors may have contributed to the job dissatisfaction experienced by these two employees?

CASE STUDY 5.2

KEEPING SUZANNE CHALMERS

Thomas Chan hung up the telephone and sighed. The vice-president of software engineering at Advanced Photonics Ltd. (APL) had just spoken to Suzanne Chalmers, who had called to arrange a meeting with Chan later that day. She didn't say what the meeting was about, but Chan almost instinctively knew that Suzanne was going to quit after working at APL for the past four years. Chalmers is a software engineer in Internet Protocol (IP), the software that directs fibre-optic light through APL's routers. It was very specialized work, and Suzanne was one of APL's top talents in that area.

Thomas Chan had been through this before. A valued employee would arrange a private meeting. The meeting would begin with a few pleasantries, then the employee would announce that he or she wanted to quit. Some employees would say they

were leaving because of the long hours and stressful deadlines. They would say they needed to decompress, get to know the kids again, or whatever. But that's not usually the real reason. Almost every organization in this industry is scrambling to keep up with technological advances and the competition. They would just be leaving one stressful job for another one.

Also, many of the people who leave APL join a start-up company a few months later. These start-up firms can be pressure cookers where everyone works 16 hours each day and has to perform a variety of tasks. For example, engineers in these small firms might have to meet customers or work on venture capital proposals rather than focus on specialized tasks related to their knowledge. APL has over 1,000 employees, so it is easier to assign people to work that matches their technical competencies.

No, the problem isn't the stress or long hours, Chan thought. The problem is money—too much money. Most of the people who leave are millionaires. Suzanne Chalmers is one of them. Thanks to generous share options that have skyrocketed on the Toronto and NASDAQ stock markets, many employees at APL have more money than they can use. Most are under 40 years old, so are too young to retire. But their financial independence gives them less reason to remain with APL.

The Meeting

The meeting with Suzanne Chalmers took place a few hours after the telephone call. It began like the others, with the initial pleasantries and brief discussion about progress on the latest fibre-optic router project. Then Suzanne made her well-rehearsed statement: "Thomas, I've really enjoyed working here, but I'm going to leave Advanced Photonics." Suzanne took a breath, then looked at Chan. When he didn't reply after a few seconds, she continued: "I need to take time off. You know, get away to recharge my batteries. The project's nearly done and the team can complete it without me. Well, anyway, I'm thinking of leaving."

Chan spoke in a calm voice. He suggested that Suzanne should take an unpaid leave for two or maybe three months, complete with paid benefits, then return refreshed. Suzanne politely rejected that offer, saying that she needed to get away from work for a while. Thomas then asked Suzanne whether she was unhappy with her work environment—whether she was getting the latest computer technology to do her work and whether there were problems with co-workers. The workplace was fine, Susanne replied. The job was getting a bit routine at times, but she had a comfortable workplace with excellent co-workers.

Chan then apologized for the cramped work space, due mainly to the rapid increase in the number of people hired over the past year. He suggested that if Suzanne took a couple of months off, APL would have a larger work space with a better view of the park behind the campus-like building when she returned. She politely thanked Chan for that offer, but it wasn't what she needed. Besides, it wouldn't be fair to have a large workspace when other team members worked in smaller quarters.

Chan was running out of tactics, so he tried his last hope: money. He asked whether Suzanne had had higher offers. Suzanne replied that she regularly received calls from other companies, and some of them offered more money. Most were start-up firms that offered a lower salary but higher potential gains in share options. Chan knew from market surveys that Suzanne was already paid well in the industry. He also knew that APL couldn't compete on share option potential. Employees working in start-up firms sometimes saw their shares increase by five or ten times their initial value, whereas shares at APL and other large firms increased more slowly. However, Chan promised Suzanne that he would recommend that she receive a significant raise—maybe 25 percent more—and more share options. Chan added that Chalmers was one of APL's most valuable employees and that the company would suffer if she left the firm.

The meeting ended with Chalmers promising to consider Chan's offer of higher pay and share options. Two days later, Chan received her resignation in writing. Five months later, Chan learned that after a few months travelling with her husband, Chalmers had joined a start-up software firm in the area.

Discussion Questions

1. Why didn't money motivate Suzanne Chalmers to stay with APL?

2. If you were Thomas Chan, what strategy, if any, would you use to motivate Suzanne Chalmers to stay at Advanced Photonics Ltd.?

3. What innate drives seem to be motivating Suzanne Chalmers?

Copyright © 2001 Steven L. McShane.

A QUESTION OF FEEDBACK

Purpose   This exercise is designed to help you understand the importance of feedback, including problems that occur with imperfect communication in the feedback process.

Materials   The instructor will distribute a few pages of exhibits to one person on each team. The other students will require a pencil with eraser and blank paper. Movable chairs and tables in a large area are helpful.

Instructions

- *Step 1:* The class is divided into pairs of students. Each pair is ideally located in a private area, away from other students and where one person can write. One student is given the pages of exhibits from the instructor. The other student in each pair is not allowed to see these exhibits.
- *Step 2:* The student holding the materials will describe each of the exhibits and the other student's task is to accurately replicate each exhibit. The pair of students can compare the replication with the original at the end of each drawing. They may also switch roles for each exhibit, if they wish. If roles are switched, the instructor must distribute exhibits separately to each student so that they are not seen by the other person. Each exhibit has a different set of limitations, as described below:

  Exhibit 1: The student describing the exhibit cannot look at the other student or his/her diagram. The student drawing the exhibit cannot speak or otherwise communicate with the person describing the exhibit.

  Exhibit 2: The student describing the exhibit may look at the other student's diagram. However, he/she may only say "Yes" or "No" when the student drawing the diagram asks a specific question. In other words, the person presenting the information can only use these words for feedback and only when asked a question by the writer.

  Exhibit 3: (optional—if time permits) The student describing the exhibit may look at the other student's diagram and may provide any feedback at any time to the person replicating the exhibit.
- *Step 3:* The class will gather to debrief this exercise. This may include discussion on the importance of feedback, and the characteristics of effective feedback for individual motivation and learning.

MEASURING YOUR EQUITY SENSITIVITY

Purpose   This self-assessment is designed to help you to estimate your level of equity sensitivity.

Instructions   Read each of the statements below and circle the response that you believe best reflects your position regarding each statement. Then use the scoring key in Appendix B to calculate your results. This exercise is completed alone so students assess themselves honestly without concerns of social comparison. However, class discussion will focus on equity theory and the effect of equity sensitivity on perceptions of fairness in the workplace.

Equity Preference Questionnaire

To what extent do you agree or disagree that...	Strongly Agree ▼	Agree ▼	Neutral ▼	Disagree ▼	Strongly Disagree ▼
1. I prefer to do as little as possible at work while getting as much as I can from my employer.	1	2	3	4	5
2. I am most satisfied at work when I have to do as little as possible.	1	2	3	4	5
3. When I am at my job, I think of ways to get out of work.	1	2	3	4	5
4. If I could get away with it, I would try to work just a little bit slower than the boss expects.	1	2	3	4	5
5. It is really satisfying to me when I can get something for nothing at work.	1	2	3	4	5
6. It is the smart employee who gets as much as he/she can while giving as little as possible in return.	1	2	3	4	5
7. Employees who are more concerned about what they can get from their employer rather than what they can give to their employer are the wisest.	1	2	3	4	5
8. When I have completed my task for the day, I help out other employees who have yet to complete their tasks.	1	2	3	4	5
9. Even if I receive low wages and poor benefits from my employer, I would still try to do my best at my job.	1	2	3	4	5
10. If I had to work hard all day at my job, I would probably quit.	1	2	3	4	5
11. I feel obligated to do more than I am paid to do at work.	1	2	3	4	5
12. At work, my greatest concern is whether or not I am doing the best job I can.	1	2	3	4	5
13. A job which requires me to be busy during the day is better than a job which allows me a lot of loafing.	1	2	3	4	5
14. At work, I feel uneasy when there is little work for me to do.	1	2	3	4	5
15. I would become very dissatisfied with my job if I had little or no work to do.	1	2	3	4	5
16. All other things being equal, it is better to have a job with a lot of duties and responsibilities than one with few duties and responsibilities.	1	2	3	4	5

Source: K.S. Sauleya and A.G. Bedeian "Equity Sensitivity: Construction of a Measure and Examination of its Psychometric Properties," *Journal of Management,* 26 (September 2000), pp. 885–910. With permission of Elsevier Science.

MEASURING YOUR GROWTH NEED STRENGTH

Go to the Student CD for the interactive version of this exercise.

Purpose This self-assessment is designed to help you to estimate your level of growth need strength.

Instructions People differ in the kinds of jobs they would most like to hold. This self-assessment gives you a chance to say just what it is about a job that is most important to you. Please indicate which of the two jobs you would prefer if you had to make a choice between them. In answering each question, assume that everything else about the jobs is the same. Pay attention only to the characteristics actually listed.

Source: Adapted from the Job Diagnostic Survey, developed by J. R. Hackman and G. R. Oldham. The authors have released any copyright ownership of this scale (see J. R. Hackman and G. Oldham, *Work Redesign* (Reading, MA: Addison-Wesley, 1980), p. 275).

Applied Performance Practices

Learning Objectives

AFTER READING THIS CHAPTER, YOU SHOULD BE ABLE TO:

■ Explain how money and other financial rewards affect our needs, attitudes, and social identity.

■ Discuss the advantages and disadvantages of the four reward objectives.

■ Identify two team and four organizational level performance-based rewards.

■ Describe five ways to improve reward effectiveness.

■ Discuss the advantages and disadvantages of job specialization.

■ Diagram the job characteristics model of job design.

■ Identify three strategies to improve employee motivation through job design.

■ Define empowerment and identify strategies to support empowerment.

■ Describe the five elements of self-leadership.

■ Explain how mental imagery improves employee motivation.

Not long ago, a WestJet maintenance employee stormed into the offices of CEO and co-founder Clive Beddoe. The employee demanded to know why the boss was squandering money on a hamburgers and beer party for a select few at head office. Beddoe quickly explained the situation: "I pointed out that I paid for the party out of my own pocket," says Beddoe, grinning. "He was a little humbled, but I congratulated him on his attitude. He's like a watchdog, and he hates inequities. That's the spirit of WestJet."

WestJet's employees (called WestJetters) are a highly motivated bunch, partly because they are rewarded for the company's success through profit sharing and stock options. The average employee recently took home $9,000 based on six months of profits. Most WestJetters are also shareholders, thanks to a generous share ownership plan. "We've got employees who own the company, whose interests are directly aligned with the interests of the company," says WestJet chief financial officer Sandy Campbell.

Unlike most airlines, WestJet actually has profits to distribute, partly because employees perform a variety of tasks. It's not unusual, for example, to see pilots go into the cabin and tidy up between flights, or for flight attendants to double as reservation agents. As a result, Westjet operates with about 59 people per aircraft, compared with more than 140 at a typical full-service airline such as Air Canada.

WestJet's success is partly due to a motivated workforce that is empowered to serve customers and receives stock options. *CP/Calgary Sun/ Stuart Dryden*

Another ingredient in WestJet's success is empowering WestJetters to do what is right for customers. The company avoided an entire layer of supervisors, giving staff more freedom to make decisions. "We empower our people to do whatever it takes to satisfy a customer in their best judgment," explains WestJet sales manager Judy Goodman. "Whatever they think is appropriate, they are free to do." The result is that even though WestJet is Canada's second largest airline, it accounts for only 0.3% of all complaints submitted by passengers to the Canadian government's Air Travel Complaints Commissioner.[1] ■

www.westjet.com

WestJet was founded less than a decade ago, yet it has already become one of North America's most successful airlines. While many factors have contributed to this success, the opening story points out that rewards, job design, empowerment, and self-leadership play a large role. This chapter looks at each of these applied performance practices. The chapter begins with an overview of the meaning of money, the different types of rewards and their objectives, and the characteristics of effective reward implementation. Next, we look at the dynamics of job design, specific job design strategies to motivate employees, and the effectiveness of recent job design interventions. We then consider the elements of empowerment as well as conditions that support empowerment. The final part of this chapter explains how employees manage their own performance through the five elements of self-leadership: personal goal setting, constructive thought patterns, designing natural rewards, self-monitoring, and self-reinforcement.

THE MEANING OF MONEY IN THE WORKPLACE

Money and other financial rewards are a fundamental part of the employment relationship. Organizations distribute money and other benefits in exchange for an employee's availability, competencies, and behaviours. Rewards try to align individual goals with corporate objectives and to provide a return for the individual's contribution. This concept of economic exchange can be found across cultures. The word for "pay" in Malay and Slovak means to replace a loss; in Hebrew and Swedish it means making equal.[2]

But money is not just an economic medium of exchange in the employment relationship. It is a symbol with much deeper and more complex meaning.[3] It affects our needs, our emotions, and our self-perception. As one scholar wrote: "Money is probably the most emotionally meaningful object in contemporary life: only food and sex are its close competitors as common carriers of such strong and diverse feelings, significance, and strivings."[4]

Money and Employee Needs

Money is an important factor in satisfying individual needs. It is strongly linked to the fulfillment of existence needs because it allows us to buy food and shelter. It is also a symbol of status, which relates to the innate drive to acquire (see Chapter 5).[5] Financial gain also symbolizes personal accomplishments and, consequently, relates to growth needs. People with a high need for achievement are not motivated primarily by money, but they do value money as a source of feedback and a representation of goal achievement. Money is a way of "keeping score" of their success. Money seems to have gained importance in people's lives. One major survey reported that compensation is one of the top three factors that attract individuals to work for an organization. Another survey reported that 35.8 percent of people working in southern Saskatchewan identified pay as the single most important influence on their overall job satisfaction.[6]

Money Attitudes and Values

Money tends to create strong emotions and attitudes. Some people are preoccupied with money. Others are nervous with money and its responsibilities. One

Anyone who doubts the motivating effect of money should see the enthusiasm of IKEA employees in Seattle on Excellence Day. Each year, the retailer shares the day's revenue with employees, so employees are particularly eager to help customers with their purchases. IKEA recently offered a similar bonus for employees around the globe, resulting in a $2,500 bonus for each full-time employee (prorated for part-time staff) in Canada. "IKEA employees worked tirelessly throughout the day and well into the night, showing the same enthusiasm that has helped make the company so successful," says IKEA Canada's president of "Big Thank You Bonus" day. Stephen Benson (shown in photo) certainly appreciated the money because it reduced the amount owing on his Yamaha Virago motorcycle. "It's the bike that IKEA bought," says Benson.[7] Under what conditions would money *not* motivate employees? *S. Oatway, Calgary Herald. Used with permission.*
www.ikea.com

large-scale study revealed that money generates a variety of emotions, most of which are negative, such as anxiety, depression, anger, and helplessness.[8] Money is associated with greed, avarice and, occasionally, generosity. Some OB scholars have identified several underlying attitudes towards money, collectively known as the "money ethic."[9] People with a strong money ethic believe that money is not evil, that it is a symbol of achievement, respect, and power, and that it should be budgeted carefully.

Cultural values seem to influence attitudes toward money. One recent study reported that "belief in the wonders of money" was higher among Canadian university students than among students in Singapore, Hong Kong, or Hawaii. Another study found that Canadians with more money reported higher levels of happiness than those with less money, mainly because money affords more freedom.[10] Other research indicates that people in countries with a long-term orientation (such as China, Hong Kong, Japan) give money a high priority in their lives.[11] In contrast, Scandinavians, Australians, and New Zealanders have strong egalitarian values that discourage people from openly talking about money or displaying their personal wealth.

Money and Social Identity

People tend to identify themselves in terms of their ownership and management of money. Some individuals see themselves as hoarders or worriers of money, whereas others will tell you they are shopaholics and spendthrifts. A recent study of Canadian managers concluded that pay influences the person's "self" (such as gauging performance, reducing anxiety) as well as social self (such as symbolizing status). Research on marital relationships shows that couples tend to adopt polarized roles (and, consequently, self-identities) regarding their management and expenditure of money.[12] The same polar relationships might exist in the workplace.

Men are more likely than women to emphasize money in their self-concept. One large-scale survey of people in 43 countries revealed that men attach more importance or value to money than women in every country except India, Norway, and Transkei. Two recent public opinion polls found that money was a much higher priority for men than for women.[13] Why do men identify more with money? Some writers suggest that men are more likely to believe that money equals power and that power is the path to respect. Other research has found that, compared with women, men are more confident managing their money and are more likely to use money as a tool to influence and impress others.[14]

The bottom line is that money and other financial rewards do much more than pay employees back for their contributions. They fulfill a variety of needs, influence emotions, and shape or represent a person's self-identity. This knowledge is important to remember when distributing rewards in the workplace. Over the next few pages, we look at various reward objectives and how to improve the implementation of performance-based rewards.

REWARD PRACTICES

Organizations apply a variety of rewards to attract, motivate, and retain employees. Each reward relates to specific objectives, namely membership and seniority, job status, competencies, and performance. Each reward objective has both advantages and disadvantages, as Exhibit 6.1 illustrates.

Membership and Seniority-based Rewards

Membership and seniority represent the largest part of most paycheques. Employees receive fixed hourly wages or salaries, and many benefits are the same for everyone or increase with seniority. Large Japanese firms typically increase every employee's pay rate for each year on the job or age. Membership and seniority-based rewards tend to attract job applicants with security needs, reduce stress, and

EXHIBIT 6.1   Reward objectives, advantages, and disadvantages

Reward objective	Sample rewards	Advantages	Disadvantages
Membership/seniority	• Fixed pay • Most employee benefits • Paid-time off	• May attract applicants • Minimizes stress of insecurity • Reduces turnover	• Doesn't directly motivate performance • May discourage poor performers from leaving • Golden handcuffs may undermine performance
Job status	• Promotion-based pay increase • Status-based benefits	• Tries to maintain internal equity • Minimizes pay discrimination • Motivates employees to compete for promotions	• Encourages political tactics to increase job worth • Creates psychological distance between employees and executives
Competencies	• Pay increase based on competency • Skill-based pay	• Improves workforce flexibility • Tends to improve quality • Consistent with employability	• Subjective measurement of competencies • Skill-based pay plans are expensive
Task performance	• Commissions • Merit pay • Gainsharing • Profit sharing • Stock options	• Motivate task performance • Attract performance-oriented applicants • Organizaational rewards create an ownership culture • Pay variability may avoid layoffs during downturns	• May weaken motivation of job itself • May distance reward giver from receiver • May discourage creativity • Viewed as quick fixes, but don't solve real causes

sometimes improve loyalty.[15] However, they do not directly motivate job performance; on the contrary, they discourage poor performers from seeking out work better suited to their abilities. Instead, the good performers are lured to better-paying jobs. Last, as we learned in Chapter 4, some of these rewards are golden handcuffs that undermine job performance by creating continuance commitment.

Job Status-based Rewards

Almost every organization rewards employees to some extent based on the status of the jobs they occupy. According to one estimate, 73 percent of Canadian firms rely on **job evaluation** to evaluate (or justify) the worth of each job within the organization.[16] Jobs have more value and are placed in higher pay grades if they require more skill and effort, have more responsibility, and have difficult working conditions. Organizations that don't rely on job evaluation still tend to reward job status based on pay survey information about the external labour market. People in some higher status jobs are also rewarded with larger offices, company-paid vehicles, and exclusive dining rooms.

> **job evaluation**
> Systematically evaluating the worth of jobs within an organization by measuring their required skill, effort, responsibility, and working conditions. Job evaluation results create a hierarchy of job worth.

Job status-based pay motivates employees to compete for promotions, and tries to make pay levels fair across different jobs (called *internal equity*). For example, the Hong Kong government recently brought in job evaluation experts from Canada to determine whether people in female-dominated civil service jobs are paid the same as people in male-dominated jobs with similar value (as measured by job evaluation ratings). However, job status-based rewards have also received heavy criticism.[17] One concern is that rewarding people for the worth of their jobs is inconsistent with the model of market-responsive organizations which have few layers of hierarchy and encourage initiative in everyone. Status-based rewards motivate employees to compete with each other, rather than focus their energy on customer service and other market needs. They also tend to reward functional specialization (e.g., marketing, finance) rather than the organization's central goals of anticipating and responding to market needs. Last, job evaluation systems motivate employees to increase their pay rate by exaggerating job duties and hoarding resources.

Competency-based Rewards

Organizations are shifting from rewarding job status to rewarding employees for their skills, knowledge, and other competencies that lead to superior performance.[18] National Bank of Canada made this transition by reducing the number of pay grades and rewarding employees more for their competency development within those wider pay bands. Each salary band has segments ranging from learning phase to excellence. While job status is still a large part of compensation, employees at the Montreal-based financial institution are now motivated more to improve their skills within each band instead of waiting for promotion within a tall career ladder.[19] *Skill-based pay* is a variation of competency-based rewards.[20] The employee's pay rate depends on the number of skill modules that he or she has mastered, not on the specific job performed on a particular day.

Competency-based rewards improve workforce flexibility because they motivate employees to acquire a variety of skills that they can apply to different jobs as demand requires. Product or service quality tends to improve because employees with multiple skills are more likely to understand the work process and know how to improve it.[21] Competency-based rewards are also consistent with employability because they reward employees who continuously learn skills that will keep them employed (see Chapter 1). One potential problem with competency-based pay is that measuring competencies can be subjective, particularly when they are personality traits or values.[22] Skill-based pay systems measure specific skills, so they are usually more objective and accurate. However, they are expensive because employees spend more time learning new tasks.

Performance-based Rewards

Performance-based rewards have existed since Babylonian days in the 20th century BC, but their popularity has increased dramatically in Canada and other countries over the past decade.[23] Some of the most popular individual, team, and organizational performance-based rewards are summarized in Exhibit 6.2 and described over the next page or two.

Individual rewards Individual incentives come in many forms, but Statistics Canada estimates that the most common incentives in Canada are bonuses/awards and commissions.[24] Awards and bonuses provide a reward for accomplishing a specific task or performance goal. For instance, employees at A. L. I. Technologies in Richmond, B.C., received free Whistler ski weekends for completing important projects. *Commissions* pay people based on sales volume rather than units produced. The income of real estate agents is partly or completely from commissions. Although less common in Canada, a third individual incentive is *piece rate* pay, which rewards people for the number of units produced.

gainsharing plan
A reward system that rewards team members for reducing costs and increasing labour efficiency in their work process.

Team rewards A decade ago, most institutional brokers on Wall Street were paid individual commissions. Today, the top dozen firms have shifted to salary and bonuses determined by team and organizational performance. Similar changes are happening in retail brokerages as Merrill Lynch and other firms on Wall Street and elsewhere shift from individual to more team-based reward systems.[25]

One of the most popular team-based rewards is the **gainsharing plan**. Gainsharing plans tend to improve team dynamics and pay satisfaction. They also create a reasonably strong E-to-P expectancy (see Chapter 5) because much of the

EXHIBIT 6.2

Types of performance-based rewards

- Organizational rewards
  - Stock ownership
  - Stock options
  - Profit sharing
  - Scorecard
- Team rewards
  - Bonus
  - Gainsharing
  - Open book
- Individual rewards
  - Award/bonus
  - Commissions
  - Piece rate

Opening the Books at Tien Wah Press

Tien Wah Press (TWP) is in a competitive business that needs to continuously improve productivity. That's why the printing company keeps its 3,000 employees in Malaysia, Singapore, and Indonesia informed about production costs, and rewards them for productivity improvements.

Every three months, TWP opens its books to employees. The operations manager at each plant describes the company's performance over the previous quarter. The briefing provides details about labour costs, wages, overtime, transportation, factory overheads, building maintenance, repair and replacement consumable, paper stock balance, printing materials, and sales as well as profit and loss.

"This briefing serves to explain to the employees how well or badly we are doing and it gives areas where the company has weaknesses that can be rectified and where its strengths are," says TWP human resource manager Datuk Kalam Azad Mohd Taib.

With this financial information, employees can see how their costs affect the company's performance. This, in turn, affects their pay cheque through TWP's flexible wage system (FWS). This reward system consists of a base salary plus merit and profit sharing scheme (MPS). The more ideas employees come up with to discover ways to reduce costs, the higher their future pay cheque.

Tien Wah Press practises open book management by showing its financial performance every three months to employees in Malaysia, Singapore, and Indonesia.
Courtesy of Tien Wah Press

"The union committee is free to make a calculation on what probable amount of MPS the employees are likely to get based on the formula given in the collective agreement," explains Kalam Azad.

Source: Based on H. Hamid, "Tien Wah's Flexi-Wage a Success," *Business Times (Malaysia),* December 7, 2000.
www.tienwah.com

---

cost reduction and labour efficiency is within the team's control. In other words, team members quickly learn that their work efficiencies increase the size of the gainsharing bonus.[26] Inland Group of Companies recently experienced the benefits of gainsharing when employees reduced costs by $9 million within the plan's first two years. The Edmonton, Alberta concrete and aggregates business distributed $2.5 million of those gains to employees. Employees at Hibernia Management and Development Co., Ltd. in Newfoundland and at many of Canada's mining companies also participate in gainsharing plans.[27]

open-book management

Involves sharing financial information with employees and encouraging them to recommend ideas that improve those financial results.

A variation of gainsharing is **open-book management**, which encourages employees to think of financial performance as a game they can play and win. Employees learn the rules of the game through training to improve their financial literacy. They also receive monthly or quarterly financial data and operating results so they can keep track of the organization's performance. Employees contribute to the "game" by recommending ways to reduce costs and improve the work unit's (or organization's) financial results.[28] GLOBAL Connections 6.1 describes how open book practices seem to work well at Tien Wah Press's printing plants in Malaysia, Singapore, and Indonesia. Supervisors provide financial information to employees every three months, and the reward system motivates employees to suggest ideas for productivity improvement.[29]

profit sharing
A reward system that pays bonuses to employees based on the previous year's level of corporate profits.

employee stock ownership plans (ESOPs)
A reward system that encourages employees to buy shares of the company.

stock options
A reward system that gives employees the right to purchase company shares at a future date at a predetermined price.

balanced scorecard
A reward system that pays bonuses to executives for improved measurements on a composite of financial, customer, internal processes, and employee factors.

Organizational rewards   WestJet, described in the opening story to this chapter, relies on two organizational level rewards to motivate employees: profit sharing and employee stock ownership. **Profit sharing plans** pay bonuses to employees based on the previous year's level of corporate profits. These plans are most often found in firms that use teams and face plenty of competition.[30] **Employee stock ownership plans (ESOPs)** encourage employees to buy shares in the company, usually at a discounted price. Employees are subsequently rewarded through dividends and market appreciation of those shares.

A third organizational level reward that has received plenty of media attention is stock options. **Stock options** give employees the right to purchase company stock at a future date at a predetermined price.[31] For example, Telus Corporation in Burnaby, B. C. recently granted 100 stock options to each of its employees at a purchase price of $34.88 with vesting in two years. Telus employees can purchase the shares two years later from the company at $34.88 and sell them at a profit if the stock exchange price is above that amount. If the market price is below $34.88, employees have eight years to purchase the stock at the predetermined price. The Conference Board of Canada estimates that less than 10 percent of mid- to large-sized businesses in Canada currently provide stock options to nonmanagement employees.[32]

Another organizational level reward strategy is the **balanced scorecard**.[33] This performance measurement system rewards people (typically executives) for improving performance on a composite of financial, customer, internal processes, and employee factors. The better the measurement improvements, the larger the bonus awarded. For instance, Nova Scotia Power developed an executive-level scorecard that calculates improvements in internal costs, customer loyalty, earnings, and employee commitment. Most categories have multiple indicators of performance. Nova Scotia Power's corporate scorecard was later cascaded down to subunits. In other words, the company's division managers now have scorecards that identify critical work processes in those subunits, but are strategically linked to factors on the corporate scorecard.[34]

How effective are organizational level rewards? ESOPs, stock options, and balanced scorecards tend to create an "ownership culture" in which employees feel aligned with the organization's success. According to one study, productivity rises by 4 percent annually at ESOP firms, compared to only 1.5 percent at non-ESOP firms. Balanced scorecards have the added benefit of aligning rewards to several specific measures of organizational performance. Profit sharing tends to create less ownership culture, but it has the advantage of automatically adjusting employee compensation with the firm's prosperity, thereby reducing the need for layoffs or negotiated pay reductions during recessions.[35]

The main problem with ESOPs, stock options, and profit sharing (less so with balanced scorecards) is that employees often perceive a weak connection between individual effort and corporate profits or the value of company shares. Even in small firms, the company's stock price or profitability is influenced by economic conditions, competition, and other factors beyond the employee's immediate control. This results in a low E-to-P expectancy (see Chapter 5), which weakens employee motivation. These organizational level rewards also fail to motivate employees when profits are negligible or in "bear" markets, when stock prices decline.

Improving Reward Effectiveness

Performance-based rewards have been criticized on the grounds that they undermine the intrinsic motivation of performing the job, discourage creativity, and create relationship problems. Many corporate leaders also use rewards as quick fixes, rather than carefully diagnosing the real causes of the undesirable behaviour. For example, one company hands out cash to employees who arrive early at company meetings and fines those who arrive late. The company would be better off identifying the causes of lateness and changing the conditions, rather than using money to force a solution to the problem.[36]

These concerns do not necessarily mean that we should abandon performance-based pay. On the contrary, the top performing companies around the world are more likely to have performance-based rewards.[37] Reward systems do motivate most employees, but only under the right conditions. Here are some of the more important strategies to improve reward effectiveness.

Link rewards to performance Employees with better performance should be rewarded more than those with poorer performance.[38] This simple principle is a logical conclusion of both behaviour modification (Chapter 2) and expectancy theory (Chapter 5), yet it seems to be unusually difficult to apply. A large survey of U.S. and Canadian firms reported that one-third paid rewards to people who didn't meet minimum performance standards. This occurs partly because job performance is difficult to measure and organizational politics biases the evaluation process. A Canadian study also recently found that managers rely on different criteria when estimating the performance levels of employees. Some emphasize task performance, others focus on organizational citizenship, and still others place most of the weight on counterproductive behaviours. The result is inconsistent performance evaluation.[39]

How can we improve the pay-for-performance linkage? First, inconsistencies and bias can be minimized by introducing gainsharing, ESOPs, and other plans that rely on objective performance measures. Second, when subjective measures of performance are necessary, companies should rely on multiple sources of information. In other words, use 360-degree feedback to minimize biases from any single source (see Chapter 3). Third, companies need to apply rewards soon after the performance occurs, and in a large enough dose (such as a bonus rather than pay increase) that employees experience positive emotion when they receive the reward.[40]

Ensure that rewards are relevant Companies need to align rewards with performance within the employee's control. The more employees see a "line of sight" between their daily actions and the reward, the more they are motivated to improve performance.[41] The balanced scorecard at Nova Scotia Power does this. The corporate scorecard for Nova Scotia Power executives includes measures

within their control; the scorecard developed for each subunit includes measures relevant to those subunits. Reward systems also need to correct for situational factors. Salespeople in one region may have higher sales because the economy is stronger there than elsewhere, so sales bonuses need to be adjusted for these economic factors.

Use team rewards for interdependent jobs   Organizations should use team (or organizational) rewards rather than individual rewards when employees work in highly interdependent jobs.[42] One reason is that individual performance is difficult to measure in these situations. For example, you can't determine how well one employee in a chemical processing plant contributes to the quality of the liquid produced. It is a team effort. A second reason is that team rewards tend to make employees more cooperative and less competitive. People see that their bonuses or other incentives depend on how well they work with co-workers, and they act accordingly.

The third reason for having team rewards is that they support employee preferences for team-based work arrangements. This was found in a study of Xerox customer service representatives. The Xerox employees assigned to teams with purely team bonuses eventually accepted and preferred a team structure, whereas those put in teams without team rewards did not adapt as well to the team structure.[43]

Ensure rewards are valued   It seems obvious that rewards work best when they are valued. Yet, recall from Chapter 5 that companies sometimes make false assumptions about what employees want, with unfortunate consequences. The solution, of course, is to ask employees what they value. Campbell Soup's Canadian distribution centre did this a few years ago. Executives thought the employees would ask for more money in a special team reward program. Instead, distribution staff said the most valued reward was a leather jacket with the Campbell Soup logo on the back.[44]

Watch out for unintended consequences   Performance-based reward systems sometimes have an unexpected—and undesirable—effect on employee behaviours.[45] Consider the pizza company that decided to reward its drivers for on-time delivery. The plan got more hot pizzas to customers on time, but it also increased the accident rates of its drivers because the incentive motivated them to drive recklessly.[46] Connections 6.2 describes a few other examples where reward systems had unintended consequences. The solution here is to carefully think through the consequences of specific rewards and, where possible, test incentives in a pilot project before applying them across the organization.

At the beginning of this chapter, we said that money and other financial rewards have a complex effect on the needs, emotions, and social identity of employees. But money isn't the only thing that motivates people to join an organization and perform effectively. "The reward of doing a job well is in having done the job," says Richard Currie, president of Toronto-based George Weston Ltd. "The money is a byproduct." Rafik O. Loutfy, a Xerox research centre director, agrees with this assessment. "Our top stars say they want to make an impact—that's the most important thing," he says. "Feeling they are contributing and making a difference is highly motivational for them."[47] In other words, George Weston, Xerox, and other companies motivate employees mainly by designing interesting and challenging jobs, which we discuss next.

When Rewards Go Wrong

There is an old saying that "what gets rewarded, gets done." But what companies reward isn't always what they had intended employees to do. Here are a few dramatic examples:

- Toyota rewards its dealerships based on customer satisfaction surveys, not just car sales. What Toyota discovered, however, is that this motivates dealers to increase satisfaction scores, not customer satisfaction. One Toyota dealership received high ratings because it offered free detailing to every customer who returned a "Very Satisfied" survey. The dealership even had a special copy of the survey showing clients which boxes to check off. This increased customer ratings, but not customer satisfaction.

- A building design company implemented an incentive plan that encouraged its engineers to design buildings so they are built below budget. One creative employee achieved this by simply scaling the building's walls and ceilings down by an inch or two. This saved thousands of dollars for the company and earned the engineer a sizeable bonus, until the company and client discovered the shrunken results.

- Stock options are supposed to motivate executives to focus on shareholder value. Instead, this incentive motivates some corporate leaders to keep the stock's price high in the short term through dodgy accounting practices and misrepresentation of the company's state of affairs. Experts believe the spectacular failures at Enron and Worldcom occurred partly because stock options motivated executives to hide bad news about falling revenue until it was too late to correct the problem. The unintended consequences of stock options might also be apparent at IBM where stock-optioned executives have spent almost $39 billion repurchasing IBM stock from the market over the past five years. This was significantly more than the $33 billion IBM invested in its entire research and development budget over that same time span. The buyback rewarded IBM executives through improved

Customer service incentives may have rewarded the wrong behaviour at Toyota dealerships. *Copyright © John Thoeming.*

stock prices, but probably didn't help IBM's long-term development of new products and services.

- Donnelly Mirrors (now part of Canada's Magna International empire) introduced a gainsharing plan that motivated employees to reduce labour but not material costs. Employees at the automobile parts manufacturer knew they worked faster with sharp grinding wheels, so they replaced the expensive diamond wheels more often. This action reduced labour costs, thereby giving employees the gainsharing bonus. However, the labour savings were easily offset by much higher costs for diamond grinding wheels.

Sources: D. Wessel, "Boardroom Sins Continue to Emerge—Stock Options Gave Executives Incentives to Boost Near-Term Share Prices," *Wall Street Journal*, June 21, 2002, p. A1; J. A. Byrne, "How To Fix Corporate Governance," *Business Week*, May 6, 2002, p. 68; D.S. Hilzenrath, "Financial 'Performance' Options Getting a Second Look," *Washington Post*, April 1, 2001, p. H1; C. Teasdale, "Not all Firms Find Variable Pay Plans Pay Off," *St. Louis Business Journal*, September 28, 1998; F. F. Reichheld, *The Loyalty Effect* (Boston, MA: Harvard University Press, 1996), p. 236; D. R. Spitzer, "Power Rewards: Rewards That Really Motivate," *Management Review*, May 1996, pp. 45–50.
www.toyota.com

JOB DESIGN PRACTICES

job design
The process of assigning tasks to a job, including the interdependency of those tasks with other jobs.

Organizational behaviour scholars generally agree that the deepest "passion" for performing a job well comes from the work itself. **Job design** refers to the process of assigning tasks to a job, including the interdependency of those tasks with other jobs. A *job* is a set of tasks performed by one person. Some jobs have very few tasks, each requiring limited skill or effort. Other jobs involve very complex tasks requiring highly trained trades people or professionals. Job design is constantly shifting due to technological change and trends in psychological contracts. Employability means that employees are no longer hired into specific jobs indefinitely. Instead, they hold generic titles (associates, team members) and are expected to perform several clusters of tasks.[48]

Whether the change occurs through information technology or workforce flexibility, job design often produces an interesting conflict between the employee's motivation and ability to complete the work. To understand this issue more fully, we begin by describing early job design efforts aimed at increasing work efficiency through job specialization.

Job Design and Work Efficiency

job specialization
The result of division of labour in which each job now includes a subset of the tasks required to complete the product or service.

Cindy Vang sits in a blue vinyl chair at Medtronic's assembly line in Minneapolis, Minnesota. Using a pair of tweezers, she loads 275 feedthroughs—tiny needle-like components for pacemakers and neurostimulators—onto a slotted storage block. She fills a block in about 15 minutes, then places the completed block on a shelf, and loads the next block.[49] Cindy Vang works in a job with a high degree of **job specialization**. Job specialization occurs when the work required to build a pacemaker—or any other product or service—is subdivided into separate jobs assigned to different people. Each resulting job includes a very narrow subset of tasks, usually completed in a short "cycle time." Cycle time is the time required to complete the task before starting over with a new work unit. For Cindy Vang, the cycle time for loading each feedthrough is a few seconds.

The economic benefits of dividing work into specialized jobs have been described and applied for at least two centuries. Over 2,300 years ago, both the Chinese philosopher Mencius and Greek philosopher Plato noted that division of labour improves work efficiency. In 1436 A.D., the waterways of Venice became an assembly line loading 10 galleons in just six hours. Over two hundred years ago, economist Adam Smith described a small factory where 10 pin makers collectively produced as many as 48,000 pins per day because they performed specialized tasks, such as straightening, cutting, sharpening, grinding, and whitening the pins. In contrast, Smith explained that if these 10 people worked alone, they would collectively produce no more than 200 pins per day.[50]

Why does job specialization potentially increase work efficiency? One reason is that employees have fewer tasks to juggle and therefore spend less time changing activities. They also require fewer physical and mental skills to accomplish the assigned work, so less time and resources are needed for training. A third reason is that employees practise their tasks more frequently with shorter work cycles, so jobs are mastered quickly. Last, work efficiency increases because employees with specific aptitudes or skills can be matched more precisely to the jobs for which they are best suited.[51]

scientific management
Involves systematically partitioning work into its smallest elements and standardizing tasks to achieve maximum efficiency.

Scientific management   One of the strongest advocates of job specialization was Frederick Winslow Taylor, an industrial engineer who introduced the principles of **scientific management** in the early 1900s.[52] Scientific management involves systematically partitioning work into its smallest elements and standardizing tasks to achieve maximum efficiency. According to Taylor, the most effective companies have detailed procedures and work practices developed by engineers, enforced by supervisors, and executed by employees. Even the supervisor's tasks should be divided: one person manages operational efficiency, another manages inspection, and another is the disciplinarian. Through scientific management, Taylor also popularized many organizational practices that are commonly found today, such as goal setting, employee training, and incentive systems.

There is ample evidence that scientific management has improved efficiency in many work settings. One of Taylor's earliest interventions was at a ball bearing factory where 120 women each worked 55 hours per week. Through job specialization and work efficiency analysis, Taylor increased production by two-thirds using a work force of only 35 women working fewer than 45 hours per week. Taylor also doubled the employees' previous wages. No doubt some of the increased productivity can be credited to improved training, goal setting, and work incentives, but job specialization has also contributed to the success of scientific management.

Problems with job specialization Job specialization is often applied successfully, but it doesn't always improve job performance. The reason is that job specialization ignores the effects of job content on employees.[53] Some jobs—such as Cindy Vang's task of loading feedthroughs—are so specialized that they are tedious, trivial, and socially isolating. Job specialization was supposed to let companies buy cheap, unskilled labour. Instead, many have to offer higher wages— some call it *discontentment pay*—to compensate for the job dissatisfaction of narrowly defined work.[54] Job specialization also costs more in terms of higher turnover, absenteeism, sabotage, and mental health problems. Work quality is often lower with highly specialized jobs because employees see only a small part of the process. As one observer of automobile assembly line work reports: "Often [employees] did not know how their jobs related to the total picture. Not knowing, there was no incentive to strive for quality—what did quality even mean as it related to a bracket whose function you did not understand."[55]

Perhaps the most important reason why job specialization has not been as successful as expected is that it ignores the motivational potential of jobs. As jobs become specialized, the work tends to become easier to perform but is less motivating. As jobs become more complex, work motivation increases but the ability to master the job decreases. Maximum job performance occurs somewhere between these two extremes, where most people can eventually perform the job tasks efficiently, yet the work is still interesting.

Job Design and Work Motivation

Industrial engineers may have overlooked the motivational effects of job characteristics, but that is now the central focus of many job design changes. Organizational behaviour scholar Frederick Herzberg is credited with shifting the spotlight when he introduced **motivator-hygiene theory**.[56] Motivator-hygiene theory proposes that employees experience job satisfaction when they fulfill growth and esteem needs (called *motivators*), and experience dissatisfaction when they have poor working conditions, job security, and other factors related to lower order needs (called *hygienes*). Herzberg argued that only the characteristics of the job itself will motivate employees, whereas the hygiene factors merely prevent dissatisfaction. It might seem rather obvious to us today that the job itself is a source of motivation, but it was radical thinking when Herzberg proposed the idea in the 1950s.

Motivator-hygiene theory didn't find much research support, but Herzberg's ideas generated new thinking about the motivational potential of the job itself.[57] Out of subsequent research emerged the **job characteristics model**, shown in

motivator-hygiene theory
Herzberg's theory stating that employees are primarily motivated by growth and esteem needs, not by lower-level needs.

job characteristics model
A job design model that relates the motivational properties of jobs to specific personal and organizational consequences of these properties.

EXHIBIT 6.3

The job characteristics model

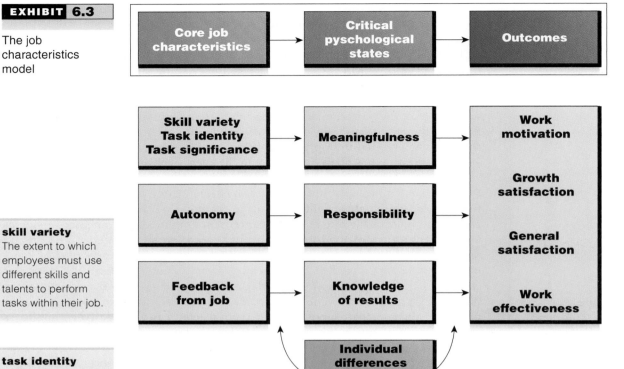

Source: J. R. Hackman and G. Oldham, *Work Redesign* (Reading, MA: Addison-Wesley, 1980), p. 90. Used with permission.

skill variety
The extent to which employees must use different skills and talents to perform tasks within their job.

task identity
The degree to which a job requires completion of a whole or identifiable piece of work.

task significance
The degree to which the job has a substantial impact on the organization and/or larger society.

autonomy
The degree to which a job gives employees the freedom, independence, and discretion to schedule their work and determine the procedures used in completing it.

Exhibit 6.3.[58] The job characteristics model identifies five core job dimensions that produce three psychological states. Employees who experience these psychological states tend to have higher levels of internal work motivation (motivation from the work itself), job satisfaction (particularly satisfaction with the work itself), and work effectiveness.

Core Job Characteristics

The job characteristics model identifies five core job characteristics (see Exhibit 6.3). Under the right conditions, employees are more motivated and satisfied when jobs have higher levels of these characteristics.

- *Skill variety*—**Skill variety** refers to using different skills and talents to complete a variety of work activities. For example, sales clerks who normally only serve customers might be assigned the additional duties of stocking inventory and changing storefront displays.
- *Task identity*—**Task identity** is the degree to which a job requires completion of a whole or identifiable piece of work, such as doing something from beginning to end, where it is easy to see how one's work fits into the whole product

Jousting and winemaking don't usually occur in the same place, but that doesn't stop Mike Just from practising both crafts. The New Zealander apprenticed in Germany, where he learned the fine art of winemaking and the thrill of wearing his own set of armour at festivals in the old German castles. When not wielding his sword, Just enjoys being involved in the entire winemaking process at Lawson's Dry Hills Winery in New Zealand "What I really like about this job is that you can start with a raw product and carry it right through to marketing the finished product, all on one site," Just explains. "[W]e plant vines here, we pick them, we make the wine on site and bottle it, then sell it to customers who come in."[61] Based on the job characteristics model, why is Mike Just highly motivated by his work? *J. Tannock, © Marlborough Express.*
www.lawsondryhills.co.nz

or service. An employee who assembles an entire computer modem rather than just solder in the circuitry would develop a stronger sense of ownership or identity with the final product.

- *Task significance*—**Task significance** is the degree to which the job has a substantial impact on the organization and/or larger society. For instance, Medtronic executives realize that Cindy Vang (described earlier) and many other employees have low skill variety, so they have special sessions where patients give testimonials to remind staff of their task significance. "We have patients who come in who would be dead if it wasn't for us," says a Medtronic production supervisor. Little wonder that 86 percent of Medtronic employees say their work has special meaning and 94 percent feel pride in what they accomplish.[59]
- *Autonomy*—Jobs with high levels of **autonomy** provide freedom, independence, and discretion in scheduling the work and determining the procedures to be used to complete the work. In autonomous jobs, employees make their own decisions rather than relying on detailed instructions from supervisors or procedure manuals.
- *Job feedback*—**Job feedback** is the degree to which employees can tell how well they are doing based on direct sensory information from the job itself. Airline pilots can tell how well they land their aircraft and physicians can see whether their operations have improved the patient's health. Some research suggests that task feedback has an important effect on reducing role ambiguity and improving job satisfaction.[60]

Critical Psychological States

job feedback
The degree to which employees can tell how well they are doing based on direct sensory information from the job itself.

The five core job characteristics affect employee motivation and satisfaction through three critical psychological states.[62] One of these is *experienced meaningfulness*—the belief that one's work is worthwhile or important. Skill variety, task identity, and task significance directly contribute to the job's meaningfulness. If the job has high levels of all three characteristics, employees are likely to feel that their job is highly meaningful. Meaningfulness drops as the job loses one or more of these characteristics.

Work motivation and performance increase when employees feel personally accountable for the outcomes of their efforts. Autonomy directly contributes to this feeling of *experienced responsibility*. Employees must be assigned control of their work environment to feel responsible for their successes and failures. The third critical psychological state is *knowledge of results*. Employees want information about the consequences of their work effort. Knowledge of results can originate from co-workers, supervisors, or clients. However, job design focuses on knowledge of results from the work itself.

Individual Differences

Job redesign doesn't increase work motivation for everyone in every situation. Employees must have the required skills and knowledge to master the more challenging work. Otherwise, job redesign tends to increase stress and reduce job performance. A second condition is that employees must be reasonably satisfied with their work environment (e.g., working conditions, job security, salaries) before job redesign affects work motivation. A third condition is that employees must have strong growth needs, whereas improving the core job characteristics will have little motivational effect on people who are primarily focused on existence or relatedness needs.[63]

Increasing Work Motivation through Job Design

Three main strategies potentially increase the motivational potential of jobs: job rotation, job enlargement, and job enrichment. This section also identifies several ways to implement job enrichment.

job rotation
The practice of moving employees from one job to another.

Job rotation   **Job rotation** is the practice of moving employees from one job to another. Consider a large "one hour" photo finishing retail outlet where one employee interacts with customers, another operates the photo finishing machine, and a third puts the finished product into envelopes and files them for pick-up. Job rotation would occur when employees move around those three jobs every few hours or days.

Moving employees around different jobs might reduce job boredom, but most organizations introduce job design mainly to develop a flexible work force. Rotation helps employees become multi-skilled, so they can fluidly shift work duties based on needs and demands. For instance, faced with cutbacks and increased workloads, Ryerson University librarians reorganized themselves from specialist to more generic jobs and rotated through four work areas.[64] A third reason for introducing job rotation is to reduce the incidence of repetitive strain injuries. Carrier Corp. uses job rotation for this reason. The air conditioning manufacturer identified complementary jobs so now employees move around to different jobs to use different muscles, thereby reducing strain on one muscle.[65]

job enlargement
Increasing the number of tasks employees perform within their job.

Job enlargement   Rather than rotating employees through different jobs, **job enlargement** combines several tasks into one job. This might involve combining two or more complete jobs into one, or just adding one or two more tasks to an existing job. Either way, the job's skill variety has increased because there are more tasks to perform. For example, WestJet flight attendants have enlarged jobs because they perform a variety of tasks rather than the more narrowly defined job duties of their counterparts at Air Canada.

A recent example of job enlargement is video journalists. As Exhibit 6.4 illustrates, a traditional news team consists of a camera operator, a sound and lighting specialist, and the journalist who writes and presents or narrates the story. A single video journalist performs all these tasks. The Canadian Broadcasting Corporation introduced video journalists a few years ago at CBET (a Windsor, Ontario affiliate of CBC) to reduce costs. The project was so successful that they are now found at CBC *Newsworld*, and CBC *Venture*. CNN is also moving towards video journalists. "[C]orrespondents would do well to learn how to shoot and edit . . .

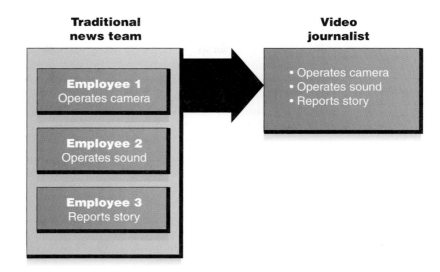

EXHIBIT 6.4

Job enlargement of
video journalists

and smart shooters and editors will learn how to write and track," CNN executives wrote in a recent memo to employees. "CNN will always value exceptional ability, [but] the more multi-talented a newsgatherer, the more opportunity the News Group will provide that person."[66]

Job enlargement significantly improves work efficiency and flexibility. However, research suggests that simply giving employees more tasks won't affect motivation, performance, or job satisfaction. Instead, these benefits result only when skill variety is combined with more autonomy and job knowledge.[67] In other words, employees are motivated when they have a variety of tasks *and* have the freedom and knowledge to structure their work to achieve the highest satisfaction and performance. These job characteristics are at the heart of job enrichment.

job enrichment
Employees are given more responsibility for scheduling, coordinating, and planning their own work.

Job enrichment   **Job enrichment** occurs when employees are given more responsibility for scheduling, coordinating, and planning their own work. Although some writers suggest that job enrichment is any strategy that increases one or more of the core job characteristics, Herzberg strongly argued that jobs are enriched only through autonomy and the resulting feelings of responsibility.[68] Two ways to enrich jobs are clustering tasks into natural groups and establishing client relationships.

Clustering tasks into natural groups involves stitching highly interdependent tasks into one job. An example of forming a natural work unit would be assembling an entire computer modem rather than just some parts of it. The video journalist job was described earlier as job enlargement because it combines several tasks. However, it is also an example of job enrichment because video journalism naturally groups tasks together to complete an entire product (i.e. a news clip). By forming natural work units, jobholders have stronger feelings of responsibility for an identifiable body of work. They feel a sense of ownership and, therefore, tend to increase job quality. Forming natural work units increases task identity and task significance because employees perform a complete product or service and can more readily see how their work affects others.

A second job enrichment strategy, called establishing client relationships, involves putting employees in *direct contact* with their clients rather than using the supervisor as a go-between. The key factor is direct communication with clients. These clients submit work and provide feedback directly to the employee rather than through a supervisor. By being directly responsible for specific clients, employees have more information and can make decisions affecting those clients.[69] Nova Scotia Power applies this form of job enrichment in its rural districts. At one time, installing and disconnecting service, reading meters, and collecting overdue accounts were assigned to people in different jobs. Now one employee completes all of these tasks for the same client and works directly with the client. By being directly responsible for specific clients, employees have more information and can make decisions affecting those clients.[70]

Research suggests that these and other job enrichment interventions are generally effective. In particular, employees with high growth needs in enriched jobs have higher job satisfaction and work motivation, along with lower absenteeism and turnover. Productivity is also higher when task identity and job feedback are improved. Product and service quality tend to improve because job enrichment increases the jobholder's felt responsibility and sense of ownership over the product or service. Quality improvements are most apparent when employees complete a natural work unit or establish client relationships.[71]

Forming natural task groups and establishing client relationships are common ways to enrich jobs, but the heart of the job enrichment philosophy is to give employees more autonomy over their work. This basic idea is at the core of one of the most widely mentioned—and most widely misunderstood—practices, known as empowerment.

EMPOWERMENT PRACTICES

When Clive Beddoe cofounded WestJet Airlines Ltd., he wanted to create an organization where employees had the freedom to serve customers rather than follow strict rules. Beddoe explains that most other airlines in the world have a military mindset. "You see it even in their flight uniforms and the autocratic way their companies behave," Beddoe points out. "Manuals and polices have to be followed exactly and, while that's necessary in the cockpit, it's not the best way when it comes to customer service." Beddoe emphasizes that WestJet is the opposite. "Here, we empower our employees and encourage them to be free-thinking and to do whatever it takes in whatever way they feel it's appropriate to solve customer problems."[72]

WestJet's success is partly due to the fact that it empowers its employees. **Empowerment** is a term that has been loosely tossed around in corporate circles and has been the subject of considerable debate among academics. However, the most widely accepted definition is that empowerment is a psychological concept represented by four dimensions: self-determination, meaning, competence, and impact regarding the individual's role in the organization.[73]

First, empowered employees experience freedom, independence, and discretion over their work activities (self-determination). Second, they care about their work and believe that what they do is important (meaning). Third, empowered people have feelings of self-efficacy, meaning that they are confident about their ability to perform the work well and have a capacity to grow with new challenges (competence). Fourth, empowered employees view themselves as active participants in the organization; that is, their decisions and actions have an influence on the company's success (impact). Empowerment consists of all four dimensions. If any

empowerment

A psychological concept in which people experience more self-determination, meaning, competence, and impact regarding their role in the organization.

Employees at Rand Merchant Bank were recently handed a booklet entitled The Complete Book of Rules. But instead of a long list of "do's and don'ts," all the pages inside were blank. The message that the South African financial institution wanted to convey is that employees are empowered to make their own decisions. "We trust that in any given situation an employee who has freedom to make choices will inherently do the best for the company," explains Rand chairman Paul Harris. Empowerment practices seem to work: Rand Merchant Bank is rated the best company to work for in South Africa and tends to outperform the marketplace in terms of earnings.[74] In what way does Rand's "Book of Rules" symbolize and support empowerment? *Courtesy of Rand Merchant Bank.* **www.rmb.co.za**

dimension weakens, the employee's sense of empowerment will weaken.

From this definition, you can see that empowerment is not a personality trait, although personality might influence the extent to which someone feels empowered. People also experience degrees of empowerment, which can vary from one work environment to the next. Empowerment is not the same as employee involvement (or participation), although the two concepts overlap in some ways. Employee involvement can range from making suggestions to having complete ownership of the decision. Empowerment describes the latter; it is the highest level of involvement. It refers to transferring the power to decide and act on situations.

Creating Empowerment

Chances are you have heard corporate leaders say they are "empowering" the workforce. What these executives really mean is that they are changing the work environment to support empowerment.[75] There are numerous individual, job design, and organizational factors that support empowerment. At the individual level, employees must possess the necessary competencies to be able to perform the work as well as handle the additional decision-making requirements. While other individual factors have been proposed (e.g., locus of control), they do not seem to have any real effect on whether employees feel empowered.[76]

Job characteristics clearly influence the dynamics of empowerment.[77] To generate beliefs about self-determination, employees must work in jobs with a high degree of autonomy with minimal bureaucratic control. To maintain a sense of meaningfulness, jobs must have high levels of task identity and task significance. And to maintain a sense of self-confidence, jobs must provide sufficient feedback.

Organizational factors also influence empowerment beliefs. Employees experience more empowerment in organizations where information and other resources are easily accessible. Empowerment also requires a learning orientation culture. In other words, empowerment flourishes in organizations that appreciate the value of the employee learning, and accept reasonable mistakes as a natural part of the learning process. Last, empowerment requires corporate leaders who trust employees and are willing to take the risks that empowerment creates. "Sometimes you get burned when you trust people," admits WestJet CEO Clive Beddoe, "but most times you don't."[78]

With the right individuals, job characteristics, and organizational environment in place, empowerment can have a noticeable effect on motivation and performance. For instance, a study of Canadian bank employees concluded that empowerment improved customer service and tended to reduce conflict between employees and their supervisors. A study of Canadian nurses reported that empowerment is associated with higher trust in management, which ultimately influences job satisfaction, belief, and acceptance of organizational goals and values, and affective organizational commitment.[79] Empowerment allows employees to apply their knowledge directly and with more responsiveness to problems and opportunities. It also tends to increase personal initiative because employees identity with and assume more psychological ownership of their work.

PRACTISING SELF-LEADERSHIP

WestJet Airlines has been mentioned several times throughout this chapter because the company illustrates how to improve employee performance through rewards, job design, and empowerment practices. WestJet is also a symbol for another increasingly important applied performance practice, called self-leadership. "What occurred to me," says WestJet CEO Clive Beddoe, "is we had to overcome the inherent difficulty of trying to manage people and to hone the process into one where people wanted to manage themselves."[80]

self-leadership
The process of influencing oneself to establish the self-direction and self-motivation needed to perform a task.

Clive Beddoe recognizes that empowerment requires employees who motivate themselves and direct their own behaviour most of the time. Indeed, corporate leaders identify self-motivation as one of the most important features to look for in new hires.[81] These corporate leaders are placing more emphasis on **self-leadership**—the process of influencing oneself to establish the self-direction and self-motivation needed to perform a task.[82] This concept includes a toolkit of behavioural activities borrowed from social learning theory (Chapter 3) and goal setting (Chapter 5). It also includes constructive thought processes that have been extensively studied in sports psychology. Overall, self-leadership takes the view that individuals mostly

Elements of
self-leadership

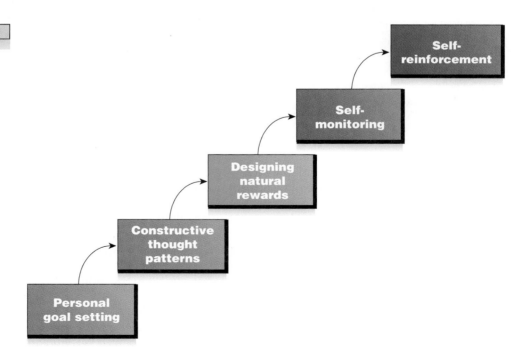

Sirius Consulting Group has been growing in leaps and bounds because it picks employees who apply self-leadership practices. "Here, you manage your own workload, set deadlines and project plans," says Siobhan MacDonald, senior account manager at the Ottawa-based firm that matches 4,000 independent IT professionals to clients. Sirius account managers are responsible for filing a monthly sales report and attending a brief weekly meeting, but otherwise they set their own hours. The proof of this self-leadership is in the six-figure paycheques that many account managers earn. "If you're self-motivated and a hard worker, there's no ceiling on what you can produce," MacDonald advises.[85] Along with self-set goals, what other self-leadership practices would improve the job performance of account managers? *Courtesy of Sirius Consulting Group.*
www.sirius.ca

regulate their own actions through these behavioural and cognitive (thought) activities.

Although we are in the early stages of understanding the dynamics of self-leadership, Exhibit 6.5 (facing page) identifies the five main elements of this process. These elements, which generally follow each other in a sequence, include personal goal setting, constructive thought patterns, designing natural rewards, self-monitoring, and self-reinforcement.[83]

Personal Goal Setting

The first step in self-leadership is to set goals for your own work effort. This applies the ideas we learned in Chapter 5 on goal setting, such as identifying goals that are specific, results-oriented, and challenging. The main difference between personal goal setting and our previous discussion is that goals are set alone, rather than assigned by or jointly decided with a supervisor. One recent study found that employees are more focused when they set their own goals. Other research reports that students who rely on personal goal setting used more effective and sophisticated learning strategies and developed stronger feelings of self-efficacy.[84]

Constructive Thought Patterns

Before beginning a task and while performing it, employees should engage in positive (constructive) thoughts about that work and its accomplishment. In particular, employees are more motivated and better prepared to accomplish a task after they have engaged in positive self-talk and mental imagery.

self-talk
Talking to ourselves about our own thoughts or actions for the purpose of increasing our self-efficacy and navigating through decisions in a future event.

Positive self-talk   Do you ever talk to yourself? Most of us do, according to a study of University of Waterloo students.[86] **Self-talk** refers to any situation in which we talk to ourselves about our own thoughts or actions. Some of this internal communication assists the decision-making process, such as weighing the advantages of a particular choice. Self-leadership is mostly interested in evaluative self-talk, in which you evaluate your capabilities and accomplishments.

The problem is that most evaluative self-talk is negative; we criticize much more than we encourage or congratulate ourselves. Negative self-talk undermines our self-efficacy, which, in turn, undermines our potential for performing a particular task.[87] In contrast, positive self-talk creates a "can do" belief and thereby increases motivation by raising our E-to-P expectancy. We often hear that professional athletes "psyche" themselves up before an important event. They tell themselves they can achieve their goal and that they have practised enough to reach that goal. They are motivating themselves through self-talk.

Mental imagery   You've probably heard the phrase, "I'll cross that bridge when I come to it!" Self-leadership takes the opposite view. It suggests that we need to mentally practise a task and imagine successfully performing it beforehand. This process is known as **mental imagery.**[88]

As you can see from this definition, mental imagery has two parts. One part involves mentally practising the task, anticipating obstacles to goal accomplishment, and working out solutions to those obstacles before they occur. By mentally walking through the activities required to accomplish the task, we begin to see problems that may occur. We can then imagine what responses would be best for each contingency.[89]

While one part of mental imagery helps us to anticipate things that could go wrong, the other part involves visualizing successful completion of the task. We imagine the experience of completing the task and the positive results that follow. Everyone daydreams and fantasizes about being in a successful situation. You might imagine yourself being promoted to your boss's job, receiving a prestigious award, or taking time off work. This visualization increases goal commitment and motivates us to complete the task effectively.

mental imagery
Mentally practicing a task and visualizing its successful completion.

Designing Natural Rewards

Self-leadership recognizes that employees actively craft their jobs. To varying degrees, they can alter tasks and work relationships to make the work more motivating.[90] One way to build natural rewards into the job is to alter the way a task is accomplished. People often have enough discretion in their jobs to make slight changes to suit their needs and preferences. For instance, you might try out a new software program to design an idea, rather than sketch the image with a pencil. By using the new software, you are adding challenge to a task that may otherwise have been mundane.

Self-Monitoring

Self-monitoring is the process of keeping track of one's progress toward a goal. In the section on job design, we learned that feedback from the job itself communicates whether we are accomplishing the task successfully. Self-monitoring includes the notion of consciously checking that naturally occurring feedback at regular intervals. It also includes designing artificial feedback where natural feedback does not occur. Salespeople might arrange to receive monthly reports on sales levels in their territory. Production staff might have gauges or computer feedback systems installed so they can see how many errors are made on the production line. Research suggests that people who have control over when they receive performance feedback perform their tasks better than those with feedback assigned by others.[91]

Self-Reinforcement

Self-leadership includes the social learning theory concept of self-reinforcement. Self-reinforcement occurs whenever an employee has control over a reinforcer but doesn't "take" the reinforcer until completing a self-set goal (see Chapter 3).[92] A common example is taking a break after reaching a pre-determined stage of your work. The work break is a self-induced form of positive reinforcement. Self-reinforcement also occurs when you decide to do a more enjoyable task after completing a task that you dislike. For example, after slogging through a difficult report, you might decide to spend time doing a more pleasant task, such as catching up on industry news by scanning Web sites.

Self-Leadership in Practice

It's too early to say that every component of self-leadership is useful, but evidence suggests that these practices generally improve self-efficacy, motivation, and performance. Studies in sports psychology indicate that self-set goals and constructive thought processes improve individual performance. For example, young ice skaters who received self-talk training improved their performance one year later. Self-talk and mental imagery have also improved the performance of tennis players and female college swimmers. Indeed, studies show that almost all Olympic athletes rely on mental rehearsal and positive self-talk to achieve their performance goals.[93]

One study reported that new employees in a Canadian organization who practised self-set goals and self-reinforcement had higher internal motivation. Another study found that airline employees who received constructive thought training experienced better mental performance, enthusiasm, and job satisfaction than co-workers who did not receive this training. A third study found that mental imagery helped supervisors and process engineers in an Ontario pulp and paper mill to transfer what they learned in an interpersonal communication skills class back on the job.[94]

People with a high degree of conscientiousness and internal locus of control are more likely to apply self-leadership strategies. However, one of the benefits of self-leadership is that it can be learned. Training programs have helped employees to improve their self-leadership skills. Organizations can also encourage self-leadership by providing sufficient autonomy and establishing rewards that reinforce self-leadership behaviours. Employees are also more likely to engage in self-monitoring in companies that emphasize continuous measurement of performance.[95] Overall, self-leadership promises to be an important concept and practice for improving employee motivation and performance.

Self-leadership, job design, empowerment, and rewards are valuable approaches to improving employee performance. However, performance is also affected by work-related stress. As we learn in the next chapter, too much stress is causing numerous problems with employee performance and well-being, but there are also ways to combat this epidemic.

CHAPTER SUMMARY

Money and other financial rewards are a fundamental part of the employment relationship. They have the potential to fulfill existence, relatedness, and growth needs. Money generates various emotions and attitudes, which vary across cultures. People (particularly men) also tend to identify themselves with their wealth.

Organizations reward employees for their membership and seniority, job status, competencies, and performance. Membership-based rewards may attract job applicants and seniority-based rewards reduce turnover, but these reward objectives tend to discourage turnover among those with the lowest performance. Rewards based on job status try to maintain internal equity and motivate employees to compete for promotions. However, job status-based rewards are inconsistent with market responsiveness, encourage employees to compete with each other, and can lead to organizational politics. Competency-based rewards are becoming increasingly popular because they improve workforce flexibility and are consistent with the emerging idea of employability. But competency-based rewards tend to be subjectively measured and can result in higher costs as employees spend more time learning new skills.

Awards/bonuses, commissions, and other individual performance-based rewards have existed for centuries and are widely used. Many companies are shifting to team-based rewards such as gainsharing plans, and to organizational rewards such as employee stock ownership plans (ESOPs), stock options, profit sharing, and balanced scorecards. ESOPs and stock options create a ownership culture, but employees often perceive a weak connection between individual performance and the organizational reward.

Financial rewards have a number of limitations, but there are several ways to improve reward effectiveness. Organizational leaders should ensure that rewards are linked to work performance, aligned with performance within the employee's control, valued by employees, do not have unintended consequences, and that team rewards are used where jobs are interdependent.

Job design refers to the process of assigning tasks to a job, including the interdependency of those tasks with other jobs. Job specialization subdivides work into separate jobs for different people. This increases work efficiency because employees master the tasks quickly, spend less time changing tasks, require less training, and can be matched more closely with the jobs best suited to their skills. However, job specialization may reduce work motivation, create mental health problems, lower product or service quality, and increase costs through discontentment pay, absenteeism, and turnover.

Contemporary job design strategies reverse job specialization through job rotation, job enlargement, and job enrichment. The job characteristics model is a template for job redesign that specifies core job dimensions, psychological states, and individual differences. Organizations introduce job rotation to reduce job boredom, develop a more flexible workforce, and reduce the incidence of repetitive strain injuries. Two ways to enrich jobs are clustering tasks into natural groups and establishing client relationships.

Empowerment is a psychological concept represented by four dimensions: self-determination, meaning, competence, and impact regarding the individual's role in the organization. Individual characteristics seem to have a minor influence on empowerment. Job design is a major influence, particularly autonomy, task identity, task significance, and job feedback. Empowerment is also supported at the organizational level through a learning orientation culture, sufficient information and resources, and corporate leaders who trust employees.

Self-leadership is the process of influencing oneself to establish the self-direction and self-motivation needed to perform a task. This includes personal goal setting, constructive thought patterns, designing natural rewards, self-monitoring, and self-reinforcement. Constructive thought patterns include self-talk and mental imagery. Self-talk refers to any situation in which a person talks to him- or herself about his or her own thoughts or actions. Mental imagery involves mentally practising a task and imagining performing it successfully beforehand.

KEY TERMS

Autonomy, p. 180

Balanced scorecard, p. 174

Employee stock ownership plan (ESOP), p. 174

Empowerment, p. 184

Gainsharing plan, p. 172

Job characteristics model, p. 179

Job design, p. 177

Job enlargement, p. 182

Job enrichment, p. 183

Job evaluation, p. 171

Job feedback, p. 181

Job rotation, p. 182

Job specialization, p. 178

Mental imagery, p. 188

Motivator-hygiene theory, p. 179

Open-book management, p. 173

Profit-sharing, p. 174

Scientific management, p. 178

Self-leadership, p. 186

Self-talk, p. 187

Skill variety, p. 180

Stock options, p. 174

Task identity, p. 180

Task significance, p. 180

DISCUSSION QUESTIONS

1. As a consultant, you have been asked to recommend either a gainsharing plan or a profit-sharing plan for employees who work in the four regional distribution and warehousing facilities of a large retail organization. Which reward system would you recommend? Explain your answer.

2. You are a member of a team responsible for developing performance measures for your college or university department/faculty based on the balanced scorecard approach. Identify one performance measurement for each of the following factors: financial, customer, internal processes and employee.

3. Inuvik Tire Corp. has redesigned its production facilities around a team-based system. However, the company president believes that employees will not be motivated unless they receive incentives based on their individual performance. Give three explanations why Inuvik Tire should introduce team-based rather than individual rewards in this setting.

4. What can organizations do to increase the effectiveness of financial rewards?

5. Most of us have watched pizzas being made while waiting in a pizzeria. What level of job specialization do you usually notice in these operations? Why does this high or low level of specialization exist? If some pizzerias have different levels of specialization than others, identify the contingencies that might explain these differences.

6. Can a manager or supervisor "empower" an employee? Discuss fully.

7. Describe a time when you practised self-leadership to successfully perform a task. With reference to each step in the self-leadership process, describe what you did to achieve this success.

8. Can self-leadership replace formal leadership in an organizational setting?

CASE STUDY 6.1

THE REGENCY GRAND HOTEL

By Lisa Ho, under the supervision of Steven L. McShane.

The Regency Grand Hotel is a five-star hotel in Bangkok. The hotel was established fifteen years ago by a local consortium of investors and has been operated by a Thai general manager throughout this time. The hotel is one of Bangkok's most prestigious hotels and its 700 employees enjoyed the prestige of being associated with the hotel. The hotel provides good welfare benefits, above market rate salary, and job security. In addition, a good year-end bonus amounting to four months' salary was rewarded to employees regardless of the hotel's overall performance during the year.

Recently, the Regency was sold to a large American hotel chain that was very keen to expand its operations into Thailand. When the acquisition was announced, the general manager decided to take early retirement when the hotel changed ownership. The American hotel chain kept all of the Regency employees, although a few were transferred to other positions. John Becker, an American with 10 years of management experi-

ence with the hotel chain, was appointed the new general manager of the Regency Grand Hotel. Becker was selected because of his previous successes in integrating newly acquired hotels in the United States. In most of the previous acquisitions, Becker took over operations with poor profitability and low morale.

Becker is a strong believer in empowerment. He expects employees to go beyond guidelines/standards to consider guest needs on a case by case basis. That is, employees must be guest-oriented at all times so they can provide excellent customer service. From his U.S. experience, Becker has found that empowerment increases employee motivation, performance, and job satisfaction, all of which contribute to the hotel's profitability and customer service ratings. Soon after becoming general manager of the Regency Grand, Becker introduced the practice of empowerment to replicate the successes that he had achieved back home.

The Regency Grand hotel has been very profitable since it opened 15 years ago. The employees have always worked according to management's instructions. Their responsibility was to ensure that the instructions from their managers were carried out diligently and conscientiously. Innovation and creativity were discouraged under the previous management. Indeed, employees were punished for their mistakes and discouraged from trying out ideas that had not been approved by management. As a result, employees were afraid to be innovative and to take risks.

Becker met with the Regency's managers and department heads to explain that empowerment would be introduced in the hotel. He told them that employees would be empowered with decision-making authority so that they could use their initiative, creativity, and judgment to satisfy guest needs or handle problems effectively and efficiently. However, he stressed that the more complex issues and decisions were to be referred to superiors, who were to coach and assist rather than provide direct orders. Furthermore, Becker stressed that mistakes were allowed but the same mistakes would not be tolerated more than twice. He advised his managers and department heads not to discuss minor issues or problems with him and not to consult with him about minor decisions. Nevertheless, he told them that they were to discuss important/major issues and decisions with him. He concluded the meeting by asking for feedback. Several managers and department heads told him that they liked the idea and would support it, while others simply nodded their heads. Becker was pleased with the response, and was eager to have his plan implemented.

In the past, the Regency had emphasized administrative control, resulting in many bureaucratic procedures throughout the organization. For example, the front counter employees needed to seek approval from their manager before they could upgrade guests to another category of room. The front counter manager would then have to write and submit a report to the general manager justifying the upgrade. Soon after his meeting with the managers, Becker reduced the number of bureaucratic rules at the Regency and allocated more decision-making authority to front-line employees. This action upset those who had previously had decision-making power over these issues. As a result, several of these employees left the hotel.

Becker also began spending a large portion of his time observing and interacting with the employees at the front desk, lobby, restaurants, and various departments. This direct interaction with Becker helped many employees to understand what he wanted and expected of them. However, the employees had a lot of difficulty trying to distinguish between a major and minor issue or decision. More often than not, supervisors would reverse employee decisions by stating that they were major issues requiring management approval. Employees who displayed initiative and made good decisions in satisfying the needs of the guests rarely received any positive feedback from their supervisors. Eventually, most of these employees lost confidence in making decisions, and reverted back to relying on their superiors for decision making.

Not long after the practice of empowerment was implemented, Becker realized that his subordinates were consulting him more frequently than before. Most of them came to him with minor issues and consulted with him on minor decisions. He had to spend most of his time attending to his subordinates. Soon he began to feel very frustrated and exhausted, and often would tell his secretary that "unless the hotel is on fire, don't let anyone disturb me."

Becker thought that the practice of empowerment would benefit the overall performance of the hotel. However, contrary to his expectations, the business and overall performance of the hotel began to deteriorate. There were an increasing number of guest complaints. In the past, the hotel had minimal guest complaints. Now there was a significant number of formal written complaints every month. Many other guests voiced their dissatisfaction to hotel employees. The number of mistakes made by employees had increased. Becker was very upset when he realized that two of the local newspapers and an overseas newspaper had published negative feedback on the hotel on service standards. He was most distressed when an international travel magazine had voted the hotel as "one of Asia's nightmare hotels."

The stress levels of the employees continuously mounted after the introduction of the practice of empowerment. Absenteeism due to illness was increasing at an alarming rate. In addition, the employee turnover rate had reached an all-time high. The good working relationships that had been established under the old management had been severely strained. The employees were no longer united and supportive of each other. They were quick to point fingers at or to backstab one another when mistakes were made and when problems occurred.

Discussion Questions

1. Identify the symptoms indicating that problems exist in this case.

2. Diagnose the problems in this case using organizational behaviour concepts.*

3. Recommend solutions that overcome or minimize the problems and symptoms in this case.

*Your instructor might restrict this case analysis to topics in this chapter, or may ask you to consider other topics in this book to analyze this case.

Note: This case is based on true events, but the industry and names have been changed.

TEAM EXERCISE 6.2

IS STUDENT WORK ENRICHED?

Purpose   This exercise is designed to help students learn how to measure the motivational potential of jobs and to evaluate the extent that jobs should be further enriched.

Instructions   Being a student is like having a job in several ways. You have tasks to perform and someone (such as your instructor) oversees your work. Although few people want to be students most of their lives (the pay is too low!), it may be interesting to determine how enriched your job is as a student.

- *Step 1*: Students are placed into teams (preferably 4 or 5 people).
- *Step 2*: Working alone, each student completes both sets of measures in this exercise. Then,

using the guidelines below, they individually calculate the score for the five core job characteristics as well as the overall motivating potential score for the job.

- *Step 3*: Members of each team compare their individual results. The group should identify differences of opinion for each core job characteristic. They should also note which core job characteristics have the lowest scores and recommend how these scores could be increased.
- *Step 4*: The entire class will now meet to discuss the results of the exercise. The instructor may ask some teams to present their comparisons and recommendations for a particular core job characteristic.

Job Diagnostic Survey							
Circle the number on the right that best describes student work.	**Very Little** ▼		**Moderately** ▼			**Very Much** ▼	
1. To what extent does student work permit you to decide on your own how to go about doing the work?	1	2	3	4	5	6	7
2. To what extent does student work involve doing a whole or identifiable piece of work, rather than a small portion of the overall work process?	1	2	3	4	5	6	7
3. To what extent does student work require you to do many different things, using a variety of your skills/talents?	1	2	3	4	5	6	7
4. To what extent are the results of your work as a student likely to significantly affect the lives and well-being of other people (e.g., within your school, your family, society)?	1	2	3	4	5	6	7
5. To what extent does working on student activities provide information about your performance?	1	2	3	4	5	6	7

Job Diagnostic Survey (cont.)

Circle the number on the right that best describes student work.	Very Inaccurate ▼			Uncertain ▼			Very Accurate ▼
6. Being a student requires me to use a number of complex and high-level skills	1	2	3	4	5	6	7
7. Student work is arranged so that I do NOT have the chance to do an entire piece of work from beginning to end.	7	6	5	4	3	2	1
8. Doing the work required of students provides many chances for me to figure out how well I am doing.	1	2	3	4	5	6	7
9. The work students must do is quite simple and repetitive.	7	6	5	4	3	2	1
10. The work of a student is one where a lot of other people can be affected by how well the work gets done.	1	2	3	4	5	6	7
11. Student work denies me any chance to use my personal initiative or judgment in carrying out the work.	7	6	5	4	3	2	1
12. Student work provides me the chance to completely finish the pieces of work I begin.	1	2	3	4	5	6	7
13. Doing student work by itself provides very few clues about whether or not I am performing well.	7	6	5	4	3	2	1
14. As a student, I have considerable opportunity for independence and freedom in how I do the work.	1	2	3	4	5	6	7
15. The work I perform as a student is NOT very significant or important in the broader scheme of things.	7	6	5	4	3	2	1

Source: Adapted from the Job Diagnostic Survey, developed by J. R. Hackman and G. R. Oldham. The authors have released any copyright ownership of this scale (see J. R. Hackman and G. Oldham, *Work Redesign* (Reading, MA: Addison-Wesley, 1980), p. 275).

Calculating The Motivating Potential Score

Scoring Core Job Characteristics: Use the following set of calculations to estimate the motivating potential score for the job of being a student. Use your answers from the Job Diagnostic Survey that you completed above.

Skill Variety (SV)
$$\frac{\text{Question } 3 + 6 + 9 = \underline{\quad\quad}}{3}$$

Task Identity (TI)
$$\frac{\text{Question } 2 + 7 + 12 = \underline{\quad\quad}}{3}$$

Task Significance (TS)
$$\frac{\text{Question } 4 + 10 + 15 = \underline{\quad\quad}}{3}$$

Autonomy
$$\frac{\text{Question } 1 + 11 + 14 = \underline{\quad\quad}}{3}$$

Job Feedback
$$\frac{\text{Question } 5 + 8 + 13 = \underline{\quad\quad}}{3}$$

Calculating Motivating Potential Score (MPS): Use the following formula and the results above to calculate the motivating potential score. Notice that skill variety, task identity, and task significance are averaged before being multiplied by the score for autonomy and job feedback.

$$\left(\frac{SV + TI + TS}{3}\right) \times \text{Autonomy} \times \text{Job Feedback}$$

$$\left(\frac{\_\_ + \_\_ + \_\_}{3}\right) + \_\_\_\_ + \_\_\_\_ = \_\_\_\_$$

SELF-ASSESSMENT EXERCISE | 6.3

WHAT IS YOUR ATTITUDE TOWARD MONEY?

Purpose This exercise is designed to help you to understand the types of attitudes toward money and to assess your attitude toward money.

Instructions Read each of the statements below and circle the response that you believe best reflects your position regarding each statement. Then use the scoring key in Appendix B to calculate your re-sults. This exercise is completed alone so students can assess themselves honestly without concerns of social comparison. However, class discussion will focus on the meaning of money, including the dimensions measured here and other aspects of money that may have an influence on behaviour in the workplace.

Money Attitude Scale

To what extent do you agree or disagree that. . .	Strongly Disagree ▼	Disagree ▼	Neutral ▼	Agree ▼	Strongly Agree ▼
1. I sometimes purchase things because I know they will impress other people.	1	2	3	4	5
2. I regularly put money aside for the future.	1	2	3	4	5
3. I tend to get worried about decisions involving money.	1	2	3	4	5
4. I believe that financial wealth is one of the most important signs of a person's success.	1	2	3	4	5
5. I keep a close watch on how much money I have.	1	2	3	4	5
6. I feel nervous when I don't have enough money.	1	2	3	4	5
7. I tend to show more respect to people who are wealthier than I am.	1	2	3	4	5
8. I follow a careful financial budget.	1	2	3	4	5
9. I worry about being financially secure.	1	2	3	4	5
10. I sometimes boast about my financial wealth or how much money I make.	1	2	3	4	5
11. I keep track of my investments and financial wealth.	1	2	3	4	5
12. I usually say "I can't afford it," even when I can afford something.	1	2	3	4	5

Sources: Adapted from J.A. Roberts and C.J. Sepulveda, "Demographics and Money Attitudes: A Test of Yamauchi and Templer's (1982) Money Attitude Scale in Mexico," *Personality and Individual Differences*, 27 (July 1999), pp. 19–35; K. Yamauchi and D. Templer, "The Development of a Money Attitudes Scale," *Journal of Personality Assessment*, 46 (1982), pp. 522–528.

ASSESSING YOUR SELF-LEADERSHIP

 Go to the Student CD for the interactive version of this exercise.

Purpose This exercise is designed to help you understand self-leadership concepts and to assess your self-leadership tendencies.

Instructions Indicate the extent to which each statement in this instrument describes you very well or does not describe you at all. Complete each item honestly to get the best estimate of your level of overall self-leadership as well as scores on each of the subscales.

STUDENT EMPOWERMENT SCALE

 Go to the Student CD for the interactive version of this exercise.

Purpose This exercise is designed to help you understand the dimensions of empowerment and to assess your level of empowerment as student.

Instructions Empowerment is a concept that applies to people in a variety of situations. This instrument is specifically adapted to your position as a student at this college or university. Indicate the extent to which you agree or disagree with each statement in this instrument, then request the results, which provide an overall score as well as scores on each of the four dimensions of empowerment. Complete each item honestly to get the best estimate of your level of empowerment.

Online LearningCentre with POWERWEB After studying the preceding material, be sure to check out our Online Learning Centre at

www.mcgrawhill.ca/college/mcshane

for more in-depth information and interactivities that correspond to this chapter.

CHAPTER 7

Work-Related Stress and Stress Management

Learning Objectives

AFTER READING THIS CHAPTER, YOU SHOULD BE ABLE TO:

- Define stress and describe the stress experience.

- Outline the stress process from stressors to consequences.

- Identify the different types of stressors in the workplace.

- Explain why a stressor might produce different stress levels in two people.

- Discuss the physiological, psychological, and behavioural effects of stress.

- Identify five ways to manage workplace stress.

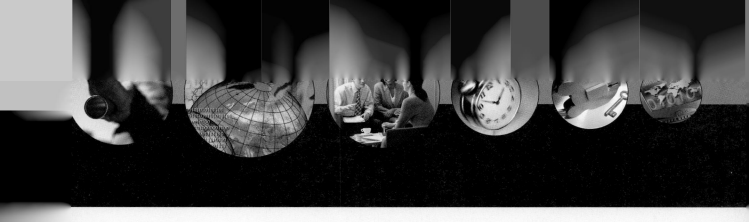

Sylvia Noreen thought that working at a small hospital in Prince Edward Island would reduce the stress she had experienced as a nurse in Ontario for 17 years. Instead, she discovered that Stewart Memorial Hospital nurses in Tyne Valley also experience unacceptable stress levels due to budget cuts and staff shortages. "There can be a lot of demands made on you," says Noreen. "The workload can get quite strenuous at times." With no vacations during her first year at Stewart, Noreen's scheduled days off were precious time to recharge her batteries. Unfortunately, those moments were fewer than she had hoped. "We're faced with being called back on our days off," Noreen says. "It is trying at times."

Canadian nurses and other health care workers are feeling some of the highest levels of stress and burnout of any occupation across the country. With Montreal-area emergency rooms filled to 167 percent, nurses at St. Luc Hospital in Montreal recently walked out twice briefly to protest the work overload. "There is exhaustion and the inability of five to do the work of eight, or 12 to do the work of 20," said Jennie Skene, president of the Quebec nurses' union.

The problem isn't just overwork, say some nurses; it's the inability to achieve the minimum standards of professional care that nurses set for themselves. "Most people went into nursing because they care about the patient, and you can't give the care you want to give," complains a nurse in Ontario. "So I think that's the biggest thing why people get burnt out and don't care as much."

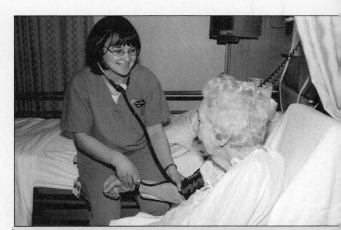

Amanda Coffin, shown here at the Queen Elizabeth Hospital in Charlottetown, just recently became a registered nurse, but is already feeling the stress of nurse shortages. *Jim Day, Charlottetown Guardian.*

Amanda Coffin, who graduated from nursing at the University of Prince Edward Island less than one year ago, has already discovered that her profession suffers stress from underfunding and nurse shortages. "It is going to get worse before it gets better is what I hear from other staff,'" says Coffin, who has witnessed two wards close at the Queen Elizabeth Hospital in Charlottetown where she works. "It's stressful because it was always constant moving of the patients."[1]

www.cna-nurses.ca

Nursing is a stressful job that has both short- and long-term effects on employees in this profession. But work-related stress is becoming an epidemic in almost every occupation in Canada. According to a recent survey, 41 percent of Canadians experience more stress than almost any other country among the 15 OECD members in the study. A Conference Board of Canada survey reports a similar level of stress (46 percent) due to the challenges of balancing work and family demands, nearly double the rate reported a decade earlier (27 percent). Another study, sponsored by the Canadian Heart and Stroke Foundation, reported that almost one-third of employees regularly have difficulty coping with the demands of their jobs.[2]

Chronic work-related stress is not just a Canadian affliction. Over half of American employees say they work under a great deal of stress. Japan's Institute of Life and Living reports that 68 percent of Japanese often feel worried and anxious, up from 37 percent a decade earlier. Nearly two-thirds of Australian employees say they are under extreme stress at work. An international study reported that people born after 1955 are up to three times as likely to experience stress-related disorders as were their grandparents. At the Escorts Heart Institute in Delhi, India, routine cardiac screenings indicate that most executives are in the advanced stages of stress. "Corporate India is finally waking up to the fact that a lot of human potential is being drained away because of stress and burnout," says Shekhar Bajaj, CEO of the Indian consumer electronics manufacturer Bajaj Electricals.[3]

In this chapter, we look at the dynamics of work-related stress and how to manage it. The chapter begins by describing the stress experience. Next, the causes and consequences of stress are examined, along with the factors that cause some people to experience stress when others do not. The final section of this chapter looks at ways to manage work-related stress from either an organizational or individual perspective.

WHAT IS STRESS?

stress

An individual's adaptive response to a situation that is perceived as challenging or threatening to the person's well-being.

Stress is an adaptive response to a situation that is perceived as challenging or threatening to a person's well-being.[4] As we shall see, stress is the person's reaction to a situation, not the situation itself. Moreover, we experience stress when something is perceived to interfere with our well-being, that is, with our innate drives and need fulfillment. Stress has both psychological and physiological dimensions. Psychologically, people perceive a situation and interpret it as challenging or threatening. This cognitive appraisal leads to a set of physiological responses, such as higher blood pressure, sweaty hands, and faster heart beat.

We often hear about stress as a negative consequence of modern living. People are stressed from overwork, job insecurity, information overload, and the increasing pace of life. These events produce *distress*—the degree of physiological, psychological, and behavioural deviation from healthy functioning.[5] There is also a positive side of stress, called *eustress*, that refers to the healthy, positive, constructive outcome of stressful events and the stress response. Eustress is the stress experience in moderation, enough to activate and motivate people so they can achieve goals, change their environments, and succeed in life's challenges.[6] In other words, we need some stress to survive. However, most research focuses on distress, because it is a significant concern in organizational settings. Employees frequently experience enough stress to hurt their job performance and increase their risk of mental and physical health problems. Consequently, our discussion will focus more on distress than on eustress.

General Adaptation Syndrome

The stress experience was first documented fifty years ago by Dr. Hans Selye, the Montreal-based pioneer in stress research.[7] Selye determined that people have a fairly consistent physiological response to stressful situations. This response, called the **general adaptation syndrome,** provides an automatic defence system to help us cope with environmental demands. Exhibit 7.1 illustrates the three stages of the general adaptation syndrome: alarm, resistance, and exhaustion. The line in this exhibit shows the individual's energy and ability to cope with the stressful situation.

Alarm reaction   In the alarm reaction stage, the perception of a threatening or challenging situation causes the brain to send a biochemical message to various parts of the body, resulting in an increased respiration rate, blood pressure, heartbeat, muscle tension, and other physiological responses. The individual's energy level and coping effectiveness initially decrease in response to the initial shock. Extreme shock, however, may result in incapacity or death because the body is unable to generate enough energy quickly enough. In most situations, the alarm reaction alerts the person to the environmental condition and prepares the body for the resistance stage.

Resistance   A person's ability to cope with the environmental demand rises above a normal state during the resistance stage because the body has activated various biochemical, psychological, and behavioural mechanisms. For example, we have a higher than normal level of adrenaline during this stage, which gives the body more energy to overcome or remove the source of stress. However, our resistance is directed to only one or two environmental demands, so that we become more vulnerable to other sources of stress. This explains why people are more likely to catch a cold or other illness when they have been working under pressure.

Exhaustion   People have a limited resistance capacity and, if the source of stress persists, they will eventually move into the exhaustion stage as this capacity diminishes. In most work situations, the general adaptation syndrome process

general adaptation syndrome

A model of the stress experience, consisting of three stages: alarm reaction, resistance, and exhaustion.

EXHIBIT 7.1

Selye's general adaptation syndrome

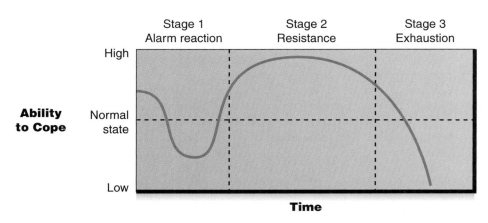

Source: Adapted from H. Selye, *The Stress of Life*, (New York: McGraw-Hill, 1956).

Intense bartering and the high stakes of a wrong decision take their toll on energy traders. Many wear out after just 10 years. "The money is so good, it's worth being obsessed and not taking vacations," says Robin Conner, a 30-year-old trader at Reliant Energy in Houston, where this photo was taken. "But it can wear you out." Axia Energy trader Ken Merideth has the same feelings. "I am so burned out at the end of the day, I don't even want to make a decision about what to eat for dinner," he admits.[9] Based on your knowledge of the general adaptation syndrome, why would these energy traders "wear out" after 10 years? Copyright © Smiley N. Pool/The Houston Chronicle. **www.reliant.com**

ends long before total exhaustion. Employees resolve tense situations before the destructive consequences of stress become manifest, or they withdraw from the stressful situation, rebuild their survival capabilities, and return later to the stressful environment with renewed energy. However, people who frequently experience the general adaptation syndrome have increased risk of long-term physiological and psychological damage.[8]

The general adaptation syndrome describes the stress experience, but this is only part of the picture. To effectively manage work-related stress, we must understand its causes and consequences as well as individual differences in the stress experience.

STRESSORS: THE CAUSES OF STRESS

Stressors, the causes of stress, include any environmental conditions that place a physical or emotional demand on the person.[10] There are numerous stressors in organizational settings and other life activities. Exhibit 7.2 lists the four main types of work-related stressors: interpersonal, role-related, task control, and organizational and physical environment stressors.

Interpersonal Stressors

Among the four types of stressors, interpersonal stressors are likely the most pervasive in the contemporary workplace. The trend toward teamwork generates interpersonal stressors because employees must interact more with co-workers. Bad bosses, office politics, and various types of interpersonal conflict also take their toll on employees. For example, one recent study found that employees immediately experienced stress from organizational politics events.[11] Other interpersonal stressors include sexual harassment, workplace violence, and bullying.

Sexual harassment   Nicole Curling's new job with Victoria Tea Company in Toronto was extremely stressful. The stress wasn't from long hours or difficult work; it was from her boss's persistent attempts to kiss and fondle her. The Ontario Human Rights Commission awarded Curling $40,000 in emotional distress damages, but the harassment and subsequent legal battle were overwhelming. "It's a gruelling, gruelling experience," she says.[12]

Nicole Curling has experienced the stress of **sexual harassment**—unwelcome conduct of a sexual nature that detrimentally affects the work environment or leads to adverse job-related consequences for its victims. According to Statistics Canada, nearly one in every four Canadian women has been sexually harassed on the job, mostly by co-workers and supervisors. Sexual harassment includes situations where a person's employment or job performance is conditional on

stressors
The causes of stress, including any environmental conditions that place a physical or emotional demand on the person.

sexual harassment
Unwelcome conduct of a sexual nature that detrimentally affects the work environment or leads to adverse job-related consequences for its victims.

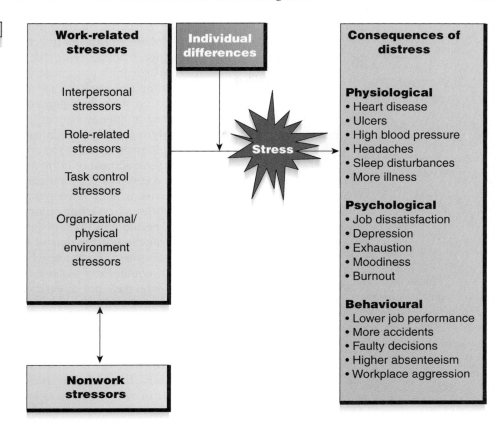

EXHIBIT 7.2

Causes and
consequences
of stress

unwanted sexual relations (called *quid pro quo*). However, the Supreme Court of Canada and other legal decision makers have also concluded that sexual harassment occurs in a *hostile work environment*, that is, when sexual conduct (such as posting pornographic material) unreasonably interferes with an individual's work performance or creates an intimidating, hostile, or offensive working environment. This leads to complications—and interpersonal stress—because men have a narrower interpretation than women do over what constitutes hostile work environment sexual harassment.[13]

Canadian corporate leaders increasingly recognize that sexual harassment (and other forms of harassment) is a serious concern. But harassment is more than a legal issue; it is a serious interpersonal stressor.[14] Victims of sexual harassment experience trauma from quid pro quo harassment and tense co-worker relations in a hostile work environment. Moreover, as Nicole Curling discovered, they are expected to endure more stress while these incidents are investigated. This is particularly true in Japan and other countries where women who complain of harassment are sometimes stigmatized by friends and co-workers. "Companies don't want to hire 'dangerous women' who make a fuss about sexual harassment," says Moeko Tanaka, the pen name of a Japanese woman who won a case of harassment against a prefecture governor.[15]

Workplace violence The most serious interpersonal stressor is the rising wave of physical violence in the workplace.[16] We immediately think about the United

States, where 1,000 employees are murdered on the job each year and 2 million others experience lesser forms of violence.[17] But the International Labour Organization reports that Canadian employees are more at risk with the fourth highest incidence of workplace assault and sexual harassment among the 32 countries studied. The report discovered that one percent of American women were assaulted in the workplace, compared with four percent of Canadian women. Canadian men had a slightly higher incidence of workplace assault than their U.S. counterparts. One recent study reported that almost all emergency department staff at St. Paul's Hospital in Vancouver have experienced physical assault, 55 percent of them within the past year. Almost one-third of these employees said they experienced extreme stress as a result of the incident.[18]

Employees who experience violence usually have symptoms of severe distress after the traumatic event.[19] A recent Canadian study reported that both workplace violence and sexual harassment generate emotions of fear and anxiety. It is not uncommon for primary victims to take long-term disability. Some never return to work. Workplace violence is also a stressor to those who observe the violence. After a serious workplace incident, counsellors assist many employees, not just the direct victims. Even employees who have not directly experienced or observed violence may show signs of stress if they work in high-risk jobs.

Workplace bullying   Susan Morgan had a relatively trouble-free job as beverage room manager at the Marine Pub in Coquitlam, B.C., until the pub owners hired a new kitchen manager, Gus Mellios. Over the next two years, Morgan and other staff experienced frequent verbal abuse from Mellios, including rudeness, yelling, and swearing whenever food was returned. The owners knew about these tirades, but were either silent or sided with Mellios. Morgan quit, sued the owners, and eventually won her case.[20]

Canadian courts have reinforced the view that employers have an obligation to treat employees with civility, decency, respect, and dignity. In other words, Canadians have a right to a workplace free of bullying. **Workplace bullying** refers to offensive, intimidating, or humiliating behaviour that degrades, ridicules, or insults another person at work.[21] Research indicates that most victims experience stress and its consequences following incidents of bullying. They also have more absenteeism and, back on the job, have impaired decision making, lower work performance, and more work errors.[22]

A recent Canadian study found that 12 percent of the public and service sector employees surveyed experienced workplace incivility, including rude behaviour, name-calling, and yelling. Five percent of hospital workers in Finland and 40 percent of federal court employees in Michigan say they have experienced bullying. People with higher authority are more likely to engage in bullying or incivility toward employees in lower positions. Women are more likely than men to be targets of bullying.[23] Bullying has become enough of a concern that Scandinavian countries have passed laws against it.

Some organizations have also taken steps to minimize the incidence of incivility. For example, Quaker Oats explicitly advises in its code of conduct that employees must treat each other with consideration, respect, and dignity. Past behaviour is the best predictor of future behaviour, so companies should carefully screen applicants in terms of past incidents. Feedback, particularly the 360-degree variety (see Chapter 5), lets employees know when their behaviour is out of line. Last, organizations should have a grievance, mediation, or other conflict

workplace bullying

Offensive, intimidating, or humiliating behaviour that degrades, ridicules, or insults another person at work.

resolution process that employees trust when they become victims of workplace bullying.[24]

Role-Related Stressors

Role-related stressors include conditions where employees have difficulty understanding, reconciling, or performing the various roles in their lives. Three types of role-related stressors are role conflict, role ambiguity, and work intensification. **Role conflict** refers to the degree of incongruity or incompatibility of expectations associated with the person's role.[25] Some people experience stress when they have two roles that conflict with each other (called *interrole conflict*). The nurses described in the opening story to this chapter experience interrole conflict because they struggle to maintain humanistic caring and preserve the nurse-patient relationship in a cost-efficient managed care environment controlled by others.[26] Role conflict also occurs when an employee receives contradictory messages from different people about how to perform a task (called *intrarole conflict*) or work with organizational values and work obligations that are incompatible with his or her personal values (called *person-role conflict*).[27]

Role ambiguity refers to the lack of clarity and predictability of the outcomes of one's behaviour. Role ambiguity produces low role perceptions, which we learned in Chapter 2 has a direct effect on job performance. It is also a source of stress in a variety of situations, such as joining an organization or working in a new joint venture, because task and social expectations are uncertain.[28]

Work overload   A third role-related stressor is *work overload*—working more hours and more intensely during those hours. In 1930, noted economist John Maynard Keynes predicted that by 2030 the average employee would be working a 15-hour work week. At the time, Kellogg's, the American cereal company, had switched from eight-hour to six-hour work shifts in order to employ more people during the Depression and give employees more time off.[29] But Keynes' prediction is a far cry from the number of hours employees work today. Although official paid work hours are lower than the early 1900s, total work hours have moved consistently upward over the past 20 years.

Equally significant, Canadians are working more *unofficial* hours beyond their paid hours of work. According to a recent Ipsos-Reid poll, 81 percent of white-collar employees in Canada accept business calls at home, 65 percent check their work e-mail after hours, and 59 percent check their work voice-mail after hours. A recent survey of 31,500 Canadians revealed that nearly one-quarter of employees work more than 50 hours per week, compared with only 10 percent a decade ago.[30] Some writers claim this rising workload is due to the pressure from globalization for more efficiency, and from employees' own desire to keep up with the Jones' in wealth and consumption. Whatever the cause, it has produced higher stress levels.[31] As GLOBAL Connections 7.1 describes, work overload is such a problem in Japan that death from overwork has its own name—*karoshi*.

Task-Control Stressors

One of the most important findings emerging from stress research is that employees are more stressed when they lack control over how and when they perform their tasks as well as over the pace of work activity.[32] Work is potentially more stressful

role conflict
Conflict that occurs when people face competing demands.

role ambiguity
Uncertainty about job duties, performance expectations, level of authority, and other job conditions.

Karoshi: Death by Overwork in Japan

Nobuo Miuro was under a lot of pressure from his employer to get a new restaurant ready for its launch. The interiors fitter from Tokyo worked late, sometimes until 4:30 in the morning. After one such marathon, Miuro caught a few hours of sleep, then returned for another long day. But he didn't get very far. The 47-year old suddenly took ill and keeled over while picking up his hammer and nails. He died a week later. The coroner's verdict was that Miuro died of "*karoshi*"—death by overwork.

Karoshi accounts for nearly 10,000 deaths each year in Japan. Japan's Ministry of Health found that employees worked an average of 80 hours per week for the six months prior to karoshi, rising to 100 hours per week during the last month. Research indicates that these long work hours cause an unhealthy lifestyle, such as smoking, poor eating habits, lack of physical exercise, and sleeplessness. This results in weight gain which, along with stressful working conditions, damages the cardiovascular system and leads to strokes and heart attacks.

Karoshi came to the public spotlight in the 1970s when Japan's economy was booming, but the country's current recession is making matters worse. Companies are laying off employees and loading the extra work onto those who remain. Performance-based expecta-tions are replacing lifetime employment guarantees, putting further pressure on employees to work long hours. Many also blame Japan's "samurai spirit" culture, which idolizes long work hours as the ultimate symbol of company loyalty and personal fortitude. "Being exhausted is considered a virtue," explains a Japanese psychiatrist.

So far, only 17 percent of Japanese firms offer over-stressed employees some form of counselling. However, the Japanese government has launched an advertising campaign encouraging people to call a "karoshi hotline" for anonymous help. The families of deceased workaholics, including Nobuo Miuro's relatives, are also taking action by suing the employers for lack of due care.

Sources: Y. Liu, "Overtime Work, Insufficient Sleep, and Risk of Non-Fatal Acute Myocardial Infarction in Japanese Men," *Occupational and Environmental Medicine*, 59 (July 2002), pp. 447–51; D. Ibison, "Overwork Kills record Number of Japanese," *Financial Times*, May 29, 2002, p. 12; "Trend of Caring for Employees Waning among Japan's Companies," *Japan Weekly Monitor*, May 14, 2001; C. Fukushi, "Workplace Stress Taking Toll on Women's Health," *Daily Yomiuri*, April 21, 2001; S. Efron, "Jobs Take a Deadly Toll on Japanese," *Los Angeles Times*, April 12, 2000, p. A1; M. Millett, "Death Of A Salaryman," *The Age (Melbourne)*, April 11, 2000, p. 15; E. Addley and L. Barton, "Who Said Hard Work Never Hurt Anybody?" *The Guardian (UK)*, March 13, 2001.
www.workhealth.org

when it is paced by a machine, involves monitoring equipment, or the work schedule is controlled by someone else. A recent Statistics Canada study of 12,000 Canadians reported that employees in production, sales, and service jobs have higher psychological stress because of their lack of work control.[33]

Organizational and Physical Environment Stressors

Organizational and physical environment stressors come in many forms. Organizations create stress by altering the psychological contract (see Chapter 4), reducing job security, and restructuring and downsizing employment. "When you announce downsizing, you immediately get higher levels of stress, tension and aggression," says Gerry Smith, vice-president of organizational health for Warren Shepell Consultants in Vancouver. "You find more interpersonal conflicts at work between employees and management and there's a reduction in services and friendliness to customers and clients."[34]

Some stressors are found in the physical work environment, such as excessive noise, poor lighting, and safety hazards. For example, a study of textile workers in a noisy plant found that their levels of stress measurably decreased when supplied with ear protectors. Another study reported that clerical employees experience significantly higher stress levels in noisy open offices than in quiet areas.[35] People working in dangerous work environments also experience potentially higher stress levels.

Work–Nonwork Stressors

The stress model shown earlier in Exhibit 7.2 has a two-way arrow, indicating that stressors from work spill over into nonwork and vice versa. There are three types of these work–nonwork stressors: time-based, strain-based, and role-based conflict.[37]

Time-based conflict   Jennifer Kelly knows all about the stress of trying to balance time at work with family. The graphic designer works 52 hours a week, sleeps about six hours a night and, in her words, is "frazzled and tired." With clients all over the world, Kelly has a 24/7 schedule, leaving little time for family. "When I'm with them (the kids), I'm so tired sometimes that I can't take them anywhere or do anything fun," admits Kelly.[38]

Jennifer Kelly has to contend with *time-based conflict*—the challenge of balancing the time demanded by work with family and other nonwork activities. This stressor is particularly noticeable in employees who hold strong family values and weakest in people whose values emphasize a work-life imbalance.[39] Time-based conflict relates back to the work overload stressor described earlier. As Canadians work longer hours (and more intensely during those hours), they have little time or energy left for themselves and family. For instance, a Conference Board of Canada study reported that 46 percent of employees reported moderate to high stress due to work-life conflict, compared to 27 percent in a survey a decade earlier.[40]

Inflexible work schedules, business travel, and rotating shift schedules also take a heavy toll because they prevent employees from effectively juggling work and nonwork.[41] Time-based conflict is more acute for women than for men because housework and childcare represent a "second shift" for many women in dual career families.[42] Until men increase their contribution to homemaking and business learns to accommodate the new social order, many of these "supermoms" will continue to experience superstress.

Ken Wiley, a faller in the Queen Charlotte Islands, knows that logging is a risky business. Wiley got badly cut when his saw kicked back on him, and broke his cheekbone when hit by a falling tree. Both his father and grandfather died in logging accidents, and this photo shows him wearing a hockey jersey worn by a fellow logger killed recently. Safety experts say the death toll could get worse because organizational change and uncertainty are creating more stress. "There is job loss and a complete change in the way companies do business," says Cary White, a safety officer with the B. C. Workers' Compensation Board. "[T]hat is a major contributing factor in accidents . . . the person has so many things on their mind they had difficulty concentrating on the job."[36] What can forest products companies do to minimize deaths and injuries due to organizational stressors? *Mark van Manen/Vancouver Sun*
www.worksafebc.com

Strain-based conflict   *Strain-based conflict* occurs when stress from one domain spills over into the other. Relationship problems, financial difficulties, and loss of a loved one usually top the list of nonwork stressors. New responsibilities, such as marriage, birth of a child, and a mortgage are also stressful to most of us. Stress at work also spills over to an employee's personal life and often becomes the foundation of stressful relations with family and friends. In support of this, one study found that fathers who experience stress at work engage in dysfunctional parenting behaviours which then lead to their children having behaviour problems in school.[43]

Role behaviour conflict   A third work–nonwork stressor, called *role behaviour conflict*, occurs when people are expected to enact different work and nonwork roles. People who act logically and impersonally at work have difficulty switching to a more compassionate behavioural style in their personal lives. For example, one study found that police officers were unable to shake off their professional role when they left the job. This was confirmed by their spouses, who reported that the officers would handle their children in the same manner as they would people in their job.[44]

Stress and Occupations

Several studies have tried to identify which jobs have more stressors than others.[45] These lists are not in complete agreement, but Exhibit 7.3 identifies a representative sample of jobs and their relative level of stressors. You should view this information with some caution, however. One problem with rating occupations in terms of their stress levels is that a particular occupation may have considerably different tasks and job environments across organizations and societies. A police officer's job may be less stressful in a small town, for instance, than in a large city where crime rates are higher and the organizational hierarchy more formal.

Another important point to remember when looking at Exhibit 7.3 is that a major stressor to one person is insignificant to another. In this respect, we must be careful not to conclude that people in high-stressor occupations actually experience higher stress than people in other occupations. Some jobs expose people to more serious stressors, but careful selection and training can result in stress levels no different from those experienced by people in other jobs. The next section discusses individual differences in stress.

EXHIBIT 7.3   Stressors in occupations

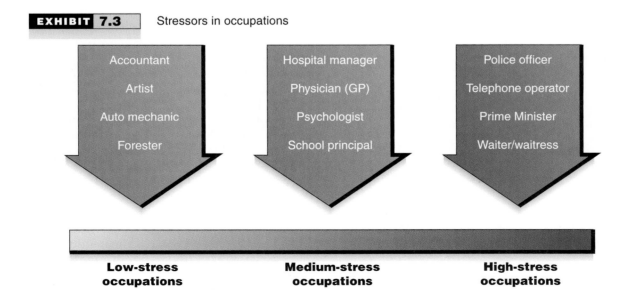

Low-stress occupations	Medium-stress occupations	High-stress occupations
Accountant	Hospital manager	Police officer
Artist	Physician (GP)	Telephone operator
Auto mechanic	Psychologist	Prime Minister
Forester	School principal	Waiter/waitress

INDIVIDUAL DIFFERENCES IN STRESS

Exhibit 7.2, shown earlier in this chapter, indicated that individual characteristics moderate the extent to which people experience stress or exhibit a specific stress outcome in a given situation. Two people may be exposed to the same stressor, such as having too many deadlines, yet they experience different stress levels or stress symptoms.[46]

People exposed to the same stressors might have different stress symptoms for three reasons. First, each of us perceives the same situation differently. People with high self-efficacy, for instance, are less likely to experience stress consequences in that situation because the stressor is less threatening.[47] Self-efficacy refers to a person's belief that he or she has the ability, motivation, and situational factors to complete a task successfully (see Chapter 3). Similarly, some people have personalities that make them more optimistic, whereas others are more pessimistic (see Chapter 4). Those with pessimistic dispositions tend to develop more stress symptoms, probably because they interpret the situation in a negative light.[48]

A second reason why some people have more stress symptoms than others in the same situation is that people have different threshold levels of resistance to a stressor. Younger employees generally experience fewer and less severe stress symptoms than older employees because they have a larger store of energy to cope with high stress levels. This explains why exercise and healthy lifestyles are discussed later in this chapter as ways to manage stress. As we shall learn later, people who exercise regularly and have healthy lifestyles (e.g., diet, sleep) are also less likely to experience negative stress outcomes.

A third reason why people may experience the same level of stress and yet exhibit different stress outcomes is that they use different coping strategies.[49] Some employees tend to ignore the stressor, hoping it will go away. This is usually an ineffective approach, which would explain why they experience higher stress levels. There is some evidence (although still inconclusive) that women cope with stress better than men. Specifically, women are more likely to seek emotional support from others in stressful situations, whereas men try to change the stressor or use less effective coping mechanisms.[50] However, we must remember that this is not true for all women or men.

Work Stress and Type A/Type B Behaviour Pattern

For several years, scholars proposed that people with a **Type B behaviour pattern** experience less stress in the same situation than people with a **Type A behaviour pattern**. Type A people are hard-driving, competitive individuals with a strong sense of time urgency. They tend to be impatient, lose their temper, talk rapidly, and interrupt others during conversations.[51] In contrast, Type B people are less competitive and less concerned about time limitations. They tend to work steadily, take a relaxed approach to life, and be even-tempered. Although scholars are now less convinced about the importance of Type A/Type B behaviour pattern in understanding work-related stress, some research continues to report that Type A people experience higher job stress.[52]

Work Stress and Workaholism

More than 30 years after the term was coined, workaholism has gained attention in the literature on stress and other topics. Scholars are still debating the precise

type A behaviour pattern
A behaviour pattern associated with people having premature coronary heart disease; type As tend to be impatient, lose their temper, talk rapidly, and interrupt others.

type B behavior puattern
A behaviour pattern of people with low risk of coronary heart disease; type Bs tend to work steadily, take a relaxed approach to life, and be even-tempered.

How Workaholic are Canadians?

Staring out from the cover of *Confessions of a Street Addict*, James Cramer looks like a dangerous man. In fact, he admits that he was an addict. "I had many of the problems you see in addicts—they can't stay away, they need more and more, they love the adrenaline and then it takes control of their lives," says Cramer.

James Cramer's "street" is Wall Street and his addiction is to his work. The cofounder of TheStreet.com and Smart Money magazine is a repentant workaholic who had the symptoms that scholars have associated with this affliction. He was obsessed with market trades, became a tyrant in the office whenever a stock went south, and lost touch with his family. Even casual gatherings were evaluated by whether they added value to his work. "You might get together with me for a drink and I would be thinking 'Why am I wasting my time?'" Cramer recalls.

How many Canadians are as workaholic as James Cramer? The question is difficult to answer because of disagreement among scholars regarding definition and measurement of workaholism. According to a recent Statistics Canada study, 27 percent of adult Canadians say they are workaholics. Men and women about equally identify themselves as workaholics. Not surprisingly, over half of employees working more than 60 hours per week consider themselves workaholics. Those who report being workaholics in the Statistics Canada study worry more, experience more stress, and are less happy with life (although they also say they enjoy their jobs).

The Statistics Canada study relies on a single item self-report, so probably overestimates the number of traditional workaholics in this country. A potentially better estimate comes from a study by Professor Ron Burke at York University of over 500 MBA alumni. Relying on academic conceptualization and measurement, Burke was able to group respondents into the three types of workaholism. The study found that 16 percent of the MBA alumni surveyed are traditional workaholics, 19 percent are enthusiastic workaholics, and 14 percent are work enthusiasts.

Sources: A, Kemeny, "Driven to Excel: A Portrait of Canada's Workaholics," *Canadian Social Trends*, Spring 2002, pp. 2–7; J. J. Cramer, *Confessions of a Street Addict* (New York: Simon & Schuster, 2002); J. Langton, "Wall Street Made me a Monster," *Evening Standard*, May 27, 2002; R. J. Burke, "Workaholism among Women Managers: Personal and Workplace Correlates," *Journal of Managerial Psychology*, 15 (2000), pp. 520–34; R. J. Burke, "Workaholism and Extra-work Satisfactions," *International Journal of Organizational Analysis*, 7 (1999), pp. 352–64.
www.statcan.ca

---

workaholic

A person who is highly involved in work, feels compelled to work, and has a low enjoyment of work.

definition, but they generally agree that there are several components of workaholism and different types of workaholics. One type of **workaholic** fits the classic definition, namely, a person who is highly involved in work, feels compelled or driven to work because of inner pressures, and has low enjoyment at work. These stereotypic workaholics exhibit compulsive behaviour and are preoccupied with work, often to the exclusion and detriment of their health, intimate relationships, and participation in child rearing.[53]

Along with stereotypic workaholics, the academic literature identifies two other workaholic types: *enthusiastic workaholics* and *work enthusiasts*. Enthusiastic workaholics have high levels of all three components—high work involvement, drive to succeed, and work enjoyment. Work enthusiasts have high work involvement and work enjoyment, but low drive to succeed.[54] Connections 7.2 describes two estimates of the degree of workaholism in Canada.

Workaholism is relevant to our discussion of stress because traditional workaholics tend to have more prone to stress and burnout. Research has found that stereotypic workaholics tend to have a Type A behaviour pattern. They have significantly higher scores on depression, anxiety, and anger than do nonworkaholics, as well as lower job and career satisfaction. Workaholics of both sexes report more health complaints than do work enthusiasts.[55] There is still some debate whether the other forms of workaholism—enthusiastic workaholics and work enthusiasts—are good or bad for the individual and organization.

CONSEQUENCES OF DISTRESS

The general adaptation syndrome introduced at the beginning of this chapter describes how chronic stress diminishes the individual's resistance, resulting in adverse consequences for both the employee and the organization. Let's look at the main physiological, psychological, and behavioural consequences.

Physiological Consequences

Stress takes its toll on the human body.[56] Studies have found that medical students who are anxious about their exams are more susceptible to colds and other illnesses. Many people experience tension headaches due to stress. Others get muscle pain and related back problems. These physiological ailments are attributed to muscle contractions that occur when people are exposed to stressors.

Cardiovascular disease is one of the most disturbing effects of stress in modern society.[57] Strokes and heart attacks, rare a century ago, are now one of the leading causes of death among Canadian adults. Stress also influences hypertension (high blood pressure). Hypertension has decreased in recent years due to better lifestyle and medical treatment, but it remains one of the top ailments in older Canadians.[58]

Medical researchers believe that the long-term effect of stress on heart disease goes something like this: Whenever people are stressed, their blood pressure goes up and down. That frequent pressure causes injury to the blood vessel walls, which eventually makes them constrict and function abnormally. Over time, this leads to heart disease. Unfortunately, we often can't tell when we are physiologically stressed. For example, researchers have found that people think they are in a low-stress state when, in fact, their palms are sweating and their blood pressure has increased.[59]

job burnout
The process of emotional exhaustion, depersonalization, and reduced personal accomplishment resulting from prolonged exposure to stress.

Psychological Consequences

Stress produces various psychological consequences, including job dissatisfaction, moodiness, and depression.[60] Emotional fatigue is another psychological consequence of stress and is related to job burnout.

Job burnout Job burnout refers to the process of emotional exhaustion, cynicism, and reduced efficacy (lower feelings of personal accomplishment) resulting from prolonged exposure to stress.[61] The phrase "job burnout" didn't exist 40 years ago; now it's heard in everyday conversations. Job burnout is a complex process that includes the dynamics of stress, coping strategies, and stress consequences. Burnout is caused by excessive demands made on people who serve or frequently interact with others. In other words, burnout is mainly due to interpersonal and role-related stressors.[62] For this reason, it is most common in helping occupations (e.g., nurses, teachers, police officers).

© 2001 Randy Glasbergen.
www.glasbergen.com

"It's a smoke detector. The boss thinks I might be headed for a burnout."

Copyright © Randy Glasbergen. Reprinted with special permission from www.glasbergen.com

The job burnout
process

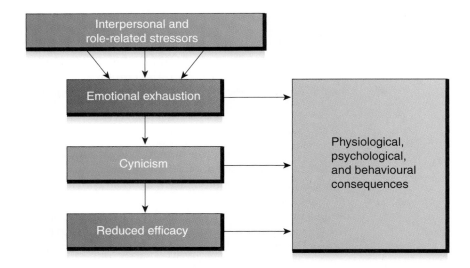

Exhibit 7.4 diagrams the relationship among the three components of job burnout. *Emotional exhaustion* is the first stage and plays a central role in the burnout process.[63] It is characterized by a lack of energy, tiredness, and a feeling that one's emotional resources are depleted. Emotional exhaustion is sometimes called *compassion fatigue* because the employee no longer feels able to give as much support and caring to clients.

Cynicism (also called *depersonalization*) follows emotional exhaustion and is identified by an indifferent attitude toward work and treating others as objects rather than people. Burned-out employees become emotionally detached from clients and cynical about the organization. This detachment goes to the point of callousness, far beyond the level of detachment normally required in helping occupations. Cynicism is also apparent when employees follow rules and regulations strictly rather than try to understand the client's needs and search for a mutually acceptable solution.

Reduced professional efficacy (also called *reduced personal accomplishment)*, the final component of job burnout, refers to feelings of diminished confidence in one's ability to perform the job well. In other words, a person's self-efficacy declines (see Chapter 3). In these situations, employees develop a sense of learned helplessness because they no longer believe that their efforts make a difference. The model shows that cynicism tends to cause reduced professional efficacy, although some experts now think lower professional efficacy and cynicism occur at the same time as a result of emotional exhaustion.[64]

Behavioural Consequences

When stress becomes distress, job performance falls and workplace accidents are more common. High stress levels impair our ability to remember information, make effective decisions, and take appropriate action.[65] You have probably experienced this in an exam or emergency work situation. You forget important information, make mistakes, and otherwise "draw a blank" under intense pressure.

Overstressed employees also tend to have higher levels of absenteeism. One reason is that stress makes people sick. The other reason is that absenteeism is a coping mechanism. At a basic level, we react to stress through fight or flight. Absenteeism is a form of flight—temporarily withdrawing from the stressful situation so that we have an opportunity to reenergize. Companies may try to minimize absenteeism, but it sometimes helps employees avoid the exhaustion stage of the stress experience (see Exhibit 7.1 earlier in this chapter).[66]

Workplace aggression Workplace aggression is more than the serious interpersonal stressor described earlier. It is also an increasingly worrisome consequence of stress.[67] Aggression represents the "fight" (instead of flight) reaction to stress. In its mildest form, employees engage in verbal conflict. They "fly off the handle" and are less likely to empathize with co-workers. Occasionally, the combination of an individual's background and workplace stressors escalate this conflict into more dangerous levels of workplace hostility.

Co-worker aggression represents a relatively small proportion of workplace violence, but these behaviours are neither random nor inconsequential. Like most forms of organizational behaviour, co-worker aggression is caused by both the person and the situation.[68] While certain individuals are more likely to be aggressive, we must also remember that employee aggression is also a consequence of extreme stress.[69] In particular, employees are more likely to engage in aggressive behaviour if they believe they have been treated unfairly, experience other forms of frustration beyond their personal control, and work in physical environments that are stressful (e.g., hot, noisy).

MANAGING WORK-RELATED STRESS

A few years ago, Mary Parniak was under a lot of pressure. The Baxter Corp. executive in Mississauga, Ontario, was involved in a messy corporate audit, faced a number of critical decisions involving ethical dilemmas, and was trying to adjust to a new boss. "I was on the brink of a stress-induced burnout," recalls Parniak. "I began to behave in ways that weren't normal for me, things like crying on the job or feeling that if one more person walked into my office I was going to scream." Fortunately, a colleague recognized the symptoms and urged Parniak to get some help before it was too late. Working with an industrial psychologist once a week for several months, Parniak learned to maintain a better balance in her life.[70]

Mary Parniak was fortunate. She was able to manage her stress before matters got worse. Unfortunately, many of us deny the existence of our stress until it is too late. This avoidance strategy creates a vicious cycle because the failure to cope with stress becomes another stressor on top of the one that created the stress in the first place. The solution is to discover the toolkit of effective stress management strategies identified in Exhibit 7.5, and to determine which ones are best for the situation.[71] As we look at each approach, keep in mind that both the organization and employees share joint responsibility for effective stress management. Moreover, managing stress often includes more than one of these strategies.

Remove the Stressor

From this list of stress management strategies, some writers argue that the *only* way companies can effectively manage stress is by removing the stressors that

EXHIBIT 7.5

Stress management
strategies

cause unnecessary tension and job burnout. Other stress management strategies may keep employees "stress-fit," but they don't solve the fundamental causes of stress.[72]

One way for organizations to manage stress is to investigate the main causes of stress in their workplace. Good Hope Hospital in the UK conducted such an audit by asking staff to complete confidential questionnaires to identify when and how they experience stress.[73] Another recommendation is to change the corporate culture and reward systems so they support a work–life balance and no longer reinforce dysfunctional workaholism. More generally, research has found that one of the most powerful ways to remove workplace stressors is to empower employees so that they have more control over their work and work environment (see Chapter 6).[74] Role-related stressors can be minimized by selecting and assigning employees to positions that match their competencies. Noise and safety risks are stressful, so improving these conditions would also go a long way to minimize stress in the workplace. Workplace bullying can be minimized through clear guidelines of behaviour and feedback for those who violate those standards.

Employees can also take an active role in removing stressors. If stress is due to ambiguous role expectations, for example, we might seek out more information from others to clarify these expectations. If a particular piece of work is too challenging, we might break it into smaller sets of tasks so that the overall project is less threatening or wearing. We can also minimize workplace violence by learning to identify early warning signs of aggression in customers and co-workers and by developing interpersonal skills that dissipate aggression.

Family-friendly and work–life initiatives   Given the high levels of work–life conflict in Canada that we read about earlier, you would think that organizations around the country are scrambling to create a family-friendly workplace that aims to improve work–life balance. Not so, according to a recent study of 31,500 Canadians, which concluded that work schedules may have deteriorated over the past decade. Many companies claim to offer a work–life balance, yet Canadians are working more hours than ever and some employees complain that much of the rhetoric doesn't match corporate practices.[75] Five of the most common work–life balance initiatives

As a new mom, Jennifer Hong (right) was eager to spend some time with her baby Kayln, so she half-jokingly asked her friend Beatrice Gautier (left) what she thought of sharing her job at Ceridian Canada Ltd. Gautier jumped at the opportunity. "It's something I'd wanted to do for years and I'd been looking for the ideal partner," says Gauthier. Today, Hong and Gautier share the same office and job, each working two or three days of the week. Both say job sharing has reduced stress and improved their lives. "In effect [Ceridian was] getting two highly skilled and motivated people for the price of one, so it was a win all round, for us, for the company and for our clients," says Hong.[77] What other activities would encourage employees at Ceridian Canada to balance their work with nonwork? *Mark van Manen/Vancouver Sun.*
www.ceridian.ca

are flexible work time, job sharing, telecommuting, personal leave, and childcare facilities.[76]

■ *Flexible work time*—Some firms are flexible about the hours, days, and amount of time employees want to work. For example, Kraft Canada's work–life program gives employees the freedom to rearrange their work schedule to accommodate family events, from attending their kids' sports activities to caring for elderly parents.[78]

■ *Job sharing*—Job sharing splits a career position between two people so they experience less time-based stress between work and family. They typically work different parts of the week with some overlapping work time in the weekly schedule to coordinate activities.[79]

■ *Telecommuting*—Chapter 1 described the increasing number of employees telecommuting. This reduces the time and stress of commuting to work and makes it easier to fulfill family obligations, such as temporarily leaving the home-office to pick the kids up from school. Research suggests that telecommuters experience a healthier work–life balance.[80] However, telecommuting may increase stress for those who crave social interaction. It also isn't a solution for child care.

■ *Personal leave programs*—Employers with strong work–life values offer extended maternity, paternity, and personal leaves to care for a new family or take advantage of a personal experience. Governments across Canada offer paid maternity leave. Increasingly, employees require personal leave to care for elderly parents who need assistance.

■ *Childcare support*—On-site child care centres have existed since World War II, when women worked in war factories. In 1964, Toronto's Riverdale Hospital became one of the first organizations in the post-war era to have a child care centre. Soon after opening the centre, the number of female applicants jumped 40 percent and absenteeism dropped significantly. Today, child care facilities are found at the National Bank of Canada, Husky Injection Molding Systems, and many other companies.[81]

Withdraw from the Stressor

Removing the stressor may be the ideal solution, but it is often not feasible. An alternative strategy is to permanently or temporarily remove employees from the stressor. Permanent withdrawal occurs when employees are transferred to jobs that better fit their competencies and values.

Temporary withdrawal strategies Temporarily withdrawing from stressors is the most frequent way employees manage stress. Nortel Networks has a relaxation

Keep the Stress-Busting Siesta in Modern Spain

Maria Jose Mateo is defying a force that has ruled Spain for centuries. The 29-year-old bank employee is trying to stay awake during the afternoon. She and many other Spaniards are giving up their siesta—a two or three-hour mid-afternoon break when employees head home for a hot meal, followed by a restful nap.

Customers in other European countries increasingly expect Spanish employees to answer the telephone throughout the day. Companies are also discouraging these long breaks to increase productivity. TotalFina, the French oil company, gives its Spanish managers and salespeople coupons for nearby fast-food outlets—a hint that they should have a power lunch, not a power nap. Commuting is also killing siestas. Employees don't have time to commute twice each day through traffic-clogged Madrid and Barcelona.

Ironically, the siesta is disappearing just when people in other countries are discovering the health benefits of a midday power nap. American studies report that the nervous system needs a long break at night and a shorter one somewhere between 2 p.m. and 5 p.m. in the afternoon. A smattering of American firms, such as Burlington Northern Santa Fe Railway, have established napping policies. Kodak, PepsiCo, IBM, and Pizza Hut offer courses teaching employees how to take power naps at work. Deloitte Consulting has gone as far as setting up nap rooms.

Fede Busquet, a former tanning-salon owner, may have found a solution to Spain's siesta dilemma. Busquet realized that Spaniards still need their siesta when he noticed rows of parked cars along Barcelona's streets with men sleeping inside around midday. He thought these people might prefer a more comfortable place for a power nap near their office.

Busquet set up two dozen parlours where, for 1,000 pesetas (US $7), customers get a 10-minute massage in an ergonomic chair, then an hour in that same chair

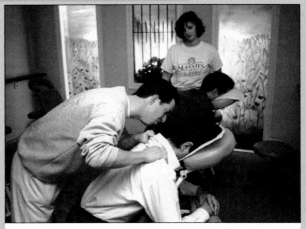

Masseurs Remco Rafina, left, and Eva Pacheco give two people a special siesta massage in a newly opened massage parlor in Madrid. For $7.6 Euros (CDN $12) customers get a 10-minute massage in an ergonomic chair, then an hour in that same chair to sleep or rest. Those in a hurry can stay half as long for half the price. *AP Photo/Paul White*

to sleep or rest. Those in a hurry can stay half as long for half the price. Business is booming. It seems that Spaniards still need their midday siesta, but something quicker and closer to the office.

Sources: L. Stevens, "Believers in the Midday Doze are Stripping Away Stigma of Siestas," *Fort Worth Star-Telegram*, March 24, 2001; R. Hogan, "A Daytime Nap Could Make You More Productive," *Los Angeles Times*, January 15, 2001; S. M. Handelsblatt, "Stressed Out and Stranded in Barcelona?" *Wall Street Journal Europe*, August 4, 2000, p. 32; R. Boudreaux, "Spaniards Are Missing Their Naps," *Los Angeles Times*, March 28, 2000; D. Woolls, "Spanish Entrepreneur Finds Market Niche in Siesta Deprived," *Deseret News*, March 22, 1999.

room complete with comfy chairs and comedy videos where employees can temporarily escape from the hassles of work. With more open offices and less privacy, some employees are finding that the washrooms are the best place to retreat.[82] Siestas provide midday sleep breaks for employees in Spain and other Mediterranean countries. However, GLOBAL Connections 7.3 describes how Spanish employees are under pressure to give up their cherished siesta due to globalization and urbanization, just as other countries discover the benefits of these power naps.

Days off and vacations represent somewhat longer temporary withdrawals from stressful conditions. One study of a police and emergency responses services department in western Canada found that this leisure time significantly improved the employee's ability to cope with work-related stress.[83] A few Canadian firms offer paid sabbaticals to long-service employees. This includes McDonald's of Canada, which offers salaried employees an eight-week paid sabbatical after 10 years of service. "[The sabbatical] allows our employees to take the time to do things they wouldn't normally have an opportunity to do and to breathe, explore, enjoy their loved ones and do some special things," says a McDonald's of Canada spokesperson.[84]

Change Stress Perceptions

Employees often experience different levels of stress in the same situation because they perceive it differently. Consequently, stress can be minimized by changing perceptions of the situation. This does not involve ignoring risks or other stressors. Rather, we can strengthen our self-efficacy and self-esteem so that job challenges are not perceived as threatening. Humour can also improve our perceptions by taking some psychological weight off the situation. "Workplace pressures will keep increasing," says a clinical psychologist at Vancouver-based telecommunications company Telus Corp. "A lot of things aren't going to change, so we have to change people's perception."[85]

Several elements of self-leadership described in Chapter 6 can alter employee perceptions of job-related stressors. For example, mental imagery can reduce the uncertainty of future work activities. A study of newly hired accountants reported that personal goal-setting and self-reinforcement can also reduce the stress that people experience when they enter new work settings.[86] Positive self-talk can change stress perceptions by increasing our self-efficacy and developing a more optimistic outlook, at least in that situation.

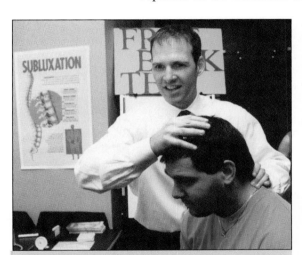

A few years ago, the Town of Richmond Hill launched a comprehensive wellness program to help employees reduce stress and improve their health. The Town conducts health risk assessment reviews, provides awareness sessions on a variety to health topics, and holds clinics on allergies and other ailments. Employees also receive free or subsidized memberships to various fitness clubs. In its first four years, the Town of Richmond Hill's wellness initiative has produced favourable results. "[W]e're seeing tremendous successes pointing to a healthier and productive workforce as well as reduced healthcare costs and absenteeism," says Joan Wade, the municipality's manager of employee benefits and occupational health and safety and wellness.[89] In your opinion, why don't more Canadian employers offer comprehensive wellness plans?
Courtesy of the Town of Richmond Hill.
www.town.richmond-hill.on.ca

Control the Consequences of Stress

Coping with workplace stress also involves controlling its consequences. For this reason, many Canadian companies have fitness centres where employees can keep in shape. Research indicates that physical exercise reduces the physiological consequences of stress by helping employees lower their respiration, muscle tension, heartbeat, and stomach acidity.[87] Another way to control the physiological consequences of stress is through relaxation and meditation. Generally, these activities decrease the individual's heart rate, blood pressure, muscle tension, and breathing rate.[88]

While fitness and relaxation/meditation are still important, many firms have shifted to the broader approach of wellness programs, which educate and support employees in better nutrition and fitness, regular sleep, and other good health habits. One recent survey reported that 67 percent of Canadian employers offer single-issue wellness initiatives (such as smoking cessation programs), but only 17 percent of employers offered more comprehensive wellness plans.[90] Magna International is in the latter group. The Toronto-based global auto-parts manufacturer has presentations on a particular health topic every two months, then sets up clinics the next month where employees meet one-on-one with health advisors on that topic.[91]

Many large employers offer **employee assistance programs (EAPs).** EAPs are counselling services that help employees overcome personal or organizational stressors and adopt more effective coping mechanisms. Most EAPs are "broad-brush" programs that counsel employees on any work or personal problems. Family problems often represent the largest percentage of EAP referrals, although this varies with industry and location. For instance, all of Canada's major banks provide post-trauma stress counselling for employees after a robbery, particularly when a weapon was visible.[92] EAPs can be one of the most effective stress management interventions when the counselling helps employees to understand the stressors, and acquire and practise stress management skills.[93]

Receive Social Support

Social support from co-workers, supervisors, family, friends, and others is one of the more effective stress management practices.[94] Social support refers to the person's interpersonal transactions with others and involves providing either emotional or informational support to buffer the stress experience.

Social support reduces stress in at least three ways.[95] First, employees improve their perception that they are valued and worthy. This, in turn, increases their self-esteem and perceived ability to cope with the stressor (e.g., "I can handle this crisis because my colleagues have confidence in me"). Second, social support provides information to help employees interpret, comprehend, and possibly remove the stressor. For instance, social support might reduce a new employee's stress because co-workers describe ways to handle difficult customers. Finally, emotional support from others can directly help to buffer the stress experience. This last point reflects the idea that "misery loves company." People seek out and benefit from the emotional support of others when they face threatening situations.[96]

Social support is an important way to cope with stress that everyone can practise by maintaining friendships. This includes helping others when they need a little support from the stressors of life. Organizations can facilitate social support by providing opportunities for social interaction among employees as well as their families. People in leadership roles also need to practise a supportive leadership style when employees work under stressful conditions and need this social support. Mentoring relationships with more senior employees may also help junior employees cope with organizational stressors.

employee assistance programs (EAPs) Counselling services that help employees overcome personal or organizational stressors and adopt more effective coping mechanisms.

CHAPTER SUMMARY

Stress is an adaptive response to a situation that is perceived as challenging or threatening to a person's well-being. Distress describes high stress levels that have negative consequences, whereas eustress describes the moderately low stress levels needed to activate people. The stress experience, called the general adaptation syndrome, involves moving through three stages: alarm, resistance, and exhaustion. The stress model shows that stress is caused by stressors. However, the effect of these stressors depends on individual characteristics. Stress affects a person's physiological and psychological well-being, and is associated with several work-related behaviours.

Stressors are the causes of stress and include any environmental conditions that place a physical or emotional demand on the person. Stressors are found in the physical work environment, the employee's various life roles, interpersonal relations, and organizational activities and conditions. Conflicts between work and nonwork obligations are a frequent source of employee stress.

Two people exposed to the same stressor may experience different stress levels because they perceive the situation differently, have different threshold stress levels, or use different coping strategies. Workaholics and employees with Type A behaviour patterns tend to experience more stress than other employees.

Intense or prolonged stress can cause physiological symptoms, such as high blood pressure, ulcers, sexual dysfunction, headaches, and coronary heart disease. Behavioural symptoms of stress include lower job performance, poorer decisions, more workplace accidents, higher absenteeism, and more workplace aggression. Psychologically, stress reduces job satisfaction and increases moodiness, depression, and job burnout. Job burnout refers to the process of emotional exhaustion, cynicism, and reduced efficacy resulting from prolonged exposure to stress. It is mainly due to interpersonal and role-related stressors and is most common in helping occupations.

Many interventions are available to manage work-related stress. Some directly remove unnecessary stressors or remove employees from the stressful environment. Others help employees alter their interpretation of the environment so that it is not viewed as a serious stressor. Wellness programs encourage employees to build better physical defences against stress experiences. Social support provides emotional, informational, and material resource support to buffer the stress experience.

KEY TERMS

Employee assistance programs (EAPs), p. 218

General adaptation syndrome, p. 201

Job burnout, p. 211

Role ambiguity, p. 205

Role conflict, p. 205

Sexual harassment, p. 202

Stress, p. 200

Stressors, p. 202

Type A behaviour pattern, p. 209

Type B behaviour pattern, p. 209

Workaholic, p. 210

Workplace bullying, p. 204

DISCUSSION QUESTIONS

1. Several Web sites—including www.unitedmedia.com/comics/dilbert/ and www.cartoonwork.com—use humour to illustrate problems that people experience at work. Scan through these and other Web sites and determine what types of work-related stressors are described.

2. Is being a full-time college or university student a stressful role? Why or why not? Contrast your response with other students' perspectives.

3. Police officer and waiter are often cited as high-stress jobs, whereas accountant and forester are low-stress jobs. Why should we be careful about describing these jobs as involving high or low stress?

4. Two recent graduates join the same major newspaper as journalists. Both work long hours and have tight deadlines to complete their stories. They are under constant pressure to scout out new leads and be the first to report new controversies. One journalist is increasingly fatigued and despondent, and has taken several days of sick leave. The other is getting the work done and seems to enjoy the challenges. Use your knowledge of stress to explain why these two journalists are reacting differently to their jobs.

5. Do people with Type A personalities make better employees? Why or why not? Do people with Type A personalities make better executives? Why or why not?

6. A friend says he is burned out by his job. What questions might you ask this friend to determine whether he is really experiencing job burnout?

7. What should organizations do to reduce employee stress? What responsibility does an employee have to manage stress effectively?

8. A Canadian technology firm pays employees' membership fees at a local fitness facility. What is your opinion of this employer-provided benefit? Is this program an expense? An investment? Explain your perspective.

C A S E   S T U D Y   **7.1**

A TYPICAL DAY FOR JOE HANSEN, MANAGING DIRECTOR

By Hazel Bothma, University of Cape Town, South Africa.

Meet Joe Hansen, managing director of Magical Connections, Cape Town, South Africa. Shadow him for a day and see the challenges and stressors he faces in his daily work.

Buzz. Joe turns over and switches the alarm off. It's 6:00 a.m. and he tosses with the idea of going for a run. However, last night, like many nights before that, he stayed up working til late in the evening, so he decides to postpone the run and catch another 30 minutes sleep. Fate intervenes within five minutes as he hears his 18-month-old daughter start to cry. Joe looks over at his wife, and decides to let her sleep. She had to take care of their daughter last night, as he had to work until 11:00 p.m. Dragging himself out of bed, he fetches his wailing daughter and goes to the kitchen to prepare her bottle. While in the kitchen he balances his daughter on his lap, turns on his laptop, and grimaces as his machine shows him 42 new e-mails. He thinks back to the time before e-mail and cellular phones were popular. Although he would be the first to admit that he couldn't do without these new technologies he realizes that in ways the division of boundaries between work and nonwork have become blurred. Joe realizes that, like many of his colleagues in the IT sector, he finds it hard to separate work life from home life. His daughter now feeding quietly in her cot gives Joe the opportunity to start responding to the e-mails and deleting much of the junk mail he receives. At 6:45 he jumps in the shower, still feeling tired, preparing himself for a day of work. As he combs his hair he notices the first touch of grey—38, he thinks wryly to himself, and starting to show. He wonders if his late hours and pressure from his work are the culprits. It's now 7:15 and Joe needs to get to the office. No time for breakfast. Instead he gulps down his second strong cup of coffee, promising himself that starting tomorrow he will make time to eat before work.

As Joe starts driving to work, the early morning traffic beginning to grow, he thinks that at least he is not on his way to the airport for one of his frequent business trips, which leave him exhausted and with piles of work to complete once back. Hardly ten minutes into the drive to work, his cellular phone rings. It's Justin, one of his team managers, requesting a meeting with him today to discuss why some of the teams are not reaching their targets. Joe thinks back to his first job at one of the major banks. Teamwork was non-existent and being then at the bottom of the managerial rung, he was hardly ever consulted or asked to make decisions. All this has changed, especially within the informational technology sector. Joe's company, Magical Connections, where he is managing director, has very few managers, and most of the 22 staff work in teams. A far cry from his days in the bank, when he was one of 500 employees, faceless in a hierarchical company. Many of the people Joe worked with in the banking industry are still there. For Joe it remains a constant challenge to keep competent staff who leave almost every two years for other IT companies, or even to seek work elsewhere in South Africa. Despite this challenge of people constantly moving in the industry, Joe does not miss the way work used to be organized in the bank, and likes the way his company is structured. The division of labour within Magical Connections helps its progress, tasks are divided logically, and the frustration of a huge bureaucracy is something he does not miss.

As Joe walks into the office, he is met with Alan, who is pacing up and down the reception floor. Their company is urgently waiting for new parts from Taiwan to arrive. Alan explains that although the parts have landed at the port in Durban, customs are holding them up, as some document seems to be missing. The companies that have been promised the various parts have been ringing Alan to find out where they are. Alan looks near the breaking point as he explains heatedly to Joe the pressure of having to deal with irate customers who want everything now. Joe is empathic with Alan as he too constantly faces pressure from all sides. After a brief meeting with Alan brainstorming solutions to this crisis, Joe eagerly helps himself to his third cup of coffee, hoping the caffeine will perk him up, and although it's only 10:00 in the morning, he finds a cigarette in his desk drawer, and goes outside to smoke. He is well aware of the health risks, not to speak about the wrath he would face if his wife found out, but as always the day seems packed with obstacles and Joe uses this five minutes to be on his own.

At 11:00 Joe sits down with one of teams to discuss their targets. Justin, one of the team members, starts the meeting off by accusing Sharon of not performing adequately and thereby jeopardizing the team's target. Justin rants on that he is tired of having to work even harder to make up for Sharon's poor performance. As Joe listens, he realizes that Justin's antagonistic nature is not helping the meeting, and Joe is aware that without good interpersonal skills from all team members the effective working of the team is only hindered. Added to this he is going to have to ascertain what is causing Sharon not to meet her targets. Joe makes a mental note to try and organize some training on interpersonal skills for all teams. It is imperative for Magical Connections that teams be effective, as this also translates into remaining competitive at both a national and global level. If their company is to stay afloat in this highly competitive environment, remaining competitive is the cornerstone of their survival.

Dan, Joe's old school friend, phones him up at 1:00 to see if he would like to join him for lunch. Joe laughs down the phone and reminds Dan that he has not had a lunch break in the past two years. He thinks longingly of a quiet lunch, good food and company, but knows that he has too much to do. Justin is still angry about poor team performance, and Joe knows he needs to deal with this issue as soon as possible. Dan laughs back at him and tells him that as M.D. he should be delegating more and enjoying some time off. He has a point, Joe thinks. Empowerment is still a relatively new concept in South Africa, but Joe knows that if he delegated more of his work to younger staff and allowed them to make more decisions, it would free up more of his time to think about long-term strategy for his company. But today is not the day for a lunch-break, so a hamburger and chips from the canteen will have to do.

At 2:30 p.m. Fiona walks into his office and tells Joe she intends to leave the company. Joe's heart sinks. She is one of the brightest employees they have. This means that again their company will have to try and attract a new person, and of course retain them. The recruitment and selection of a new person will be time consuming and Joe makes a mental note to start this process.

At 4:00 p.m. Joe finds himself lying on a massage table having a massage in his office. It is a relatively new idea that the company brought in a month ago on recommendations from some employees. All employees are entitled to a 30-minute massage once a week. With gentle music floating in his office, the smell of aromatherapy oils lingering in the air, Joe feels his knots being worked under the masseur's able hands and feels the release of his tension. What a great idea this has turned out to be.

With a bulging briefcase Joe manages to leave the office at 6:00 p.m.—aware that his wife has been looking after their daughter all day and will now be exhausted and desperate for him to come home and help. He has six new computer journals he needs to read, and a page of Web sites that he needs to explore. The almost constant pressure to keep abreast of the flood of information within this industry is an overwhelming feature of Joe's life. Added to this Joe realizes that next week he needs to undertake a vendor computer-training course, which will keep him out of the office. For Joe the constant need for retraining is a necessity to stay abreast.

As Joe starts his 20-minute drive home he puts a new CD on and starts humming to his favourite track. The humming soon changes to a full-throated bellow as he sings the chorus out aloud and makes drumming noises on the steering wheel. However, a phone call with another work-related issue interrupts this pleasant interlude. As he ends the call, Joe thinks to himself that this weekend he is going to take his wife and daughter away for a weekend. Perhaps to the mountains where they can relax as a family, and he can spend some time talking to his wife. He grins to himself, no cell phone and no laptop. With that comforting thought he thinks about the challenges he faces tomorrow and in the future. Magical Connections needs to stay fast, flexible, responsive, resilient, and creative, and Joe looks forward to being one of the people doing just that. Despite the challenges of his job, Joe loves his work and finds it challenging and rewarding.

Discussion Questions

1. Identify the stressors facing Joe.
2. How do you think Joe could go about managing his stress more effectively?
3. Would it be fair to argue that employees within the IT sector experience higher levels of stress than, say, employees within the banking or manufacturing sector?

TEAM EXERCISE 7.2

STRESSED OUT OR "NO PROBLEM"?

Purpose This exercise is designed to help students understand how people can have different stress reactions to the same stressors.

Instructions

- *Step 1:* Students individually indicate their responses to each of the incidents on the scoring sheet.
- *Step 2:* The instructor places students into groups (typically 4 or 5 people) to compare their results. For each incident, group members should discuss why each person feels more or less stress. They should pay particular attention to the reasons why some students would feel little stress. Specifically, they should examine the extent that each person (a) perceives the situation differently, (b) has more or less tolerance to stressors due to health or need to cope with other problems, and (c) would use different coping strategies to deal with any stress related to the incident.
- *Step 3:* After group members have diagnosed these results, the instructor brings the class together to compare results and discuss why people react differently to stressors.

Circle the number on the right that best describes the extent to which you would feel stressed in this situation.	Very Little ▼		Moderately ▼			Very Much ▼	
1. Your final exam for Economics 200 is in 48 hours and a bad flu and other assignments have prevented you from studying for it. You know that the instructor will not accept your illness and other assignments as an excuse to have the examination at another time.	1	2	3	4	5	6	7
2. You started work last month as a sales clerk in a small clothing store (men's or women's) and have been asked to mind the store while the other two clerks take their lunch break elsewhere in the shopping mall. During this usually slow time, four customers walk in, each one of them wanting your immediate attention.	1	2	3	4	5	6	7

Circle the number on the right that best describes the extent to which you would feel stressed in this situation.	Very Little ▼		Moderately ▼			Very Much ▼	
3. You and two friends are driving in an older van with snow tires to a ski resort in the Canadian Rockies. You took over driving duty at 8 p.m., two hours ago. Your friends are asleep in the back seat while you approach a steep pass. It has been snowing so heavily that you must drive at a crawl to see where you are going and avoid sliding off the road. You passed the last community 30 miles back and the resort is 40 miles ahead (nearly two hours at your current speed).	1	2	3	4	5	6	7
4. You work as an accountant in a large insurance company and, for the past month, have received unwanted attention several times each week from your supervisor, a married person of the opposite sex. The supervisor regularly touches your shoulder and comments on your looks. You are sure that they are advances rather than just friendly gestures.	1	2	3	4	5	6	7
5. You and your spouse purchased your first home one year ago, a detached house with mortgage payments that your spouse barely covers with his/her take-home pay. The economy has since entered a deep recession and the company informed you today that you will be laid off in two months.	1	2	3	4	5	6	7

Source: Copyright © 2000. Steven L. McShane.

S E L F - A S S E S S M E N T   E X E R C I S E   7.3

TIME STRESS SCALE

Purpose This self-assessment is designed to help you to identify your level of time-related stress.

Instructions Read each of the statements below and circle "Yes" or "No." Then use the scoring key in Appendix B to calculate your results. This exercise is completed alone so students can assess themselves honestly without concerns of social comparison. However, class discussion will focus on the time-stress scale.

1. Yes No   Do you plan to slow down in the coming year?

2. Yes No   Do you consider yourself a workaholic?

3. Yes No   When you need more time, do you tend to cut back on your sleep?

4. Yes No   At the end of the day, do you often feel that you have not accomplished what you had set out to do?

5. Yes No   Do you worry that you don't spend enough time with your family or friends?

6. Yes No   Do you feel that you're constantly under stress trying to accomplish more than you can handle?

7. Yes No   Do you feel trapped in a daily routine?

8. Yes No   Do you feel that you just don't have time for fun any more?

9. Yes No   Do you often feel under stress when you don't have enough time?

10. Yes No   Would you like to spend more time alone?

Source: Statistics Canada's 1998 General Social Survey. Cited in P. DeMont, "Too Much Stress, Too Little Time," *Ottawa Citizen,* November 12, 1999.

BEHAVIOUR ACTIVITY PROFILE — THE TYPE "A" SCALE

 Go to the Student CD for the interactive version of this exercise.

Purpose This self-assessment is designed to help you to identify the extent to which you follow a Type "A" behaviour pattern.

Instructions Each of us displays certain kinds of behaviours, thought patterns of personal characteristics. In this self-assessment, select the number that you feel best describes where you are between each pair of words or phrases. The best answer for each set of descriptions is the response that most nearly describes the way you feel, behave, or think. Answer these in terms of your regular or typical behaviour, thoughts, or characteristics. The results show your relative position on the Type "A" and Type "B" behaviour pattern continuum.

Copyright © 1982 Michael T. Matteson and John M. Ivanevich. Used with permission.

WORK ADDICTION RISK TEST

 Go to the Student CD for the interactive version of this exercise.

Purpose This self-assessment is designed to help you to identify the extent to which you are a workaholic.

Instructions This instrument presents several statements, and asks you to indicate the extent to which each statement is true of your work habits. You need to be honest with yourself for a reasonable estimate of your level of workaholism.

Copyright © Sage Publications. All rights reserved. Used with permission of Sage Publications, Inc.

PERCEIVED STRESS SCALE

 Go to the Student CD for the interactive version of this exercise.

Purpose This self-assessment is designed to help you to estimate your perceived general level of stress.

Instructions The questions in this scale ask you about your feelings and thoughts during the last month. In each case, please indicate how often you felt or thought a certain way. You need to be honest with yourself for a reasonable estimate of your general level of stress.

Copyright © Sage Publications. All rights reserved. Used with permission of Sage Publications, Inc.

After studying the preceding material, be sure to check out our Online Learning Centre at
www.mcgrawhill.ca/college/mcshane
for more in-depth information and interactivities that correspond to this chapter.

Online LearningCentre with POWERWEB

THE ROYAL BANK OF CANADA VIGNETTES

Purpose This exercise is designed to help you understand perceptual issues when working in a diverse work force.

Instructions The instructor will play a few vignettes portraying actual events at The Royal Bank of Canada. For each vignette, the class will follow these steps:

- *Step 1:* Watch the vignette, keeping in mind the questions presented below.
- *Step 2:* The instructor will stop the videotape at the appropriate place and the class will discuss the vignette, guided by the following questions (the instructor may ask additional questions):

    (a) What is your reaction to this incident?
    (b) What is the main issue in this vignette?
    (c) What perceptual problems might exist here?
    (d) What solutions, if any, would you recommend?

- *Step 3:* After discussing the vignette, the instructor will play the video follow-up so that the class can hear what The Royal Bank of Canada recommends in this situation.

Source: Royal Bank of Canada.

CAREER COACH PROGRAM

Money can solve a lot of problems, but for high tech companies desperate to hang on to their highly skilled employees, money alone doesn't cut it. Somebody else can always offer more. That's why the race is on to find new ways to keep staff happy.

Sixty hour weeks. Unrealistic bosses. Demanding customers. Families unseen for days. In the world of high tech, these are common complaints heard around the water cooler. Dy4 is no exception. The Kanata, Ontario designer of computers for harsh climates, is stretching employees to the limit with rapid growth and product backlogs. To recruit and retain the best employees, Dy4 has introduced a Career Coach Program that helps employees target those areas causing friction.

"The main issue is that they've lost a sense of control in their work place," says Daniel O'Connor, the founder of Keepers Inc. that runs the career coach program. "And what that leaves them feeling is very disempowered and subject to the whims of the industry, the whims of their managers, the whims of the company and that's a pretty discouraging feeling."

O'Connor is working with Grant, who manages one of Dy4's product lines. Grant gets anxiety attacks thinking about the number of meetings he must attend each day while trying to get his product out on time. But is Grant completely powerless? Maybe he's a pushover. Does he ever say no? O'Connor gets Grant to think about the things that lead to all these meetings. But it takes time. A few weeks later, O'Connor discovers that Grant has 10 meetings and is backlogged with 600 e-mail messages.

Ernie is an engineer at Dy4 who is worried about work/life balance. O'Connor encouraged him to track his time for a week and then look at how his life is divided into a pie chart. Dy4 got a huge 61 hour slice of Ernie's pie last week. His family got the crumbs. To turn things around, O'Connor gets Ernie to set some goals, such as going out with his wife at least once every two weeks and eating dinner with the family at least five nights a week. So far, Ernie only gets home one or two nights each week by dinner time.

It's a slow start, but Dy4 employees are moving in the right direction. And as it takes hold, the Career Coach Program helps Dy4 keep its talent from looking elsewhere for work.

THE SPEED TRAP

E-mail, cell phones, and fax machines have put us on the fast track. But are we accelerating beyond our endurance? Are we speeding to a standstill? Rather than ease our burdens, these communication devices have increased our technostress. Tim Breen, a busy copy centre manager, points out that technology moves far faster than we do, and trying to keep up can wear us out, both mentally and physically.

The mad rush to squeeze more work activities into the day, with no time left for personal pursuits, led small business owner Sandra Erickson to seek help. She turned to time management consultant Mark Ellwood who teaches clients how to get balance into their lives.

"Eric," a patient at the Homewood Health Centre in Guelph, Ontario wishes he had sought help earlier. A casualty of a 13-to-16 hour workday regime, the former construction executive found himself going into a tailspin. After climbing into the top income bracket, Eric was diagnosed as clinically depressed, and lost his job.

Psychiatrist Dr. Beth Reade says that there is a limit, even for the most high-energy people, on how much we can do. We have to set our priorities and learn to say no, she says.

Japan has officially recognized overwork as a disease. It's called *karoshi* and 10,000 workers die of it each year. One victim, 23-year-old Yoshiko, was a graphic artist who died on the job suddenly due to a brain haemorrhage. According to her parents, who are suing their daughter's former employer, Yoshiko worked herself to death.

Although France has legislated a 35-hour work week, four out of 10 businesses have workers on the job for more than 10 hours a day. Labour inspector Gerard Filoche says that a 13 percent unemployment rate means employers can coerce employees to work unreasonable hours.

Discussion Questions

1. While watching this documentary, identify the various incidents with the stressor categories described in this chapter. Which stressors seem to be more common?

2. What strategies identified in this program that help employees minimize or avoid unnecessary stress at work and in their lives?

3. Are there any sources of work-related stress that this documentary overlooks? What are they?

Source: "The Speed Trap," CBC *Witness*, January 6, 2000, © 90th Parallel Productions.

EMPLOYEE LOYALTY

Not so long ago, life was simple. Companies offered secure, even lifetime employment. Workers were loyal to the company. Well, a few million layoffs later, that deal is history. But companies still need loyal staff and they need young people that will stay with them.

Joel Baglole is a case in point. Baglole received an internship at the *Toronto Star* and later was offered a full-time job. Baglole happily accepted the position, but quit six weeks later when the prestigious *Wall Street Journal* offered him a job. "[The *Toronto Star*] paid me and I worked hard and so that's the way I looked at it," explains Baglole. "I didn't feel like I owed them anything over and above what I'd already given them."

John Honderich has a different view. "We thought that we had made the investment in his being here in terms of what was happening," says the *Toronto Star* publisher. "I think that loyalty has become the forgotten value in the work place today," he adds. "I place a great deal of importance on loyalty because it's a glue that's made this particular organization work and it's been part of the history. We've been around for 108 years. And so when you have a long history and long tradition, loyalty has obviously been part of it."

Honderich and other employers believe that the younger generation of employees don't have loyalty. "They're always looking for the next. And that just seems to be the way they're programmed. That seems to be more the, the mode today."

But Baglole thinks the problem is employers, not young people. "Every day I hear about people... bumped down, demoted, laid off, forced into retirement, given the golden handshake," he says. What's the solution? According to Baglole, companies need to increase job security. "Start hiring long term. ...Welcome to the team. You're a valued employee. Here are your benefits. Here's your pension. Here's your corporate credit card. Welcome to the team."

Joseph Polarski's computer consulting company in Toronto is trying to create loyalty through job security, just like Polarski experienced at IBM in the past. "I come from the IBM culture where there was a commitment," he says. "I still dream of that culture. I believe it was an excellent culture and I want to have it back."

The *Toronto Star's* John Honderich is also trying to improve loyalty through training and company shares. But *The Star*, which laid off 200 staffers recently, shies away from job security. "You never can say never to lay-offs. You never can say, because what's going to happen? I mean, this company survived for 108 years and we'd like to think we're going to survive for another 108 years but there's no guarantees."

That's one thing Honderich and Baglole agree on: "I mean, there are no guarantees in life," Baglole acknowledges.

Discussion Questions

1. Which, if any, of the five strategies to build organizational commitment would be effective in this situation involving Joel Baglole?

2. Explain how Joel Baglole's psychological contract is influenced by organizational loyalty in this situation.

Source: L. Buckner, "Employee Loyalty," CBC *Venture*, March 6, 2001.

BALANCING WORK AND LIFE

Work–life balance is the hottest topic among human resource executives these days, and for good reason. Most Canadians have a serious lack of balance, which is costing employers plenty. "We've seen an alarming increase in the amount of stress leave that people are on," says Nora Spinks, one of Canada's leading experts on work–life balance. "It's one of the fastest growing short-term disabilities that there is, that employers are now having to look at."

Companies have introduced several practices to minimize the damage to time-stressed staff, such as fitness programs, career breaks, daycare centres, flex-time, job sharing, telework, and so on. But a major Canadian study has reported that Canadians are still stressed.

"If we look at about a decade ago only about ten percent of the workforce was working a 50 hour plus week," explains Carleton University business professor Linda Duxbury. "We now see that about one in four people are working that many hours." The study also discovered that over one-third of professional and managerial men and women say that the way they're trying to cope is simply by not having kids.

University of Guelph professor Peter Hausdorf says that part of the problem is that employers don't want to deal with the main cause of poor work–life balance: workload. "[Employers] seem reluctant to deal with the fact that the issue is ... workload and what they would rather do is focus on other aspects. So [they'll] have fitness facilities to deal with stress. These are all good things but they're not dealing with the core issue, which is the volume of work."

Courtney Pratt, CEO of Toronto Hydro, admits his company is pushing staff too hard, but he doesn't see much choice while Toronto hydro prepares for privatization. "But when you get into a crunch like we're in, there's not a whole lot you can do other than I think you have to empathize with people," Pratt admits. "You do whatever you can to try and give them the time off that they need but quite frankly, we need their intellectual horse-power right now and it's not an option."

Linda Duxbury sees the issue differently: "Excuse me, but how can you afford to continue to operate this way?" she warns. "Look at your absenteeism. Look at your turnover. Look at your prescription and benefit costs. Look at your succession planning." Nora Spinks notes that the need to keep good staff is another reason to encourage work–life balance: "If you're competing for the same people that somebody else is, and now offering flexibility and support of work environments and stress-free opportunities, people are going to be attracted to there before they're attracted to an organization where it's rigid, it's structured, it's high stress."

Discussion Questions

1. Explain how companies that encourage work–life balance might be more successful than those pushing more hours of work out of their staff.

2. What other topics in the first two parts of this book explain how work–life balance may improve organizational effectiveness?

Source: Dianne Buckner, "Balancing Work and Life," CBC *Venture*, April 7, 2002.

GRIN AND BARE IT

Summary written by Bernadette Cross, University of Newcastle, Australia

For many centuries it was considered inappropriate in the Japanese culture to use the face as a tool for conveying emotion. The mind was all that was important, and the ideal was a face that showed nothing. Expression was in fact regarded as part of scandalous behaviour. For example, smiling was considered useful only for cheating or hiding the self. Instead, the Japanese are accustomed to interpreting subtlety. This is symbolized in their oldest national theatre, Noh theatre, in which a mask with no expression is worn by the main character. Used to no dialogue in the performance and no expression on the mask, Japanese people are much better than Westerners at understanding subtle expressions, such as a tilt of the head.

However, Japan is changing, including its cultural norms toward emotional expression. The "new, user-friendly Japan" wants to be able to smile on demand. Conveying particular emotions during work is now known to improve production, profitability, and success. Japan's business leaders are realizing that business improves when employees display specific emotions in the workplace. Consequently, many employees are being sent off to "Smile Schools." These schools teach people how to express an array of emotions, from being sad at a funeral to smiling at a customer in a department store.

Tokyo's largest department store wants its employees to smile more at customers, so it is holding special classes, led by Yoshihiko Kadokawa, founder of the Smile Amenities Institute. This video program observes employees at the department store learn the subtle—and often difficult—task of displaying a sincere smile.

Discussion Questions

1. Discuss why employees in Japan tend to show few emotions at work.

2. What training methods do these Smile Schools use to teach students how to display positive emotions? In your opinion, do these training methods work?

3. Given that Japanese employees have traditionally hidden their true emotions at work, do you think Smile School will reduce emotional dissonance? Why or why not?

CHAPTER 8

Foundations of Team Dynamics

Learning Objectives

AFTER READING THIS CHAPTER, YOU SHOULD BE ABLE TO:

- Define teams.

- Distinguish teams from informal groups.

- Outline the model of team effectiveness.

- Identify six organizational and team environmental elements that influence team effectiveness.

- Explain the influence of the team's task, composition, and size on team effectiveness.

- Describe the five stages of team development.

- Identify four factors that shape team norms.

- List six factors that influence team cohesiveness.

- Discuss the limitations of teams.

- Explain how companies minimize social loafing.

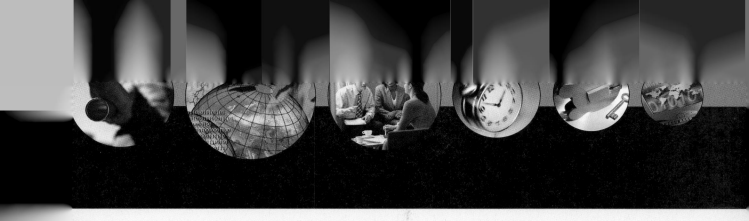

From 1995 to 2000, Outboard Marine Corp.'s (OMC) share of the outboard engine market plummeted from 55 to just 23 percent. The maker of Evinrude and Johnson outboard motors suffered from engine quality problems and inefficient production methods. Montreal-based Bombardier Inc. purchased the American company and created a team-based transformation that surprised competitors and allies alike.

Bombardier manufacturing executive Roch Lambert led the turnaround team, consisting of former OMC manufacturing experts as well as specialists in plant maintenance, finance, marketing, and quality control from Bombardier's Canadian operations. The team's audacious goal was to completely reconfigure OMC's manufacturing process. Less than one year later, it now produces the highest-quality Evinrude and Johnson engines ever made.

In rapid order, the turnaround team scrutinized the engine drawings, inventory system, and manufacturing process to identify faults and required changes. OMC's manufacturing operations were spread around four plants throughout the United States, which increased production costs and time. Lambert's team closed two plants and relocated production to a new building in Sturtevant, Wisconsin. Equipment was moved into the building just hours after the previous owner had moved out.

Montreal-based Bombardier Inc. relied on teams to transform money-losing Outboard Marine Corp. into a high quality manufacturer of Johnson and Evinrude outboard engines. *Jack Orton/Journal Sentinel Inc., reproduced with permission*

Bombardier initially selected 300 people from the 6,000 applications for the Sturtevant production facility. In particular, the company looked for "team players" with problem-solving skills, rather than looking first at prior work experience such as engine assembly. Quality control, such as ensuring the previous assembler's work achieved the required standards, was built into everyone's job. Bombardier's team-based approach is paying off as dealers who had abandoned the Johnson and Evinrude brands are now flocking back.[1]

www.bombardier.com

teams
Groups of two or more people who interact and influence each other, are mutually accountable for achieving common objectives, and perceive themselves as a social entity within an organization.

groups
Two or more people with a unifying relationship.

Teams are replacing individuals as the basic building blocks of organizations. In the opening story, Bombardier relied on teams to transform Outboard Motor Corporation and to improve product quality in the manufacturing process. TVA Group, Canada's largest producer and distributor of French-language television programs, has shifted to team-based projects and is giving more recognition to teams than to individuals. Dofasco is so focused on teams that it carefully selects applicants with team skills. "We're not just looking for technical ability," explains an executive at the Hamilton, Ontario steel company. "We're (looking for people who can) work on teams and solve problems."[2]

Teams are groups of two or more people who interact and influence each other, are mutually accountable for achieving common goals associated with organizational objectives, and perceive themselves as a social entity within an organization.[3] All teams exist to fulfill some purpose, such as assembling a product, providing a service, designing a new manufacturing facility, or making an important decision. Team members are held together by their interdependence and need for collaboration to achieve common goals. All teams require some form of communication so members can coordinate and share common objectives. Team members also influence each other, although some members have more influence than others regarding the team's goals and activities.

All teams are **groups**, because they consist of people with a unifying relationship. But not all groups are teams; some groups are just people assembled together, without necessarily being interdependent or having an organizationally-focused objective.[4] For example, the friends you meet for lunch wouldn't be called a team because they have little or no task interdependence (each person could just as easily eat lunch alone) and no organizational purpose beyond their social interaction. Although the terms "group" and "team" are used interchangeably in this book, our main focus is on teams. This is partly because most of the discussion is about groups that perform organizationally-related tasks, and partly because the term "teams" has largely replaced "groups" in business language.[5]

This chapter looks at the complex conditions that make teams more or less effective in organizational settings. After introducing the different types of teams in organizational settings, we present a model of team effectiveness. Most of the chapter examines each part of this model, including team and organizational environment, team design, and the team processes of development, norms, roles, and cohesiveness.

The Chrysler Division of DaimlerChrysler has created three types of executive and professional teams to get new products to market faster and more in line with customer needs. The product strategy team—led by the Chrysler Group President—analyzes customer trends, new design ideas, technological innovation, and the economic environment to determine which new vehicle line to develop and build. The six product innovation teams are responsible for design, manufacturing, and marketing issues for Chrysler's five product groups and transmission processes. Chrysler's 50 component parts teams will ensure that vehicle groups share components. For example, one team plans to reduce the use of 27 different batteries to about five types of batteries across Chrysler products.[6] In your opinion, why is Chrysler organizing people into teams for these activities? © Alan Levenson/Getty Images
www.daimlerchrysler.com

TYPES OF TEAMS AND INFORMAL GROUPS

There are many types of teams and other groups in organizational settings. Exhibit 8.1 categorizes groups in terms of their permanence (teams versus informal groups) and formality in the organization.

EXHIBIT 8.1

Types of teams
and groups

	Permanent	**Temporary**
Formal teams	Production team Management team	Task force Skunkworks team
Informal groups	Friendship group	Community of practice

Permanent and Temporary Teams

Permanent work teams are responsible for a specific set of tasks or work processes in the organization. Most departments are relatively permanent teams because employees directly interact and coordinate work activities with each other.[7] In the opening story to this chapter, Bombardier organized Outboard Motor Corp. employees into permanent teams responsible for different parts of the manufacturing process. Management teams are also relatively permanent because these groups of people work together indefinitely.

Along with permanent teams, organizations rely on relatively temporary teams to make decisions or complete short-term projects. Companies bring together employees from various departments to design a product, solve a client's problem, or search for new opportunities. *Task forces* (also called project teams) are temporary teams that investigate a particular problem and disband when the decision is made. For instance, Reko Automation & Machine Tool Inc in Windsor, Ontario put together 35 teams to review each of the company's quality standards. These teams disbanded after the task was completed and the company achieved the required quality standards in only 10 months.[8]

skunkworks

Temporary teams consisting of employees borrowed from several functional areas to develop new products, services, or procedures.

Skunkworks **Skunkworks** are usually (but not always) temporary teams formed spontaneously to develop products or solve complex problems. They are initiated by an innovative employee (a *champion*) who borrows people and resources (called *bootlegging*) to help the organization.[9] Some skunkworks are isolated from the rest of the organization, and are able to ignore the more bureaucratic rules governing other organizational units. The earliest corporate Intranets started as skunkworks, championed by employees with a UNIX computer and free software from universities to create a Web server. Skunkworks are responsible for several innovations at 3M Corp. One example is a special micro-surface mouse pad that has become a commercial success. "Management had no idea the project was being worked on, until it was ready to be launched," explains a 3M executive. "Some lab, some manufacturing, and some marketing people got together as an informal team to do it."[10]

A skunkworks team helped to make Vancouver-based Ballard Power Systems a global leader in fuel cell technology. Geoffrey Ballard, founder of Vancouver-based Ballard Power Systems, wanted to develop a project to demonstrate the company's fuel cell technology in buses. Unfortunately, Ballard had stepped down as CEO of his company, and the current executives and board rejected his idea. Undaunted, he proceeded with the project by borrowing people and resources throughout the company. The successful project proved crucial to Ballard Power's ability to attract several automotive partners.[11]

Informal Groups

informal groups
Two or more people who form a unifying relationship around personal rather than organizational goals.

Along with formal work teams, organizations consist of **informal groups.** Informal groups are not initiated by the organization and usually do not perform organizational goals (thus they are "informal"). Instead, they exist primarily for the benefit of their members. Some informal groups, such as the group you meet for lunch, exist primarily to satisfy the drive to bond. These groups are relatively permanent because they are held together by lasting friendships and by the structure of formal teams.

communities of practice
Informal groups bound together by shared expertise and passion for a particular activity or interest.

Communities of practice are groups bound together by shared expertise and passion for a particular activity or interest.[12] For instance, Schlumberger Ltd. has communities of practice on deep-water drilling, horizontal drilling, deviated wells, and other areas of expertise. Employees are connected to the oil-field services firm's Web portal where they share knowledge on their daily experiences.[13] In most organizations, communities of practice are informal groups that congregate in person or cyberspace to share knowledge. People who have a common passion for environmental concerns, for example, might meet twice each month over lunch to share their knowledge. Other communities interact entirely through list servers and Web sites where participants exchange information on specific technical issues. Many communities of practice extend beyond organizational boundaries, so they represent a source of knowledge acquisition.

Why informal groups exist　People often join informal groups because of the innate drive to bond. Indeed, some writers suggest that group formation is hardwired through the evolutionary development of the human species.[14] As we learned in Chapter 5, people invest considerable time and effort forming and maintaining relationships without any special circumstances or ulterior motives. Similarly, social identity theory (see Chapter 3) says that we define ourselves by our group affiliations. If we belong to work teams or informal groups that are viewed favourably by others, we tend to view ourselves more favourably. We are motivated to become members of groups that are similar to ourselves because this reinforces our social identity.[15]

Some groups form because they accomplish tasks that cannot be achieved by individuals working alone. When groups are successful, it is easier to attract new members. Finally, informal groups tend to form in stressful situations because we are comforted by the physical presence of other people and are therefore motivated to be near them.[16] This explains why soldiers huddle together in battle, even though they are taught to disperse under fire. It also explains why employees tend to congregate when they hear that the company has been sold or that some people may be laid off.

A MODEL OF TEAM EFFECTIVENESS

team effectiveness
The extent to which a team achieves its objectives, achieves the needs and objectives of its members, and sustains itself over time.

Why are some teams more effective than others? This question has challenged organizational researchers for some time and, as you might expect, numerous models of team effectiveness have been proposed over the years.[17] **Team effectiveness** refers to how the team affects the organization, individual team members, and the team's existence.[18] First, most teams exist to serve some purpose relating to the organization or other system in which the group operates. In the opening story to this chapter, Roch Lambert's team was responsible for designing and implementing a new manufacturing centre for Bombardier's recently acquired company, Outboard Motor Corp. Some informal groups also have task-oriented goals (although not organizationally mandated goals), such as sharing information in an informal community of practice.

Second, team effectiveness considers the satisfaction and well-being of its members. People join groups to fulfill their personal needs, so it makes sense that effectiveness is partly measured by this need fulfillment. Finally, team effectiveness includes the team's viability—its ability to survive. It must be able to maintain the commitment of its members, particularly during the turbulence of the team's development. Without this commitment, people leave and the team falls apart. A team must also secure sufficient resources and find a benevolent environment in which to operate.

Exhibit 8.2 presents the model of team effectiveness that we will examine closely over the rest of this chapter. We begin by looking at elements of the team's and organization's environment that influence team design, processes, and outcomes.

ORGANIZATIONAL AND TEAM ENVIRONMENT

Our discussion of team effectiveness logically begins with the contextual factors that influence the team's design, processes, and outcomes.[19] There are many elements in the organizational and team environment that influence team effectiveness. Six of the most important elements are reward systems, communication systems, physical space, organizational environment, organizational structure, and organizational leadership.

- *Reward systems*—Research indicates that team members tend to work together more effectively when they are at least partly rewarded for team performance.[20]

EXHIBIT 8.2

A model of team effectiveness

Organizational and team environment
- Reward systems
- Communication systems
- Physical space
- Organizational environment
- Organizational structure
- Organizational leadership

Team design
- Task characteristics
- Team size
- Team composition

Team processes
- Team development
- Team norms
- Team roles
- Team cohesiveness

Team effectiveness
- Achieve organizational goals
- Satisfy member needs
- Maintain team survival

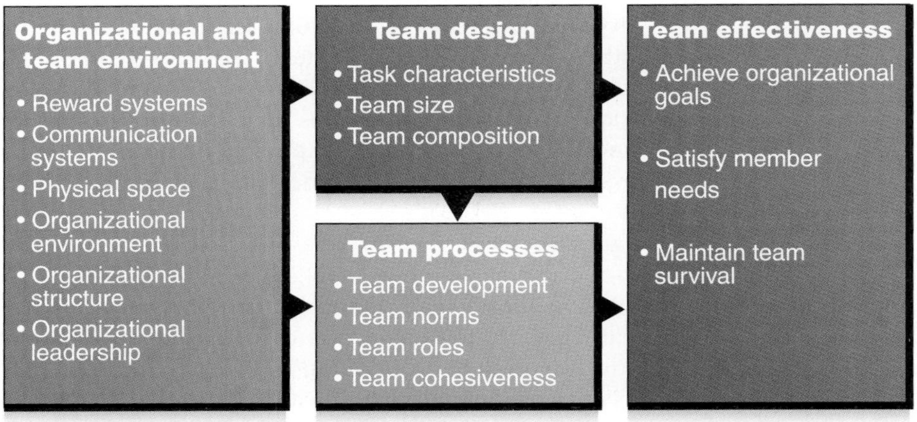

This doesn't mean that everyone on the team should receive the same amount of pay based on the team's performance. On the contrary, rewards tend to work better in Canada and other western societies when individual pay is based on a combination of individual and team performance. For instance, American Skandia rewards its best customer service representatives with an individual bonus. But, recognizing that individuals rarely work alone, the U.S. operations of the Swedish insurance company also rewards the employee's team for that individual's achievement.[21]

■ *Communications systems*—A poorly designed communication system can starve a team of valuable information and feedback, or it may swamp it with information overload.[22] As we will learn in Chapter 9, communication systems are particularly important when team members are geographically dispersed. Even when team members are co-located (work in the same physical space), that space should be arranged to encourage rather than discourage face-to-face dialogue.

■ *Physical space*—The layout of an office or manufacturing facility does more than improve communication among team members. It also shapes employee perceptions about being together as a team and influences the team's ability to accomplish tasks. That's why Trojan Technologies Inc. in London, Ontario chose a building and furniture that allow teams to organize quickly and communicate effectively. "Nothing gets built without a team and office design needs to facilitate teamwork," explains Trojan president Hank Vander Laan.[23]

■ *Organizational environment*—Team success depends on the company's external environment. If the organization cannot secure resources, for instance, the team cannot fulfill its performance targets. Similarly, high demand for the team's output creates feelings of success, which motivates team members to stay with the team. A competitive environment can motivate employees to work together more closely.

■ *Organizational structure*—Many teams fail because the organizational structure does not support them. Teams work better when there are few layers of management and teams are given autonomy and responsibility for their work. This structure encourages interaction with team members rather than with supervisors. Teams also flourish when employees are organized around work processes rather than specialized skills. This structure increases interaction among team members.[24]

■ *Organizational leadership*—Teams require ongoing support from senior executives to align rewards, organizational structure, communication systems, and other elements of team context. They also require team leaders or facilitators who provide coaching and support. Team leaders are also enablers, meaning that they ensure their teams have the authority to solve their own problems and the resources to accomplish their tasks.[25] Leaders also maintain a value system that supports team performance more than individual success.

TEAM DESIGN FEATURES

Putting together a team is rather like designing a mini-organization. There are several elements to consider, and the wrong combination will undermine team effectiveness. Three of the main structural elements to consider when designing teams are task characteristics, team size, and team composition. As we saw earlier in the team effectiveness model (Exhibit 8.2), these design features affect team effectiveness directly as well as indirectly through team processes. For example, the skills and diversity of team members affect team cohesiveness, but they also have a direct effect on how well the team performs its task. Similarly, the type of work performed by the team (task characteristics) may influence the types of roles that emerge, but it also has a direct effect on the satisfaction and well-being of team members.

Task Characteristics

Teams are generally more effective when tasks are clear and easy to implement, because team members can learn their roles more quickly.[26] In contrast, teams with ill-defined tasks require more time to agree on the best division of labour and the correct way to accomplish the goal. These are typically more complex tasks requiring diverse skills and backgrounds, which further strain the team's ability to develop and form a cohesive unit.

task interdependence
The degree to which a task requires employees to share common inputs or outcomes, or to interact in the process of executing their work.

New Balance Athletic Shoe Inc. is competing against low-wage factories in Asia through technology and a team-based organization. Well-trained employees at New Balance's five factories in Massachusetts and Maine operate computerized equipment, running up to 20 sewing-machine heads at once. Everyone works in teams of five or six people, performing a half-dozen jobs, switching tasks every few minutes, and picking up the slack for one another. New employees receive 22 hours of classroom instruction on teamwork and other techniques and get continuous training on the factory floor. This combination of teams and technology allows New Balance to produce a pair of shoes in 24 minutes, compared with nearly three hours in Asian factories.[30] What level of task interdependence among team members seems to occur at New Balance? © Mark Garfinkel/Boston Herald
www.newbalance.com

Task interdependence **Task interdependence** is a critically important task characteristic because it relates to the definition of teams (i.e. that they interact and influence each other and are mutually accountable). Task interdependence exists when team members must share common inputs to their individual tasks, need to interact in the process of executing their work, or receive outcomes (such as rewards) that are partly determined by the performance of others.[27] The higher the level of task interdependence, the greater the need for teams rather than individuals working alone. Teams are well suited to highly interdependent tasks because people coordinate better when working together than separately. Moreover, recent evidence indicates that task interdependence creates an additional sense of responsibility among team members which motivates them to work together rather than alone.[28] This is why companies organize employees around work processes. Each team is responsible for highly interdependent tasks, so they coordinate the work more efficiently than individuals working in specialized departments.

Exhibit 8.3 illustrates the three levels of task interdependence.[29] *Pooled interdependence* is the lowest level of interdependence (other than independence), in which individuals operate independently except for reliance on a common resource or authority. Employees share a common payroll, cafeteria, and other organizational resources. In most cases, they can work well alone rather than in teams if pooled interdependence is the highest relationship among them.

Sequential interdependence occurs when the output of one person becomes the direct input for

Levels of task
interdependence

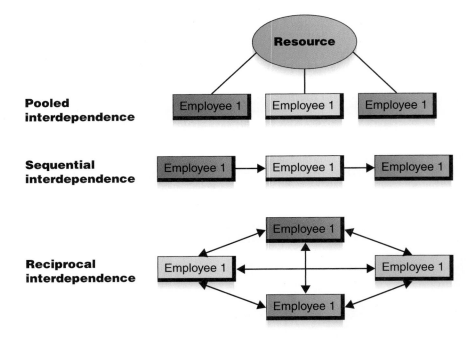

another person or unit. This interdependent linkage is found in fish processing plants. Fish are handled by the slitter, then passed to the gutter, who then passes their work to the slimers, who then send their work to the grader.[31] Although employees in this production line process usually work alone, they are sufficiently interdependent that Toyota and other companies create teams around these processes. *Reciprocal interdependence* is the highest level of interdependence, in which work output is exchanged back and forth among individuals. Employees with reciprocal interdependence should almost always be organized into teams to facilitate coordination in their interwoven relationship.

Team Size

St. Luke's is a highly successful British advertising agency that relies on self-directed work teams to serve clients. The London-based firm is so team-oriented that it refuses to participate in industry awards that recognize individual achievement. One way that St. Luke's supports team dynamics is through the "35 rule" which says that no team shall have more than 35 members. "When any one group becomes larger than 35 people, it has to split apart, as an amoeba would," explains Andy Law, St. Luke's CEO and co-founder.[32]

Team size is an important concern at St. Luke's. Some writers claim that team size should be limited to 10 people or less, making St. Luke's limit of 35 team members far too high. In reality, the optimal team size depends on several factors, such as the number of people required to complete the work and the amount of coordination needed to work together. The general rule is that teams should be large enough to provide the necessary competencies and perspectives to perform the work, yet small enough to maintain efficient coordination and the meaningful involvement of each member.[33]

Larger teams are typically less effective because members consume more time and effort coordinating their roles and resolving differences. Individuals have less opportunity to participate and, consequently, are less likely to feel that they are contributing to the team's success. Larger work units tend to break into informal subgroups around common interests and work activities, leading members to form stronger commitments to their subgroup than to the larger team. Pharmaceutical giant Pfizer Inc. tries to avoid large teams at its research centres by organizing five to seven scientists into "families" and grouping about 10 families into a "tribe" of 70 people.[34]

Team Composition

Steve Currie vividly recalls his job interview at the Flight Centres travel agency in Toronto. After an initial telephone screening, Currie and about 30 other applicants attended a session where groups of four applicants were given several challenges. One task was to figure out how to survive on a desert island after a shipwreck. After lunch, candidates who performed well on these role-play exercises were given formal interviews.[35]

Flight Centres travel agency has a strong team orientation, so it carefully selects people with the necessary motivation *and* competencies to work together. With respect to motivation, every member must have sufficient drive to perform the task in a team environment. Team members must be motivated to agree on the goal, work together rather than alone, and abide by the team's rules of conduct. Employees with a collectivist orientation—those who value duty to groups to which they belong, and to group harmony (see Chapter 2)—tend to perform better in work teams, whereas those with a low collectivist orientation tend to perform better alone.[36]

Along with the motivation to work in teams, employees must possess the skills and knowledge necessary to accomplish the team's objectives.[37] Each person needs only some of the necessary skills, but the entire group must have the full set of competencies. Team members also need to be able to work well with others. Research suggests that high performing team members demonstrate more cooperative behaviour toward others and generally have more emotional intelligence to manage their emotions (see Chapter 4). Researchers also emphasize the importance of training employees in ways to communicate and coordinate with each other in a team environment.[38] Connections 8.1 describes how Sean Loutitt, the chief pilot at Calgary-based Kenn Borek Air Ltd., considered each of these team composition issues when he selected crew members to rescue an ailing American doctor from an Antarctic research station in winter.

homogeneous teams
Teams that include members with common technical expertise, demographics (age, gender), ethnicity, experiences, or values.

heterogeneous teams
Teams that include members with diverse personal characteristics and backgrounds.

Team diversity   Another important dimension of team composition is the diversity of team members.[39] **Homogeneous teams** include members with common technical expertise, demographics (age, gender), ethnicity, experiences, or values, whereas **heterogeneous teams** have members with diverse personal characteristics and backgrounds. Should teams be homogeneous or heterogeneous? Both have advantages and disadvantages, so their relative effectiveness depends on the situation. Heterogeneous teams experience more conflict and take longer to develop. They are susceptible to "faultlines"—hypothetical dividing lines that may split a team into subgroups along gender, ethnic, professional, or other dimensions. In some situations, these faultlines may eventually split the team apart.[40] In contrast, members of homogeneous teams experience higher satisfaction, less

Team Composition Helps Calgary Crew Succeed in Daring Antarctic Rescue

As chief pilot of Calgary-based Kenn Borek Air Ltd., Sean Loutitt had flown people and supplies to Antarctica many times during the southern hemisphere summer. But when asked to rescue an ailing doctor from Amundsen-Scott research station at the South Pole in late April, wintertime in Antarctica, Loutitt knew that the success of this risky mission would depend on picking the right people for his team. "[We] want the person to be a team player," Loutitt recalls in his choice of co-pilot Mark Carey and flight engineer Norm Wong. "I mean, we all have to pull together and work together." Three other staff from Kenn Borek Air were also chosen as the back-up crew in a second plane.

No one had previously flown to Antarctica so late into the southern hemisphere winter, when the continent is in complete darkness and extremely cold. The U.S. Air Force attempted a rescue, but abandoned the idea because its three Hercules cargo planes could not fly at temperatures below -55 C and would require more fuel to get out than the research station could spare. Temperatures at Amundsen-Scott research station regularly dip to -70 C, a temperature at which metal snaps like a twig and airplane fuel turns to jelly.

Using rugged twin-Otter planes built for the Canadian Arctic, the two crews flew for five days from Calgary to Chile, then to the British base station of Rothera on Antarctica's coast. While the backup plane waited in Rothera, Sean Loutitt and his team flew their fully loaded plane with a replacement physician through 2,500 kilometres of darkness to the South Pole research station.

Research station staff braved -71 C temperatures to clear the snowy runway and cheer the Twin Otter as it landed. Special heaters kept the plane from freezing over while the rescue team slept, but the wing flaps were frozen and the plane's skis were stuck to the ice

Sean Loutitt (far right) carefully picked team members Mark Carey and Norm Wong (both on left) for a daring rescue mission to an Antarctic research station during winter. The team is shown here during that trip with Canadian researchers Jennifer and John Bird, who work at the station. *Copyright John Bird*

when they returned to the plane. Creative "bush maintenance" got the flaps working and the plane free, but without knowing whether the instrumentation was actually working. Only several hours later, when a pink line of light appeared along the horizon, did the crew know that they were heading in the right direction, back to Rothera station. "All of us are pretty proud," says Loutitt about the rescue. "It was a big team effort."

Sources: T. Clark, "Flight into Darkness," *W-Five* (CTV Television), December 2, 2001; L. Abraham, "Teamwork Key in South Pole Rescue," *Regina Leader-Post*, April 28, 2001, p. D13; M. Reid, "Tired Rescue Team finally Flying Home," *Calgary Herald*, April 26, 2001.
www.borekair.com

conflict, and better interpersonal relations. Consequently, homogeneous teams tend to be more effective on tasks requiring a high degree of cooperation and coordination, such as emergency response teams or string quartets.

Although heterogeneous teams are more difficult to develop, they are generally more effective than homogeneous teams in executive groups and in other situations involving complex problems that require innovative solutions.[41] This is because people from different backgrounds see a problem or opportunity from different perspectives. For example, one recent study found that all-male teams were less effective than mixed gender teams on some tasks because all-male teams tended to make decisions that were too aggressive.[42]

Heterogeneous team members also solve complex problems more easily because they usually have a broader knowledge base. However, the benefits of diversity occur primarily when the team tries to reach consensus (rather than voting) and each member actively tries to understand and incorporate other members' viewpoints. A senior executive at Monsanto Corp. sums up this view: "Every time I have put together a diverse group of people, that team has always come up with a more breakthrough solution than any homogeneous group working on the same problem."[43]

Finally, a team's diversity may give it more legitimacy or allow its members to obtain a wide network of cooperation and support in the organization. When teams represent various professions or departments, they are more likely to represent the organization's diverse interests and perspectives. As a result, other employees are more likely to accept and support the team's decisions and actions.

TEAM PROCESSES

Our discussion so far has presented two sets of elements in the team effectiveness model: (1) organizational and team environment and (2) team design. The next few pages introduce the third set of team effectiveness elements, collectively known as team processes. These processes—team development, norms, roles, and cohesiveness—are influenced by both team design and organizational and team environment factors.

TEAM DEVELOPMENT

A few years ago, the National Transportation Safety Board (NTSB) in the United States studied the circumstances under which airplane cockpit crews were most likely to have accidents and related problems. What they discovered was startling: 73 percent of all incidents took place on the crew's first day, and 44 percent occurred on the crew's very first flight together. This isn't an isolated example. NASA studied pilot fatigue after the pilots returned from multiple-day trips. Not surprisingly, fatigued pilots made more errors in NASA flight simulators. But the NASA researchers were surprised to discover that fatigued crews who had worked together made fewer errors than rested crews who had not yet flown together.[44]

The NTSB and NASA studies reveal that team members must resolve several issues and pass through several stages of development before emerging as an effective work unit. They must get to know each other, understand their roles, discover which behaviours are appropriate and which are inappropriate, and learn how to coordinate their work or social activities. The longer team members work together, the better they develop common mental models, mutual understanding, and effective performance routines to complete the work. For this reason, Budd Canada resisted union demands for a new work schedule that would create new work teams. "Even though the individual level of skills could be good, people who work together as a team regularly are always slightly ahead of a team that is put together on an ad hoc basis," explains Budd Canada executive Winston Wong.[45]

The five-stage model of team development shown in Exhibit 8.4 provides a general outline of how teams evolve by forming, storming, norming, performing, and eventually adjourning.[46] The model shows teams progressing from one stage to the next in an orderly fashion, but the dotted lines also illustrate that they might

Stages of team
development

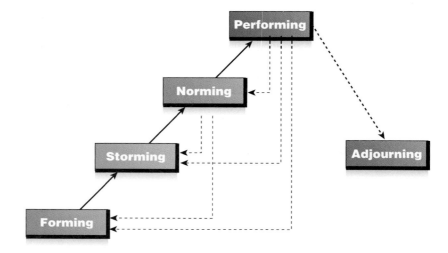

fall back to an earlier stage of development as new members join or other conditions disrupt the team's maturity.

1. *Forming*—The first stage of team development is a period of testing and orientation in which members learn about each other and evaluate the benefits and costs of continued membership. People tend to be polite during this stage and will defer to the existing authority of either a formal or informal leader who must provide an initial set of rules and structures for interaction. Members experience a form of socialization as they try to find out what is expected of them and how they will fit into the team.

2. *Storming*—The storming stage is marked by interpersonal conflict as members become more proactive and compete for various team roles. Coalitions may form to influence the team's goals and means of goal attainment. Members try to establish norms of appropriate behaviour and performance standards. This is a tenuous stage in the team's development, particularly when the leader is autocratic and lacks the necessary conflict-management skills.

3. *Norming*—During the norming stage, the team develops its first real sense of cohesion as roles are established and a consensus forms around group objectives. Members have developed relatively similar mental models, so they have common expectations and assumptions about how the team's goals should be accomplished. They have developed common team-based mental models that allow them to interact more efficiently so they can move into performing, the next stage.[47]

4. *Performing*—The team becomes more task-oriented in the performing stage. Team members have learned to coordinate and resolve conflicts more efficiently. Further coordination improvements must occasionally be addressed, but the greater emphasis is on task accomplishment. In high-performance teams, members are highly cooperative, have a high level of trust in each other, are committed to group objectives, and identify with the team. There is a climate of mutual support in which team members feel comfortable about taking risks, making errors, or asking for help.[48]

5. *Adjourning*—Most work teams and informal groups eventually end. Task forces disband when their project is completed. Informal work groups may

reach this stage when several members leave the organization or are reassigned elsewhere. Some teams adjourn as a result of layoffs or plant shutdowns. Whatever the cause of team adjournment, members shift their attention away from task orientation to a socio-emotional focus as they realize that their relationship is ending.

The team development model is a useful framework for thinking about how teams develop. At the same time, we must keep in mind that it is not a perfect representation of the dynamics of team development.[49] The model does not explicitly show that some teams remain in a particular stage longer than others, or that team development is a continuous process. As membership changes and new conditions emerge, teams cycle back to earlier stages in the developmental process to regain the equilibrium or balance lost by the change (as shown by the dotted lines in Exhibit 8.4).

TEAM NORMS

norms

The informal rules and expectations that groups establish to regulate the behaviour of their members.

Have you ever noticed how employees in some departments almost run for the exit door the minute the work day ends, whereas people in the same jobs elsewhere seem to be competing for who can stay at work the longest? These differences are partly due to **norms**—the informal rules and expectations that groups establish to regulate the behaviour of their members. Norms apply only to behaviour, not to private thoughts or feelings. Moreover, norms exist only for behaviours that are important to the team.[50]

Norms guide the way team members deal with clients, how they share resources, whether they are willing to work longer hours, and many other behaviours in organizational life. Some norms ensure that employees support organizational goals, whereas other norms might conflict with organizational objectives. For example, the level of employee absence from work is partly influenced by absence norms in the workplace. In other words, employees are more likely to take off work if they work in teams that support this behaviour.[51]

Conformity to Team Norms

Everyone has experienced peer pressure at one time or another. Co-workers grimace if we are late for a meeting or make sarcastic comments if we don't have our part of the project completed on time. In more extreme situations, team members may try to enforce their norms by temporarily ostracizing deviant co-workers or threatening to terminate their membership. This heavy-handed peer pressure isn't as rare as you might think. One survey revealed that 20 percent of employees have been pressured by their colleagues to slack off at work. Half the time, the peer pressure occurred because colleagues didn't want to look like poor performers when compared with their more productive co-workers.[52]

Norms are also directly reinforced through praise from high-status members, more access to valued resources, or other rewards available to the team.[53] But team members often conform to prevailing norms without direct reinforcement or punishment because they identify with the group and want to align their behaviour with the team's values. This effect is particularly strong in new members because they are uncertain of their status and want to demonstrate their membership in the team. GLOBAL Connections 8.2 provides an extreme example of the consequences of team norms and conformity in organizational settings.

Elite New Zealand Prison Team's "Culture of Obedience"

Members of a special emergency response team congregated at dawn for a covert mission. The 16 hand-picked and specially trained members based at Paparua Prison, New Zealand, were supposed to reduce prison violence, prevent drugs from entering prisons, and improve prisoner compliance. But the mission on this day was different. The response team was hunting for an escapee—a rooster belonging to a member of the response team that had escaped to a neighbouring farm.

This is just one of the bizarre incidents about the special unit, dubbed the "Goon Squad" by adversaries. The team worked independently of the prison officers and had its own distinctive black uniforms. Unfortunately, a government report also concluded that the team developed a distinctive set of norms, some of which violated Corrections Department policies.

A government investigation heard claims that the team falsified time sheets, juggled the work roster for personal gain, used department vehicles for personal use, used unnecessary intimidation on inmates, disci-

plined staff inappropriately, and hunted wayward roosters on company time. The special unit also conducted missions in the outside community even though its mandate was restricted to the prison. "Our focus moved to a policeman's role, which we should not have been doing," admits one former member.

None of its members complained during the unit's existence because of "a culture of obedience." For example, when one member refused to go to a party, others in the unit allegedly went to his home, restrained him, hit him over the head with an axe handle, handcuffed him, and dragged him along to the party.

"The most chilling thing about the team was an apparent fear of authority among members, leading to a culture of obedience and silence," says an executive member of the Howard League for Penal Reform. "In effect, they became a law unto themselves."

Sources: Y. Martin, "Goon Squad," *The Press (Christchurch),* June 9, 2001, p. 2; "'Goon Squad' Prison Staff Disciplined," *New Zealand Press Association,* May 23, 2001; Y. Martin, "Crack Prison Team Members Guilty of Serious Misconduct," *The Press (Christchurch),* May 24, 2001, p. 1. **nz.realisticpolitics.com/ goonsquadaction.htm**

How Team Norms Develop

Norms develop as team members learn that certain behaviours help them function more effectively.[54] Some norms develop when team members or outsiders make explicit statements that seem to aid the team's success or survival. For example, the team leader might frequently express the importance of treating customers with respect and courtesy. A second factor triggering the development of a new norm is a critical event in the team's history. A team might develop a strong norm to keep the work area clean after a co-worker slips on metal scraps and seriously injures herself.

Team norms are most strongly influenced by events soon after the team is formed.[55] Future behaviours are influenced by the way members of a newly formed team initially greet each other, where they locate themselves in a meeting, and so on. A fourth influence on team norms is the beliefs and values that members bring to the team. For example, bargaining groups develop norms about appropriate bargaining behaviour based on each member's previous bargaining experience.[56]

Troubleshooting Dysfunctional Team Norms

Although many team norms are deeply anchored, there are ways to change them or minimize their influence on employee behaviour. One approach is to introduce performance-oriented norms as soon as the team is created. Another strategy is to select members who will bring desirable norms to the group. If the organization wants to emphasize safety, then it should select team members who already value safety.

Selecting people with positive norms may be effective in new teams, but not when adding new members to existing teams with counterproductive norms. A better strategy for existing teams is to explicitly discuss the counterproductive norm with team members using persuasive communication tactics (see Chapter 12).[57] For example, the surgical team of a small Ontario hospital had developed a norm of arriving late for operations. Patients and other hospital staff often waited 30 minutes or more for the team to arrive. The hospital CEO eventually spoke to the surgical team about their lateness and, through moral suasion, convinced team members to arrive for operating room procedures no more than five minutes late for their appointments.[58]

Team-based reward systems can sometimes weaken counterproductive norms. Unfortunately, the pressure to conform to the counterproductive norm is sometimes stronger than the financial incentive.[59] For instance, employees working in a pyjama factory were paid under a piece-rate system. Some individuals in the group were able to process up to 100 units per hour and thereby earn more money, but they all chose to abide by the group norm of 50 units per hour.[60]

Finally, a dysfunctional norm may be so deeply ingrained that the best strategy is to disband the group and replace it with people having more favourable norms. Companies should seize the opportunity to introduce performance-oriented norms when the new team is formed, and select members who will bring desirable norms to the group.

TEAM ROLES

role
A set of behaviours that people are expected to perform because they hold certain positions in a team and organization.

Every work team and informal group has two sets of roles that help it to survive and be more productive. A **role** is the set of behaviours that people are expected to perform because they hold certain positions in a team and organization.[61] One set of roles helps focus the team on its objectives, such as giving and seeking information, elaborating ideas, coordinating activities, and summarizing the discussion or past events (see Exhibit 8.5). The other set of roles tries to maintain good working relations among team members. These relationship-oriented roles include resolving conflicts among team members, keeping communication channels open, reinforcing positive behaviours of other team members, and making team members aware of group process problems when they emerge.

team cohesiveness
The degree of attraction people feel toward the team and their motivation to remain members.

Some team roles are formally assigned to specific people. For example, team leaders are usually expected to initiate discussion, ensure that everyone has an opportunity to present their views, and help the team reach agreement on the issues discussed. But team members often take on various roles informally. Some people like to encourage colleagues to participate more actively. Others prefer to mediate conflicts that may arise among team members. As noted earlier, these preferences are usually worked out during the storming stage of team development. The critical point is that team members need to ensure that these roles are fulfilled so that the team can function effectively.

TEAM COHESIVENESS

Team cohesiveness—the degree of attraction people feel toward the team and their motivation to remain members—is usually an important factor in a team's success.[62] Employees feel cohesiveness when they believe the team will help them achieve their personal goals, fulfill their need for affiliation or status, or provide

EXHIBIT 8.5   Roles for team effectiveness

Role activities	Description	Example
Task-oriented roles		
Initiator	Identifies goals for the meeting, including ways to work on those goals	"The main purpose of this meeting is to solve the problem our client is having with this product."
Information seeker	Asks for clarification of ideas or further information to support an opinion	"Jang, why do you think the client is using the product incorrectly?"
Information giver	Shares information and opinions about the team's task and goals	"Let me tell you what some of my clients did to overcome this problem."
Coordinator	Coordinates subgroups and pulls together ideas	"Susan, will you be meeting with Shaheem's group this week to review common issues with the client?"
Evaluator	Assesses the team's functioning against a standard	"So far, we have resolved three of the client's concerns, but we still have a tough one to wrestle with."
Summarizer	Acts as the team's memory	Person takes notes of meeting and summarizes the discussion when requested.
Orienter	Keeps the team focused on its goals	"We seem to be getting off on a tangent; let's focus on why the product isn't operating properly for our client."
Relationship-oriented roles		
Harmonizer	Mediates intragroup conflicts and reduces tension	"Courtney, you and Brad may want to look at your positions on this; they aren't as different as they seem."
Gatekeeper	Encourages and facilitates participation of all team members	"James, what do you think about this issue?"
Encourager	Praises and supports the ideas of other team members, thereby showing warmth and solidarity to the group	"Tracy, that's a wonderful suggestion. I think we will solve the client's problem sooner than we expected."

Sources: Adapted from information in K. D. Benne and P. Sheats, "Functional Roles of Group Members," *Journal of Social Issues*, 4 (1948), pp. 41–49.

social support during times of crisis or trouble. Cohesiveness is an emotional experience, not just a calculation of whether to stay or leave the team. It exists when team members make the team part of their social identity (see Chapter 3). Cohesiveness is the glue or *esprit de corps* that holds the group together and ensures that its members fulfill their obligations.[63]

Influences on Team Cohesiveness

Several factors influence team cohesiveness: member similarity, team size, member interaction, difficult entry, team success, and external competition or challenges. For the most part, these factors reflect the individual's social identity with the group and beliefs about how team membership will fulfill personal needs.[64] Several of these factors are related to our earlier discussion about why people join informal groups and how teams develop. Specifically, teams become more cohesive as they reach higher stages of development and are more attractive to potential members.

Member similarity Homogeneous teams become cohesive more easily than heterogeneous teams. People in homogeneous teams have similar backgrounds and values, so they find it easier to agree on team objectives, the means to fulfill those objectives, and the rules applied to maintain group behaviour. This, in turn, leads to greater trust and less dysfunctional conflict within the group.[65] In contrast, diverse teams are susceptible to the previously described "faultlines" that psychologically impede cohesiveness, particularly during the early stages of development. The dilemma here is that heterogeneous teams are usually better than homogeneous teams at completing complex tasks or solving problems requiring creative solutions.

Team size Smaller teams tend to be more cohesive than larger teams because it is easier for a few people to agree on goals and coordinate work activities. The smallest teams aren't always the most cohesive, however. Small teams are less cohesive when they lack enough members to perform the required tasks. Thus, team cohesiveness is potentially greatest when teams are as small as possible, yet large enough to accomplish the required tasks.

Member interaction Teams tend to be more cohesive when team members interact with each other fairly regularly. This occurs when team members perform highly interdependent tasks and work in the same physical area.[66] As we noted earlier, Trojan Technologies in London, Ontario has strengthened team cohesiveness by providing office space and furniture that allow employees to quickly form teams in the same physical area. Similarly, Chatelain Architects encourages team interaction with an open office space consisting of low partitions and no special acoustical barriers. "We are always moving around, teaming up and working at other people's desks," says Chatelain executive Jill Miernicki. "It's a very dynamic environment."[67]

Somewhat difficult entry Teams tend to be more cohesive when entry to the team is restricted. The more élite the team, the more prestige it confers on its members, and the more the members tend to value their membership in the unit. Existing team members are also more willing to welcome and support new members after they have "passed the test," possibly because they have shared the same entry experience. One issue is how difficult the initiation should be for entry into the team. Research suggests that severe initiations can potentially lead to humiliation and psychological distance from the group, even for those who successfully endure the initiation.[68]

Team success Cohesiveness increases with the team's level of success.[69] Individuals are more likely to attach their social identity to successful teams than to those with a string of failures. Moreover, team members are more likely to believe the group will continue to be successful, thereby fulfilling their personal goals (continued employment, pay bonus, etc.) Team leaders can increase cohesiveness by regularly communicating and celebrating the team's successes. Notice that this can create a spiral effect. Successful teams are more cohesive and, under certain conditions, increased cohesiveness increases the team's success.

External competition and challenges   Team cohesiveness tends to increase when members face external competition or a valued objective that is challenging.[70] This might include the threat from an external competitor or friendly competition from other teams. These conditions tend to increase cohesiveness because employees value the team's ability to overcome the threat or competition if they can't solve the problem individually. They also value their membership as a form of social support. We need to be careful about the degree of external threat, however. Evidence suggests that teams seem to be less effective when external threats are severe. Although cohesiveness tends to increase, external threats are stressful and cause teams to make less effective decisions under these conditions.[71]

Consequences of Team Cohesiveness

Every team must have some minimal level of cohesiveness to maintain its existence.[72] People who belong to high cohesion teams are motivated to maintain their membership and to help the team work effectively. Compared with low cohesion teams, high cohesion team members spend more time together, share information more frequently, and are more satisfied with each other. They provide each other with better social support in stressful situations.[73]

Members of high cohesion teams are generally more sensitive to each other's needs and develop better interpersonal relationships, thereby reducing dysfunctional conflict. When conflict does arise, they tend to resolve these differences swiftly and effectively. For example, a recent Canadian study reported that cohesive recreational hockey teams engaged in more constructive conflict—that is, team members tried to resolve their differences cooperatively—whereas less cohesive teams engaged in more combative conflict.[74]

Cohesiveness and team performance   With better cooperation and more conformity to norms, high cohesion teams usually perform better than low cohesion teams.[76] However, the relationship is a little more complex. Exhibit 8.6 illustrates how the effect of cohesiveness on team performance depends on the extent that team norms are consistent with organizational goals. Cohesive teams will likely have lower task performance when norms conflict with organizational objectives, because cohesiveness motivates employees to perform at a level more consistent with group norms.[77]

Trevor Pound was looking forward to lying on a Mexican beach for his 30th birthday. But the software engineer's crucial role in a major project at Mitel, the Ottawa-based high technology company, put those February vacation plans on hold. Pound barely mentioned his disappointment, but fellow team members at the communications systems firm wanted to make up for his loss. Nearly a dozen co-workers spent a weekend transforming Pound's drab grey cubicle into a colourful oasis. They brought in a five-foot-wide beach umbrella, a beach chair, a heat lamp, a ukulele, some beach toys, a dozen tropical plants, and over 100 kilograms of sand. The culprits even supplied colourful shorts and a Hawaiian style shirt. The result: Pound celebrated his birthday in an almost tropical setting on that cold winter day. More important, the practical joke expressed the team's support for his loss of personal time.[75] How else do cohesive team members support each other? © *John Major/Ottawa Citizen*
www.mitel.com

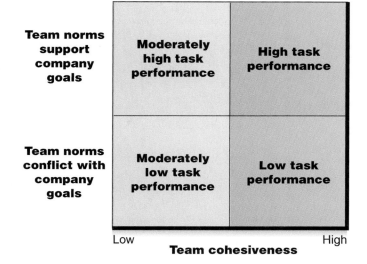

EXHIBIT 8.6

Effect of team cohesiveness on task performance

	Low ——— Team cohesiveness ——— High
Team norms support company goals	Moderately high task performance | High task performance
Team norms conflict with company goals	Moderately low task performance | Low task performance

THE TROUBLE WITH TEAMS

Scholars and business leaders have long recognized that teams can be a competitive advantage. Yet, it is easy to lose sight of the fact that teams aren't always needed.[78] Sometimes, a quick and decisive action by one person is more appropriate. Some tasks are also performed just as easily by one person as by a group. "Teams are overused," admits Philip Condit, CEO of Boeing, Inc. The aircraft manufacturer makes extensive use of teams, but knows that they aren't necessary for everything that goes on in organizations. Management guru Peter Drucker agrees. "The now-fashionable team in which everybody works with everybody on everything from the beginning rapidly is becoming a disappointment," he says.[79]

A second problem is that teams take time to develop and maintain. Scholars refer to these hidden costs as **process losses**—resources (including time and energy) expended toward team development and maintenance rather than the task.[80] It is much more efficient for an individual to work out an issue alone that to resolve differences of opinion with other people. The process loss problem becomes apparent when adding new people to the team. The group has to recycle through the team development process to bring everyone up to speed. The software industry even has a name for this. "Brooks's Law" says that adding more people to a late software project only makes it later. Researchers point out that the cost of process losses may be offset by the benefits of teams. Unfortunately, few companies conduct a cost-benefit analysis of their team activities.[81]

A third problem is that teams require the right environment to flourish. Many companies forget this point by putting people in teams without changing anything else. As we noted earlier, teams require appropriate rewards, communication systems, team leadership, and other conditions. Without these, the shift to a team structure could be a waste of time. At the same time, critics suggest that changing these environmental conditions to improve teamwork could result in higher costs than benefits for the overall organization.[82]

process losses
Resources (including time and energy) expended toward team development and maintenance rather than the task.

Social Loafing

social loafing
A situation in which people exert less effort (and usually perform at a lower level) when working in groups than when working alone.

Perhaps the best known limitation of teams is the risk of productivity loss due to **social loafing**. Social loafing occurs when people exert less effort (and usually perform at a lower level) when working in groups than when working alone.[83] A few scholars question whether social loafing is very common, but students can certainly report many instances of this problem in their team projects!

Social loafing is most likely to occur in large teams when individual output is difficult to identify. This particularly includes situations in which team members work alone toward a common output pool (i.e. they have low task interdependence). Under these conditions, employees aren't as worried that their performance will be noticed. Social loafing is less likely to occur when the task is interesting, because individuals have a higher intrinsic motivation to perform their duties. It is less common when the group's objective is important, possibly because individuals experience more pressure from other team members to perform well. Finally, social loafing is less common among members with a strong collectivist value, because they value group membership and believe in working toward group objectives (see Chapter 4).[84]

How to minimize social loafing   By understanding the causes of social loafing, we can identify ways to minimize this problem. Some of the strategies listed below reduce social loafing by making each member's performance more visible. Other strategies increase each member's motivation to perform his or her tasks within the group.[85]

- *Form smaller teams*—Splitting the team into several smaller groups reduces social loafing because each person's performance becomes more noticeable and important for team performance. A smaller group also potentially increases cohesiveness, so would-be shirkers feel a greater obligation to perform fully for their team.
- *Specialize tasks*—It is easier to see everyone's contribution when each team member performs a different work activity. For example, rather than pooling their effort for all incoming customer inquiries, each customer service representative might be assigned a particular type of client.
- *Measure individual performance*—Social loafing is minimized when each member's contribution is measured. Of course, individual performance is difficult to measure in some team activities, such as problem-solving projects in which the team's performance depends on one person discovering the best answer.
- *Increase job enrichment*—Social loafing is minimized when team members are assigned more motivating jobs, such as those requiring more skill variety or having direct contact with clients. However, this minimizes social loafing only if members have a strong growth need strength (see Chapter 6). More generally, however, social loafing is less common among employees with high job satisfaction.
- *Select motivated employees*—Social loafing can be minimized by carefully selecting job applicants who are motivated by the task and have a collectivist value orientation. Those with collectivist values are motivated to work harder for the team because they value their membership in the group.

This chapter has laid the foundation for our understanding of team dynamics. To build an effective team requires time, the right combination of team members, and the right environment. We will apply these ingredients of environment and team processes in the next chapter, which looks at high performance teams, including self-directed teams and virtual teams.

CHAPTER SUMMARY

Teams are groups of two or more people that interact and influence each other, are mutually accountable for achieving common objectives, and perceive themselves as a social entity within an organization. All teams are groups because they consist of people with a unifying relationship, but not all groups are teams, because they don't have purposive interaction.

Traditional departments are typically permanent work teams because employees directly interact and coordinate work activities with each other. Organizations also rely on task forces, skunkworks, and other relatively temporary teams to make decisions or complete short-term projects. Informal groups exist primarily for the benefit of their members rather than for the organization. Communities of practice may be teams or informal groups in which members are bound together by shared expertise or passion for a particular activity or interest.

Team effectiveness includes the group's ability to survive, achieve its system-based objectives, and fulfill the needs of its members. The model of team effectiveness considers the team and organizational environment, team design, and team processes. The team or organizational environment influences team effectiveness directly, as well as through team design and team processes. Six elements in the organizational and team environment that influence team effectiveness are reward systems, communication systems, physical space, organizational environment, organizational structure, and organizational leadership.

Three team design elements are task characteristics, team size, and team composition. Teams work best when tasks are clear, easy to implement, and require a high degree of interdependence. Teams should be large enough to perform the work, yet small enough for efficient coordination and meaningful involvement. Effective teams are composed of people with the competencies and motivation to perform tasks in a team environment. Heterogeneous teams operate best on complex projects and problems requiring innovative solutions.

Teams develop through the stages of forming, storming, norming, performing, and eventually adjourning. However, some teams remain in a particular stage longer than others, and team development is a continuous process. Teams develop norms to regulate and guide member behaviour. These norms may be influenced by critical events, explicit statements, initial experiences, and members' pregroup experiences. Team members also have roles—a set of behaviours they are expected to perform because they hold certain positions in a team and organization.

Cohesiveness is the degree of attraction people feel toward the team and their motivation to remain members. Cohesiveness increases with member similarity, smaller team size, higher degree of interaction, somewhat difficult entry, team success, and external challenges. Teams need some level of cohesiveness to survive, but high cohesive units have higher task performance only when their norms do not conflict with organizational objectives.

Teams are not always beneficial or necessary. Moreover, they have hidden costs, known as process losses, and require particular environments to flourish. Teams often fail because they are not set up in supportive environments. Social loafing is another potential problem with teams. This is the tendency for individuals to perform at a lower level when working in groups than when alone. Social loafing can be minimized by making each member's performance more visible and increasing each member's motivation to perform his or her tasks within the group.

KEY TERMS

Communities of practice, p. 234

Groups, p. 232

Heterogeneous teams, p. 239

Homogeneous teams, p. 239

Informal groups, p. 234

Norms, p. 243

Process losses, p. 249

Role, p. 245

Skunkworks, p. 233

Social loafing, p. 250

Task interdependence, p. 237

Team cohesiveness, p. 245

Team effectiveness, p. 235

Teams, p. 232

DISCUSSION QUESTIONS

1. Informal groups exist in almost every form of social organization. What types of informal groups exist in your classroom? Why are students motivated to belong to these informal groups?

2. What are "communities of practice"? How can they contribute to organizational performance? Individual performance?

3. You have been asked to lead a complex software project over the next year that requires the full-time involvement of approximately 100 people with diverse skills and backgrounds. Using your knowledge of team size, how can you develop an effective team under these conditions?

4. You have been put in charge of a cross-functional task force that will develop enhanced Internet banking services for retail customers. The team includes representatives from marketing, information services, customer service, and accounting, all of whom will move to the same location at headquarters for three months. Describe the behaviours you might observe during each stage of the team's development.

5. You have just been transferred from the Regina office to the Saskatoon office of your company, a Canada-wide sales organization of electrical products for developers and contractors. In Regina, team members regularly called customers after a sale to ask whether the products arrived on time and whether they are satisfied. But when you moved to the Saskatoon office, no one seemed to make these follow-up calls. A recently hired co-worker explained that other co-workers discouraged her from making those calls. Later, another co-worker suggested that your follow-up calls were making everyone else look lazy. Give three possible reasons why the norms in Saskatoon might be different from those in the Regina office, even though the customers, products, sales commissions, and other characteristics of the workplace are almost identical.

6. Describe a time when you were part of a work team or an informal group. Using Exhibit 8.5 as a guide, identify the role(s) you performed and the specific behaviours you demonstrated in each role. What role did you enjoy the most? Why? What are the implications of this information to you? To your organization?

7. You have been assigned to a class project with five other students, none of whom you have met before. To what extent would team cohesiveness improve your team's performance on this project? What actions would you recommend to build team cohesiveness among student team members in this situation?

8. "The now-fashionable team in which everybody works with everybody on everything from the beginning rapidly is becoming a disappointment." Discuss three problems associated with teams.

CASE STUDY   8.1

TREETOP FOREST PRODUCTS

Treetop Forest Products Ltd. is a sawmill operation in British Columbia that is owned by a major forest products company, and operates independently of headquarters. It was built 30 years ago, and completely updated with new machinery five years ago. Treetop receives raw logs from the area for cutting and planing into building-grade lumber, mostly 2-by-4 and 2-by-6 pieces of standard lengths. Higher-grade logs leave Treetop's sawmill department in finished form and are sent directly to the packaging department. The remaining 40 percent of sawmill output are cuts from lower grade logs, and require further work by the planing department.

Treetop has one general manager, 16 supervisors and support staff, and 180 unionized employees.

The unionized employees are paid an hourly rate specified in the collective agreement, and management and support staff are paid a monthly salary. The mill is divided into six operating departments: boom, sawmill, planer, packaging, shipping, and maintenance. The sawmill, boom, and packaging departments operate a morning shift starting at 6 a.m. and an afternoon shift starting at 2 p.m. Employees in these departments rotate shifts every two weeks. The planer and shipping departments operate only morning shifts. Maintenance employees work the night shift (starting at 10 p.m.).

Each department, except for packaging, has a supervisor on every work shift. The planer supervisor is responsible for the packaging department on the morning shift, and the sawmill supervisor is responsible for the packaging department on the afternoon shift. However, the packaging operation is housed in a building that is separate from the other departments, so supervisors seldom visit the packaging department. This is particularly true for the afternoon shift, because the sawmill supervisor is the furthest distance from the packaging building.

Packaging Quality

Ninety percent of Treetop's product is sold on the international market through Westboard Co., a large marketing agency. Westboard represents all forest products mills owned by Treetop's parent company as well as several other clients in the region. The market for building-grade lumber is very price competitive, because many mills sell the same product. However, some differentiation does occur in product packaging and presentation and buyers look closely at the packaging when deciding whether to buy from Treetop or another mill.

To encourage its clients to package their products better, Westboard sponsors a monthly package quality award. The marketing agency samples and rates its clients' packages daily, and the sawmill with the highest score at the end of the month is awarded a plaque. Package quality is a combination of how the lumber is piled (e.g., defects turned in), where the bands and dunnage are placed, how neatly the stencil and seal are applied, the stencil's accuracy, and how neatly and tightly the plastic wrap is attached.

Treetop Forest Products has won Westboard's packaging quality award several times over the past few years, and received high ratings in the months that it didn't win. However, the mill's ratings have started to decline over the past couple of years, and several clients have complained about the appearance of the finished product. A few large customers switched to competitors' lumber, saying that the decision was based on the substandard appearance of Treetop's packaging when it arrived in their lumber yard.

Bottleneck in Packaging

The planing and sawmilling departments have significantly increased productivity over the past couple of years. The sawmill operation recently set a new productivity record on a single day. The planer operation has increased productivity to the point where last year it reduced operations to just one (rather than two) shifts per day. These productivity improvements are due to better operator training, fewer machine breakdowns, and better selection of raw logs. (Sawmill cuts from high-quality logs do not usually require planing work.)

Productivity levels in the boom, shipping, and maintenance departments have remained constant. However, the packaging department has recorded decreasing productivity over the past couple of years, with the result that a large backlog of finished product is typically stockpiled outside the packaging building. The morning shift of the packaging department is unable to keep up with the combined production of the sawmill and planer departments, so the unpackaged output is left for the afternoon shift. Unfortunately, the afternoon shift packages even less product than the morning shift, so the backlog continues to build. The backlog adds to Treetop's inventory costs and increases the risk of damaged stock.

Treetop has added Saturday overtime shifts as well as extra hours before and after the regular shifts for the packaging department employees to process this backlog. Last month, the packaging department employed 10 percent of the work force but accounted for 85 percent of the overtime. This is frustrating to Treetop's management, because time and motion studies recently confirmed that the packaging department is capable of processing all the daily sawmill and planer production without overtime. Moreover, with employees earning one and a half or two times their regular pay on overtime, Treetop's cost competitiveness suffers.

Employees and supervisors at Treetop are aware that people in the packaging department tend to extend lunch by 10 minutes and coffee breaks by 5 minutes. They also typically leave work a few minutes before the end of shift. This abuse has worsened recently, particularly on the afternoon shift. Employees who are temporarily assigned to the packaging department also seem to participate in this time loss pattern after a few days. Although they are punctual and productive in other departments, these temporary employees soon adopt the packaging crew's informal schedule when assigned to that department.

Discussion Questions

1. Based on your knowledge of team dynamics, explain why the packaging department is less productive than other teams at Treetop.

2. How should Treetop change the nonproductive norms that exist in the packaging group?

3. What structural and other changes would you recommend that may improve this situation in the long term?

TEAM TOWER POWER

Purpose This exercise is designed to help you understand team roles, team development, and other issues in the development and maintenance of effective teams.

Materials The instructor will provide enough Lego pieces or similar materials for each team to complete the assigned task. All teams should have identical (or very similar) amount and type of pieces. The instructor will need a measuring tape and stopwatch. Students may use writing materials during the design stage (Stage 2 below). The instructor will distribute a "Team Objectives Sheet" and "Tower Specifications Effectiveness Sheet" to all teams.

Instructions

■ *Step 1*: The instructor will divide the class into teams. Depending on class size and space available, teams may have between 4 to 7 members, but all should be approximately the same size.

■ *Step 2*: Each team is given 20 minutes to design a tower that uses only the materials provided, is freestanding, and provides an optimal return on investment. Team members may wish to draw their tower on paper or a flip chart to assist the tower's design. Teams are free to practise building their tower during this stage. Preferably, teams are assigned to their own rooms so the design can be created

privately. During this stage, each team will complete the Team Objectives Sheet distributed by the instructor. This sheet requires the Tower Specifications Effectiveness Sheet, also distributed by the instructor.

■ *Step 3*: Each team will show the instructor that it has completed its Team Objectives Sheet. Then, with all teams in the same room, the instructor will announce the start of the construction phase. The time elapsed for construction will be closely monitored and the instructor will occasionally call out time elapsed (particularly if there is no clock in the room).

■ *Step 4:* Each team will advise the instructor as soon as it has completed its tower. The team will write down the time elapsed that the instructor has determined. It may be asked to assist the instructor by counting the number of blocks used and height of the tower. This information is also written on the Team Objectives Sheet. Then, the team calculates its profit.

■ *Step 5*: After presenting the results, the class will discuss the team dynamics elements that contribute to team effectiveness. Team members will discuss their strategy, division of labour (team roles), expertise within the team, and other elements of team dynamics.

Source: Several published and online sources describe variations of this exercise, but there is no known origin to this activity.

TEAM ROLES PREFERENCES SCALE

Purpose This self-assessment is designed to help you to identify your preferred roles in meetings and similar team activities.

Instructions Read each of the statements below and circle the response that you believe best reflects your position regarding each statement.

Then use the scoring key in Appendix B to calculate your results for each team role. This exercise is completed alone so students can assess themselves honestly without concerns of social comparison. However, class discussion will focus on the roles that people assume in team settings. This scale only assesses a few team roles.

After studying the preceding material, be sure to check out our Online Learning Centre at

www.mcgrawhill.ca/college/mcshane

for more in-depth information and interactivities that correspond to this chapter.

CHAPTER 9

Developing High-Performance Teams

Learning Objectives

AFTER READING THIS CHAPTER, YOU SHOULD BE ABLE TO:

- Identify the characteristics of self-directed work teams.

- Describe the four conditions in sociotechnical systems theory for high-performance SDWTs.

- Summarize three challenges to the implementation of SDWTs.

- Distinguish virtual teams from conventional teams.

- Explain why virtual teams have become so popular in organizations.

- Describe the role of communication systems, task structure, team size, and team composition in virtual team effectiveness.

- Summarize the three levels of trust in teams.

- Outline the four types of team building.

- Identify three reasons why team building tends to fail.

TRW Canada is a model of a team-based organization. Nestled in the quiet community of Tillsonburg, Ontario, the maker of automobile suspension components relies on self-directed work teams to operate the company's 20 cells (manufacturing processes). These teams are expected to think like a small business, and are given considerable autonomy to do so. TRW Canada still has supervisors, but instead of the traditional command-and-control jobs of the past, they serve as team advisors, and operate as a link between team and management.

Each team is responsible for scheduling production, certifying skills, assigning daily jobs, hiring employees, managing materials, and training. Six coordinators on each team oversee those tasks as well as their normal production duties. For example, the team's training coordinator conducts an annual training needs analysis and works with the human resources group to enroll team members in training programs. A special plant-wide team evaluates the six coordinators on each team each year and rewards the team when all six coordinators pass an annual performance assessment.

TRW Canada's reliance on self-directed work teams is paying off. Over the past five years, the company has increased sales per employee by 179 percent and cut inventory and scrap costs by nearly 50 percent. *Industry Week* magazine recognized TRW Canada as one of North America's best manufacturing plants—the only Canadian plant to receive this distinction.

TRW Canada is one of Canada's most successful manufacturing plants, thanks to its reliance on self-directed teams to get the job done.
Reprinted with permission of TRW 2000

Employees also appreciate TRW Canada's team structure. "There's a certain excitement," explains Beth Penner, a member of the stabilizer link team. "We are much more involved in everyday decisions and feel much more part of a team."[1]

www.trwauto.com

T eams have become the main building blocks of organizations. The previous chapter presented the foundations of team dynamics, including types of teams and the main elements of team effectiveness. This chapter extends our discussion of teams by focusing on two types of high-performance teams: self-directed work teams and virtual teams. After introducing self-directed work teams, we examine the elements of sociotechnical systems theory to understand how these teams operate more effectively in an empowered environment. We also discuss the challenges facing self-directed work teams. Next, we look at the trend toward virtual teams, including why these teams have become so popular. The team effectiveness model in Chapter 8 is then applied to identify the team environment, design, and processes that support high-performance virtual teams. We also look at the important topic of trust in virtual teams and other groups. The last section reviews various teambuilding strategies.

SELF-DIRECTED WORK TEAMS (SDWTs)

**self-directed
work teams
(SDWTs)**

Cross-functional work groups organized around work processes, that complete an entire piece of work requiring several interdependent tasks, and that have substantial autonomy over the execution of these tasks.

When Bayer Inc. consolidated five companies in four years, the health care and chemical company decided it was time to restructure its Canadian warehouse operations into self-directed work teams. All warehouse employees now work in a team-based environment and have the same job title: warehouse operator. They are expected to share work activities by learning the four skill levels representing the previous job categories (e.g., picker, forklift operator). "It took nearly two years to develop and institute this transformation, but it has been worth it," says a Bayer executive. "From the outset, employees took ownership of their respective jobs [and] supported the warehouse team concept."[2]

Bayer, Inc., TRW Canada, and many other organizations are following the trend toward **self-directed work teams (SDWTs)**. By most estimates, over two-thirds of medium and large organizations in North America use SDWT structures for part of their operations.[3] These formal groups complete an entire piece of work requiring several interdependent tasks and have substantial autonomy over the execution of these tasks. SDWTs vary somewhat from one firm to the next, but generally they have the features listed in Exhibit 9.1.[4]

EXHIBIT 9.1

Attributes of self-directed work teams pick-up

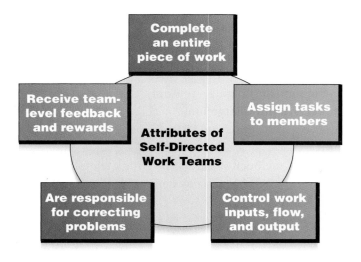

Complete an entire piece of work

Receive team-level feedback and rewards

Assign tasks to members

**Attributes of
Self-Directed
Work Teams**

Are responsible for correcting problems

Control work inputs, flow, and output

Jabil Circuits relies on self-directed work teams at its manufacturing operations in St. Petersburg, Florida and Auburn Hills, Michigan. "Our manufacturing environment is team-oriented," says Jabil Circuits' operations manager in Michigan. "Employees are organized into teams of from three to 14 or 15 people." Each production team is responsible for a specific customer group. For example, one team makes circuit boards that go into car dashboards. Team members have a high degree of autonomy to stop production when they see quality problems. They are also cross-trained to perform several tasks so they can cover for each other.[6] What advantages and potential problems would Jabil Circuits have with its team-based organizational structure? *M. Guss, Tampa Tribune* **www.jabil.com**

First, SDWTs complete an entire piece of work, whether it's a product, a service, or part of a larger product or service. For example, self-directed work teams at TRW Canada are responsible for an entire manufacturing process. Second, the team—not supervisors—assigns tasks that individual team members perform. In other words, the team plans, organizes, and controls work activities with little or no direct involvement from a higher status supervisor.

Third, SDWTs control most work inputs, flow, and output. "[Teams] have total authority to make all decisions: I mean total, complete authority on every aspect of business," explains Dennis W. Bakke, CEO and cofounder of electrical power company AES Corp.[5] Fourth, SDWTs are responsible for correcting work flow problems as they occur. In other words, the teams maintain their own quality and logistical control. Last, SDWTs receive team-level feedback and rewards. This recognizes and reinforces the fact that the team—not individuals—is responsible for the work, although team members may also receive individual feedback and rewards.

You may have noticed from this description that members of SDWTs have enriched and enlarged jobs (see Chapter 6). The team's work includes all the tasks required to make an entire product or provide a service. The team is also mostly responsible for scheduling, coordinating, and planning these tasks.[7] Self-directed work teams were initially designed around production processes. However, they are also found in administrative and service activities, automobile service centres, city government administration, and customer assistance teams in courier services.[8] These service tasks are well suited to self-directed work teams because employees have interdependent tasks and decisions require the knowledge and experience of several people.[9]

Sociotechnical Systems Theory and SDWTs

sociotechnical systems (STS) theory
A theory stating that effective work sites have joint optimization of their social and technological systems, and that teams should have sufficient autonomy to control key variances in the work process.

How do companies create successful self-directed work teams? To answer this question, we need to look at **sociotechnical systems (STS)** theory, the main source of current SDWT practices. STS theory was introduced during the 1940s at Britain's Tavistock Institute, where Eric Trist, Fred Emery, and their colleagues had been studying the effects of technology on coal mining in the United Kingdom.[10]

The Tavistock researchers observed that the new coal mining technology (called the "long wall" method) led to lower, not higher, job performance. They analyzed the causes of this problem and established the idea that organizations need "joint optimization" between the social and technical systems of the work unit. In other words, they needed to introduce technology in a way that created the best structure for semi-autonomous work teams. Moreover, the Tavistock group concluded that teams should be sufficiently autonomous so they could control the main "variances" in the system. This means that the team has to control the factors that have the greatest impact on quality, quantity, and the cost of the product or service. From this overview of STS, we can identify four main conditions for high-performance SDWTs (see Exhibit 9.2).[11]

SDWT is a primary work unit   STS suggests that SDWTs work best in a primary work unit that makes a product, provides a service, or otherwise completes an entire work process. By making an entire product or service together, the team is independent enough from other work units that it can make adjustments without affecting or being affected too much by others. At the same time, employees within a primary work unit perform interdependent subtasks so they have the sense of performing a common task.[12]

SDWT has collective self-regulation   STS advocates a team-based structure in which employees in the primary work unit have sufficient autonomy to manage the work process. STS writers call it **collective self-regulation,** which means that the team can decide how to divide up work among its members as well as how to coordinate that work. Collective self-regulation is a central feature in self-directed work teams and refers to a team-based version of autonomy in job enrichment (see Chapter 6). This condition gives SDWTs the freedom to respond more quickly and effectively to their environment. It also motivates team members through feelings of empowerment. This is apparent in GLOBAL Connections 9.1, which describes self-directed teams at The Patchwork Traditional Food Company. The gourmet food maker in northern Wales is operated entirely by self-directed teams that decide their own work schedules, production and post-production activities, and are involved in product development.

SDWTs control key variances   STS says that high-performance SDWTs have control over "key variances." These variances are the disturbances or interruptions that occur in a work process, such as the mixture of ingredients in soup manufacturing or the courteousness of service at an airline reservations call centre. By controlling these factors, work teams control the quantity and quality of output in the work process. In contrast, STS has little advantage when the causes

collective self-regulation
Team-based structure in which employees in the primary work unit have enough autonomy to manage the work process.

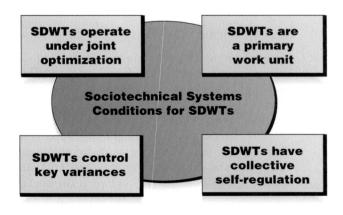

EXHIBIT 9.2

Sociotechnical systems conditions for SDWTs

Welsh Firm's Success due to Self-Directed Teams

Twenty years ago, Margaret Carter started selling pâté and other food products to local pubs as a way of supporting herself and her children after her divorce. Today, her Welsh company, The Patchwork Traditional Food Company, is a bustling operation whose 30 employees manufacture gourmet foods for clients throughout the United Kingdom and continental Europe.

Carter says that the company's two ingredients for success are making its products by hand in small batches and relying on self-directed work teams. "We've had the self-directed teams for about 15 years, and the idea is that nobody has titles and staff are empowered to make their own decisions," she says. The production team calls itself The Motley Crew; the post-production team is known as The Musketeers.

Once each week, team members gather for a 59:59 meeting (which lasts no more than 59 minutes and 59 seconds) to discuss problems that occurred during the previous week and goals for the forthcoming week.

Each team decides its own production schedules and work patterns, is able to recruit collectively, and is involved in everything from designing new packaging to product development. Team members become multi-skilled and eventually get rotated into the roles of team leader and communication officer.

Each team also has a daily "huddle" meeting. "In the morning everybody arrives in their various teams and the first thing they do is have something called a huddle," Carter explains. "So for 10 minutes everybody discusses the workload for the day and the issues that have arisen from the previous day." To maintain a team focus and to remove any status differences, staff conduct their morning huddle away from individual desks. "They stand in a circle away from their desks so there is no control issue," says Carter, who now spends much of her time speaking to other businesses about implementing self-directed work teams.

Source: Based on D. Devine, "Recipe For Making Things Happen," *Western Mail*, July 10, 2002, p. 9. www.patchwork-pate.co.uk

www.patchwork-pate.co.uk

of good or poor performance are due mainly to technology, supplies, or other factors beyond the team's control.

SDWTs operate under joint optimization   Perhaps the most crucial feature of STS is **joint optimization**—the notion that a balance must be struck between social and technical systems to maximize the operation's effectiveness.[13] Production demands and social dynamics must be compatible. In particular, the technological system should be implemented in a way that encourages or facilitates team dynamics, job enrichment, and meaningful feedback.

This idea of joint optimization was quite radical in the 1940s, a time when many thought there was only one best way to install technology in the workplace, and that jobs must be designed around this structure alone. STS, on the other hand, says that companies have considerable latitude in how they introduce technology. In particular, it assumes that technology is flexible enough to support a semi-autonomous, team-based structure.

Applying Sociotechnical Systems Theory   Shell Canada, Pratt & Whitney Canada, Nortel Networks, and several other Canadian organizations have applied sociotechnical systems to establish a better environment for team-based work." In most of these and other operations, STS produced higher quality products and a more satisfied workforce. For example, L. L. Bean applied STS principles when redesigning its order fulfillment centre. "The technology here is very simple," says the executive responsible for operations in Maine. "The innovative part is adapting it to create a new sociotechnical norm in the new facility."[14] These team-based structures worked because corporate leaders diagnosed and redesigned the technological structure to ensure that it supported a team-based work environment.

joint optimization
The balance that is struck between social and technical systems to maximize an operation's effectiveness.

Celestica Inc. operates in a competitive environment where technology and employees need careful alignment. To achieve this alignment, the Canadian high-technology manufacturer adopted sociotechnical systems (STS) as its template for corporate renewal. Employee study teams mapped work process flows and identified key variances—disturbances or interruptions that occur in a work process. Several changes were introduced that addressed each of the key variances. Permanent self-directed work teams of 15 to 40 people were established to complete each work process. As a result of STS, productivity and quality doubled and job satisfaction increased significantly. As one employee explains: "What I like about the STS process is that the change has been driven by the employees—those responsible for execution—as opposed to management dictating how it's going to be."[15] To what extent has Celestica applied the four STS conditions necessary for successful self-directed work teams? *Courtesy of Celestica Inc.*
www.celestica.com

In spite of its long-term success, STS is not very helpful at identifying how to optimally align social and technical systems. Volvo's Uddevalla plant in Sweden may have demonstrated this point.[16] The Uddevalla plant replaced the traditional assembly line with fixed workstations at which teams of approximately 20 employees assemble and install components in an unfinished automobile chassis. This technological structure creates a strong team orientation, but the team's productivity was among the *lowest* in the automobile industry because the technological design was not flexible enough. (It takes 50 hours to produce a car at Uddevalla versus 25 hours at a traditional Volvo plant and 13 hours at a Toyota plant.) In its attempt to accommodate the social system, Volvo's production system may have become too inefficient technologically.

Challenges to SDWTs

Even where sociotechnical systems theory indicates that self-directed work teams are appropriate, corporate leaders need to recognize and overcome at least three potential barriers: cross-cultural issues, management resistance, and employee and labour union resistance.

Cross-cultural issues   SDWTs are more difficult to implement in high power distance cultures. Employees in these cultures are more comfortable when supervisors give them directions, whereas low power distance employees value their involvement in decisions. Mexico has a very high power distance value system, which explains why firms have difficulty implementing self-directed work teams there. One study reported that Mexican employees expect managers to make decisions affecting their work, whereas SDWTs emphasize self-initiative and individual responsibility within teams. Some writers suggest that SDWTs may be more difficult to apply in China, where traditional cultural values tend to support a rigid social hierarchy.[17] SDWTs may also be more difficult to implement in cultures with high individualism and low collectivism because employees are less comfortable collaborating and working interdependently with co-workers.[18]

Management resistance   The poet Robert Frost once wrote, "The brain is a wonderful organ; it starts working the moment you get up in the morning and does not stop until you get into the office."[19] Frost's humour highlights the fact that many organizations expect employees to park their brains at the door. It's not surprising, then, to learn that supervisors and higher-level managers are often the main source of resistance to the transition to self-directed work teams.[20] Their main worry is losing power when employees gain power through empowered teams. Some are concerned that their jobs will lose value, and others believe that they will not have any jobs at all.

Another problem is that supervisors do not know how to become "hands-off" facilitators of several work teams rather than "hands-on" supervisors of several employees.[21] This was one of the biggest stumbling blocks to self-directed work teams at TRW Canada, described in the opening vignette to this chapter. Many supervisors kept slipping back into their command-and-control supervisory styles. As one TRW employee explains: "One of the toughest things for some of them was to shift from being a boss to a coach, moving from saying, 'I know what's good for you' to 'How can I help you?'"[22] Research suggests that supervisors are less likely to resist self-directed work teams when they have worked in a high-involvement workplace and received considerable training in their new facilitation role.[23]

Employee and labour union resistance Employees sometimes oppose SDWTs because the teams require new skills or appear to require more work. Many feel uncomfortable as they explore their new roles, and they may be worried that they lack the skills to adapt to the new work requirements. Labour unions supported the early experiments in sociotechnical change in Europe and India, but some Canadian and American unions have reservations about SDWTs.[24] One concern is that teams improve productivity at the price of higher stress levels among employees, which is sometimes true. Another concern is that SDWTs require more flexibility because they reverse work rules and remove job categories that unions have negotiated over the years. Labour union leaders are therefore concerned that it will be a difficult battle to regain these hard-fought union member rights.

In spite of these challenges, self-directed work teams offer enormous potential for organizations when they are implemented under the right conditions, as specified by sociotechnical systems theory. Meanwhile, information technologies and knowledge-work have enabled virtual teams to become more popular. The next section examines this new breed of team, including strategies to create high-performance virtual teams.

VIRTUAL TEAMS

virtual teams
Teams whose members operate across space, time, and organizational boundaries and are linked through information technologies to achieve organizational tasks.

Gordon Currie doesn't let a few kilometres get in the way of his business. Currie lives in Dawson Creek, British Columbia, but the clients of his Web-design company are all based in the United States. What started out as a hobby 12 years ago is now a global business with clients that have included Virgin Records and Hitachi. Currie's team members are even more geographically diverse than his clients. "I currently have four [team members], and I have not met face to face with any of them," confides Currie. "I have one from Sweden, two from California, and one from Australia. I went out and hired them on the Net."[25]

Gordon Currie and his colleagues are part of the growing trend toward virtual teams. **Virtual teams** are teams whose members operate across space, time, and organizational boundaries and are linked through information technologies to achieve organizational tasks.[26] As with all teams, virtual teams are made up of groups of two or more people who interact and influence each other, are mutually accountable for achieving common goals associated with organizational objectives, and perceive themselves as a social entity within an organization (see Chapter 8).

However, virtual teams have two features that distinguish them from conventional teams. First, conventional team members are co-located (work in the same physical area), whereas virtual team members are separated by distance and sometimes by time. Team members may be spread across a city or located anywhere around the planet. Second, because of their lack of co-location, members of virtual teams depend on information technologies to communicate and coordinate their work effort. Conventional teams might also use information technology, but they are still able to communicate face to face at most times during the workday.[27]

Virtual teams may be permanent or temporary. They might operate as permanently distributed departments, or as bootlegged skunkworks temporarily set up to develop a new product or service. Unlike most conventional teams, virtual teams are also dispersed geographically, organizationally, and temporally. Some virtual teams operate across organizations but within one city. Others operate within one company but across several countries, cultures, and time zones.[28]

Andy Bearsley (left) and Matt Fox-Wilson know all about virtual teams. The New Zealand computer graphics programmers and their three employees are scattered from Auckland to Rotorua, while their clients are all located in North America. "We are fairly distributed," says Fox-Wilson. "It doesn't matter where an employee works as long as they come in once a week and they can get access to our server for source code." Initially it took some convincing for U.S. and Canadian firms to sign a contract with a team on the other side of the Pacific. But the work paid off for both parties and the duo's firm, Ambient Design, now has contracts with Ottawa-based Corel, Adobe, and other major software firms.[32] What conditions are needed to make Ambient Design's virtual team work effectively?
P. Estcourt, New Zealand Herald
www.ambient-design.com

Why Companies Form Virtual Teams

Virtual teams have become one of the most significant developments in organizations over the past decade. "Virtual teams are now a reality," says Frank Waltmann, head of learning at pharmaceutical company Novartis.[29] New information technologies offer one explanation why virtual teams are more common. Internet, intranets, instant messaging, virtual whiteboards, and other products have made it easier than in the past to communicate with and coordinate people at a distance. Distance isn't irrelevant yet and (as we shall learn in this section) information technologies have not yet achieved the level of face-to-face communication, but computer connectivity has strengthened bonds among people in different locations to such an extent that they can now feel like a team.[30]

The shift from production-based to knowledge-based work has also made virtual teamwork feasible. Information technologies allow people to exchange knowledge work, such as software code, product development plans, and ideas for strategic decisions. In contrast, it is still very difficult (although not completely impossible) to rely on virtual teams for production work, in which people develop physical objects.[31]

Information technologies and knowledge-based work make virtual teams *possible*, but two other factors—knowledge management and globalization—make them increasingly *necessary*. Knowledge has become the currency of competitive advantage, so organizations need to seek out this knowledge wherever it is available. Virtual teams are a natural part of the knowledge management process because they encourage employees to share and use knowledge when geography limits more direct forms of collaboration. Moreover, as companies cross industry boundaries (for example, when Internet providers move into the entertainment business), they must depend on virtual teams to leverage the knowledge potential across these groups.

Globalization is the other reason why virtual teams are increasingly necessary. As we described in Chapter 1, globalization has become the new reality in many organizations. Companies are opening businesses overseas, forming tight alliances with companies located elsewhere, and serving customers who want global support. These global conditions require a correspondingly global response in the form of virtual teams, which coordinate these operations.[33]

Designing High-Performance Virtual Teams

Virtual teams are a variation of teams, so the team effectiveness model in Chapter 8 provides a useful template to identify the features of high-performance virtual teams.[34] Exhibit 9.3 outlines the key design issues for virtual teams that we discuss over the next couple of pages.

Virtual team environment Reward systems, communication systems, organizational environment, organizational structure, and leadership influence the effectiveness of all teams, including virtual teams.[35] However, communication systems are particularly important because, unlike conventional teams, virtual teams cannot rely on face-to-face meetings whenever they wish. As we will learn in Chapter 11, face-to-face communication transfers the highest volume and complexity of information and offers the timeliest feedback. In contrast, e-mail, telephone, and other information technologies fall far behind in their ability to exchange information. "Having a four- to five-hour discussion is hard to do by phone, especially where you need to read body language," says an executive at accounting giant PricewaterhouseCoopers.[36] Even video conferencing, which seems similar to face-to-face communication, actually communicates much less than we realize.

EXHIBIT 9.3

Designing high-performance virtual teams

Team Design Element	Special Virtual Team Requirements
Team environment	• Virtual teams need several communication channels available to offset lack of face-to-face communication
Team tasks	• Virtual teams operate better with structured rather than complex and ambiguous tasks
Team size and composition	• Virtual teams usually require smaller team size than conventional teams • Virtual team members must have skills in communicating through information technology and in processing multiple threads of conversation • Virtual team members are more likely than conventional team members to require cross-cultural awareness and knowledge
Team processes	• Virtual team development and cohesiveness require some face-to-face interaction, particularly when the team forms

To become a high-performance virtual team, an organization needs to provide a variety of communication media, and virtual team members need to creatively combine these media to match the task demands.[37] For instance, virtual team members rely on e-mail to coordinate routine tasks, but can quickly switch to videoconferencing and electronic whiteboards when emergencies arise. The lack of face-to-face communication isn't all bad news for virtual teams. Working through e-mail or intranet systems can also minimize status differences due to language skills. Team members whose first language is not English may be overwhelmed into silence in face-to-face meetings, but have time to craft persuasive messages in cyberspace.[38]

Virtual team tasks   Scholars suggest that virtual teams operate best with structured tasks that require only moderate levels of task interdependence.[39] Consider the task structure of client service engineers at BakBone Software. Each day, Bakbone engineers in San Diego pick up customer support problems that have been passed on from colleagues in Maryland and England. At the end of the workday, they pass some of these projects on to BakBone co-workers in Tokyo. The assignments sent on to Tokyo must be stated clearly because overseas co-workers can't ask questions in the middle of San Diego's night.

This structured task arrangement at BakBone works well in virtual teams. In contrast, complex and ambiguous tasks require an enormous amount of consultation and coordination in real time, which virtual teams have difficulty processing due to lack of face-to-face communication. "You don't have the time for open-ended conversation [in a virtual team]," admits BakBone engineer Roger Rodriguez "You can't informally brainstorm with someone."[40] Generally, complex and ambiguous tasks should be assigned to co-located teams.

Virtual team size and composition   The problems of team size we learned about in Chapter 8 are amplified in virtual teams because of limited opportunities for face-to-face communication and social bonding. Even with the benefit of video conferencing tools, team size becomes an issue at lower numbers than it does for conventional teams due to the limits of information technologies.

High-performance virtual teams apply the team composition issues described in Chapter 8, but virtual team members also require special skills in communication systems. In particular, they need to coordinate through e-mail without creating undesirable emotions and must juggle several independent "threads" of electronic conversation (rather like the seemingly random threads in virtual chat rooms).

Virtual teams are more likely than conventional teams to include people across cultures, so team members must also be aware of cross-cultural issues. For example, one study reported that virtual teams of American and Belgian college students were easily confused by differing conventions about commas vs. decimal points in numbers (e.g., $2.953 million versus $2,953 million). They also experienced cultural differences in socializing. The American students were willing to socialize after they completed the assignment, whereas the Belgian students were more interested in developing a relationship with their partners before beginning work on the project.[41]

Team processes   High-performance teams apply the many recommendations in Chapter 8 regarding team development, norms, roles, and cohesiveness. Team development and cohesiveness are particular concerns because virtual teams lack the face-to-face interaction that supports these processes.[42] There is no "virtual" solution to this dilemma, so many practitioners recommend that virtual team members meet face to face, particularly when the team is formed. The ability to "put a face" to remote colleagues seems to strengthen the individual's emotional bond to the team. "[E]ven if the work of global teams will be primarily virtual, we usually start with a face-to-face meeting," explains an executive at microprocessor manufacturer Advanced Micro Devices.[43]

Siemens discovered the importance of face-to-face contact in virtual teams when the German high-technology company's 70 Enterprise Networks group employees in the United States were required to work from home. Productivity dropped and turnover increased, until Siemens management diagnosed the problem and identified a solution. While still dispersed around the country, Siemens Enterprise Networks employees now meet face to face each year at an annual four-day work-and-play gathering. The annual session provides a much-needed social connection, which has contributed to lower turnover and higher team cohesiveness. "We feel [the annual meeting is] essential," explains a Siemens executive. "This keeps a touchstone back to other human beings. Cliques can form and people bond, even over the miles."[44]

Team Trust

Our discussion of virtual teams would be incomplete without emphasizing the importance of trust in team dynamics. Any relationship—including the relationship among virtual team members—depends on a certain degree of trust between the parties.[45] **Trust** occurs when we have positive expectations about another party's intentions and actions toward us in risky situations (see Chapter 4). A high level of trust occurs when the other party's actions affect you in situations where you are vulnerable, but you believe they will not adversely affect your needs.

To understand how trust relates to virtual teams, we need to understand that people experience the three levels of trust illustrated in Exhibit 9.4.

trust
Positive expectations about another party's intentions and actions toward us in risky situations.

- *Calculus-based trust*—This minimal level of trust refers to an expected consistency of behaviour based on deterrence. Each party believes that the other

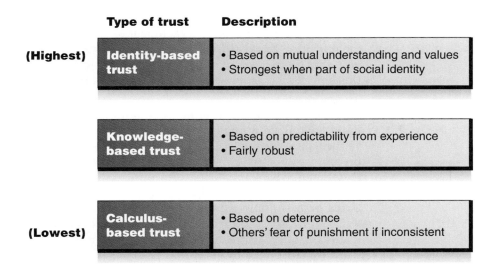

EXHIBIT 9.4

Levels of trust in teams

	Type of trust	Description
(Highest)	**Identity-based trust**	• Based on mutual understanding and values • Strongest when part of social identity
	Knowledge-based trust	• Based on predictability from experience • Fairly robust
(Lowest)	**Calculus-based trust**	• Based on deterrence • Others' fear of punishment if inconsistent

will deliver on its promises because punishments will be administered if they fail. For example, most employees trust each other at least at a minimum level because co-workers could get fired if they attempt to undermine another employee's work effort. This ability to punish others who violate expected behaviour is calculus-based trust.

- *Knowledge-based trust*—Knowledge-based trust is grounded on the other party's predictability. This predictability develops from meaningful communication and experience with the other party. The better you know fellow team members, the more accurately you can predict what they will do in the future. Similarly, the more consistent the leader's behaviour—the more he or she "walks the talk"—the more employees are willing to trust that person.[46]
- *Identification-based trust*—This third type of trust is based on mutual understanding and the emotional bond between the parties. Identification occurs when one party thinks like, feels like, and responds like the other party. High-performance teams exhibit this level of trust. By sharing the same values, employees understand what to expect from each other.

Calculus-based trust is the weakest of the three because it is easily broken when expectations are violated and sanctions subsequently applied against the violating party. It is difficult to develop a strong level of trust based only on the threat of punishment if one party fails to deliver on its promises. Generally, calculus-based trust alone cannot sustain a team's relationship, particularly among members of a virtual team, and with the team leader. "Trust is a basic premise of work relationships," advises a PricewaterhouseCoopers executive. "If you manage by watching people work, then virtual teaming isn't a good choice."[47]

Knowledge-based trust is more stable than calculus-based trust because it is developed over time. Suppose another member of your virtual team submitted documentation to you on schedule in the past, but it arrived late today. Knowledge-based trust would be dented, but not broken. Through knowledge-based trust, you "know" that this tardiness is probably an exception because it deviates from the co-worker's past actions.

Identification-based trust is the most robust of the three. Because an individual holds the same values as other team members, he or she is more likely to forgive transgressions. Social identity theory explains why this is so. Recall from Chapter 3 that social identity theory refers to the phenomenon whereby people define themselves in terms of their attachment to various groups (see Chapter 3). Having identification-based trust with team members means that we identify ourselves with that group. As a result, we would be reluctant to acknowledge a violation of this high-level trust because it would strike at the heart of our self-image.

Dynamics of trust in teams   A common misconception is that team members build trust from a low level when they first join the team. According to recent studies, the opposite is actually more likely to occur. People typically join a virtual or conventional team with a high level—*not* a low level—of trust in their new teammates.[48] New members form positive expectations about work in the team and want to identify with the work unit. However, this trust is fragile because it is based on assumptions rather than well-established experience. As a result, trust tends to decrease rather than increase, according to recent studies on virtual teams. In other words, if new team members experience trust violations, their trust is pushed to a lower level. Employees who join the team with identification-based trust tend to drop back to knowledge-based or perhaps calculus-based trust. Declining trust is particularly challenging in virtual teams because research identifies clear communication among team members as an important condition for sustaining trust.

TEAM BUILDING

Québec-based L'Union Canadienne and Calgary-based Sovereign General are located in different parts of Canada and do business in different parts of the insurance industry, so when they agreed to merge, one of the pressing issues was to ensure that the combined management develop into a high-performance team. Along with working through the details to develop an integrated culture, executives went through a teambuilding exercise in which some took the role of challengers, some of collaborators, and some of communicators. "The important thing is to make people aware of the roles they assume, and how they will function as part of the new team," explains Hugh Mitchell, a partner at Montréal-based Universalia, the management consulting firm that facilitated the teambuilding session.[49]

Executives at L'Union Canadienne and Sovereign General engaged in one of many forms of **team building**—any formal activity intended to improve the development and functioning of a work team. Most team building accelerates the team development process, which, in turn, might reshape team norms or strengthen cohesiveness. Team building is sometimes applied to newly established teams, but is more common among existing teams that have regressed to earlier stages of team development. Team building is therefore most appropriate when the team experiences high membership turnover or members have lost sight of their respective roles and team objectives.[50]

team building
Any formal activity intended to improve the development and functioning of a team.

Types of Team Building

There are four main types of team building: role definition, goal setting, problem solving, and interpersonal processes.[51] Role definition team building encourages team members to describe their perceptions of their roles as well as their role expectations of other team members. After discussing these perceptions, team members revise their roles and work toward a common mental model of their responsibilities.[52]

Some team building interventions clarify the team's performance goals, increase the team's motivation to accomplish these goals, and establish a mechanism for systematic feedback on the team's goal performance. This is very similar to individual goal setting, described in Chapter 5, except that the goals are applied to teams. Research suggests that goal setting is an important dimension of team building.[53]

A third type of team building examines the team's task-related decision-making process and identifies ways to make it more effective.[54] Each stage of decision making is examined, such as how the team identifies problems and searches for alternatives (see Chapter 10). To improve their problem-solving skills, some teams participate in simulation games that require team decisions in hypothetical situations.[55] As well as helping team members make better decisions, these teambuilding activities tend to improve interpersonal processes.

The fourth type of team building is interpersonal processes that try to build trust and open communication among team members by resolving hidden agendas and misperceptions. This includes **dialogue** sessions where team members

dialogue
A process of conversation among team members in which they learn about each other's mental models and assumptions, and eventually form a common model for thinking within the team.

Extreme Teambuilding in Asia

Perched on a narrow beam eight metres above the ground, Wu Xi never stopped thinking about the possibility of falling. The 30-year-old engineer at Ericsson Cyberlab in Singapore was roped together with five colleagues as they scaled their way up a 25-metre pyramid. "I was so scared, but I couldn't give up," says Wu. "My team members held onto me very firmly and they kept encouraging me."

Throughout Asia, companies are discovering the benefits of unusual teambuilding activities outside the typical office environment. Wu Xi and her co-workers climbed over rock walls, inched across planks, scaled cargo nets, and performed other daunting tasks to improve team dynamics at the Swedish telecommunication firm's Asian research unit. "We all made it to the top with lots of difficulties," explains Ericsson Cyberlab director Andreas Fasbender. "But the best part was that you could really achieve more as a team."

Anker Bir took a different approach to team building. Employees at the Indonesian brewery spent a day in sophisticated gear stalking their rivals with laser guns at Laser Quest in Surabaya. Team members worked together to protect a box, a king or a queen, or to fight a superpowerful vampire with unlimited lives and ammunition.

Endro Hariyadi, an Anker Bir account representative, says that employees are more comfortable at work

Employees at Ericsson Cyberlab in Singapore scale great heights to build team spirit. © H-Y How, *Straits Times (Singapore)*

after they blast away at each other with laser guns. "We're all friends here, even if we don't get along well in the office," he jokes.

Sources: D. Goh, "Firms Strike Out for Adventure Learning," *Sunday Times (Singapore)*, April 8, 2001, pp. 7, 29; F. Whaley, "Shooting for Success," *Asian Business*, February 2000, p. 48. **www.cyberlab.com.sg**

---

engage in conversations to develop a common mental model of the ideal team process. As they gain awareness of each other's models and assumptions, members eventually begin to form a common model for thinking within the team.[56] Although dialogue is potentially effective, most organizations tend to rely on wilderness team building, paintball wars, and obstacle course challenges to improve interpersonal processes. Most interpersonal process team building activities have distinctively American foundations. However, as GLOBAL Connections 9.2 describes, they are also gaining acceptance in Asia.

Is Team Building Effective?

Team building activities have become more popular as companies increasingly rely on teams to get the work done. Some organizations are even experimenting with offbeat team-building activities in the hope that these sessions will improve team dynamics. Coca-Cola executives in China participated in a team-building program that included fire walking. Deloitte Consulting sent some of its California employees on a three-day extreme adventure race. Among other things, the experience included sleeping in garbage bags on the dew-soaked ground and huddling together in "puppy piles" to stay warm. Staffordshire County Council in the U.K.

sent a team of employees to the fire brigade for the day, where they learned to navigate through a smoke-filled room and battle a controlled towering inferno. '"Faced with danger, people have to work together," explains a Staffordshire employee. "They have no other choice."[57]

Are these and more traditional team-building programs effective? Is the money well spent? So far, the answer is an equivocal "maybe." Studies suggest that some team building activities are successful, but just as many fail to build high-performance teams.[58] One problem is that corporate leaders assume team-building activities are general solutions to general team problems. No one bothers to diagnose the team's specific needs (e.g., problem solving, interpersonal processes) because the team-building intervention is assumed to be a broad-brush solution. In reality, as we just learned, there are different types of team-building activities for different team needs. This mismatch can potentially lead to ineffective team building.[59]

Another problem is that corporate leaders tend to view team building as a one-shot medical inoculation that every team should receive when it is formed. In truth, team building is an ongoing process, not a three-day jumpstart. Some experts suggest, for example, that wilderness experiences often fail because they rarely include follow-up consultation to ensure that team learning is transferred back to the workplace.[60]

Last, we must remember that team building occurs on the job, not just on an obstacle course or in a national park. Organizations should encourage team members to reflect on their work experiences and to experiment with just-in-time learning for team development.

CHAPTER SUMMARY

Self-directed work teams (SDWTs) complete an entire piece of work that requires several interdependent tasks and have substantial autonomy over the execution of these tasks. Sociotechnical systems theory (STS) is the template typically used to determine whether SDWTs will operate effectively. STS identifies four main conditions for high-performance SDWTs.

First, SDWTs must be a primary work unit, that is, an intact team that makes a product, provides a service, or otherwise completes an entire work process. Second, the team must have collective self-regulation, meaning that it must have sufficient autonomy to manage the work process. Third, high-performance SDWTs have control over "key variances." This refers to the idea that teams control the disturbances or interruptions that create quality problems in the work process. Fourth, STS states that a balance must be struck between social and technical systems to maximize the operation's effectiveness.

Sociotechnical systems theory has been widely supported since its origins in the 1950s. However, it is not very helpful at identifying the optimal alignment of the social and technical system. Moreover,

SDWTs face several barriers to implementation. These high-performance teams tend to operate best in cultures with low power distance and high collectivism. Supervisors often resist SDWTs because of fears that empowering teams will remove the power of supervisors. Supervisors must also adjust from their traditional hands-on "command-and-control" style to being hands-off facilitators. Employees oppose SDWTs when they worry that they lack the skills to adapt to the new work requirements. Labour unions sometimes oppose SDWTs because of the risk of higher stress and the need to remove job categories that unions have negotiated over the years.

Virtual teams are teams whose members operate across space, time, and organizational boundaries and are linked through information technologies to achieve organizational tasks. The main difference between virtual and conventional teams is that virtual teams are not co-located and that they rely on information technologies rather than face-to-face interaction.

Virtual teams are becoming more common because information technology and knowledge-based work make it easier to collaborate from a distance. Virtual teams are becoming increasingly necessary because they are a natural part of the knowledge management process. Moreover, as companies globalize, they must rely more on virtual teams than co-located teams so they can coordinate operations at distant sites.

Several elements in the team effectiveness model stand out as important issues for virtual teams. High-performance virtual teams require a variety of communication media, and virtual team members need to creatively combine these media to match task demands. Virtual teams operate better with structured rather than complex and ambiguous tasks. They usually cannot maintain as large a team as is possible in conventional teams. Members of virtual teams require special skills in communication systems and should be aware of cross-cultural issues. Virtual team members should also meet face to face, particularly when the team forms, to help team development and cohesiveness.

Trust is important in team dynamics, particularly in virtual teams. Trust occurs when we have positive expectations about another party's intentions and actions toward us in risky situations. The minimum level of trust is calculus-based trust, which is based on deterrence. Teams cannot survive with this level of trust. Knowledge-based trust is a higher level of trust and is grounded on the other party's predictability. The highest level of trust, called identity-based trust, is based on mutual understanding and the emotional bond between the parties. When most employees join a team they have a high level of trust, which tends to decline over time.

Team building is any formal activity intended to improve the development and functioning of a work team. Four team-building strategies are role definition, goal setting, problem solving, and interpersonal processes. Some team building events succeed, but companies often fail to consider the contingencies of team building.

KEY TERMS

Collective self-regulation, p. 260

Dialogue, p. 269

Joint optimization, p. 261

Self-directed work team (SDWT), p. 258

Sociotechnical system theory (STS), p. 259

Team building, p. 269

Trust, p. 267

Virtual teams, p. 263

DISCUSSION QUESTIONS

1. How do self-directed work teams differ from conventional teams?

2. Advanced Telecom Ltd. has successfully introduced self-directed work teams (SDWTs) at its operations throughout Canada. The company now wants to introduce SDWTs at its plants in Singapore and Mexico. What potential cross-cultural challenges might Advanced Telecom experience as it introduces SDWTs in these countries?

3. A chicken processing company wants to build a processing plant designed around sociotechnical systems principles. In a traditional chicken processing plant, employees work in separate departments—cleaning and cutting, cooking, packaging, and warehousing. The cooking and packaging processes are controlled by separate workstations in the traditional plant. How would the company change this operation according to sociotechnical systems design?

4. What can organizations do to reduce management resistance to self-directed work teams?

5. Why are virtual teams becoming increasingly necessary?

6. Suppose the instructor for this course assigned you to a project team consisting of three other students who are currently taking similar courses in Ireland, Singapore, and Brazil. All students speak English and have similar knowledge of the topic. Use your knowledge of virtual teams to discuss the problems that your team might face, compared with a team of local students who can meet face to face.

7. What can virtual teams do to sustain trust among team members?

8. "Team building activities have become more popular as companies increasingly rely on teams to get the work done." What problems may arise that could lead to ineffective team building results?

THE SHIPPING INDUSTRY ACCOUNTING TEAM

For the past five years, I have been working at McKay, Sanderson, and Smith Associates, a mid-sized accounting firm in Halifax that specializes in commercial accounting and audits. My speciality is accounting practices for shipping companies, ranging from small fishing fleets to a couple of the big firms with ships on the St. Lawrence Seaway.

About 18 months ago, McKay, Sanderson, and Smith Associates became part of a large merger involving two other accounting firms across Canada. These firms have offices in Montreal, Ottawa, Toronto, Calgary, and Vancouver. Although the other two accounting firms were much larger than McKay, all three firms agreed to avoid centralizing the business around one office in Toronto. Instead, the new firm—called Goldberg, Choo, and McKay Associates—would rely on teams across the country to "leverage the synergies of our collective knowledge" (an oft-cited statement from the managing partner soon after the merger).

The effects of the merger came home to me a year ago when my boss (a senior partner and vice-president of the merger firm) announced that I would be working more closely with three people from the other two firms to collectively become the firm's new shipping industry accounting team. The other "team members" were Rochelle in Montreal, Thomas in Toronto, and Brad in Vancouver. I had met Rochelle briefly at a meeting in Montreal during the merger, but have never met Thomas or Brad, although I knew they were shipping accounting professionals at the other firms.

Initially, the shipping "team" activities involved e-mailing each other about new contracts and prospective clients. Later, we were asked to submit joint monthly reports on accounting statements and issues. Normally, I submitted my own monthly reports, which summarize activities involving my own clients. Coordinating the monthly report with three other people took much more time, particularly since different accounting documentation procedures across the three firms were still being resolved. It took numerous e-mails and a few telephone calls to work out a reasonable monthly report style.

During this aggravating process, it became apparent—to me at least—that this "team" business was costing me more time than it was worth. Moreover, Brad in Vancouver didn't have a clue as to how to communicate with the rest of us. He rarely replied to e-mails. Instead, he often used the telephone voice-mail system, which resulted in lots of telephone tag. Brad arrives at work at 9 a.m. in Vancouver (and is often late!), which is early afternoon in Halifax. I work from 8 a.m. to 4 p.m., a flexible arrangement so I can chauffeur my kids after school to sports and music lessons. So Brad and I have a window of less than three hours to share information.

The biggest nuisance with the shipping specialist accounting team started two weeks ago when the firm asked the four of us to develop a new strategy for attracting more shipping firm business. This new strategic plan is a messy business. Somehow, we have to share our thoughts on various approaches, agree on a new plan, and write a unified submission to the managing partner. Already, the project is taking most of my time just in writing and responding to e-mails, and talking in conference calls (which none of us did much before the team was formed).

Thomas and Rochelle have already had two or three "misunderstandings" via e-mail about their different perspectives on delicate aspects of the strategic plan. The worst of these disagreements required a conference call that all of us had to resolve. Except for the most basic matters, it seems that we can't even understand each other, let alone agree on key issues. I have come to the conclusion that I would never want Brad to work in my Halifax office (thank goodness, he's on the other side of the country). While Rochelle and I seem to agree on most points, the overall team can't form a common vision or strategy. I don't know how Rochelle, Thomas, or Brad feel, but I would be quite happy to work somewhere that did not require any of these long-distance team headaches.

Discussion Questions

1. What type of team was formed here? Was it necessary, in your opinion?

2. Use the team effectiveness model in Chapter 8 and related information in this chapter to identify the strengths and weaknesses of this team's environment, design, and processes.

3. Assuming that these four people must continue to work as a team, recommend ways to improve the team's effectiveness.

TEAM-TRUST EXERCISE

Purpose This exercise is designed to help you understand the role of interpersonal trust in the development and maintenance of effective teams.

Materials The instructor will provide the same 15 objects for each team as well as for the model.

Instructions

- *Step 1*: The instructor will divide the class into teams of approximately 10 people.
- *Step 2*: Each team receives 15 objects from the instructor. The same 15 objects are arranged in a specific way on a table at the front of the room (or elsewhere, as designated by the instructor). The table is behind a screened area so that the arrangements cannot be seen by participants from their work areas. The goal of each team is to duplicate the *exact* arrangement (e.g., location, overlap, spacing) of the objects on the table, using its own matching set of objects, within 20 minutes (or other time limit given by the instructor). Participants are allowed one 30-second opportunity at the beginning of the exercise to view the screened table. They may not write, draw, or talk while viewing the screened table. However, each team has *up to two saboteurs*. These are people who have been selected by the instructor (either before the exercise or through notes distributed to all participants). Saboteurs will use any reasonable method to prevent the team from producing an accurate configuration of objects in their work area. They are forbidden to reveal their identities.
- *Step 3:* At the end of the time limit, the instructor will evaluate each team's configuration and decide which one is the most accurate. The class members will then evaluate their experience in the exercise in terms of team development and other aspects of team dynamics.

Source: This exercise is based on ideas discussed in G. Thompson and P. Pearce, "The Team-Trust Game," *Training and Development*, May 1992, pp. 42–43.

EGG DROP EXERCISE

Purpose This exercise is designed to help you understand the dynamics of high-performance teams.

Materials The instructor will provide various raw materials with which to complete this task. The instructor will also distribute a cost sheet to each team, and will post the rules for managers and workers. Rule violations will attract penalties that increase the cost of production.

Team Task The team's task is to design and build a protective device that will allow a raw egg (provided by the instructor) to be dropped from a great height without breaking. The team wins if its egg does not break, using the lowest priced device.

Instructions

- *Step 1*: The instructor will divide the class into teams, with approximately 6 people on each team. Team members will divide into roles of "managers" and "workers." The team can have as many people as it thinks is needed for managers and workers as long as all team members are assigned to one of these roles. Please note from the cost sheet that managers and workers represent a cost to your project's budget.
- *Step 2*: Within the time allotted by the instructor, each team's managers will design the device to protect the egg. Workers and managers will then purchase supplies from the store, and workers will then build the egg protection device. Team members should read the rules carefully to avoid penalty costs.

Source: This exercise, which is widely available in many forms, does not seem to have any known origin.

THE TEAM PLAYER INVENTORY

By Theresa Kline, University of Calgary

Purpose This exercise is designed to help you estimate the extent to which you are positively predisposed to work in teams.

Instructions Read each of the statements below and circle the response that you believe best indicates the extent to which you agree or disagree with that statement. Then use the scoring key in Appendix B to calculate your results for each scale. This exercise is completed alone so students can assess themselves honestly without concerns of social comparison. However, class discussion will focus on the characteristics of individuals who are more or less compatible with working in self-directed work teams.

The Team Player Inventory					
To what extent to do you agree or disagree that...?	Completely disagree ▼	Disagree somewhat ▼	Neither agree nor disagree ▼	Agree somewhat ▼	Completely agree ▼
1. I enjoy working on team projects.	☐	☐	☐	☐	☐
2. Team project work easily allows others not to 'pull their weight'.	☐	☐	☐	☐	☐
3. Work that is done as a team is better than the work done individually.	☐	☐	☐	☐	☐
4. I do my best work alone rather than in a team.	☐	☐	☐	☐	☐
5. Team work is overrated in terms of the actual results produced.	☐	☐	☐	☐	☐
6. Working in a team gets me to think more creatively.	☐	☐	☐	☐	☐
7. Teams are used too often when individual work would be more effective.	☐	☐	☐	☐	☐
8. My own work is enhanced when I am in a team situation.	☐	☐	☐	☐	☐
9. My experiences working in team situations have been primarily negative.	☐	☐	☐	☐	☐
10. More solutions or ideas are generated when working in a team situation than when working alone.	☐	☐	☐	☐	☐

Source: T. J. B. Kline, "The Team Player Inventory: Reliability and Validity of a Measure of Predisposition Towards Organizational Team Working Environments," *Journal for Specialists in Group Work*, 24 (1999), pp. 102–12.

After studying the preceding material, be sure to check out our Online Learning Centre at
www.mcgrawhill.ca/college/mcshane
for more in-depth information and interactivities that correspond to this chapter.

Online LearningCentre with POWERWEB

CHAPTER 10

Decision Making and Creativity

Learning Objectives

AFTER READING THIS CHAPTER, YOU SHOULD BE ABLE TO:

- Diagram the rational model of decision making.

- Explain why people have difficulty identifying problems and opportunities.

- Contrast the rational model with how people actually evaluate and choose alternatives.

- Explain how emotions and intuition influence our selection of alternatives.

- Outline the causes of escalation of commitment to a poor decision.

- Describe four benefits of employee involvement in decision making.

- Identify four contingencies that affect the optimal level of employee involvement.

- Outline the four steps in the creative process

- Describe the characteristics of employees and the workplace that support creativity.

- Identify five problems facing teams when making decisions.

- Describe the five structures for team decision making.

- Explain why brainstorming may be more effective than scholars believed until recently.

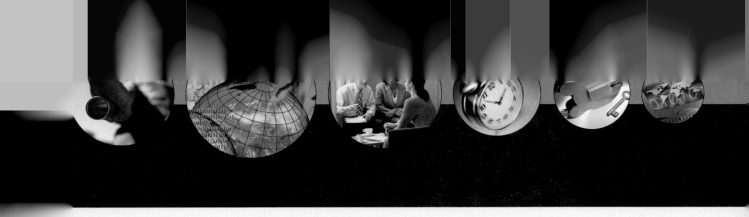

Bruce Poon Tip's first trip to Thailand was a disappointment—a fluffy trip "on a coach tour with five-star hotels and in air-conditioned buses." So the former University of Calgary student returned a couple of years later on a $10-a-day budget and stayed with local hill tribes. "I was disgusted by what I had thought this country was about, and what it really was about," recalls Poon Tip. "That was when I knew others would want authentic travel experiences."

With this revelation, Poon Tip decided to launch G.A.P Adventures, a Toronto-based company that sells authentic travel packages to exotic places with an emphasis on sustainability. Travellers stay at locally-run guest houses rather than four-star hotels, eat in local restaurants instead of all-you can-eat American-style buffets, and abandon air-conditioned coaches for public transit. It was such a crazy idea when Poon Tip launched the company that he couldn't convince his mother to help him fund the business. Yet today, G.A.P Adventures employs 85 staff and offers 10,000 travellers over 800 different itineraries in more than 100 countries.

G.A.P continues to develop creative ideas in the industry. The company's Australian office managed the ground operations and transportation for the Survivor series in that country. In exchange, G.A.P secured the use of the property for spin-off tours. Poon Tip is also launching Real Traveller, which puts more emphasis on adventure and less on sustainability.[1] ■

www.gap.ca

Creativity and astute decision making have helped Bruce Poon Tip (shown) and his company, G. A. P Adventures, to become an innovator in the travel industry. *Courtesy of G. A. P Adventures, Toronto*

decision making
A conscious process of making choices among one or more alternatives with the intention of moving toward some desired state of affairs

Bruce Poon Tip and his staff make thousands of decisions that keep G.A.P Adventures at the forefront of innovation in the travel industry. **Decision making** is a conscious process of making choices among one or more alternatives with the intention of moving toward some desired state of affairs.[2] This chapter begins by outlining the "rational" model of decision making. Then we examine this model more critically by recognizing how people identify problems and opportunities, choose among alternatives, and evaluate the success of their decisions differently from the rational model. The next section looks at the contingencies of employee involvement in decision making. This is followed by a close examination of the factors that support creativity in decision making, including the characteristics of creative people, work environments that support creativity, and creative activities. The final section of this chapter extends the discussion of creativity in team settings. Specifically, we look at various factors that restrict effective team decision making and creativity, then we examine team structures that help to overcome these constraints.

THE "RATIONAL" DECISION-MAKING MODEL

How do people make decisions in organizational settings? We can begin to answer this question by looking at the traditional "rational" model of decision making shown in Exhibit 10.1.[3] Throughout this chapter, we'll see that this rational model *does not* represent how people actually make decisions. However, it does provide a useful template for examining various parts of the decision process.

According to the rational model, the first step in the decision-making process is to identify a problem or recognize an opportunity. A *problem* is the deviation between the current and desired situation—the gap between "what is" and "what ought to be."[4] This deviation is a *symptom* of more fundamental root causes that needs to be corrected.[5] An *opportunity* is a deviation between current expectations and a potentially better situation that was not previously expected. In other words, decision makers realize that certain decisions may produce results beyond current goals or expectations.

EXHIBIT 10.1

Rational model of decision making

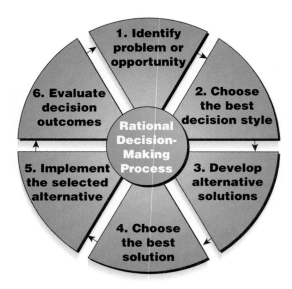

programmed decision

The process whereby decision makers follow standard operating procedures to select the preferred solution without the need to identify or evaluate alternative choices.

The second step is to determine the most appropriate decision style.[6] One important issue is whether this is a **programmed** or **nonprogrammed decision**.[7] A programmed decision follows standard operating procedures. There is no need to explore alternative solutions because the optimal solution has already been identified and documented. At many call centres, for example, staff rely on programmed decisions in a computer database. The database narrows down the customer's problem with a set of questions, then presents a ready-made solution. In contrast, nonprogrammed decisions include all steps in the decision model because the problems are new, complex, or ill-defined. In these cases, decision makers must search for alternatives and possibly develop unique solutions. Programmed decisions eventually drive out nonprogrammed decisions because we rely on past solutions as problems reappear.

The third step in the rational decision model is to develop a list of possible solutions.[8] This usually begins by searching for ready-made solutions, such as practices that have worked well on similar problems. If an acceptable solution cannot be found, then decision makers design a custom-made solution or modify an existing one. The fourth step involves choosing the best alternative. In a purely rational process, this would involve identifying all factors against which the alternatives are judged, assigning weights reflecting the importance of those factors, rating each alternative on those factors, then calculating each alternative's total value from the ratings and factor weights.[9] The fifth step in the rational model is to implement the selected alternative. This is followed by the sixth step, which involves evaluating whether the gap has narrowed between "what is" and "what ought to be." Ideally, this information should come from systematic benchmarks, so that relevant feedback is objective and easily observed.

nonprogrammed decision

The process applied to unique, complex, or ill-defined situations whereby decision makers follow the full decision-making process, including a careful search for and/or development of unique solutions.

Problems with the Rational Decision-Making Model

The rational model seems so logical, yet it is rarely practised. One reason is that the rational model assumes people are efficient and logical information processing machines. But as the next few pages will reveal, people have difficulty recognizing problems, they cannot (or will not) simultaneously process the huge volume of information needed to identify the best solution, and they have difficulty recognizing when their choices have failed. The second reason the rational model doesn't fit reality is that it focuses on logical thinking and completely ignores the fact that emotions also influence—perhaps even dominate—the decision-making process. As we shall discover in this chapter, emotions both support and interfere with our quest to make better decisions.[10] With these points in mind, let's look again at each step of decision making, but with more detail about what really happens.

IDENTIFYING PROBLEMS AND OPPORTUNITIES

When Albert Einstein was asked how he would save the world in one hour, he replied that he would spend the first 55 minutes defining the problem and the last five minutes solving it.[11] Problem identification is the first and arguably the most important step in decision making. But problems and opportunities do not appear on our desks as well-labelled objects. Instead, decision makers must somehow translate masses of information into evidence that something is wrong or that an opportunity is available. This translation occurs through both the rational and emotional centres of the brain.[12]

Recall from Chapter 4 that we process perceptual information both logically and emotionally. In a split second, the emotional centre classifies situations as good or bad and assigns corresponding emotional markers (anger, surprise, delight, etc.) to the situation based on this quick evaluation. The emotional markers are then sent to the rational centre where they influence the slower logical analysis of the situation. Both the emotional markers and the logical analysis determine whether you perceive something as a problem, as an opportunity, or as irrelevant. Your emotional reaction and rational analysis of the situation also depend on which information you receive and how it is presented.

Let's say that a worried-looking colleague tells you that the company's salesperson in Atlantic Canada has just quit. You might immediately become worried or frustrated, possibly in reaction to the other person's emotional display. In other words, your emotional brain centre quickly assigned these emotional markers to the news about the salesperson quitting. Meanwhile, the rational part of your brain is working through the situation and eventually concludes that this event isn't so bad after all. The salesperson's performance has been mediocre, and you already know of an excellent salesperson at another company who wants to join your company in that region. What initially felt like a problem was really an opportunity once it was based on your rational analysis of the situation. The initial emotions of worry or frustration might have been wrong in this situation, but sometimes your emotions provide a good indicator of problems or opportunities. Later, we'll see how emotions can be valuable allies in the quest to identify problems and to choose the best solution.

Perceptual Biases and Diagnostic Skill Failures

Along with weighing the emotional and rational evaluations of a situation, decision makers have to deal with imperfect perceptions. As we learned in Chapter 3, selective attention mechanisms cause relevant information to be unconsciously screened out. Moreover, employees, clients, and others with vested interests try to influence the decision maker's perceptions so that it is more or less likely that information is perceived as a problem or opportunity.[13] Another perceptual challenge, also noted in Chapter 3, is that people see problems or opportunities through their *mental models*. These working models of the world help us to make sense of our environment, but they also perpetuate assumptions that blind us to new realities. Connections 10.1 describes how narrow mental models are the source of several famous missed opportunities.

Another barrier to effective problem finding is that decision makers have imperfect diagnostic skills.[14] A common diagnostic error is the tendency to define problems in terms of their solutions. Someone who says, "The problem is that we need more control over our suppliers," has fallen into this trap. Notice that this statement focuses on a solution (controlling suppliers), whereas proper

© 1998 Randy Glasbergen.

"My team has created a very innovative solution, but we're still looking for a problem to go with it."

Copyright © Randy Glasbergen. Reprinted with special permission from www.glasbergen.com

Famous Missed Opportunities

Mental models create road maps that guide our decisions. Unfortunately, these maps also potentially block our ability to see emerging problems and opportunities. Here are a few famous examples:

- *L.A. Confidential* director Brian Helgeland approached Hollywood studios about a new film featuring a lowly squire in 14th century England who aspires to be a knight. The squire and his street-smart colleagues (including Geoffrey Chaucer) would do battle on contemporary themes such as youth, freedom, and equality. The entire film would be set to 1970s rock music. The Hollywood studios weren't impressed. "When I pitched it, I couldn't sell it," laments Helgeland. "Some people would laugh and then say, 'What are you really here for?'" Undeterred, Helgeland eventually convinced Columbia Pictures to back the project. The film, *A Knight's Tale*, recouped its $41 million costs in just three weeks and went on to become one of the more successful films of the year.

- Graphical user interfaces, mice, windows, pull-down menus, laser printing, distributed computing, and Ethernet technologies weren't invented by Apple, Microsoft, or IBM. These essential elements of contemporary personal computing originated in the 1970s from researchers at Xerox PARC. Unfortunately, Xerox executives were so focused on their photocopier business that they didn't bother to patent most of these inventions. Xerox has successfully applied some of its laser technology, but the lost value of Xerox PARC's other computing discoveries is much larger than the entire photocopier industry today.

- In 1995, IDEO founder David Kelley was given a personal demonstration of a new mobile computing interface that required the user to learn special shorthand writing. Based on his company's experience designing everything from the Apple mouse to stand-up toothpaste tubes, Kelley wasn't impressed. He advised the visitor that this product would have difficulty in the marketplace because

Brian Helgeland's film *A Knight's Tale* paid for itself in just three weeks even though most Hollywood studio executives rejected the proposal. © *Photofest*

people won't take time to learn a new way to use a computer. Three years later, in spite of Kelley's predictions, the Palm PDA became one of world's most popular computing devices.

- When the World Wide Web burst onto the cyberspace scene in the early 1990s, Bill Gates wondered what all the fuss was about. Even as late as 1996, the Microsoft founder lampooned investors for their love-in with companies that made Internet products. However, Gates eventually realized the error in his mental model of computing. Making up for lost time, Microsoft bought Hotmail and other Web-savvy companies, and added Internet support to its Windows operating system.

Sources: C. Sim, "Battling the Odds," *KrisWorld* (Singapore Airlines Inflight Magazine), September 2001, pp. 8–10; T. Kelley and J. Littman, *The Art of Innovation* (N.Y.: Random House, 2001), pp. 165–166; B. Campbell and M. Conron, "Xerox Ready to Hit Another Home Run," *Ottawa Citizen*, June 28, 1999; O. Port, "Xerox Won't Duplicate Past Errors," *Business Week*, September 29, 1997, p. 98; T. Abate, "Meet Bill Gates, Stand-Up Comic," *San Francisco Examiner*, March 13, 1996, p. D1. **www.ideo.com**

diagnosis would determine the cause of symptoms before jumping to solutions. The tendency to focus on solutions is based on the human bias for action as well as the need to reduce uncertainty.[15]

Decision makers also focus on solutions because they have a preferred set of actions that have worked well in the past. Some executives are known for cutting the workforce whenever they face problems; others introduce a new customer service program as their favourite solution to a variety of problems. The point here is that decision makers tend to look at problems from the perspective of the ready-made solutions that worked for them in the past.

Identifying Problems and Opportunities More Effectively

Recognizing problems and opportunities will always be a challenge, but the process can be improved by being aware of these perceptual and diagnostic limitations. By recognizing how mental models restrict a person's understanding of the world, decision makers learn to openly consider other perspectives of reality. Perceptual and diagnostic weaknesses can also be minimized by discussing the situation with colleagues. Decision makers discover blind spots in problem identification by hearing how others perceive certain information and diagnose them.[16] Opportunities also become apparent when outsiders explore this information from their different mental models.

EVALUATING AND CHOOSING ALTERNATIVES

According to the rational model of decision making, people rely on logic to evaluate and choose alternatives. This rational process assumes that decision makers have well-articulated and agreed-on organizational goals, that they efficiently and simultaneously process facts about all alternatives and the consequences of those alternatives, and that they choose the alternative with the highest pay-off.

Nobel-prize winning organizational scholar Herbert Simon questioned these assumptions half a century ago. He argued that people engage in **bounded rationality** because they process limited and imperfect information, and rarely select the best choice.[17] Simon and other OB researchers subsequently demonstrated that how people evaluate and choose alternatives differs from the rational model in several ways, as illustrated in Exhibit 10.2. These differences are so significant that even economists are now shifting from the rational model to the bounded rationality model in their theories and assumptions.[18] Let's look at these differences in terms of goals, information processing, and maximization.

bounded rationality
Processing limited and imperfect information and satisficing rather than maximizing when choosing among alternatives.

Problems with Goals

We need clear goals to choose the best solution. Goals identify "what ought to be" and therefore provide a standard against which each alternative is evaluated. The reality, however, is that organizational goals are often ambiguous or in conflict with each other. For instance, one survey recently found that 25 percent of managers and employees feel decisions are delayed because of the difficulty agreeing on what they want the decision to achieve.[19]

Problems with Information Processing

People do not make perfectly rational decisions because they don't process information very well. One problem is that decision makers can't possibly think through all the alternatives and the outcomes of those alternatives. Consequently, they look at only a few alternatives and only some of the main outcomes of those alternatives.[20] For example, there may be dozens of computer brands to choose

EXHIBIT 10.2   Rational model assumptions versus organizational behaviour findings about choosing decision alternatives

Rational decision model assumptions

Observations from organizational behaviour

Rational decision model assumptions	Observations from organizational behaviour
Decision makers use goals that are clear, compatible, and agreed upon.	Decision makers use goals that are ambiguous, are in conflict, and lack consensus.
Decision makers can process information about all alternatives and their outcomes.	Decision makers have limited information-processing abilities.
Decision makers evaluate all alternatives simultaneously.	Decision makers evaluate alternatives sequentially.
Decision makers evaluate alternatives against a set of absolute standards.	Decision makers evaluate alternatives against an implicit favourite alternative.
Decision makers process factual information.	Decision makers process perceptually distorted information.
Decision makers choose the alternative with the highest payoff (maximizing).	Decision makers choose the alternative that is good enough (satisficing).

from and dozens of features to consider, yet people typically evaluate only a few brands and a few features.

A related problem is that decision makers typically look at alternatives sequentially rather than examining all alternatives at the same time. As a new alternative comes along, it is immediately compared to an **implicit favourite**. An implicit favourite is an alternative that the decision maker prefers and that is used as a comparison against which other choices are judged. There are two problems with this sequential implicit favourite process. First, people often form an implicit favourite based on limited information long before the formal process of evaluating alternatives begins. Second, people unconsciously try to make their implicit favourite come out the winner in most comparisons.[21] They do this by distorting information and changing the importance of decision criteria.

A recent study of Canadian auditing students illustrates how people distort information and decision criteria to support their implicit favourite.[22] Students were given a detailed case and asked to determine whether a company's financial problems were "significant" enough to be reported in the audit. Students who decided that the company was in financial trouble distorted the available information to make the financial problems appear worse, whereas those who preferred not to report the problems minimized any reference to the negative information. Moreover, students who wanted to report the company's financial problems used a

implicit favourite
The decision maker's preferred alternative against which all other choices are judged.

vague definition of "significant," whereas students who didn't want to report the problems used a precise and harsher definition of this criterion. In short, these students developed a preference about whether to report the company's problems, then distorted information and their decision criterion to support this preference.

Problems with Maximization

satisficing
Selecting a solution that is satisfactory or "good enough" rather than optimal or "the best."

Decision makers tend to select the alternative that is acceptable or "good enough," rather than the best possible solution. In other words, they engage in **satisficing** rather than maximizing. Satisficing occurs because it isn't possible to identify all the possible alternatives, and information about available alternatives is imperfect or ambiguous. Satisficing also occurs because, as mentioned already, decision makers tend to evaluate alternatives sequentially. They evaluate alternatives one at a time against the implicit favourite and eventually select an option that is good enough to satisfy their needs or preferences.[23]

Emotions and Making Choices

Herbert Simon and other OB scholars demonstrated that the rational brain centre does not evaluate alternatives nearly as well as is assumed by the rational model of decision making. However, they neglected to mention another glaring weakness with the rational model, namely, that it completely ignores the effect of emotions on human decision making.[24] Just as both the rational and emotional brain centres alert us to problems, these processes also influence our choice of alternatives.

Scholars are just beginning to understand the effects of emotions on decision making. We know that while the rational brain centre processes (imperfectly, as we just learned) information about the various choices, the emotional centre more quickly creates emotional markers that attract us to some alternatives and repel us from others. Some research suggests that the decision maker's reliance on logic or emotions depends on whether the object chosen is supposed to produce emotions. For instance, one recent study reported that subjects relied more on their emotions to evaluate computer game software (which is supposed to produce excitement and other emotions), but more on perceptions and logical analysis to evaluate spell-checker software (which is not intended to produce emotions). Other research suggests that our general moods can assist or hinder the decision-making process. Specifically, people engage in more perceptual biases (such as halo effect and fundamental attribution error) when they are in a positive mood, whereas they tend to evaluate alternatives more accurately when in a neutral or negative mood.[25] Overall, we need to be aware that emotions and logical analysis work alongside each other and together to influence our choices.

Intuition and Making Choices

Greg McDonald felt uneasy about a suspicious-looking crack in the rock face, so the veteran Potash Corp. of Saskatchewan miner warned a co-worker to stay away from the area. "There was no indication there was anything wrong—just a little crack," McDonald recalled. A few minutes later, the ceiling in that mine shaft 1,000 metres underground caved in. Fortunately, the co-worker heeded McDonald's advice. "If he had been there, he would be dead," McDonald said in an interview following a near-sleepless night after the incident.[26]

The gut instinct that helped Greg McDonald save his co-worker's life is also the subject of considerable discussion in organizational behaviour. Most people—whether underground miners in Saskatchewan or corporate executives in Toronto—will tell you they pay attention to their intuition when making decisions. **Intuition** is the ability to know when a problem or opportunity exists and to select the best course of action without conscious reasoning.[27] Some scholars warn us that intuition is merely wishful thinking that can have disastrous results. In spite of these warnings, most professionals and executives say they rely on intuition, particularly in combination with more rational decision making.[28] Notice that intuition rarely occurs alone. Decision makers analyze the available information, then turn to their intuition to complete the process.

Should we rely on intuition or view it with caution? The answer is "both." It is true that we sometimes justify biased and nonsystematic decision making as intuition. When deciding to invest in a new business, for example, decision makers run the risk of following their emotions rather than looking at the evidence. However, there is also increasing research evidence that intuition is the conduit through which people use their tacit knowledge. Tacit knowledge is subtle information acquired through observation and experience that is not clearly understood and therefore cannot be explicitly communicated (see Chapter 3). This knowledge incorporates logical reasoning that has become habit over time. Thus, intuition allows us to draw on our vast storehouse of unconscious knowledge.[29]

intuition
The ability to know when a problem or opportunity exists and select the best course of action without conscious reasoning.

Choosing Solutions More Effectively

It is very difficult to get around the human limitations of making choices, but a few strategies may help. Some companies systematically evaluate alternatives by identifying relevant factors and scoring each alternative on those criteria. For example, a cross-functional committee at Dow Chemical relies on a systematic evaluation process to decide which information technology projects to pursue.[30] This process potentially minimizes the implicit favourite and satisficing problems that occur when relying on general subjective judgments. However, there is still a risk that decision makers will bias the criteria so the preferred choice ultimately receives the highest score. Intuition also has to be taken into account within this rational process. We need to be careful that "gut feelings" are not merely perceptual distortions and false assumptions, but intuition does seem to have a role in making sound choices.[31]

Another issue is how to work with our emotions when making choices. Many of us have made bad decisions in emotional haste, and many have tried to make "rational" choices when we should have paid more attention to our emotions. The first recommendation here is that we need to be constantly aware that decisions are influenced by both rational and emotional processes. With this awareness, some decision makers deliberately revisit important issues so they can look at the information in different moods and allow their initial emotions to subside. Others practise **scenario planning**, in which they anticipate emergencies long before they occur, so that alternative courses of action are evaluated without the pressure and emotions that occur during real emergencies.[32]

scenario planning
A systematic process of thinking about alternative futures, and what the organization should do to anticipate and react to those environments.

EVALUATING DECISION OUTCOMES

Contrary to the rational model, decision makers aren't completely honest with themselves when evaluating the effectiveness of their decisions. One concern is that after making a choice, decision makers tend to support their choice by forgetting or downplaying the negative features of the selected alternative and emphasizing its positive features. This perceptual distortion, known as **postdecisional justification,** results from the need to maintain a positive self-identity.[33] Postdecisional justification gives people an excessively optimistic evaluation of their decisions, but only until they receive very clear and undeniable information to the contrary. Unfortunately, it also inflates the decision maker's initial evaluation of the decision, so reality often comes as a painful shock when objective feedback is finally received.

Escalation of Commitment

A second problem when evaluating decision outcomes is **escalation of commitment**. Escalation of commitment is the tendency to repeat an apparently bad decision or allocate more resources to a failing course of action.[34] There are plenty of escalation examples around the world. Tokyo's Metropolitan Transport Bureau promised to build a 29-kilometre high-speed subway loop under the city in record time and at enormous profit. Instead, the multi-billion dollar project was seriously over-budget, more than three years overdue, and won't be profitable until 2040, if ever. Denver's International Airport was supposed to include a state-of-the-art automated baggage handling system. Instead, the project was eventually abandoned, causing the airport to open 16 months late and $2 billion over budget. Connections 10.2 describes how the PacifiCat project in British Columbia escalated to twice the original cost and produced three ferries that could not be sold. Escalation also occurred years ago when the British government continued funding the Concorde supersonic jet long after its lack of commercial viability was apparent. To this day, some scholars refer to escalation of commitment as the "Concorde fallacy."[35]

Causes of escalating commitment Why are people led deeper and deeper into failing projects? Organizational behaviour scholars have identified several reasons, including self-justification, gambler's fallacy, perceptual blinders, and closing costs.

■ *Self-justification*—Escalation of commitment often occurs because people try to save face and engage in impression management to look successful (see Chapter 12).[36] Those who are personally identified with the decision tend to persist because that demonstrates confidence in their own decision-making ability. The B.C. Ferries PacifiCat project probably escalated because it was the former premier's pet project. It was difficult to cancel a symbol of his personal success as a government leader.

■ *Gambler's fallacy*—Many projects result in escalation of commitment because decision makers underestimate their risk and overestimate their probability of success. They become victims of the so-called "gambler's fallacy" by having inflated expectations of their ability to control problems that may arise. In other words, decision makers falsely believe that luck is on their side, so they invest more in a losing course of action.

■ *Perceptual blinders*—Escalation of commitment sometimes occurs because decision makers do not see the problems soon enough. Through perceptual defence (see Chapter 3), they unconsciously screen out or explain away negative

---

postdecisional justification

Justifying choices by unconsciously inflating the quality of the selected option and deflating the quality of the discarded options.

escalation of commitment

The tendency to repeat an apparently bad decision or allocate more resources to failing course of action.

PacifiCats: An Escalation of Commitment

In the mid-1990s, B.C. Ferries—the government agency that operates the ferry system in British Columbia—decided to design and build three catamaran-style ferries to carry passengers and vehicles across the 24 kilometre strait between the city of Vancouver and Vancouver Island. The premier of British Columbia promised that these "PacifiCats" would travel faster than conventional ferries and cost $210 million "right down to the toilet paper."

Instead, costs ballooned to nearly $500 million as the project fell more than two years behind schedule. The first two PacifiCats were plagued by so many mechanical problems that each ferry was under repair half the time. A more devastating discovery was that the PacifiCats had a massive wake that caused ecological and property damage along the shoreline, making them unsuitable for B.C. waters.

These problems were not unforeseen. During the project's first year, a marine engineer warned that the PacifiCats were not economically feasible and could endanger the public. Soon after, a British shipping journal reported that the ferries would cost much more to build than the original estimates. By the fifth year, the B.C. auditor general slammed the project, saying that the B.C. Ferries' board of directors had endorsed the project under government pressure. The board apparently raised concerns about the PacifiCats both before and many times after their decision.

Almost six years after the PacifiCat project was announced, a new premier cancelled the program and put the three ferries up for sale at less than one-quarter of their cost. So far, there are no offers. The former premier, who had supported the PacifiCats until he

The BC Government's ill-fated "PacifiCat" program illustrates the risks of escalation of commitment.
© R. Allen/Vancouver Province.

stepped down for other reasons, was one of the few people to criticize terminating the project.

Sources: R. Mickleburgh, "Study Urges big Changes for Troubled B.C. Ferries," *Globe and Mail*, December 18, 2001, p. A1; "Liberals Scrap Aggressive Campaign to Sell Three Fast Ferries," *Canadian Press*, November 1, 2001; K. Fraser, "Ferry-Tale Alarms," *Vancouver Province*, June 14, 2000; P. Willcocks, "Fast Ferries may Sell for Under $40 Million Each," *Vancouver Sun*, May 31, 2000; K. Lunman, "B.C. Admits Failure, Puts Fast Ferries up for Sale," *Globe and Mail*, March 14, 2000, p. A1; C. McInnes, "Victoria Sinks Fast Ferries," *Vancouver Sun*, March 14, 2000; K. Lunman, "B.C. NDP Blasted in Report on Ferries," *Globe and Mail*, October 29, 1999, p. A7.
www.bcferries.bc.ca

information. Serious problems initially look like random errors along the trend line to success. Even when they see that something is wrong, the information is sufficiently ambiguous that it can be misinterpreted or justified.

■ *Closing costs*—Even when a project's success is in doubt, decision makers will persist because the costs of ending the project are high or unknown. Terminating a major project may involve large financial penalties, a bad public image, or personal political costs. This is probably another explanation why the B.C. Ferries PacifiCat program escalated. Keeping the three ferries in storage would have cost $9 million and leave a reminder of the government's mistake.

Evaluating Decision Outcomes More Effectively

One effective way to minimize escalation of commitment and postdecisional justification is to separate decision choosers from decision evaluators. This tends to avoid the problem of saving face because the person responsible for evaluating the decision is not connected to the original decision. For example, one study found that banks were more likely to take action against bad loans after the executive responsible for signing the original loan was transferred elsewhere.[37] In other words, the bank cut its losses only when someone else took over the loan portfolio. Similarly, the B.C. Ferries PacifiCat project was cancelled only after the premier who started the project had stepped down as leader.

A second strategy is to publicly establish a preset level at which the decision is abandoned or re-evaluated.[38] This is similar to a stop-loss order in the stock market, whereby the stock is sold if it falls below a certain price. The problem with this solution is that conditions are often so complex that it is difficult to identify an appropriate point to abandon a project.[39] Finally, projects might have less risk of escalation if several people are involved. Team members continuously monitor each other and might notice problems sooner than someone working alone on the project. Employee involvement offers these and other benefits to the decision-making process, as we learn next.

EMPLOYEE INVOLVEMENT IN DECISION MAKING

employee involvement
The degree to which employees influence how their work is organized and carried out.

In this world of rapid change and increasing complexity, individuals in key decision-making positions are rarely able to identify problems or opportunities or choose alternatives alone. As one respected scholar recently wrote, "the new organizational realities are that top-down decision making is not sufficiently responsive to the dynamic organizational environment. Employees must be actively involved in decisions—or completely take over many decisions." **Employee involvement** (also called *participative management*) refers to the degree to which employees influence how their work is organized and carried out.[40] At the lowest level, participation involves asking employees for information. They do not make recommendations and might not even know what the problem is about. At a moderate level of involvement, employees are told about the problem and asked to provide recommendations to the decision maker. At the highest level of involvement, the entire decision-making process is handed over to employees. They identify the problem, choose the best alternative, and implement their choice.[41]

Various levels and forms of employee involvement exist throughout every Canadian organization. Each year, a cross-section of staff at Québec-based MAC Closures participates in a two-day retreat to draft the company's strategic plan for the following year. At Zenon Environmental Inc., employees decide on corporate changes affecting them through the firm's "Employee Parliament." And when Brossard, Québec-based Enerfin, Inc. ran into financial trouble, employees identified and implemented productivity and quality improvements that saved the cooling systems company from possible extinction.[42]

codetermination
A form of employee involvement required by some governments that typically operates at the work site as works councils and at the corporate level as supervisory boards.

Some countries require employee involvement at both the work site and corporate levels through a process of **codetermination**. In Sweden, Norway, and some other European countries, for instance, employee representatives sit on supervisory boards, making decisions about executive salaries and recommendations about the company's direction. At the same time, employers must consult with employee representation committees (called works councils) regarding matters of employment staffing, work processes, and individual dismissals.[43]

Benefits of Employee Involvement

For the past half century, organizational behaviour scholars have advised that employee involvement potentially improves decision making quality and commitment.[44] Involving employees potentially improves decision quality by recognizing problems more quickly and defining them more accurately. Employees are, in many respects, the sensors of the organization's environment. When the organization's activities do not align with customer expectations, employees are usually the first to know. Employee involvement ensures that everyone in the organization is quickly alerted to these problems.

Employee involvement can also improve the number and quality of solutions generated. In a well-managed meeting, team members create *synergy* by pooling their knowledge to form new alternatives. In other words, several people working together can generate more and better solutions than if these people worked alone. A third benefit is that employee involvement often improves the likelihood of choosing the best alternative. This occurs because the decision is reviewed by people with diverse perspectives and a broader representation of values.

Along with improving decision quality, employee involvement tends to strengthen employee commitment to the decision. Rather than viewing themselves as agents of someone else's decision, staff members feel personally responsible for its success. Employee involvement also increases perceptions of fairness because they participate in the allocation of resources and rewards in the project.[45] Consequently, employees are more motivated to implement the decision and are less likely to resist changes resulting from it.[46]

Contingencies of Employee Involvement

If employee involvement is so wonderful, why don't companies leave all decisions to employees further down the hierarchy? The answer is that the appropriateness and effectiveness of employee involvement depends on the situation. The employee involvement model, shown in Exhibit 10.3, indicates that the optimal level of employee involvement is contingent on the decision structure, source of decision knowledge, decision commitment, and risk of conflict in the decision process.

■ *Decision structure*—At the beginning of this chapter, we learned that some decisions are programmed whereas others are nonprogrammed. Programmed decisions are less likely to need employee involvement because the solutions are already worked out from past experience. In other words, the benefits of employee involvement increase with the novelty and complexity of the problem or opportunity.

■ *Source of decision knowledge*—Subordinates should be involved in some level of decision making when the leader lacks sufficient knowledge and subordinates have additional information to improve decision quality. In many cases, employees are closer to customers and production activities, so they often know where the company can save money, improve product or service quality, and realize opportunities. This is particularly true for complex decisions where employees are more likely to possess relevant information.[47]

■ *Decision commitment*—Participation tends to improve employee commitment to the decision. If employees are unlikely to accept a decision made without their involvement, then some level of participation is usually necessary.

■ *Risk of conflict*—Two types of conflict undermine the benefits of employee involvement. First, if employee goals and norms conflict with the organization's

EXHIBIT 10.3

Model of employee involvement in decision making

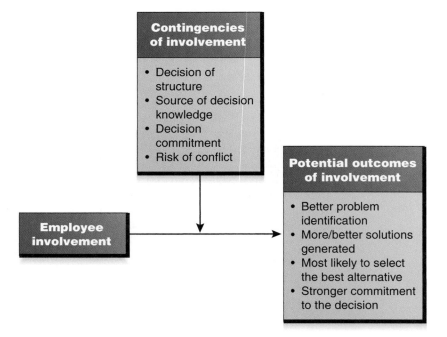

goals, then only a low level of employee involvement is advisable. Second, the degree of involvement depends on whether employees will reach agreement on the preferred solution. If conflict is likely, then high involvement (i.e. where employees make the decision alone) is probably ineffective.

Employee involvement is an important component of the decision-making process. In order to make the best decisions, we need to involve the people with the most valuable information who will gain commitment to implement the decision. Another important component of decision making is creativity, which we discuss next.

CREATIVITY

creativity
The capacity to develop an original product, service, or idea that makes a socially recognized contribution.

G.A.P Adventures, described in the opening vignette to this chapter, doesn't just embrace employee involvement to make good decisions; it also encourages creativity in the decision-making process. Walk into G.A.P's offices and you will notice that employees bounce weird ideas off each other and debate the merits of alternatives. **Creativity** refers to developing an original product, service, or idea that makes a socially recognized contribution.[48] Although there are unique conditions for creativity that we discuss over the next few pages, it is really an integral part of the decision-making process described earlier in the previous chapter. We rely on creativity to find problems, identify alternatives, and implement solutions. Creativity is not something saved for special occasions.

The Creative Process Model

One of the earliest and most influential models of creativity is shown in Exhibit 10.4.[49] The first stage is *preparation*—the person or group's effort to acquire

EXHIBIT 10.4

The creative
process model

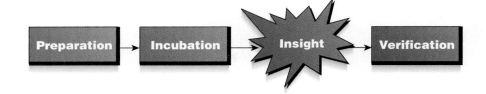

knowledge and skills regarding the problem or opportunity.[50] Preparation involves developing a clear understanding of what you are trying to achieve through a novel solution, then actively studying information seemingly related to the topic.

The second stage, called *incubation*, is the stage of reflective thought. We put the problem aside, but our mind is still working on it in the background.[51] The important condition here is to maintain a low-level awareness by frequently revisiting the problem. Incubation does not mean that you forget about the problem or issue. Incubation assists **divergent thinking**. Divergent thinking involves reframing the problem in a unique way and generating different approaches to the issue. This contrasts with *convergent thinking*, which refers to calculating the conventionally accepted "right answer" to a logical problem.[52] Divergent thinking breaks us away from existing mental models so we can apply concepts or processes from completely different areas of life. Consider the following classic example: Years ago, the experimental bulbs in Thomas Edison's lab kept falling off their fixtures until a technician wondered whether the threaded caps that screwed down tightly on kerosene bottles would work on light bulbs. They did, and the design remains to this day.[53]

Insight, the third stage of creativity, refers to the experience of suddenly becoming aware of a unique idea.[54] These flashes of inspiration don't keep a particular schedule; they might come to you at any time of day or night. They are also fleeting and can be quickly lost if not documented. For this reason, many creative people keep a journal or notebook nearby at all times, so that they can jot down these ideas before they disappear.[55] Insights are merely rough ideas. Their usefulness still requires *verification* through conscious evaluation and experimentation. Thus, while verification is labelled as the final stage of creativity, it is really the beginning of a long process of experimentation and further creativity.

Creative People and Work Environments

Minnesota Mining & Manufacturing Co. (3M) introduces an average of 10 new products every week and generates 30 percent of its annual revenues from products developed within the previous four years.[56] The company achieves these impressive goals by finding creative people and putting them in an environment that encourages creative ideas. In other words, 3M executives have learned that creativity is a function of both the person and the situation.

Characteristics of creative people Everyone is creative, but some people seem to be more creative than others. Four of the main features of creative people are intelligence, subject-matter knowledge and experience, persistence, and inventive thinking style. First, creative people have above-average intelligence to synthesize information and analyze ideas, as well as to apply their ideas.[57] Like the fictional sleuth Sherlock Holmes, creative people recognize the significance of

---

divergent thinking

Involves reframing the problem in a unique way and generating different approaches to the issue.

Mike Lazaridis faced plenty of industry doubters when he first proposed the idea of a handheld wireless communication device a decade ago. Then his company, Research in Motion (RIM), worked through numerous failures before getting closer to Lazaridis' vision. "Mike is one of the most tenacious people I've ever met," says a former Ericsson executive. "[He] keeps grinding towards his goal until he gets there. There were eight or nine failures before BlackBerry. He took lots of at-bats before he hit his home run." Through this persistence, RIM has become a leader in wireless communication.[60] What other individual characteristics would make Mike Lazaridis a creative person? *CP/Kitchener Waterloo Record/Rick Koza*
www.rim.net

small bits of information and are able to connect them in ways that no one else could imagine. Then, they have the capacity to evaluate the potential usefulness of their ideas.

Persistence is the second feature of creative people. The fact is that innovations derive more from trial and error than from intelligence and experience. Persistence drives creative people to continue developing and testing after others have given up.[58] In other words, people who develop more creative products and services are those who develop more ideas that don't work. Thomas Edison emphasized this point in his famous statement that genius is 1 percent inspiration and 99 percent perspiration. Edison and his staff discovered hundreds of ways *not* to build a light bulb before they got it right! This persistence is based on a high need for achievement and moderate or high degree of self-confidence.[59]

A third feature of creative people is that they possess sufficient knowledge and experience on their subject. Creativity experts explain that discovering new ideas requires knowledge of the fundamentals. For example, the Beatles produced most of their songs only after they had played together for several years. They developed extensive experience singing and adapting the music of other people before their creative talents soared.[61]

Although knowledge and experience may be important in one sense, they can also undermine creativity because people develop mental models that lead to "mindless behaviour," when they stop questioning their assumptions.[62] This explains why some corporate leaders like to hire people from other industries and areas of expertise. For instance, Geoffrey Ballard, founder of Vancouver-based Ballard Power Systems, hired a chemist to develop a better battery. When the chemist protested that he didn't know anything about batteries, Ballard replied: "That's fine. I don't want someone who knows batteries. They know what won't work."[63] Ballard explained that he wanted to hire people who would question and investigate what experts had stopped questioning.

The fourth characteristic of creative people is their inventive thinking style. Creative types are divergent thinkers and risk-takers. They are not bothered about making mistakes or working with ambiguous information. They take a broad view of problems, don't like to abide by rules or status, and are less concerned about social approval of their actions.[64]

Organizational conditions supporting creativity   Hiring creative people is only part of the creativity equation. Organizations also need to maintain a work environment that supports the creative process for everyone.[65] One of the most important conditions is that the organization has a *learning orientation*; that is, leaders recognize that employees make reasonable mistakes as part of the creative process.[66] "In our new product development department, the most damaging thing to creativity is if someone has a fear of failure," warns Jim Pratt, CEO Vancouver-based Sepp's Gourmet Foods. "So you have to remove that from your culture. We try to create a culture that says, 'It's okay to fail.'"[67]

The job's intrinsic motivation, which was discussed in Chapter 6, is another important condition for creativity.[68] Employees tend to be more creative when they believe their work has a substantial impact on the organization and/or larger society (i.e. task significance). Creativity also increases with autonomy—the freedom to pursue novel ideas without bureaucratic delays. Creativity is about changing things, and change is only possible when employees have the authority to experiment. Creativity is an ongoing learning process, so employees need access to fairly continuous feedback from the job and other sources. More generally, jobs encourage creativity when they are challenging and aligned with the employee's competencies.[69] Challenging work pushes employees to draw on their fullest potential.

Along with supporting a learning orientation and intrinsically motivating jobs, creative companies foster open communication and provide sufficient resources. They provide a reasonable level of job security, which explains why creativity suffers during times of downsizing and corporate restructuring.[70] Organizational support extends to the roles of project leaders and co-workers.[71] Project leaders must apply enough pressure to complete the project, yet give individuals and teams enough freedom and time with plenty of support. Extreme time pressures, unrealistic goals, and ongoing distractions are well-known creativity inhibitors.[72] While we need some pressure to produce, companies also need to minimize pressure when it strangles creative output. Team members and other co-workers further improve creativity when they trust each other, communicate well, and are committed to the assigned project. In contrast, creativity is undermined when co-workers criticize new ideas, are competitive, and engage in political tactics to achieve personal goals.

Activities that Encourage Creativity

Along with hiring creative people and giving them a supportive work environment, organizations have introduced numerous activities that attempt to crank up the creative potential. One set of activities encourages employees to redefine the problem. One way to redefine problems is to look at abandoned projects. After a few months of neglect, these projects might be seen in new ways.[73] Another strategy involves asking people unfamiliar with the issue (preferably with different expertise) to explore the problem with you. You state the objectives and give some facts, then let the other person ask questions to further understand the situation. By verbalizing the problem, listening to questions, and hearing what others think, you are more likely to form new perspectives on the issue.[74]

A second set of creativity activities, known as *associative play*, ranges from art classes to impromptu story telling. Wedgwood, the Irish-based tableware company, brought together its overseas executives in a workshop where they tore up magazines, pasted up pictures, and selected music that represented what they thought the Wedgwood brand should become. Employees at Telus Corp., the Burnaby, B.C.-based telecommunications provider, worked with an improvisational theatre troupe to act out goofy roles as machines, animals, and other characters. "A necessity for organizations is to empower people to take risks," explains Jay Ono, who led the corporate improv program at Telus. "To foster risk-taking, you need a supportive environment where people aren't afraid to express themselves."[75]

EDS executives don't seem to mind if James Wang (centre), Jim Sugarman, and Gwendolyn Chan look like they are playing rather than working. That's because the computer service firm developed four eSpace innovation centres where playing with rubber balls, Lego blocks, and other toys are all part of the creative process. "The toys give you something to do while you're reflecting and thinking and they trigger new ideas," explains a team leader at the innovation centre in Detroit. Another EDS staffer adds: "We're all about collaboration and creativity and inspiration, and the toys are props to stimulate the thought process."[76] How would this associative play improve creativity at EDS? *Morris Richardson II/The Detroit News*
www.eds.com

Another associative play activity, called *morphological analysis*, involves listing different dimensions of a system and the elements of each dimension, then looking at each combination. This encourages people to carefully examine combinations that initially seem nonsensical. Tyson Foods, the world's largest poultry producer, applied this activity to identify new ways to serve chicken for lunch. The marketing and research team assigned to this task focused on three categories: occasion, packaging, and taste. Next, the team worked through numerous combinations of items in the three categories. This created unusual ideas, such as cheese chicken pasta (taste) in pizza boxes (packaging) for concessions at baseball games (occasion). Later, the team looked more closely at the feasibility of these combinations and sent them to customer focus groups for further testing.[77]

A third set of activities that encourage creativity in organizations is known as cross-pollination.[78] Many creative firms mix together employees from different past projects so they can share new knowledge with each other. Cross-pollination also occurs through formal information sessions where people from different parts of the organization share their knowledge. Mitel, the Ottawa-based communications systems designer, holds Demo Days—internal trade shows where Mitel teams exhibit their projects and are encouraged to steal ideas from other groups within the organization.[79]

CONSTRAINTS ON TEAM DECISION MAKING AND CREATIVITY

Cross-pollination highlights the fact that creativity and decision making rarely occur alone. Under certain conditions, teams are more effective than individuals at identifying problems, choosing alternatives, and evaluating their decisions. "Teams are the heart of the IDEO method," advises Tom Kelley, general manager IDEO, the California industrial design firm that is renowned for its creative practices. "We believe it's how innovation and much of business take place in the world."[80] In spite of the potential benefits of teams, team dynamics can interfere with creativity and decision making. In this section, we look at the main factors that restrict effective creativity and decision making in team settings. In the final section of this chapter, we look at specific team structures that try to overcome these constraints.

Time Constraints

There's a saying that "committees keep minutes and waste hours." This reflects the fact that teams take longer than individuals to make decisions.[81] Unlike individuals, teams require extra time to organize, coordinate, and socialize. The larger the group, the more time required to make a decision. Team members need time to learn about each other and build rapport. They need to manage an imperfect communication process so that they can understand each other's ideas. They also need to co-ordinate roles and rules of order within the decision process.

Another time constraint found in most team structures is that only one person can speak at a time.[82] This problem, known as **production blocking**, causes participants to forget potentially creative ideas by the time it is their turn to speak. Team members who concentrate on remembering their fleeting thoughts end up ignoring what others are saying, even though their statements could trigger more creative ideas.

Evaluation Apprehension

Individuals are reluctant to mention ideas that seem silly because they believe (often correctly) that other team members are silently evaluating them.[83] This **evaluation apprehension** is based on an individual's desire to create a favourable self-presentation and the need to protect one's self-esteem. It is most common in meetings attended by people with different levels of status or expertise, or when members formally evaluate each other's performance throughout the year (as in 360 degree feedback). Evaluation apprehension is a problem when a group wants to generate creative ideas, because innovative ideas often sound bizarre or illogical when presented, so employees are afraid to mention them in front of co-workers.

Conformity to Peer Pressure

Chapter 8 described how cohesiveness leads individual members to conform to the team's norms. This control keeps the group organized around common goals, but it may also cause team members to suppress their dissenting opinions about discussion issues, particularly when a strong team norm is related to the issue. When someone does state a point of view that violates the majority opinion, other members might punish the violator or try to prove that his or her opinion is incorrect. It's not surprising, then, that nearly half the managers surveyed in one study say they give up in team decisions because of pressure from others to conform to the team's decision.[84] Conformity can also be subtle. To some extent, we depend on others' opinions to validate our own views. If co-workers don't agree with us, then we begin to question our own opinions even without overt peer pressure.[85]

Groupthink

Groupthink is the tendency of highly cohesive groups to value consensus at the price of decision quality.[86] Groupthink goes beyond the problem of conformity. There are strong social pressures on individual members to maintain harmony by avoiding conflict and disagreement. They suppress doubts about decision alternatives preferred by the majority or group leader. Team members want to maintain this harmony because their self-identity is enhanced by membership in a powerful decision-making body that speaks with one voice.[87] Team harmony also helps members cope with the stress of making crucial top-level decisions.

High cohesiveness isn't the only cause of groupthink. Groupthink is also more likely to occur when the team is isolated from outsiders, the team leader is opin-

production blocking
A time constraint in team decision making due to the procedural requirement that only one person may speak at a time.

evaluation apprehension
When individuals are reluctant to mention ideas that seem silly because they believe (often correctly) that other team members are silently evaluating them.

groupthink
The tendency of highly cohesive groups to value consensus at the price of decision quality.

ionated (rather than impartial), the team is under stress due to an external threat, the team has experienced recent failures or other decision-making problems, and the team lacks clear guidance from corporate policies or procedures. Several symptoms of groupthink have been identified and are summarized in Exhibit 10.5. In general, teams overestimate their invulnerability and morality, become closed-minded to outside and dissenting information, and experience several pressures toward consensus.[88]

Group Polarization

group polarization

The tendency of teams to make more extreme decisions than individuals working alone.

Group polarization refers to the tendency of teams to make more extreme decisions than individuals working alone.[89] Suppose that a group of people meets to decide on the future of a new product. Individual team members might come to the meeting with various degrees of support or opposition to the product's future. Yet, by the end of the meeting, chances are that the team will agree on a more extreme solution than the average person had when the meeting began. One reason for the extreme preference is that team members become comfortable with more extreme positions when they realize that co-workers also support the same position. Persuasive arguments favouring the dominant position convince doubtful members and help form a consensus around the extreme option. Finally, individuals feel less personally responsible for the decision consequences because the decision is made by the team.

Social support, persuasion, and shifting responsibility explain why teams make more *extreme* decisions, but why do they usually make riskier decisions? The answer is that decision makers maintain overly positive emotions that create an illusion of control. They become victims of the "gambler's fallacy," that they can

EXHIBIT 10.5   Symptoms of groupthink

Groupthink symptom	Description
Illusion of invulnerability	The team feels comfortable with risky decisions because possible weaknesses are suppressed or glossed over.
Assumption of morality	There is such an unquestioned belief in the inherent morality of the team's objectives that members do not feel the need to debate whether their actions are ethical.
Rationalization	Underlying assumptions, new information, and previous actions that seem inconsistent with the team's decision are discounted or explained away.
Stereotyping of outgroups	The team stereotypes or oversimplifies the external threats on which the decision is based; "enemies" are viewed as purely evil or moronic.
Self-censorship	Team members suppress their doubts to maintain harmony.
Illusion of unanimity	Self-censorship results in harmonious behaviour, so individual members believe that they alone have doubts; silence is automatically perceived as evidence of consensus.
Mindguarding	Some members become self-appointed guardians to prevent negative or inconsistent information from reaching the team.
Pressuring of dissenters	Members who happen to raise their concerns about the decision are pressured to fall into line and be more loyal to the team.

Source: Based on I. L. Janis, *Groupthink: Psychological Studies of Policy Decisions and Fiascoes*, 2nd ed. (Boston: Houghton Mifflin, 1982), p. 244.

beat the odds. For example, team members tend to think, "This strategy might be unsuccessful 80 percent of the time, but it will work for us!" Thus, team members are more likely to favour the risky option.[90] The result of group polarization is that teams sometimes choose riskier alternatives than an individual would choose.

TEAM STRUCTURES FOR CREATIVITY AND DECISION MAKING

So far, we have learned that teams potentially make better decisions than individuals in a number of situations, but team dynamics can seriously interfere with the decision-making process. Fortunately, scholars have identified a number of general rules and specific team structures to minimize this dilemma. One general rule is that neither the team leader nor any other participant dominates the process. This limits the adverse effects of conformity and lets other team members generate more creative and controversial ideas.[91] Another practice is to maintain an optimal team size. The group should be large enough that members possess the collective knowledge to resolve the problem, yet small enough that the team doesn't consume too much time or restrict individual input.[92] Team norms are also important to ensure that individuals engage in critical thinking rather than follow the group's implicit preferences.

Team structures also help to minimize the problems described over the previous few pages. Five team structures potentially improve creativity and decision making in team settings: constructive conflict, brainstorming, electronic brainstorming, Delphi technique, and nominal group technique.

Constructive Conflict

constructive conflict

Any situation where people debate their different opinions about an issue in a way that keeps the conflict focused on the task rather than people.

Constructive conflict occurs when team members debate their different perceptions about an issue in a way that keeps the conflict focused on the task rather than people. Through dialogue, participants learn about other points of view, which encourages them to re-examine their basic assumptions about a problem and its possible solution. Constructive conflict is *constructive* because employees discuss their different opinions without generating negative emotions toward each other. This can occur if participants focus on facts rather than people and avoid statements that threaten the esteem and well-being of other team members.[93]

Some companies try to generate constructive conflict by having some team members serve as devil's advocates.[94] A devil's advocate is a team member selected to take the position opposite the group's preference. The idea is to point out the weaknesses and potential problems with the preference so that it is carefully scrutinized. This strategy sounds good in theory, but it doesn't work well in practice. Research studies report that devil's advocates often support the team's preferred choice more than they find problems with it.[95] If a team member supports the group's position, it is difficult for that person to take a critical role against that position.

Rather than rely on contrived dissent such as devil's advocacy, corporate leaders need to form decision-making teams that authentically engage in constructive conflict. Researchers have identified three strategies to achieve authentic constructive conflict. First, decision-making groups need to be heterogeneous.[96] As we learned in previous chapters, heterogeneous teams are better than homogeneous teams at perceiving issues and potential solutions from different perspectives. "Every time I have put together a diverse group of people, that team has always come up with a more breakthrough solution than any homogeneous group working on the same problem," says an executive at chemical giant Monsanto.[97]

Second, these heterogeneous team members need to meet often enough to allow meaningful discussion over contentious issues. The team's diversity won't generate constructive conflict if the team leader makes most of the decisions alone. Only through dialogue can team members better understand different perspectives, generate more creative ideas, and improve decision quality. Third, effective teams generate constructive conflict when individual members take on different discussion roles. Some participants are action-oriented, others insist on reviewing details, one or two might try to minimize dysfunctional conflict, and so on. In other words, team members cover the various roles required to support team dynamics.

Brainstorming

brainstorming

A freewheeling, face-to-face meeting where team members generate as many ideas as possible, piggyback on the ideas of others, and avoid evaluating anyone's ideas during the idea-generation stage.

In the 1950s, advertising executive Alex Osborn wanted to find a better way for teams to generate creative ideas.[98] Osborn's solution, called **brainstorming**, requires team members to abide by four rules. Osborn believed that these rules encourage divergent thinking while minimizing evaluation apprehension and other team dynamics problems.

▪ *Speak freely*—Brainstorming welcomes wild and wacky ideas because these become the seeds of divergent thinking in the creative process. Crazy suggestions are sometimes crazy only because they break out of the mould set by existing mental models.

▪ *No criticism*—Team members are more likely to contribute wild and wacky ideas if no one tries to mock or criticize them. Thus, a distinctive rule in brainstorming is that no one is allowed to criticize any ideas that are presented.

▪ *Provide as many ideas as possible*—Brainstorming is based on the idea that quantity breeds quality. In other words, teams generate better ideas when they generate many ideas. This relates to the belief that divergent thinking occurs after traditional ideas have been exhausted. Therefore, the group should think of as many possible solutions as they can and go well beyond the traditional solutions to a problem.

▪ *Build on the ideas of others*—Team members are encouraged to "piggyback" or "hitch-hike," that is, to combine and improve on the ideas already presented. Building on existing ideas encourages the synergy of team processes, mentioned earlier in this chapter as a benefit of employee involvement.

Brainstorming is the most popular team structure for encouraging creative ideas. Yet, for several years, organizational behaviour researchers have warned that this practice has several limitations. One concern is that brainstorming rules do not completely remove evaluation apprehension; employees still know that others are silently evaluating the quality of their ideas. Production blocking and related time constraints prevent all ideas from being presented. Some research also reports that individuals working alone produce more potential solutions to a problem than if they work together brainstorming.[99]

Rather than deterring organizations from using brainstorming, these findings should remind us that brainstorming is effective only under the right conditions. GLOBAL Connections 10.3 describes how IDEO, the California-based industrial design firm, thrives on brainstorming by creating the right environment and

IDEO Catches a Brainstorm

No one does brainstorming as well—or as often—as the folks at IDEO. Engineers at the California-based industrial design firm that created 3Com's Palm V and the stand-up toothpaste tube attend an average of 24 brainstorm sessions each year. A few participate in as many as 80 brainstorms annually.

IDEO's brainstorms are scheduled, face-to-face meetings that generate ideas, usually about designing products. A typical session lasts about one hour and is attended by the design team as well as other IDEO engineers with relevant skills. For instance, one brainstorming session to design better ski goggles invited engineers who knew about foam, clear plastics, and manufacturing processes. Clients are also included in some sessions.

Since it was founded in 1978, IDEO has developed a clear set of brainstorming rules: defer judgment, build on the ideas of others, one conversation at a time, stay focused on the topic, and encourage wild ideas. These rules are prominently displayed throughout the meeting room and violators are given friendly reminders. A good IDEO brainstorming session produces about 100 ideas. Each idea is numbered to push for quantity and to keep track of the discussion. The creative sparks are aided by studying similar products as well as a treasure chest of unique materials brought to the session.

Newcomers at IDEO quickly discover that brainstorming requires special interpersonal skills, not just rules and props. "The skills for successful brainstorming develop in an individual over time," explains an IDEO engineer. "I consider myself a good brainstormer but only a fair facilitator. A year ago, I was a good brainstormer and a poor facilitator."

Sources: T. Kelley, *The Art of Innovation* (N.Y.: Currency Doubleday, 2001), pp. 55–66; A. Hargadon and R. I. Sutton, "Building an Innovation Factory," *Harvard Business Review*, 78 (May-June 2000), pp. 157–66; R. Garner, "Innovation for Fun and Profit," *Upside Magazine*, March 2000; P. Sinton, "Teamwork the Name of the Game for IDEO," *San Francisco Chronicle*, February 23, 2000; E. Brown, "A Day at Innovation U.," *Fortune*, April 12, 1999, pp. 163–65; R. I. Sutton and A. Hargadon, "Brainstorming Groups in Context: Effectiveness in a Product Design Firm," *Administrative Science Quarterly*, 41 (December 1996), pp. 685–718.
www.ideo.com

structure to make these sessions productive. Evaluation apprehension may be a problem for brainstorming in student research experiments, but it is less of a problem at IDEO where high-performing teams have a lot of trust and support risky thinking. IDEO's brainstorming facilitators also stretch the collective effort by pushing for more than 150 ideas in an hour.

Another issue with the earlier critiques of brainstorming is that they overlooked other benefits of brainstorming beyond the number of ideas produced. Brainstorming participants interact and participate directly, thereby increasing decision acceptance and team cohesiveness. Brainstorming rules tend to keep the team focused on the required task. There is some evidence that effective brainstorming sessions provide valuable nonverbal communication that spreads enthusiasm. Team members share feelings of optimism and excitement which may encourage a more creative climate. Clients are often involved in brainstorming sessions, so these positive emotions may produce higher customer satisfaction than if people are working alone on the product.[100] Overall, brainstorming may prove more valuable to creativity than some of the earlier research studies indicated.

Electronic Brainstorming

electronic brainstorming
Using special computer software, participants share ideas while minimizing the team dynamics problems inherent in traditional brainstorming sessions.

DuPont Canada, CIBC, IBM Canada, and many other firms have tried to improve team decision making through **electronic brainstorming**. With the aid of groupware (special computer software for groups), electronic brainstorming lets participants share ideas while minimizing many of the problems in team dynamics described earlier. A facilitator begins the process by posting a question. Partici-

Rocco Di Giovanni (top right in photo) has observed time and time again how electronic brainstorming can improve team decision making. As manager of Mohawk College's Procor Decision Support Centre in Hamilton, Ontario, Di Giovanni facilitates electronic meetings of business and community groups using GroupSystems.com software. Up to 15 participants sit at special desks where computer terminals are recessed to provide anonymity. Participants type in comments or ideas relating to a trigger question asked by the facilitator. Soon after, the typed information appears anonymously on a screen at the front of the room. The posted information encourages participants to enter more ideas. Eventually, the group votes electronically for each idea. Considering the strong evidence of the benefits of electronic brainstorming, why isn't it used more often in organizational decision making? *Steven L. McShane*
www.mohawkc.on.ca/dept/bid/procor.htm

pants then enter their answers or ideas on their computer terminal. Soon after, everyone's ideas are posted anonymously and randomly on the computer screens or at the front of the room. Participants eventually vote electronically on the ideas presented. Face-to-face discussion usually follows the electronic brainstorming process.

Research indicates that electronic brainstorming generates more ideas than traditional brainstorming, and that participants are more satisfied, motivated, and confident about the decision-making exercise than in other team structures.[101] One reason for these favourable outcomes is that electronic brainstorming significantly reduces production blocking. Participants are able to document their ideas as soon as the ideas pop into their heads, rather than waiting their turn to communicate.[102] The process also supports creative synergy because participants can easily develop new ideas from those generated by other people. Electronic brainstorming also minimizes the problem of evaluation apprehension because ideas are posted anonymously. "The equipment allows them to throw some crazy ideas out without people knowing they are the author of it," explains David Lindsay, the civil servant who organized a brainstorming session among Ontario government cabinet ministers.[103]

Despite these numerous advantages, electronic brainstorming is not widely used by corporate leaders. One possible reason is that it might be too structured and technology-bound for some executives. Furthermore, some decision makers may feel threatened by the honesty of statements generated through this process, and by their inability to control the discussion. A third explanation is that electronic brainstorming may work best for certain types of decisions, but not for others. For example, electronic brainstorming may be less effective than face-to-face meetings, where effective decision making is less important than social bonding and emotional interaction.[104] Overall, electronic brainstorming can significantly improve decision making under the right conditions, but more research is required to identify those conditions.

Delphi Technique

The **Delphi technique** systematically pools the collective knowledge of experts on a particular subject to make decisions, predict the future, or identify opposing views (called *dissensus*).[105] Delphi groups do not meet face-to-face; in fact, partic-

Delphi technique
A structured team decision-making process of systematically pooling the collective knowledge of experts on a particular subject to make decisions, predict the future, or identify opposing views.

ipants are often located in different parts of the world and may not know each other's identity. Moreover, like electronic brainstorming, participants do not know who "owns" the ideas submitted. Typically, Delphi group members submit possible solutions or comments regarding an issue to the central convener. The compiled results are returned to the panel for a second round of comments. This process may be repeated a couple more times until consensus or dissensus emerges. The Delphi technique helped an electricity supply company understand how to respond to customers who don't pay their bills. It was also used by rehabilitation counsellors to reach consensus on rehabilitation credentialling.[106]

Nominal Group Technique

nominal group technique
A structured team decision-making process whereby team members independently write down ideas, describe and clarify them to the group, and then independently rank or vote on them.

Nominal group technique is a variation of traditional brainstorming and Delphi technique that tries to combine individual efficiencies with team dynamics.[107] The method is called *nominal* because participants form a group *in name only* during two stages of decision making. This process, shown in Exhibit 10.6, first involves the individual, then the group, and finally the individual again.

After the problem is described, team members silently and independently write down as many solutions as they can. During the group stage, participants describe their solutions to the other team members, usually in a round-robin format. As with brainstorming, there is no criticism or debate, although members are encouraged to ask for clarification of the ideas presented. In the final stage, participants silently and independently rank or vote on each proposed solution. Ranking is preferred because this forces each person to carefully review all of the alternatives presented.[108] Nominal group technique prefers voting or ranking over reaching consensus to avoid the dysfunctional conflict that comes with debate.

Nominal group technique tends to produce more and better quality ideas than traditional interacting groups.[109] Due to its high degree of structure, nominal group technique usually maintains a high task orientation and relatively low potential for conflict within the team. However, team cohesiveness is generally lower in nominal decisions because the structure minimizes social interaction. Production blocking and evaluation apprehension still occur to some extent.

Throughout this chapter, we have learned how people make decisions, involve employees in the decision process, improve creativity, and solve problems more effectively in teams. In each of these topics, decisions require plenty of information sharing, which we discuss in the next chapter on communication in organizations.

EXHIBIT 10.6

Nominal group technique

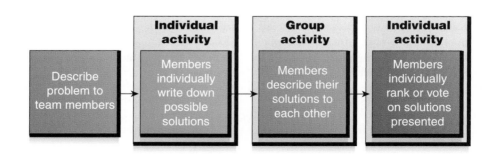

CHAPTER SUMMARY

Decision making is a conscious process of making choices among one or more alternatives with the intention of moving toward some desired state of affairs. The rational decision-making model includes identifying problems and opportunities, choosing the best decision style, developing alternative solutions, choosing the best solution, implementing the selected alternative, and evaluating decision outcomes.

Emotions, perceptual biases, and poor diagnostic skills affect our ability to identify problems and opportunities. We can minimize these challenges by being aware of the human limitations and discussing the situation with colleagues. Evaluating and choosing alternatives is often challenging because organizational goals are ambiguous or in conflict, human information processing is incomplete and subjective, and people tend to satisfice rather than maximize. Emotions shape our preferences for alternatives, and general moods support or hinder our careful evaluation of alternatives. Most people also rely on intuition to help them evaluate and choose alternatives.

Solutions can be chosen more effectively by systematically identifying and weighting the factors used to evaluate alternatives, cautiously using intuition where we possess enough tacit knowledge on the issue, and considering whether our emotions make sense in the situation. Scenario planning can help to make future decisions without the pressure and emotions that occur during real emergencies.

Postdecisional justification and escalation of commitment make it difficult to accurately evaluate decision outcomes. Escalation is mainly caused by self-justification, the gambler's fallacy, perceptual blinders, and closing costs. These problems are minimized by separating decision choosers from decision evaluators, establishing a preset level at which the decision is abandoned or re-evaluated, relying on more systematic and clear feedback about the project's success, and involving several people in decision making.

Employee involvement (or participation) refers to the degree that employees influence how their work is organized and carried out. The level of participation may range from an employee providing specific information to management without knowing the problem or issue, to complete involvement in all phases of the decision process. Employee involvement may lead to higher decision quality and commitment, but several contingencies need to be considered, including the decision structure, source of decision knowledge, decision commitment, and risk of conflict.

Creativity refers to developing an original product, service, or idea that makes a socially recognized contribution. The four creativity stages are preparation, incubation, insight, and verification. Incubation assists divergent thinking, which involves reframing the problem in a unique way and generating different approaches to the issue.

Four of the main features of creative people are intelligence, subject-matter knowledge and experience, persistence, and inventive thinking style. Creativity is also strengthened for everyone when the work environment supports a learning orientation, the job has high intrinsic motivation, the organization provides a reasonable level of job security, and project leaders provide appropriate goals, time pressure, and resources. Three types of activities that encourage creativity are redefining the problem, associative play, and cross-pollination.

Team decisions are impeded by time constraints, evaluation apprehension, conformity to peer pressure, groupthink, and group polarization. Production blocking—where only one person typically speaks at a time—is a form of time constraint on teams. Evaluation apprehension occurs when employees believe that others are silently evaluating them, so they avoid stating seemingly silly ideas. Conformity keeps team members aligned with team goals, but it also tends to suppress dissenting opinions. Groupthink is the tendency of highly cohesive groups to value consensus at the price of decision quality. Group polarization refers to the tendency of teams to make more extreme decisions than individuals working alone.

Three rules that minimize team decision-making problems are ensuring that the team leader does not dominate, maintaining an optimal team size, and ensuring that team norms support critical thinking. Five team structures that potentially improve creativity and team decision making are constructive conflict, brainstorming, electronic brainstorming, Delphi technique, and nominal group technique. Constructive conflict occurs when team members debate their different perceptions about an issue in a way that keeps the conflict focused on the task rather than people. Brainstorming requires team members to speak freely, avoid criticism, provide as many ideas as possible, and build on the ideas of others. Electronic brainstorming uses computer software to share ideas while minimizing team dynamics problems. Delphi technique systematically pools the collective knowledge of experts on a particular subject without face-to-face meetings. In nominal group technique, participants write down ideas alone, describe these ideas in a group, then silently vote on these ideas.

KEY TERMS

Bounded rationality, p. 282

Brainstorming, p. 298

Codetermination, p. 288

Constructive conflict, p. 297

Creativity, p. 290

Decision making, p.278

Delphi technique, p. 301

Divergent thinking, p. 291

Electronic brainstorming, p. 299

Employee involvement, p. 288

Escalation of commitment, p. 286

Evaluation apprehension, p. 295

Group polarization, p. 296

Groupthink, p. 295

Implicit favourite, p. 283

Intuition, p. 285

Nominal group technique, p. 301

Nonprogrammed decision, p. 279

Postdecisional justification, p. 286

Production blocking, p. 295

Programmed decision, p.279

Satisficing, p. 284

Scenario planning, p. 285

DISCUSSION QUESTIONS

1. "The rational model (of decision-making) seems so logical, yet it is rarely practised in reality." Do you agree or disagree with this statement? Discuss your perspective.

2. A major software developer in Vancouver is experiencing an increasing number of customer complaints and a general trend toward lower sales. Describe three reasons why executives in this organization might be slow to realize that a problem exists or to identify the root cause(s) of these symptoms.

3. Describe a time when you repeated a bad decision or continued to support a failing course of action. What happened? Why did you do what you did?

4. A management consultant is hired by a manufacturing firm to determine the best site for its next production facility. The consultant has had several meetings with the company's senior executives regarding the factors to consider when making its recommendation. Discuss three decision-making problems that might prevent the consultant from choosing the best site location.

5. The Chinese word for business is "Sheng-yi," which literally means "to give birth to ideas." Explain how creativity is an inherent part of business decision-making.

6. Two characteristics of creative people are that they have relevant experience and are persistent in their quest. Does this mean that the people with the most experience and the highest need for achievement are the most creative? Explain your answer.

7. What can instructors do to foster creativity in a university or college learning environment?

8. Cornerbrook Technologies Ltd. wants to use brainstorming with its employees and customers to identify new uses for its technology. Advise Cornerbrook's president about the potential benefits of brainstorming, as well as its potential limitations.

CASE STUDY 10.1

EMPLOYEE INVOLVEMENT CASES

Case 1: The Sugar Substitute Research Decision

You are the head of research and development (R&D) for a major Canadian beer company. While working on a new beer product, one of the scientists in your unit seems to have tentatively identified a new chemical compound that has few calories but tastes closer to sugar than current sugar substitutes. The company has no foreseeable need for this product, but it could be patented and licensed to manufacturers in the food industry.

The sugar substitute discovery is in its preliminary stages and would require considerable time and resources before it would be commercially viable. This means that it would necessarily take some resources away from other projects in the lab. The sugar substitute project is beyond your technical expertise, but some of the R&D lab researchers are familiar with that field of chemistry. As with most forms of research, it is difficult to determine the amount of research required to further identify and perfect the sugar substitute. You do not know how much demand is expected for this product. Your department has a decision process for funding projects that are behind schedule. However, there are no rules or precedents about funding projects that would be licensed but not used by the organization.

The company's R&D budget is limited and other scientists in your work group have recently complained that they require more resources and financial support to get their projects completed. Some of these other R&D projects hold promise for future beer sales. You believe that most researchers in the R&D unit are committed to ensuring that the company's interests are achieved.

Case 2: Coast Guard Cutter Decision Problem

You are the captain of a 72-metre Coast Guard cutter, with a crew of 16, including officers. Your mission is general at-sea search and rescue. At 2:00 a.m., while enroute to your home port after a routine 28-day patrol, you receive word from the nearest Coast Guard station that a small plane has crashed 100 kilometres offshore. You obtain all the available information concerning the location of the crash, inform your crew of the mission, and set a new course at maximum speed for the scene to commence a search for survivors and wreckage.

You have now been searching for 20 hours. Your search operation has been increasingly impaired by rough seas, and there is evidence of a severe storm building. The atmospherics associated with the deteriorating weather have made communications with the Coast Guard station impossible. A decision must be made shortly about whether to abandon the search and place your vessel on a course that would ride out the storm (thereby protecting the vessel and your crew, but relegating any possible survivors in the plane to almost certain death from exposure) or to continue a potentially futile search and the risks it would entail.

Before losing communications, you receive an update weather advisory concerning the severity and duration of the storm. Although your crew members are extremely conscientious about their responsibilities, you believe that they would be divided on the decision of leaving or staying.

Discussion Questions (both cases)

1. To what extent should your subordinates be involved in this decision? Select one of the following levels of involvement:

   ■ *No involvement*: You make the decision alone without any participation from subordinates.

   ■ *Low involvement*: You ask one or more subordinates for information relating to the problem, but you don't ask for their recommendations and might not mention the problem to them.

   ■ *Medium involvement*: You describe the problem to one or more subordinates (alone or in a meeting) and ask for any relevant information as well as their recommendations on the issue. However, you make the final decision, which might or might not reflect their advice.

   ■ *High involvement*: You describe the problem to subordinates. They discuss the matter, identify a solution without your involvement (unless they invite your ideas), and implement that solution. You have agreed to support their decision.

2. What factors led you to choose this level of employee involvement rather than the others?

3. What problems might occur if less or more involvement occurred in this case (where possible)?

Sources: The Sugar Substitute Research Decision is written by Steven L. McShane, © 2002. The Coast guard cutter case is adapted from V.H. Vroom and A. G. Jago, *The New Leadership: Managing Participation in Organizations* (Englewood Cliffs, N.J.: Prentice Hall, 1988).© 1987 V. H. Vroom and A. G. Jago. Used with permission of the authors.

WHERE IN THE WORLD ARE WE?

Purpose   This exercise is designed to help you understand the potential advantages of involving others in decisions rather than making decisions alone.

Materials   Students require an unmarked copy of the map of Canada with grid marks (Exhibit 2). Students are not allowed to look at any other maps or use any other materials. The instructor will provide a list of communities located somewhere on Exhibit 2. The instructor will also provide copies of the answer sheet after students have individually and in teams estimated the locations of communities.

Instructions

■   *Step 1*: Write down in Exhibit 1 the list of communities identified by your instructor. Then, working alone, estimate the location in Exhibit 2 of these communities, all of which are in Canada. For example, mark a small "1" in Exhibit 2 on the spot where you believe the first community is located. Mark a small "2" where you think the second community is located, and so on. Please be sure to number each location clearly, with numbers small enough to fit within one grid space.

■   *Step 2*: The instructor will organize students into approximately equal sized teams (typically 5 or 6 people per team). Working with your team members, reach a consensus on the location of each community listed in Exhibit 1. The instructor might provide teams with a separate copy of this map, or each member can identify the team's numbers using a different coloured pen on their individual maps. The team's decision for each location should occur by consensus, not voting or averaging.

■   *Step 3*: The instructor will provide or display an answer sheet, showing the correct locations of the communities. Using this answer sheet, students will count the minimum number of grid squares between the location they individually marked and the true location of each community. Write the number of grid squares in the second column of Exhibit 1, then add up the total. Next, count the minimum number of grid squares between the location the team marked and the true location of each community. Write the number of grid squares in the third column of Exhibit 1, then add up the total.

■   *Step 4*: The instructor will ask for information about the totals and the class will discuss the implication of these results for employee involvement and decision making.

EXHIBIT 1   List of selected communities in Canada

Number	Community	Individual distance in grid units from the true location	Team distance in grid units from the true location
1			
2			
3			
4			
5			
6			
7			
8			
		Total:	Total:

© 2002 Steven L. McShane

Map of Canada

WINTER SURVIVAL EXERCISE

Purpose This exercise is designed to help you understand the potential advantages of involving others in decisions rather than making decisions alone.

Instructions

- *Step 1:* Read the "Situation" below. Then, working alone, rank the 12 items shown in the chart below according to their importance to your survival. In the "Individual Ranking" column, indicate the most important item with "1," using "12" as the least important. Keep in mind the reasons why each item is or is not important.

- *Step 2:* The instructor will divide the class into small teams (4 to 6 people). Each team will rank the items in the second column. Team rankings should be based on consensus, not simply averaging the individual rankings.

- *Step 3:* When the teams have completed their rankings, the instructor will provide the expert's ranking, which can be entered in the third column.

- *Step 4:* Each student will compute the absolute difference (i.e. ignore minus signs) between the individual ranking and the expert's ranking, record this information in column four, and total the absolute values at the bottom of column four.

- *Step 5:* In column five, record the absolute difference between the team's ranking and the expert's ranking, and sum these absolute scores at the bottom. A class discussion will follow regarding the implications of these results for employee involvement and decision making.

Situation You have just crash-landed somewhere in the woods of southern Manitoba or possibly northern Minnesota. It is 11:32 a.m. in mid-January. The small plane in which you were travelling crashed onto a small lake. The pilot and co-pilot were killed. Shortly after the crash, the plane sank completely into the lake with the pilot's and co-pilot's bodies inside. Everyone else on the flight escaped to land dry and without serious injury.

The crash came suddenly before the pilot had time to radio for help or inform anyone of your position. Since your pilot was trying to avoid the storm, you know the plane was considerably off course. The pilot announced shortly before the crash that you were 70 kilometres northwest of a small town that is the nearest known habitation.

You are in a wilderness area made up of thick woods broken by many lakes and rivers. The snow depth varies from above the ankles in windswept areas to more than knee-deep where it has drifted. The last weather report indicated that the temperature would reach minus 10 degrees Celsius in the daytime and minus 25 degrees at night. There is plenty of dead wood and twigs in the area around the lake. You and the other surviving passengers are dressed in winter clothing appropriate for city wear—suits, pantsuits, street shoes, and overcoats. While escaping from the plane, your group salvaged the 12 items listed in the chart below. Assume that the number of persons in the group is the same as the number in your group, and that you have agreed to stay together.

Items	Step 1 Your individual ranking	Step 2 Your team's ranking	Step 3 Survival expert's ranking	Step 4 Difference between steps 1 and 3	Step 5 Difference between steps 2 and 3
Winter survival tally sheet					
Ball of steel wool					
Newspapers					
Compass					
Hand axe					
Cigarette lighter					
45-caliber pistol					
Section air map					
Canvas					
Shirt and pants					
Can of shortening					
Whiskey					
Chocolate bars					
Total					

(The lower the score, the better)   Your score   Team score

Source: Adapted from "Winter Survival" in D. Johnson and F. Johnson, *Joining Together*, 3rd ed. (Englewood Cliffs, NJ: Prentice Hall, 1984).

TEAM EXERCISE 10.4

THE HOPPING ORANGE

Purpose To help students understand the dynamics of creativity and team problem solving.

Instructions You will be placed in teams of six students. One student serves as the official timer for the team and must have a watch, preferably with stopwatch timer. The instructor will give each team an orange (or similar object) with a specific task involving use of the orange. The objective is easily understood and non-threatening, and will be described by the instructor at the beginning of the exercise. Each team will have a few opportunities to achieve the objective more efficiently.

CREATIVITY BRAINBUSTERS

Purpose To help students understand the dynamics of creativity and team problem solving.

Instructions This exercise may be completed alone or in teams of three or four people. If teams are formed, students who already know the solutions to one or more of these problems should identify themselves and serve as silent observers. When finished (or, more likely, when time is up), the instructor will review the solutions and discuss the implications of this exercise. In particular, be prepared to discuss what you needed to solve these puzzles and what may have prevented you from solving them more quickly (or at all).

1. Double Circle Problem

Draw two circles, one inside the other, with a single line, with neither circle touching the other (as shown below). In other words, you must draw both of these circles without lifting your pen (or other writing instrument).

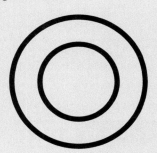

2. Nine Dot Problem

Below are nine dots. Without lifting your pencil, draw no more than four straight lines that pass through all nine dots.

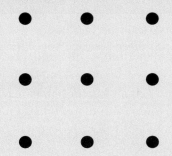

3. Nine Dot Problem Revisited

Referring to the nine dot exhibit above, describe how, without lifting your pencil, you could pass a pencil line through all dots with three (3) or fewer straight lines.

4. Word Search

In the following line of letters, cross out five letters so that the remaining letters, without altering their sequence, spell a familiar English word.

FCIRVEEALTETITVEERS

5. Burning Ropes

You have two pieces of rope of unequal lengths and a box of matches. In spite of their different lengths, each piece of rope takes one hour to burn; however, parts of each rope burn at unequal speeds. For example, the first half of one piece might burn in ten minutes. Use these materials to accurately determine when 45 minutes has elapsed.

MEASURING YOUR CREATIVE PERSONALITY

Purpose This self-assessment is designed to help you to measure the extent to which you have a creative personality.

Instructions Listed below is an adjective checklist with 30 words that may or may not describe you. Put a mark in the box beside the words that you think accurately describe you. Please DO NOT mark the boxes for words that do not describe you. When finished, you can score the test using the scoring key in Appendix B. This exercise is completed alone so students can assess themselves without concerns of social comparison. However, class discussion will focus on how this scale might be applied in organizations, and the limitations of measuring creativity in work settings.

Adjective Checklist

Affected	☐	Honest	☐	Reflective	☐
Capable	☐	Humorous	☐	Resourceful	☐
Cautious	☐	Individualistic	☐	Self-confident	☐
Clever	☐	Informal	☐	Sexy	☐
Commonplace	☐	Insightful	☐	Sincere	☐
Confident	☐	Intelligent	☐	Snobbish	☐
Conservative	☐	Inventive	☐	Submissive	☐
Conventional	☐	Mannerly	☐	Suspicious	☐
Dissatisfied	☐	Narrow interests	☐	Unconventional	☐
Egotistical	☐	Original	☐	Wide interests	☐

Source: Adapted from and based on information in H. G. Gough and A. B. Heilbrun, Jr., *The Adjective Check List Manual* (Palo Alto, Calif." Consulting Psychologists Press, 1965); and H. G. Gough.

TESTING YOUR CREATIVE BENCH STRENGTH

 Go to the Student CD for the interactive version of this exercise.

Purpose This self-assessment is designed to help you determine how well you engage in divergent thinking to identify problems and their solutions creatively.

Instructions This self-assessment consists of 12 questions that require divergent thinking to identify the answers. Answer each question in the space provided. When finished, look at the correct answer for each question, along with an explanation.

DECISION MAKING STYLE INVENTORY

 Go to the Student CD for the interactive version of this exercise.

Purpose This self-assessment is designed to help you estimate your preferred style of decision making.

Instructions The statements in this self-assessment describe how individuals go about making important decisions. Please indicate whether you agree or disagree with each statement. Answer each item as truthfully as possible so that you get an accurate estimate of your decision making style. This exercise is completed alone so students assess themselves honestly without concerns of social comparison. However, class discussion will focus on the decision-making style that people prefer in organizational settings.

11

Communicating in Teams and Organizations

Learning Objectives

AFTER READING THIS CHAPTER, YOU SHOULD BE ABLE TO:

- Explain the importance of communication and diagram the communication process.

- Describe problems with communicating through electronic mail.

- Identify two ways in which nonverbal communication differs from verbal communication.

- Identify two conditions requiring a channel with high media richness.

- Identify four common communication barriers.

- Discuss how men and women communicate differently.

- Outline the key elements of active listening.

- Summarize four communication strategies in organizational hierarchies.

Hiram Walker & Sons Ltd has a stately headquarters in Walkerville, Ontario, but CEO Ian Gourlay prefers to spend much of his time out and about. Chances are, you'll see Gourlay walking through the distillery, addressing a community reception, or attending meetings around the organization. Having the CEO stop by the distillery is something of a novelty to its 400 staff. "They find that unusual, I don't," says Gourlay, who adds that employees are becoming accustomed to seeing him and learning about him.

Hiram Walker employees are also discovering the benefits of a CEO who wanders around the workplace. "He sees what we're up against and what we're trying to do," says Gary Lajoie, plant superintendent of finished goods.

Pearse Flynn also knows the value of direct communication with employees. The CEO of Damovo in Glasgow, Scotland, and former head of Ottawa-based Newbridge Networks (now part of the French telecommunications company Alcatel) would hand out sticky notes at the end of some meetings and asked employees to write down what was on their minds after he left the room. "I guarantee you, you do five of those and you'll know what the issues are in the organization," he advises.

Even as a senior Alcatel executive overseeing 40,000 employees around the world, Flynn kept a gruelling pace to maintain personal communication. "I make so much of my decisions from the fact that I chat with people, and I pick up what's really going on in people's minds," he says.[1] ■

www.canadianclubwhisky.com

Hiram Walker president Ian Gourlay, shown here with utility operator Rose Kenney, values face-to-face communication to find out what is really happening in the Walkerville, Ontario company.
Windsor Star

communication
The process by which information is transmitted and understood between two or more people.

communication competence
A person's ability to identify appropriate communication patterns in a given situation and to achieve goals by applying that knowledge.

Ian Gourlay and Pearse Flynn believe in the power of communication. **Communication** refers to the process by which information is transmitted and *understood* between two or more people. We emphasize the word *understood* because transmitting the sender's intended meaning is the essence of good communication. Ian Gourlay, Pearse Flynn, and leaders of other large organizations require innovative strategies to keep communication pathways open. Smaller businesses may have fewer structural bottlenecks, but they, too, can suffer from subtle communication barriers.

In a knowledge-based economy, employees require a high level of communication competence. **Communication competence** refers to a person's ability to identify appropriate communication patterns in a given situation and to achieve goals by applying that knowledge.[2] Competent communicators quickly learn the meaning listeners take from certain words and symbols, and they know which communication medium is best in a particular situation. Moreover, competent communicators use this knowledge to communicate in ways that achieve personal, team, and organizational objectives. Someone with high communication competence would quickly determine that an e-mail is the best way to convey a particular message to a co-worker rather than a written memo or telephone call. Communication competence is particularly vital for executives. According to one recent study, Canadian CEOs spend most of their time and energy on communicating and meeting with employees, or spending time with customers. This is consistent with earlier research findings that corporate leaders spend almost 80 percent of their day communicating.[3]

Communication plays an important role in knowledge management (see Chapter 1).[4] Employees are the organization's brain cells, and communication is the nervous system that carries this information and shared meaning to vital parts of the organizational body. Effective communication brings knowledge into the organization and disseminates it quickly to employees who require that information. Effective communication minimizes the "silos of knowledge" problem that undermines an organization's potential. This, in turn, allows employees to make more informed decisions about corporate actions. For instance, British Telecom encourages employees to generate "knowledge moments"—occasions where they have communicated information to co-workers that has resulted in better decisions.[5]

Along with decision making and knowledge management, effective communication coordinates work activities.[6] Through dialogue, co-workers develop common mental models—the broad world views that people rely on to guide their perceptions and behaviours—so they can synchronize interdependent work activities through common expectations and assumptions.[7] Finally, communication is the glue that bonds people together. It fulfills the drive to bond (see Chapter 5) and, as part of the dynamics of social support, eases work-related stress (see Chapter 7). It's not surprising, therefore, that surveys of Canadian and American employees report that workplace communication has a significant effect on job satisfaction and loyalty.[8]

This chapter begins by presenting a model of the communication process and discussing several communication barriers. Next, the different types of communication channels, including computer-mediated communication, are described, followed by which factors to consider when choosing a communication medium. The chapter then presents some options for communicating in organizational hierarchies and describes the pervasive organizational grapevine. The latter part of the chapter examines cross-cultural and gender differences in communication, and strategies to improve interpersonal communication.

A MODEL OF COMMUNICATION

The communication model presented in Exhibit 11.1 provides a useful "conduit" metaphor for thinking about the communication process.[9] According to this model, communication flows through channels between the sender and receiver. The sender forms a message and encodes it into words, gestures, voice intonations, and other symbols or signs. Next, the encoded message is transmitted to the intended receiver through one or more communication channels (media). The receiver senses the incoming message and decodes it into something meaningful. Ideally, the decoded meaning is what the sender had intended.

In most situations, the sender looks for evidence that the other person received and understood the transmitted message. This feedback may be a formal acknowledgment, such as a "Yes, I know what you mean," or indirect evidence from the receiver's subsequent actions. Notice that feedback repeats the communication process. Intended feedback is encoded, transmitted, received, and decoded from the receiver to the sender of the original message.

This model recognizes that communication is not a free-flowing conduit.[10] Rather, the transmission of meaning from one person to another is hampered by *noise*—the psychological, social, and structural barriers that distort and obscure the sender's intended message. If any part of the communication process is distorted or broken, neither the sender nor the receiver will have a common understanding of the message.

COMMUNICATION CHANNELS

A critical part of the communication model is the channel through which information is transmitted. There are two main types of channels: verbal and nonver-

EXHIBIT 11.1

The communication process model

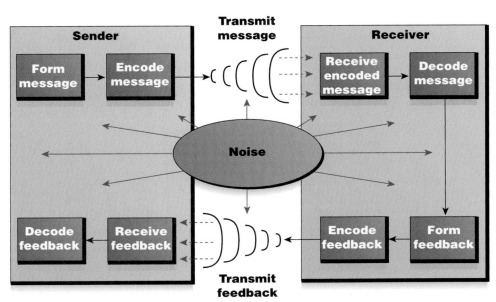

bal. *Verbal communication* includes any oral or written means of transmitting meaning through words. *Nonverbal communication*, which we discuss later, is any part of communication that does not use words.

Verbal Communication

Different forms of verbal communication should be used in different situations. Face-to-face interaction is usually better than written methods for transmitting emotions and persuading the receiver. This is because nonverbal cues accompany oral communications, such as voice intonations and use of silence. Moreover, in face-to-face settings, the sender receives immediate feedback from the receiver and can adjust the emotional tone of the message accordingly.

Written communication is more appropriate for recording and presenting technical details. This is because ideas are easier to follow when written down than when communicated aurally. Traditionally, written communication has been slow to develop and transmit, but electronic mail and other computer-mediated communication channels have significantly improved written communication efficiency.[11]

Electronic Mail

Electronic mail (e-mail) is revolutionizing the way we communicate in organizational settings. Trillions of e-mail messages are transmitted each year, and it's easy to understand their popularity.[12] Messages are quickly formed, edited, and stored. Information can be appended and transmitted to many people with a simple click of a mouse. E-mail is asynchronous (messages are sent and received at different times), so there is no need to coordinate a communication session. This technology also allows fairly random access of information: you can select any message in any order and skip to different parts of a message.

E-mail tends to be the preferred medium for coordinating work (e.g., confirming a co-worker's production schedule) and for sending well-defined information for decision making. Although e-mail reduces the amount of face-to-face and telephone communication, it tends to significantly increase the overall volume of information transmitted, particularly from employees to people further up the organizational hierarchy.[13] Some social and organizational status differences still exist with e-mail, but they are less apparent than in face-to-face or telephone communication. E-mail also reduces many selective attention biases because it hides our age, race, weight, and other features that can be observed in face-to-face meetings.

Problems with e-mail   Anyone who has used e-mail knows that it has several problems and limitations. Perhaps the most obvious of these is that e-mail contributes to information overload. Many e-mail users are overwhelmed by hundreds of messages each week, many of which are either unnecessary or irrelevant to the receiver. This occurs because e-mails can be easily created and copied to thousands of people through group mailbox systems.

A second problem is that e-mail is an ineffective medium for communicating emotions. For example, the emotion of sarcasm is difficult to convey through e-mail because the verbal message requires contrasting nonverbal cues. The result is that email can produce faster misunderstanding, not necessarily better communication. "Every fight that goes on [at Disney] seems to start with a misunderstanding over an e-mail," says Disney CEO Michael Eisner.[14] E-mail aficionados try to clarify the emotional tone of their messages by combining ASCII characters to form graphic faces called emoticons or "smileys." An entire lexicon of emoticons has developed, including those illustrated in Exhibit 11.2. However, some experts warn that smileys still do not easily solve the difficult task of communicating emotions through e-mail.[15]

A third problem is that e-mail seems to diminish our politeness and respect for others. This is mostly evident through the increased frequency of **flaming**. Flaming is the act of sending an emotionally charged message to others. Over half the people questioned in one survey said they receive abusive flame-mail and that men are both the most frequent victims and perpetrators.[16] The main cause of flaming is that people can post e-mail messages before their emotions subside, whereas the sender of a traditional memo or letter would have time for sober second thoughts. Presumably, flaming and other e-mail problems will become less common as employees receive training on how to use this communication medium.[17] For example, employees eventually learn the largely unwritten and evolving code of conduct for communicating on the Internet, called *netiquette*.

A fourth problem is that e-mail lacks the warmth of human interaction.[18] As employees increasingly cocoon themselves through information technology, they lose the social support of human contact that can keep their stress in check. Realizing this and other limitations of e-mail, some British companies are banning e-mail one day each week. As GLOBAL Connections 11.1 describes, these firms believe that some things are better discussed in person than in cyberspace.

Other Computer-Mediated Communication

IBM executives weren't surprised when a recent survey indicated that IBM employees rated co-workers as one of the two most credible or useful sources of information. What *did* surprise IBM executives was that the other equally credible and important source of information was IBM's intranet.[19] Intranets, extranets, instant messaging, and other forms of computer-mediated communication have fuelled the hyperfast world of corporate information sharing.[20] Geographically

flaming
The act of sending an emotionally charged message to others.

EXHIBIT 11.2	Icon	Meaning	Icon	Meaning
	:-)	Happy	0:-)	Angel (I'm being good)
Icons of emotion (emoticons) in e-mail messages	:-}	Smirk	:-p	Tongue sticking out
	:-(	Unhappy	:-x	Oops!
	<:-)	Dumb question	{ }	Hug

Source: Based on R. Peck, "Learning to Speak Computer Lingo," *(New Orleans) Times-Picayune*, June 5, 1997, p. E1; R. Weiland, "The Message Is the Medium," *Incentive*, September 1995, p. 37.

British Firms Encourage Live Conversation with "E-Mail-Free Fridays"

The revolution started on a Friday. A maverick executive at the offices of Camelot, the British lottery agency, issued a startling edict: no more e-mails on the last day of the work week unless totally, absolutely necessary. Staff, it seemed, were forgetting how to talk to each other.

"We needed to make staff more aware of other forms of communication," explains Camelot spokeswoman Jenny Dowden. "If there were elements of the business where you could talk face-to-face instead of sending an e-mail, we wanted to encourage people to do that."

Nestlé Rowntree also decided it was time to discourage e-mail in favour of more personal conversations. By introducing "fewer e-mail Fridays," the British confectioner hopes its employees will think more carefully about whether they need to copy messages to so many people and whether there are better ways of getting the message across.

"A no e-mail Friday does two things," explains Andrew Harrison, the marketing director for Nestlé Rowntree. "It removes needless information flow across the organization and it forces people to talk face-to-face and agree on plans mutually. An e-mail ban begins to build a culture of designing and delivering ideas together."

How effective are these edicts to ban or minimize e-mail on Fridays? Camelot restricted its e-mail ban to four Fridays and is "still in the process of reviewing the results." But Dowden says the 50 e-mails she typically receives dropped to three or four on Fridays. Nestlé Rowntree executives also say they are noticing changing communication patterns. "People have started to think about how and what they are communicating and are re-finding their voices," says one Nestlé manager.

Sources: J. Arlidge, "Office Staff Log off for Email-Free Fridays," *The Observer (London),* August 12, 2001; N. Muktarsingh, "Companies Rediscover The Power Of Speech," *Mail on Sunday (London),* July 22, 2001, p. 8; O. Burkeman, "Post Modern," *The Guardian (London),* June 20, 2001. **www.camelotplc.com**

---

dispersed work teams can coordinate their work more efficiently through instant messaging software and intranets. Suppliers are networked together so tightly through computer-mediated technology that customers see them as one organization (see Chapter 17).

Instant messaging *Instant messaging* appears to be the "next great thing" in technology-based communication. Ernst & Young, UBS Warburg, Paine Webber, and other companies have already implemented instant messaging as a preferred communication strategy. Instant messaging software connects two or more specific people and pushes the messages at each of them. If you send an instant message to a co-worker who is connected, your message will instantly pop up on the co-worker's computer monitor (or other communications device). Instant messages are much briefer than e-mail, often relying on acronyms (such as R U THR for "Are you there?").[21]

For example, if you require information for a client, you might log into the instant message service that connects to dozens of other employees in your area. Your message would pop up on their computer instantly and the information you require could be available within minutes. "No other communications technology operates in situations like that in a time-efficient manner," says Andy Konchan, an executive at the financial planning firm UBS Warburg. "Clients are often taken aback by the speed with which we can now respond to specialized or unusual queries." UBS Warburg has thousands of instant messaging channels representing different knowledge or client interests. The company's 13,000 employees connect to the channels most closely aligned with their area of work.[22]

You might think that emerging computer-mediated technologies further increase information overload. This is true for some forms of technology, but pre-

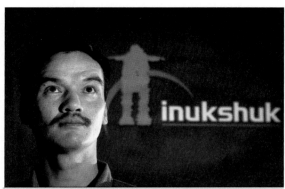

Like most executives, Adamee Itorcheak carries a laptop computer and cellular telephone almost everywhere he goes. The difference is that Itorcheak lives in Iqaluit, the capital city of Nunavut Territory in northern Canada, and his travels include traditional Inuit hunting trips in the Arctic wilderness. As president of Nunavut's largest Internet service provider and a partner in a high-speed wireless service, Itorcheak is probably the most wired person in the region. He is also wiring together most people in Nunavut, from fish plant workers in Pangnirtung to a fishing guide in Clyde River. Through online forums and chat rooms, the people of Nunavut are becoming a more closely knit community. "Here in this huge territory, 20,000 people live in scattered groups," explains Itorcheak. "The Internet is the only way to bring us all together."[23] What are the limitations of Internet-based communication for people who rarely communicate face-to-face? *Nick Didlick/Vancouver Sun*

www.inukshuk.ca

liminary evidence suggests that Internet-based communication actually *reduces* overload because it offers greater control over the amount of information flow. We decide how much information to receive from the Internet and intranet, whereas there is almost no control over the number of voice mails, e-mails, faxes, and paper-based memos we receive. This is supported by a survey of executives in 11 countries. Half of them said the Internet is reducing information overload; only 19 percent claim that it is making matters worse.[24]

Nonverbal Communication

Computer-mediated communication is changing the face of organizations, but it hasn't yet replaced nonverbal communication. Nonverbal communication includes facial gestures, voice intonation, physical distance, and even silence. This communication channel is necessary when physical distance or noise prevent effective verbal exchanges, and the need for immediate feedback precludes written communication. But even in close face-to-face meetings, most information is communicated nonverbally.[25] Nonverbal communication is also important in emotional labour—the effort, planning, and control needed to express organizationally desired emotions (see Chapter 4). Employees make extensive use of nonverbal cues to transmit prescribed feelings to customers, co-workers, and others.

Nonverbal communication differs from verbal communication in a couple of ways. First, it is less rule-bound than verbal communication. We receive a lot of formal training on how to understand spoken words, but very little to understand the nonverbal signals that accompany them. Consequently, nonverbal cues are more ambiguous and more susceptible to misinterpretation. Second, verbal communication is typically conscious, whereas most nonverbal communication is automatic and unconscious. We normally plan the words we say or write, but rarely plan every blink, smile, or other gesture during a conversation. Indeed, many of these facial expressions communicate the same meaning across cultures precisely because they are hard-wired unconscious or preconscious responses to human emotions.[26] For example, pleasant emotions cause the brain centre to widen the mouth, whereas negative emotions produce constricted facial expressions (squinting eyes, pursed lips, etc.).

emotional contagion

The automatic and unconscious tendency to mimic and synchronize our nonverbal behaviours with other people.

Emotional contagion   One of the most fascinating effects of emotions on nonverbal communication is the phenomenon called **emotional contagion**. Emotional contagion is the automatic process of "catching" or sharing another person's emotions by mimicking their facial expressions and other nonverbal behaviour. Consider what happens when you see a co-worker accidentally bang his or her head against a filing cabinet. Chances are, you wince and put your hand on your own head as if *you* had hit the cabinet. Similarly, while listening to someone describe a positive event, you tend to smile and exhibit other emotional displays of happiness. While some of our nonverbal communication is planned, emotional contagion represents unconscious behaviour—we automatically mimic and synchronize our nonverbal behaviours with other people.[27]

Emotional contagion serves three purposes. First, mimicry provides continuous feedback, communicating that we understand and empathize with the sender. To consider the significance of this, imagine if employees remained expressionless after watching a co-worker bang his or her head! Such a lack of parallel behaviour conveys a lack of understanding or caring. Second, mimicking the nonverbal behaviours of other people seems to be a way of receiving emotional meaning from those people. If a co-worker is angry with a client, your tendency to frown and show anger while listening helps you share that emotion more fully. In other words, we receive meaning by expressing the sender's emotions as well as by listening to the sender's words.

Last, emotional contagion is associated with the drive to bond that was described in Chapter 5. Social solidarity is built out of each member's awareness of a collective sentiment. Through nonverbal expressions of emotional contagion, people see that others share the same emotions. This strengthens team cohesiveness by providing evidence of member similarity.[28]

CHOOSING THE BEST COMMUNICATION CHANNELS

Employees perform better if they can quickly determine the best communication channels for the situation and are flexible enough to use different methods, as the occasion requires.[29] But which communication channels are most appropriate? We partly answered this question in our evaluation of the different communication channels. However, two additional contingencies worth noting are media richness and symbolic meaning.

Media Richness

Soon after Ernst & Young encouraged its employees around the globe to form virtual teams, the accounting firm realized that e-mail and voice mail weren't sufficient for these groups. "Try coming to an agreement on the verbiage of a legal contract with a team of lawyers and engineers representing multiple interests using only the telephone and e-mail," says John Whyte, Ernst & Young's chief information officer. "You can spend weeks sorting through fragmented e-mail conversations or individual phone calls and voice mails." Now employees discuss complex issues through special software that provides a virtual whiteboard on the computer screen and allows real-time chat (instant messaging). It's not quite as good as face-to-face meetings, but much better than the previous patchwork of e-mail and telephone calls.[30]

Ernst & Young discovered that some issues require more **media richness** than e-mail and telephone messages can offer. Media richness refers to the medium's *data-carrying capacity*—the volume and variety of information that can be transmitted.[31] Face-to-face meetings have the highest data-carrying capacity because the sender simultaneously uses multiple communication channels (verbal and nonverbal), the receiver can provide immediate feedback, and the information exchange can be

media richness
The data-carrying capacity of a communication medium, including the volume and variety of information it can transmit.

customized to suit the situation. Real-time chat would be somewhat lower in the hierarchy, and e-mail further below chat software. Financial reports and other impersonal documents are the leanest media because they allow only one form of data transmission (e.g., written), the sender does not receive timely feedback from the receiver, and the information exchange is standardized for everyone.

Exhibit 11.3 shows that rich media are better than lean media when the communication situation is nonroutine and ambiguous. Nonroutine situations require rich media because the sender and receiver have little common experience and, therefore, need to transmit a large volume of information with immediate feedback. During unexpected emergencies, for instance, you should use face-to-face meetings to coordinate work activities quickly and minimize the risk of misunderstanding and confusion. Lean media may be used in routine situations because the sender and receiver have common expectations through shared mental models.[32] Ambiguous issues, such as Ernst & Young's contract work, also require rich media because the parties must share large amounts of information with immediate feedback to resolve multiple and conflicting interpretations of their observations and experiences. For instance, research indicates that product development presents several ill-defined issues, so team members work better with face-to-face communication than with leaner media.[33]

EXHIBIT 11.3   A hierarchy of media richness

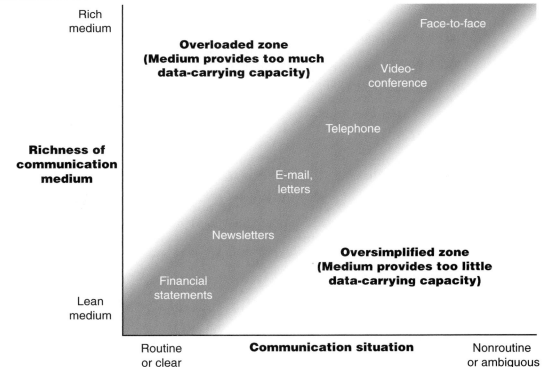

Source: Based on R. Lengel and R. Daft, "The Selection of Communication Media as an Executive Skill," *Academy of Management Executive* 2, no. 3 (August 1988), p. 226; R. L. Daft and R. H. Lengel, "Information Richness: A New Approach to Managerial Behavior and Organization Design," *Research in Organizational Behavior*, 1984, p. 199.

What happens when we choose the wrong level of media richness for the situation? When the situation is routine or clear, then using a rich medium—such as holding a special meeting—would be a waste of time. On the other hand, if a unique and ambiguous issue is handled through lean media, such as e-mail, then issues would take longer to resolve and misunderstandings are more likely to occur. These are the problems that employees at Ernst & Young experienced.

One last point about media richness is that we need to consider previous experience with both the media and the other person in the information exchange. People who have plenty of experience with a particular communication medium can "push" the amount of media richness normally possible through that information channel. Using a medium efficiently seems to allow more information flow than what is possible for people who are new to the medium. Similarly, we can sometimes rely on leaner media when communicating with people who are familiar to us. This familiarity means that the sender and receiver often share common mental models, which reduces the volume of information transmitted.[34]

Symbolic Meaning of the Medium

"The medium is the message."[35] This famous phrase by the late Canadian communications guru Marshall McLuhan means that the sender's choice of communication channel transmits meaning beyond the message content. For example, a personal meeting with an employee may indicate that the issue is important, whereas a brief handwritten note may suggest less importance.

The difficulty we face when choosing a communication medium is that its symbolic meaning may vary from one person to the next. Some people view e-mail as a symbol of professionalism, some see it as evidence of the sender's efficiency, while others might view an e-mail message as a low-status clerical activity because it involves typing.[36] Overall, we must be sensitive to the symbolic meaning of the selected communication medium to ensure that it amplifies rather than contradicts the meaning found in the message content.

COMMUNICATION BARRIERS (NOISE)

In spite of the best intentions of sender and receiver to communicate, several barriers inhibit the effective exchange of information. As author George Bernard Shaw once wrote, "The greatest problem with communication is the illusion that it has been accomplished." Four pervasive communication barriers (called "noise" earlier in Exhibit 11.1) are perceptions, filtering, language, and information overload. Later, we will also investigate cross-cultural and gender communication barriers.

Perceptions

As we learned in Chapter 3, the perceptual process determines what messages we select or screen out, as well as how the selected information is organized and interpreted. This can be a significant source of noise in the communication process if the sender and receiver have different perceptual frames and mental models. For example, a plant superintendent in a concrete block plant picked up a piece of broken brick while talking with the supervisor. This action had no particular meaning to the superintendent—just something to toy with during the conversation. Yet as soon as the senior manager had left, the supervisor ordered one half-hour of overtime for the entire crew to clean up the plant. The supervisor mistakenly perceived the superintendent's actions as a signal that the plant was messy.[37]

Filtering

Some messages are filtered or stopped altogether on their way up or down the organizational hierarchy.[38] Filtering may involve deleting or delaying negative information, or using less harsh words so that events sound more favourable. Employees and supervisors usually filter communication to create a good impression of themselves to superiors. Filtering is most common when the organization rewards employees who communicate mainly positive information and among employees with strong career mobility aspirations.[39]

Language

Words and gestures carry no inherent meaning, so the sender must ensure that the receiver understands these symbols and signs. Lack of mutual understanding is a common reason why messages are distorted. Two potential language barriers are jargon and ambiguity.

jargon
The technical language and acronyms as well as recognized words with specialized meaning in specific organizations or groups.

Jargon   "Hi Jack, I've worked out a klugey solution to the UI issue," an employee e-mails a colleague in the next cubicle. "We need to get granular on this. Unfortunately, I'm OOF next week, so you'll have to burn up a few cycles on it. I'm worried that the blue-badges on this project will go totally nonlinear when they realize the RTM date is slipping."[40]

If you understood most of the previous paragraph, you probably work at Microsoft or some other high technology company where employees communicate through Microspeak. This **jargon** includes technical language and acronyms as well as recognized words with specialized meaning in specific organizations or social groups. Microspeak and other jargon might baffle most of us, but it potentially increases communication efficiency when both sender and receiver understand this specialized language. Jargon also shapes and maintains an organization's cultural values as well as symbolizing an employee's social-identity in a group (see Chapter 3).[41]

However, jargon can also be a barrier to effective communication. One example is an incident at Sea Launch, the Long Beach, California-based multinational venture that launches satellites. During a test of a countdown protocol devised by the American staff, the Russian scientists involved with the project suddenly became moody and distant. When Sea Launch's mission control director Steve Thelin eventually asked why they were acting this way, the Russians complained that no one had told them who "Roger" was. Everyone had a good laugh

© 2001 Ted Goff

"That's my commendation for deciphering all the sales talk when we needed to upgrade the computer."

when Thelin explained that "Roger" is jargon used by the Americans to indicate that they understood what the other person in a transmission is saying.[42]

Ambiguity   Most languages—and certainly the English language—include some degree of ambiguity because the sender and receiver interpret the same word or phrase differently. If a co-worker says, "Would you like to check the figures again?," the employee may be politely *telling* you to double-check the figures. But this message is sufficiently ambiguous that you may think the co-worker is merely *asking* if you want to do this. The result is a failure to communicate.

However, ambiguity is sometimes used deliberately in work settings. Corporate leaders rely on metaphors and other ambiguous language to describe ill-defined or complex ideas.[43] Ambiguity is also used to avoid conveying or creating undesirable emotions. For example, one recent study reported that people rely on more ambiguous language when communicating with people who have different values and beliefs. In this case, ambiguity minimizes the risk of conflict.[44] The brokerage industry also relies on ambiguous language when advising clients to get rid of their stock in a particular company. Brokers are reluctant to use the word "sell" because it criticizes the company's performance, yet some of these companies are current or future clients. "'Hold' means 'sell'" admits one veteran of the brokerage industry. "It's a kind of 'meta' language where you have to look into the meaning behind the word."[45]

Information Overload

Every day, Dave MacDonald is flooded with up to 100 e-mail messages. The Xerox Canada executive is also bombarded with voice mail, faxes, memos, and other pieces of information. "Without some kind of system in place, I'd spend practically all my time trying to sort through it and not get much of anything else done," says MacDonald.[46]

Dave MacDonald is not alone. Canadian office workers send and receive an average of 169 e-mails, phone calls, voice-mails, faxes, paper documents, and other messages each day! One survey reports that 49 percent of managers in several other countries feel they are fairly often or regularly incapable of processing this infoglut. More than 40 percent of them say that receiving so much information weakens their decision-making ability, delays important decisions, and makes it difficult to concentrate on their main tasks. Some medical experts also warn that being bombarded with electronic information is causing memory loss in young people.[47]

Marshall McLuhan predicted more than 30 years ago that employees would become overloaded with messages. "One of the effects of living with electric information is that we live in a state of information overload," said McLuhan. "There's always more than you can cope with."[48] **Information overload** occurs when the volume of information received exceeds the person's capacity to process it. Employees have a certain *information processing capacity*, that is, the amount of information they can process in a fixed unit of time. At the same time, jobs have a varying *information load*, that is, the amount of information to be processed per unit of time.[49]

As Exhibit 11.4 illustrates, information overload occurs whenever the job's information load exceeds the individual's information processing capacity. Information overload creates noise in the communication system because information

information overload

A condition in which the volume of information received exceeds the person's capacity to process it.

Dynamics of
information overload

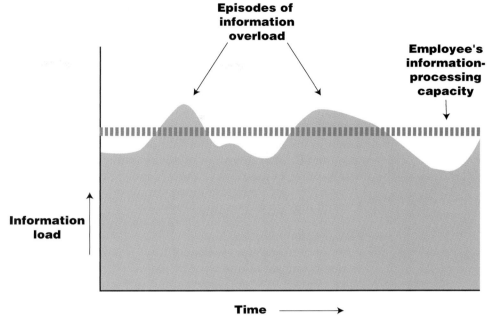

gets overlooked or misinterpreted when people can't process it fast enough. It has also become a common cause of workplace stress.

Information overload is minimized in two ways: by increasing our information processing capacity and reducing the job's information load.[50] We can increase information processing capacity by learning to read faster, scanning documents more efficiently, and removing distractions that slow information processing speed. Time management also increases information processing capacity. When information overload is only temporary, we can increase information processing capacity by working longer hours.

We can reduce information load by buffering, summarizing, or omitting the information. Buffering occurs when assistants screen the person's messages and forward only those considered essential reading. Summarizing condenses information into fewer words, for example, reading abstracts and executive summaries rather than the entire document. Omitting is the practice of ignoring less important information. For example, some e-mail software programs have a filtering algorithm that screens out unwanted junk mail (called "spam").

Perceptions, filtering, language, and information overload are not the only sources of noise in the communication process, but they are probably the most common. Noise also occurs when we communicate across cultures or genders, both of which are discussed next.

CROSS-CULTURAL AND GENDER COMMUNICATION

In a world of increasing globalization and cultural diversity, organizations face new opportunities as well as communication challenges. Employees must become more sensitive and competent in cross-cultural communication. They must also overcome their reluctance to communicate with co-workers from another cultural group. These communication competencies are also gaining importance as companies increasingly work with clients, suppliers, and joint venture partners from other countries.

Language is the most obvious cross-cultural barrier.[51] Words are easily misunderstood in verbal communication, either because the receiver has a limited vocabulary or the sender's accent makes it difficult for the receiver to understand the sound. The ambiguity of language that we discussed earlier becomes a bigger concern across cultures because sender and receiver have different values and interpretations of the language. For example, a French executive might call an event a "catastrophe" as a casual exaggeration, but someone in Germany would take that literally as an earthshaking event. Similarly, one study of more than 200 commission and task force reports concluded that First Nations people and Canadian government representatives were often talking about different things even though they used the same words.[52]

Mastering the same language improves one dimension of cross-cultural communication, but problems may still occur when interpreting voice intonation.[53] A deep voice symbolizes masculinity in North America, but African men often express their emotions using a high-pitched voice. Middle Easterners sometimes speak loudly to show sincerity and interest in the discussion, whereas Japanese people tend to speak softly to communicate politeness or humility. These different cultural norms may cause one person to misinterpret the other.

Nonverbal Differences

Nonverbal communication is more important in some cultures than in others. For example, people in Japan interpret more of a message's meaning from nonverbal cues than verbal ones. "A lot of Japanese is either unspoken or communicated through body language," explains Henry Wallace, the Scottish-born CEO of Mazda Corp. in Japan.[54] To avoid offending or embarrassing the receiver (particularly outsiders), Japanese people will often say what the other person wants to hear (called *tatemae*) but send more subtle nonverbal cues indicating the sender's true feelings (called *honne*).[55] A Japanese colleague might politely reject your business proposal by saying: "I will think about that" while sending nonverbal signals that he or she is not really interested. This difference explains why Japanese employees may prefer direct conversation to e-mail and other media that lack nonverbal cues.

Most nonverbal cues are specific to a particular culture and may have a completely different meaning to people raised in other cultures. For example, most of us shake our head from side to side to say "No," but a variation of head shaking means "I understand" to some people from India. Filipinos raise their eyebrows to give an affirmative answer, yet Arabs interpret this expression (along with clicking one's tongue) as a negative response. Most Canadians are taught to maintain eye contact with the speaker to show interest and respect, yet First Nations people in Canada, Australian Aborigines, and others learn at an early age to show respect by looking down when an older or more senior person is talking to them.[56]

Even the common handshake communicates different meanings across cultures. Westerners tend to appreciate a firm handshake as a sign of strength and warmth in a friendship or business relationship. In contrast, many Asians and Middle Easterners favour a loose grip and regard a firm clench as aggressive. Germans prefer one good handshake stroke, whereas anything less than five or six strokes may symbolize a lack of trust in Spain. If this isn't confusing enough, people from some cultures view any touching in public—including handshakes—as a sign of rudeness.

Silence and conversational overlaps Communication includes the silence between our words and gestures. However, the meaning of silence varies from one culture to another. In Japan, people tend to show respect for the speaker by remaining silent for a few seconds after the person has spoken to contemplate what has just been said.[57] To them, silence is an important part of communication (called *haragei*) because it preserves harmony and is more reliable than talk. Silence is shared by everyone and belongs to no one, so it becomes the ultimate form of interdependence. Moreover, Japanese value empathy, which can only be demonstrated by understanding others without using words.

In contrast, most people in Canada view silence as a *lack* of communication and often interpret long breaks as a sign of disagreement. For example, after presenting their proposal to a potential Japanese client, a group of American consultants expected to be bombarded with questions. Instead, their proposal was greeted with a long silence. As the silence continued, most of the consultants concluded that the Japanese client disapproved, so they prepared to pack and leave. But the lead consultant gestured them to stop, because the client's face and posture seemed to indicate interest rather than rejection. He was right: when the client finally spoke, it was to give the consulting firm the job.[58]

Conversational overlaps also send different messages in different cultures. Japanese usually stop talking when they are interrupted, whereas talking over the other person's speech is more common in Brazil and some other countries. The reason is that talking while someone is speaking to you is considered quite rude in Japan, whereas Brazilians are more likely to interpret this as the person's interest and involvement in the conversation.

Gender Differences in Communication

Popular press books have depicted gender differences in communication as varying so widely that it makes men and women seem like completely different life forms. In reality, men and women have similar communication practices, but there are subtle distinctions that can occasionally lead to misunderstanding and conflict.[59] One distinction is that men are more likely than women to view conversations as negotiations of relative status and power.[60] They assert their power by directly giving advice to others (e.g., "You should do the following") and using combative language. There is also evidence that men interrupt women far more often than vice versa and that they dominate talk time in conversations with women.

Men tend to engage in "report talk," in which the primary function of the conversation is impersonal and efficient information exchange. This may explain why men tend to quantify information (e.g., "It took us six weeks"). Women also engage in report talk, particularly when conversing with men. But conversations among women tend to have a higher incidence of relationship building through "rapport talk." Thus, women use more intensive adverbs ("I was *so happy* that he completed the report") and hedge their statements ("It seems to be . . ."). Rather than asserting status, women use indirect requests such as "Have you considered . . .?" Similarly, women apologize more often and seek advice from others more quickly than men do. Finally, research fairly consistently indicates that women are more sensitive than men to nonverbal cues in face-to-face meetings.[61]

Both men and women usually understand each other, but these subtle differences are occasional irritants. For instance, female scientists in Canada have complained that adversarial interaction among male scientists makes it difficult for women to participate in meaningful dialogue.[62] Another irritant occurs when women seek empathy but receive male dominance in response. Specifically, women sometimes discuss their personal experiences and problems to develop closeness with the receiver. But when men hear problems, they quickly suggest solutions because this asserts their control over the situation. As well as frustrating a woman's need for common understanding, the advice actually says: "You and I are different; you have the problem and I have the answer." Meanwhile, men become frustrated because they can't understand why women don't appreciate their advice.

IMPROVING INTERPERSONAL COMMUNICATION

Effective interpersonal communication depends on the sender's ability to get the message across and the receiver's performance as an active listener. In this section, we outline these two essential features of effective interpersonal communication.

Getting Your Message Across

This chapter began with the statement that effective communication occurs when the other person receives and understands the message. To accomplish this difficult task, the sender must learn to empathize with the receiver, repeat the message, choose an appropriate time for the conversation, and be descriptive rather than evaluative.

- *Empathize*—Recall from Chapter 3 that empathy is a person's ability to understand and be sensitive to the feelings, thoughts, and situation of others. In conversations, this involves putting yourself in the receiver's shoes when encoding the message. For instance, should you be sensitive to words that may be ambiguous or trigger the wrong emotional response?
- *Repeat the message*—Rephrase the key points a couple of times. The saying "Tell them what you're going to tell them; tell them; then tell them what you've told them" reflects this need for redundancy.
- *Use timing effectively*—Your message competes with other messages and noise, so find a time when the receiver is less likely to be distracted by these other matters.
- *Be descriptive*—Focus on the problem, not the person, if you have negative information to convey. People stop listening when the information attacks their self-esteem. Also, suggest things the listener can do to improve, rather than pointing to him or her as a problem.

Active Listening

Darryl Heustis admits that he isn't always good at listening to other people. "I've had the unique ability to start formulating my response before the person is through with the question," Heustis sheepishly admits. Fortunately, Heustis, who is the vice-president for medical affairs at the Jerry L. Pettis Memorial VA Medical

Centre in Loma Linda, California, and his colleagues have completed training that helps them to more actively listen to what others are saying. "Now, I've learned to practise my listening skills and observation skills. I've improved at watching people carefully, looking for body language and other signals of what they're feeling."[63]

Darryl Heustis and other executives are discovering that listening is at least as important as talking. As one sage wisely wrote: "Nature gave people two ears but only one tongue, which is a gentle hint that they should listen more than they talk."[64] Listening is a process of actively sensing the sender's signals, evaluating them accurately, and responding appropriately. These three components of listening—sensing, evaluating, and responding—reflect the listener's side of the communication model described at the beginning of this chapter.[65] Listeners receive the sender's signals, decode them as intended, and provide appropriate and timely feedback to the sender. Active listeners constantly cycle through sensing, evaluating, and responding during the conversation and engage in various activities to improve these processes (see Exhibit 11.5).

Sensing Sensing is the process of receiving signals from the sender and paying attention to them. These signals include the words spoken, the nature of the sounds (speed of speech, tone of voice, etc.), and nonverbal cues. Active listeners improve sensing by postponing evaluation, avoiding interruptions, and maintaining interest.

- *Postpone evaluation*—Many listeners become victims of first impressions (see Chapter 3). They quickly form an opinion of the speaker's message and subsequently screen out important information. Active listeners, on the other hand, try to stay as open-minded as possible by delaying evaluation of the message until the speaker has finished.
- *Avoid interruptions*—Interrupting the speaker's conversation has two adverse effects on the sensing process. First, it disrupts the speaker's idea, so the listener does not receive the entire message. Second, interruptions tend to

EXHIBIT 11.5

Components of active listening

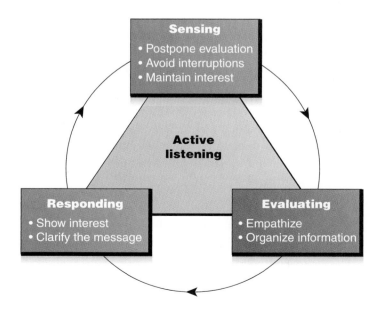

second-guess what the speaker is trying to say, which contributes to the problem of evaluating the speaker's ideas too early.

■ *Maintain interest*—As with any behaviour, active listening requires motivation. Too often, we close our minds soon after a conversation begins because the subject is boring. Instead, active listeners maintain interest by taking the view—probably an accurate one—that there is always something of value in a conversation; it's just a matter of actively looking for it.

Evaluating This component of listening includes understanding the message meaning, evaluating the message, and remembering the message. To improve their evaluation of the conversation, active listeners empathize with the speaker and organize information received during the conversation.

■ *Empathize*—Active listeners try to understand and be sensitive to the speaker's feelings, thoughts, and situation. Empathy is a critical skill in active listening because the listener can then accurately interpret the verbal and nonverbal cues in the conversation from the other person's point of view.

■ *Organize information*—Listeners process information three times faster than the average rate of speech (450 words per minute versus 125 words per minute), so they are easily distracted. Active listeners use this spare time to organize the information into key points. In fact, it's a good idea to imagine that you must summarize what people have said after they are finished speaking.[66]

Responding Responding, the third component of listening, refers to the listener's development and display of behaviours that support the communication process. Responsiveness is feedback to the sender, which motivates and directs the speaker's communication. Active listeners do this by showing interest and clarifying the message.

■ *Show interest*—Active listeners show interest by maintaining sufficient eye contact and sending back channel signals such as "Oh, really!" and "I see" during appropriate breaks in the conversation.

■ *Clarify the message*—Active listeners provide feedback by rephrasing the speaker's ideas at appropriate breaks ("So you're saying that...?"). This further demonstrates interest in the conversation and helps the speaker determine whether you understand the message.

COMMUNICATING IN ORGANIZATIONAL HIERARCHIES

So far, we have focused on "micro-level" issues in the communication process, namely, in the dynamics of sending and receiving information between two people in various situations. But in this era of knowledge as competitive advantage, corporate leaders also need to maintain an open flow of communication up, down, and across the organization. In this section, we discuss four "macro-level" communication strategies: newsletters/e-zines, workspace design, employee surveys, and management by walking around.

Work Space Design

One of the most prominent trends in organizations these days is redesigning offices to encourage spontaneous communication. Connections 11.2 describes

Communicating in (Office) Space

There's nothing like a wall to prevent employees from talking to each other. That's why Intuit Canada's new building in Edmonton, Alberta, features plenty of open office space. The site also features almost two dozen meeting rooms so employees can chat privately when necessary. These changes make more efficient use of space, but their main thrust is to provide direct line-of-sight among employees so that they share knowledge more easily.

Some companies have taken open office communication to the extreme. In Vancouver, the new offices of advertising firm Lanyon Phillips feature open rectangular workstations and semi-open area pods for meetings. "So often in offices, people are stuck in little rabbit holes and you feel like you could be the only one in the building," explains company chairman Peter Lanyon. "In this space, you can see from one end to the other. You get the sense of being connected with other people."

At eBay Canada's offices in Toronto, privacy is non-existent except for the telephone booths near the front entrance. Even CEO Lorna Borenstein's desk is out in the open, indistinguishable from those of her staff. "It looks a little New Agie," says Borenstein, "but it works like a well-oiled machine."

Eric Legere, the Canadian who led the design of GlaxoSmithKline's new offices in Hong Kong, realized that it is culturally difficult to move executives out of their offices in Asia. "Getting rid of all the private offices was never on the table for us," admits a GlaxoSmithKline Hong Kong executive. Instead, Legere created smaller offices with more "breakout" areas, such as bright cafés, enlarged meeting rooms and corridors, plus booth-like "touchdown stations" and "quiet rooms."

Sources: K. MacNamara, "eBay Canada's CEO has 1,000-Watt Smile, `Super' Career Plan," *National Post*, May 6, 2002, p. PW4; J. Krich, "Office Politics," *Asian Wall Street Journal*, September 28, 2001, p. W1; R. Turchansky, "$14M Digs for Growing Software Company," *Edmonton Journal*, February 1, 2001.

Intuit Canada's new call centre in Edmonton, Alberta, has plenty of open space to encourage employee communication. *B. Gavriloff, Edmonton Journal*

www.intuit.com/canada

how some Canadian firms have completely removed closed offices, whereas others maintain some privacy for senior staff, but improve office design so employees have more "breakout" spaces for coincidental communication episodes.

Do these open space offices actually improve communication? Anecdotal evidence lends support to the thesis that people communicate more often with fewer walls between them. However, scientific research also suggests that open office design potentially increases employee stress due to the loss of privacy and personal space.[67] Some employees at the offices of TBWA Chiat/Day resorted to making telephone calls in bathroom stalls and under their desks after the Los-Angeles advertising firm moved to open offices. The firm has since reverted to a "nesting" model that consists of some private individual space as well as open space for collaboration.

According to an analysis of 13,000 employee surveys in 40 major organizations, workspace contributes to individual performance primarily by providing a place to concentrate on work without distraction. The second most important influence of workspace on performance is how it facilitates informal communication with co-workers. The point here is that workspace needs to provide a balance between its ability to give employees a place to concentrate and its influence on social interaction.[68]

Newsletters and E-zines

A decade ago, Hughes Software Systems (HSS) in India had 50 employees. If HSS wanted to share company news, it gathered its employees together for a meeting. Today, HSS employs 1,300 people, so it depends on various electronic and paper media to keep everyone informed. Employees receive hard-copy newsletters about company developments, but they also receive timely information through HSS's intranet. If that's not enough, HSS has an electronic message board called "Junk," where employees share their views on everything from the quality of cafeteria food to ways to get around the electronic blockades HSS has placed on sports Web sites.[69]

Hughes Software Systems and other large organizations are increasingly applying a multi-pronged communication strategy to share information with employees. This strategy typically includes both print-based newsletters and web-based electronic newsletters, called e-zines. For example, Hewlett-Packard (HP) posts late-breaking company news every day in its intranet-based publication called *hpNow*. HP employees also receive a print magazine several times each year called *Invent*, which features longer, more in-depth articles. HP and other firms have discovered that one communication medium is not enough. Online sources offer instant communication, but many employees still have difficulty reading long articles on a computer screen. Print articles are slower and more costly, but they are more portable and it is easier to read long articles.[70]

Employee Surveys

Most of Canada's "best" companies to work for conduct regular employee opinion surveys. Most of them survey employees to monitor worker morale. However, many firms also use these surveys to involve employees in decisions on everything from dress codes to pension plans.[71] Companies also depend on 360-degree feedback surveys, which communicate employee attitudes toward specific managers.

Management by Walking Around

management by walking around (MBWA)
A communication practice in which executives get out of their offices and learn from others in the organization through face-to-face dialogue.

The opening vignette to this chapter described how Hiram Walker CEO Ian Gourlay and Damovo CEO Pearse Flynn engage in **management by walking around** (MBWA). Coined several years ago at Hewlett-Packard, MBWA means that executives should get out of their offices and learn from others in the organization through face-to-face dialogue.[72] MBWA minimizes filtering because execu-

The uncertain future of Mitsubishi Motors Australia Ltd. (MMAL) has kept CEO Tom Phillips busy as a corporate communicator. When rumours circulated that Mitsubishi headquarters in Japan would shut down the Adelaide-based automaker, Phillips met employees on the assembly line to dispel those myths. When MMAL received a large capital injection, Phillips called a meeting (shown in photo) with every employee attending to announce the deal. As the plant thumped to rock music, Phillips led MMAL's 3,200 employees in a Mexican wave, then told them their future looked stronger than ever. A few months later, when Mitsubishi officially ruled out closing the Adelaide plant, Phillips was quick to communicate the good news to everyone. "I'm going down the (assembly) line tomorrow to shake hands and slap backs," said Phillips when he received the good news.[74] Why should corporate leaders personally meet with employees rather than send a memo under these circumstances? *Russell Millard/The Advertiser (Adelaide)* **www.mitsubishi-motors.com.au**

tives listen directly to employees. It also helps executives acquire a deeper meaning and quicker understanding of internal organizational problems.

MBWA can take many forms. Ian Gourlay likes to visit the production floor to listen to employees. Pearse Flynn hands out sticky notes which are later returned with anonymous employee comments. Along with attending weekly connect breaks where executives mingle with employees, Greg Aasen, chief operating officer and cofounder of PMC-Sierra in Vancouver, does his MBWA by running with employees during lunch. "Even the senior guys I've worked with for 10 years, they tell you a lot more running out on the trails than they would in your office. It's less intimidating, I guess," says Aasen.[73]

COMMUNICATING THROUGH THE GRAPEVINE

Whether or not executives get out of their offices, employees will always rely on the oldest communication channel: the corporate **grapevine**. The grapevine is an unstructured and informal network founded on social relationships rather than organizational charts or job descriptions. According to some estimates, 75 percent of employees typically receive news from the grapevine before they hear about it through formal channels.[75]

Grapevine Characteristics

Early research identified several unique features of the grapevine.[76] It transmits information very rapidly in all directions throughout the organization. The typical pattern is a cluster chain, whereby a few people actively transmit rumours to many others. The grapevine works through informal social networks, so it is more active when employees have similar backgrounds and are able to communicate easily. Many rumours seem to have at least a kernel of truth, possibly because rumours are transmitted through media-rich communication channels (e.g., face to face) where employees are motivated to communicate effectively. Nevertheless, the grapevine distorts information by deleting fine details and exaggerating key points of the story.

The problem with some of these earlier findings is that they might not be representative of the grapevine in this era of information technology. E-mail and instant messaging have replaced the traditional water cooler as the main place where people share gossip. Social networks have expanded as employees communicate with each other around the globe, not just around the next cubicle. Vault.com and other public Web sites have become virtual water coolers by posting anonymous comments about specific companies for all to view. This technology extends gossip to anyone, not just employees connected to social networks.

grapevine
An unstructured and informal communication network founded on social relationships rather than organizational charts or job descriptions.

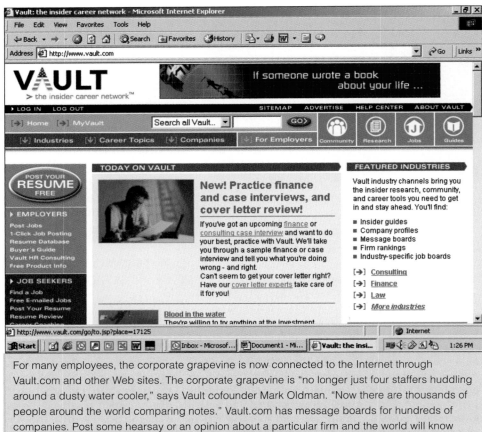

For many employees, the corporate grapevine is now connected to the Internet through Vault.com and other Web sites. The corporate grapevine is "no longer just four staffers huddling around a dusty water cooler," says Vault cofounder Mark Oldman. "Now there are thousands of people around the world comparing notes." Vault.com has message boards for hundreds of companies. Post some hearsay or an opinion about a particular firm and the world will know about it in seconds. "[W]ith the power of the Internet, there is more of a global and real-time flow to rumours and gossip," says Oldman. Vault.com estimates that up to 9% of Goldman Sachs employees check in with Vault's Goldman board during any given week. Partners at McKinsey & Co. actively respond to rumours and queries posted on the consulting firm's message board at Vault.com.[77] In your opinion, how does the Internet potentially change the pattern and accuracy of grapevine information? *Reprinted with permission of Vault.com—The Insider Career Network* **www.vault.com**

Grapevine Advantages and Disadvantages

Should the grapevine be encouraged, tolerated, or quashed? The difficulty in answering this question is that the grapevine has both advantages and disadvantages. One benefit is that the grapevine helps employees make sense of their workplace when information is not available through formal channels.[78] It is also the main conduit through which organizational stories and other symbols of the organization's culture are communicated (see Chapter 16).

A third advantage of the grapevine is that the social interaction relieves anxiety.[79] This explains why rumour mills are most active during times of uncertainty. Finally, the grapevine is associated with the drive to bond. Being a recipient of gossip is a sign of inclusion, according to evolutionary psychologists. Trying to quash the grapevine is, in some respects, an attempt to undermine natural human needs for interaction.[80]

The grapevine is not always beneficial. Morale tumbles when management is slower than the grapevine in communicating information, because it suggests a lack of sincerity and concern for employees. Moreover, grapevine information may become sufficiently distorted that it escalates rather than reduces employee anxieties. This is most likely to occur when the original information is transmitted through several people rather than by one or two people.

Companies have tried to learn the identities of people who post anonymous rumours on Web sites, but their quest usually fails. City officials in Cascavel, Brazil have banned employees from engaging in spreading office gossip, but the grapevine will always exist.[81] A better strategy is to listen to the grapevine as a signal of employee anxiety, then correct the cause of the anxiety. Some companies also listen to the grapevine and step in to correct blatant errors and fabrications.

CHAPTER SUMMARY

Communication refers to the process by which information is transmitted and *understood* between two or more people. Communication supports knowledge management, decision making, work coordination, and the drive to bond. The communication process involves forming, encoding, and transmitting the intended message to a receiver, who then decodes the message and provides feedback to the sender. Effective communication occurs when the sender's thoughts are transmitted to and understood by the intended receiver.

Electronic mail (e-mail) is a powerful way to communicate, and it has changed communication patterns in organizational settings. However, e-mail also contributes to information overload, is an ineffective channel for communicating emotions, tends to reduce politeness and respect in the communication process, and lacks the warmth of human interaction. Some forms of computer-mediated communication give employees the freedom to communicate effectively from any location.

Nonverbal communication includes facial gestures, voice intonation, physical distance, and even silence. Employees make extensive use of nonverbal cues when engaging in emotional labour because these cues help to transmit prescribed feelings to customers, co-workers, and others. Emotional contagion refers to the automatic and unconscious tendency to mimic and synchronize our nonverbal behaviours with other people. The most appropriate communication medium depends on its data-carrying capacity (media richness) and its symbolic meaning to the receiver. Nonroutine and ambiguous situations require rich media.

Several barriers create noise in the communication process. People misinterpret messages because of perceptual biases. Some information is filtered out

as it gets passed up the hierarchy. Jargon and ambiguous language are barriers when the sender and receiver have different interpretations of the words and symbols used. People also screen out or misinterpret messages due to information overload.

Globalization and workforce diversity have brought new communication challenges. Words are easily misunderstood in verbal communication and employees are reluctant to communicate across cultures. Voice intonation, silence, and other nonverbal cues have different meaning and importance in other cultures. There are also some communication differences between men and women, such as the tendency for men to exert status and engage in report talk in conversations, whereas women use more rapport talk and are more sensitive than men to nonverbal cues.

To get a message across, the sender must learn to empathize with the receiver, repeat the message, choose an appropriate time for the conversation, and be descriptive rather than evaluative. Listening includes sensing, evaluating, and responding. Active listeners support these processes by postponing evaluation, avoiding interruptions, maintaining interest, empathizing, organizing information, showing interest, and clarifying the message.

Some companies try to encourage informal communication through workspace design, although open offices run the risk of increasing stress and reducing the ability to concentrate on work. Many organizations also rely on a combination of print newsletters and intranet-based e-zines to communicate corporate news. Employee surveys are widely used to measure employee attitudes or involve employees in corporate decisions. Some executives also engage in management by walking around to facilitate communication across the organization.

In any organization, employees rely on the grapevine, particularly during times of uncertainty. The grapevine is an unstructured and informal network founded on social relationships rather than organizational charts or job descriptions. Although early research identified several unique features of the grapevine, some of these features may be changing as the Internet plays an increasing role in grapevine communication.

KEY TERMS

Communication, p. 314
Communication competence, p. 314
Emotional contagion, p. 319

Flaming, p. 317
Grapevine, p. 333
Information overload, p. 324
Jargon, p. 323

Management by walking around (MBWA), p. 332
Media richness, p. 320

DISCUSSION QUESTIONS

1. What is the role of communication in an effective organization?
2. "Electronic mail (e-mail) is revolutionizing the way we communicate in organizational settings." What are the advantages and limitations of communicating via e-mail?
3. Marshall McLuhan coined the popular phrase "The medium is the message." What does this phrase mean, and why should we be aware of it when communicating in organizations?
4. Describe a time when you experienced difficulty communicating cross-culturally. What did you do to facilitate effective communication? What was the outcome?
5. Explain why men and women are sometimes frustrated with each other's communication behaviours.
6. What, if any, is the receiver's responsibility to ensure communication is effective?
7. A Canadian executive recently admitted that she deliberately "leaks" information through the organizational grapevine before communicating the information through formal channels. The reason, she explains, is that this gives employees an opportunity to think about the information. "[B]y the time the message is formally announced, everybody has had a chance to think about it and feel like they're on the inside track." Discuss the advantages and limitations of this communication strategy.
8. This chapter makes several distinctions between communication in Japan and Canada. Discuss three distinctions between communication in these two cultures.

C A S E   S T U D Y   11.1

BRIDGING THE TWO WORLDS—THE ORGANIZATIONAL DILEMMA

By William Todorovic, University of Waterloo.

I had been hired by a Toronto based company, ABC Limited, and it was my first day of work. I was 26 years old, and I was now the manager of ABC's customer service group, which looked after customers, logistics, and some of the raw material purchasing. My superior, George, was the vice-president of the company. ABC manufactured most of its products from aluminum, a majority of which were destined for the construction industry.

As I walked around the shop floor, the employees appeared to be concentrating on their jobs, barely noticing me. Management held daily meetings in which various production issues were discussed. No one from the shop floor was invited to the meetings, unless there was a specific problem. Later I also learned that management had separate washrooms and separate lunchrooms as well as other perqs, which floor employees did not have. Most of the floor employees felt that management, although polite on the surface, did not really feel they had anything to learn from the floor employees.

John, who worked on the aluminum slitter, a crucial operation required before any other operations could commence, had had a number of unpleasant encounters with George. As a result, George usually sent written memos to the floor in order to avoid a direct confrontation with John. Because the directions in the memos were complex, these memos were often more than two pages long.

One morning, as I was walking around, I noticed that John was very upset. Feeling that perhaps there was something I could do, I approached John and asked him if I could help. He indicated that everything was just fine. From the looks of the situation, and John's body language, I felt that he was willing to talk, but John knew this was not the way things were done at ABC. Tony, who worked at the machine next to John's, then cursed and said that the office guys only cared about schedules, not about the people down on the floor. I just looked at him, and then said that I had only begun working here last week, but thought I could address some of their issues. Tony gave me a strange look, shook his head, and went back to his machine. I could still hear him swearing as I left. Later I realized that most of the office staff were also offended by Tony's language.

On the way back to my office, Lesley, a recently hired engineer from Russia, approached me and pointed out that the employees were not accustomed to management talking to them. Management only issued orders and made demands. As we discussed the different perceptions between office and floor staff, we were interrupted by a very loud lunch bell, which startled me. I was happy to join Lesley for lunch, but she asked me why I was not eating in the office lunchroom. I replied that if I was going to understand how ABC worked, I had to get to know all the people better. In addition, I realized that this was not how things were done at ABC, and wondered about the nature of the apparent division between the management and the floor. In the lunchroom, the other workers were amazed to see me there, commenting that I was still new and had not learned the ropes yet.

After lunch, when I asked George, my supervisor, about his recent confrontation with John, George was surprised that John had got upset, and

exclaimed, "I just wanted John to know that he had done a great job, and as a result, we will be able to ship one large order from the west coast on time. If fact, I thought I was complimenting him."

Earlier, Lesley had indicated that certain behaviour was expected from management, and therefore from me. I reasoned that I didn't think this behaviour worked, and besides, it's not what I believed or how I cared to behave. For the next couple of months, I simply walked around the floor and took every opportunity to talk to the shop floor employees. Often when the employees related specific information about their workplaces, I felt that it went over my head. Frequently I had to write down the information and revisit it later. I made a point of listening to them, identifying where they were coming from, and trying to understand them. I needed to keep my mind open to new ideas. Because the shop employees expected me to make requests and demands, I made a point of not doing any of that. Soon enough, the employees became friendly, and started to accept me as one of their own, or at least as a different type of management person.

During my third month of work, the employees showed me how to improve the scheduling of jobs, especially those on the aluminum slitter. In fact, the greatest contribution was made by John who demonstrated better ways to combine the most common slitting sizes, and reduce waste by retaining some of the "common-sized" material for new orders. Seeing the opportunity, I programmed a spreadsheet to calculate and track inventory. This, in addition to better planning and forecasting allowed us to reduce our new order turnarounds from four to five weeks to in by 10 a.m. out by 5 p.m. on the same day.

By the time I had been employed at ABC for four months, I realized that members from other departments were coming to me and asking me to relay messages to the shop employees. When I asked why they were delegating this task to me, they stated that I spoke the same language as the shop employees. Increasingly, I became the messenger for the office to shop floor communication.

One morning, George called me into his office and complimented me on the level of customer service and the improvements that had been achieved. As we talked, I mentioned that we could not have done it without John's help. "He really knows his stuff, and he is good," I said. I suggested that we consider him for some type of promotion.

Also, I hoped that this would be a positive gesture that would improve communication between the office and shop floor.

George turned and pulled a flyer out of his desk; "Here's a management skills seminar. Do you think we should send John to it?"

"That's a great idea," I exclaimed, "Perhaps it would be good if he were to receive the news from you directly, George." George agreed, and after discussing some other issues, we departed company.

That afternoon, John came into my office, upset and ready to quit. "After all my effort and work, you guys are sending me for training seminars. So, am I not good enough for you?"

Discussion Questions

1. What barriers to effective communication existed in ABC Limited? How did the author deal with these? What would you do differently?

2. Identify and discuss why John was upset at the end of the case. What do you recommend the writer should do then?

TEAM EXERCISE 11.2

ANALYZING THE ELECTRONIC GRAPEVINE

Purpose This exercise is designed to help you understand the dynamics of grapevine communication.

Instructions This activity is usually conducted in between classes as a homework assignment. The instructor will divide the class into teams (although this activity can also be conducted by individuals). Each team will be assigned a large organization that has active posting on electronic grapevine Web sites such as Vault.com.

During the assignment, each team reads through recent postings of messages about the organization. Based on these raw comments, the team should be prepared to answer the following questions in the next class (or whenever the exercise will be debriefed in class):

1. What are the main topics in recent postings about this organization? Are they mostly good or bad news? Why?

2. To what extent do these postings seem to present misinformation or conflicting information?

3. Should corporate leaders intervene in these rumours? If so, how?

TEAM EXERCISE 11.3

TINKER TOY COMMUNICATION

Purpose This exercise is designed to help you understand the importance of media richness and related issues that affect communicating effectively.

Materials This activity requires one student on each team to have a cellular telephone that he/she is willing to use for this exercise. Alternatively, in-house land-line telephones or walkie-talkies may be used. The instructor will provide each team with a set of pieces from Tinker Toy, Lego, Mega Blocks, straws, or other materials suitable for building. Each pair of teams must have identical pieces in shape, size, and colour. This activity also requires either two large rooms or one large room and a few smaller rooms.

Instructions

■ *Step 1:* The instructor will divide the class into an even number of teams, each with 4 to 5 students. Teams should have the same number of members where possible. Remaining students can serve as observers. Teams are paired (e.g.,

Team 1A, with Team 1B, Team 2A with Team 2B, etc.) and each team in the pair receives the identical set of building materials as the other. For example, Team 1A would have the same set of materials as Team 1B. Teams should check their materials to be sure the paired team has identical pieces. Each team must have a member with a cellular telephone. Each team should have the telephone number of its paired team.

- *Step 2:* The "A" teams in each pair are moved to another room near the class (or to several small rooms) while the "B" teams remain in the classroom. Ideally, each team would be assigned to its own small tutorial room with paired teams located beside each other. In most classes, the instructor would have only two rooms, with one team from each pair in each room.

- *Step 3:* The "A" teams build a sculpture using *all* of the pieces provided. The instructor will set a time limit for this construction (typically about 10 minutes). The "B" teams are located in another room and must not observe this construction. Ideally, the "A" team's structure should be able to be moved into the classroom at the end of the exercise.

- *Step 4:* When the "A" team members have completed their structure, the "B" team members try to replicate the "A" team's structure would seeing it. The "A" team telephones the corresponding "B" team and verbally describes the structure over the telephone. Only one person from each team may communicate with the other team throughout this exercise. However, the "B" Team communicator would convey the message to other "B" Team members who are building the replicated structure. The instructor will limit the time allowed for the "B" team to replicate the structure (about 15 minutes).

- *Step 5:* If the "A" team structures are sturdy enough, they should be brought into the classroom and placed beside the "B" team's replication. The class might want to rate each replication for its similarity to the original structure. The class will then discuss the factors that influence communication in this situation, including the importance of communication media, language, and perceptions.

© 2001 Steven L. McShane. This is a variation of an exercise discussed in C. Olofson, "Monster Board Has Fun," *Fast Company*, Issue 16 (August 1998), p. 50.

TEAM EXERCISE 11.4

A NOT-SO-TRIVIAL CROSS-CULTURAL COMMUNICATION GAME

Purpose This exercise is designed to develop and test your knowledge of cross-cultural differences in communication and etiquette.

Materials The instructor will provide one set of question/answer cards to each pair of teams.

Instructions

- *Step 1:* The class is divided into an even number of teams. Ideally, each team would have three students. (Two or four student teams are possible if matched with an equal-sized team.) Each team is then paired with another team and the paired teams (team "A" and Team "B") are assigned a private space away from other matched teams.

- *Step 2:* The instructor will hand each pair of teams a stack of cards with the multiple choice questions face down. These cards have questions and answers about cross-cultural differences in communication and etiquette. No books or other aids are allowed.

- *Step 3:* The exercise begins with a member of Team A picking up one card from the top of the pile and asking the question on that card to both people on Team B. The information given to Team B includes the question and all alternatives listed on the card. Team B has 30 seconds after the question and alternatives have been read to give an answer. Team B earns one point if the correct answer is given. If Team B's answer is incorrect, however, Team A earns that point. Correct answers to each question are indicated on the card and, of course, should not be revealed until the question is correctly answered or time is up. Whether or not Team B answers correctly, it picks up the next card on the pile and asks it of members of Team A. In other words, cards are read alternatively to each team. This procedure is repeated until all the cards have been read or time has elapsed. The team receiving the most points wins.

Important note: The textbook provides very little information pertaining to the questions in this exercise. Rather, you must rely on past learning, logic, and luck to win.

© 2001 Steven L. McShane.

SELF-ASSESSMENT EXERCISE 11.5

ACTIVE LISTENING SKILLS INVENTORY

Purpose This self-assessment is designed to help you estimate your strengths and weaknesses on various dimensions of active listening

Instructions Think back to face-to-face conversations you have had with a co-worker or client in the office, hallway, factory floor, or other setting. Indicate the extent to which each item describes your behaviour during those conversations. Answer each item as truthfully as possible so you get an accurate estimate of where your active listening skills need improvement. Then use the scoring key in Appendix B to calculate your results for each scale. This exercise is completed alone so students can assess themselves honestly without concerns of social comparison. However, class discussion will focus on the important elements of active listening.

Circle the best response to the right that indicates the extent to which each statement describes you when listening to others.

Score

1. I keep an open mind about the speaker's point of view until he/she has finished talking. — Not at all — A little — Somewhat — Very much — _____

2. While listening, I mentally sort out the speaker's ideas in a way that makes sense to me. — Not at all — A little — Somewhat — Very much — _____

3. I stop the speaker and give my opinion when I disagree with something he/she has said. — Not at all — A little — Somewhat — Very much — _____

4. People can often tell when I'm not concentrating on what they are saying. — Not at all — A little — Somewhat — Very much — _____

5. I don't evaluate what a person is saying until he/she has finished talking. — Not at all — A little — Somewhat — Very much — _____

6. When someone takes a long time to present a simple idea, I let my mind wander to other things. — Not at all — A little — Somewhat — Very much — _____

7. I jump into conversations to present my views rather than wait and risk forgetting what I wanted to say. — Not at all — A little — Somewhat — Very much — _____

8. I nod my head and make other gestures to show I'm interested in the conversation. — Not at all — A little — Somewhat — Very much — _____

9. I can usually keep focused on what people are saying to me even when they don't sound interesting. — Not at all — A little — Somewhat — Very much — _____

10. Rather than organize the speaker's ideas, I usually expect the person to summarize them for me. — Not at all — A little — Somewhat — Very much — _____

11. I always say things like "I see" or "uh-huh" so people know that I'm really listening to them. — Not at all — A little — Somewhat — Very much — _____

12. While listening, I concentrate on what is being said and regularly organize the information. — Not at all — A little — Somewhat — Very much — _____

13. While the speaker is talking, I quickly determine whether I like or dislike his/her ideas. — Not at all — A little — Somewhat — Very much — _____

14. I pay close attention to what people are saying even when they are explaining something I already know. — Not at all — A little — Somewhat — Very much — _____

15. I don't give my opinion until I'm sure the other person has finished talking. — Not at all — A little — Somewhat — Very much — _____

After studying the preceding material, be sure to check out our Online Learning Centre at

www.mcgrawhill.ca/college/mcshane

for more in-depth information and interactivities that correspond to this chapter.

CHAPTER 12

Power and Influence in the Workplace

Learning Objectives

AFTER READING THIS CHAPTER, YOU SHOULD BE ABLE TO:

- Define the meaning of power and counterpower.

- Describe the five bases of power in organizations.

- Explain how information relates to power in organizations.

- Discuss the four contingencies of power.

- Explain how romantic relationships relate to power dynamics in organizations.

- Summarize the eight types of influence tactics.

- Discuss three contingencies to consider when deciding which influence tactic to use.

- Distinguish influence from organizational politics.

- Describe the organizational conditions and personal characteristics that support organizational politics.

- Identify ways to minimize organizational politics.

As a corporate road warrior, Jane Buckley knows that she needs to take more than her suitcase and computer on important business trips. The corporate director of strategic solutions for Compass Group, the Vancouver-based food services management provider, also carries one of the most important business tools: her golf clubs. "Our company cares who it does business with and likes to establish long-term relationships with clients," explains Buckley. "Golf is one way of establishing those personal connections."

Canadians play over 64 million rounds of golf each year, and many of those sessions result in valuable business connections and deals. Traditionally, men have done most of this networking, but women are now developing their golfing skills to assist their power and influence in organizations. "Women should be aware of where the networking is happening, and if they do feel that a lot of connections and networking with people are happening on the links, then by all means get involved with that," advises Sharon Crozier, director of the University of Calgary's Counselling & Student Development Centre.

Judith MacBride, director of human resources management research for the Conference Board of Canada, agrees. "We've heard so many times that a lot of business, a lot of networking and deal-making, gets done on the golf course," she says. The Conference Board of Canada's research indicates that many women feel their career success has been restricted because they are not on the golf course with their male colleagues. This is consistent with a U.S. survey reporting that almost 50 percent of women in senior executive positions say that exclusion from informal networks is a major barrier to the career advancement of women. More startling was that only 15 percent of male CEOs saw this as a problem. In other words, male CEOs fail to see that networking is one of the main reasons why women are held back in their careers.[1] ■

www.compassgroupcanada.hcareers.ca

Jayne Buckley, an executive with Compass Group in Vancouver, travels with her golf clubs to support the power of networking with colleagues and clients. *C. Price, Vancouver Province*

Golfing might not be the first thing that comes to mind when discussing organizational power and influence. Yet playing golf and engaging in other informal networks can make a difference to an individual's career progress and, in some cases, their ability to fulfill job duties. The reality is that no one escapes from organizational power and influence. They exist in every business and, according to some writers, in every decision and action.[2]

This chapter unfolds as follows: First, we define power and present a basic model depicting the dynamics of power in organizational settings. We then discuss the five bases of power, as well as information as a power base. Next, we look at the contingencies needed to translate those sources into meaningful power. Our discussion of power finishes with a look at recent studies on how office romances complicate power dynamics in organizations. The latter part of the chapter examines the various types of influence in organizational settings, as well as the contingencies of effective influence strategies. The final section of this chapter looks at the distinction between influence and organizational politics, as well as ways of minimizing dysfunctional politics.

THE MEANING OF POWER

power
The capacity of a person, team, or organization to influence others.

counterpower
The capacity of a person, team, or organization to keep a more powerful person or group in the exchange relationship.

Power is the capacity of a person, team, or organization to influence others.[3] Power is not the act of changing others' attitudes or behaviour; it is only the *potential* to do so. People frequently have power they do not use; they might not even know they have power.

The most basic prerequisite of power is that one person or group believes it is dependent on another person or group for something of value.[4] This relationship is shown in Exhibit 12.1, where Person A has power over Person B because Person A controls something that Person B needs to achieve his or her goals. You might have power over others by controlling a desired job assignment, useful information, important resources, or even the privilege of being associated with you! To make matters more complex, power is ultimately a perception, so people might gain power simply by convincing others that they have something of value. Thus, power exists when others believe that you control resources that they want.[5]

Although power requires dependence, it is really more accurate to say that the parties are *interdependent*. One party may be more dependent than the other, but the relationship exists only when both parties have something of value to offer the other. Exhibit 12.1 shows a dotted line to illustrate the weaker party's (Person B's) power over the dominant participant (Person A). This **counterpower,** as it is

EXHIBIT 12.1

Dependence in the power relationship

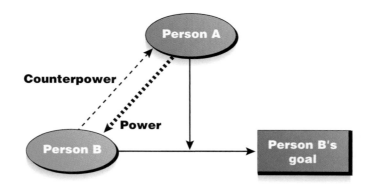

known, is strong enough to maintain Person A's participation in the exchange relationship. For example, executives have power over subordinates by controlling their job security and promotional opportunities. At the same time, employees have counterpower because they can control their ability to work productively, thereby creating a positive impression of the supervisor to his or her boss. Counterpower usually motivates executives to apply their power judiciously, so the relationship is not broken.

A Model of Power in Organizations

Power involves more than just dependence. As we see in Exhibit 12.2, the model of power includes both power sources and contingencies. It indicates that power is derived from five sources: legitimate, reward, coercive, expert, and referent. The model also shows that these sources yield power only under certain conditions. The four contingencies of power include the employee's or department's substitutability, centrality, discretion, and visibility. Finally, as we will discuss later, the type of power applied affects the type of influence the powerholder has over the other person or work unit.

SOURCES OF POWER IN ORGANIZATIONS

Over 40 years ago, French and Raven listed five sources of power within organizations: legitimate, reward, coercive, expert, and referent.[6] Many researchers have studied these five power bases and searched for others, but for the most part, French and Raven's list remains intact.[7] The first three power bases are derived from the powerholder's position; that is, the person receives these power bases because of the specific authority or roles they are assigned in the organization. The latter two sources of power originate from the powerholder's own characteristics. In other words, that person brings those power bases to the organization.[8]

legitimate power
The capacity to influence others through formal authority.

Legitimate Power

Legitimate power is an *agreement* among organizational members that people in certain roles can request certain behaviours of others. This perceived right comes partly from formal job descriptions and partly from informal rules of conduct.

Used with permission of Rapid Phase Group, www.madameve.co.sa

A model of power within organizations

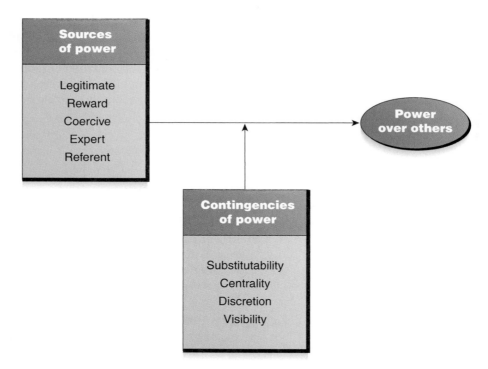

Executives have considerable legitimate power, but all employees also have this power, based on company rules and government laws.[9] For example, an organization might give employees the right to request customer files if this information is required for their job.

Legitimate power depends on more than job descriptions. It also depends on mutual agreement from those expected to abide by this authority. Your boss's power to make you work overtime depends partly on you agreeing to this power. Classic stories of shipboard mutinies, such as *The Caine Mutiny* and *Mutiny on the Bounty*, illustrate this point. Today, employees question their boss's right to make them stay late, perform unsafe tasks, and other activities. Thus, legitimate power is a person's authority to make discretionary decisions as long as his or her followers accept that discretion.[10]

People in high power distance cultures (i.e. those who accept an unequal distribution of power—see Chapter 2) are more likely to comply with legitimate power than are people in low power distance cultures. Legitimate power is also stronger in some organizations than in others. A 3M scientist might continue to work on a project after being told by superiors to stop working on it, because the 3M culture supports an entrepreneurial spirit, which includes ignoring your boss's authority from time to time.[11]

More generally, employees are becoming less tolerant of legitimate power. They increasingly expect to be involved in decisions rather than being told what to do. "People won't tolerate the command-and-control mode," says Bank of Montreal CEO Tony Comper.[12] Thus, the command style of leadership that often guided employee behaviour in the past must be replaced by other forms, particularly expert and referent power, which are described below.

The Caine Mutiny is a classic Pulitzer Prize-winning novel and film about the limits of legitimate power. Captain Queeg (Humphrey Bogart, seated centre) is a hard disciplinarian who shapes up the crew of the *Caine*, a battered minesweeper during World War II. However, Queeg's judgment and focus have been impaired by too much combat. After Queeg makes several critical mistakes and forces the crew to search for missing strawberries, some officers fear that their captain is a danger to himself and the crew. Sure enough, a beleaguered Queeg panics during a storm at sea, so two key officers—Lt. Keefer (Fred MacMurray, standing centre) and Lt. Maryk (Van Johnson, seated right)—stage a mutiny and assume command. The story illustrates how Queeg's orders and competence tested the limits of his legitimate power over crew members. What "mutinies" have you heard about in more recent organizational settings? What commands triggered employees to refuse to obey their boss? *Archive Photos Getty Images*

Reward Power

Reward power is derived from a person's ability to control the allocation of rewards valued by others and to remove negative sanctions (i.e. negative reinforcement). Managers have formal authority that gives them power over the distribution of organizational rewards such as pay, promotions, time off, vacation schedules, and work assignments. Employees also have reward power over their bosses through the use of 360 degree feedback systems (see Chapter 5). Employee feedback affects the supervisor's promotions and other rewards, so they tend to behave differently toward employees after 360-degree feedback is introduced.

Coercive Power

Coercive power is the ability to apply punishment. Managers have coercive power through their authority to reprimand, demote, and fire employees. Labour unions might use coercive power tactics, such as withholding services, to influence management in collective agreement negotiations. Team members sometimes apply sanctions, ranging from sarcasm to ostracism, to ensure that co-workers conform to team norms. Many firms rely on the coercive power of team members to control co-worker behaviour. For example, 44 percent of production employees at the CAMI automobile plant in Ingersoll, Ontario, believe that team members use coercive power to improve co-worker performance. One employee at a forge plant that relies on self-directed work teams sums up the use of peer pressure this way: "They say there are no bosses here, but if you screw up, you find one pretty fast!"[13]

Expert Power

For the most part, legitimate, reward, and coercive power originate from the position held by the person wielding the power. In contrast, *expert power* originates from within the person: it is an individual's or work unit's capacity to influence others by possessing knowledge or skills that they value. Employees are gaining expert power as our society moves from an industrial to a knowledge-based economy. The reason is that employee knowledge becomes the means of production, not some machine the owner controls. And without this control over production, owners are more dependent on employees to achieve their corporate objectives.

Referent Power

referent power
The capacity to influence others based on the identification and respect they have for the powerholder.

People have **referent power** when others identify with them, like them, or otherwise respect them. Like expert power, referent power comes from within the person. It is largely a function of that person's interpersonal skills and usually develops slowly. Referent power is usually associated with charismatic leadership. *Charisma* is often defined as a form of interpersonal attraction whereby followers develop a respect for and trust in the charismatic individual.[14]

Information and Power

Information is power.[15] This phrase is increasingly relevant in a knowledge-based economy. Information power derives from either the legitimate or expert sources of power described above and exists in two forms: (a) control over the flow and interpretation of information given to others and (b) the perceived ability to cope with organizational uncertainties.

Control over information flow   SAP, the German business-software company, recently introduced a communications system that broadcasts the latest company news on the car radios of SAP employees, through its intranet site, and in regular e-mails sent directly from SAP's chairman. SAP employees appreciate this direct communication. However, the company's middle managers have objected to these initiatives because they undermine their power as the gatekeepers of company information.[16] Traditionally, SAP's middle managers have been communication "traffic cops." Their job was to distribute, regulate, and filter out information throughout the organizational hierarchy. This right to control information flow is a form of legitimate power and is most common in highly bureaucratic firms. The wheel formation in Exhibit 12.3 depicts this highly centralized control over information flow. The information gatekeeper in the middle of this configuration—such as the middle managers at SAP—can influence others through the amount, type, and quality of information they receive.

EXHIBIT 12.3

Power through the control of information

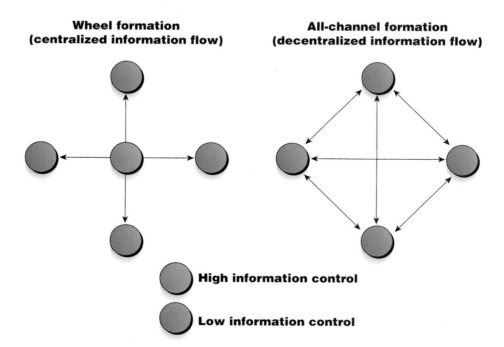

**Wheel formation
(centralized information flow)**

**All-channel formation
(decentralized information flow)**

High information control

Low information control

The problem facing these information gatekeepers is that this centralized information control structure is incompatible with knowledge management and team-based organizations. Consequently, SAP and other organizations are encouraging more knowledge sharing by moving toward the all-channel communication structure (see Exhibit 12.3) in which all employees have relatively equal access to information. This allows employees and self-directed work teams to make better decisions. In its purest form, the all-channel network may seem chaotic, so large organizations with bureaucratic cultures tend to slip back into the wheel pattern. The wheel pattern also re-emerges because, as we saw at SAP, it confers more power on those who distribute the information.[17]

Coping with uncertainty   Not many people have the job of "coolhunter." But that's what Keith Whitham does at Bozell Worldwide Canada Inc. Whitham is a strategic planner in the Toronto ad agency's future-planning department. His job is to spot "cool" consumer trends among people in various age groups. To do this, he spends most of his time absorbing magazines and newspapers, keeping an eye on the Internet, and talking to people. "You have to be an information junkie," Whitham explains, "but there is no substitute for getting out there among the people who make the buying decisions." Whitham's knowledge helps clients cope with the uncertainty of fads and longer-term shifts in buying behaviour. The danger of this work is the cost of a wrong prediction. "This is my calling, but heaven help me if I make the wrong call," says Whitham.[18]

Organizations operate in changing environments, so they depend on Keith Whitham and others who have the capacity to reduce the uncertainty of future events. The more firms can cope with the uncertainty of future events, the more easily they can achieve their goals.[19] Individuals and work units acquire power by helping the organization to cope with uncertainty. Coping includes any activity that effectively deals with environmental uncertainties affecting the organization. A groundbreaking study of Canadian breweries and container companies identified three general strategies to help organizations cope with uncertainty. These coping strategies are arranged in a hierarchy of importance, with the first being the most powerful:[20]

■ *Prevention*—The most effective strategy is to prevent environmental changes from occurring. For example, financial experts acquire power by preventing an organization from experiencing a cash shortage or defaulting on loans.
■ *Forecasting*—The next best strategy is to predict environmental changes or variations. In this respect, marketing specialists gain power by predicting changes in consumer preferences.
■ *Absorption*—People and work units also gain power by absorbing or neutralizing the impact of environmental shifts as they occur. An example is the ability of maintenance crews to come to the rescue when machines break down and the production process stops.

CONTINGENCIES OF POWER

Let's say you have expert power by virtue of your ability to forecast and possibly even prevent dramatic changes in the organization's environment. Does this expertise mean that you are influential? Not necessarily. As we saw earlier in Exhibit 12.2, power bases generate power only under certain conditions. The four conditions—called the contingencies of power—include substitutability, centrality, discretion, and visibility.[21] These are not sources of power; rather, they determine the extent to which people can leverage their power bases. You may have lots of expert power, but you won't be able to influence others with this power base if the contingency factors are not in place.

Substitutability

Substitutability refers to the availability of alternatives. Power is strongest when someone has a monopoly over a valued resource. Conversely, power decreases as the number of alternative sources of the critical resource increases. Substitutability refers to substitutions of the resource itself, not only to other sources that offer the resource. For instance, labour unions are weakened when companies introduce technologies that replace the need for their union members. At one time, a strike by telephone employees would have shut down operations, but computerized systems and other technological innovations now ensure that telephone operations continue during labour strikes and reduce the need for telephone operators during normal operations. Technology is a substitute for employees and, consequently, reduces union power.

How do people and work units increase their power through nonsubstitutability? There are several ways, although not all of them are ethical. We describe some of them here for your information—not necessarily for you to practise.

- *Controlling tasks*—Professions have legislation that prevents outsiders from performing certain tasks within their domain. Lawyers keep paralegals out of certain activities, and doctors keep nurses, midwives, and others away from certain interventions. Government laws require public corporations to use the services of chartered accountants in audits.
- *Controlling knowledge*—Professions control access to the knowledge of their work domain, such as through restricted enrollment in educational programs. Knowledge is also restricted on the job. Several years ago, maintenance workers in a French tobacco processing plant became very powerful because they controlled the knowledge required to repair the tobacco machines.[22] The maintenance manuals had mysteriously disappeared and the machines had been redesigned enough so that only the maintenance staff knew how to fix them if they broke down (which they often did). Knowing the power of nonsubstitutability, maintenance staff carefully avoided documenting the repair procedures and didn't talk to production employees about their trade knowledge.
- *Controlling labour*—People gain power by controlling the availability of their labour. Labour unions attempt to organize as many people as possible within a particular trade or industry so that employers have no other source of labour supply.[23] When unionized workers produce almost all of a particular product or service in a society, then the union has an easier time increasing wages. The union's power during a strike is significantly weakened when the employer can continue production through outside contractors or other non-union facilities.
- *Differentiation*—Differentiation occurs when an individual or work unit claims to have a unique resource—such as raw materials or knowledge—that the organization would want. By definition, the uniqueness of this resource means that no one else has it. The tactic here isn't so much the nonsubstitutability of the resource, but making organizational leaders believe that the resource is unique.

Some people claim that consultants use this tactic. They take skills and knowledge that many consulting firms can provide and wrap them into a package (with the latest buzz words, of course) so that it looks like a service no one else can offer.

Centrality

centrality
The degree and nature of interdependence between the powerholder and others.

While most airline employees have been restless for wage increases after years of modest gains, pilots have the most power to negotiate pay increases. "They have such power because they can ground the airline and in a couple of weeks it will have lost its profits for the entire year," says an airline investment analyst in London.[24] Airline pilots have considerable power because of their **centrality** in the organization. Centrality refers to the degree and nature of interdependence between the powerholder and others.[25] Airline pilots have high centrality because (a) their actions affect many people and (b) their actions quickly affect other people. Think about your own centrality for a moment: If you decided not to show up for work or school tomorrow, how many people would be affected, and how much time would pass before they were affected? If you have high centrality, most people in the organization would be adversely affected by your absence, and they would be affected quickly.

City of Toronto employees picked an ideal time to leverage their power by going on strike in early summer, 2002. Tourism and the recreation of city residents were immediately affected by closed public swimming pools and cancelled Toronto Islands ferry services. The Pope's visit in mid-summer also put pressure on government officials to end the strike quickly. But the biggest factor was undoubtedly the stench of garbage that permeated the city. Without garbage collection, illegal dumps sprang up, and the heat of summer made living in Toronto a nightmare to many residents. "I can smell this through two doors, air conditioning, cologne and my own gym socks," quipped one resident. "I thought there was nothing stinkier than my gym socks. I was really wrong."[26] What contingencies of power gave the City of Toronto employees so much power in this strike? *CP/Kevin Frayer*
www.city.toronto.on.ca

Discretion

The freedom to exercise judgment—to make decisions without referring to a specific rule or receiving permission from someone else—is another important contingency of power in organizations. Consider the plight of first-line supervisors. It may seem that they have legitimate power over employees, but this power is often curtailed by specific rules. They must administer programs developed from above and follow specific procedures in their implementation. They administer rewards and punishments, but must abide by precise rules regarding their distribution. Indeed, supervisors are often judged not on their discretionary skills, but on their ability to follow prescribed rules and regulations. This lack of discretion makes supervisors largely powerless even though they may have access to some of the power bases described earlier in this chapter. "Middle managers are very much 'piggy-in-the-middle'," complains a middle manager at Britain's National Health System. "They have little power, only what senior managers are allowed to give them."[27]

Visibility

Power does not flow to unknown people in the organization. Those with valuable knowledge or higher authority will yield power only when others are aware of these power bases. Only when a person's or work unit's source of power is visible—when it is known to others—will that source of power be meaningful.[28] One way to increase visibility is to take people-oriented jobs and work on projects that require frequent interaction with senior executives. "You can take visibility in steps," advises Kerstin Schultz, senior director of Global Operations at the pharmaceutical firm Searle. "You can start by making yourself visible in a small group, such as a staff meeting. Then when you're comfortable with that, seek out larger arenas."[29]

Employees also gain visibility by being, quite literally, visible. Some people strategically take offices or cubicles where co-workers pass most often (such as closest to the elevator or office lunch room). Many professionals display their educational diplomas and awards on office walls to remind visitors of their expertise.[30] Other people play the game of "face time"—spending more time at work and showing that they are working productively. One female engineer working on a colour laser printer project made a habit of going to the office once each week at 2 a.m., after her boss once saw her working at that hour. "[A]fter the reaction I got from my manager I decided it was important to do that early morning work in the office," explains the engineer. "It is better to be seen here if you are going to work in the middle of the night."[31]

Another way to increase visibility is through **mentoring**—the process of learning the ropes of organizational life from a senior person within the company. Mentors give protégés more visible and meaningful work opportunities, and open doors for them to meet more senior people in the organization. Mentors also teach these newcomers influence tactics that are supported by the organization's senior decision makers.[32]

mentoring
The process of learning the ropes of organizational life from a senior person with the company.

Networking and Power

The opening vignette to this chapter introduced the notion that golfing—or other venues for informal networking—can make a difference in your career. This reflects the often-heard statement: "It's not what you know, but who you know that counts!" In other words, employees get ahead not just by developing their competencies. They also need to engage in **networking**—cultivating social relationships with others to accomplish their goals.

Networking increases a person's power in three ways.[33] First, networks consist of people who trust each other, which increases the flow of information among those within the network. The more you network, the more likely you will receive valuable information that increases your expert power in the organization. Second, people tend to identify more with partners within their own networks, which increases referent power among people within each network. This network-based referent power may lead to more favourable decisions by others in the network.

Finally, networking increases a person's visibility, and, possibly, centrality, which are important contingencies of power. Networkers are better known in the organization, so their talents are more readily recognized. One recent study also found that networkers with high self-monitoring personalities tend to locate themselves in strategic positions in informal networks, so they can gain centrality.[34] For example, you might be regarded as the main person who distributes

networking
Cultivating social relationships with others to accomplish one's goals.

information in the network, or who keeps the network connected through informal gatherings.

Networking is a natural part of the informal organization, yet it can create a formidable barrier to those who are not actively connected to it.[35] As the opening vignette to this chapter indicated, women are excluded from powerful networks because they do not participate in golf games and other male-dominated social events. That's what Deloitte & Touche executives discovered when they investigated why so many junior female recruits left the accounting and consulting firm before reaching partnership level. Deloitte & Touche now relies on mentoring, formal women's network groups, and measuring career progress to ensure that female staff members have the same career development opportunities as their male colleagues.[36]

Office Romance and Power

Most contemporary workplaces employ almost as many women as men. They work long hours together, often on collaborative projects requiring frequent interaction. The long days also make it more difficult to meet people outside the workplace. It's little wonder that so many romantic relationships today are started in the workplace. A few recent surveys have estimated that over 40 percent of employees in Canada and other countries have dated a co-worker. One poll also found that one-quarter of Canadian employees say they have had intimate relations with a co-worker.[37]

The problem with this trend is that office romances don't mix very well with organizational power. One concern is that co-workers tend to think one or both employees in the relationship abuse their power by favouring each other, particularly where one person in the relationship has higher status. Almost 70 percent of employees in one recent survey said they dislike workplace romances between supervisors and subordinates because they can foster favouritism.[38]

A more serious concern is that nearly one-quarter of sexual harassment cases result from workplace romances that went sour.[39] "A lot of sexual harassment complaints result from consensual relationships that went bad," advises a lawyer who specializes in sexual harassment cases. "One of them decides to break it off. The other continues to pursue and it becomes something other than consensual, and the person claims he or she is being sexually harassed."[40] The risk of sexual harassment is potentially greater in a supervisor-subordinate relationship. If the subordinate ends the relationship, the supervisor might create a hostile work environment through subtle day-to-day decisions. Even when the jilted supervisor acts appropriately, the subordinate may still feel intimidated by the former partner's power over work and career decisions.

INFLUENCING OTHERS

influence
Any behaviour that attempts to alter another person's attitudes or behaviour.

So far, we have focused on the sources and contingencies of power. But power is only the *capacity* to influence others. It is the potential to change someone's attitudes and behaviour. **Influence**, on the other hand, refers to any *behaviour* that actually attempts to alter someone's attitudes or behaviour.[41] Influence is power in motion. It applies one or more power bases to get people to alter their beliefs, feelings, and activities. Consequently, our interest in the remainder of this chapter is in how people use power to influence others.

Influence tactics are woven through the social fabric of all organizations. This is because influence is an essential process through which people coordinate their efforts and act in concert to achieve organizational objectives. Some experts say that influencing others on matters of organizational value is central to the definition of leadership (see Chapter 14).[42] Influence operates down, across, and up the corporate hierarchy; executives ensure that subordinates complete required tasks; employees influence co-workers to help them with their job requirements; and subordinates engage in upward influence tactics so corporate leaders can make decisions compatible with subordinates' needs and expectations.

Types of Influence Tactics

Organizational behaviour scholars have devoted considerable attention to the various types of influence tactics found in organizational settings. Unfortunately, they do not agree on a definitive list of influence tactics. A groundbreaking study 25 years ago identified eight main influence strategies, but recent evidence suggests that some of these strategies overlap.[43] The original list also seems to have a Western bias that ignores influence tactics used in non-Western cultures.[44] With these caveats in mind, let's look at the following influence tactics identified in the most recent literature (see Exhibit 12.4): silent authority, assertiveness, exchange, coalition formation, upward appeal, ingratiation and impression management, persuasion, and information control.

Silent authority   The silent application of authority occurs when someone complies with a request because of the requester's legitimate power as well as the target person's role expectations. A common example occurs when you comply with your boss's request to complete a particular task. If the task is within your job scope and your boss has the right to make this request, then this influence strategy operates without negotiation, threats, persuasion, or other tactics.

EXHIBIT 12.4   Types of influence tactics in organizations

Influence Tactic	Description
Silent authority	Influencing behaviour through legitimate power without explicitly referring to that power base
Assertiveness	Actively applying legitimate and coercive power through pressure or threats
Exchange	Promising benefits or resources in exchange for the target person's compliance
Coalition formation	Forming a group that attempts to influence others by pooling the resources and power of its members
Upward appeal	Gaining support from one or more people with higher authority or expertise
Ingratiation/impression management	Attempting to increase liking by, or perceived similarity to, some targeted person
Persuasion	Using logical arguments, factual evidence, and emotional appeals to convince people of the value of a request
Information control	Explicitly manipulating someone else's access to information for the purpose of changing their attitudes and/or behaviour

Some scholars overlook silent authority as an influence strategy, but it is the most common form of influence in high power distance cultures. Employees comply with supervisor requests without question because they respect the supervisor's higher authority in the organization. Silent authority also occurs when leaders influence subordinates through role modelling. One study reported that Japanese managers typically influence subordinates by engaging in the behaviours they want employees to mimic.[45]

Assertiveness   In contrast to silent authority, assertiveness might be called "vocal authority" because it involves actively applying legitimate and coercive power to influence others. Assertiveness includes persistently reminding the target of his or her obligations, frequently checking the target's work, confronting the target, and using threats of sanctions to force compliance. Assertiveness typically applies or threatens to apply punishment if the target does not comply. Explicit or implicit threats range from job loss to losing face by letting down the team. Extreme forms of assertiveness include blackmailing colleagues, for instance, threatening to reveal the other person's previously unknown failures unless he or she complies with your request.

Exchange   Exchange activities involve the promise of benefits or resources in exchange for the target person's compliance with your request. This tactic also includes reminding the target of past benefits or favours with the expectation that the target person will now make up for that debt. The *norm of reciprocity* is a central and explicit theme in exchange strategies. According to the norm of reciprocity, individuals are expected to help those who have helped them.[46] Negotiation, which we discuss more fully in Chapter 13, is also an integral part of exchange influence activities. For instance, you might negotiate with your boss for a day off in return for working a less desirable shift at a future date.

Earlier in this chapter, we looked at networking as a way to increase your power. Networking is also an exchange influence strategy because it tends to build up exchange credits. Active networkers help colleagues in the short term because it may prove valuable in the future. Networking nurtures allies and sponsors, thereby making it easier to get approval for projects and other initiatives later on.

coalition
A group that attempts to influence people outside the group by pooling the resources and power of its members.

Coalition formation   When people lack sufficient power alone to influence others in the organization, they might form a **coalition** of people who support the proposed change. A coalition is influential in three ways. First, it pools the power and resources of many people, so the coalition potentially has more influence than if each person operated alone. Second, by symbolizing the legitimacy of the issue, the coalition's mere existence can be a source of power. In other words, a coalition creates a sense that the issue deserves attention because it has broad support.[47] Third, coalitions tap into the power of the social identity process introduced in Chapter 3. A coalition is essentially an informal group that advocates a new set of norms and behaviours. If the coalition has a broad-based membership (i.e. its members come from various parts of the organization), then other employees are more likely to identify with that group and, consequently, accept the ideas the coalition is proposing.[48]

Consider the following example: Cindy Casselman, a Xerox communications manager, applied a coalition influence strategy on her boss to gain support for an intranet system (called WebBoard). When her boss rejected her initial request for

WebBoard, Casselman quietly assembled a coalition of people who would benefit from this intranet system. The informal group included an executive who wanted an intranet site to test his unit's work on virtual document delivery systems and another executive who wanted WebBoard to showcase Xerox's new networked PCs. With these and other supporters, Casselman's boss had no choice but to allow and partially fund the initiative. Casselman's coalition concentrated the power of several people and symbolized popular support for her WebBoard initiative.[49]

Upward appeal   Have you ever had a disagreement with a colleague in which one of you eventually says, "I'm sure the boss (or teacher) will agree with me on this. Let's find out!" This tactic—called **upward appeal**—is a form of coalition in which one or more members is someone with higher authority or expertise. Upward appeal ranges from a formal alliance to the perception of informal support from someone with higher authority or expertise. Upward appeal also includes relying on the authority of the firm as an entity without approaching anyone further up the hierarchy. For instance, one study reported that Japanese managers remind employees of their obligation to support the organization's objectives.[50] By reminding the target that your request is consistent with the organization's overarching goals, you are implying support from senior executives without formally involving anyone with higher authority in the situation.

upward appeal
A type of coalition in which one or more members is someone with higher authority or expertise.

Ingratiation and impression management   Upward appeals, assertiveness, and coalitions are somewhat (or very!) forceful ways to influence other people. At the opposite extreme is a "soft" influence tactic called **ingratiation**. Ingratiation includes any attempt to increase liking by, or perceived similarity to, some targeted person.[51] Flattering your boss in front of others, helping co-workers with their work, exhibiting similar attitudes (e.g., agreeing with your boss's proposal to change company policies), and seeking the other person's counsel (e.g., asking for their "expert" advice) are all examples of ingratiation. Ingratiation is potentially influential because it increases the perceived similarity of the source of ingratiation to the target person. This similarity causes the target person to form more favourable opinions of the ingratiator. For example, if you ingratiate your boss, he or she is more likely to notice your good performance and attribute any performance problems to the situation rather than to your ability or motivation.

ingratiation
Any attempt to increase the extent to which a target person likes us or perceives that he or she is similar to us.

Notice that many ingratiation tactics are desirable behaviours that relate to organizational citizenship and information sharing.[52] However, people who are obvious in their ingratiation risk losing any influence because their behaviours are considered insincere and self-serving. The terms "apple polishing" and "brown-nosing" are applied to those who ingratiate to excess. This explains why some studies report that people who engage in ingratiation are less likely to get promoted.[53]

Ingratiation is part of a larger influence tactic known as impression management. **Impression management** is the practice of actively shaping our public images.[54] Many impression management activities are done routinely to satisfy the basic norms of social behaviour, such as the way we dress and how we behave toward colleagues and customers.[55] Other impression management tactics are done deliberately. An extreme example of impression management occurs when people pad their résumés. One study of 1.86 million background checks by a reference checking firm revealed that about 25 percent of applicants falsify information about work experience and education.[56] GLOBAL Connections 12.1 describes an extreme example of impression management by a technology entrepreneur in Singapore.

impression management
The practice of actively shaping our public images.

Taking Impression Management to the Extreme

By any standard, Dennis Lee's résumé is impressive. The 29-year-old co-founder of elipva, a Singapore high-technology start-up firm, says he is a renowned artificial intelligence researcher, the author of several books, and the recipient of numerous awards. One press release from elipva proudly announced that Lee and MIT professor Andersen Dula had won the "Innovator 2000 Award" from the Massachusetts Institute of Technology and AT&T.

Another press release stated that Lee had won a Stanford University award in connection with Pattie Maes, a renowned MIT researcher in the field of intelligent agents. A third announcement said that Lee had received a rare artificial intelligence award sponsored by the prestigious American Association for Artificial Intelligence (AAAI) and Stanford University. A photo of the AAAI award appeared on Lee's personal Web site. Lee's résumé also lists books he wrote, published by well-known publishers. Copies of at least one of these volumes were distributed to the media.

The problem with Dennis Lee's résumé is that it was an elaborate misrepresentation. MIT Media Labs couldn't find any Andersen Dula and the school didn't hand out an innovation award to Lee. MIT intelligent agents researcher Pattie Maes does exist, but she did not collaborate with Lee on any work. Lee's books looked homemade and carried incorrect publisher names, although no one noticed when copies were distributed. Soon after firing Lee for these falsehoods, elipva also reported that some of Mr Lee's published writings had been copied from other sources with no credit given.

Lee hasn't explained why he fabricated his past to such an extreme, but his mastery of impression management certainly worked effectively, for a while. These

High-tech entrepreneur Dennis Lee got carried away with impression management. *Straits Times (Singapore)*

imaginary achievements helped Lee gain recognition in the media, the venture capital community, and the Singapore Internet community. Lee became so respected that he was invited to speak at the Internet World Asia conference and was nominated as "Internet Visionary of the Year" at the Internet World Asia Industry Awards.

Sources: J. Lien, "Some Vital Questions on elipva Still Unanswered," *Business Times (Singapore)*, June 5, 2001, p. 12; J. Jaucius, "Internet Guru's Credentials a True Work of Fiction," *Ottawa Citizen*, June 12, 2001; W.F. Tang, "Technopreneur Sacked, Probe Confirms Fraud," *Business Times (Singapore)*, May 24, 2001, pp. 1, 2; "BT Search Sparks Probe," *Business Times (Singapore)*, May 20, 2001; J. Lien, "Technopreneur Suspended over Alleged Fake Claims," *Business Times (Singapore)*, May 19, 2001, pp. 1, 2; "Surprise MIT Award for S'porean," Straits Times (Singapore), November 28, 2000, p. 15.

www.elipva.com

---

persuasion

Using logical arguments, facts, and emotional appeals to encourage people to accept a request or message.

Persuasion **Persuasion** is one of the most common influence strategies in organizations, and is considered an important characteristic of leader effectiveness.[57] The literature on influence strategies has typically described persuasion as the use of reason through factual evidence and logical arguments. However, recent studies have begun to recognize that emotion is as important as logic in attitude and behaviour change.[58] Thus, persuasion involves using logical arguments, factual evidence, and emotional appeals to convince people that a request is practical and will result in positive outcomes.

The effectiveness of persuasion as an influence tactic depends on the characteristics of the persuader, message content, communication medium, and the audience being persuaded.[59] What makes one person more persuasive than another? One factor is the person's perceived expertise. Persuasion attempts are more successful when listeners believe the speaker is knowledgeable about the topic. People are also more persuasive when they demonstrate credibility, such as when the persuader does not seem to profit from the persuasion attempt and states a few points against his or her own position.[60]

Message content is more important than the messenger when the issue is important to the audience. Persuasive message content acknowledges several points of view so the audience does not feel cornered by the speaker.[61] The message should also be limited to a few strong arguments, which are repeated a couple of times, but not too often.[62] The message content should use emotional appeals (such as graphically showing the unfortunate consequences of a bad decision), but only in combination with logical arguments so the audience doesn't feel manipulated.[63] Also, emotional appeals should always be accompanied with specific recommendations to overcome the threat. Finally, message content is more persuasive when the audience is warned about opposing arguments. This **inoculation effect** causes listeners to generate counter-arguments to the anticipated persuasion attempts, which makes the opponent's subsequent persuasion attempts less effective.

Two other considerations when persuading people are the medium of communication used and the characteristics of the audience. Generally, persuasion works best in face-to-face conversations and through other media-rich communication channels. The personal nature of face-to-face communication increases the persuader's credibility, and the richness of this channel provides faster feedback, letting the persuader know that the influence strategy is working. Not everyone is influenced in the ways described above. It is more difficult to persuade people who have high self-esteem and whose attitudes (the ones you are trying to change) are strongly connected to their self-identity.[64]

Information control   Persuasion typically involves selectively presenting information, whereas information control involves explicitly manipulating someone else's *access* to information for the purpose of changing their attitudes and/or behaviour.[65] This tactic is quite common. One poll reported that almost one-half of British employees believe people keep their colleagues in the dark about work issues if it helps their own cause.[66] Information control is frequently used as an upward influence strategy through the process of filtering (see Chapter 11). Specifically, lower level employees screen out information flowing up the hierarchy so that higher level executives make decisions that are consistent with the preferences of lower level employees. Employees also engage in information control by organizing meeting agendas to suit their personal interests. For example, they might place a particular issue near the bottom of the agenda so the committee either doesn't get to it or is too fatigued to make a final judgment. Others arrange meetings so they control who attends.[67]

Contingencies of Influence Tactics

Research has generally found that "soft" tactics such as friendly persuasion and subtle ingratiation are more acceptable than "hard" tactics such as upward appeal and assertiveness.[68] Soft tactics rely on personal power bases (expert and referent power) which tend to build commitment to the influencer's request. For example, co-workers tend to "buy in" to your ideas when you apply effective ingratiation and impression management tactics or use persuasion based on expertise. In con-

inoculation effect

A persuasive communication strategy of warning listeners that others will try to influence them in the future and that they should be wary about the opponent's arguments.

trast, hard influence tactics rely on position power (legitimate, reward, and coercion) which tend to produce compliance or resistance in others. Hard tactics tend to undermine trust, which can hurt future relationships. For example, coalitions are often successful, but their effect may be limited when the group's forcefulness is threatening.[69]

Aside from the general preference for soft rather than hard tactics, the most appropriate influence strategy depends on a few contingencies. One consideration is the influencer's power base.[70] Those with expertise may be more successful using persuasion whereas those with a strong legitimate power base may be more successful applying silent authority. A related contingency is whether the person being influenced is higher, lower, or at the same level in the organization. Although employees have some legitimate power over their bosses, they may face adverse career consequences by being too assertive with this power. Similarly, it may be more acceptable for supervisors to control information access than for employees to control what information they distribute to co-workers and people at higher levels in the organization.

A third contingency is cultural values and expectations. Canadian managers and subordinates alike often rely on ingratiation because it minimizes conflict and supports a trusting relationship. In contrast, managers in Hong Kong and other high power distance cultures tend to rely less on ingratiation, possibly because this tactic disrupts the more distant roles that managers and employees expect in these cultures.[71] At the same time, exchange tactics tend to be more common and effective in Asian cultures than in Canada because the importance of interpersonal relationships ("guanxi") strengthens the norm of reciprocity.[72]

The appropriateness of various influence tactics has also changed with emerging employment relationships and the expectations of younger employees. Decentralizing authority, empowerment, and the increased emphasis on teams are challenging traditional applications of power through hierarchical control. Employees increasingly influence the organization's future, but without formal sources of legitimate, reward, and coercive power. Furthermore, employees are increasingly wary of leaders who rely exclusively on their formal sources of legitimate, reward, and coercive power. The result is the rising emphasis on more subtle influence tactics. Supervisors likely applied silent authority and assertiveness more a few decades ago than they do today because of these shifting expectations.[73]

Gender differences in influence tactics Men and women seem to differ in their use of influence tactics. Direct impression management tactics are apparently used more often by men than by women. Men are more likely to advertise their achievements and take personal credit for the successes of others reporting to them. Women are more reluctant to force the spotlight on themselves, preferring instead to share the credit with others. At the same time, women are more likely to apologize—personally take blame—even for problems they didn't cause. Men are more likely to assign blame and less likely to assume it.[74]

Some research suggests that women generally have difficulty exerting some forms of influence in organizations, and this has limited their promotional opportunities. In particular, women are viewed as *less* (not more) influential when they try to directly influence others by exerting their authority or expertise. In job interviews, for example, direct and assertive female job applicants were less likely to be hired than were male applicants using the same influence tactics. Similarly, women who directly disagreed in conversations were less influential than women who agreed with the speaker.[75] These findings suggest that women may face problems applying "hard" influence tactics such as assertiveness. Instead, until stereotypes change, women need to rely on softer and more indirect influence strategies, such as ingratiation.

INFLUENCE TACTICS AND ORGANIZATIONAL POLITICS

You might have noticed that organizational politics has not been mentioned yet, even though you probably thought that some of the practices or examples described over the past few pages were political tactics. The phrase was carefully avoided because, for the most part, "organizational politics" is in the eye of the beholder. I might perceive your attempt to influence our boss as normal behaviour whereas someone else might perceive your tactic as brazen organizational politics. This is why scholars mainly discuss influence tactics as behaviours and organizational politics as perceptions. The influence tactics described earlier are behaviours that might be considered organizational politics, or might be considered normal behaviour. It all depends on the observer's perception of the situation.

organizational politics
Behaviours that others perceive as self-serving tactics for personal gain at the expense of other people and possibly the organization.

When are influence tactics perceived as organizational politics? Most scholars say that influence tactics are viewed as **organizational politics** when observers perceive that the tactics are self-serving behaviours to gain self-interests, advantages, and benefits at the expense of others that are sometimes contrary to the interests of the entire organization or work unit.[76] These perceptions depend on the specific influence tactics observed, but they also vary with the perceiver's position and personal characteristics. A recent study of officers and civilian staff at the Royal Canadian Mounted Police (RCMP) in Ottawa reported that lower level employees had higher perceptions of organizational politics than did employees at higher levels in the organization. Employees who felt they had less control over their work environment also had higher perceptions that the organization was political.[77]

While influence is sometimes beneficial to the organization, organizational politics is usually considered less desirable. Indeed, employees who believe their organization is steeped in organizational politics have lower job satisfaction, organizational commitment, and organizational citizenship, as well as high levels of work-related stress. Organizational politics also increases the incidence of "neglect" behaviours, such as reducing work effort, paying less attention to quality, and increasing absenteeism and lateness (see EVLN model in Chapter 4).[78]

Over one-third of management and non-management employees recently surveyed claim that organizational politics is the most common reason for decision-making delays. Another survey estimates that business leaders spent nearly one-fifth of their time dealing with organizational politics.[79] They say this time is consumed addressing several problems created by political behaviours, such as lack of trust, reduced willingness to collaborate, reduced knowledge sharing, and misuse of organizational resources.

Conditions Supporting Organizational Politics

Organizational politics flourish under the right conditions.[80] One of those conditions is scarce resources. When budgets are slashed, people rely on political tactics to safeguard their resources and maintain the status quo. This happened at Exponential Technology, a company working on a superfast chip for Apple's Macintosh. When Apple's future became uncertain, the company hired a second group of engineers to develop a similar chip for the Intel-compatible market. But with budget restrictions, the Mac-compatible engineers did their best to run the new group out of town. "It got really ugly," recalls Exponential CEO Rick Shriner. "It came down to a battle for limited resources." To reduce the political infighting, Shriner moved the Intel group to another city.[81]

Along with resource scarcity, office politics flourish when resource allocation decisions are ambiguous, complex, or lack formal rules.[82] This occurs because decision makers are given more discretion over resource allocation, so potential recipients of those resources use political tactics to influence the factors that should be considered in the decision. Organizational change encourages political behaviours for this reason. Change creates uncertainty and ambiguity as the company moves from an old set of rules and practices to a new set. During these times, employees act politically to protect their valued resources, position, and self-image.

Organizational politics also becomes commonplace when it is tolerated and transparently supported by the organization.[83] Companies sometimes promote people who are the best politicians, not necessarily the best talent, to run the company. If left unchecked, organizational politics can paralyze an organization as people focus more on protecting themselves than on fulfilling their roles. Political activity becomes self-reinforcing unless the conditions supporting political behaviour are altered.

Personal characteristics   Several personal characteristics affect a person's motivation to engage in organizational politics.[84] Some people have a strong need for personal as opposed to socialized power (see Chapter 5). They seek power for its own sake, and use political tactics to acquire more power. People with an internal locus of control are more likely than those with an external locus of control to engage in political behaviours. This does not mean that internals are naturally political; rather, they are more likely to use influence tactics when political conditions are present because, unlike externals, they feel very much in charge of their own destiny.

Machiavellian values	Some individuals have strong **Machiavellian values.** Machiavellianism is named after Niccolo Machiavelli, the 16th-century Italian political philosopher who wrote *The Prince*, a famous treatise about political behaviour. People with high Machiavellian values are comfortable getting more than they deserve, and believe that deceit is a natural and acceptable way to achieve this goal. They seldom trust co-workers and tend to use cruder influence tactics, such as bypassing their boss or being assertive, to get their own way.[85] We can see these characteristics in GLOBAL Connections 12.2, where a manager blatantly used political tactics to replace his boss as the top non-elected official of a city government.

Machiavellian values
The belief that deceit is a natural and acceptable way to influence others.

Minimizing Organizational Politics and Its Consequences

The conditions that fuel organizational politics also give us some clues about how to control dysfunctional political activities.[86] One strategy to keep organizational politics in check is to introduce clear rules and regulations to specify the use of scarce resources. Corporate leaders also need to actively support the all-channel communication structure described earlier in this chapter so that political employees do not misuse power through information control. As mentioned, organiza-

The Organizational Politics of Replacing Your Boss

Lyn Metcalf, chief executive of the City of South Perth, Western Australia, created a general manager's position and recommended to city council that David Moylan was a good candidate for the job. This was a fateful recommendation because a few months later, Moylan's political tactics helped to remove Metcalf and promote Moylan to his boss's job as chief executive.

Almost as soon as Moylan was appointed general manager, he tried to convince city councillors that South Perth's administration required a major overhaul. Metcalf disagreed, saying that the organization just needed some "fine tuning" to get it running well. What Metcalf didn't know was that part of Moylan's proposed restructuring plan was to combine the chief executive position with the general manager job that Moylan had just accepted.

Soon after Moylan's appointment, Metcalf took sick leave to recover from a back operation, leaving another executive as acting CEO. Almost as soon as Metcalf left, Moylan produced a report to city councillors blaming Metcalf's leadership style and philosophy for the current problems, explaining that a new leader was needed for the proposed restructuring. During the subsequent Western Australian government inquiry into these events, Metcalf saw Moylan's report, calling it "a knife stuck well and truly in me. (It) sounds like a bit of an assassination."

Without authorization from South Perth council, Moylan apparently took the initiative to visit Metcalf at his home during the sick leave to offer Metcalf the option of significantly reduced pay or quitting with a severance payment. Metcalf negotiated a large severance. Other city executives also left due to the proposed restructuring that Moylan orchestrated.

The city then searched for a permanent CEO to replace Metcalf. Moylan was a frontrunner even though

South Perth city general manager David Moylan was able to oust his boss, take his job, and introduce his restructuring plan through organizational politics.
Kerris Berrington, News Limited

he lacked the specialist skills for the position. Soon after, Moylan sent a memo to councillors explaining why he was the best person for the job. A few months after he was appointed general manager, Moylan moved into the chief executive's job. Less than one year later, however, he was ousted when a Western Australian government inquiry concluded that his tactics were exercised without the approval of elected officials.

Sources: J. Kelly, "Probe Tells of Secret Council Deals," *Sunday Times (Perth)*, November 26, 2000, p. 1; J. Kelly, "Paid Off then Promoted," *Sunday Times (Perth)*, November 19, 2000, p. 5.
www.southperth.wa.gov.au

tional politics can become a problem during times of organizational change. Effective organizational change practices—particularly education and involvement—can minimize uncertainty and, consequently, politics, during the change process (see Chapter 17).

Organizational politics is either supported or punished, depending on team norms and the organization's culture. Thus, leaders need to actively manage group norms to curtail self-serving influence activities. They also need to support organizational values, such as altruism and customer-focus, that oppose political tactics. One of the most important strategies is for leaders to become role models of organizational citizenship rather than symbols of successful organizational politicians.

Along with minimizing organizational politics, companies can limit the adverse effects of political perceptions by giving employees more control over their work and keeping them informed about organizational events. Research has found that employees who are kept informed about what is going on in the organization and who are involved in organizational decisions are less likely to experience stress, job satisfaction, and absenteeism as a result of organizational politics.[87]

CHAPTER SUMMARY

Power is the capacity to influence others. It exists when one party perceives that he or she is dependent on the other for something of value. However, the dependent person must also have counterpower—some power over the dominant party—to maintain the relationship.

There are five power bases. Legitimate power is an agreement among organizational members that people in certain roles can request certain behaviours of others. Reward power is derived from the ability to control the allocation of rewards valued by others and to remove negative sanctions. Coercive power is the ability to apply punishment. Expert power is the capacity to influence others by possessing knowledge or skills that they value. People have referent power when others identify with them, like them, or otherwise respect them.

Information plays an important role in organizational power. Employees gain power by controlling the flow of information that others need, and by being able to cope with uncertainties related to important organizational goals.

Four contingencies determine whether these power bases translate into real power. Individuals and work units are more powerful when they are nonsubstitutable, that is, when there are no alternatives. Employees, work units, and organizations reduce substitutability by controlling tasks, knowledge, and labour, and by differentiating themselves from competitors. A second contingency is centrality. People have more power when they have high centrality, that is, the number of people affected and how quickly others are affected by their actions. Discretion, the third contingency of power, refers to the freedom to exercise judgment. Power increases when people have freedom to use their power. The fourth contingency, visibility, refers to the idea that power increases to the extent that a person's or work unit's competencies are known to others.

Networking involves cultivating social relationships with others to accomplish one's goals. This activity increases an individual's expert and referent power as well as visibility and possibly centrality. However, networking can limit opportunities for people outside the network, as many women in senior management positions have discovered.

Workplace romance has a complex effect on power in organizations. Co-workers tend to believe that employees in a sexual relationship will abuse their power. If the relationship ends, power imbalances between the two employees may lead to sexual harassment.

Influence refers to any behaviour that attempts to alter someone's attitudes or behaviour. Influence operates down, across, and up the corporate hierarchy, applies one or more power bases, and is an essential process through which people achieve organizational objectives. The most widely studied influence tactics are silent authority (influence through passive application of legitimate power), assertiveness (actively applying legitimate and coercive power), exchange (promising benefits or resources in exchange for compliance), coalition formation (a group formed to support a particular change), upward appeal (a coalition in which one or more members is someone with higher authority or expertise), ingratiation (any attempt to increase liking by, or perceived similarity to, some targeted person) and impression management (actively shaping our public images), persuasion (using logical arguments, factual evidence, and emotional appeals to convince people), and information control (explicitly manipulating access to information).

"Soft" influence tactics such as friendly persuasion and subtle ingratiation are more acceptable than "hard" tactics such as upward appeal and assertiveness. However, the most appropriate influence tactic also depends on the influencer's power base; whether the person being influenced is higher, lower, or at the same level in the organization; and the cultural values and expectations regarding influence behaviour. Research also indicates that some influence tactics that are effective for men are ineffective for women.

Organizational politics refers to influence tactics that others perceive to be self-serving behaviours to gain self-interests, advantages, and benefits at the expense of others and sometimes contrary to the interests of the entire organization or work unit. Organizational politics is more prevalent when scarce resources are allocated using complex and ambiguous decisions, and when the organization tolerates or rewards political behaviour. Individuals with a high need for personal power, an internal locus of control, and strong Machiavellian values have a higher propensity to use political tactics.

Organizational politics can be minimized by providing clear rules for resource allocation, establishing a free flow of information, using education and involvement during organizational change, supporting team norms and a corporate culture that discourage dysfunctional politics, and having leaders who role-model organizational citizenship rather than political savvy.

KEY TERMS

Centrality, p. 351

Coalition, p. 355

Counterpower, p. 344

Impression management, p. 356

Influence, p. 353

Ingratiation, p. 356

Inoculation effect, p. 358

Legitimate power, p. 345

Machiavellian values, p. 361

Mentoring, p. 352

Networking, p. 352

Organizational politics, p. 360

Persuasion, p. 357

Power, p. 344

Referent power, p. 347

Substitutability, p. 350

Upward appeal, p. 356

DISCUSSION QUESTIONS

1. What role does counterpower play in the power relationship? Give an example where you have counterpower at school or work.

2. "Employees are becoming less tolerant of legitimate power." What are the limitations of legitimate power?

3. List the eight influence tactics described in this chapter in terms of how often they are used by students to influence the instructor. Which influence tactic is applied most often, which is applied second most often, etc.? Why is each influence tactic relatively common or uncommon in student-instructor relations?

4. You have just been hired as a special assistant to the deputy minister of health in a provincial government. You have worked in another province in a similar capacity and have several years of experience in the area of government health policy. Discuss your level of power as a special assistant in terms of the four contingencies of power described in this chapter. Your answer should specify any assumptions you make.

5. How does networking increase a person's power? What networking strategies could you initiate *now* to potentially enhance your future career success?

6. How do cultural differences impact the following influence tactics: a) Silent authority and b) Upward appeal?

7. The author of a popular business book wrote, "Office politics is a demotivator that should be eliminated." He argues that when companies allow politics to determine who gets ahead, employees put their energy into political behaviour rather than job performance. Discuss the author's comments about organizational politics.

8. This book frequently emphasizes that successful companies engage in knowledge management. What influence tactics were described in this chapter that directly interfere with knowledge management objectives?

FOREIGN EXCHANGE CONFRONTATION

I worked in the foreign exchange (FX) back office, where deals done by our 150 dealers were checked, payment instructions were added, and queries addressed. My job was to resolve problems arising from deals. Much of the time this meant going upstairs and talking to the dealers.

Now, you never told a dealer that he or she was wrong, even when handling dealers who, throughout the whole of my placement, were never right. You just briefly stated what the problem was and asked them to kindly look into it.

This particular incident involves Nick, one of the men who always made mistakes. This time he had mixed up the currencies on a deal. The payment was due in half an hour, so it was important to get him to amend the deal. I went up to see him, but Lee, also from the back office, was already talking to him about something else. Because my problem was urgent, I waited for Lee to finish. When Lee left, Nick glanced at me and then, to my surprise, left his desk and went over to another dealer, John, from whom we had heard juicy comments for quite a while. A group of dealers assembled and I could hear and see from their behaviour that they were not discussing business.

I went over and discovered that the reason for their behaviour was two pages from *The Sun* newspaper filled with pictures of posing, naked women. Something inside me just snapped. I told Nick that my job was actually meant as a service to the dealers, to help make them aware of errors before it cost them money. I explained how much work I had to do and how much other dealers appreciated my corrections, so by ignoring me he was not only wasting my time, but his own colleagues' right to the service the back office offers. And with his error-statistics, I would imagine he had better things to do than to stare at page three girls.

I turned around, left my sheet of paper on his desk and departed.

My main emotion both then and now is anger. I felt I had been patient and taken much more rude behaviour than was acceptable. The way Nick ignored me to go and look at photos of semi-clad women in a newspaper was the straw that broke the camel's back. I also felt helpless and vulnera-

ble. They were discussing female anatomy in detail in a room with almost all men, and I knew my views were in the minority. I was afraid any reaction from me would be ridiculed. Writing about it now, I also feel proud for having had the courage to tell him off.

The Foreign Exchange dealers, nearly all men, were the most arrogant group of people I have ever come across in my life. If I had not gradually come to understand some of the reasons for their behaviour, an outburst like the one I have just described would have come much earlier. You need to appreciate the fact that the FX department is, at the moment, one of the best departments result-wise in this firm, which creates a feeling of invulnerability and extreme self-importance among those working there. I did not feel that this was a valid excuse for their behavior; still, I learned to accept it.

The back-office policy was to accept any amount of rudeness from the dealers, and then let it all come out afterwards when you were safely back at your desk. This policy was no good as it only helped to increase the hostility between the dealers and the back office. My telling off the dealer meant that I had broken the main taboo in the office. Over several weeks, I realized that this earned me a lot of respect. I had done something many of my colleagues had wanted to do for years, but dared not. The risk was smaller for me as I was only there for a short while. So, I achieved respect both from the back office and from some of the dealers. And perhaps, even more important, I respected myself more for having done what I felt was right.

Discussion Questions

1. Describe the power bases and contingencies of power held by Nick and the "back-office" person during this incident.

2. How did the back-office person's power change after this incident? Why?

Source: Adapted from Y. Gabriel, "An Introduction to the Social Psychology of Insults in Organizations," *Human Relations*, 51 (November 1998), pp. 1329–54.

BUDGET DELIBERATIONS

By Sharon Card, Saskatchewan Institute of Applied Science & Technology

Purpose This exercise is designed to help you understand some of the power dynamics and influence tactics that occur across hierarchical levels in organizations.

Materials This activity works best when one small room leads to a larger room, which leads to a larger area.

Instructions These exercise instructions are based on a class size of about 30 students. The instructor may adjust the size of the first two groups slightly for larger classes. The instructor will organize students as follows: A few (3–4) students are assigned the position of executives. Preferably, they are located in a secluded office or corner of a large classroom. Another 6–8 students are assigned positions as middle managers. Ideally, these people will be located in an adjoining room or space, allowing privacy for the executives. The remaining students represent the non-management employees in the organization. They are located in an open area outside the executive and management rooms.

Rules Members of the executive group are free to enter the space of either the middle management or nonmanagement groups and to communicate whatever they wish, whenever they wish. Members of the middle management group may enter the space of the nonmanagement group whenever they wish, but must request permission to enter the executive group's space. The executive group can refuse the middle management group's request. Members of the nonmanagement group are not allowed to disturb the top group in any way unless specifically invited by members of the executive group. The nonmanagement group does have the right to request permission to communicate with the middle management group. The middle management group can refuse the lower group's request.

Task Your organization is in the process of preparing a budget. The challenge is to balance needs with the financial resources. Of course, the needs are greater than the resources. The instructor will distribute a budget sheet showing a list of budget requests and their costs. Each group has control over a portion of the budget and must decide how to spend the money over which they have control. Non-management has discretion over a relatively small portion and the executive group has discretion over the greatest portion. The exercise is finished when the organization has negotiated a satisfactory budget, or until the instructor calls time out. The class will then debrief with the following questions and others the instructor might ask.

Discussion Questions

1. What can we learn from this exercise about power in organizational hierarchies?

2. How is this exercise similar to relations in real organizations?

3. How did students in each group feel about the amount of power they held?

4. How did they exercise their power in relations with the other groups?

UPWARD INFLUENCE SCALE

Purpose   This exercise is designed to help you understand several ways of influencing people further up the organizational hierarchy as well as to estimate your preferred upward influence tactics.

Instructions   Read each of the statements below and circle the response that you believe best indicates how often you engaged in that behaviour over the past six (6) months. Then use the scoring key in Appendix B to calculate your results. This exercise is completed alone so students can assess themselves honestly without concerns of social comparison. However, class discussion will focus on the types of influence in organizations and the conditions under which particular influence tactics are most and least appropriate.

Upward Influence Scale				
How often in the past six months have you engaged in the behaviours?	**Never** ▼	**Seldom** ▼	**Occasionally** ▼	**Frequently** ▼	**Almost Always** ▼
1. I obtain the support of my co-workers in persuading my manager to act on my request.	1	2	3	4	5
2. I offer an exchange in which I will do something that my manager wants if he or she will do what I want.	1	2	3	4	5
3. I act very humble and polite while making my request.	1	2	3	4	5
4. I appeal to higher management to put pressure on my manager.	1	2	3	4	5
5. I remind my manager of how I have helped him or her in the past and imply that now I expect compliance with my request.	1	2	3	4	5
6. I go out of my way to make my manager feel good about me, before asking him or her to do what I want.	1	2	3	4	5
7. I use logical arguments in order to convince my manager.	1	2	3	4	5
8. I have a face-to-face confrontation with my manager in which I forcefully state what I want.	1	2	3	4	5
9. I act in a friendly manner toward my manager before making my request.	1	2	3	4	5
10. I present facts, figures, and other information to my manager in support of my position.	1	2	3	4	5
11. I obtain the support and cooperation of my subordinates to back up my request.	1	2	3	4	5

(continued)

How often in the past six months have you engaged in the behaviours?	Never ▼	Seldom ▼	Occasionally ▼	Frequently ▼	Almost Always ▼
Upward Influence Scale (cont.)					
12. I obtain the informal support of higher management to back me.	1	2	3	4	5
13. I offer to make a personal sacrifice such as giving up my free time if my manager will do what I want.	1	2	3	4	5
14. I very carefully explain to my manager the reasons for my request.	1	2	3	4	5
15. I verbally express my anger to my manager in order to get what I want.	1	2	3	4	5
16. I use a forceful manner. I try such things as making demands, setting deadlines, and expressing strong emotion.	1	2	3	4	5
17. I rely on the chain of command—on people higher up in the organization who have power over my supervisor.	1	2	3	4	5
18. I mobilize other people in the organization to help me in influencing my supervisor.	1	2	3	4	5

Source: C. Schriesheim and T. Hinkin, "Influence Tactics Used by Subordinates: A Theoretical and Empirical Analysis and Refinement of the Kipnis, Schmidt, and Wilkinson subscales," *Journal of Applied Psychology*, 75 (1990), pp. 246–57

SELF-ASSESSMENT EXERCISE 12.4

PERCEPTIONS OF POLITICS SCALE (POPS)

 Go to the Student CD for the interactive version of this exercise.

Purpose This self-assessment is designed to help you to assess the degree to which you view your work environment as politically charged.

Instructions This scale consists of several statements that might or might not describe the school where you are attending classes. These statements refer to the administration of the school, not the classroom. Please indicate the extent to which you agree or disagree with each statement.

MACHIAVELLIANISM SCALE

Go to the Student CD for the interactive version of this exercise.

Purpose   This self-assessment is designed to help you to assess the degree to which you have a Machiavellian personality.

Instructions   Indicate the extent to which you agree or disagree that each statement in this instrument describes you. Complete each item honestly to get the best estimate of your level of Machiavellianism.

CHAPTER 13

Conflict and Negotiation in the Workplace

Learning Objectives

AFTER READING THIS CHAPTER, YOU SHOULD BE ABLE TO:

- Distinguish task-related from socioemotional conflict.

- Discuss the advantages and disadvantages of conflict in organizations.

- Identify six sources of organizational conflict.

- Outline the five interpersonal styles of conflict management.

- Summarize six structural approaches to managing conflict.

- Outline four situational influences on negotiations.

- Compare and contrast the three types of third-party dispute resolution.

For almost two years after Air Canada acquired its archrival Canadian Airlines, a solid wall divided pilots from the two airlines. One door at Pearson Airport led to the large crew room where the 2,400 Air Canada pilots prepare for their flights. Another door further up the hallway led to a much smaller room for the 1,200 former Canadian Airlines pilots.

The physical wall dividing the two rooms was probably knocked down when Air Canada finally scheduled the two pilot groups to work in the same cockpits two years after the merger, but the psychological wall of conflict is as strong as ever. "There will always be a wall there in our eyes," admits Robert Cohen, a Canadian Airlines first officer with 13 years of experience at the former airline. "We will not mingle with those people and the feeling is mutual. They [Air Canada pilots] don't even want us in their system. It's evident."

Conflict between Air Canada and Canadian Airlines pilots continues as they battle over seniority rights. Many Air Canada pilots believe the Canadian Airlines pilots should be placed at the bottom of the seniority list because they would have had no seniority if Air Canada hadn't rescued Canadian from bankruptcy. Canadian Airlines pilots, on the other hand, believe they are entitled to the same rights and seniority because the two airlines merged. The outcome is critical because seniority determines what aircraft and routes pilots fly as well as their days off, vacation, pay, and pensions. "For a pilot, seniority is everything," says Peter Foster, spokesman for the Air Canada Pilots Association.

The two pilot groups tried to negotiate a single seniority list, but the effort failed after one day. A subsequent arbitration decision discounted the seniority of Canadian Airlines pilots by an average of more than nine years, which outraged the Canadian Airlines pilots. A federal labour board later agreed with Canadian Airlines pilots and suspended the arbitration decision, but this action upset the Air Canada pilots.

"I've never seen this kind of hostility," says Christine Hayvice, a 27-year Canadian Airlines employee and spokesperson for the labour union representing the former Canadian ticket agents and reservation staff. Her group is also battling over seniority rights with the labour union representing Air Canada ticket agents and reservation staff.[1] ∎

www.aircanada.ca

Conflict between Air Canada pilots and former Canadian Airlines pilots has created tension and ill feeling as they battle over seniority rights.
CP/Tannis Toohey

conflict

The process in which one party perceives that its interests are being opposed or negatively affected by another.

Conflict is a process in which one party perceives that its interests are being opposed or negatively affected by another party.[2] The opening story illustrates a classic conflict situation because the interests of Canadian Airlines pilots are likely opposed to the interests of Air Canada pilots. The more one pilot group gets what it wants, the more it interferes with what the other pilot group wants to get.

This chapter looks at the dynamics of conflict in organizational settings. We begin by describing the conflict process and discussing the consequences and sources of conflict in organizational settings. Five conflict management styles are then described, followed by a discussion of the structural approaches to conflict management. The last two sections of this chapter introduce two procedures for resolving conflict: negotiation and third-party resolution.

THE CONFLICT PROCESS

When describing an incident involving conflict, we are usually referring to the observable part of conflict—the angry words, shouting matches, and actions that symbolize opposition. But this *manifest conflict* is only a small part of the conflict process. As Exhibit 13.1 illustrates, the conflict process begins with the sources of conflict.[3] Incompatible goals, different values, and other conditions lead one or both parties to perceive that conflict exists. We will look closely at these sources of conflict later in this chapter because understanding and changing the root causes are the key to effective conflict management.

Conflict Perceptions and Emotions

At some point, the sources of conflict lead one or both parties to perceive that conflict exists. They also experience various conflict-laden emotions toward the other party. For example, Air Canada and Canadian Airlines pilots were frustrated and angry with each other over the seniority conflict.

EXHIBIT 13.1   The conflict process

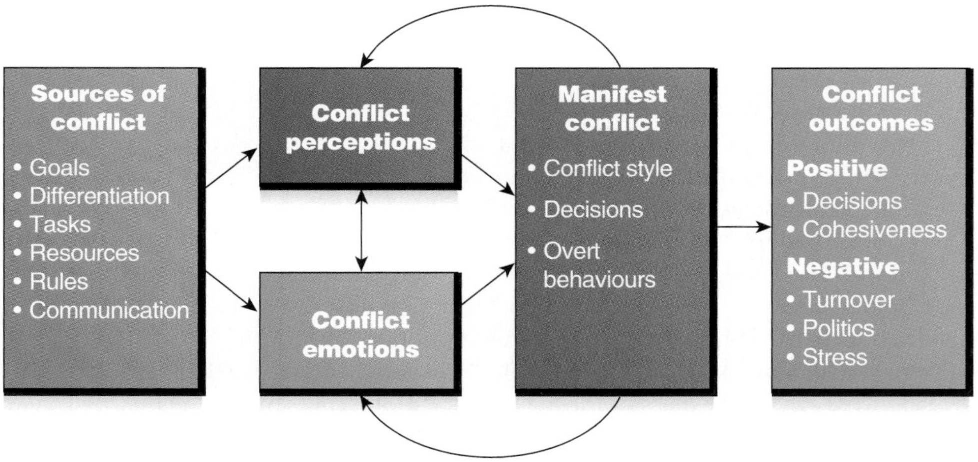

Task-related versus socioemotional conflict   When asked what Toyota Motor Company does to make great cars, one engineer replied, "Lots of conflict."[4] Toyota employees know that conflict is not always bad. Successful organizations encourage mild forms of conflict without having it escalate into an emotional battle among employees or work units. The key is to create *task-related conflict*, and to prevent it from escalating into *socioemotional conflict*.[5] Task-related conflict occurs when people disagree about task issues, such as goals, key decision areas, procedures, and the appropriate choice for action. The conflict is separate from them, an object "out there" that must be addressed. This conflict is potentially healthy and valuable because it makes people rethink their perspectives of reality. As long as the conflict remains focused on the issue, new ideas may emerge and the conflict remains controlled.

Unfortunately, conflict often becomes personal. Rather than focusing on the issue, each party perceives the other party as the problem. With socioemotional conflict, differences are viewed as personal attacks rather than attempts to resolve an issue. The discussion becomes emotionally charged, which introduces perceptual biases and distorts information processing.

Manifest Conflict

Conflict perceptions and emotions usually manifest themselves in the decisions and overt behaviours of one party toward the other. These conflict episodes may range from subtle nonverbal behaviours to war-like aggression. For example, one source stated that there have been "fights in the terminals" and "scuffles on the crew bus" between Air Canada and Canadian Airlines pilots as a result of their conflict.[6] Conflict is also manifested by the style each side uses to resolve the conflict, such as whether one side tries to defeat the other or to find a mutually beneficial solution. Conflict management styles will be described later in this chapter. At this point, you should know that these styles influence each side's decisions and behaviours. Consequently, they play a critical role in determining whether the conflict will escalate or be quickly resolved.

Conflict escalation cycle   The conflict process in Exhibit 13.1 shows arrows looping back from manifest conflict to conflict perceptions and emotions. These loops represent the fact that the conflict process is really a series of episodes that potentially link together into an escalation cycle or spiral.[7] It doesn't take much to start this conflict cycle—just an inappropriate comment, a misunderstanding, or an undiplomatic action. These behaviours communicate to the other party in a way that creates a perception of conflict. If the first party did not intend to demonstrate conflict, then the second party's response may create that perception.

If the conflict remains task-related, both parties may resolve the conflict through logical analysis. However, the communication process has enough ambiguity that a wrong look or word may trigger an emotional response by the other side and set the stage for socioemotional conflict. These distorted beliefs and emotions reduce each side's motivation to communicate, making it more difficult for them to discover common ground and ultimately resolve the conflict.[8] The parties then rely more on stereotypes and emotions to reinforce their perceptions of the other party. Some structural conditions increase the likelihood of conflict escalation. Employees who are more confrontational and less diplomatic also tend to escalate conflict.[9]

Conflict Outcomes

conflict management
Interventions that alter the level and form of conflict in ways that maximize its benefits and minimize its dysfunctional consequences.

Angela regards herself as a nice person, but conflict with another employee put her in touch with the darker side of her personality. "I never thought I had this black spot in my soul until this person made my life hell," says the projects officer at a consulting firm. The colleague was a good friend until he accused Angela of "stealing" an important client. Relations deteriorated as the colleague responded by spreading malicious and untrue gossip about Angela. Angela complained, but her superiors didn't act on it for several months. The colleague was eventually fired.[10]

This real-life incident illustrates how misunderstandings and disagreements escalate into socioemotional conflict, which results in negative outcomes for the organization. "The conflict was bad for business," Angela recalls, "because it affected staff decisions and took the focus off making money." Socioemotional conflict increases frustration, job dissatisfaction, and stress. In the longer term, this leads to increased turnover and absenteeism.[11]

These symptoms are showing up among executives at Walt Disney Corp. Disney CEO Michael Eisner apparently supports an environment where executives battle each other over scarce resources. Insiders claim that several people have left Disney because the constant conflict has worn them down.[12] At the intergroup level, conflict with people outside the team may lead to groupthink. The conflict increases cohesiveness within the group, but members value consensus so much that it undermines decision quality.[13]

Given these problems, it's not surprising that people normally associate **conflict management** with reducing or removing conflict. Conflict management isn't necessarily about minimizing conflict, however.[14] It refers to interventions that alter the level and form of conflict in ways that maximize its benefits and minimize its dysfunctional consequences. This sometimes means increasing the level of task-related conflict. Task-related conflict helps people to recognize problems, identify a variety of solutions, and better understand the relevant issues. This *constructive conflict* encourages people to learn about other points of view, which helps them to re-examine their basic assumptions about a problem and its possible solution.[15]

Conflict is also beneficial where intergroup conflict improves team dynamics within those units. Teams increase their cohesiveness and task orientation when they face an external threat. Under conditions of moderate conflict, this motivates team members to work more efficiently toward these goals, thereby increasing the team's productivity.

Southwest Airlines is best known as a "fun" place to work, but the company also encourages lots of debate among its employees so the best ideas get scrutinized. "I find it helpful to encourage people to express differing points of view and bring evidence to support their points of view to the table," says Jim Parker, Southwest's incoming CEO. Parker is shown here at left with Southwest's founder and past CEO Herb Kelleher as well as executive vice-president Colleen Barrett. "It's usually through that constructive conflict of ideas that the better idea will emerge."[16] What conditions must apply to ensure that conflict remains task oriented and doesn't become socioemotional? *L. M. Otero/Associated Press*
www.iflyswa.com

SOURCES OF CONFLICT IN ORGANIZATIONS

If you see manifest conflict in organizations, it is most likely caused by one or more of the six conditions shown in Exhibit 13.2.

Incompatible Goals

A common source of conflict is goal incompatibility.[17] Goal incompatibility occurs when one employee's or department's personal or work goals seem to interfere with another person's or department's goals. This source of conflict is clearly apparent at Air Canada. The pilots have conflicting goals—each wants to receive the highest possible seniority to improve their career and job status. But if Canadian Airlines pilots receive the seniority levels they want, then the Air Canada pilots will necessarily receive seniority lower than what they would prefer, which would deny Canadian Airlines pilots any seniority. The point here is that people with divergent goals are more likely to experience conflict.

Differentiation

Not long ago, a British automotive company proposed a friendly buyout of an Italian firm. Executives at both companies were excited about the opportunities of sharing distribution channels and manufacturing technologies. But the grand vision of a merged company turned to a nightmare as executives began meeting over the details. Their backgrounds and experiences were so different that they were endlessly confused and constantly apologizing to the other side for oversights and misunderstandings. At one meeting—the last, as it turned out—the president of the Italian firm stood up and, smiling sadly, said, "I believe we all know what is the problem here . . . it seems your forward is our reverse; your down, our up; your right, our wrong. Let us finish now, before war is declared."[18]

These automobile executives discovered that conflict is often caused by different values and beliefs because of unique backgrounds, experiences, or training.

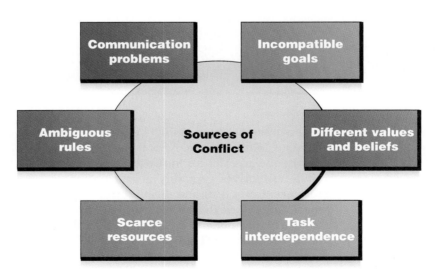

EXHIBIT 13.2

Sources of conflict in organizations

Working through Culture Clashes in the Renault-Nissan Partnership

Carlos Ghosn experienced more than his share of cross-cultural conflict when French carmaker Renault made him president of its partner, Nissan Motor Co. in Japan. "Certainly many of you have felt the effects of intra-company cultural clashes as your business has become globalized," said the Brazilian-born Renault executive to an audience of automobile executives, consultants, and media. "The results are a waste of talent and a waste of energy."

Ghosn and other French executives were irritated that Nissan's executives seem to lack a "sense of urgency" to stop seven years of financial losses at Japan's second largest carmaker. "Even though the evidence is against them, [Nissan executives] sit down and they watch the problem a little bit longer," complains Ghosn.

The Japanese executives were equally disturbed by the French practice of evaluating performance issues across work units. "In a big Japanese company, everyone has their own pigeonhole and their own responsibilities which never impinge on anyone else's, and which means no one questions a colleague's work," explains an anonymous Nissan source.

Conflicts even simmered over traditions involving lunches and meetings. The French executives believe they work better after long lunches, whereas the Japanese executives shovel down their food and get back to work as a show of loyalty. Meanwhile, the Japanese are fond of long meetings because they make their opinions seem valued by the company. This irritates the French executives, who prefer quicker decision making.

The good news is that Ghosn seems to be defeating the dysfunctional conflict and saving the Japanese car company through a set of challenging, measurable

Carlos Ghosn (shown) experienced plenty of cross-cultural conflict when the Renault executive was transferred to Japan as president of Nissan Motor Co.
© Reuters NewMedia Inc./Corbis

objectives called the "Nissan Revival Plan." The plan is a superordinate goal that rallied staff and encouraged them to put aside their cultural differences. "We all knew that in order to develop a plan that would work, we would have to treat natural cultural suspicions and culture clashes as a luxury for rich people," Ghosn explains.

Sources: Y. Kageyama, "Renault Manager Crosses Cultural Divide to Turn around Nissan," *Associated Press State & Local Wire*, June 25, 2001; O. Morgan, "Nissan's Boy from Brazil puts Accent on Profits," *The Observer* (UK), May 27, 2001, p. 7; F. Kadri, "Renault-Nissan Two Years on: Being Bi-national is Not so Simple," *Agence France-Presse*, April 1, 2001; A.R. Gold, M. Hirano, and Y. Yokoyama, "An Outsider Takes on Japan: An Interview with Nissan's Carlos Ghosn," *McKinsey Quarterly*, January 2001, p. 95; "Nissan's Ghosn Calls Cultural Clashes 'A Luxury for the Rich'" *PR Newswire*, January 18, 2000. **www.nissan.co.jp**

Mergers often produce conflict because they bring together people with divergent corporate cultures. Employees fight over the "right way" to do things because of their unique experiences in the separate companies. The British and Italian automobile executives probably also experienced conflict due to their different national cultures. Cultural diversity makes it difficult to understand or accept the beliefs and values that other people hold toward organizational decisions and events. The partnership of French automaker Renault and Japanese automaker Nissan, described in GLOBAL Connections 13.1, provides another rich illustration of conflict due to both national and corporate cultural differences.

Many companies are also experiencing the rising incidence of cross-generational conflict.[19] Generation gaps have always existed, but generational conflict is more common today because employees across age groups work together more than ever before. Younger and older employees have different needs, different expectations, and somewhat different values. This differentiation appears in many types of conflict. For example, younger and older employees at Techneglas Inc. recently experienced conflict with each other over a proposed work schedule. Younger employees value more time off, so they wanted 12-hour shifts with bigger blocks of time off work. But many of the older Techneglas employees insisted on sticking to the current 8-hour shift schedule because it lets them work overtime with less fatigue. "The old people don't have a life," snaps one of the younger Techneglas employees. "Their jobs are their lives."[20]

Task Interdependence

Conflict tends to increase with the level of task interdependence. Task interdependence exists when team members must share common inputs to their individual tasks, need to interact in the process of executing their work, or receive outcomes (such as rewards) that are partly determined by the performance of others (see Chapter 8). The higher the level of task interdependence, the greater the risk of conflict, because there is a greater chance that each side will disrupt or interfere with the other side's goals.[21]

Other than complete independence, employees tend to have the lowest risk of conflict when working with others in a pooled interdependence relationship (i.e. where people share a common resource but do not work directly with each other). The potential for conflict is higher in sequential interdependence work relationships, such as an assembly line. The highest risk of conflict tends to occur in reciprocal task interdependence situations. With reciprocal interdependence, employees are highly dependent on each other and, consequently, have a higher probability of interfering with each other's work and personal goals.

Scarce Resources

Scarce resources generate conflict because scarcity motivates people to compete with others who also need those resources to achieve their objectives.[22] Conflict between Air Canada and Canadian Airlines pilots would be nonexistent if everyone could receive the highest salaries, enjoy the longest vacations, and choose any airplane to fly on any schedule they want. Instead, pilots must share scarce resources at Air Canada. Those with the highest seniority get the highest pay with the best airplanes and schedules; those with the lowest seniority get what's left over.

Ambiguous Rules

Ambiguous rules—or the complete lack of rules—breed conflict. This occurs because uncertainty increases the risk that one party intends to interfere with the other party's goals. Ambiguity also encourages political tactics. In some cases, employees enter a free-for-all battle to win decisions in their favour. This explains why conflict is more common during mergers and acquisitions. Employees from both companies have conflicting practices and values, and few rules have developed to minimize the manoeuvring for power and resources.[23] When clear rules exist, on the other hand, employees know what to expect from each other because they have agreed to abide by those rules.

Communication Problems

Conflict often occurs due to the lack of opportunity, ability, or motivation to communicate effectively. Let's look at each of these causes. First, when two parties lack the opportunity to communicate, they tend to use stereotypes to explain past behaviours and anticipate future actions. Unfortunately, stereotypes are sufficiently subjective that emotions can negatively distort the meaning of an opponent's actions, thereby escalating perceptions of conflict. Moreover, without direct interaction, the two sides have less empathy for each other.

Second, some people lack the necessary skills to communicate in a diplomatic, nonconfrontational manner. When one party communicates its disagreement in an arrogant way, opponents are more likely to heighten their perception of the conflict. Arrogant behaviour also sends a message that one side intends to be competitive rather than cooperative. This may lead the other party to reciprocate with a similar conflict management style.[24] Consequently, as we explained earlier, ineffective communication often leads to an escalation in the conflict cycle.

Ineffective communication can also lead to a third problem: less motivation to communicate in the future. For example, an accountant was verbally abused by an information services manager soon after he was hired. Since then, he has avoided the manager, leaving some problems undetected and unresolved. Another employee reported that the relationship with his manager deteriorated to such an extent that for five months they communicated only by e-mail.[25] These reactions aren't surprising. Socioemotional conflict is uncomfortable, so people are less motivated to interact with others in a conflicting relationship.

Unfortunately, less communication can further escalate the conflict because there is less opportunity to empathize with the opponent's situation and opponents are more likely to rely on distorted stereotypes of the other party. In fact, conflict tends to further distort these stereotypes through the process of social identity (see Chapter 3). We begin to see competitors less favourably so that our self-identity can remain strong during these uncertain times.[26]

The lack of motivation to communicate also explains (along with different values and beliefs, described earlier) why conflict is more common in cross-cultural relationships. People tend to feel uncomfortable or awkward interacting with co-workers from different cultures, so they are less motivated to engage in dialogue with them.[27] With limited communication, people rely more on stereotypes to fill in missing information. They also tend to misunderstand each other's verbal and nonverbal signals, further escalating the conflict.

win–win orientation
The belief that the parties will find a mutually beneficial solution to their disagreement.

win–lose orientation
The belief that the conflicting parties are drawing from a fixed pie, so the more one party receives, the less the other party will receive.

INTERPERSONAL CONFLICT MANAGEMENT STYLES

The six structural conditions described above set the stage for conflict. The conflict process identified earlier in Exhibit 13.1 illustrated that these sources of conflict lead to perceptions and emotions. Some people enter a conflict with a **win–win orientation.** This is the perception that the parties will find a mutually beneficial solution to their disagreement. They believe that the resources at stake are expandable rather than fixed if the parties work together to find a creative solution. Other people enter a conflict with a **win–lose orientation.** They adopt the belief that the parties are drawing from a fixed pie, so the more one party receives, the less the other party will receive.

Conflict tends to escalate when the parties develop a win–lose orientation because they rely on power and politics to gain advantage. A win–lose orientation may occasionally be appropriate when the conflict really is over a fixed resource, but few organizational conflicts are due to perfectly opposing interests with fixed resources. To varying degrees, the opposing groups can gain by believing that their positions aren't perfectly opposing and that creative solutions are possible. For instance, a supplier and customer may initially think they have opposing interests—the supplier wants to receive more money for the product, whereas the customer wants to pay less money for it. Yet, further discussion may reveal that the customer would be willing to pay more if the product could be provided earlier than originally arranged. The vendor may actually value that earlier delivery because it saves inventory costs. By looking at the bigger picture, both parties can often discover common ground.

Adopting a win–win or win–lose orientation influences our conflict management style, that is, our actions toward the other person. Researchers have categorized five interpersonal styles of approaching the other party in a conflict situation. The most recent variation of this model appears in Exhibit 13.3. Each conflict resolution style can be placed in a two-dimensional grid reflecting the person's degree of concern for his or her own interests and concern for the other

EXHIBIT 13.3

Interpersonal
conflict management
styles

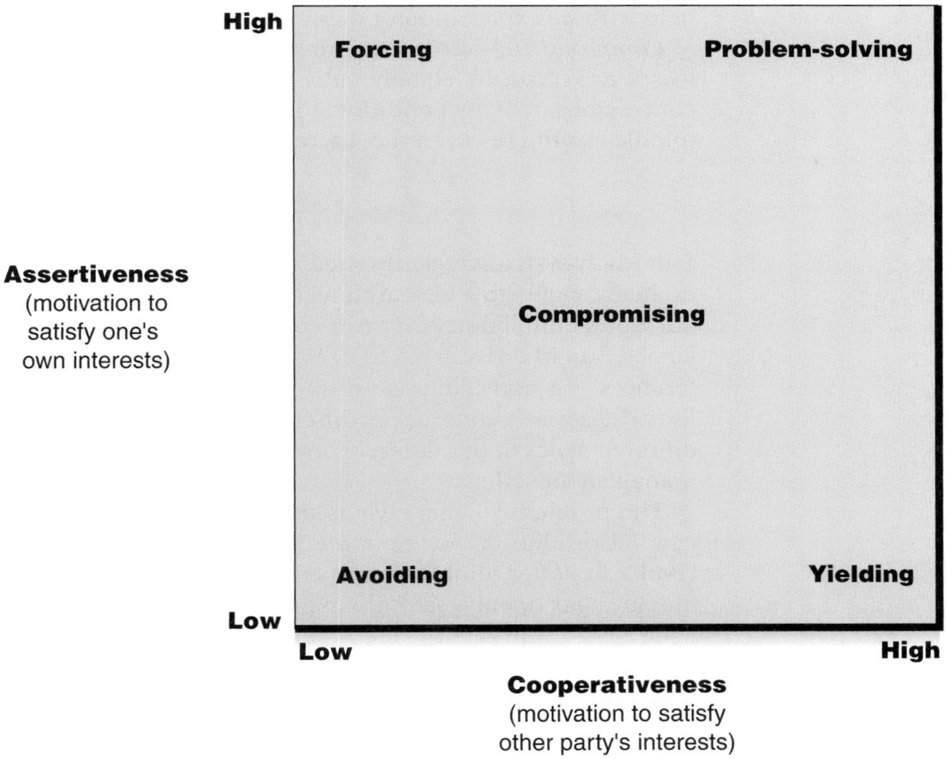

Source: C. K. W. de Dreu, A. Evers, B. Beersma, E. S. Kluwer, and A. Nauta, "A Theory-based Measure of Conflict Management Strategies in the Workplace," *Journal of Organizational Behavior*, 22 (2001), pp. 645–68. For earlier variations of this model, see: T. L. Ruble and K. Thomas, "Support For a Two-Dimensional Model of Conflict Behavior," *Organizational Behavior and Human Performance*, 16 (1976), p. 145.

party's interests. Problem solving is the only style that represents a purely win–win orientation. The other four styles represent variations of the win–lose approach. For effective conflict management, we should learn to apply different conflict management styles to different situations.[28]

- *Problem solving*—Problem solving tries to find a mutually beneficial solution for both parties. Information sharing is an important feature of this style because both parties need to identify common ground and potential solutions that satisfy both (or all) of them.
- *Avoiding*—Avoiding tries to smooth over or avoid conflict situations altogether. It reflects a low concern for both self and the other party; in other words, avoiders try to suppress thinking about the conflict. For example, some employees will rearrange their work area or tasks to minimize interaction with certain co-workers.[29]
- *Forcing*—Forcing tries to win the conflict at the other's expense. This style, which has the strongest win–lose orientation, relies on some of the "hard" influence tactics described in Chapter 12, particularly assertiveness, to get one's own way.
- *Yielding*—Yielding involves giving in completely to the other side's wishes, or at least cooperating with little or no attention to your own interests. This style involves making unilateral concessions, unconditional promises, and offering help with no expectation of reciprocal help.
- *Compromising*—Compromising involves looking for a position in which your losses are offset by equally valued gains. It involves matching the other party's concessions, making conditional promises or threats, and actively searching for a middle ground between the interests of the two parties.[30]

Choosing the Best Conflict Management Style

Sun Microsystems recently sued memory chip maker Kingston Technology over exclusive rights to a new architecture in memory modules. When the court threw out Sun's complaint, Kingston cofounder David Sun had another idea; he challenged Sun Microsystems CEO Scott McNealy to a game of golf to settle their differences.[31] A golf game is an unusual way to resolve conflict, but this incident illustrates how people apply different conflict management styles. Ideally, we use different styles under different conditions, but most of us have a preferred conflict management style.

The problem solving style is usually recognized as the preferred approach to conflict resolution. For example, the problem solving conflict management style results in better joint venture performance.[32] The parties discuss concerns more quickly and openly, seek their partner's opinions, and explain their course of action more fully than where a non-problem solving style is used. However, this style really only works under certain conditions. It is best when the parties do not have perfectly opposing interests and when they have enough trust and openness to share information. Problem solving is usually desirable because organizational conflicts are rarely win–lose situations. There is usually some opportunity for mutual gain if the parties search for creative solutions.[33]

You might think that avoiding is an ineffective conflict management strategy, but research suggests that it is the best approach when conflict has become socioemotional.[34] At the same time, conflict avoidance should not be a long-term solu-

John Risley doesn't mind creating conflict, if that's what it takes to change Canada's seafood industry. The entrepreneur who built Halifax-based Clearwater Fine Foods from a one-truck lobster operation into one of the world's leading privately-owned marketers of shellfish, believes that the future of Canada's seafood industry depends on modernization and integration. Risley recently overthrew the board of Newfoundland's Fisheries Products International Ltd. and replaced it with his own slate of directors. The plan was to merge FPI with Clearwater and install Risley as the new CEO, but the Newfoundland government prevented the merger, partly as a result of the conflict. But that setback hasn't stopped Risley from moving forward in other ways. "With Risley, you either like the guy or hate him," says one investment analyst. "And so far there are quite a few people out there who believe in him."[35] What conflict management style does John Risley seem to be using here? Is it the best style in this situation? *CP/Andrew Vaughan*
www.clearwaterfinefoods.ca

tion, because it increases the other party's frustration. The forcing approach to conflict resolution is usually inappropriate because organizational relationships rarely involve complete opposition. However, forcing may be necessary when you know you are correct and the dispute requires a quick solution. For example, a forcing style may be necessary when the other party engages in unethical conduct because any degree of unethical behaviour is unacceptable. The forcing style may also be necessary when the other party would take advantage of more cooperative strategies.

The yielding style may be appropriate when the other party has substantially more power or the issue is not as important to you as to the other party. On the other hand, yielding behaviours may give the other side unrealistically high expectations, thereby motivating them to seek more from you in the future. In the long run, yielding may produce more conflict rather than resolve it. The compromising style may be best when there is little hope for mutual gain through problem solving, both parties have equal power, and both are under time pressure to settle their differences. However, compromise is rarely a final solution and may cause the parties to overlook options for mutual gain.

Cultural and Gender Differences in Conflict Management Styles

Cultural differences are more than just a source of conflict. Cultural background also affects the conflict management style we prefer using.[36] This is because we are more comfortable with conflict management styles that are consistent with our personal and cultural value system. Some research suggests that people from collectivist cultures—where people value group harmony and duty to groups to which they belong—are motivated to maintain harmonious relations. Consequently, they tend to rely on avoidance or problem solving to resolve disagreements.[37] In contrast, people from low collectivist cultures more frequently apply a compromising or forcing style. People from high collectivist cultures can be competitive with people outside their group, but they are generally more likely than people from low collectivist cultures to avoid confrontation, where possible.

Some writers suggest that men and women also tend to rely on different conflict management styles.[38] Generally speaking, women pay more attention than men do to the relationship between the parties. Consequently, women tend to adopt a problem solving style in business settings, and are more willing to compromise to protect the relationship. Men tend to be more competitive and take a short-term orientation to the relationship. Of course, we must be cautious about these observations because gender has a weak influence on conflict management style.

STRUCTURAL APPROACHES TO CONFLICT MANAGEMENT

Conflict management styles refer to how we approach the other party in a conflict situation. But conflict management also involves altering the underlying structural causes of potential conflict. The main structural approaches are identified in Exhibit 13.4. Although this section discusses ways to reduce conflict, we should keep in mind that conflict management sometimes calls for increasing conflict. This occurs mainly by reversing the strategies described over the next few pages.[39]

Emphasizing Superordinate Goals

superordinate goal

A common objective held by conflicting parties that is more important than their conflicting departmental or individual goals.

Carlos Ghosn, described earlier in this chapter, was able to minimize conflict between French and Japanese executives partly by focusing everyone on the "Nissan Revival Plan" as a **superordinate goal**. Superordinate goals are common objectives held by conflicting parties that are more important than the departmental or individual goals on which the conflict is based. By increasing commitment to corporate-wide goals, employees place less emphasis and therefore feel less conflict with co-workers regarding competing individual or departmental level goals.[40] Superordinate goals also potentially reduce the problem of differentiation because they establish a common frame of reference. Heterogeneous team members still perceive different ways to achieve corporate objectives, but superordinate goals ensure they mutually understand and agree on the objectives themselves.

Several research studies indicate that focusing on superordinate goals weakens dysfunctional conflict. One study revealed that marketing managers in Hong Kong, China, Japan, and the United States were more likely to develop a problem solving conflict management style when executives aligned departmental goals with corporate objectives. A U.S. study found that the most effective executive teams consistently apply a superordinate goal strategy. They frame their decisions as collaborations, thereby drawing attention and commitment away from sub-level goals.[41]

EXHIBIT 13.4

Structural approaches to conflict management

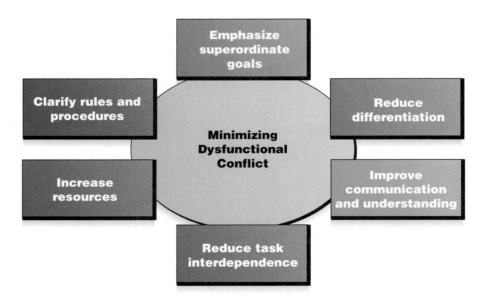

Executives at Tivoli Systems discovered the importance of superordinate goals after participating in an exercise called "Paper Airplanes, Inc." Each team at the Austin, Texas, company had 30 minutes to manufacture and sell as many standard-specific planes as possible. The teams initially performed poorly because participants focused on their individual goals. "[T]he biggest problem [was] that you couldn't just focus on your part," explains Tivoli executive Bill Jones (left in photo). Teams eventually won the exercise after their members focused on the organization's success more than their individual tasks. Now the exercise is a reminder that Tivoli employees need to focus on superordinate goals rather than departmental differences. "[W]hen things come up we refer to the exercise to help everyone get on the same page," says Brent Vance (right in photo).[42] In what other ways might the Paper Airplanes exercise reduce dysfunctional conflict? *Ed Lallo*
www.tivoli.com

Reducing Differentiation

Another way to minimize dysfunctional conflict is to reduce the differences that produced the conflict in the first place.[43] The Manila Diamond Hotel in the Philippines accomplishes this by rotating staff across different departments. "In Manila Diamond, there is no turf mentality," explains the hotel's marketing manager. "We all work together. We even share each other's jobs whenever necessary." Similarly, Hibernia Management and Development Co. in Newfoundland reduced the "destructive differences" between hourly and salaried personnel by putting employees on salary rather than hourly wages.[44]

Improving Communication and Understanding

Communication is critical to effective conflict management. This can range from casual gatherings among employees who rarely meet otherwise, to formal processes where differences are identified and discussed. Multinational peace-keeping forces work together more effectively when troops eat and socialize together.[45] By improving the opportunity, ability, and motivation to share information, employees develop less extreme perceptions of each other than if they rely on stereotypes and emotions. Direct communication provides a better understanding of the other person's or department's work environment and resource limitations. Ongoing communication is particularly important where the need for functional specialization makes it difficult to reduce differentiation.[46]

Interdepartmental communication includes socializing over a game of ping pong or foosball. "The more informal communication that happens between various groups in companies, the better they work together as a team," explains Jamey Harvey, CEO of software maker iKimbo. "Marketing actually understands the intense pressure the development team is under to develop software on time. And the development team understands that the marketing team is spending money that's going to be wasted if the product doesn't come out on time."[47]

Some of the teambuilding activities described in Chapter 9 reduce conflict because they help participants understand each other. Siemens AG's nuclear power division in Germany and French nuclear giant Framatome SA took this route when they merged recently. Senior executives at both firms were sent to a retreat an hour outside Paris where they spent a few days in canoe races and blindfolded three-legged races. The consulting firm that operates the retreat also spends time with each group to review the cultural differences between French and German executives.[48]

dialogue
A process of conversation among team members in which they learn about each other's mental models and assumptions, and eventually form a common model for thinking within the team.

Another teambuilding activity that can minimize conflict is the **dialogue** meeting, in which the disputing parties discuss their differences. Dialogue helps participants understand each other's mental models and fundamental assumptions so they can create a common thinking process and mental models for the team (see Chapter 8).[49] Several companies, including Xerox Canada, Toyota, Sony, Microsoft, Dell Computer, and Hewlett-Packard have introduced yet another conflict-busting activity called drum circles. As Connections 13.2 describes, participants in this unique teambuilding activity use drums and other percussion instruments to learn the process of working together. It teaches harmony, not only musically, but in how employees communicate and understand each other.

Reducing Task Interdependence

Conflict increases with the level of interdependence, so minimizing dysfunctional conflict might involve reducing the level of interdependence between the parties. If cost effective, this might occur by dividing the shared resource so that each party has exclusive use of part of it. Sequentially or reciprocally interdependent jobs might be combined so that they form a pooled interdependence. For example, rather than having one employee serve customers and another operate the cash register, each employee could handle both customer activities alone. Buffers also help to reduce task interdependence between people. Buffers include resources, such as adding more inventory between people who perform sequential tasks. We also find human buffers in organizations—people who intervene between highly interdependent people or work units.[50]

Increasing Resources

An obvious way to reduce conflict due to resource scarcity is to increase the amount of resources available. Corporate decision makers might quickly dismiss this solu-

Drumming Out Their Differences

Dozens of businesspeople pour into an auditorium where drums of all types—Latin American congas, African doumbeks, and Brazilian surdos—line the room. The participants anxiously take their seats. Few have played drums before, but they will all play in harmony tonight. They will learn to cooperate and coordinate through the beat of their drums.

Leading the two-hour drumming session is Doug Sole, co-owner of Soul Drums in Toronto. He starts by pointing randomly to individuals, asking them to play a beat that others will imitate. The rhythm intensifies as others join in, then falls apart into a cacophony. "We're having a communication problem here," Sole interrupts. "If we all start banging our own thing, it's going to be chaos." Sole begins again, and repeats the process until the auditorium is filled with the hypnotic beat of strangers working together.

Drum circles represent a metaphor for cooperation, coordination, communication, and teamwork in nontraditional corporate structures. They focus participants on the process of working together, not just on the outcome of achieving a goal. "It forced us to listen to, be dependent on, and have fun with each other," explains Kathleen Ross, an executive at Arbitron, a Maryland-based media research firm whose employees have participated in drum circles.

Onye Onyemaechi, a Nigerian master drummer in California, says that employees often work side-by-side for years without really getting to know one another. He warns that this lack of unity and understanding hinders the organization's potential, whereas drum circles begin the process of creating harmony among these strangers. "Drum circles bring people together to realize their common base," he advises.

"Drum circles thrive on collaborative creativity, and that is so important in the Internet world," says Christine Stevens, founder of Upbeat Drum Circles in Fort Collins,

Doug Sole and other drum circle facilitators build cooperation and mutual understanding with drumsticks and boomwhackers. *Gary Diggens, Soul Drums Ltd.; Doug Sole, Mel Bay Productions, Pacific Missouri*

Colorado. "Drum circles involve creativity and sharing, but they also demonstrate that things need to be coordinated to sound good."

Sources: S. Terry, "Lost in the Rhythm," *Christian Science Monitor*, May 23, 2001, p. 11; R. Segall, "Catch The Beat," *Psychology Today*, July 2000; M. K. Pratt, "A Pound of Cure," *Fast Company*, April 2000; A. Georgiades, "Business Heeds the Beat," *Toronto Star*, August 4, 1999. **www.souldrums.com**

tion because of the costs involved. However, they need to carefully compare these costs with the costs of dysfunctional conflict arising out of resource scarcity.

Clarifying Rules and Procedures

Some conflicts arise from ambiguous decision rules regarding the allocation of scarce resources. Consequently, these conflicts can be minimized by establishing rules and procedures. Rules clarify the distribution of resources, such as when students can use the laser printer or for how long they can borrow library books.

Consider the following situation that occurred when Armstrong World Industries, Inc. brought in consultants to implement a client/server network. Information systems employees at the flooring and building materials company experienced conflict with the consultants over who was in charge. Another conflict occurred when the consultants wanted to work long hours and take Fridays off to fly home. Armstrong minimized these conflicts by spelling out as much as possible in the contract each party's responsibilities and roles. Issues that were unclear or overlooked in the contract were clarified by joint discussion between two senior executives at the companies.[51]

Rules establish changes to the terms of interdependence, such as an employee's hours of work or a supplier's fulfillment of an order. In most cases, the parties affected by these rules are involved in the process of deciding the terms of interdependence. By redefining the terms of interdependence, the strategy of clarifying rules is part of the larger process of negotiation.

RESOLVING CONFLICT THROUGH NEGOTIATION

negotiation

Occurs whenever two or more conflicting parties attempt to resolve their divergent goals by redefining the terms of their interdependence.

Think back through yesterday's events. Maybe you had to work out an agreement with other students about what tasks to complete for a team project. Chances are you shared transportation with someone, so you had to clarify the timing of the ride. Then perhaps there was the question of who made dinner. Each of these daily events created potential conflict, and they were resolved through negotiation. **Negotiation** occurs whenever two or more conflicting parties attempt to resolve their divergent goals by redefining the terms of their interdependence.[52] In other words, people negotiate when they think that discussion can produce a more satisfactory arrangement (at least for them) in their exchange of goods or services.

As you can see, negotiation is not an obscure practice reserved for labour and management bosses hammering out a collective agreement. Everyone negotiates—every day. Most of the time, you don't even realize that you are in negotiations.[53] Negotiation is particularly evident in the workplace because employees work interdependently with each other. They negotiate with their supervisors over next month's work assignments, with customers over the sale and delivery schedules of their product, and with co-workers over when to have lunch. And yes, they occasionally negotiate with each other in labour disputes and collective agreements.

Some writers suggest that negotiations are more successful when the parties adopt a problem-solving style, whereas others caution that this conflict management style is sometimes costly.[54] We know that any win–lose style (forcing, yielding, etc.) is unlikely to produce the optimal solution, because the parties have not shared the information they need to discover a mutually satisfactory solution. On the other hand, we must be careful about adopting an openly problem-solving style until mutual trust has been established.

The concern with the problem-solving style is that information is power, so information sharing gives the other party more power to leverage a better deal if the opportunity occurs. Skilled negotiators often adopt a *cautiously* problem-solving style at the outset by sharing information slowly and determining whether the other side will reciprocate. In this respect, they try to establish trust with the other party.[55] They switch to one of the win–lose styles only when it becomes apparent that a win–win solution is not possible or that the other party is unwilling to share information cooperatively.

Bargaining Zone Model of Negotiations

The negotiation process moves each party along a continuum with an area of potential overlap called the *bargaining zone.*[56] Exhibit 13.5 displays one possible bargaining zone situation. This linear diagram illustrates a purely win–lose situation—one side's gain will be the other's loss. However, the bargaining zone model can also be applied to circumstances in which both sides potentially gain from the negotiations. As this model illustrates, the parties typically establish three main negotiating points. The *initial offer point* is the team's opening offer to the other party. This may be its best expectation or a pie-in-the-sky starting point. The *target point* is the team's realistic goal or expectation for a final agreement. The *resistance point* is the point beyond which the team will not make further concessions.

The parties begin negotiations by describing their initial offer point for each item on the agenda. In most cases, the participants know that this is only a starting point which will change as both sides offer concessions. In win–lose situations, neither the target nor the resistance points are revealed to the other party. However, people try to discover the other side's resistance point because this knowledge helps them determine how much they can gain without breaking off negotiations.

On the other hand, when the parties have a win–win orientation, the objective is to find a creative solution that keeps everyone close to their initial offer points. They can, hopefully, find an arrangement by which each side loses relatively little value on some issues and gains significantly more on other issues. For example, a supplier might want to delay delivery dates, whereas delivery times are not important to the business customer. If the parties share this information, they can quickly agree to a delayed delivery schedule, thereby costing the customer very little and gaining the supplier a great deal. On other items (financing, order size,

EXHIBIT 13.5   Bargaining zone model of negotiations

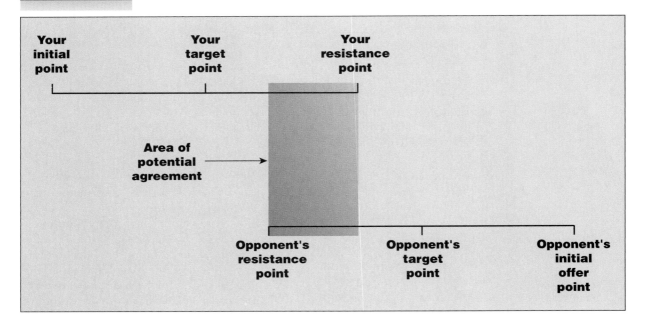

etc.), the supplier might give something with minimal loss even though it is a significant benefit to the business customer.

Situational Influences on Negotiations

The effectiveness of negotiating depends on both the situation and the behaviours of the negotiators. Four of the most important situational factors are location, physical setting, time, and audience.

Location   It is easier to negotiate on your own turf because you are familiar with the negotiating environment and are able to maintain comfortable routines.[57] Also, there is no need to cope with travel-related stress or depend on others for resources during the negotiation. Of course, you can't walk out of negotiations as easily when on your own turf, but this is usually a minor issue. Considering the strategic benefits of home turf, many negotiators agree to neutral territory. Telephones, video conferences, and other forms of information technology potentially avoid territorial issues, but skilled negotiators usually prefer the media richness of face-to-face meetings.[58]

Physical setting   The physical distance between the parties and formality of the setting can influence their orientation toward each other and the disputed issues.[59] So can the seating arrangements. People who sit face to face are more likely to develop a win–lose orientation toward the conflict situation. In contrast, some negotiation groups deliberately intersperse participants around the table to convey a win–win orientation. Others arrange the seating so that both parties face a white board, reflecting the notion that both parties face the same problem or issue.

Time passage and deadlines   The more time people invest in negotiations, the stronger their commitment to reaching an agreement. This increases the motivation to resolve the conflict, but it also fuels the escalation of commitment problems described in Chapter 10. For example, the more time put into negotiations, the stronger the tendency to make unwarranted concessions so that the negotiations do not fail.

Time deadlines may be useful to the extent that they motivate the parties to complete negotiations. However, time deadlines may become a liability when exceeding deadlines is costly.[60] Negotiators make concessions and soften their demands more rapidly as the deadline approaches. Moreover, time pressure inhibits a problem-solving conflict management style, because the parties have less time to exchange information or present flexible offers.

Audience characteristics   Most negotiators have audiences—anyone with a vested interest in the negotiation outcomes, such as executives, other team members, or the general public. Negotiators tend to act differently when their audience observes the negotiation or has detailed information about the process, compared with situations in which the audience only sees the end results.[61] When the audience has direct surveillance over the proceedings, negotiators tend to be more competitive, less willing to make concessions, and more likely to engage in political tactics against the other party.[62] This "hard-line" behaviour shows the audience that the negotiator is working for their interests. With their audience watching, negotiators also have more interest in saving face. Sometimes, audiences are drawn into the negotiations by acting as a source of indirect appeals. The general public often takes on this role when groups negotiate with governments.[63]

Negotiator Behaviours

Negotiator behaviours play an important role in resolving conflict. Four of the most important behaviours are setting goals, gathering information, communicating effectively, and making concessions.

■ *Preparation and goal-setting*—Research has consistently reported that people have more favourable negotiation results when they prepare for the negotiation and set goals.[64] In particular, negotiators should carefully think through their initial offer, target, and resistance points. They need to consider alternative strategies in case the negotiation fails. Negotiators also need to check their underlying assumptions, as well as goals and values. Equally important is the need to research what the other party wants from the negotiation.

■ *Gathering information*—"Seek to understand before you seek to be understood." This popular philosophy from management guru Stephen Covey applies to effective negotiations. It means that we should spend more time listening closely to the other party and asking them for details of their position.[66] One way to improve the information gathering process is to have a team of people participate in negotiations. Asian companies tend to have large negotiation teams for this purpose.[67] With more information about an opponent's interests and needs, negotiators are better able to discover low-cost concessions or proposals that will satisfy the other side.

■ *Communicating effectively*—Effective negotiators communicate in a way that maintains effective relationships between the parties.[68] Specifically, they minimize socioemotional conflict by focusing on issues rather than people. Effective negotiators also avoid irritating statements such as "I think you'll agree that this is a generous offer." Third, effective negotiators are masters of persuasion. This does not involve misleading the other party. Rather, as discussed in Chapter 12, negotiators structure the content of their message so that it is accepted by others, not merely understood.[69]

■ *Making concessions*—Concessions are important because they (1) enable the parties to move toward the area of potential agreement, (2) symbolize each party's motivation to bargain in good faith, and (3) tell the other party of the relative importance of the negotiating items.[70] How many concessions should you make? This varies with the other party's expectations and the level of trust between you. For instance, many Chinese negotiators are wary of people who

Paul Tellier is a master negotiator with several recommendations for making deals come together. But Tellier has one recommendation above all others: preparation. "You have to be prepared every which way about the people, the subject, and your fallback position," advises the former CEO of Bombardier Inc. and former CEO of CN, two of North America's largest and most successful transportation companies. Part of the preparation process is to anticipate and practice unexpected issues that may arise. "Before walking into the room for the actual negotiation, I ask my colleagues to throw some curve balls at me," says Tellier.[65] In what other ways can people prepare for negotiations? *CP/Venelle Schneider*

www.cn.ca

change their position during the early stages of negotiations. Similarly, some writers warn that Russian negotiators tend to view concessions as a sign of weakness, rather than a sign of trust.[71] Generally, the best strategy is to be moderately tough and give just enough concessions to communicate sincerity and motivation to resolve the conflict.[72] Being too tough can undermine relations between the parties; giving too many concessions implies weakness and encourages the other party to use power and resistance.

THIRD-PARTY CONFLICT RESOLUTION

third-party conflict resolution
Any attempt by a relatively neutral person to help the parties resolve their differences.

Most of this chapter has focused on people directly involved in a conflict, yet many disputes in organizational settings are resolved with the assistance of a third party, such as your boss. **Third-party conflict resolution** is any attempt by a relatively neutral person to help parties resolve their differences. There are generally three types of third-party dispute resolution activities: arbitration, inquisition, and mediation. These activities can be classified by their level of control over the process and their control over the decision (see Exhibit 13.6).[73]

■ *Arbitration*—Arbitrators have high control over the final decision, but low control over the process.[74] Executives engage in this strategy by following previously-agreed rules of due process, listening to arguments from the disputing employees, and making a binding decision. Arbitration is applied as the final stage of grievances by unionized employees, but it is also becoming more common in nonunion conflicts. Some Canadian and American firms offer arbitration, in which peers serve as arbitrators.

■ *Inquisition*—Inquisitors control all discussion about the conflict. Like arbitrators, they have high decision control because they choose the form of conflict resolution. However, they also have high process control because they choose which information to examine, how to examine it, and generally decide how the conflict resolution process shall be handled.

EXHIBIT 13.6

Types of third-party intervention

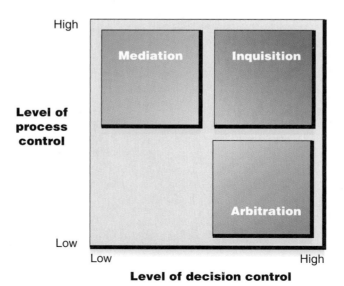

▓ *Mediation*—Mediators have high control over the intervention process. In fact, their main purpose is to manage the process and context of interaction between the disputing parties. However, the parties make the final decision about how to resolve their differences. Thus, mediators have little or no control over the conflict resolution decision.

Choosing the Best Third-Party Intervention Strategy

Team leaders, executives, and co-workers regularly intervene in disputes between employees and departments. Sometimes they adopt a mediator role; other times they serve as arbitrators. However, research suggests that people in positions of authority (e.g., managers) usually adopt an inquisitional approach whereby they dominate the intervention process as well as make a binding decision.[75] Managers like the inquisition approach because it is consistent with the decision-oriented nature of managerial jobs, gives them control over the conflict process and outcome, and tends to resolve disputes efficiently.

However, in organizational settings the inquisitional approach to third-party conflict resolution is usually the least effective.[76] One problem is that leaders who take an inquisitional role tend to collect only limited information about the problem using this approach, so their imposed decision may produce an ineffective solution to the conflict. Moreover, employees tend to think that the procedures and outcomes of inquisitions are unfair because they have little control over this approach.

Which third-party intervention is most appropriate in organizations? The answer depends partly on the situation.[77] For example, arbitration is much less popular in Hong Kong than in North America. But, generally speaking, for everyday disputes between two employees, the mediation approach is usually best because it gives employees more responsibility for resolving their own disputes; the third-party representative merely establishes an appropriate context for conflict resolution. Although not as efficient as other strategies, mediation potentially offers the highest level of employee satisfaction with the conflict process and outcomes.[78] When employees cannot resolve their differences, arbitration seems to work best because the predetermined rules of evidence and other processes create a higher sense of procedural fairness. Moreover, arbitration is preferred where the organization's goals should take priority over individual goals.

alternative dispute resolution (ADR)
A third-party dispute resolution process that includes mediation, typically followed by arbitration.

Alternative dispute resolution   TRW Inc. and several other firms take third-party resolution one step further through a comprehensive **alternative dispute resolution (ADR)** process. ADR combines third-party dispute resolution in an orderly sequence. ADR typically begins with a meeting between the employee and employer to clarify and negotiate their differences. If this fails, a mediator is brought in to help the parties reach a mutually agreeable solution. If mediation fails, the parties submit their case to an arbitrator whose decision may be either binding or voluntarily accepted by the employer. Although most ADR systems rely on professional arbitrators, some firms prefer peer arbitrations, which include a panel of co-workers and managers who are not involved in the dispute.[79]

ADR is useful in nonunion settings where a formal grievance process does not already exist. Although still rare in Canada, ADR is increasingly found in employee-employer disputes involving potentially legalistic processes. For instance, Workers Compensation agencies in some Canadian provinces encourage employees and employers to participate in an ADR process rather than proceeding directly to a quasi-judicial arbitration. ADR is more conciliatory and helps the parties solve their own problems.

Whether resolving conflict through third-party dispute resolution or direct negotiation, we need to recognize that many solutions come from the sources of conflict that were identified earlier in this chapter. This may seem obvious, but in the heat of conflict, people often focus on each other rather than on the underlying causes. Recognizing these conflict sources is the role of effective leadership, which is discussed in the next chapter.

CHAPTER SUMMARY

Conflict is the process by which one party perceives that its interests are being opposed or negatively affected by another party. The conflict process begins with the sources of conflict. These sources lead one or both sides to perceive a conflict and to experience conflict emotions. This, in turn, produces manifest conflict, such as behaviours toward the other side.

When conflict is task-related, the parties view the conflict experience as something separate from them. Disputes are much more difficult to resolve when they produce socioemotional conflict, where the parties perceive each other as the problem. The conflict process often escalates through a series of episodes and shifts from task-related to socioemotional conflict.

Conflict management maximizes the benefits and minimizes the dysfunctional consequences of conflict. Conflict is beneficial in the form of constructive conflict because it makes people think more fully about issues. Positive conflict also increases team cohesiveness when conflict is with another group. The main problems with conflict are that it may lead to job stress, dissatisfaction, and turnover. Dysfunctional intergroup conflict may undermine decision making.

Conflict tends to increase when people have incompatible goals, differentiation (different values and beliefs), interdependent tasks, scarce resources, ambiguous rules, and problems communicating with each other. Conflict is more common in a multicultural work force because of greater differentiation and communication problems among employees.

People with a win–win orientation believe the parties will find a mutually beneficial solution to their disagreement. Those with a win–lose orientation adopt the belief that the parties are drawing from a fixed pie. The latter tends to escalate conflict. Among the five interpersonal conflict management styles, only problem solving represents a purely win–win orientation. The four other styles—avoiding, forcing, yielding, and compromising—adopt some variation of a win–lose orientation. Women and people with high collectivism tend to use a problem solving or avoidance style more than men and people with low collectivism.

Structural approaches to conflict management include emphasizing superordinate goals, reducing differentiation, improving communication and understanding, reducing task interdependence, increasing resources, and clarifying rules and procedures. These elements can also be altered to stimulate conflict.

Negotiation occurs whenever two or more conflicting parties attempt to resolve their divergent goals by redefining the terms of their interdependence. Negotiations are influenced by several situational factors, including location, physical setting, time passage and deadlines, and audience. Important negotiator behaviours include preparation and goal setting, gathering information, communicating effectively, and making concessions.

Third-party conflict resolution is any attempt by a relatively neutral person to help parties resolve their differences. The three main forms of third-party dispute resolution are mediation, arbitration, and inquisition. Managers tend to use an inquisition approach, although mediation and arbitration are more appropriate, depending on the situation. Alternative dispute resolution applies mediation, but may also involve negotiation and eventually arbitration.

KEY TERMS

Alternative dispute resolution, p. 391

Conflict management, p. 374

Conflict, p. 372

Dialogue, p. 384

Negotiation, p. 386

Superordinate goals, p. 382

Third-party conflict resolution, p. 390

Win–lose orientation, p. 378

Win–win orientation, p. 378

DISCUSSION QUESTIONS

1. Distinguish task-related conflict from socioemotional conflict and explain where these two forms fit into the conflict-escalation cycle.

2. "All conflict is dysfunctional." Do you agree or disagree with this statement? Discuss.

3. During an employment interview an interviewee was asked: "Tell us about a time when you experienced conflict with a co-worker. What happened and what was the outcome of the conflict situation?" The interviewee replied, "I have never experienced conflict with anyone at work." What is your reaction to the interviewee's statement? What are your recommendations to the interviewers?

4. What effect does the increasing cultural diversity of the workforce have on the potential for conflict in organizations? Explain your answer. Identify two examples from your own experience when differing values or beliefs resulted in conflict in an organizational or educational setting. What was the outcome of each conflict you identified?

5. This chapter describes five conflict management styles. Discuss situations in which each of these styles would be best used to resolve conflicts among students (such as in projects) and between students and the instructor.

6. You have recently been appointed team leader of a cross-functional team. What approach could you implement as your team is formed to minimize dysfunctional conflict?

7. Suppose you head one of five divisions in a multinational organization and are about to begin this year's budget deliberations at headquarters. What are the characteristics of your audience in these negotiations and what effect might they have on your negotiation behaviour?

8. Managers tend to use an inquisitional approach to resolving disputes between employees and departments. Describe the inquisitional approach and discuss its appropriateness to organizational settings.

CASE STUDY 13.1

CONFLICT IN CLOSE QUARTERS

A team of psychologists at Moscow's Institute for Biomedical Problems (IBMP) wanted to learn more about the dynamics of long-term isolation in space. This knowledge would be applied to the International Space Station, a joint project of several countries that would send people into space for more than six months and eventually include a trip to Mars taking up to three years.

IBMP set up a replica of the Mir space station in Moscow. They then arranged for three international researchers from Japan, Canada, and Austria to spend 110 days isolated in a chamber the size of a train car. This chamber joined a smaller chamber where four Russian cosmonauts had already completed half of their 240 days of isolation. This was the first time an international crew had been involved in the studies. None of the participants spoke English as their first language, yet they communicated in English throughout their stay, at varying levels of proficiency.

Judith Lapierre, a French Canadian, was the only female in the experiment. Along with a PhD in public health and social medicine, Lapierre had studied space sociology at the International Space

University in France, and conducted isolation research in the Antarctic. This was her fourth trip to Russia, where she had learned the language. The mission was supposed to have a second female participant from the Japanese space program, but she was not selected by IBMP.

The Japanese and Austrian participants viewed the participation of a woman as a favourable factor, says Lapierre. For example, to make the surroundings more comfortable, they rearranged the furniture, hung posters on the wall, and put a tablecloth on the kitchen table. "We adapted our environment, whereas the Russians just viewed it as something to be endured," she explains. "We decorated for Christmas, because I'm the kind of person who likes to host people."

New Year's Eve Turmoil

Ironically, it was at one of those social events, the New Year's Eve party, that events took a turn for the worse. After drinking vodka (allowed by the Russian space agency), two of the Russian cosmonauts got into a fistfight that left blood splattered on the chamber walls. At one point, a colleague hid the knives in the station's kitchen because of fears that the two Russians were about to stab each other. The two cosmonauts, who generally did not get along, had to be restrained by other men. Soon after that brawl, the Russian commander grabbed Lapierre, dragged her out of view of the television monitoring cameras, and kissed her aggressively—twice. Lapierre fought him off, but the message didn't register. He tried to kiss her again the next morning.

The next day, the international crew complained to IBMP about the behaviour of the Russian cosmonauts. The Russian institute apparently took no action against any of the aggressors. Instead, its psychologists replied that the incidents were part of the experiment. They wanted crew members to solve their personal problems with mature discussion, without asking for outside help. "You have to understand that Mir is an autonomous object, far away from anything," Vadim Gushin, the IBMP psychologist in charge of the project explained after the experiment ended in March. "If the crew can't solve problems among themselves, they can't work together."

Following IBMP's response, the international crew wrote a scathing letter to the Russian institute and the space agencies involved in the experiment. "We had never expected such events to take place in a highly controlled scientific experiment where individuals go through a multistep selection process," they wrote. "If we had known . . . we would not have joined it as subjects." The letter also complained about IBMP's response to their concerns.

Informed of the New Year's Eve incident, the Japanese space program convened an emergency meeting on January 2nd to address the incidents. Soon after, the Japanese team member quit, apparently shocked by IBMP's inaction. He was replaced with a Russian researcher on the international team. Ten days after the fight—a little over a month after the international team began the mission—the doors between the Russian and international crew's chambers were barred at the request of the international research team. Lapierre later emphasized that this action was taken because of concerns about violence, not the incident involving her.

A Stolen Kiss or Sexual Harassment

By the end of the experiment in March, news of the fistfight between the cosmonauts and the commander's attempts to kiss Lapierre had reached the public. Russian scientists attempted to play down the kissing incident by saying that it was one fleeting kiss, a clash of cultures, and a female participant who was too emotional.

"In the West, some kinds of kissing are regarded as sexual harassment. In our culture it's nothing," said Russian scientist Vadim Gushin in one interview. In another interview, he explained: "The problem of sexual harassment is given a lot of attention in North America but less in Europe. In Russia it is even less of an issue, not because we are more or less moral than the rest of the world; we just have different priorities."

Judith Lapierre says the kissing incident was tolerable compared to this reaction from the Russian scientists who conducted the experiment. "They don't get it at all," she complains. "They don't think anything is wrong. I'm more frustrated than ever. The worst thing is that they don't realize it was wrong."

Norbert Kraft, the Austrian scientist on the international team, also disagreed with the Russian interpretation of events. "They're trying to protect themselves," he says. "They're trying to put the fault on others. But this is not a cultural issue. If a woman doesn't want to be kissed, it is not acceptable."

Discussion Questions

1. Identify the different conflict episodes that exist in this case. Who was in conflict with whom?

2. What are the sources of conflict for these incidents?

3. What conflict management style(s) did Lapierre, the international team, and Gushin use to resolve these conflicts? What style(s) would have worked best in these situations?

4. What conflict management interventions were applied here? Did they work? What alternative strategies would work best in this situation and in the future?

The facts of this case have been pieced together by Steven L. McShane from the following sources: G. Sinclair Jr., "If you Scream in Space, Does Anyone Hear?" *Winnipeg Free Press*, May 5, 2000, p. A4; S. Martin, "Reining in the Space Cowboys," *Globe & Mail*, April 19, 2000, p. R1; M. Gray, "A Space Dream Sours," *Maclean's*, April 17, 2000, p. 26; E. Niiler, "In Search of the Perfect Astronaut," *Boston Globe*, April 4, 2000, p. E4; J. Tracy, "110-Day Isolation Ends in Sullen ... Isolation," *Moscow Times*, March 30, 2000, p. 1; M. Warren, "A Mir Kiss?" *Daily Telegraph* (London), March 30, 2000, p. 22; G. York, "Canadian's Harassment Complaint Scorned," *Globe and Mail*, March 25, 2000, p. A2; S. Nolen, "Lust in Space," *Globe and Mail*, March 24, 2000, p. A3.

T E A M   E X E R C I S E   13.2

UGLI ORANGE ROLE PLAY

Purpose This exercise is designed to help you understand the dynamics of interpersonal and intergroup conflict as well as the effectiveness of negotiation strategies under specific conditions.

Materials The instructor will distribute roles for Dr. Roland, Dr. Jones and a few observers. Ideally, each negotiation should occur in a private area away from other negotiations.

Instructions

■ *Step 1:* The instructor will divide the class into an even number of teams of three people each, with one participant left over for each team formed (e.g., six observers if there are six teams). Half the teams will take the role of Dr. Roland and the other half will be Dr. Jones. The instructor will distribute roles after these teams have been formed.

■ *Step 2:* Members within each team are given 10 minutes (or other time limit stated by the instructor) to learn their roles and decide negotiating strategy.

■ *Step 3:* After reading their roles and discussing strategy, each Dr. Jones team is matched with a Dr. Roland team to conduct negotiations. Observers will receive observation forms from the instructor, and two observers will be assigned to watch the paired teams during prenegotiations and subsequent negotiations.

■ *Step 4:* As soon as Roland and Jones reach agreement or at the end of the time allotted for the negotiation (whichever comes first), the Roland and Jones teams report to the instructor for further instruction.

■ *Step 5:* At the end of the exercise, the class will congregate to discuss the negotiations. Observers, negotiators and instructors will then discuss their observations and experiences and the implications for conflict management and negotiation.

This exercise was developed by Robert J House, Wharton Business School, University of Pennsylvania. A similar incident is also attributed to earlier writing by R. R. Blake and J. S. Mouton.

THE DUTCH TEST FOR CONFLICT HANDLING

Purpose   This self-assessment is designed to help you to identify your preferred conflict management style.

Instructions   Read each of the statements below and circle the response that you believe best reflects your position regarding each statement. Then use the scoring key in Appendix B to calculate your results for each conflict management style. This exercise is completed alone so students assess themselves honestly without concerns of social comparison. However, class discussion will focus on the different conflict management styles and the situations in which each is most appropriate.

Dutch Test for Conflict Handling					
When I have a conflict at work, I do the following:	Not at All ▼				Very Much ▼
1. I give in to the wishes of the other party.	1	2	3	4	5
2. I try to realize a middle-of-the-road solution.	1	2	3	4	5
3. I push my own point of view.	1	2	3	4	5
4. I examine issues until I find a solution that really satisfies me and the other party.	1	2	3	4	5
5. I avoid confrontation about our differences.	1	2	3	4	5
6. I concur with the other party.	1	2	3	4	5
7. I emphasize that we have to find a compromise solution.	1	2	3	4	5
8. I search for gains.	1	2	3	4	5
9. I stand for my own and others' goals and interests.	1	2	3	4	5
10. I avoid differences of opinion as much as possible.	1	2	3	4	5
11. I try to accommodate the other party.	1	2	3	4	5
12. I insist we both give in a little.	1	2	3	4	5
13. I fight for a good outcome for myself.	1	2	3	4	5
14. I examine ideas from both sides to find a mutually optimal solution.	1	2	3	4	5
15. I try to make differences loom less severe.	1	2	3	4	5
16. I adapt to the parties' goals and interests.	1	2	3	4	5
17. I strive whenever possible towards a fifty-fifty compromise.	1	2	3	4	5
18. I do everything to win.	1	2	3	4	5
19. I work out a solution that serves my own as well as others' interests as good as possible.	1	2	3	4	5
20. I try to avoid a confrontation with the other.	1	2	3	4	5

Source: C. K. W. de Dreu, A. Evers, B. Beersma, E. S. Kluwer, and A. Nauta, "A Theory-based Measure of Conflict Management Strategies in the Workplace," *Journal of Organizational Behavior*, 22 (2001), pp. 645–68.

After studying the preceding material, be sure to check out our Online Learning Centre at

www.mcgrawhill.ca/college/mcshane

for more in-depth information and interactivities that correspond to this chapter.

14

Leadership in Organizational Settings

Learning Objectives

AFTER READING THIS CHAPTER, YOU SHOULD BE ABLE TO:

- Define leadership.

- List seven competencies of effective leaders.

- Describe the people-oriented and task-oriented leadership styles.

- Outline the path–goal theory of leadership.

- Discuss the importance of Fiedler's contingency model of leadership.

- Contrast transactional with transformational leadership.

- Describe the four elements of transformational leadership.

- Identify three reasons why people inflate the importance of leadership.

- Explain how societal culture influences our perceptions of effective leaders.

- Discuss similarities and differences in the leadership styles of women and men.

The world has changed, and so has our concept of effective leadership. That's what consultants Booz Allen & Hamilton and the World Economic Forum's Strategic Leadership Project recently reported. Based on interviews with 6,000 executives and employees in several countries, they found that effective leaders subordinate their own egos and, instead, nurture leadership in others throughout an organization. "The trick to leadership often is listening to the leaders around you," advises Rick Antonson, president and CEO of Tourism Vancouver.

Cynthia Trudell also recognizes this emerging view of leadership. "I believe the ability to listen is as fundamental as any other skill in the ability to lead," says the Canadian executive who previously led the Saturn division of General Motors and is now president of Brunswick Corp.'s Sea Ray Group. Trudell also emphasizes that leaders must be able to move others in a new direction through passion. "A great leader is one who has vision, perseverance, and the capacity to inspire others," she says.

This new image is a far cry from the "command-and-control" leaders of yesteryear who took centre stage and pretended to have all the answers. "I don't think that dictatorial leaders will survive," warns United Airlines executive Anne Keating. "It's an old-fashioned way of leading people." Wal King, CEO of Leighton Constructions, agrees. "Leadership style has gone from an autocratic style to encouraging participation to achieve a common outcome."

Others emphasize that leadership is partly determined by personal characteristics. "In my mind, trust, ethics and honesty comprise the new 'leadership currency,'" says Gary Irvin, CEO of FORUM Credit Union. Rich Teerlink, the recently retired CEO of Harley-Davidson, offers a more detailed list of leadership values: "Tell the truth. Be fair. Keep your promises. Respect individuality. If leaders live by those, they can be successful."[1]

www.searay.com

"A great leader is one who has vision, perseverance, and the capacity to inspire others," says Cynthia Trudell, the Canadian executive who is president of Brunswick Corp.'s Sea Ray Group.
CP/Nina Long

leadership

Influencing, motivating, and enabling others to contribute toward the effectiveness and success of the organizations of which they are members.

What is leadership? The opening vignette illustrates that our concept of leadership is changing, but it remains a complex issue that stirs up plenty of interest and discussion. Reviews of the leadership literature state that scholars do not sufficiently agree on the definition of leadership.[2] However, at a meeting at the University of Calgary a few years ago, 54 scholars from 38 countries reached a consensus that **leadership** is the ability to influence, motivate, and enable others to contribute toward the effectiveness and success of the organizations of which they are members.[3]

Leaders apply various forms of influence—from subtle persuasion to direct application of power—to ensure that followers have the motivation and role clarity to achieve specified goals. Leaders also arrange the work environment—such as allocating resources and altering communication patterns—so that employees can achieve corporate objectives more easily. However leadership is defined, only 8 percent of executives in large firms think their organizations have enough of it.[4] Most are concerned about a lack of leadership talent.

Leadership isn't restricted to the executive suite. Anyone in the organization may be a leader.[5] Indeed, the emerging view, as we read in the opening vignette to this chapter, is that effective leaders teach and empower their employees to take leadership roles. "We're quite serious when we talk about leadership even to a bench worker on the assembly line," says an executive at General Semiconductor, a global high-technology company. "Lots of people will say, 'Oh, I'm not a leader,' but when we point out that the essence of leadership is influence, they realize everyone has leadership qualities and responsibilities."[6]

Effective self-directed work teams, for example, consist of members who share leadership responsibilities or otherwise allocate this role to a responsible coordinator. Similarly, research indicates that technology champions—employees who overcome technical and organizational obstacles to introduce technological change in their area of the organization—are most successful when they possess the traits and enact the behaviours we associate with effective leadership.[8] The point here is that anyone can be a leader at an appropriate time and place.

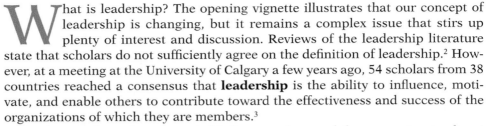

Newfoundland Power Inc. depends on leadership in each of its employees. "When there is a truck on the side of the road, there are two guys who are working without supervision. We trust them," explains Newfoundland Power CEO Philip Hughes. "Both of these guys has to have leadership qualities or nothing will happen." The power utility has dramatically improved customer service by recognizing that leadership is not restricted to the executive suite. "If there is a storm, there is no handbook or manual," Hughes explains. "The employees have to be part construction worker, part electrician and part journey person. This takes teamwork and leadership."[7] How can corporate leaders leverage the power of leadership throughout the organization? *Photo courtesy The Telegram*
www.newfoundlandpower.com

PERSPECTIVES OF LEADERSHIP

Leadership has been contemplated since the days of Greek philosophers and it is one of the most popular research topics among organizational behaviour scholars. This has resulted in an enormous volume of leadership literature, most of which can be spit into the five perspectives shown in Exhibit 14.1. Although some of these perspectives are currently more popular than others, each helps us to more fully understand this complex issue.

EXHIBIT 14.1

Perspectives of
leadership

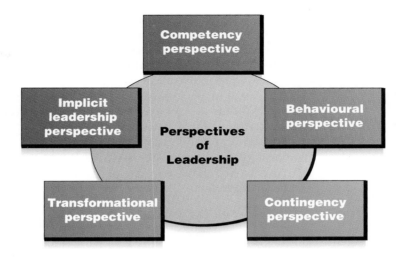

Some scholars have studied the traits or competencies of great leaders, whereas others have looked at their behaviours. More recent studies have looked at leadership from a contingency approach by considering the appropriate leader behaviours in different settings. Currently, the most popular perspective is that leaders transform organizations through their vision, communication, and ability to build commitment. An emerging perspective suggests that leadership is mainly a perceptual bias. We distort reality and attribute events to leaders because we feel more comfortable believing that a competent individual is at the organization's helm.[9] This chapter explores each of these five perspectives of leadership. In the final section, we also look at cross-cultural and gender issues in organizational leadership.

COMPETENCY (TRAIT) PERSPECTIVE OF LEADERSHIP

Kathleen Taylor, head of worldwide operations at Four Seasons Hotels and Resorts, is highly regarded for her leadership characteristics. "There's a combination of being very intelligent with a practical sense of common sense," says her boss, Isadore Sharp, who is founder and CEO of the Toronto-based hotel chain. "She's very self-confident with great humility," Sharp said. "She has a great sense of fairness and sensitivity while being very direct with a high measure of integrity."[10]

Isadore Sharp's comments indicate that effective leaders possess certain characteristics. Since the beginning of recorded civilization, people have been interested in the personal characteristics that distinguish great leaders from the rest of us. The ancient Egyptians demanded authority, discrimination, and justice from their leaders. The Greek philosopher Plato called for prudence, courage, temperance, and justice.[11]

For the first half of the 20th century, organizational behaviour scholars used scientific methods to determine whether certain personality traits and physical characteristics (particularly, the person's height and weight) actually distinguish leaders from lesser souls. A major review in the late 1940s concluded that no consistent list of traits could be distilled from the hundreds of studies conducted up to that time. A subsequent review suggested that a few traits are consistently associated with effective leaders, but that most are unrelated to effective leadership.[12] These conclusions caused many scholars to give up their search for the personal characteristics that distinguish effective leaders.

In the early 1990s, leadership scholars began to re-examine the trait approach, but with more emphasis on specific *competencies*. Competencies encompass a broader range of personal characteristics—such as knowledge, skills, abilities, and values—that were not considered by earlier studies on leadership traits. The recent studies coincided with the increasing popularity of competency-based practices in organizations, such as the competency-based rewards described in Chapter 6.[13] Recent leadership literature identifies seven competencies that are characteristic of effective leaders.[14] These competencies are listed in Exhibit 14.2 and briefly described below.

▪ *Emotional intelligence*—Effective leaders have a high level of emotional intelligence.[15] They have the ability to perceive and express emotion, assimilate emotion in thought, understand and reason with emotion, and regulate emotion in themselves and others (see Chapter 4).[16] Emotional intelligence requires a strong self-monitoring personality (see Chapter 2) because leaders must be sensitive to situational cues and readily adapt their own behaviour appropriately.[17] It also requires the ability to empathize with others and possess the social skills necessary to build rapport as well as network with others. Moreover, the contingency leadership perspective described later in this chapter assumes that effective leaders are high self-monitors so they can adjust their behaviour to match the situation.

▪ *Integrity*—This refers to the leader's truthfulness and tendency to translate words into deeds. Several large-scale studies have reported that integrity is the most important leadership characteristic. Employees want honest leaders whom they can trust.[18]

EXHIBIT 14.2 Seven competencies of effective leaders	**Leadership trait**	**Description**
	Emotional intelligence	The leader's ability to perceive and express emotion, assimilate emotion in thought, understand and reason with emotion, and regulate emotion in oneself and others
	Integrity	The leader's truthfulness and tendency to translate words into deeds
	Drive	The leader's inner motivation to pursue goals
	Leadership motivation	The leader's need for socialized power to accomplish team or organizational goals
	Self-confidence	The leader's belief in his or her own leadership skills and ability to achieve objectives
	Intelligence	The leader's above-average cognitive ability to process enormous amounts of information
	Knowledge of the business	The leader's understanding of the company's environment to make more intuitive decisions

Sources: Most elements of this list were derived from S. A. Kirkpatrick and E. A. Locke, "Leadership: Do Traits Matter?" *Academy of Management Executive*, 5 (May 1991), pp. 48–60. Several of these ideas are also discussed in H. B. Gregersen, A. J. Morrison, and J. S. Black, "Developing Leaders for the Global Frontier," *Sloan Management Review*, 40 (Fall 1998), pp. 21–32; R. J. House and R. N. Aditya, "The Social Scientific Study of Leadership: Quo Vadis?" *Journal of Management*, 23 (1997), pp. 409–73.

▪ *Drive*—Leaders have a high need for achievement (see Chapter 5). This drive refers to the inner motivation that leaders possess to pursue their goals and encourage others to move forward with theirs. Drive inspires an unbridled inquisitiveness and a need for constant learning.

▪ *Leadership motivation*—Leaders have a strong need for power because they want to influence others (see Chapter 5). However, they tend to have a need for "socialized power" because their motivation is constrained by a strong sense of altruism and social responsibility.[19] In other words, effective leaders try to gain power so they can influence others to accomplish goals that benefit the team or organization.

▪ *Self-confidence*—Kathleen Taylor and other leaders believe in their leadership skills and ability to achieve objectives. They possess the self-efficacy that they are capable to lead others.[20]

▪ *Intelligence*—Leaders have above-average cognitive ability to process enormous amounts of information. Leaders aren't necessarily geniuses; rather, they have a superior ability to analyze alternate scenarios and identify potential opportunities.

▪ *Knowledge of the business*—Effective leaders know the business environment in which they operate. This helps their intuition recognize opportunities and understand their organization's capacity to capture those opportunities.

Competency (Trait) Perspective Limitations and Practical Implications

One concern with the competency perspective is that it assumes great leaders have the same personal characteristics, all of which are equally important in all situations. This is probably a false assumption; leadership is far too complex to have a universal list of traits that apply to every condition. Some competencies might not be important all the time. Moreover, research suggests that alternative combinations of competencies may be equally successful. In other words, people with two different sets of competencies might be equally good leaders.[21]

A few scholars have also warned that some personal characteristics might only influence our perception that someone is a leader, not whether that person really makes a difference to the organization's success.[22] People who exhibit integrity, self-confidence, and other traits are called leaders because they fit our stereotype of an effective leader. Or we might see a successful person, call that person a leader, and then attribute self-confidence and other unobservable traits that we consider essential for great leaders. We will discuss this perceptual distortion more fully toward the end of the chapter.

Aside from these limitations, the competency perspective recognizes that some people possess personal characteristics that offer them a higher potential to be great leaders. The most obvious implication of this is that organizations are relying increasingly on competency-based methods to hire people for future leadership positions.[23] Leadership talents are important throughout the organization, so this recommendation should extend to all levels of hiring, not just senior executives. Companies also need to determine which behaviours represent these competencies so that employees with leadership talents can be identified early for promotion.

The competency perspective of leadership does not necessarily imply that great leaders are born, rather than developed. On the contrary, competencies only indicate leadership potential, not leadership performance. People with these characteristics become effective leaders only after they have developed and mastered the necessary leadership behaviours. People with somewhat lower leadership competencies may become very effective leaders because they have leveraged their potential more fully. This means that companies must do more than hire people with certain competencies. They must also develop their potential through leadership development programs and practical experience in the field.

BEHAVIOURAL PERSPECTIVE OF LEADERSHIP

In the 1940s and 1950s, scholars from Ohio State University launched an intensive research investigation to answer the question: What behaviours make leaders effective? Questionnaires were administered to subordinates, asking them to rate their supervisors on a large number of behaviours. These studies, along with similar research at the University of Michigan and Harvard University, distilled two clusters of leadership behaviours from more than 1,800 leadership behaviour items.[24]

One cluster represented people-oriented behaviours. This included showing mutual trust and respect for subordinates, demonstrating a genuine concern for their needs, and having a desire to look out for their welfare. Leaders with a strong people-oriented style listen to employee suggestions, do personal favours for employees, support their interests when required, and treat employees as equals.

The other cluster represented a task-oriented leadership style and included behaviours that define and structure work roles. Task-oriented leaders assign employees to specific tasks, clarify their work duties and procedures, ensure that they follow company rules, and push them to reach their performance capacity. They establish stretch goals and challenge employees to push beyond those high standards.

Choosing Task- versus People-Oriented Leadership

Should leaders be task-oriented or people-oriented? This is a difficult question to answer because each style has its advantages and disadvantages. People-oriented leadership is associated with higher job satisfaction among subordinates, as well as lower absenteeism, grievances, and turnover. However, job performance tends to be lower than for employees with task-oriented leaders.[25] Task-oriented leadership, on the other hand, seems to increase productivity and team unity. Canadian university students apparently value task-oriented instructors because they want clear objectives and well-prepared lectures that abide by the unit's objectives.[26]

One problem with task-oriented leadership is that it is associated with lower job satisfaction as well as higher absenteeism and turnover among subordinates. This is an increasing concern because today's workforce is less receptive to "command-and-control" leadership. Employees want to participate in decisions rather than receive them without question.[27] Another problem with the task-oriented leadership style is knowing how far to challenge employees. As Connections 14.1 describes, some bosses are friendly tyrants while others cross the line as bullies.

Behavioural leadership scholars reported that these two styles are independent of each other. Some people are high or low on both styles; others are high on one style and low on the other. Most are somewhere in between. Early scholars concluded that the most effective leaders exhibit high levels of both task-oriented and people-oriented behaviours.[28] Out of this hypothesis developed a popular leadership development program, called the **Leadership Grid®** (formerly known as the *Managerial Grid*).[29] Participants assess their current levels of task-oriented and people-oriented leadership, then work with trainers to achieve maximum levels of concern for both people and production (task).

Leadership Grid®
A leadership model that assesses leadership effectiveness in terms of the person's level of task-oriented and people-oriented style.

When Tough Taskmasters Become Bullying Bosses

Dominic D'Alessandro has a reputation for stellar business acumen and high levels of passion and intensity. But the CEO of Toronto-based Manulife Financial Corp. is also known as a tough taskmaster. "He always set the bar very high. Once you'd cleared it, he'd raise it even higher," says a former employee. D'Alessandro admits he's very demanding, but believes it is good for the organization. "I don't apologize for it," he says. "I'm no more demanding of people who work with me than I am of myself."

D'Alessandro may be a tough taskmaster, but other executives have slipped into the harsher role of a bullying boss. According to former staff at Livent Inc., senior managers at the Toronto-based theatre company bullied and verbally abused employees to work harder. Timothy Lloyd was under such intense pressure and verbal abuse from his boss at Imperial Parking in Calgary that he successfully sued for constructive dismissal (i.e. the company violated the employment relationship).

The CEO of Cerner Corp. gained notoriety after he warned staff in an e-mail that layoffs would occur and time clocks would be installed unless they worked well beyond the usual 40-hour work week. "The pizza man should show up at 7:30 p.m. to feed the starving teams working late," the e-mail stated. "The lot should be half-full on Saturday mornings ... You have two weeks. Tick, tock." Cerner's shareholders apparently dislike bossy leaders. The medical software firm's stock dropped by 22 percent when the abusive e-mail became public.

Rob Hain, CEO of Toronto-based AIM Funds Management Inc., is well aware of the problems with task-oriented bosses who push too hard. "You can't make 1,200 people do something," says Hain, who prefers to

Dominic D'Alessandro agrees that he is a tough boss, but says he is just as demanding of himself as he is of others. *CP/Kevin Frayer*

delegate decisions to staff and emphasizes his preference for work-life balance. "If you have to show a report card at the end of the day about how much blood you've spilled on the street, then why would anyone want to work for you?"

Sources: M. Johne, "When Bullies go to Work," *Globe and Mail*, April 17, 2002, p. C1; K. Macklem, "The Anti-Establishment CEO," *Maclean's*, December 17, 2001; R. McQueen, "AIM's Rob Hain has his Clients Scoped Out," *National Post*, July 16, 2001, p. C10; D. Hayes and J.A. Karash, "Harsh E-Mail Roils Cerner," *Kansas City Star*, March 24, 2001, p. A1; A. Clark, "An Epic from Livent," *Maclean's*, March 1, 1999, pp. 40–41;
www.manulife.ca

The problem with the behavioural leadership perspective, as subsequent research has discovered, is that it implies that high levels of both styles are best in all situations. In reality, the best leadership style depends on the situation.[30] On a positive note, the behavioural perspective laid the foundation for two of the main leadership styles—people-oriented and task-oriented—found in many contemporary leadership theories. These contemporary theories adopt a contingency perspective, which we describe next.

CONTINGENCY PERSPECTIVE OF LEADERSHIP

The contingency perspective of leadership is based on the idea that the most appropriate leadership style depends on the situation. Most (though not all) contingency leadership theories assume that effective leaders must be both insightful and flexible.[31] They must be able to adapt their behaviours and styles to the immediate situation. This isn't easy to do, however. Typically, leaders have a preferred style. It takes considerable effort for leaders to learn when and how to alter their styles to match the situation. As we noted earlier, leaders must have a high emotional intelligence, particularly a self-monitoring personality, so they can diagnose the circumstances and match their behaviours accordingly.[32]

Path–Goal Theory of Leadership

path–goal leadership theory
A contingency theory of leadership based on expectancy theory of motivation that relates several leadership styles to specific employee and situational contingencies.

Several contingency theories have been proposed over the years, but **path–goal leadership theory** has withstood scientific critique better than the others. The theory has its roots in the expectancy theory of motivation (see Chapter 5).[33] Early research incorporated expectancy theory into the study of how leader behaviours influence employee perceptions of expectancies (paths) between employee effort and performance (goals). Based on this perspective, scholars developed and refined path–goal theory as a contingency leadership model.[34]

Path–goal theory states that effective leaders influence employee satisfaction and performance by making their need satisfaction contingent on effective job performance. Leaders strengthen the performance-to-outcome expectancy and valences of those outcomes by ensuring that employees who perform their jobs well have a higher degree of need fulfillment than employees who perform poorly.

Effective leaders strengthen the effort-to-performance expectancy by providing the information, support, and other resources necessary to help employees complete their tasks.[35] For instance, the best performing self-directed work teams at Xerox had leaders who gave first priority to arranging organizational support for the team.[36] In other words, path–goal theory advocates **servant leadership**.[37] Servant leaders do not view leadership as a position of power; rather, they are coaches, stewards, and facilitators. Leadership is an obligation to understand employee needs and to facilitate their work performance. Servant leaders ask, "How can I help you?" rather than expecting employees to serve them.

servant leadership
The belief that leaders serve followers by understanding their needs and facilitating their work performance.

Leadership styles   Exhibit 14.3 presents the path–goal theory of leadership. This model highlights four leadership styles and several contingency factors leading to three indicators of leader effectiveness. The four leadership styles are:[38]

■ *Directive*—These are clarifying behaviours that provide a psychological structure for subordinates. The leader clarifies performance goals, the means to reach those goals, and the standards against which performance will be judged. It also includes judicious use of rewards and disciplinary actions. Directive leadership is the same as the task-oriented leadership described earlier and echoes our discussion in Chapter 2 on the importance of clear role perceptions in employee performance.

■ *Supportive*—These behaviours provide psychological support for subordinates. The leader is friendly and approachable, makes the work more pleasant, treats employees with equal respect, and shows concern for the status, needs, and well-being of employees. Supportive leadership is the same as the people-oriented leadership described earlier and reflects the benefits of social support to help employees cope with stressful situations (see Chapter 7).

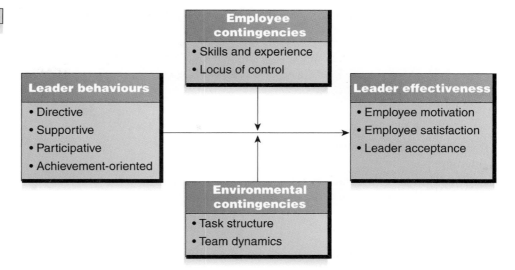

EXHIBIT 14.3

Path–goal
leadership theory

Employee contingencies
- Skills and experience
- Locus of control

Leader behaviours
- Directive
- Supportive
- Participative
- Achievement-oriented

Leader effectiveness
- Employee motivation
- Employee satisfaction
- Leader acceptance

Environmental contingencies
- Task structure
- Team dynamics

Participative—These behaviours encourage and facilitate subordinate involvement in decisions beyond their normal work activities. The leader consults with employees, asks for their suggestions, and takes these ideas into serious consideration before making a decision. Participative leadership relates to involving employees in decisions (see Chapter 10).

Achievement-oriented—These behaviours encourage employees to reach their peak performance. The leader sets challenging goals, expects employees to perform at their highest level, continuously seeks improvement in employee performance, and shows a high degree of confidence that employees will assume responsibility and accomplish challenging goals. Achievement-oriented leadership applies goal-setting theory (Chapter 5) as well as positive expectations in self-fulfilling prophecy (Chapter 3).

The path–goal model contends that effective leaders are capable of selecting the most appropriate behavioural style (or styles) for that situation. Leaders might use more than one style at a time. For example, they might be both supportive and participative in a specific situation.

Contingencies of Path–Goal Theory

As a contingency theory, path–goal theory states that each of these four leadership styles will be effective in some situations but not in others. The path–goal leadership model specifies two sets of situational variables that moderate the relationship between a leader's style and effectiveness: (1) employee characteristics and (2) characteristics of the employee's work environment. Several contingencies have already been studied within the path–goal framework, and the model is open for more variables in the future.[39] However, we will examine only four contingencies here (see Exhibit 14.4).

Skill and experience A combination of directive and supportive leadership is best for employees who are (or perceive themselves to be) inexperienced and

EXHIBIT 14.4   Selected contingencies of path–goal theory

	Directive	Supportive	Participative	Achievement-oriented
Employee contingencies				
Skill and experience	Low	Low	High	High
Locus of control	External	External	Internal	Internal
Environmental contingencies				
Task structure	Nonroutine	Routine	Nonroutine	?
Team dynamics	Negative norms	Low cohesion	Positive norms	?

unskilled. Directive leadership gives subordinates information about how to accomplish the task, whereas supportive leadership helps them cope with the uncertainties of unfamiliar work situations. Directive leadership is detrimental when employees are skilled and experienced because it introduces too much supervisory control.

Locus of control   Recall from Chapter 2 that people with an internal locus of control believe that they have control over their work environment. Consequently, these employees prefer participative and achievement-oriented leadership styles and may become frustrated with a directive style. In contrast, people with an external locus of control believe their performance is due more to luck and fate, so they tend to be more satisfied with directive and supportive leadership.

Task structure   Leaders should adopt the directive style when the task is non-routine, because this style minimizes role ambiguity, which tends to occur in these complex work situations (particularly for inexperienced employees).[40] The directive style is ineffective when employees have routine and simple tasks because the manager's guidance serves no purpose and may be viewed as unnec-essarily close control. Employees in highly routine and simple jobs may require supportive leadership to help them cope with the tedious nature of the work and lack of control over the pace of work. Participative leadership is preferred for employees performing nonroutine tasks because the lack of rules and proce-dures gives them more discretion to achieve challenging goals. The participative style is ineffective for employees in routine tasks because they lack discretion over their work.

Team dynamics   Cohesive teams with performance-oriented norms act as a substitute for most leader interventions. High team cohesiveness substitutes for supportive leadership, whereas performance-oriented team norms substitute for directive and possibly achievement-oriented leadership. Thus, when team cohe-siveness is low, leaders should use the supportive style. They should apply a direc-tive style to counteract team norms that oppose the team's formal objectives. For example, the team leader may need to use legitimate power if team members have developed a norm to "take it easy" rather than get a project completed on time.

Practical Implications and Limitations of Path–Goal Theory

Path–goal theory has received considerable research support, certainly more than other contingency leadership models.[41] However, one or two contingencies (i.e. task structure) have found limited research support. Other contingencies and leadership styles in the path–goal leadership model haven't received scholarly investigation at all.[42] For example, some cells in Exhibit 14.4 have question marks because we do not yet know how those leadership styles apply to those contingencies. A recently expanded model adds new leadership styles and contingencies, but they have not yet been tested. Until further study comes along, it is unclear whether certain contingencies should be considered when choosing the best leadership style.

Another concern is that as path–goal theory expands, the model may become too complex for practical use. Although the model provides a detailed representation of the complexity of leadership, it may become too cumbersome for training people in leadership styles. Few people would be able to remember all the contingencies and appropriate leadership styles for those contingencies. In spite of these limitations, path–goal theory remains a relatively complete and robust contingency leadership theory.

Other Contingency Theories

At the beginning of this chapter we noted that numerous leadership theories have developed over the years. Most of them are found in the contingency perspective of leadership. Some overlap with the path–goal model in terms of leadership styles, but most use simpler and more abstract contingencies. We will very briefly mention only two here because of their popularity and historical significance to the field.

Situational leadership model   One of the most popular contingency theories among trainers is the **situational leadership model**, developed by Paul Hersey and Ken Blanchard.[43] The model suggests that effective leaders vary their style with the "readiness" of followers. (An earlier version of the model called this "maturity.") Readiness refers to the employee's or work team's ability and willingness to accomplish a specific task. Ability refers to the extent to which the follower has the skills and knowledge to perform the task without the leader's guidance. Willingness refers to the follower's self-motivation and commitment to perform the assigned task. The model compresses these distinct concepts into a single situational condition.

The situational leadership model also identifies four leadership styles—telling, selling, participating, and delegating—that Hersey and Blanchard distinguish in terms of the amount of directive and supportive behaviour provided. For example, "telling" has high task behaviour and low supportive behaviour. The situational leadership model has four quadrants with each quadrant showing the leadership style that is most appropriate under different circumstances.

In spite of its popularity, at least three reviews have concluded that the situational leadership model lacks empirical support.[44] Only one part of the model apparently works, namely that leaders should use "telling" (i.e. directive style) when employees lack motivation and ability. (Recall this is also documented in path–goal theory.) The model's elegant simplicity is attractive and entertaining, but other parts don't represent reality very well. The most recent review also concluded that the theory has logical and internal inconsistencies.

situational leadership model
Developed by Hersey and Blanchard, suggests that effective leaders vary their style with the "readiness" of followers.

Fiedler's contingency model
Developed by Fred Fiedler, suggests that leader effectiveness depends on whether the person's natural leadership style is appropriately matched to the situation.

Fiedler's contingency model   The earliest contingency theory of leadership, called **Fiedler's contingency model**, was developed by Fred Fiedler and his associates.[45] According to this model, leader effectiveness depends on whether the person's natural leadership style is appropriately matched to the situation. The theory examines two leadership styles that essentially correspond to the previously described people-oriented and task-oriented styles. Unfortunately, Fiedler's model relies on a questionnaire that does not measure either leadership style very well.

Fiedler's model suggests that the best leadership style depends on the level of *situational control*, that is, the degree of power and influence that the leader possesses in a particular situation. Situational control is affected by three factors in the following order of importance: leader-member relations, task structure, and position power.[46] Leader-member relations is the degree to which employees trust and respect the leader and are willing to follow his or her guidance. Task structure refers to the clarity or ambiguity of operating procedures. Position power is the extent to which the leader possesses legitimate, reward, and coercive power over subordinates. These three contingencies form the eight possible combinations of *situation favourableness* from the leader's viewpoint. Good leader-member relations, high task structure, and strong position power create the most favourable situation for the leader because he or she has the most power and influence under these conditions.

Fiedler has gained considerable respect for pioneering the first contingency theory of leadership. However, his theory has fared less well. As mentioned, the leadership style scale used by Fiedler has been widely criticized. There is also no scientific justification for placing the three situational control factors in a hierarchy. Moreover, it seems that leader-member relations is actually an indicator of leader effectiveness (as in path–goal theory) rather than as a situational factor. Finally, the theory considers only two leadership styles whereas other models present a more complex and realistic array of behaviour options. These concerns explain why the theory has limited empirical support.[47]

Changing the situation to match the leader's natural style   Fiedler's contingency model may have become a historical footnote, but it does make an important and lasting contribution by suggesting that leadership style is related to an individual's personality and, consequently, is relatively stable over time. Leaders might be able to alter their style temporarily, but they tend to use a preferred style in the long term. More recent scholars have also proposed that leadership styles are "hard-wired" more that most contingency leadership theories assume.[48]

If leadership style is influenced by a person's personality, then organizations should engineer the situation to fit the leader's dominant style, rather than expecting leaders to change their style with the situation. A directive leader might be assigned inexperienced employees who need direction rather than seasoned people who work less effectively under a directive style. Alternatively, companies might transfer supervisors to workplaces where their dominant style fits best. For instance, directive leaders might be parachuted into work teams with counterproductive norms, whereas leaders who prefer a supportive style should be sent to departments where employees face work pressures and other stressors.

leadership substitutes
A theory that identifies contingencies that either limit the leader's ability to influence subordinates or make that particular leadership style unnecessary.

Leadership substitutes   So far, we have looked at theories that recommend using different leadership styles in various situations. But one theory, called **leadership substitutes**, identifies contingencies that either limit the leader's ability to

Fortunato Restagno (front) and his three colleagues at Pursue Associates rely on leadership substitutes more than traditional supervision to get their work done. Everyone at the Kitchener, Ontario graphics start-up firm stays focused on organizational objectives through common values, a performance-based reward system, formal training, and guidance from co-workers. The result is an efficient team that creates the motion signage showing airline logos with moving text in Toronto's Pearson International Airport.[53] What other leadership substitutes might help teams lead themselves without direct supervision? © *Kitchener-Waterloo Record*
www.pursueassociates.com

influence subordinates or make that particular leadership style unnecessary. When substitute conditions are present, employees are effective without a formal leader who applies a particular style. Although the leadership substitute model requires further refinement, there is general support for the overall notion that some conditions neutralize or substitute for leadership styles.[49]

Several conditions have been identified in the literature that might substitute for task-oriented or people-oriented leadership. For example, performance-based reward systems keep employees directed toward organizational goals, so they probably replace or reduce the need for task-oriented leadership. Task-oriented leadership is also less important when employees are skilled and experienced. Notice how these propositions are similar to path–goal leadership theory, namely that directive leadership is unnecessary—and may be detrimental—when employees are skilled or experienced.[50]

Leadership substitutes have become more important as organizations remove supervisors and shift toward team-based structures. In fact, an emerging concept is that effective leaders help team members learn to lead themselves through leadership substitutes.[51] Some writers suggest that co-workers are powerful leader substitutes in these organizational structures. Co-workers instruct new employees, thereby providing directive leadership and they also provide social support, which reduces stress among fellow employees (see Chapter 7). Teams with norms that support organizational goals may substitute for achievement-oriented leadership, because employees encourage (or pressure) co-workers to stretch their performance levels.[52]

Self-leadership has also been discussed as a potentially valuable leadership substitute in self-directed work teams.[54] Recall from Chapter 6 that self-leadership is the process of influencing oneself to establish the self-direction and self-motivation needed to perform a task.[55] It includes self-set goals, self-reinforcement, constructive thought processes, and other activities that influence a person's own motivation and behaviour. As employees become more proficient in self-leadership, they presumably require less leadership from others to keep them focused and energized toward organizational objectives.

TRANSFORMATIONAL PERSPECTIVE OF LEADERSHIP

When Rick George became CEO of Suncor Energy Inc. in 1991, he soon realized why Suncor was called "the unluckiest oil company in Canada." It experienced a devastating fire and crippling labour dispute at a time when it was one of the world's highest-cost oil producers. At a time when Suncor managers were ready to jump ship, George began communicating a vague but promising future to employees. He gave subordinates the power to improve productivity and, as the company's financial position stabilized, to expand production. Then George did something that still shocks some in Canada's oil patch; he urged employees and the industry to become environmentally friendly. Today, just about every Suncor employee can proudly repeat "Rick's mantra," which is to increase production, reduce costs, and reduce the environmental footprint.[56]

Rick George is a **transformational leader.** Through his vision and actions, he transformed Suncor Energy from a troubled company into one of the leaders in Canada's oil industry. Transformational leaders such as Rick George, Terry Matthews (Mitel and Newbridge Networks), Julia Levy (QLT), and Isadore Sharp (Four Seasons Hotels and Resorts) dot the Canadian landscape. These people are agents of change. They develop a vision for the organization or work unit, inspire and collectively bond employees to that vision, and give them a "can do" attitude that makes the vision achievable.[57]

Transformational versus Transactional Leadership

Transformational leadership is different from **transactional leadership**. Transactional leadership is "managing"—helping organizations achieve their current objectives more efficiently, such as by linking job performance to valued rewards and ensuring that employees have the resources needed to get the job done.[58] The contingency and behavioural theories described earlier adopt the transactional perspective because they focus on leader behaviours that improve employee performance and satisfaction. In contrast, transformational leadership is about "leading"—changing the organization's strategies and culture so they have a better fit with the surrounding environment.[59] Transformational leaders are change agents who energize and direct employees to a new set of corporate values and behaviours.

Organizations require both transactional and transformational leadership. Transactional leadership improves organizational efficiency, whereas transformational leadership steers companies onto a better course of action. Transformational leadership is particularly important in organizations that require significant alignment with the external environment. Canadian research suggests that organizations that drive societal change—such as environmental organizations—are highly receptive contexts for transformational leadership.[60] Unfortunately, too many leaders get trapped in the daily managerial activities that represent transactional leadership.[61] They lose touch with the transformational aspect of effective leadership. Without transformational leaders, organizations stagnate and eventually become seriously misaligned with their environments.

Transformational versus Charismatic Leadership

One topic that has generated some confusion and controversy is the distinction between transformational and charismatic leadership.[62] A few writers use the words charismatic and transformational leadership interchangeably, as if they have the same meaning. However, charismatic leadership differs from transformational leadership. *Charisma* is a form of interpersonal attraction whereby followers develop a respect for and trust in the charismatic individual. Charismatic

transformational leadership
A leadership perspective that explains how leaders change teams or organizations by creating, communicating, and modelling a vision for the organization or work unit, and inspiring employees to strive for that vision.

transactional leadership
Leadership that helps organizations achieve their current objectives more efficiently, such as linking job performance to valued rewards and ensuring that employees have the resources needed to get the job done.

leadership therefore extends beyond behaviours to personal traits that provide referent power over followers.[63] Transformational leadership, on the other hand, is mainly about behaviours that people use to lead the change process. The remainder of this section will focus on transformational leadership because it offers more specific behavioural implications.

Elements of Transformational Leadership

There are several descriptions of transformational leadership, but most include the four elements illustrated in Exhibit 14.5. These elements include creating a strategic vision, communicating the vision, modelling the vision, and building commitment toward the vision.

Creating a strategic vision   Transformational leaders are the brokers of dreams.[64] They shape a strategic vision of a realistic and attractive future that bonds employees together and focuses their energy toward a superordinate organizational goal. Strategic vision represents the substance of transformational leadership and reflects a future for the company or work unit that is ultimately accepted and valued by organizational members. Strategic vision creates a "higher purpose" or superordinate goal that energizes and unifies employees.[65] A strategic vision might originate with the leader, but it is just as likely to emerge from employees, clients, suppliers, or other constituents. It typically begins as an abstract idea that becomes progressively clearer through critical events and discussions with staff about strategic and operational plans.[66]

There is some evidence that visions are the most important part of transformational leadership.[67] Visions offer the motivational benefits of goal setting, but they are more than mundane goals. Visions are compelling future states that bond employees and motivate them to strive for those objectives. Visions are typically described in a way that distinguishes them from the current situation, yet makes the goal both appealing and achievable.

Communicating the vision   If vision is the substance of transformational leadership, then communicating that vision is the process. Canadian CEOs say that the most important leadership qualities are being able to build and share their vision for the organization.[68] Transformational leaders communicate meaning and elevate the importance of the visionary goal to employees. They frame mes-

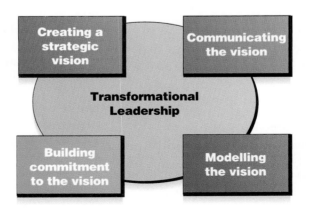

sages around a grand purpose with emotional appeal that captivates employees and other corporate stakeholders. Framing helps transformational leaders establish a common mental model so that the group or organization will act collectively toward the desirable goal.[69] Arthur Blank, the co-founder of home improvement retail giant Home Depot, likes to remind employees that they are "in the business of making people's dreams come true."[70] Blank helps employees see their role toward customers in a different light, one that is much more meaningful and motivating than "selling hammers and nails."

Transformational leaders also bring their visions to life through symbols, metaphors, stories, and other vehicles that transcend plain language.[71] Metaphors borrow images of other experiences, thereby creating richer meaning of the vision that has not yet been experienced. When George Cohon, the ebullient CEO of McDonald's Canada, faced the difficult challenge of opening restaurants in Moscow, he frequently reminded his team members that they were establishing "hamburger diplomacy." In the mid-1800s, when ocean transportation was treacherous, Samuel Cunard emphasized that he was creating an "ocean railway." At the time, railroads provided one of the safest forms of transportation, and Cunard's metaphor reinforced the notion to employees and passengers alike that Halifax-based Cunard Steamship Lines would provide equally safe transportation across the Atlantic Ocean.[72]

Modelling the vision   Transformational leaders not only talk about a vision; they enact it. They "walk the talk" by stepping outside the executive suite and doing things that symbolize the vision.[73] Moreover, transformational leaders are reliable and persistent in their actions. They stay on course, thereby legitimizing the vision and providing further evidence that they can be trusted. Leaders walk the talk through significant events, but they also alter mundane activities—meeting agendas, office locations, executive schedules—so they are consistent with the vision and its underlying values. "If you talk about speed in action, yet procrastinate on difficult decisions, you are not believable," warns Percy Barnevik, former CEO of the Swiss/Swedish electrical conglomerate ABB. "I and the members of my executive committee must 'walk the talk' and live up to what we say."[74]

Leaders walk the talk through significant events, but they also alter mundane activities—meeting agendas, office locations, executive schedules—so they are consistent with the vision and its underlying values. Modelling the vision is important because employees and other stakeholders are executive watchers who look for behaviours to symbolize values and expectations. The greater the consistency between the leader's words and actions, the more employees will believe and follow the leader. Walking the talk also builds employee trust because trust is partly determined by the consistency of the person's actions.[76]

As a transformational leader, Rick George doesn't just form a vision for the company's future. He actively communicates that vision. "You can't over-communicate, whether it's your vision, your values and beliefs, or your goals and objectives," George advises. George has also successfully transformed the Calgary-based energy company by walking the talk. "The example you set at the top is probably the most important thing a CEO does in terms of what you ask people to do," says George. "You have got to walk that same line yourself."[75] How might Rick George and other leaders communicate and model their vision in ways that would bring about meaningful change? *Courtesy of Suncor Energy Inc.*

www.suncor.ca

Mauricio Botelho Transforms Embraer into a World Leader

Brazilian aircraft maker Embraer started out as a branch of the Brazilian government responsible for building training aircraft for the nation's airforce. Like its counterparts in many nations, the Brazilian Air Force wanted the latest technology, so it invested heavily in research and development. However, Embraer became so costly to run that during an economic crisis, the Brazilian government had to sell it to private-sector investors. The government retained only 1 percent ownership plus veto power over executive decisions.

At about that time, Embraer hired Mauricio Novis Botelho to serve as its chief executive officer. Botelho's vision was to remake the struggling operation into a profitable business. Botelho started his efforts at transformation by creating efficiency. The company cut half its workforce and more than one-third of its administrative expenses. At the same time, it slashed its 14-month production lead time to nine months.

When greater efficiency created the conditions for survival, Botelho could turn more of his attention to the remaining employees. He was concerned that the layoffs had destroyed morale and created persistent anxiety. Seeing that the company had to continue slashing costs, Botelho brought together union and management representatives to negotiate a 10 percent cut in pay and benefits. Botelho expressed pride in his employees' willingness to make this sacrifice: "It shows how committed people are to the future."

That commitment has begun to bear fruit. New aircraft designs have won contracts, and the company has been profitable for several years. Sales have grown, and as the company has become one of the world's largest aircraft manufacturers, Embraer has hired employees, surpassing earlier employment levels. Today, Embraer is Brazil's leading exporter, and most observers give the credit to Botelho's leadership.

Sources: "Brazil's Best Companies," *LatinFinance*, March 1, 2001, p. S24; F. Shalom, "Meet Bombardier's Challenger," *Montreal Gazette*, February 3, 2001; Larry Rohter, "Brazil's Hot Commodity? Not Coffee or Soccer," *New York Times*, December 31, 2000, sec. 3, p. 1; S. Evers, "The Jane's Interview," *Jane's Defence Weekly*, November 6, 1996. **www.embraer.com**

Building commitment toward the vision   Transforming a vision into reality requires employee commitment. Transformational leaders build this commitment in several ways. Their words, symbols, and stories build a contagious enthusiasm that energizes people to adopt the vision as their own. Leaders demonstrate a "can do" attitude by enacting their vision and staying on course. Their persistence and consistency reflect an image of honesty, trust, and integrity. Finally, leaders build commitment by involving employees in the process of shaping the organization's vision.

Evaluating the Transformational Leadership Perspective

Transformational leaders do make a difference, according to organizational behaviour studies.[77] Subordinates are more satisfied and have higher affective organizational commitment under transformational leaders. They also perform their jobs better, engage in more organizational citizenship behaviours, and make better or more creative decisions. One Canadian study also reported that organizational commitment and financial performance seem to increase in bank branches where the branch manager completed a transformational leadership training program.[78] GLOBAL Connections 14.2 illustrates the effect of transformational leadership on organizational performance. It describes how Mauricio Novis Botelho's leadership transformed Embraer from a bureaucratic (and almost bankrupt) government-owned business to one of the leading aircraft manufacturers in the world.

Transformational leadership is currently the most popular leadership perspective, but it faces a number of challenges. One problem is that some writers engage in circular logic by defining transformational leadership in terms of the leader's success.[79] They suggest that leaders are transformational when they successfully bring about change, rather than whether they engage in certain behaviours we call transformational. Another concern is that the transformational leadership model seems to be universal rather than contingency-oriented. Only very recently have writers begun to explore the idea that transformational leadership is more appropriate in some situations than others.[80] For instance, transformational leadership is probably more appropriate when organizations need to adapt than when environmental conditions are stable. Preliminary evidence suggests that the transformational leadership perspective is relevant across cultures. However, there may be specific elements of transformational leadership, such as the way visions are formed and communicated, that are more appropriate in North America than in other cultures.[81]

IMPLICIT LEADERSHIP PERSPECTIVE

Competency, behaviour, contingency, and transformational leadership perspectives make the basic assumption that leaders "make a difference." Certainly, there is evidence that senior executives do influence organizational performance.[82] However, leaders might have less influence than most of us would like to believe. Some leadership experts suggest that three perceptual processes cause people to inflate the importance of leadership in explaining organizational events. These processes, collectively called **implicit leadership theory** (also known as the "romance of leadership"), include attribution errors, stereotyping, and the need for situational control.[83]

implicit leadership theory
A theory stating that perceptual processes that cause people to inflate the importance of leadership in explaining organizational events.

Attributing Leadership

People have a strong need to attribute the causes of events around them so they can feel more confident about how to control them in the future. The fundamental attribution error is a common perceptual bias in this attribution process (see Chapter 3). Fundamental attribution error is the tendency to attribute the behaviour of other people to their own motivation and ability rather than to situational factors. In the context of leadership, it causes employees to believe that organizational events are due more to the motivation and ability of their leaders than to environmental conditions. Leaders are given credit or blame for the company's success or failure because employees do not readily see the external forces that also influence these events. Leaders reinforce this belief by taking credit for organizational successes.[84]

Stereotyping Leadership

To some extent, people rely on stereotypes to determine whether their boss is an effective leader. Each of us has preconceived notions about the features and behaviours of an effective leader. These leadership perceptions are partly based on cultural values, so an effective leader in one country might not seem as effective to employees in

"A year ago, I was a skinny, green-haired, skate boarding CEO of a dot-com company. But that didn't work out."

another country. We rely on stereotypes partly because a leader's success might not be known for months or possibly years. Consequently, employees depend on immediate information to decide whether the leader is effective. If the leader fits the mould, then employees are more confident that he or she is effective.[85]

Need for Situational Control

A third perceptual distortion of leadership suggests that people want to believe leaders make a difference. There are two basic reasons for this belief.[86] First, leadership is a useful way for us to simplify life events. It is easier to explain organizational successes and failures in terms of the leader's ability than by analyzing a complex array of other forces. For example, there are usually many reasons why a company fails to change quickly enough in the marketplace, yet we tend to simplify this explanation down to the notion that the company president or some other corporate leader was ineffective.

Second, there is a strong tendency in Canada and similar cultures to believe that life events are generated more from people than from uncontrollable natural forces.[87] This illusion of control is satisfied by believing that events result from the rational actions of leaders. In short, employees feel better believing that leaders make a difference, so they actively look for evidence that this is so.

The implicit leadership perspective questions the importance of leadership, but it also provides valuable advice to improve leadership acceptance. This approach highlights the fact that leadership is a perception of followers as much as the actual behaviours and characteristics of people calling themselves leaders. Potential leaders must be sensitive to this fact, understand what followers expect, and act accordingly. Individuals who do not make an effort to fit leadership prototypes will have more difficulty bringing about necessary organizational change.[88]

CROSS-CULTURAL AND GENDER ISSUES IN LEADERSHIP

Along with the five perspectives of leadership presented throughout this chapter, we need to keep in mind that societal cultural values and practices affect what leaders do. Culture shapes the leader's values and norms, which influence his or her decisions and actions. These cultural values also shape the expectations that followers have of their leaders. Someone who acts inconsistently with these cultural expectations is more likely to be perceived as an ineffective leader. Moreover, leaders who deviate from those values may experience various forms of influence to get them to conform with the leadership norms and expectations of that society. In other words, implicit leadership theory described in the previous section of this chapter explains differences in leadership practices across cultures.

Over the past few years, 150 researchers from dozens of countries have worked together on Project GLOBE (Global Leadership and Organizational Behaviour Effectiveness) to identify the effects of cultural values on leadership.[89] The project organized countries into ten regional clusters, of which Canada is grouped into the "Anglo" cluster with the United States, Australia, New Zealand, and Great Britain. The results of this massive investigation are just beginning to appear, but preliminary work suggests that some features of leadership are universal and some differ across cultures.

Specifically, the GLOBE Project reports that "charismatic visionary" is a universally-recognized concept, and that middle managers around the world believe that it is characteristic of effective leaders. Charismatic visionary represents a cluster of concepts including visionary, inspirational, performance-orientation, integrity, and decisiveness.[90] In contrast, participative leadership is perceived as characteristic of effective leadership in low power distance cultures, but less so in high power distance cultures. For instance, one study reported that Mexican employees expect managers to make decisions affecting their work. Mexico is a high power distance culture, so followers expect leaders to apply their authority rather than delegate their power most of the time.[91] One GLOBE study also revealed that Iranian managers identified leadership dimensions that reflected Iran's cultural and religious heritage and were not identified in GLOBE studies of other cultures. In summary, there are similarities and differences in the concept and preferred practice of leadership across cultures.

Gender Differences in Leadership

Do women lead differently than men? Most Canadian CEOs think so. A recent survey revealed that 76 percent of male and female chief executives believe that the leadership and management skills of women differ markedly from those of their male counterparts, with women generally seen as consensus builders better able to "nurture strong interpersonal relationships."[92]

These perceptions are consistent with the views of several writers who suggest that women have an interactive style that includes more people-oriented and participative leadership.[93] They suggest that women are more relationship-oriented, cooperative, nurturing, and emotional in their leadership roles. They further assert that these qualities make women particularly well suited to leadership roles at a time when companies are adopting a stronger emphasis on teams and employee involvement. These arguments are consistent with sex role stereotypes: men tend to be more task-oriented whereas women are more people-oriented.

Are these stereotypes true? Do women adopt more people-oriented and participative leadership styles? The answer is no to the first, yes to the second. Leadership studies in field settings have generally found that male and female leaders do not differ in their levels of task-oriented or people-oriented leadership. The main explanation why men and women do not differ on these styles is that real-world jobs require similar behaviour from male and female job incumbents.[94]

However, women do adopt a participative leadership style more readily than their male counterparts. Scholars suggest that women may be more participative because their upbringing has made them more egalitarian and less status oriented. There is also some evidence that women have somewhat better interpersonal skills than men, and this translates into their relatively greater use of the participative leadership style. A third explanation is that subordinates expect female leaders to be more participative, based on their own sex stereotypes. If a female manager tries to be more autocratic, subordinates are more likely to complain (or use some other influence tactic) because they expect the female executive or team leader to be participative.[95]

Evaluating female leaders   For several years, OB scholars warned that female leaders are evaluated slightly less favourably than equivalent male leaders, and that this difference is almost completely due to sex stereotype bias. Specifically, women are evaluated negatively when they adopt a stereotypically male leadership style (i.e. autocratic) and occupy traditionally male-dominated positions.

These negative evaluations suggest that women "pay the price" for entering traditionally male leadership jobs and for adopting a male-stereotypic leadership style.[96] It also lends further support to our earlier point on why women adopt a more participative style.

However, as the opening story to this chapter emphasized, the perceptions of effective leaders are shifting. Followers increasingly expect leaders to support and empower them. These leadership styles are more consistent with how many women prefer to lead and how followers stereotype female leaders. Consequently, several recent surveys reported that women are rated higher than men on most leadership dimensions, including the emerging leadership qualities of coaching, teamwork, and empowering employees.[97]

Whether women or men are better leaders depends, of course, on the individual and on specific circumstances. We should also be careful about perpetuating the apparently false assumption that female leaders are less task-oriented or more people-oriented. At the same time, both male and female leaders must be sensitive to the fact that followers have expectations about how leaders should act, and negative evaluations may go to leaders who deviate from those expectations.

CHAPTER SUMMARY

Leadership is a complex concept that is defined as the ability to influence, motivate, and enable others to contribute toward the effectiveness and success of the organizations of which they are members. Leaders use influence to motivate followers, and arrange the work environment so that they do the job more effectively. Leaders exist throughout the organization, not just in the executive suite.

The competency perspective tries to identify the characteristics of effective leaders. Recent writing suggests that leaders have emotional intelligence, integrity, drive, leadership motivation, self-confidence, above-average intelligence, and knowledge of the business. The behavioural perspective of leadership identified two clusters of leader behaviour, people-oriented and task-oriented. People-oriented behaviours include showing mutual trust and respect for subordinates, demonstrating a genuine concern for their needs, and having a desire to look out for their welfare. Task-oriented behaviours include assigning employees to specific tasks, clarifying their work duties and procedures, ensuring that they follow company rules, and pushing them to reach their performance capacity.

The contingency perspective of leadership takes the view that effective leaders diagnose the situation and adapt their style to fit that situation. The path–goal model is the prominent contingency theory that identifies four leadership styles—directive, supportive, participative, and achievement-oriented

—and several contingencies relating to the characteristics of the employee and of the situation.

Two other contingency leadership theories include the situational leadership model and Fiedler's contingency theory. Research support is quite weak for both theories. However, a lasting element of Fiedler's theory is the idea that leaders have natural styles and, consequently, companies need to change the leader's environment to suit their style. Leadership substitutes identify contingencies that either limit the leader's ability to influence subordinates or make that particular leadership style unnecessary. This idea will become more important as organizations remove supervisors and shift toward team-based structures.

Transformational leaders create a strategic vision, communicate that vision through framing and use of metaphors, model the vision by "walking the talk" and acting consistently, and build commitment toward the vision. This contrasts with transactional leadership, which involves linking job performance to valued rewards and ensuring that employees have the resources needed to get the job done. Contingency and behavioural perspectives adopt the transactional view of leadership.

According to the implicit leadership perspective, people inflate the importance of leadership through attribution, stereotyping, and fundamental needs for human control. Implicit leadership theory is evident across cultures because cultural values shape the behaviours that followers expect of their leaders. Cultural values also influence the leader's personal values, which in turn influence his or her leadership practices. The GLOBE Project data reveal that there are similarities and differences in the concept and preferred practice of leadership across cultures.

Generally, women do not differ from men in the degree of people-oriented or task-oriented leadership. However, female leaders more often adopt a participative style. Research also suggests that people evaluate female leaders based on gender stereotypes, which may result in higher or lower ratings, depending on the leadership style they use.

KEY TERMS

Fiedler's contingency model, p. 410

Implicit leadership theory, p. 416

Leadership Grid ®, p. 404

Leadership substitutes, p. 410

Leadership, p. 400

Path–goal leadership theory, p. 406

Servant leadership, p. 406

Situational leadership model, p. 409

Transactional leadership, p. 412

Transformational leadership, p. 412

DISCUSSION QUESTIONS

1. Why is it important for organizations to value and support leadership demonstrated at all levels in an organization?

2. Find two recent newspaper ads for management or executive positions. Identify four selection factors that the hiring organizations will use to select effective managers and/or executives.

3. Consider your favourite instructor. What people-oriented and task-oriented leadership behaviours has he or she used effectively? In general, do you think students prefer an instructor who is more people-oriented or task-oriented? Explain your answer.

4. Your employees are skilled and experienced customer service representatives who perform non-routine tasks, such as solving unique customer problems or special needs with the company's equipment. Use path–goal theory to identify the most appropriate leadership style(s) you should use in this situation. Be sure to fully explain your answer and discuss why other styles are inappropriate.

5. Discuss the accuracy of the following statement: "Contingency theories don't work because they assume leaders can adjust their style to the situa-

tion. In reality, leaders have a preferred leadership style that they can't easily change."

6. Transformational leadership is currently the most popular perspective of leadership. However, it is far from perfect. Discuss three concerns with transformational leadership.

7. You have recently been promoted to a supervisory position in Mexico. You will be responsible for supervising a group of approximately 20 employees from Mexico responsible for installing a telecommunications infrastructure in a remote area. What behaviours will your employees expect from you in this leadership role? How do cultural differences influence your response?

8. You hear two people debating the merits of women as leaders. One person claims that women make better leaders than men because women are more sensitive to their employees' needs and involve them in organizational decisions. The other person counters that although these leadership styles may be increasingly important, most women have trouble gaining acceptance as leaders when they face tough situations in which a more autocratic style is required. Discuss the accuracy of these comments.

JEREMIAH BIGATALLIO'S LEADERSHIP CHALLENGE

By Alvin Turner, Brock University.

Jeremiah Bigatallio was eager to start his new job at InterContinental Communication, a high tech company in Toronto. Jeremiah, a civil engineer, joined the organization because it was a relatively young, growing, and dynamic organization that claimed in a brochure five years ago that its work environment had been modelled on Microsoft's. Jeremiah was hired as director of engineering services to supervise a staff of twenty-five. The staff includes ten engineers, seven technicians and eight lab assistants.

Mr. Bigatallio's predecessor was John Angle, who was fired for just cause. The official reason for his dismissal was not made public, but it was well known that he was having trouble managing his staff as well as interacting with other departments. First, most of the engineers did not get along with one another; some have not spoken to each other for more than two years. Second, the technicians disliked the engineers because they were seen as arrogant prima donnas who were only concerned about themselves. The engineers had no respect for or confidence in the technicians. They felt that the technicians were a group of bungling incompetents who should all be sent back to trade school. Third, both of these teams were in almost complete harmony in their contempt for the lab assistants, feeling that all of them were lacking in initiative, vastly over-paid, vastly under-qualified, and more concerned with abusing overtime privileges and being promoted than achieving and maintaining minimum productivity standards.

Other line and staff department heads were very upset with John Angle. The head of corporate financial control was dissatisfied with him because his department was constantly over budget allocations, particularly because of the excessive amount of overtime worked by his staff. He did not keep good records and did not submit accounting information on time. A recent audit revealed major financial irregularities of more than $300,000 in salaries. There are also concerns about the potential misappropriation of $250,000 of a Human Resources Development Canada jobs grant program. People in other departments (research and development, manufacturing, quality assurance) were very displeased with John Angle because the internecine warfare ongoing in his department made it difficult to work with anyone in engineering. This lack of communication, and frequent substandard lathes, dies, and design surveys resulted in backlogged work and unnecessary overtime expenses. And when communication did occur, the engineering unit's performance was generally unreliable.

John Angle believed in self-directing and autonomous work teams. Consequently, he believed in empowering his subordinates to make decisions and feel responsible for the successes of the department as well as their own successes. John provided little or no direction or support for his subordinates. He did not articulate his vision, leadership style, or expectations to his subordinates. He felt that they were highly trained professionals who should know what was expected of them and be "willing to do the right thing." He also felt that by being self-regulating and solving their own problems as they arose, employees would learn from their own mistakes. He saw this as the best way for employees to grow and develop on the job and for the organization to realize maximum output from workers.

John Angle viewed himself as a progressive liberal thinker whose new-age leadership style would transform and motivate employees to achieve great things. He believed that sharing power would enhance employees' self-worth and energize them. He also believed in maintaining a convivial work atmosphere. Thus, absenteeism and lateness were overlooked. Angle was also fairly lax in enforcing work rules and work productivity standards. As a consequence of this laxity, employees took advantage of the situation and worked at their leisure. They were frequently late or absent and (mis)managed other aspects of their own work schedule. They also took frequent coffee breaks and tended to work a substantially higher amount of overtime than other employees in the organization.

When Jeremiah was hired, he was told that he had the full confidence of the CEO and his vice-presidents to clean up the mess in the engineering department. He was given four months to fix all the existing problems in the department.

On his first day on the job, Jeremiah sat down in his office and typed on his laptop, 'What type of leadership style should I use on this diverse team of individuals?' Then he stopped to retrieve a note from his pocket that he had found under his door that morning. It said: "Try changing our overtime around here and we will cut you down to size!"

Discussion Questions

1. In what way was John Angle's leadership style ineffective? In what way may the existing span of control be considered too broad or too narrow? What impact does the existing structure have on a manager's leadership style?

2. Use the Path–Goal Leadership model to identify the best leadership style(s) for Jeremiah Bigatallio in this situation at InterContinental Communication.

3. What other type of leadership style could Jeremiah use in leading his staff? Explain why and how you believe the style you have selected will be effective in resolving the conflicts and other problems within the engineering department and between other departments.

TEAM EXERCISE 14.2

LEADERSHIP DIAGNOSTIC ANALYSIS

Purpose   To help students learn about the different path–goal leadership styles and when to apply each style.

Instructions

- *Step 1:* Students individually write down two incidents in which someone had been an effective leader over them. The leader and situation might be from work, a sports team, a student work group, or any other setting where leadership might emerge. For example, students might describe how their supervisor in a summer job pushed them to reach higher performance goals than they would have done otherwise. Each incident should state the actual behaviours that the leader used, not just general statements (e.g., "My boss sat down with me and we agreed on specific targets and deadlines, then he said several times over the next few weeks that I was capable of reaching those goals.") Each incident requires only two or three sentences.

- *Step 2:* After everyone has written their two incidents, the instructor will form small groups (typically between 4 or 5 students). Each team will answer the following questions for each incident presented in that team:

  1. Which path–goal theory leadership style(s) —directive, supportive, participative, or achievement-oriented—did the leader apply in this incident?

  2. Ask the person who wrote the incident about the conditions that made this leadership style (or these styles, if more than one was used) appropriate in this situation? The team should list these contingency factors clearly and, where possible, connect them to the contingencies described in path–goal theory. (Note: the team might identify path–goal leadership contingencies that are not described in the book. These, too, should be noted and discussed.)

- *Step 3:* After the teams have diagnosed the incidents, each team will describe to the entire class the most interesting incidents as well as its diagnosis of that incident. Other teams will critique the diagnosis. Any leadership contingencies not mentioned in the textbook should also be presented and discussed.

LEADERSHIP DIMENSIONS INSTRUMENT

Purpose   This assessment is designed to help you to understand two important dimensions of leadership and to identify which of these dimensions is more prominent in your supervisor, team leader, coach, or other person to whom you are accountable.

Instructions   Read each of the statements below and circle the response that you believe best describes your supervisor. You may substitute "supervisor" with anyone else to whom you are accountable, such as a team leader, CEO, course instructor, or sports coach. Then use the scoring key in Appendix B to calculate the results for each leadership dimensions. After completing this assessment, be prepared to discuss in class the distinctions between these leadership dimensions.

My supervisor...	Strongly Disagree ▼	Disagree ▼	Neutral ▼	Agree ▼	Strongly Agree ▼
1. Focuses attention on irregularities, mistakes, exceptions and deviations from what is expected of me.	1	2	3	4	5
2. Engages in words and deeds that enhance his/her image of competence.	1	2	3	4	5
3. Monitors performance for errors needing correction.	1	2	3	4	5
4. Serves as a role model for me.	1	2	3	4	5
5. Points out what I will receive if I do what is required.	1	2	3	4	5
6. Instills pride in being associated with him/her.	1	2	3	4	5
7. Keeps careful track of mistakes.	1	2	3	4	5
8. Can be trusted to help me overcome any obstacle.	1	2	3	4	5
9. Tells me what to do to be rewarded for my efforts.	1	2	3	4	5
10. Makes me aware of strongly held values, ideals, and aspirations which are shared in common.	1	2	3	4	5
11. Is alert for failure to meet standards.	1	2	3	4	5
12. Mobilizes a collective sense of mission.	1	2	3	4	5
13. Works out agreements with me on what I will receive if I do what needs to be done.	1	2	3	4	5
14. Articulates a vision of future opportunities.	1	2	3	4	5
15. Talks about special rewards for good work.	1	2	3	4	5
16. Talks optimistically about the future.	1	2	3	4	5

Source: Items and dimensions are adapted from D. N. Den Hartog, J. J. Van Muijen and P. L. Koopman, "Transactional Versus Transformational Leadership: An Analysis of the MLQ," *Journal of Occupational & Organizational Psychology*, 70 (March 1997), pp. 19–34. Den Hartog et al. label transactional leadership as "rational-objective leadership" and label transformational leadership as "inspirational leadership." Many of their items may have originated from B. M. Bass and B. J. Avolio, *Manual for the Multifactor Leadership Questionnaire*. (Palo Alto, CA: Consulting Psychologists Press, 1989).

G.A.P TRAVEL

In less than ten years, G.A.P Adventures has grown from a two-person operation to more than 70 employees, with over $12 million in sales. Now founder and CEO Bruce Poon Tip is working to make his company corporate and professional without losing its high involvement style. But along the way, Poon Tip has made more than his share of tough decisions.

This program begins by showing G.A.P Adventures staff at a spring retreat, where Poon Tip makes a surprise announcement: He has just hired Dave Bowen, formerly marketing director of G.A.P's biggest U.S. competitor. Poon Tip is counting on Bowen to instill some corporate discipline at G.A.P without quashing employees' enthusiasm. The staff have some bluntly stated concerns, such as Bowen's aggressive style and high expectations.

Bowen's first assignment is to work with marketing assistant Natalie Lauzon to revamp G.A.P's annual brochure. They will have disagreements along the way. For the first time in G.A.P's history, Poon Tip is handing over the job to someone else. The brochure is a travel company's bible, the text from which all sales flow. There are lots of changes required, and the two have less than four months.

Bowen's ideas about what is considered good material in the brochure are different than G.A.P employees'. One G.A.P staffer wants to include a warning about uncomfortable bus rides in the brochure. "What we're doing is we're telling them, just like we say on the front of the page, if you want the comforts of home, stay there," he explains. But Bowen disagrees. "It's a negative. So I think it causes a lot more harm for people that are thinking about it."

Poon Tip is no longer involved in the brochure, but he has his hands full with other matters. One concern is that Exodus Travel, a U.K. adventure company that partners with G.A.P, has been bought by a large competitor. The company has not contacted G.A.P and rumours are flowing that G.A.P is going to be dumped as a partner. At the same time, the Australian and New Zealand dollars took steep dives, so the Australian office is screaming that they want G.A.P to re-cost the whole brochure.

Months later, Poon Tip announces that G.A.P is splitting into two companies to keep the G.A.P image pure. Some staff have left G.A.P, and others with more corporate backgrounds have moved in. "Always surprises with G.A.P," Poon Tip promises. "We can never just be a normal company."

Discussion Questions

1. How well does the rational model of decision making represent G.A.P's process of resolving the problems that arise in this program?

2. To what degree are G.A.P employees involved in decision making? Are there apparent benefits to this involvement?

3. This program shows how a new manager (Dave Bowen) tries to improve G.A.P. Discuss the influence tactics and leadership styles that Bowen uses to transform G.A.P.

Source: D. Buckner, "G.A.P Travel," CBC *Venture*, June 23, 2002.

FORECASTING IN BUSINESS

High up in a Calgary office tower, half a dozen perfectly serious people are busily helping the Royal Bank of Canada prepare for extraordinary events in the old industry that might never happen. Judith Dwarkin of the Canadian Energy Research Institute and a participant in the Royal Bank sessions rhymes off the possibilities: "Nation states practise predatory economic policies. We have trading blocks, globalization disintegrates, conflict and strife are rampant and terrorism is not particularly well controlled. The world lurches through four recessions."

Over in Vancouver, Finning International is working through a similar exercise. For two years now, the industrial equipment distributor has been paying their consultant to scare them with various scenarios, such as what if a price war broke out, started by the equipment manufacturers all copying each other's machines? "[We're looking at] various scenarios that we've put together, areas obviously where there are significant pitfalls and you want to avoid those," says Finning vice-president Brian Bell.

Both companies are engaging in scenario planning—imagining the worst things that might happen and how the company can prevent or respond to those conditions. In these unpredictable times, businesses are exploring alternatives to traditional forecasting, looking for ways to prepare for whatever might happen next. "We live on shifting ground and that we need to learn to live on shifting ground and to operate in a world where surprises do appear," says Dwarkin.

Recent terrorist activities have prompted Canadian executives to look more closely at the unthinkable. The question is whether executives will continue to conduct "what if" scenario sessions if and when life returns to normal. Executives admit that no one can really forecast the future. But scenario planning helps executives to practise their decisions beforehand, so they are at least somewhat prepared for the unexpected. "I think that's one of the important things from a business perspective...not to be blindsided by further substantial changes in your business environment without having had at least a little bit of forethought about them," explains Brian Bell.

Discussion Questions

1. Based on the human problems with decision making described in the textbook, how does scenario planning improve the decision-making process?

2. Scenario planning occurs in teams rather than with the top executive only. What are the benefits of team rather than individual decision making in scenario planning?

Source: H. Gould, "Scenario Planning (Forecasting in Business)," CBC *Venture*, April 21, 2002.

15

Organizational Structure and Design

Learning Objectives

AFTER READING THIS CHAPTER, YOU SHOULD BE ABLE TO:

- Describe three types of coordination in organizational structures.

- Explain why firms can have flatter structures than previously believed.

- Discuss the dynamics of centralization and formalization as organizations get larger and older.

- Contrast functional structures with divisional structures.

- Explain why geographic divisional structures are becoming less common than other divisional structures.

- Outline the features and advantages of the matrix structure.

- Describe four features of team-based organizational structures.

- Discuss the advantages of the network structure.

- Summarize three contingencies of organizational design.

- Explain how organizational strategy relates to organizational structure.

Flight Centre is ranked as the Number 1 place to work in Canada. It is also a runaway success story in the travel industry, with continuous profitability and over 600 retail shops in several countries. What's the secret to Flight Centre's success? According to chief executive and cofounder Graham Turner, Flight Centre's unique "tribal" organizational structure facilitates easy replication and fuels organic growth.

Each Flight Centre retail shop, as well as each administrative group, represents a family. "If you look at a family structure, then the manageable size for people to get along and understand each other is three to seven people, and that's what we call a family," Turner explains. Between seven to 10 families in an area form a village with a village leader. "In a village, people co-operate with each other—the basic unit is still the family but when they need to, the families cooperate with each other," Turner says. "It might be that one store—or one family—has someone sick for a while, so another family will lend them a person until things get back to normal."

Three or four villages form a tribe, which is comparable to regional operations and special divisions of a company. "In a tribe you've got formal functions—you've got a chief, for example. That's the level when you have to start having a bureaucracy." As a tribe becomes overpopulated with Flight Centre families and villages, it splits into smaller tribes.

Flight Centre is highly decentralized. Each tribe (region) has control of its own recruitment, marketing, and training. Tribes also have the freedom to buy services from other Flight Centre business units, or to buy holiday packages from outside wholesalers instead. Further decentralization occurs down to each Flight Centre shop. The shop's team leader takes 10 percent of the shop's profit and may own up to 20 percent of the shop. The team structure is supported by a reward system in which the shop is its own profit centre and employees take a share of those profits on top of their guaranteed base salary. This tribal structure seems to work well in an industry that has to pay attention to local markets and change quickly in a dynamic environment.[1] ■

www.flightcentre.ca

Flight Centre has a "tribal" structure that organizes employees around families, villages, and tribes. *AAP Image/ Dave Hunt*

organizational structure
The division of labour as well as the patterns of coordination, communication, work flow, and formal power that direct organizational activities.

organizational design
The process of creating and modifying organizational structures.

There is something of a revolution occurring in how organizations are structured. Driven by global competition and facilitated by information technology, Flight Centre and many other companies are throwing out the old organizational charts and trying out new designs that they hope will achieve organizational objectives more effectively. **Organizational structure** refers to the division of labour as well as the patterns of coordination, communication, work flow, and formal power that direct organizational activities. An organizational structure reflects its culture and power relationships.[2] Our knowledge of this subject provides the tools to engage in **organizational design**, that is, to create and modify organizational structures.

Organizational structures are frequently used as tools for change. Structures support or inhibit communication and relationships across the organization.[3] They also serve as mechanisms that either support change or make change initiatives more difficult. Structures establish new communication patterns and align employee behaviour with the corporate vision. They establish new communication patterns and refreeze the change initiatives. For example, Ford Motor Company restructured its many business units so that employees are closer to specific types of customers, such as luxury car buyers (Jaguar, Volvo), services (Hertz, e-commerce), and Ford's mainstream car buyers.[4]

We begin this chapter by considering the two fundamental processes in organizational structure: division of labour and coordination. This is followed by a detailed investigation of the four main elements of organizational structure: span of control, centralization, formalization, and departmentalization. The latter part of the chapter examines the contingencies of organizational design, including organizational size, technology, external environment, and strategy.

DIVISION OF LABOUR AND COORDINATION

All organizational structures include two fundamental requirements: the division of labour into distinct tasks and the coordination of that labour so that employees are able to accomplish common goals.[5] Organizations are groups of people who work interdependently toward some purpose (see Chapter 1). To efficiently accomplish their goals, these groups typically divide the work into manageable chunks, particularly when there are many different tasks to perform. They also introduce various coordinating mechanisms to ensure that everyone is working effectively toward the same objectives.

Division of Labour

Division of labour refers to the subdivision of work into separate jobs assigned to different people. Subdivided work leads to job specialization, because each job now includes a narrow subset of the tasks necessary to complete the product or service (see Chapter 6). For example, designing and building the Confederation Bridge spanning Prince Edward Island and New Brunswick required thousands of specific tasks that were divided among thousands of people. Tasks were also divided vertically, such as having supervisors coordinate work while employees performed the work.

Work is divided into specialized jobs because it potentially increases work efficiency.[6] Job incumbents can master their tasks quickly because work cycles are very short and less time is wasted changing from one task to another. Training costs are reduced because employees require fewer physical and mental skills to accomplish the assigned work. Finally, job specialization makes it easier to match people with specific aptitudes or skills to the jobs for which they are best suited.

Coordinating Work Activities

As soon as people divide work among themselves, coordinating mechanisms are needed to ensure that everyone works in concert.[7] Every organization—from the two-person corner convenience store to the largest corporate entity—uses one or more of the following coordinating mechanisms: informal communication, formal hierarchy, and standardization (see Exhibit 15.1).

Coordination through informal communication All organizations use informal communication as a coordinating mechanism.[8] This includes sharing information on mutual tasks as well as forming common mental models so that employees synchronize work activities using the same mental road map.[9] Informal communication permits considerable flexibility because employees transmit a large volume of information through face-to-face communication and other media-rich channels (see Chapter 11). Consequently, informal communication is a vital coordinating mechanism in nonroutine and ambiguous situations.

Coordination through informal communication is easiest in small firms and work units where employees face few communication barriers. Emerging information technologies have further leveraged this coordinating mechanism in large organizations, even when employees are scattered around the globe. Larger organizations can also support informal communication by forming temporary cross-functional teams and moving team members into a common physical area (called *co-locating*). For example, **platform teams** (also called *concurrent engineering teams*) are project teams consisting of people from marketing, design, manufacturing, customer service, and other areas.[10] These employees are typically co-located to improve cross-functional coordination, whereas more formal and less flexible coordinating mechanisms develop products through several departments.

Larger organizations also encourage coordination through informal communication by creating *integrator roles*. These people are responsible for coordinating a

platform teams
Temporary teams consisting of people from marketing, design, and other areas, who are responsible for developing a product or service.

EXHIBIT 15.1 Coordinating mechanisms in organizations

Form of coordination	Description	Subtypes
Informal communication	Sharing information on mutual tasks; forming common mental models to synchronize work activities	• Direct communication • Integrator roles
Formal hierarchy	Assigning legitimate power to individuals, who then use this power to direct work processes and allocate resources	• Direct supervision • Corporate structure
Standardization	Creating routine patterns of behaviour or output	• Standardized skills • Standardized processes • Standardized output

Sources: Based on information in D. A. Nadler and M. L. Tushman, *Competing by Design: The Power of Organizational Architecture* (New York: Oxford University Press, 1997), chap. 6; H. Mintzberg, *The Structuring of Organizations* (Englewood Cliffs, NJ: Prentice Hall, 1979), chap. 1; J. Galbraith, *Designing Complex Organizations* (Reading, MA: Addison-Wesley, 1973), pp. 8–19.

work process by encouraging employees in each work unit to share information and informally coordinate work activities. Integrators do not have authority over the people involved in that process, so they must rely on persuasion and commitment. At Procter & Gamble, brand managers coordinate work among marketing, production, and design groups.[11]

Coordination through formal hierarchy Informal communication is the most flexible form of coordination, but it can be time-consuming. Consequently, as organizations grow, they develop a second coordinating mechanism in the shape of a formal hierarchy. Hierarchy assigns legitimate power to individuals, who then use this power to direct work processes and allocate resources (see Chapter 12). In other words, work is coordinated through direct supervision.

Any organization with a formal structure coordinates work to some extent through the formal hierarchy. For instance, team leaders at Sierra Systems in Vancouver coordinate work by ensuring that employees in their group remain on schedule and that their tasks are compatible with tasks completed by others in the group. The team leader has direct authority to reassign people to different work activities and to resolve conflicts by dictating solutions. The formal hierarchy also coordinates work among executives through the division of organizational activities. If the organization is divided into geographic areas, the structure gives the heads of those regional groups legitimate power over executives responsible for production, customer service, and other activities in those areas. If the organization is divided into product groups, then the heads of those groups have the right to coordinate work across regions.

The formal hierarchy has traditionally been applauded as the optimal coordinating mechanism for large organizations. Henri Fayol, an early scholar on the subject, argued that organizations are most effective when managers exercise their authority and employees receive orders from only one supervisor. Coordination should occur through the chain of command; that is, up the hierarchy and across to the other work unit.[12] Coordination through formal hierarchy may have been popular with classic organizational theorists, but it is often a very inefficient coordinating mechanism. Later in this chapter, we will learn that there are limits to how many employees a supervisor can coordinate. Furthermore, the chain of command is rarely as fast or accurate as direct communication between employees. And, as recent scholars have warned, today's educated and individualistic workforce is less tolerant of rigid structures and legitimate power.[13]

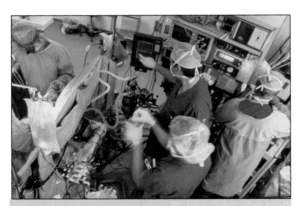

Led by Dr. Tirone David, this open-heart surgery team at Toronto General Hospital is divided into specialized jobs so each person has the required competencies for each position. To some extent, surgical work is coordinated through informal communication. However, much of the work activity can occur without discussion because team members also coordinate through standardization of skills. Through extensive training, each medical professional has learned precise role behaviours so that his or her task activities are coordinated with others on the surgical team. What other types of organizations make extensive use of skill standardization to coordinate work? *Charles Ledford/Black Star/Time Pix*

www.uhn.ca

Coordination through standardization Standardization—creating routine patterns of behaviour or output—is the third means of coordination. Many organizations try to improve the quality and consistency of a product or service by standardizing work activities through job descriptions and procedures.[14] This coordinates work requiring routine and simple tasks, but not in complex and ambiguous situations. In these situations, companies might coordinate work by standardizing the individual's or team's goals and product or service output (e.g., customer satisfaction, production efficiency). For instance, to coordinate the work of salespeople, companies assign sales targets rather than specific behaviours.

When work activities are too complex to standardize through procedures or goals, companies often coordinate work effort by extensively training employees or hiring people who have learned precise role behaviours from educational programs. This form of coordination is used in hospital operating rooms. Surgeons, nurses, and other operating room professionals coordinate their work more through training than through goals or company rules.

Division of labour and coordination of work are the two fundamental ingredients of all organizations. How work is divided, who makes decisions, which coordinating mechanisms are emphasized, and other issues are related to the four elements of organizational structure.

ELEMENTS OF ORGANIZATIONAL STRUCTURE

Every company is configured in terms of four basic elements of organizational structure. This section introduces three of them: span of control, centralization, and formalization. The fourth element—departmentalization—is presented in the next section.

Span of Control

span of control
The number of people directly reporting to the next level in the hierarchy.

Span of control refers to the number of people directly reporting to the next level in the hierarchy. As we mentioned earlier, Henri Fayol strongly recommended the formal hierarchy as the primary coordinating mechanism. Consequently, he and other theorists at the time prescribed a relatively narrow span of control, typically no more than 20 employees per supervisor and 6 supervisors per manager. These prescriptions were based on the assumption that managers simply cannot monitor and control any more subordinates closely enough.

Today, we know better. The best performing manufacturing facilities currently have an average of 31 employees per supervisor. This is a much wider span of control than past scholars had recommended. Yet these operations plan to stretch this span to an average of 75 employees per supervisor over the next few years.[15]

What's the secret here? Did Fayol and others miscalculate the optimal span of control? The answer is that early scholars thought in terms of Frederick Taylor's scientific management model (see Chapter 6). They believed that employees should "do" the work, and supervisors and other management personnel should monitor employee behaviour and make most of the decisions. This division of labour limited the span of control. It is very difficult to directly supervise 75 people. It is much easier to *oversee* 75 subordinates who are grouped into several self-directed work teams. Employees manage themselves, thereby releasing supervisors from the time-consuming tasks of monitoring behaviour and making everyone else's decisions.[16]

Consolidated Diesel's manufacturing facility in Whitakers, North Carolina, illustrates this point. The plant's 1,700 employees produce 650 engines each day in four different models, each of which can be configured in any of more than 3,500 different ways. While comparable plants might have one supervisor for every 25 employees, Consolidated Diesel has one for every 100 employees. The company is able to operate with a much wider span of control because production employees are organized into self-directed work teams that are responsible for their own areas.[17]

The underlying principle here is that the span of control depends on the presence of other coordinating mechanisms. Self-directed work teams supplement direct supervision with informal communication and specialized knowledge. This also explains why dozens of surgeons and other medical professionals may report to the head surgeon in a major hospital. The head surgeon doesn't engage in much direct supervision because the standardized skills of the medical staff coordinate the unit's work. A wider span of control is also possible when employees perform similar tasks or have routine jobs. In these situations, the organization relies more on standardizing work processes to coordinate work, thereby reducing the need for hands-on supervision.[18]

Tall and flat structures   The Development Bank of South Africa increased employee productivity by restructuring and flattening the organization. In particular, the government-owned financial institution slashed the number of managers from 74 to 27 and cut out one of its four management layers. "[T]he essence of transformation was not to shift the chairs, but to ensure that some of the chairs came out of the room," says a bank executive.[19]

Ducks Unlimited Canada recently flattened its organizational structure by removing layers of management. The Winnipeg-based environmental conservation group wanted to help empower employees, making it easier for the professionals in the field to make decisions quickly without having to go up and down the proverbial hierarchy. "I think by having that flattened structure there is more job enrichment," says Cheryl Barber, Ducks Unlimited Canada's human resources administrator. "People feel that they are in control of what they are doing and that also helps to retain the employees."[24] What conditions should corporate leaders consider when determining the optimal number of layers of management?
Courtesy of Ducks Unlimited Canada/D. Langhorst
www.ducks.ca

The Development Bank of South Africa joins a long list of companies that are moving toward flatter organizational structures. Royal Mail, which delivers mail throughout Great Britain, went from 16 layers of management to six layers. Varian X-Ray Tube Products reduced its five management tiers down to three.[20] This trend toward delayering—moving from a tall to a flat structure—is partly in response to the recommendations of management gurus. For example, Tom Peters challenged corporate leaders to cut the number of layers to three within a facility and to five within the entire organization.[21]

The main arguments in favour of delayering are that it potentially cuts overhead costs and puts decision makers closer to front-line staff and information about customer needs. "[C]orporations have come to realize that they need to have fewer layers of management if they are to communicate daily with their organizations and if they are to become closer to the customer," advises Lawrence A Bossidy, CEO of AlliedSignal.[22] However, some organizational experts warn that corporate leaders may be cutting out too much hierarchy. They argue that the much-maligned "middle managers" serve a valuable function by controlling work activities and managing corporate growth. Moreover, companies will always need hierarchy because someone has to make quick decisions and be a source of appeal over conflicts.[23]

One last point before leaving this topic: The size of an organization's hierarchy depends on both the average span of control and the number of people employed by the organization. As shown in Exhibit 15.2, a tall structure has many hierarchical levels, each with a relatively narrow span of control, whereas a flat structure has few levels, each with a wide span of control[25] Larger organizations that depend on hierarchy for coordination necessarily develop taller structures. For instance, Microsoft is considered a high-involvement organization, yet it has at least seven levels of corporate hierarchy to coordinate its tens of thousands of employees.[26]

Centralization and Decentralization

centralization

The degree to which formal decision authority is held by a small group of people, typically those at the top of the organizational hierarchy.

Centralization and decentralization represent a second element of organizational design. **Centralization** means that formal decision-making authority is held by a small group of people, typically those at the top of the organizational hierarchy. Most organizations begin with centralized structures, because the founder makes most of the decisions and tries to direct the business toward his or her vision. But as organizations grow, they diversify and their environments become more complex. Senior executives aren't able to process all the decisions that significantly influence the business. Consequently, larger organizations tend to *decentralize*, that is, they disperse decision authority and power throughout the organization.

Although larger firms tend to decentralize, this is not necessarily true of every part of the organization. Nestlé's marketing department is decentralized, yet some

EXHIBIT 15.2   Span of control and tall/flat structures

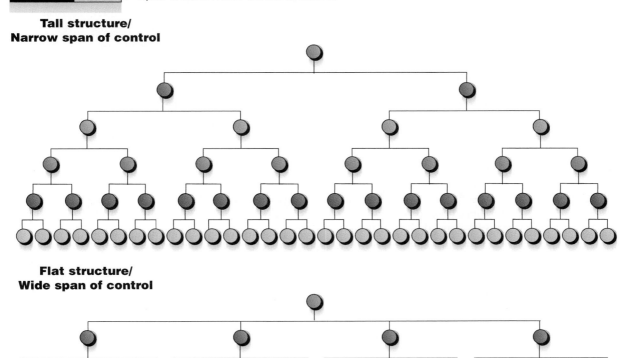

**Tall structure/
Narrow span of control**

**Flat structure/
Wide span of control**

parts of the giant Swiss food company are centralized. "If you are too decentralized, you can become too complicated—you get too much complexity in your production system," explains Nestlé CEO Peter Brabeck. Nestlé centralizes its production, logistics, and supply chain management to leverage the economies of scale of a large organization.[27] Also, firms tend to rapidly centralize during times of turbulence and organizational crisis. When the problems are over, leaders tend to decentralize decision making slowly, if at all.

Formalization

Have you ever wondered why McDonald's hamburgers in St. Jerome, Québec, look and taste the same as the MacDonald's hamburgers in Singapore? The reason is that the fast-food company has engineered out all variation through formalization. **Formalization** is the degree to which organizations standardize behaviour through rules, procedures, formal training, and related mechanisms.[28] In other words, formalization represents the establishment of standardization as a coordinating mechanism.

McDonald's Restaurants has a formalized structure because it prescribes every activity in explicit detail. Each McDonald's franchise must dole out five perfect drops of mustard, a quarter ounce of onions, and two pickles—three if they're small—on each hamburger. Drink cups are filled with ice up to a point just below the arches on their sides. Cooking and bagging fries are explained in 19 steps. Employees who work on the grill must put the hamburger patties in six rows of six patties each. A Big Mac is supposed to be assembled in 25 seconds from the time it appears on the order screen.[29]

Older companies tend to become more formalized because work activities become routinized, making them easier to document into standardized practices. Larger companies formalize as a coordinating mechanism, because direct supervision and informal communication among employees do not operate as easily. External influences, such as government safety legislation and strict accounting rules, also encourage formalization.

Problems with formalization   Formalization may increase efficiency, but it can also create problems. Rules and procedures reduce organizational flexibility, so employees follow prescribed behaviours even when the situation clearly calls for a customized response. Some work rules become so convoluted that organizational efficiency would decline if they were actually followed as prescribed. Labour unions sometimes call work-to-rule strikes, in which their members closely follow the formalized rules and procedures established by an organization. This tactic increases union power, because the company's productivity falls significantly when employees follow the rules that are supposed to guide their behaviour.

Another concern is that although employees with very strong security needs and a low tolerance for ambiguity like working in highly formalized organizations, others become alienated and feel powerless in these structures. Finally, rules and procedures have been known to take on a life of their own in some organizations. Rules become the focus of attention, not the organization's ultimate objectives of producing a product or service and serving its dominant stakeholders.

Mechanistic versus Organic Structures

You may have noticed that organizations seem to cluster around their span of control, centralization, and formalization. Some companies, such as McDonald's,

formalization
The degree to which organizations standardize behaviour through rules, procedures, formal training, and related mechanisms.

The Extreme Organic Structure of St. Luke's

A few years ago, American advertising company Chiat/Day was acquired by a larger firm, which intended to lay off most of Chiat/Day's 35 London staff. But these employees had other plans. They held a retreat to design their concept of the ideal organization, then they applied that ideal model to their newly-formed advertising agency, called St. Luke's.

Named after the patron saint of artists, St. Luke's is a highly organic structure fashioned after a medieval guild. "We wanted to do something radical," explains St. Luke's co-founder David Abraham. "Many ad agencies have a very hierarchical structure and exist only to benefit shareholders that you never meet or owners with little direct involvement, so we created a corporate structure to match our ideals."

St. Luke's doesn't have any bosses or corporate hierarchy—just apprentices and practitioners. David Abraham and Andy Law are the company's main co-founders (Law is also company chairman), but no one reports to either of them. "Neither of us can tell people what to do," explains Law. "In fact, we report to them. We have to tell everybody openly all the time what we're doing." A five-member board elected by employees governs the agency, but almost all the 115 people now employed at St. Luke's are company owners and have equal say in how the company is run.

Anyone who joins St. Luke's contractually agrees to be flexible in their job duties, including moving to different tasks based on feedback from peers. The company's headquarters—a converted toffee factory in London—supports this organic structure because it doesn't have any offices. The only work spaces, other than the front reception and cafeteria, are client rooms with visual themes to support creative thinking.

"Working without a formal structure presents pressures—ambiguity is stressful," explains Abraham. Still, Britain's most unusual ad agency has become its most successful. St. Luke's has grown 25 percent faster than any competitor, and has been recognized as Britain's top advertising agency.

Sources: A. Law, "Creating the Most Frightening Company on Earth: An Interview with Andy Law of St. Luke's," *Harvard Business Review*, 78 (September–October 2000), p. 142; A. Law, *Creative Company* (New York: John Wiley & Sons, 2000); J. P. Flintoff, "Keeping Faith in St Luke," *Guardian* (London), September 19, 1998, p. 22; F. Jebb, "Don't Call Me Sir," *Management Today*, August 1998, pp. 44–47; H. Jones, "Selling Space," *Design Week*, April 10, 1998, pp. 18–21; A. R. Sorkin, "Gospel According to St. Luke's," *New York Times*, February 12, 1998, pp. D1, D7; S. Caulkin, "The Advertising Gospel According To St Luke's," *Observer* (London), August 24, 1997, p. 8; M. Carter, "In St Luke's We Trust," *The Independent* (London), April 21, 1997, p. 6.
www.stlukes.co.uk

mechanistic structure

An organizational structure with a narrow span of control and high degrees of formalization and centralization.

organic structure

An organizational structure with a wide span of control, little formalization, and decentralized decision making.

have a **mechanistic structure**.[30] Mechanistic structures are characterized by a narrow span of control and high degree of formalization and centralization. They have many rules and procedures, limited decision making at lower levels, tall hierarchies of people in specialized roles, and vertical rather than horizontal communication flows. Tasks are rigidly defined, and are altered only when sanctioned by higher authorities.

Companies with an **organic structure** have the opposite characteristics. They have a wide span of control, little formalization, and decentralized decision making. Tasks are fluid, adjusting to new situations and organizational needs. The organic structure values knowledge and takes the view that information may be located anywhere in the organization rather than among senior executives. Thus, communication flows in all directions with little concern for the formal hierarchy. St. Luke's is an extreme example of a company with an organic structure. As described in GLOBAL Connections 15.1, the award-winning British advertising agency is completely decentralized, and has minimal hierarchy and formalization.

Mechanistic structures operate best in stable environments because they rely on efficiency and routine behaviours. However, as we have emphasized throughout this book, most organizations operate in a world of dramatic change. Information technology, globalization, a changing workforce, and other factors have strengthened the need for more organic structures that are flexible and responsive to these changes. Moreover, organic structures are more consistent with knowledge management because they emphasize information sharing rather than hierarchy and status.[31]

FORMS OF DEPARTMENTALIZATION

Span of control, centralization, and formalization are important elements of organizational structure, but most people think about organizational charts when the discussion of organizational structure arises. The organizational chart is the fourth element in the structuring of organizations, called departmentalization. Departmentalization specifies how employees and their activities are grouped together. It is a fundamental strategy for coordinating organizational activities because it influences organizational behaviour in the following ways.[32]

- Departmentalization establishes the "chain of command," that is, the system of common supervision among positions and units within the organization. It establishes formal work teams, as described in Chapter 8. Departmentalization typically determines which positions and units must share resources. Thus, it establishes interdependencies among employees and subunits.
- Departmentalization usually creates common measures of performance. Members of the same work team, for example, share common goals and budgets, giving the company standards against which to compare subunit performance.
- Departmentalization encourages coordination through informal communication among people and subunits. With common supervision and resources, members within each configuration typically work near each other so they can use frequent and informal interaction to get the work done.

There are almost as many organizational charts as there are businesses, but we can identify five pure types of departmentalization: simple, functional, divisional, matrix, and team-based. Few companies fit exactly into any of these categories, but they are a useful framework for discussing more complex hybrid forms of departmentalization. Later, we will look at various forms of network structure.

functional structure
An organizational structure that organizes employees around specific knowledge or other resources.

"Shipwrecked or not, Bradley, we must maintain the chain of command."

Edward Smith/SMI133/Artizans Syndicate

Simple Structure

Most companies begin with a *simple structure*.[33] They employ only a few people and typically offer only one distinct product or service. Hierarchy is minimal—usually just employees reporting to the owners. Employees are grouped into broadly defined roles because economies of scale are insufficient to assign them to specialized roles. Simple structures are flexible, yet they usually depend on the owner's direct supervision to coordinate work activities. Consequently, this structure is very difficult to operate under complex conditions.

Functional Structure

A **functional structure** organizes employees around specific knowledge or other resources. Employees with marketing expertise are grouped into a marketing unit, those with production skills are located in manufacturing, engineers are found in product development, and so on. Organizations with functional structures are typically centralized to coordinate their activities effectively. Standardization of work processes is the most common form of coordination used in a functional structure. Most organizations use functional structures at some level or at some time in their development.

Advantages and disadvantages   An important advantage of functional structures is that they foster professional identity and clarify career paths. They permit greater specialization so that the organization has expertise in each area. Direct supervision is easier, because managers have backgrounds in that functional area and employees approach them with common problems and issues. Finally, functional structures create common pools of talent that typically serve everyone in the organization. This creates an economy of scale that would not exist if functional specialists were spread over different parts of the organization.[34]

Functional structures also have limitations.[35] Because people are grouped together with common interests and backgrounds, these designs tend to emphasize subunit goals over superordinate organizational goals. Employees in purchasing, accounting, engineering, and other functional units are less likely to give priority to the company's product or service than to the goals of their own department. Unless people are transferred from one function to the next, they fail to develop a broader understanding of the business. A related concern is that functional structures emphasize differences across work units. For this reason, functional structures tend to have higher dysfunctional conflict and poorer coordination with other work units. Together, these problems require substantial formal controls and coordination when functional structures are used.

Divisional Structure

divisional structure

An organizational structure that groups employees around geographic areas, clients, or outputs.

A **divisional structure** groups employees around geographic areas, clients, or outputs (products/services). Divisional structures are sometimes called *strategic business units* (SBUs), because normally they are more autonomous than functional structures and may operate as subsidiaries rather than departments of the enterprise. Exhibit 15.3 illustrates the three pure forms of divisional structure.[36] *Geographic divisionalized structures* organize employees around distinct areas of the country or globe. Exhibit 15.3(*a*) illustrates a geographic divisionalized structure similar to McDonald's Restaurants' global structure. *Product/service structures* organize work around distinct outputs. Exhibit 15.3(*b*) illustrates this type of structure at Bombardier. The Montreal-based transportation leader divides its workforce mainly into product divisions, ranging from recreational to aerospace products. *Client structures* represent the third form of divisional structure, in which employees are organized around specific customer groups. Exhibit 15.3(*c*) illustrates the client structure that Microsoft has adopted.[37]

Which form of divisionalization should large organizations adopt? The answer depends mainly on the company's market strategy, which in turn is influenced by the primary source of environmental diversity or uncertainty.[38] If the organization's environment is most diverse geographically, then a geographic form of divisionalization would work best. Consider the shifting organizational structure of

EXHIBIT 15.3   Three types of divisional structure

(a) Geographic structure

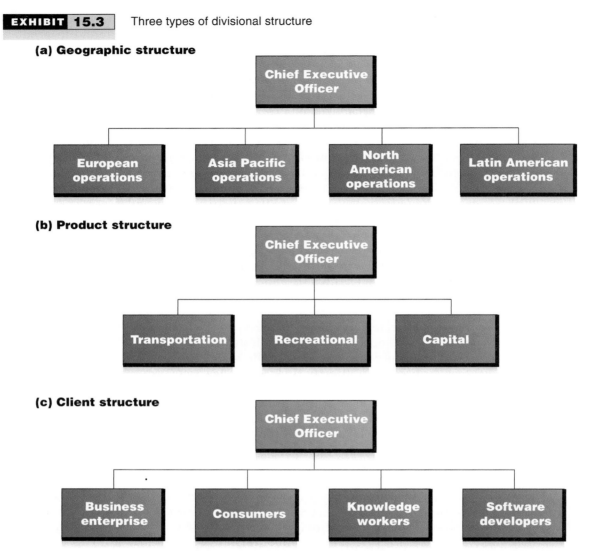

(b) Product structure

(c) Client structure

Note: Diagram (a) is similar to the geographic divisional structure of McDonald's; diagram (b) shows the product/service division at Bombardier Inc.; diagram (c) shows the customer groups at Microsoft Corporation.

Nortel Networks over the past two decades. Nortel was a telecommunications equipment provider in the 1980s, and most of its customers were telephone companies, most of which were either owned or highly regulated by governments. Nortel organized geographically because it had to cater to different regulations and needs across regions. But as the telephone industry deregulated, and as Nortel expanded into several product areas, the Brampton, Ontario, company shifted to more of a product-based structure. Deregulation meant that Nortel could standardize its products globally, so there was less need for a structure that emphasized geography. Today, Nortel Networks is mainly organized around three customer-based divisions—optical long-haul networks, metro and enterprise networks, and wireless networks—because customers represent the highest form of diversity in Nortel's market environment.[39]

In the past, Nortel Networks and other large organizations with international operations typically adopted a geographic divisionalized structure. McDonald's, Coca-Cola, Nestlé, and other food companies are still organized by region because consumer tastes vary across cultures. However, most divisionalized companies are moving away from geographical structures for three reasons.[40] First, information technology reduces the need for local representation. Clients can purchase online and communicate with businesses from almost anywhere in the world, making local representation less critical. Second, geographical structures are waning because freer trade has reduced government intervention in some products, and consumer preferences in many product and service areas are becoming more similar (converging) around the world. Third, business customers are becoming more global, and they want one global point of purchase, not one in every country or region. Axa Group is moving toward global profit centres for its services (e.g., reinsurance) because clients increasingly expect the London-based insurer to provide global (not regional) expertise and support.[41]

Advantages and disadvantages   The divisional form is a building block structure, because it accommodates growth relatively easily. Related products or clients can be added to existing divisions with little need for additional learning, whereas increasing diversity may be accommodated by sprouting a new division. Organizations typically reorganize around divisional structures as they expand into distinct products, services, and domains of operation, because coordinating functional units becomes too unwieldy with increasing diversity.[42]

Organizations tend to adopt divisional structures as they grow and become more complex, but this structural configuration is not perfect. The most common complaint is that divisional structures duplicate and insufficiently use their resources. Another problem is that this structure creates "silos of knowledge" because functional specialists are spread throughout the various business units. Consequently, new knowledge and practices in one part of the organization are not shared elsewhere. Divisional structures also tend to reduce cooperation across groups. Nortel Networks recognized this problem, so it developed a special communication program, called "Come Together," to remind employees of their responsibility to work more closely with employees from other divisions.[43]

Matrix Structure

When Wolfgang Kemna became head of SAP America, he soon discovered that the German software giant's U.S. subsidiary was too inward looking. "What I found was a highly defocused company," says Kemna. Much of the problem was due to the fact that SAP America's organizational structure was configured around the company's main product, whereas SAP actually has five main software applications—such as customer relationship management and supply chain management. Moreover, SAP's products require unique marketing and application in different industries. So, Kemna and his executive team introduced a **matrix structure** that organizes employees around both the five main software applications and various industry groups.[44]

A matrix structure overlays two organizational forms in order to leverage the benefits of both. SAP America relies on a matrix structure that balances power

matrix structure
A type of departmentalization that overlays a divisionalized structure (typically a project team) with a functional structure.

between its product and client groups or divisions. Many global corporations adopt a matrix structure that combines geographical with product divisions. The product-based structure allows the company to exploit global economies of scale, whereas the geographic structure keeps knowledge close to the needs of individual countries. Asea Brown Boveri (ABB) is widely known for this global matrix structure. The Swiss/Swedish manufacturer of industrial electrical systems has country managers as well as managers responsible for specific product lines.[45]

Instead of combining two divisional structures, some matrix structures overlap a functional structure with project teams.[46] As Exhibit 15.4 illustrates, employees are assigned to a cross-functional project team, yet they also belong to a permanent functional unit (e.g., engineering, marketing, etc.) to which they return when a project is completed.

Matrix structures create the unusual situation where employees have two bosses. A project team member would report to the project leader on a daily basis, but also report to the functional leader (engineering, marketing, etc.) Some companies give these managers equal power; more often, each has authority over different elements of the employee's or work unit's tasks.[47] Matrix structures that combine two divisionalized forms also have a dual-boss reporting system, but only for some employees. The manager of ABB's transformer plant in Canada would report to both the Canadian country manager and the global manager of ABB's transformer business. Only about 500 plant managers and group leaders at ABB have two bosses due to the matrix structure. The other 200,000 ABB employees work in direct authority structures below the matrix structure.

EXHIBIT 15.4   A simplified matrix structure

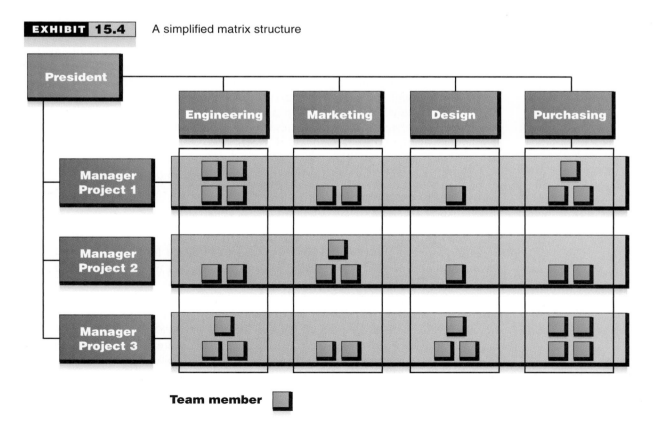

Team member ▢

Advantages and disadvantages   Matrix structures usually optimize the use of resources and expertise, making them ideal for project-based organizations with fluctuating workloads.[48] When properly managed, they improve communication efficiency, project flexibility, and innovation compared with purely functional designs. Matrix structures focus technical specialists on the goals of serving clients and creating marketable products. Yet, by maintaining a link to their functional unit, employees are able to interact and coordinate with others in their technical specialty.

In spite of these advantages, matrix structures have several well-known problems.[49] One concern is that they require more coordination than functional or pure divisional structures. The existence of two bosses can also dilute accountability. Royal Dutch/Shell has moved away from a matrix design for these reasons. Matrix structures also tend to generate conflict, organizational politics, and stress. In project-based firms, for example, project leaders must have a general management orientation and conflict resolution skills to coordinate people with diverse functional backgrounds. They also need good negotiation and persuasive communication skills to gain support from functional leaders. Employees who feel comfortable in structured bureaucracies tend to have difficulty adjusting to the relatively fluid nature of matrix structures. Stress is a common symptom of poorly managed matrix structures, because employees must cope with two managers with potentially divergent needs and expectations.

Team-based (Lateral) Structure

About a decade ago, The Criterion Group adopted a team-based organization to improve quality and efficiency. The New Zealand manufacturer of ready-to-assemble furniture now has just one layer of eight managers between the managing director and production staff. Criterion's 140 employees are organized into self-directed work teams with their own performance indicators and activity-based costing systems.[50]

**team-based
organization**

A type of departmentalization with a flat hierarchy and relatively little formalization, consisting of self-directed work teams responsible for various work processes.

The Criterion Group has embraced the **team-based organizational structure**. Some writers call this a *lateral structure* because, with few organizational levels, it is very flat and relies on extensive lateral communication.[51] The team-based organizational structure, which is illustrated in Exhibit 15.5, has a few features that distinguish it from other organizational forms. First, it uses self-directed work teams rather than individuals as the basic organizational building block. Second, teams are typically organized around work processes, such as making a specific product or serving a specific client group.

A third distinguishing feature of team-based organizational structures is that they have a very flat hierarchy, usually with no more than two or three management levels. The Criterion Group and other organizations delegate most supervisory activities to the team by having members take turns as the coordinator. Finally, this type of structure has very little formalization. Almost all day-to-day decisions are made by team members rather than someone further up the organizational hierarchy. Teams are given relatively few rules about how to organize their work. Instead, the executive team typically assigns output goals to the team, such as the volume and quality of product or service, or productivity improvement targets for the work process. Teams are then encouraged to use available resources and their own initiative to achieve those objectives.

EXHIBIT 15.5   Team-based (lateral) structure

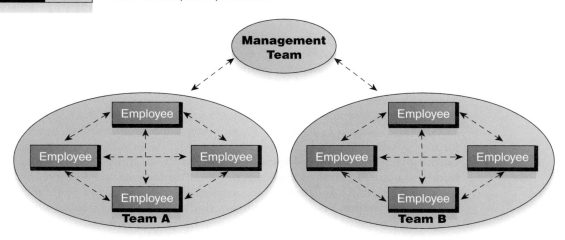

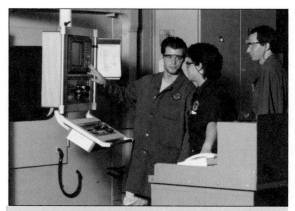

Pratt & Whitney Canada's Halifax plant has no middle managers, no supervisors, no executive washrooms, no executive parking spaces, and no fancy job titles. Instead, a team of six executives sets overall plant objectives for manufacturing turbine blades and related aircraft engine parts. The operation's 450 employees belong to self-directed work teams that are almost completely responsible for meeting those objectives. Employees also belong to special task forces to review plant rules and evaluate job applicants. Together with extensive use of robotics technology, these team practices have dramatically improved operating efficiency, job satisfaction, and admiration from others in the industry.[52] What are the main features of team-based organizational structures? *Courtesy of Pratt & Whitney Canada* **www.pwc.ca**

Team-based structures are usually found within the manufacturing operations of larger divisionalized structures. For example, aircraft components maker Pratt & Whitney has a divisionalized structure, but some of the manufacturing plants within those divisions have team-based organizational structures. Much less common are companies with a team-based structure from top to bottom.

Advantages and disadvantage   The team-based organization is an increasingly popular structure because it is usually more responsive and flexible.[53] Teams empower employees and reduce reliance on a managerial hierarchy, thereby reducing costs. A cross-functional team structure improves communication and cooperation across traditional boundaries. With greater autonomy, this structure also allows quicker and more informed decision making.[54] Some hospitals have shifted from functional departments to cross-functional teams for this reason. Teams composed of nurses, radiologists, anaesthetists, a pharmacology representative, possibly social workers, a rehabilitation therapist, and other specialists communicate and coordinate more efficiently, thus reducing delays and errors.[55]

One concern with team-based structures is that they can be costly to maintain due to the need for ongoing interpersonal skills training. Teamwork potentially takes more time to coordinate than formal hierarchy during the early stages of team development (see Chapter 8). Employees may experience more stress due to increased ambiguity in their roles. Team leaders also experience more stress due to increased conflict, loss of functional power, and unclear career progression ladders.[56]

Network Structures

To the outside world, Cisco Systems is one company. But the world's leading provider of business-to-business computer networks is mostly a constellation of suppliers, contract manufacturers, assemblers, and other partners connected through an intricate web of computer technology. Cisco's network springs into action as soon as a customer places an order (usually through the Internet). Suppliers send the required materials to assemblers who ship the product directly to the client, usually the same day. Seventy percent of Cisco's product is outsourced this way. In many cases, Cisco employees never touch the product. "Partnerships are key to the new world strategies of the 21st century," says a Cisco senior vice-president. "Partners collapse time because they allow you to take on more things and bring them together quicker."[57]

Cisco is a living example of the **network structure**. A network structure (also known as a *modular structure*) is an alliance of several organizations for the purpose of creating a product or serving a client.[58] As Exhibit 15.6 illustrates, this collaborative structure typically consists of several satellite organizations beehived around a "hub" or "core" firm. The core firm "orchestrates" the network process and provides one or two other core competencies, such as marketing or product development. For instance, Cisco mainly designs and markets new prod-

network structure

An alliance of several organizations for the purpose of creating a product or serving a client.

EXHIBIT 15.6

A network structure

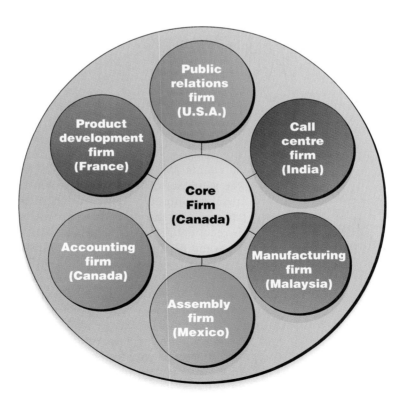

ucts. Nike, another network organization, mainly provides marketing expertise for its sports footwear and apparel.

The core firm might be the main contact with customers, but most of the product or service delivery and support activities are farmed out to satellite organizations located anywhere in the world. Extranets (web-based networks with partners) and other technologies ensure that information flows easily and openly between the core firm and its array of satellites. For instance, Nokia, the Finnish company, entered the U.S. video display market with only five employees. All the major tasks—marketing, sales, logistics, and technical support—were contracted out to specialists around the country. This diverse network was then connected through information technology to a common database.[59] "The traditional idea of the unit of business has always been the company," explains Jayson Myers, chief economist at the Alliance of Manufacturers and Exporters Canada. "Now, it's the network, going beyond one company and encompassing all its suppliers and many of its customers."[60]

One of the main forces pushing toward a network structure is the recognition that an organization has only a few *core competencies*. A core competency is a knowledge base that exists throughout the organization and provides a strategic advantage. As companies discover their core competency, they "unbundle" non-critical tasks to other organizations that have a core competency at performing those tasks. For instance, Mitel Networks decided that its core competency is designing Internet protocol-based communications equipment, not manufacturing that equipment. Consequently, the Ottawa-based high technology firm recently outsourced its manufacturing and repair business to BreconRidge Manufacturing Solutions.[61]

Companies are also more likely to form network structures when technology is changing quickly and production processes are complex or varied.[62] Many firms cannot keep up with the hyperfast changes in information technology, so they outsource their entire information systems departments to IBM, EDS, and other firms that specialize in information systems services. Similarly, many high-technology firms form networks with Toronto-based Celestica Inc. because Celestica has expertise in diverse production processes.

Virtual corporations   The network structures that exist at Cisco Systems, Mitel Networks, Nike, Dell Computer, and other firms generally perform a patterned set of tasks for all clients. When you order a computer from Dell, the network partners follow the same set of transactions as the next person who orders a computer. The specific computer configuration may change, but the relationships among the partners and the production process are fairly standardized until the partnership is reconfigured every few years.

In contrast, some network structures—known as **virtual corporations** (also called *cellular organizations*)—represent several independent companies that form unique partnership teams to provide customized products or services, usually to specific clients, for a limited time.[63] host universal is a good example of this. The British advertising firm (which spells its name all lower case) has no employees or clients. Instead, it serves a specific project by forming a unique team of partners, who then disband when the project is finished. "At host we have no clients or employees, which enables us to pull the most effective teams together from our network without foisting redundant skills, fees and hierarchy onto clients," explains founding partner Steve Hess.[64]

virtual corporations
Network structures representing several independent companies that form unique partnership teams to provide customized products or services, usually to specific clients, for a limited time.

Virtual corporations exist temporarily and reshape themselves quickly to fit immediate needs. When an opportunity emerges, a unique combination of partners in the alliance form a virtual corporation that works on the assignment until it is completed. Virtual corporations are self-organizing, meaning that they rearrange their own communication patterns and roles to fit the situation. The relationship among the partners is mutually determined rather than imposed by a core firm.

Advantages and disadvantages   For several years, scholars have argued that organizational leaders must develop a metaphor of organizations as plasma-like organisms rather than rigid machines.[65] Network structures come close to the organism metaphor because they offer the flexibility to realign their structure with changing environmental requirements. If customers demand a new product or service, the core firm forms new alliances with other firms offering the appropriate resources. For example, by finding partners with available plant facilities, Cisco Systems expanded its business much more rapidly than if it had built its own production facilities. When Cisco's needs change, it isn't saddled with nonessential facilities and resources. Network structures also offer efficiencies because the core firm becomes globally competitive as it shops worldwide for subcontractors with the best people and the best technology at the best price. Indeed, the pressures of global competition have made network structures more vital, and computer-based information technology has made them possible.[66]

A potential disadvantage of network structures is that they expose the core firm to market forces. Other companies may bid up the price for subcontractors, whereas the short-term cost would be lower if the company hired its own employees to provide this function. Another problem is that although information technology makes worldwide communication much easier, it will never replace the degree of control organizations have when manufacturing, marketing, and other functions are in-house. The core firm can use arm's-length incentives and contract provisions to maintain the subcontractor's quality, but these actions are relatively crude compared with those used to maintain the performance of in-house employees.

CONTINGENCIES OF ORGANIZATIONAL DESIGN

Organizational theorists and practitioners are interested not only in the elements of organizational structure, but also in the contingencies that determine or influence the optimal design. In this section, we introduce four contingencies of organizational design: size, technology, environment, and strategy.

Organizational Size

Larger organizations have considerably different structures than smaller organizations.[67] As the number of employees increases, job specialization increases due to a greater division of labour. Larger firms also have more elaborate coordinating mechanisms to manage the greater division of labour. They are more likely to use standardized work processes and outputs to coordinate work activities. These coordinating mechanisms create an administrative hierarchy and greater formalization. As organizations have gotten larger, informal communication has traditionally decreased as a coordinating mechanism. However, emerging computer technologies and increased emphasis on empowerment have caused informal communication to regain its importance in large firms.[68]

Larger organizations also tend to be more decentralized. As we noted earlier in this chapter, neither founders nor senior managers have sufficient time or expertise to process all the decisions that significantly influence the business as it grows. Therefore, decision-making authority is pushed down to lower levels, where incumbents are able to cope with the narrower range of issues under their control.[69]

Technology

Based on the open systems model (see Chapter 1), we know that an organization's structure needs to be aligned with its dominant technology. Two important technological contingencies that influence the best type of organizational structure are the variety and analyzability of work activities.[70] *Variety* refers to the number of exceptions to standard procedure that can occur in the team or work unit. *Analyzability* refers to the extent to which transforming input resources to outputs can be reduced to a series of standardized steps.

Some jobs are routine, meaning that employees perform the same tasks all the time and, when exceptions do occur, rely on set rules (standard operating procedures). Almost everything is predictable. These situations, such as automobile assembly lines, have highly formalized and centralized as well as standardized work processes.

When employees perform tasks with high variety and low analyzability, they apply their skills to unique situations with little opportunity for repetition. Research project teams operate under these conditions. These situations call for an organic structure, one with low formalization, highly decentralized decision-making authority, and coordination mainly through informal communication among team members.

High variety and high analyzability tasks have many exceptions to routines, but these exceptions can usually be resolved through standard procedures. Maintenance groups and engineering design teams experience these conditions. Work units that fall into this category should use an organic structure, but it is possible to have somewhat greater formalization and centralization due to the analyzability of problems.

Skilled trades people tend to work in situations with low variety and low analyzability. Their tasks involve few exceptions but the problems that arise are difficult to resolve. This situation allows more centralization and formalization than in a purely organic structure, but coordination must include informal communication among the skilled employees so that unique problems can be resolved.

External Environment

The best structure for an organization depends on its external environment. The external environment includes anything outside the organization, including most stakeholders (e.g., clients, suppliers, government), resources (e.g., raw materials, human resources, information, finances), and competitors. Four relatively distinct characteristics of external environments influence the type of organizational structure best suited to a particular situation: dynamism, complexity, diversity, and hostility.[71]

■   *Dynamic vs stable environments*—Dynamic environments have a high rate of change, leading to novel situations and a lack of identifiable patterns. Organic structures are better suited to this type of environment so the organization can adapt more quickly to changes.[72] Network and team-based structures seem to be most effective in dynamic environments, because they usually have these features. In contrast, stable environments are characterized by regular cycles of activity and steady changes in supply and demand for inputs and outputs. Events are more predictable, enabling the firm to apply rules and procedures. Thus, more mechanistic structures tend to work best under these conditions.

■ *Complex versus simple environments*—Complex environments have many elements whereas simple environments have few things to monitor. Decentralized structures seem to be better suited to complex environments, because these subunits are close to their local environment and are able to make more informed choices. GLOBAL Connections 15.2 describes how Coca-Cola CEO Douglas Daft decentralized the world's largest soft drink maker because consumers around the world have different tastes. Daft and other corporate leaders decentralize to make the organization more entrepreneurial and responsive to the local environments in which they operate.

■ *Diverse versus integrated environments*—Organizations located in diverse environments have a greater variety of products or services, clients, and regions. In contrast, an integrated environment has only one client, product, and geographic area. The more diversified the environment, the more the firm needs to use a divisionalized form aligned with that diversity. If it sells a single product around the world, a geographic divisionalized structure would align best with the firm's geographic diversity.

■ *Hostile versus munificent environments*—Firms located in a hostile environment face resource scarcity and more competition in the marketplace. Typically, hostile environments are dynamic ones because access to resources and demand for outputs can't be predicted. Organic structures tend to be best in hostile environments. However, when the environment is extremely hostile—such as when there is a severe shortage of supplies or lower market share—organizations tend to temporarily centralize so that decisions can be made more quickly and executives feel more comfortable being in control.[73] Ironically, centralization may result in lower-quality decisions during organizational crises, because top management has less information, particularly when the environment is complex.

Organizational Strategy

Although size, technology, and environment influence the optimal organizational structure, these contingencies do not necessarily determine structure. Instead, there is increasing evidence that corporate leaders formulate and implement strategies that shape both the characteristics of these contingencies as well as the organization's resulting structure. **Organizational strategy** refers to the way the organization positions itself in its setting in relation to its stakeholders, given the organization's resources, capabilities, and mission.[74] The idea that an organization interacts with, rather than being totally determined by, its environment is known as **strategic choice**.[75] In other words, organizational leaders take steps to define and manipulate their environments, rather than let the organization's fate be entirely determined by external influences.

The notion of strategic choice can be traced back to the work of Alfred Chandler in the early 1960s.[76] Chandler's proposal was that structure follows strategy. He observed that organizational structures follow the growth strategy developed

organizational strategy
The way an organization positions itself in its setting in relation to its stakeholders, given the organization's resources, capabilities, and mission.

strategic choice
The idea that an organization interacts with its environment rather than being totally determined by it.

Coca-Cola Decentralizes for Diverse Consumers

One of Douglas Daft's first actions as Coca-Cola's CEO was to cut half the staff at the soft drink maker's Atlanta headquarters and move the regional chieftains closer to their local markets. Daft has spent most of his career working at Coke's far flung operations, so he knows how centralized decision making has hampered Coke's ability to serve local needs. For example, Coke was several months behind its rivals in launching a new carbonated tea in north-east China: "We had the formula, we had the flavour, we had done all the taste-testing," complains Daft, "but Atlanta kept saying 'are you sure?'"

Coke executives in Atlanta had previously decided everything from the timing of promotions to filming commercials for faraway markets. They assumed Coke had global appeal, so centralized control was appropriate. But Daft argues otherwise. "You can't pander to similarities between people: you have to find the differences." Daft believes it will be easier for Coke executives to anticipate and respond to those differences through a more decentralized organizational structure.

Coke's decentralization makes sense in terms of the diverse consumer tastes around the planet, but the company stumbled in the process because it didn't have a control system to replace centralized supervision over brand marketing. Some local managers weren't ready to act on their own. Others took their newfound freedom too far with very un-Coke-like ads, such as skinny-dippers in Italy and an angry grandmother in the U.S.

Coke's solution wasn't to centralize again. Instead, the company developed a global marketing group with 100 people around the world who design marketing strategy for the company's core brands. The local operations then have the freedom to develop their own marketing campaigns within that architecture. "We haven't swung back," insists Stephen Jones, Coke's chief mar-

Coca-Cola decentralized its structure because consumer tastes vary in different parts of the world. *AFP/CORBIS*

keting officer. "The local markets are still accountable, but now they have guidance, process and strategy."

Sources: J. F. Peltz, "Cola Wars," *Hamilton Spectator*, April 13, 2002, p. B1; B. McKay, "Coke Hunts for Talent to Re-Establish Its Marketing Might," *Wall Street Journal*, March 6, 2002, p. B4; P.R. Chowdhury, "The Unbottling Of Coke," *Business Today*, January 2001; P. O'Kane, "Coca Cola's Canny Man," *The Herald* (Glasgow), June 18, 2000, p. 3; "Debunking Coke," *The Economist*, February 12, 2000; "World has Changed at Coca-Cola as 6,000 Lose Jobs," *National Post*, January 27, 2000, p. C10.
www.coca-cola.com

by the organization's decision makers. Moreover, he noted that organizational structures change only after decision makers decide to do so. This point recognizes that the link between structure and the contingency factors described earlier is mediated by organizational strategy.

Chandler's thesis that structure follows strategy has become the dominant perspective of business policy and strategic management. An important aspect of this view is that organizations can choose the environments in which they want to operate. Some businesses adopt a *differentiation strategy* by bringing unique products to the market or attracting clients who want customized goods and services. They try to distinguish their outputs from those provided by other firms through marketing, providing special services, and innovation. Others adopt a *cost leader-*

ship strategy, in which they maximize productivity and are thereby able to offer popular products or services at a competitive price.[77]

The type of organizational strategy selected leads to the best organizational structure to adopt.[78] Organizations with a cost leadership strategy should adopt a mechanistic, functional structure with high levels of job specialization and standardized work processes. This is similar to the routine technology category described earlier because both maximize production and service efficiency. A differentiation strategy, on the other hand, requires more customized relations with clients. A matrix or team-based structure that is less centralized and formalized is most appropriate here because it enables technical specialists to coordinate their work activities more closely with the client's needs. Overall, it is now apparent that organizational structure is influenced by size, technology, and environment, but the organization's strategy may reshape these elements and loosen their connection to organizational structure.

CHAPTER SUMMARY

Organizational structure refers to the division of labour as well as the patterns of coordination, communication, work flow, and formal power that direct organizational activities. All organizational structures divide labour into distinct tasks and coordinate that labour to accomplish common goals. The primary means of coordination are informal communication, formal hierarchy, and standardization.

The four basic elements of organizational structure include span of control, centralization, formalization, and departmentalization. At one time, scholars suggested that firms should have a tall hierarchy with a narrow span of control. Today, most organizations have the opposite because they rely on informal communication and standardization, rather than direct supervision, to coordinate work processes.

Centralization means that formal decision authority is held by a small group of people, typically senior executives. Many companies decentralize as they become larger and more complex because senior executives lack the necessary time and expertise to process all the decisions that significantly influence the business. Companies also tend to become more formalized over time because work activities become routinized. Formalization increases in larger firms because standardization works more efficiently than informal communications and direct supervision.

A functional structure organizes employees around specific knowledge or other resources. This fosters greater specialization and improves direct supervision, but makes it more difficult for people to see the organization's larger picture or to coordinate across departments. A divisional structure groups employees around geographic areas, clients, or outputs. This

structure accommodates growth and focuses employee attention on products or customers rather than tasks. However, this structure creates silos of knowledge and duplication of resources.

The matrix structure combines two structures to leverage the benefits of both types of structure. However, this approach requires more coordination than functional or pure divisional structures, may dilute accountability, and increases conflict. Team-based structures are very flat, have low formalization and organize self-directed teams around work processes rather than functional specialties. A network structure is an alliance of several organizations for the purpose of creating a product or serving a client. Virtual corporations are network structures that can quickly reorganize themselves to suit the client's requirements.

The best organizational structure depends on the firm's size, technology, and environment. Generally, larger organizations are decentralized and more formalized, with greater job specialization and elaborate coordinating mechanisms. The work unit's technology—including variety of work and analyzability of problems—influences the decision whether to adopt an organic or mechanistic structure. We need to consider whether the external environment is dynamic, complex, diverse, or hostile.

Although size, technology, and environment influence the optimal organizational structure, these contingencies do not necessarily determine structure. Rather, organizational leaders formulate and implement strategies to define and manipulate their environments. It is these strategies, rather than the other contingencies, that directly shape the organization's structure.

KEY TERMS

Centralization, p. 433

Divisional structure, p. 437

Formalization, p. 434

Functional structure, p. 436

Matrix structure, p. 439

Mechanistic structure, p. 435

Network structure, p. 443

Organic structure, p. 435

Organizational design, p. 428

Organizational strategy, p. 448

Organizational structure, p. 428

Platform teams, p. 429

Span of control, p. 431

Strategic choice, p. 448

Team-based organizational structure, p. 441

Virtual corporations, p. 444

DISCUSSION QUESTIONS

1. Why are organizations moving toward flatter structures?
2. What form of coordination is most likely to be used in a cross-functional project team? A football team?
3. Why is the use of geographic divisional structures declining?
4. From an employee perspective, what are the advantages and disadvantages of working in a matrix structure?
5. What competencies do employees require to effectively function in a team-based structure?

6. Some writers believe that a network structure is an effective design for global competition. Is this true, or are there situations for which this organizational structure may be inappropriate?
7. Suppose that you have been hired as a consultant to diagnose the environmental characteristics of your college or university. How would you describe the school's external environment? Is the school's existing structure appropriate for this environment?
8. What do we mean by "structure follows strategy"?

CASE STUDY 15.1

THE RISE AND FALL OF PMC AG

Founded in 1930, PMC AG is a German manufacturer of high-priced sports cars. During the early years, PMC was a small consulting engineering firm that specialized in solving difficult automotive design problems for clients. At the end of World War II, however, the son of PMC's founder decided to expand the business beyond consulting engineering. He was determined that PMC would build its own precision automobiles.

In 1948, the first PMC prototypes rolled out of the small manufacturing facility. Each copy was handmade by highly-skilled craftspeople. For several years, parts and engine were designed and built by other companies and assembled at the PMC plant. By the 1960s, however, PMC had begun to design and build its own parts.

PMC grew rapidly during the 1960s to mid-1980s. The company designed a completely new car in the early 1960s, launched a lower-priced model in 1970, and added a mid-priced model in 1977. By the mid-1980s, PMC had become very profitable as its name became an icon for wealthy entrepreneurs and jetsetters. In 1986, the year of highest production, PMC sold 54,000 cars. Nearly two-thirds of these were sold in North America.

PMC's Structure

PMC's organizational structure expanded with its success. During the early years, the company consisted only of an engineering department and a production department. By the 1980s, employees were divided into more than 10 functional departments representing different stages of the production process as well as upstream (e.g., design, purchasing) and downstream (e.g., quality control, marketing) activities. Employees worked exclusively in one department. It was almost considered mutiny for an employee to voluntarily move into another department.

PMC's production staff were organized into a traditional hierarchy. Front-line employees reported to work group leaders, who reported to supervisors, who reported to group supervisors in each area. Group supervisors reported to production managers, who reported to production directors, who reported to PMC's executive vice-president of manufacturing. At one point, nearly 20 percent of production staff members were involved in supervisory tasks. In the early 1990s, for example, there were 48 group supervisors, 96 supervisors, and 162 work group leaders supervising about 2,500 front-line production employees.

PMC's Craft Tradition

PMC had a long tradition and culture that supported craft expertise. This appealed to Germany's skilled workforce because it gave employees an opportunity to test and further develop their skills. PMC workers were encouraged to master long work cycles, often as much as 15 minutes per unit. Their ideal was to build as much of the automobile as possible alone. For example, a few masters were able to assemble an entire engine. Their reward was to personally sign their name on the completed component.

The design engineers worked independently of the production department, with the result that production employees had to adjust designs to fit the available parts. Rather than being a nuisance, the production employees viewed this as a challenge that would further test their well-developed craft skills. Similarly, manufacturing engineers occasionally redesigned the product to fit manufacturing capabilities.

To improve efficiency, a moving track assembly system was introduced until 1977. Even then, the emphasis on craft skills was apparent. Employees were encouraged to quickly put all the parts on the car, knowing that highly-skilled troubleshooting craftspeople would discover and repair defects after the car came off the line. This was much more costly and time consuming than assembling the vehicle correctly the first time, but it provided yet another challenging set of tasks for skilled craftspeople. And to support their position, PMC vehicles were known for their lack of defects by the time they were sold to customers.

The End of Success?

PMC sports cars filled a small niche in the automobile market for those who wanted a true sports car just tame enough for everyday use. PMCs were known for their superlative performance based on excellent engineering technology, but they were also becoming very expensive. Japanese sports cars were not quite in the same league as a PMC, but the cost of manufacturing the Japanese vehicles was a small fraction of the cost of manufacturing a vehicle at PMC.

This cost inefficiency hit PMC's sales during the late 1980s and early 1990s. First, Germany's currency appreciated against the U.S. dollar, which made PMC sports cars even more expensive in the North American market. By 1990, PMC was selling half the number of cars it had sold just four years earlier. Then the North American recession hit, driving PMC sales down further. In 1993, PMC sold just 14,000 vehicles. And although sales rebounded to 20,000 by 1995, the high price tag put PMCs out of reach of many potential customers. It was clear to PMC's founding family that changes were needed, but they weren't sure where to begin.

Discussion Questions

1. Describe PMC's organizational structure in terms of the four organizational design features (i.e. span of control, centralization, formalization, and departmentalization.

2. Discuss the problems with PMC's current structure.

3. Identify and justify an organizational structure that, in your opinion, would be more appropriate for PMC.

Source: Written by Steven L. McShane based on information from several sources about "PMC." The company name and some details of actual events have been altered to provide a fuller case discussion.

ORGANIZATIONAL STRUCTURE AND DESIGN: THE CLUB ED EXERCISE

By Cheryl Harvey and Kim Morouney, Wilfrid Laurier University

Purpose This exercise is designed to help you understand the issues you need to consider when designing organizations at various stages of growth.

Materials Each student team should have enough overhead transparencies or flip chart sheets to display several organizational charts.

Instructions Each team discusses the scenario presented. The first scenario is presented below. The instructor will facilitate discussion and advise teams when to begin the next step. This exercise may take place over one or two class sessions.

■ *Step 1*: Students are placed in teams (typically 4 or 5 people).
■ *Step 2:* After reading Scenario #1 presented below, each team will design an organizational chart (departmentalization) that is most appropriate for this situation. Students should be able to describe the type of structure drawn and to explain why it is appropriate. The structure should be drawn on an overhead transparency or flip chart for others to see during later class discussion. The instructor will set a fixed time (e.g., 15 minutes) to complete this task.

Scenario #1 Determined never to shovel snow again, you are establishing a new resort business on a small Caribbean island. The resort is under construction and is scheduled to open one year from now. You decide it is time to draw up an organizational chart for this new venture, called Club Ed.

■ *Step 3*: At the end of the time allowed, the instructor will present Scenario #2 and each team will be asked to draw another organizational chart to suit that situation. Again, students should be able to describe the type of structure drawn and explain why it is appropriate.
■ *Step 4*: At the end of the time allowed, the instructor will present Scenario #3 and each team will be asked to draw another organizational chart to suit that situation.
■ *Step 5*: Depending on the time available, the instructor might present a fourth scenario. The class will gather to present their designs for each scenario. During each presentation, teams should describe the type of structure drawn and explain why it is appropriate.

Source: Adapted from C. Harvey and K. Morouney, *Journal of Management Education*, 22 (June 1998), pp. 425–29. Used with permission of the authors.

IDENTIFYING YOUR PREFERRED ORGANIZATIONAL STRUCTURE

Purpose This exercise is designed to help you understand how an organization's structure influences the personal needs and values of people working in that structure.

Instructions Personal values influence how comfortable you are working in different organizational structures. You might prefer an organization with clearly defined rules or no rules at all. You might prefer a firm where almost any employee can make important decisions, or where important decisions are screened by senior executives. Read each statement and indicate the extent to which you would like to work in an organization with that characteristic. When finished, use the scoring key in Appendix B to calculate your results. This self-assessment is completed alone so students can complete this self-assessment honestly without being concerned about social comparisons. However, class discussion will focus on the elements of organizational design and their relationship to personal needs and values.

Organizational Structure Preference Scale

I would like to work in an organization where. . .   Score

1. A person's career ladder has several steps toward higher status and responsibility.   Not at all   A little   Somewhat   Very much   _____

2. Employees perform their work with few rules to limit their discretion.   Not at all   A little   Somewhat   Very much   _____

3. Responsibility is pushed down to employees who perform the work.   Not at all   A little   Somewhat   Very much   _____

4. Supervisors have few employees, so they work closely with each person.   Not at all   A little   Somewhat   Very much   _____

5. Senior executives make most decisions to ensure that the company is consistent in its actions.   Not at all   A little   Somewhat   Very much   _____

6. Jobs are clearly defined so there is no confusion over who is responsible for various tasks.   Not at all   A little   Somewhat   Very much   _____

7. Employees have their say on issues, but senior executives make most of the decisions.   Not at all   A little   Somewhat   Very much   _____

8. Job descriptions are broadly stated or nonexistent.   Not at all   A little   Somewhat   Very much   _____

9. Everyone's work is tightly synchronized around top management operating plans.   Not at all   A little   Somewhat   Very much   _____

10. Most work is performed in teams without close supervision.   Not at all   A little   Somewhat   Very much   _____

11. Work gets done through informal discussion with co-workers rather than through formal rules.   Not at all   A little   Somewhat   Very much   _____

12. Supervisors have so many employees that they can't watch anyone very closely.   Not at all   A little   Somewhat   Very much   _____

13. Everyone has clearly understood goals, expectations, and job duties.   Not at all   A little   Somewhat   Very much   _____

14. Senior executives assign overall goals, but leave daily decisions to front-line teams.   Not at all   A little   Somewhat   Very much   _____

15. Even in a large company, the CEO is only three or four levels above the lowest position.   Not at all   A little   Somewhat   Very much   _____

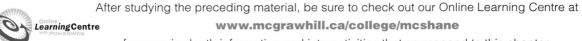

After studying the preceding material, be sure to check out our Online Learning Centre at

www.mcgrawhill.ca/college/mcshane

for more in-depth information and interactivities that correspond to this chapter.

Organizational Culture

Learning Objectives

AFTER READING THIS CHAPTER, YOU SHOULD BE ABLE TO:

- Describe the elements of organizational culture.

- Discuss the importance of organizational subcultures.

- List four categories of artifacts through which corporate culture is deciphered.

- Identify three functions of organizational culture.

- Discuss the conditions under which cultural strength can improve corporate performance.

- Discuss the effect of organizational culture on business ethics.

- Compare and contrast four strategies for merging organizational cultures.

- Identify five strategies to strengthen an organization's culture.

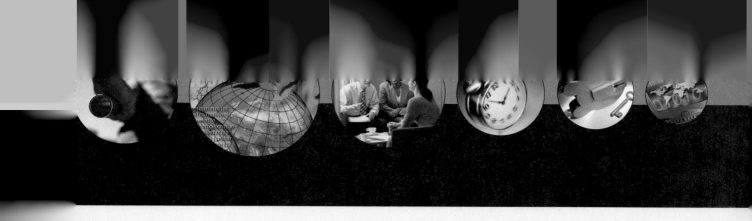

Corporate culture is one of the main drivers of employee commitment and engagement. That's what Vancouver City Savings Credit Union (VanCity) discovered when it surveyed its staff a few years ago. "Employees wanted to know the organization was truly going to live up to its values and stay true to its commitments," says Donna Wilson, VanCity's vice-president of human resources.

VanCity has paid attention to its corporate culture for many years. For example, the company introduced Canada's first ethically screened mutual fund in 1986 and is well-known for its strong sense of social responsibility. But the company's culture had never been written down, and VanCity's 1,500 staff needed a clearer understanding of these values. So, 130 VanCity staff—from the board of directors to employee representatives in every branch—gathered to articulate what the organization stood for. At the end of the process, everyone agreed that VanCity had three dominant cultural values: integrity, innovation, and responsibility.

The process didn't stop with a values statement posted in every branch. VanCity leaders meet staff in all departments and branches twice yearly to discuss the company's cultural values. VanCity's values also figure into the decision-making process. "Even on the formal business plan, notations are made where actions demonstrate the commitment to corporate values, and rewards are being given out for behaviours supporting the values," explains Donna Wilson.

Vancouver City Savings Credit Union has applied a values-based business model to improve customer and employee relations. *Courtesy of VanCity.*

Thanks to its corporate culture, VanCity is rated as one of Canada's best companies to work for, and as one of the 10 most respected businesses in British Columbia. "[Values] define our company clearly in the financial services market in British Columbia, and give us a national and international profile few other regionally based companies anywhere in the world enjoy," says VanCity CEO Dave Mowat.[1] ▪

www.vancity.com

organizational culture

The basic pattern of shared assumptions, values, and beliefs considered to be the correct way of thinking about and acting on problems and opportunities facing the organization.

VanCity has rediscovered the power of organizational culture. **Organizational culture** is the basic pattern of shared assumptions, values, and beliefs that are considered to be the correct way of thinking about and acting on problems and opportunities facing an organization. It defines what is important and unimportant in the company. You might think of it as the organization's DNA—invisible to the naked eye, yet a powerful template that shapes what happens in the workplace.[2]

This chapter begins by examining the elements of organizational culture and how culture is deciphered through artifacts. This is followed by a discussion of the relationship between organizational culture and corporate performance, including the effects of cultural strength, fit, and adaptability. Then we turn to the issue of mergers and corporate culture. The last section looks at specific strategies for maintaining a strong organizational culture.

ELEMENTS OF ORGANIZATIONAL CULTURE

As Exhibit 16.1 illustrates, the assumptions, values, and beliefs that represent organizational culture operate beneath the surface: they are not directly observed, yet their effects are everywhere. Assumptions reveal the deepest part of organizational culture because they are unconscious and taken for granted. Assumptions are the shared mental models, the broad world-views or theories-in-use that

EXHIBIT 16.1

Elements of organizational culture

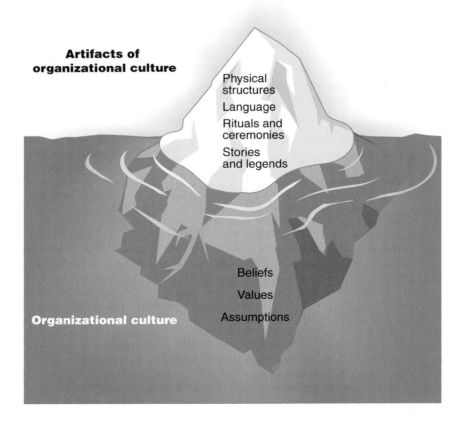

people rely on to guide their perceptions and behaviours (see Chapter 3). At VanCity, for example, employees assume that the company's integrity to customers and staff is one of the keys to the company's survival and success. These assumptions are ingrained. In other high technology companies, employees might assume less security and involvement.

An organization's cultural beliefs and values are somewhat easier than assumptions to decipher because people are aware of them. *Beliefs* reflect an individual's perceptions of reality. Values are more stable, long-lasting beliefs about what is important. They help us define what is right or wrong, or good or bad, in the world (see Chapter 2).[3] For example, Telus Corp. chief executive Darren Entwistle is transforming the Vancouver-based telecommunications company's culture into one that emphasizes efficiency. In contrast, the corporate culture of Ottawa-based MDS Nordion places more emphasis on work-life balance. "Our approach to employee health is results-oriented, emphasizing a supportive culture," says MDS Nordion CEO John Morrison.[4]

We can't determine an organization's cultural values just by asking employees and other people about them. Values are socially desirable, so what people say they value (called *espoused values*) may differ from what they truly value (*enacted values*).[5] Espoused values do not represent an organization's culture. Rather, they establish the public image that corporate leaders want to display. Enacted values, on the other hand, are values-in-use. They are the values that guide individual decisions and behaviour in the workplace.

Content of Organizational Culture

Organizations differ in their cultural content, that is, the relative ordering of beliefs, values, and assumptions. Consider the following companies and their apparent dominant cultures:

- *Northwood Technologies*—The culture of this Ottawa-based software developer is atypical for the high technology business because it values work-life balance. "When I came here I couldn't believe how well people were treated, and it was so refreshing to know that not every high-tech is as insane as many of the others I've encountered," says a Northwood employee. "I've seen a complete change in myself just from coming to this organization. It's everything to do with culture."[6]
- *Q-Media*—A thrifty culture has kept this Vancouver-based software packaging and distribution company in business. Q-Media relies on higher-cost small manufacturing runs, whereas its U.S. competitors have more lucrative large contracts. To survive, Q-Media employees focus on reducing costs. Profit and loss are calculated daily and full-time staff receive a share of cost savings. "We had to be thrifty," explains Q-Media CEO Robert Lawrie "I would argue it is our core asset, although it never shows up in our balance sheet."[7]
- *Brown & Brown*—Aggressive is too mild a word to describe the corporate culture of Brown & Brown, Inc. The unofficial mascot of this Daytona Beach, Florida-based insurance company is a cheetah. On the back cover of a recent annual report, in Latin, is the warning "No Egg-Sucking Dogs," a not-so-subtle reminder that poor performers will not be tolerated. This is not an idle threat. At its annual sales meeting, managers of poorly performing divisions are led to a podium by employees dressed as medieval executioners, while a

Research in Motion (RIM) has a fast-paced, entrepreneurial, yet supportive, culture. Employees at the Waterloo, Ontario pioneer in wireless digital assistants (think Blackberry) are in a constant race to beat competitors at the latest technology. At the same time, RIM's culture emphasizes having fun, including barbeques, Popsicle days, and special events. For example, RIM's entire work force recently took an afternoon off to watch the latest Star Wars movie! "This is a fun, creative, intense and inclusive corporate culture," explains RIM co-CEO Jim Balsillie (right). "It's a collegial culture," adds Mike Lazaridis, RIM's other co-CEO (left).[9] How would you try to determine whether Research in Motion really has these cultural values? *Kitchener-Waterloo Record*
www.rim.net

funeral dirge plays over loudspeakers. These managers have to explain to an audience of 1,000 employees why they failed to meet their annual goals. "It does sound a bit harsh, but that's the culture," says Brown & Brown's chief executive. "This is not a warm and fuzzy world."[8]

Employee-friendly. Thrifty. Aggressive. How many corporate cultural values are there? No one knows for certain. There are dozens of individual and cross-cultural values, so there are likely as many organizational values. Some writers and consultants have attempted to classify organizational cultures into a few categories with catchy labels such as "mercenaries" and "communes." Although these typologies might reflect the values of a few organizations, they oversimplify the diversity of cultural values in organizations. Worse, they tend to distort rather than clarify our attempts to diagnose corporate culture.

Organizational Subcultures

When discussing organizational culture, we are actually referring to the *dominant culture,* that is, the themes shared most widely by the organization's members. However, organizations also comprise *subcultures* located throughout their various divisions, geographic regions, and occupational groups.[10] Some subcultures enhance the dominant culture by espousing parallel assumptions, values, and beliefs; others are called *countercultures* because they directly oppose the organization's core values.

Subcultures, particularly countercultures, potentially create conflict and dissension among employees, but they also serve two important functions.[11] First, they maintain the organization's standards of performance and ethical behaviour. Employees who hold countercultural values are an important source of surveillance and critique of the dominant order. They encourage constructive conflict and more creative thinking about how the organization should interact with its environment. Subcultures prevent employees from blindly following one set of values and thereby help the organization to abide by society's ethical values.

The second function of subcultures is that they are the spawning grounds for emerging values that keep the firm aligned with the needs of customers, suppliers, society, and other stakeholders. Companies eventually need to replace their dominant values with ones that are more appropriate for the changing environment. If subcultures are suppressed, the organization may take longer to discover and adopt values aligned with the emerging environment.

DECIPHERING ORGANIZATIONAL CULTURE THROUGH ARTIFACTS

artifacts

The observable symbols and signs of an organization's culture.

We can't directly see an organization's cultural assumptions, values, and beliefs. Instead, as Exhibit 16.1 illustrated earlier, we can indirectly decipher organizational culture through **artifacts**. Artifacts are the observable symbols and signs of an organization's culture, such as the way visitors are greeted, the physical layout, and how employees are rewarded.[12] Understanding an organization's culture requires painstaking assessment of many artifacts because they are subtle and often ambiguous.[13] The process is very much like an anthropological investigation of a new society. Some scholars extract organizational values from the narratives of everyday corporate life;[14] others survey employees, observe workplace behaviour, and study written documents. We probably need to do all of these things to accurately assess an organization's culture.

Although this book tries to present accurate examples, we should remain cautious about public statements regarding a company's culture. Most often, these statements are based on no more than a journalist's quick scan or the company's own public relations pronouncements of its espoused values. With this in mind, let's consider four broad categories of artifacts: organizational stories and legends, rituals and ceremonies, language, physical structures and symbols.

Four Seasons Hotels and Resorts hires, trains, and rewards employees for superior customer service. Yet founder Isadore Sharp will tell you that the company's legendary service is also ingrained in Four Seasons' corporate culture. There is certainly evidence of the customer service value in stories and legends. One story recounts an incident in which rock star Rod Stewart called Four Seasons staff while he was a guest to find someone to play the bagpipes in his suite. The employees were able to find a bagpipe player, even though Stewart phoned in the request at *midnight*![16] In what ways do these stories and legends support organizational culture? *Courtesy of Four Seasons Hotels and Resorts*
www.fourseasons.com

Organizational Stories and Legends

In the late 1980s, so the story goes, executives at Maritime Life Assurance Co. were poring over the plans for a new head office in Halifax. The crowning glory of the architectural design was a spectacular ocean view from the ninth-floor offices. Naturally, the architects designed the space for the executive suite. But Maritime's CEO believed that this would be inconsistent with the company's culture. Instead, the plum location went to the employees in the form of an elegant, wood-panelled cafeteria. The executives had to park their offices elsewhere.[15]

This story from Maritime Life Assurance Co. story illustrates one of the company's core values—that employee well-being and satisfaction come before executive status. Stories and legends about past corporate incidents serve as powerful social prescriptions of the way things should (or should not) be done. They provide a realistic human side to corporate expectations, individual performance standards, and assumptions about the way things should work around the organization.

Not all stories and legends are positive. Some are retold to demonstrate what's wrong with the corporate culture. For instance, General Motors (GM) employees who rejected the automaker's dominant culture liked to tell about how dozens of GM people arrived at the airport to meet a senior executive. An executive's status was symbolized by the number of vehicles leaving the airport with the executive.[17] This story didn't just symbolize respect for authority; it was repeated because it highlighted the decadence and waste that characterized GM's dominant culture.

Organizational stories and legends are most effective at communicating cultural values when they describe real people, are assumed to be true, and are known by employees throughout the organization. Stories are also prescriptive—they advise people what to do or not to do.[18] Research on organizational stories reveals that they tend to answer one or more of the following questions: How does the boss react to mistakes? What events are so important that people get fired? Who, if anyone, can break the rules? How do people rise to the top of this organization? How much help can employees expect from the organization for transfers and other events? How will the organization deal with crises?[19]

Rituals and Ceremonies

Soon after moving from IBM to Digital Equipment Corporation (acquired by Hewlett-Packard through its merger with Compaq Computer) several years ago, Peter DeLisi noticed that Digital employees seemed to fight a lot with each other. "Shouting matches were a frequent occurrence, and I came to conclude that Digital people didn't like one another," he recalls. Eventually, DeLisi learned that Digital employees didn't dislike each other; they were engaging in the ritual of "pushing back"—defending ideas until truth ultimately prevailed.[20]

"Pushing back" at Digital Computer was a ritual that reflected the firm's belief that constructive conflict is useful. **Rituals** are the programmed routines of daily organizational life that dramatize the organization's culture. Along with shouting matches at Digital, rituals include how visitors are greeted, how often senior executives visit subordinates, how people communicate with each other, how much time employees take for lunch, and so on. **Ceremonies** are more formal artifacts than rituals. Ceremonies are planned activities conducted specifically for the benefit of an audience. This would include publicly rewarding (or punishing) employees, or celebrating the launch of a new product or newly won contract.[21]

rituals
The programmed routines of daily organizational life that dramatize the organization's culture.

Organizational Language

The language of the workplace speaks volumes about the company's culture. How employees address co-workers, describe customers, express anger, and greet stakeholders are all verbal symbols of cultural values. Employees at The Container Store compliment each other about "being Gumby," meaning that they are being as flexible as the once-popular green toy—going outside their regular job to help a customer or another employee. (A human-sized Gumby is displayed at the retailer's headquarters.)[22]

ceremonies
Planned and usually dramatic displays of organizational culture, conducted specifically for the benefit of an audience.

Organizational leaders also use phrases, metaphors, and other special vocabularies to symbolize the company's culture.[23] Of course, metaphors and catchphrases often reflect the leader's *espoused values*—the values that leaders want people to believe exist—rather than *enacted values*—the company's true values (see Chapter 2).

Language also highlights values held by organizational subcultures. This was recently apparent to consultants working at Whirlpool. They kept hearing employees talk about the appliance company's "PowerPoint culture." This phrase, which names Microsoft's presentation software, is a critique of Whirlpool's hierarchical culture in which communication is one-way (from executives to employees.) PowerPoint presentations tend be one-way conversations from the presenter to the audience, and Whirlpool employees see themselves as the "audience" with limited opportunity to voice opinions or concerns to senior management (the "presenters").[24]

Physical Structures and Symbols

Walk into Mountain Equipment Co-op's (MEC) retail outlet in Toronto (as well as most other cities where MEC has outlets) and you will quickly realize that this company means business about being green. Three large pine slabs near the entrance say: Tread Lightly. Leave No Trace. Take Only Memories. Concrete floors and beams are made from recycled slag (a byproduct of coal-fired generating stations that usually ends up in landfill). Wood beams are recycled from demolished buildings. The roof holds a 10,000-square-foot garden with four-inch-thick soil that insulates the building while adding greenery to Toronto's downtown. "Every aspect of the building was questioned," explains an executive at the Toronto architectural firm that designed the building. "It's a very unusual retail store—it's like an experiment in environmental solutions."[25]

Mountain Equipment Co-op reveals its culture through the design of its retail outlets throughout Canada. In many organizations, the size, shape, location, and age of buildings might suggest the company's emphasis on teamwork, environmental friendliness, flexibility, or any other set of values. These structures may be deliberately designed to shape the culture, or they may be incidental artifacts of the existing culture.[26]

Even if the building doesn't make much of a statement, there is a treasure trove of physical artifacts inside. Desks, chairs, office space, and wall hangings (or lack of them) are just a few of the items that might convey cultural meaning. Stroll through the Vancouver offices of Crystal Decisions and you'll see all the classic markers of a high-tech haven—warehouse-sized windows, comfy couches, foosball, and billiards tables.[27] Each of these artifacts alone might not say much, but put enough of them together and the company's cultural values become easier to decipher.

ORGANIZATIONAL CULTURE AND PERFORMANCE

Does organizational culture affect corporate performance? Bob Gett thinks so. The chief executive officer of consulting firm Viant, Inc. prefers to be called "chief cultural officer" because he believes a strong corporate culture shapes an organization's success. Several writers on this subject also conclude that a strong corporate culture is good for business.[28] Generally, they argue that culture serves three important functions.

First, corporate culture is a deeply embedded form of social control that influences employee decisions and behaviour.[29] Culture is pervasive and operates unconsciously. You might think of it as an automatic pilot, directing employees in ways that are consistent with organizational expectations. Second, corporate culture is the "social glue" that bonds people together and makes them feel part of the organizational experience.[30] Employees are motivated to internalize the organization's dominant culture because it fulfills their need for social identity. This social glue is increasingly important as a way to attract new staff and retain top performers.

Finally, corporate culture assists the sense-making process.[31] It helps employees understand organizational events. They can get on with the task at hand rather than spend time trying to figure out what is expected of them. Employees can also communicate more efficiently and reach higher levels of cooperation with each other because they share common mental models of reality.

Organizational Culture Strength and Fit

Each of these functions of organizational culture assumes that a strong culture is better than a weak one. A *strong organizational culture* exists when most employees across all subunits hold the dominant values of the organization. The values are also institutionalized through well-established artifacts, thereby making it difficult for those values to change. Furthermore, strong cultures are long-lasting. In many cases, they can be traced back to the beliefs and values established by the company's founder.[32] In contrast, companies have weak cultures when the dominant values are short lived and held mainly by a few people at the top of the organization.

These benefits don't necessarily mean that companies with strong cultures have higher performance. On the contrary, studies have found only a modestly positive relationship between culture strength and success.[33] One reason for the weak relationship is that a strong culture increases organizational performance only when the cultural content is appropriate for the organization's environment (see Exhibit 16.2). GLOBAL Connections 16.1 describes how Infosys Technologies has been successful partly because its culture is aligned with the demands of its environment in the global software marketplace. This "valley culture" values employees as the source of competitive advantage, egalitarian workplace practices, and high levels of quality service. Without these cultural values, Infosys would have difficulty keeping talented software engineers or attracting global clients.

When a firm's strong culture is misaligned with its environment, employees have difficulty anticipating and responding to the needs of customers or other dominant stakeholders. Lego seems to face this problem.[34] The Danish maker of Lego blocks has a fiercely independent culture which has created problems in an era of increasing globalization. Until recently, Lego refused to license products through partnerships with movie studios. When one executive proposed a partnership with Lucasfilms to make Star Wars products, other executives were horrified, arguing that this "wasn't the Lego way." One executive threatened, "Over my dead body will you be launching Star Wars in Europe." Lego's chief executive eventually approved the deal and Lego Star Wars became the company's most successful product launch in recent memory. Yet Lego's corporate culture nearly killed this important initiative.

EXHIBIT 16.2

Organizational culture and performance

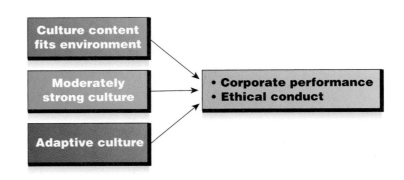

Silicon Valley Culture Aligns Infosys with Its Environment

Infosys Technologies has an impressive 17-hectare campus. Around the massive green courtyard connecting the six low-rise buildings, you can see employees playing on the miniature golf green, cooling off in the mammoth swimming pool, or munching on a freshly made Domino's pizza from one of the two huge food courts. There is also a huge video-wall, a leading edge training centre, and a complete medical centre. Not bad, even by Silicon Valley standards.

But Infosys isn't located in Silicon Valley, or even in North America. India's third largest information technology firm has its headquarters 25 kilometres south of Bangalore. To compete and survive in the global marketplace, Infosys has built a campus and adopted a culture that matches its Silicon Valley clients and competitors. This "valley culture" values employees as a scarce resource, so providing a lavish workplace is a worthwhile investment to become the employer of choice. Such "culture and caring aspects are really the emotional glue that hold employees together," explains Hema Ravichandar, Infosys' head of human resources.

Infosys also has an egalitarian culture, somewhat unusual in Indian companies. "Everyone has e-mail access," says Infosys CEO Narayana Murthy. "Everyone eats in the same canteen. We all share the same gymnasium. So there is much less hierarchical mindset than in the traditional company." Infosys became the first Indian company to offer employee stock options, another artifact of this egalitarian culture.

Customer focus through quality is another cultural value that has helped Infosys succeed in the global

Infosys has a strong "valley culture" that is aligned with its external environment. *James Bagnall and Sanjay Chetty Naidu/The Ottawa Citizen*

marketplace. "We're symbolic of the coming of age of Indian companies and technology," says Infosys president Nandan Nilekani. "We focus on customer service and deadlines, and that's a valley kind of culture. It's exciting. Incredibly exciting."

Sources: "Islands of Quality," *The Economist*, June 2, 2001, p. 17; J. Bagnall, "The Modern Face of India," *Ottawa Citizen*, March 5, 2001, p. B2; J. Slater, "The Battle to Retain IT Talent," *Far Eastern Economic Review*, Feb 15, 2001, p. 70; R. Sukumar, "Infosys: Wealth and Values," *Business Today*, January 7, 2001, p. 131; S. Bodow, "Murthy's Law," *Business 2.0*, November 28, 2000; M. McDonald, "Software Companies In India Turn Problem Into Tidy Profits," *San Jose Mercury*, January 2, 2000 **www.infy.com**

A second concern as to why companies with strong cultures aren't necessarily more effective is that strong cultures lock decision makers into mental models that can blind them to new opportunities and unique problems. When an organization's culture intensely emphasizes customer service, for example, employees tend to see problems as customer service problems, even though some are really problems about efficiency or technology. Thus, strong cultures might cause decision makers to overlook or incorrectly define subtle misalignments between the organization's activities and the changing environment.[35]

Finally, very strong cultures tend to suppress dissenting subcultural values. In the long term, this prevents organizations from nurturing new cultural values that should become dominant values as the environment changes. In the short term, a strong culture might undermine constructive conflict (see Chapter 13). Thus, corporate leaders need to recognize that healthy organizations have subcultures with dissenting values which may produce dominant values in the future.

Adaptive Cultures

So far, we have learned that strong cultures are more effective when cultural values are aligned with the organization's environment. Also, no corporate culture should be so strong that it blinds employees to alternative viewpoints or completely suppresses dissenting subcultures. One last point is that organizations are more likely to succeed when they have an adaptive culture.[36] An **adaptive culture** exists when employees focus on the changing needs of customers and other stakeholders, and support initiatives to keep pace with these changes.

> **adaptive culture**
> An organizational culture in which employees focus on the changing needs of customers and other stakeholders, and support initiatives to keep pace with these changes.

Organizational culture experts are starting to piece together the elements of adaptive cultures.[37] First and foremost, adaptive cultures have an external focus. Employees hold a common mental model, that the organization's success depends on continuous change to support stakeholders. Nortel Networks shifted from telephones to Internet gear. Nokia moved from toilet paper and rubber boots to mobile telephones. Both of these firms have maintained an adaptive culture because employees believe that change is both necessary and inevitable to keep pace with a changing external environment.

Second, employees in adaptive cultures pay as much attention to organizational processes as they do to organizational goals. They engage in continuous improvement of internal processes (production, customer service, etc.) to serve external stakeholders. Third, employees in adaptive cultures have a strong sense of ownership. They assume responsibility for the organization's performance. In other words, they believe in "it's our job" rather than "it's not my job." Fourth, adaptive cultures are proactive and quick. Employees seek out opportunities, rather than wait for them to arrive. They act quickly to learn through discovery rather than engage in "paralysis by analysis."

Organizational Culture and Business Ethics

Along with other forms of performance, an organization's culture can potentially influence ethical conduct. In fact, Canadian executives identify organizational culture as one of the three main influences on ethical conduct at work. (The other two are executive leadership and personal commitment to ethical principles.)[38] This makes sense because, as we learned in Chapter 2, good behaviour is driven by ethical values. An organization can guide the conduct of its employees by embedding ethical values in its dominant culture.

The relationship between ethics and organizational culture can be found in companies accused of serious discrimination or sexual harassment. These firms typically have a "gendered culture" that supports discriminatory organizational rules and maintains assumptions that limit the career potential of women.[39] In extreme cases, the corporate culture reinforces perceptions of female staff as sexual objects, which increases the frequency of harassment. Thus, companies require more than policies and practices to repair sexual discrimination and harassment problems; they must change the underlying culture into one that views men and women as equal partners in the enterprise.

Organizational culture is also a potential source of ethical problems when it applies excessive control over employees. All organizations require some control to ensure that employee actions are aligned with organizational objectives. But as Connections 16.2 describes, a few organizations imprint their cultural values so strongly on employees that they risk becoming corporate cults. They take over

When Corporate Culture Becomes a Corporate Cult

Andrew Brenner is still troubled by an interview he had a few years ago for a legal job at Microsoft. "All the lawyers seemed to think it was a foregone conclusion Microsoft would take over the world," says Brenner. Ultimately, Brenner decided not to pursue the job. "It's a very strong culture. Too strong for me."

While many writers seem to celebrate organizations with strong cultures, a few are worried that some firms are becoming corporate cults. A recent book on the subject suggests that employees are victims of corporate cults when they work crushingly long hours, have few friends outside the workplace, develop emotional attitudes about their job, and have difficulty distinguishing "who I am" from "what I do."

Microsoft has been accused of being a corporate cult. Some employees practically live at the software giant's campus in Redmond, Washington. "There's people working here 24 hours a day," says a Microsoft manager. "It's set up so you never have to go home." Consultancy McKinsey & Company apparently has an equally strong culture. Says one senior McKinseyite:

"It's like being a Catholic. Once baptized, there is no escape." A reporter from Britain's *Financial Times* newspaper suggests that the firm's training for new recruits looks more like a brainwashing camp. "It's as if they are Moonies," says the journalist. "That's slightly scary."

Razorfish, an Internet professional services organization, also has the characteristics of a corporate cult. "We've been accused of creating a cult-like atmosphere here, but to us there's Razorfish and not-Razorfish," says Len Sellers, managing director of Razorfish's San Francisco office.

Sellers defends the strong culture at Razorfish, but he also describes how it has taken over his life. "I used to be an avid sailor, but haven't been on a boat in a year," he admits. "I used to have girlfriends, but they left out of boredom and frustration. I used to have a cat, but it moved in with a neighbour. It's one thing when a girlfriend leaves, but it's another when a cat goes."

Sources: T. C. Doyle, "New Economy, New Culture," *VarBusiness*, July 10, 2000, p. 26; J. Useem, "Welcome to the New Company Town," *Fortune*, January 10, 2000, pp. 62–70; D. Arnott, *Corporate Cults* (NY: AMACOM, 1999); "The Cult of The Firm," *The Express On Sunday (UK)*, August 15, 1999. **www.microsoft.com**

employee lives and rob their individualism. Thus, an organization's culture should be consistent with society's ethical values and the culture should not be so strong that it undermines individual freedom.

MERGING ORGANIZATIONAL CULTURES

Corporate culture was on the minds of executives at Billiton plc in South Africa and BHP in Australia when they met to discuss a proposed merger into the world's largest mining company. "Obviously one of the questions when you get into a merger is: Is one culture going to dominate or do you create a new one?" says Tom Brown, BHP's human resources director. "Lots of mergers have failed to realize what they purported to be because they failed to look at the people or culture side of the business." To ensure that the BHP-Billiton merger wasn't another casualty, the two firms set up a committee to address the cultural issues and plan integration of the two firms. The committee began by taking a "cultural swab" from both companies. What they found was two businesses in cultural transition, so it was possible to form a composite culture that took the best of both firms.[40]

From a corporate cultural perspective, the BHP-Billiton merger started on the right track. Unfortunately, it is also the exception. Mergers and acquisitions in Canada and the United States had an equity value of more than $5 trillion over the past four years—nearly equal to the combined annual gross domestic products of Japan and Germany. Yet, more than two-thirds of these combined firms underperformed their industry peers in following years. The main problem is that corporate leaders are so focused on the financial or marketing logistics of a merger that they fail to conduct due-diligence audits on their respective corporate cultures.[41]

The corporate world is littered with mergers that failed or had a difficult gestation because of clashing organizational cultures. For example, Quebecor felt the side effects of imposing its "tight ship" culture on SunMedia. Morale apparently plummeted and turnover increased because staff at *The Toronto Sun* and other SunMedia newspapers had difficulty adjusting to Quebecor's harsh values.[42] "It's the people stuff that trips up mergers," says an executive at AstraZeneca U.S., one of the world's largest pharmaceutical companies after the merger of Astra AB and Zeneca Group PLC. "You can do the deal because it looks really good on paper, but if you don't engage the minds of the people from each culture, you won't get the productivity you need to be successful."[43]

bicultural audit
Diagnoses cultural relations between companies prior to a merger and determines the extent to which the cultural clashes will likely occur.

Bicultural Audit

Organizational leaders can minimize these cultural collisions and fulfill their duty of due diligence by conducting a bicultural audit, similar to what BHP and Billiton did prior to their merger. A **bicultural audit** diagnoses cultural relations between the companies and determines the extent to which cultural clashes will likely occur.[44] "The process [of addressing cultural issues] really starts during due diligence" advises Barry Griswell, CEO of The Principal Financial Group, which acquired Bankers Trust Australia. BT Funds Management CEO Ian Martin agrees. "Cultural considerations have been high on our agenda throughout our integration with The Principal," says Martin. "Management on both sides has been sensitive to, and interested in, the unique cultures of each organization."[45]

The bicultural audit process begins with interviews, questionnaires, focus groups, and observation to identify cultural differences between the merging companies. This includes carefully examining artifacts of each organization—the office layout, how customers are billed, how decisions are made, how information is shared, and so on. Next, the bicultural audit data are analyzed to determine which differences between the two firms will result in conflict and which cultural values provide common ground on which to build a cultural foundation in the merged organization. The final stage of the bicultural audit involves identifying strategies and preparing action plans to bridge the cultures of the two organizations.

Before Abitibi-Price agreed to merge with Stone Consolidated, the pulp-and-paper firm developed the Merging Cultures Evaluation Index (MCEI), an evaluation system that would help the company compare its culture with other companies in the industry. The MCEI analyzed several dimensions of corporate culture, such as concentration of power versus diffusion of power, innovation versus tradition, wide versus narrow flow of information, and consensus versus authoritative decision making. Abitibi and Stone executives completed the questionnaire to assess their own culture, then compared the results. The MCEI results, along with financial and infrastructural information, served as the basis for Abitibi-Price to merge with Stone Consolidated to become Montreal-based Abitibi-Consolidated, the world's largest pulp-and-paper firm.[46] In what other ways should executives conduct a bicultural audit prior to a merger? *CP/Ryan Remiorz*
www.abicon.com

Strategies to Merge Different Organizational Cultures

In some cases, the bicultural audit results in a decision to end merger talks because the two cultures are too different to merge effectively. For instance, GE Capital has rejected potential acquisitions when it became apparent that the other firm's cultural values were incompatible. Nortel Networks also walked away from a joint venture with Cisco Systems because it wasn't comfortable with the other firm's cultural values.[47] However, even with substantially different cultures, two companies may form a workable union if they apply the appropriate merger strategy. The four main strategies for merging different corporate cultures are assimilation, deculturation, integration, and separation (see Exhibit 16.3).[48]

Assimilation   Assimilation occurs when employees at the acquired company willingly embrace the cultural values of the acquiring organization. This tends to occur when the acquired company has a weak culture that is dysfunctional, and the acquiring company's culture is strong and focused on clearly defined values. Sun Microsystems has acquired many smaller organizations using this strategy. The California high-technology company refuses to digest larger firms because it is much more difficult to apply Sun's aggressive culture.[49] Culture clash is rare with assimilation because the acquired firm's culture is weak and its employees are looking for better cultural alternatives.

Deculturation   Assimilation is rare. Employees usually resist organizational change, particularly when they are asked to throw away personal and cultural values. Under these conditions, some acquiring companies apply a *deculturation* strategy by imposing their culture and business practices on the acquired organization. The acquiring firm strips away artifacts and reward systems that support the old culture. People who cannot adopt the acquiring company's culture are often terminated.

This happened when Anderson Exploration Ltd. (now part of Devon Exploration) acquired Home Oil Co. Ltd. Both oil firms had headquarters in Calgary, but were different in every other way. Home Oil valued status and splendour, with a bit of extravagance thrown in. The firm had an executive dining room, two floors of executive offices, a small fleet of planes, and expensive art. Anderson's founder,

EXHIBIT 16.3   Strategies for merging different organizational cultures

Merger strategy	Description	Works best when:
Assimilation	Acquired company embraces acquiring firm's culture.	Acquired firm has a weak culture.
Deculturation	Acquiring firm imposes its culture on unwilling acquired firm.	Rarely works—may be necessary only when acquired firm's culture doesn't work but employees don't realize it.
Integration	Combining the two or more cultures into a new composite culture.	Existing cultures can be improved.
Separation	Merging companies remain distinct entities with minimal exchange of culture or organizational practices.	Firms operate successfully in different businesses requiring different cultures.

Source: Based on ideas in K. W. Smith, "A Brand-New Culture for the Merged Firm," *Mergers and Acquisitions*, 35 (June 2000), pp. 45–50; A. R. Malekazedeh and A. Nahavandi, "Making Mergers Work by Managing Cultures," *Journal of Business Strategy*, May–June 1990, pp. 55–57.

J. C. Anderson, soon replaced Home Oil's culture with the efficient and lean values that dominated Anderson Exploration. "They had a culture, we had a culture," says Anderson with characteristic bluntness. "Ours worked, theirs didn't. At the end of the day, we've got to have this combined organization being a lot closer to our culture."[50]

Deculturation may be necessary when the acquired firm's culture doesn't work but employees aren't convinced of this. However, this strategy rarely works because it increases the risk of socioemotional conflict (see Chapter 13). Employees from the acquired firm resist the cultural intrusions from the buying firm, thereby delaying or undermining the merger process.

Integration   A third strategy is to integrate the corporate cultures of both organizations. This involves combining the two or more cultures into a new composite culture that preserves the best features of the previous cultures. Integration is slow and potentially risky, because there are many forces preserving the existing cultures. However, this strategy should be considered when the companies have relatively weak cultures, or when their cultures include several overlapping values. Integration also works best when people realize that their existing cultures are ineffective and are, therefore, motivated to adopt a new set of dominant values.

Separation   A separation strategy occurs where the merging companies agree to remain distinct entities with minimal exchange of culture or organizational practices. This strategy is most appropriate when the two merging companies are in unrelated industries or operate in different countries, because the most appropriate cultural values tend to differ by industry and national culture. Distinct cultures within an organization can also lead to the separation strategy of demerging. For instance, some energy companies have split into two entities—one for the slow-moving utility business and another for the volatile exploration and trading businesses that require a different culture.

CHANGING AND STRENGTHENING ORGANIZATIONAL CULTURE

Whether merging two cultures or reshaping the firm's existing values, corporate leaders need to understand how to change and strengthen the organization's dominant culture. Indeed, some organizational scholars conclude that the only way to ensure any lasting change is to realign cultural values with those changes. In other words, changes "stick" when they become "the way we do things around here."[51]

Changing organizational culture requires the change management toolkit that we will learn about in the next chapter (Chapter 17). Corporate leaders need to make employees aware of the urgency for change. Then they need to "unfreeze" the existing culture by removing artifacts that represent that culture and "refreeze" the new culture by introducing artifacts that communicate and reinforce the new values.

Strengthening Organizational Culture

Artifacts communicate and reinforce the new corporate culture, but we also need to consider ways to further strengthen that culture. Five approaches that are commonly cited in the literature are the actions of founders and leaders, introducing

EXHIBIT 16.4

Strategies for
strengthening
organizational
culture

culturally consistent rewards, maintaining a stable work force, managing the cultural network, and selecting and socializing new employees (see Exhibit 16.4).

Actions of founders and leaders   Founders establish an organization's culture.[52] You can see this at Four Seasons Hotels and Resorts where founder Isadore Sharp has created a culture that emphasizes mutual respect and customer service. Founders develop the systems and structures that support their personal values. Typically, they are also the visionaries whose energetic style provides a powerful role model for others to follow.

In spite of the founder's influence, subsequent leaders can break the organization away from the founder's values if they apply the transformational leadership concepts that were described in Chapter 14. Transformational leaders alter and strengthen organizational culture by communicating and enacting their vision of the future.[53] For example, Carly Fiorina is trying to change Hewlett-Packard's culture because she believes H-P employees hide behind their corporate culture to avoid tough decisions. "The phrase 'The H-P Way' became a way of resisting change and resisting radical ideas," argues Fiorina. "One of the things I've been able to do as an outsider is challenge it."[54]

Introducing culturally consistent rewards   Reward systems strengthen corporate culture when they are consistent with cultural values.[55] For example, Husky Injection Molding Systems has an unusual stock incentive program that supports its environmentalist culture. Employees earn 1/20th of a company share for each seedling they plant, one share for each month of car pooling, and so on. The idea is to align rewards to the cultural values the company wants to reinforce.

Maintaining a stable work force   An organization's culture is embedded in the minds of its employees. Organizational stories are rarely written down; rituals and ceremonies do not usually exist in procedure manuals; organizational metaphors are not found in corporate directories. Thus, organizations depend on a stable work force to communicate and reinforce the dominant beliefs and

Ray Anderson admits he didn't pay much attention to environmentalism when he launched Atlanta-based Interface Inc. in the 1970s. But after reading *The Ecology of Commerce* in 1994, Anderson's newfound environmental values have reshaped the culture of the world's largest floor covering company. "[W]e've got a company full of people who've really bought in to that vision," says Anderson, shown here at a speech in Ottawa. Today, Interface has solar-powered looms, a weaving plant that uses recycled plastics, and an R&D department that experiments with hemp, sugar cane, and other renewable resources. Most of the company's 8,000 employees on four continents have received environmental training, and many of them have created environmental organizations in their communities.[56] In what ways do founders and leaders influence their organization's culture? *Pierre Roussel/The Ottawa Citizen*
www.interfaceinc.com

values. The organization's culture can disintegrate during periods of high turnover and precipitous downsizing because the corporate memory leaves with these employees.[57] Conversely, corporate leaders who want to change the corporate culture have accelerated the turnover of senior executives and older employees who held the previous culture in place.

Managing the cultural network   Organizational culture is learned, so an effective network of cultural transmission is necessary to strengthen the company's underlying assumptions, values, and beliefs. According to Max De Pree, former CEO of furniture manufacturer Herman Miller Inc., every organization needs "tribal storytellers" to keep the organization's history and culture alive.[58] The cultural network exists through the organizational grapevine. It is also supported through frequent opportunities for interaction so employees can share stories and re-enact rituals. Senior executives must tap into the cultural network, sharing their own stories and creating new ceremonies and other opportunities to demonstrate shared meaning. Company magazines and other media can also strengthen organizational culture by communicating cultural values and beliefs more efficiently.

Selecting and socializing employees   People at Bristol-Myers recently noticed that executives hired from the outside weren't as successful as those promoted from within. Within a year, many quit or were fired. Ben Dowell, who runs Bristol-Myers' Center for Leadership Development, looked closely at the problem and arrived at the following conclusion: "What came through was, those who left were uncomfortable in our culture or violated some core area of our value system." From this discovery, Bristol-Myers assessed its culture—it's team-oriented, consistent with the firm's research and development roots. Now applicants are carefully screened to ensure they have compatible values.[59]

Bristol-Myers and a flock of other organizations strengthen their corporate cultures by hiring people with beliefs, values, and assumptions similar to those cultures. They realize that a good fit of personal and organizational values makes it easier for employees to adopt the corporate culture. A good person-organization fit also improves job satisfaction and organizational loyalty because new hires with values compatible to the corporate culture adjust more quickly to the organization.[60]

Job applicants are also paying more attention to corporate culture during the hiring process. According to one survey, job applicants ask corporate culture questions more than any other topic, aside from pay and benefits.[61] Companies realize that employees must feel comfortable with the company's values, not just the job duties and hours of work. Thus, job applicants need to look at corporate culture artifacts when deciding whether to join a particular organization. By diagnosing the company's dominant culture, they are more likely to determine whether its values are compatible with their own.

Along with selecting people with compatible values, companies maintain strong cultures through the effective socialization of new employees (see Chapter 9). By communicating the company's dominant values, job candidates and new hires are more likely to internalize these values quickly and deeply. For example, IKEA holds "Culture Days" during which employees reacquaint themselves with the Scandinavian home furnishing company's dominant values: thrift, hard work, fair play, and inventiveness.[62]

Throughout this chapter, we have learned that organizational culture is pervasive and powerful. For corporate leaders, it is either a force for change or an insurmountable barrier to it. For employees, it is either the glue that bonds people or a force that drives them away from the organization. So many artifacts communicate and reinforce the existing culture that it requires a monumental effort to replace the current values. Transformational leadership can assist this process, as can the effective management of change, which we explore in the next chapter.

CHAPTER SUMMARY

Organizational culture is the basic pattern of shared assumptions, values, and beliefs that govern behaviour within a particular organization. Assumptions are the shared mental models or theories-in-use that people rely on to guide their perceptions and behaviours. Beliefs represent an individual's perceptions of reality. Values are more stable, long-lasting beliefs about what is important. They help us define what is right or wrong, or good or bad, in the world. Culture content refers to how beliefs, values, and assumptions are ordered.

Organizations have subcultures as well as the dominant culture. Some subcultures enhance the dominant culture, whereas countercultures have values that oppose the organization's core values. Subcultures maintain the organization's standards of performance and ethical behaviour. They are also the source of emerging values that replace aging core values.

Artifacts are the observable symbols and signs of an organization's culture. Four broad categories of artifacts include organizational stories and legends, rituals and ceremonies, language, physical structures and symbols. Understanding an organization's culture requires a painstaking assessment of many artifacts because they are subtle and often ambiguous.

Organizational culture has three main functions. It is a deeply embedded form of social control. It is also the "social glue" that bonds employees together and makes them feel part of the organizational experience. Third, corporate culture helps employees make sense of the workplace.

Companies with strong cultures generally perform better than those with weak cultures, but only when the cultural content is appropriate for the organization's environment. Also, the culture should not be so strong that it drives out dissenting values, which may form emerging values for the future. Organizations should have adaptive cultures so that employees focus on the need for change and support initiatives and leadership that keep pace with these changes.

Organizational culture relates to business ethics in two ways. First, corporate cultures can support society's ethical values, thereby reinforcing ethical conduct. Second, some cultures are so strong that they rob a person's individualism and discourage constructive conflict.

Mergers should include a bicultural audit to diagnose the compatibility of the organizational cultures. The four main strategies for merging different corporate cultures are integration, deculturation, assimilation, and separation.

Organizational culture is very difficult to change. However, this can be done by creating an urgency for change and replacing artifacts that support the old culture with artifacts aligned more with the desired future culture. Organizational culture may be strengthened through the actions of founders and leaders, introducing culturally consistent rewards, maintaining a stable work force, managing the cultural network, and selecting and socializing employees.

KEY TERMS

Adaptive culture, p. 464

Artifacts, p. 459

Bicultural audit, p. 466

Ceremonies, p. 460

Organizational culture, p. 456

Rituals, p. 460

DISCUSSION QUESTIONS

1. Can an employee be productive and satisfied in an organization if the individual's values differ from the values of the organization? Discuss.
2. Some people suggest that the most effective organizations have the strongest cultures. What do we mean by the "strength" of organizational culture, and what possible problems are there with a strong organizational culture?
3. The CEO of a Canadian manufacturing firm wants everyone to support the organization's dominant culture of lean efficiency and hard work. The CEO has introduced a new reward system to reinforce this culture and personally interviews all professional and managerial applicants to ensure that they bring similar values to the organization. Some employees who criticized these values had their careers sidelined until they left. Two mid-level managers were fired for supporting contrary values, such as work-life balance. Based on your knowledge of organizational subcultures, what potential problems is the CEO creating?

4. Identify at least two artifacts you have observed in your department or faculty from each of the four broad categories:
   a) Organizational stories and legends
   b) Rituals and ceremonies
   c) Language
   d) Physical structures and symbols.
5. "Organizations are more likely to succeed when they have an adaptive culture." What can an organization do to foster an adaptive culture?
6. What role, if any, should organizational culture play in the feasibility assessment of an organizational merger?
7. Explain how transformational leadership strengthens corporate culture.
8. Suppose you are asked by senior officers of a Canadian city to identify ways to reinforce a new culture of teamwork and collaboration. The senior executive group clearly supports these values, but it wants everyone in the organization to embrace them. Identify four types of activities that would strengthen these cultural values.

CASE STUDY 16.1

ASSETONE BANK

AssetOne Bank is one of Asia's largest financial institutions, but it had difficulty entering the personal investment business where several other companies dominate the market. To gain entry to this market, AssetOne decided to acquire TaurusBank, a much smaller financial institution that had aggressively developed investment funds (unit trusts) and online banking in the region. Taurus was owned by a European conglomerate that wanted to exit the financial sector, so the company was quietly put up for sale. The opportunity to acquire Taurus seemed like a perfect fit to AssetOne's executives, who saw the purchase as an opportunity to finally gain a competitive position

in the personal investment market. In particular, the acquisition would give AssetOne valuable talent in online banking and investment fund businesses.

Negotiations between AssetOne and TaurusBank occurred secretly, except for communication with government regulatory agencies, and took several months as AssetOne's executive team deliberated over the purchase. When AssetOne finally decided in favour of the acquisition, employees of both companies were notified only a few minutes before the merger was announced publicly. During the public statement, AssetOne's CEO boldly announced that TaurusBank would become a "seamless extension of AssetOne." He explained that, like AssetOne, Taurus employees would learn the value of detailed analysis and cautious decision making.

The comments by AssetOne's CEO shocked many employees at Taurus, which was an aggressive and entrepreneurial competitor in online banking and personal investments. Taurus was well known for its edgy marketing, innovative products, and tendency to involve employees to generate creative ideas. The company didn't hesitate to hire people from other industries who would bring different ideas to the investment and online banking business. AssetOne, on the other hand, promoted its executives almost completely from within the ranks. Every member of the senior executive team had started at AssetOne. The company also emphasized decision making at the top so they could maintain better control and consistency.

Frustration was apparent within a few months after the merger. Several Taurus executives quit after the repeated failure of AssetOne's executive team to decide quickly on critical online banking initiatives. For example, at the time of the acquisition, Taurus was in the process of forming affinity alliances with several companies. Yet, six months later, AssetOne's executive team had still not decided whether to proceed with these partnerships.

The biggest concerns occurred in the investment fund business where 20 of TaurusBank's 60 fund managers were lured away by competitors within the first year. Some left for better opportunities. Six fund managers left with the Taurus executive in charge of the investment fund business, who joined an investment firm that specializes in investment funds. Several employees left Taurus after AssetOne executives insisted that all new investment funds must be approved by AssetOne's executive group. Previously, Taurus had given the investment fund division the freedom to launch new products without needing the approval of the entire executive team.

Two years later, AssetOne's CEO admitted that the acquisition of TaurusBank had not given them the opportunities that they had originally hoped for. AssetOne had more business in this area, but many of the more talented people in investment funds and online banking had left the firm. Overall, the merged company had not kept pace with other innovative financial institutions in the market.

Discussion Questions

1. Based on your understanding of mergers and organizational culture, discuss the problems that occurred in this case.

2. What strategies would you recommend to AssetOne's executives to avoid these corporate culture clashes in future mergers and acquisitions?

Copyright © 2002 Steven L. McShane

TEAM EXERCISE 16.2

ORGANIZATIONAL CULTURE METAPHORS

By David L. Luechauer, Butler University and Gary M. Shulman, Miami University

Purpose Both parts of this exercise are designed to help you understand, assess, and interpret organizational culture using metaphors.

Part A: Assessing Your School's Culture

Instructions A metaphor is a figure of speech that contains an implied comparison between a word or phrase that is ordinarily used for one thing but can be applied to another. Metaphors also carry a great deal of hidden meaning—they say a lot about what we think and feel about that object. Therefore, this activity asks you to use several metaphors to define the organizational culture of your university, college, or institute. (Alternatively, the instructor might ask students to assess another organization that most students know about.)

■ *Step 1*: The class will be divided into teams of 4 to 6 members.

■ *Step 2*: Each team will reach consensus on which words or phrases should be inserted in the blanks of the statements presented below. This information should be recorded on a flip chart or overhead acetate for class presentation. The instructor will provide 15 to 20 minutes for teams to determine which words best describe the college's culture.

If our school were an animal, it would be a _____ because _____.

If our school were a food, it would be _____ because _____.

If our school were a place, it would be _____ because _____.

If our school were a season, it would be _____ because _____.

If our school were a TV show or movie, it would be _____ because _____.

■ *Step 3:* The class will listen to each team present the metaphors that it believes symbolizes the school's culture. For example, a team that picks winter for a season might mean they are feeling cold or distant about the school and its people.

■ *Step 4:* The class will discuss the discussion questions stated below.

Discussion Questions for Part A

1. How easy was it for your group to reach consensus regarding these metaphors? What does that imply about the culture of your school?

2. How do you see these metaphors in action? In other words, what are some critical school behaviours or other artifacts that reveal the presence of your culture?

3. Think of another organization to which you belong (e.g., work, religious congregation). What are its dominant cultural values, how

do you see them in action, and how do they affect the effectiveness of that organization?

Part B: Analyzing and Interpreting Cultural Metaphors

Instructions Previously, you completed a metaphor exercise to describe the corporate culture of your school. That exercise gave you a taste of how to administer such a diagnostic tool and draw inferences from the results generated. This activity builds on that experience and is designed to help refine your ability to analyze such data and make suggestions for improvement. Five work teams (4 to 7 members/mixed gender in all groups) of an organization located in Cincinnati completed the metaphor exercise similar to the exercise in which you participated in class (see Part A above). Their responses are shown in the table below. Working in teams, analyze the information in this table and answer these questions:

Discussion questions for Part B

1. In your opinion, what are the dominant cultural values in this organization? Explain your answer.

2. What are the positive aspects of this type of culture?

3. What are the negative aspects of this type of culture?

4. What is this organization's main business, in your opinion? Explain your answer.

5. These groups all reported to one manager. What advice would you give to her about this unit?

Metaphor Results of Five Teams in a Cincinnati Organization					
Team	Animal	Food	Place	TV Show	Season
1	Rabbit	Big Mac	Casino	48 Hrs. (movie)	Spring
2	Horse	Taco	Racetrack	Miami Vice	Spring
3	Elephant	Ribs	Circus	Roseanne	Summer
4	Eagle	Big Mac	Las Vegas	CNN	Spring
5	Panther	Chinese	New York	LA Law	Racing

Source: Adapted from D. L. Luechauer and G. M. Shulman, "Using A Metaphor Exercise To Explore The Principles Of Organizational Culture," *Journal of Management Education*, 22 (December 1998), pp. 736–44. Used with permission of the authors.

CORPORATE CULTURE PREFERENCE SCALE

Purpose   This self-assessment is designed to help you to identify a corporate culture that fits most closely with your personal values and assumptions.

Instructions   Read each pair of statements in the Corporate Culture Preference Scale and circle the statement that describes the organization you would prefer to work in. Then use the scoring key in Appendix B to calculate your results for each sub-scale. This exercise is completed alone so students can assess themselves honestly without concerns of social comparison. However, class discussion will focus on the importance of matching job applicants to the organization's dominant values.

Corporate Culture Preference Scale

I would prefer to work in an organization:

1a. Where employees work well together in teams.	**OR**	1b. That produces highly respected products or services.
2a. Where top management maintains a sense of order in the workplace.	**OR**	2b. Where the organization listens to customers and responds quickly to their needs.
3a. Where employees are treated fairly.	**OR**	3b. Where employees continuously search for ways to work more efficiently.
4a. Where employees adapt quickly to new work requirements.	**OR**	4b. Where corporate leaders work hard to keep employees happy.
5a. Where senior executives receive special benefits not available to other employees.	**OR**	5b. Where employees are proud when the organization achieves its performance goals.
6a. Where employees who perform the best get paid the most.	**OR**	6b. Where senior executives are respected.
7a. Where everyone gets their jobs done like clockwork.	**OR**	7b. That is on top of new innovations in the industry.
8a. Where employees receive assistance to overcome any personal problems.	**OR**	8b. Where employees abide by company rules.
9a. That is always experimenting with new ideas in the marketplace.	**OR**	9b. That expects everyone to put in 110 percent for peak performance.
10a. That quickly benefits from market opportunities.	**OR**	10b. Where employees are always kept informed of what's happening in the organization.
11a. That can quickly respond to competitive threats.	**OR**	11b. Where most decisions are made by the top executives.
12a. Where management keeps everything under control.	**OR**	12b. Where employees care for each other.

Copyright © 2000 Steven L. McShane

After studying the preceding material, be sure to check out our Online Learning Centre at
www.mcgrawhill.ca/college/mcshane
for more in-depth information and interactivities that correspond to this chapter.

CHAPTER 17

Organizational Change

Learning Objectives

- Describe the elements of Lewin's force field analysis model.

- Outline six reasons people resist organizational change.

- Discuss six strategies to minimize resistance to change.

- Outline the conditions for effectively diffusing change from a pilot project.

- Describe the action research approach to organizational change.

- Outline the "Four-D" model of appreciative inquiry and explain how this approach differs from action research.

- Explain how parallel learning structures assist the change process.

- Discuss four ethical issues in organizational change.

A decade ago, Telus Corp. was a monopoly in western Canada, Bell Canada was a partner in long distance telephone services, and cable companies were in an unrelated business. Today, due to deregulation and technological change, the Vancouver-based telecommunications firm competes directly with Bell Canada and cable companies for the same customers.

"That's a massive change in the competitive dynamic," says CEO Darren Entwistle, who was hired to turn Telus into a more performance-oriented company. "And we need to ensure that our organization is geared appropriately in terms of our operating efficiency and effectiveness to compete successfully within that competitive dynamic."

Entwistle brought in a new executive team, quickly opened Telus operations in Ontario, restructured the workforce, introduced personal development reviews and a new reward system to improve employee performance, and worked toward instilling a new set of company values and direction. "We're trying to create what we call a high-performance culture," explains Mary Pat Barry, head of Telus internal communications. "It's now a different organization than it was—one that's more appropriate to the new economy."

This change process hasn't been easy for many Telus employees. "People are really stressed out," warns Rod Hiebert, president of the labour union representing Telus staff. Complaining that Entwistle is changing Telus too quickly, Hiebert and his union have urged shareholders to fire Telus' entire senior management team and replace it with "stable, experienced management."

Darren Entwistle (shown in photo) was hired as CEO of Telus Corp to ensure the Vancouver-based telecommunications company remained competitive in a turbulent environment. *CP/Kevin Frayer*

But others say the Telus workforce is long overdue for change. "[I]t's a workforce that's been low in productivity and has consistently resisted any change over the years," explains telecommunications consultant Eamon Hoey. However, Entwistle says that Telus employees generally support the change process. "I do think the employees of this organization understand the need for change," says Entwistle, who points to surveys indicating that employees overwhelmingly support the company's leadership, productivity drive, and strategic direction.[1]

www.telus.com

force field analysis
Lewin's model of systemwide change that helps change agents diagnose the forces that drive and restrain proposed organizational change.

Change is difficult enough in small firms. At Telus Corp. and other large organizations, it requires monumental effort and persistence. Organizational change is also very messy. The change process that Darren Entwistle launched at Telus illustrates that organizational transformations are buffeted by uncertain consequences, organizational politics, and various forms of employee resistance.

This chapter examines ways to bring about meaningful change in organizations. We begin by introducing Lewin's model of change and its component parts. This includes sources of resistance to change, ways to minimize this resistance, and stabilizing desired behaviours. Next, this chapter examines three approaches to organizational change—action research, appreciative inquiry, and parallel learning structures. The last section of this chapter considers both cross-cultural and ethical issues in organizational change.

LEWIN'S FORCE FIELD ANALYSIS MODEL

Social psychologist Kurt Lewin developed the force field analysis model to help us understand how the change process works (see Exhibit 17.1).[2] Although developed over 50 years ago, Lewin's **force field analysis** model remains the best way of viewing this process.

One side of the force field model represents the *driving forces* that push organizations toward a new state of affairs. Chapter 1 described some of the driving forces in the external environment, including globalization, information technology, and a changing workforce. Along with these external forces, some corporate leaders create driving forces within the organization, for instance, by increasing competition across company departments and encouraging new practices and values that the leader believes are inherently better.

The other side of Lewin's model represents the *restraining forces*, which maintain the status quo. These restraining forces are commonly called "resistance to change" because they appear as employee behaviours that block the change process. Stability occurs when the driving and restraining forces are roughly in equilibrium, that is, they are of approximately equal strength in opposite directions.

unfreezing
The first part of the change process whereby the change agent produces disequilibrium between the driving and restraining forces.

EXHIBIT 17.1

Lewin's force field analysis model

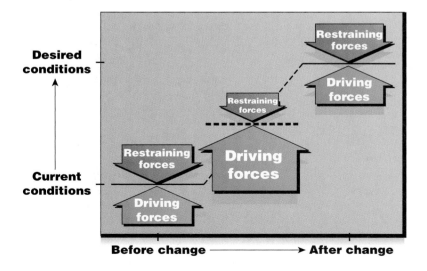

refreezing
The latter part of the change process in which systems and conditions are introduced that reinforce and maintain the desired behaviours.

Lewin's force field model emphasizes that effective change occurs by **unfreezing** the current situation, moving to a desired condition, and then **refreezing** the system so that it remains in this desired state. Unfreezing involves producing disequilibrium between the driving and restraining forces. As we will describe later, this may occur by increasing the driving forces, reducing the restraining forces, or having a combination of both. Refreezing occurs when the organization's systems and structures are aligned with the desired behaviours. They must support and reinforce the new role patterns and prevent the organization from slipping back into the old way of doing things. Over the next few pages, we use Lewin's model to understand why change is blocked and how the process can evolve more smoothly.

Restraining Forces

BP Norge, the Norwegian subsidiary of British Petroleum, faced more resistance from employees than from the infamous North Sea weather when it introduced self-directed work teams (SDWTs) on its drilling rigs. Many skeptical employees claimed that previous attempts to create SDWTs didn't work. Others were convinced that they already had SDWTs, so why change anything? Several people complained that SDWTs required more responsibility, so they wanted more status and pay. Still others were worried that they lacked the skills to operate in SDWTs. Some BP Norge supervisors were slow to embrace SDWTs because they didn't want to give away their cherished power.[3]

In his two tumultuous years as CEO, Jacques Nasser (left) heaped a lot of change on employees at Ford Motor Company. He tried to shift the automaker from engineering prowess to "cyber-savviness," from quality to efficiency, and from an old-boys' club to a performance-focused competitor. In one year, Nasser rammed through a performance review system that took General Electric nearly a decade to implement. The changes were too much for many Ford employees. Some engineers grumbled that quality has declined; employees stung by the performance system launched age discrimination lawsuits. "When you induce change, you get a reaction," explains a senior Ford executive. "I have letters from employees congratulating us. I have letters from employees doing the opposite." In the latter group was the Ford family, who replaced Nasser with William Clay Ford (right) as CEO.[6] How can corporate leaders change their organizations quickly without experiencing the level of resistance experienced at Ford? *AP/Wide World*
www.ford.com

BP Norge isn't the only company where employees block organizational change. In one survey, 43 percent of executives identified employee resistance as the main reason their organization is not more productive.[4] This resistance takes many forms, including passive noncompliance, complaints, absenteeism, turnover, and collective action (e.g., strikes, walkouts). In some situations (such as at Telus Corp.), employees resist change by trying to remove the chief change agent.[5]

Some organizational behaviour scholars suggest that employee resistance is a symptom, not a problem, in the change process. In other words, change agents need to investigate and remove the causes of resistance, which are usually the underlying restraining forces.[7] For example, rather than directly dealing with incidences of passive noncompliance, leaders need to understand why employees are not changing their behaviour in the desired ways. In some situations, employees may be worried about the *consequences* of change, such as how the new conditions will take away their power and status. In other situations, employees show resistance because of concerns about the *process* of change itself, such as the effort required to break old habits and learn new skills. The main reasons people resist change are shown in Exhibit 17.2 and are described below. They include direct costs, saving face, fear of the unknown, breaking routines, incongruent organizational systems, and incongruent team dynamics:[8]

- *Direct costs*—People tend to block actions that result in either higher direct costs or lower benefits than the existing situation. For instance, some Telus employees likely resisted change because it threatened their job security and career development potential.

- *Saving face*—Some people resist change as a political strategy to "prove" that the decision is wrong or that the person encouraging change is incompetent. For example, senior executives in a manufacturing firm bought a computer other than the system recommended by the information systems department. Soon after the system was in place, several information systems employees let minor implementation problems escalate to show that senior management had made a poor decision.

- *Fear of the unknown*—People resist change because they are worried that they cannot adopt the new behaviours. This fear of the unknown increases the *risk* of personal loss. For example, one company owner wanted sales staff to telephone rather than personally visit prospective customers. With no experience in telephone sales, they complained about the changes. Some even avoided the training program that taught them how to make telephone sales. "The salespeople were afraid of failing," explained the owner. "Each of them was very successful in the field, but they had never been exposed to a formalized telephone lead development program."[9]

- *Breaking routines*—Chapter 1 described how organizations need to unlearn, not just learn.[10] This means employees need to abandon behavioural routines that are no longer appropriate. Unfortunately, people are creatures of habit. They like to stay within their comfort zones by continuing routine role patterns that make life predictable.[11] Consequently, many people resist organiza-

EXHIBIT 17.2

Forces resisting organizational change

tional changes that force employees out of their comfort zones and require investing time and energy learning new role patterns.

■ *Incongruent organizational systems*—Rewards, selection, training, and other control systems ensure that employees maintain desired role patterns. Yet the organizational systems that maintain stability also discourage employees from adopting new ways.[12] The implication, of course, is that organizational systems must be altered to fit the desired change. Unfortunately, control systems can be difficult to change, particularly when they have supported role patterns that worked well in the past.[13]

■ *Incongruent team dynamics*—Teams develop and enforce conformity to a set of norms that guide behaviour (see Chapter 8). However, conformity to existing team norms may discourage employees from accepting organizational change. Team norms that conflict with the desired changes need to be altered.

UNFREEZING, CHANGING, AND REFREEZING

According to Lewin's force field analysis model, effective change occurs by unfreezing the current situation, moving to a desired condition, and then refreezing the system so it remains in this desired state. Unfreezing occurs when the driving forces are stronger than the restraining forces. This occurs by making the driving forces stronger, weakening or removing the restraining forces, or a combination of both. Thus, driving forces must increase enough to motivate change.

Change rarely occurs by increasing driving forces alone, however, because the restraining forces often adjust to counterbalance the driving forces. It is rather like the coils of a mattress. The harder corporate leaders push for change, the stronger the restraining forces push back. This antagonism threatens the change effort by producing tension and conflict within the organization.

The preferred option is to both increase the driving forces and reduce or remove the restraining forces. Increasing the driving forces creates an urgency for change, and reducing the restraining forces minimizes resistance to change. "The only way to have people change is because they choose to," explains Carly Fiorina, chief executive of Hewlett-Packard. "You cannot force change onto people—not lasting change, not real change."[14]

Creating an Urgency for Change

Today's business environment is changing so rapidly that it would leave anyone breathless. This point was emphasized in Chapter 1. Specifically, in the 1920s, companies stayed on the S&P 500 list an average of 67 years. Today, the average company life cycle on the S&P 500 is about 12 years. In other words, your grandparents could work for the same organization all of their lives, whereas you will likely outlive two or three companies.[15]

These environmental pressures are the driving forces that push employees out of their comfort zones. They energize people to face the risks that change creates. In many organizations, however, external driving forces are hardly felt by anyone below the top executives. Corporate leaders tend to buffer employees from the external environment, yet are surprised when change does not occur. Worse, they rely on contrived threats rather than the external driving forces to support the change effort.

Thus, the change process must begin by informing employees about competitors, changing consumer trends, impending government regulations, and other driving

Companies with an adaptive culture respond more quickly to the driving forces for change. Corning, Inc. is one of those companies. Once known for its Pyrex, Revere metal cookware, and Corelle laminated glass tableware, Corning is now a leader in fibre-optic technology, pumping out optical technologies at breathtaking speed. The company relies on a "destroy-and-create" strategy in which employees are motivated to develop a better product or practice before the competition does. For example, just weeks after completing a new state-of-the-art fibre-optics manufacturing facility, Corning's designers were asked to create a next-generation plant that would outperform it. "We've told them to go off and make obsolete that $1 billion we just spent," says Corning's vice president for optical communications.[18] Why would employees in adaptive cultures be more responsive to environmental driving forces for change? *AP/Wide World*
www.corning.com

forces.[16] For instance, James Donald had to communicate the urgency for change when he took over Pathmark Stores. The New Jersey-based supermarket chain was in financial trouble, but few of the company's 28,000 employees knew about these problems. To get employees ready for change and avoid bankruptcy, Donald prepared a video that told everyone about Pathmark's tremendous debt. Some employees quit, fearing that the company wasn't going to make it. But the remaining 99 percent quickly committed to getting the company back to health.[17]

Customer-driven change

Dissatisfied customers represent a compelling driving force for change because of the adverse consequences for the organization's survival and success. Customers also provide a human element that further energizes employees to change current behaviour patterns.[19] Joel Kocher, CEO of Micron Electronics, engaged in customer-driven change in his previous job as an executive at a computer manufacturing firm. At a large employee meeting, Kocher read an angry customer letter. Some employees responded defensively by suggesting the customer had installed or used the computer equipment incorrectly, or that the problem is never as serious as the customer says.

Then, to everyone's surprise, Kocher brought the customer who wrote the letter into the meeting. "We actually brought the customer to the meeting, to personalize it for every single person in the room," says Kocher. "And it was very, very interesting to see the metamorphosis that occurred within the context of these several hundred people when you actually had a customer talking about how their foul-up had hurt this person and hurt their business."[20]

Reducing the Restraining Forces

Effective change involves more than making employees aware of the driving forces. It also involves reducing or removing the restraining forces. Exhibit 17.3 identifies six ways to overcome employee resistance. Communication, training, employee involvement, and stress management try to reduce the restraining forces and, if feasible, should be attempted first.[21] However, negotiation and coercion are necessary for people who will clearly lose something from the change and when the speed of change is critical.

Communication   Communication is the highest priority and first strategy required for any organizational change. It reduces the restraining forces by keep-

EXHIBIT 17.3   Methods for dealing with resistance to change

Strategy	Example	When used	Problems
Communication	Customer complaint letters are shown to employees.	When employees don't feel an urgency for change or don't know how the change will affect them.	Time-consuming and potentially costly.
Training	Employees learn how to work in teams as the company adopts a team-based structure.	When employees need to break old routines and adopt new role patterns.	Time-consuming and potentially costly.
Employee involvement	Company forms a task force to recommend new customer service practices.	When the change effort needs more employee commitment, some employees need to save face, and/or employee ideas would improve decisions about the change strategy.	Very time-consuming. May also lead to conflict and poor decisions if employees' interests are incompatible with organizational needs.
Stress management	Employees attend sessions to discuss their worries about the change.	When communication, training, and involvement do not sufficiently ease employee worries.	Time-consuming and potentially expensive. Some methods may not reduce stress for all employees.
Negotiation	Employees agree to replace strict job categories with multiskilling in return for increased job security.	When employees will clearly lose something of value from the change and would not otherwise support the new conditions. Also necessary when the company must change quickly.	May be expensive, particularly if other employees want to negotiate their support. Also tends to produce compliance, but not commitment to the change.
Coercion	Company president tells managers to get on board and accept the change or leave.	When other strategies are ineffective and the company needs to change quickly.	Can lead to more subtle forms of resistance, as well as long-term antagonism with the change agent.

Sources: Adapted from J. P. Kotter and L. A. Schlesinger, "Choosing Strategies for Change," *Harvard Business Review*, 57 (1979), pp. 106–14; P. R. Lawrence, "How to Deal with Resistance to Change," *Harvard Business Review* (May–June 1954), pp. 49–57.

ing employees informed about what to expect from the change effort. Although time consuming and costly, communication can potentially reduce fear of the unknown and develop team norms that are more consistent with the change effort. For instance, a major survey reported that high-performing organizations had strong downward communication practices in explaining and promoting major changes.

Communication improves the change process in at least two ways. First, it is the conduit through which employees typically learn about the driving forces for change. Whether through town hall meetings with senior management or by directly meeting with disgruntled customers, employees become energized to change. Second, communication clarifies an otherwise uncertain future. The more corporate leaders communicate their images of the future, the more easily employees can visualize their own role in that future.[22]

Scotiabank relied on a specific communication strategy to move employees toward a more customer-focused financial institution.[23] Employees participated in learning map sessions, which give a visual representation of the company's desired future. Scotiabank's corporate newsletter provided further details from the learning maps and the need for a more customer-focused company. Finally, the bank opened a toll-free telephone line so employees could receive more information on demand, as well as feedback their experiences. As a result, every Scotiabank branch in Canada implemented the bank's new sales delivery model on or ahead of schedule with strong employee buy-in.

Training   Training is an important process in most change initiatives because employees need to learn new knowledge and skills. When a company introduces a new sales database, for instance, representatives need to learn how to adapt their previous behaviour patterns to benefit from the new system. Coaching is a variation of training that provides more personalized feedback and direction during the learning process. GLOBAL Connections 17.1 describes how an executive at Unilever's Elida Fabergé factory in Seacroft, UK, brought about significant change by hiring team coaches to train employees. Coaching and other forms of training are time consuming, but they help employees break routines by having them learn new role patterns.

Some training programs, such as action learning projects (see Chapter 3), can also minimize employee resistance caused by saving face. This is because employees actively guide the change process through this learning process. In Ford Motor Co.'s "Capstone" action learning program, for instance, global teams of six mid-level Ford executives are formed and given six months to tackle a strategic challenge, At the end of six months, team members present their findings and receive feedback from senior Ford executives as well as fellow participants.[24]

Employee involvement   Employee involvement can be an effective way to reduce the restraining forces because it creates psychological ownership of the decision (see Chapter 10). Rather than viewing themselves as agents of someone else's decision, staff members feel personally responsible for its success. Employee involvement also minimizes resistance to change by reducing problems of saving face and fear of the unknown. "It is important to have employees take ownership of this," says Colleen Arnold, an executive at IBM Global Services. "It won't work if it's just coming from the top 10 people in the company."[25]

Employee involvement is fairly easy to apply in small organizations, but how do large firms involve everyone? One solution is to have representative employees directly involved in the change process. Celestica, Inc. followed this change strategy when it was spun off from IBM. Nearly two dozen design teams at the Toronto-based high technology manufacturer targeted specific change initiatives by diagnosing Celestica's work processes against the company's critical success factors. Numerous study teams then developed recommendations and implementation strategies in the areas that required change.[26]

Search conferences (sometimes called *future search conferences*) are another way to involve a large number of employees and other stakeholders in the change process. Search conferences are large group sessions, usually lasting a few days, in which participants identify environmental trends and establish strategic solutions for those conditions.[27] Experts on various topics are sometimes brought in to speak during lunch or dinner. Search conferences "put the entire system in the

search conferences
Systemwide group sessions, usually lasting a few days, in which participants identify environmental trends and establish strategic solutions for those conditions.

Coaching for Change at Unilever's Elida Fabergé Factory in Seacroft

Gary Calveley announced a bold vision soon after he arrived as works director at Unilever's Elida Fabergé factory in Seacroft, UK. Calveley wanted the facility to apply European quality practices, win the Best Factory award, and become the safest Unilever site in Europe. What's surprising isn't that Calveley set such audacious goals; the surprise is that the plant actually achieved them in three years!

One of the key strategies in Elida Fabergé's success was the introduction of team coaches to guide the change process. Calveley recruited Gene Toner as an independent change agent, who then recruited 10 people with coaching skills from the fields of sports, policing, teaching, and psychology. Two were appointed from inside the company.

The coaching process began with "lots of tension and questioning" as employees openly wondered why they needed coaches when experts already worked on the production line. To address these doubts, Calveley worked with a theatre company to produce a play portraying current and past work in the factory, and how it could be improved using European quality management practices. After watching the play, coaches guided employees through the process of finding ways to turn this vision of a quality-focused factory into a reality.

The theatrical production helped employees realize that, just like sports coaches, the coaches were there to guide employees toward their goals. Another contributing factor to the coaches' role was the variable pay system Calveley negotiated with the union. The new reward system tied pay increases to measurable goals in each employee's personal development plan (PDP). The coaches worked with employees to develop

Change consultant Gene Toner (left) and plant manager Gary Calveley (right) introduced coaching to make Unilever's Elida Fabergé factory the best in Europe.
Dean Smith/The Camera Crew

these PDPs and provided feedback so they could reach them. This made the coaches valuable allies to both employees and management in the change process.

"[O]nce the targets had been set and people were committed to them, they started coming to the coaches," recalls one coach. "[T]hey came in early, stayed late, or came over during stoppages—it was a bit of a turnaround from being seen as a nuisance factor before." Only three employees out of the workforce of 600 got no pay increase in the first year. And by the third year, the entire plant had achieved Calveley's audacious goals.

Source: Adapted from P. Baker, "Change Catalysts," *Works Management*, 54 (July 2001), pp. 18–21.
www.unilever.com

room," meaning that they try to involve as many employees and other stakeholders as possible associated with the organizational system. For example, Richmond Savings, now part of Coast Capital Savings Credit Union, was able to involve all 400 employees in a six-day search conference to create a new vision for the Vancouver-based financial institution.

Various organizations, such as the Toronto District School Board, Richmond Savings Credit Union, Microsoft, and the Canadian Nature Federation have used search conferences to assist the change process.[28] However, this change strategy is only as good as the people participating. If the ideas lack creativity or foresight, then very little of the effort will produce meaningful results for the organization.[29] Moreover, search conferences and other forms of employee involvement require follow-up action by decision makers. If employees do not see meaningful deci-

To develop a meaningful strategy, the Toronto District School Board (TDSB) hosted a search conference that included students, staff, families, and community members. "This conference will bring together people who do not always have the opportunity to meet and plan for our students," said Marguerite Jackson, TDSB's director of education. "Together we will focus on collaborative planning for the future of education in our city." During the three-day event, small teams of participants looked at perceived societal, economic, technological, political, and environmental trends (left photo). These trends were then organized into themes plastered on coloured paper across an entire wall (right photo). According to the organizers, the search conference enabled a large number of diverse people to discover their common ground and to work on creating the future they envision together. What conditions would make search conferences most effective for organizational change? *Reprinted with permission of the Toronto District School Board* **www.tdsb.on.ca**

sions and actions resulting from these meetings, they begin to question the credibility of the process and are more cynical of similar change strategies in the future

Stress management   The opening story to this chapter suggested that many Telus employees experienced stress due to dramatic changes at the Vancouver-based telecommunications company. Organizational change is a stressful experience for many people because it threatens self-esteem and creates uncertainty about the future.[30] Communication, training, and employee involvement can reduce some of these stressors, but companies also need to introduce stress management practices to help employees cope with the changes. Stress management minimizes resistance by removing some of the direct costs and fear of the unknown of the change process. Stress also saps energy, so minimizing stress potentially increases employee motivation to support the change process.

Negotiation   As long as people resist change, organizational change strategies will require some influence tactics.[31] Recall from Chapter 12 that influence refers to any *behaviour* that tries to alter someone's attitudes or behaviour. Negotiation is a form of exchange, which involves the promise of benefits or resources in exchange for the target person's compliance with influencer's request. This strategy potentially activates those who would otherwise lose out from the change. However, it merely gains compliance rather than commitment to the change effort, so might not be effective in the long term.

Coercion   If all else fails, leaders rely on coercion to change organizations. Coercion, which refers to the assertive influence tactic described in Chapter 12, can include persistently reminding people of their obligations, frequently monitoring behaviour to ensure compliance, confronting people who do not change, and using threats of sanctions to force compliance. Firing people who will not support the change is an extreme step, but it is not uncommon. According to some reports, nearly two-thirds of large company turnarounds include replacing some or all senior management.[32]

For example, Montreal-based Dorel Industries replaced the top management of its juvenile products division (called Dorel Cosco) because management was stuck in the mindset that their division was performing well enough. Dorel Industries CEO Martin Schwartz and his executive team saw plenty of room for improvement at the Dorel Cosco division. "The problem was that the previous top management [at Dorel Cosco] had all its concentration on the top line and not on the bottom line," says Schwartz. "Their attitude was that as long as we were better than the competition, [profitability would take care of itself]. In our attitude, that's not good enough." One year later, the Dorel Cosco division's performance had improved significantly under the guidance of a new management team.[33]

Replacing staff is a radical form of organizational "unlearning" (see Chapter 1) because replacing executives removes knowledge of the organization's past routines. This potentially opens up opportunities for new practices to take hold.[34] At the same time, coercion is a risky strategy because survivors (employees who are not fired) may have less trust in corporate leaders and engage in more political tactics to protect their own job security. More generally, various forms of coercion may change behaviour through compliance, but they won't develop commitment to the change effort (see Chapter 12).

Refreezing the Desired Conditions

Unfreezing and changing behaviour patterns won't result in lasting change. People are creatures of habit, so they easily slip back into past patterns. Therefore, leaders need to refreeze the new behaviours by realigning organizational systems and team dynamics with the desired changes.[35] This stabilization does not occur automatically: organizational leaders must continuously restabilize the desired behaviours.

If the change process is supposed to encourage efficiency, then rewards should be realigned to motivate and reinforce efficient behaviour.[36] Telus Corp., described at the beginning of this chapter, introduced performance-based reward systems to refreeze employee behaviours oriented toward performance and customer service. Feedback systems help employees learn how well they are moving toward the desired objectives, and provide a permanent architecture to support the new behaviour patterns in the long term. "I'm a firm believer that you change what you measure," says Carol Lavin Bernick, president of the Alberto-Culver Co. North America.[37]

STRATEGIC VISIONS, CHANGE AGENTS, AND DIFFUSING CHANGE

Kurt Lewin's force field analysis model provides a rich understanding of the dynamics of organizational change. But it overlooks three other ingredients in effective change processes: strategic visions, change agents, and diffusing change. Every successful change requires a clear, well-articulated vision of the desired future state. You can see the importance of strategic vision in the change process at Telus Corp,

From its headquarters in St. John's, Newfoundland, CHC Helicopter Corp. has become the world's largest helicopter services company with 350 aircraft in 60 bases around the world. CHC employees have experienced considerable change throughout the company's recent growth spurt, but the turbulence has been eased by the company's well-established strategic vision. CHC clearly lays out its four principles: (1) safety is first and foremost, (2) customers must receive value through quality service, (3) the workplace must promote teamwork, and (4) CHC must build on its strengths to sustain profitable growth.[40] Why are strategic visions and guiding principles an important part of managing change? *Courtesy of CHC Helicopter Corp.* **www.chc.ca**

described in the opening vignette to this chapter. Darren Entwistle began the turnaround with a clear vision of a more performance-oriented, customer-focused organization. This vision provides a sense of direction and establishes the critical success factors against which the real changes are evaluated. It also minimizes employee fear of the unknown and provides a better understanding about what behaviours employees must learn for the future state.[38] Although some executives say that strategic visions are too "fluffy," most executives in large organizations believe a clear vision of the proposed change is the most important feature of successful change initiatives.[39]

Change Agents

Organizational change also requires change agents to help form, communicate, and build commitment toward the desired future state. A **change agent** is anyone who possesses enough knowledge and power to guide and facilitate the change effort. Some organizations rely on external consultants to serve as change agents. However, change agents are typically people within the organization who possess the leadership competencies necessary to bring about meaningful change. Corporate executives certainly need to be change agents. However, as companies rely increasingly on self-directed work teams, most employees will become change agents from time to time.

Effective change agents are transformational leaders (see Chapter 14).[41] They form a vision of the desired future state, communicate that vision in ways that are meaningful to others, behave in ways that are consistent with the vision, and build commitment to the vision.

change agent
Anyone who possesses enough knowledge and power to guide and facilitate the change effort.

Diffusing Change

Change agents often test the transformation process with a pilot project, and then diffuse what has been learned from this experience to other parts of the organization. The reason is that pilot projects are more flexible and less risky than centralized, organization-wide programs.[42] Scholars have identified several conditions that effectively diffuse change from the pilot project to the rest of the organization.[43] Diffusion is more likely to occur when the pilot project is successful within one or two years and receives visibility (e.g., favourable news media coverage). These conditions tend to increase top management support for the change program and persuade other managers to introduce the change effort in their operations. Successful diffusion also depends on labour union support and active involvement in the diffusion process.

Another important condition is that the diffusion strategy not be described too abstractly, because this makes the instructions too vague to introduce the change elsewhere. Neither should the strategy be stated too precisely, because it might not seem relevant to other areas of the organization. Finally, without producing excessive turnover in the pilot group, people who have worked under the new system should be moved to other areas of the organization, so they can transfer their knowledge and commitment of the change effort to work units that have not yet experienced it.

THREE APPROACHES TO ORGANIZATIONAL CHANGE

So far, we have looked at the dynamics of change that occur every day in organizations. However, organizational change agents and consultants also apply various approaches to or mental models of organizational change. This section introduces three of the leading approaches to organizational change: action research, appreciative inquiry, and parallel learning structures.

Action Research Approach

action research
A data-based, problem-oriented process that diagnoses the need for change, introduces the intervention, and then evaluates and stabilizes the desired changes.

Along with introducing the force field model, Kurt Lewin recommended an **action research** approach to the change process. Action research takes the view that meaningful change is a combination of action orientation (changing attitudes and behaviour) and research orientation (testing theory).[44] On the one hand, the change process needs to be action-oriented because the ultimate goal is to bring about change. An action orientation involves diagnosing current problems and applying interventions to resolve those problems.[45] On the other hand, the change process is a research study because change agents apply a conceptual framework (such as team dynamics or organizational culture) to a real situation. As with any good research, the change process involves collecting data to diagnose problems more effectively and to systematically evaluate how well the theory works in practice.

Within this dual framework of action and research, the action research approach adopts an open systems view. It recognizes that organizations have many interdependent parts, so change agents need to anticipate both the intended and unintended consequences of their interventions. Action research is also a highly participative process because open systems change requires both the knowledge and commitment of members within that system. Overall, action research is a data-based, problem-oriented process that diagnoses the need for change, introduces the intervention, and then evaluates and stabilizes the desired changes (see Exhibit 17.4).[46]

process consultation
Involves helping the organization solve its own problems by making it aware of organizational processes, the consequences of those processes, and the means by which they can be changed.

■ *Form client-consultant relationship*—Action research usually assumes that the change agent originates outside the system (such as a consultant), so the process begins by forming the client-consultant relationship. Consultants need to determine the client's readiness for change, including whether people are motivated to participate in the process, are open to meaningful change, and possess the abilities to complete the process. Many change management consultants prefer to adopt a **process consultation** role rather than one as a technical expert. Process consultants help people within the system to solve their own problems by making them aware of organizational processes, the consequences of those processes, and the means by which they can be changed.[47]

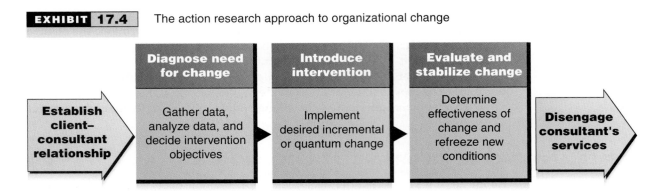

EXHIBIT 17.4   The action research approach to organizational change

- *Diagnose the need for change*—Action research is a problem-oriented activity that carefully diagnoses the problem through systematic analysis of the situation. Organizational diagnosis identifies the appropriate direction for the change effort by gathering and analyzing data about an ongoing system, such as through interviews and surveys of employees and other stakeholders.[48] Organizational diagnosis also involves employees in the process of deciding on the appropriate change method, the schedule for these actions, and the expected standards of successful change.

- *Introduce intervention*—This stage in the action research model applies one or more actions to correct the problem. It may include any of the prescriptions mentioned in this textbook, such as building more effective teams, managing conflict, building a better organizational structure, or changing the corporate culture. An important issue is how quickly the changes should occur.[49] Some experts recommend *incremental change* in which the organization fine-tunes the system and takes small steps toward a desired state. Others claim that *quantum change* is often required, in which the system is overhauled decisively and quickly. Quantum change, such as at Telus Corp. (see opening vignette to this chapter), is usually traumatic for employees and offers little opportunity for correction. But incremental change is also risky when the organization is seriously misaligned with its environment, because it can threaten its survival.

- *Evaluate and stabilize change*—Action research recommends evaluating the effectiveness of the intervention against the standards established in the diagnostic stage. Unfortunately, even when these standards are clearly stated, the effectiveness of an intervention might not be apparent for several years, or might be difficult to separate from other factors. If the activity has the desired effect, then the change agent and the participants need to stabilize the new conditions. This refers to the refreezing process that we described earlier, redesigning rewards, information systems, team norms, and other conditions so they support the new values and behaviours.

The action research approach to organizational change has dominated thinking ever since it was introduced in the 1940s. However, some experts complain that the problem-oriented nature of action research—in which something is wrong that must be fixed—focuses on the negative dynamics of the group or system rather than its positive opportunities and potential. This concern has led to the development of a more positive approach to organizational change, called appreciative inquiry.

Appreciative Inquiry Approach

Appreciative inquiry tries to break out of the problem-solving mentality by reframing relationships around the positive and the possible.[50] It takes the view that organizations are creative entities in which people are capable of building synergy beyond their individual capabilities. To avoid dwelling on the group's own shortcomings, the process usually directs its inquiry toward successful events and successful organizations. This external focus becomes a form of behavioural modelling, but it also increases open dialogue by redirecting the group's attention away from its own problems. Appreciative inquiry is especially useful when participants are aware of their "problems" or already suffer from enough negativity in their relationships. The positive orientation of appreciative inquiry enables groups to overcome these negative tensions and build a more hopeful perspective of their future by focusing on what is possible.

Exhibit 17.5 outlines the "Four-D" model appreciative inquiry, which was developed in Harare, Zimbabwe, by a group working with the U.S. Agency for International Development and the Save the Children Fund.[52] The process begins with *discovery*—identifying the positive elements of the observed events or organization. This might involve documenting positive customer experiences elsewhere in the organization. Or it might include interviewing members of another organization to discover its fundamental strengths. As participants discuss their findings, they shift into the *dreaming* stage by envisioning what might be possible in an ideal organization. By directing their attention to a theoretically ideal organization or situation, participants feel safer revealing their hopes and aspirations than if they were discussing their own organization or predicament.

As participants make their private thoughts public to the group, the process shifts into the third stage, called *designing*. Designing involves the process of dialogue (see Chapter 9), in which participants listen with selfless receptivity to each other's models and assumptions and eventually form a collective model for thinking within the team.[53] In effect, they create a common image of what should be. As this model takes shape, group members shift the focus back to their own situation. In the final stage of appreciative inquiry, called *delivering*, participants establish specific objectives and direction for their own organization based on their model of what will be.

The Hunter Douglas Window Fashions Division (WFD) relied on appreciative inquiry to create a collective vision, reinstill a sense of community among employees, and build leadership within the organization. The business unit sent an advisory team to a weeklong training program where they learned about the Four-D process. The WFD advisory team then described appreciative inquiry and its rationale to employees through a series of town hall meetings. The discovery phase consisted of over 500 interviews with employees, customers, suppliers, and community members. These results were reviewed at an Appreciative Summit where WFD employees worked through the dream, design, and deliver stages. A second wave of interviews became background data for a subsequent search conference-type of strategic planning summit. WFD executives say that appreciative inquiry improved productivity and cross-departmental collaboration, and created a "can-do" attitude toward the company's quality management initiative.[51] What problems might occur if Hunter Douglas relied on action research rather than appreciative inquiry to facilitate this change process? *Courtesy of Amanda Trosten-Bloom*
www.hunterdouglas.com

EXHIBIT 17.5   The appreciative inquiry process

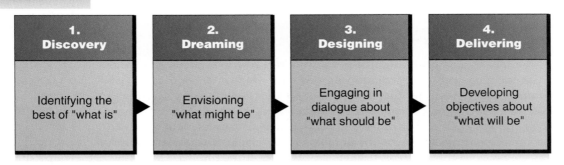

Sources: Based on J. M. Watkins and B. J. Mohr, *Appreciative Inquiry: Change at the Speed of Imagination* (San Francisco: Jossey-Bass, 2001), pp. 25, 42–45; D. Whitney and C. Schau, "Appreciative Inquiry: An Innovative Process for Organization Change," *Employment Relations Today*, 25 (Spring 1998), pp. 11–21; F. J. Barrett and D. L. Cooperrider, "Generative Metaphor Intervention: A New Approach for Working with Systems Divided by Conflict and Caught in Defensive Perception," *Journal of Applied Behavioral Science*, 26 (1990), p. 229.

Appreciative inquiry in practice   Appreciative inquiry is a relatively new approach to organization change, but several organizations have already applied its basic principles. Chrysler Canada practised a form of appreciative inquiry by beginning each meeting with a success story. "We had found that too often we would dwell on our mistakes and failures, subsequently spiralling around them," says a Chrysler Canada executive. Writing success stories helped Chrysler's managers see themselves and their colleagues in a more positive and optimistic light. At first, people were hard pressed to think of successes, but they eventually realized that these gems of experience existed every day in their part of the operation.[54]

AVON Mexico also applied appreciative inquiry to develop employment opportunities for women in the top ranks. A team of employees and consultants interviewed people for their stories illustrating best practices in gender equality at AVON Mexico. These stories were presented at two-day sessions, and participants built on these best practices to discover how AVON could extend these experiences. Over the next few years, the company won the Catalyst award for gender equality, its profit increased dramatically (attributed partly to the appreciative inquiry process), and women found their way into more senior positions at AVON Mexico.[55]

Appreciative inquiry has garnered much interest among organizational change scholars and practitioners. Indeed, this approach has become so popular that some consultants are quick to label anything with a positive orientation as a form of appreciative inquiry. Another concern is that research has not yet examined the contingencies of this approach.[56] Specifically, we don't yet know the conditions in which appreciative inquiry is the best approach to organizational change, and under what conditions it is less effective. Overall, appreciative inquiry has much to offer the organizational change process, but we are just beginning to understand its potential and limitations.

Parallel Learning Structure Approach

Parallel learning structures are highly participative arrangements, composed of people from most levels of the organization who follow the action research model

parallel learning structures
Highly participative groups constructed alongside (i.e. parallel to) the formal organization with the purpose of increasing the organization's learning and producing meaningful organizational change.

Royal Dutch/Shell Changes through Parallel Learning Structures

A few years ago, competitors were threatening Royal Dutch/Shell's market share. The oil company's executives in London and The Hague spent two years reorganizing, downsizing, and educating several layers of management, but this top-down approach had minimal effect. Managers in charge of Shell's operations for a particular country resisted changes that threatened their autonomy, and headquarters managers couldn't break out of the routines that had worked for them in the past.

So Steve Miller, head of Shell's worldwide oil products business, decided to apply a parallel learning structure and change the company from the bottom up. He and his executive team held several five-day workshops, each attended by six country teams of front-line people (e.g., gas station managers, truck drivers, marketing professionals). Participants at these "retailing boot camps" learned about worrisome competitive trends in their regions and were taught powerful marketing tools to identify new opportunities. The teams then returned home to study their market and develop proposals for improvement. For example, a team in South Africa proposed ways to increase liquid gas market share. The Malaysian team developed plans to increase gasoline sales in that country.

Four months later, the teams returned for a second workshop where each proposal was critiqued by Miller's executive team in "fishbowl" sessions with the other teams watching. Videotapes from these sessions became socialization tools for other employees back in the home country. Each team had sixty days to put its ideas into action, then return for a third workshop to analyze what worked and what didn't.

These workshops, along with field tours and several other grassroots activities, had a tremendous effect. Front-line employees developed an infectious enthusiasm and a stronger business approach to challenging the competition. "I can't overstate how infectious the optimism and energy of these committed employees was on the many managers above them," says Miller. The change process also resulted in solid improvements in profitability and market share in most regions where employees had attended the sessions.

Sources: R. Pascale, M. Millemann, and L. Gioja, *Surfing on the Edge of Chaos* (London: Texere, 2000); R. T. Pascale, "Leading From a Different Place," In J. A. Conger, G. M. Spreitzer, and E. E. Lawler III (Eds.), *The Leader's Change Handbook* (San Francisco: Jossey-Bass, 1999), pp. 301–20; D. J. Knight, "Strategy in Practice: Making it Happen," *Strategy & Leadership*, 26 (July-August 1998), pp. 29–33; R. T. Pascale, "Grassroots Leadership—Royal Dutch/Shell," *Fast Company*, Issue 14 (April-May 1998), pp. 110–20.
www.shell.com

to produce meaningful organizational change. They are social structures developed alongside the formal hierarchy with the purpose of increasing the organization's learning.[57] Ideally, parallel learning structure participants are sufficiently free from the constraints of the larger organization that they can more effectively solve organizational issues.

Celestica Inc. relied on a parallel learning structure to introduce a more sociotechnically-designed, team-based organization. Nearly two dozen teams of employees targeted specific change initiatives by diagnosing work processes against the Toronto-based high technology manufacturer's critical success factors. Numerous study teams then developed recommendations and implementation strategies in the areas that required change.[58] This high involvement strategy increased the quality of decisions made during the change process, employee knowledge of the changes, and employee commitment to those changes.

GLOBAL Connections 17.2 describes how Royal Dutch/Shell's retail boot camp teams also represent a form of parallel structure because they work outside the normal structure. These teams represent various countries and establish a more entrepreneurial approach to getting things done at Shell. The retail teams are separated from the traditional hierarchy, making it easier to instill new attitudes, role patterns, and work behaviours.

CROSS-CULTURAL AND ETHICAL ISSUES IN ORGANIZATIONAL CHANGE

One significant concern with organizational change that originates from North America is that it potentially conflicts with cultural values in some other countries.[59] A few scholars point out that change practices in North America assume a linear model of change, as shown earlier in the force field analysis, that is punctuated by tension and overt conflict. Indeed, some organizational change practices encourage the open display of conflict. But these assumptions are incompatible with cultures that view change as a natural cyclical process with harmony and equilibrium as the objectives.[60]

For instance, people in many Asian countries try to minimize conflict in order to respect others and save face.[61] These concerns do not mean that western-style change interventions are necessarily ineffective elsewhere. Rather, it suggests that we need to develop a more contingency-oriented perspective with respect to the cultural values of its participants.

Ethical Concerns with Organizational Change

Some organizational change practices also face ethical problems.[62] One ethical concern is threats to the privacy rights of individuals. The action research model is built on the idea of collecting information from organizational members, yet this requires employees to provide personal information and emotions that they may not want to divulge. The scientific nature of the data collection exercise may mislead employees into believing that their information is confidential when, in reality, executives can sometimes identify the opinions of individual employees.[63]

A second ethical concern is that some change activities potentially increase management's power by inducing compliance and conformity in organization members. This power shift occurs because change creates uncertainty and re-establishes management's position in directing the organization. Moreover, action research is a system-wide activity that requires employee participation rather than allowing individuals to get involved voluntarily. Indeed, one of the challenges of consultants is to "bring onside" those who are reluctant to engage in the process.

A third concern is that some organizational change interventions undermine an individual's self-esteem. The unfreezing process requires participants to disavow their existing beliefs, sometimes including their own competence at certain tasks or interpersonal relations. Some specific change practices involve direct exposure to personal critique by co-workers as well as public disclosure of one's personal limitations and faults.

The ethical concern of violating self-esteem apparently occurred at SaskTel a few years ago. The Regina-based telecommunications company brought in consultants to improve team dynamics. Instead, the 20 SaskTel employees involved in the project claim the consultants isolated them in an office suite with paper taped over its glass walls so no one could see inside, and quarantined them in small cubicles, preventing them from talking to each other. The employees eventually united and forced SaskTel to get rid of the consultants. "Team members regularly received insults in front of the group," recalls Kathryn Markus, a seven-year SaskTel manager. "The isolation, long hours, and purposeless activity left me feeling abandoned, betrayed, and frightened." Markus and several other SaskTel employees took sick leave when they abandoned the project.[64]

A fourth ethical concern is the change management consultant's role in the change process. Ideally, consultants should occupy "marginal" positions with the clients they are serving. This means that they must be sufficiently detached from the organization to maintain objectivity and avoid having the client become too dependent on them.[65] However, some consultants tend to increase, rather than decrease, clients' dependence for financial gain. Others have difficulty maintaining neutrality because they often come to the situation with their own biases and agendas.

Organizational change is a complex process with a variety of approaches and issues. Many corporate leaders have promised more change than they were able to deliver because they underestimated the time and challenges involved. Yet, the dilemma is that most organizations operate in hyper-fast environments that demand continuous and rapid adaptation. Successful organizations have mastered the complex dynamics of moving people through the continuous process of change.

ORGANIZATIONAL BEHAVIOUR: A FINAL WORD

Nearly 100 years ago, industrialist Andrew Carnegie said: "Take away my people, but leave my factories, and soon grass will grow on the factory floors. Take away my factories, but leave my people, and soon we will have a new and better factory." Carnegie's statement reflects the message woven throughout this textbook, that organizations are not buildings or machinery or financial assets. Rather, organizations are the people in them. They are human entities—full of life, sometimes fragile, always exciting.

CHAPTER SUMMARY

Lewin's force field analysis model states that all systems have driving and restraining forces. Change occurs through the process of unfreezing, changing, and refreezing. Unfreezing produces disequilibrium between the driving and restraining forces. Refreezing realigns the organization's systems and structures with the desired behaviours.

Restraining forces are manifested as employee resistance to change. The main reasons why people resist change are direct costs, saving face, fear of the unknown, breaking routines, incongruent organizational systems, and incongruent team dynamics. Resistance to change may be minimized by keeping employees informed about what to expect from the change effort (communicating); teaching employees valuable skills for the desired future (training); involving them in the change process; helping them to cope with the stress of change; negotiating trade-offs with those who will clearly lose from the change effort; and using coercion (sparingly and as a last resort).

Organizational change also requires driving forces. This means that employees need to have an urgency to change by becoming aware of the environmental conditions that demand change in the organization. The change process also requires refreezing the new behaviours by realigning organizational systems and team dynamics with the desired changes.

Every successful change requires a clear, well-articulated vision of the desired future state. Strategic visions are guided by a change agent—anyone who possesses enough knowledge and power to guide and facilitate the change effort. Change agents rely on transformational leadership to develop a vision, communicate that vision, and build commitment to the vision of a desirable future state. The change process also often applies a diffusion process in which change begins as a pilot project and eventually spreads to other areas of the organization.

Organizational change agents and consultants apply various approaches to organizational change. Action research has been the dominant approach over the past half-century. It is a highly participative, open-systems approach emphasizing that meaningful change is a combination of action orientation (changing attitudes and behaviour) and research orientation (testing theory). It is a data-based, problem-oriented process that diagnoses the need for change, introduces the intervention, and then evaluates and stabilizes the desired changes.

Another approach is appreciative inquiry, which focuses participants on the positive and possible. It tries to break out of the problem-solving mentality that dominates the action research model. The four stages of appreciative inquiry include discovery, dreaming, designing, and delivering. A third approach, called parallel learning structures, relies on social structures developed alongside the formal hierarchy whose purpose is to increase the organization's learning. They are highly participative arrangements, composed of people from most levels of the organization who follow the action research model to produce meaningful organizational change.

One significant concern with organizational change originating from North America is that it potentially conflicts with the cultural values in some other countries. Moreover, organizational change practices can raise one or more ethical concerns, including increasing management's power over employees, threatening individual privacy rights, undermining individual self-esteem, and making clients dependent on the change consultant.

KEY TERMS

Action research, p. 489

Appreciative inquiry, p. 491

Change agent, p. 488

Force field analysis, p. 478

Parallel learning structure, p. 492

Process consultation, p. 489

Refreezing, p. 479

Search conferences, p. 485

Unfreezing, p. 478

DISCUSSION QUESTIONS

1. Chances are that the school you are attending is currently undergoing some sort of change to adapt more closely to its environment. Discuss the external forces that are driving these changes. What internal drivers for change also exist?

2. Use Lewin's force field analysis to describe the dynamics of organizational change at Royal Dutch/Shell, as described in Connections 17.2 (see page 493).

3. Employee resistance is a *symptom*, not a *problem* in the change process." What are some of the real problems that may underlie employee resistance?

4. What can organizations do to create an environment where employees are more likely to experience a sense of urgency for change?

5. What are the potential pitfalls of using coercion as a method of implementing change?

6. Web Circuits, Inc. is a Montreal-based manufacturer of computer circuit boards for high-technology companies. Senior management wants to introduce value-added management practices to reduce production costs and remain competitive. A consultant has recommended that the company start with a pilot project in one department and when successful, diffuse these practices to other areas of the organization. Discuss the advantages of this recommendation and identify three conditions (other than the pilot project's success) that would make diffusion of the change effort more successful.

7. Suppose that you are vice-president of branch services at Bank of Toronto. You notice that several branches have consistently low customer service ratings even though there are no apparent differences in resources or staff characteristics. Describe an appreciative inquiry process in one of these branches that might help to overcome these problems.

8. What potential ethical concerns are associated with organizational change? How should organizations deal with these concerns?

TRANSACT INSURANCE CORPORATION

TransAct Insurance Corporation (TIC) provides automobile insurance in the parts of Canada where private insurance is permitted. Last year, a new president was brought in by TIC's board of directors to improve the company's competitiveness and customer service. After spending several months assessing the situation, the new president introduced a strategic plan to improve TIC's competitive position. He also replaced three vice-presidents. Jim Leon was hired as vice-president of Claims, TIC's largest division, with 1,500 employees, 50 claims centre managers, and five regional directors.

Jim immediately met with all claims managers and directors, and visited employees at TIC's 50 claims centres. As an outsider, this was a formidable task, but his strong interpersonal skills and uncanny ability to remember names and ideas helped him through the process. Through these visits and discussions, Jim discovered that the claims division had been managed in a relatively authoritarian, top-down manner. He could also see that morale was very low and employee-management relations were guarded. High workloads and isolation (adjusters work in tiny cubicles) were two other common complaints. Several managers acknowledged that the high turnover among claims adjusters was partly due to these conditions.

Following discussions with TIC's president, Jim decided to make morale and supervisory leadership his top priority. He initiated a divisional newsletter with a tear-off feedback form for employees to register their comments. He announced an open-door policy in which any Claims Division employee could speak to him directly and confidentially without going first to the immediate supervisor. Jim also fought organizational barriers to initiate a flex-time program so employees could design work schedules around their needs. This program later became a model for other areas of TIC.

One of Jim's most pronounced symbols of change was the "Claims Management Credo" outlining the philosophy that every claims manager would follow. At his first meeting with the complete claims management team, Jim presented a list of what he thought were the important philosophies and actions of effective managers. The management group was asked to select and prioritize items from this list and were told that the resulting list would be the division's management philosophy and all managers would be held accountable for abiding by its principles. Most claims managers were uneasy about this process, but they also understood that the organization was under competitive pressure and that Jim was using this exercise to demonstrate his leadership.

The claims managers developed a list of 10 items, such as encouraging teamwork, fostering a trusting work environment, setting clear and reasonable goals, and so on. The list was circulated to senior management in the organization for their comments and approval, and sent back to all claims managers for their endorsement. Once this was done, a copy of the final document was sent to every claims division employee. Jim also announced plans to follow up with an annual survey to evaluate each claims manager's performance. This concerned the managers, but most of them believed that the credo exercise was a result of Jim's initial enthusiasm and that he would be too busy to introduce a survey after settling into the job.

One year after the credo had been distributed, Jim announced that the first annual survey would be conducted. All claims employees would complete the survey and return it confidentially to the human resources department, where the survey results would be compiled for each claims centre manager. The survey asked the extent to which the manager had lived up to each of the 10 items in the credo. Each form also provided space for comments.

Claims centre managers were surprised that a survey would be conducted, but they were even more worried about Jim's statement that the results would be shared with employees. What "results" would employees see? Who would distribute these results? What happens if a manager gets poor ratings from his or her subordinates? "We'll work out the details later," said Jim in response to these questions. "Even if the survey results aren't great, the information will give us a good baseline for next year's survey."

The claims division survey had a high response rate. In some centres, every employee completed and returned a form. Each report showed the claim centre manager's average score for each of the 10 items as well as how many employees rated the manager at each level of the five-point scale. The reports also included every comment made by employees at that centre.

No one was prepared for the results of the first survey. Most managers received moderate or poor ratings on the 10 items. Very few managers averaged above 3.0 (out of a 5-point scale) on more than a couple of items. This suggested that, at best, employees were ambivalent about whether their claims centre manager had abided by the 10 management philosophy items. The comments were even more devastating than the ratings. Comments ranged from mildly disappointed to extremely critical of their claims manager. Employees also described their longstanding frustration with TIC, high workloads, and isolated working conditions. Several people bluntly stated that they were skeptical about the changes that Jim had promised. "We've heard the promises before, but now we've lost faith," wrote one claims adjuster.

The survey results were sent to each claims manager, the regional director, and employees at the claims centre. Jim instructed managers to discuss the survey data and comments with their regional manager and directly with employees. The claims centre managers were shocked to learn that the reports included individual comments. They had assumed the reports would exclude comments and only show averaged scores for all employees at the centre. Some managers went to their regional director, complaining that revealing the personal comments would ruin their careers. Many directors sympathized, but the results were already available to employees.

When Jim heard about these concerns, he agreed that the results were lower than expected and that the comments should not have been shown to employees. After discussing the situation with his directors, he decided that the discussion meetings between claims managers and their employees should proceed as planned. To delay or withdraw the reports would undermine the credibility and trust that Jim was trying to develop with employees. However, the regional director attended the meeting in each claims centre to minimize direct conflict between the claims centre manager and employees.

Although many of these meetings went smoothly, a few created harsh feelings between managers and their employees. The source of some comments were easily identified by their content, and this created a few delicate moments in several sessions. A few months after these meetings, two claims centre managers quit and three others asked for transfers back to nonmanagement positions in TIC. Meanwhile, Jim wondered how to manage this process more effectively, particularly since employees expected another survey the following year.

Discussion Questions

1. Identify the forces pushing for change and the forces restraining the change effort in this case.

2. Was Jim Leon successful at bringing about change? Why or why not?

3. What should Jim Leon do now?

© Copyright 2000. Steven L. McShane and Terrance J. Bogyo. This case is based on actual events, but names, industry, and some characteristics have been changed to maintain anonymity.

TEAM EXERCISE 17.2

STRATEGIC CHANGE INCIDENTS

Purpose This exercise is designed to help you identify strategies to facilitate organizational change in various situations.

Instructions

- *Step 1:* The instructor will place students into teams, and each team will be assigned one of the scenarios presented below.

- *Step 2:* Each team will diagnose its assigned scenario to determine the most appropriate set of change management practices. Where appropriate, these practices should (a) create an urgency to change, (b) minimize resistance to change, and (c) refreeze the situation to support the change initiative. Each of these scenarios is based on real events that occurred in Canada and elsewhere.

■ *Step 3:* Each team will present and defend its change management strategy. Class discussion regarding the appropriateness and feasibility of each strategy will occur after all teams assigned the same scenario have presented. The instructor will then describe what the organizations actually did in these situations.

Scenario 1: Greener Telco

The board of directors at a large telephone company wants its executives to make the organization more environmentally friendly by encouraging employees to reduce waste in the workplace. The government and other stakeholders for the company expect this action to be taken and to be publicly successful. The goal of this initiative is to significantly reduce the use of paper, refuse, and other waste throughout the company's many widespread offices. Unfortunately, a survey indicates that employees do not value environmental objectives and do not know how to "reduce, reuse, recycle." As the executive responsible for this change, you have been asked to develop a strategy that

might bring about meaningful behavioural change toward these environmental goals. What would you do?

Scenario 2: Go Forward Airline

A major airline had experienced a decade of rough turbulence, including two bouts of bankruptcy protection, ten chief executives, and morale so low that employees ripped off company logos from their uniforms out of embarrassment. Service was terrible and the airplanes rarely arrived at or left the terminal on time. This was costing the airline significant amounts of money in passenger layovers. Managers were paralyzed by anxiety and many had been with the firm so long that they didn't know how to set strategic goals that worked. One-fifth of all flights were losing money and overall the company was near financial collapse (just three months away from defaulting on payroll obligations). You and the newly-hired CEO must get employees to quickly improve operational efficiency and customer service. What actions would you take to bring about these changes in time?

TEAM EXERCISE 17.3

APPLYING LEWIN'S FORCE FIELD ANALYSIS

Purpose This exercise is designed to help you understand how to diagnose situations using force field analysis, and to identify strategies to facilitate organizational change.

Instructions This exercise involves diagnosing the situation described below, identifying the forces for and against change, and recommending strategies to reduce resistance to change. The exercise is described as a team activity, although the instructor may choose to have it completed individually. Also, the instructor may choose a situation other than the one presented here.

■ *Step 1:* Students will form teams of 4 or 5 people and everyone will read the following situation. (Note: If your school has a full trimester system, then imagine the situation below as though your school currently has a semester system):

   "Like most postsecondary institutions in Canada, your college/university has two

semesters (beginning in September and January) as well as a 6-week "Intersession" from early May to mid-June. Instructors typically teach their regular load of courses during the two semesters. Intersession is taught mainly by part-time faculty, although some full-time faculty teach for extra pay. After carefully reviewing costs, student demand, and competition from other institutions, senior administration has decided that your college/university should switch to a trimester curriculum. In a trimester system, courses are taught in three equal semesters—September to December, January to April, and May to early August. Faculty must teach any two semesters in which their courses are offered (for universities) or all three semesters (for colleges). Senior administration has determined that this change will allow the institution to admit more students without building additional classrooms or other facilities. Moreover, market surveys indicate that over 50 percent of current students would continue their studies in the new summer semester and the institution would attract more full-fee students from other countries. The provincial government looks very favourably on the trimester plan because it increases the efficiency of college/university resources and eases the significant shortage of spaces available. (There are many more applicants to your college/university than people admitted for the foreseeable future.) The faculty association has not yet had time to state its position on this proposed change."

- *Step 2:* Using Lewin's Force Field Analysis model below, identify the forces that seem to support the change and the forces that likely oppose the change to a trimester system. Team members should consider all possible sources of support and resistance, not just those stated in the situation above.
- *Step 3:* For each source of resistance, identify one or more strategies that would most effectively manage change. Recall from the textbook that the change management strategies include: communication, training, employee involvement, stress management, negotiation, and coercion.
- *Step 4:* The class will discuss each team's results.

Force Field
Analysis Model

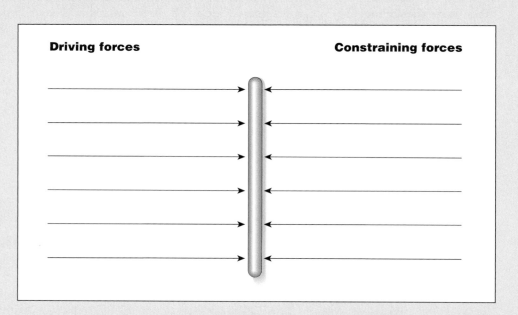

Driving forces   Constraining forces

TOLERANCE OF CHANGE SCALE

Purpose This exercise is designed to help you understand how people differ in their tolerance of change.

Instructions Read each of the statements below and circle the response that best fits your personal belief. Then use the scoring key in Appendix B of this book to calculate your results. This self-assessment is completed alone so students can rate themselves honestly without concerns of social comparison. However, class discussion will focus on the meaning of the concept measured by this scale and its implications for managing change in organizational settings.

Tolerance of Change Scale

To what extent does each statement describe you? Indicate your level of agreement by marking the appropriate response on the right.

	Strongly Agree ▼	Moderately Agree ▼	Slightly Agree ▼	Neutral ▼	Slightly Disagree ▼	Moderately Disagree ▼	Strongly Disagree ▼
1. An expert who doesn't come up with a definite answer probably doesn't know too much.	☐	☐	☐	☐	☐	☐	☐
2. I would like to live in a foreign country for a while.	☐	☐	☐	☐	☐	☐	☐
3. There is really no such thing as a problem that can't be solved.	☐	☐	☐	☐	☐	☐	☐
4. People who fit their lives into a schedule probably miss most of the joy of living.	☐	☐	☐	☐	☐	☐	☐
5. A good job is one where it is always clear what is to be done and how it is to be done.	☐	☐	☐	☐	☐	☐	☐
6. It is more fun to tackle a complicated problem than to solve a simple one.	☐	☐	☐	☐	☐	☐	☐
7. In the long run, it is possible to get more done by tackling small, simple problems rather than large, complicated ones.	☐	☐	☐	☐	☐	☐	☐
8. Often the most interesting and stimulating people are those who don't mind being different and original.	☐	☐	☐	☐	☐	☐	☐
9. What we are used to is always preferable to what is unfamiliar.	☐	☐	☐	☐	☐	☐	☐
10. People who insist on a yes or no answer just don't know how complicated things really are.	☐	☐	☐	☐	☐	☐	☐
11. A person who leads an even, regular life in which few surprises or unexpected happenings arise really has a lot to be grateful for.	☐	☐	☐	☐	☐	☐	☐
12. Many of our most important decisions are based on insufficient information.	☐	☐	☐	☐	☐	☐	☐
13. I like parties where I know most of the people more than ones where all or most of the people are complete strangers.	☐	☐	☐	☐	☐	☐	☐
14. Teachers or supervisors who hand out vague assignments give one a chance to show initiative and originality.	☐	☐	☐	☐	☐	☐	☐
15. The sooner everyone acquires similar values and ideals, the better.	☐	☐	☐	☐	☐	☐	☐
16. A good teacher is one who makes you wonder about your way of looking at things.	☐	☐	☐	☐	☐	☐	☐

Source: Adapted from S. Budner, "Intolerance of Ambiguity as a Personality Variable," *Journal of Personality*, 30 (1962), pp. 29–50.

After studying the preceding material, be sure to check out our Online Learning Centre at **www.mcgrawhill.ca/college/mcshane** for more in-depth information and interactivities that correspond to this chapter.

SAS INSTITUTE

SAS Institute is a profitable software company, but not because it applies the industry practice of driving employees to work 24/7 schedules. SAS has a completely different culture, one that values employee well-being. Even employees admit that the company indulges them.

SAS prides itself on providing such amenities as a health care centre, where employees can take themselves and their children in times of illness, thus reducing their time away from work. On-site day care centres enforce a cultural belief that family is important to the company. In order to reduce stress and increase the likelihood of having a balanced and happy worker, SAS provides breakout rooms where employees can escape at any time of the day.

Exercise opportunities are provided, with three gymnasiums, an aquatics centre, three outdoor playing fields, and miles of walking trails through woodlands. Furthermore, a 35-hour workweek is instilled so that at 5 p.m., practically all offices are empty, because the company encourages everyone to go home. The belief that a home and personal life are an integral part of a successful work life makes this culture stand out from the rest.

Discussion Questions

1. Describe the organizational culture at SAS Institute. Is this culture appropriate for SAS's environment?

2. Describe three categories of artifacts through which organizational culture is communicated at SAS.

Source: Last segment of "The Speed Trap," CBC *Witness*, January 6, 2000.

WENDY'S RESTAURANTS OF CANADA

Employees at Wendy's Restaurants of Canada are about to be swept up in a tide of extraordinary change. To boost profits, Wendy's needed a fundamental makeover from the top down. It wanted to break down the military style of management and, in its place, create a culture of vulnerability and trust. Wendy's vice-president, Chris Park, says that he wants managers to realize that they don't have to be in control all the time, that they can let go and take support from their team members.

Wendy's brought together 160 restaurant managers from across Canada to an Ontario resort where New Mexico-based Pecos River guided them into a new way of working with their employees. The course included trust falls, tightrope walking with a partner, sessions where they "revealed their inner selves," and discussions about the new culture at Wendy's. As the day wore on, the lessons from Pecos River began to sink in. Employees felt the mutual support and increased their willingness to depend on others.

Craig Stapon is responsible for leading the change in Wendy's six Winnipeg restaurants. Stapon joined Wendy's as district manager just before the course began, and he wants to make his mark. During the Pecos River course, Stapon and his restaurant managers shared their inner thoughts and discussed their vision of the new Wendy's. But Craig's vision wasn't quite what some of the other managers saw. When Craig suggested that everyone should be "normalized" by working Monday to Friday, Edie Helfrick shot back that Stapon was seeing everything his way. "There's going to be big changes, I know that," she said, "but it's his changes—it's what he wants."

A few weeks after the retreat, Craig Stapon tried to get his Winnipeg managers "on board" with the change. He introduced a magic wand so managers can be honest during the weekly meetings. He also used these meetings to openly evaluate managers on their commitment to the change process. But some managers suggested that Stapon isn't promoting the change in a positive way.

Craig Stapon and other Wendy's managers are discovering that it's a struggle to change the old corporate culture with a new philosophy. It's a long, difficult journey to create a company that's truly trusting and supportive. But Chris Parks believes that at least they've taken the first step. "Pecos River is really a working model of ... getting a commitment from everybody who is working together to support each other."

Discussion Questions

1. What changes did executives at Wendy's Restaurants of Canada expect to result from the Pecos River program? Did these changes occur in the Winnipeg restaurants?

2. Was there any resistance to change among the Winnipeg restaurant managers? If so, what form of resistance did it take?

3. What change management strategies did Craig Stapon use among the Winnipeg managers? Were these strategies effective? Why or why not?

Source: T. Notar, "Wendy's Restaurants of Canada," CBC *Venture*, September 1992.

CASE 1   Arctic Mining Consultants

Tom Parker enjoyed working outdoors. At various times in the past, he had worked as a ranch hand, high steel rigger, headstone installer, prospector, and geological field technician. Now 43, Parker is a geological field technician and field coordinator with Arctic Mining Consultants. He has specialized knowledge and experience in all nontechnical aspects of mineral exploration, including claim staking, line cutting and grid installation, soil sampling, prospecting, and trenching. He is responsible for hiring, training, and supervising field assistants for all Arctic Mining Consultants' programs. Field assistants are paid a fairly low daily wage (no matter how long they work, which may be up to 12 hours or more) and are provided meals and accommodation. Many of the programs are operated by a project manager who reports to Parker.

Parker sometimes acts as a project manager, as he did on a job that involved staking 15 claims near Eagle Lake, British Columbia. He selected John Talbot, Greg Boyce, and Brian Millar, all of whom had previously worked with Parker, as the field assistants. To stake a claim, the project team marks a line with flagging tape and blazes along the perimeter of the claim, cutting a claim post every 500 metres (called a "length"). The 15 claims would require almost 100 kilometres of line in total. Parker had budgeted seven days (plus mobilization and demobilization) to complete the job. This meant that each of the four stakers (Parker, Talbot, Boyce, and Millar) would have to complete a little over seven "lengths" each day. The following is a chronology of the project.

Day 1

The Arctic Mining Consultants crew assembled in the morning and drove to Eagle Lake, where they were flown by helicopter to the claim site. On arrival, they set up tents at the edge of the area to be staked, and agreed on a schedule for cooking duties. After supper, they pulled out the maps and discussed the job—how long it would take, the order in which the areas were to be staked, possible helicopter landing spots, and areas that might be more difficult to stake.

Parker pointed out that with only a week to complete the job, everyone would have to average seven and a half lengths per day. "I know that is a lot," he said, "but you've all staked claims before and I'm confident that each of you is capable of it. And it's only for a week. If we get the job done in time, there's a $300 bonus for each man." Two hours later, Parker and his crew members had developed what seemed to be a workable plan.

Day 2

Millar completed six lengths, Boyce six lengths, Talbot eight, and Parker eight. Parker was not pleased with Millar's or Boyce's production. However, he didn't make an issue of it, thinking that they would develop their "rhythm" quickly.

Day 3

Millar completed five and a half lengths, Boyce four, and Talbot seven. Parker, who was nearly twice as old as the other three, completed eight lengths. He also had enough time left to walk over and check the quality of the stakes that Millar and Boyce had completed, then walk back to his own area for helicopter pickup back to the tent site.

That night Parker exploded with anger. "I thought I told you that I wanted seven and a half lengths a day!" he shouted at Boyce and Millar. Boyce said that he was slowed down by unusually thick underbrush in his assigned area. Millar said that he had done his best and would try to pick up the pace. Parker did not mention that he had inspected their work. He explained that as far as he was concerned, the field assistants were supposed to finish their assigned area for the day, no matter what.

Talbot, who was sharing a tent with Parker, talked to him later. "I think that you're being a bit hard on them, you know. I know that it has been more by luck than anything else that I've been able to do my quota. Yesterday I only had five lengths done after the first seven hours and there was only an hour before I was supposed to be picked up. Then I hit a patch of really open bush, and was able to do three lengths in 70 minutes. Why don't I take Millar's area tomorrow and he can have mine? Maybe that will help."

"Conditions are the same in all of the areas," replied Parker, rejecting Talbot's suggestion. "Millar just has to try harder."

Day 4

Millar did seven lengths and Boyce completed six and a half. When they reported their production that evening, Parker grunted uncommunicatively. Parker and Talbot did eight lengths each.

Day 5

Millar completed six lengths, Boyce six, Talbot seven and a half, and Parker eight. Once again Parker blew up, but he concentrated his diatribe on Millar. "Why don't you do what you say you are going to do? You know that you have to do seven and a half lengths a day. We went over that when we first got here, so why don't you do it? If you aren't willing to do the job then you never should have taken it in the first place!"

Millar replied by saying that he was doing his best, that he hadn't even stopped for lunch, and that he didn't know how he could possibly do any better. Parker launched into him again: "You have got to work harder! If you put enough effort into it, you will get the area done!"

Later Millar commented to Boyce, "I hate getting dumped on all the time! I'd quit if it didn't mean that I'd have to walk 80 kilometres to the highway. And besides, I need the bonus money. Why doesn't he pick on you? You don't get any more done than me; in fact, you usually get less. Maybe if you did a bit more he wouldn't be so bothered about me."

"I only work as hard as I have to," Boyce replied.

Day 6

Millar raced through breakfast, was the first one to be dropped off by the helicopter, and arranged to be the last one picked up. That evening the production figures were Millar eight and a quarter lengths, Boyce seven, and Talbot and Parker eight each. Parker remained silent when the field assistants reported their performance for the day.

Day 7

Millar was again the first out and last in. That night, he collapsed in an exhausted heap at the table, too tired to eat. After a few moments, he announced in an abject tone, "Six lengths. I worked like a dog all day and I only got a lousy six lengths!" Boyce completed five lengths, Talbot seven, and Parker seven and a quarter.

Parker was furious. "That means we have to do a total of 34 lengths tomorrow if we are to finish this job on time!" With his eyes directed at Millar, he added: "Why is it that you never finish the job? Don't you realize that you are part of a team, and that you are letting the rest of the team down? I've been checking your lines and you're doing too much blazing (clearing underbrush) and wasting too much time making picture-perfect claim posts! If you worked smarter, you'd get a lot more done!"

Day 8

Parker cooked breakfast in the dark. The helicopter dropoffs began as soon as morning light appeared on the horizon. Parker instructed each assistant to complete 8 lengths and, if they finished early, to help the others. Parker said that he would finish the other 10 lengths. Helicopter pickups were arranged for one hour before dark.

By noon, after working as hard as he could, Millar had only completed three lengths. "Why bother," he thought to himself, "I'll never be able to do another five lengths before the helicopter comes, and I'll catch the same amount of abuse from Parker for doing six lengths as for seven and a half." So he sat down and had lunch and a rest. "Boyce won't finish his eight lengths either, so even if I did finish mine, I still wouldn't get the bonus. At least I'll get one more day's pay this way."

That night, Parker was livid when Millar reported that he had completed five and a half lengths. Parker had done ten and a quarter lengths, and Talbot had completed eight. Boyce proudly announced that he finished seven and a half lengths, but sheepishly added that Talbot had helped him with some of it. All that remained were the two and a half lengths that Millar had not completed.

The job was finished the next morning and the crew demobilized. Millar has never worked for Arctic Mining Consultants again, despite being offered work several times by Parker. Boyce sometimes does staking for Arctic, and Talbot works full time with the company.

CASE 2   A Window on Life

For Gilles LaCroix, there is nothing quite as beautiful as a handcrafted wood-framed window. LaCroix's passion for windows goes back to his youth in St. Jean, Québec, where he was taught how to make residential windows by an elderly carpenter. He learned about the characteristics of good wood, the best tools to use, and how to choose the best glass from local suppliers. LaCroix apprenticed with the carpenter in his small workshop and, when the carpenter retired, was given the opportunity to operate the business himself.

LaCroix hired an apprentice as he built up business in the local area. His small operation soon expanded as the quality of windows built by LaCroix Industries Ltd. became better known. Within eight years, the company was employing nearly 25 people and the business had moved to larger facilities to accommodate the increased demand from southern Québec. In these early years, LaCroix spent most of his time in the production shop, teaching new apprentices the unique skills he had mastered and applauding the journeymen for their accomplishments. He would constantly repeat the point that LaCroix products had to be of the highest quality because they gave families a "window on life."

After 15 years, LaCroix Industries was employing over 200 people. A profit-sharing program was introduced to give employees a financial reward for their contribution to the organization's success. Due to the company's expansion, headquarters had to be moved to another area of town, but the founder never lost touch with the work force. Although new apprentices were now taught entirely by the master carpenters and other craftspeople, LaCroix would still chat with plant and office employees several times each week.

When a second work shift was added, LaCroix would show up during the evening break with coffee and boxes of doughnuts and discuss how the business was doing and how it had become so successful through quality workmanship. Production employees enjoyed the times he would gather them together to announce new contracts with developers from Montréal and Toronto. After each announcement, LaCroix would thank everyone for making the business a success. They knew that LaCroix quality had become a standard of excellence in window manufacturing across Canada.

It seemed that almost every time he visited, LaCroix would repeat the now well-known phrase that LaCroix products had to be of the highest quality because they provided a window on life to so many families. Employees never grew tired of hearing this from the company founder. However, it gained extra meaning when LaCroix began posting photos of families looking through LaCroix windows. At first, LaCroix would personally visit developers and homeowners with a camera in hand. Later, as the "window on life" photos became known by developers and customers, people would send in photos of their own families looking through elegant front windows made by LaCroix Industries. The company's marketing staff began using this idea, as well as LaCroix's famous phrase, in their advertising. After one such marketing campaign, hundreds of photos were sent in by satisfied customers. Production and office employees took time after work to write personal letters of thanks to those who had submitted photos.

As the company reached the quarter-century mark, LaCroix, now in his mid-fifties, realized that

the organization's success and survival depended on expansion into the United States. After consulting with employees, LaCroix made the difficult decision to sell a majority share to Build-All Products, Inc., a conglomerate with international marketing expertise in building products. As part of the agreement, Build-All brought in a vice-president to oversee production operations while LaCroix spent more time meeting with developers around North America. LaCroix returned to the plant and office at every opportunity, but often this would be only once a month.

Rather than visiting the production plant, Jan Vlodoski, the new production vice-president, would rarely leave his office in the company's downtown headquarters. Instead, production orders were sent to supervisors by memorandum. Although product quality had been a priority throughout the company's history, less attention had been paid to inventory controls. Vlodoski introduced strict inventory guidelines and outlined procedures on using supplies for each shift. Goals were established for supervisors to meet specific inventory targets. Whereas employees previously could have tossed out several pieces of warped wood, they would now have to justify this action, usually in writing.

Vlodoski also announced new procedures for purchasing production supplies. LaCroix Industries had highly trained purchasing staff who worked closely with senior craftspeople when selecting suppliers, but Vlodoski wanted to bring in Build-All's procedures. The new purchasing methods removed production leaders from the decision process and, in some cases, resulted in trade-offs that LaCroix's employees would not have made earlier. A few employees quit during this time, saying that they did not feel comfortable about producing a window that would not stand the test of time. However, unemployment was high in St. Jean, so most staff members remained with the company.

After one year, inventory expenses had decreased by approximately 10 percent, but the number of defective windows returned by developers and wholesalers had increased markedly. Plant employees knew that the number of defective windows would increase as they used lower-quality materials to reduce inventory costs. However, they heard almost no news about the seriousness of the problem until Vlodoski sent a memo to all production staff saying that quality had to be maintained. During the latter part of the first year under Vlodoski, a few employees had the opportunity to personally ask LaCroix about the changes and express their concerns. LaCroix apologized, saying that due to his travels to new regions, he had not heard about the problems, and that he would look into the matter.

Exactly 18 months after Build-All had become majority shareholder of LaCroix Industries, LaCroix called together five of the original staff in the plant. The company founder looked pale and shaken as he said that Build-All's actions were inconsistent with his vision of the company and, for the first time in his career, he did not know what to do. Build-All was not pleased with the arrangement either. Although LaCroix windows still enjoyed a healthy market share and were competitive for the value, the company did not quite provide the minimum 18 percent return on equity that the conglomerate expected. LaCroix asked his longtime companions for advice.

CASE 3 Big Screen's Big Failure

By Fiona McQuarrie, University College of the Fraser Valley

Bill Brosnan stared at the financial statements in front of him and shook his head. The losses from *Conquistadors*, the movie that was supposed to establish Big Screen Studios as a major Hollywood power, were worse than anyone had predicted. In fact, the losses were so huge that Brosnan's predecessor, Buck Knox, had been fired as a result of this colossal failure. Brosnan had wanted to be the head of a big movie production company for as long as he could remember, and was thrilled to have been chosen by the board of directors to be the new president. But he had never expected that the first task in his dream job would be to deal with the fallout from one of the most unsuccessful movies ever made.

The driving force behind *Conquistadors* was its director, Mark Frazier. Frazier had made several profitable movies for other studios and had a reputation for being a maverick with a "vision." He was a director with clearly formulated ideas of what his movies should look like, and he also had no hesitation about being forceful with producers, studios, actors, and technical staff to ensure that his idea came to life as he had envisioned it. For several years, while Frazier had been busy on other projects, he had also been working on a script about two Spanish aristocrats in the 16th century who set out for America to find riches and gold, and encounter many amazing adventures on their travels. Frazier was something of an amateur historian, which led to his interest in the real-life stories of the Spanish conquistadors and bringing those stories to life for a 21st century audience. But he also felt that creating an epic tale like this would establish him as a serious writer and filmmaker in the eyes of Hollywood, some of whose major powers had dismissed his past work as unimaginative or clichéd.

At the time Big Screen Studios approached Frazier to see if he would be interested in working for them, the company was going through a rough spot. Through several years of hard work and mostly successful productions, Buck Knox, the president of Big Screen, had established Big Screen as a studio that produced cost-efficient and profitable films. The studio also had a good reputation for being supportive of the creative side of filmmaking; actors, writers, directors, and producers generally felt that Big Screen trusted them enough to give them autonomy in making decisions appropriate for their productions. (Other studios had reputations for keeping an overly tight rein on production budgets and for dictating choices based on cost rather than artistic considerations.) However, in the last two years Big Screen had invested in several major productions—a musical, a horror film, and the sequel to a wildly successful film adaptation of a comic book—that for various reasons had all performed well below expectations. Knox had also heard through the grapevine that several of the studio's board members were prepared to join together to force him out of the presidency if Big Screen did not come up with a hit soon.

Knox knew that Frazier was being wooed by several other studios for his next project, and decided to contact Frazier to see if he was interested in directing any of the productions Big Screen was considering in the next year or so. After hearing Knox's descriptions of the upcoming productions, Frazier said, "What I'd really be interested in doing is directing this script I've been writing." He described the plot of *Conquistadors* to Knox, and Knox was enchanted by the possibilities—two strong male lead characters, a beautiful woman the men encountered in South America whose affections they fought over, battles, sea voyages, and challenging journeys over mountains and through jungles. However, Knox could also see that this movie might be extremely expensive to produce. He expressed this concern to Frazier, and Frazier replied, "Yes, but it will be an investment that will pay off. I know this movie will work. And I've mentioned it to two other studios and they are interested in it. I would prefer to make it with Big Screen, but if I have to, I will go somewhere else to get it made. That is how strongly I believe in it. However, any studio I work with has to trust me. I won't make the film without adequate financial commitment from the studio, I want final approval over casting, and I won't make the film if I don't get final cut." ("Final cut" means the director, not the studio, edits the version of the movie that is released to theatres, and that the studio cannot release a version of the movie that the director does not approve.)

Knox told Frazier that he would get back to him later that week, and asked Frazier not to commit to any other project until then. He spent several days mulling over the possibilities. Like Frazier, he believed that *Conquistadors* could be a huge success. It certainly sounded like it had more potential than anything else Big Screen had in development. However, Knox was still concerned about the potential cost, and the amount of control over the project that Frazier was demanding. Frazier's reputation as a maverick meant that he would likely not compromise on his demands.

Knox was also concerned about his own vulnerability if the movie failed. But on the other hand, Big Screen needed a big hit, and it needed one soon. Big Screen would look very bad if it turned down *Conquistadors* and the movie became a gigantic hit for some other studio. Frazier had a respectable track record of producing moneymakers, so even if he might be difficult to work with, the end product was usually successful. At the end of the week, Knox phoned Frazier and told him that Big Screen was willing to produce *Conquistadors*. Frazier thanked Knox, and added, "This film is going to redeem me, and it's going to redeem Big Screen as well."

Pre-production on the film started almost immediately, after Frazier and the studio negotiated a budget of $50 million. This was slightly higher than Knox had anticipated, but he believed it was not an excessive amount to permit Frazier to realize the grand vision he had described. Knox further reassured himself by assigning John Connor, one of his trusted vice-presidents, to act as the studio's liaison with Frazier and to be executive producer on the film. Connor was a veteran of many years in the movie production industry and was experienced in working with directors and budgets. Knox trusted Connor to be able to make Frazier contain the costs of the production within the agreed-upon limits.

The first major problem the film encountered involved casting. The studio gave Frazier final approval over casting as he had requested. Frazier's first signing was Cole Rogan, a famous action star, to be one of the male leads. The studio did not object to this choice; in fact, Knox and Connor felt that Rogan was an asset because he had a reputation as a star who could "open" a film (in other words, audiences would come to a movie just because he was in it). However, Frazier then decided to cast Frank Monaco as the other male lead. Monaco had made only a few films to date, and those were fluffy romantic comedies. Frazier said that Monaco would bring important qualities of vulnerability and innocence to the role, which would be a strong contrast to Rogan's rugged machismo. However, Connor told Knox, he saw two major problems with Monaco's casting: Monaco had never proven himself in an epic adventure role, and he was an accomplished enough actor that he would make the rather wooden Rogan look bad. Knox told Connor to suggest to Frazier that Rogan's role be recast. Unfortunately, it turned out that Frazier had signed Rogan to a "pay or play" deal, meaning that if the studio released Rogan from the project, the studio would have to pay him a considerable sum of money. Knox was somewhat bothered that Frazier had made this deal with Rogan without consulting either him or Connor, but he told Connor to instruct Frazier to release Rogan and recast the role, and the studio would just accept the payment to Rogan as part of the production costs. Although Frazier complained, he did as the studio asked and chose Marty Jones as a replacement, an actor who had had some success in films but mostly in supporting roles. However, Jones was thrilled to be cast in a major role, and Connor felt that he would be capable of playing the part convincingly.

A few weeks after casting was completed, Connor called Knox and asked to see him immediately. "Buck," he told him once he arrived at Knox's office, "we have a really big problem." Connor said that Frazier was insisting the majority of the production be filmed in the jungles of South America, where most of the action took place, rather than on a studio soundstage or in a more accessible location that resembled the South American locale. Not only that, but Frazier was also insisting that he needed to bring along most of the crew who had worked on his previous films, rather than staffing the production locally. "Why does he want that? That's going to cost a hell of a lot," Knox said. "I know," Connor said, "but he says it's the only way that the film is going to work. He says it just won't be the same if the actors are in a studio or in some swamp in the southern U.S. According to him, the actors and the crew need to be in the real location to truly understand what the conquistadors went through, and audiences won't believe it's a real South American jungle if the film isn't made in one."

Knox told Connor that Frazier had to provide an amended budget to reflect the increased costs before he would approve the location filming. Connor took the request to Frazier, who complained that the studio was weakening on its promise to support the film adequately, and added that he might be tempted to take the film to another studio if he was not allowed to film on location in South America. After a few weeks, he produced an amended budget of $75 million. Knox was horrified that the budget for Conquistadors had grown one and a half times the orignial budget after only a few weeks. He told Connor that he would only accept the amended budget under two conditions: one, that Connor would go on the location shoot to ensure that costs stayed within the amended budget, and two, that if the costs exceeded Frazier's estimates, he would have to pay any excess himself. Frazier again complained that the studio was attempting to compromise his vision, but grudgingly accepted the modified terms.

Frazier, Connor, and the cast and crew then headed off to the South American jungles for a scheduled two-month shoot. Immediately it became apparent that there was more trouble. Connor, who reported daily to Knox, told him after two weeks had passed that Frazier was shooting scenes several times over—not because the actors or the crew were making mistakes, or because there was something wrong with the scene, but because the output just didn't meet his artistic standards. This attention to detail meant that the filming schedule was nearly a week behind after only the first week's work. Also, because the filming locations were so remote, the cast and crew were spending nearly four hours of a scheduled seven-hour work day travelling to and from location, leaving only three hours in which they could work at regular pay rates. Work beyond those hours meant they had to be paid overtime, and as Frazier's demanding vision required shooting ten or twelve hours each day, the production was incurring huge overtime costs. As if that wasn't bad enough, the "rushes" (the finished film produced each day) showed that Monaco and Jones didn't have any chemistry as a pair, and Gia Norman, the European actress Frazier had cast as the love interest, had such a heavy accent that most of her lines couldn't be understood.

Knox told Connor that he was coming to the location right away to meet with Frazier. After several days of very arduous travel, Knox, Connor, and Frazier met in the canvas tent that served as the director's "office" in the middle of the jungle. Knox didn't waste any time with pleasantries. "Mark," he told Frazier, "there is no way you can bring this film in for the budget you have promised or within the deadline you agreed to. John has told me how this production is being managed, and it's just not acceptable. I've done some calculations, and at the rate you are going, this picture is going to cost $85 million and have a running time of four and a half hours. Big Screen is not prepared to support that. We need a film that's a commercially viable length, and we need it at a reasonable cost."

"It needs to be as long as it is," replied Frazier, "because the story has to be told. And if it has to cost this much, it has to cost this much. Otherwise it will look like crap and no one will buy a ticket to see it."

"Mark," replied Knox, "we are prepared to put $5 million more into this picture, and that is it. You have the choice of proceeding under those terms, and keeping John fully appraised of the costs so that he can help you stay within the budget. If you don't agree to that, you can leave the production, and we will hire another director and sue you for breach of contract."

Frazier looked as though he was ready to walk into the jungle and head back to California that very minute, but the thought of losing his dream project was too much for him. He muttered, "OK, I'll finish it."

Knox returned to California, nursing several nasty mosquito bites, and Connor stayed in the jungle and reported to him regularly. Unfortunately, it didn't seem like Frazier was paying much attention to the studio's demands. Connor estimated that the shoot would run three months rather than two, and that the total cost of the shoot would be $70 million. This only left $10 million of the budget for post-production, distribution, and marketing, which was almost nothing for an epic adventure. To add to Knox's problems, he got a phone call from Richard Garrison, the chairman of Big Screen's board of directors. Garrison had heard gossip about what was going on with *Conquistadors* in the jungles of South America, and wanted to know what Knox was going to do to curb Frazier's excesses. Knox told Garrison that Frazier was operating under clearly understood requirements, and that Connor was on the set to monitor the costs. Unfortunately, Knox thought, Connor was doing a good job of reporting, but he didn't seem to be doing much to correct the problems he was observing.

Frazier eventually came back to California after three and a half months of shooting, and started editing the several hundred hours of film he had produced. Knox requested that Frazier permit Connor or himself to participate in the editing, but Frazier retorted that permitting that would infringe on his right to "final cut," and refused to allow anyone associated with the studio to be in the editing room. Knox scheduled a release date for the film in six months' time, and asked the studio's publicity department to start working on an ad campaign for the film, but not much could be done on either of these tasks without at least a rough cut of the finished product.

Three weeks into the editing, Connor called Knox. "I heard from Mark today," he said. "He wants to do some reshoots." "Is that a problem?" Knox asked. "No," said Connor, "most of it is interior stuff that we can do here. But he wants to add a prologue. He says that the story doesn't make sense without more development of how the two lead characters sailed from Spain to South America. He wants to hire a ship."

"He wants to WHAT?" exclaimed Knox.

"He wants to hire a sailing ship, like the conquistadors travelled on. There's a couple of tall ships that would do, but the one he wants is in drydock in Mexico, and would cost at least a million to make seaworthy and sail up to southern California. And that's on top of the cost of bringing the actors and crew back for a minimum of a week. I suggested to him that we try some special effects or a computerized animation for the scenes of the ship on the ocean, and shoot the shipboard scenes in the studio, but he says that won't be the same and it needs to be authentic."

At this point, Knox was ready to drive over to the editing studios and take care of Frazier himself. Instead, he called Garrison and explained the situation. "I won't commit any more money to this without the board's approval. But we've already invested $80 million into this already, so is a few more million that much of a deal if it gets the damn thing finished and gets Frazier out of our hair? If we tell him no, we'll have to basically start all over again, or just dump the whole thing and kiss $80 million goodbye." At the other end of the line, Garrison sighed, and said, "Do whatever you have to do to get it done."

Knox told Connor to authorize the reshoots, with a schedule of two months and the expectation that Frazier would have a rough cut of the film ready for the studio executives to view in three months. However, because of the time Frazier had already spent in editing, Knox had to change the release date, which meant changing the publicity campaign as well—and releasing the film at the same time that one of Big Screen's major competitors was releasing another epic adventure that was considered a surefire hit. However, Knox felt he had no choice. If he didn't enforce some deadline, Frazier might sit in the editing room and tinker with his dream forever.

Connor supervised the reshoots, and reported that they went as well as could be expected. The major problem was that Gia Norman had had plastic surgery on her nose after the first shoot was completed, and looked considerably different than she had in the jungles of South America. However, creative lighting, makeup, and costuming managed to minimize the change in her appearance. By all accounts, the (very expensive) sailing ship looked spectacular in the rushes, and Frazier was satisfied that his vision had been sufficiently dramatized.

Amazingly, Frazier delivered the rough cut of the film at the agreed-upon time. Knox, Connor, Garrison, and the rest of the studio's executives crowded into the screening room to view the realization of Frazier's dream. Five and a half hours later, they were in shock. No one could deny that the movie looked fantastic, and that it was an epic on a grand scale, but there was no way the studio could release a five and a half hour long film commercially, plus Frazier had agreed to produce a movie that was two and a half hours long at most. Knox was at his wits' end. He cornered Garrison in the hallway outside the screening room. "Will you talk to Mark? He won't listen to me, he won't listen to John. But we can't release this. It won't work." Garrison agreed, and contacted Frazier the next day. He reported back to Knox that Frazier, amazingly, had agreed to cut the film to two hours and fifteen minutes. Knox, heartened by this news, proceeded with the previously set release date, which by now was a month away, and got the publicity campaign going.

Two days before the scheduled release date, Frazier provided an advance copy of his shortened version of *Conquistadors* for a studio screening. Knox had asked him to provide a copy sooner, but Frazier said that he could not produce anything

that quickly. As a consequence, the version of the film that the studio executives were seeing for the first time was the version that had already had thousands of copies duplicated for distribution to movie theatres all across North America. In fact, those copies were on their way by courier to the theatres as the screening started.

At the end of the screening, the studio executives were stunned. Yes, the movie was shorter, but now it made no sense. Characters appeared and disappeared randomly, the plot was impossible to follow, and the dialogue did not make sense at several key points in the small parts of plot that were discernible. The film was a disaster. Several of the executives present voiced the suspicion that Frazier had deliberately edited the movie this way to get revenge on the studio for not "respecting" his vision and forcing him to reduce the film's length. Others suggested that Frazier was simply a lunatic who never should have been given so much autonomy in the first place.

Knox, Garrison, and Connor held a hastily-called meeting the next morning. What could the studio do? Recall the film and force Frazier to produce a more coherent shorter version? Recall the film and release the five-and-a-half hour version? Or let the shorter version be released as scheduled and hope that it wouldn't be too badly received? Knox argued that the film should be recalled and Frazier should be forced to produce the product he agreed to produce. Connor said that he thought Frazier had been doing his best to do what the studio wanted, based on what Connor saw on the set, and that making Frazier cut the movie so short compromised the vision that Frazier wanted to achieve. He said the studio should release the long version and present it as a "special cinematic event." Garrison, as chairman of the board, listened to both sides, and after figuring out the costs of recalling and/or reediting the film—not to mention the less tangible costs of further worsening the film's reputation—said, "Gentlemen, we really don't have any choice. *Conquistadors* will be released tomorrow."

Knox immediately cancelled the critics' screenings of *Conquistadors* scheduled for that afternoon, so that bad reviews would not appear on the day of the film's release. Despite that preemptive step and an extensive advertising campaign, *Conquistadors* was a complete and utter flop. On a total outlay of

$90 million, the studio recouped less than $9 million. The reviews of the film were terrible, and audiences stayed away in droves. The only place *Conquistadors* was even close to successful was in some parts of Europe, where film critics called the edited version an example of American studios' crass obsession with making money by compromising the work of a genius. The studio attempted to capitalize on this note of hope by releasing the five-and-a-half hour version of *Conquistadors* for screening at some overseas film festivals and cinema appreciation societies, but the revenues from these screenings were so small that they made no difference to the overall financial results.

Three months after *Conquistadors* was released, Garrison called Knox in and told him he was fired.

Garrison told Knox the board appreciated what a difficult production *Conquistadors* had been to manage, but that the costs of the production had been unchecked to a degree that the board no longer had confidence in Knox's ability to operate Big Screen Studios efficiently. Connor was offered a very generous early retirement package, and accepted it. The board then hired Bill Brosnan, a vice-president at another studio, as Knox's replacement.

After reviewing *Conquistadors'* financial records and the notes that Knox had kept throughout the production, Brosnan was determined that a disaster like this would not undermine his career as it had Knox's. But what could he do to ensure that would not happen?

CASE 4   Intelligentsia

By Roy L. Kirby, Ph.D., Carleton University

Note to Students: This case includes several additional online documents in the "Intelligentsia File" at www.mcgrawhill.ca/college/mcshane. The relevance of each online document to its section of this case is indicated in bold throughout this case.

Company Background

General Engineering was a well-respected engineering company, founded in 1935, with business interests in many areas of "old" technology, known for meeting the needs of small rural communities for utility services. After a long history of solid service in heavy electric motor repair, local power line installation, and telephone line maintenance, things began to change. In the recent past, newer services have included alternative sources of electric power (such as solar panels and wind generators, plus ordinary gasoline powered small generators), and two-way radio communication for farms. Three years ago, as part of a movement to update the company's business, they began to diversify into contract work on fibre-optic communications networks for downtown businesses. This led to much grander ideas about company success in the 21st century. Six months ago the company owners bought out MCP Systems Research, Inc., a small but vital company with smart ideas and tremendous talent in wireless communications, plus Internet-based commerce. The new name of the merged businesses is Intelligentsia Systems Incorporated.

In addition to existing General Engineering markets, the company saw major opportunities in a wide range of state of the art services: Internet server supply (ISP), Web domains, and interactive TV with shopping capabilities (e-commerce). However, the priority for new business strategy is to develop wireless telephone and data supply (Wireless Internet Service Provider, *WISP*) to new housing developments in distant suburbs, through Wireless local area networks, or WLAN's, where developers, given promises about wireless service by Intelligentsia, have taken the brave step of omitting land lines and have installed transmission towers instead, often concealed in the trees. They are marketing these new wireless areas as environmentally "green," aiming at young, technologically aware homebuyers who seek to be chic. There have been legal challenges by a local cable company on the grounds of unfair competition, but the ex-CEO of General Engineering, Pat Chuchinniwat, who was brought into General Engineering as a change agent three years ago, shrugged them off as meaningless when he announced the merger. "They wouldn't spend the money to supply cable service to rural suburbs—it's too far and too expensive. Wireless is the way to go and the cable companies know it, this far out in the country." said Pat, who has a reputation for frank talk and efficiency, even corporate bullying, but smiles cheerily through it all and loves the publicity, the talk shows, and the news cameras. "The number of cell phone subscribers soared 22% last year in Canada to a record 11 million users, with 22 million forecast by 2005. However, usage will soon reach a plateau. We will face fierce competition from companies such as Telus, Rogers, Bell, and Microcell if we aim only for voice transmission; users are spending less than ever—nationally, figures are down from an average of $75 per month in 1995 to less than $50 at present. No one has reached the market penetration that they enjoy in Japan and in Europe, but even *they* are finding it difficult to make a profit, due to competition and the high costs of installing the infrastructure.

The real challenge is to boost our revenue stream by diversifying into wireless data services. Intelligentsia will leap over the voice telephony bandwagon and go for the next generation: the fastest networks we can offer for text messaging, access from home to corporate intranets, downloading movies. That, and "no-wire" suburbs are our targets. We offer services that no one else does; we offer wireless plans cheaply; we support the electronic house, complete with net-coupled service for the wired household. Anyone buying a new house today will have at least some knowledge of "smart" wireless data networks for the home office and kids too. So? We will offer packaged home wiring installation for new construction by local developers. Kitchen appliances are already available that will connect to the Net and keep a record of your grocery needs. Home theater, security systems—all lie within our reach! Futuristic? Yes—but isn't that where we are headed? Anyone outside the range of telephone companies or cable companies is our customer, " Pat said in a speech to an enthusiastic board a year ago.

The merger had put Pat in the CEO's seat at Intelligentsia, but the CEO of MCP became, under the merger negotiations, chair of the board. Pat knows that support for this ambitious plan will be supported strongly by the ex-MCP president—and ex-MCP staff. Unfortunately for many others, the merger will bring a significant reduction in staff requirements. Two companies may need twelve VP's, but this new, unified organization needs only seven, plus the CEO. Technical staff is not affected; indeed, recruitment will begin soon to make the new services available, opening up markets. Small rural General Engineering offices will begin closing as Intelligentsia goes to an e-commerce approach, with all bills being paid by e-mail, telephone and so on. One of CEO Chuchinniwat's pet projects is a cutting-edge laboratory set up three years ago to exploit / explore new technologies. This lab has been expensive and criticized as being too far-out by the executive committees, but it has produced some unique results under the controversial, charismatic Dr. Ute Klemper. (**See online Document #1 for details of a recent incident involving Dr. Klemper.**)

The merger will make it possible to bring some of the basic research, including applications of encryption technology, to the marketplace, and some say that Chuchinniwat needed this merger to satisfy the General Engineering family owners, who plan to take the company public in two years' time. Pat Chuchinniwat has set out the basic ethical premises of Intelligentsia as an honest dealer with a value system that has solid meaning for customers and staff alike, and has mentioned many times the need for the company to be a good corporate citizen. There are environment committees, charity committees, community service groups, and policies that guide the retention of staff, flexible working hours for parents of young families, harassment guidelines and training, encouragement to see cultural diversity as a source of innovation and last, a performance appraisal system that requires constructive ongoing communication as opposed to only annual events.

Needless to say, some of the staff of General Engineering, until three years ago a solid, traditional, value-based company, are worried about losing their jobs as the new initiatives are implemented and the business takes a whole new direction. They have good reason to be worried; one of the people recruited (by the ex-CEO of MCP) from outside to make these changes is Sandy Bartlett, (ex-VP of Finance of FlatIron Appliances), a well-known and much-feared brute force in the downsizing business. "Dracula" Bartlett is the nickname, earned over many mergers and cutbacks. Bartlett is now VP of Corporate Services—a wide range of powers as yet largely undefined—but Sandy has wasted no time in setting out a territory of power. The ex-VP of Public Relations of General Engineering, J. Bradson Hyde, is not taking signals and threats to reorganize and restructure passively and is getting ready for a fight for corporate power and career survival, with an ambitious spouse driving this aggressive stand from behind the scenes.

The Natchez Associates Investigation

Your company, Natchez Associates Inc., specializes in the expert management of knowledge workers and in problem-solving consulting at a skilled, sophisticated level. As one of their more promising young interns, you support R. J. Renaldo, a senior consultant. The VP of Human Resources at Intelligentsia, Merritt Hadley, has brought in Natchez Associates to help make the merger go smoothly as the two companies make the transition toward a different organizational culture. Fortunately you have a mentor from your recent days as a student at the Sprock-Carrolton School of Management, and this person, Jean-Marie Rock, has been supportive of you since your graduation *summa cum laude* a few years ago. You take lunch occasionally and keep in touch through e-mail. (**See online Document #2 for some of this correspondence.**)

On your first day at Intelligentsia, you sit in the pleasant, if bare, office with the view of the artificial lake and fountain, and ponder the future. Your job is to ease this transition and maintain the cohesion of the new firm by handling problems before they become crises. The local media has already been snooping around looking for any scandal or sign of staff cutbacks. Already the General Engineering oldsters are talking about opening discussions with union organizers at the Communications Workers of Canada in an attempt to scare Intelligentsia executives and thus slow things down. On the other hand, the MCP staff, knowledge workers all, are keen and *ready to roll* on what they see as the opportunity to grab new skills and move up in the world. Unwritten career plans for some are ambitious: With any luck, within five or six years they will move on, become stakeholders in an IPO and will bank the millions that can follow. There are massive egos here, but massive talent too; some are concerned about the ethics of market domination through locking up a niche in the new electronic universe, and some see this not as expediency but as sharp business, period. The merger has brought two companies together under one organization but there are different value scales here. You already foresee all the people problems that accompany the marriage of the traditional Old School slowness and opposition to change, seen by many as solid and trustworthy—and the sharp business approaches of MCP, loved by them as new and dramatically exciting, but seen as *shallow* by General Engineering employees, some of whom are looking for a buy-out already. In both groups, frustration with each other is widespread.

You let these background considerations play across your mind, and then decide to get a look at a similar situation. You already know that Iowa's Prairie Net expects to sign up 10,000 customers by the end of 2002; and questions have been raised about their ability to provide the broadband width they say they can. They rely a great deal on the 900 MHZ and 2.4GHz frequency bands although they are looking at even higher frequencies in the 5 to 8 GHZ bands. You fire up the computer and, as the web browser comes to life, you look up Platinum Communications Corporation, based in Okotoka, Alberta, founded in 2000. You find information on the *Globe and Mail* site.

Here you find confirmation that the ideas of Intelligentsia's board are based in reality. Platinum, a start-up company, is going after a wireless market that the large telephone and cable companies have so far neglected in rural communities. They have ignored small towns because providing service past the so-called "last mile" means high infrastructure costs to serve what they see, relatively speaking, as a handful of subscribers. Platinum Communications has a technology that is capable of 1.4 megabytes per second data transmission rate. How do they do it? They transmit from the 52-storey Calgary Tower to antennas that then distribute the signal to subscribers. This way, Platinum avoids the high costs of renting existing land lines from the Telco's. The range varies between ten and twenty-four kilometres. Industry analysts like this strategy because Platinum has identified an unserved market and the demand is there.

You think to yourself, "Show Time, Folks!" open up the e-mail program, and find a message from Bev Harris about testing done on managers. It seems that Harris is warning you about the quality of some managers. This is alarming but informative. There are references to Lindsay Peebles that are quite important. You start to make notes, but you have barely looked at that message before you decide to look up the personnel file of key employees.

The first thing you find is a set of notes e-mailed to you about a conversation between Dr. Smith and Dr. Klemper, head of the encryption laboratory. "Well, now, here's a people problem if ever I saw one," you think; "hardest of problems, but it has to be addressed. Let's look at the folder. It reads like a play . . . , I'll call it the Smith/Klemper conflict," and you file the attachment under Incident Files, on your hard drive. (**See online Document #3 for details of the Smith/Klemper conflict**.)

But there was more. It seemed that Klemper had been receiving attention from a coach in people skills and communication/interpersonal skills, since Klemper had quite a reputation for being an ego-driven scientist who claimed unique results but did not deny being a very demanding master. You find the report in Klemper's personnel file but you save it in your own special personnel file. (**See online Document #4 for Dr. Klemper's executive coaching report**.)

You decide to look at anything you can find on this Smith character and find a self assessment on the extent to which Smith feels valued at work—it now seems clear that Smith is a submissive and feeling person, while Klemper is an aggressive logical thinker. "Hmm," you think—"I should look over the Myers Briggs test materials. Could help me understand these people.

"OK, now let's look at this green folder here. . . . Who is the Peebles person?? There are files on needs for power and affiliation—now let me see . . . that's the McClelland material, isn't it?" (**See online Document #5 for details of Lindsay Peebles**.)

"Who's this Pat Kelly person? Some team leader, eh? But I'd better wait and get into it fully." The green folder is thin, but it lays out the events of an emotionally bitter interaction between Pat and a team member called Niam. Pat has really gotten into a spat with Niam, who thinks that Pat is an oldster who is not needed and is unwelcome as a supervisor. However, Pat is quite disrespectful to the boss, Kim—who gets quite frustrated by Pat's apparent unwillingness to adapt to the team-based culture now espoused by Intelligentsia. (**See online Document #6 for details of the conflict between Pat Kelly and Niam Lacey**.)

You continue through the files and find something concrete on the new business. This looks important—something about Decisions, Decisions—a bounded rationality case about the Olympics. You file it for later study. (**See online Document #7 for the bounded rationality case about the Olympics**.)

You are getting tired but are almost through filing these notes that will add so much to your understanding and diagnosis of the Intelligentsia situation. You now scan a set of files about Rand Smith. Rand is an ESTJ on the Myers Briggs Type Inventory, and his report says:

> The SJ combination is found in just fewer than 40% of the general population. These people exist to be useful to their social unit. Must belong, and must earn that belonging; must be the givers, the caretakers.
>
> Education fits the SJ well, and many teachers are SJ types. Rand probably took care of others at school, providing support and assistance in the completion of tasks and the understanding of factual data or assignments. Rand may very well enjoy that part of work to do with the development of others, through training, development, and collaboration where Rand is the expert. Dislikes dependency on others—will want independence and may experience guilt if accepts dependence "too easily," in Rand's own terms of reference.
>
> SJ's can be rather pessimistic . . .

At this point, you give up reading and file everything away.

Monday Morning Management Meeting

A week later, you attend the company's Monday morning management meeting. After introducing the new encryption specialist, Rand explains that he has heard rumours about one or more employees apparently trying to undermine his e-commerce security project. Before any discussion begins, Rand immediately takes the offensive.

"Look, I have to work with these people," Rand begins. "I try hard to let them know I care enough to keep an eye on things. However, if there is any nasty business going on, especially with this Net encryption project, I warn this committee to be careful. I have learned from an old pal, a head-hunter, that some employees are grumbling about leaking information about this project to the competition."

Raising his voice, Rand continues: "If we have a problem, we solve it, right? Isn't that our way? Isn't that what we have always done as a management team? Are we agreed that I fire 'em at the first sign of a leak? I assume everyone is with me on that? That's the policy, right?"

Around the table, a few heads nodded in agreement.

"Yeah, Rand, you do what you gotta do."

" I'm with you, Rand."

"Okay by me."

" Right, if you see a problem then it must be a problem."

"OK, I suppose; I'll go along with the rest of the committee."

Liam Xu and Chris Tyler, two other managers at the meeting, shuffled through the agenda materials and said nothing. However, the rest soon came onside, as Rand had predicted they would, and there was consensus: some employees might have been putting the project at risk and Rand had to deal with it. The new encryption specialist was silent, pondering the differences between Ute Klemper and Rand Smith.

Sam Goodrich was silent, too, thinking it was just as well that although Smith had gotten the director's job—no surprise—Smith was welcome to it. "My spouse was right about Rand—and the jokes that Rand is a modern day barbarian might not be far off the truth. There's trouble ahead on this project—I think I'll look elsewhere in the company, but I'd better get out of here pretty soon."

After the management committee meeting had ended, Chris Tyler spoke quietly to Liam Xu as they sat holding coffees. "Well, Liam, I'm not quite sure what happened in there. Did Rand just get the entire committee to let him fire anyone he thinks might threaten the project? I don't even know if there is any threat, but I suppose we had no choice. Have a muffin?"

CASE 5   Perfect Pizzeria

Perfect Pizzeria in Southville, deep in southern Illinois, is the chain's second-largest franchise. The headquarters is located in Phoenix, Arizona. Although the business is prospering, it has employee and managerial problems.

Each operation has one manager, an assistant manager, and from two to five night managers. The managers of each pizzeria work under an area supervisor. There are no systematic criteria for being a manager or becoming a manager trainee. The franchise has no formalized training period for the manager. No college education is required. The managers for whom the case observer worked during a four-year period were relatively young (ages 24 to 27), and only one had completed college. They came from the ranks of night managers,

assistant managers, or both. The night managers were chosen for their ability to perform the duties of the regular employees. The assistant managers worked a two-hour shift during the luncheon period five days a week to gain knowledge about bookkeeping and management. Those who were becoming managers remained at that level unless they expressed interest in investing in the business.

The employees were mostly college students, with a few high school students performing the less challenging jobs. Because Perfect Pizzeria was located in an area with few job opportunities, it had a relatively easy task of filling its employee quotas. All the employees, with the exception of the manager, were employed part time. Consequently, they earned only the minimum wage.

The Perfect Pizzeria system is devised so that food and beverage costs and profits are set up according to a percentage. If the percentage of food unsold or damaged in any way is very low, the manager gets a bonus. If the percentage is high, the manager does not receive a bonus; rather, he or she receives only his or her normal salary.

There are many ways the percentage can fluctuate. Because the manager cannot be in the store 24 hours a day, some employees make up for their paycheques by helping themselves to the food. When a friend comes in to order a pizza, extra ingredients are put on the friend's pizza. Occasional nibbles by 18 to 20 employees throughout the day at the meal table also raise the percentage figure. An occasional bucket of sauce may be spilled or a pizza accidentally burned. Sometimes the wrong size of pizza may be made.

In the event of an employee mistake or a burned pizza by the oven person, the expense is supposed to come from the individual. Because of peer pressure, the night manager seldom writes up a bill for the erring employee. Instead, the establishment takes the loss and the error goes unnoticed until the end of the month when inventory is taken. That's when the manager finds out that the percentage is high and that there will be no bonus.

In the present instance, the manager took retaliatory measures. Previously, each employee was entitled to a free pizza, salad, and all the soft drinks he or she could drink for every 6 hours of work. The manager raised this figure from 6 to 12 hours of work. However, the employees had been receiving these 6-hour benefits for a long time. Therefore, they simply took advantage of the situation whenever the manager or the assistant was not in the building. Although the night managers theoretically had complete control of the operation in the evenings, they did not command the respect that the manager or assistant manager did. That was because night managers received the same pay as the regular employees, could not reprimand other employees, and were basically the same age or sometimes even younger than the other employees.

Thus, apathy grew within the pizzeria. There seemed to be a further separation between the manager and his workers, who had started out being a closely knit group. The manager made no attempt to alleviate the problem, because he felt it would iron itself out. Either the employees who were dissatisfied would quit or they would be content to put up with the new regulations. As it turned out, there was a rash of employee dismissals. The manager had no problem filling the vacancies with new workers, but the loss of key personnel was costly to the business.

With the high turnover, the manager found he had to spend more time in the building supervising and sometimes taking the place of inexperienced workers. This was in direct violation of the franchise regulation, which stated that a manager would act as a supervisor and at no time take part in the actual food preparation. Employees were not placed under strict supervision with the manager working alongside them. The operation no longer worked smoothly because of differences between the remaining experienced workers and the manager concerning the way in which a particular function should be performed.

Within two months, the manager was again free to go back to his office and leave his subordinates in charge of the entire operation. During this two-month period, in spite of the differences between experienced workers and the manager, the unsold/damaged food percentage had returned to the previous low level and the manager received a bonus each month. The manager felt that his problems had been resolved and that conditions would remain the same, since the new personnel had now been properly trained.

It didn't take long for the new employees to become influenced by the other employees. Immediately after the manager returned to his supervisory role, the unsold/damaged food percentage began to rise. This time the manager took a bolder step. He cut out any benefits that the employees had—no free pizzas, salads, or drinks. With the job market at an even lower ebb than usual, most employees were forced to stay. The appointment of a new area supervisor made it impossible for the manager to "work behind the counter," because the supervisor was centrally located in Southville.

The manager tried still another approach to alleviate the rising unsold/damaged food percentage problem and maintain his bonus. He placed a notice on the bulletin board, stating that if the percentage remained at a high level, a lie detector test would be given to all employees. All those found guilty of taking or purposefully wasting food or drinks would be immediately terminated. This did not have the desired effect on the employees, because they knew if they were all subjected to the test, all would be found guilty and the manager would have to dismiss all of them. This would leave him in a worse situation than ever.

Even before the following month's percentage was calculated, the manager knew it would be high. He had evidently received information from one of the night managers about the employees' feelings toward the notice. What he did not expect was that the percentage would reach an all-time high. That is the state of affairs at the present time.

Source: J. E. Dittrich and R. A. Zawacki, *People and Organizations*. (Plano, Texas: Business Publications, 1981), pp. 126–128. Used by permission of Irwin/McGraw-Hill.

CASE 6   Trivac Industries Ltd.

TriVac Industries Ltd., a Kitchener, Ontario-based manufacturer of centralized vacuum systems, was facing severe cash flow problems due to increasing demand for its products and rapid expansion of production facilities. Steve Heinrich, TriVac's founder and majority shareholder, flew to Germany to meet with the management of Rohrtech Gmb to discuss the German company's willingness to become a majority shareholder of TriVac Industries in exchange for an infusion of much-needed cash. A deal was struck whereby Rohrtech would become majority shareholder while Heinrich would remain as TriVac's president. One of Rohrtech's senior executives would become the chairperson of TriVac's board of directors and Rohrtech would appoint two other board members.

This relationship worked well until Rohrtech was acquired by a European conglomerate two years later. Rohrtech's new owner wanted more precise financial information and controls placed on its holdings, including TriVac Industries, but Heinrich resented this imposition and refused to provide the necessary information. Relations between Rohrtech and TriVac Industries quickly soured to the point where Heinrich refused to let Rohrtech representatives into the TriVac Industries plant. He also instituted legal proceedings to regain control of the company.

According to the original agreement between TriVac and Rohrtech, any party who possessed over two-thirds of a company's shares could force the others to sell their shares to the majority shareholder. Heinrich owned 29 percent of TriVac's shares whereas Rohrtech owned 56 percent. The remaining 15 percent of TriVac Industries shares were held by Tex Weston, TriVac's vice-president of sales and marketing. Weston was one of TriVac's original investors and a long-time executive at TriVac Industries, but he had remained quiet throughout most of the battle between Rohrtech and Heinrich. However, Weston finally agreed to sell his shares to Rohrtech, thereby forcing Heinrich to give up his shares. When Heinrich's bid for control failed, Rohrtech purchased all remaining shares and TriVac's board of directors (now dominated by Rohrtech) fired Heinrich as president. The board immediately appointed Weston as TriVac Industries' new president.

Searching for a New COO

Several months before Heinrich was fired as president, the chairman of TriVac's board of directors privately received instructions from Rohrtech to hire an executive search firm in Toronto to identify possible outside candidates for the new position of chief operating officer (COO) at TriVac Industries. The successful candidate would be hired after the conflict with Heinrich had ended (presumably with Heinrich's departure). The COO would report to the president (the person eventually replacing Heinrich) and would be responsible for the day-to-day management of the company. Rohrtech's management correctly believed that most of TriVac's current managers were loyal to Heinrich and, by hiring an outsider, the German firm would gain more inside control over its Canadian subsidiary (TriVac).

The executive search firm identified several qualified executives interested in the COO position and a short list of three candidates were interviewed by TriVac's chairman and another Rohrtech representative. One of these candidates, Kurt Devine, was vice-president of sales at an industrial packaging firm in Montréal, Québec, and, at 52 years old, was looking for one more career challenge before retirement. The Rohrtech representatives explained the current situation and said that they were offering stable employment after the problem with Heinrich was resolved so that the COO could help settle TriVac's problems. When Devine expressed his concern about rivalry with internal candidates, the senior Rohrtech manager stated: "We have a controller, but he is not our choice. The sales manager is capable, but he is located in British Columbia and doesn't want to move to Ontario."

One week after Heinrich was fired and Weston was appointed president, TriVac's chairman invited Devine to a meeting at a posh hotel attended by the chairman, another Rohrtech manager on TriVac's board of directors, and Weston. The chairman explained the recent events at TriVac Industries and formally invited Devine to accept the position of chief operating officer. After discussing salary and details about job duties, Devine asked the others whether he had their support as well as the support of TriVac's employees. The two Rohrtech representatives said "Yes" while Weston remained silent. When the chairman left the room to get a bottle of wine to toast the new COO, Devine asked Weston how long he had known about the decision to hire him. Weston replied: "Just last week when I became president. I was surprised....I don't think I would have hired you."

Confrontation with Tom O'Grady

Devine began work at TriVac Industries in early October and, within a few weeks, noticed that the president and two other TriVac Industries managers were not giving him the support he needed to accomplish his work. For example, Weston would call the sales people almost daily yet spoke to Devine only when Devine approached him first. The vice-president of sales, who lived in Vancouver, rarely communicated with Devine whereas Tom O'Grady, the vice-president of finance and administration, seemed to resent his presence the most. O'Grady had been promoted from the posi-

tion of controller in October and now held the highest rank at TriVac Industries below Devine. After Heinrich's departure, TriVac's board of directors had placed O'Grady in charge of day-to-day operations until Devine took over.

Devine depended on O'Grady for general operations information because he had more knowledge than anyone else about many aspects of the business. However, O'Grady provided incomplete information on many occasions and would completely refuse to educate the COO on some matters. O'Grady was also quick to criticize many of Devine's decisions and made indirect statements to Devine about his appropriateness as a COO. He also mentioned that he and other TriVac managers didn't want the German company (Rohrtech) to interfere with their company.

Devine would later learn about other things O'Grady had said and done to undermine his position. For example, O'Grady actively spoke to office staff and other managers about the problems with Devine and encouraged them to tell the president about their concerns. Devine overheard O'Grady telling another manager that Devine's memoranda were a "complete joke" and that "Devine didn't know what he was talking about most of the time." On one occasion, O'Grady let Devine present incorrect information to resellers (companies that sold TriVac products to customers) even though O'Grady knew that it was incorrect "just to prove what an idiot Rohrtech had hired."

Just six weeks after joining TriVac Industries, Devine confronted O'Grady with his concerns. O'Grady was quite candid with the COO, saying everyone felt that Devine was a "plant" by Rohrtech and was trying to turn TriVac Industries into a branch office of the German company. He said that some employees would quit if Devine did not leave because they wanted TriVac Industries to maintain its independence from Rohrtech. In a later meeting with Devine and Weston, O'Grady repeated these points and added that Devine's management style was not appropriate for TriVac Industries. Devine responded that he had not received any support from TriVac Industries since the day he had arrived even though Rohrtech had sent explicit directions to Weston and other TriVac Industries managers that he was to have complete support in managing the company's daily operations. Weston told the two men that they should work together and that, of course, Devine was the more senior person.

Decision by TriVac's Board of Directors

As a member of TriVac's board of directors, Weston included Devine's performance on the January meeting's agenda, and invited O'Grady to provide comments at that meeting. Based on this testimony, the board decided to remove Devine from the COO job and give him a special project instead. O'Grady was immediately named acting COO. The chairman and other Rohrtech representatives on TriVac's Board were disappointed that events did not unfold as they had hoped, but they agreed to remove Devine rather than face the mass exodus of TriVac managers that Weston and O'Grady had warned about.

In late April, Devine attended a morning meeting of TriVac's board of directors to present his interim report on the special project. The board agreed to give Devine until mid-June to complete the project. However, the board recalled Devine into the boardroom in the afternoon and Weston bluntly asked Devine why he didn't turn in his resignation? Devine replied: "I can't think of a single reason why I should. I will not resign. I joined your company six months ago as a challenge. I have not been allowed to do my job. My decision to come here was based on support from Rohrtech and on a great product." The next day, Weston came to Devine's office with a letter of termination signed by the chairman of TriVac's board of directors.

CASE 7 Westray

The Westray Mine Explosion: A teaching case by Caroline O'Connell and Albert Mills, Saint Mary's University.

It was the sixth of February 1996. Carl Guptill sat at his kitchen table nursing a cup of coffee. He was a beefy man with long hair, often tucked through the back of a baseball cap. The next day he would testify at the Commission of Inquiry into the Westray Mine explosion and friends had been phoning to offer their support. One caller, a geologist from nearby Antigonish, hadn't been in touch since working with Guptill at a mine in Guysborough County more than five years ago, but he wanted Carl to know he was thinking of him.

Carl Guptill's thoughts drifted back to another kitchen table—Roy Feltmate's. Roy, a longtime friend, had worked on B crew at the Westray Mine. In April of 1992, three months after he had left his job at Westray, Guptill met up with Roy and four other members of B crew, at Feltmate's home. Talk quickly turned to safety at the mine. Conditions had continued to deteriorate and the men believed that an explosion or a cave-in was inevitable. They calculated their odds of being the

crew underground when it happened at 25 per cent. The men made Guptill promise that if they died in the mine, he would "go public" and tell the world what he knew. Mike MacKay implored him to "do it for our widows."

On May 9, 1992, a few short weeks after that kitchen meeting, the odds caught up with Roy Feltmate, Mike MacKay, Randy House, Robbie Fraser and 22 other members of B crew. At 5:20 a.m. an explosion ripped through the Westray Mine. All 26 miners underground died. Fifteen bodies were recovered but 11 bodies, including Roy Feltmate's and Mike MacKay's remained in the mine. Guptill would keep his promise to them.

One Miner's Tale

Carl Guptill had worked in hard rock mines in Nova Scotia before hiring on at Westray. At the Gay's River Mine, he had chaired the health and safety committee and at the Forest Hill Mine he'd been a shift supervisor to a crew of 35 or more men. He had completed an advanced management course at Henson College, the continuing education arm of Halifax's Dalhousie University. He was mine rescue certified and had been captain of a mine rescue team. As both a miner and a supervisor, he'd enjoyed a good working relationship with Albert McLean, the provincial mine inspector. Guptill put safety first and believed he'd made that clear to Roger Parry, the underground manager at Westray, when Parry interviewed him for a job.

After only a few shifts, Guptill began to question safety practices at Westray. Farm tractors, which shouldn't even be used underground, were loaded beyond their capacity. Combustible coal dust was allowed to build up underground; levels of explosive methane gas were too high and the methanometers that detected the gas were rigged to circumvent their intended purpose of warning miners when gas levels were dangerous. In addition, miners worked 12-hour shifts, often without breaks. The batteries for miners' headlamps could not sustain their charge and were often dim or out by the end of a shift. There were no underground toilets and miners relieved themselves in unused corners of the mine.

Complaints fell on deaf ears. One supervisor answered Guptill's concerns with the comment that "they got a few thousand applications up on top, men willing to come down here and take your place." On only his 13th shift, Guptill's supervisor ordered him to continue working after his lamp had dimmed. In the dark, Guptill stumbled and a steel beam he was attempting to move landed on him and injured him. After three days in hospital, he called Roger Parry. The conversation quickly turned into a shouting match. Guptill then contacted Claude White, the provincial director of mine safety. White, in turn, sent him to mine inspector Albert McLean. Shortly thereafter Guptill met with McLean, John Smith, the man responsible for inspection of electrical and mechanical equipment in mines, and Fred Douche, in charge of mine rescue. In this meeting Carl Guptill spoke of his accident and of the many safety violations he had observed in his short time working at Westray. Guptill expected that his report would result in a shutdown of the mine and a complete investigation. Weeks later, having heard nothing, he again called inspector Albert

McLean. The two met once more, this time in a local motel room, instead of the labour department's offices. McLean kept the television on high volume throughout the meeting. Puzzled, Guptill later concluded that McLean was fearful he would tape the meeting. McLean told Guptill that the other men had not backed up his complaints and that as inspector, he could do little. He did offer to "put in a good word" for Guptill with management if he wanted to return to work. This was the story Carl Guptill told the Commission of Inquiry.

A Snapshot of Mining in Picot County

The four communities of Trenton, New Glasgow, Westville and Stellarton run into each other to make up Pictou County, Nova Scotia. All told, 25,000 people live there, descendants of Scots who landed with the ship *Hector* and immigrants from the other British Isles and Europe who followed Britain's General Mining Association overseas in the early nineteenth century. Hardy stock, they had mined the county's 25 seams of coal for generations. One historian estimated that nearly 600 residents had lost their lives in coal mines, as many as had been killed in both world wars. Although full of coal, the seams were considered among the most dangerous in the world; the beds were uneven and the ash content was high. The mines were subject to rock falls and flooding. Most significant were the high levels of explosive methane gas.

At their peak in 1875, Pictou coal mines produced 250,000 tons of coal a year and employed over 1600 men and boys. The last mine operating in Pictou was the small, privately operated Drummond Mine, which closed in 1984. By the mideighties, the only coal mines left in Nova Scotia were operating under heavy federal subsidy in Cape Breton, an economically depressed area in the northernmost part of the province. Cape Breton mines might have met the same fate as those in Pictou had they not been in the territory of a powerful federal member of parliament as the oil crisis in the Middle East dominated headlines and economies in the 1970's. Under OPEC, oil from the Middle East was subject both to price hikes and embargoes. This rejuvenated the dying Cape Breton coal industry and coal rebounded as a source of energy in Nova Scotia. In the late 1980's and early 1990's, a similar opportunity presented itself to the industry in Pictou. An evolving environmental agenda was driving power generation. The provincial electrical utility, Nova Scotia Power Corporation, was seeking to lower its sulphur dioxide emissions. It needed an alternative to high-sulphur Cape Breton coal. Enter Clifford Frame, Curragh Resources, and Westray.

Politics and Big Guns

Clifford Frame, a big man who drove big cars, raised cattle and smoked expensive cigars, was a self-made tycoon in the style of a previous era. In his youth he had turned down a chance to play for the New York Rangers farm team. Instead he got a degree in mine engineering and worked his way from the pit to the corner office. After rising to the post of president of Denison Mines, he'd been fired in 1985 after a very public project failure in British Columbia. He formed Curragh Resources in 1985 and had early success reviving a lead-zinc mine in the Yukon. In 1987, the industry publication the *Northern Miner* named him "Mining Man of the Year." That same year he incorporated Westray Coal and a year later, in 1988 he bought out Suncor's coal rights in Pictou County. In his time at Denison, Frame had come to know key political players in Ottawa. Through these connections he was introduced to Elmer MacKay, then federal representative for Pictou, and minister of public works. Frame aggressively sought federal and political support for his operation. Pictou County was burdened by a 20 percent unemployment rate and Frame promised that his mine would employ at least 250 people in jobs paying $35,000 to $60,000 for 15 years. Economic spin-offs in neighbouring communities would total in the millions of dollars. Politicians, including then Premier John Buchanan, supported Frame. Perhaps the project's greatest advocate was local provincial MLA (Member of the Legislative Assembly) Donald Cameron, who became minister of economic development as the project evolved and ultimately was elected premier, his position at the time of the explosion. Frame successfully negotiated a $12 million equity loan with the provincial government as well as an $8 million interim loan when federal negotiations lagged.

He also struck a so-called "take or pay" agreement that guaranteed a market for Westray coal. Under this contract, the Nova Scotia government would buy 275,000 tons of coal if other buyers did not materialize. Westray would pay back any revenues from this agreement without interest at the end of 15 years. The federal government proved a tougher sell and discussions dragged out over three years. Ultimately the federal government came through with a loan guarantee of $85 million and an interest buydown of nearly $27 million. This was much less than the amount originally sought by Frame but much more than the government's policies usually allowed for such projects. Harry Rogers, a federal deputy minister, was involved in the negotiations and would later describe Clifford Frame as "... personally abrasive and abusive ... Probably the most offensive person I have met in business or in government." However a deal was finally struck and in September of 1991, at Westray's official opening, politicians from both levels of government lined up to congratulate each other and the company.

Rules of the Game

Mining is dangerous work. The first regulations to protect the safety of miners date back to 1873 and provided for the inspection of mines. In 1881, legislation allowed for the certification of miners and mine officials. The new rules also called for gas testing and banned smoking underground. This legislation followed a disaster in which 60 miners died and made Nova Scotia mines the safest in the world, according to one mining historian. In 1923 the age limit for working underground was raised from 12 to 16. (It would not be raised to age 18 until 1951.) By 1927, the maximum allowable level of methane in a mine was 2.5 per cent. At the time of the Westray explosion, a methane reading of 2.5 per cent required the removal of all workers from the site, while a reading of 1.25 per cent mandated the shutdown of electricity that could spark an explosion.

At the time the Westray mine exploded, the regulation of coal mining in Nova Scotia fell primarily under the *Coal Mines Regulation Act*, a 160-page piece of legislation considered 30 years out of date. An example of its anachronisms could be found in section 94, which outlined the duties of stablemen who tended the horses underground. The section provided for care of the horses and cleanliness of the stables. A further indication of just how out of date the legislation was, and how limited its power to deter unsafe behaviours, was the fine schedule. The maximum fine that could be levied under the *Act* was $200. More applicable to the modern mine, it also regulated the qualifications required for various levels of mining competency, including miners, managers, owners and inspectors. Most significantly, for Westray, the legislation regulated maximum allowable levels of methane. It also stipulated the removal of highly combustible coal dust and the spreading of limestone dust to neutralize its effects. The *Act* included provisions for roof supports and the prohibition of tobacco products and matches underground; it permitted worker inspections of the mines and limited shift duration to eight hours. All would become issues for public scrutiny after the explosion.

Operating as a parallel was the provincial *Occupational Health and Safety Act* enacted in 1986. It imposed on employers the obligation to ensure workplace safety and to provide appropriate training, equipment, facilities and supervision. This legislation also required employees to take safety precautions, to wear appropriate clothing or equipment and to cooperate with employers, regulators, and other employees in these goals. The *Act* also mandated joint occupational health and safety committees for workplaces with designated numbers of employees. These committees made up of both employer and worker representatives were charged with educating the workplace on safety issues, maintaining records, inspecting the workplace, and responding to complaints. A key element of this legislation was a worker's right to refuse unsafe work and not to be discriminated against, or punished for doing so. The *Act* also provided that the legislation itself must be available for inspection by workers so that they would be aware of their rights. It also required employers to report to the regulators any accident resulting in an injury.

When this legislation was passed, responsibility for its enforcement was transferred from the provincial department of mines and energy to the department of labour. Inspectors also retained jurisdiction over the *Coal Mines Regulation Act*. Both *Acts* authorized inspectors to order a work stoppage and the *Coal Mines Regulation Act*, under section 64, specifically empowered an inspector to order a dangerous mine closed.

A Day in the Life[1]

The continuous miner roared, cutting coal from the face of the mine and loading it into shuttle cars for transport to a conveyor belt. A huge machine, it allowed previously unheard of quantities of coal to be mined in a day. Pictou miners knew it was a far cry from the pick and shovels of their grandfather's mines and the explosives of their father's mines. The men at work that day were the usual mixed bag of experienced miners and untried "newbies." Like most days at Westray, even those with underground experience had gained it in hard rock mines, not coal mines. There were simply not enough certified coal minters in the area to fill the jobs. Claude White had granted the company an exemption under the *Coal Mines Regulation Act* to use hard rock miners in their place. Lenny Bonner and Shaun Comish were old friends and veterans of hard rock mining. They had been hired together and their pit talk this morning centred on a recent accident in the mine. A young kid, Matthew Sears, had his leg crushed when he tried to replace a roller on the conveyor belt. As he stood on the belt, it started up without the usual warning and his leg was jammed in a large roller. The men in the mine at the time had reported that Ralph Melanson kept pulling the safety cable to stop the belt, but it kept restarting. Sears had been through five operations since the accident and would be months off work. "Poor kid," said one to the other, "he told me that his first day on the job he didn't even know how to turn his lamp on." Roger Parry had sent him down alone to meet his crew and he'd stood there, shocked by how dark it was.

[1]All events described in this section are based on the sworn testimony of miners and other witnesses to the Commission of Inquiry. They are told here as if they happened on one workday. Except for this change in chronology they are an accurate depiction of work underground at Westray as described by the parties.

Both Bonner and Comish recalled their first day at Westray. Without any orientation, they'd been issued their self-rescuers and sent underground. At the time they had laughed because neither of them understood most of what Roger Parry said to them. Between his British accent and his wad of chewing tobacco, all meaning was lost. Both men had progressed quickly underground from installing arches on the roadway and roof supports in the rooms being mined to operating equipment—drills, the bolter, the shuttle car. Neither had received any specific instruction. As Comish put it, "I got on it and [he] showed me what levers to move and what was your brake and what was your throttle and away you go." He recalled with some nostalgia the mine in Ontario where he had learned to drive a scoop tram in a designated training are, away from production. Both men knew that at Westray, the more equipment a miner could operate, the higher his pay.

The continuous miner had come to a stop. This meant the methanometer or "sniffer" had detected too much gas. Comish pressed the reset button a few times to no effect. Bonner was running the shuttle car and waited. Comish overpowered the trip switch and kept filling the shuttle car. He disliked overriding a safety measure that was really for his own protection but he'd been shown how to do it and he understood what was expected. The mine's bonus system was simple: more coal meant more money. As he did every four days when he was back underground, Comish thought about quitting; he thought again about the roof over his family's heads and the food on their plates, sighed and got back to work. Some days, there was no need to override the sniffer. Comish recalled working in the Southwest section of the mine one shift when the methanometer wasn't working. Comish had turned to Donnie Dooley and joked, "If we get killed, I'll never speak to you again." Despite the jokes and the camaraderie, Comish couldn't escape the feeling that things weren't quite right. He decided that this day he just didn't want to be in the mine. He planned to tell his supervisor that he had to leave at five to get his car fixed—a harmless white lie.

Some of the men underground that day wondered when Eugene Johnson would be back from Montréal. His name had been selected from a draw to go to a ceremony where the industry association would give out the John T. Ryan award honouring Westray as the safest coal mine in Canada. The award was based on reported accident statistics. Johnson and his wife were scheduled to see a National Hockey League game along with Clifford Frame and his wife. The men were sure he'd have some stories from his trip.

Bonner asked Comish if Wayne Cheverie was underground that day. Neither could recall seeing him at the beginning of the shift. With no tag system in the deployment area, there was no way of knowing at any given time who or how many people were underground. Lenny Bonner thought back to his time at the Gay's River Mine. The tag system there had been stringently enforced. One day, he'd forgotten to tag out, meaning that his tag was on the board and therefore, he was officially still underground. Although his shift boss had watched him leave the property, he could not remove a miner's tag from the board. Instead, Bonner had driven back, tagged out and his shift boss had been required to wait since he could not leave until all men under his charge were accounted for.

The men were interested in Wayne Cheverie because he had been making a lot of noise about safety lately. Even back in September at the official opening of the mine, he had buttonholed government mine inspector Albert McLean after the ceremonies. Cheverie reported that he had told McLean many of his concerns about roof conditions and the lack of stone dust and asked him point blank if he had the power to shut the mine down. McLean told him no. Cheverie knew the outcome for other miners who had complained—harassment and intimidation. However, it was well known among the men that Cheverie was coming to the end of his rope. He was not only talking about complaining to the department of labour, but he was also threatening to go to the media. Recently, after refusing work, Cheverie had been told by Arnie Smith, his direct supervisor, that if he left the mine, he'd be fired. His response, "Fired or dead, Arnie, that's not much of a choice, is it?" Bonner understood how Cheverie felt. A chunk of the mine's roof had fallen on his head one day. Bonner had gone home with a sore leg and back and an egg on his head. He'd had to fight with management to get paid for the day. Roger Parry had said, "We don't pay people for going home sick." Bonner had replied, "If you call the roof coming in and chunks of coal hitting you on the head and the back and almost killing you, you call that 'going home sick'!" Eventually he had been paid for the shift. He reflected that at least he was better off than that poor kid Todd MacDonald. On MacDonald's first day of work, there'd been a roof fall and the kid had been buried up to his waist. He was flat on his back, facing the roof, as if he'd watched it fall instead of running the hell out of there.

Bonner and Comish and a few of the other men stopped work for a quick and belated break. They often didn't get to their lunches until after their shifts. Bonner sat down with his lunch pail but jumped up again quickly. He had picked a spot too close to a pile of human waste but in the dark had not noticed it until the stink hit him. Back when he'd first started work at the mine, Bonner had spoken to mine manager Gerald Phillips about installing underground toilets. Phillips had told him that he was considering a number of different models. In the meantime, Bonner felt demeaned, like an animal forced to crouch on the ground like a dog. As it turned out, their lunch break was short-lived anyway. Shaun Comish had warned the others that he saw a light approaching and the men had scattered like rats, fearing that Roger Parry was on his way down. With his usual profanities he would send them back to work.

Disaster

Within minutes of the explosion neighbours and family members began to gather at the mine site. Within hours, local, national and international media had set up equipment and reporters in the community centre that served as their hub. Family members, in an arena directly across from the centre, where they awaited news of their loved ones, resented the prying cameras and intrusive questions. For six days they waited, they cried, they drank coffee, they smoked cigarettes, and comforted their children and each other with hopes of a triumphant rescue.

Family and community, producers and reporters, along with viewers everywhere grew to know Colin Benner as the "face of Westray." He had been appointed to the position of president of operations in April and had been responsible for the Westray Mine less than one month when it blew up. He had just barely begun the processes that he hoped would help dig Westray out of its financial hole. Production was short, with the mine failing to provide the 60,000 tons a month to Nova Scotia Power for which it had contracted. Sales in the previous six months had reached $7.3 million but costs had exceeded $13 million. Benner had also heard rumblings about safety, about discontent among the miners and about the heavy-handed techniques of Gerald Phillips and Roger Parry.

All this however, was put aside as he dealt with the crisis. He served as media liaison, updating on the progress of the rescue efforts. By the sixth day he was showing the strain and it was with obvious sorrow on May 14th that he announced the search was being discontinued as their was no hope that anyone could have survived the blast. It was simply too dangerous for the rescue crews to continue.

Search for Truth

On May 15th, just the day after Colin Benner had announced that the search for the miners had been suspended, Premier Donald Cameron appointed Justice Peter Richard to a commission of inquiry into the explosion. His terms of reference were broad and mandated him to look into all aspects of the establishment, management, and regulation of the Westray Mine. They specifically empowered the Inquiry to determine if any "neglect had caused or contributed to the occurrence" and if the events could have been prevented. A tangled web of legal proceedings held up the inquiry for more than three years. In that time both provincial charges and criminal charges were laid, then withdrawn, against the company and its managers. The inquiry heard its first testimony on November 6th, 1995. Justice Richard also undertook substantial studies on coal mining and mine safety to prepare for the task. He visited mines in Canada and the United States and consulted with experts in South Africa, Great Britain and Australia. He commissioned technical reports from six experts in subjects that included mining ventilation and geotechnology. He commissioned academic studies in history, economics, psychology and political science. These reports provided him with insight into the history of mining in Pictou, the multiplier effect of large-scale employment on the communities, the impact of production bonuses on miners' behaviour and the role of ministerial responsibility in the public sector. The Inquiry heard 71 witnesses in 76 days of testimony and produced 16,815 pages of transcripts; it entered 1579 exhibits into evidence after examining 800 boxes of documents. The total cost of the inquiry was nearly $5 million.

Justice Richard's findings are contained in a three-volume, 750-page report entitled, "The Westray Story: A Predictable Path to Disaster." He released his report on December 1st, 1997. His key conclusion was that the explosion was both predictable and preventable. He acknowledged the 20/20 vision that accompanies hindsight but in specific, detailed, and readable prose he isolated the many factors that contributed to an explosion that cost 26 men their lives, left over 20 women widows and over 40 children fatherless. He set the tone of his report by quoting the French sociologist and inspector general of mines, Frederic Le Play (1806-1882) who said, "The most important thing to come out of a mine is the miner." Justice Richard, in the preface to his report, noted that "the *Westray Story* is a complex mosaic of actions, omissions, mistakes, incompetence, apathy, cynicism, stupidity, and neglect." He noted with some dismay the overzealous political sponsorship of Westray's start-up but he clearly implicated management as the entity most responsible through its arrogance, its lack of training, its tacit and overt support of unsafe practices, and its production bonus system. Only Colin Benner and Graham Clow, the mining engineer consultant, were singled out for praise. Each had attended the inquiry without subpoena and at his own expense. They were the only Curragh executives to testify. Benner, in particular, offered key testimony on his plans for the mine. He had struck a Mine Planning Task Force to address the safety and production problems in the mine. His goal had been to design a safe and achievable mine plan that incorporated human relations and mutual respect among workers and managers. His plans had been cut short by the explosion. Justice Richard also noted the many failures of the provincial inspectorate, describing it as "markedly derelict." He singled out inspector Albert McLean for his incompe-

tence and lack of diligence, but did not spare his supervisors, to whom McLean's failings should have been obvious. Finally, he vindicated Carl Guptill. He concluded that McLean's treatment of him was a "disservice to a miner with legitimate complaints."

Epilogue

In 1993, a review by Coopers and Lybrand of Nova Scotia's labour department's management and practices unit recommended sweeping changes to the department which included staff training, development, and performance reviews. In 1997, a revised *Occupational Health and Safety Act* became law. In 1995 all criminal charges against Westray and mine officials were stayed for procedural reasons. In 1998, in embarrassed response to the findings of the Commission of Inquiry, the Canadian Institute of Mining, Metallurgy and Petroleum (CIM) rescinded the John T. Ryan award for safety, presented to the late Eugene Johnson on behalf of Westray on the eve of the explosion. In 1999 the federal leader of the NDP introduced a private member's bill in the House of Commons to amend the *Criminal Code* to hold corporations, executives and directors liable for workplace deaths. The bill died on the order paper after an election call. In 2001 the Nova Scotia Court of Appeal denied the Westray Families Group the right to sue the provincial government, concluding that such a lawsuit contravened provincial workers' compensation legislation. This was upheld in 2002 by the Supreme Court of Canada. In May of 2002, ten years after the explosion and despite all lobbying and legislative efforts, Parliament was still considering the issue of corporate criminal liability.

Albert McLean and others were fired from their positions in the department of labour. Donald Cameron won a provincial election in 1993 but was defeated in 1998. Shortly thereafter he accepted a posting in Boston as Consul General to the United States. It was reported that Gerald Phillips had been charged with attempted homicide in Honduras as a result of an injury to a young man caught up in a protest to prevent a mine operation that threatened his village. A Vancouver-based mining company subsequently hired Phillips in 1998. Although Curragh Resources dissolved into bankruptcy as a result of the explosion,

Clifford Frame continued to attract investors and at last report was continuing to develop mines. Roger Parry was last known to be driving a bus in Alberta. Many miners left Pictou County and looked for work in western and northern Canada. Carl Guptill operates an aquaculture business on Nova Scotia's eastern shore. Some of the "Westray widows" have moved, remarried, and rebuilt their lives while others remain frozen in loss. The bodies of 11 miners remain underground.

Sources

Jobb, D. (1994). *Calculated Risk: Greed, Politics and the Westray Tragedy.* Halifax, Nimbus.

Richard, J.K.P. (1997) *The Westray Story: A predictable path to disaster: Report of the Westray Mine Public Inquiry.* Halifax, Province of Nova Scotia.

Transcripts of the Westray Mine Public Inquiry Commission. Indexed at http://alts.net/ns1625/950013index.html

Wilde, G. (1997) *Risk awareness and risk acceptance at the Westray coal mine.* Report to the Westray Mine Public Inquiry

Theory Building and Systematic Research Methods

People need to make sense of their world, so they form theories about the way the world operates. A **theory** is a general set of propositions that describes interrelationships among several concepts. We form theories for the purpose of predicting and explaining the world around us.[1] What does a good theory look like? First, it should be stated as clearly and simply as possible so that the concepts can be measured and there is no ambiguity about the theory's propositions. Second, the elements of the theory must be logically consistent with each other, because we cannot test anything that doesn't make sense. Finally, a good theory provides value to society; it helps people understand their world better than they could have without the theory.[2]

Theory building is a continuous process that typically includes the inductive and deductive stages shown in Exhibit A.1.[3] The inductive stage draws on personal experience to form a preliminary theory, and the deductive stage uses the scientific method to test the theory.

The inductive stage of theory building involves observing the world around us, identifying a pattern of relationships, and then forming a theory from these personal observations. For example, you might casually notice that new employees want their supervisor to give direction, whereas this leadership style irritates long-service employees. From these observations, you form a theory about the effectiveness of directive leadership. (See Chapter 14 for a discussion of this leadership style.)

Positivism Versus Interpretivism

Research requires an interpretation of reality, and researchers tend to perceive reality in one of two ways. A common view, called **positivism**, is that reality exists independent of people. It is "out there" to be discovered and tested. Positivism is the foundation for most quantitative research (statistical analysis). It assumes that we can measure variables and that these variables have fixed relationships with other vari-

EXHIBIT A.1

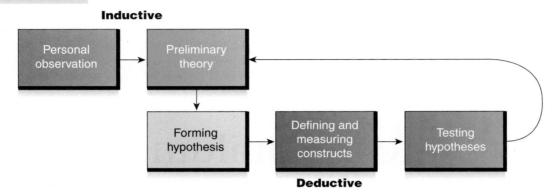

ables. For example, the positivist perspective says that we could study whether a supportive style of leadership reduces stress, and if we find evidence of it, then someone else studying leadership and stress would "discover" the same relationship.

Interpretivism takes a different view of reality. It suggests that reality comes from shared meaning among people in that environment. For example, supportive leadership is a personal interpretation of reality, not something that can be measured across time and people. Interpretivists rely mainly on qualitative data, such as observation and nondirective interviews. They particularly listen to the language people use to understand the common meaning that people give toward various events or phenomena. For example, they might argue that you need to experience and observe supportive leadership to effectively study it; moreover, you can't really predict relationships because the specific situation shapes reality.[4]

Most OB scholars identify themselves somewhere between the extreme views of positivism and interpretivism. Many believe that inductive research should begin from an interpretivist angle. We should enter a new topic with an open mind and search for the shared meaning of people in that situation. In other words, researchers should let the participants define reality rather than let the researcher's preconceived notions shape that reality. This process involves gathering qualitative information and

letting this information shape their theory.[5] After the theory emerges, researchers shift to a positivist perspective by quantitatively testing relationships with that theory.

Theory Testing: The Deductive Process

Once a theory has been formed, we shift into the deductive stage of theory building. This process includes forming hypotheses, defining and measuring constructs, and testing hypotheses (see Exhibit A.1). **Hypotheses** make empirically testable declarations that certain variables and their corresponding measures are related in a specific way proposed by the theory. For instance, to find support for the directive leadership theory described earlier, we need to form and then test a specific hypothesis from that theory. One such hypothesis might be: "New employees are more satisfied with supervisors who exhibit a directive rather than nondirective leadership style." Hypotheses are indispensable tools of scientific research, because they provide the vital link between the theory and its empirical verification.

Defining and measuring constructs   Hypotheses are testable only if we can define and then form measurable indicators of the concepts stated in those hypotheses. Consider the hypothesis in the previous paragraph about new employees and directive leadership. To test this hypothesis, we first need to define the concepts, such as "new employees," "directive leadership," and "supervisor." These are known as **constructs**, because they are abstract ideas constructed by the researcher that can be linked to observable information. Organizational behaviour scholars developed the construct called *directive leadership* to help them understand the different effects that leaders have on followers. We can't directly see, taste, or smell directive leadership; we rely instead on indirect indicators that it exists, such as observing someone giving directions, maintaining clear performance standards, and ensuring that procedures and practices are followed.

As you can see, defining constructs well is very important, because these definitions become the foundation for finding or developing acceptable measures of those constructs. We can't measure directive leadership if we only have a vague idea about what this concept means. The better the definition is, the better our chances are of applying a measure that adequately represents that construct. However, even with a good definition, constructs can be difficult to measure, because the empirical representation must capture several elements of the definition. A measure of directive leadership must be able to identify not only people who give directions, but also those who maintain performance standards and ensure that procedures are followed.

Testing hypotheses The third step in the deductive process is to collect data for the empirical measures of the variables. Following our directive leadership example, we might conduct a formal survey in which new employees describe the behaviour of their supervisors and their attitudes toward their supervisor. Alternatively, we might design an experiment in which people work with someone who applies either a directive or nondirective leadership style. When the data have been collected, we can use various procedures to statistically test our hypotheses.

A major concern in theory building is that some researchers might inadvertently find support for their theory simply because they use the same information used to form the theory during the inductive stage. Consequently, the deductive stage must collect new data that are completely independent of the data used during the inductive stage. For instance, you might decide to test your theory of directive leadership by studying employees in another organization. Moreover, the inductive process may have relied mainly on personal observation, whereas the deductive process might use survey questionnaires. By studying different samples and using different measurement tools, we minimize the risk of conducting circular research.

Using the Scientific Method

Earlier, we said that the deductive stage of theory building follows the scientific method. The **scientific method** is the systematic, controlled, empirical, and critical investigation of hypothetical propositions about the presumed relationships among natural phenomena.[6] There are several elements to this definition, so let's look at each one. First, scientific research is systematic and controlled because researchers want to rule out all but one explanation for a set of interrelated events. To rule out alternative explanations, we need to control them in some way, such as by keeping them constant or removing them entirely from the environment.

Second, we say that scientific research is empirical because researchers need to use objective reality—or as close as they can get to it—to test theory. They measure observable elements of the environment, such as what a person says or does, rather than relying on their own subjective opinion to draw conclusions. Moreover, scientific research analyzes these data using acceptable principles of mathematics and logic.

Finally, scientific research involves critical investigation. This means that the study's hypotheses, data, methods, and results are openly described so that other experts in the field can properly evaluate this research. It also means that scholars are encouraged to critique and build on previous research. Eventually, the scientific method encourages the refinement and eventually the replacement of one theory with another that better suits our understanding of the world.

Grounded Theory: An Alternative Approach

The scientific method dominates the positivist approach to systematic research, but another approach, called **grounded theory**, dominates research when qualitative methods are used.[7] Grounded theory is a process of developing knowledge through the constant interplay of data collection, analysis, and theory development. It relies mainly on qualitative methods to form categories and variables, analyze relationships among these concepts, and form a model based on that observations and analysis. Grounded theory combines the inductive stages of theory development by cycling back and forth between data collection and analysis to converge into a robust explanatory model. This ongoing reciprocal process results in theory that is grounded in the data (thus the name, grounded theory).

Like the scientific method, grounded theory is a systematic and rigorous process of data collection and analysis. It requires specific steps and documentation, and adopts a positivist view by assuming that the results can be generalized to other settings. However, grounded theory also takes an interpretivist view by building categories and variables from the perceived realities of the subjects rather than from an assumed universal truth.[8] It also recognizes that personal biases are not easily removed from the research process.

Selected Issues in Organizational Behaviour Research

There are many issues to consider in theory building, particularly when we use the deductive process to test hypotheses. Some of the more important issues are sampling, causation, and ethical practices in organizational research.

Sampling in Organizational Research   When finding out why things happen in organizations, we typically gather information from a few sources and then draw conclusions about the larger population. If we survey several employees and find out that older employees are more loyal to their company, then we would like to generalize this statement to all older employees in our population, not just those whom we surveyed. Scientific inquiry generally requires researchers to engage in **representative sampling**—that is, sampling a population in such a way that we can extrapolate the results of that sample to the larger population.

One factor that influences representativeness is whether the sample is selected in an unbiased way from the larger population. Let's suppose you want to study organizational commitment among employees in your organization. A casual procedure might result in sampling too few employees from the head office and too many located elsewhere in the country. If head office employees actually are more loyal than employees located elsewhere, then the biased sampling would cause the results to underestimate the true level of loyalty among employees in the company. If you repeat the process again next year, but somehow overweight employees from the head office, the results might wrongly suggest that employees have increased their organizational commitment over the past year, when in reality, the only change may be the direction of sampling bias.

How do we minimize sampling bias? The answer is to randomly select the sample. A randomly drawn sample gives each member of the population an equal probability of being chosen, so it is less likely that a subgroup within that population would dominate the study's results.

The same principle applies to randomly assigning subjects to groups in experimental designs. If we want to test the effects of a team development training program, we need to randomly place some employees in the training group and randomly place others in a group that does not receive training. Without this random selection, each group might have different types of employees, so we wouldn't know whether it is the training explains the differences between the two groups. Moreover, if employees respond differently to the training program, we couldn't be sure that the training program results are representative of the larger population. Of course, random sampling does not necessarily produce a perfectly representative sample, but we do know that this is the best approach to ensure unbiased selection.

The other factor that influences representativeness is sample size. Whenever we select a portion of the population, there will be some error in our estimate of the population values. The larger the sample, the less error will occur in our estimate. Let's suppose you want to find out how employees in a 500-person firm feel about smoking in the workplace. If you asked 400 of those employees, the information would provide a very good estimate of how the entire work force in that organization feels. If you survey only 100 employees, the estimate might deviate more from the true population. If you ask only 10 people, the estimate could be quite different from what all 500 employees feel.

Notice that sample size goes hand in hand with random selection. You must have a sufficiently large sample size for the principle of randomization to work effectively. In our example of attitudes toward smoking, a random selection would have little value if our sample consisted of only 10 employees from the 500-person organization. The reason is that these 10 people probably wouldn't capture the diversity of employees throughout the organization. In fact, the more diverse the population, the larger the sample size should be, to provide adequate representation through random selection.

Causation in Organizational Research   Theories present notions about relationships among constructs. Often, these propositions suggest a causal relationship, namely, that one variable has an effect on another variable. When discussing causation, we refer to variables as being independent or dependent. Independent variables are the presumed causes of dependent variables, which are the presumed effects. In our earlier example of directive leadership, the main independent variable (there might be others) would be the supervisor's directive or nondirective leadership style, because we presume that it causes the dependent variable (satisfaction with supervision).

In laboratory experiments (described later), the independent variable is always manipulated by the experimenter. In our research on directive leadership, we might have subjects (new employees) work with supervisors who exhibit directive or nondirective leadership behaviours.

If subjects are more satisfied under the directive leaders, then we would be able to infer an association between the independent and dependent variables.

Researchers must satisfy three conditions to provide sufficient evidence of causality between two variables.[9] The first condition of causality is that the variables are empirically associated with each other. An association exists whenever one measure of a variable changes systematically with a measure of another variable. This condition of causality is the easiest to satisfy, because there are several well-known statistical measures of association. A research study might find, for instance, that heterogeneous groups (in which members come from diverse backgrounds) produce more creative solutions to problems. This might be apparent because the measure of creativity (such as number of creative solutions produced within a fixed time) is higher for teams that have a high score on the measure of group heterogeneity. They are statistically associated or correlated with each other.

The second condition of causality is that the independent variable precedes the dependent variable in time. Sometimes, this condition is satisfied through simple logic. In our group heterogeneity example, it doesn't make sense to say that the number of creative solutions caused the group's heterogeneity, because the group's heterogeneity existed before it produced the creative solutions. In other situations, however, the temporal relationship among variables is less clear. One example is the ongoing debate about job satisfaction and organizational commitment. Do companies develop more loyal employees by increasing their job satisfaction, or do changes in organizational loyalty cause changes in job satisfaction? Simple logic does not answer these questions; instead, researchers must use sophisticated longitudinal studies to build up evidence of a temporal relationship between these two variables.

The third requirement for evidence of a causal relationship is that the statistical association between two variables cannot be explained by a third variable. There are many associations that are obviously not causally related. For example, there is a statistical association between the number of storks in an area and the birth rate in that area. We know that storks don't bring babies, so something else must be causing the association between these two variables. The real explanation is that there is a higher incidence of both storks and birth rates in rural areas.

In other studies, the third variable effect is less apparent. Many years ago, before polio vaccines were available, a study in the United States reported a surprisingly strong association between consumption of a certain soft drink and the incidence of polio. Was polio caused by drinking this pop, or did people with polio have a unusual craving for this beverage? Neither. Both polio and consumption of the pop drink were caused by a third variable: climate. There was a higher incidence of polio in the summer months and in warmer climates, and people drink more liquids in these climates.[10] As you can see from this example, researchers have a difficult time supporting causal inferences, because third variable effects are sometimes difficult to detect.

Ethics in Organizational Research   Organizational behaviour researchers need to abide by the ethical standards of the society in which the research is conducted. One of the most important ethical considerations is the individual subject's freedom to participate in the study. For example, it is inappropriate to force employees to fill out a questionnaire or attend an experimental intervention for research purposes only. Moreover, researchers have an obligation to tell potential subjects about any potential risks inherent in the study so that participants can make an informed choice about whether or not to be involved.

Finally, researchers must be careful to protect the privacy of those who participate in the study. This usually includes letting people know when they are being studied as well as guaranteeing that their individual information will remain confidential (unless permission to publish identities is otherwise granted). Researchers maintain anonymity through careful security of data. The research results usually aggregate data in numbers large enough that they do not reveal the opinions or characteristics of any specific individual. For example, we would report the average absenteeism of employees in a department rather than state the absence rates of each person. When sharing data with other researchers, it is usually necessary to specially code each case so that individual identities are not known.

Research Design Strategies

So far, we have described how to build a theory, including the specific elements of empirically testing that theory within the standards of scientific inquiry. But what are the different ways of designing a research study so that we get the data necessary to achieve our research objectives? There are many strategies, but they mainly fall under three headings: laboratory experiments, field surveys, and observational research.

Laboratory Experiments

A **laboratory experiment** is any research study in which independent variables and variables outside the researcher's main focus of inquiry can be controlled to some extent. Laboratory experiments are usually located outside the everyday work environment, such as a classroom, simulation lab, or any other artificial setting in which the researcher can manipulate the environment. Organizational behaviour researchers sometimes conduct experiments in the workplace (called *field experiments*) in which the independent variable is manipulated. However, the researcher has less control over the effects of extraneous factors in field experiments than in laboratory situations.

Advantages of laboratory experiments   There are many advantages of laboratory experiments. By definition, this research method offers a high degree of control over extraneous variables that would otherwise confound the relationships being studied. Suppose we wanted to test the effects of directive leadership on the satisfaction of new employees. One concern might be that employees are influenced by how much leadership is provided, not just the type of leadership style. An experimental design would allow us to control how often the supervisor exhibited this style so that this extraneous variable does not confound the results.

A second advantage of lab studies is that the independent and dependent variables can be developed more precisely than in a field setting. For example, the researcher can ensure that supervisors in a lab study apply specific directive or nondirective behaviours, whereas real-life supervisors would use a more complex mixture of leadership behaviours. By using more precise measures, we are more certain that we are measuring the intended construct. Thus, if new employees are more satisfied with supervisors in the directive leadership condition, we are more confident that the independent variable was directive leadership rather than some other leadership style.

A third benefit of laboratory experiments is that the independent variable can be distributed more evenly among participants. In our directive leadership study, we can ensure that approximately half of the subjects have a directive supervisor, whereas the other half have a nondirective supervisor. In natural settings, we might have trouble finding people who have worked with a nondirective leader and, consequently, we couldn't determine the effects of this condition.

Disadvantages of laboratory experiments
With these powerful advantages, you might wonder why laboratory experiments are the least appreciated form of organizational behaviour research.[11] One obvious limitation of this research method is that it lacks realism and, consequently, the results might be different in the real world. One argument is that laboratory experiment subjects are less involved than their counterparts in an actual work situation. This is sometimes true, although many lab studies have highly motivated participants. Another criticism is that the extraneous variables controlled in the lab setting might produce a different effect of the independent variable on the dependent variables. This might also be true, but remember that the experimental design controls variables in accordance with the theory and its hypotheses. Consequently, this concern is really a critique of the theory, not the lab study.

Finally, there is the well-known problem that participants are aware they are being studied and this causes them to act differently than they normally would. Some participants try to figure out how the researcher wants them to behave and then deliberately try to act that way. Other participants try to upset the experiment by doing just the opposite of what they believe the researcher expects. Still others might act unnaturally simply because they know they are being observed. Fortunately, experimenters are well aware of these potential problems and are usually (although not always) successful at disguising the study's true intent.

Field Surveys

Field surveys collect and analyze information in a natural environment—an office, factory, or other existing location. The researcher takes a snapshot of reality and tries to determine whether elements of that situation (including the attitudes and behaviours of people in that situation) are associated with each other as hypothesized. Everyone does some sort of field research. You might think that people from some provinces are better drivers than others, so you "test" your theory by looking at the way people with out-of-province license plates drive. Although your methods of data collection might not satisfy scientific standards, this is a form of field research because it takes information from a naturally occurring situation.

Advantages and disadvantages of field surveys   One advantage of field surveys is that the variables often have a more powerful effect than they would in a laboratory experiment. Consider the effect of peer pressure on the behaviour of members within the team. In a natural environment, team members would form very strong cohesive bonds over time, whereas a researcher would have difficulty replicating this level of cohesiveness and corresponding peer pressure in a lab setting.

Another advantage of field surveys is that the researcher can study many variables simultaneously, thereby permitting a fuller test of more complex theories. Ironically, this is also a disadvantage of field surveys, because it is difficult for the researcher to contain his or her scientific inquiry. There is a tendency to shift from deductive hypothesis testing to more inductive exploratory browsing through the data. If these two activities become mixed together, the researcher can lose sight of the strict covenants of scientific inquiry.

The main weakness with field surveys is that it is very difficult to satisfy the conditions for causal conclusions. One reason is that the data are usually collected at one time, so the researcher must rely on logic to decide whether the independent variable really preceded the dependent variable. Contrast this with the lab study in which the researcher can usually be confident that the independent variable was applied before the dependent variable occurred. Increasingly, organizational behaviour studies use longitudinal research to provide a better indicator of temporal relations among variables, but this is still not as precise as the lab setting. Another reason why causal analysis is difficult in field surveys is that extraneous variables are not controlled as they are in lab studies. Without this control, there is a higher chance that a third variable might explain the relationship between the hypothesized independent and dependent variables.

Observational Research

In their study of brainstorming and creativity, Robert Sutton and Andrew Hargadon observed 24 brainstorming sessions at IDEO, a product design firm in Palo Alto, California. They also attended a dozen "Monday morning meetings," conducted 60 semi-structured interviews with IDEO executives and designers, held hundreds of informal discussions with these people, and read through several dozen magazine articles about the company.[12]

Sutton's and Hargadon's use of observational research and other qualitative methods was quite appropriate for their research objectives, which were to re-examine the effectiveness of brainstorming beyond the number of ideas generated. Observational research generates a wealth of descriptive accounts about the drama of human existence in organizations. It is a useful vehicle for learning about the complex dynamics of people and their activities, such as brainstorming. (The results of Sutton and Hargadon's study are discussed in Chapter 10.)

Participant observation takes the observation method one step further by having the observer take part in the organization's activities. This experience gives the researcher a fuller understanding of the activities compared to just watching others participate in those activities.

In spite of its intuitive appeal, observational research has a number of weaknesses. The main problem is that the observer is subject to the perceptual screening and organizing biases that we discuss in Chapter 3 of this textbook. There is a tendency to overlook the routine aspects of organizational life, even though they may prove to be the most important data for research purposes. Instead, observers tend to focus on unusual information, such as activities that deviate from what the observer expects. Because observational research usually records only what the observer notices, valuable information is often lost.

Another concern with the observation method is that the researcher's presence and involvement may influence the people whom he or she is studying. This can be a problem in short-term observations, but in the long term people tend to return to their usual behaviour patterns. With ongoing observations, such as Sutton and Hargadon's study of brainstorming sessions at IDEO, employees eventually forget that they are being studied.

Finally, observation is usually a qualitative process, so it is more difficult to empirically test hypotheses with the data. Instead, observational research provides rich information for the inductive stages of theory building. It helps us to form ideas about the way things work in organizations. We begin to see relationships that lay the foundation for new perspectives and theory. We must not confuse this inductive process of theory building with the deductive process of theory testing.

B

Scoring Keys for Self-Assessment Exercises

The following pages provide scoring keys for self-assessments that are fully presented in this textbook. Other self-assessments summarized in this book are scored on the student CD.

CHAPTER 2
Scoring Key for Self-Monitoring Scale

Scoring Instructions: Use the table below to assign numbers to each box you checked. Insert the number for each statement on the appropriate line below the table. For example, if you checked "Somewhat false" for statement #1 ("In social situations, I have the ability…"), you would write a "2" on the line with "(1)" underneath it. After assigning numbers for all 12 statements, add up your scores to estimate your affective and continuance school commitment.

For statement items 1, 2, 3, 4, 5, 6, 7, 8, 10, 11, 13		For statement items 9, 12	
Very true	= 6	Very true	= 1
Somewhat true	= 5	Somewhat true	= 2
Slightly more true than false	= 4	Slightly more true than false	= 3
Slightly more false than true	= 3	Slightly more false than true	= 4
Somewhat false	= 2	Somewhat false	= 5
Very false	= 1	Very false	= 6

Sensitive to Expressive Behaviour of Others

$$\underset{(2)}{\_\_\_} + \underset{(4)}{\_\_\_} + \underset{(5)}{\_\_\_} + \underset{(6)}{\_\_\_} + \underset{(8)}{\_\_\_} + \underset{(11)}{\_\_\_} = \underset{(A)}{\_\_\_}$$

Ability to Modify Self-presentation

$$\underset{(1)}{\_\_\_} + \underset{(3)}{\_\_\_} + \underset{(7)}{\_\_\_} + \underset{(9)}{\_\_\_} + \underset{(10)}{\_\_\_} + \underset{(12)}{\_\_\_} + \underset{(13)}{\_\_\_} = \underset{(B)}{\_\_\_}$$

Self-monitoring Total Score

$$\underset{(A)}{\_\_\_} + \underset{(B)}{\_\_\_} = \underset{Total}{\_\_\_}$$

Interpreting your Score: Self-monitoring consists of two dimensions: (a) sensitivity to expressive behaviour of others and (b) ability to modify self-presentation. These two dimensions as well as the total score are defined in the following table, along with the range of scores for high, medium, and low levels of each scale.

Self-monitoring Dimension and Definition	Score Interpretation
Sensitive to Expressive Behaviour of Others: This scale indicates the extent that you are aware of the feelings and perceptions of others, as expressed by their facial expressions, subtle statements, and other behaviours.	High: 25–36 Medium: 18–24 Low: Below 18

Self-monitoring Dimension and Definition	Score Interpretation
Ability to Modify Self-presentation: This scale indicates the extent to which you are adept at modifying your behaviour in a way that is most appropriate for the situation or social relationship.	High: 30–42 Medium: 21–29 Low: Below 21
Self-monitoring Total: Self-monitoring refers to an individual's level of sensitivity to the expressive behaviour of others and the ability to adapt appropriately to these situational cues.	High: 55–78 Medium: 39–54 Low: Below 39

CHAPTER 3
Scoring Key for Assessing Your General Self-Efficacy

Scoring Instructions: To calculate your score on the new general self-efficacy scale, use the following guideline to assign numbers to each box you checked: Strongly agree = 5; Agree = 4; Neutral = 3; Disagree = 2; Strongly disagree = 1. Then add up the numbers to determine your total score.

Interpreting your Score: Self-efficacy refers to a person's belief that he or she has the ability, motivation, and resources to complete a task successfully. This particular scale is called a "general" self-efficacy scale because it estimates a person's self-efficacy in a broad range of situations. The average general self-efficacy score varies from one group of people to the next. For example, managers tend to have a somewhat higher general self-efficacy than young undergraduate psychology students. The following table allows you to compare your general efficacy score to the range of scores among undergraduate psychology students in the United States (77% female; average age = 23).

General Self-efficacy	
Score	**Interpretation**
Above 34	High level of general self-efficacy
32–34	Above average level of general self-efficacy
28–31	Average level of general self-efficacy
24–27	Below average level of general self-efficacy
Below 24	Low level of general self-efficacy

CHAPTER 4
Scoring Key for School Commitment Scale

Scoring Instructions: Use the table below to assign numbers to each box you checked. Insert the number for each statement on the appropriate line below the table. For example, if you checked "Moderately disagree" for statement #1 ("I would be very happy…"), you would write a "2" on the line with "(1)" underneath it. After assigning numbers for all 12 statements, add up your scores to estimate your affective and continuance school commitment.

For statement items 1, 2, 3, 4, 6, 8, 10, 11, 12	For statements items 5, 7, 9
Strongly agree = 7	Strongly agree = 1
Moderately agree = 6	Moderately agree = 2
Slightly agree = 5	Slightly agree = 3
Neutral = 4	Neutral = 4
Slightly disagree = 3	Slightly disagree = 5
Moderately disagree = 2	Moderately disagree = 6
Strongly disagree = 1	Strongly disagree = 7

Affective Commitment ____ + ____ + ____ + ____ + ____ + ____ = _____
                          (1)   (3)   (5)   (7)   (9)   (11)

Continuance Commitment ____ + ____ + ____ + ____ + ____ + ____ = _____
                           (2)   (4)   (6)   (8)   (10)   (12)

Interpreting your Affective Commitment Score: This scale measures both affective commitment and continuance commitment. Affective commitment refers to a person's emotional attachment to, identification with, and involvement in a particular organization. In this scale, the organization is the school where you are a student. How high or low is your affective commitment? The ideal would be to compare your score with the collective results of other students in your class. You can also compare your score with the following results, which are based on a sample of Canadian employees.

Affective Commitment	
Score	**Interpretation**
Above 37	High level of affective commitment
32–36	Above average level of affective commitment
28–31	Average level of affective commitment
20–27	Below average level of affective commitment
Below 20	Low level of affective commitment

Interpreting your Continuance Commitment Score: Continuance commitment occurs when employees believe it is in their interest to stay with the organization. People with a high continuance commitment have a strong calculative bond with the organization. In this scale, the organization is the school where you are a student. How high or low is your continuance commitment? The ideal would be to compare your score with the collective results of other students in your class. You could also compare your score with the following results, which are based on a sample of Canadian employees.

Continuance Commitment	
Score	Interpretation
Above 32	High level of continuance commitment
26–31	Above average level of continuance commitment
21–25	Average level of continuance commitment
13–20	Below average level of continuance commitment
Below 12	Low level of continuance commitment

CHAPTER 5
Scoring Key for Equity Sensitivity

Scoring Instructions: To score this scale, called the Equity Preference Questionnaire (EPQ), complete the three steps below:

Step 1: Write your circled numbers for the items indicated below and add them up.

$$\underline{} + \underline{} + \underline{} + \underline{} + \underline{} + \underline{} + \underline{} + \underline{} = \underline{}$$
(1)   (2)   (3)   (4)   (5)   (6)   (7)   (10)   Subtotal A

Step 2: The remaining items in the Equity Preference Questionnaire need to be reverse-scored. To calculate a reverse score, subtract the direct score from 6. For example, if you circled 4 in one of these items, the reverse score would be 2 (i.e. 6 − 4 = 2). If you circled 1, the reverse score would be 5 (i.e. 6 − 1 = 5). Calculate the *reverse score* for each of the items indicated below and write them in the space provided. Then calculate Subtotal B by adding up these reverse scores.

$$\underline{} + \underline{} + \underline{} + \underline{} + \underline{} + \underline{} + \underline{} + \underline{} = \underline{}$$
(8)   (9)   (11)   (12)   (13)   (14)   (15)   (16)   Subtotal B

Step 3: Calculate the total score by summing Subtotal A and Subtotal B.

$$\underline{} + \underline{} = \underline{}$$
Subtotal A   Subtotal B   TOTAL

Interpreting your Score: The Equity Preference Questionnaire measures the extent to which you are a "Benevolent," "Equity sensitive," or "Entitled." Generally, people who score as follows fall into one of these categories:

EPQ Score	Equity Preference Category
59–80	Benevolents—are tolerant of situations where they are underrewarded.
38–58	Equity Sensitives—want an outcome/input ratio equal to the ratio of the comparison other.
16–37	Entitleds—want to receive proportionately more than others (i.e. like to be overrewarded).

CHAPTER 6
Scoring Key for the Money Attitude Scale

Scoring Instructions: This instrument presents three dimensions with a smaller set of items from the original Money Attitude Scale. To calculate your score on each dimension, write the number you circled in the scale to the corresponding item number in the scoring key below. For example, write the number you circled in the scale's first statement ("I sometimes purchase things...") on the line above "Item 1." Then add up the numbers for that dimension. The money attitude total score is calculated by adding up all scores and all dimensions.

Money Attitude		
Dimension	Calculation	Your Score
Money as Power/Prestige	____ + ____ + ____ + ____ = ____ Item 1 Item 4 Item 7 Item 10	
Retention Time	____ + ____ + ____ + ____ = ____ Item 2 Item 5 Item 8 Item 11	
Money Anxiety	____ + ____ + ____ + ____ = ____ Item 3 Item 6 Item 9 Item 12	
Money Attitude Total	Add up all dimension scores =	____

Interpreting your Score: The three Money Attitude Scale dimensions measured here, as well as the total score, are defined as follows:
Money as Power/Prestige: People with higher scores on this dimension tend to use money to influence and impress others.

Retention Time: People with higher scores on this dimension tend to be careful financial planners.

Money Anxiety: People with higher scores on this dimension tend to view money as a source of anxiety.

Money Attitude Total: This is a general estimate of how much respect and attention you give to money.

The following table shows how a sample of MBA students scored on the Money Attitude Scale. The table shows percentiles, that is, the percentage of people with the same or lower score. For example, the table indicates that a score of "12" on the retention scale is quite low because only 20 percent of students would have scored at this level or lower (80 percent scored higher). However, a score of "12" on the prestige scale is quite high because 80 percent of students scored at or below this number (only 20 percent scored higher).

Percentile (% with scores at or below this number)	Prestige Score	Retention Score	Anxiety Score	Total Money Score
Average score	9.89	14.98	12.78	37.64
Highest score	17	20	18	53
90	13	18	16	44
80	12	17	15	42
70	11	17	14	40
60	10	16	14	39
50	10	15	13	38
40	9	14	12	36
30	8	14	11	34
20	7	12	10	32
10	7	11	8	29
Lowest score	4	8	6	23

CHAPTER 7
Scoring Key for Time Stress Scale

Scoring Instructions: To estimate how time-stressed you are, add up the number of items where you circled "Yes." Scores range from 0 to 10.

Interpreting your Score: One of the major causes of stress in today's fast-paced life is the lack of time to fulfill our obligations. Severely time-stressed people are constantly under pressure to complete work, don't have enough time in the day, and feel trapped in a daily routine. Statistics Canada estimates that 25 percent of men and 29 percent of women in their 20s are severely time stressed. Statistics Canada offers the following guidelines for interpreting your time-stress score:

Time Stress	
Score	**Interpretation**
7–10	You seem to be severely time stressed.
5–6	You seem to be moderately time stressed.
0–4	You seem to experience little or no time stress.

CHAPTER 8
Scoring Key for the Team Roles Preferences Scale

Scoring Instructions: Write the scores circled for each item on the appropriate line below (statement numbers are in brackets), and add up each scale.

Encourager _____ + _____ + _____ = _____
           (6)   (9)   (11)

Gatekeeper _____ + _____ + _____ = _____
          (4)   (10) (13)

Harmonizer _____ + _____ + _____ = _____
         (3)   (8)   (12)

Initiator _____ + _____ + _____ = _____
        (1)   (5)   (14)

Summarizer _____ + _____ + _____ = _____
         (2)   (7)   (15)

Interpreting your Score: The five team role dimensions measured here are defined as follows, along with the range of scores for high, medium, and low levels of each role. These norms are based on results from a sample of MBA students.

Team Role and Definition	Interpretation
Encourager: People who score high on this dimension have a strong tendency to praise and support the ideas of other team members, thereby showing warmth and solidarity to the group.	High: 12 and above Medium: 9–11 Low: 8 and below
Gatekeeper: People who score high on this dimension have a strong tendency to encourage all team members to participate in the discussion.	High: 12 and above Medium: 9–11 Low: 8 and below
Harmonizer: People who score high on this dimension have a strong tendency to mediate intragroup conflicts and reduce tension.	High: 11 and above Medium: 9–10 Low: 8 and below

Team Role and Definition	Interpretation
Initiator: People who score high on this dimension have a strong tendency to identify goals for the meeting, including ways to work on those goals.	High: 12 and above Medium: 9–11 Low: 8 and below
Summarizer: People who score high on this dimension have a strong tendency to keep track of what was said in the meeting (i.e. act as the team's memory).	High: 10 and above Medium: 8–9 Low: 7 and below

CHAPTER 9
Scoring Key for the Team Player Inventory

Scoring Instructions: To calculate your score on the Team Player Inventory, use the table below to assign numbers to each box that you checked. Then add up the numbers to determine your total score.

For statement items 1, 3, 6, 8, 10	For statement items 2, 4, 5, 7, 9
Completely agree = 5	Completely agree = 1
Agree somewhat = 4	Agree somewhat = 2
Neither agree nor disagree = 3	Neither agree nor disagree = 3
Disagree somewhat = 2	Disagree somewhat = 4
Completely disagree = 1	Completely disagree = 5

Interpreting your Score: The Team Player Inventory estimates the extent to which you are positively predisposed to working on teams. The higher your score, the more you enjoy working in teams and believe that teamwork is beneficial. The following table allows you to compare your Team Player Inventory score against the norms for this scale. These norms are derived from undergraduate psychology students at a Canadian university.

Team Player Inventory	
Score	**Interpretation**
40–50	You have a strong predisposition or preference for working in teams.
21–39	You are generally ambivalent about working in teams.
10–20	You have a low predisposition or preference for working in teams.

CHAPTER 10
Scoring Key for Assessing Your Creative Disposition

Scoring Instructions: Assign plus one (+1) point beside the following words if you put a check mark beside them: Capable, Clever, Confident, Egotistical, Humorous, Individualistic, Informal, Insightful, Intelligent, Inventive, Original, Reflective, Resourceful, Self-Confident, Sexy, Snobbish, Unconventional, Wide Interests.

Assign negative one (–1) point beside the following words if you put a check mark beside them: Affected, Cautious, Commonplace, Conservative, Conventional, Dissatisfied, Honest, Mannerly, Narrow Interests, Sincere, Submissive, Suspicious.

Words without a check mark receive a zero. Add up the total score, which will range from –12 to +18.
Interpreting your Score: This instrument estimates your creative potential as a personal characteristic. The scale recognizes that creative people are intelligent, persistent, and possess an inventive thinking style. Creative personality varies somewhat from one occupational group to the next. The exhibit below provides norms based on undergraduate and graduate university students.

Creative Disposition	
Score	**Interpretation**
Above +9	You have a high creative disposition.
+1 to +9	You have an average creative disposition.
Below +1	You have a low creative disposition.

CHAPTER 11
Scoring Key for the Active Listening Skills Inventory

Scoring Instructions: Use the table below to score the response you circled for each statement. Write the score for each item on the appropriate line below the table (statement numbers are in brackets), and add

For statement items 3, 4, 6, 7, 10, 13	For statement items 1, 2, 5, 8, 9, 11, 12, 14, 15
Not at all = 3	Not at all = 0
A little = 2	A little = 1
Somewhat = 1	Somewhat = 2
Very much = 0	Very much = 3

up each subscale. For example, if you checked "A little" for statement #1 ("I keep an open mind…"), you would write a "1" on the line with "(1)" underneath it. Then calculate the overall Active Listening Inventory score by summing all subscales.

Avoiding
Interruption (AI)   ____ + ____ + ____ = ____
                     (3)   (7)   (15)

Maintaining
Interest (MI)   ____ + ____ + ____ = ____
                     (6)   (9)   (14)

Postponing
Evaluation (PE)   ____ + ____ + ____ = ____
                     (1)   (5)   (13)

Organizing
Information (OI)   ____ + ____ + ____ = ____
                     (2)   (10)   (12)

Showing
Interest (SI)   ____ + ____ + ____ = ____
                     (4)   (8)   (11)

Active Listening (total score):   ____

Interpreting your Score: The five active listening dimensions and the overall active listening scale measured here are defined below, along with the range of scores for high, medium, and low levels of each dimension based on a sample of MBA students:

Active Listening Dimension and Definition	Score Interpretation
Avoiding Interruption: People with high scores on this scale have a strong tendency to let the speaker finish his or her statements before responding.	High: 8–9 Medium: 6–7 Low: Below 5
Maintaining Interest: People with high scores on this dimension have a strong tendency to remain focused and concentrate on what the speaker is saying even when the conversation is boring or the information is well known.	High: 6–9 Medium: 3–5 Low: Below 3
Postponing Evaluation: People with high scores on this dimension have a strong tendency to keep an open mind and avoid evaluating what the speaker is saying until the speaker has finished.	High: 7–9 Medium: 4–6 Low: Below 4
Organizing Information: People with high scores on this dimension have a strong tendency to actively organize the speaker's ideas into meaningful categories.	High: 8–9 Medium: 5–7 Low: Below 5

Active Listening Dimension and Definition	Score Interpretation
Showing Interest: People with high scores on this dimension have a strong tendency to use nonverbal gestures or brief verbal acknowledgements to demonstrate that they are paying attention to the speaker.	High: 7–9 Medium: 5–6 Low: Below 5
Active Listening (total): People with high scores on this dimension have a strong tendency to actively sense the sender's signals, evaluate them accurately, and respond appropriately.	High: Above 31 Medium: 26–31 Low: Below 26

Note: The Active Listening Inventory does not explicitly measure two other dimensions of active listening, namely, empathizing and providing feedback. Empathizing is difficult to measure; providing feedback involves behaviours that are similar to showing interest.

CHAPTER 12
Scoring Key for the Upward Influence Scale

Scoring Instructions: To calculate your scores on the Upward Influence Scale, write the number circled for each statement on the appropriate line below (statement numbers are in brackets), and add up each scale.

Assertiveness   ____ + ____ + ____ = ____
                     (8)   (15)   (16)

Exchange   ____ + ____ + ____ = ____
                     (2)   (5)   (13)

Coalition Formation ____ + ____ + ____ = ____
                     (1)   (11)   (18)

Upward Appeal   ____ + ____ + ____ = ____
                     (4)   (12)   (17)

Ingratiation   ____ + ____ + ____ = ____
                     (3)   (6)   (9)

Persuasion   ____ + ____ + ____ = ____
                     (7)   (10)   (14)

Interpreting your Score: Influence refers to any behaviour that tries to alter someone's attitudes or behaviour. There are several types of influence, including the following six measured by this instrument: assertiveness, exchange, coalition formation, upward appeal, ingratiation, and persuasion. This instrument assesses your preference for using each type of influence on your boss or other people at higher levels in the organization. Each scale has a potential score ranging from

3 to 15 points. Higher scores indicate that the person has a higher preference for that particular tactic. The six upward influence dimensions measured here are defined below, along with the range of scores for high, medium, and low levels of each tactic.

Influence Tactic and Definition	Score Interpretation
Assertiveness: Assertiveness involves actively applying legitimate and coercive power to influence others. This tactic includes persistently reminding others of their obligations, frequently checking their work, confronting them, and using threats of sanctions to force compliance.	High: 8–15 Medium: 5–7 Low: 3–4
Exchange: Exchange involves the promise of benefits or resources in exchange for the target person's compliance with your request. This tactic also includes reminding the target of past benefits or favours with the expectation that the target will now make up for that debt. Negotiation is also part of the exchange strategy.	High: 10–15 Medium: 6–9 Low: 3–5
Coalition Formation: Coalition formation occurs when a group of people with common interests band together to influence others. This tactic pools the power and resources of many people, so the coalition potentially has more influence than if each person operated alone.	High: 11–15 Medium: 7–10 Low: 3–6
Upward Appeal: Upward appeal occurs when you rely on support from a higher-level person to influence others. In effect, this is a form of coalition in which one or more members is someone with higher authority or expertise.	High: 9–15 Medium: 6–8 Low: 3–5
Ingratiation: Flattering your boss in front of others, helping your boss with his or her work, agreeing with your boss' ideas, and asking for your boss's advice are all examples of ingratiation. This tactic increases the perceived similarity of the ingratiating person to the target person.	High: 13–15 Medium: 9–12 Low: 3–8
Persuasion: Persuasion refers to using logical and emotional appeals to change others' attitudes. According to several studies, it is also the most common upward influence strategy.	High: 13–15 Medium: 9–12 Low: 3–8

CHAPTER 13
Scoring Key for The Dutch Test for Conflict Handling

Scoring Instructions: Write the number circled for each item on the appropriate line below (statement number is under the line), and add up each subscale.

Conflict Handling		
Dimension	Calculation	Your Score
Yielding	_____ + _____ + _____ + _____ = _____ Item 1 Item 6 Item 11 Item 16	
Compromising	_____ + _____ + _____ + _____ = _____ Item 2 Item 7 Item 12 Item 17	
Forcing	_____ + _____ + _____ + _____ = _____ Item 3 Item 8 Item 13 Item 18	
Problem Solving	_____ + _____ + _____ + _____ = _____ Item 4 Item 9 Item 14 Item 19	
Avoiding	_____ + _____ + _____ + _____ = _____ Item 5 Item 10 Item 15 Item 20	

Interpreting your Score: The five conflict handling dimensions are defined below, along with the range of scores for the high, medium, and low levels of each dimension:

Conflict Handling Dimension and Definition	Score Interpretation
Yielding: Yielding involves giving in completely to the other side's wishes, or at least cooperating with little or no attention to your own interests. This style involves making unilateral concessions, unconditional promises, and offering help with no expectation of reciprocal help.	High: 14–20 Medium: 9–13 Low: 4–8
Compromising: Compromising involves looking for a position in which your losses are offset by equally valued gains. It involves matching the other party's concessions, making conditional promises or threats, and actively searching for a middle ground between the interests of the two parties.	High: 17–20 Medium: 11–16 Low: 4–10
Forcing: Forcing involves trying to win the conflict at the other's expense. It includes "hard" influence tactics, particularly assertiveness, to get one's own way.	High: 15–20 Medium: 9–14 Low: 4–8

Conflict Handling Dimension and Definition	Score Interpretation
Problem Solving: Problem solving tries to find a mutually beneficial solution for both parties. Information sharing is an important feature of this style because both parties need to identify common ground and potential solutions that satisfy both (or all) of them.	High: 17–20 Medium: 11–16 Low: 4–10
Avoiding: Avoiding tries to smooth over or avoid conflict situations altogether. It reflects a low concern for both self and the other party. In other words, avoiders try to suppress thinking about the conflict.	High: 13–20 Medium: 8–12 Low: 4–7

CHAPTER 14
Scoring Key for Leadership Dimensions Instrument

Transactional Leadership

Scoring Instructions: Add up scores for the odd numbered items (i.e. 1, 3, 5, 7, 9, 11, 13, 15) Maximum score is 40.

Interpreting your Score: Transactional leadership is "managing"—helping organizations achieve their current objectives more efficiently, such as by linking job performance to valued rewards and ensuring that employees have the resources needed to get the job done. The following table shows the range of scores for high, medium, and low levels of transactional leadership.

Transactional Leadership	
Score	**Interpretation**
32–40	The person you evaluated seems to be a highly transactional leader.
25–31	The person you evaluated seems to be a moderately transactional leader.
Below 25	The person you evaluated seems to display few characteristics of a transactional leader.

Transformational Leadership:

Scoring Instructions: Add up scores for the even numbered items (i.e. 2, 4, 6, 8, 10, 12, 14, 16). Maximum score is 40. Higher scores indicate that your supervisor has a strong inclination toward transformational leadership.

Interpreting your Score: Transformational leadership involves changing teams or organizations by creating, communicating, and modelling a vision for the organization or work unit, and inspiring employees to strive for that vision. The following table shows the range of scores for high, medium, and low levels of transformational leadership.

Transformational Leadership	
Score	**Interpretation**
32–40	The person you evaluated seems to be a highly transformational leader.
25–31	The person you evaluated seems to be a moderately transformational leader.
Below 25	The person you evaluated seems to display few characteristics of a transformational leader.

CHAPTER 15
Scoring Key for the Organizational Structure Preference Scale

Scoring Instructions: Use the table below to assign numbers to each response you circled. Insert the number for each statement on the appropriate line below the table. For example, if you checked "Not at all" for item #1 ("A person's career ladder. . ."), you would write a "0" on the line with "(1)" underneath it. After assigning numbers for all 15 statements, add up the scores to estimate your degree of preference for a tall hierarchy, formalization, and centralization. Then calculate the overall score by summing all scales.

For statement items 2, 3, 8, 10, 11, 12, 14, 15	For statement items 1, 4, 5, 6, 7, 9, 13
Not at all = 3	Not at all = 0
A little = 2	A little = 1
Somewhat = 1	Somewhat = 2
Very much = 0	Very much = 3

Tall Hierarchy (H)	___ + (1)	___ + (4)	___ + (10)	___ + (12)	___ = (15)	___ (H)
Formalization (F)	___ + (2)	___ + (6)	___ + (8)	___ + (11)	___ = (13)	___ (F)
Centralization (C)	___ + (3)	___ + (5)	___ + (7)	___ + (9)	___ = (14)	___ (C)
Total Score (Mechanistic)	___ + (H)	___ + (F)	___ = (C)	___ Total		

Interpreting your Score: The three organizational structure dimensions and the overall score are defined below, along with the range of scores for high, medium, and low levels of each dimension, and are based on a sample of MBA students:

Organizational Structure Dimension and Definition	Interpretation
Tall Hierarchy: People with high scores on this dimension prefer to work in organizations with several levels of hierarchy and a narrow span of control (few employees per supervisor).	High: 11–15 Medium: 6–10 Low: Below 6
Formalization: People with high scores on this dimension prefer to work in organizations where jobs are clearly defined, with limited discretion.	High: 12–15 Medium: 9–11 Low: Below 9
Centralization: People with high scores on this dimension prefer to work in organizations where decision making occurs mainly among top management rather than being spread out to lower level staff.	High: 10 to 15 Medium: 7 to 9 Low: Below 7
Total Score (Mechanistic): People with high scores on this scale prefer to work in mechanistic organizations, whereas those with low scores prefer to work in organic organizational structures. Mechanistic structures are characterized by a narrow span of control and high degree of formalization and centralization. Organic structures have a wide span of control, little formalization, and decentralized decision making.	High: 30–45 Medium: 22–29 Low: Below 22

CHAPTER 16
Scoring Key for the Corporate Culture Preference Scale

Scoring Instructions: In each space below, write in a "1" if you circled the statement and "0" if you did not. Then add up the scores for each subscale.

Control Culture	___ (2a)	+ ___ (5a)	+ ___ (6b)	+ ___ (8b)	+ ___ (11b)	+ ___ (12a)	= ___
Performance Culture	___ (1b)	+ ___ (3b)	+ ___ (5b)	+ ___ (6a)	+ ___ (7a)	+ ___ (9b)	= ___
Relationship Culture	___ (1a)	+ ___ (3a)	+ ___ (4b)	+ ___ (8a)	+ ___ (10b)	+ ___ (12b)	= ___
Responsive Culture	___ (2b)	+ ___ (4a)	+ ___ (7b)	+ ___ (9a)	+ ___ (10a)	+ ___ (11a)	= ___

Interpreting your Score: These corporate cultures may be found in many organizations, but they represent only four of many possible organizational cultures. Also, keep in mind that none of these subscales is inherently good or bad. Each is effective in different situations. The four corporate cultures are defined below, along with the range of scores for high, medium, and low levels of each dimension and are based on a sample of MBA students:

Corporate Culture Dimension and Definition	Score Interpretation
Control Culture: This culture values the role of senior executives in leading the organization. Its goal is to keep everyone aligned and under control.	High: 3–6 Medium: 1–2 Low: 0
Performance Culture: This culture values individual and organizational performance and strives for effectiveness and efficiency.	High: 5–6 Medium: 3–4 Low: 0–2
Relationship Culture: This culture values nurturing and well-being. It considers open communication, fairness, teamwork, and sharing a vital part of organizational life.	High: 6 Medium: 4–5 Low: 0–3
Responsive Culture: This culture values its ability to keep in tune with the external environment, including being competitive and realizing new opportunities.	High: 6 Medium: 4–5 Low: 0–3

CHAPTER 17
Scoring Key for the Tolerance of Change Scale

Scoring Instructions: Use the table below to assign numbers to each box you checked. For example, if you checked "Moderately disagree" for statement #1

For statement items 2, 4, 6, 8, 10, 12, 14, 16	For statement items 1, 3, 5, 7, 9, 11, 13, 15
Strongly agree = 7	Strongly agree = 1
Moderately agree = 6	Moderately agree = 2
Slightly agree = 5	Slightly agree = 3
Neutral = 4	Neutral = 4
Slightly disagree = 3	Slightly disagree = 5
Moderately disagree = 2	Moderately disagree = 6
Strongly disagree = 1	Strongly disagree = 7

("An expert who doesn't come up ..."), you would write a "2" beside that statement. After assigning numbers for all 16 statements, add up your scores to estimate your tolerance for change.

Interpreting your Score: This measurement instrument is formally known as the "tolerance of ambiguity" scale. Although it was developed forty years ago, the instrument is still used today in research. People with a high tolerance of ambiguity are comfortable with uncertainty, sudden change, and new situations. These are characteristics of the hyperfast changes occurring in many organizations today. The exhibit below indicates the range of scores for high, medium, and low tolerance for change. These norms are based on results for MBA students.

Tolerance for Change	
Score	**Interpretation**
81–112	You seem to have a high tolerance for change.
63–80	You seem to have a moderate level of tolerance for change.
Below 63	You seem to have a low degree of tolerance for change. Instead, you prefer stable work environments.

The number following each definition indicates the chapter in which the term receives the fullest description.

A

ability Both the natural aptitudes and learned capabilities required to successfully complete a task. (2)

action learning A variety of experiential learning activities in which employees are involved in a "real, complex, and stressful problem," usually in teams, with immediate relevance to the company. (3)

action research A data-based, problem-oriented process that diagnoses the need for change, introduces the intervention, and then evaluates and stabilizes the desired changes. (17)

adaptive culture An organizational culture in which employees focus on the changing needs of customers and other stakeholders, and support initiatives to keep pace with those changes. (16)

alternative dispute resolution (ADR) A third-party dispute resolution process that includes mediation, typically followed by arbitration. (13)

appreciative inquiry An organizational change strategy that directs the group's attention away from its own problems and focuses participants on the group's potential and positive elements. (17)

artifacts The observable symbols and signs of an organization's culture. (16)

attitudes The cluster of beliefs, assessed feelings, and behavioural intentions toward an object. (4)

attribution process The perceptual process of deciding whether an observed behaviour or event is caused largely by internal or by external factors. (3)

autonomy The degree to which a job gives employees the freedom, independence, and discretion to schedule their work and determine the procedures used in completing it. (6)

B

balanced scorecard A reward system that pays bonuses to executives for improved measurements on a composite of financial, customer, internal process, and employee factors. (6)

behaviour modification A theory that explains learning in terms of the antecedents and consequences of behaviour. (3)

bicultural audit Diagnoses cultural relations between companies prior to a merger and determines the extent to which cultural clashes will be likely to occur. (16)

"Big Five" personality dimensions The five abstract dimensions representing most personality traits: conscientiousness, agreeableness, neuroticism, openness to experience, and extroversion (CANOE). (2)

bounded rationality Processing limited and imperfect information and satisficing rather than maximizing when choosing among alternatives. (10)

brainstorming A freewheeling, face-to-face meeting where team members generate as many ideas as possible, piggyback on the ideas of others, and avoid evaluating anyone's ideas during the idea-generation stage. (10)

C

care principle The moral principle stating that we should benefit those with whom we have special relationships. (2)

centrality The degree and nature of interdependence between the power-holder and others. (12)

centralization The degree to which formal decision authority is held by a small group of people, typically those at the top of the organizational hierarchy. (15)

ceremonies Planned and usually dramatic displays of organizational culture, conducted specifically for the benefit of an audience. (16)

change agent Anyone who possesses enough knowledge and power to guide and facilitate the organizational change effort. (17)

coalition An informal group that attempts to influence people outside the group by pooling the resources and power of its members. (12)

codetermination A form of employee involvement required by some governments that typically operates at the work site as works councils and at the corporate level as supervisory boards. (10)

cognitive dissonance Occurs when people perceive an inconsistency between their beliefs, feelings, and behaviour. (4)

collective self-regulation Team-based structure in which employees in the primary work unit have enough autonomy to manage the work process. (9)

collectivism The extent to which people value duty to groups to which they belong, and to group harmony. (2)

communication The process by which information is transmitted and understood between two or more people. (11)

communication competence A person's ability to identify appropriate communication patterns in a given situation and to achieve goals by applying that knowledge. (11)

communities of practice Informal groups bound together by shared expertise and passion for a particular activity or interest. (1, 8)

competencies The abilities, values, personality traits, and other characteristics of people that lead to superior performance. (2)

conflict The process in which one party perceives that its interests are being opposed or negatively affected by another party. (13)

conflict management Interventions that alter the level and form of conflict in ways that maximize its benefits and minimize its dysfunctional consequences. (13)

conscientiousness A "Big Five" personality dimension that characterizes people who are careful, dependable, and self-disciplined. (2)

constructive conflict Any situation where people debate their differing opinions about an issue in a way that keeps the conflict focused on the task rather than people. (10)

constructs Abstract ideas constructed by researchers that can be linked to observable information. (Appendix A)

contact hypothesis The theory that as individuals interact with one another they rely less on stereotypes about each other. (3)

contingency approach The idea that a particular action may have different consequences in different situations. (1)

contingent work Any job in which the individual does not have an explicit or implicit contract for long-term employment, or one in which the minimum hours of work can vary in a nonsystematic way. (1)

continuance commitment A bond felt by an employee that motivates him or her to stay only because leaving would be costly. (4)

corporate social responsibility (CSR) An organization's moral obligation toward its stakeholders. (1)

counterpower The capacity of a person, team, or organization to keep a more powerful person or group in the exchange relationship. (12)

counterproductive work behaviours (CWBs) Potentially harmful voluntary behaviours enacted on an organization's property or employees. (2)

creativity The capacity to develop an original product, service, or idea that makes a socially recognized contribution. (10)

D

decision making A conscious process of making choices among one or more alternatives with the intention of moving toward some desired state of affairs. (10)

Delphi technique A structured team decision-making process of systematically pooling the collective knowledge of experts on a particular subject to make decisions, predict the future, or identify opposing views. (10)

dialogue A process of conversation among team members in which they learn about each other's mental models and assumptions, and eventually form a common model for thinking within the team. (9, 13)

distributive justice The perceived fairness in outcomes we receive relative to our contributions and the outcomes and contributions of others. (5)

distributive justice principle The moral principle stating that people who are similar should be rewarded similarly, and those dissimilar should be rewarded differently. (2)

divergent thinking Involves reframing a problem in a unique way and generating different approaches to the issue. (10)

divisional structure An organizational structure that groups employees around geographic areas, clients, or outputs. (15)

E

effort-to-performance (E→P) expectancy The individual's perceived probability that his or her effort will result in a particular level of performance. (5)

electronic brainstorming Using special computer software, participants share ideas while minimizing the team dynamics problems inherent in traditional brainstorming sessions. (10)

emotional contagion The automatic and unconscious tendency to mimic and synchronize one's own nonverbal behaviours with those of other people. (11)

emotional dissonance The conflict between required and true emotions. (4)

emotional intelligence (EI) The ability to perceive and express emotion, assimilate emotion and thought, understand and reason with emotion, and regulate emotion in oneself and others (4)

emotional labour The effort, planning, and control needed to express organizationally desired emotions during interpersonal transactions. (4)

emotions Psychological and physiological episodes toward an object, person, or event that create a state of readiness. (4)

empathy A person's ability to understand and be sensitive to the feelings, thoughts, and situations of others. (3)

employability An employment relationship in which people are expected to continually develop their skills to remain employed. (1)

employee assistance programs (EAPs) Counselling services that help employees overcome personal or organizational stressors and adopt more effective coping mechanisms. (7)

employee involvement The degree to which employees influence how their work is organized and carried out. (10)

employee stock ownership plans (ESOPs) A reward system that encourages employees to buy shares of the company. (6)

empowerment A psychological concept in which people experience more self-determination, meaning, competence, and impact regarding their role in the organization. (6)

equity sensitivity One's outcome–input preferences and reaction to various outcome–input ratios. (5)

equity theory Theory that explains how people develop perceptions of fairness in the distribution and exchange of resources. (5)

ERG theory Alderfer's motivation theory of three instinctive needs arranged in a hierarchy, in which people progress to the next higher need when a lower one is fulfilled, and regress to a lower need if unable to fulfill a higher one. (5)

escalation of commitment The tendency to repeat an apparently bad decision or allocate more resources to a failing course of action. (10)

ethical sensitivity A personal characteristic that enables people to recognize the presence and determine the relative importance of an ethical issue. (2)

ethics The study of moral principles or values that determine whether actions are right or wrong and outcomes are good or bad. (1, 2)

evaluation apprehension When individuals are reluctant to mention ideas that seem silly because they believe (often correctly) that other team members are silently evaluating them. (10)

executive coaching A helping relationship using behavioural methods to assist clients in identifying and achieving goals for their professional performance and personal satisfaction. (5)

existence needs A person's physiological and physically related safety needs, such as the need for food, shelter, and safe working conditions. (5)

exit-voice-loyalty-neglect (EVNL) model The four ways, as indicated in the name, employees respond to job dissatisfaction. (4)

expectancy theory The motivation theory based on the idea that work effort is directed toward behaviours that people believe will lead to desired outcomes. (5)

extinction Occurs when the target behaviour decreases because no consequence follows it. (13)

extroversion A "Big Five" personality dimension that characterizes people who are outgoing, talkative, sociable, and assertive. (2)

F

feedback Any information that people receive about the consequences of their behaviour. (5)

Fiedler's contingency model Developed by Fred Fiedler, suggests that leader effectiveness depends on whether the person's natural leadership style is appropriately matched to the situation. (14)

field surveys A research design strategy that involves collecting and analyzing information in a natural environment, an office, a factory, or other existing location. (Appendix A)

flaming The act of sending an emotionally charged electronic mail message to others. (11)

force field analysis Lewin's model of systemwide change that helps change agents diagnose the forces that drive and restrain proposed organizational change. (17)

formalization The degree to which organizations standardize behaviour through rules, procedures, formal training, and related mechanisms. (17)

frustration-regression process A process whereby a person who is un-

able to satisfy a higher need becomes frustrated and regresses to the next lower need level. (5)

functional structure An organizational structure that organizes employees around specific knowledge or other resources. (15)

fundamental attribution error The tendency to attribute the behaviour of other people more to internal than to external factors. (3)

G

gainsharing plan A reward system that rewards team members for reducing costs and increasing labour efficiency in their work process. (6)

general adaptation syndrome A model of the stress experience, consisting of three stages: alarm reaction, resistance, and exhaustion. (7)

globalization When an organization extends its activities to other parts of the world, actively participates in other markets, and competes against organizations located in other countries. (1)

goal setting The process of motivating employees and clarifying their role perceptions by establishing performance objectives. (5)

goals The immediate or ultimate objectives that employees are trying to accomplish from their work effort. (5)

grafting The process of acquiring knowledge by hiring individuals or buying entire companies. (1)

grapevine An unstructured and informal communication network founded on social relationships rather than organizational charts or job descriptions. (11)

grounded theory A process adopted in most qualitative research of developing knowledge through the constant interplay of data collection, analysis, and theory development. (1, Appendix A)

group polarization The tendency of teams to make more extreme decisions than individuals working alone. (10)

groups Two or more people with a unifying relationship. (8)

groupthink The tendency of highly cohesive groups to value consensus at the price of decision quality. (10)

growth needs A person's needs for self-esteem through personal achieve-

ment as well as for self-actualization. (5)

H

halo error A perceptual error whereby our general impression of a person, usually based on one prominent characteristic, colours the perception of other characteristics of that person. (3)

heterogeneous teams Teams that include members with diverse personal characteristics and backgrounds. (8)

homogeneous teams Teams that include members with common technical expertise, demographics (age, gender), ethnicity, experiences, or values. (8)

hypotheses Statements making empirically testable declarations that certain variables and their corresponding measures are related in a specific way proposed by theory. (Appendix A)

I

implicit favourite The decision maker's preferred alternative against which all other choices are judged. (10)

implicit leadership theory A theory stating that perceptual processes cause people to inflate the importance of leadership in explaining organizational events. (14)

impression management The practice of actively shaping one's public image. (12)

individual rights principle The moral principle stating that every person is entitled to legal and human rights. (2)

individualism The extent to which a person values independence and personal uniqueness. (2)

influence Any behaviour that attempts to alter another person's attitudes or behaviour. (12)

informal groups Two or more people who form a unifying relationship around personal rather than organizational goals. (8)

information overload A condition in which the volume of information received exceeds the person's capacity to process it. (11)

ingratiation Any attempt to increase the extent to which a target person likes us or perceives that he or she is similar to us. (12)

inoculation effect   A persuasive communication strategy of warning listeners that others will try to influence them in the future and that they should be wary about the opponent's arguments. (12)

intellectual capital   The sum of an organization's human capital, structural capital, and relationship capital. (1)

interpretivism   The view held in many qualitative studies that reality comes from shared meaning among people in that environment. (Appendix A)

introversion   A "Big Five" personality dimension that characterizes people who are territorial and solitary. (2)

intuition   The ability to know when a problem or opportunity exists and select the best course of action without conscious reasoning. (10)

J

jargon   The technical language and acronyms as well as recognized words with specialized meanings in specific organizations or groups. (11)

job burnout   The process of emotional exhaustion, depersonalization, and reduced personal accomplishment resulting from prolonged exposure to stress. (7)

job characteristics model   A job design model that relates the motivational properties of jobs to specific personal and organizational consequences of those properties. (6)

job design   The process of assigning tasks to a job, including the interdependency of those tasks with other jobs. (6)

job enlargement   Increasing the number of tasks employees perform within their job. (6)

job enrichment   Employees are given more responsibility for scheduling, coordinating, and planning their own work. (6)

job evaluation   Systematically evaluating the worth of jobs within an organization by measuring their required skill, effort, responsibility, and working conditions. Job evaluation results create a hierarchy of job worth. (6)

job feedback   The degree to which employees can tell how well they are doing based on direct sensory information from the job itself. (6)

job rotation   The practice of moving employees from one job to another. (6)

job satisfaction   A person's attitude regarding his or her job and work content. (2, 4)

job specialization   The result of division of labour in which each job includes a subset of the tasks required to complete the product or service. (6, 17)

Johari Window   The model of personal and interpersonal understanding that encourages disclosure and feedback to increase the open area and reduce the blind, hidden, and unknown areas of oneself. (3)

joint optimization   The balance that is struck between social and technical systems to maximize an operation's effectiveness. (9)

K

knowledge management   Any structured activity that improves an organization's capacity to acquire, share, and use knowledge in ways that improve its survival and success. (1)

L

laboratory experiment   Any research study in which independent variables and variables outside the researcher's main focus of inquiry can be controlled to some extent. (Appendix A)

leadership   Influencing, motivating, and enabling others to contribute toward the effectiveness and success of the organizations of which they are members. (14)

Leadership Grid®   A leadership model that assesses leadership effectiveness in terms of the person's level of task-oriented and people-oriented style. (14)

leadership substitutes   A theory that identifies contingencies that either limit the leader's ability to influence subordinates or make that particular leadership style unnecessary. (14)

learning   A relatively permanent change in behaviour that occurs as a result of a person's interaction with the environment. (3)

learning orientation   The extent to which an organization or individual supports knowledge management, particularly opportunities to acquire knowledge through experience and experimentation. (3)

legitimate power   The capacity to influence others through formal authority. (12)

locus of control   A personality trait referring to the extent to which people believe events are within their control. (2)

M

Machiavellian values   The belief that deceit is a natural and acceptable way to influence others. (12)

management by objectives (MBO)   A participative goal-setting process in which organizational objectives are cascaded down to work units and individual employees. (5)

management by walking around (MBWA)   A communication practice in which executives get out of their offices and learn from others in the organization through face-to-face dialogue. (11)

matrix structure   A type of departmentalization that overlays a divisionalized structure (typically a project team) with a functional structure. (15)

mechanistic structure   An organizational structure with a narrow span of control and high degrees of formalization and centralization. (15)

media richness   The data-carrying capacity of a communication medium, including the volume and variety of information it can transmit. (11)

mental imagery   Mentally practising a task and visualizing its successful completion. (6)

mental models   The broad worldviews or "theories in-use" that people rely on to guide their perceptions and behaviours. (3)

mentoring   The process of learning the ropes of organizational life from a senior person within the company. (12)

moral intensity   The degree to which an issue demands the application of ethical principles. (2)

motivation   The forces within a person that affect his or her direction, intensity, and persistence of voluntary behaviour. (2, 5)

motivator–hygiene theory   Herzberg's theory stating that employees are primarily motivated by growth and esteem needs, not by lower-level needs. (6)

Myers-Briggs Type Indicator (MBTI) A personality test that measures each of the traits in Jung's model. (2)

N

need for achievement (nAch) A learned need in which people want to accomplish reasonably challenging goals through their own efforts, like being successful in competitive situations, and desiring unambiguous feedback regarding their success. (5)

need for affiliation (nAff) A learned need in which people seek approval from others, conform to their wishes and expectations, and avoid conflict and confrontation. (5)

need for power (nPow) A learned need in which people want to control their environment, including people and material resources, to benefit either themselves (personalized power) or others (socialized power). (5)

needs Deficiencies that energize or trigger behaviours to satisfy those needs. (5)

needs hierarchy theory Maslow's motivation theory of five instinctive needs arranged in a hierarchy, whereby people are motivated to fulfill a higher need as a lower one becomes gratified. (5)

negative affectivity (NA) The tendency to experience negative emotions. (4)

negative reinforcement Occurs when the removal or avoidance of a consequence increases or maintains the frequency or future probability of a behaviour. (3)

negotiation Occurs whenever two or more conflicting parties attempt to resolve their divergent goals by redefining the terms of their interdependence. (13)

network structure An alliance of several organizations for the purpose of creating a product or serving a client. (15)

networking Cultivating social relationships with others to accomplish one's goals. (12)

nominal group technique A structured team decision-making process whereby team members independently write down ideas, describe and clarify them to the group, and then independently rank or vote on them. (10)

nonprogrammed decision The process applied to unique, complex, or ill-defined situations whereby decision makers follow the full decision-making process, including a careful search for and/or development of unique solutions. (10)

norms The informal rules and expectations that groups establish to regulate the behaviour of their members. (8)

O

open-book management Involves sharing financial information with employees and encouraging them to recommend ideas that improve those financial results. (6)

open systems Organizations that take their sustenance from the environment and, in turn, affect that environment through their output. (1)

organic structure An organizational structure with a wide span of control, little formalization, and decentralized decision making. (15)

organizational behaviour (OB) The study of what people think, feel, and do in and around organizations. (1)

organizational citizenship Behaviours that extend beyond the employee's normal job duties. (2)

organizational commitment The employee's emotional attachment to, identification with, and involvement in a particular organization. (4)

organizational culture The basic pattern of shared assumptions, values, and beliefs governing the way employees within an organization think about and act on problems and opportunities. (1, 16)

organizational design The process of creating and modifying organizational structures. (15)

organizational learning The knowledge management process in which organizations acquire, share, and use knowledge to succeed. (1)

organizational memory The storage and preservation of intellectual capital. (1)

organizational politics Behaviours that others perceive as self-serving tactics for personal gain at the expense of other people and possibly the organization. (12)

organizational strategy The way an organization positions itself in its setting in relation to its stakeholders, given the organization's resources, capabilities, and mission. (15)

organizational structure The division of labour and the patterns of coordination, communication, work flow, and formal power that direct organizational activities. (15)

organizations Groups of people who work interdependently toward some purpose. (1)

P

parallel learning structures Highly participative groups constructed alongside (i.e. parallel to) the formal organization with the purpose of increasing the organization's learning and producing meaningful organizational change. (17)

path–goal leadership theory A contingency theory of leadership based on expectancy theory of motivation that relates several leadership styles to specific employee and situational contingencies. (14)

perception The process of selecting, organizing, and interpreting information in order to make sense of the world around us. (3)

performance-to-outcome (P→O) expectancy The perceived probability that a specific behaviour or performance level will lead to specific outcomes. (5)

personality The relatively stable pattern of behaviours and consistent internal states that explain a person's behavioural tendencies. (2)

persuasion Using logical arguments, facts, and emotional appeals to encourage people to accept a request or message. (12)

platform teams Temporary teams consisting of people from marketing, design, and other areas, who are responsible for developing a product or service. (15)

positive affectivity (PA) The tendency to experience positive emotional states. (4)

positive reinforcement Occurs when the introduction of a consequence increases or maintains the frequency or future probability of a behaviour. (3)

positivism   A view held in quantitative research in which reality exists independent of the perceptions and interpretations of people. (Appendix A)

postdecisional justification   Justifying choices by unconsciously inflating the quality of the selected option and deflating the quality of the discarded options. (10)

power   The capacity of a person, team, or organization to influence others. (12)

power distance   The extent to which people accept unequal distribution of power in a society. (2)

prejudice   The unfounded negative emotions toward people belonging to a particular stereotyped group. (3)

primacy effect   A perceptual error in which we quickly form an opinion of people based on the first information we receive about them. (3)

procedural justice   The fairness of the procedures used to decide the distributions of resources. (5)

process consultation   Involves helping the organization solve its own problems by making it aware of organizational processes, the consequences of those processes, and the means by which they can be changed. (17)

process losses   Resources (including time and energy) expended toward team development and maintenance rather than the task. (8)

production blocking   A time constraint in team decision making due to the procedural requirement that only one person may speak at a time. (10)

profit sharing   A reward system that pays bonuses to employees based on the previous year's level of corporate profits. (6)

programmed decision   The process whereby decision makers follow standard operating procedures to select the preferred solution without the need to identify or evaluate alternative choices. (10)

projection bias   A perceptual error in which an individual believes that other people have the same beliefs and behaviours that we do. (3)

psychological contract   The individual's beliefs about the terms and conditions of a reciprocal exchange agreement between that person and another party. (4)

punishment   Occurs when a consequence decreases the frequency or future probability of a behaviour. (3)

R

recency effect   A perceptual error in which the most recent information dominates one's perception of others. (3)

referent power   The capacity to influence others based on the identification and respect they have for the power holder. (12)

refreezing   The latter part of the change process in which systems and conditions are introduced that reinforce and maintain the desired behaviours. (17)

relatedness needs   A person's needs to interact with other people, receive public recognition, and feel secure around other people. (5)

representative sampling   The process of sampling a population in such a way that one can extrapolate the results of that sample to the larger population. (Appendix A)

rituals   The programmed routines of daily organizational life that dramatize the organization's culture. (16)

role   A set of behaviours that people are expected to perform because they hold certain positions in a team and organization. (8)

role ambiguity   Uncertainty about job duties, performance expectations, level of authority, and other job conditions. (7)

role conflict   Conflict that occurs when people face competing demands. (7)

role perceptions   A person's beliefs about what behaviours are appropriate or necessary in a particular situation, including the specific tasks that make up the job, their relative importance, and the preferred behaviours to accomplish those tasks. (2)

S

satisfaction-progression process   A process whereby people become in-

creasingly motivated to fulfill a higher need as a lower need is gratified. (5)

satisficing   Selecting a solution that is satisfactory, or "good enough" rather than optimal or "the best." (10)

scenario planning   A systematic process of thinking about alternative futures, and what the organization should do to anticipate and react to those environments. (10)

scientific management   Involves systematically partitioning work into its smallest elements and standardizing tasks to achieve maximum efficiency. (6)

scientific method   A set of principles and procedures that help researchers to systematically understand previously unexplained events and conditions. (1)

search conferences   Systemwide group sessions, usually lasting a few days, in which participants identify environmental trends and establish strategic solutions for those conditions. (17)

selective attention   The process of filtering information received by our senses. (3)

self-directed work teams (SDWTs)   Cross-functional work groups organized around work processes, that complete an entire piece of work requiring several interdependent tasks, and that have substantial autonomy over the execution of those tasks. (9)

self-efficacy   A person's belief that he or she has the ability, motivation, and resources to complete a task successfully. (3)

self-fulfilling prophecy   Occurs when our expectations about another person cause that person to act in a way that is consistent with those expectations. (3)

self-leadership   The process of influencing oneself to establish the self-direction and self-motivation needed to perform a task. (6)

self-monitoring   A personality trait referring to an individual's level of sensitivity and ability to adapt to situational cues. (2)

self-serving bias   A perceptual error whereby people tend to attribute their favourable outcomes to internal factors and their failures to external factors. (3)

self-talk Talking to ourselves about our own thoughts or actions for the purpose of increasing our self-efficacy and navigating through decisions in a future event. (6)

servant leadership The belief that leaders serve followers by understanding their needs and facilitating their work performance. (14)

sexual harassment Unwelcome conduct of a sexual nature that detrimentally affects the work environment or leads to adverse job-related consequences for its victims. (7)

situational leadership model Developed by Hersey and Blanchard, suggests that effective leaders vary their style with the "readiness" of followers. (14)

skill variety The extent to which employees must use different skills and talents to perform tasks within their job. (6)

skill-based pay Pay structures in which employees earn higher pay rates according to the number of skill modules they have mastered. (6)

skunkworks Temporary teams consisting of employees borrowed from several functional areas to develop new products, services, or procedures. (8)

social identity theory A model that explains self-perception and social perception in terms of the person's unique characteristics (personal identity) and membership in various social groups (social identity). (3)

social learning theory A theory stating that much learning occurs by observing others and then modelling the behaviours that lead to favourable outcomes and avoiding the behaviours that lead to punishing consequences. (3)

social loafing A situation in which people exert less effort (and usually perform at a lower level) when working in groups than when working alone. (8)

sociotechnical systems (STS) theory A theory stating that effective work sites have joint optimization of their social and technological systems, and that teams should have sufficient au-

tonomy to control key variances in the work process. (9)

span of control The number of people directly reporting to the next level in the organizational hierarchy. (15)

stakeholders Shareholders, customers, suppliers, governments, and any other groups with a vested interest in the organization. (1)

stereotyping The process of assigning traits to people based on their membership in a social category. (3)

stock options A reward system that gives employees the right to purchase company shares at a future date at a predetermined price. (6)

strategic choice The idea that an organization interacts with its environment rather than being totally determined by it. (15)

stress An individual's adaptive response to a situation that is perceived as challenging or threatening to the person's well-being. (7)

stressors The causes of stress, including any environmental conditions that place a physical or emotional demand on the person. (7)

substitutability The extent to which people dependent on a resource have alternatives. (12)

superordinate goal A common objective held by conflicting parties that is more important than their conflicting departmental or individual goals. (13)

T

tacit knowledge Knowledge embedded in our actions and ways of thinking, and transmitted only through observation and experience. (3)

task identity The degree to which a job requires completion of a whole or an identifiable piece of work. (6)

task interdependence The degree to which a task requires employees to share common inputs or outcomes, or to interact in the process of executing their work. (8)

task performance Goal-directed activities that are under that individual's control. (2)

task significance The degree to which the job has a substantial impact

on the organization and/or larger society. (6)

team-based organization A type of departmentalization with a flat hierarchy and relatively little formalization, consisting of self-directed work teams responsible for various work processes. (15)

team building Any formal activity intended to improve the development and functioning of a team. (9)

team cohesiveness The degree of attraction people feel toward the team and their motivation to remain members. (8)

team effectiveness The extent to which a team achieves its objectives, achieves the needs and objectives of its members, and sustains itself over time. (8)

teams Groups of two or more people who interact and influence each other, are mutually accountable for achieving common objectives, and perceive themselves as a social entity within an organization. (8)

teleworking Working from home, usually with a computer connection to the office; also called *telecommuting*. (1)

theory A general set of propositions that describes interrelationships among several concepts. (Appendix A)

third-party conflict resolution Any attempt by a relatively neutral person to help the parties resolve their differences. (13)

360-degree feedback Performance feedback received from a full circle of people around an employee. (5)

transactional leadership Leadership that helps organizations achieve their current objectives more efficiently, such as linking job performance to valued rewards and ensuring that employees have the resources needed to get the job done. (14)

transformational leadership A leadership perspective that explains how leaders change teams or organizations by creating, communicating, and modelling a vision for the organization or work unit, and inspiring employees to strive for that vision. (14)

trust Positive expectations about another party's intentions and actions in risky situations. (4, 9)

type A behaviour pattern A behaviour pattern associated with people having premature coronary heart disease; type As tend to be impatient, lose their temper, talk rapidly, and interrupt others. (7)

type B behaviour pattern A behaviour pattern associated with people having a low risk of coronary heart disease; type Bs tend to work steadily, take a relaxed approach to life, and be even-tempered. (7)

U

uncertainty avoidance The degree to which people tolerate ambiguity or feel threatened by ambiguity and uncertainty. (2)

unfreezing The first part of the change process whereby the change agent produces disequilibrium between the driving and restraining forces. (17)

upward appeal A type of coalition in which one or more members is someone with higher authority or expertise. (12)

utilitarianism The moral principle stating that decision makers should seek the greatest good for the greatest number of people when choosing among alternatives. (2)

V

valence The anticipated satisfaction or dissatisfaction that an individual feels toward an outcome. (5)

value system An individual's hierarchical arrangement of values. (2)

values Stable, long-lasting beliefs about what is important in a variety of situations. (1, 2)

values congruence A situation wherein two or more entities have similar value systems. (2)

variable interval schedule A behaviour modification schedule that reinforces behaviour after it has occurred for a varying length of time around some average. (2)

variable ratio schedule A behaviour modification schedule that reinforces behaviour after it has occurred a varying number of times around some average. (2)

virtual corporations Network structures representing several independent companies that form unique partnership teams to provide customized products or services, usually to specific clients, for a limited time. (15)

virtual teams Teams whose members operate across space, time, and organizational boundaries and linked through information technologies to achieve organizational tasks. (1, 9)

W

win–lose orientation The belief that conflicting parties are drawing from a fixed pie, so the more one party receives, the less the other party will receive. (13)

win–win orientation The belief that the parties will find a mutually beneficial solution to their disagreement. (13)

workaholic A person who is highly involved in work, feels compelled to work, and has a low enjoyment of work. (7)

workplace bullying Offensive, intimidating, or humiliating behaviour that degrades, ridicules, or insults another person at work. (7)

NOTES

CHAPTER ONE

1. "Four Seasons Hotels and Resorts Makes Fortune—100 Best Companies to Work for in America," *PR Newswire*, January 23, 2002; J. Higley, "Head of the Class," *Hotel & Motel Management*, November 2001, pp. 92 ff; L. Bilmes. "Scoring Goals for People and Company," *Financial Times*, November 26, 2001; "A Fanaticism For People," *Business Today*, April 2001; B. Dexter, "A 'No-bull' Hotel Chain," *Toronto Star*, April 12, 2001, p. L3; J. Webster, "Group Therapy," *Catering And Hotel Keeper*, March 22, 2001, p. 32 ff; S. Ondrasek, "Four Seasons makes Local Debut," *Prague Post*, February 7, 2001; K. Hanson, "Perks Help Keep Four Seasons Staff Pampering Guests," *National Post*, January 13, 2001, p. D8.

2. M. Warner, "Organizational Behaviour Revisited," *Human Relations*, 47 (October 1994), pp. 1151–66. The various historical sources are described in: T. Takala, "Plato on Leadership," *Journal of Business Ethics*, 17 (May 1998), pp. 785–98; R. Kanigel, *The One Best Way: Frederick Winslow Taylor and the Enigma of Efficiency* (Viking: NY, 1997); M. Weber, *The Theory of Social and Economic Organization*, A. M. Henderson and T. Parsons (trans.), (N. Y.: Oxford University Press, 1947); N. Machiavelli, *The Prince and the Discourses*, (N.Y.: Modern Library, 1940); F. J. Roethlisberger and W. J. Dickson, *Management and the Worker*, (Cambridge, MA: Harvard University Press, 1939); A. Smith, *The Wealth of Nations* (London: Dent, 1910).

3. L. E. Greiner, "A Recent History of Organizational Behaviour," in *Organizational Behaviour*, ed. S. Kerr (Columbus, Ohio: Grid, 1979), pp. 3–14.

4. T. Barrett, "'Just Show Me the Trucks,' say Tourists," *Edmonton Journal*, May 10, 2002, p. J9; C. Varcoe, "Oilsands Boom," *Victoria Times Colonist*, December 24, 2001; S. Hume, "An Energy Odyssey," *Vancouver Sun*, June 8, 2001.

5. B. Schlender, "The Three Faces of Steve," *Fortune*, November 9, 1998.

6. R. N. Stern and S. R. Barley, "Organizations as Social Systems: Organization Theory's Neglected Mandate," *Administrative Science Quarterly*, 41 (1996), pp. 146–62; D. Katz and R. L. Kahn, *The Social Psychology of Organizations* (New York: Wiley, 1966), Chapter 2.

7. J. Pfeffer, *New Directions for Organization Theory*, (New York: Oxford University Press, 1997), pp. 7–9.

8. P. R. Lawrence and N. Nohria, *Driven: How Human Nature Shapes Our Choices*, (San Francisco: Jossey-Bass, 2002), Chapter 6.

9. S. A. Mohrman, C. B. Gibson, and A. M. Mohrman Jr., "Doing Research that is Useful to Practice: A Model and Empirical Exploration," *Academy of Management Journal*, 44 (April 2001), pp. 357–375. This view also appears in P. R. Lawrence, "Historical Development of Organizational Behaviour," in L. W. Lorsch (ed.) *Handbook of Organizational Behaviour*, (Englewood Cliffs, N.J.: Prentice Hall, 1987), pp. 1–9. For a contrary view, see A. P. Brief and J. M. Dukerich, "Theory in Organizational Behaviour: Can It Be Useful?" *Research in Organizational Behaviour*, 13 (1991), pp. 327–52.

10. M. S. Myers, *Every Employee a Manager*, (New York:McGraw Hill, 1970). The phrase "adult supervision" as a derogatory term for managers is mentioned in: T. A. Stewart, "Just Think: No Permission Needed," *Fortune*, January 8, 2001, p. 190.

11. D. MacDonald, "Good Managers Key to Buffett's Acquisitions," *Montreal Gazette*, November 16, 2001; D. Yankelovich, "Got to Give to Get," *Mother Jones*, Vol. 22 (July 1997), pp. 60–63. The results of the Watson Wyatt study are reported in B. N. Pfau and I. T. Kay, *The Human Capital Edge* (New York: McGraw-Hill, 2002); B. N. Pfau and I. T. Kay, "The Five Key Elements of a Total Rewards and Accountability Orientation," *Benefits Quarterly*, 18 (Third Quarter 2002), pp. 7–15.

12. B. Duff-Brown, "Service Centers Booming in India," *Chicago Tribune*, July 9, 2001, p. 6; M. Landler, "Hi, I'm in Bangalore (but I Can't Say So)," *New York Times*, March 21, 2001, p. A1.

13. H. Schachter, "The 21st Century CEO," *Profit*, 18 (April 1999), pp. 25–35; M. A. Hitt, B. W. Keats, and S. M. DeMarie, "Navigating in the New Competitive Landscape: Building Strategic Flexibility and Competitive Advantage in the 21st Century," *Academy of Management Executive*, 12 (November 1998), pp. 22–42. For discussion of the diverse meanings of "globalization," see: M. F. Guillén, "Is Globalization Civilizing, Destructive or Feeble? A Critique of Five Key Debates in the Social Science Literature," *Annual Review of Sociology*, 27 (2001), pp. 235–60.

14. J. Garten, *The Mind of the CEO* (NY: Perseus, 2001), Chapter 3.

15. Cited in: P. Verburg, "New Kid on the Beach," *Canadian Business*, 72 (February 12, 1999), pp. 52–56.

16. J. Bagnall, "SiGe Siren Song," *Ottawa Citizen*, December 6, 2001, p. E3.

17. For excellent coverage of the benefits and challenges of globalization for Canadians and people in other countries, see: R. P. Chaykowski (ed.) *Globalization and the Canadian Economy: The Implications for Labour Markets, Society and the State*, (Kingston, Ont.: School of Policy Studies, Queen's University, 2001).

18. R. Martin, "The Virtue Matrix: Calculating the Return on Corporate Responsibility," *Harvard Business Review*, 68 (March 2002), pp. 68–75.

19. C. Higgins and L. Duxbury, *The 2001 National Work–Life Conflict Study: Report One, Final Report* (Ottawa: Health Canada, March 2002); J. Foley, "Has Work Intensified in Canada?" *Proceedings of the Annual Conference of the Administrative Sciences Association*

of Canada, *Human Resource Management Division*, 23 (9) (2002), pp. 24–32; A. Dastmalchian and P. Blyton, "Workplace Flexibility and the Changing Nature of Work: An Introduction," *Canadian Journal of Administrative Sciences*, 18 (2001), pp. 1–4; T. H. Wagar, "Consequences of Work Force Reduction: Some Employer and Union Evidence," *Journal of Labor Research*, 22 (Fall 2001), pp. 851–62.

20. C. Kleiman, "Work Issues the Same the Whole World Over," *Seattle Times*, September 2, 2001.

21. P. R. Sparrow, "Reappraising Psychological Contracting: Lessons For The Field Of Human-Resource Development From Cross-Cultural And Occupational Psychology Research," *International Studies of Management & Organization*, 28 (March 1998), pp. 30–63; R. Schuler and N. Rogovsky, "Understanding Compensation Practice Variations Across Firms: The Impact Of National Culture," *Journal of International Business Studies*, 29 (1998), pp. 159–77.

22. R. House, M. Javidan, P. Hanges, P. Dorfman, "Understanding Cultures and Implicit Leadership Theories Across the Globe: An Introduction to Project GLOBE," *Journal of World Business*, 37 (Spring 2002), pp. 3–10; R. House, M. Javidan, and P. Dorfman, "Project GLOBE: An Introduction," *Applied Psychology: An International Journal*, 50 (2001), pp. 489–505.

23. R.D. Foster, "Internet takes Ancient Craft Global," *Christian Science Monitor*, September 7, 2001, p. 7.

24. R. P. Gephart, Jr., "Introduction to the Brave New Workplace: Organizational Behavior in the Electronic Age," *Journal of Organizational Behavior*, 23 (2002), pp. 327–44; R. E. Rice and U. E. Gattiker, "New Media and Organizational Structuring," In F. M. Jablin and L. L. Putnam (eds.) *The New Handbook of Organizational Communication* (Thousand Oaks, CA: Sage, 2001), pp. 544–81.

25. K. Voigt, "Virtual Work: Some Telecommuters Take Remote Work To the Extreme," *Wall Street Journal Europe*, February 1, 2001, p. 1.

26. P. Chisholm, "Redesigning Work," *Maclean's*, March 5, 2001, pp. 34–38. The AT&T and Canadian surveys are reported in: "AT&T Telework Survey Indicates Productivity is Up," *AT&T news release*, August 6, 2002; Ipsos-Reid, *Canadian Families and the Internet*, Report to The Royal Bank of Canada, January 2002. The advantages and disadvantages, and contingencies of telework are nicely detailed in: L. Duxbury and C. Higgins, "Telework: A Primer for the Millennium Introduction," In C. L. Cooper and R. J. Burke (eds.) *The New World of Work: Challenges and Opportunities* (Oxford: Blackwell, 2002), pp. 157–99.

27. D-G Tremblay "Telework: Work Organization and Satisfaction of Teleworkers," *Proceedings of the Annual Conference of the Administrative Sciences Association of Canada, Human Resource Management Division*, 23 (9) (2002), pp. 73–83; N. B. Kurland and D. E. Bailey, "Telework: The Advantages and Challenges of Working Here, There, Anywhere, and Anytime," *Organizational Dynamics*, 28 (Autumn 1999), pp. 53–68; A. Mahlon, "The Alternative Workplace: Changing Where and How People Work," *Harvard Business Review*, 76 (May-June 1998), pp. 121–30.

28. J. Lipnack and J. Stamps, *Virtual Teams: People Working Across Boundaries with Technology*, (New York: John Wiley & Sons, 2001); D. J. Armstrong and P. Cole, "Managing Distances and Differences in Geographically Distributed Work Groups," In S. E. Jackson and M. N. Ruderman (Eds.) *Diversity in Work Teams: Research Paradigms for a Changing Workplace*. (Washington, DC: American Psychological Association, 1995), pp. 187–215.

29. T. R. Kayworth and D. E. Leidner, "Leadership Effectiveness in Global Virtual Teams," *Journal of Management Information Systems*, 18 (Winter 2001/2002), pp. 7–40; B. L. Kelsey, "Managing in Cyberspace: Strategies for Developing high-Performance Virtual Team," Paper presented at the 2001 Annual Conference of the Administrative Sciences Association of Canada, Organizational Behaviour Division, London, Ontario, June 2001; J. S. Lureya and M. S. Raisinghani "An Empirical Study of Best Practices in Virtual Teams," *Information & Management*, 38 (2001) pp. 523–44; D. L. Duarte and N. T. Snyder, *Mastering Virtual Teams: Strategies, Tools, and Techniques that Succeed, 2nd ed.* (San Francisco, CA: Jossey-Bass, 2000).

30. C. Cobb, "Canadians want Diverse Society: Poll," *Ottawa Citizen*, February 18, 2002, p. A5. The McDonald's Canada quotation appears in: F. McNair, "Employers Reach Out to Reflect Society," *Edmonton Journal*, July 10, 2002, p. F6.

31. Statistical information comes from census information at the Statistics Canada Web site (www.statcan.ca). Also see: J. Duncanson, "Mostly White, Mostly Male: Why Police Are Reaching Out Again," *Toronto Star*, March 6, 1999, p. 1; R. A. Wanner, "Prejudice, Profit or Productivity: Explaining Returns to Human Capital among Male Immigrants to Canada," *Canadian Ethnic Studies*, 30 (September 1998), pp. 24–55; V. M. Esses and R. C. Gardner, "Multiculturalism in Canada: Context and Current Status," *Canadian Journal of Behavioural Science*, 28 (July 1996), pp. 145–52.

32. N. Glazer, "American Diversity and the 2000 Census," *The Public Interest*, June 22, 2001, pp. 3–18. The problem of ethnic diversity in Canada is discussed in: E. Kishibe, "Defining Societies of One," *The Globe and Mail*, July 5, 2001, p. A20; N. Bissoondath, "There's No Place Like Home," *New Internationalist*, Issue 305 (September 1998). The perpetual foreigner problem is discussed in: F. H. Wu, *Yellow: Race in America Beyond Black and White*, (New York: Basic, 2002), pp. 79–129.

33. P. Rich, "Doctors, Women, Mothers, Wives," *Medical Post*, 34 (December 1, 1998), pp. Suppl. 48–51; D. Mangan, "Remember When...A Women Doctor was a Rarity?" *Medical Economics*, 75 (May 11, 1998), pp. 225–26.

34. C. Loughlin and J. Barling, "Young Workers' Work Values, Attitudes, and Behaviours," *Journal of Occupational and Organizational Psychology*, 74 (2001), pp. 543–58.

35. Most writers define Generation-X as people born immediately after the baby boom generation ended (1964) through to around 1977. The exception is University of Toronto professor David Foot who describes Gen-Xers as people born from 1960 to 1964 (the end of the baby boom). See B. Losyk, "Generation X: What They Think and

What They Plan To Do," *The Futurist*, Vol. 31 (March-April 1997), pp. 29–44. For a discussion of Generation-X at work and as a consumer in Canada, see: R. Barnard, D. Cosgrave, J. Welsh, *Chips and Pop* (Toronto: Malcolm Lester Books, 1998).

36. N. Mui, "Here Come the Kids," *New York Times*, February 4, 2001, p. 1; R. Zemke and B. Filipczak, *Generations at Work: Managing the Clash of Veterans, Boomers, Xers, and Nexters in Your Workplace*, (N. Y.: Amacom, 2000); B.R. Kupperschmidt, "Multigeneration Employees: Strategies for Effective Management," *Health Care Manager*, September 2000, pp. 65–76; S. Hays, "Generation X and the Art of the Reward," *Workforce*, 78 (November 1999), pp. 44–48; B. Losyk, "Generation X: What They Think and What They Plan to Do," *The Futurist*, Vol. 31 (March-April 1997), pp. 29–44.

37. W. Chow, "Banana Magazine Starting to Bear Fruit," *Vancouver Sun*, May 31, 2002.

38. D. C. Lau and J. K. Murnighan, "Demographic Diversity and Faultlines: The Compositional Dynamics of Organizational Groups," *Academy of Management Review*, 23 (April 1998), pp. 325–40; G. Robinson and K. Dechant, "Building a Business Case for Diversity," *Academy of Management Executive*, 11 (August 1997), pp. 21–31; J. R. W. Joplin and C. S. Daus, "Challenges of Leading a Diverse Workforce," *Academy of Management Executive*, 11 (August 1997), pp. 32–47.

39. "Mixing Nationalities in the Workplace," *Guardian* (London), November 11, 1999, p. 23.

40. D. van Knippenberg and S. A. Haslam, "Realizing the Diversity Dividend: Exploring the Subtle Interplay Between Identity, Ideology and Reality," In S. A. Haslam, D. van Knippenberg, M. Platow, & N. Ellemers (Eds.) *Social Identity at Work: Developing Theory for Organizational Practice*, (New York: Taylor & Francis, in press); R. J. Ely and D. A. Thomas, "Cultural Diversity at Work: The Effects of Diversity Perspectives on Work Group Processes and Outcomes," *Administrative Science Quarterly*, 46 (June 2001), pp. 229–73.

41. R. J. Burke, "Organizational Transitions," In C. L. Cooper and R. J. Burke (eds.) *The New World of Work:*

Challenges and Opportunities (Oxford: Blackwell, 2002), pp. 3–28; F. Patterson, "Developments in Work Psychology: Emerging Issues and Future Trends," *Journal of Occupational and Organizational Psychology*, 74 (November 2001), pp. 381–90.

42. W. R. Boswell, L. M. Moynihan, M. V. Roehling, and M. A. Cavanaugh, "Responsibilities in the 'New Employment Relationship': An Empirical Test of an Assumed Phenomenon," *Journal of Managerial Issues*, 13 (Fall 2001), pp. 307–27; M. V. Roehling, M. A. Cavanaugh, L. M. Moynihan, and W. R. Boswell, 39 (2000) "The Nature of the New Employment Relationship(s): A Content Analysis of the Practitioner and Academic Literatures," *Human Resource Management*, pp. 305–20; J. Dionne-Proulx, J-C. Bernatchez, and R. Boulard, "Attitudes and Satisfaction Levels Associated with Precarious Employment," *International Journal of Employment Studies*, 6 (1998), pp. 91–114; P. Cappelli et al, *Change at Work* (New York: Oxford University Press, 1997).

43. D. G. Gallagher, "Contingent Work Contracts: Practice and Theory," In C. L. Cooper and R. J. Burke (eds.) *The New World of Work: Challenges and Opportunities* (Oxford: Blackwell, 2002), pp. 115–36; A. E. Polivka, "Contingent and Alternative Work Arrangements, Defined," *Monthly Labor Review*, 119 (October 1996), pp. 3–10; S. Nollen and H. Axel, *Managing Contingent Workers* (New York: AMACOM, 1996), pp. 4–9.

44. P. Kulig, "Temporary Employment Changing the Character of Canada's Labour Force," *Canadian HR Reporter*, November 16, 1998, pp. 1, 15; K. Barker and K. Christensen (Eds.) *Contingent Work: American Employment in Transition* (Ithaca, N.Y.: ILR Press, 1998).

45. D. H. Pink, "Land of the Free," *Fast Company*, May 2001, pp. 125–33; S. B. Gould, K. J. Weiner, and B. R. Levin, *Free Agents: People and Organizations Creating a New Working Community*, (San Francisco: Jossey-Bass, 1997); C. von Hippel, S. L. Mangum, D. B. Greenberger, R. L. Heneman, and J. D. Skoglind, "Temporary Employment: Can Organizations and Employees Both Win?" *Academy of Management Executive*, 11 (February 1997), pp.

93–104; W. J. Byron, S. J., "Coming to Terms with the New Corporate Contract," *Business Horizons*, January-February 1995, pp. 8–15.

46. J. Walsh and S. Deery, "Understanding the Peripheral Workforce: Evidence from the Service Sector," *Human Resource Management Journal*, 9 (1999), pp. 50–63.

47. Y-S. Park and R.J. Butler, "The Safety Costs of Contingent Work: Evidence from Minnesota," *Journal of Labor Research*, 22 (Fall 2001), pp. 831–49; D. M. Rousseau and C. Libuser, "Contingent Workers in High Risk Environments," *California Management Review*, 39 (Winter 1997), pp. 103–23.

48. A. Sagie and D. Elizur, "Work Values: A Theoretical Overview and a Model of Their Effects," *Journal of Organizational Behaviour*, 17 (1996), pp. 503–14; W. H. Schmidt and B. Z. Posner, *Managerial Values in Perspective* (New York: American Management Association, 1983).

49. Cited in T. Schubert, "Stop Bad Vibes Rising," *New Zealand Management*, 47 (September 2000), pp. 32–35.

50. For early writing on values in the context of organizations, see: E. H. Schein, *Organizational Culture and Leadership* (San Francisco, Calif.: Jossey-Bass, 1985); G. Hofstede, *Culture's Consequences: International Differences in Work-Related Values* (Beverly Hills, CA: Sage, 1980); A.M. Pettigrew, "On Studying Organizational Cultures," *Administrative Science Quarterly*, 24 (1979), pp. 570–81; G.W. England, "Personal Value Systems of American Managers," *Academy of Management Journal*, 10, (1967), pp. 53–68; W.D. Guth and R. Tagiuri, "Personal Values and Corporate Strategy," *Harvard Business Review*, 43 (1965), pp. 123–32.

51. B. R. Agle and C. B. Caldwell, "Understanding Research on Values in Business," *Business and Society*, 38 (September 1999), pp. 326–87; B. M. Meglino and E. C. Ravlin, "Individual Values in Organizations: Concepts, Controversies, and Research," *Journal of Management*, 24 (May 1998), pp. 351–89.

52. J. B. Izzo and P. Withers, *Values Shift* (Toronto: Prentice-Hall Canada,

2000); B. R. Agle and C. B. Caldwell, "Understanding Research on Values in Business," *Business and Society*, 38 (September 1999), pp. 326–87; P. Mc-Donald and J. Gandz, "Getting Value from Values," *Organizational Dynamics*, Winter 1992, pp. 64–77.

53. The role of values as a control system is discussed in: M. G. Murphy and K. M. Davey, "Ambiguity, Ambivalence and Indifference in Organisational Values," *Human Resource Management Journal*, 12 (2002), pp. 17–32; T.M. Begley, "Articulating Corporate Values through Human Resource Policies," *Business Horizons*, July, 2000; J.C. Mc-Cune, "Exporting Corporate Culture," *Management Review*, 88 (December 1999), pp. 52–56; M.S. Fenwick, H.L. DeCieri, and D.E. Welch, "Cultural and Bureaucratic Control in MNEs: The Role of Expatriate Performance Management," *Management International Review*, 39 (1999), Special Issue #3.

54. S.R. Chatterjee; C.A.L. Pearson, "Indian Managers in Transition: Orientations, Work Goals, Values and Ethics," *Management International Review*, 40 (January 2000), pp. 81–95.

55. This cynicism of executive ethics is beautifully captured in: D. Olive, "How Celebrity CEOs Failed to Deliver," *Toronto Star*, August 24, 2002, p. A1.

56. D. Staples, "God, Markets, Mergers and Money: Part II," *Ottawa Citizen*, August 1, 2002; M. Gordon, "WorldCom ex-CEO Ebbers knew Hundreds of Millions Shifted: Company Lawyers," *Canadian Press*, July 11, 2002; C. Varcoe and L. Schmidt, "CEOs Under Siege," *Calgary Herald*, July 6, 2002; A. Swift, "Cinar's Disgraced Founders Animate Board Coup at Annual Meeting," *Kitchener-Waterloo Record*, April 29, 2002; C. Muschi, "Signs of Life at Cinar," *Montreal Gazette*, October 14, 2000; M. Acharya, "OSC Hearings Promise Dirt on Mining Scandals," *Toronto Star*, February 28, 2000.

57. Cited in S. Zadek, The *Civil Corporation: The New Economy of Corporate Citizenship* (London: Earthscan, 2001), pp. 50–51.

58. R. J. Adams, "Good Corporate Citizenship in the 21st Century," *Workplace Gazette*, 4 (2001), pp. 50–54; Vector Re-search, "Analysis of the Public Opinion Poll Conducted for the Canadian Democracy and Corporate Accountability Commission," unpublished report, Toronto, 2001. Milton Friedman's quotation is cited in F. T. McCarthy, "Doing Well by Doing Good," *Economist*, April 22, 2000.

59. Canadian Democracy And Corporate Accountability Commission, *The New Balance Sheet: Corporate Profits and Responsibility in the 21st Century, Final Report* (Toronto, January 2002); S. Zadek, The *Civil Corporation: The New Economy of Corporate Citizenship* (London: Earthscan, 2001); S. G. Scott and V. R. Lane, "A Stakeholder Approach to Organizational Identity," *Academy of Management Review*, 25 (January 2000), pp. 43–62; A. A. Atkinson, J. H. Waterhouse, and R. B. Wells, "A Stakeholder Approach to Strategic Performance Measurement," *Sloan Management Review*, 38 (Spring 1997), pp. 25–37; G. T. Savage, T. W. Nix, C. J. Whitehead, and J. D. Blair, "Strategies for Assessing and Managing Organizational Stakeholders," *Academy of Management Executive*, 5, (May 1991), pp. 61–75; R. E. Freeman, *Strategic Management: A Stakeholder Approach* (Marshfield, MA: Pitman Publishing, 1984).

60. S. Zadek, The *Civil Corporation: The New Economy of Corporate Citizenship* (London: Earthscan, 2001), Chapter 9.

61. G. Livingston, "HBC Denies Sweatshop Allegation," *Ottawa Citizen*, May 15, 2002, p. F8.

62. D. Keeler, "Spread the Love and Make it Pay," *Global Finance*, 16 (May 2001), p. 20 ff.

63. Keeler, "Spread the Love and Make it Pay."

64. D. Mowat, "The VanCity Difference—A Case for the Triple Bottom Line Approach to Business," *Corporate Environmental Strategy*, 9 (February 2002) pp. 24–29; Vancouver City Savings Credit Union, *The VanCity Social Report, 1998–99* (Vancouver: Vancouver City Savings Credit Union, 2000)

65. M. N. Zald, "More Fragmentation? Unfinished Business in Linking the Social Sciences and the Humanities," *Administrative Science Quarterly*, 41 (1996), pp. 251–61.

66. For recent applications of evotionary psychology in organizational behaviour, see: P. R. Lawrence and N. Nohria, *Driven: How Human Nature Shapes Our Choices*, (San Francisco: Jossey-Bass, 2002); C. Loch, M. Yaziji, and C. Langen, "The Fight for the Alpha Position: Channeling Status Competition in Organizations," *European Management Journal*, 19 (February 2001), pp. 16–25; B. D. Pierce and R. White, "The Evolution of Social Structure: Why Biology Matters," *Academy of Management Review*, 24 (October 1999), pp. 843–53; N. Nicholson, "Evolutionary Psychology: Toward a New View of Human Nature and Organizational Society," *Human Relations*, 50 (September 1997), pp. 1053–78.

67. T. S. Kuhn, *The Structure of Scientific Revolutions* (Chicago: University of Chicago Press, 1970).

68. C. Heath and S. B. Sitkin, "Big-B versus Big-O: What is Organizational about Organizational Behaviour?" *Journal of Organizational Behaviour*, 22 (2001), pp. 43–58.

69. A. Strauss and J. Corbin (Eds.). *Grounded Theory in Practice*. (London: Sage Publications, 1997); B. G. Glaser and A. Strauss. *The Discovery of Grounded Theory: Strategies for Qualitative Research*. (Chicago, IL: Aldine Publishing Co, 1967).

70. For an excellent critique of the "one best way" approach by past scholars, see: P. F. Drucker, "Management's New Paradigms," *Forbes*, October 5, 1998, pp. 152–77.

71. H. L. Tosi and J. W. Slocum, Jr., "Contingency Theory: Some Suggested Directions," *Journal of Management*, 10 (1984), pp. 9–26.

72. D. M. Rousseau and R. J. House, "Meso Organizational Behaviour: Avoiding Three Fundamental Biases," In C. J. Cooper and D. M. Rousseau (Eds.) *Trends in Organizational Behaviour*, Vol. 1, (Chichester, UK: John Wiley & Sons, 1994), pp. 13–30.

73. H. Trinca, "Her Way," *Boss Magazine*, October 9, 2000.

74. R. T. Pascale, M. Millemann, and L. Gioja, *Surfing the Edge of Chaos* (NY: Crown, 2000); P. Senge et al, *The Dance of Change*, (NY: Currency Doubleday, 1999), pp. 137–48; A. De Geus, *The Living Company*. (Boston: Harvard Busi-

ness School Press, 1997); A. Waring, *Practical Systems Thinking*, (Boston: International Thomson Business Press, 1997); P. M. Senge, *The Fifth Discipline: The Art and Practice of the Learning Organization* (New York: Doubleday Currency, 1990), Chapter 4; F. E. Kast and J. E. Rosenweig, "General Systems Theory: Applications for Organization and Management," *Academy of Management Journal*, 1972, pp. 447–65.

75. R. Mitchell, "Feeding the Flames," *Business 2.0*, May 1, 2001.

76. V. P. Rindova and S. Kotha, "Continuous 'Morphing': Competing through Dynamic Capabilities, Form, and Function," *Academy of Management Journal*, 44 (2001), pp. 1263–80; R.T. Pascale, M. Millemann, and L. Gioja, *Surfing on the Edge of Chaos* (London: Texere, 2000).

77. R. Martin, "The Virtue Matrix: Calculating the Return on Corporate Responsibility," *Harvard Business Review*, 68 (March 2002), pp. 68–75.

78. M. L. Tushman, M. B. Nadler, and D. A. Nadler, *Competing by Design : The Power of Organizational Architecture* (New York: Oxford University Press, 1997).

79. G. F. B. Probst, "Practical Knowledge Management: A Model That Works," *Prism* (Second Quarter 1998), pp. 17–23; G. Miles, Grant, R. E. Miles, V. Perrone, and L. Edvinsson, "Some Conceptual And Research Barriers To The Utilization Of Knowledge," *California Management Review*, 40 (Spring 1998), pp. 281–88; E. C. Nevis, A. J. DiBella, and J. M. Gould, "Understanding Organizations as Learning Systems," *Sloan Management Review*, 36 (Winter 1995), pp. 73–85; G. Huber, "Organizational Learning: The Contributing Processes and Literature." *Organizational Science*, 2 (1991), pp. 88–115.

80. H. Saint-Onge and D. Wallace, *Leveraging Communities of Practice for Strategic Advantage*, (Boston: Butterworth-Heinemann, 2003), pp. 9–10; L. A. Joia, "Measuring Intangible Corporate Assets Linking Business Strategy With Intellectual Capital," *Journal of Intellectual Capital*, 1 (2000), pp. 68–84; T. A. Stewart, *Intellectual Capital: The New Wealth of Organizations* (New York: Currency/Doubleday, 1997); H. Saint-Onge, "Tacit Knowledge: The Key to the Strategic Alignment of Intellectual Capital," *Strategy & Leadership*, 24 (March/April 1996), pp. 10–14.

81. Relationship capital was initially called customer capital in the knowledge management literature. However, its concept is evolving to relationships among external stakeholders. For example, see: D. Halloran, "Putting Knowledge Management Initiatives into Action at Motorola," Presentation by Motorola vice-president and director of human resources Dan Halloran at The Future of Business in the New Knowledge Economy Conference, March 22–23, 2000, Pan Pacific Hotel, Singapore.

82. N. Bontis, "Assessing Knowledge Assets: A Review of the Models Used to Measure Intellectual Capital," *International Journal of Management Reviews*, 3 (2001), pp. 41–60; P.N. Bukh, H.T. Larsen, and J. Mouritsen, "Constructing Intellectual Capital Statements," *Scandinavian Journal of Management*, 17 (March 2001), pp. 87–108.

83. There is no complete agreement on the meaning of organizational learning (or learning organization), and the relationship between organizational learning and knowledge management is still somewhat ambiguous. For discussion on this point, see: B. R. McElyea, "Knowledge Management, Intellectual Capital, and Learning Organizations: A Triad of Future Management Integration," *Futurics*, 26 (2002), pp. 59–65.

84. P. Tam, "Hot Jobs in a Cool Economy," *Ottawa Citizen*, April 18, 2002. The practice of grafting in knowledge management is discussed in: Huber, "Organizational Learning," *Organizational Science*.

85. L. Falkenberg, J. Woiceshyn and J. Karagianis, "Knowledge Acquisition Processes For Technology Decisions," *Proceedings of the Academy of Management 2002 Annual Conference*, Technology and Innovation Management Division, pp. J1–J6.

86. A. L. Brown, "In Economic Slowdown, Wal-Mart Counts on its Cultural Roots," *Detroit News*, June 9, 2001; L. Wah, "Behind the Buzz," *Management Review*, 88 (April 1999), pp. 16–19; C. W. Wick and L. S. Leon, "From Ideas to Actions: Creating a Learning Organization." *Human Resource Management*, 34 (Summer 1995), pp. 299–311; D. Ulrich, T. Jick, and M. Von Glinow, "High Impact Learning: Building and Diffusing Learning Capability." *Organizational Dynamics*, 22 (Autumn 1993), pp. 52–66. This is similar to "synthetic learning" described in D. Miller, "A Preliminary Typology of Organizational Learning: Synthesizing the Literature," *Journal of Management*, 22 (1996), pp. 485–505.

87. C. O'Dell and C. J. Grayson, "If Only We Knew What We Know: Identification And Transfer Of Internal Best Practices," *California Management Review*, 40 (Spring 1998), pp. 154–174; R. Ruggles, "The State Of The Notion: Knowledge Management In Practice," *California Management Review*, 40 (Spring 1998), pp. 80–89; G. S. Richards and S. C. Goh, "Implementing Organizational Learning: Toward a Systematic Approach," *The Journal of Public Sector Management*, (Autumn 1995), pp. 25–31.

88. Saint-Onge and Wallace, *Leveraging Communities of Practice for Strategic Advantage*, pp. 12–13; Etienne C Wenger and William M Snyder, "Communities of Practice: The Organizational Frontier," *Harvard Business Review* 78 (January-February 2000), pp. 139–45; C. O'Dell and C. J. Grayson, "If Only We Knew What We Know: Identification And Transfer Of Internal Best Practices," *California Management Review*, 40 (Spring 1998), pp. 154–74.

89. Saint-Onge and Wallace, *Leveraging Communities of Practice for Strategic Advantage*, Chapter 5.

90. G. Barker, "High Priest of the PC," *The Age*, April 4, 2001; N. Way, "Talent War," *Business Review Weekly*, August 18, 2000, p. 64.

91. Stewart, *Intellectual Capital*, Chapter 7.

92. B.P. Sunoo "The Sydney Challenge," *Workforce*, September 2000, pp. 70–76

93. D. Lei, J. W. Slocum, and R. A. Pitts, "Designing Organizations for Competitive Advantage: The Power of Unlearning and Learning," *Organizational Dynamics*, 27 (Winter 1999), pp. 24–38; M. E. McGill and J. W. Slocum, Jr., "Unlearn the Organization," *Organizational Dynamics*, 22 (2) (1993), pp. 67–79.

CHAPTER TWO

1. K. MacQueen, "The Anti-Retailer: Vancouver's Mountain Equipment Co-op Succeeds in Spite of Itself," *Maclean's*, April 29, 2002, p. 30; L. Hendry, "Friend of the Earth," *Winnipeg Free Press*, March 16, 2002, p. A16; A. Samuel, "Mountain Coop's Web Election a Bold Climb Toward Revitalizing Democracy," *Vancouver Sun*, March 13, 2002, p. A15; H. Shaw, "Mountain keeps Profit at Sea Level," *National Post*, June 28, 2001, p. C2.

2. S. Roccas, L. Sagiv, S. H. Schwartz, and A. Knafo, "The Big Five Personality Factors and Personal Values," *Personality and Social Psychology*, 28 (June 2002), pp. 789–801.

3. C. C. Pinder, *Work Motivation in Organizational Behaviour*, (Upper Saddle River, NJ: Prentice-Hall, 1998); E. E. Lawler III, *Motivation in Work Organizations* (Monterey, Calif.: Brooks/Cole, 1973), pp. 2–5.

4. N. DeBono, "Workforce Tipped Scales in City's Favour," *London Free Press*, February 9, 2002.

5. J. P. Briscoe and D. T. Hall, "Grooming and Picking Leaders Using Competency Frameworks: Do They Work? An Alternative Approach and New Guidelines for Practice," *Organizational Dynamics*, 28 (Autumn 1999), pp. 37–52; Hay Group et. al. *Raising the Bar: Using Competencies to Enhance Employee Performance* (Scottsdale, AZ: American Compensation Association, 1996); L. M. Spencer and S. M. Spencer, *Competence at Work: Models for Superior Performance* (New York: Wiley, 1993); R. Boyatzis, *The Competent Manager: A Model for Effective Performance* (New York: John Wiley & Sons, 1982).

6. Royal Bank of Canada's competencies are described at their Web site on August 28, 2002: http://www.rbc.com/fastforward/bf_key_comp.html. Two examples of the three competency set are found in: T. Hellström, "Knowledge and Competence Management at Ericsson: Decentralization and Organizational Fit," *Journal of Knowledge Management*, 4 (2000). Other writers have also organized competencies into these three categories. See, for example: D. Goleman, "Emotional Intelligence: Issues in Paradigm Building," In C. Cherniss and D. Goleman (eds.), *The Emotionally Intelligent Workplace* (San Francisco: Jossey-Bass, (2001), p. 23.

7. R. Jacobs, "Using Human Resource Functions to Enhance Emotional Intelligence," In C. Cherniss and D. Goleman (eds.), *The Emotionally Intelligent Workplace* (San Francisco: Jossey-Bass, (2001), pp. 161–63; J. Sandberg, "Understanding Human Competence at Work: An Interpretative Approach," *Academy of Management Journal*, 43 (January 2000), pp. 9–25; T. Hoffmann, "The Meanings of Competency," *Journal of European Industrial Training*, 23 (1999), pp. 275–85.

8. J. R. Edwards, "Person-Job Fit: A Conceptual Integration, Literature Review, and Methodological Critique," *International Review of Industrial and Organizational Psychology*, 6 (1991), pp. 283–357; J. E. Hunter and R. F. Hunter, "Validity and Utility of Alternative Predictors of Job Performance," *Psychological Bulletin*, 96 (1984), pp. 72–98.

9. J. Baxter, "Canadian Firms 'Underinvest' in Employees," *Ottawa Citizen*, October 26, 2001.

10. B. Power, "Hanging Around Truly Mandatory in Course," *Halifax Herald*, January 25, 2002.

11. B. Riggs and M. E. Thyfault, "The Modern Call Center—Customer Relationships And Loyalty Take Center Stage," *InformationWeek*, October 4, 1999.

12. The converse of this statement is that role ambiguity undermines job performance. For evidence of this, see: A. Nygaard and R. Dahlstrom, "Role Stress and Effectiveness in Horizontal Alliances," *Journal of Marketing*, 66 (April 2002), pp. 61–82.

13. L. Ramsay, "Time to Examine the Exam," *National Post*, October 18, 1999, p. C15.

14. Gary Johns discusses situational factors both in terms of constraints on behaviour and on the complexities of organizational research. See G. Johns, "Commentary: In Praise of Context," *Journal of Organizational Behaviour*, 22 (2001), pp. 31–42; Also see S. B. Bacharach and P. Bamberger, "Beyond Situational Constraints: Job Resources Inadequacy and Individual Performance at Work," *Human Resource Management Review*, 5 (1995), pp. 79–102; K. F. Kane (ed.), "Special Issue: Situational Constraints and Work Performance," *Human Resource Management Review*, 3 (Summer 1993), pp. 83–175.

15. J. H. Sheridan, "Lockheed Martin Corp.," *Industry Week*, 247 (October 19, 1998), pp. 54–56.

16. J. P Campbell, "The Definition and Measurement of Performance in the New Age," In D. R. Ilgen and E. D. Pulakos (eds.) *The Changing Nature of Performance: Implications for Staffing, Motivation, and Development* (San Francisco: Jossey-Bass, 1999), pp. 399–429; J. P. Campbell, R. A. McCloy, S. H. Oppler, and C. E. Sager, "A Theory of Performance," In N. Schmitt, W. C. Borman, and Associates (eds.) *Personnel Selection in Organizations* (San Francisco: Jossey-Bass, 1993), pp. 35–70.

17. D. W. Organ, "Organizational Citizenship Behaviour: It's Construct Clean-up Time," *Human Performance*, 10 (1997), pp. 85–97; D. W. Organ, "The Motivational Basis of Organizational Citizenship Behaviour," *Research in Organizational Behaviour*, 12 (1990), pp. 43–72. Early reference to organizational citizenship (extra-role behaviours) is found in: C. I. Barnard, *The Functions of the Executive* (Cambridge, Mass.: Harvard University Press, 1938), pp. 83–84; D. Katz and R. L. Kahn, *The Social Psychology of Organizations* (New York: Wiley, 1966), pp. 337–40.

18. J. A. LePine, A. Erez, and D. E. Johnson, "The Nature and Dimensionality of Organizational Citizenship Behaviour: A Critical Review and Meta-Analysis," *Journal of Applied Psychology*, 87 (February 2002), pp. 52–65; L. Van Dyne and J. A. LePine, "Helping and Voice Extra-Role Behaviours: Evidence Of Construct and Predictive Validity," *Academy of Management Journal*, 41 (1998), pp. 108–119; R. N. Kanungo and J. A. Conger, "Promoting Altruism as a Corporate Goal," *Academy of Management Executive*, 7, no. 3 (1993), pp. 37–48.

19. M. Rotundo and P. Sackett, "The Relative Importance of Task, Citizenship, and Counterproductive Performance to Global Ratings of Job Performance: A Policy-Capturing Approach," *Journal of Applied Psychology*, 87 (February 2002), pp. 66–80.

20. P. E. Spector and S. Fox "An Emotion-Centered Model of Voluntary Work Behaviour: Some Parallels between Counterproductive Work Behaviour and Organizational Citizenship Behaviour," *Human Resource Management Review*, 12 (2002), pp. 269–92; S. Fox, P. E. Spector, and D. Miles, "Counterproductive Work Behaviour (CWB) in Response to Job Stressors and Organizational Justice: Some Mediator and Moderator Tests for Autonomy and Emotions," *Journal of Vocational Behaviour*, 59 (2001) pp. 291–309.

21. D. Yankelovich, "Got to Give to Get," *Mother Jones*, Vol. 22 (July 1997), pp. 60–63.

22. For specific Canadian examples of staff shortages, see: K. Jaimet, "Forecast Calls for Weather Expert Drought," *National Post*, April 11, 2002; C. Nuttall-Smith, "The Energy Boom: Is B.C. Ready?" *Vancouver Sun*, June 2, 2001; P. Withers, "Running on Empty," *B.C. Business*, 29 (May 2001), pp. 50–57.

23. P. Bailey, "St. Paul's Hospital Forced to Shut Doors to Emergency After All Beds were Taken," *Vancouver Sun*, November 15, 2001.

24. N. Cockburn, "Healthy Job Market for Nursing Grads," *Edmonton Journal*, June 7, 2002. "Nursing Shortage Closes The Pas Hospital Unit," *CBC News Manitoba*, April 5, 2002.

25. "War for Talent II: Seven Ways to Win," *Fast Company*, 42 (January 2001).

26. S. M. Jacoby, "Most Workers Find A Sense Of Security In Corporate Life," *Los Angeles Times*, September 7, 1998, p. B5.

27. T. Romita, "The Talent Search," *Business 2.0*, June 12, 2001; K. Dobbs, "Knowing How to Keep your Best and Brightest," *Workforce*, 80 (April 2001), pp. 56–60.

28. T. R. Mitchell, B. C. Holtom, and T. W. Lee, "How to Keep your Best Employees: Developing an Effective Retention Policy," *Academy of Management Executive*, 15 (November 2001), pp. 96–108.

29. G. Kean, "Too Much Money Spent On Sick Leave, Says Board Association," *Western Star*, November 29, 2001; V. Lu, "Rising Sick Days Cost Billions," *Toronto Star*, August 15, 1999.

Canadian absenteeism data are from: Statistics Canada. "Work Absences," *The Daily*, July 4, 2002. For data comparing absenteeism in Canada and other OECD countries, see: R. M. Leontaridi and M. E. Ward, "Dying to Work? An Investigation into Work-related Stress, Quitting Intentions, and Absenteeism," Paper presented at the Royal Economic Society 2002 Annual Conference, University of Warwick, Coventry, UK, March 2002.

30. D. F. Colemen and N. V. Schaefer, "Weather and Absenteeism," *Canadian Journal of Administrative Sciences*, 7, no. 4 (1990), pp. 35–42; S. R. Rhodes and R. M. Steers, *Managing Employee Absenteeism* (Reading, Mass.: Addison-Welsey, 1990).

31. D. A. Harrison and J. J. Martocchio, "Time for Absenteeism: A 20-Year Review of Origins, Offshoots, and Outcomes," *Journal of Management*, 24 (Spring 1998), pp. 305–50; R. D. Hackett and P. Bycio, "An Evaluation of Employee Absenteeism as a Coping Mechanism Among Hospital Nurses," *Journal of Occupational & Organizational Psychology*, 69 (December 1996) pp. 327–38; R. G. Ehrenberg, R. A. Ehrenberg, D. I. Rees, and E. L. Ehrenberg, "School District Leave Policies, Teacher Absenteeism, and Student Achievement," *Journal of Human Resources*, 26 (Winter 1991), pp. 72–105; I. Ng, "The Effect of Vacation and Sick Leave Policies on Absenteeism," *Canadian Journal of Administrative Sciences* 6 (December 1989), pp. 18–27; V. V. Baba and M. J. Harris, "Stress and Absence: A Cross-Cultural Perspective," *Research in Personnel and Human Resources Management, Supplement*, 1 (1989), pp. 317–37.

32. B. A. Agle and C. B. Caldwell, "Understanding Research on Values in Business," *Business and Society*, 38 (September 1999), pp. 326–87; J. J. Dose, "Work Values: An Integrative Framework and Illustrative Application to Organizational Socialization," *Journal of Occupational and Organizational Psychology*, 70 (September 1997), pp. 219–240; A. Sagie and D. Elizur, "Work Values: A Theoretical Overview and a Model of Their Effects," *Journal of Organizational Behaviour*, 17 (1996), pp. 503–14; S. H. Schwartz, "Are there Universal Aspects

in the Structure and Contents of Human Values?" *Journal of Social Issues*, 50 (1994), pp. 19–45; W. H. Schmidt and B. Z. Posner, *Managerial Values in Perspective* (New York: American Management Association, 1983); M. Rokeach, *The Nature of Human Values* (New York: The Free Press, 1973).

33. D. Lubinski, D. B. Schmidt, & C. P. Benbow, "A 20-year Stability Analysis of the Study of Values for Intellectually Gifted Individuals from Adolescence to Adulthood," *Journal of Applied Psychology*, 81 (1996), pp. 443–51; M. Rokeach, *Understanding Human Values* (New York: Free Press, 1979).

34. For a recent study of values and leadership, see: C. P. Egri and S. Herman, "Leadership in the North American Environmental Sector: Values, Leadership Styles, and Contexts of Environmental Leaders and Their Organizations," *Academy of Management Journal*, 43 (August 2000), pp. 571–604. For other studies on the effects of values, see: Meglino and Ravlin, "Individual Values in Organizations."

35. S. H. Schwartz, G. Melech, A. Lehmann, S. Burgess, M. Harris, and V. Owens, "Extending the Cross-Cultural Validity of the Theory of Basic Human Values With a Different Method of Measurement," *Journal of Cross-Cultural Psychology*, 32 (September 2001), pp. 519–42; P. Stern, T. Dietz, and G. A. Guagnano, "A Brief Inventory of Values," *Educational and Psychological Measurement*, 58 (December 1998), pp. 984–1001; S. H. Schwartz, "Value Priorities and Behaviour: Applying a Theory of Integrated Value Systems," In C. Seligman, J. M. Olson, & M. P. Zanna (Eds.), *The Psychology of Values: The Ontario Symposium, Vol. 8*, (Hillsdale, NJ: Lawrence Erlbaum, 1996), pp. 1–24; S. H. Schwartz, "Are there Universal Aspects in the Structure and Contents of Human Values?" *Journal of Social Issues*, 50 (1994), pp. 19–45; S. H. Schwartz, "Universals in the Content and Structure of Values: Theoretical Advances and Empirical Tests in 20 Countries," *Advances in Experimental Social Psychology*, 25 (1992), pp. 1–65.

36. Meglino and Ravlin, "Individual Values in Organizations"; C. Argyris and D. A. Schön, *Organizational Learn-*

ing: A Theory of Action Perspective (Reading, MA: Addison-Wesley, 1978).

37. P. Pruzan, "The Question of Organizational Consciousness: Can Organizations have Values, Virtues and Visions?" *Journal of Business Ethics*, 29 (February 2001), pp. 271–284.

38. S. R. Chatterjee; C. A. L. Pearson, "Indian Managers in Transition: Orientations, Work Goals, Values and Ethics," *Management International Review*, January 2000, pp. 81–95; K. F. Alam, "Business Ethics in New Zealand Organizations: Views from the Middle and Lower Level Managers," *Journal of Business Ethics*, 22 (November 1999), pp. 145–53.

39. T. Treadgold, "Love In A Hot Climate," *Business Review Weekly*, January 17, 2002, p. 17; H. Trinca, "The McKinsey Rapport," *BOSS Magazine*, March 9, 2001, p. 34.

40. A. E. M. Van Vianen, "Person-Organization Fit: The Match Between Newcomers' And Recruiters' Preferences For Organizational Cultures," *Personnel Psychology*, 53 (Spring 2000), pp. 113–49; B. A. Agle and C. B. Caldwell, "Understanding Research on Values in Business," *Business and Society*, 38 (September 1999), pp. 326–87.

41. S. Whittaker, "Bringing your Own Values to Work," *Ottawa Citizen*, April 7, 2001, p. J1.

42. D. Arnott, *Corporate Cults* (NY: AMACOM, 1999); K. M. Eisenhardt, J. L. Kahwajy, and L. J. Bourgeois, III "Conflict and Strategic Choice: How Top Management Teams Disagree," *California Management Review*, 39 (Winter 1997), pp. 42–62.

43. T. A. Joiner, "The Influence of National Culture and Organizational Culture Alignment on Job Stress and Performance: Evidence from Greece," *Journal of Managerial Psychology*, 16 (2001), pp. 229–42; Z. Aycan, R. N. Kanungo, and J. B. P. Sinha, "Organizational Culture And Human Resource Management Practices: The Model of Culture Fit," *Journal Of Cross-Cultural Psychology*, 30 (July 1999), pp. 501–26.

44. C. Fox, "Firms Go Warm And Fuzzy To Lure Staff," *Australian Financial Review*, May 15, 2001, p. 58.

45. D. Oyserman, H. M. Coon, and M. Kemmelmeier, "Rethinking Individualism and Collectivism: Evaluation of Theoretical Assumptions and Meta-Analyses," *Psychological Bulletin*, 128 (2002), pp. 3–72; F. S. Niles, "Individualism-Collectivism Revisited," *Cross-Cultural Research*, 32 (November 1998), pp. 315–41; C. P. Earley and C. B. Gibson, "Taking Stock In Our Progress On Individualism-Collectivism: 100 Years Of Solidarity And Community," *Journal of Management*, 24 (May 1998), pp. 265–304; J. A. Wagner III, "Studies of Individualism-Collectivism: Effects of Cooperation in Groups," *Academy of Management Journal*, 38 (1995), pp. 152–72; H. C. Triandis, *Individualism and Collectivism* (Boulder, CO: Westview, 1995).

46. D. Oyserman et al., "Rethinking Individualism and Collectivism."

47. M. Voronov and J. A. Singer, "The Myth of Individualism-Collectivism: A Critical Review," *Journal of Social Psychology*, 142 (August 2002), pp. 461–80; M. H. Bond, "Reclaiming the Individual from Hofstede's Ecological Analysis—A 20-Year Odyssey: Comment on Oyserman et al. (2002)" *Psychological Bulletin*, 128 (2002), pp. 73–77.

48. K. L. Newman and S. D. Nolan, "Culture and Congruence: The Fit Between Management Practices and National Culture," *Journal of International Business Studies*, 27 (1996), pp. 753–79; G. Hofstede, "Cultural Constraints in Management Theories," *Academy of Management Executive*, 7 (1993), pp. 81–94; G. Hofstede, *Culture's Consequences: International Differences in Work-Related Values* (Beverly Hills, CA: Sage, 1980).

49. M. Erez and P. Christopher Earley, *Culture, Self-Identity, and Work* (New York: Oxford University Press, 1993), pp. 126–27.

50. G. Hofstede, *Cultures and Organizations: Software of the Mind*, (New York: McGraw-Hill, 1991), p. 124. Hofstede used the terms "masculinity" and "femininity" for achievement and nurturing orientation, respectively. We have adopted the latter to minimize the sexist perspective of these concepts. The achievement and nurturing orientation labels are also used in G. R. Jones, J. M. George, and C. W. L. Hill, *Contemporary Management* (Burr Ridge, IL: Irwin/McGraw-Hill, 1998), pp. 112–13.

51. For counterarguments, see: G. Hofstede, "Attitudes, Values and Organizational Culture: Disentangling the Concepts," *Organization Studies*, 19 (June 1998), pp. 477–92.

52. M. Voronov and J. A. Singer, "The Myth of Individualism-Collectivism: A Critical Review," *Journal of Social Psychology*, 142 (August 2002), pp. 461–80; S.S. Sarwono and R.W Armstrong, "Microcultural Differences and Perceived Ethical Problems: An International Business Perspective," *Journal of Business Ethics*, 30 (March 2001), pp. 41–56; C.J. Robertson, "The Global Dispersion of Chinese Values: A Three-Country Study of Confucian Dynamism," *Management International Review*, 40 (Third Quarter 2000), pp. 253–68; J.S. Osland, A. Bird, J. Delano, and M. Jacob, "Beyond Sophisticated Stereotyping: Cultural Sensemaking in Context," *Academy of Management Executive*, 14 (February 2000), pp. 65–79. The research on Canada's 13 cultural groups is found in: M. Adams, *Better Happy than Rich?* (Toronto: Viking, 2001).

53. P. Brent, "Store Wars," *National Post*, October 16, 2001; B. Simon, "Canada Warms to Wal-Mart," *New York Times*, September 1, 2001, p. 1; J. Heinzl, "Wal-Mart's Cheer Fades," *Globe and Mail*, February 15, 1997.

54. M. Adams, "What Makes Us Different," *Globe and Mail*, July 4, 2001; Adams, *Better Happy than Rich?*

55. C. Cobb, "Canadians want Diverse Society: Poll," *Ottawa Citizen*, February 18, 2002, p. A5.

56. K. May, "Canadian Nationalism Growing: Study," *Ottawa Citizen*, June 5, 2002, p. A8.

57. H. MacLennan, *Two Solitudes* (Toronto: MacMillan of Canada, 1945).

58. E. Grabb, J. Curtis, and D. Baer, "Defining Moments and Recurring Myths: Comparing Canadians and Americans after the American Revolution," *Canadian Review of Sociology and Anthropology*, 37 (November 2000), pp. 373–419; D. M. Taylor and L. Dube, L. "Two Faces of Identity: The 'I' and the 'We'," *Journal of Social Issues*, 42 (1986), pp. 81-98; R. N. Kanungo and J. K. Bhatnagar, "Achievement Orientation and Occupational Values: A Comparative Study of Young French

and English Canadians," *Canadian Journal of Behavioural Science*, 12 (1978), pp. 384–92.

59. N. Chiasson, L. Dube, and J-P. Blondin, "Happiness: A Look Into the Folk Psychology of Four Cultural Groups," *Journal of Cross-Cultural Psychology*, 27 (November 1996), pp. 673–91; M. Major, M. McCarrey, P. Mercier, and Y. Gasse, "Meanings of Work And Personal Values Of Canadian Anglophone And Francophone Middle Managers," *Canadian Journal of Administrative Sciences*, 11 (September 1994), pp. 251–63.

60. Z. Wu and D. E. Baer, "Attitudes Toward Family and Gender Roles: A Comparison of English and French Canadian Women," *Journal of Comparative Family Studies*, 27 (Autumn 1996), pp. 437–52. The quotation, by Seymour Lipset, is also cited from this source.

61. L. Redpath and M. Nielsen. "A Comparison of Native Culture, Nonnative Culture and New Management Ideology." *Canadian Journal of Administrative Sciences*, vol. 14 (September 1997): 327–39; I. Chapman, D. McCaskill, and D. Newhouse, *Management in Contemporary Aboriginal Organizations* (Peterborough, Ont.: Trent University, 1992), Administrative Studies Working Paper Series #92-04.

62. R. Walker, "Nunavut Politics: When Caribou Culture meets Westminster," *Christian Science Monitor*, April 28, 2000.

63. R. B. Anderson, "Entrepreneurship and Aboriginal Canadians: A Case Study in Economic Development," *Journal of Developmental Entrepreneurship*, 7 (April 2002), pp. 45–65; J. Stackhouse, "Norma Rae of the Okanagan," *Globe and Mail*, November 8, 2001, p. A14.

64. C. Savoye, "Workers say Honesty is Best Company Policy," *Christian Science Monitor*, June 15, 2000.

65. P. L. Schumann "A Moral Principles Framework for Human Resource Management Ethics," *Human Resource Management Review*, 11 (Spring-Summer 2001), pp. 93–111; M. G. Velasquez, *Business Ethics*, 4th ed. (Upper Saddle River, N.J.: Prentice Hall, 1998), Chapter 2.

66. R. Berenbeim, "The Search for Global Ethics," *Vital Speeches of the Day*, 65 (January 1999), pp. 177–78.

67. Velasquez, *Business Ethics*, p. 123; Schumann "A Moral Principles Framework for Human Resource Management Ethics," p. 104.

68. D. R. May and K. P. Pauli, "The Role of Moral Intensity in Ethical Decision Making," *Business and Society*, 41 (March 2002), pp. 84–117; B.H. Frey, "The Impact of Moral Intensity on Decision Making in a Business Context," *Journal of Business Ethics*, 26 (August 2000), pp. 181–95; J. M. Dukerich, M. J. Waller, E. George, and G. P. Huber "Moral Intensity and Managerial Problem Solving," *Journal of Business Ethics*, 24 (March 2000), pp. 29–38; T. J. Jones, "Ethical Decision Making by Individuals in Organizations: An Issue Contingent Model," *Academy of Management Review*, 16 (1991), pp. 366–95.

69. J. R. Sparks and S. D. Hunt, "Marketing Researcher Ethical Sensitivity: Conceptualization, Measurement, and Exploratory Investigation," *Journal of Marketing*, 62 (April 1998), pp. 92–109.

70. B. Stoneman and K.K. Holliday, "Pressure Cooker," *Banking Strategies*, January-February, 2001, p. 13; Alam, "Business Ethics in New Zealand Organizations"; K. Blotnicky, "Is Business in Moral Decay?" *Halifax Chronicle-Herald*, June 11, 2000; D. McDougall and B. Orsini, "Fraudbusting Ethics," *CMA Management*, 73 (June 1999), pp. 18–21; J. Evensen, "Ethical Behaviour In Business And Life Is Its Own Reward," *Deseret News* (Salt Lake City, UT), October 19, 1997. For a discussion of the situational effects on ethical conduct, see: C. J. Thompson, "A Contextualist Proposal for the Conceptualization and Study of Marketing Ethics," *Journal of Public Policy and Marketing*, 14 (1995), pp. 177–91.

71. V. Kirsch, "Sometimes the Lines between Right and Wrong can Become a Little Blurred," *Guelph Mercury*, October 18, 1999, p. B1; L. Young, "Ethics Training is the Key," *Canadian HR Reporter*, June 14, 1999, p. 2; M. Acharya, "A Matter of Business Ethics," *Kitchener-Waterloo Record*, March 23, 1999, p. C2.

72. M. S. Schwartz, "The Nature of the Relationship Between Corporate Codes of Ethics and Behaviour," *Journal of Business Ethics*, 32 (August 2001), pp. 247–62; J. S. Adams and A. Tashchian, "Codes of Ethics as Signals for Ethical Behaviour," *Journal of Business Ethics*, 29 (February 2001), pp. 199–211; M. A. Clark and S. L. Leonard, "Can Corporate Codes of Ethics Influence Behaviour?" *Journal of Business Ethics*, 17 (April 1998), pp. 619–30.

73. L. Young, "Employer Ethics Codes Lack Supports Needed for Success," *Canadian HR Reporter*, April 19, 1999, pp. 1, 11. For a discussion of additional ethical practices, see "Doing Well by Doing Good," *Economist*, April 22, 2000.

74. R. N. Kanungo "Ethical Values of Transactional and Transformational Leaders," *Canadian Journal of Administrative Sciences*, 18 (December 2001), pp. 257–65; E. Aronson, "Integrating Leadership Styles and Ethical Perspectives," *Canadian Journal of Administrative Sciences*, 18 (December 2001), pp. 244–256; M. Mendonca "Preparing for Ethical Leadership in Organizations," *Canadian Journal of Administrative Sciences*, 18 (December 2001), pp. 266–76.

75. S. Roccas, L. Sagiv, S. H. Schwartz, and A. Knafo, "The Big Five Personality Factors and Personal Values," *Personality and Social Psychology*, 28 (June 2002), pp. 789–801.

76. R. T. Hogan, "Personality and Personality Measurement," In M. D. Dunnette and L. M. Hough (eds.) *Handbook of Industrial and Organizational Psychology*, 2nd ed, Vol. 2 (Palo Alto, CA: Consulting Psychologists Press, 1991), pp. 873–919. Also see: W. Mischel, *Introduction to Personality* (New York: Holt, Rinehart, & Winston, 1986).

77. H. M. Weiss and S. Adler, "Personality and Organizational Behaviour," *Research in Organizational Behaviour*, 6 (1984), pp. 1–50.

78. R.R. McCrae et al., "Nature over Nurture: Temperament, Personality, and Life Span Development," *Journal of Personality and Social Psychology*, 78 (2000), pp. 173-86.

79. H. C. Triandis and E. M. Suh, "Cultural Influences on Personality," *Annual Review of Psychology*, 53 (2002), pp. 133–60; D. C. Funder, "Personality,"

Annual Review of Psychology, 52 (2001), pp. 197–221; R. R. McCrae et al., "Nature over Nurture: Temperament, Personality, and Life Span Development," *Journal of Personality and Social Psychology*, 78 (2000), pp. 173–86; W. Revelle, "Personality Processes," *Annual Review of Psychology*, 46 (1995), pp. 295–328.

80. R. M. Guion and R. F. Gottier, "Validity of Personality Measures in Personnel Selection," *Personnel Psychology*, 18 (1965), pp. 135–64. Also see N. Schmitt, R. Z. Gooding, R. D. Noe, and M. Kirsch, "Meta-Analyses of Validity Studies Published Between 1964 and 1982 and the Investigation of Study Characteristics," *Personnel Psychology*, 37 (1984), pp. 407–22.

81. P. G. Irving, "On the Use of Personality Measures in Personnel Selection," *Canadian Psychology*, 34 (April 1993), pp. 208–14.

82. K. M. DeNeve and H. Cooper,"The Happy Personality: A Meta-Analysis of 137 Personality Traits and Subjective Well-Being," *Psychological Bulletin*, 124 (September 1998), pp. 197–229; M. K. Mount and M. R. Barrick, "The Big Five Personality Dimensions: Implications for Research and Practice in Human Resources Management," *Research in Personnel and Human Resources Management*, 13 (1995), pp. 153–200; B. M. Bass, *Stogdill's Handbook of Leadership: A Survey of Theory and Research*, 3rd ed. (New York: Free Press, 1990); J. L. Holland, *Making Vocation Choices: A Theory of Careers* (Englewood Cliffs, NJ: Prentice Hall, 1973).

83. C. Daniels, "Does This Man Need a Shrink?" *Fortune*, February 5, 2001, pp. 205.

84. This historical review, and the trait descriptions in this section are discussed in: R. J. Schneider and L. M. Hough, "Personality and Industrial/Organizational Psychology," *International Review of Industrial and Organizational Psychology*, 10 (1995), pp. 75–129; M. K. Mount and M. R. Barrick, "The Big Five Personality Dimensions: Implications for Research and Practice in Human Resources Management," *Research in Personnel and Human Resources Management*, 13 (1995), pp. 153–200; J. M. Digman, "Personality Structure: Emergence of the Five-Fac-

tor Model," *Annual Review of Psychology*, 41 (1990), pp. 417–40.

85. G. M. Hurtz and J. J. Donovan, "Personality and Job Performance: The Big Five Revisited," *Journal of Applied Psychology*, 85 (December 2000), pp. 869–79; M. K. Mount, M. R. Barrick, and J. P. Strauss, "Validity of Observer Ratings of the Big Five Personality Factors," *Journal of Applied Psychology*, 79 (1994), pp. 272–80; R. P. Tett, D. N. Jackson, and M. Rothstein, "Personality Measures as Predictors of Job Performance: A Meta-Analytic Review," *Personnel Psychology*, 44 (1991), pp. 703–42.

86. J. M. Howell and C. A. Higgins, "Champions of Change: Identifying, Understanding, and Supporting Champions of Technological Innovations," *Organizational Dynamics*, Summer 1990, pp. 40–55.

87. T. A. Judge and R. Ilies, "Relationship of Personality to Performance Motivation: A Meta-Analytic Review," *Journal of Applied Psychology*, 87 (August 2002), pp. 797–807; L. A. Witt, L. A. Burke, and M. R. Barrick, "The Interactive Effects of Conscientiousness and Agreeableness on Job Performance," *Journal of Applied Psychology*, 87 (February 2002), pp. 164–69; M. Dalton and M. Wilson, "The Relationship of the Five-Factor Model of Personality to Job Performance for a Group of Middle Eastern Expatriate Managers," *Journal of Cross-Cultural Psychology*, March 2000, pp. 250–58; K. P. Carson and G. L. Stewart, "Job Analysis and the Sociotechnical Approach to Quality: A Critical Examination," *Journal of Quality Management*, 1 (1996), pp. 49–64; Mount and Barrick, "The Big Five Personality Dimensions," pp. 177–78.

88. I. B. Myers, *The Myers-Briggs Type Indicator*. (Palo Alto, CA: Consulting Psychologists Press, 1987); C. G. Jung, *Psychological Types* (Translated by H. G. Baynes, revised by R.F.C. Hull). (Princeton, NJ: Princeton University Press, 1971). (Original work published in 1921).

89. L.R. Offermann and R.K. Spiros "The Science and Practice of Team Development: Improving the Link," *Academy of Management Journal*, 44 (April 2001), pp. 376–92.

90. G. Potts, "Oklahoma City Employers Use Personality Tests to Improve

Placement," *Daily Oklahoman*, February 26, 2001.

91. C. Caggiano, "Psycho Path," *Inc.*, 20 (July 1998), pp. 76–85.

92. W. L. Johnson et al., "A Higher Order Analysis of the Factor Structure of the Myers-Briggs Type Indicator," *Measurement and Evaluation in Counseling and Development*, 34 (July 2001), pp. 96–108; D. W. Salter and N. J. Evans, "Test-Retest of the Myers-Briggs Type Indicator: An Examination of Dominant Functioning," *Educational & Psychological Measurement*, 57 (August 1997), pp. 590–97; W. L. Gardner and M. J. Martinko, "Using the Myers-Briggs Type Indicator to Study Managers: A Literature Review and Research Agenda," *Journal of Management*, 22 (1996), pp. 45–83; M. H. McCaulley, "The Myers-Briggs Type Indicator: A Measure for Individuals and Groups," *Measurement and Evaluation in Counseling and Development*, 22 (1990), pp. 181–95.

93. J. A. Edwards, K. Lanning, and K. Hooker, "The MBTI and Social Information Processing: An Incremental Validity Study," *Journal of Personality Assessment*, 78 (June 2002), pp. 432–50; R. Farnsworth, E. Gilbert and D. Armstrong, "Exploring The Relationship Between The Myers-Briggs Type Indicator And The Baron Emotional Quotient Inventory: Applications For Professional Development Practices," *Proceedings of the Annual Conference of the Administrative Sciences Association of Canada, Human Resources Division*, 23 (9) (2002), pp. 16–23; Gardner and Martinko, "Using the Myers-Briggs Type Indicator to Study Managers."

94. P. E. Spector et al, "Do National Levels of Individualism and Internal Locus of Control Relate to Well-being: An Ecological Level International Study," *Journal of Organizational Behaviour*, 22 (2001), pp. 815–32; S. S. K. Lam and J. Schaubroeck, "The Role of Locus of Control in Reactions to Being Promoted and to Being Passed Over: A Quasi Experiment," *Academy of Management Journal*, 43 (February 2000), pp. 66–78; J. M. Howell and B. J. Avolio, "Transformational Leadership, Transactional Leadership, Locus of Control, and Support for Innovation: Key Predictors of Consolidated-Busi-

ness-Unit Performance," *Journal of Applied Psychology*, 78 (1993), pp. 891–902; D. Miller and J.-M. Toulouse, "Chief Executive Personality and Corporate Strategy and Structure in Small Firms," *Management Science*, 32 (1986), pp. 1389–1409; P. E. Spector, "Behaviour in Organizations as a Function of Employee's Locus of Control," *Psychological Bulletin*, 91 (1982), pp. 482–97.

95. M. Snyder, *Public Appearances/Private Realities: The Psychology of Self-Monitoring* (New York: W. H. Freeman, 1987).

96. A. Mehra, M. Kilduff, and D. J. Brass, "The Social Networks of High and Low Self-monitors: Implications for Workplace Performance," *Administrative Science Quarterly*, 46 (March 2001), pp. 121–46; M. A. Warech, J. W. Smither, R. R. Reilly, R. E. Millsap, and S. P. Reilly "Self-Monitoring and 360-Degree Ratings," *Leadership Quarterly*, 9 (Winter 1998), pp. 449–73; M. Kilduff and D. V. Day, "Do Chameleons Get Ahead? The Effects of Self-Monitoring on Managerial Careers," *Academy of Management Journal*, 37 (1994), pp. 1047–60; R. J. Ellis and S. E. Cronshaw, Self-Monitoring and Leader Emergence: A Test of Moderator Effects. *Small Group Research*, 23 (1992), pp. 113–29; S. J. Zaccaro, R. J. Foti, and D. A. Kenny, "Self-Monitoring and Trait-Based Variance in Leadership: An Investigation of Leader Flexibility Across Multiple Group Situations," *Journal of Applied Psychology*, 76 (1991), pp. 308–15.

97. T. Snyder, "Take This Job and Love It," *Chatelaine*, October 1999, p. 97.

98. J. Holland, *Making Vocational Choices: A Theory of Careers* (Englewood Cliffs, N. J.: Prentice Hall, 1973).

99. A. Furnham, "Vocational Preference and P-O Fit: Reflections on Holland's Theory of Vocational Choice," *Applied Psychology: An International Review*, 50 (2001), pp. 5–29; G. D. Gottfredson and J. L. Holland, "A Longitudinal Test of The Influence of Congruence: Job Satisfaction, Competency Utilization, and Counterproductive Behaviour," *Journal of Counseling Psychology*, 37, (1990), pp. 389–98.

100. Furnham, "Vocational Preference and P-O Fit"; J. Arnold, "The Psychology of Careers in Organizations," *International Review of Industrial and Organizational Psychology*, 12 (1997), pp. 1–37.

101. R.A. Young and C.P. Chen, "Annual Review: Practice and Research in Career Counseling and Development—1998," *Career Development Quarterly*, December 1999, p. 98.

CHAPTER THREE

1. M. Orton, "'You Feel Very Isolated'," *Ottawa Citizen*, July 25, 2002; R. Ross, "System Favours the Few, the Male," *Toronto Star*, May 20, 2002, p. E1; H. Sokoloff, "'Geek' Culture Turns Women Off Computer Studies: Report," *National Post*, March 19, 2002, p. A1; D. Rucker, "Barrier Breakers," *Oilweek*, April 2, 2001, p. 30ff.

2. Plato, *The Republic*, trans. D. Lee (Harmondsworth, England: Penguin, 1955), Part VII, Section 7.

3. S. F. Cronshaw and R. G. Lord, "Effects of Categorization, Attribution, and Encoding Processes on Leadership Perceptions," *Journal of Applied Psychology*, 72 (1987), pp. 97–106.

4. R. H. Fazio, D. R. Roskos-Ewoldsen, and M. C. Powell, "Attitudes, Perception, and Attention," In P. M. Niedenthal and S. Kitayama, (eds.) *The Heart's Eye: Emotional Influences in Perception and Attention* (San Diego,CA: Academic Press, 1994), pp. 197–216.

5. D. Goleman, *Vital Lies, Simple Truths: The Psychology of Deception* (New York: Touchstone, 1985); M. Haire and W. F. Grunes, "Perceptual Defenses: Processes Protecting an Organized Perception of Another Personality," *Human Relations*, 3 (1950), pp. 403–12.

6. C. N. Macrae, G. V. Bodenhausen, A. M. Schloerscheidt, and A. B. Milne, "Tales of the Unexpected: Executive Function and Person Perception." *Journal of Personality and Social Psychology*, 76 (1999), pp. 200–13; J. M. Beyer et al., "The Selective Perception of Managers Revisited," *Academy of Management Journal*, 40 (June 1997), pp. 716–37; C. N. Macrae and G. V. Bodenhausen, "The Dissection of Selection in Person Perception: Inhibitory Processes in Social Stereotyping," *Journal of Personality & Social Psychology*, 69 (1995), pp. 397–407; J. P. Walsh, "Selectivity and Selective Perception: An Investigation of Managers' Belief Structures and Information Processing," *Academy of Management Journal*, 31 (1988), pp. 873–96; D. C. Dearborn and H. A. Simon, "Selective Perception: A Note on the Departmental Identification of Executives," *Sociometry*, 21 (1958), pp. 140–44.

7. J. Rupert, "We Haven't Forgotten about Her," *Ottawa Citizen*, December 6, 1999; W. Burkan, "Developing Your Wide-Angle Vision; Skills for Anticipating the Future," *Futurist*, 32 (March 1998), pp. 35–38. For splatter vision applied to professional bird watchers, see E. Nickens, "Window on the Wild," *Backpacker*, 25 (April 1997), pp. 28–32.

8. D. Gurteen, "Knowledge, Creativity and Innovation," *Journal of Knowledge Management*, 2 (September 1998), p. 5; C. Argyris and D. A. Schön, *Organizational Learning II*. (Reading, MA: Addison-Wesley, 1996); P. M. Senge, *The Fifth Discipline: The Art and Practice of the Learning Organization* (New York: Doubleday Currency, 1990), Chapter 10; P. N. Johnson-Laird, *Mental Models* (Cambridge: Cambridge University Press, 1984). Mental models are widely discussed in the philosophy of logic. For example, see: J. L. Aronson, "Mental Models And Deduction," *American Behavioural Scientist*, 40 (May 1997), pp. 782–97.

9. "What are Mental Models?" *Sloan Management Review*, 38 (Spring 1997), p. 13; P. Nystrom and W. Starbuck, "To Avoid Organizational Crises, Unlearn," *Organizational Dynamics*, 12 (Winter 1984), pp. 53–65.

10. M. A. Hogg and D. J. Terry, "Social Identity and Self-categorization Processes in Organizational Contexts," *Academy of Management Review*, 25 (January 2000), pp. 121–40; B. E. Ashforth and F. Mael, "Social Identity Theory and the Organization," *Academy of Management Review*, 14 (1989), pp. 20–39; H. Tajfel, *Social Identity and Intergroup Relations* (Cambridge: Cambridge University Press, 1982). The process of self-identity in the social context is self-categorization theory, but self-categorization and social identity concepts have blended together so much that this section labels both as social identity theory.

11. The interaction between personal and social identity is quite complex, as researchers are now discovering. See

J.A. Howard, "Social Psychology of Identities," *Annual Review of Sociology*, 26 (2000), pp. 367–93.

12. J. E. Dutton, J. M. Dukerich, and C. V. Harquail, "Organizational Images And Member Identification," *Administrative Science Quarterly*, 39 (June 1994), pp. 239–63. For recent research on the selection of identity groups, see B. Simon and C. Hastedt, "Self-Aspects as Social Categories: The Role of Personal Importance and Valence," *European Journal of Social Psychology*, 29 (1999), pp. 479–87.

13. J. W. Jackson and E. R. Smith, "Conceptualizing Social Identity: A New Framework And Evidence For The Impact Of Different Dimensions," *Personality & Social Psychology Bulletin*, 25 (January 1999), pp. 120–35.

14. C.N. Macrae and G.V. Bodenhausen, "Social Cognition: Thinking Categorically about Others," *Annual Review of Psychology*, 51 (2000), pp. 93–120; S. T. Fiske, "Stereotyping, Prejudice, and Discrimination," In D. T. Gilbert, S. T. Fiske, & G. Lindzey (Eds.), *Handbook of Social Psychology, 4th ed.*, (New York: McGraw-Hill, 1998), pp. 357–411; W. G. Stephan and C. W. Stephan, *Intergroup Relations* (Boulder, CO: Westview, 1996), Chapter 1; L. Falkenberg, "Improving the Accuracy of Stereotypes within the Workplace," *Journal of Management*, 16 (1990), pp. 107–18.

15. M. Billig, "Henri Tajfel's 'Cognitive Aspects of Prejudice' and the Psychology of Bigotry," *British Journal of Social Psychology*, 41 (2002), pp. 171–88.

16. C. N. Macrae and G. V. Bodenhausen, "Social Cognition: Thinking Categorically about Others," *Annual Review of Psychology*, 51 (2000), pp. 93–120.

17. J. C. Turner and S. A. Haslam, "Social Identity, Organizations, and Leadership," In M. E. Turner, *Groups at Work: Theory and Research*, (Mahwah, NJ: Lawrence Erlbaum Associates, 2001), pp. 25–65; P. J. Oaks, S. A. Haslam, and J. C. Turner, *Stereotyping and Social Reality*. (Cambridge, MA: Blackwell, 1994). The recent Canadian study is found in: L. Sinclair and Z. Kunda, "Motivated Stereotyping of Women: She's Fine if She Praised Me but Incompetent if She Criticized Me," *Personality and Social Psychology*

Bulletin, 26 (November 2000), pp. 1329–42.

18. S. Johnston, "Oil's Well For Gutsy Women," *Edmonton Sun*, March 7, 1999, p. SE8.

19. F. T McAndrew et al., "A Multicultural Study of Stereotyping in English-Speaking Countries," *Journal of Social Psychology*, August 2000, pp. 487–502; S. Madon et al., "The Accuracy and Power of Sex, Social Class, and Ethnic Stereotypes: A Naturalistic Study in Person Perception," *Personality & Social Psychology Bulletin*, 24 (December 1998), pp. 1304–18; Y. Lee, L. J. Jussim, and C. R. McCauley (Eds.), *Stereotype Accuracy: Toward Appreciating Group Differences*. (Washington, DC: American Psychological Association, 1996). For early discussion of stereotypes, see W. Lippmann, *Public Opinion*. (New York: Macmillan, 1922).

20. D. L. Stone and A. Colella, "A Model of Factors Affecting the Treatment of Disabled Individuals in Organizations," *Academy of Management Review*, 21 (1996), pp. 352–401.

21. C. Stangor and L. Lynch, "Memory for Expectancy-Congruent and Expectancy-Incongruent Information: A Review of the Social and Social Development Literatures," *Psychological Bulletin*, 111 (1992), pp. 42–61; C. Stangor, L. Lynch, C. Duan, and B. Glass, "Categorization of Individuals on the Basis of Multiple Social Features," *Journal of Personality and Social Psychology*, 62 (1992), pp. 207–18.

22. M. Hewstone, M. Rubin, and H. Willis, "Intergroup Bias," *Annual Review of Psychology*, 53 (2002), pp. 575–604; Fiske, "Stereotyping, Prejudice, and Discrimination"; S. O. Gaines and E. S. Reed, "Prejudice: From Allport to DuBois," *American Psychologist*, 50 (February 1995), pp. 96–103.

23. Y. Zacharias, "Woman Wins Discrimination Case against Canadian Tire," *Vancouver Sun*, March 22, 2002, p. D3. For research on prejudicial attitudes in Ontario hospitals, see: R. Hagey et al., "Immigrant Nurses' Experience of Racism," *Journal of Nursing Scholarship*, 33 (Fourth Quarter 2001), pp. 389ff.

24. P. M. Buzzanell, "Reframing the Glass Ceiling as a Socially Constructed Process: Implications for Understand-

ing and Change," *Communication Monographs*, 62 (December 1995), pp. 327–54; M. E. Heilman, "Sex Stereotypes and their Effects in the Workplace: What We Know and What We Don't Know," *Journal of Social Behaviour & Personality*, 10 (1995) pp. 3–26.

25. K. Kawakami and J. F. Dovidio, "Implicit Stereotyping: How reliable is It? *Personality and Social Psychology Bulletin*, 27 (2001), pp. 212–25; J. A. Bargh, "The Cognitive Monster: The Case Against the Controllability of Automatic Stereotype Effects," In S. Chaiken and Y. Trope (eds.) *Dual Process Theories in Social Psychology*. (New York: Guilford, 1999), pp. 361–82.

26. J. W. Sherman, A. Y. Lee, G. R. Bessenoff, and L. A. Frost, "Stereotype Efficiency Reconsidered: Encoding Flexibility under Cognitive Load," *Journal of Personality and Social Psychology*, 75 (1998), pp. 589–606; C. N. Macrae, A. B. Milne, and G. V. Bodenhausen, "Stereotypes as Energy-Saving Devices: A Peek Inside the Cognitive Toolbox," *Journal of Personality and Social Psychology*, 66 (1994), pp. 37–47; S. T. Fiske, "Social Cognition and Social Perception," *Annual Review of Psychology*, 44 (1993), pp. 155–94.

27. M. Bendick Jr., M. L. Egan, and S. M. Lofhjelm, "Workforce Diversity Training: From Anti-Discrimination Compliance to Organizational Development HR," *Human Resource Planning*, 24 (2001), pp. 10–25.

28. A. P. Brief et. al., "Beyond Good Intentions: The Next Steps Toward Racial Equality In The American Workplace," *Academy of Management Executive*, 11 (November 1997), pp. 59–72; M. J. Monteith, "Self-Regulation of Prejudiced Responses: Implications for Progress in Prejudice-Reduction Efforts," *Journal of Personality and Social Psychology*, 65 (1993), pp. 469–85.

29. B. Parks, "Club Swinging a Sticky Situation in NHL," *Star-Ledger* (Newark, NJ), March 28, 2000, p. 61; L. Hornby, "Racism Meeting Hits Home With Leafs Players," *Toronto Sun*, September 27, 1999, p. 81; K. C. Johnson, "When Words Collide," *Chicago Tribune*, May 2, 1999, p. 7.

30. F. Glastra, M. Meerman, P. Schedler, and S. De Vries, "Broadening the Scope of Diversity Management: Strategic Implications in the Case of

the Netherlands," *Relations Industrielles*, 55 (Fall 2000), pp. 698–721; J.S. Osland, A. Bird, J. Delano, and M. Jacob, "Beyond Sophisticated Stereotyping: Cultural Sensemaking in Context," *Academy of Management Executive*, 14 (February 2000), pp. 65–79.

31. S. Brickson, "The Impact of Identity Orientation Individual and Organizational Outcomes in Demographically Diverse Settings," *Academy of Management Review*, 25 (January 2000), pp. 82–101; Z. Kunda and P. Thagard, "Forming Impressions from Stereotypes, Traits, and Behaviours: A Parallel-Constraint Satisfaction Theory," *Psychological Review*, 103 (1996), pp. 284–308. For a recent application of the contact hypothesis and education in a non-work setting, see: P. W. Corrigan et al., "Three Strategies for Changing Attributions about Severe Mental Illness," *Schizophrenia Bulletin*, 27 (2001), pp. 187ff.

32. B. Whitaker, "United Parcel's School for Hard Hearts, Sort Of," *New York Times*, July 26, 2000; M. J. Reid, "Profit Motivates Corporate Diversity," *San Francisco Examiner*, March 15, 1998, p. W42.

33. F. J. Flynn, J. a. Chatman, and S. E. Spataro, "Getting to Know You: The Influence of Personality on Impressions and Performance of Demographically Different People in Organizations," *Administrative Science Quarterly*, 46 (September 2001), pp. 414–42; F. Linnehan and A. M. Konrad, "Diluting Diversity: Implications for Intergroup Inequality in Organizations," *Journal of Management Inquiry*, 8 (December 1999), pp. 399–414; M. B. Brewer and R. J. Brown, "Intergroup Relations," In D. T. Gilbert, S. T. Fiske, & G. Lindzey (Eds.), *Handbook of Social Psychology, Vol. 2*, (New York: McGraw-Hill, 1998), pp. 554–94.

34. B. F. Reskin, "The Proximate Causes of Employment Discrimination," *Contemporary Sociology*, 29 (March 2000), pp. 319–28.

35. H. H. Kelley, *Attribution in Social Interaction* (Morristown, N.J.: General Learning Press, 1971).

36. H. H. Kelley, "The Processes of Causal Attribution," *American Psychologist*, 28 (1973), pp. 107–28; J. M. Feldman, "Beyond Attribution Theory: Cognitive Processes in Performance Appraisal," *Journal of Applied Psychology*, 66 (1981), pp. 127–48.

37. J. D. Ford, "The Effects of Causal Attributions on Decision Makers' Responses to Performance Downturns," *Academy of Management Review*, 10 (1985), pp. 770–786; M. J. Martinko and W. L. Gardner, "The Leader/Member Attribution Process," *Academy of Management Review*, 12 (1987), pp. 235–49.

38. J. Martocchio and J. Dulebohn, "Performance Feedback Effects in Training: the Role of Perceived Controllability," *Personnel Psychology*, 47 (1994), pp. 357–73; J. M. Crant and T. S. Bateman, "Assignment of Credit and Blame for Performance Outcomes," *Academy of Management Journal*, 36 (1993), pp. 7–27; D. R. Norris and R. E. Niebuhr, "Attributional Influences on the Job Performance–Job Satisfaction Relationship," *Academy of Management Journal*, 27 (1984), pp. 424–31.

39. H. J. Bernardin and P. Villanova, "Performance Appraisal," in *Generalising from Laboratory to Field Settings*, ed. E. A. Locke (Lexington, Mass.: Lexington Books, 1986), pp. 43–62; and S. G. Green and T. R. Mitchell, "Attributional Processes of Leader–Member Interactions," *Organizational Behaviour and Human Performance*, 23 (1979), pp. 429–58.

40. P. J. Taylor and J. L. Pierce, "Effects of Introducing a Performance Management System on Employees' Subsequent Attitudes and Effort," *Public Personnel Management*, 28 (Fall 1999), pp. 423–52.

41. J. R. Bettman and B. A. Weitz, "Attributions in the Board Room: Causal Reasoning in Corporate Annual Reports," *Administrative Science Quarterly*, 28 (1983), pp. 165–83.

42. P. Rosenthal and D. Guest, "Gender Difference in Managers' Causal Explanations for Their Work Performance: A Study in Two Organizations," *Journal of Occupational & Organizational Psychology*, 69 (1996) pp. 145–51.

43. "The Motive Isn't Money," *Profit*, 14 (Spring 1995) pp. 20–29

44. J. M. Darley and K. C. Oleson, "Introduction to Research on Interpersonal Expectations," In *Interpersonal Expectations: Theory, Research, and Applications* (Cambridge, UK: Cambridge University Press, 1993), pp. 45–63; D. Eden, *Pygmalion in Management* (Lexington, Mass.: Lexington, 1990); L. Jussim, "Self-Fulfilling Prophecies: A Theoretical and Integrative Review," *Psychological Review*, 93 (1986), pp. 429–45.

45. Similar models are presented in R. H. G. Field and D. A. Van Seters, "Management by Expectations (MBE): The Power of Positive Prophecy," *Journal of General Management*, 14 (Winter 1988), pp. 19–33; D. Eden, "Self-Fulfilling Prophecy as a Management Tool: Harnessing Pygmalion," *Academy of Management Review*, 9 (1984), pp. 64–73.

46. M. J. Harris and R. Rosenthal, "Mediation of Interpersonal Expectancy Effects: 31 Meta-Analyses," *Psychological Bulletin*, 97 (1985), pp. 363–86.

47. D. Eden, "Interpersonal Expectations in Organizations," In *Interpersonal Expectations: Theory, Research, and Applications* (Cambridge, UK: Cambridge University Press, 1993), pp. 154–78.

48. J-F. Manzoni, "The Set-Up-to-Fail Syndrome," *Harvard Business Review*, 76 (March-April 1998), pp. 101–13; J. S. Livingston, "Retrospective Commentary," *Harvard Business Review*, 66 (September-October 1988), p. 125.

49. D. Eden et al., "Implanting Pygmalion Leadership Style through Workshop Training: Seven Field Experiments," *Leadership Quarterly*, 11 (2000), pp. 171–210; S. Oz and D. Eden, "Restraining the Golem: Boosting Performance by Changing the Interpretation of Low Scores," *Journal of Applied Psychology*, 79 (1994), pp. 744–54.

50. S. S. White and E. A. Locke, "Problems with the Pygmalion Effect and Some Proposed Solutions," *Leadership Quarterly*, 11 (Autumn 2000), pp. 389–415. This source also cites recent studies on the failure of traditional Pygmalion training. For an early application of self-efficacy in self-fulfilling prophecy, see K. S. Crawford, E. D. Thomas, J. J. and Fink, "Pygmalion at Sea: Improving the Work Effectiveness of Low Performers," *Journal of Applied Behavioural Science*, 16 (1980), pp. 482–505.

51. A. D. Stajkovic and F. Luthans, "Social Cognitive Theory And Self-Efficacy: Going Beyond Traditional Motivational And Behavioural Approaches," *Organizational Dynamics*, 26 (Spring 1998), pp. 62–74; A. Bandura, *Self-Efficacy: The Exercise of Control* (W. H. Freeman & Co., 1996); M. E. Gist and T. R. Mitchell, "Self-Efficacy: A Theoretical Analysis of Its Determinants and Malleability," *Academy of Management Review*, 17 (1992), pp. 183–211; R. F. Mager, "No Self-Efficacy, No Performance," *Training*, 29 (April 1992), pp. 32–36.

52. T. Hill, P. Lewicki, M. Czyzewska, and A. Boss, "Self-Perpetuating Development of Encoding Biases in Person Perception," *Journal of Personality and Social Psychology*, 57 (1989), pp. 373–87; C. L. Kleinke, *First Impressions: The Psychology of Encountering Others* (Englewood Cliffs, N.J.: Prentice Hall, 1975).

53. O. Ybarra, "When First Impressions Don't Last: The Role of Isolation and Adaptation Processes in the Revision of Evaluative Impressions," *Social Cognition*, 19 (October 2001), pp. 491–520.

54. D. D. Steiner and J. S. Rain, "Immediate and Delayed Primacy and Recency Effects in Performance Evaluation," *Journal of Applied Psychology*, 74 (1989), pp. 136–42; R. L. Heneman and K. N. Wexley, "The Effects of Time Delay in Rating and Amount of Information Observed in Performance Rating Accuracy," *Academy of Management Journal*, 26 (1983), pp. 677–86.

55. W. H. Cooper, "Ubiquitous Halo," *Psychological Bulletin*, 90 (1981), pp. 218–44; K. R. Murphy, R. A. Jako, and R. L. Anhalt, "Nature and Consequences of Halo Error: A Critical Analysis," *Journal of Applied Psychology*, 78 (1993), pp. 218–25.

56. T. H. Feeley, "Evidence of Halo Effects in Student Evaluations of Communication Instruction," *Communication Education*, 51 (July 2002), pp. 225–36; S. Kozlowski, M. Kirsch, and G. Chao, "Job Knowledge, Ratee Familiarity, Conceptual Similarity, and Halo Error: An Exploration," *Journal of Applied Psychology*, 71 (1986), pp. 45–49.

57. C. J. Jackson and A. Furnham, "Appraisal Ratings, Halo, and Selection: A Study Using Sales Staff," *European Journal of Psychological Assessment*, 17 (2001), pp. 17–24; W. K. Balzer, and L. M. Sulsky, "Halo and Performance Appraisal Research: A Critical Examination," *Journal of Applied Psychology*, 77 (1992), pp. 975–85.

58. R. L Gross and S. E Brodt, "How Assumptions of Consensus Undermine Decision Making," *Sloan Management Review*, January 2001, pp. 86–94; G. G. Sherwood, "Self-Serving Biases in Person Perception: A Re-examination of Projection as a Mechanism of Defense," *Psychological Bulletin*, 90 (1981), pp. 445–59.

59. W. G. Stephen and K.A. Finlay, "The Role of Empathy in Improving Intergroup Relations," *Journal of Social Issues*, 55 (Winter 1999), pp. 729–43; C. Duan and C. E. Hill, "The Current State of Empathy Research," *Journal of Counseling Psychology*, 43 (1996), pp. 261–74.

60. S. K. Parker and C. M. Axtell, "Seeing Another Viewpoint: Antecedents and Outcomes of Employee Perspective Taking," *Academy of Management Journal*, 44 (December 2001), pp. 1085–100.

61. F. Shalom, "Catching the Next Wave at Pratt," *Montreal Gazette*, July 27, 2002. The importance of coaching and feedback in developing empathy is described in: D. Goleman, "What Makes a Leader?" *Harvard Business Review*, 76 (November-December 1998), pp. 92–102.

62. T. W. Costello and S. S. Zalkind, *Psychology in Administration: A Research Orientation* (Englewood Cliffs, N.J.: Prentice Hall, 1963), pp. 45–46.

63. J. Luft, *Group Processes* (Palo Alto, Calif.: Mayfield Publishing, 1984). For a variation of this model, see J. Hall, "Communication Revisited," *California Management Review*, 15 (Spring 1973), pp. 56–67.

64. L. C. Miller and D. A. Kenny, "Reciprocity of Self-Disclosure at the Individual and Dyadic Levels: A Social Relations Analysis," *Journal of Personality and Social Psychology*, 50 (1986), pp. 713–19.

65. D. M. Harris and R. L. DeSimone, *Human Resource Development* (Fort Worth, TX: Harcourt Brace, 1994), p. 54; B. Bass and J. Vaughn, *Training in Industry: The Management of Learning* (Belmont, Calif.: Wadsworth, 1966), p. 8; W. McGehee and P. W. Thayer, *Training in Business and Industry* (New York: Wiley, 1961), pp. 131–34.

66. G. F. B. Probst, "Practical Knowledge Management: A Model That Works," *Prism* (Second Quarter 1998), pp. 17–23; G. Miles, Grant, R. E. Miles, V. Perrone, and L. Edvinsson, "Some Conceptual And Research Barriers To The Utilization Of Knowledge," *California Management Review*, 40 (Spring 1998), pp. 281–88; E. C. Nevis, A. J. DiBella, and J. M. Gould, "Understanding Organizations as Learning Systems," *Sloan Management Review*, 36 (Winter 1995), pp. 73–85; D. Ulrich, T. Jick, and M. Von Glinow, "High Impact Learning: Building and Diffusing Learning Capability." *Organizational Dynamics*, 22 (Autumn 1993), pp. 52–66; G. Huber, "Organizational Learning: The Contributing Processes and Literature," *Organizational Science*, 2 (1991), pp. 88–115.

67. Watson Wyatt, *Playing to Win: Strategic Rewards in the War for Talent—Fifth Annual Survey Report 2000/2001* (Washington, DC: Watson Wyatt, 2001).

68. W. L. P. Wong and D. F. Radcliffe, "The Tacit Nature of Design Knowledge," *Technology Analysis & Strategic Management*, December 2000, pp. 493–512; R. Madhavan and R. Grover, "From Embedded Knowledge To Embodied Knowledge: New Product Development As Knowledge Management," *Journal of Marketing*, 62 (October 1998), pp. 1–12; D. Leonard and S. Sensiper, "The Role Of Tacit Knowledge In Group Innovation," *California Management Review*, 40 (Spring 1998), pp. 112–32; I. Nonaka and H. Takeuchi, *The Knowledge-Creating Company* (New York: Oxford University Press, 1995); R. K. Wagner and R. J. Sternberg, "Practical Intelligence in Real-World Pursuits: The Role of Tacit Knowledge," *Journal of Personality and Social Psychology*, 49 (1985), pp. 436–58.

69. A. Lam "Tacit Knowledge, Organizational Learning and Societal Institutions: An Integrated Framework," *Organization Studies*, 21 May, 2000.

70. M. J. Kerr, "Tacit Knowledge as a Predictor of Managerial Success: A Field Study," *Canadian Journal of Behavioural Science*, 27 (1995) pp. 36–51.

71. W. F. Dowling, "Conversation with B. F. Skinner," *Organizational Dynamics*, Winter 1973, pp. 31–40.

72. R. G. Miltenberger, *Behaviour Modification: Principles and Procedures* (Pacific Grove, CA: Brooks/Cole, 1997); J. Komaki, T. Coombs, and S. Schepman, "Motivational Implications of Reinforcement Theory," In R. M. Steers, L. W. Porter, & G. A. Bigley (Eds.), *Motivation and Leadership at Work*, (New York: McGraw-Hill, 1996), pp. 34–52; H. P. Sims and P. Lorenzi, *The New Leadership Paradigm: Social Learning and Cognition in Organizations* (Newbury Park, CA: Sage, 1992), Part II.

73. F. Luthans and R. Kreitner, *Organizational Behaviour Modification and Beyond* (Glenview, Ill.: Scott, Foresman, 1985); pp. 85–88; and T. K. Connellan, *How to Improve Human Performance* (New York: Harper & Row, 1978), pp. 48–57.

74. Miltenberger, *Behaviour Modification*, Chapter 4–6.

75. T. C. Mawhinney and R. R. Mawhinney, "Operant Terms and Concepts Applied to Industry," in *Industrial Behaviour Modification: A Management Handbook*, ed. R. M. O'Brien, A. M. Dickinson, and M. P. Rosow (New York: Pergamon Press, 1982), p. 117; R. Kreitner, "Controversy in OBM: History, Misconceptions, and Ethics," in L. W. Frederiksen (Ed.), *Handbook of Organizational Behaviour Management*, (New York: Wiley, 1982), pp. 76–79.

76. Luthans and Kreitner, *Organizational Behaviour Modification and Beyond*, pp. 53–54.

77. K. D. Butterfield, L. K. Trevino, and G. A. Ball, "Punishment from the Manager's Perspective: A Grounded Investigation and Inductive Model," *Academy of Management Journal*, 39 (1996), pp. 1479–1512; L. K. Trevino, "The Social Effects of Punishment in Organizations: A Justice Perspective," *Academy of Management Review*, 17 (1992), pp. 647–76.

78. G. P. Latham and V. L. Huber, "Schedules of Reinforcement: Lessons from the Past and Issues for the Future," *Journal of Organizational Behaviour Management*, 13 (1992), pp. 125–49.

79. F. Luthans and A. D. Stajkovic, "Reinforce for Performance: The Need to Go Beyond Pay and Even Rewards," *Academy of Management Executive*, 13 (May 1999), pp. 49–57; Alexander D. Stajkovic and F. Luthans, "A Meta-Analysis of the Effects of Organizational Behaviour Modification on Task Performance, 1975–95," *Academy of Management Journal*, Vol. 40 (October 1997), pp. 1122–49.

80. K. Maeshiro, "School Attendance Pays," *Los Angeles Daily News*, January 28, 2002, p. AV1; P. Eaton-Robb, "For Employees, Solutions That Work," *Providence Journal*, January 10, 2001, p. E1; D. Behar, "Firm Launches Lottery to Beat 'Sickies' Plague," *Daily Mail (UK)*, January 8, 2001, p. 27; G. Masek, "Dana Corp.," *Industry Week*, October 19, 1998, p. 48.

81. D. Brown, "Corp. Culture Change Combats Absenteeism," *Canadian HR Reporter*, November 29, 1999, pp. 1, 16; R. Curren, "Lottery Helps Solve Absenteeism," *Winnipeg Free Press*, November 6, 1999. Updated information provided by Ms. Roxann Good, NOVA Chemicals Ltd., July 2000.

82. "New Warnings on the Fine Points of Safety Incentives," *Pay for Performance Report*, September 2002; G. A. Merwin, J. A. Thomason, and E. E. Sanford, "A Methodological and Content Review of Organizational Behaviour Management in the Private Sector: 1978–1986," *Journal of Organizational Behaviour Management*, 10 (1989), pp. 39–57; T. C. Mawhinney, "Philosophical and Ethical Aspects of Organizational Behaviour Management: Some Evaluative Feedback," *Journal of Organizational Behaviour Management*, 6 (Spring 1984), pp. 5–31.

83. J. A. Bargh and M. J. Ferguson, "Beyond Behaviourism: On the Automaticity of Higher Mental Processes," *Psychological Bulletin*, 126 (2000), pp. 925–45.

84. A. Bandura, *Social Foundations of Thought and Action: A Social Cognitive Theory* (Englewood Cliffs, N.J.: Prentice Hall, 1986).

85. A. Pescuric and W. C. Byham, "The New Look of Behaviour Modeling," *Training & Development*, 50 (July 1996), pp. 24–30; H. P. Sims, Jr., and C. C. Manz, "Modeling Influences on Employee Behaviour," *Personnel Journal*, January 1982, pp. 58–65.

86. L. K. Trevino, "The Social Effects of Punishment in Organizations: A Justice Perspective," *Academy of Management Review*, 17 (1992), pp. 647–76; M. E. Schnake, "Vicarious Punishment in a Work Setting," *Journal of Applied Psychology*, 71 (1986), pp. 343–45.

87. M. Foucault, *Discipline and Punish: The Birth of the Prison*. (Harmondsworth: Penguin, 1977).

88. L. K. Trevino, "The Social Effects of Punishment in Organizations: A Justice Perspective," *Academy of Management Review*, 17 (1992), pp. 647–76; M. E. Schnake, "Vicarious Punishment in a Work Setting," *Journal of Applied Psychology*, 71 (1986), pp. 343–45.

89. A. W. Logue, *Self-Control: Waiting Until Tomorrow for What You Want Today*. (Englewood Cliffs, NJ: Prentice-Hall, 1995); A. Bandura, "Self-Reinforcement: Theoretical and Methodological Considerations," *Behaviourism*, 4 (1976), pp. 135–55.

90. C. A. Frayne, "Improving Employee Performance Through Self-Management Training," *Business Quarterly*, 54 (Summer 1989), pp. 46–50.

91. D. Woodruff, "Putting Talent to the Test," *Wall Street Journal Europe*, November 14, 2000, p. 25. The simulation events described here were experienced by the author of this article, but we reasonably assume that Mandy Chooi, who also completed the simulation, went through similar events in her simulation.

92. S. Gherardi, D. Nicolini, F. Odella, "Toward a Social Understanding Of How People Learn In Organizations," *Management Learning*, 29 (September 1998), pp. 273–97; Ulrich, Jick, and Von Glinow, "High Impact Learning."

93. D. A. Kolb, R. E. Boyatzis, and C. Mainemelis, "Experiential Learning Theory: Previous Research and New Directions," In R. J. Sternberg and L. F. Zhang (Eds.), *Perspectives on Thinking, Learning, and Cognitive Styles*. (Mahwah, NJ: Lawrence Erlbaum, 2001), pp. 227–48; D.A. Kolb, *Experiential Learning* (Englewood Cliffs, NJ: Prentice-Hall, 1984).

94. The learning orientation concept is the focus of current attention in marketing: See M. A. Farrell, "Developing a Market-Oriented Learning Organization," *Australian Journal of Management*, 25 (September 2000); W.E. Baker and J.M. Sinkula, "The Synergistic Effect of Market Orientation and Learning Orientation," *Journal of the Academy of Marketing Science*, 27 (1999), pp. 411–27.

95. R. Farson and R. Keyes, "The Failure-Tolerant Leader," *Harvard Business Review*, 80 (August 2002), pp. 64–71; J. Jusko, "Always Lessons To Learn," *Industry Week*, February 15, 1999, p. 23.

96. L. Ferenc, "Mock Disaster Tests Region's Resources," *Toronto Star*, May 30, 2002, p. B7; "York Region Conducts Emergency Exercise with Town of Newmarket and GO Transit," Town of Newmarket news release, May 29, 2002.

97. R. W. Revans, *The Origin and Growth of Action Learning* (London: Chartwell Bratt, 1982), pp. 626–27.

98. V.J. Marsick, "The Many Faces of Action Learning," *Management Learning*, 30 (June 1999), pp. 159–76.

99. R. M. Fulmer, P. Gibbs, and J. B. Keys, "The Second Generation Learning Organizations: New Tools For Sustaining Competitive Advantage," *Organizational Dynamics*, 27 (Autumn 1998), pp. 6–20; A. L. Stern "Where the Action Is," *Across the Board*, Vol. 34 (September 1997), pp. 43–47; R. W. Revans, "What Is Action Learning?" *Journal of Management Development*, 15 (1982), pp. 64–75.

100. R.M. Fulmer, P.A. Gibbs and M. Goldsmith, "Developing Leaders: How Winning Companies Keep on Winning," *Sloan Management Review*, October 2000, pp. 49–59; J. A. Conger and K. Xin, "Executive Education in the 21st Century," *Journal of Management Education*, (February 2000), pp. 73–101.

101. T. T. Baldwin, C. Danielson, and W. Wiggenhorn, "The Evolution of Learning Strategies in Organizations: From Employee Development to Business Redefinition," *Academy of Management Executive*, 11 (November 1997), pp. 47–58.

CHAPTER FOUR

1. "Why is SaskTel a Great Place to Plan Your Career?" SaskTel Web site (www.sasktel.com); "Sharing What We've Learned: SaskTel International In Tanzania and Beyond," Presentation by Garry Simmons, President of SaskTel International, at the Transdisciplinary Seminar series, University of Regina, February 27, 2002; R. Yerema, *Canada's Top 100 Employers, 2002* (Toronto: MediaCorp Canada, 2002), pp. 249–52; A. Kyle, "Deal Taps Native Workforce," *Saskatoon Star-Phoenix*, December 1, 2001; "No Layoffs, Plenty of Loyalty," *Maclean's*, November 5, 2001.

2. S. Schwartz, "More than Coffee and Tea," *Montreal Gazette*, March 18, 2002.

3. The meaning of emotions is still being debated, so its definition varies somewhat across sources. The definition presented here is constructed from information in the following sources: N. M. Ashkanasy, W. J. Zerbe, C. E. J. Hartel "Introduction: Managing Emotions in a Changing Workplace," In N. M. Ashkanasy, W. J. Zerbe, C. E. J. Hartel (Eds.) *Managing Emotions in the Workplace* (Armonk, N.Y.: M. E. Sharpe, 2002), pp. 3–18; H. M. Weiss, "Conceptual and Empirical foundations for the Study of Affect at Work," In R. G. Lord, R. J. Klimoski, & R. Kanfer (Eds.) *Emotions in the Workplace* (San Francisco: Jossey-Bass, 2002), pp. 20–63; S. Kitayama and P. M. Niedenthal, "Introduction," In P. M. Niedenthal and S. Kitayama, *The Heart's Eye: Emotional Influences in Perception and Attention* (San Diego, CA: Academic Press, 1994), pp. 6–7.

4. R. Kanfer and R. J. Klimoski, "Affect and Work: Looking Back to the Future," In R. G. Lord, R. J. Klimoski, & R. Kanfer (Eds.) *Emotions in the Workplace* (San Francisco: Jossey-Bass, 2002), pp. 473–90; J. M. George and A. P. Brief, "Motivational Agendas in the Workplace: The Effects of Feelings on Focus of Attention and Work Motivation," *Research in Organizational Behaviour*, 18 (1996), pp. 75–109.

5. R. B. Zajonc, "Emotions," In D.T. Gilbert, S.T. Fiske, and L. Gardner (eds.) *Handbook of Social Psychology* (New York: Oxford University Press, 1998), pp. 591–634; K. Oatley and J. M. Jenkins, "Human Emotions: Function and Dysfunction," *Annual Review of Psychology*, 43 (1992), pp. 55–85.

6. H. M. Weiss and R. Cropanzano, "Affective Events Theory: A Theoretical Discussion of the Structure, Causes, and Consequences of Affective Experiences at Work," *Research in Organizational Behavior*, 18 (1996), pp. 1–74; P. Shaver, J. Schwartz, D. Kirson, and C. O'Connor, "Emotion Knowledge: Further Exploration of a Prototype Approach," *Journal of Personality and Social Psychology*, 52 (1987), pp. 1061–86.

7. R. J. Larson, E. Diener, and R. E. Lucas, "Emotion: Models, Measures, and Differences," In R. G. Lord, R. J. Klimoski, & R. Kanfer (Eds.) *Emotions in the Workplace* (San Francisco: Jossey-Bass, 2002), pp. 64–113.

8. A. P. Brief, *Attitudes In and Around Organizations* (Thousand Oaks, CA: Sage, 1998); J. M. George and G. R. Jones, "Experiencing Work: Values, Attitudes, and Moods," *Human Relations*, 50 (April 1997), pp. 393–416; J. M. Olson and M. P. Zama, "Attitudes and Attitude Change," *Annual Review of Psychology*, 44 (1993), pp. 117–54. There is ongoing debate about whether attitudes represent only feelings or all three components described here. However, those who adopt the single factor perspective still refer to beliefs as the cognitive *component* of attitudes. For example, see: I. Ajzen "Nature and Operation of Attitudes," *Annual Review of Psychology*, 52 (2001), pp. 27–58.

9. M. D. Zalesny and J. K. Ford, "Extending the Social Information Processing Perspective: New Links to Attitudes, Behaviours, and Perceptions," *Organizational Behaviour and Human Decision Processes*, 52 (1992), pp. 205–46; G. Salancik and J. Pfeffer, "A Social Information Processing Approach to Job Attitudes and Task Design," *Administrative Science Quarterly*, 23 (1978), pp. 224–53.

10. C. J. Armitage and M. Conner, "Efficacy of the Theory of Planned Behaviour: A Meta-analytic Review," *British Journal of Social Psychology*, 40 (2001), pp. 471–99.

11. J. D. Morris, C-M Woo, J. A. Geason, and J-Y Kim, "The Power of Affect: Predicting Intention," *Journal of Advertising Research*, 42 (May/June

2002), pp. 7–17; M. Perugini and R. P. Bagozzi "The Role of Desires and Anticipated Emotions in Goal-Directed Behaviours: Broadening and Deepening the Theory of Planned Behaviour," *British Journal of Social Psychology*, 40 (March 2001), pp. 79–98; C. D. Fisher, "Mood and Emotions while Working: Missing Pieces of Job Satisfaction?" *Journal of Organizational Behavior*, 21 (2000), pp. 185–202. For a review of the predictability of the traditional attitude model, see: Armitage and Conner, "Efficacy of the Theory of Planned Behaviour."

12. The emotional centre is the limbic centre where the innate drives reside. The rational centre is the prefrontal cerebral cortex. Signals are transferred in both directions between these brain centres. Neural connections suggest a much stronger signal from the emotional centre to the rational centre than vice versa. See D. S. Massey, "A Brief History of Human Society: The Origin and Role of Emotion in Social Life," *American Sociological Review*, 67 (February 2002), pp. 1–29; P. R. Lawrence and N. Nohria, *Driven: How Human Nature Shapes Our Choices*, (San Francisco: Jossey-Bass, 2002), pp. 44–47, 168–70; R. Hastie, "Problems For Judgment And Decision Making," *Annual Review of Psychology*, 52 (2001), pp. 653–83; A. Damasio, *The Feeling of What Happens* (New York: Harcourt Brace and Co., 1999).

13. Weiss and Cropanzano, "Affective Events Theory."

14. Weiss and Cropanzano, "Affective Events Theory," pp. 52–57.

15. L. Festinger, *A Theory of Cognitive Dissonance* (Evanston, Ill.: Row, Peterson, 1957); G. R. Salancik, "Commitment and the Control of Organizational Behaviour and Belief," in B. M. Staw and G. R. Salancik (eds.) *New Directions in Organizational Behaviour*, (Chicago: St. Clair, 1977), pp. 1–54.

16. T. A. Judge, E. A. Locke, and C. C. Durham, "The Dispositional Causes of Job Satisfaction: A Core Evaluations Approach," *Research in Organizational Behaviour*, 19 (1997), pp. 151–88; A. P Brief, A. H. Butcher, and L. Roberson, "Cookies, Disposition, and Job Attitudes: The Effects of Positive Mood-Inducing Events and Negative Affectivity

on Job Satisfaction in a Field Experiment," *Organizational Behaviour and Human Decision Processes*, 62 (1995), pp. 55–62.

17. C. M. Brotheridge and A. A. Grandey, "Emotional Labor and Burnout: Comparing Two Perspectives of 'People Work'," *Journal of Vocational Behavior*, 60 (2002), pp. 17–39; A. P. Brief and H. M.Weiss, "Organizational Behavior: Affect in the Workplace," *Annual Review of Psychology*, 53 (2002), pp. 279–307; R. D. Iverson and S. J. Deery, "Understanding the "Personological" Basis of Employee Withdrawal: The Influence of Affective Disposition on Employee Tardiness, Early Departure, and Absenteeism," *Journal of Applied Psychology*, 86 (October 2001), pp. 856–66.

18. C. Dormann and D. Zapf, "Job Satisfaction: A Meta-Analysis of Stabilities," *Journal of Organizational Behavior*, 22 (2001), pp. 483–504; J. Schaubroeck, D. C. Ganster, and B. Kemmerer, "Does Trait Affect Promote Job Attitude Stability?" *Journal of Organizational Behaviour*, 17 (1996), pp. 191–196; R. D. Arvey, B. P. McCall, T. L. Bouchard, and P. Taubman, "Genetic Differences on Job Satisfaction and Work Values," *Personality and Individual Differences*, 17 (1994), pp. 21–33.

19. D. Matheson, "A Vancouver Cafe Where Rudeness is Welcomed," Canada AM, *CTV Television*, January 11, 2000; R. Corelli, "Dishing out Rudeness," *Maclean's*, January 11, 1999, p. 44.

20. J. A. Morris and D. C. Feldman, "The Dimensions, Antecedents, and Consequences of Emotional Labour," *Academy of Management Review*, 21 (1996), pp. 986–1010; B. E. Ashforth and R. H. Humphrey, "Emotional Labour in Service Roles: The Influence of Identity," *Academy of Management Review*, 18 (1993), pp. 88–115.

21. K. McArthur, "Air Canada tells Employees to Crack a Smile more Often," *Globe and Mail*, March 14, 2002, p. B1; G. Van Moorsel, "Call Centres Deserve Ringing Endorsement," *London Free Press*, October 27, 2001.

22. A. A. Grandey and A. L. Brauburger, "The Emotion Regulation Behind the Customer Service Smile," In R. G. Lord, R. J. Klimoski, & R. Kanfer (Eds.) *Emotions in the Workplace* (San

Francisco: Jossey-Bass, 2002), pp 260–94; J. A. Morris and D. C. Feldman, "Managing Emotions in the Workplace," *Journal of Managerial Issues*, 9 (Fall 1997), pp. 257–74.

23. J.S. Sass, "Emotional Labour as Cultural Performance: The Communication of Caregiving in a Nonprofit Nursing Home," *Western Journal of Communication*, 64 (Summer 2000), pp. 330–358; R. I. Sutton, "Maintaining Norms about Expressed Emotions: The Case of Bill Collectors," *Administrative Science Quarterly*, 36 (1991), pp. 245–68.

24. J. Strasburg, "The Making of a Grand Hotel," *San Francisco Chronicle*, March 25, 2001, p. B1.

25. E. Forman, "'Diversity Concerns Grow as Companies Head Overseas,' Consultant Says," *Fort Lauderdale Sun-Sentinel*, June 26, 1995.

26. J. Schaubroeck and J. R. Jones, "Antecedents of Workplace Emotional Labour Dimensions and Moderators of their Effects on Physical Symptoms," *Journal of Organizational Behaviour*, 21 (2000), 163–83; R. Buck, "The Spontaneous Communication of Interpersonal Expectations," In *Interpersonal Expectations: Theory, Research, and Applications* (Cambridge, UK: Cambridge University Press, 1993), pp. 227–41. The quotation from George Burns comes from the Buck source. However, this line has also been attributed to Groucho Marx.

27. W. J. Zerbe, "Emotional Dissonance and Employee Well-Being," In N. M. Ashkanasy, W. J. Zerbe, C. E. J. Hartel (Eds.) *Managing Emotions in the Workplace* (Armonk, N.Y.: M. E. Sharpe, 2002), pp. 189–214; K. Pugliesi, "The Consequences of Emotional Labour: Effects on Work Stress, Job Satisfaction, and Well-Being," *Motivation & Emotion*, 23 (June 1999), pp. 125–54; A. S. Wharton, "The Psychosocial Consequences Of Emotional Labour," *Annals of the American Academy of Political & Social Science*, 561 (January 1999), pp. 158–76.

28. C. M. Brotheridge and A. A. Grandey, "Emotional Labor and Burnout: Comparing Two Perspectives of 'People Work'," *Journal of Vocational Behavior*, 60 (2002), pp. 17–39. This observation is also identified in: N. M.

Ashkanasy and C. S. Daus, "Emotion in the Workplace: The New Challenge for Managers," *Academy of Management Executive*, 16 (February 2002), pp. 76–86.

29. D. Flavelle, "Firms Try To Rope Winners By Hiring Out Of The Herd," *Toronto Star*, January 30, 2000; G. Pitts, "Hotel Chain Hires for Attitude," *Globe and Mail*, June 3, 1997, p. B13.

30. T. Schwartz, "'How Do You Feel?'" *Fast Company*, June 2000, p. 296; J. Stuller, "Unconventional Smarts," *Across the Board*, 35 (January 1998), pp. 22–23.

31. J. D. Mayer, P. Salovey, D. R. Caruso, "Models of Emotional Intelligence," In R. J. Sternberg (Ed.). *Handbook of Human Intelligence, 2nd ed.*, (New York: Cambridge University Press, 2000), p. 396. This definition is also recognized in: C. Cherniss, "Emotional Intelligence and Organizational Effectiveness," In C. Cherniss and D. Goleman, (Eds.), *The Emotionally Intelligent Workplace* (San Francisco: Jossey-Bass, 2001), pp. 3–12.

32. Mayer et al., "Models of Emotional Intelligence," pp. 396–420; J. D. Mayer P. Salovey, "What is Emotional Intelligence?" In P. Salovey & D. Sluyter (Eds). *Emotional Development and Emotional Intelligence: Implications for Educators* (New York: Basic Books, 1997), pp. 3–33. R. J. Grossman, "Emotions at Work," *Health Forum Journal*, 43 (September-October, 2000), pp. 18–22; D. Swift, "Do Doctors have an Emotional Handicap?," *Medical Post*, March 9, 1999, p. 30.

33. R. J. Grossman, "Emotions at Work," *Health Forum Journal*, 43 (September-October, 2000), pp. 18–22; D. Swift, "Do Doctors have an Emotional Handicap?," *Medical Post*, March 9, 1999, p. 30.

34. A brief history of emotional intelligence is presented in: D. Goleman, "Emotional Intelligence: Issues in Paradigm Building," In C. Cherniss and D. Goleman, (Eds.), *The Emotionally Intelligent Workplace* (San Francisco: Jossey-Bass, 2001), pp. 13–26; S. Newsome, A. L. Day, and V. M. Catano, "Assessing the Predictive Validity of Emotional Intelligence," *Personality and Individual Differences*, 29 (December 2000), pp. 1005–16.

35. P. J. Jordan, N. M. Ashkanasy, C. E. J. Hartel, and G. S. Hooper, "Workgroup Emotional Intelligence: Scale Development and Relationship to Team Process Effectiveness and Goal Focus," *Human Resource Management Review*, 12 (2002), pp. 195–214; C-S Wong and K. S. Law, "The Effects of Leader and Follower Emotional Intelligence on Performance and Attitude: An Exploratory Study," *Leadership Quarterly*, 13 (2002), pp. 243–74; L. T. Lam and S. L. Kirby, "Is Emotional Intelligence An Advantage? An Exploration Of The Impact Of Emotional And General Intelligence On Individual Performance," *Journal of Social Psychology*, 142 (February 2002), pp. 133–43; N. S. Schutte et al., "Emotional Intelligence and Interpersonal Relations," *Journal of Social Psychology*, 141 (August 2001), pp. 523–36; S. Fox and P.E. Spector, "Relations of Emotional Intelligence, Practical Intelligence, General Intelligence, and Trait Affectivity with Interview Outcomes: It's Not All Just G," *Journal of Organizational Behaviour*, 21 (2000), pp. 1099–379.

36. D. Dawda and S.D. Hart, "Assessing Emotional Intelligence: Reliability and Validity of the Bar-On Emotional Quotient Inventory (EQ-i) in University Students," *Personality and Individual Differences*, 28 (2000), pp. 797–812.

37. J. Brown, "School Board, Employment Centres Test Emotional Intelligence," *Technology in Government*, 8 (April 2001), p. 9; R. J. Grossman, "Emotions at Work," *Health Forum Journal*, 43 (September-October, 2000), pp. 18–22.

38. "Emotional Intelligence (EQ) Gets Better with Age," EQi News Release, March 3, 1997.

39. H. M. Weiss, "Deconstructing Job Satisfaction: Separating Evaluations, Beliefs and Affective Experiences," *Human Resource Management Review*, 12 (2002), pp. 173–94. There is still some debate about this definition, because some definitions include emotion as an element or indicator of job satisfaction, whereas this definition views emotion as a cause of job satisfaction. For discussion of this point, see: Brief and Weiss, "Organizational Behavior: Affect in the Workplace."

40. E. A. Locke, "The Nature and Causes of Job Satisfaction," in M. Dun-

nette (Ed.) *Handbook of Industrial and Organizational Psychology*, (Chicago: Rand McNally, 1976), pp. 1297–1350. Our definition takes the view that job satisfaction is a "collection of attitudes," not several "facets" of job satisfaction. For details of this issue, see: Weiss, "Deconstructing Job Satisfaction."

41. S. Foster, "Good Job, Lots of Cash, Great Life," *Regina Leader-Post*, June 8, 2002.

42. "Workplace Satisfaction Hits 82 Percent," *Vancouver Sun*, November 1, 1999; S. Lambert, "Annual Poll Finds We're a Happy Lot," *Toronto Star*, October 10, 1998, p. B2. This is similar to Gallup polls in the United States, which have reported consistently for the past decade that at least 85 percent of Americans are satisfied with their job. See: F. Newport, "Most American Workers Satisfied With Their Jobs," *Gallup News Service*, August 29, 2002.

43. International Survey Research, *Employee Satisfaction in the World's 10 Largest Economies: Globalization or Diversity?* (Chicago: ISR, 2002); "Ipsos-Reid Global Poll Finds Major Differences in Employee Satisfaction Around the World," Ipsos-Reid News Release, January 8, 2001.

44. R. Laver, "The Best & Worst Jobs," *Maclean's*," May 31, 1999, pp. 18–23.

45. The problems with measuring attitudes and values across cultures is discussed in: P. E. Spector et al, "Do National Levels of Individualism and Internal Locus of Control Relate to Well-being: An Ecological Level International Study," *Journal of Organizational Behavior*, 22 (2001), pp. 815–32; G. Law, "If You're Happy & You Know It, Tick The Box," *Management-Auckland*, 45 (March 1998), pp. 34–37.

46. M. Troy, "Motivating your Workforce: A Home Depot Case Study," *DSN Retailing Today*, June 10, 2002, p. 29.

47. W. H. Turnley and D. C. Feldman, "The Impact of Psychological Contract Violations on Exit, Voice, Loyalty, and Neglect," *Human Relations*, 52 (July 1999), pp. 895–922; M. J. Withey and W. H. Cooper, "Predicting Exit, Voice, Loyalty, and Neglect," *Administrative Science Quarterly*, 1989, 34, 521–39.

48. T. R. Mitchell, B. C. Holtom, and T. W. Lee, "How to Keep your Best Em-

ployees: Developing an Effective Retention Policy," *Academy of Management Executive*, 15 (November 2001), pp. 96–108. The idea of "triggering events" leading to exit is also brought forward in: B. Dyck and F. A. Starke, "The Formation of Breakaway Organizations: Observations and a Process Model," *Administrative Science Quarterly*, 44 (December 1999), pp. 792–822.

49. A. A. Luchak, "What Kind of Voice do Loyal Employees Use?" *British Journal of Industrial Relations*, in press; L. Van Dyne and J. A. LePine, "Helping and Voice Extra-role Behaviors: Evidence of Construct and Predictive Validity. *Academy of Management Journal*, 41 (1998), pp. 108–19.

50. The confusion regarding loyalty was pointed out over a decade ago in Withey and Cooper, "Predicting Exit, Voice, Loyalty, and Neglect" and is equally confusing today. In addition to the interpretation presented here, loyalty has been defined as situations where dissatisfied employees are less loyal, including engaging in fewer organizational citizenship behaviours. See: W. H. Turnley and D. C. Feldman, "The Impact of Psychological Contract Violations on Exit, Voice, Loyalty, and Neglect," *Human Relations*, 52 (July 1999), pp. 895–922.

51. J. Zhou and J. M. George, "When Job Dissatisfaction Leads to Creativity: Encouraging the Expression of Voice," *Academy of Management Journal*, 44 (August 2001), pp. 682–96; J. D. Hibbard, N. Kumar, and L. W. Stern, "Examining the Impact of Destructive Acts in Marketing Channel Relationships," *Journal of Marketing Research*, 38 (February 2001), pp. 45–61; Dyck and Starke, "The Formation of Breakaway Organizations."

52. R. D. Hackett and P. Bycio, "An Evaluation of Employee Absenteeism as a Coping Mechanism Among Hospital Nurses," *Journal of Occupational & Organizational Psychology*, 69 (December 1996), pp. 327–38;

53. M. J. Withey and I. R. Gellatly, "Exit, Voice, Loyalty And Neglect: Assessing The Influence of Prior Effectiveness and Personality," *Proceedings of the Administrative Sciences Association of Canada, Organizational Behavior Division*, 20 (1999), pp. 110–19; M. J. Withey and I. R. Gellatly, "Situational

and Dispositional Determinants of Exit, Voice, Loyalty and Neglect," *Proceedings of the Administrative Sciences Association of Canada*. Saskatoon, Saskatchewan, June 1998.

54. B. M. Staw and S. G. Barsade, "Affect and Managerial Performance: A Test of the Sadder-but-Wiser vs. Happier-and-Smarter Hypotheses," *Administrative Science Quarterly* 38 (1993), pp. 304–31; M. T. Iaffaldano and P. M. Muchinsky, "Job Satisfaction and Job Performance: A Meta-Analysis," *Psychological Bulletin*, 97 (1985), pp. 251–73; D. P. Schwab and L. L. Cummings, "Theories of Performance and Satisfaction: A Review," *Industrial Relations*, 9 (1970), pp. 408–30.

55. T. A. Judge, C. J. Thoresen, J. E. bono, and G. K. Patton, "The Job Satisfaction-Job Performance Relationship: A Qualitative and Quantitative Review," *Psychological Bulletin*, 127 (2001), pp. 376–407.

56. Judge et al, "The Job Satisfaction-Job Performance Relationship," pp. 377–81.

57. Judge et al, "The Job Satisfaction-Job Performance Relationship," pp. 389, 391.

58. T. Kirchofer, "Firm Takes Boat of Confidence," *Boston Herald*, March 20, 2001, p. 27.

59. "Happy, Passionate Employees Key to Good Business, Top Executives Say," *Ascribe News*, April 16, 2001; S. OndraSek, "Four Seasons makes Local Debut," *Prague Post*, February 7, 2001.

60. J. I. Heskett, W. E. Sasser, and L. A. Schlesinger, *The Service Profit Chain*, (N.Y.: Free Press, 1997). For recent support of this model, see D. J. Koys, "The Effects of Employee Satisfaction, Organizational Citizenship Behaviour, and Turnover on Organizational Effectiveness: A Unit-Level, Longitudinal Study," *Personnel Psychology*, 54 (April 2001), pp. 101–14

61. A. J. Rucci, S. P. Kirn, and R. T. Quinn, "The Employee-Customer-Profit Chain At Sears," *Harvard Business Review*, 76 (January-February 1998), pp. 83–97.

62. K. Gwinner, D. Gremier, and M. Bitner, "Relational Benefits in Services Industries: The Customer's Perspective," *Journal of the Academy of Marketing Science*, 26 (1998), pp. 101–14.

63. S. Franklin, *The Heroes: A Saga of Canadian Inspiration* (Toronto: McClelland & Stewart, 1967), pp. 53–59.

64. R. T. Mowday, L. W. Porter, and R. M. Steers, *Employee Organization Linkages: The Psychology of Commitment, Absenteeism, and Turnover* (New York: Academic Press, 1982).

65. C. W. Mueller and E. J. Lawler, "Commitment to Nested Organizational Units: Some Basic Principles and Preliminary Findings," *Social Psychology Quarterly*, (December 1999), pp. 325–46; T. E. Becker, R. S. Billings, D. M. Eveleth, and N. L. Gilbert, "Foci and Bases of Employee Commitment: Implications for Job Performance," *Academy of Management Journal*, 39 (1996), pp. 464–82.

66. J. P. Meyer, "Organizational Commitment," *International Review of Industrial and Organizational Psychology*, 12 (1997), pp. 175–228. Along with affective and continuance commitment, Meyer identifies "normative commitment," which refers to employee feelings of obligation to remain with the organization. This commitment has been excluded so that students focus on the two most common perspectives of commitment.

67. R. D. Hackett, P. Bycio, and P. A. Hausdorf, "Further Assessments of Meyer and Allen's (1991) Three-Component Model of Organizational Commitment," *Journal of Applied Psychology*, 79 (1994), pp. 15–23.

68. International Survey Research, "UK Employees Lack Commitment," News release, September 3, 2002; Z. Olijnyk, "Win the Loyalty Game," *Canadian Business*, December 10, 2001, pp. 74ff; Watson Wyatt, "Survey Says Employee Commitment Declining," News release, March 14, 2000. In contrast, the Gallup Organization has reported consistently high loyalty ratings for the past decade among American workers. See: D.W. Moore, "Most American Workers Satisfied With Their Job," *Gallup News Service*, August 31, 2001

69. J. P. Meyer, D. J. Stanley, L. Herscovitch, and L. Topolnytsky, "Affective, Continuance, and Normative Commitment to the Organization: A Meta-analysis of Antecedents, Correlates, and Consequences," *Journal of Vocational Behavior*, 61 (2002), pp. 20–52; M. Riketta, "Attitudinal Organi-

zational Commitment and Job Performance: A Meta-Analysis," *Journal of Organizational Behavior*, 23 (2002), pp. 257–66; F. F. Reichheld, "Lead for Loyalty," *Harvard Business Review*, 79 (July-August 2001), p. 76; D. S. Bolon, "Organizational Citizenship Behavior Among Hospital Employees: A Multidimensional Analysis Involving Job Satisfaction And Organizational Commitment," *Hospital & Health Services Administration*, 42 (Summer 1997), pp. 221–41; Meyer, "Organizational Commitment," pp. 203–15; F. F. Reichheld, *The Loyalty Effect* (Boston: Harvard Business School Press, 1996), Chapter 4.

70. P. Arab, "CIBC Takeover of Merrill Lynch Brokerage Makes Bank Biggest Brokerage," *Canadian Press*, November 22, 2001; P. Mackey, "Old Ireland Tries New Hooks," *Computerworld*. April 23, 2001, p. 46.

71. A. A. Luchak, "What Kind of Voice do Loyal Employees Use?" *British Journal of Industrial Relations*, in press; A. A. Luchak and I. R. Gellatly, "What Kind of Commitment Does a Final-Earnings Pension Plan Elicit?" *Relations Industrielles*, 56 (Spring 2001), p. 394–417; H. L. Angle and M. B. Lawson, Organizational Commitment And Employees' Performance Ratings: Both Type Of Commitment And Type Of Performance Count," *Psychological Reports*, 75 (1994), pp. 1539–51; J. P. Meyer, S. V. Paunonen, I. R. Gellatly, R. D. Goffin, and D. N. Jackson, "Organizational Commitment and Job Performance: It's the Nature of the Commitment That Counts," *Journal of Applied Psychology*, 74 (1989), pp. 152–56.

72. J. P. Meyer and N. J. Allen, *Commitment in the Workplace: Theory, Research, and Application*, (Thousand Oaks, CA: Sage, 1997), Chapter 4.

73. J. E Finegan, "The Impact of Person and Organizational Values on Organizational Commitment," *Journal of Occupational and Organizational Psychology*, 73 (June 2000), pp. 149–69; E. W. Morrison and S. L. Robinson, "When Employees Feel Betrayed: A Model of How Psychological Contract Violation Develops," *Academy of Management Review*, 22 (1997), pp. 226–56.

74. L. Rhoades, R. Eisenberger, and S. Armeli, "Affective Commitment to the Organization: The Contribution of Perceived Organizational Support," *Journal of Applied Psychology*, 86 (October 2001), pp. 825–36.

75. C. Hendry, Chris and R. Jenkins, "Psychological Contracts And New Deals," *Human Resource Management Journal*, 7 (1997), pp. 38–44; D. M. Noer, *Healing the Wounds* (San Francisco: Jossey-Bass, 1993); S. Ashford, C. Lee, and P. Bobko, "Content, Causes, and Consequences of Job Insecurity: A Theory-Based Measure and Substantive Test," *Academy of Management Journal*, 32 (1989), pp. 803–29.

76. D. Steinhart, "Where Pink Slips are not Part of Corporate Culture," *National Post*, October 5, 2001.

77. T. S. Heffner and J. R. Rentsch, "Organizational Commitment and Social Interaction: A Multiple Constituencies Approach," *Journal of Vocational Behavior*, 59 (2001), pp. 471–90.

78. A. Dastmalchian and M. Javidan, "High-Commitment Leadership: A Study of Iranian Executives," *Journal of Comparative International Management*, 1 (1998), pp. 23–37.

79. R. J. Lewicki and B. B. Bunker, "Developing and Maintaining Trust in Work Relationships," In R. M. Kramer and T. R. Tyler (Eds.) *Trust in Organizations:Frontiers of Theory and Research*, (Thousand Oaks, CA: Sage, 1996), pp. 114–39; S. L. Robinson, "Trust and Breach of the Psychological Contract," *Administrative Science Quarterly*, 41 (1996), pp. 574–99; J. M. Kouzes and B. Z. Posner, *The Leadership Challenge* (San Francisco: Jossey-Bass, 1987), pp. 146–52.

80. J. Beatty, "Tense Employees Wonder Who will Go," *Victoria Times Colonist*, November 29, 2001.

81. R. Deruyter, "Some Auto Workers Upset by Forced Overtime," *Kitchener-Waterloo Record*, March 15, 2002.

82. P. Kruger, "Betrayed by Work," *Fast Company*, November 1999, p. 182.

83. E. W. Morrison and S. L. Robinson, "When Employees Feel Betrayed: A Model of How Psychological Contract Violation Develops," *Academy of Management Review*, 22 (1997), pp. 226–56.

84. S. L. Robinson, M. S. Kraatz, and D. M. Rousseau, "Changing Obligations and the Psychological Contract: A Longitudinal Study," *Academy of Management Journal*, 37 (1994), pp. 137–52; D. M. Rousseau and J. M. Parks, "The Contracts of Individuals and Organizations," *Research in Organizational Behavior*, 15 (1993), pp. 1–43.

85. P. Herriot, W. E. G. Manning, and J. M. Kidd, "The Content of the Psychological Contract," *British Journal of Management*, 8 (1997), pp. 151–62.

86. J. McLean Parks and D. L. Kidder, "'Till Death Us Do Part...' Changing Work Relationships in the 1990s," In C. L. Cooper and D. M. Rousseau (Eds.) *Trends in Organizational Behavior*, Vol. 1 (Chichester, UK: Wiley, 1994), pp.112–36.

87. P. G. Irving, T. F. Cawsey, R. Cruikshank, "Organizational Commitment Profiles: Implications for Turnover Intentions and Psychological Contracts," *Proceedings of the Administrative Sciences Association of Canada, Organizational Behavior Division*, 23 (5) (2002), pp. 21–30.

88. W. H. Whyte, *Organization Man* (New York: Simon & Schuster, 1956).

89. C. Hendry and R. Jenkins, "Psychological Contracts and New Deals," *Human Resource Management Journal*, 7 (1997), pp. 38–44; P. Herriot and C. Pemberton, *New Deals: The Revolution in Managerial Careers* (John Wiley & Sons, 1995), Chapter 3; W. H. Whyte, *The Organization Man* (New York: Simon and Schuster, 1956), p.129.

90. R. J. Burke, "Organizational Transitions," In C. L. Cooper and R. J. Burke (eds.) *The New World of Work: Challenges and Opportunities* (Oxford: Blackwell, 2002), pp. 3–28; F. Patterson, "Developments in Work Psychology: Emerging Issues and Future Trends," *Journal of Occupational and Organizational Psychology*, 74 (November 2001), pp. 381–90.

91. J. C. Meister, "The Quest For Lifetime Employability," *Journal of Business Strategy*, 19 (May-June 1998), pp. 25–28; T. A. Stewart, "Gray Flannel Suit? Moi?" *Fortune*, March 16, 1998, pp. 76–82; A. Rajan, "Employability in the Finance Sector: Rhetoric vs Reality," *Human Resource Management Journal*, 7 (1997), pp. 67–78.

92. W. R Boswell, L. M. Moynihan, M. V. Roehling, and M. A. Cavanaugh, "Responsibilities in the "New Employ-

ment Relationship": An Empirical Test of an Assumed Phenomenon," *Journal of Managerial Issues*, 13 (Fall 2001), pp. 307–327.

93. J. Lyon, "How Safe is Your Job?" *Canadian Banker*, February 1997, pp. 12–15. The job security poll is reported in: M. Debock, "Job-Market Survey Reveals Loyalty Split," *Montreal Gazette*, July 22, 2002.

94. L. Uchitelle, "As Job Cuts Spread, Tears Replace Anger," *New York Times*, August 5, 2001. Psychological contract expectations of young employees are discussed in: P. Herriot and C. Pemberton, "Facilitating New Deals," *Human Resource Management Journal*, 7 (1997), pp. 45–56; P. R. Sparrow, "Transitions in the Psychological Contract: Some Evidence from the Banking Sector." *Human Resource Management Journal*, 6 (1996), pp. 75–92.

CHAPTER FIVE

1. L. Nealin, "The Guys Behind the Clodhoppers," *Airlines Magazine* (WestJet's Inflight Magazine), April 2002, pp. 47–49; D. McMurdy, "Building Future on Sweet Idea," *National Post*, February 11, 2002, p. FP1; S. Heinrich, "They're Laughing all the Way to the Bank," *National Post*, October 29, 2001, p. FP12; G. Kirbyson, "Now Clodhopper Fans Tasting Homey Tale Along with Candy," *Winnipeg Free Press*, August 22, 2001, p. B5.

2. C. C. Pinder, *Work Motivation in Organizational Behaviour* (Upper Saddle River, NJ: Prentice-Hall, 1998); E. E. Lawler III, *Motivation in Work Organizations* (Monterey, Calif.: Brooks/Cole, 1973), pp. 2–5.

3. "Towers Perrin Study Finds, Despite Layoffs and Slow Economy, a New, More Complex Power Game is Emerging Between Employers and Employees," *Business Wire*, August 30, 2001.

4. T. H. Wagar, "Consequences of Work Force Reduction: Some Employer and Union Evidence," *Journal of Labor Research*, 22 (Fall 2001), pp. 851–62; R. J. Burke and C. L. Cooper (eds.) *The Organization in Crisis: Downsizing, restructuring, and Privatization* (Oxford: Blackwell Publishers, 2000); R. Burke, "Downsizing and Restructuring in Organizations: Research Findings and Lessons Learned—Introduction," *Cana-*

dian Journal of Administrative Sciences, 15 (December 1998), pp. 297–99.

5. R. Zemke and B. Filipczak, *Generations at Work: Managing the Clash of Veterans, Boomers, Xers, and Nexters in Your Workplace*, (NY: AMACOM, 2000); B. Losyk, "Generation X: What They Think and What They Plan to Do," *The Futurist*, Vol. 31 (March-April 1997), pp. 29–44; B. Tulgan, *Managing Generation X: How to Bring Out the Best in Young Talent* (Oxford: Capstone, 1996).

6. C. C. Pinder, *Work Motivation in Organizational Behaviour*, Chapter 3.

7. A. H. Maslow, "A Theory of Human Motivation," *Psychological Review*, 50 (1943), pp. 370–96; A. H. Maslow, *Motivation and Personality* (New York: Harper & Row, 1954).

8. For recent examples of Maslow's continued popularity, see: M. Witzel, "Motivations that Push our Buttons," *Financial Times*, August 14, 2002, p. 9; P. Kelley, "Revisiting Maslow," *Workspan*, 45 (May 2002), pp. 50–56.

9. M. A. Wahba and L. G. Bridwell, "Maslow Reconsidered: A Review of Research on the Need Hierarchy Theory," *Organizational Behaviour and Human Performance*, 15 (1976), pp. 212–40.

10. C. P. Alderfer, *Existence, Relatedness, and Growth* (New York: The Free Press, 1972).

11. J. P. Wanous and A. A. Zwany, "A Cross-Sectional Test of Need Hierarchy Theory," *Organizational Behaviour and Human Performance*, 18 (1977), pp. 78–97.

12. E. A. Locke, "Motivation, Cognition, and Action: An Analysis of Studies of Task Goals and Knowledge," *Applied Psychology: An International Review*, 49 (2000), pp. 408–29; S. A. Haslam, C. Powell, and J. Turner, "Social Identity, Self-categorization, and Work Motivation: Rethinking the Contribution of the Group to Positive and Sustainable Organisational Outcomes," *Applied Psychology: An International Review*, 49 (July 2000), pp. 319–39.

13. P. R. Lawrence and N. Nohria, *Driven: How Human Nature Shapes Our Choices*, (San Francisco: Jossey-Bass, 2002), p. 10.

14. Lawrence and Nohria, *Driven*, p. 261.

15. Lawrence and Nohria, *Driven*, Chapter 4 to Chapter 7.

16. Lawrence and Nohria, *Driven*, pp. 66–68.

17. R. E. Baumeister and M. R. Leary, "The Need to Belong: Desire for Interpersonal Attachments as a Fundamental Human Motivation," *Psychological Bulletin*, 117 (1995), pp. 497–529.

18. C. Greeno, "End of Road for Truck-Spring Manufacturer," *Kitchener-Waterloo Record*, June 29, 2002, p. B1.

19. Lawrence and Nohria, *Driven*, p. 136.

20. The emotional centre is the limbic centre where the innate drives reside. The rational centre is the prefrontal cerebral cortex. Although signals can run in both directions between these brain centres, neural connections suggest a much stronger signal from the emotional centre to the rational centre than vice versa. See D. S. Massey, "A Brief History of Human Society: The Origin and Role of Emotion in Social Life," *American Sociological Review*, 67 (February 2002), pp. 1–29; Lawrence and Nohria, *Driven*, pp. 44–47, 168–70.

21. Lawrence and Nohria, *Driven*, p. 47.

22. For critiques of various evolutionary psychology theories, see: P. R. Ehrlich, "Human Natures, Nature Conservation, and Environmental Ethics," *Bioscience*, 52 (January 2002), pp. 31–43; L. R. Caporael, "Evolutionary Psychology: Toward a Unifying Theory and a Hybrid Science," *Annual Review of Psychology*, 52 (2001), pp. 607–28.

23. For example, see: J. Langan-Fox and S. Roth, "Achievement Motivation and Female Entrepreneurs," *Journal of Occupational and Organizational Psychology*, 68 (1995), pp. 209–18; H. A. Wainer and I. M. Rubin, "Motivation of Research and Development Entrepreneurs: Determinants of Company Success, Part I," *Journal of Applied Psychology*, 53 (June 1969), pp. 178–84.

24. R. Amit, K. R. MacCrimmon, C. Zietsma and J. M. Oesch, "Does Money Matter? Wealth Attainment as the Motive for Initiating Growth-Oriented Technology Ventures," *Journal of Business Venturing*, 16 (March 2001), pp.119–43; D. C. McClelland, *The Achieving Society* (New York: Van Nostrand Reinhold, 1961); M. Patchen,

Participation, Achievement, and Involvement on the Job (Englewood Cliffs, NJ: Prentice-Hall, 1970).

25. D. C. McClelland, "Retrospective Commentary," *Harvard Business Review*, 73 (January-February 1995), pp. 138–39; D. McClelland and R. Boyatzis, "Leadership Motive Pattern and Long-Term Success in Management," *Journal of Applied Psychology*, 67 (1982), pp. 737–43.

26. R. J. House and R. N. Aditya, "The Social Scientific Study of Leadership: Quo Vadis?" *Journal of Management*, 23 (1997), pp. 409–73; D. C. McClelland and D. H. Burnham, "Power Is the Great Motivator," *Harvard Business Review*, 73 (January-February 1995), pp. 126–39 (reprinted from 1976).

27. D. Vredenburgh and Y. Brender, "The Hierarchical Abuse of Power in Work Organizations," *Journal of Business Ethics*, 17 (September 1998), pp. 1337–47; McClelland and Burnham, "Power Is the Great Motivator."

28. D. G. Winter, "A Motivational Model of Leadership: Predicting Long-term Management Success from TAT Measures of Power Motivation and Responsibility," *Leadership Quarterly*, 2 (1991), pp. 67–80.

29. House and Aditya, "The Social Scientific Study Of Leadership: Quo Vadis?"

30. D. C. McClelland and D. G. Winter, *Motivating Economic Achievement* (New York: The Free Press, 1969); and D. Miron and D. McClelland, "The Impact of Achievement Motivation Training on Small Business," *California Management Review* 21 (1979), pp. 13–28.

31. Lawrence and Nohria, *Driven*, Chapter 11.

32. A. Tomlinson, "Top Shops Deliver More than Flashy Perks," *Canadian HR Reporter*, January 28, 2002, pp. 1, 3.

33. A, Kohn, *Punished by Rewards* (N.Y.: Houghton Mifflin, 1993).

34. Human Resources Development Canada, "PanCanadian Petroluem," *Work-Life Balance in Canadian Workplaces*, July 2001. http://labour.hrdc-drhc.gc.ca/worklife/pancanadian-en.cfm.

35. Expectancy theory of motivation in work settings originated in V. H. Vroom, *Work and Motivation* (New York: Wiley, 1964). The version of expectancy theory presented here was developed by Edward Lawler. Lawler's model provides a clearer presentation of the model's three components. P-to-O expectancy is similar to "instrumentality" in Vroom's original expectancy theory model. The difference is that instrumentality is a correlation whereas P-to-O expectancy is a probability. See: D. A. Nadler and E. E. Lawler, "Motivation: A Diagnostic Approach," in . J. R. Hackman, E. E. Lawler III, and L. W. Porter (Eds.) *Perspectives on Behaviour in Organizations*, 2nd ed., (New York: McGraw-Hill, 1983), pp. 67–78; J. P. Campbell, M. D. Dunnette, E. E. Lawler, and K. E. Weick, *Managerial Behaviour, Performance, and Effectiveness* (New York: McGraw-Hill, 1970), pp. 343–48; E. E. Lawler, *Motivation in Work Organizations* (Monterey, Calif.: Brooks/Cole, 1973), Chapter 3.

36. Nadler and Lawler, "Motivation: A Diagnostic Approach," pp. 70–73.

37. K. A. Karl, A. M. O'Leary-Kelly, and J. J. Martoccio, "The Impact of Feedback and Self-Efficacy on Performance in Training," *Journal of Organizational Behaviour* 14 (1993), pp. 379–94; T. Janz, "Manipulating Subjective Expectancy Through Feedback: A Laboratory Study of the Expectancy-Performance Relationship," *Journal of Applied Psychology*, 67 (1982), pp. 480–85.

38. K. May, "Managers Rewarded for Presiding over $1B Bungle," *Ottawa Citizen*, January 27, 2000.

39. J. B. Fox, K. D. Scott, and J. M. Donohoe, "An Investigation into Pay Valence and Performance in a Pay-for-Performance Field Setting," *Journal of Organizational Behaviour*, 14 (1993), pp. 687–93.

40. W. Van Eerde and H. Thierry, "Vroom's Expectancy Models and Work-Related Criteria: A Meta-Analysis," *Journal of Applied Psychology*, 81 (1996), pp. 575–86; T. R. Mitchell, "Expectancy Models of Job Satisfaction, Occupational Preference and Effort: A Theoretical, Methodological, and Empirical Appraisal," *Psychological Bulletin*, 81 (1974), pp. 1053–77.

41. C. L. Haworth and P. E. Levy, "The Importance of Instrumentality Beliefs in the Prediction of Organizational Citizenship Behaviours," *Journal of Vocational Behavior*, 59 (August 2001), pp. 64–75; M. L. Ambrose and C. T. Kulik, "Old Friends, New Faces: Motivation Research in the 1990s," *Journal of Management*, 25 (May 1999), pp. 231–92; K. C. Snead and A. M. Harrell, "An Application of Expectancy Theory to Explain a Manager's Intention to Use a Decision Support System," *Decision Sciences*, 25 (1994), pp. 499–513.

42. Elenkov, "Can American Management Concepts Work In Russia?"; N. A. Boyacigiller and N. J. Adler, "The Parochial Dinosaur: Organizational Science in a Global Context," *Academy of Management Review*, 16 (1991), pp. 262–90; N. J. Adler, *International Dimensions of Organizational Behaviour*, 3rd ed. (Cincinnati: South-Western, 1997), Chapter 6.

43. D. H. B. Welsh, F. Luthans, and S. M. Sommer, "Managing Russion Factory Workers: The Impact of U.S.-Based Behavioural and Participative Techniques," *Academy of Management Journal*, 36 (1993), pp. 58–79; T. Matsui and I. Terai, "A Cross-Cultural Study of the Validity of the Expectancy Theory of Motivation," *Journal of Applied Psychology*, 60 (1979), pp. 263–65.

44. For recent OB writing incorporating emotions in the topic of employee motivation, see: E. L. Zurbriggen and T. S. Sturman, "Linking Motives and Emotions: A Test of McClelland's Hypotheses," *Personality & Social Psychology Bulletin*, 28 (April 2002), pp. 521–35; P. E. Spector and S. Fox "An Emotion-Centered Model of Voluntary Work Behavior: Some Parallels between Counterproductive Work Behavior and Organizational Citizenship Behavior," *Human Resource Management Review*, 12 (2002), pp. 269–92; J. Brockner and E. T. Higgins "Regulatory Focus Theory: Implications for the Study of Emotions at Work," *Organizational Behavior and Human Decision Processes*, 86 (September 2001) pp. 35–66; M. Perugini and R. P. Bagozzi "The Role of Desires and Anticipated Emotions in Goal-Directed Behaviours: Broadening and Deepening the Theory of Planned Behaviour," *British Journal of Social Psychology*, 40 (March 2001), pp. 79–98.

45. David Beardsley, "This Company Doesn't Brake For (Sacred) Cows," *Fast Company*, 16 (August 1998), pp. 66.

46. For recent research on the effectiveness of goal setting, see: L. A. Wilk and W. K. Redmon, "The Effects of Feedback and Goal Setting on the Productivity and Satisfaction of University Admissions Staff," *Journal of Organizational Behaviour Management*, Vol. 18 (1998), pp. 45–68; K. H. Doerr and T. R. Mitchell, "Impact of Material Flow Policies and Goals on Job Outcomes," *Journal of Applied Psychology*, 81 (1996), pp. 142–52; A. A. Shikdar and B. Das, "A Field Study of Worker Productivity Improvements." *Applied Ergonomics*, 26 (February 1995), pp. 21–27; M. D. Cooper and R. A. Phillips, "Reducing Accidents Using Goal Setting and Feedback: A Field Study," *Journal of Occupational & Organizational Psychology*, 67 (1994), pp. 219–40.

47. T. H. Poister and G. Streib, "MBO in Municipal Government: Variations on a Traditional Management Tool," *Public Administration Review*, 55 (1995), pp. 48–56.

48. R. Kaiser, "Human Touch Selling Online," *Chicago Tribune*, September 10, 2001, p. CN1; F. Knowles, "CDW Chief Gung-Ho," *Chicago Sun-Times*, April 23, 2001, p. 51.

49. E. A. Locke and G. P. Latham, *A Theory of Goal Setting and Task Performance* (Englewood Cliffs, N.J.: Prentice Hall, 1990); A. J. Mento, R. P. Steel, and R. J. Karren, "A Meta-analytic Study of the Effects of Goal Setting on Task Performance: 1966–1984," *Organizational Behaviour and Human Decision Processes*, 39 (1987), pp. 52–83; M. E. Tubbs, "Goal-setting: A Meta-analytic Examination of the Empirical Evidence," *Journal of Applied Psychology*, 71 (1986), pp. 474–83. Some practitioners rely on the acronym "SMART" goals, referring to goals that are specific, measurable, acceptable, relevant, and timely. However, this list overlaps key elements (e.g., specific goals *are* measurable and timely) and overlooks the key elements of challenging and feedback-related.

50. K. Tasa, T. Brown, and G. H. Seijts, "The Effects of Proximal, Outcome and Learning Goals on Information Seeking and Complex Task Performance" *Proceedings of the Annual Conference of the Administrative Sciences Association of Canada, Organizational Behaviour Division*, 23 (5) (2002), pp. 11–20.

51. Locke, "Motivation, Cognition, and Action"; I. R. Gellatly and J. P. Meyer, "The Effects of Goal Difficulty on Physiological Arousal, Cognition, and Task Performance," *Journal of Applied Psychology*, 77 (1992), pp. 694–704; A. Mento, E. A. Locke, and H. Klein, "Relationship of Goal Level to Valence and Instrumentality," *Journal of Applied Psychology*, 77 (1992), pp. 395–405.

52. J. T. Chambers, "The Future of Business," *Executive Excellence*, 17 (February 2000), pp. 3–4; K. R. Thompson, W. A. Hochwarter, and N. J. Mathys, "Stretch Targets: What Makes them Effective?" *Academy of Management Executive*, Vol. 11 (August 1997), pp. 48–60; S. Sherman, "Stretch Goals: The Dark Side of Asking for Miracles," *Fortune*, 132 (November 13, 1995), pp. 231–32.

53. M. E. Tubbs, "Commitment as a Moderator of the Goal-Performance Relation: A Case for Clearer Construct Definition," *Journal of Applied Psychology*, 78 (1993), pp. 86–97.

54. H. J. Klein, "Further Evidence of the Relationship Between Goal Setting and Expectancy Theory," *Organizational Behaviour and Human Decision Processes*, 49 (1991), pp. 230–57.

55. J. Wegge, "Participation in Group Goal Setting: Some Novel Findings and a Comprehensive Model as a New Ending to an Old Story," *Applied Psychology: An International Review*, 49 (2000), pp. 498–516; Locke and Latham, *A Theory of Goal Setting and Task Performance*, Chapters 6 and 7; E. A. Locke, G. P. Latham, and M. Erez, "The Determinants of Goal Commitment," *Academy of Management Review*, 13 (1988), pp. 23–39.

56. R. W. Renn and D. B. Fedor, "Development and Field Test of a Feedback Seeking, Self-Efficacy, and Goal Setting Model of Work Performance," *Journal of Management*, 27 (2001) pp. 563–83.

57. A. N. Kluger & A. DeNisi, "The Effects of Feedback Interventions on Performance: A Historical Review, A Meta-Analysis, and a Preliminary Feedback Intervention Theory," *Psychological Bulletin*, 119 (March 1996), pp. 254–84; A. A. Shikdar and B. Das, "A Field Study of Worker Productivity Improvements," *Applied Ergonomics*, 26 (1995), pp. 21–27; L. M. Sama and R. E. Kopelman, "In Search of a Ceiling Effect on Work Motivation: Can Kaizen Keep Performance 'Risin'?" *Journal of Social Behaviour & Personality*, 9 (1994), pp. 231–37.

58. R. Waldersee and F. Luthans, "The Impact of Positive and Corrective Feedback on Customer Service Performance," *Journal of Organizational Behaviour*, 15 (1994), pp. 83–95; P. K. Duncan and L. R. Bruwelheide, "Feedback: Use and Possible Behavioural Functions," *Journal of Organizational Behaviour Management*, 7 (Fall 1985), pp. 91–114; J. Annett, *Feedback and Human Behaviour* (Baltimore: Penguin, 1969).

59. R. D. Guzzo and B. A. Gannett, "The Nature of Facilitators and Inhibitors of Effective Task Performance," In F. D. Schoorman & B. Schneider (eds.) *Facilitating Work Effectiveness*, (Lexington, Mass.: Lexington Books, 1988), p. 23; R. C. Linden and T. R. Mitchell, "Reactions to Feedback: The Role of Attributions," *Academy of Management Journal*, 1985, pp. 291–308.

60. P. M. Posakoff and J. Fahr, "Effects of Feedback Sign and Credibility on Goal Setting and Task Performance," *Organizational Behaviour and Human Decision Processes*, 44 (1989), pp. 45–67.

61. A. Tomlinson, "Top Shops Deliver More than Flashy Perks," *Canadian HR Reporter*, January 28, 2002, pp. 1, 3; I. Wilkinson, "Few Rules Rule," *BC Business*, January 2002, pp. 25ff; "Creo Named One of Canada's Top Employers," *CCN Newswire*, December 19, 2001.

62. For discussion of multi-source feedback, see: L. E. Atwater, D. A. Waldman, and J. F. Brett, "Understanding and Optimizing Multisource Feedback," *Human Resource Management*, 41 (Summer 2002), pp. 193–208; W. W. Tornow and M. London, *Maximizing the Value of 360-degree Feedback: A Process for Successful Individual and Organizational Development* (San Francisco: Jossey-Bass, 1998).

63. S. Brutus and M. Derayeh, "Multisource Assessment Programs in Orga-

nizations: An Insider's Perspective," *Human Resource Development Quarterly*, 13 (July 2002), pp. 187ff.

64. D. A. Waldman and L. E. Atwater, "Attitudinal and Behavioral Outcomes of an Upward Feedback Process," *Group & Organization Management*, 26 (June 2001), pp. 189–205.

65. The problems with 360-degree feedback are discussed in: M.A. Peiperl, "Getting 360 Degree Feedback Right," *Harvard Business Review*, 79 (January 2001), pp. 142–147; A. S. DeNisi and A. N. Kluger, "Feedback Effectiveness: Can 360-Degree Appraisals be Improved?" *Academy of Management Executive*, 14 (February 2000), pp. 129–39; J. Ghorpade, "Managing Five Paradoxes of 360-Degree Feedback," *Academy of Management Executive*, 14 (February 2000), pp. 140–50; B. Usher and J. Morley, "Overcoming the Obstacles to a Successful 36-Degree Feedback Program," *Canadian HR Reporter*, February 8, 1999, p. 17.

66. S. Watkins, "Ever Wanted To Review The Boss?" *Investor's Business Daily*, August 10, 2001, p. A1.

67. R. R. Kilburg, *Executive Coaching: Developing Managerial Wisdom in a World of Chaos.*, (Washington D.C.: American Psychological Association, 2000), p. 65.

68. D. Goleman, *The Emotionally Intelligent Workplace*, (San Francisco: Jossey-Bass, 2001); J. H. Eggers and D. Clark, "Executive Coaching that Wins," *Ivey Business Journal*, 65 (September 2000), pp. 66ff.

69. S. Berglas, "The Very Real Dangers of Executive Coaching," *Harvard Business Review*, 80 (June 2002), pp. 80–86.

70. M.C. Andrews and K.M. Kacmar, "Confirmation and Extension of the Sources of Feedback Scale in Service-based Organizations," *Journal of Business Communication*, 38 (April 2001), pp. 206–226.

71. N. Zurell, "Built for Speed," *Intelligent Enterprise*, September 3, 2002, p. 14.

72. L. Hollman, "Seeing the Writing On the Wall," *Call Center*, August 2002, p. 37.

73. M. London, "Giving Feedback: Source-Centered Antecedents and Consequences of Constructive and Destructive Feedback," *Human Resource Management Review*, 5 (1995), pp. 159–88; D. Antonioni, "The Effects of Feedback Accountability on 360-Degree Appraisal Ratings," *Personnel Psychology*, 47 (1994), pp. 375–90; S. J. Ashford and G. B. Northcraft, "Conveying More (or Less) Than We Realize: The Role of Impression Management in Feedback Seeking," *Organizational Behaviour and Human Decision Processes*, 53 (1992), pp. 310–34; E. W. Morrison and R. J. Bies, "Impression Management in the Feedback-Seeking Process: A Literature Review and Research Agenda," *Academy of Management Review*, 16 (1991), pp. 522–41.

74. J. R. Williams, C. E. Miller, L. A. Steelman, and P. E. Levy, "Increasing Feedback Seeking in Public Contexts: It Takes Two (or More) to Tango," *Journal of Applied Psychology*, 84 (December 1999), pp. 969–76; G. B. Northcraft and S. J. Ashford, "The Preservation of Self in Everyday Life: The Effects of Performance Expectations and Feedback Context on Feedback Inquiry," *Organizational Behaviour and Human Decision Processes*, 47 (1990), pp. 42–64.

75. P. M. Wright, "Goal Setting and Monetary Incentives: Motivational Tools that Can Work Too Well," *Compensation and Benefits Review*, 26 (May-June, 1994), pp. 41–49.

76. F. M. Moussa, " Determinants and Process of the Choice of Goal Difficulty," *Group & Organization Management*, 21 (1996), pp. 414–38.

77. Some scholars suggest that goal setting is the best supported and most practical work motivation theory. See: C. C. Pinder, *Work Motivation in Organizational Behavior* (Upper Saddle River, NJ: Prentice-Hall, 1998), p. 384.

78. K. Gagne, "One Day at a Time," *Workspan*, February 2002, pp. 20ff.

79. D. T. Miller, "Disrespect and the Experience of Injustice," *Annual Review of Psychology*, 52 (2001), pp. 527–53; R. Cropanzano and M. Schminke, "Using Social Justice to Build Effective Work Groups," In M. E. Turner (ed.) *Groups at Work: Theory and Research* (Mahwah, New Jersey: Lawrence Erlbaum Associates, 2001), pp. 143–71; J. Greenberg and E. A. Lind, "The Pursuit of Organizational Justice: From Conceptualization to Implication to Application," In C. L. Cooper and E. A. Locke (Eds.) *Industrial and Organizational Psychology: Linking Theory with Practice* (London: Blackwell, 2000), pp. 72–108.

80. "Commission Withdraws Complaint in Light of Pay Equity Agreement," *M2 Presswire*, September 24, 1999; C. Silverthorn, "Rights Commission Launches Investigation into Safeway Pay Practices," *Canadian Press Newswire*, January 9, 1998.

81. R. Cropanzano and M. Schminke, "Using Social Justice to Build Effective Work Groups," In M. E. Turner (ed.) *Groups at Work: Theory and Research* (Mahwah, New Jersey: Lawrence Erlbaum Associates, 2001), pp. 143–71;

82. R. Cropanzano and J. Greenberg, "Progress in Organizational Justice: Tunneling Through the Maze," In C. L. Cooper and I. T. Robertson (Eds.) *International Review of Industrial and Organizational Psychology* (New York: Wiley, 1997), pp. 317–72; R. T. Mowday, "Equity Theory Predictions of Behaviour in Organizations," in *Motivation and Work Behaviour*, 5th ed., ed. R. M. Steers & L. W. Porter (New York: McGraw-Hill, 1991), pp. 111–31; J. S. Adams, "Toward an Understanding of Inequity," *Journal of Abnormal and Social Psychology*, 67 (1963), pp. 422–36.

83. G. Blau, "Testing the Effect of Level and Importance of Pay Referents on Pay Level Satisfaction," *Human Relations*, 47 (1994), pp. 1251–68; C. T. Kulik and M. L. Ambrose, "Personal and Situational Determinants of Referent Choice," *Academy of Management Review*, 17 (1992), pp. 212–37; J. Pfeffer, "Incentives in Organizations: The Importance of Social Relations," in *Organization Theory: From Chester Barnard to the Present and Beyond*, ed. O. E. Williamson (New York: Oxford University Press, 1990), pp. 72–97.

84. T. P. Summers and A. S. DeNisi, "In Search of Adams' Other: Reexamination of Referents Used in the Evaluation of Pay," *Human Relations*, 43 (1990), pp. 497–511.

85. J. S. Adams, "Inequity in Social Exchange," in *Advances in Experimental Psychology*, ed. L. Berkowitz (New York: Academic Press, 1965), pp. 157–89.

86. Y. Cohen-Charash and P. E. Spector "The Role of Justice in Organiza-

tions: A Meta-Analysis," *Organizational Behaviour and Human Decision Processes*, 86 (November 2001), pp. 278–321.

87. J. Barling, C. Fullagar, and E. K. Kelloway, *The Union and Its Members: A Psychological Approach* (New York: Oxford University Press, 1992).

88. J. Greenberg, "Cognitive Reevaluation of Outcomes in Response to Underpayment Inequity," *Academy of Management Journal*, 32 (1989), pp. 174–184; E. Hatfield and S. Sprecher, "Equity Theory and Behaviour in Organizations," *Research in the Sociology of Organizations*, 3 (1984), pp. 94–124.

89. Cited in *Canadian Business*, February 1997, p. 39.

90. M. N. Bing and S. M. Burroughs, "The Predictive and Interactive Effects of Equity Sensitivity in Teamwork-oriented Organizations," *Journal of Organizational Behaviour*, 22 (2001), pp. 271–90; K. S. Sauleya and A. G. Bedeian "Equity Sensitivity: Construction of a Measure and Examination of its Psychometric Properties," *Journal of Management*, 26 (September 2000), pp. 885–910; P. E Mudrack, E. S. Mason, and K. M. Stepanski, "Equity Sensitivity and Business Ethics," *Journal of Occupational and Organizational Psychology*, 72 (December 1999), pp. 539–60; R. P. Vecchio, "An Individual-Differences Interpretation of the Conflicting Predictions Generated by Equity Theory and Expectancy Theory," *Journal of Applied Psychology*, 66 (1981), pp. 470–81.

91. The meaning of these three groups has evolved over the years. These definitions are based on W. C. King, Jr. and E. W. Miles, "The Measurement of Equity Sensitivity," *Journal of Occupational and Organizational Psychology*, 67 (1994), pp. 133–42.

92. M. Wenzel, "A Social Categorization Approach to Distributive Justice: Social Identity as the Link Between Relevance of Inputs and Need for Justice," *British Journal of Social Psychology*, 40 (2001), pp. 315–35.

93. C. Viswesvaran and D. S. Ones, "Examining the Construct of Organizational Justice: A Meta-Analytic Evaluation of Relations with Work Attitudes and Behaviours," *Journal of Business Ethics*, 38 (July 2002), pp. 193–203;

J. A. Colquitt, D. E. Conlon, M. W. Wesson, L. H. Porter, and K. Y. Ng, "Justice at the Millennium: A Meta-Analytic Review of 25 Years of Organizational Justice Research," *Journal of Applied Psychology*, 86 (2001), 425–45; Y. Cohen-Charash and P. E. Spector "The Role of Justice in Organizations: A Meta-Analysis," *Organizational Behaviour and Human Decision Processes*, 86 (November 2001), pp. 278–321.

94. Several types of justice have been identified and there is some debate whether they represent forms of procedural justice or are distinct from procedural and distributive justice. The discussion here adopts the former view, which seems to dominate the literature. See C. Viswesvaran and D. S. Ones, "Examining the Construct of Organizational Justice: A Meta-Analytic Evaluation of Relations with Work Attitudes and Behaviours," *Journal of Business Ethics*, 38 (July 2002), pp. 193–203.

95. Greenberg and Lind, "The Pursuit of Organizational Justice," pp. 79–80. for recent evidence of the voice effect, see: E. A. Douthitt and J. R. Aiello, "The Role of Participation and Control in the Effects of Computer Monitoring on Fairness Perceptions, Task Satisfaction, and Performance," *Journal of Applied Psychology*, 86 (October 2001), pp. 867–74.

96. L. B. Bingham, "Mediating Employment Disputes: Perceptions of Redress at the United States Postal Service," *Review of Public Personnel Administration*, 17 (Spring 1997), pp. 20–30; R. Folger and J. Greenberg, "Procedural Justice: An Interpretive Analysis of Personnel Systems," *Research in Personnel and Human Resources Management* 3 (1985), pp. 141–83.

97. R. Hagey et al., "Immigrant Nurses' Experience of Racism," *Journal of Nursing Scholarship*, 33 (Fourth Quarter 2001), pp. 389ff. K. Roberts and K. S. Markel, "Claiming in the Name of Fairness: Organizational Justice and the Decision to File for Workplace Injury Compensation," *Journal of Occupational Health Psychology*, 6 (October 2001), pp. 332–47.

98. D. T. Miller, "Disrespect and the Experience of Injustice," *Annual Review of Psychology*, 52 (2001), pp.

534–35; 543–45; J. A. Colquitt, D. E. Conlon, M. W. Wesson, L. H. Porter, and K. Y. Ng, "Justice at the Millennium: A Meta-Analytic Review of 25 Years of Organizational Justice Research," *Journal of Applied Psychology*, 86 (2001), 425–45.

99. S. Fox, P. E. Spector, and D. Miles, "Counterproductive Work Behaviour (CWB) in Response to Job Stressors and Organizational Justice: Some Mediator and Moderator Tests for Autonomy and Emotions," *Journal of Vocational Behaviour*, 59 (2001) pp. 291–309; L. Greenberg and J. Barling, "Employee Theft," In C. L. Cooper & D. M. Rousseau (eds.) *Trends in Organizational Behaviour*, 3 (1996), pp. 49–64.

100. D. P. Skarlicki and R. Folger, "Retaliation in the Workplace: The Roles of Distributive, Procedural, and Interactional justice," *Journal of Applied Psychology*, 82 (1997), pp. 434–43.

101. N. D. Cole and G. P. Latham, "Effects of Training in Procedural Justice on Perceptions of Disciplinary Fairness by Unionized Employees and Disciplinary Subject Matter Experts," *Journal of Applied Psychology*, 82 (1997), pp. 699–705; D. P. Skarlicki and G. P. Latham, "Increasing Citizenship Behavior Within a Labor Union: A Test of Organizational Justice Theory," *Journal of Applied Psychology*, 81 (1996), pp. 161–69.

CHAPTER SIX

1. N. de Bono, "WestJet Airlines Brings its Discount Prices," *London Free Press*, February 2, 2002; T. Hogue "The Little Airline that Could," *Hamilton Spectator*, N. de Bono, "WestJet Airlines Brings its Discount Prices," *London Free Press*, December 29, 2001, p. M2; P. Fitzpatrick, "Air Travel Complaints soar 35%," *National Post*, November 30, 2001, p. A4; P. Verburg, "Prepare for Takeoff," *Canadian Business*, December 25, 2000, pp. 94–99.

2. M. C. Bloom and G. T. Milkovich, "Issues in Managerial Compensation Research," In C. L. Cooper & D. M. Rousseau (eds.) *Trends in Organizational Behaviour, Vol. 3* (Chicester, UK: John Wiley & Sons, 1996), pp. 23–47.

3. T. Kinni, "Why We Work," *Training*, 35 (August 1998), pp. 34–39; A. Furnham and M. Argyle, *The Psychology of Money* (London: Routledge, 1998); T.

L-P. Tang, "The Meaning of Money Revisited," *Journal of Organizational Behaviour*, 13 (March 1992), pp. 197–202.

4. Cited in T. R. Mitchell and A. E. Mickel, "The Meaning of Money: An Individual-Difference Perspective," *Academy of Management Review*, (July 1999), pp. 568–78.

5. C. Loch, M. Yaziji, and C. Langen, "The Fight for the Alpha Position: Channeling Status Competition in Organizations," *European Management Journal*, 19 (February 2001), pp. 16–25. For discussion of the drive to acquire, see: P. R. Lawrence and N. Nohria, *Driven: How Human Nature Shapes Our Choices*, (San Francisco: Jossey-Bass, 2002), Chapter 4.

6. S. Foster, "Good Job, Lots of Cash, Great Life," *Regina Leader-Post*, June 8, 2002; Watson Wyatt Worldwide, *Playing to Win: Strategic Rewards in the War for Talent—Fifth Annual Survey Report 2000/2001*, (Chicago: Watson Wyatt Worldwide, 2001).

7. H. Meyer, "IKEA Seattle: The Little Store that Could," *Corporate Meetings & Incentives*, 21 (September 2002), pp. 16ff; A. Crawford, "Unique IKEA Promotion Rewards Front-Line Workers," *Calgary Herald*, October 25, 1999.

8. A. Furnham and R. Okamura, "Your Money or Your Life: Behavioural and Emotional Predictors of Money Pathology," *Human Relations*, 52 (September 1999), pp. 1157–77.

9. T. L-P. Tang, J. K. Kim, and D. S-H. Tang, "Does Attitude toward Money Moderate the Relationship between Intrinsic Job Satisfaction and Voluntary Turnover?" *Human Relations*, 53 (February 2000), pp. 213–45; Thomas Li-Ping Tang and Jwa K Kim, "The Meaning of Money among Mental Health Workers: The Endorsement of Money Ethic as Related to Organizational Citizenship Behaviour, Job Satisfaction, and Commitment," *Public Personnel Management*, 28 (Spring 1999), pp. 15–26.

10. S. H. Ang, "The Power of Money: A Cross-Cultural Analysis of Business-Related Beliefs," *Journal of World Business*, 35 (March 2000), pp. 43–60. The importance of money in Canada and its relationship to life happiness are discussed in: M. Adams, *Better Happy than Rich?* (Toronto: Viking, 2001).

11. L. S. Hoon and V. K. G. Lim, "Attitudes Towards Money and Work—Implications for Asian Management Style Following the Economic Crisis," *Journal of Managerial Psychology*, 16 (2001), pp. 159–72; A.K. Kau, S.J. Tan and J. Wirtz, *Seven Faces of Singaporeans: Their Values, Aspirations, and Lifestyles*. (Singapore: Prentice Hall, 1998); A. Furnham, B. D. Kirkcaldy, and R. Lynn, "National Attitudes to Competitiveness, Money, and Work Among Young People: First, Second, and Third World Differences," *Human Relations*, 47 (January 1994), pp. 119–32.

12. O. Mellan, "Men, Women & Money," *Psychology Today*, 32 (February 1999), pp. 46–50. For the Canadian study, see: H. Das, "The Four Faces of Pay: An Investigation into How Canadian Managers View Pay," *International Journal of Commerce & Management*, 12 (2002), pp. 18–40.

13. R. Lynn, *The Secret of the Miracle Economy*. (London: SAE, 1991), cited in A. Furnham and R. Okamura, "Your Money or Your Life: Behavioural and Emotional Predictors of Money Pathology," *Human Relations*, 52 (September 1999), pp. 1157–77. The recent public opinion polls are cited in: M. Steen, "Study Looks at What Good Employees Want from a Company," *San Jose Mercury*, December 19, 2000; J. O'Rourke, "Show Boys the Money and Tell Girls You Care," *Sydney Morning Herald*, December 10, 2000.

14. M. Steen, "Study Looks at What Good Employees Want from a Company," *San Jose Mercury*, December 19, 2000; O. Mellan, "Men, Women & Money," *Psychology Today*, 32 (February 1999), pp. 46–50; V. K. G. Lim and T. S. H. Teo, "Sex, Money and Financial Hardship: An Empirical Study of Attitudes Towards Money among Undergraduates in Singapore," *Journal of Economic Psychology*, 18 (1997), pp. 369–386; A. Furnham, "Attitudinal Correlates and Demographic Predictors of Monetary Beliefs and Behaviours," *Journal of Organizational Behavior*, 17 (1996), 375–88.

15. J. M. Newman and F. J. Krzystofiak, "Value-Chain Compensation," *Compensation and Benefits Review*, 30 (May 1998), pp. 60–66. Japanese pay practices are described in: H. Y. Park, "A Comparative Analysis of Work In-

centives in U.S. and Japanese Firms," *Multinational Business Review*, 4 (Fall 1996), pp. 59–70.

16. R. J. Long, "Job Evaluation in Canada: Has its Demise Been Greatly Exaggerated?" *Proceedings of the Annual Conference of the Administrative Sciences Association of Canada, Human Resource Management Division*, 23 (9) (2002), pp. 61–72. For more details about job status-based compensation, see: R. J. Long, *Compensation in Canada: Strategy, Practice, and Issues*, 2nd ed. (Toronto: ITP Nelson Publishers, 2002), Chapter 9.

17. E. E. Lawler, III, *Rewarding Excellence: Pay Strategies for the New Economy* (San Francisco: Jossey-Bass, 2000), pp. 30–35, 109–19; M. Quaid, *Job Evaluation: The Myth of Equitable Assessment* (Toronto: University of Toronto Press, 1993); S. L. McShane, "Two Tests of Direct Gender Bias in Job Evaluation Ratings," *Journal of Occupational Psychology*, 63 (1990), pp. 129–40. The pay equity study in Hong Kong is described in: Q. Chan and C. Wan, "Equal Pay Under the Microscope," *South China Morning Post*, May 31, 2001, p. 4.

18. R. Shareef, "A Midterm Case Study Assessment of Skill-Based Pay in the Virginia Department of Transportation," *Review of Public Personnel Administration*, 18 (Winter 1998), pp. 5–22; D. Hofrichter, "Broadbanding: A 'Second Generation' Approach," *Compensation & Benefits Review*, 25 (September/October 1993), pp. 53–58.

19. M. Messin and S. St-Onge, "Widening Salary Bands at the National Bank of Canada," *Workplace Gazette*, 3 (Summer 2000), pp. 82–85.

20. B. Murray and B. Gerhart, "Skill-Based Pay and Skill Seeking," *Human Resource Management Review*, 10 (Autumn 2000), pp. 271–87; J.R. Thompson and C.W. LeHew, "Skill-Based Pay as an Organizational Innovation," *Review of Public Personnel Administration*, 20 (Winter 2000), pp. 20–40; D-O. Kim and K. Mericle, "From Job-based Pay to Skill-based Pay in Unionized Establishments: A Three-Plant Comparative Analysis," *Relations Industrielles*, 54 (Summer 1999), pp. 549–80; E. E. Lawler III, "From Job-Based to Competency-Based Organizations," *Journal*

of Organizational Behaviour, 15 (1994), pp. 3–15.

21. E. E. Lawler III, G. E. Ledford, Jr., and L. Chang, "Who Uses Skill-Based Pay, and Why," *Compensation and Benefits Review*, 25 (March-April 1993), pp. 22–26.

22. E.E. Lawler III, "Competencies: A Poor Foundation for The New Pay," *Compensation & Benefits Review*, November/December 1996, pp. 20, 22–26.

23. E. B. Peach and D. A. Wren, "Pay for Performance from Antiquity to the 1950s," *Journal of Organizational Behaviour Management*, 1992, pp. 5–26.

24. "Human Resources Practices: Survey Results," *Worklife Report*, 13 (January 2001), p. 6.

25. Lawler, *"Rewarding Excellence*, Chapter 9; J. S. DeMatteo, L. T. Eby, and E. Sundstrom, "Team-Based Rewards: Current Empirical Evidence and Directions for Future Research," In B. M. Staw and L. L. Cummings (Eds.) *Research in Organizational Behaviour*, 20 (1998), pp. 141–83; P. Pascarella, "Compensating Teams," *Across the Board*, 34 (February 1997), pp. 16–23; D. G. Shaw and C. E. Schneier, "Team Measurement and Rewards: How Some Companies are Getting it Right," *Human Resource Planning*, (1995) pp. 34–49. The team-based rewards on Wall Street are described in: F. Russo, "Aggression Loses Some Of Its Punch," *Time*, July 30, 2001.

26. L.R. Gomez-Mejia, T.M. Welbourne, R.M. Wiseman, "The Role of Risk Sharing and Risk Taking under Gainsharing," *Academy of Management Review*, 25 (July 2000), pp. 492–507; D. P. O'Bannon and C. L. Pearce, "An Exploratory Examination of Gainsharing in Service Organizations: Implications for Organizational Citizenship Behaviour and Pay Satisfaction," *Journal of Managerial Issues*, 11 (Fall 1999), pp. 363–78; C. Cooper and B. Dyck, "Improving the Effectiveness of Gainsharing: The Role of Fairness and Participation," *Administrative Science Quarterly*, 37 (1992), pp. 471–90.

27. "Inland Group Uses Gainsharing to Become a 'World Class' Company," *Pay for Performance Report*, August 2002; "Canadian Companies Encourage Employees With Innovative Bonus Plans," *Coal International*, March/April 2002,

p. 68; "How Hibernia Helped Its Hourly Employees Make a Leap to PFP," *Pay for Performance Report*, January 2000.

28. J. Case, "Opening the Books," *Harvard Business Review*, 75 (March-April 1997), pp. 118–27; T. R. V. Davis, "Open-Book Management: Its Promise and Pitfalls," *Organizational Dynamics*, Winter 1997, pp. 7–20; J. Case, *Open Book Management: The Coming Business Revolution* (New York: Harper Business, 1995).

29. H. Hamid, "Tien Wah's Flexi-Wage a Success," *Business Times (Malaysia)*, December 7, 2000.

30. T. H. Wagar, and R. J. Long, "Profit Sharing in Canada: Incidence and Predictors," *1995 ASAC Conference, Human Resources Division*, 16 (9) (1995), pp. 97–105.

31. J. M. Newman and M. Waite, "Do Broad-Based Stock Options Create Value?" *Compensation and Benefits Review*, 30 (July 1998), pp. 78–86.

32. G. Bellett, "Worker-Friendly Policies Connect with Telus Staff: Stock Options, Education Raise Employees' Worth," *Edmonton Journal*, February 20, 2002, p. F6; "Giving Stock to More Employees Improves Corporate Performance," *Canadian HR Report*, March 26, 2001; B. Lewis, "Exec Perk Goes to All at Telus," *Vancouver Province*, March 2, 2001.

33. R. S. Kaplan and D. P. Norton, *The Strategy-Focused Organization* (Cambridge, MA: Harvard Business School Press, 2001).

34. Nova Scotia Power's balanced scorecard is described in: P. R. Niven, *Balanced Scorecard Step-by-Step: Maximizing Performance and Maintaining Results* (New York: John Wiley & Sons, 2002); Kaplan and Norton, *The Strategy-Focused Organization*, pp. 121–23.

35. S.J. Marks, "Incentives that Really Reward and Motivate," *Workforce*, 80 (June 2001), pp. 108–114; "A Fair Day's Pay," *Economist*, May 8, 1999, p. 12; D. Bencivenga, "Employee-Owners Help Bolster The Bottom Line," *HRMagazine*, 42 (February 1997), pp. 78–83; J. Chelius and R. S. Smith, "Profit Sharing and Employment Stability," *Industrial and Labour Relations Review*, 43 (1990), pp. 256s–73s.

36. M.D. Mumford, "Managing Creative People: Strategies and Tactics for Innovation," *Human Resource Management Review*, 10 (Autumn 2000), pp. 313–51; M. O'Donnell and J. O'Brian, "Performance-Based Pay in the Australian Public Service," *Review of Public Personnel Administration*, 20 (Spring 2000), pp. 20–34; A. Kohn, "Challenging Behaviourist Dogma: Myths About Money and Motivation," *Compensation and Benefits Review*, 30 (March 1998), pp. 27–33; A. Kohn, *Punished by Rewards* (Boston: Houghton Mifflin, 1993); B. Nelson, *1001 Ways to Reward Employees* (New York: Workman Publishing, 1994), p. 148; W. C. Hamner, "How to Ruin Motivation With Pay," *Compensation Review*, 7, no. 3 (1975), pp. 17–27.

37. B. N. Pfau and I. T. Kay, "The Five Key Elements of a Total Rewards and Accountability Orientation," *Benefits Quarterly*, 18 (Third Quarter 2002), pp. 7–15; B. N. Pfau And I. T. Kay, *The Human Capital Edge* (New York: McGraw-Hill, 2002); J. Pfeffer, *The Human Equation* (Boston: Harvard Business School Press, 1998). For an early summary of research supporting the motivational value of performance-based rewards, see: E. E. Lawler, III, *Pay and Organizational Effectiveness: A Psychological View* (New York: McGraw-Hill, 1971).

38. Lawler, *"Rewarding Excellence*, pp. 77–79; S. Kerr, "Organization Rewards: Practical, Cost-neutral Alternatives that You May Know, But Don't Practice," *Organizational Dynamics*, 28 (Summer 1999), pp. 61–70.

39. M. Rotundo and P. Sackett, "The Relative Importance of Task, Citizenship, and Counterproductive Performance to Global Ratings of Job Performance: A Policy-Capturing Approach," *Journal of Applied Psychology*, 87 (February 2002), pp. 66–80; "New Survey Finds Variable Pay Has Yet to Deliver on Its Promise," *Pay for Performance Report*, March 2000, p. 1. The politics of pay is discussed in: D. Collins, *Gainsharing and Power? Lessons from Six Scanlon Plans*, (Ithaca: Cornell University Press, 1998); K. M. Bartol and D. C. Martin, "When Politics Pays: Factors Influencing Managerial Compensation Deci-

sions," *Personnel Psychology*, 43 (1990), pp. 599–614.

40. Kerr, "Organization Rewards."

41. Lawler, *Rewarding Excellence*, p. 77; "New Survey Finds Variable Pay 'Has Yet to Deliver on Its Promise'," *Pay for Performance Report*, March 2000, p. 1.

42. DeMatteo, et al, "Team-Based Rewards."

43. R. Wageman, "Interdependence and Group Effectiveness," *Administrative Science Quarterly*, 40 (1995), pp. 145–80.

44. "Dream Teams," *Human Resources Professional*, November 1994, pp. 17–19.

45. S. Kerr, "On the Folly of Rewarding A, While Hoping for B," *Academy of Management Journal*, 18 (1975), pp. 769–83.

46. D. R. Spitzer, "Power Rewards: Rewards That Really Motivate," *Management Review*, May 1996, pp. 45–50.

47. D. MacDonald, "Good Managers Key to Buffett's Acquisitions," *Montreal Gazette*, November 16, 2001; P.M. Perry, "Holding Your Top Talent," *Research Technology Management*, 44 (May 2001), pp. 26–30.

48. G. L. Dalton, "The Collective Stretch: Workforce Flexibility" *Management Review*, 87 (December 1998), pp. 54–59; C. Hendry and R. Jenkins, "Psychological Contracts and New Deals," *Human Resource Management Journal*, 7 (1997), pp. 38–44.

49. D. Whitford, "A Human Place to Work," *Fortune*, January 8, 2001, pp. 108–19.

50. A. Smith, *The Wealth of Nations* (London: Dent, 1910). Earlier examples are described in "Scientific Management: Lessons from Ancient History through the Industrial Revolution," www.accel-team.com.

51. M. A. Campion, "Ability Requirement Implications of Job Design: An Interdisciplinary Perspective," *Personnel Psychology*, 42 (1989), pp. 1–24; H. Fayol, *General and Industrial Management*, trans. C. Storrs (London: Pitman, 1949); E. E. Lawler III, *Motivation in Work Organizations* (Monterey, Calif.: Brooks/Cole, 1973), Chapter 7.

52. For a review of Taylor's work and life, see R. Kanigel, *The One Best Way: Frederick Winslow Taylor and the Enigma of Efficiency* (Viking: NY, 1997). Also see C. R. Littler, "Taylorism, Fordism, and Job Design," in *Job Design: Critical Perspectives on the Labour Process*, ed. D. Knights, H. Willmott, and D. Collinson (Aldershot, U.K.: Gower Publishing, 1985), pp. 10–29; F. W. Taylor, *The Principles of Scientific Management* (New York: Harper & Row, 1911).

53. E. E. Lawler III, *High-Involvement Management* (San Francisco: Jossey-Bass, 1986), Chapter 6; and C. R. Walker and R. H. Guest, *The Man on the Assembly Line* (Cambridge, Mass.: Harvard University Press, 1952).

54. W. F. Dowling, "Job Redesign on the Assembly Line: Farewell to Blue-Collar Blues?" *Organizational Dynamics*, Autumn 1973, pp. 51–67; Lawler, *Motivation in Work Organizations*, p. 150.

55. M. Keller, *Rude Awakening* (New York: Harper Perennial, 1989), p. 128.

56. F. Herzberg, B. Mausner, and B. B. Snyderman, *The Motivation to Work*, (New York: Wiley, 1959).

57. S. K. Parker, T. D. Wall, and J. L. Cordery, "Future Work Design Research and Practice: Towards an Elabourated Model of Work Design," *Journal of Occupational and Organizational Psychology*, 74 (November 2001), pp. 413–40. A decisive critique of Herzberg's theory is: N. King, "Clarification and Evaluation of the Two Factor Theory of Job Satisfaction," *Psychological Bulletin*, 74 (1970), pp. 18–31.

58. J. R. Hackman and G. Oldham, *Work Redesign* (Reading, Mass.: Addison-Wesley, 1980).

59. D. Whitford, "A Human Place to Work," *Fortune*, January 8, 2001, pp. 108–119.

60. M.C. Andrews and K.M. Kacmar, "Confirmation and Extension of the Sources of Feedback Scale in Service-based Organizations," *Journal of Business Communication*, 38 (April 2001), pp. 206–26.

61. T. Nicholson, "The Vintage Makers—Part One," *Marlborough Express*, January 31, 2001.

62. G. Johns, J. L. Xie, and Y. Fang, "Mediating and Moderating Effects in Job Design," *Journal of Management*, 18 (1992), pp. 657–76.

63. P. E. Spector, "Higher-Order Need Strength as a Moderator of the Job Scope–Employee Outcome Relationship: A Meta Analysis," *Journal of Occupational Psychology*, 58 (1985), pp. 119–27.

64. R. M. Malinski, "Job Rotation in an Academic Library: Damned if You Do and Damned If You Don't!" *Library Trends*, March 22, 2002, pp. 673ff.

65. S. Shepard, "Safety Program at Carrier Plant in Collierville Paying Dividends," *Memphis Business Journal*, May 25, 2001, p. 38. One recent Canadian study reported that job rotation had no effect on work attitudes or stress. See: J. Godard, "High Performance and the Transformation Of Work? The Implications of Alternative Work Practices for the Experience and Outcomes of Work," *Industrial & Labour Relations Review*, 54 (July 2001), pp. 776–805.

66. M. Grotticelli, "CNN Moves to Small-format ENG," *Broadcasting & Cable*, May 14, 2001, p. 46. Information about video journalists at CBC is found in: S. Yaffe and L. Rice-Barker, "CBC: Regs Don't make Sense," *Playback*, January 24, 2000, p. 1; "Windsor's Enterprise Going Where no TV News Station has Gone Before," *Broadcaster*, 54 (April 1995), pp. 12–14; H. Enchin, "Video Players," *Globe and Mail*, December 6, 1994, p. B22.

67. N. G. Dodd and D. C. Ganster, "The Interactive Effects of Variety, Autonomy, and Feedback on Attitudes and Performance," *Journal of Organizational Behaviour*, 17 (1996), pp. 329–47; M. A. Campion and C. L. McClelland, "Follow-up and Extension of the Interdisciplinary Costs and Benefits of Enlarged Jobs," *Journal of Applied Psychology*, 78 (1993), pp. 339–51.

68. This point is emphasized in C. Pinder, *Work Motivation* (Glenview, Ill.: Scott, Foresman, 1984), pp. 244; and F. Herzberg, "One More Time: How Do You Motivate Employees? *Harvard Business Review*, 46 (January-February 1968), pp. 53–62. For a full discussion of job enrichment, also see R. W. Griffin, *Task Design: An Integrative Ap-*

proach (Glenview, IL: Scott Foresman, 1982); J. R. Hackman, G. Oldham, R. Janson, and K. Purdy, "A New Strategy for Job Enrichment," *California Management Review*, 17(4) (1975), pp. 57–71.

69. Hackman and Oldham, *Work Redesign*, pp. 137–138.

70. L. R. Comeau, "Re-engineering for a More Competitive Tomorrow," *Canadian Business Review*, Winter 1994, pp. 51–52.

71. R. Saavedra and S.K. Kwun, "Affective States in Job Characteristics Theory," *Journal of Organizational Behaviour*, 21 (2000), pp. 131–46; P. Osterman, "How Common is Workplace Transformation and Who Adopts It?" *Industrial and Labour Relations Review*, 47 (1994), pp. 173–88; D. E. Bowen and E. E. Lawler III, "The Empowerment of Service Workers: What, Why, How, and When," *Sloan Management Review*, Spring 1992, pp. 31–39; P. E. Spector and S. M. Jex, "Relations of Job Characteristics from Multiple Data Sources with Employee Affect, Absence, Turnover Intentions, and Health," *Journal of Applied Psychology*, 76 (1991), pp. 46–53; Y. Fried and G. R. Ferris, "The Validity of the Job Characteristics Model: A Review and Meta-analysis," *Personnel Psychology*, 40 (1987), pp. 287–322

72. B. Lewis, "WestJet—A Crazy Idea that Took Off," *Vancouver Province*, October 21, 2001.

73. This definition is based mostly on G. M. Spreitzer and R. E. Quinn, *A Company of Leaders: Five Disilines for Unleashing the Power in Your Workforce* (San Francisco: Jossey-Bass, 2001), pp 13–21; G. M. Spreitzer, "Psychological Empowerment in the Workplace: Dimensions, Measurement, and Validation," *Academy of Management Journal*, 38 (1995), pp. 1442–65. However, most elements of this definition appear in other discussions of empowerment. See, for example: S. T. Menon, "Employee Empowerment: An Integrative Psychological approach," *Applied Psychology: An International Review*, 50 (2001), pp. 153–80; W.A. Randolph, "Re-Thinking Empowerment: Why is it so Hard to Achieve?," *Organizational Dynamics*, 29 (November 2000), pp. 94–107; R. Forrester, "Empowerment: Rejuvenating a Potent Idea," *Academy*

of Management Executive, 14 (August 2000), pp. 67–80; J. A. Conger and R. N. Kanungo, "The Empowerment Process: Integrating Theory and Practice," *Academy of Management Review*, 13 (1988), pp. 471–82. I would also like to extend my thanks to Angus Buchanan for helping me to rediscover the details of the empowerment literature.

74. "Job Satisfaction Means More Than Pay," *Business Day (South Africa)*, December 6, 2000, p. 14; S. Planting, "Mirror, Mirror ... Here Are The Fairest Of Them All," *Financial Mail (South Africa)*, November 24, 2000, p. 48.

75. R. Forrester, "Empowerment: Rejuvenating a Potent Idea," *Academy of Management Executive*, 14 (August 2000), pp. 67–90. The positive relationship between these conditions (sometimes called structural empowerment conditions) and psychological empowerment is found in: H. K. S. Laschinger, J. Finegan, and J. Shamian, "Promoting Nurses' Health: Effect of Empowerment on Job Strain and Work Satisfaction," *Nursing Economics*, 19 (March/April 2001), pp. 42–52

76. C. S. Koberg, R. W. Boss, J. C. Senjem, and E. A. Goodman, "Antecedents and Outcomes of Empowerment," *Group and Organization Management*, 24 (1999), pp. 71–91.

77. T. D. Wall, J. L. Cordery, and C. W. Clegg, "Empowerment, Performance, and Operational Uncertainty: A Theoretical Integration," *Applied Psychology: An International Review*, 51 (2002), pp. 146–72; W. A. Randolph and M. Sashkin, "Can Organizational Empowerment Work in Multinational Settings? *Academy of Management Executive*, 16 (February 2002), pp. 102–116; J. Yoon, "The Role of Structure and Motivation for Workplace Empowerment: The Case of Korean Employees," *Social Psychology Quarterly*, 64 (June 2001), pp. 195–206; B. J. Niehoff, R. H. Moorman, G. Blakely, and J. Fuller, "The Influence of Empowerment and Job Enrichment on Employee Loyalty in a Downsizing Environment," *Group and Organization Management*, 26 (March 2001), pp. 93–113; K. Blanchard, J. P. Carlos, and A. Randolph, *The 3 Keys to Empowerment: Release the Power Within People*

For Astonishing Results. (San Francisco: Berrett-Koehler, 1999).

78. P. Verburg, "Prepare for Takeoff," *Canadian Business*, December 25, 2000, pp. 94–99. The organizational factors affecting empowerment are discussed in: P. A. Miller, P. Goddard, and H. K. Spence Laschinger, "Evaluating Physical Therapists' Perception Of Empowerment Using Kanter's Theory Of Structural Power In Organizations," *Physical Therapy*, 81 (December 2001), pp. 1880–88; G. M. Spreitzer and R. E. Quinn, *A Company of Leaders: Five Disiplines for Unleashing the Power in Your Workforce* (San Francisco: Jossey-Bass, 2001); J. Godard, "High Performance and the Transformation Of Work? The Implications of Alternative Work Practices for the Experience and Outcomes of Work," *Industrial & Labour Relations Review*, 54 (July 2001), pp. 776–805; G. M. Spreitzer, "Social Structural Characteristics of Psychological Empowerment," *Academy of Management Journal*, 39 (April 1996), pp. 483–504.

79. H. K. S. Laschinger, J. Finegan, and J. Shamian, "The Impact of Workplace Empowerment, Organizational Trust on Staff Nurses' Work Satisfaction and Organizational Commitment," *Health Care Management Review*, 26 (Summer 2001), pp. 7–23; J-C. Chebat and P. Kollias, "The Impact of Empowerment on Customer Contact Employees' Role in Service Organizations," *Journal of Service Research*, 3 (August 2000), pp. 66–81.

80. P. Verburg, "Prepare for Takeoff," *Canadian Business*, December 25, 2000, pp. 94–99.

81. T. Romita, "The Talent Search," *Business 2.0*, June 12, 2001.

82. C. P. Neck and C. C. Manz, "Thought Self-Leadership: The Impact of Mental Strategies Training on Employee Cognition, Behaviour, and Affect," *Journal of Organizational Behaviour*, 17 (1996), pp. 445–67.

83. C. C. Manz and H. P. Sims, Jr. *Superleadership: Leading Others to Lead Themselves* (Englewood Cliffs, NJ: Prentice-Hall, 1989); C. C. Manz, "Self-Leadership: Toward an Expanded Theory of Self-Influence Processes in Organizations," *Academy of Management Review*, 11 (1986), pp. 585–600.

84. O. J. Strickland and M. Galimba, "Managing Time: The Effects of Personal Goal Setting on Resource Allocation Strategy and Task Performance," *Journal of Psychology*, 135 (July 2001), pp. 357–67; P. R. Pintrich, "The Role of Goal Orientation in Self-Regulated Learning," In M. Boekaerts, P. R. Pintrich, & M. Zeidner (Eds.), Handbook of Self-Regulation (New York: Academic, 2000), pp. 452–502; H. P. Sims, Jr. and C. C. Manz, *Company of Heroes: Unleashing the Power of Self-Leadership* (New York: Wiley, 1996); A. M. Saks, R. R. Haccoun, and D. Laxer, "Transfer Training: A Comparison of Self-Management and Relapse Prevention Interventions," *ASAC 1996 Conference Proceedings, Human Resources Division*, 17 (9) (1996), pp. 81–91; M. E. Gist, A. G. Bavetta, and C. K. Stevens, "Transfer Training Method: Its Influence on Skill Generalization, Skill Repetition, and Performance Level," *Personnel Psychology*, 43 (1990), pp. 501–23.

85. R. Seymour, "Canada's Best Bosses," *Profit Magazine*, June 2001.

86. R. M. Duncan and J. A. Cheyne, "Incidence and Functions of Self-reported Private Speech in Young Adults: A Self-verbalization Questionnaire," *Canadian Journal of Behavioural Science*, 31 (April 1999), pp. 133–36. For an organizational behaviour discussion of constructive thought patterns, see: C. P. Neck and C. C. Manz, "Thought Self-Leadership: The Influence of Self-Talk and Mental Imagery on Performance," *Journal of Organizational Behaviour*, 13 (1992), pp. 681–99.

87. G. E. Prussia, J. S. Anderson, and C. C. Manz, "Self-leadership and Performance Outcomes: The Mediating Influence of Self-efficacy," *Journal of Organizational Behaviour*, September 1998, pp. 523–38; Neck and Manz, "Thought Self-Leadership: The Impact of Mental Strategies Training on Employee Cognition, Behaviour, and Affect."

88. Early scholars seem to distinguish mental practice from mental imagery, whereas recent literature combines mental practice with visualizing positive task outcomes within the meaning of mental imagery. For recent discussion of this concept, see: C. P. Neck, G. L. Stewart, and C. C. Manz, "Thought

Self-Leadership as a Framework for Enhancing the Performance of Performance Appraisers," *Journal of Applied Behavioural Science*, 31 (September 1995), pp. 278–302; W. P. Anthony, R. H. Bennett III, E. N. Maddox, and W. J. Wheatley, "Picturing the Future: Using Mental Imagery to Enrich Strategic Environmental Assessment," *Academy of Management Executive*, 7 (2) (1993), pp. 43–56.

89. L. Morin and G. Latham, "The Effect of Mental Practice and Goal Setting as a Transfer of Training Intervention on Supervisors' Self-efficacy and Communication Skills: An Exploratory Study," *Applied Psychology: An International Review*, 49 (July 2000), pp. 566–78; J. E. Driscoll, C. Cooper, and A. Moran, "Does Mental Practice Enhance Performance?" *Journal of Applied Psychology*, 79 (1994), pp. 481–92.

90. A. Wrzesniewski and J. E. Dutton, "Crafting a Job: Revisioning Employees as Active Crafters of their Work," *Academy of Management Review*, 26 (April 2001), pp. 179–201; Manz, "Self-Leadership: Toward an Expanded Theory of Self-Influence Processes in Organizations."

91. M. I. Bopp, S. J. Glynn, and R. A. Henning, "Self-Management of Performance Feedback During Computer-Based Work by Individuals and Two-Person Work Teams," Paper presented at the APA-NIOSH conference, March 1999.

92. A. W. Logue, *Self-Control: Waiting Until Tomorrow for What You Want Today*. (Englewood Cliffs, NJ: Prentice-Hall, 1995).

93. J. Bauman, "The Gold Medal Mind," *Psychology Today*, 33 (May 2000), pp. 62–69; K. E. Thiese and S. Huddleston, "The Use Of Psychological Skills By Female Collegiate Swimmers," *Journal of Sport Behaviour*, December 1999, pp. 602–10; D. Landin and E. P. Hebert, "The Influence of Self-talk on the Performance of Skilled Female Tennis Players," *Journal of Applied Sport Psychology*, 11 (September 1999), pp. 263–82; C. Defrancesco and K. L. Burke, "Performance Enhancement Strategies Used in a Professional Tennis Tournament," *International Journal of Sport Psychology*, 28 (1997), pp. 185–95; S. Ming and G. L. Martin,

"Single-Subject Evaluation of a Self-Talk Package for Improving Figure Skating Performance," *Sport Psychologist*, 10 (1996), pp. 227–38.

94. Morin and Latham, "The Effect of Mental Practice and Goal Setting as a Transfer of Training Intervention on Supervisors' Self-efficacy and Communication Skills"; A. M. Saks and B. E. Ashforth, "Proactive Socialization and Behavioural Self-Management." *Journal of Vocational Behaviour*, 48 (1996), pp. 301–23; Neck and Manz, "Thought Self-Leadership: The Impact of Mental Strategies Training on Employee Cognition, Behaviour, and Affect."

95. A.L. Kazan, "Exploring the Concept of Self-Leadership: Factors Impacting Self-Leadership of Ohio Americorps Members," *Dissertation Abstracts International*, 60 (June 2000); S. Ross, "Corporate Measurements Shift from Punishment to Rewards," *Reuters*, February 28, 2000; M. Castaneda, T. A. Kolenko, and R. J. Aldag, "Self-Management Perceptions and Practices: A Structural Equations Analysis," *Journal of Organizational Behaviour* 20 (1999), pp. 101–20; G. L. .Stewart, K. P. Carson, and R. L. Cardy, "The Joint Effects of Conscientiousness and Self-Leadership Training on Employee Self-Directed Behaviour in a Service Setting," *Personnel Psychology*, 49 (1996), pp. 143–64.

CHAPTER SEVEN

1. J. Day, "Nursing Trouble," *Charlottetown Guardian*, March 9, 2002; J. Davenport and A. Hanes, "Nurses Demand Relief," *Montreal Gazette*, February 21, 2002; J. Blythe, A. Baumann, and P. Giovannetti, "Nurses' Experiences of Restructuring in Three Ontario Hospitals," *Journal of Nursing Scholarship*, 33 (First Quarter 2001), pp. 61–68.

2. "Canadian Workers Among the Most Stressed," *Worklife*, 14 (2) (2002), pp. 8–9; R. M. Leontaridi and M. E. Ward, "Dying to Work? An Investigation into Work-related Stress, Quitting Intentions, and Absenteeism," Paper presented at the Royal Economic Society 2002 Annual Conference, University of Warwick, Coventry, UK, March 2002; S. Lem, "Snowed Under By Stress," *London Free Press*, February 3, 2000, p. C4; J. MacBride-King, and K. Bachmann, "Is work-life balance still

an issue for Canadians and their employers? You bet it is," (Ottawa: Conference Board of Canada, 1999).

3. "CareerBuilder Survey Finds Growing Worker Disenchantment, Long Hours and Stress," *PR Newswire*, August 30, 2001; "Good Bosses are Hard to Find," Morgan & Banks news release, August 2000; S. Efron, "Jobs Take a Deadly Toll on Japanese," *Los Angeles Times*, April 12, 2000, p. A1; N. Chowdhury and S. Menon, "Beating Burnout," *India Today*, June 9, 1997, p. 86; Cross-National Collaborative Group, "The Changing Rate of Major Depression: Cross-National Comparisons," *JAMA: The Journal of the American Medical Association*, 268 (December 2, 1992), pp. 3098–105.

4. R. S. DeFrank and J. M. Ivancevich, "Stress on the Job: An Executive Update," *Academy of Management Executive*, 12 (August 1998), pp. 55–66; J. C. Quick and J. D. Quick, *Organizational Stress and Prevention Management* (New York: McGraw-Hill, 1984).

5. J. C. Quick, J. D. Quick, D. L. Nelson, and J. J. Hurrell, Jr., *Preventive Stress Management in Organizations*, (Washington, DC: American Psychological Association, 1997).

6. B. L. Simmons and D. L. Nelson, "Eustress at Work: The Relationship Between Hope and Health in Hospital Nurses," *Health Care Management Review*, 26 (October 2001), pp. 7–18.

7. H. Selye, *Stress without Distress* (Philadelphia: J. B. Lippincott, 1974).

8. S. E. Taylor, R. L. Repetti, and T. Seeman, "Health Psychology: What Is an Unhealthy Environment and How Does It Get Under the Skin?" *Annual Review of Psychology*, 48 (1997), pp. 411–47.

9. G. Hassell, "Energy Trading Fast, Furious And Lucrative," *Houston Chronicle*, May 20, 2001, p. 25.

10. K. Danna and R. W. Griffin, "Health and Well-being in the Workplace: A Review and Synthesis of the Literature," *Journal of Management*, Spring 1999, pp. 357–84; Quick and Quick, *Organizational Stress and Prevention Management*, p. 3.

11. E. Vigoda, "Stress-Related Aftermaths to Workplace Politics: The Relationships Among Politics, Job Distress, and Aggressive Behavior in Organiza-

tions," *Journal of Organizational Behavior*, 23 (2002), pp. 571–91. For the effects of conflict and teams on stress, see: P. E. Spector and S. M. Jex, "Development of Four Self-Report Measures of Job Stressors and Strain: Interpersonal Conflict at Work Scale, Organizational Constraints Scale, Quantitative Workload Inventory, and Physical Symptoms Inventory," *Journal of Occupational Health Psychology*, 3 (1998), pp. 356–367; D. F. Elloy and A. Randolph, "The Effect Of Superleader Behavior On Autonomous Work Groups In A Government Operated Railway Service," *Public Personnel Management*, 26 (June 1997), pp. 257ff.

12. "Commission Powerless To Enforce Judgment," *London Free Press*, February 21, 2000, p. A7.

13. S. I. Paish and A. A. Alibhai, *Act, Don't React: Dealing With Sexual Harassment in Your Organization* (Vancouver: Western Legal Publications, 1996). H. Johnson, "Work-Related Sexual Harassment," *Perspectives on Labour and Income*, Winter 1994, pp. 9–12; For a discussion of these two forms of sexual harassment from the U.S. perspective, see: V. Schultz, "Reconceptualizing Sexual Harassment," *Yale Law Journal*, 107 (April 1998), pp. 1683–1805. Research on gender differences in what constitutes sexual harassment is found in: M. Rotundo, D-H. Nguyen, and P. R. Sackett, "A Meta-Analytic Review of Gender Differences in Perceptions of Sexual Harassment," *Journal of Applied Psychology*, 86 (October 2001), pp. 914–22.

14. L. J. Munson, C. Hulin, and F. Drasgow, "Longitudinal Analysis of Dispositional Influences and Sexual Harassment: Effects on Job and Psychological Outcomes," *Personnel Psychology*, (Spring 2000), pp. 21–46; L. F. Fitzgerald, F. Drasgow, C. L. Hulin, M. J. Gelfand, and V. Magley, "The Antecedents and Consequences of Sexual Harassment in Organizations: A Test of an Integrated Model," *Journal of Applied Psychology*, 82 (1997), pp. 578–89; C. S. Piotrkowski, "Gender Harassment, Job Satisfaction, and Distress among Employed White and Minority Women," *Journal of Occupational Health Psychology*, 3 (January 1998), pp. 33–43; J. Barling, I. Dekker, C. A. Loughlin, E. K. Kelloway, C. Ful-

lagar, and D. Johnson, "Prediction and Replication of the Organizational and Personal Consequences of Workplace Sexual Harassment," *Journal of Managerial Psychology*, 11 (5) (1996), pp. 4–25.

15. H.W. French, "Fighting Sex Harassment, and Stigma, in Japan," *New York Times*, July 15, 2001, p.1.

16. J. H. Neuman and R. A. Baron, "Workplace Violence and Workplace Aggression: Evidence Concerning Specific Forms, Potential Causes, and Preferred Targets," *Journal of Management*, 24 (May 1998), pp. 391–419.

17. G. Lardner, Jr., "Violence at Work Is Largely Unreported," *Washington Post*, July 27, 1998, p. A2.

18. J. M. Christenson et al., "Violence in the Emergency Department: A Survey of Health Care Workers," *Canadian Medical Association Journal*, 161 (November 16, 1999), pp. 1245–48. The ILO study is cited in J. D. Leck, "Violence in the Workplace: A New Challenge," *Optimum*, 31 (November 2001); "ILO Survey Reveals Extent of Violence at Work," *Agence France Presse*, July 19, 1998.

19. J. D. Leck, "How Violence is Costing the Canadian Workplace," *HR Professional*, February/March 2002; J. Barling, A. G. Rogers, and E. K. Kelloway, "Behind Closed Doors: In-Home Workers' Experience of Sexual Harassment and Workplace Violence," *Journal of Occupational Health Psychology*, 6 (July 2001), pp. 255–69; M. Kivimaki, M. Elovainio, and J. Vahtera, "Workplace Bullying and Sickness Absence in Hospital Staff," *Occupational & Environmental Medicine*, 57, (October 2000), pp. 656–60; J. Barling, "The Prediction, Experience, and Consequences of Workplace Violence," In G. R. VandenBos and E. Q. Bulatao (Eds.), *Violence on the Job: Identifying Risks and Developing Solutions* (Washington, DC: American Psychological Association, 1996), pp. 29–49.

20. *Morgan v. Chukal Enterprises Ltd.*, Supreme Court of British Columbia, BCSC 1163, July 28, 2000. (Available online at www.courts.gov.bc.ca). See also *Lloyd v. Imperial Parking Ltd.*, [1997] 3 W.W.R. 697 (Alta. Q.B.).

21. H. Cowiea et al., "Measuring Workplace Bullying," *Aggression and Violent*

Behavior, 7 (2002), pp. 33–51; C.M. Pearson, L.M. Andersson, and C.L. Porath "Assessing and Attacking Workplace Incivility," *Organizational Dynamics*, 29 (November 2000), pp. 123–37.

22. Kivimaki et al., "Workplace Bullying and Sickness Absence in Hospital Staff"; P. McCarthy and M. Barker, "Workplace Bullying Risk Audit", *Journal of Occupational Health and Safety, Australia and New Zealand*, 16 (2000), pp. 409–418; M. O'Moore, E. Seigne, L. McGuire, and M. Smith, "Victims of Bullying at Work in Ireland," *Journal of Occupational Health and Safety* 14 (1998), pp. 569–74; G. Namie, U.S. "Hostile Workplace Survey" http://www.bullybusters.org/home/twd/bb/res /surv2000.html.

23. Information about Joanne Leck's current research on the incidence of workplace bully is cited in S. Hickman, "Making Work A Better Place," *HK MBA Alumni Connections*, University of Ottawa, August 2000, p. 3. The University of Michigan study of workplace bullying is cited in: M. Fletcher Stoeltje, "Jerks at Work," *San Antonio Express-News*, August 31, 2001, p. F1. M. Kivimaki, M. Elovainio, and J. Vahtera, "Workplace Bullying and Sickness Absence in Hospital Staff," *Occupational & Environmental Medicine*, 57 (October 2000), pp. 656–60; S. Einarsen, "Harassment and Bullying at Work: A Review of the Scandinavian Approach," *Aggression and Violent Behavior*, 5 (2000), pp. 379–401.

24. Pearson et al., "Assessing and Attacking Workplace Incivility."

25. R. J. House and J. R. Rizzo "Role Conflict and Ambiguity as Critical Variables in a Model of Organizational Behavior," *Organizational Behavior and Human Performance*, 7 (June 1972), pp. 467–505. Also see: M. Siegall and L. L. Cummings, "Stress and Organizational Role Conflict," *Genetic, Social, and General Psychology Monographs*, 12 (1995), pp. 65–95; E. K. Kelloway and J. Barling, "Job Characteristics, Role Stress and Mental Health," *Journal of Occupational Psychology* 64 (1991), pp. 291–304; R. L. Kahn, D. M. Wolfe, R. P. Quinn, J. D. Snoek, and R. A. Rosenthal, *Organizational Stress: Studies in Role Conflict and Ambiguity* (New York: Wiley, 1964).

26. M. C. Turkel, "Struggling to Find a Balance: The Paradox between Caring and Economics," *Nursing Administration Quarterly*, 26 (Fall 2001), pp. 67–82.

27. G. R. Cluskey and A. Vaux, "Vocational Misfit: Source of Occupational Stress Among Accountants," *Journal of Applied Business Research*, 13 (Summer 1997), pp. 43–54; J. R. Edwards, "An Examination of Competing Versions of the Person-Environment Fit Approach to Stress," *Academy of Management Journal*, 39 (1996), pp. 292–339; B. E. Ashforth and R. H. Humphrey, "Emotional Labor in Service Roles: The Influence of Identity," *Academy of Management Review*, 18 (1993), pp. 88–115.

28. A. Nygaard and R. Dahlstrom, "Role Stress and Effectiveness in Horizontal Alliances," *Journal of Marketing*, 66 (April 2002), pp. 61–82; A. M. Saks and B. E. Ashforth, "Proactive Socialization and Behavioral Self-Management." *Journal of Vocational Behavior*, 48 (1996), pp. 301–23; D. L. Nelson and C. Sutton, "Chronic Work Stress and Coping: A Longitudinal Study and Suggested New Directions," *Academy of Management Journal*, 33 (1990), pp. 859–69.

29. B. K. Hunnicutt, *Kellogg's Six-Hour Day* (Philadelphia,: Temple University Press, 1996); J. B. Schor, *The Overworked American: The Unexpected Decline of Leisure* (New York: Basic, 1991).

30. C. Higgins and L. Duxbury, *The 2001 National Work–Life Conflict Study: Report One, Final Report* (Ottawa: Health Canada, March 2002); "Workin' Past 9 to 5—New Study Finds Many Canadian White-Collar Workers Tied to Job Around the Clock," Ipsos-Reid news release, March 27, 2001 (Ipsos-Reid survey of 1,000 Canadians conducted for Workopolis in January-February 2001); K. Hall, "Hours Polarization at the End of the 1990s," *Perspectives on Labour and Income*, Summer 1999, pp. 28–37.

31. J. Foley, "Haw Work Intensified in Canada?" *Proceedings of the Annual Conference of the Administrative Sciences Association of Canada, Human Resource Management Division*, 23 (9) (2002), pp. 24–32; K. Isaksson, C. Hogstedt, C. Eriksson, and T. Theorell.

(Eds.) *Health Effects of the New Labour Market*. (New York: Kluwer Academic, 2000). See also: A. R. Hochschild, *The Time Bind: When Work Becomes Home and Home Becomes Work*. (New York : Metropolitan Books, 1997).

32. J. Vahtera, M. Kivimaki, J. Pentti, and T. Theorell, "Effect of Change in the Psychosocial Work Environment on Sickness Absence: A Seven Year Follow Up of Initially Healthy Employees," *Journal of Epidemiology & Community Health*, 54 (July 2000), pp. 482–83; L. D Sargent and D. J. Terry "The Effects of Work Control and Job Demands on Employee Adjustment and Work Performance," *Journal of Occupational and Organizational Psychology*, 71 (September 1998), pp. 219–36; M. G. Marmot, H. Bosma H. Hemingway, E. Brunner, and S. Stansfeld, "Contribution of Job Control And Other Risk Factors To Social Variations In Coronary Heart Disease Incidence," *Lancet*, 350 (July 26, 1997), pp. 235–39; P. M. Elsass and J. F. Veiga, "Job Control And Job Strain: A Test Of Three Models," *Journal of Occupational Health Psychology*, 2 (July 1997), pp. 195–211; R. Karasek and T. Theorell, *Healthy Work: Stress, Productivity, and the Reconstruction of Working Life* (New York: Basic Books, 1990).

33. P. Fayerman, "Job Stress Linked to Control, Says Statistics Canada," *Vancouver Sun*, January 18, 1999, pp. B1, B3.

34. G. Bellett, "Employees Rage at Changes," *Victoria Times-Colonist*, March 3, 2002. Several articles on the effects of downsizing and restructuring are presented in: R. J. Burke and C. L. Cooper (Eds.) *The Organization in Crisis: Downsizing, Restructuring, and Privatization* (Oxford, UK: Blackwell, 2000).

35. G. Evans and D. Johnson, "Stress and Open-Office Noise," *Journal of Applied Psychology*, 85 (2000), pp. 779–783; S. Melamed and S. Bruhis, "The Effects of Chronic Industrial Noise Exposure on Urinary Cortisol, Fatigue, and Irritability: A Controlled Field Experiment," *Journal of Occupational and Environmental Medicine*, 38 (1996), pp. 252–56.

36. G. Hamilton, "Death in the Woods," *Vancouver Sun*, July 24, 2002.

37. C. S. Bruck, T. D. Allen, and P. E. Spector "The Relation between Work–Family Conflict and Job Satisfaction: A Finer-Grained Analysis," *Journal of Vocational Behavior*, 60 (2002), 336–53; G. A. Adams, L. A. King, and D. W. King, "Relationships of Job and Family Involvement, Family Social Support, and Work-Family Conflict with Job and Life Satisfaction," *Journal of Applied Psychology*, 81 (August 1996), pp. 411–20; J. H. Greenhaus and N. Beutell, N., "Sources of Conflict between Work and Family Roles," *Academy of Management Review*, 10 (1985), pp. 76–88.

38. L. Washburn, "Sleepless In America," *Bergen Record*, March 28, 2001, p. A1.

39. R. J. Burke, "Workaholism in Organizations: The Role of Organizational Values," *Personnel Review*, 30 (October 2001), pp. 637–45; D.S. Carlson, "Work-Family Conflict in the Organization: Do Life Role Values Make a Difference?" *Journal of Management*, September, 2000.

40. J. MacBride-King and K. Bachmann, *Is Work-Life Balance still an Issue for Canadians and their Employers? You Bet it Is.* (Ottawa: Conference Board of Canada.), cited in K. L. Johnson, D. S. Lero, and J. A. Rooney, *Work-Life Compendium 2001* (Guelph, Ont.: Centre for Families, Work and Well-Being, University of Guelph 2001). Also see: J. A. Frederick and J. E. Fast, "Enjoying Work: An Effective Strategy in the Struggle to Juggle?" *Canadian Social Trends*, Summer 2001, pp. 8–11.

41. M. Shields, "Shift Work and Health," *Health Reports (Statistics Canada)*, 13 (Spring 2002), pp. 11–34; Higgins and Duxbury, *The 2001 National Work–Life Conflict Study;* M. Jamal and V. V. Baba, "Shiftwork and Department-Type Related to Job Stress, Work Attitudes and Behavioral Intentions: A Study of Nurses," *Journal of Organizational Behavior*, 13 (1992), pp. 449–64; C. Higgins, L. Duxbury, and R. Irving, "Determinants and Consequences of Work-Family Conflict," *Organizational Behavior and Human Decision Processes*, 51 (February 1992), pp. 51–75.

42. D.L Nelson and R.J Burke, "Women Executives: Health, Stress, and Success," *Academy of Management Executive*, 14 (May 2000), pp. 107–21; C. S. Rogers, "The Flexible Workplace: What Have we Learned?" *Human Resource Management*, 31 (Fall 1992), pp. 183–199; L. E. Duxbury and C. A. Higgins, "Gender Differences in Work–Family Conflict," *Journal of Applied Psychology*, 76 (1991), pp. 60–74; A. Hochschild, *The Second Shift* (New York: Avon, 1989). One somewhat different view is that time-based conflict and other work-family conflict stressors reflect the gendered assumptions about work (male) and family (female) duties. As men and women break down their gendered roles, work-family conflicts might become less troublesome. See: M. Runté and A. J. Mills, "The Discourse Of Work-Family Conflict: A Critique," *Proceedings of the Annual Conference of the Administrative Sciences Association of Canada, Gender and Diversity in Organizations Division*, 23 (11) (2002), pp. 21–32.

43. M. P. Leiter and M. J. Durup, "Work, Home, and In-Between: A Longitudinal Study of Spillover," *Journal of Applied Behavioral Science*, 32 (1996), pp. 29–47; W. Stewart and J. Barling, "Fathers' Work Experiences Effect on Children's Behaviors via Job-Related Affect and Parenting Behaviors," *Journal of Organizational Behavior*, 17 (1996), pp. 221–32; C. A. Beatty, "The Stress of Managerial and Professional Women: Is the Price too High?" *Journal of Organizational Behavior*, 17 (1996), pp. 233–51. Also see: D. L. Morrison and R. Clements, "The Effect of One Partner's Job Characteristics on the Other Partner's Distress: A Serendipitous, but Naturalistic, Experiment," *Journal of Occupational and Organizational Psychology*, 70 (December 1997), pp. 307–24; C. Higgins, L. Duxbury, and R. Irving, "Determinants and Consequences of Work–Family Conflict," *Organizational Behavior and Human Decision Processes*, 51 (February 1992), pp. 51–75.

44. A. S. Wharton and R. J. Erickson, "Managing Emotions on the Job and at Home: Understanding the Consequences of Multiple Emotional Roles," *Academy of Management Review*, 18 (1993), pp. 457–86. For a recent discussion of role conflict and spillover between work and nonwork, see: S. M. MacDermid, B. L. Seery, and H. M. Weiss, "an Emotional Examination of the Work-family Interface," In R. G. Lord, R. J. Klimoski, & R. Kanfer (Eds.) *Emotions in the Workplace* (San Francisco: Jossey-Bass, 2002), pp. 402–27.

45. "Office Workers more Stressed than Nurses," *The Independent (London)*, August 7, 2000, p. 8; B. Keil, "The 10 Most Stressful Jobs In NYC," *New York Post*, April 6, 1999, p. 50; International Labor Office, *World Labor Report* (Geneva: ILO, 1993), Chapter 5; Karasek and Theorell, *Healthy Work*.

46. Quick et al., *Preventive Stress Management in Organizations*, Chapter 3.

47. J. A. Roberts, R. S. Lapidus, and L. B. Chonko, "Salespeople and Stress: The Moderating Role of Locus of Control on Work Stressors and Felt Stress," *Journal of Marketing Theory & Practice*, 5 (Summer 1997), pp. 93–108; J. Schaubroeck and D. E. Merritt, "Divergent Effects of Job Control on Coping with Work Stressors: The Key Role of Self-Efficacy," *Academy of Management Journal*, 40 (June 1997), pp. 738–54; A. O'Leary and S. Brown, "Self-Efficacy and the Physiological Stress Response," In J. E. Maddux (ed.) *Self-Efficacy, Adaptation, and Adjustment: Theory, Research, and Application* (New York : Plenum Press, 1995.)

48. S. C. Segerstrom, S. E. Taylor, M. E. Kemeny, and J. L.. Fahey, "Optimism is Associated with Mood, Coping, and Immune Change in Response to Stress," *Journal of Personality & Social Psychology*, 74, (June 1998), pp. 1646–655.

49. K. R. Parkes, "Personality and Coping as Moderators of Work Stress Processes: Models, Methods and Measures," *Work & Stress*, 8 (April 1994) pp. 110–129; S. J. Havlovic and J. P. Keenen, "Coping with Work Stress: The Influence of Individual Differences," In P. L. Perrewé (ed.) Handbook on Job Stress [Special Issue], *Journal of Social Behavior and Personality*, 6 (1991), pp. 199–212.

50. B. C. Long and S. E. Kahn (eds.), *Women, Work, and Coping : A Multidisciplinary Approach to Workplace Stress* (Montreal : McGill-Queen's University Press, 1993); E. R. Greenglass, R. J. Burke, and M. Ondrack, "A Gen-

der-Role Perspective of Coping and Burnout," *Applied Psychology: An International Review* 39 (1990), pp. 5–27; T. D. Jick and L. F. Mitz, "Sex Differences in Work Stress," *Academy of Management Review*, 10 (1985), pp. 408–20.

51. M. Friedman and R. Rosenman, *Type A Behavior and Your Heart* (New York: Knopf, 1974). For more recent discussion, see P. E. Spector and B. J. O'Connell, "The Contribution of Personality Traits, Negative Affectivity, Locus of Control and Type A to the Subsequent Reports of Job Stressors and Job Strains," *Journal of Occupational and Organizational Psychology*, 67 (1994), pp. 1–11; K. R. Parkes, Personality and Coping as Moderators of Work Stress Processes: Models, Methods and Measures. *Work & Stress*, 8 (April 1994) pp. 110–29.

52. B. D. Kirkcaldy, R. J. Shephard, and A. F. Furnham, "The Infuence of Type A Behaviour and Locus Of Control upon Job Satisfaction and Occupational Health," *Personality and Individual Differences*, in press; A. L. Day and S. Jreige, "Examining Type A Behavior Pattern to Explain the Relationship Between Job Stressors and Psychosocial Outcomes," *Journal of Occupational Health Psychology*, 7 (April 2002), pp. 109–20.

53. C. P. Flowers and B. Robinson, "A Structural And Discriminant Analysis of the Work Addiction Risk Test," *Educational and Psychological Measurement*, 62 (June 2002) pp. 517–26; R. J. Burke, "Workaholism among Women Managers: Personal and Workplace Correlates," *Journal of Managerial Psychology*, 15 (2000), pp. 520–34; R. J. Burke, "Workaholism and Extra-work Satisfactions," *International Journal of Organizational Analysis*, 7 (1999), pp. 352–64; J. T. Spence and A. S. and Robbins, "Workaholism: Definition, Measurement and Preliminary Results," *Journal of Personality Assessment*, 58 (1992), pp. 160–78. The origin of the term "workaholism" is attributed to W. Oates, *Confessions of a Workaholic*. (New York: World, 1971). Toronto clinical psychological Barbara Killinger provided one of the earliest descriptions of the traditional workaholic in: B. Killinger, *Workaholics: The Respectable Addicts*. (Toronto: Key Porter Books, 1991).

54. R. J. Burke, "Workaholism among Women Managers: Personal and Workplace Correlates," *Journal of Managerial Psychology*, 15 (2000), pp. 520–34;. Other typologies of workaholics have been proposed in: B. E. Robinson, "A Typology of Workaholics With Implications for Counsellors," *Journal of Addictions & Offender Counseling*, 21 (October 2000), pp. 34ff.

55. R. J. Burke, "Workaholism among Women Managers: Personal and Workplace Correlates," *Journal of Managerial Psychology*, 15 (2000), pp. 520–34; B. E. Robinson, "The Work Addition Risk Test: Development of a Tentative Measure of Workaholism," *Perceptual and Motor Skills*, 88 (1999), pp. 199–210; R. J. Burke and G. MacDermid, "Are Workaholics Job Satisfied and Successful in their Careers?" *Career Development International*, 4 (1999), pp. 277–82.

56. D. Ganster, M. Fox, and D. Dwyer, "Explaining Employees' Health Care Costs: A Prospective Examination of Stressful Job Demands, Personal Control, and Physiological Reactivity," *Journal of Applied Psychology, 86* (May 2001), pp. 954–64; S. Cohen, D. A. Tyrrell, and A. P. Smith, "Psychological Stress and Susceptibility to the Common Cold," *New England Journal of Medicine*, 325 (August 29, 1991), pp. 654–56.

57. S. A. Everson et al., "Stress-Induced Blood Pressure Reactivity and Incident Stroke in Middle-Aged Men," *Stroke*, 32 (June 2001), pp. 1263–70; R. J. Benschop, et al., "Cardiovascular and Immune Responses to Acute Psychological Stress in Young and Old Women: A Meta-Analysis," *Psychosomatic Medicine*, 60 (May-June 1998), pp. 290–96; H. Bosma, R. Peter, J. Siegrist, and M. Marmot, "Two Alternative Job Stress Models and the Risk of Coronary Heart Disease," *American Journal of Public Health*, 88 (January 1998), pp. 68–74.

58. Statistics Canada, *How Healthy Are Canadians*, (*Health Reports* special issue) (Ottawa: Statistics Canada, 2001); "Health Among Older Adults," *Health Reports*, 11 (Winter 1999), pp. 47–61.

59. D. K. Sugg, "Study Shows Link Between Minor Stress, Early Signs of Coronary Artery Disease," *Baltimore Sun*, December 16, 1997, p. A3.

60. R. C. Kessler, "The Effects of Stressful Life Events on Depression," *Annual Review of Psychology*, 48 (1997), pp. 191–214; H. M. Weiss and R. Cropanzano, "Affective Events Theory: A Theoretical Discussion of the Structure, Causes, and Consequences of Affective Experiences at Work," *Research in Organizational Behavior*, 18 (1996), pp. 1–74.

61. C. Maslach, W. B. Schaufeli, and M. P. Leiter, "Job Burnout," *Annual Review of Psychology*, 52 (2001), pp. 397–422; R. T. Lee and B. E. Ashforth, "A Meta-analytic Examination of the Correlates of the Three Dimensions of Job Burnout," *Journal of Applied Psychology*, 81 (1996) pp. 123–33; R. J. Burke, "Toward a Phase Model of Burnout: Some Conceptual and Methodological Concerns," *Group and Organization Studies* 14 (1989), pp. 23–32; C. Maslach, *Burnout: The Cost of Caring* (Englewood Cliffs, N.J.: Prentice Hall, 1982).

62. C. L. Cordes and T. W. Dougherty, "A Review and Integration of Research on Job Burnout," *Academy of Management Review*, 18 (1993), pp. 621–56.

63. R. T. Lee and B. E. Ashforth, "A Further Examination of Managerial Burnout: Toward an Integrated Model," *Journal of Organizational Behavior*, 14 (1993), pp. 3–20.

64. Maslach et al, "Job Burnout," p. 405. However, there is also recent support for the three-stage model presented here. See: S. Toppinen-Tanner, R. Kalimo, and P. Mutanen, "The Process of Burnout in White-Collar and Blue-Collar Jobs: Eight-Year Prospective Study of Exhaustion," *Journal of Organizational Behavior*, 23 (2002), pp. 555–70.

65. M. Jamal, "Job Stress and Job Performance Controversy: An Empirical Assessment;" *Organizational Behavior and Human Performance*, 33 (1984), pp. 1–21; G. Keinan, "Decision Making under Stress: Scanning of Alternatives under Controllable and Uncontrollable Threats," *Journal of Personality and Social Psychology*, 52 (1987), pp. 638–44; S. J. Motowidlo, J. S. Packard, and M. R. Manning, "Occupational Stress: Its Causes and Consequences for Job Performance," *Journal of Applied Psychology*, 71 (1986), pp. 618–29.

66. R. D. Hackett and P. Bycio, "An Evaluation of Employee Absenteeism as a Coping Mechanism Among Hospital Nurses," *Journal of Occupational & Organizational Psychology*, 69 (December 1996) pp. 327–38; V. V. Baba and M. J. Harris, "Stress and Absence: A Cross-Cultural Perspective," *Research in Personnel and Human Resources Management*, Supplement 1 (1989), pp. 317–37.

67. DeFrank and Ivancevich, "Stress on the Job: An Executive Update;" Neuman and Baron, "Workplace Violence and Workplace Aggression."

68. H. Steensma, "Violence in the Workplace: The Explanatory Strength of Social (In)justice Theories," In M. Ross and D. T. Miller (Eds.) *The Justice Motive in Everyday Life*. (New York: Cambridge University Press, 2002), pp. 149–167; L. Greenberg and J. Barling, "Predicting Employee Aggression Against Coworkers, Subordinates and Supervisors: The Roles of Person Behaviors and Perceived Workplace Factors," *Journal of Organizational Behavior*, 20 (1999), pp. 897–913; M. A. Diamond, "Administrative Assault: A Contemporary Psychoanalytic View of Violence and Aggression in the Workplace," *American Review of Public Administration*, 27 (September 1997), pp. 228–47.

69. Neuman and Baron, "Workplace Violence and Workplace Aggression"; L. Berkowitz, *Aggression: Its Causes, Consequences, and Control*. (New York: McGraw-Hill, 1993).

70. R. Andrew, "Years of Living Dangerously," *CA Magazine*, March 1999, pp. 26–30.

71. Siegall and Cummings, "Stress and Organizational Role Conflict," *Genetic, Social, & General Psychology Monographs*; Havlovic and Keenen, "Coping with Work Stress: the Influence of Individual Differences."

72. T. Newton, J. Handy, and S. Fineman, *Managing Stress: Emotion and Power at Work* (Newbury Park, CA: Sage, 1995).

73. N. Elkes, "Hospital Tackles Health of Stressed-Out Staff," *Birmingham Evening Mail* (UK), August 24, 2001, p. 73.

74. Burke, "Workaholism and Extrawork Satisfactions"; N. Terra, "The Pre-vention of Job Stress by Redesigning Jobs and Implementing Self-Regulating Teams," In L. R. Murphy (ed.) *Job Stress Interventions* (Washington, DC: American Psychological Association, 1995); T. D. Wall and K. Davids, "Shopfloor Work Organization and Advanced Manufacturing Technology," *International Review of Industrial and Organizational Psychology*, 7 (1992), pp. 363–98; Karasek and Theorell, *Healthy Work*.

75. Higgins and Duxbury, *The 2001 National Work–Life Conflict Study*, p. xiv. For discussion of the importance of leadership rhetoric versus real support, see: M. Blair-Loy and A. S. Wharton, "Employees' Use of Work-Family Policies and the Workplace Social Context," *Social Forces*, 80 (March 2002), pp. 813–45.

76. C. Avery and D. Zabel. *The Flexible Workplace: A Sourcebook of Information and Research* (Westport, CT: Quorum, 2000)

77. G. Bellett, "Why Job-Sharing Needs Three Partners," *Vancouver Sun*, February 16, 2002, p. E1.

78. V. Galt, "Kraft Canada Cooks up a Tempting Workplace," *Globe and Mail*, August 5, 2002, p. B1.

79. B. S. Watson, "Share and Share Alike," *Management Review*, 84 (October 1995), pp. 50–52.

80. E. J. Hill, B. C. Miller, S. P. Weiner, J. Colihan, "Influences of the Virtual Office on Aspects of Work and Work/Life Balance," *Personnel Psychology*, 51 (Autumn 1998), 667–83; A. Mahlon, "The Alternative Workplace: Changing Where and How People Work," *Harvard Business Review*, (May-June 1998), pp. 121–30.

81. B. Livesey, "Provide and Conquer," *Report on Business Magazine*, March 1997, pp. 34–44; K. Mark, "Balancing Work and Family," *Canadian Banker*, January-February 1993, pp. 22–24; Bureau of Municipal Research, *Work-Related Day Care—Helping to Close the Gap* (Toronto: BMR, 1981).

82. S. Hale, "Execs Embrace Wide-Open Spaces," *Los Angeles Times*, May 13, 2001; P. DeMont, "Too Much Stress, Too Little Time," *Ottawa Citizen*, November 12, 1999.

83. Y. Iwasaki, R. C. Mannell, B. J. A. Smale and J. Butcher, "A Short-Term Longitudinal Analysis of Leisure Coping Used by Police and Emergency Response Service Workers," *Journal of Leisure Research*, 34 (July 2002), pp. 311–39.

84. A. Gordon, "Perks and Stock Options are Great, But It's Attitude that Makes the Difference," *Globe and Mail*, January 28, 2000; A. Vincola, "Working Sabbaticals Offer Employees more than Rejuvenation," *Canadian HR Reporter*, November 15, 1999, pp. 11, 13; L. Ramsay, "Good for the Employee, Good for the Employer," *National Post*, July 30, 1999, p. C15. For recent American experiences with corporate sabbaticals, see: P. Paul, "Time Out," *American Demographics*, 24 (June 2002).

85. S. Felix, "Taking the Sting Out of Stress," *Benefits Canada*, 22 (November 1998), pp. 21–24.

86. A. M. Saks and B. E. Ashforth, "Proactive Socialization and Behavioral Self-Management." *Journal of Vocational Behavior*, 48 (1996), pp. 301–323; M. Waung, "The Effects of Self-Regulatory Coping Orientation on Newcomer Adjustment and Job Survival," *Personnel Psychology*, 48 (1995), pp. 633–50; J. E. Maddux (ed.) *Self-Efficacy, Adaptation, and Adjustment : Theory, Research, and Application* (New York : Plenum Press, 1995.)

87. A. J. Daley and G. Parfitt, "Good Health—Is it Worth It? Mood States, Physical Well-Being, Job Satisfaction and Absenteeism in Members and Non-Members of British Corporate Health and Fitness Clubs," *Journal of Occupational and Organizational Psychology*, 69 (1996), pp. 121–34; L. E. Falkenberg, "Employee Fitness Programs: Their Impact on the Employee and the Organization," *Academy of Management Review*, 12 (1987), pp. 511–22; R. J. Shephard, M. Cox, and P. Corey, "Fitness Program Participation: Its Effect on Workers' Performance," *Journal of Occupational Medicine*, 23 (1981), pp. 359–63.

88. A. S. Sethi, "Meditation for Coping with Organizational Stress," in *Handbook of Organizational Stress Coping Strategies*, A. S. Sethi and R. S. Schuler (Cambridge, Mass.: Ballinger, 1984) pp. 145–65; M. T. Matteson and J. M. Ivancevich, *Managing Job Stress and*

Health (New York: The Free Press, 1982), pp. 160–66.

89. "Town of Richmond Hill receives first Well Workplace Award," *Benefits Canada*, February 2002; "Richmond Hill First Recipient of Workplace Wellness Award," *Canada NewsWire*, January 14, 2002.

90. M. Moralis, "Canada all Talk, No Action on Wellness," *Canadian HR Reporter*, April 22, 2002, pp. 23, 29. For a more detailed discussion of stress and wellness in organizations, see: K. Danna and R.W. Griffin, "Health and Well-being in the Workplace: A Review and Synthesis of the Literature," *Journal of Management*, 25 (May 1999), pp. 357–384.

91. L. Cassiani and D. Brown, "Investing in Wellness," *Canadian HR Reporter*, October 23, 2000, p. 20.

92. J. McCoy, "Company Stress Programs 'a Sham'," *Ottawa Citizen*, Monday November 15, 1999; S. MacDonald, and S. Wells, "The Prevalence and Characteristics of Employee Assistance, Health Promotion and Drug Testing Programs in Ontario," *Employee Assistance Quarterly*, 10 (1994), pp. 25–60; R. Loo and T. Watts, "A Survey of Employee Assistance Programs in Medium and Large Canadian Organizations," *Employee Assistance Quarterly*, 8 (1993), pp. 65–71.

93. J. J. L. van der Klink, R. W. B. Blonk, A. H. Schene, and F. J. H. van Dijk, "The Benefits of Interventions for Work-related Stress," *American Journal of Public Health*, 91 (February 2001), pp. 270–76; T. Rotarius, A. Liberman, and J.S. Liberman, "Employee Assistance Programs: A Prevention and Treatment Prescription for Problems in Health Care Organizations," *Health Care Manager*, 19 (September 2000), pp. 24–31.

94. P.D. Bliese and T.W. Britt, "Social Support, Group Consensus, and Stressor-Strain Relationships: Social Context Matters," *Journal of Organizational Behavior*, 22 (2001), pp. 425–36; B.N. Uchino, J. T. Cacioppo, and J. K. Kiecolt-Glaser, "The Relationship Between Social Support and Physiological Processes: A Review with Emphasis on Underlying Mechanisms and Implications for Health," *Psychological Bulletin*, 119 (May 1996), pp. 488–531; M.

R. Manning, C. N. Jackson, and M. R. Fusilier, "Occupational Stress, Social Support, And The Costs Of Health Care," *Academy of Management Journal*, 39 (June 1996), pp. 738–50.

95. J. S. House, *Work Stress and Social Support* (Reading, Mass.: Addison-Wesley, 1981); S. Cohen and T. A. Wills, "Stress, Social Support, and the Buffering Hypothesis," *Psychological Bulletin* 98 (1985), pp. 310–57.

96. S. Schachter, *The Psychology of Affiliation* (Stanford, Calif.: Stanford University Press, 1959).

CHAPTER EIGHT

1. G. Bylinsky, "Bombardier: A New Plant Saves Old Brand Names," (Elite Factories), *Fortune*, September 2, 2002, pp. 172ff; R. Barrett, "New Owner Hopes Outboard Motors Make a Splash," *Milwaukee Journal Sentinel*, January 20, 2002, p. 1D; L. Klink, "Bombardier to Hire up to 700," *Milwaukee Journal Sentinel*, September 2, 2001, p. 32.

2. A. Swift, "Management Method Catching On," *London Free Press*, March 8, 2000; I. Bloomstone, "Everyone Wins when Workers Participate," *Montreal Gazette*, June 21, 1999, p. F3; M. Greissel, "Dofasco Supports Research at the University of British Columbia," *Iron Age New Steel*, 14 (May 1998), pp. 64–68.

3. Very similar variations of this definition are found in: E. Sundstrom, "The Challenges of Supporting Work Team Effectiveness," In E. Sundstrom and Associates (Eds.) *Supporting Work Team Effectiveness* (San Francisco, CA: Jossey-Bass, 1999), pp. 6–9; S. G. Cohen and D. E. Bailey, "What Makes Teams Work: Group Effectiveness Research From The Shop Floor To The Executive Suite," *Journal of Management*, 23 (May 1997), pp. 239–90; M. A. West, "Preface: Introducing Work Group Psychology," In M. A. West (Ed.) *Handbook of Work Group Psychology*, (Chichester, UK: Wiley, 1996), p. xxvi; S. A. Mohrman, S. G. Cohen, and A. M. Mohrman, Jr., *Designing Team-Based Organizations: New Forms for Knowledge Work* (San Francisco: Jossey-Bass, 1995), pp. 39–40; J. R. Katzenbach and K. D. Smith, "The Discipline of Teams," *Harvard Business Review*, 71

(March–April 1993), pp. 111–20;); M. E. Shaw, *Group Dynamics*, 3rd ed. (New York: McGraw-Hill, 1981), p. 8.

4. L. R. Offermann and R. K. Spiros "The Science and Practice of Team Development: Improving the Link," *Academy of Management Journal*, 44 (April 2001), pp. 376–392. David Nadler similarly distinguishes "crowds" from "groups" and "teams." See D. A. Nadler, "From Ritual to Real Work: The Board as a Team," *Directors and Boards*, 22 (Summer 1998), pp. 28–31.

5. The preference for using the term "team" rather than "group" is also discussed in: Cohen and Bailey, "What Makes Teams Work"; R. A. Guzzo and M. W. Dickson, "Teams in Organizations: Recent Research on Performance and Effectiveness," *Annual Review of Psychology*, 47 (1996), pp. 307–38.

6. S. Carney, "DaimlerChrysler Launches Product Teams," *The Detroit News*, July 13, 2001, p. 1; J. Dixon, "Lean, Mean Is Theme for Chrysler," *Detroit Free Press*, July 12, 2001; E. Garsten, "Chrysler Has New Product Process," *AP Online*, July 12, 2001. E. Garsten, "Chrysler Has New Product Process," *AP Online*, July 12, 2001.

7. G. E. Huszczo, *Tools for Team Excellence* (Palo Alto, CA: Davies-Black, 1996, pp. 9–15; R. Likert, *New Patterns of Management* (New York: McGraw-Hill, 1961), pp. 106–08.

8. B. Meyer, "Reko Finds Hidden Potential while Getting ISO 9001," *Windsor Star*, September 17, 2001.

9. T. Peters, *Thriving on Chaos* (New York: Knopf, 1987), pp. 211–18; T. Kidder, *Soul of a New Machine* (Boston: Little, Brown, 1981); T. Peters and N. Austin, *A Passion for Excellence* (New York: Random House, 1985), Chapters 9 and 10.

10. S. Zesiger, "Dial 'M' For Mystique," *Fortune*, January 12, 1998, p. 175; R. Hertzberg, "No Longer a Skunkworks," *Internet World*, November 3, 1997; R. Lim, "Innovation, Innovation, Innovation," *Business Times* (Singapore), October 27, 1997, p. 18.

11. T. Koppel, *Powering the Future* (Toronto: John Wiley & Sons, 1999)

12. H. Saint-Onge and D. Wallace, *Leveraging Communities of Practice for Strategic Advantage*, (Boston: Butter-

worth-Heinemann, 2003); E. C. Wenger and W. M. Snyder, "Communities of Practice: The Organizational Frontier," *Harvard Business Review*, 78 (January–February 2000), pp. 139–45; J. W. Botkin, *Smart Business: How Knowledge Communities can Revolutionize your Company* (New York: Free Press, 1999).

13. M. Finlay, "Panning for Gold," *ComputerUser*, July 1, 2001.

14. P. R. Lawrence and N. Nohria, *Driven: How Human Nature Shapes Our Choices*, (San Francisco: Jossey-Bass, 2002); B. D. Pierce and R. White, "The Evolution of Social Structure: Why Biology Matters," *Academy of Management Review*, 24 (October 1999), pp. 843–53.

15. J. C. Turner and S. A. Haslam, "Social Identity, Organizations, and Leadership," In M. E. Turner (Ed.) *Groups at Work: Theory and Research* (Mahwah, N. J.: Lawrence Erlbaum Associates, 2001), pp. 25–65; M. A. Hogg and D. J. Terry, "Social Identity and Self-Categorization Processes in Organizational Contexts," *Academy of Management Review*, 25 (January 2000), pp. 121–40.

16. A. S. Tannenbaum, *Social Psychology of the Work Organization* (Belmont, CA.: Wadsworth, 1966), p. 62; S. Schacter, *The Psychology of Affiliation* (Stanford, Calif.: Stanford University Press, 1959), pp. 12–19.

17. R. Forrester and A. B. Drexler, "A Model for Team-based Organization Performance," *Academy of Management Executive*, 13 (August 1999), pp. 36–49; M. A. West, C. S. Borrill, and K. L. Unsworth, "Team Effectiveness in Organizations," *International Review of Industrial and Organizational Psychology*, 13 (1998), pp. 1–48; R.A. Guzzo and M.W. Dickson, "Teams in Organizations: Recent Research on Performance and Effectiveness," *Annual Review of Psychology*, 47 (1996), pp. 307–38.

18. J. R. Hackman, R. Wageman, T. M. Ruddy, and C. L. Ray, "Team Effectiveness in Theory and in Practice," In C. L. Cooper and E. A. Locke (Eds.) *Industrial and Organizational Psychology: Linking Theory with Practice* (Oxford, U.K.: Blackwell, 2000), pp. 109–29; M. R. Barrick, G. L. Stewart, M. J. Neubert, and M. K. Mount, "Relating

Member Ability and Personality to Work-Team Processes and Team Effectiveness," *Journal of Applied Psychology*, 83 (1998), pp. 377–91; West et al, "Team Effectiveness in Organizations;" Mohrman, Cohen, and Mohrman, Jr., *Designing Team-Based Organizations*, pp.58–65; J. E. McGrath, "Time, Interaction, and Performance (TIP): A Theory of Groups," *Small Group Research*, 22 (1991), pp. 147–74; G. P. Shea and R. A. Guzzo, "Group Effectiveness: What Really Matters?" *Sloan Management Review*, 27 (1987), pp. 33–46.

19. J. N. Choi, "External Activities and Team Effectiveness: Review and Theoretical Development," *Small Group Research*, 33 (April 2002), pp. 181–208.

20. E. E. Lawler, III, *Rewarding Excellence: Pay Strategies for the New Economy* (San Francisco: Jossey-Bass, 2000), pp. 207–14; S. Sarin and V. Mahajan, "The Effect of Reward Structures on the Performance of Cross-Functional Product Development Teams," *Journal of Marketing*, 65 (April 2001), pp. 35–53; J. S. DeMatteo, L. T. Eby, and E. Sundstrom, "Team-Based Rewards: Current Empirical Evidence and Directions for Future Research," *Research in Organizational Behaviour*, 20 (1998), pp. 141–83.

21. L. A. Yerkes, "Motivating Workers in Tough Times," *Incentive*, October 2001. pp. 120–21

22. P. Bordia "Face-To-Face Versus Computer-Mediated Communication: A Synthesis of the Experimental Literature," *Journal of Business Communication*, 34 (January 1997), pp. 99–120; A. D. Shulman, "Putting Group Information Technology in its Place: Communication and Good Work Group Performance," In S. R. Clegg, C. Hardy, and W. R. Nord (Eds.) *Handbook of Organization Studies*, (London: Sage, 1996), pp. 357–74; J. E. McGrath and A. B. Hollingshead, *Groups Interacting with Technology*, (Thousand Oaks, CA: Sage, 1994).

23. A. Smith, "Perfect Fits Vander Laan," *London Free Press*, May 3, 1999, p. 11. Work space design and team dynamics are discussed in J. Wineman and M. Serrato, "Facility design for high-performance teams," In E. Sundstrom and Associates (eds.) *Supporting Work Team Effectiveness* (San Francisco: Jossey-Bass, 1999), pp. 271–98.

24. R. Wageman, "Case Study: Critical Success Factors for Creating Superb Self-Managing Teams at Xerox," *Compensation and Benefits Review*, 29 (September–October 1997), pp. 31–41; D. Dimancescu and K. Dwenger, "Smoothing the Product Development Path," *Management Review*, 85 (January 1996), pp. 36–41.

25. E. F. McDonough III, "Investigation of Factors Contributing to the Success of Cross-Functional Teams," *Journal of Product Innovation Management*, 17 (May 2000), pp. 221–35; A. Edmondson, "Psychological Safety and Learning Behaviour in Work Teams," *Administrative Science Quarterly*, 44 (1999), pp. 350–83; D. G. Ancona and D. E. Caldwell, "Demography and Design: Predictors of New Product Team Performance," *Organization Science*, 3 (August 1992), pp. 331–41.

26. M. A. Campion, E. M. Papper, and G. J. Medsker, "Relations Between Work Team Characteristics and Effectiveness: A Replication and Extension," *Personnel Psychology*, 49 (1996), pp. 429–52; S. Worchel and S. L. Shackelford, "Groups Under Stress: The Influence of Group Structure and Environment on Process and Performance," *Personality & Social Psychology Bulletin*, 17 (1991), pp. 640–47; E. Sundstrom, K. P. De Meuse, and D. Futrell, "Work Teams: Applications and Effectiveness," *American Psychologist*, 45 (1990), pp. 120–33.

27. R. Wageman, "The Meaning of Interdependence," In M.E. Turner (Ed.), *Groups at Work: Theory and Research* (Mahwah, N.J.: Lawrence Erlbaum Associates, 2001), pp. 197–217.

28. G. van der Vegt, B. Emans, and E. van de Vliert, "Motivating Effects of Task and Outcome Interdependence in Work Teams," *Group & Organization Management*, 23 (June 1998), pp. 124–43; R. C. Liden, S. J. Wayne, and L. K. Bradway, "Task Interdependence as a Moderator of the Relation Between Group Control and Performance," *Human Relations*, 50 (1997), pp. 169–81; R. Wageman, "Interdependence and Group Effectiveness," *Administrative Science Quarterly*, 40 (1995), pp.145–80; M. A. Campion, G. J. Medsker, and A. C. Higgs, "Relations Between Work Group Characteristics and Effectiveness: Implications for De-

signing Effective Work Groups," *Personnel Psychology*, 46 (1993), pp. 823–50; M. N. Kiggundu, "Task Interdependence and the Theory of Job Design," *Academy of Management Review*, 6 (1981), pp. 499–508.

29. J. D. Thompson, *Organizations in Action* (New York: McGraw-Hill, 1967), pp. 54–56.

30. J. Kurlantzick, "New Balance Stays a Step Ahead," *U.S. News & World Report*, July 2, 2001, p. 34; A. Bernstein, "Low-Skilled Jobs: Do They Have To Move?" *Business Week*, February 26, 2001, p. 92; G. Gatlin, "Firm Boasts of New Balance of Power," *The Boston Herald*, January 24, 2001, p. 27.

31. K. H. Doerr, T. R. Mitchell, and T. D. Klastorin, "Impact of Material Flow Policies and Goals on Job Outcomes," *Journal of Applied Psychology*, 81 (1996), pp. 142–52.

32. A. Muoio, "Growing Smart," *Fast Company*, Issue 16 (August 1998); A. R. Sorkin, "Gospel According to St. Luke's," *New York Times*, February 12, 1998, p. D1.

33. G. R. Hickman and A. Creighton-Zollar, "Diverse Self-Directed Work Teams: Developing Strategic Initiatives For 21st Century Organizations," *Public Personnel Management*, 27 (Spring 1998), pp. 187–200; J. R. Katzenbach and D. K. Smith, *The Wisdom of Teams: Creating the High-Performance Organization* (Boston: Harvard University Press, 1993), pp. 45–47; G. Stasser, "Pooling of Unshared Information During Group Discussion," in S. Worchel, W. Wood, and J. A. Simpson (Eds.), *Group Process and Productivity*, (Newbury Park, Calif.: Sage, 1992), pp. 48–67.

34. T. Willmert, "Smart Workplace Design Should Bring People, and their Ideas, Together," *Minneapolis Star Tribune*, January 28, 2001, p. D11.

35. D. Flavelle, "Firms Try To Rope Winners By Hiring Out Of The Herd," *Toronto Star*, January 30, 2000.

36. L. T. Eby and G. H. Dobbins, "Collectivist Orientation in Teams: An Individual and Group-Level analysis," *Journal of Organizational Behaviour*, 18 (1997), pp. 275–95; P. C. Earley, "East Meets West Meets Mideast: Further Explorations of Collectivistic and Individualistic Work Groups," *Academy of*

Management Journal, 36 (1993), pp. 319–48.

37. Mohrman, Cohen, and Mohrman, Jr., *Designing Team-Based Organizations*, pp. 248–54; M. J. Stevens and M. A. Campion, "The Knowledge, Skill and Ability Requirements for Teamwork: Implications for Human Resources Management," *Journal of Management*, 20 (1994) pp. 503–30; A. P. Hare, *Handbook of Small Group Research*, 2nd ed. (New York: The Free Press, 1976), pp. 12–15.

38. S. Sonnentag, "Excellent Performance: The Role of Communication and Cooperation Processes," *Applied Psychology: An International Review*, 49 (July 2000), pp. 483–97; B. Buzaglo and S. Wheelan, "Facilitating Work Team Effectiveness: Case Studies from Central America," *Small Group Research*, 30 (1999), pp. 108–129; B. Schultz, "Improving Group Communication Performance: An Overview of Diagnosis and Intervention," In L. Frey, D. Gouran, and M. Poole (Eds.), *Handbook of Group Communication Theory and Research* (Thousand Oaks, CA: Sage, 1999), pp. 371–94; M. R. Barrick, G. L. Stewart, M. J. Neubert, and M. K. Mount, "Relating Member Ability and Personality to Work-Team Processes and Team Effectiveness," *Journal of Applied Psychology*, 83 (1998), pp. 377–91.

39. D. C. Hambrick, S. C. Davison, S. A. Snell, and C. C. Snow, "When Groups Consist Of Multiple Nationalities: Towards A New Understanding of the Implications," *Organization Studies*, 19 (1998), pp. 181–205; F. J. Milliken and L. L. Martins, "Searching for Common Threads: Understanding the Multiple Effects of Diversity in Organizational Groups," *Academy of Management Review*, 21 (1996), pp. 402–33; J. K. Murnighan and D. Conlon, "The Dynamics of Intense Work Groups: A Study of British String Quartets," *Administrative Science Quarterly*, 36 (1991), pp. 165–86.

40. P. C. Earley and E. Mosakowski, "Creating Hybrid Team Cultures: An Empirical Test of Transnational Team Functioning," *Academy of Management Journal*, 43 (February 2000), pp. 26–49; D. C. Lau and J. K. Murnighan, "Demographic Diversity and Faultlines: The Compositional Dynamics of Organiza-

tional Groups," *Academy of Management Review*, 23 (April 1998), pp. 325–40.

41. L. H. Pelled, K. M. Eisenhardt, and K. R. Xin, "Exploring the Black Box: An Analysis of Work Group Diversity, Conflict, and Performance," *Administrative Science Quarterly*, 44 (March 1999), pp. 1–28; K. Y. Williams and C. A. O' Reilly III, "Demography and Diversity in Organizations: A Review of 40 Years of Research," *Research in Organizational Behaviour*, 20 (1998), pp. 77–140; B. Daily, A. Wheatley, S. R. Ash, and R. L. Steiner, "The Effects of a Group Decision Support System on Culturally Diverse and Culturally Homogeneous Group Decision Making," *Information & Management*, 30 (1996), pp. 281–89; W. E. Watson, K. Kumar, and L. K. Michaelson, "Cultural Diversity's Impact on Interaction Process and Performance: Comparing Homogeneous and Diverse Task Groups," *Academy of Management Journal*, 36 (1993), pp. 590–602.

42. J.A. LePine, J.R. Hollenbeck, D.R. Ilgen, J. A. Colquitt, A. Ellis "Gender Composition, Situational Strength, and Team Decision-Making Accuracy: A Criterion Decomposition Approach," *Organizational Behaviour and Human Decision Processes*, 88 (2002), pp. 445–75.

43. Linda Tucci "Owens Drake Consulting Fosters Systematic Change," *St. Louis Business Journal*, May 25, 1998. For the importance of consensus and understanding in heterogeneous decision making groups, see: S. Mohammed and E. Ringseis, "Cognitive Diversity and Consensus in Group Decision Making: The Role of Inputs, Processes, and Outcomes," *Organizational Behaviour and Human Decision Processes*, 85 (July 2001), pp. 310–35.

44. The NTSB and NASA studies are summarized in: J. R. Hackman, "New Rules For Team Building," *Optimize*, July 1, 2002, pp. 50ff.

45. R. Deruyter, "Budd Workers Reject Shift Change," *Kitchener-Waterloo Record*, June 1, 2002.

46. B. W. Tuckman and M. A. C. Jensen, "Stages of Small-Group Development Revisited," *Group and Organization Studies*, 2 (1977), pp. 419–42. For a humorous and somewhat cynical

discussion of team dynamics through these stages, see: H. Robbins and M. Finley, *Why Teams Don't Work* (Princeton, NJ: Peterson's/Pacesetters, 1995), Chapter 21.

47. J. E. Mathieu and G. F. Goodwin, "The Influence of Shared Mental Models on Team Process and Performance," *Journal of Applied Psychology*, 85 (April 2000), pp. 273–84; J. A. Cannon-Bowers, S. I. Tannenbaum, E. Salas, and C. E. Volpe, "Defining Competencies and Establishing Team Training Requirements," In Guzzo, Salas, and Associates (Eds.) *Team Effectiveness and Decision Making in Organizations*, (San Francisco: Jossey-Bass, 1995), pp. 333–80.

48. A. Edmondson, "Psychological Safety and Learning Behaviour in Work Teams," *Administrative Science Quarterly*, 44 (1999), pp. 350–83.

49. D. L. Miller, "Synergy in Group Development: A Perspective on Group Performance," *Proceedings of the Annual ASAC Conference, Organizational Behaviour Division* 17, pt. 5 (1996), pp. 119–28; S. Worchel, D. Coutant-Sassic, and M. Grossman, "A Developmental Approach to Group Dynamics: A Model and Illustrative Research," in *Group Process and Productivity*, ed. Worchel et al., pp. 181–202; C. J. G. Gersick, "Time and Transition in Work Teams: Toward a New Model of Group Development," *Academy of Management Journal*, 31 (1988), pp. 9–41.

50. D. C. Feldman, "The Development and Enforcement of Group Norms," *Academy of Management Review*, 9 (1984), pp. 47–53; L. W. Porter, E. E. Lawler, and J. R. Hackman, *Behaviour in Organizations* (New York: McGraw-Hill, 1975), pp. 391–94.

51. I. R. Gellatly, "Individual and Group Determinants of Employee Absenteeism: Test of a Causal Model," *Journal of Organizational Behaviour*, 16 (1995), pp. 469–85; G. Johns, "Absenteeism Estimates by Employees and Managers: Divergent Perspectives and Self-Serving Perceptions," *Journal of Applied Psychology*, 79 (1994), pp. 229–39.

52. "Employees Terrorized by Peer Pressure in the Workplace," Morgan & Banks news release, September 2000. Also see: B. Latané, "The Psychology of Social Impact," *American Psychologist*, 36 (1981), pp. 343–56; C. A. Kiesler and S. B. Kiesler, *Conformity* (Reading, Mass.: Addison-Wesley, 1970).

53. Porter, Lawler, and Hackman, *Behaviour in Organizations*, pp. 399–401.

54. Feldman, "The Development and Enforcement of Group Norms," pp. 50–52.

55. Katzenbach and Smith, *The Wisdom of Teams*, pp. 121–23.

56. K. L. Bettenhausen and J. K. Murnighan, "The Development of an Intragroup Norm and the Effects of Interpersonal and Structural Challenges," *Administrative Science Quarterly*, 36 (1991), pp. 20–35.

57. R. S. Spich and K. Keleman, "Explicit Norm Structuring Process: A Strategy for Increasing Task-Group Effectiveness," *Group & Organization Studies*, 10 (March 1985), pp. 37–59.

58. L. Y. Chan and B. E. Lynn, "Operating in Turbulent Times: How Ontario's Hospitals are Meeting the Current Funding Crisis," *Health Care Management Review*, 23 (June 1998), p. 7.

59. D. I. Levine, "Piece Rates, Output Restriction, and Conformism," *Journal of Economic Psychology*, 13 (1992), pp. 473–89.

60. L. Coch and J. R. P. French, Jr., "Overcoming Resistance to Change," *Human Relations*, 1 (1948), pp. 512–32.

61. D. Katz and R. L. Kahn, *The Social Psychology of Organizations* (New York: John Wiley & Sons, 1966), Chapter 7; J. W. Thibault and H. H. Kelley, *The Social Psychology of Groups* (New York: John Wiley & Sons, 1959), Chapter 8.

62. D. Vinokur-Kaplan, "Treatment Teams that Work (and Those that Don't): An Application of Hackman's Group Effectiveness Model to Interdisciplinary Teams in Psychiatric Hospitals," *Journal of Applied Behavioral Science*, 31 (1995), pp. 303–27; Shaw, *Group Dynamics*, pp. 213–26; P. S. Goodman, E. Ravlin, and M. Schminke, "Understanding Groups in Organizations," *Research in Organizational Behaviour*, 9 (1987), pp. 121–73.

63. J. R. Kelly and S. G. Barsade, "Mood and Emotions in Small Groups and Work Teams," *Organizational Behaviour and Human Decision Processes*, 86 (September 2001), pp. 99–130; S. Lembke and M. G. Wilson, "Putting the 'Team' into Teamwork: Alternative Theoretical Contributions for Contemporary Management Practice," *Human Relations*, 51 (July 1998), pp. 927–44; B. E. Ashforth and R. H. Humphrey, "Emotion in the Workplace: A Reappraisal," *Human Relations*, 48 (1995), pp. 97–125.

64. K. M. Sheldon and B. A. Bettencourt, "Psychological Need-Satisfaction and Subjective Well-Being within Social Groups," *British Journal of Social Psychology*, 41 (2002), pp. 25–38; N. Ellemers, R. Spears, and B. Doosje, "Self And Social Identity," *Annual Review of Psychology*, 53 (2002), pp. 161–86; A. Lott and B. Lott, "Group Cohesiveness as Interpersonal Attraction: A Review of Relationships with Antecedent and Consequent Variables," *Psychological Bulletin*, 64 (1965), pp. 259–309.

65. S. E. Jackson, "Team Composition in Organizational Settings: Issues in Managing an Increasingly Diverse Work Force," in Worchel et al. (eds.), *Group Process and Productivity*, pp. 138–73; J. Virk, P. Aggarwal, and R. N. Bhan, "Similarity versus Complementarity in Clique Formation," *Journal of Social Psychology*, 120 (1983), pp. 27–34.

66. M. B. Pinto, J. K. Pinto, and J. E. Prescott, "Antecedents and Consequences of Project Team Cross-Functional Cooperation," *Management Science*, 39 (1993), pp. 1281–96; W. Piper, M. Marrache, R. Lacroix, A. Richardson, and B. Jones, "Cohesion as a Basic Bond in Groups," *Human Relations*, 36 (1983), pp. 93–108.

67. M. Frase-Blunt, "The Cubicles Have Ears. Maybe They Need Earplugs," *Washington Post*, March 6, 2001, p. HE7.

68. J. E. Hautaluoma and R. S. Enge, "Early Socialization into a Work Group: Severity of Initiations Revisited," *Journal of Social Behaviour & Personality*, 6 (1991) pp. 725–48; E. Aronson and J. Mills, "The Effects of Severity of Initiation on Liking for a Group," *Journal of Abnormal and Social Psychology*, 59 (1959), pp. 177–81.

69. B. Mullen and C. Copper, "The Relation Between Group Cohesiveness and Performance: An Integration," *Psy-*

chological Bulletin, 115 (1994), pp. 210–27; Shaw, *Group Dynamics*, p. 215.

70. The positive and negative effective of external threats on teams is discussed in: M. E. Turner and T. Horvitz, "The Dilemma of Threat: Group Effectiveness and Ineffectiveness under Adversity," In M. E. Turner (Ed.) *Groups at Work: Theory and Research* (Mahwah, NJ: Lawrence Erlbaum Associates, 2001), pp. 445–70.

71. M. Rempel and R. J. Fisher, "Perceived Threat, Cohesion, And Group Problem Solving In Intergroup Conflict," *International Journal of Conflict Management*, 8 (1997), pp. 216–34.

72. J. M. McPherson and P. A. Popielarz, "Social Networks and Organizational Dynamics," *American Sociological Review*, 57 (1992), pp. 153–70; Piper et al., "Cohesion as a Basic Bond in Groups," pp. 93–108.

73. C. A. O'Reilly III, D. F. Caldwell, and W. P. Barnett, "Work Group Demography, Social Integration, and Turnover," *Administrative Science Quarterly*, 34 (1989), pp. 21–37.

74. P. J. Sullivan and D. L. Feltz, "The Relationship Between Intrateam Conflict and Cohesion Within Hockey Teams," *Small Group Research*, 32 (June 2001), pp. 342–55.

75. J. Pappone, "Sometimes Life's Truly a Beach ...," *Ottawa Citizen*, February 3, 2000.

76. R. D. Banker, J. M. Field, R. G. Schroeder, and K. K. Sinha, "Impact of Work Teams on Manufacturing Performance: A Longitudinal Study," *Academy of Management Journal*, 39 (1996), pp. 867–90; D. Vinokur-Kaplan, "Treatment Teams That Work (And Those That Don't): An Application Of Hackman's Group Effectiveness Model To Interdisciplinary Teams In Psychiatric Hospitals," *Journal of Applied Behavioral Science*, 31 (September 1995), pp. 303–27; Mullen and Copper, "The Relation Between Group Cohesiveness and Performance," *Psychological Bulletin*; C. R. Evans and K. L. Dion, "Group Cohesion and Performance: A Meta-Analysis," *Small Group Research*, 22 (1991), pp. 175–86.

77. K. L. Gammage, A. V. Carron, and P. A. Estabrooks, "Team Cohesion and Individual Productivity: The Influence of the Norm for Productivity and the Identifiability of Individual Effort," *Small Group Research*, 32 (February 2001), pp. 3–18; C. Langfred, "Is Group Cohesiveness a Double-edged Sword? An Investigation of the Effects of Cohesiveness on Performance," *Small Group Research*, 29 (1998), pp. 124–43.

78. E. A. Locke et al., "The Importance of the Individual in an Age of Groupism," M. E. Turner (Ed.) *Groups at Work: Theory and Research* (Mahwah, N. J.: Lawrence Erlbaum Associates, 2001), pp. 501–28; Robbins and Finley, *Why Teams Don't Work*, Chapter 20; "The Trouble with Teams," *Economist*, January 14, 1995, p. 61; A. Sinclair, "The Tyranny of Team Ideology," *Organization Studies*, 13 (1992), pp. 611–26.

79. P. Panchak, "The Future Manufacturing," *Industry Week*, 247 (September 21, 1998), pp. 96–105; B. Dumaine, "The Trouble with Teams," *Fortune*, September 5, 1994, pp. 86–92.

80. I. D. Steiner, *Group Process and Productivity*, (New York: Academic Press, 1972).

81. D. Dunphy and B. Bryant, "Teams: Panaceas or Prescriptions for Improved Performance?" *Human Relations*, 49 (1996), pp. 677–99. For discussion of Brooke's Law, see: M. A. Cusumano "How Microsoft Makes Large Teams Work Like Small Teams," *Sloan Management Review*, 39 (Fall 1997), pp. 9–20.

82. R. Cross, "Looking Before You Leap: Assessing the Jump to Teams in Knowledge-based Work," *Business Horizons*, September, 2000.

83. M. Erez and A. Somech "Is Group Productivity Loss the Rule or the Exception? Effects of Culture and Group-Based Motivation," *Academy of Management Journal*, 39 (1996), pp. 1513–37; S. J. Karau and K. D. Williams, "Social Loafing: A Meta-Analytic Review and Theoretical Integration," *Journal of Personality and Social Psychology*, 65 (1993), pp. 681–706; J. M. George, "Extrinsic and Intrinsic Origins of Perceived Social Loafing in Organizations," *Academy of Management Journal*, 35 (1992), pp. 191–202; R. Albanese and D. D. Van Fleet, "Rational Behaviour in Groups: The Free-Riding Tendency," *Academy of Management Review*, 10 (1985), pp. 244–55.

84. M. Erez and A. Somech "Is Group Productivity Loss the Rule or the Exception? Effects of Culture and Group-Based Motivation," *Academy of Management Journal*, 39 (1996), pp. 1513–37; P. C. Earley, "Social Loafing and Collectivism: A Comparison of the U.S. and the People's Republic of China," *Administrative Science Quarterly*, 34 (1989), pp. 565–81.

85. T. A. Judge and T. D. Chandler, "Individual-level Determinants of Employee Shirking," *Relations Industrielles*, 51 (1996), pp. 468–86; J. M. George, "Asymmetrical Effects Of Rewards and Punishments: The Case of Social Loafing," *Journal of Occupational and Organizational Psychology*, 68 (1995), pp. 327–38; R. E. Kidwell and N. Bennett, "Employee Propensity to Withhold Effort: A Conceptual Model to Intersect Three Avenues of Research," *Academy of Management Review*, 19 (1993), pp. 429–56; J. A. Shepperd, "Productivity Loss in Performance Groups: A Motivation Analysis," *Psychological Bulletin*, 113 (1993), pp. 67–81.

CHAPTER NINE

1. J. Jusko, "Always Lessons To Learn," *Industry Week*, February 15, 1999, pp. 23–27; T. Stevens, "TRW Canada, Ltd.," *Industry Week*, October 19, 1998, pp. 76–78.

2. R. Robertson, "Pain Relief," *Materials Management and Distribution*, April 1997.

3. E.E. Lawler, *Organizing for High Performance* (San Francisco: Jossey-Bass, 2001); S. G. Cohen, G. E. Ledford, Jr., and G. M. Spreitzer, "A Predictive Model of Self-Managing Work Team Effectiveness," *Human Relations*, 49 (1996), pp. 643–76.

4. The SDT attributes discussed here are discussed in Yeatts and Hyten, *High-Performing Self-Managed Work Teams*; B. L. Kirkman and D. L. Shapiro, "The Impact Of Cultural Values On Employee Resistance To Teams: Toward A Model Of Globalized Self-Managing Work Team Effectiveness," *Academy of Management Review*, 22 (July 1997), pp. 730–57; Mohrman et al., *Designing Team-Based Organizations*.

5. L. Rittenhouse, "Dennis W. Bakke—Empowering a Workforce with Princi-

ples," *Electricity Journal*, January, 1998, pp. 48–59.

6. J. King, "Employers Quickly Hire Circuit Board Assemblers," *Detroit News*, October 15, 2000, p. 1; J-A. Johnston, "The Faces of Productivity," *Tampa Tribune*, September 4, 2000, p. 7.

7. P. S. Goodman, R. Devadas, and T. L. G. Hughson, "Groups and Productivity: Analyzing the Effectiveness of Self-Managing Teams," in J. P. Campbell, R. J. Campbell, and Associates (eds.), *Productivity in Organizations*, (San Francisco: Jossey-Bass, 1988), pp. 295–327.

8. The automobile service centres, city government, and courier service examples of SDWTs are described in: C. R. Emery and L. D. Fredendall, "The Effect of Teams on Firm Profitability and Customer Satisfaction," *Journal of Service Research*, 4 (February 2002), pp. 217–29; S. Simpson, "Ilg Repaying Emotional Debt To City," *Hartford Courant*, December 15, 2001, p. B1; J. Childs, "Five Years and Counting: The Path to Self-Directed Work Teams," *Hospital Materiel Management Quarterly*, 18 (May 1997), pp. 34–43.

9. D. Tjosvold, *Teamwork for Customers* (San Francisco: Jossey-Bass, 1993); D. E. Bowen and E. E. Lawler III, "The Empowerment of Service Workers: What, Why, How, and When," *Sloan Management Review*, Spring 1992, pp. 31–39.

10. E. L. Trist, G. W. Higgin, H. Murray, and A. B. Pollock, *Organizational Choice* (London: Tavistock, 1963). The origins of SDTs from sociotechnical systems research is also noted in R. Beckham, "Self-Directed Work Teams: The Wave of the Future?" *Hospital Material Management Quarterly*, 20 (August 1998), pp. 48–60.

11. The main components of sociotechnical systems are discussed in M. Moldaschl and W. G. Weber, "The 'Three Waves' of Industrial Group Work: Historical Reflections on Current Research on Group Work," *Human Relations*, 51 (March 1998), pp. 347–88; W. Niepce and E. Molleman, "Work Design Issues In Lean Production From A Sociotechnical Systems Perspective: Neo-Taylorism Or The Next Step In Sociotechnical Design?" *Human Relations*, 51 (March 1998), pp. 259–87.

12. E. Ulich and W. G. Weber, "Dimensions, Criteria, and Evaluation of Work Group Autonomy," In M. A. West (Ed.) *Handbook of Work Group Psychology* (Chichester, UK: John Wiley & Sons, 1996), pp. 247–82.

13. C. C. Manz and G. L. Stewart, "Attaining Flexible Stability by Integrating Total Quality Management and Socio-technical Systems Theory," *Organization Science*, 8 (1997), pp. 59–70; K. P. Carson and G. L. Stewart, "Job Analysis and the Sociotechnical Approach to Quality: A Critical Examination," *Journal of Quality Management*, 1 (1996), pp. 49–65.

14. K. Kane, "L.L. Bean Delivers the Goods," *Fast Company*, Issue 10 (August 1997), p. 104.

15. M. Evans, T. Hamilton, L. Surtees and S. Tuck, "The Road to a Billion," *Globe and Mail*, January 6, 2000; R. Dyck and N. Halpern, "Team-based Organizations Redesign at Celestica," *Journal for Quality & Participation*, 22 (September–October 1999), pp. 36–40.

16. L. Fuxman, "Teamwork in Manufacturing: The Case of the Automotive Industry," *International Journal of Commerce & Management*, 9 (1999), pp. 103–30; P. S. Adler and R. E. Cole, "Designed for Learning: A Tale of Two Auto Plants," *Sloan Management Review*, 34 (Spring 1993), pp. 85–94; J. P. Womack, D. T. Jones, and D. Roos, *The Machine that Changed the World* (New York: MacMillan, 1990).

17. X. Chen and W. Barshes, "To Team or Not to Team?" *The China Business Review*, 27 (March–April 2000), pp. 30–34; C. E. Nicholls, H. W. Lane, and M. B. Brechu, "Taking Self-Managed Teams to Mexico," *Academy of Management Executive*, 13 (August 1999), pp. 15–25.

18. C. Robert and T.M. Probst, "Empowerment and Continuous Improvement in the United States, Mexico, Poland, and India," *Journal of Applied Psychology*, 85 (October 2000), pp. 643–58; B. L. Kirkman and D. L. Shapiro, "The Impact Of Cultural Values On Employee Resistance To Teams: Toward A Model Of Globalized Self-Managing Work Team Effectiveness," *Academy of Management Review*, 22 (July 1997), pp. 730–57; C. Pavett and T. Morris, "Management Styles Within

A Multinational Corporation: A Five Country Comparative Study." *Human Relations*, 48 (1995) pp. 1171–91; M. Erez and P. C. Earley, *Culture, Self-Identity, and Work*, (New York: Oxford University Press, 1993), pp. 104–12.

19. This quotation is found at: www .quoteland.com

20. J.D. Orsburn and L. Moran, *The New Self-directed Work Teams: Mastering the Challenge*, (New York: McGraw-Hill, 2000), Chapter 11; C. C. Manz, D. E. Keating, and A. Donnellon, "Preparing for an Organizational Change to Employee Self-Management: The Managerial Transition," *Organizational Dynamics*, 19 (Autumn 1990), pp. 15–26.

21. G. T. Fairhurst, S. Green, and J. Courtright, "Inertial Forces And The Implementation Of A Socio-Technical Systems Approach: A Communication Study," *Organization Science*, 6 (1995), pp.168–85; Manz et al., "Preparing for an Organizational Change to Employee Self-Management," pp. 23–25.

22. J. Jusko, "Always Lessons To Learn," *Industry Week*, February 15, 1999, pp. 23–30. Similar comments are reported in: D. Stafford, "Sharing the Driver's Seat," *Kansas City Star*, June 11, 2002, p. D1; R. Cross, "Looking Before You Leap: Assessing the Jump to Teams in Knowledge-based Work," *Business Horizons*, September, 2000.

23. M. Fenton-O'Creevy, "Employee Involvement and the Middle Manager: Saboteur or Scapegoat?" *Human Resource Management Journal*, 11 (2001), pp. 24–40.

24. R. Yonatan and H. Lam, "Union Responses to Quality Improvement Initiatives: Factors Shaping Support and Resistance," *Journal of Labor Research*, 20 (Winter 1999), pp. 111–31; D. I. Levine, *Reinventing the Workplace* (Washington, D.C.: Brookings, 1995), pp. 66–69; I. Goll and N. B. Johnson, "The Influence of Environmental Pressures, Diversification Strategy, and Union/Nonunion Setting on Employee Participation," *Employee Responsibilities and Rights Journal*, 10 (1997), pp. 141–54; R. Hodson, "Dignity in the Workplace under Participative Management: Alienation and Freedom Revisited," *American Sociological Review*, 61 (1996), pp. 719–38.

25. A. Ford, "Web Ace Turns Hobby into Global Winner," *Vancouver Province*, February 15, 2000.

26. J. Lipnack and J. Stamps, *Virtual Teams: People Working Across Boundaries with Technology*, (New York: John Wiley & Sons, 2001); A. M. Townsend, S. M. deMarie, and A. R. Hendrickson, "Virtual Teams and the Workplace of the Future," *Academy of Management Executive*, 12 (August 1998), 17–29.

27. B. S. Bell and W. J. Kozlowski, "A Typology of Virtual Teams: Implications for Effective Leadership," *Group & Organization Management*, 27 (March 2002), pp. 14–49

28. B. S. Bell and W. J. Kozlowski, "A Typology of Virtual Teams: Implications for Effective Leadership," *Group & Organization Management*, 27 (Mar 2002), pp. 14–49; D. L. Duarte and N. T. Snyder, *Mastering Virtual Teams: Strategies, Tools, and Techniques that Succeed, 2nd ed.* (San Francisco, CA: Jossey-Bass, 2000), pp. 4–8.

29. S. Murray, "Pros and Cons of Technology: The Corporate Agenda: Managing Virtual Teams," *Financial Times* (London) May 27, 2002, p. 6.

30. G. Gilder, *Telecosm: How Infinite Bandwidth Will Revolutionize Our World* (N.Y.: Free Press, 2001); J. S. Brown, "Seeing Differently: A Role for Pioneering Research," *Research Technology Management*, 41 (May-June 1998), pp. 24–33.

31. A. M. Townsend, S. M. DeMarie, and A. R. Hendrickson, "Virtual Teams: Technology and the Workplace of the Future," *Academy of Management Executive*, 12 (August 1998), pp. 17–29.

32. M. Foreman, "US Pays for Designers to Stay Home," *New Zealand Herald*, November 21, 2000.

33. Y. L. Doz, J. F. P. Santos, and P. J. Williamson, "The Metanational Advantage," *Optimize*, May 2002, pp. 45ff; J. S. Lureya and M. S. Raisinghani, "An Empirical Study of Best Practices in Virtual Teams," *Information & Management*, 38 (2001) pp. 523–44.

34. B. L. Kelsey, "Managing in Cyberspace: Strategies for Developing high-Performance Virtual Team," Paper presented at the 2001 Annual Conference of the Administrative Sciences Association of Canada, Organizational Behaviour Division, London, Ontario, June 2001.

35. J. S. Lureya and M. S. Raisinghani "An Empirical Study of Best Practices in Virtual Teams," *Information & Management*, 38 (2001) pp. 523–44; K. Fisher and M. D. Fisher, *The Distance Manager* (New York: McGraw-Hill, 2000).

36. S. Gaspar, "Virtual Teams, Real Benefits," *Network World*, September 24, 2001, p. 45.

37. D. Robey, H. M. Khoo, and C. Powers, "Situated Learning in Cross-functional Virtual Teams," *Technical Communication*, (February 2000), pp. 51–66.

38. S. Murray, "Pros and Cons of Technology: The Corporate Agenda: Managing Virtual Teams," *Financial Times* (London) May 27, 2002, p. 6.

39. Lureya and Raisinghani "An Empirical Study of Best Practices in Virtual Teams."

40. S. Alexander, "Virtual Teams Going Global," *InfoWorld*, Nov 13, 2000, pp. 55–56.

41. S. Van Ryssen and S. H. Godar, "Going International Without Going International: Multinational Virtual Teams," *Journal of International Management*, 6 (2000), pp. 49–60.

42. F. G. Mangrum, M. S. Fairley, and D. L. Wieder, "Informal Problem Solving in the Technology-Mediated Work Place," *Journal of Business Communication*, 38 (July 2001), pp. 315–36; Robey et al, "Situated Learning in Cross-functional Virtual Teams;" E. J. Hill, B. C. Miller, S. P. Weiner and J. Colihan, "Influences of the Virtual Office On Aspects Of Work And Work/Life Balance," *Personnel Psychology*, 51 (Autumn 1998), pp. 667–83; S. B. Gould, K. J. Weiner, and B. R. Levin, *Free Agents: People and Organizations Creating a New Working Community* (San Francisco: Jossey-Bass, 1997), pp. 158–60.

43. L. L. Bierema, J. W. Bing, and T. J. Carter, "The Global Pendulum," *T & D*, 56 (May 2002), pp. 70–79.

44. J. Zbar, "Home Base," *Network World Fusion*, March 12, 2001.

45. D. L. Duarte and N. T. Snyder, *Mastering Virtual Teams: Strategies, Tools, and Techniques that Succeed, 2nd ed.* (San Francisco, CA: Jossey-Bass, 2000), pp. 139–55; S. L. Robinson, "Trust and Breach of the Psychological Contract," *Administrative Science Quarterly*, 41 (1996), pp. 574–99. For a discussion of the antecedents of trust, see: E. M Whitener, S. E. Brodt, M. A. Korsgaard and J. M. Werner, "Managers As Initiators Of Trust: An Exchange Relationship Framework For Understanding Managerial Trustworthy Behavior," *Academy of Management Review*, 23 (July 1998), pp. 513–30. Different foci of trust are discussed in: R. D. Costigan, S. S. Ilter, and J. J. Berman "A Multi-Dimensional Study of Trust in Organizations," *Journal of Managerial Issues*, 10 (Fall 1998), pp. 303–17.

46. Whitener et al, "Managers As Initiators Of Trust"; Bennis and Nanus, *Leaders*, pp. 43–55; Kouzes and Posner, *Credibility: How Leaders Gain and Lose It, Why People Demand It*. Knowledge-based trust is sometimes called "history-based trust" in the psychological literature. See R. M. Kramer, "Trust and Distrust in Organizations: Emerging Perspectives, Enduring Questions," *Annual Review of Psychology*, 50 (1999), pp. 569–98.

47. S. Gaspar, "Virtual Teams, Real Benefits," *Network World*, September 24, 2001, p. 45.

48. S. L. Jarvenpaa and D. E. Leidner, "Communication and Trust in Global Virtual Teams," *Organization Science*, 10 (1999), pp. 791–815; T. K. Das and B. Teng, "Between Trust and Control: Developing Confidence in Partner Cooperation in Alliances," *Academy of Management Review*, 23 (1998), pp. 491–512.

49. S. L. Jarvenpaa and D. E. Leidner, "Is Anybody out There? The Implications of Trust in Global Virtual Teams," *Journal of Management Information Systems*, 14 (1998), pp. 29–64.

50. L. Fleming, "M&As, Piecing Together Strategies," *Canadian Underwriter*, 68 (October 2001), pp. 78–79.

51. W. G. Dyer, *Team Building: Issues and Alternatives*, 2nd ed. (Reading, Mass.: Addison-Wesley, 1987); and S. J. Liebowitz and K. P. De Meuse, "The Application of Team Building," *Human Relations*, 35 (1982), pp. 1–18.

52. Sundstrom et al., "Work Teams: Applications and Effectiveness," *Ameri-*

can Psychologist, p. 128; M. Beer, *Organizational Change and Development: A Systems View* (Santa Monica, Calif.: Goodyear, 1980), pp. 143–46.

53. Beer, *Organizational Change and Development*, p. 145.

54. G. Coetzer, *A Study of the Impact of Different Team Building Techniques on Work Team Effectiveness*. Unpublished MBA research project (Burnaby, B.C.: Simon Fraser University, 1993).

55. T. G. Cummings and C. G. Worley, *Organization Development & Change*, 6th Ed. (Cincinnati: South-Western, 1997), pp. 218–19; P. F. Buller and C. H. Bell, Jr., "Effects of Team Building and Goal Setting on Productivity: A Field Experiment," *Academy of Management Journal*, 29 (1986), pp. 305–28.

56. C. J. Solomon, "Simulation Training Builds Teams Through Experience," *Personnel Journal*, 72 (June 1993), pp. 100–06.

57. M. J. Brown, "Let's Talk About It, Really Talk About It," *Journal for Quality & Participation*, 19, no. 6, (1996) pp. 26–33; E. H. Schein, "On Dialogue, Culture, and Organizational Learning," *Organizational Dynamics*, Autumn 1993, pp. 40–51; and P. M. Senge, *The Fifth Discipline* (New York: Doubleday Currency, 1990), pp. 238–49.

58. B. Oaff, "Team Games Take Turn for the Verse," *Mail on Sunday (UK)*, January 28, 2001, p. 56; K. Cross, "Adventure Capital," *Business 2.0*, July 11, 2000; C. Prystay, "Executive Rearmament: Tempering Asia's Executive Mettle," *Asian Business*, October 1996.

59. R. W. Woodman and J. J. Sherwood, "The Role of Team Development in Organizational Effectiveness: A Critical Review," *Psychological Bulletin*, 88 (1980), pp. 166–86; Sundstrom et al, "Work Teams: Applications and Effectiveness," p. 128.

60. Robbins and Finley, *Why Teams Don't Work*, Chapter 17.

61. P. McGraw, "Back from the Mountain: Outdoor Management Development Programs and How to Ensure the Transfer of Skills to the Workplace," *Asia Pacific Journal of Human Resources*, 31 (Spring 1993), pp. 52–61; G. E. Huszczo, "Training for Team Building," *Training and Development Journal*, 44 (February 1990), pp. 37–43.

CHAPTER TEN

1. K. Pearson, "The Adventurer," *Profit*, 21 (May 2002), p. 32; "G.A.P Adventures CEO at United Nations for Launch of the International Year of Ecotourism," *PR Newswire*, January 25, 2002; L. Pratt, "Adventures with Ethics," *National Post*, August 18, 2001; "Mind the G.A.P.," *CBC Venture*, November 7, 2000.

2. F. A. Shull, Jr., A. L. Delbecq, and L. L. Cummings, *Organizational Decision Making* (New York: McGraw-Hill, 1970), p. 31. Also see: J. G. March, "Understanding How Decisions Happen in Organizations," In Z. Shapira (Ed.) *Organizational Decision Making* (New York: Cambridge University Press, 1997), pp. 9–32.

3. This model is adapted from several sources: H. Mintzberg, D. Raisinghani, and A. Théorét, "The Structure of 'Unstructured' Decision Processes," *Administrative Science Quarterly* 21 (1976), pp. 246–75; H. A. Simon, *The New Science of Management Decision* (New York: Harper & Row, 1960); C. Kepner and B. Tregoe, *The Rational Manager* (New York: McGraw-Hill, 1965); W. C. Wedley and R. H. G. Field, "A Predecision Support System," *Academy of Management Review* 9 (1984), pp. 696–703.

4. B.M. Bass, *Organizational Decision Making* (Homewood, Ill.: Irwin, 1983), Chapter 3; W.F. Pounds, "The Process of Problem Finding," *Industrial Management Review*, 11 (Fall 1969), pp. 1–19; C. Kepner and B. Tregoe, *The Rational Manager* (New York: McGraw-Hill, 1965).

5. P. F. Drucker, *The Practice of Management* (New York: Harper & Brothers, 1954), pp. 353–57.

6. Wedley and Field, "A Predecision Support System," p. 696; Drucker, *The Practice of Management*, p. 357; and L. R. Beach and T. R. Mitchell, "A Contingency Model for the Selection of Decision Strategies," *Academy of Management Review*, 3 (1978), pp. 439–49.

7. I. L. Janis, *Crucial Decisions* (New York: The Free Press, 1989), pp. 35–37; Simon, *The New Science of Management Decision*, pp. 5–6.

8. Mintzberg, Raisinghani, and Théorét, "The Structure of 'Unstructured' Decision Processes," pp. 255–56.

9. B. Fischhoff and S. Johnson, "The Possibility of Distributed Decision Making," In Shapira, *Organizational Decision Making*, pp. 216–37.

10. The different view of emotions on decision making are discussed or emphasized in: N. M. Ashkanasy and C. E. J. Hartel, "Managing Emotions in Decision-Making," In N. M. Ashkanasy, W. J. Zerbe, C. E. J. Hartel (Eds.) *Managing Emotions in the Workplace* (Armonk, N.Y.: M. E. Sharpe, 2002); D. S. Massey, "A Brief History of Human Society: The Origin and Role of Emotion in Social Life," *American Sociological Review*, 67 (February 2002), pp. 1–29; J. P. Forgas and J. M. George, "Affective Influences on Judgments and Behaviour in Organizations: An Information Processing Perspective," *Organizational Behaviour and Human Decision Processes*, 86 (September 2001), pp. 3–34; N. Schwarz, "Social Judgment and Attitudes: Warmer, More Social, And Less Conscious," *European Journal of Social Psychology*, 30 (2000), pp. 149–76; P. Greenspan, "Emotional Strategies and Rationality," *Ethics*, 110 (April 2000), pp. 469–87.

11. A. Howard, "Opinion," *Computing*, July 8, 1999, p. 18.

12. Schwarz, "Social Judgment and Attitudes," pp. 149–76; R. Hastie, "Problems For Judgment And Decision Making," *Annual Review of Psychology*, 52 (2001), pp. 653–83.

13. J. E. Dutton, "Strategic Agenda Building in Organizations," In Shapira, *Organizational Decision Making*, pp. 81–107; M. Lyles and H. Thomas, "Strategic Problem Formulation: Biases and Assumptions Embedded in Alternative Decision-Making Models," *Journal of Management Studies*, 25 (1988), pp. 131–45; I. I. Mitroff, "On Systematic Problem Solving and the Error of the Third Kind," *Behavioral Science*, 9 (1974), pp. 383–93.

14. D. Domer, *The Logic of Failure* (Reading, MA: Addison-Wesley, 1996); M. Basadur, "Managing the Creative Process in Organizations," In M. A. Runco (Ed.) *Problem Finding, Problem Solving, and Creativity* (Norwood, NJ: Ablex Publishing, 1994), pp. 237–68.

15. P. C. Nutt, "Preventing Decision Debacles," *Technological Forecasting and Social Change*, 38 (1990), pp. 159–74.

16. P. C. Nutt, *Making Tough Decisions* (San Francisco: Jossey-Bass, 1989).

17. H. A. Simon, "A Behavioral Model of Rational Choice," *Quarterly Journal of Economics*, 69 (1955), pp. 99–118.

18. J. Conlisk, "Why Bounded Rationality?" *Journal of Economic Literature*, 34 (1996), pp. 669–700; B. L. Lipman, "Information Processing and Bounded Rationality: A Survey," *Canadian Journal of Economics*, 28 (1995), pp. 42–67.

19. L. T. Pinfield, "A Field Evaluation of Perspectives on Organizational Decision Making," *Administrative Science Quarterly*, 31 (1986), pp. 365–88. The recent survey, conducted by Kepner-Tregoe, is described in: D. Sandahl and C. Hewes," Decision Making at Digital Speed," *Pharmaceutical Executive*, 21 (August 2001), p. 62.

20. H. A. Simon, *Administrative Behaviour*, 2nd ed. (New York: The Free Press, 1957), pp. xxv, 80–84; and J. G. March and H. A. Simon, *Organizations* (New York: Wiley, 1958), pp. 140–41.

21. J. E. Russo, V. H. Medvec, and M. G. Meloy, "The Distortion of Information During Decisions," *Organizational Behaviour & Human Decision Processes*, 66 (1996), pp. 102–10; P. O. Soelberg, "Unprogrammed Decision Making," *Industrial Management Review*, 8 (1967), pp. 19–29.

22. F. Phillips, "The Distortion of Criteria after Decision-Making," *Organizational Behaviour and Human Decision Processes*, 88 (2002) pp. 769–84.

23. H. A. Simon, *Models of Man: Social and Rational* (New York: Wiley, 1957), p. 253.

24. N. M. Ashkanasy, W. J. Zerbe, C. E. J. Hartel "Introduction: Managing Emotions in a Changing Workplace," In N. M. Ashkanasy, W. J. Zerbe, C. E. J. Hartel (Eds.) *Managing Emotions in the Workplace* (Armonk, N.Y.: M. E. Sharpe, 2002), pp. 3–18.

25. J. P. Forgas and J. M. George, "Affective Influences on Judgments and Behaviour in Organizations: An Information Processing Perspective," *Organizational Behaviour and Human Decision Processes*, 86 (September 2001), pp. 3–34. The computer software evaluation study is found in: D. S. Kempf "Attitude Formation from Product Trial: Distinct Roles of Cognition And Affect for Hedonic and Functional Products," *Psychology and Marketing*, 16 (1999), pp. 35–50.

26. M. Lyons, "Cave-in Too Close for Comfort, Miner Says," *Saskatoon StarPhoenix*, May 6, 2002.

27. O. Behling and N. L. Eckel, "Making Sense Out of Intuition," *Academy of Management Executive*, 5 (February 1991), pp. 46–54; Nutt, *Making Tough Decisions*, p. 54; H. A. Simon, "Making Management Decisions: The Role of Intuition and Emotion," *Academy of Management Executive* (February 1987), pp. 57–64; W. H. Agor, "The Logic of Intuition," *Organizational Dynamics* (Winter 1986), pp. 5–18.

28. N. Khatri, "The Role of Intuition in Strategic Decision Making," *Human Relations*, 53 (January 2000), pp. 57–86; L. A. Burke and M. K. Miller, "Taking the Mystery Out of Intuitive Decision Making," *Academy of Management Executive*; 13 (November 1999), pp. 91–99.

29. M. D. Lieberman, "Intuition: A Social Cognitive Neuroscience Approach," *Psychological Bulletin*, 126 (2000), pp. 109–37; E. N. Brockmann and W. P. Anthony, "The Influence of Tacit Knowledge and Collective Mind on Strategic Planning," *Journal of Managerial Issues*, 10 (Summer 1998), pp. 204–22; D. Leonard and S. Sensiper, "The Role Of Tacit Knowledge In Group Innovation," *California Management Review*, 40 (Spring 1998), pp. 112–32. For a discussion of the problems with intuition in business start-ups, see: L. Broderick and M. Sponer, "The Death of Gut Instinct," *Inc.*, 23 (January 2001), pp. 38–42.

30. J. Gregoire, "Leading the Charge for Change," *CIO*, June 1, 2001. Also see: Y. Ganzach, A. H. Kluger, and N. Klayman, "Making Decisions from an Interview: Expert Measurement and Mechanical Combination," *Personnel Psychology*, 53 (Spring 2000), pp. 1–20.

31. A.M. Hayashi, "When to Trust Your Gut," *Harvard Business Review*, 79 (February 2001), pp. 59–65; E. Gubbins and B. Quinton, "Serial Entrepreneurs: They're Grrreat!" *Upstart*, January 30, 2001.

32. P. Goodwin and G. Wright, "Enhancing Strategy Evaluation in Scenario Planning: A Role for Decision Analysis," *Journal of Management Studies*, 38 (January 2001), pp. 1–16; P. J. H. Schoemaker, "Disciplined Imagination: From Scenarios to Strategic Options," *International Studies of Management & Organization*, 27 (Summer 1997), pp. 43–70; K. Van Der Heijden, *Scenarios: The Art of Strategic Conversation*. (N.Y.: Wiley, 1996). The recommendation of revisiting decisions is noted in: J. M. George, "Emotions and Leadership: The Role of Emotional Intelligence," *Human Relations*, 53 (2000), pp. 1027–55.

33. R. N. Taylor, *Behavioral Decision Making* (Glenview, Ill.: Scott, Foresman, 1984), pp. 163–66.

34. D. R. Bobocel and J. P. Meyer, "Escalating Commitment to a Failing Course of Action: Separating the Role of Choice and Justification," *Journal of Applied Psychology*, 79 (1994), pp. 360–63; G. Whyte, "Escalating Commitment in Individual and Group Decision Making: A Prospect Theory Approach," *Organizational Behaviour and Human Decision Processes*, 54 (1993), pp. 430–55; G. Whyte, "Escalating Commitment to a Course of Action: A Reinterpretation," *Academy of Management Review*, 11 (1986), pp. 311–21.

35. M. Keil and R. Montealegre, "Cutting your Losses: Extricating your Organization When a Big Project Goes Awry," *Sloan Management Review*, 41, (Spring 2000), pp. 55–68; M. Fackler, "Tokyo's Newest Subway Line a Saga of Hubris, Humiliation," *Associated Press Newswires*, July 20, 1999; P. Ayton and H. Arkes, "Call It Quits," *New Scientist*, June 20, 1998.

36. F. D. Schoorman and P. J. Holahan, "Psychological Antecedents of Escalation Behaviour: Effects of Choice, Responsibility, and Decision Consequences," *Journal of Applied Psychology*, 81 (1996), pp. 786–93.

37. B. M. Staw. K. W. Koput, and S. G. Barsade "Escalation at the Credit Window: A Longitudinal Study of Bank Executives' Recognition and Write-Off Of Problem Loans," *Journal of Applied Psychology*, 82 (1997), pp. 130–42. Also see: M. Keil and D. Robey, "Turning Around Troubled Software Projects: An Exploratory Study of the Deescalation of Commitment to Failing Courses of Action," *Journal of Management Information Systems*, 15 (Spring 1999), pp. 63–87.

38. W. Boulding, R. Morgan, and R. Staelin, "Pulling the Plug to Stop the New Product Drain," *Journal of Marketing Research*, 34 (1997), pp. 164–76; I. Simonson and B. M. Staw, "De-escalation Strategies: A Comparison of Techniques for Reducing Commitment to Losing Courses of Action," *Journal of Applied Psychology*, 77 (1992), pp. 419–26.

39. D. Ghosh, "De-Escalation Strategies: Some Experimental Evidence," *Behavioral Research in Accounting*, 9 (1997), pp. 88–112.

40. M. Fenton-O'Creevy, "Employee Involvement and the Middle Manager: Saboteur or Scapegoat?" *Human Resource Management Journal*, 11 (2001), pp. 24–40. Also see: V. H. Vroom and A. G. Jago, *The New Leadership: Managing Participation in Organizations* (Englewood Cliffs, N.J.: Prentice Hall, 1988), p. 15. The quotation in this paragraph is from: E. E. Lawler, III, *"Rewarding Excellence: Pay Strategies for the New Economy* (San Francisco: Jossey-Bass, 2000). pp. 23–24.

41. R. C. Liden and S. Arad, "A Power Perspective of Empowerment and Work Groups: Implications for Human Resources Management Research," *Research in Personnel and Human Resources Management*, 14 (1996), pp. 205–51; R. C. Ford and M. D. Fottler, "Empowerment: A Matter of Degree," *Academy of Management Executive*, 9 (August 1995), pp. 21–31; R. W. Coye and J. A. Belohlav, "An Exploratory Analysis of Employee Participation," *Group & Organization Management*, 20 (1995), pp. 4–17; Vroom and Jago, *The New Leadership*.

42. P. Fengler and T. Heaps, "Aqua Purus," *Corporate Knights*, 2002. (www .corporateknights.ca); R. Kang, "Turnarounds of the Year: Power from the People," *Profit*, November 1999, pp. 36ff; P. Delean, "These Caps are Tops," *Montreal Gazette*, September 27, 1999.

43. J. T. Addison, "Nonunion Representation in Germany," *Journal of Labor Research*, 20 (Winter 1999), pp. 73–92; G. Strauss, "Collective Bargaining, Unions, and Participation," In F. Heller, E. Pusic, G. Strauss, and B. Wilpert (Eds.) *Organizational Participation: Myth and Reality* (New York: Oxford University Press, 1998), pp.

97–143; D. I. Levine, *Reinventing the Workplace* (Washington, DC: Brookings, 1995), pp. 47–48.

44. For early writing supporting employee involvement, see: R. Likert, *New Patterns of Management* (New York: McGraw-Hill, 1961); D. McGregor, *The Human Side of Enterprise* (New York: McGraw-Hill, 1960); C. Argyris, *Personality and Organization* (New York: Harper & Row, 1957).

45. C. L. Cooper, B. Dyck, and N. Frohlich, "Improving the Effectiveness of Gainsharing: The Role of Fairness and Participation," *Administrative Science Quarterly*, 37 (1992), pp. 471–90.

46. J. P. Walsh and S-F. Tseng, "The Effects Of Job Characteristics On Active Effort At Work," *Work & Occupations*, 25 (February 1998), pp. 74–96; K. T. Dirks, L. L. Cummings, and J. L. Pierce, "Psychological Ownership in Organizations: Conditions Under Which Individuals Promote and Resist Change," *Research in Organizational Change and Development*, 9 (1996), pp. 1–23.

47. J. A. Wagner III, C. R. Leana, E. A. Locke, and D. M. Schweiger, "Cognitive and Motivational Frameworks in U.S. Research on Participation: A Meta-Analysis of Primary Effects," *Journal of Organizational Behaviour*, 18 (1997), pp. 49–65; G. P. Latham, D. C. Winters, and E. A. Locke, "Cognitive and Motivational Effects of Participation: A Mediator Study," *Journal of Organizational Behaviour*, 15 (1994), pp. 49–63; Cotton, *Employee Involvement*, Chapter 8; S. J. Havlovic, "Quality of Work Life and Human Resource Outcomes," *Industrial Relations*, 1991, pp. 469–79; K. I. Miller and P. R. Monje, "Participation, Satisfaction, and Productivity: A Meta-Analytic Review," *Academy of Management Journal*, 29 (1986), pp. 727–53.

48. A. Cummings and G. R. Oldham, "Enhancing Creativity: Managing Work Contexts for the High Potential Employee," *California Management Review*, 40 (Fall 1997), pp. 22–38; T. M. Amabile, *The Social Psychology of Creativity* (N.Y.: Springer-Verlag, 1983), pp. 32–35.

49. B. Kabanoff and J. R. Rossiter, "Recent Developments in Applied Creativity," *International Review of Indus-*

trial and Organizational Psychology, 9 (1994), pp. 283–324.

50. J. R. Hayes, "Cognitive Processes in Creativity," In J. A. Glover, R. R. Ronning, and C. R. Reynolds, (Eds.) *Handbook of Creativity* (N.Y.: Plenum, 1989), pp. 135–45.

51. R. S. Nickerson, "Enhancing Creativity," In R. J. Sternberg (Ed.) *Handbook of Creativity* (New York: Cambridge University Press, 1999), pp. 392–430; A. Hiam, "Obstacles to Creativity—and How You Can Remove Them," *Futurist*, 32 (October 1998), pp. 30–34.

52. R. T. Brown, "Creativity: What are We to Measure," In J. A. Glover, R. R. Ronning, and C. R. Reynolds (Eds.) *Handbook of Creativity* (NY: Plenum, 1989), pp. 3–32.

53. A. Hargadon and R. I. Sutton, "Building an Innovation Factory," *Harvard Business Review*, 78 (May-June 2000), pp. 157–66.

54. For a thorough discussion of insight, see: R. J. Sternberg and J. E. Davidson (Eds.) *The Nature of Insight* (Cambridge, MA: MIT Press, 1995).

55. V. Parv, "The Idea Toolbox: Techniques For Being A More Creative Writer," *Writer's Digest*, Vol. 78 (July 1998), p. 18; J. Ayan, *Aha! 10 Ways to Free Your Creative Spirit and Find Your Great Ideas* (N.Y.:Crown Trade, 1997), pp. 50–56.

56. A. Chandrasekaran, "Bye, Bye Serendipity," *Business Standard*, March 28, 2000, p. 1; K. Cottrill, "Reinventing Innovation," *Journal of Business Strategy*, March-April 1998, pp. 47–51.

57. S. Taggar, "Individual Creativity and Group Ability to Utilize Individual Creative Resources: A Multilevel Model," *Academy of Management Journal*, 45 (April 2002), pp. 315–30; R. J. Sternberg and L. A. O'Hara, "Creativity and Intelligence," In R. J. Sternberg (Ed.) *Handbook of Creativity* (N.Y.: Cambridge University Press, 1999), pp. 251–72.

58. Sutton, *Weird Ideas that Work*, pp. 8–9, Chap. 10.

59. G. J. Feist, "The Influence of Personality on Artistic and Scientific Creativity," In R. J. Sternberg (Ed.) *Handbook of Creativity* (N.Y.: Cambridge University Press, 1999), pp. 273–96; M. A. West, *Developing Creativ-*

ity in Organizations (Leicester, UK: BPS Books, 1997), pp. 10–19.

60. B. Breen, "Rapid Motion," *Fast Company*, 49 (August 2001), p. 49; L. Pratt, "Persistence in Motion," *Profit Magazine*, 20 (May 2001), pp. 18–22.

61. R. W. Weisberg, "Creativity and Knowledge: A Challenge to Theories," In Sternberg (Ed.) *Handbook of Creativity*, pp. 226–50.

62. R. I. Sutton, *Weird Ideas that Work* (New York: Free Press, 2002), pp. 121, 153–54. For other literature on creativity and knowledge, see: R. J. Sternberg, *Thinking Styles* (N.Y.: Cambridge University Press, 1997) ; R. J. Sternberg, L. A. O'Hara, and T. I. Lubart, "Creativity as Investment," *California Management Review*, 40 (Fall 1997), pp. 8–21.

63. T. Koppell, *Powering the Future* (New York: Wiley, 1999), p. 15.

64. D.K. Simonton, "Creativity: Cognitive, Personal, Developmental, and Social Aspects," *American Psychologist*, 55 (January 2000), pp. 151–58; A. Cummings and G. R. Oldham, "Enhancing Creativity: Managing Work Contexts for the High Potential Employee," *California Management Review*, 40 (Fall 1997), pp. 22–38.

65. S. Bharadwaj and A. Menon, "Making Innovation Happen in Organizations: Individual Creativity Mechanisms, Organizational Creativity Mechanisms or Both?" *Journal of Product Innovation Management*, 17 (November 2000), pp. 424–34; M.D. Mumford, "Managing Creative People: Strategies and Tactics for Innovation," *Human Resource Management Review*, 10 (Autumn 2000), pp. 313–51; T. M. Amabile, R. Conti, H. Coon, J. Lazenby, and M. Herron, "Assessing the Work Environment for Creativity," *Academy of Management Journal*, 39 (1996), pp. 1154–84; G. R. Oldham and A. Cummings, "Employee Creativity: Personal and Contextual Factors at Work," *Academy of Management Journal*, 39 (1996), pp. 607–34.

66. The learning orientation concept is the focus of current attention in marketing: See M. A. Farrell, "Developing a Market-Oriented Learning Organization," *Australian Journal of Management*, 25 (September 2000); W. E. Baker and J. M. Sinkula, "The Synergistic Effect of Market Orientation and

Learning Orientation," *Journal of the Academy of Marketing Science*, 27 (1999), pp. 411–27.

67. "It's OK to Fail," *Profit Magazine*, 18 (November 1999), pp. 25–32.

68. C. E. Shalley, L. L. Gilson, and T. C. Blum, "Matching Creativity Requirements and the Work Environment: Effects on Satisfaction and Intentions to Leave," *Academy of Management Journal*, April 2000, pp. 215–223; R. Tierney, S. M. Farmer, and G. B. Graen, "An Examination of Leadership and Employee Creativity: The Relevance of Traits and Relationships," *Personnel Psychology*, 52 (Autumn 1999), pp. 591–620; Cummings and Oldham, "Enhancing Creativity."

69. T. M. Amabile, "Motivating Creativity in Organizations: On Doing What You Love and Loving What You Do," *California Management Review*, 40 (Fall 1997), pp. 39–58.

70. T. M. Amabile, "Changes in the Work Environment for Creativity during Downsizing," *Academy of Management Journal*, 42 (December 1999), pp. 630–40.

71. Cummings and Oldham, "Enhancing Creativity."

72. T. M. Amabile, "A Model of Creativity and Innovation in Organizations," *Research in Organizational Behaviour*, 10 (1988), pp. 123–67. The survey about time pressure in advertising and marketing is summarized in "No Time For Creativity," *London Free Press*, August 7, 2001, p. D3.

73. Hiam, "Obstacles to Creativity— and How You Can Remove Them."

74. West, *Developing Creativity in Organizations*, pp. 33–35.

75. P. Luke, "Business World's a Stage," *Vancouver Province*, September 2, 2001; P. Brown, "Across the Table into the Bedroom," *The Times of London*, March 1, 2001, p. D4.

76. B. Breen, "How EDS Got Its Groove Back," *Fast Company*, Issue 51 (October 2001), pp. 106–17; C.E. Ramirez, "EDS Brainstorming Team Plots Course for Future," *Detroit News*, August 27, 2001, p. 1; M. Wendland, "EDS Plots To Ignite New Ideas," *Detroit Free Press*, March 1, 2001.

77. J. Neff, "At Eureka Ranch, Execs Doff Wing Tips, Fire Up Ideas," *Adver-*

tising Age, 69 (March 9, 1998), pp. 28–29.

78. A. G. Robinson and S. Stern, *Corporate Creativity, How Innovation and Improvement Actually Happen* (San Francisco: Berrett-Koehler Publishers, 1997).

79. D. Beardsley, "This Company Doesn't Brake For (Sacred) Cows," *Fast Company*, 16 (August 1998).

80. T. Kelley, *The Art of Innovation* (N.Y.: Currency Doubleday, 2001), p. 69.

81. V. H. Vroom and A. G. Jago, *The New Leadership*, (Englewood Cliffs, NJ: Prentice-Hall, 1988), pp. 28–29.

82. R. B. Gallupe, W. H. Cooper, M. L. Grisé, and L. M. Bastianutti, "Blocking Electronic Brainstorms," *Journal of Applied Psychology*, 79 (1994), pp. 77–86; M. Diehl and W. Stroebe, "Productivity Loss in Idea-Generating Groups: Tracking Down the Blocking Effects," *Journal of Personality and Social Psychology*, 61 (1991), pp. 392–403.

83. B. E. Irmer and P. Bordia, "Evaluation Apprehension And Perceived Benefits In Interpersonal And Database Knowledge Sharing," *Academy of Management Proceedings* 2002, pp. B1–B6.

84. P. W. Mulvey, J. F. Veiga, P. M. Elsass, "When Teammates Raise a White Flag," *Academy of Management Executive*, 10 (February 1996), pp. 40–49.

85. S. Plous, *The Psychology of Judgment and Decision Making* (Philadelphia: Temple University Press, 1993), pp. 200–02.

86. B. Mullen, T. Anthony, E. Salas, and J. E. Driskell, "Group Cohesiveness and Quality of Decision Making: An Integration of Tests of the Groupthink Hypothesis," *Small Group Research*, 25 (1994), pp. 189–204; I. L. Janis, *Crucial Decisions* (New York: Free Press, 1989), pp. 56–63; I. L. Janis, *Groupthink: Psychological Studies of Policy Decisions and Fiascoes*, 2nd ed. (Boston: Houghton Mifflin, 1982).

87. M. E. Turner and A. R. Pratkanis, "Threat, Cohesion, and Group Effectiveness: Testing a Social Identity Maintenance Perspective on Groupthink," *Journal of Personality and Social Psychology*, 63 (1992), pp. 781–96.

88. M. Rempel and R. J. Fisher, "Perceived Threat, Cohesion, And Group

Problem Solving In Intergroup Conflict," *International Journal of Conflict Management*, 8 (1997), pp. 216–34.

89. C. McGarty, J. C. Turner, M. A. Hogg, B. David, and M. S. Wetherell, "Group Polarization as Conformity to the Prototypical Group Member," *British Journal of Social Psychology*, 31 (1992), pp. 1–20; D. Isenberg, "Group Polarization: A Critical Review and Meta-analysis," *Journal of Personality and Social Psychology*, 50 (1986), pp. 1141–51; D. G. Myers and H. Lamm, "The Group Polarization Phenomenon," *Psychological Bulletin*, 83 (1976), pp. 602–27.

90. D. Friedman, "Monty Hall's Three Doors: Construction and Deconstruction of a Choice Anomaly," *American Economic Review*, 88 (September 1998), pp. 933–46; D. Kahneman and A. Tversky, "Prospect Theory: An Analysis of Decision under Risk," *Econometrica*, 47 (1979), pp. 263–91. The influence of gambler's fallacy in terms of emotions and evolutionary psychology is discussed in: N. Nicholson, "Evolutionary Psychology: Toward a New View of Human Nature and Organizational Society," *Human Relations*, 50 (September 1997), pp. 1053–78.

91. Janis, *Crucial Decisions*, pp. 244–49.

92. F. A. Schull, A. L. Delbecq, and L. L. Cummings, *Organizational Decision Making* (New York: McGraw-Hill, 1970), pp. 144–49.

93. Sutton, *Weird Ideas that Work*, Chapter 8.; A. C. Amason, "Distinguishing the Effects of Functional and Dysfunctional Conflict on Strategic Decision Making: Resolving a Paradox for Top Management Teams," *Academy of Management Journal*, 39 (1996), pp. 123–48; G. Katzenstein, "The Debate on Structured Debate: Toward a Unified Theory," *Organizational Behaviour and Human Decision Processes*, 66 (1996), pp. 316–32; D. Tjosvold, *Team Organization: An Enduring Competitive Edge* (Chichester, U.K.: Wiley, 1991).

94. J. S. Valacich and C. Schwenk, "Structuring Conflict In Individual, Face-To-Face, And Computer-Mediated Group Decision Making: Carping Versus Objective Devil's Advocacy," *Decision Sciences*, 26 (1995), pp. 369–93; D. M. Schweiger, W. R. Sandberg, and P.

L. Rechner, "Experiential Effects of Dialectical Inquiry, Devil's Advocacy, and Consensus Approaches to Strategic Decision Making," *Academy of Management Journal*, 32 (1989), pp. 745–72.

95. C. J. Nemeth, J. B. Connell, J. Rogers, and K. S. Brown, "Improving Decision Making by Means of Dissent," *Journal of Applied Social Psychology*, 31 (2001), pp. 48–58.

96. K. M. Eisenhardt, J. L. Kahwajy, and L. J. Bourgeois, III "Conflict and Strategic Choice: How Top Management Teams Disagree," *California Management Review*, 39 (Winter 1997), pp. 42–62.

97. L. Tucci "Owens Drake Consulting Fosters Systematic Change," *St. Louis Business Journal*, May 25, 1998.

98. A. F. Osborn, *Applied Imagination* (New York: Scribner, 1957).

99. B. Mullen, C. Johnson, and E. Salas, "Productivity Loss in Brainstorming Groups: A Meta-analytic Integration," *Basic and Applied Psychology*, 12 (1991), pp. 2–23.

100. R. I. Sutton and A. Hargadon, "Brainstorming Groups in Context: Effectiveness in a Product Design Firm," *Administrative Science Quarterly*, 41 (1996), pp. 685–718; P. B. Paulus and M. T. Dzindolet "Social Influence Processes in Group Brainstorming," *Journal of Personality and Social Psychology*, 64 (1993), pp. 575–86; B. Mullen, Brian, C. Johnson, and E. Salas, "Productivity Loss in Brainstorming Groups: A Meta-Analytic Integration." *Basic and Applied Psychology*, 12 (1991), pp. 2–23.

101. A. R. Dennis and J. S. Valacich, "Electronic Brainstorming: Illusions and Patterns of Productivity," *Information Systems Research*, 10 (1999), pp. 375–377; R. B. Gallupe, A. R. Dennis, W. H. Cooper, J. S. Valacich, L. M. Bastianutti, and J. F. Nunamaker, Jr., "Electronic Brainstorming and Group Size," *Academy of Management Journal*, 35 (June 1992), pp. 350–69; R. B. Gallupe, L. M. Bastianutti, and W. H. Cooper, "Unblocking Brainstorms," *Journal of Applied Psychology* 76 (1991), pp. 137–42.

102. P. Bordia "Face-To-Face Versus Computer-Mediated Communication: A Synthesis of the Experimental Literature," *Journal of Business Communi-*

cation, 34 (1997), pp. 99–120; J. S. Valacich, A. R. Dennis, and T. Connolly "Idea Generation in Computer-Based Groups: A New Ending to an Old Story," *Organizational Behaviour and Human Decision Processes*, 57 (1994), pp. 448–67; R. B. Gallupe, W. H. Cooper, M. L. Grisé, and L. M. Bastianutti, "Blocking Electronic Brainstorms," *Journal of Applied Psychology*, 79 (1994), pp. 77–86.

103. G. Crone, "Electrifying Brainstorms," *National Post*, July 3, 1999, p. D11.

104. A. Pinsoneault, H. Barki, R.B. Gallupe, and N. Hoppen. "Electronic Brainstorming: The Illusion of Productivity," *Information Systems Research*, 10 (1999) pp. 110–33; B. Kabanoff and J. R. Rossiter, "Recent Developments in Applied Creativity," *International Review of Industrial and Organizational Psychology*, 9 (1994), pp. 283–324.

105. H. A. Linstone and M. Turoff (eds.) *The Delphi Method: Techniques and Applications* (Reading, MA: Addison-Wesley, 1975).

106. C. Critcher and B. Gladstone, "Utilizing the Delphi Technique in Policy Discussion: A Case Study of a Privatized Utility in Britain," *Public Administration*, 76 (Autumn 1998), pp. 431–49; S. R. Rubin et al., "Research Directions Related to Rehabilitation Practice: A Delphi Study," *Journal of Rehabilitation*, 64 (Winter 1998), p. 19.

107. A. L. Delbecq, A. H. Van de Ven, and D. H. Gustafson, *Group Techniques for Program Planning: A Guide to Nominal Group and Delphi Processes* (Middleton, Wis.: Green Briar Press, 1986).

108. A. B. Hollingshead, "The Rank-Order Effect In Group Decision Making," *Organizational Behaviour and Human Decision Processes*, 68 (1996), pp. 181–93.

109. S. Frankel, "NGT + MDS: An Adaptation of the Nominal Group Technique for Ill-Structured Problems," *Journal of Applied Behavioral Science*, 23 (1987), pp. 543–51; and D. M. Hegedus and R. Rasmussen, "Task Effectiveness and Interaction Process of a Modified Nominal Group Technique in Solving an Evaluation Problem," *Journal of Management*, 12 (1986), pp. 545–60.

CHAPTER ELEVEN

1. T. Whipp, "Walking in the President's Shoe," *Windsor Star*, December 3, 2001; J. Boxell, "Man who Sold $7bn Newbridge in Fresh Challenge," *Financial Times (London)*, September 10, 2001; P. Tam, "The Bulldog Unchained," *Ottawa Citizen*, July 24, 2000; K. Goff, "Workers Ponder their Futures," *Ottawa Citizen*, February 24, 2000; K. Standen, "Just What the Doctor Ordered," *Ottawa Citizen*, November 3, 1999; E. Mulqueen, "The Director's Chair—Pearse Flynn, Vice-President, Newbridge," *Irish Times*, August 27, 1999, p. 64; J. Bagnall, "Shaking Newbridge to the Core," *Ottawa Citizen*, March 17, 1999.

2. N. Sriussadaporn-Charoenngam and F. M. Jablin, "An Exploratory Study of Communication Competence in Thai Organizations," *Journal of Business Communication*, 36 (October 1999), pp. 382–418; F. M. Jablin et al., "Communication Competence in Organizations: Conceptualization and Comparison across Multiple Levels of Analysis," In L. Thayer & G. Barnett (Eds.), *Organization Communication: Emerging Perspectives*, Vol. 4 (Norwood, NJ: Ablex, 1994), pp. 114–40.

3. "Canadian CEOs Love Their 'Coaching' Jobs," *London Free Press*, September 10, 1999, p. D7; H. Mintzberg, *The Nature of Managerial Work* (New York: Harper & Row, 1973); E. T. Klemmer and F. W. Snyder, "Measurement of Time Spent Communicating," *Journal of Communication*, 22 (June 1972), pp. 142–58.

4. R. T. Barker and M. R. Camarata, "The Role of Communication in Creating and Maintaining a Learning Organization: Preconditions, Indicators, and Disciplines," *Journal of Business Communication*, 35 (October 1998), pp. 443–67.

5. R. Grenier and G. Metes, "Wake Up and Smell the Syzygy," *Business Communications Review*, 28 (August 1998), pp. 57–60; "We are the World," *CIO*, 9 (August 1996), p. 24.

6. G. Calabrese, "Communication and Co-operation in Product Development: A Case Study of a European Car Producer," *R & D Management*, 27 (July 1997), pp. 239–52; C. Downs, P. Clampitt, and A. L. Pfeiffer, "Communication and Organizational Outcomes," in *Handbook of Organizational Communication*, ed. G. Goldhaber & G. Barnett (Norwood, N.J.: Ablex, 1988), pp. 171–211.

7. V. L. Shalin, and G. V. Prabhu, "A Cognitive Perspective on Manual Assembly." *Ergonomics*, 39 (1996), pp. 108–127; I. Nonaka and H. Takeuchi, *The Knowledge-Creating Company* (New York: Oxford University Press, 1995).

8. T. Wanless, "Let's Hear it for Workers!" *Vancouver Province*, June 13, 2002; L. K. Lewis and D. R. Seibold, "Communication During Intraorganizational Innovation Adoption: Predicting User's Behavioral Coping Responses to Innovations in Organizations," *Communication Monographs*, 63 (2), (1996), pp. 131–57; R. J. Burke and D. S. Wilcox, "Effects of Different Patterns and Degrees of Openness in Superior—Subordinate Communication on Subordinate Satisfaction," *Academy of Management Journal*, 12 (1969), pp. 319–26.

9. C. E. Shannon and W. Weaver, *The Mathematical Theory of Communication* (Urbana, IL: University of Illinois Press, 1949). For a more recent discussion, see: K. J. Krone, F. M. Jablin, and L. L. Putnam, "Communication Theory and Organizational Communication: Multiple Perspectives," in F. M. Jablin, L. L. Putnam, K. H. Roberts, and L. W. Porter (eds.), *Handbook of Organizational Communication: An Interdisciplinary Perspective*, (Newbury Park, Calif.: Sage, 1987), pp. 18–40.

10. S. Axley, "Managerial and Organizational Communication in Terms of the Conduit Metaphor," *Academy of Management Review*, 9 (1984), pp. 428–37.

11. J. H. E. Andriessen, "Mediated Communication and New Organizational Forms," *International Review of Industrial and Organizational Psychology*, 6 (1991), pp. 17–70; L. Porter and K. Roberts, "Communication in Organizations," in *Handbook of Industrial and Organizational Psychology*, ed. M. Dunnette (Chicago: Rand McNally, 1976), pp. 1553–89.

12. F. Moore, "Storage faces Newest Challenge—Coping with Success," *Computer Technology Review*, 21 (September 2001), p. 1; S. D. Kennedy, "Finding a Cure for Information Anxiety," *Information Today*, May 1, 2001, p. 40; M. R. Overly, "E-Policy," *Messaging Magazine*, January/February 1999. For a discussion of the merits of e-mail, see: J. Hunter and M. Allen, "Adaptation to Electronic Mail," *Journal of Applied Communication Research*, August 1992, pp. 254–74; M. Culnan and M. L. Markus, "Information Technologies," in Jablin et al., (eds.) *Handbook of Organizational Communication: An Interdisciplinary Perspective*, pp. 420–43.

13. C. S. Saunders, D. Robey, and K. A. Vaverek, "The Persistence of Status Differentials in Computer Conferencing," *Human Communications Research*, 20 (1994), pp. 443–72; D. A. Adams, P. A. Todd, and R. R. Nelson, "A Comparative Evaluation of the Impact of Electronic and Voice Mail on Organizational Communication," *Information & Management*, 24 (1993), pp. 9–21.

14. "Eisner: E-mail Is Biggest Threat," *Associated Press*, May 12, 2000; A. D. Shulman, "Putting Group Information Technology in its Place: Communication and Good Work Group Performance," In Clegg et al (eds.) *Handbook of Organization Studies*, pp. 373–408.

15. J. Jamieson, "Net Marks 20 Years of the ;-)," *Vancouver Province*, September 20, 2002; S. Schafer, "Misunderstandings @ the Office," *Washington Post*, October 31, 2000, p. E1; M. Gibbs, "Don't Say it with Smileys," *Network World*, Aug 9, 1999, p. 62.

16. A. Gumbel, "How E-mail Puts Us in a Flaming Bad Temper," *The Independent* (London), January 3, 1999, p. 14; J. Kaye, "The Devil You Know," *Computer Weekly*, March 19, 1998, p. 46; S. Kennedy, "The Burning Issue of Electronic Hate Mail," *Computer Weekly*, June 5, 1997, p. 22

17. A. C. Poe, "Don't Touch That 'Send' Button!" *HRMagazine*, 46 (July 2001), pp. 74–80. Problems with e-mail are discussed in M. M. Extejt, "Teaching Students to Correspond Effectively Electronically: Tips for Using Electronic Mail Properly," *Business Communication Quarterly*, 61 (June 1998), pp. 57–67; V. Frazee, "Is E-mail Doing More Harm than Good?" *Personnel Journal*, 75 (May 1996), p. 23.

18. J. L. Locke, "Q: Is E-Mail Degrading Public and Private Discourse?; Yes:

Electronic Mail Is Making Us Rude, Lonely, Insensitive and Dishonest," *Insight on the News*, October 19, 1998, p. 24.

19. S. Stellin, "The Intranet Is Changing Many Firms From Within," *New York Times*, January 30, 2001.

20. S. Stellin, "The Intranet Is Changing Many Firms From Within," *New York Times*, January 30, 2001; A. Mahlon, "The Alternative Workplace: Changing Where and How People Work," *Harvard Business Review*, (May–June 1998), pp. 121–30; C. Meyer and S. Davis, *Blur: The Speed of Change in the Connected Economy*, (Reading, MA: Addison-Wesley, 1998); P. Bordia "Face-To-Face Versus Computer-Mediated Communication: A Synthesis of the Experimental Literature," *Journal of Business Communication*, 34 (January 1997), pp. 99–120.

21. M. McCance, "IM: Rapid, Risky," *Richmond Times-Dispatch*, July 19, 2001, p. A1; C. Hempel, "Instant-Message Gratification is What People Want," *Ventura County Star*, April 9, 2001.

22. D. Robb, "Ready or Not...Instant Messaging has Arrived as a Financial Planning Tool," *Journal of Financial Planning*, July, 2001, pp. 12–14.

23. W. Boei, "The Most Wired Person in Nunavut," *Ottawa Citizen*, November 13, 1999; S. De Santis, "Across Tundra and Cultures, Entrepreneur Wires Arctic," *Wall Street Journal*, October 19, 1998, p. B1; T. Saito, "Internet Helps Keep Scattered Inuit in Touch," *Daily Yomiuri*, June 7, 1997.

24. "New Age Heralds End of Information Overload," *Financial News*, December 8, 1998.

25. T. E. Harris, *Applied Organizational Communication: Perspectives, Principles, and Pragmatics* (Hillsdale, NJ: Lawrence Erlbaum Associates, 1993), Chapter 5; R. E. Rice and D. E. Shook, "Relationships of Job Categories and Organizational Levels to Use of Communication Channels, Including Electronic Mail: A Meta-Analysis and Extension," *Journal of Management Studies*, 27 (1990), pp. 195–229; Sitkin et al., "A Dual-Capacity Model of Communication Media Choice in Organizations," p. 584.

26. P. Ekman and E. Rosenberg, *What the Face Reveals: Basic and Applied Studies of Spontaneous Expression Using the Facial Action Coding System*. (Oxford, England: Oxford University Press, 1997).

27. B. Parkinson, *Ideas and Realities of Emotion* (London: Routledge, 1995), pp. 182–83; E. Hatfield, J. T. Cacioppo, and R. L. Rapson, *Emotional Contagion* (Cambridge, UK: Cambridge University Press, 1993).

28. J. R. Kelly and S. G. Barsade, "Mood and Emotions in Small Groups and Work Teams," *Organizational Behavior and Human Decision Processes*, 86 (September 2001), pp. 99–130.

29. R. L. Daft, R. H. Lengel, and L. K. Tevino, "Message Equivocality, Media Selection, and Manager Performance: Implications for Information Systems," *MIS Quarterly*, 11 (1987), pp. 355–66.

30. I. Lamont, "Do Your Far-flung Users Want to Communicate as if They Share an Office?" *Network World*, November 13, 2000.

31. R. Lengel and R. Daft, "The Selection of Communication Media as an Executive Skill," *Academy of Management Executive*, 2 (1988), pp. 225–32; G. Huber and R. Daft, "The Information Environments of Organizations," in Jablin et al. (eds.), *Handbook of Organizational Communication: An Interdisciplinary Perspective*, pp. 130–64; R. Daft and R. Lengel, "Information Richness: A New Approach to Managerial Behavior and Organization Design," *Research in Organizational Behavior*, 6 (1984), pp. 191–233.

32. R. E. Rice, "Task Analyzability, Use of New Media, and Effectiveness: A Multi-Site Exploration of Media Richness," *Organization Science*, 3 (1992) pp. 475–500; J. Fulk, C. W. Steinfield, J. Schmitz, and J. G. Power, "A Social Information Processing Model of Media Use in Organizations," *Communication Research*, 14 (1987), pp. 529–52.

33. R. Madhavan and R. Grover, "From Embedded Knowledge To Embodied Knowledge: New Product Development As Knowledge Management," *Journal of Marketing*, 62 (October 1998), pp. 1–12; D. Stork and A. Sapienza, "Task and Human Messages over the Project Life Cycle: Matching Media to Messages," *Project Management Journal*, 22 (December 1992), pp. 44–49.

34. John R Carlson and Robert W. Zmud, "Channel Expansion Theory and the Experiential Nature of Media Richness Perceptions," *Academy of Management Journal*, 42 (April 1999), pp. 153–70.

35. M. McLuhan, *Understanding Media: The Extensions of Man* (New York: McGraw-Hill, 1964).

36. S. B. Sitkin, K. M. Sutcliffe, and J. R. Barrios-Choplin, "A Dual-Capacity Model of Communication Media Choice in Organizations," *Human Communication Research*, 18 (June 1992), pp. 563–98; J. Schmitz and J. Fulk, "Organizational Colleagues, Media Richness, and Electronic Mail: A Test of the Social Influence Model of Technology Use," *Communication Research*, 18 (1991), pp. 487–523.

37. M. Meissner, "The Language of Work," In R. Dubin (ed.) *Handbook of Work, Organization, and Society*, (Chicago: Rand McNally, 1976), pp. 205–79.

38. D. Goleman, R. Boyatzis, and A. McKee, *Primal Leaders* (Boston: Harvard Business School Press, 2002), pp. 92–95.

39. M. J. Glauser, "Upward Information Flow in Organizations: Review and Conceptual Analysis," *Human Relations*, 37 (1984), pp. 613–43.

40. Translation: "Hi Jack, I've worked out a rough solution to the user interface problem. We need to examine the finer details. Unfortunately, I'm away next week, so you need to devote time and energy to this problem. I'm worried that the permanent Microsoft employees on this project will get really angry when they realize that we are getting behind on the released-to-manufacturing date." See: K. Barnes, "The Microsoft Lexicon," (www.cinepad .com/mslex.htm); S. Greenhouse, "Braindump on the Blue Badge: A Guide to Microspeak," *New York Times*, August 13, 1998, p. G1.

41. L. Larwood, "Don't Struggle to Scope Those Metaphors Yet," *Group and Organization Management*, 17 (1992), pp. 249–54; L. R. Pondy, P. J. Frost, G. Morgan, and T. C. Dandridge (eds.), *Organizational Symbolism* (Greenwich, Conn.: JAI Press, 1983).

42. L. Sahagun, "Cold War Foes Find Harmony in Satellite Launch Partnership," *Los Angeles Times*, July 25, 2001, p. B1.

43. M. J. Hatch, "Exploring the Empty Spaces of Organizing: How Improvisational Jazz helps Redescribe Organizational Structure," *Organization Studies*, 20 (1999), pp. 75–100; G. Morgan, *Images of Organization*, 2nd Ed. (Thousand Oaks, CA: Sage, 1997); L. L. Putnam, Nelson Phillips, and P. Chapman, "Metaphors of Communication and Organization," In S. R. Clegg, C. Hardy, and W. R. Nord (eds.) *Handbook of Organization Studies* (London: Sage, 1996), pp. 373–408; E. M. Eisenberg, "Ambiguity as a Strategy in Organizational Communication," *Communication Monographs*, 51 (1984), pp. 227–42; R. Daft and J. Wiginton, "Language and Organization," *Academy of Management Review*, 4 (1979), pp. 179–91.

44. M. Rubini and H. Sigall, "Taking the Edge Off of Disagreement: Linguistic Abstractness and Self-Presentation to a Heterogeneous Audience," *European Journal of Social Psychology*, 32 (2002), pp. 343–51.

45. B. Robins, "Why 'Sell' is Now a Four-Letter Word," *The Age (Melbourne)*, June 16, 2001.

46. "Information Technology In The 21st Century," *Globe and Mail*, September 17, 1999.

47. J.T. Koski, "Reflections on Information Glut and Other Issues in Knowledge Productivity," *Futures*, 33 (August 2001), pp. 483–95; C. Norton and A. Nathan, "Computer-mad Generation has a Memory Crash," *Sunday Times* (London), February 4, 2001; S. Bury, "Does E-mail Make you More Productive?" *Silicon Valley North*, September 1999.

48. From "The Best of Ideas," CBC Radio program, 1967. Cited at Web site www.mcluhan4managers.com

49. A. Edmunds and A. Morris, "The Problem of Information Overload in Business Organisations: A Review of the Literature," *International Journal of Information Management*, 20 (2000), pp. 17–28; A. G. Schick, L. A. Gordon, and S. Haka, "Information Overload: A Temporal Approach," *Accounting, Or-*ganizations & Society*, 15 (1990), pp. 199–220.

50. Schick et al., "Information Overload," pp. 209–14; C. Stohl and W. C. Redding, "Messages and Message Exchange Processes," in Jablin et al. (eds.) *Handbook of Organizational Communication*, pp. 451–502.

51. G. Dutton, "One Workforce, Many Languages," *Management Review*, 87 (December 1998), pp. 42–47.

52. G. Erasmus, "Why Can't We Talk?" *Globe and Mail*, March 9, 2002; D. Woodruff, "Crossing Culture Divide Early Clears Merger Paths," *Asian Wall Street Journal*, May 28, 2001, p. 9.

53. Mead, *Cross-Cultural Management Communication*, pp. 161–62; and J. V. Hill and C. L. Bovée, *Excellence in Business Communication* (New York: McGraw-Hill, 1993), Chapter 17.

54. F. Cunningham, "A Touch of the Tartan Treatment for Mazda," *The Scotsman*, October 14, 1997, p. 27.

55. R. M. March, *Reading the Japanese Mind* (Tokyo: Kodansha International, 1996), Chapter 1; H. Yamada, *American and Japanese Business Discourse: A Comparison of Interaction Styles* (Norwood, NJ: Ablex, 1992), p. 34.

56. One writer explains that Aboriginal people tend to avoid conflict, so differences are discussed over an open campfire which absorbs some of the potential conflict, and allows people to avoid direct eye contact. See H. Blagg, "A Just Measure of Shame?" *British Journal of Criminology*, 37 (Autumn 1997), pp. 481–501. For other differences in cross-cultural communication, see: R. Axtell, *Gestures: The Do's and Taboos of Body Language around the World* (New York: Wiley, 1991); P. Harris and R. Moran, *Managing Cultural Differences* (Houston: Gulf, 1987); and P. Ekman, W. V. Friesen, and J. Bear, "The International Language of Gestures," *Psychology Today*, May 1984, pp. 64–69.

57. H. Yamada, *Different Games, Different Rules* (New York: Oxford University Press, 1997), pp. 76–79; H. Yamada, *American and Japanese Business Discourse*, Chapter 2; D. Tannen, *Talking from 9 to 5* (New York: Avon, 1994), pp. 96–97; D. C. Barnlund, *Communication Styles of Japanese and Americans: Images and Realities* (Belmont, Calif.: Wadsworth, 1988).

58. D. Goleman, What Makes a Leader?" *Harvard Business Review*, 76 (November–December 1998), pp. 92–102.

59. This stereotypic notion is prevalent throughout J. Gray, *Men Are From Mars, Women Are From Venus* (New York: HarperCollins, 1992). For a critique of this view see: J. T. Wood, "A Critical Response to John Gray's Mars and Venus Portrayals of Men and Women," *Southern Communication Journal*, 67 (Winter 2002), pp. 201–10; D. J. Canary, T. M. Emmers-Sommer, *Sex and Gender Differences in Personal Relationships* (New York: Guilford Press, 1997), Chapter 1; M. Crawford, *Talking Difference: On Gender and Language* (Thousand Oaks, CA: Sage, 1995), Chapter 4.

60. Crawford, *Talking Difference: On Gender and Language*, pp. 41–44; Tannen, *Talking from 9 to 5*; D. Tannen, *You Just Don't Understand: Men and Women in Conversation* (New York: Ballentine Books, 1990); S. Helgesen, *The Female Advantage: Women's Ways of Leadership* (New York: Doubleday, 1990).

61. A. Mulac et al., "'Uh-Huh. What's That All About?' Differing Interpretations Of Conversational Backchannels and Questions as Sources of Miscommunication Across Gender Boundaries," *Communication Research*, 25 (December 1998), pp. 641–68; G. H. Graham, J. Unruh, and P. Jennings, "The Impact of Nonverbal Communication in Organizations: A Survey of Perceptions," *Journal of Business Communication*, 28 (1991), pp. 45–61; J. Hall, "Gender Effects in Decoding Nonverbal Cues," *Psychological Bulletin*, 68 (1978), pp. 845–57.

62. P. Tripp-Knowles "A Review of the Literature on Barriers Encountered by Women in Science Academia," *Resources for Feminist Research*, 24 (Spring/Summer 1995) pp. 28–34.

63. R. J. Grossman, "Emotions at Work," *Health Forum Journal*, 43 (September–October, 2000), pp. 18–22.

64. Cited in K. Davis and J. W. Newstrom, *Human Behavior at Work: Organizational Behavior*, 7th ed. (New York: McGraw-Hill, 1985), p. 438.

65. The three components of listening discussed here are based on several recent studies in the field of marketing, including: K. de Ruyter and M. G. M. Wetzels, "The Impact of Perceived Listening Behavior in Voice-to-Voice Service Encounters," *Journal of Service Research*, 2 (February 2000), pp. 276–84; S. B. Castleberry, C. D. Shepherd, and R. Ridnour, "Effective Interpersonal Listening in the Personal Selling Environment: Conceptualization, Measurement, and Nomological Validity," *Journal of Marketing Theory and Practice*, 7 (Winter 1999), pp. 30–38; L. B. Comer and T. Drollinger, "Active Empathetic Listening and Selling Success: A Conceptual Framework," *Journal of Personal Selling & Sales Management*, 19 (Winter 1999), pp. 15–29.

66. S. Silverstein, "On The Job But Do They Listen?," *Los Angeles Times*, July 19, 1998.

67. G. Evans and D. Johnson, "Stress and Open-Office Noise," *Journal of Applied Psychology*, 85 (2000), pp. 779–783.

68. F. Russo, "My Kingdom For A Door," *Time Magazine*, October 23, 2000, p. B1. The TBWA Chiat/Day office design and its problems are described in Hulsman, "Farewell, Corner Office"; "Why Chiat/Day is Putting Down its Binoculars," *Creative Review*, April 1998, p. 67; C. Knight, "Gone Virtual," *Canadian HR Reporter*, December 16, 1996, pp. 24, 26.

69. M. Misra and P. Misra, "Hughes Software: Fun & Flexibility," *Business Today*, January 7, 2001, p. 182.

70. B. Sosnin, "Digital Newsletters 'E-volutionize' Employee Communications," *HRMagazine*, 46 (May 2001), pp. 99–107; G. Grates, "Is the Employee Publication Extinct?" *Communication World*, 17 (December 1999/January 2000), pp. 27–30.

71. A. Gordon, "Perks and Stock Options are Great, But it's Attitude that Makes the Difference," *Globe and Mail*, January 28, 2000; B. Schneider, S. D. Ashworth, A. C. Higgs, and L. Carr, "Design, Validity, and Use of Strategically Focused Employee Attitude Surveys," *Personnel Psychology*, 49 (1996), pp. 695–705; T. Geddie, "Surveys are a Waste of Time...Until You Use Them,"

Communication World, April 1996, pp. 24–26; D. M. Saunders and J. D. Leck, "Formal Upward Communication Procedures: Organizational and Employee Perspectives," *Canadian Journal of Administrative Sciences*, 10 (1993), pp. 255–68.

72. The original term is "management by *wandering* around," but this has been replaced with "walking" over the years. T. Peters and R. Waterman, *In Search of Excellence* (New York: Harper and Row, 1982), p. 122; W. Ouchi, *Theory Z* (New York: Avon Books, 1981), pp. 176–77.

73. D. Penner, "Putting the Boss out Front," *Vancouver Sun*, June 7, 2002.

74. M. Duffy, "Jobs Cloud Lifts for Staff at Mitsubishi," *The Advertiser*, April 3, 2001, p. 12; M. Duffy, "Contract a Lifeline for Mitsubishi," *Herald Sun*, April 3, 2001; Duffy, "Welcome to the Future," *The Advertiser*, November 29, 2000, p. 1; M. Duffy, "Japan Backs Mitsubishi," *The Advertiser*, November 28, 2000, pp. 1, 6; M. Duffy, "Let Us Get On With It," *The Advertiser*, November 18, 2000, p. 1.

75. "Survey Finds Good And Bad Points On Worker Attitudes," *Eastern Pennsylvania Business Journal*, May 5, 1997, p. 13.

76. G. Kreps, *Organizational Communication* (White Plains, N.Y.: Longman, 1986), pp. 202–206; W. L. Davis and J. R. O'Connor, "Serial Transmission of Information: A Study of the Grapevine," *Journal of Applied Communication Research*, 5 (1977), pp. 61–72; K. Davis, "Management Communication and the Grapevine," *Harvard Business Review*, 31 (September–October 1953), pp. 43–49.

77. J. N. Lynem, "Sex, Lies and Message Boards," *San Francisco Chronicle*, July 1, 2001, p. W1; D. E. Lewis, "Firms Try to Cope with Rumors, Gossip on Online Message Boards," *Boston Globe*, May 17, 2001; M. Schrage, "If You Can't Say Anything Nice, Say It Anonymously," *Fortune*, December 6, 1999, p. 352; S. Caudron, "Employeechat.com: Bashing HR on the Web," *Workforce*, 78 (December 1999), pp. 36–42.

78. D. Krackhardt and J. R. Hanson, "Informal Networks: The Company Behind the Chart," *Harvard Business Review*, 71 (July–August 1993), pp.

104–11; H. Mintzberg, *The Structuring of Organizations* (Englewood Cliffs, NJ: Prentice Hall, 1979), pp. 46–53.

79. M. Noon and R. Delbridge, "News from Behind My Hand: Gossip in Organizations," *Organization Studies*, 14 (1993), pp. 23–36; R. L. Rosnow, "Inside Rumor: A Personal Journey," *American Psychologist*, 46 (May 1991), pp. 484–96; C. J. Walker and C. A. Beckerle, "The Effect of State Anxiety on Rumor Transmission," *Journal of Social Behavior & Personality*, 2 (August 1987), pp. 353–60.

80. N. Nicholson, "Evolutionary Psychology: Toward a New View of Human Nature and Organizational Society," *Human Relations*, 50 (September 1997), pp. 1053–78.

81. "Odd Spot," *The Age (Melbourne)*, July 20, 2001, p. 1.

CHAPTER TWELVE

1. G. Teel, "The Ultimate Power Play for Sealing Deals," *Calgary Herald*, June 29, 2002; I. Bailey, "Golf 101: Put Down that Club, We're Making Deals over Here," *National Post*, September 27, 2001; T. Wanless, "Business and Golfing—Par for the Course," *Vancouver Province*, June 10, 2001; S. J. Wells, "Smoothing the Way," *HRMagazine* 46 (June 2001), pp. 52–58.

2. C. Hardy and S. Leiba-O'Sullivan, "The Power Behind Empowerment: Implications For Research And Practice," *Human Relations*, 51 (April 1998), pp. 451–83; R. Farson, *Management of the Absurd*, (New York: Simon & Schuster, 1996), Chapter 13; R. M. Cyert and J. G. March, *A Behavioral Theory of the Firm* (Englewood Cliffs, N.J.: Prentice Hall, 1963).

3. For a discussion of the definition of power, see: J. M. Whitmeyer, "Power through Appointment," *Social Science Research*, 29 (2000), pp. 535–55; J. Pfeffer, *New Directions in Organizational Theory* (New York: Oxford University Press, 1997), Chapter 6; J. Pfeffer, *Managing with Power* (Boston: Harvard Business University Press, 1992), pp. 17, 30; H. Mintzberg, *Power In and Around Organizations* (Englewood Cliffs, NJ: Prentice Hall, 1983), Chapter 1.

4. A. M. Pettigrew, *The Politics of Organizational Decision-Making* (London:

Tavistock, 1973); R. M. Emerson, "Power-Dependence Relations," *American Sociological Review*, 27 (1962), pp. 31–41; R. A. Dahl, "The Concept of Power," *Behavioral Science*, 2 (1957), pp. 201–18.

5. D. J. Brass and M. E. Burkhardt, "Potential Power and Power Use: An Investigation of Structure and Behaviour," *Academy of Management Journal*, 36 (1993), pp. 441–70; K. M. Bartol and D. C. Martin, "When Politics Pays: Factors Influencing Managerial Compensation Decisions," *Personnel Psychology*, 43 (1990), pp. 599–614.

6. P. P. Carson and K. D. Carson, "Social Power Bases: A Meta-Analytic Examination of Interrelationships and Outcomes," *Journal of Applied Social Psychology*, 23 (1993), pp. 1150–69; P. Podsakoff and C. Schreisheim, "Field Studies of French and Raven's Bases of Power: Critique, Analysis, and Suggestions for Future Research," *Psychological Bulletin*, 97 (1985), pp. 387–411; J. R. P. French and B. Raven, "The Bases of Social Power," in D. Cartwright (ed.) *Studies in Social Power*, (Ann Arbor, Mich.: University of Michigan Press, 1959), pp. 150–67.

7. For example, see S. Finkelstein, "Power in Top Management Teams: Dimensions. Measurement, And Validation," *Academy of Management Journal*, 35 (1992), pp. 505–38.

8. G. Yukl and C. M. Falbe, "Importance of Different Power Sources in Downward and Lateral Relations," *Journal of Applied Psychology*, 76 (1991), pp. 416–23.

9. G. A. Yukl, *Leadership in Organizations*, 3rd ed. (Englewood Cliffs, NJ: Prentice Hall, 1994), p. 13; B. H. Raven, "The Bases of Power: Origins and Recent Developments," *Journal of Social Issues*, 49 (1993), pp. 227–51.

10. C. Hardy and S. R. Clegg, "Some Dare Call It Power," In S. R. Clegg, C. Hardy, and W. R. Nord, (Eds.) *Handbook of Organization Studies* (London: Sage, 1996), pp. 622–41; C. Barnard, *The Function of the Executive*. (Cambridge, MA: Harvard University Press, 1938).

11. I. Nonaka and H. Takeuchi, *The Knowledge-Creating Company* (New York: Oxford University Press, 1995), pp. 138–39.

12. H. Schachter, "The 21st Century CEO," *Profit*, April 1999, p. 25; J. A. Conger, *Winning 'em Over* (New York: Simon & Shuster, 1998), Appendix A.

13. "Empowerment Torture to Some," *Tampa Tribune*, October 5, 1997, p. 6. Peer pressure at CAMI is described in: D. Robertson, J. Rinehart, C. Huxley, and the CAW Research Group at CAMI, "Team Concept and Kaizen: Japanese Production Management in a Unionized Canadian Auto Plant," *Studies in Political Economy*, 39 (Autumn 1992), pp. 77–107. For discussion of peer pressure, see: M. L. Loughry, "Co-workers Are Watching: Performance Implications Of Peer Monitoring," *Academy of Management Best Papers Proceedings 2002*, pp. O1–O6; J. A. LePine and L. Van Dyne, "Peer Responses to Low Performers: An Attributional Model of Helping in the Context of Groups," *Academy of Management Review*, 26 (2001), pp. 67–84; G. Sewell, "The Discipline of Teams: The Control of Team-Based Industrial Work through Electronic and Peer Surveillance," *Administrative Science Quarterly* 43 (June 1998), pp. 397–428. For a detailed discussion of coercive and reward power in network structures, see: L. D. Molm, *Coercive Power in Social Exchange*. (Cambridge: Cambridge University Press, 1997).

14. J. D. Kudisch and M. L. Poteet, "Expert Power, Referent Power, and Charisma: Toward the Resolution of a Theoretical Debate," *Journal of Business & Psychology*, 10 (Winter 1995), pp. 177–95

15. Information was identified as a form of influence, but not power, in the original French and Raven writing. Information was added as a sixth source of power in subsequent writing by Raven, but this book takes the view that information power is derived from the original five sources. See B. H. Raven, "Kurt Lewin Address: Influence, Power, Religion, and the Mechanisms of Social Control," *Journal of Social Issues*, 55 (Spring 1999), pp. 161–86; Yukl and Falbe, "Importance of Different Power Sources in Downward and Lateral Relations."

16. "Corporate Culture Instilled Online," *The Economist*, November 11, 2000.

17. D. J. Brass, "Being in the Right Place: A Structural Analysis of Individual Influence in an Organization," *Administrative Science Quarterly*, 29 (1984), pp. 518–39; N. M. Tichy, M. L. Tuchman, and C. Frombrun, "Social Network Analysis in Organizations," *Academy of Management Review*, 4 (1979), pp. 507–19; H. Guetzkow and H. Simon, "The Impact of Certain Communication Nets upon Organization and Performance in Task-Oriented Groups," *Management Science*, 1 (1955), pp. 233–50.

18. R. Colapinto, "Nine-to-Five Nirvana," *Canadian Business*, 72 (April 30, 1999), pp. 34–38.

19. C. S. Saunders, "The Strategic Contingency Theory of Power: Multiple Perspectives," *The Journal of Management Studies*, 27 (1990), pp. 1–21; D. J. Hickson, C. R. Hinings, C. A. Lee, R. E. Schneck, and J. M. Pennings, "A Strategic Contingencies' Theory of Intraorganizational Power," *Administrative Science Quarterly*, 16 (1971), pp. 216–27; J. D. Thompson, *Organizations in Action* (New York: McGraw-Hill, 1967).

20. C. R. Hinings, D. J. Hickson, J. M. Pennings, and R. E. Schneck, "Structural Conditions of Intraorganizational Power," *Administrative Science Quarterly*, 19 (1974), pp. 22–44.

21. Hickson et al., "A Strategic Contingencies' Theory of Intraorganizational Power;" Hinings et al., "Structural Conditions of Intraorganizational Power;" and R. M. Kanter, "Power Failure in Management Circuits," *Harvard Business Review*, July–August 1979, pp. 65–75.

22. M. Crozier, *The Bureaucratic Phenomenon* (London: Tavistock, 1964).

23. M. F. Masters, *Unions at the Crossroads: Strategic Membership, Financial, and Political Perspectives* (Westport, CT: Quorum Books, 1997).

24. D. Beveridge, "Job Actions Hit World's Airlines during Year's Busiest Flying Season," *Canadian Press*, July 10, 2001; M. O'Dell, "Airlines Grounded by the Rise of Pilot Power," *Financial Times (UK)*, July 3, 2001.

25. Brass and Burkhardt, "Potential Power and Power Use," pp. 441–70; Hickson et al., "A Strategic Contingencies' Theory of Intraorganizational

Power," pp. 219–21; J. D. Hackman, "Power and Centrality in the Allocation of Resources in Colleges and Universities," *Administrative Science Quarterly*, 30 (1985), pp. 61–77.

26. D. Wanagas, "Still Possible to Save some Face," *National Post*, July 6, 2002; "Medical Officer of Health Orders Garbage Cleanup," *CBC News* (online), July 5, 2002; "Toronto Tourism Industry Worried Strike Will Damage Reputation," *CBC News* (online), July 5, 2002; "Toronto Strike Keeps Growing," *CBC News* (online), July 4, 2002.

27. L. Holden, "European Managers: HRM and an Evolving Role," *European Business Review*, 12 (2000), pp. 251–60; Kanter, "Power Failure in Management Circuits," p. 68; B. E. Ashforth, "The Experience of Powerlessness in Organizations," *Organizational Behaviour and Human Decision Processes*, 43 (1989), pp. 207–42.

28. M. L. A. Hayward and W. Boeker, "Power and Conflicts Of Interest In Professional Firms: Evidence From Investment Banking," *Administrative Science Quarterly*, 43 (March 1998), pp. 1–22.

29. R. Madell, "Ground Floor," *Pharmaceutical Executive (Women in Pharma Supplement)*, June 2000, pp. 24–31.

30. Raven, "The Bases of Power," pp. 237–39.

31. L. A. Perlow, "The Time Famine: Toward a Sociology of Work Time," *Administrative Science Quarterly*, 44 (March 1999), pp. 5–31.

32. M. C. Higgins and K. E. Kram, "Reconceptualizing Mentoring at Work: A Developmental Network Perspective," *Academy of Management Review*, 26 (April 2001), pp. 264–88; B. R. Ragins, "Diversified Mentoring Relationships in Organizations: A Power Perspective," *Academy of Management Review*, 22 (1997), pp. 482–521.

33. D. Krackhardt and J. R. Hanson, "Informal Networks: The Company Behind the Chart," *Harvard Business Review*, 71 (July–August 1993), pp. 104–11; and R. E. Kaplan, "Trade Routes: The Manager's Network of Relationships," *Organizational Dynamics*, Spring 1984, pp. 37–52.

34. A. Mehra, M. Kilduff, and D. J. Brass, "The Social Networks of High and Low Self-monitors: Implications for Workplace Performance," *Administrative Science Quarterly*, 46 (March 2001), pp. 121–46.

35. M. Linehan, "Barriers to Women's Participation in International Management," *European Business Review*, 13 (2001), pp. 10–18; R. J. Burke and C. A. McKeen, "Women in Management," *International Review of Industrial and Organizational Psychology*, 7 (1992), pp. 245–83; B. R. Ragins and E. Sundstrom, "Gender and Power in Organizations: A Longitudinal Perspective," *Psychological Bulletin*, 105 (1989), pp. 51–88.

36. D. M. McCracken, "Winning the Talent War for Women: Sometimes It Takes a Revolution," *Harvard Business Review*, (November-December 2000), pp. 159–67; D. L Nelson and R. J. Burke, "Women Executives: Health, Stress, and Success," *Academy of Management Executive*, 14 (May 2000), pp. 107–21.

37. C. M. Schaefer and T. R. Tudor, "Managing Workplace Romances," *SAM Advanced Management Journal*, 66 (Summer 2001), pp. 4–10; S. Ulfelder, "Cupid hits Cubeland," *Boston Globe*, February 11, 2001, p. H1; R. Dhooma, "Taking Care of Business and Pleasure," *Toronto Sun*, September 20, 1999, p. 38; A. Kingston, "Working It," *Flare*, 21 (April 1999), pp 104, 106; E. Edmonds, "Love and Work," *Ottawa Sun*, February 14, 1999, p. S10. Also see G. N. Powell and S. Foley, "Something to Talk About: Romantic Relationships in Organizational Settings," *Journal of Management*, 24 (1998), pp. 421–28.

38. "Work Life," *Arizona Daily Star*, February 18, 2001, p. D1. For a discussion of perceived justice and office romance, see: S. Foley and G. N. Powell, "Not All is Fair in Love and Work: Coworkers' Preferences for and Responses to Managerial Interventions Regarding Workplace Romances," *Journal of Organizational Behavior*, 20 (1999), pp. 1043–56.

39. S. Ulfelder, "Cupid hits Cubeland," *Boston Globe*, February 11, 2001, p. H1. For a detailed discussion of workplace romance and sexual harassment, see: C. A. Pierce and H. Aguinis, "Link Between Workplace Romance and Sexual Harassment," *Group & Organization Management*, 26 (June 2001), pp. 206–29.

40. M. Solomon, "The Secret's Out: How to Handle the Truth of Workplace Romance," *Workforce*, 7 (July 1998), pp. 42–48. Also see C. A Pierce and H. Aguinis, "A Framework for Investigating the Link Between Workplace Romance and Sexual Harassment," *Group & Organization Management*, 26 (June 2001), pp. 206–229; N. Nejat-Bina, "Employers as Vigilant Chaperones Armed with Dating Waivers: The Intersection of Unwelcomeness and Employer Liability in Hostile Work Environment Sexual Harassment Law," *Berkeley Journal of Employment and Labor Law*, December 22, 1999, pp. 325ff.

41. A. Somech and A. Drach-Zahavy, "Relative Power and Influence Strategy: The Effects of Agent/Target Organizational Power on Superiors' Choices of Influence Strategies," *Journal of Organizational Behavior*, 23 (2002), pp. 167–79; K. Atuahene-Gima and H. Li, "Marketing's Influence Tactics in New Product Development: A Study of High Technology Firms in China," *Journal of Product Innovation Management*, 17 (2000), pp. 451–70.

42. D. Katz and R. L. Kahn, *The Social Psychology of Organizations*. (New York: Wiley, 1966), p. 301.

43. W. A. Hochwarter, A. W. Pearson, G. R. Ferris, P. L. Perrewe, and D. A. Ralston, "A Reexamination of Schriesheim and Hinkin's (1990) Measure of Upward Influence," *Educational and Psychological Measurement*, 60 (October 2000), pp. 755–71; C. Schriesheim and T. Hinkin, "Influence Tactics Used by Subordinates: A Theoretical and Empirical Analysis and Refinement of the Kipnis, Schmidt, and Wilkinson subscales," *Journal of Applied Psychology*, 75 (1990), pp. 246–257. The original research involving student essays is reported in: D. Kipnis, S. M. Schmidt, and I. Wilkinson, 1. "Intraorganizational Influence Tactics: Explorations in Getting One's Way," *Journal of Applied Psychology*, 65 (1980), pp. 440–52.

44. Some of the more thorough lists of influence tactics are presented in: L. A. McFarland, A. M. Ryan, and S. D.

Kriska, "Field Study Investigation of Applicant Use of Influence Tactics in a Selection Interview," *Journal of Psychology*, 136 (July 2002), pp. 383–98; A. Rao, K. Hashimoto, and A. Rao, "Universal and Culturally Specific Aspects of Managerial Influence: A Study of Japanese Managers," *Leadership Quarterly*, 8 (1997), pp. 295–312.

45. A. Rao, K. Hashimoto, and A. Rao, "Universal and Culturally Specific Aspects of Managerial Influence: A Study of Japanese Managers," *Leadership Quarterly*, 8 (1997), pp. 295–312. Silent authority as an influence tactic in non-Western cultures is also discussed in: S. F. Pasa, "Leadership Influence in a High Power Distance and Collectivist Culture," *Leadership & Organization Development Journal*, 21 (2000), pp. 414–26.

46. A. W. Gouldner, "The Norm of Reciprocity: A Preliminary Statement," *American Sociological Review*, 25 (1960), pp. 161–78.

47. E. A. Mannix, "Organizations as Resource Dilemmas: The Effects of Power Balance on Coalition Formation in Small Groups." *Organizational Behaviour and Human Decision Processes*, 55 (1993), pp. 1–22; A. T. Cobb, "Toward the Study of Organizational Coalitions: Participant Concerns and Activities in a Simulated Organizational Setting," *Human Relations*, 44 (1991), pp. 1057–79; W. B. Stevenson, J. L. Pearce, and L. W. Porter, "The Concept of 'Coalition' in Organization Theory and Research," *Academy of Management Review*, 10 (1985), pp. 256–68.

48. D. J. Terry, M. A. Hogg, and K. M. White, "The Theory of Planned Behaviour: Self-Identity, Social Identity and Group Norms," *British Journal of Social Psychology*, 38 (September 1999), pp. 225–44.

49. M. Warshaw, "The Good Guy's Guide to Office Politics," *Fast Company*, Issue 14 (April-May 1998), pp. 157–78.

50. Rao et al, "Universal and Culturally Specific Aspects of Managerial Influence."

51. D. Strutton and L. E. Pelton, "Effects of Ingratiation on Lateral Relationship Quality Within Sales Team Settings," *Journal of Business Research*, 43 (1998), pp. 1–12.

52. H. G. Enns, S. L. Huff, and B. R. Golden, "How CIOs Obtain Peer Commitment to Strategic IS Proposals: Barriers and Facilitators," *Journal of Strategic Information Systems*, 10 (March 2001), pp. 3–14; G. Yukl, *Leadership in Organizations (3rd ed.)*, (Englewood Cliffs, NJ: Prentice Hall, 1994).

53. D. Strutton, L. E. Pelton, and J. F. Tanner, Jr., "Shall We Gather in the Garden: The Effect of Ingratiatory Behaviors on Buyer Trust in Salespeople," *Industrial Marketing Management*, 25 (1996): 151–62; R. Thacker and S. I. Wayne, "An Examination of the Relationship Between Upward Influence Tactics and Assessments of Promotability," *Journal of Management*, 21 (1995), pp. 739–56.

54. A. Rao and S. M. Schmidt, "Upward Impression Management: Goals, Influence Strategies, and Consequences," *Human Relations*, 48 (1995), pp. 147–67; R. A. Giacalone and P. Rosenfeld (eds.), *Applied Impression Management* (Newbury Park, Calif.: Sage, 1991); and J. T. Tedeschi (ed.), *Impression Management Theory and Social Psychological Research* (New York: Academic Press, 1981).

55. W. L. Gardner III, "Lessons in Organizational Dramaturgy: The Art of Impression Management," *Organizational Dynamics*, Summer 1992, pp. 33–46; R. C. Liden and T. R. Mitchell, "Ingratiatory Behaviours in Organizational Settings," *Academy of Management Review*, 13 (1988), pp. 572–87.

56. A. Vuong, "Job Applicants Often don't Tell Whole Truth," *Denver Post*, May 30, 2001, p. C1. For a discussion of research on false résumés, see: S. L. McShane, "Applicant Misrepresentation in Résumés and Interviews," *Labor Law Journal*, 45 (January 1994), pp. 15–24.

57. L. A. McFarland, A. M. Ryan, and S. D. Kriska, "Field Study Investigation of Applicant Use of Influence Tactics in a Selection Interview," *Journal of Psychology*, 136 (July 2002), pp. 383–98; G. Yukl and J. B. Tracey, "Consequences of Influence Tactics Used with Subordinates, Peers, and the Boss," *Journal of Applied Psychology*, 77 (1992), pp. 525–35.

58. Fortunately, some recent writing on persuasion influence tactics incorporates the role of emotions. See: S. Fox and Y. Amichai-Hamburger, "The Power of Emotional Appeals in Promoting Organizational Change Programs," *Academy of Management Executive*, 15 (November 2001), pp. 84–94.

59. A. P. Brief, *Attitudes In and Around Organizations* (Thousand Oaks, CA: Sage, 1998), pp. 69–84; K. K. Reardon, *Persuasion in Practice* (Newbury Park, CA: Sage, 1991); P. Zimbardo and E. B. Ebbeson, *Influencing Attitudes and Changing Behavior* (Reading, Mass.: Addison-Wesley, 1969).

60. J. J. Jiang, G. Klein, and R. G. Vedder, "Persuasive Expert Systems: The Influence of Confidence and Discrepancy," *Computers in Human Behavior*, 16 (March 2000), pp. 99–109; J. A. Conger, *Winning 'Em Over: A New Model for Managing in the Age of Persuasion* (New York: Simon & Schuster, 1998); J. Cooper and R. T. Coyle, "Attitudes and Attitude Change," *Annual Review of Psychology*, 35 (1984), pp. 395–426.

61. E. Aronson, *The Social Animal* (San Francisco: W. H. Freeman, 1976), pp. 67–68; R. A. Jones and J. W. Brehm, "Persuasiveness of One- and Two-Sided Communications as a Function of Awareness that There Are Two Sides," *Journal of Experimental Social Psychology*, 6 (1970), pp. 47–56.

62. D. G. Linz and S. Penrod, "Increasing Attorney Persuasiveness in the Courtroom," *Law and Psychology Review* 8 (1984), pp. 1–47; R. B. Zajonc, "Attitudinal Effects of Mere Exposure," *Journal of Personality and Social Psychology Monograph*, 9 (1968), pp. 1–27; R. Petty and J. Cacioppo, *Attitudes and Persuasion: Classic and Contemporary Approaches* (Dubuque, Iowa: W. C. Brown, 1981).

63. Conger, *Winning 'Em Over*.

64. M. Zellner, "Self-Esteem, Reception, and Influenceability," *Journal of Personality and Social Psychology*, 15 (1970), pp. 87–93.

65. C. P. Egri, D. A. Ralston, C. S. Murray, and J. D. Nicholson, "Managers in the NAFTA Countries: A Cross-Cultural Comparison of Attitudes Toward Upward Influence Strategies," *Journal of International Management*, 6 (2000), pp. 149–71.

66. "Be Part of the Team if you Want to Catch the Eye," *Birmingham Post (UK)*, August 31, 2000, p. 14.

67. Y. Gabriel, "An Introduction to the Social Psychology of Insults in Organizations," *Human Relations*, 51 (November 1998), pp. 1329–54.

68. L. A. McFarland, A. M. Ryan, and S. D. Kriska, "Field Study Investigation of Applicant Use of Influence Tactics in a Selection Interview," *Journal of Psychology*, 136 (July 2002), pp. 383–98; Somech and Drach-Zahavy, "Relative Power and Influence Strategy"; R. C. Ringer and R. W. Boss, "Hospital Professionals' Use of Upward Influence Tactics," *Journal of Managerial Issues*, 12 (Spring 2000), pp. 92–108; B. H. Raven, J. Schwarzwald, and M. Koslowsky, "Conceptualizing and Measuring a Power/Interaction Model of Interpersonal Influence," *Journal of Applied Social Psychology*, 28 (1998), pp. 307–32.

69. Falbe and Yukl, "Consequences for Managers of Using Single Influence Tactics and Combinations of Tactics," pp. 638–52. The effectiveness of coalitions in marketing is described in: K. Atuahene-Gima and H. Li, "Marketing's Influence Tactics in New Product Development: A Study of High Technology Firms in China," *Journal of Product Innovation Management*, 17 (2000), pp. 451–70.

70. C. M. Falbe and G. Yukl, "Consequences for Managers of Using Single Influence Tactics and Combinations of Tactics," *Academy of Management Journal*, 35 (1992), pp. 638–52.

71. J. R. Schermerhorn, Jr. and M. H. Bond, "Upward and Downward Influence Tactics in Managerial Networks: A Comparative Study of Hong Kong Chinese and Americans," *Asia Pacific Journal of Management*, 8 (1991), pp. 147–58.

72. K. R. Xin and A. S. Tsui, "Different Strokes for Different Folks? Influence Tactics by Asian-American and Caucasian-American Managers," *Leadership Quarterly*, 7 (l996), 109–32.

73. H. G. Enns, S. L. Huff, and B. R. Golden, "How CIOs Obtain Peer Commitment to Strategic IS Proposals: Barriers and Facilitators," *Journal of Strategic Information Systems*, 10 (March 2001), pp. 3–14; R. C. Ringer and R. W. Boss, "Hospital Professionals' Use of Upward Influence Tactics," *Journal of Managerial Issues*, 12 (Spring 2000), pp. 92–108.

74. N. Martin, " Men 'Gossip more than Women to Boost their Egos'," *Daily Telegraph (UK)*, June 15, 2001, p. P13; Tannen, *Talking From 9 to 5*, Chapter 2; M. Crawford, *Talking Difference: On Gender and Language* (Thousand Oaks, CA: Sage, 1995), pp. 41–44; D. Tannen, *Talking From 9 to 5* (New York: Avon, 1995), pp. 137–41, 151–52; D. Tannen, *You Just Don't Understand: Men and Women in Conversation* (New York: Ballentine Books, 1990); S. Helgesen, *The Female Advantage: Women's Ways of Leadership* (New York: Doubleday, 1990).

75. L. L. Carli, "Gender, Interpersonal Power, and Social Influence," *Journal of Social Issues*, 55 (Spring 1999), pp. 81ff; E. H. Buttner and M. McEnally, "The Interactive Effect of Influence Tactic, Applicant Gender, and Type of Job on Hiring Recommendations," *Sex Roles*, 34 (1996), pp. 581–91; S. Mann, "Politics and Power in Organizations: Why Women Lose Out," *Leadership & Organization Development Journal*, 16 (1995), pp. 9–15.

76. E. Vigoda and A. Cohen, "Influence Tactics and Perceptions of Organizational Politics: A Longitudinal Study," *Journal of Business Research*, 55 (2002), pp. 311–24; R. Cropanzano, J. C. Howes, A. A. Grandey, and P. Toth, "The Relationship of Organizational Politics and Support to Work Behaviors, Attitudes, And Stress," *Journal of Organizational Behavior*, 18 (1997), pp. 159–80.

77. W. E. O'Connor and T. G. Morrison, "A Comparison of Situational and Dispositional Predictors of Perceptions of Organizational Politics," *Journal of Psychology*, 135 (May 2001), pp. 301–12.

78. E. Vigoda, "Stress-related Aftermaths to Workplace Politics: The Relationships Among Politics, Job Distress, and Aggressive Behavior in Organizations," *Journal of Organizational Behavior*, 23 (2002), pp. 571–91; K. M. Kacmar and R. A. Baron, "Organizational Politics: The State of the Field, Links to Related Processes, and an Agenda for Future Research," In G. R. Ferris (Ed.), *Research in Personnel and Human Resources Management*, (Greenwich, CT: JAI Press, 1999), pp. 1–39; K. M. Kacmar, D. P. Bozeman, D. S. Carlson, and W. P. Anthony, "An Examination of the Perceptions of Organizational Politics Model: Replication and Extension," *Human Relations*, 52 (1999), pp. 383–416; J. M. Maslyn and D. B. Fedor, "Perceptions of Politics: Does Measuring Different Foci Matter?" *Journal of Applied Psychology*, 84 (1998), pp. 645–53.

79. D. Sandahl and C. Hewes," Decision Making at Digital Speed," *Pharmaceutical Executive*, 21 (August 2001), p. 62; "Notes About Where We Work and How We Make Ends Meet," *Arizona Daily Star*, February 18, 2001, p. D1.

80. C. Hardy, *Strategies for Retrenchment and Turnaround: The Politics of Survival* (Berlin: Walter de Gruyter, 1990), Chapter 14; J. Gandz and V. V. Murray, "The Experience of Workplace Politics," *Academy of Management Journal*, 23 (1980), pp. 237–251.

81. P. Dillon, "Failure IS an Option," *Fast Company*, Issue 22 (February-March, 1999), pp. 154–71.

82. M. C. Andrews and K. M. Kacmar, "Discriminating Among Organizational Politics, Justice, and Support," *Journal of Organizational Behavior*, 22 (2001), pp. 347–66.

83. G. R. Ferris, G. S. Russ, and P. M. Fandt, "Politics in Organizations," in R. A. Giacalone and P. Rosenfeld (Eds.) *Impression Management in the Organization*, (Hillsdale, N.J.:Erlbaum, 1989), pp. 143–70; H. Mintzberg, "The Organization as Political Arena," *Journal of Management Studies*, 22 (1985), pp. 133–54.

84. R. J. House, "Power and Personality in Complex Organizations," *Research in Organizational Behaviour*, 10 (1988), pp. 305–57; L. W. Porter, R. W. Allen, and H. L. Angle, "The Politics of Upward Influence in Organizations," *Research in Organizational Behaviour*, 3 (1981), pp. 120–22.

85. K. S. Sauleya and A. G. Bedeian "Equity Sensitivity: Construction of a Measure and Examination of its Psychometric Properties," *Journal of Management*, 26 (September 2000), pp. 885–910; S. M. Farmer, J. M. Maslyn,

D. B. Fedor, and J. S. Goodman, "Putting Upward Influence Strategies in Context," *Journal of Organizational Behaviour*, 18 (1997), pp. 17–42; P. E. Mudrack, "An Investigation into the Acceptability of Workplace Behaviours of a Dubious Ethical Nature," *Journal of Business Ethics*, 12 (1993), pp. 517–24; and R. Christie and F. Geis, *Studies in Machiavellianism* (New York: Academic Press, 1970).

86. G. R. Ferris, et. al, "Perceptions of Organizational Politics: Prediction, Stress-Related Implications, and Outcomes," *Human Relations*, 49 (1996), p. 233–263.

87. L. A. Witt, M. C. Andrews, and K. M. Kacmar, "The Role of Participative Decisionmaking in the Organizational Politics-Job Satisfaction Relationship," *Human Relations*, 53 (2000), pp. 341–57.

CHAPTER THIRTEEN

1. S. Pigg, "Pilots get New Deadlines in Dispute over Seniority," *Toronto Star*, October 4, 2002, p. C2; S. Pigg, "Pilot Seniority Issue Reopened," *Toronto Star*, July 11, 2002, p. C12; S. Pigg, "Air Canada: An Airline Divided, *Toronto Star*, June 2, 2001, p. E1; K. McArthur, "Air Canada Pilot Seniority Feelings Run High: 'Scuffles on the Crew Bus'," *Canadian Press*, April 3, 2001; A. Swift, "Pilots for Air Canada, Canadian Airlines Begin Campaign for One Union," *Canadian Press*, January 6, 2001.

2. J. A. Wall and R. R. Callister, "Conflict and Its Management," *Journal of Management*, 21 (1995), pp. 515–558; D. Tjosvold, *Working Together to Get Things Done* (Lexington, Mass.: Lexington, 1986), pp. 114–115.

3. The conflict process is described in K. W. Thomas, "Conflict and Negotiation Processes in Organizations," In M. D. Dunnette and L. M. Hough (Eds.) *Handbook of Industrial and Organizational Psychology*, 2nd Ed., Vol. 3 (Palo Alto, CA: Consulting Psychologists Press, 1992), pp. 651–718; L. Pondy, "Organizational Conflict: Concepts and Models, *Administrative Science Quarterly*, 2 (1967), pp. 296–320.

4. A. C. Ward, "Another Look at How Toyota Integrates Product Development," *Harvard Business Review* (July-August 1998), pp. 36–49.

5. L. H. Pelled, K. R. Xin, and A. M. Weiss, "No Es Como Mi: Relational Demography And Conflict In A Mexican Production Facility," *Journal of Occupational and Organizational Psychology*, 74 (March 2001), pp. 63–84; L. H. Pelled, K. M. Eisenhardt, and K. R. Xin, "Exploring the Black Box: An Analysis of Work Group Diversity, Conflict, and Performance," *Administrative Science Quarterly*, 44 (March 1999), pp. 1–28. One recent study reported that both task-related and socioemotional conflict have a negative effect on team performance. However, the effect for task-related conflict varied considerably across studies, suggesting that it has a positive effect under specific conditions. See: C. K. W. De Dreu and L. R. Weingart, "Task Versus Relationship Conflict, Team Performance and Team Member Satisfaction: A Meta-Analysis," *Journal of Applied Psychology*, 2003, in press.

6. K. McArthur, "Air Canada Pilot Seniority Feelings Run High: 'Scuffles on the Crew Bus'," *Canadian Press*, April 3, 2001.

7. J. M. Brett, D. L. Shapiro, and A. L. Lytle, "Breaking the Bonds Of Reciprocity In Negotiations," *Academy of Management Journal*, 41 (August 1998), pp. 410–24; G. E. Martin and T. J. Bergman, "The Dynamics Of Behavioral Response To Conflict In The Workplace," *Journal of Occupational & Organizational Psychology*, 69 (December 1996), pp. 377–87; G. Wolf, "Conflict Episodes," In *Negotiating in Organizations*, ed. M. H. Bazerman and R. J. Lewicki (Beverly Hills, Calif.: Sage, 1983), pp. 135–40; L. R. Pondy, "Organizational Conflict: Concepts and Models," *Administrative Science Quarterly*, 12 (1967), pp. 296–320.

8. H. Witteman, "Analyzing Interpersonal Conflict: Nature of Awareness, Type of Initiating Event, Situational Perceptions, and Management Styles," *Western Journal of Communications*, 56 (1992), pp. 248–80; F. J. Barrett and D. L. Cooperrider, "Generative Metaphor Intervention: A New Approach for Working with Systems Divided by Conflict and Caught in Defensive Perception," *Journal of Applied Behavioral Science*, 26 (1990), pp. 219–39.

9. Wall and Callister, "Conflict and Its Management," pp. 526–33.

10. T. Wallace, "Fear & Loathing," *Boss Magazine*, April 12, 2001, p. 42.

11. C. K. W. de Dreu, P. Harinck, and A. E. M. Van Vianen, "Conflict and Performance in Groups and Organizations," *International Review of Industrial and Organizational Psychology*, 14 (1999), pp. 376–405.

12. F. Rose, "The Eisner School of Business," *Fortune*, July 6, 1998, pp. 29–30. For a more favorable interpretation of conflict at Disney, see: S. Wetlaufer, "Common Sense and Conflict: An Interview with Disney's Michael Eisner," *Harvard Business Review*, 78 (January-February 2000), pp. 114–24.

13. M. Rempel and R. J. Fisher, "Perceived Threat, Cohesion, And Group Problem Solving In Intergroup Conflict," *International Journal of Conflict Management*, 8 (1997), pp. 216–34.

14. Amason, "Distinguishing the Effects of Functional and Dysfunctional Conflict on Strategic Decision Making"; L. L. Putnam, "Productive Conflict: Negotiation as Implicit Coordination," *International Journal of Conflict Management*, 5 (1994), pp. 285–99; D. Tjosvold, *The Conflict-Positive Organization* (Reading, MA: Addison-Wesley, 1991); R. A. Baron, "Positive Effects of Conflict: A Cognitive Perspective," *Employee Responsibilities and Rights Journal*, 4 (1991), pp. 25–36.

15. K. M. Eisenhardt, J. L. Kahwajy, and L. J. Bourgeois, III "Conflict and Strategic Choice: How Top Management Teams Disagree," *California Management Review*, 39 (Winter 1997), pp. 42–62; J. K. Bouwen and R. Fry, "Organizational Innovation and Learning: Four Patterns of Dialog Between the Dominant Logic and the New Logic," *International Studies of Management and Organizations*, 21 (1991), pp. 37–51.

16. L. Goldberg, "Southwest's New Co-Pilots," Houston Chronicle, April 22, 2001, p. 1.

17. R. E. Walton and J. M. Dutton, "The Management of Conflict: A Model and Review," *Administrative Science Quarterly*, 14 (1969), pp. 73–84.

18. D.M. Brock, D. Barry, and D.C. Thomas, "'Your Forward is Our Reverse, Your Right, our Wrong': Rethinking Multinational Planning

Processes in Light of National Culture," *International Business Review*, 9 (December 2000), pp. 687–701

19. For a fuller discussion of conflict across the generations, see: R. Zemke and B. Filipczak, *Generations at Work: Managing the Clash of Veterans, Boomers, Xers, and Nexters in Your Workplace*, (N. Y.: Amacom, 1999).

20. T. Aeppel, "Power Generation: Young and Old See Technology Sparking Friction on Shop Floor," *Wall Street Journal*, April 7, 2000, p. A1.

21. K. Jelin, "A Multimethod Examination of the Benefits and Detriments of Intragroup Conflict," *Administrative Science Quarterly*, 40 (1995), pp. 245–82; P. C. Earley and G. B. Northcraft, "Goal Setting, Resource Interdependence, and Conflict Management," In M. A. Rahim (Ed.) *Managing Conflict: An Interdisciplinary Approach*, (New York: Praeger, 1989), pp. 161–70.

22. W. W. Notz, F. A. Starke, and J. Atwell, "The Manager as Arbitrator: Conflicts over Scarce Resources," In Bazerman and Lewicki (Eds.), *Negotiating in Organizations*, pp. 143–64.

23. A. Risberg, "Employee Experiences of Acquisition Processes," *Journal of World Business*, 36 (March 2001), pp. 58–84.

24. Brett et al, "Breaking the Bonds Of Reciprocity In Negotiations;" R. A. Baron, "Reducing Organizational Conflict: An Incompatible Response Approach," *Journal of Applied Psychology*, 69 (1984), pp. 272–79.

25. K. D. Grimsley "Slings and Arrows on the Job," *Washington Post*, July 12, 1998, p. H1; "Flame Throwers," *Director*, 50 (July 1997), p. 36.

26. T.A. Abma, "Stakeholder Conflict: A Case Study," *Evaluation and Program Planning*, 23 (May 2000), pp.199–210; J. W. Jackson and E. R. Smith, "Conceptualizing Social Identity: A New Framework And Evidence For The Impact Of Different Dimensions," *Personality & Social Psychology Bulletin*, 25 (January 1999), pp. 120–35.

27. D. C. Dryer and L. M. Horowitz, "When do Opposites Attract? Interpersonal Complementarity versus Similarity," *Journal of Personality and Social Psychology*, 72 (1997), pp. 592–603.

28. R. J. Lewicki and J. A. Litterer, *Negotiation* (Homewood, Ill.: Irwin, 1985), pp. 102–06; K. W. Thomas, "Toward Multi-Dimensional Values in Teaching: The Example of Conflict Behaviors," *Academy of Management Review*, 2 (1977), pp. 484–90.

29. Jehn, "A Multimethod Examination of the Benefits and Detriments of Intragroup Conflict," p. 276.

30. C. K. W. de Dreu, A. Evers, B. Beersma, E. S. Kluwer, and A. Nauta, "A Theory-based Measure of Conflict Management Strategies in the Workplace," *Journal of Organizational Behavior*, 22 (2001), pp. 645–68.

31. M. Lyster et al., "The Changing Guard," *Orange County Business Journal*, May 7, 2001, p. 31.

32. L. Xiaohua and R. Germain, "Sustaining Satisfactory Joint Venture Relationships: The Role Of Conflict Resolution Strategy," *Journal of International Business Studies*, 29 (March 1998), pp. 179–96.

33. Tjosvold, *Working Together to Get Things Done*, Chapter 2; D. W. Johnson, G. Maruyama, R. T. Johnson, D. Nelson, and S. Skon, "Effects of Cooperative, Competitive, and Individualistic Goal Structures on Achievement: A Meta-Analysis," *Psychological Bulletin*, 89 (1981), pp. 47–62; R. J. Burke, "Methods of Resolving Superior–Subordinate Conflict: The Constructive Use of Subordinate Differences and Disagreements," *Organizational Behavior and Human Performance*, 5 (1970), pp. 393–441.

34. C. K. W. De Dreu and A. E. M. Van Vianen, "Managing Relationship Conflict and the Effectiveness of Organizational Teams," *Journal of Organizational Behavior*, 22 (2001), pp. 309–28.

35. M. Tutton, "Seafood Firm on Feeding Frenzy," *Toronto Star*, June 30, 2002, p. C13; O. Bertin, "FPI Ready to Get Back to Business," *Globe and Mail*, May 17, 2002, p. B2; I. Bulmer, "Fishing Battle nears Climax," *Halifax Herald*, April 27, 2001.

36. C. H. Tinsley and J. M. Brett, "Managing Workplace Conflict in the United States and Hong Kong," *Organizational Behavior and Human Decision Processes*, 85 (July 2001), pp. 360–81; M. W. Morris and H-Y. Fu, "How does

Culture Influence Conflict Resolution? Dynamic Constructivist Analysis," *Social Cognition*, 19 (June 2001), pp. 324–49; K. Leung and D. Tjosvold (Eds.), *Conflict Management in the Asia Pacific* (Singapore: John Wiley & Sons, 1998); M. A. Rahim and A. A. Blum, (Eds.), *Global Perspectives on Organizational Conflict*, (Westport, CT: Praeger, 1995); M. Rabie, *Conflict Resolution and Ethnicity*, (Westport, CT: Praeger, 1994). For an exception to these studies, see: D. A. Cai and E. L. Fink, "Conflict Style Differences Between Individualists and Collectivists," *Communication Monographs*, 69 (March 2002), pp. 67–87.

37. C. C. Chen, X. P. Chen, and J. R. Meindl, "How Can Cooperation be Fostered? The Cultural Effects of Individualism-Collectivism," *Academy of Management Review*, 23 (1998), pp. 285–304; S. M. Elsayed-Ekhouly and R. Buda, "Organizational Conflict: A Comparative Analysis of Conflict Styles Across Cultures," *International Journal of Conflict Management*, 7 (1996), pp. 71–81; D. K. Tse, J. Francis, and J. Walls, "Cultural Differences in Conducting Intra- and Inter-Cultural Negotiations: A Sino-Canadian Comparison," *Journal of International Business Studies*, 25 (1994), pp. 537–555; S. Ting-Toomey et al., "Culture, Face Management, and Conflict Styles of Handling Interpersonal Conflict: A Study in Five Cultures," *International Journal of Conflict Management*, 2 (1991), pp. 275–96.

38. L. Karakowsky, "Toward an Understanding of Women and Men at the Bargaining Table: Factors Affecting Negotiator Style and Influence in Multi-Party Negotiations," *Proceedings of the Annual ASAC Conference, Women in Management Division*, (1996), pp. 21–30; W. C. King, Jr. and T. D. Hinson, "The Influence of Sex and Equity Sensitivity on Relationship Preferences, Assessment of Opponent, and Outcomes in a Negotiation Experiment," *Journal of Management*, 20 (1994), pp. 605–24; R. Lewicki, J. Litterer, D. Saunders, and J. Minton, (Eds.) *Negotiation: Readings, Exercises, and Cases*, (Homewood, IL: Irwin, 1993).

39. E. Van de Vliert, "Escalative Intervention in Small Group Conflicts,"

Journal of Applied Behavioral Science, 21 (Winter 1985), pp. 19–36.

40. M. B. Pinto, J. K. Pinto, and J. E. Prescott, "Antecedents and Consequences of Project Team Cross-Functional Cooperation," *Management Science*, 39 (1993), pp. 1281–97; M. Sherif, "Superordinate Goals in the Reduction of Intergroup Conflict," *American Journal of Sociology*, 68 (1958), pp. 349–58.

41. X. M. Song, J. Xile, B. Dyer, "Antecedents and Consequences of Marketing Managers' Conflict-Handling Behaviors," *Journal of Marketing*, 64 (January 2000), pp. 50–66; K. M. Eisenhardt, J. L. Kahwajy, and L.J. Bourgeois III, "How Management Teams Can Have A Good Fight," *Harvard Business Review*, July-August 1997, pp. 77–85.

42. L. Mulitz, "Flying Off over Office Politics," *InfoWorld*, November 6, 2000.

43. X.M. Song, J. Xile, and B. Dyer, "Antecedents and Consequences of Marketing Managers' Conflict-Handling Behaviors," *Journal of Marketing*, 64 (January 2000), pp. 50–66.

44. "Teamwork Polishes this Diamond," *Philippine Daily Inquirer*, October 4, 2000, p. 10; "How Hibernia Helped Its Hourly Employees Make a Leap to PFP," *Pay for Performance Report*, 64 (January 2000), pp. 50–66.

45. This strategy and other conflict management practices in joint military operations are fully discussed in E. Elron, B. Shamir, and E. Ben-Ari "Why Don't they Fight each Other? Cultural Diversity and Operational Unity in Multinational Forces," *Armed Forces & Society*, 26 (October 1999), pp. 73–97.

46. R. J. Fisher, E. Maltz, and B. J. Jaworski, "Enhancing Communication Between Marketing and Engineering: The Moderating Role of Relative Functional Identification," *Journal Of Marketing*, 61 (1997), pp. 54–70. For a discussion of minimizing conflict through understanding as "other point multiplicity," see: T. A. Abma, "Stakeholder Conflict: A Case Study," *Evaluation and Program Planning*, 23 (May 2000), pp.199–210

47. A. Zurcher, "Techies and Non-Techies Don't Always Interface Well," *Washington Post*, September 3, 2000, p. L5.

48. D. Woodruff, "Crossing Culture Divide Early Clears Merger Paths," *Asian Wall Street Journal*, May 28, 2001, p. 9.

49. L. Ellinor and G. Gerard, *Dialogue: Rediscovering the Transforming Power of Conversation*, (N.Y.: John Wiley & Sons Inc, 1998); W. N. Isaacs, "Taking Flight: Dialog, Collective Thinking, and Organizational Learning," *Organizational Dynamics*, Autumn 1993, pp. 24–39; E. H. Schein, "On Dialog, Culture, and Organizational Learning," *Organizational Dynamics*, Autumn 1993, pp. 40–51; P. M. Senge, *The Fifth Discipline* (New York: Doubleday Currency, 1990), pp. 238–49.

50. P. R. Lawrence and J. W. Lorsch, *Organization and Environment* (Homewood, Ill.: Irwin, 1969).

51. E. Horwitt, "Knowledge, Knowledge, Who's Got the Knowledge." *Computerworld*, April 8, 1996, pp. 80, 81, 84.

52. D. G. Pruitt and P. J. Carnevale, *Negotiation in Social Conflict* (Buckingham, U.K.: Open University Press, 1993), p. 2; and J. A. Wall, Jr., *Negotiation: Theory and Practice* (Glenview, Ill.: Scott, Foresman, 1985), p. 4.

53. L. Edson, "The Negotiation Industry," *Across the Board*, April 2000, pp. 14–20.

54. For a critical view of the problem solving style in negotiation, see J. M. Brett, "Managing Organizational Conflict," *Professional Psychology: Research and Practice*, 15 (1984), pp. 664–78.

55. R. E. Fells, "Overcoming The Dilemmas In Walton And Mckersie's Mixed Bargaining Strategy," *Industrial Relations* (Laval), 53 (March 1998), pp. 300–25; R. E. Fells, "Developing Trust in Negotiation," *Employee Relations*, 15 (1993), pp. 33–45.

56. L. Thompson, *The Mind and Heart of the Negotiator* (Upper Saddle River, NJ: Prentice-Hall, 1998), Chapter 2; R. Stagner and H. Rosen, *Psychology of Union–Management Relations* (Belmont, Calif.: Wadsworth, 1965), pp. 95–96, 108–10; and R. E. Walton and R. B. McKersie, *A Behavioral Theory of Labor Negotiations: An Analysis of a Social Interaction System* (New York: McGraw-Hill, 1965), pp. 41–46.

57. J. Mayfield, M. Mayfield, D. Martin, and P. Herbig, "How Location Impacts International Business Negoti-ations," *Review of Business*, 19 (December 1998), pp. 21–24; J. W. Salacuse and J. Z. Rubin, "Your Place or Mine? Site Location and Negotiation," *Negotiation Journal*, 6 (January 1990), pp. 5–10; Lewicki and Litterer, *Negotiation*, pp. 144–46.

58. For a full discussion of the advantages and disadvantages of face-to-face and alternative negotiations situations, see: M. H. Bazerman, J. R. Curhan, D. A. Moore, and K. L. Valley, "Negotiation," *Annual Review of Psychology*, 51 (2000), pp. 279–314.

59. Lewicki and Litterer, *Negotiation*, pp. 146–51; and B. Kniveton, *The Psychology of Bargaining* (Aldershot, Eng.: Avebury, 1989), pp. 76–79.

60. Pruitt and Carnevale, *Negotiation in Social Conflict*, pp. 59–61; and Lewicki and Litterer, *Negotiation*, pp. 151–54.

61. B. M. Downie, "When Negotiations Fail: Causes of Breakdown and Tactics for Breaking the Stalemate," *Negotiation Journal*, April 1991, pp. 175–86.

62. Pruitt and Carnevale, *Negotiation in Social Conflict*, pp. 56–58; Lewicki and Litterer, *Negotiation*, pp. 215–22.

63. V. V. Murray, T. D. Jick, and P. Bradshaw, "To Bargain or Not to Bargain? The Case of Hospital Budget Cuts," in *Negotiating in Organizations*, ed. Bazerman & Lewicki pp. 272–95.

64. D. C. Zetik and A. F. Stuhlmacher, "Goal Setting and Negotiation Performance: A Meta-Analysis," *Group Processes & Intergroup Relations*, 5 (January 2002), pp. 35–52; S. Doctoroff, "Reengineering Negotiations," *Sloan Management Review*, 39 (March 1998), pp. 63–71; R. L. Lewicki, A. Hiam, and K. Olander, *Think Before you Speak: The Complete Guide to Strategic Negotiation*, (New York : John Wiley & Sons, 1996); G. B. Northcraft and M. A. Neale, "Joint Effects of Assigned Goals and Training on Negotiator Performance," *Human Performance*, 7 (1994), pp. 257–72.

65. B. McRae, *The Seven Strategies of Master Negotiators* (Toronto: McGraw-Hill Ryerson, 2002), pp. 7–11.

66. M. A. Neale and M. H. Bazerman, *Cognition and Rationality in Negotiation* (New York: Free Press, 1991), pp. 29–31; L. L. Thompson, "Information Exchange in Negotiation," *Journal of*

Experimental Social Psychology, 27 (1991), pp. 161–79.

67. Y. Paik, and R. L. Tung "Negotiating with East Asians: How to Attain "Win–Win" Outcomes," *Management International Review*, 39 (1999), pp. 103–22; L. Thompson, E. Peterson, and S. E. Brodt, "Team Negotiation: An Examinaton of Integrative and Distributive Bargaining," *Journal of Personality and Social Psychology*, 70 (1996), pp. 66–78.

68. L. L. Putnam and M. E. Roloff (eds.), *Communication and Negotiation* (Newbury Park, Calif.: Sage, 1992).

69. L. Hall (ed.), *Negotiation: Strategies for Mutual Gain* (Newbury Park, Calif.: Sage, 1993); D. Ertel, "How to Design a Conflict Management Procedure that Fits Your Dispute." *Sloan Management Review*, 32 (Summer 1991), pp. 29–42.

70. Lewicki and Litterer, *Negotiation*, pp. 89–93.

71. J.J. Zhao, "The Chinese Approach to International Business Negotiation," *Journal of Business Communication*, July 2000, pp. 209–237; Paik and Tung "Negotiating with East Asians;" N. J. Adler, *International Dimensions of Organizational Behavior*, 2nd ed., (Belmont, CA: Wadsworth, 1991), pp. 180–181.

72. Kniveton, *The Psychology of Bargaining*, pp. 100–101; J. Z. Rubin and B. R. Brown, *The Social Psychology of Bargaining and Negotiation* (New York: Academic Press, 1976), Chapter 9; and Brett, "Managing Organizational Conflict," pp. 670–71.

73. A. R. Elangovan, "The Manager as the Third Party: Deciding How to Intervene in Employee Disputes," In R. Lewicki, J. Litterer, and D. Saunders (Eds.), *Negotiation: Readings, Exercises, and Cases, 3rd ed.*, (N. Y.: McGraw-Hill, 1999), pp. 458–69; L. L. Putnam, "Beyond Third Party Role: Disputes and Managerial Intervention," *Employee Responsibilities and Rights Journal*, 7 (1994), pp. 23–36; Sheppard et al., *Organizational Justice*.

74. M. A. Neale and M. H. Bazerman, *Cognition and Rationality in Negotiation* (New York: The Free Press, 1991), pp. 140–42.

75. B. H. Sheppard, "Managers as Inquisitors: Lessons from the Law," in M. Bazerman and R. J. Lewicki (Eds.), *Bargaining Inside Organizations*, (Beverly Hills, CA: Sage, 1983), pp. 193–213.

76. R. Cropanzano, H. Aguinis, M. Schminke, and D. L. Denham, "Disputant Reactions to Managerial Conflict Resolution Tactics," *Group & Organization Management*, 24 (June 1999), pp. 124–53; R. Karambayya and J. M. Brett, "Managers Handling Disputes: Third Party Roles and Perceptions of Fairness," *Academy of Management Journal*, 32 (1989), pp. 687–704.

77. A. R. Elangovan, "Managerial Intervention in Organizational Disputes: Testing a Prescriptive Model of Strategy Selection," *International Journal of Conflict Management*, 4 (1998), pp. 301–35.

78. J. P. Meyer, J. M. Gemmell, and P. G. Irving, "Evaluating the Management of Interpersonal Conflict in Organizations: A Factor-Analytic Study of Outcome Criteria," *Canadian Journal of Administrative Sciences*, 14 (1997), pp. 1–13.

79. C. Hirschman, "Order in the Hearing," *HRMagazine*, 46 (July 2001), p. 58; D. Hechler, "No Longer a Novelty: ADR Winning Corporate Acceptance," *Fulton County Daily Report*, June 29, 2001; S. L. Hayford, "Alternative Dispute Resolution," *Business Horizons*, 43 (January-February 2000), pp. 2–4.

CHAPTER FOURTEEN

1. P. Withers, "The Leadership Challenge," *BC Business*, 30 (March 2002), pp. 26ff; L. Veit, "Ethical Matters," *Credit Union Management*, 24 (June 2001), pp. 18–20; P. Gallagher, "How Can You Be a Great Leader—Drive the Vision," *Success*, 48 (April 2001), pp. 28–33; C. Fox, "CEOs Slipping Into Old Habits," *Australian Financial Review*, February 6, 2001, p. 38; p. L11; New Economy, Old Values," *Corporate Report Wisconsin*, 16 (October 2000), pp. 12ff; "Leadership A to Z. (Interview)," *Training & Development*, March 2000, p. 58; P. Clark and E. Mychasuk, "The New Leadership," *Boss Magazine*, September 11, 2000, p. 32.

2. R. A. Barker, "How Can we Train Leaders if We Do Not Know What Leadership Is?" *Human Relations*, 50 (1997), pp. 343–62; P. C. Drucker, "Forward," in F. Hesselbein et al, *The Leader of the Future* (San Francisco, CA: Jossey-Bass, 1997).

3. R. House, M. Javidan, P. Hanges, and P. Dorfman, "Understanding Cultures and Implicit Leadership Theories Across the Globe: An Introduction to Project GLOBE," *Journal of World Business*, 37 (2002), pp. 3–10; R. House, M. Javidan, and P. Dorfman, "Project GLOBE: An Introduction," *Applied Psychology: An International Review*, 50 (2001), pp. 489–505.

4. M. Groves, "Cream Rises to the Top, but From a Small Crop," *Los Angeles Times*, June 8, 1998. A recent study also reported that only 3 percent of executives in large firms agreed that their company develops leadership talent quickly and effectively. See H. Handfield-Jones, "How Executives Grow," *McKinsey Quarterly*, January 2000, pp. 116–23.

5. R. G. Isaac, W. J. Zerbe, and D. C. Pitt, "Leadership and Motivation: The Effective Application of Expectancy Theory," *Journal of Managerial Issues*, 13 (Summer 2001), pp. 212–26.

6. C.L. Cole, "Eight Values Bring Unity to a Worldwide Company," *Workforce*, 80 (March 2001), pp. 44–45.

7. M. Callahan, "Key to Success is Happy Employees, says Utility's CEO," *Western Star* (Cornerbrook, Nfld), May 18, 2002.

8. C. A. Beatty, "Implementing Advanced Manufacturing Technologies: Rules of the Road," *Sloan Management Review*, Summer 1992, pp. 49–60; J. M. Howell and C. A. Higgins, "Champions of Technological Innovation," *Administrative Science Quarterly*, 35 (1990), pp. 317–41.

9. Many of these perspectives are summarised in R. N. Kanungo, "Leadership in Organizations: Looking Ahead to the 21st Century," *Canadian Psychology*, 39 (Spring 1998), pp. 71–82.

10. J. Higley, "Head of the Class," *Hotel & Motel Management*, November 2001, pp. 92ff.

11. T. Takala, "Plato on Leadership," *Journal of Business Ethics*, 17 (May 1998), pp. 785–98.

12. R. M. Stogdill, *Handbook of Leadership* (New York: The Free Press, 1974), Chap. 5.

13. J. Kochanski, "Competency-Based Management," *Training & Develop-*

ment, October 1997, pp. 40–44; Hay Group et. al. *Raising the Bar: Using Competencies to Enhance Employee Performance* (Scottsdale, AZ: American Compensation Association, 1996); L. M. Spencer and S. M. Spencer, *Competence at Work: Models for Superior Performance* (New York: Wiley, 1993).

14. Most elements of this list were derived from S. A. Kirkpatrick and E. A. Locke, "Leadership: Do Traits Matter?" *Academy of Management Executive*, 5 (May 1991), pp. 48–60. Various leadership competencies are also discussed in: R. M. Aditya, R. J. House, and S. Kerr, "Theory and Practice of Leadership: Into the New Millennium," In C. L. Cooper and E. A. Locke (eds.) *Industrial and Organizational Psychology: Linking Theory with Practice* (Oxford, UK: Blackwell, 2000), pp. 130–65; H. B. Gregersen, A. J. Morrison, and J. S. Black, "Developing Leaders for the Global Frontier," *Sloan Management Review*, 40 (Fall 1998), pp. 21–32; R. J. House and R. N. Aditya, "The Social Scientific Study of Leadership: Quo Vadis?" *Journal of Management*, 23 (1997), pp. 409–73; R. J. House and M. L. Baetz, "Leadership: Some Empirical Generalizations and New Research Directions," *Research in Organizational Behavior* 1 (1979), pp. 341–423.

15. D. Goleman, R. Boyatzis, and A. McKee, *Primal Leaders* (Boston: Harvard Business School Press, 2002); J. George, "Emotions and Leadership: The Role of Emotional Intelligence," *Human Relations*, 53 (August 2000), pp. 1027–55; D. Goleman, What Makes a Leader?" *Harvard Business Review*, 76 (November-December 1998), pp. 92–102.

16. J. D. Mayer, P. Salovey, D. R. Caruso, "Models of Emotional Intelligence," In R. J. Sternberg (Ed.). *Handbook of Human Intelligence, 2nd ed.*, (New York: Cambridge University Press, 2000), p. 396. This definition is also recognized in: C. Cherniss, "Emotional Intelligence and Organizational Effectiveness," In C. Cherniss and D. Goleman, (Eds.), *The Emotionally Intelligent Workplace* (San Francisco: Jossey-Bass, 2001), pp. 3–12.

17. J. J. Sosik, D. Potosky, and D. I. Jung, "Adaptive Self-Regulation: Meeting Others' Expectations of Leadership and Performance," *Journal of Social Psychology*, 142 (April 2002), pp. 211–32; J. A. Kolb, "The Relationship Between Self-Monitoring And Leadership In Student Project Groups," *Journal of Business Communication*, 35 (April 1998), pp. 264–82; S. J. Zaccaro, R. J. Foti, and D. A. Kenny, "Self-Monitoring and Trait-Based Variance in Leadership: An Investigation of Leader Flexibility across Multiple Group Situations," *Journal of Applied Psychology*, 76 (1991), pp. 308–15; S. E. Cronshaw and R. J. Ellis, "A Process Investigation Of Self-Monitoring And Leader Emergence," *Small Group Research*, 22 (1991), pp. 403–20; S. J. Zaccaro, R. J. Foti, and D. A. Kenny, "Self-Monitoring And Trait-Based Variance Is Leadership: An Investigation Of Leader Flexibility Across Multiple Group Situations," *Journal of Applied Psychology*, 76 (1991): 308–15.

18. C. Savoye, "Workers say Honesty is Best Company Policy," *Christian Science Monitor*, June 15, 2000; "Canadian CEOs Give Themselves Top Marks for Leadership!" *Canada NewsWire*, September 9, 1999; J. M. Kouzes, and B. Z. Posner, *Credibility: How Leaders Gain and Lose It, Why People Demand It* (San Francisco: Jossey-Bass, 1993).

19. House and Aditya, "The Social Scientific Study of Leadership."

20. L. L. Paglis and S. G. Green, "Leadership Self-Efficacy and Managers' Motivation for Leading Change," *Journal of Organizational Behavior*, 23 (2002), pp. 215–35.

21. R. Jacobs, "Using Human Resource Functions to Enhance Emotional Intelligence," In C. Cherniss and D. Goleman (eds.), *The Emotionally Intelligent Workplace* (San Francisco: Jossey-Bass, (2001), pp. 161–63.

22. R. G. Lord and K. J. Maher, *Leadership and Information Processing: Linking Perceptions and Performance*, (Cambridge, MA: Unwin Hyman, 1991).

23. W. C. Byham, "Grooming Next-Millennium Leaders," *HRMagazine*, 44 (February 1999), pp. 46–50; R. Zemke and S. Zemke, "Putting Competencies to Work," *Training*, 36 (January 1999), pp. 70–76.

24. G. A. Yukl, *Leadership in Organizations*, 3rd ed. (Englewood Cliffs, NJ: Prentice Hall, 1994), pp. 53–75; R. Likert, *New Patterns of Management* (New York: McGraw-Hill, 1961.

25. M.D. Abrashoff, "Retention Through Redemption," *Harvard Business Review*, 79 (February 2001), pp. 136–41.

26. A. K. Korman, "Consideration, Initiating Structure, and Organizational Criteria—A Review," *Personnel Psychology*, 19 (1966), pp 349–62; E. A. Fleishman, "Twenty Years of Consideration and Structure," in E. A. Fleishman and J. C. Hunt (eds.), *Current Developments in the Study of Leadership*, (Carbondale, Ill.: Southern Illinois University Press, 1973), pp. 1–40.

27. V. V. Baba, "Serendipity in Leadership: Initiating Structure and Consideration in the Classroom," *Human Relations*, 42 (1989), pp. 509–25.

28. P. Weissenberg and M. H. Kavanagh, "The Independence of Initiating Structure and Consideration: A Review of the Evidence," *Personnel Psychology*, 25 (1972), pp. 119–30; Stogdill, *Handbook of Leadership*, Chapter 11; R. L. Kahn, "The Prediction of Productivity," *Journal of Social Issues*, 12(2) (1956), pp. 41–49;

29. R. R. Blake and A. A. McCanse, *Leadership Dilemmas—Grid Solutions* (Houston: Gulf Publishing Company, 1991); R. R. Blake and J. S. Mouton, "Management by Grid Principles or Situationalism: Which?" *Group and Organization Studies*, 7 (1982), pp. 207–10.

30. L. L. Larson, J. G. Hunt, and R. N. Osborn, "The Great Hi–Hi Leader Behavior Myth: A Lesson from Occam's Razor," *Academy of Management Journal*, 19 (1976), pp. 628–41; S. Kerr, C. A. Schriesheim, C. J. Murphy, and R. M. Stogdill, "Towards a Contingency Theory of Leadership Based upon the Consideration and Initiating Structure Literature," *Organizational Behavior and Human Performance*, 12 (1974), pp. 62–82; A. K. Korman, "Consideration, Initiating Structure, and Organizational Criteria—A Review," *Personnel Psychology*, 19 (1966), pp. 349–62.

31. R. Tannenbaum and W. H. Schmidt, "How to Choose a Leadership Pattern," *Harvard Business Review*, May–June 1973, pp. 162–80.

32. For a recent discussion of the contingency perspective of leadership and

emotional intelligence, see D. Goleman, "Leadership that Gets Results," *Harvard Business Review*, 78 (March-April 2000), pp. 78–90.

33. For a thorough study of how expectancy theory of motivation relates to leadership, see: Isaac, Zerbe, and Pitt, "Leadership and Motivation: The Effective Application of Expectancy Theory."

34. M. G. Evans, "The Effects of Supervisory Behavior on the Path–Goal Relationship," *Organizational Behavior and Human Performance*, 5 (1970), pp. 277–98; M. G. Evans, "Extensions of a Path–Goal Theory of Motivation," *Journal of Applied Psychology*, 59 (1974), pp. 172–78; R. J. House, "A Path–Goal Theory of Leader Effectiveness," *Administrative Science Quarterly*, 16 (1971), pp. 321–38.

35. R. J. House and T. R. Mitchell, "Path–Goal Theory of Leadership," *Journal of Contemporary Business*, Autumn 1974, pp. 81–97.

36. M. Fulmer, "Learning Across a Living Company: The Shell Companies' Experiences," *Organizational Dynamics*, 27 (Autumn 1998), pp. 61–69; R. Wageman, "Case Study: Critical Success Factors for Creating Superb Self-Managing Teams at Xerox," *Compensation and Benefits Review*, 29 (September-October 1997), pp. 31–41.

37. M. E. McGill and J. W. Slocum, Jr., "A Little Leadership, Please?" *Organizational Dynamics*, 39 (Winter 1998), pp. 39–49; R. J. Doyle, "The Case of a Servant Leader: John F. Donnelly, Sr." In R. P. Vecchio (ed.), *Leadership: Understanding the Dynamics of Power and Influence in Organizations*, (Notre Dame, IN: University of Notre Dame Press, 1997), pp. 439–57.

38. R. J. House, "Path–Goal Theory of Leadership: Lessons, Legacy, and a Reformulated Theory," *Leadership Quarterly*, 7 (1996), pp. 323–52.

39. J. C. Wofford and L. Z. Liska, "Path–Goal Theories of Leadership: A Meta-Analysis," *Journal of Management*, 19 (1993), pp. 857–76; J. Indvik, "Path–Goal Theory of Leadership: A Meta-Analysis," *Academy of Management Proceedings*, 1986, pp. 189–92.

40. R. T. Keller, "A Test of the Path-Goal Theory of Leadership with Need for Clarity as a Moderator in Research and Development Organizations," *Journal of Applied Psychology*, 74 (1989), pp. 208–12.

41. Wofford and Liska, "Path–Goal Theories of Leadership: A Meta-Analysis;" Yukl, *Leadership in Organizations*, pp. 102–104; and Indvik, "Path-Goal Theory of Leadership: A Meta-Analysis."

42. C. A. Schriesheim and L. L. Neider, "Path–Goal Leadership Theory: The Long and Winding Road," *Leadership Quarterly*, 7 (1996), pp. 317–21. One of the more prominent studies that found evidence against path–goal theory is: H. K. Downey, J. E. Sheridan, and J. W. Slocum, "Analysis of Relationships among Leader Behavior, Subordinate Job Performance and Satisfaction: A Path–Goal Approach, Academy of Management Journal, 18 (1975), pp. 253–62.

43. P. Hersey and K. H. Blanchard, *Management of Organizational Behavior: Utilizing Human Resources*, 5th ed. (Englewood Cliffs, N.J.: Prentice Hall, 1988).

44. C. L. Graeff, "Evolution of Situational Leadership Theory: A Critical Review," *Leadership Quarterly*, 8 (1997), pp. 153–70; W. Blank, J. R. Weitzel, and S. G. Green, "A Test of the Situational Leadership Theory," *Personnel Psychology*, 43 (1990), pp. 579–97; R. P. Vecchio, "Situational Leadership Theory: An Examination of a Prescriptive Theory," *Journal of Applied Psychology*, 72 (1987), pp. 444–51.

45. F. E. Fiedler, *A Theory of Leadership Effectiveness* (New York: McGraw-Hill, 1967); F. E. Fiedler and M. M. Chemers, *Leadership and Effective Management* (Glenview, Ill.: Scott, Foresman, 1974).

46. F.E. Fiedler, "Engineer the Job to Fit the Manager," *Harvard Business Review*, 43, no. 5 (1965), pp. 115–22.

47. For a summary of criticisms, see: Yukl, *Leadership in Organizations*, pp. 197–98.

48. N. Nicholson, *Executive Instinct* (New York: Crown, 2000).

49. P. M. Podsakoff and S. B. MacKenzie, "Kerr and Jermier's Substitutes For Leadership Model: Background, Empirical Assessment, And Suggestions For Future Research," *Leadership Quarterly*, 8 (1997), pp. 117–32; P. M. Podsakoff, B. P. Niehoff, S. B. MacKenzie, and M. L. Williams, "Do Substitutes Really Substitute for Leadership? An Empirical Examination of Kerr and Jermier's Situational Leadership Model," *Organizational Behavior and Human Decision Processes*, 54 (1993), pp. 1–44.

50. This observation has also been made by C. A. Schriesheim "Substitutes-for-Leadership Theory: Development And Basic Concepts," *Leadership Quarterly*, 8 (1997), pp. 103–108.

51. D. F. Elloy and A. Randolph, "The Effect Of Superleader Behavior On Autonomous Work Groups In A Government Operated Railway Service," *Public Personnel Management*, 26 (Summer 1997), pp. 257–72.

52. M. L. Loughry, "Coworkers Are Watching: Performance Implications Of Peer Monitoring," *Academy of Management Proceedings* 2002, pp. O1–O6.

53. "Air Travellers see K-W Firm's Handiwork," *Kitchener-Waterloo Record*, May 3, 2000.

54. C. Manz and H. Sims, *Superleadership; Getting to the Top by Motivating Others* (San Francisco, CA: Berkley Publishing, 1990).

55. C. P. Neck and C. C. Manz, "Thought Self-Leadership: The Impact of Mental Strategies Training on Employee Cognition, Behavior, and Affect," *Journal of Organizational Behavior*, 17 (1996), pp. 445–67.

56. A. Nikiforuk, "Saint or Sinner?" *Canadian Business*, May 13, 2002, pp. 54ff; C. Cattaneo, "The Man who Saved Suncor," *National Post*, September 11, 1999, p. D1.

57. J. M. Howell and B. J. Avolio, "Transformational Leadership, Transactional Leadership, Locus of Control, and Support for Innovation: Key Predictors of Consolidated-Business-Unit Performance," *Journal of Applied Psychology*, 78 (1993), pp. 891–902; J. A. Conger and R. N. Kanungo, "Perceived Behavioral Attributes of Charismatic Leadership," *Canadian Journal of Behavioral Science*, 24 (1992), pp. 86–102; J. Seltzer and B. M. Bass, "Transformational Leadership: Beyond Initiation and Consideration," *Journal of Management*, 16 (1990), pp. 693–703.

58. B. J. Avolio and B. M. Bass, "Transformational Leadership, Charisma,

and Beyond," in J. G. Hunt, H. P. Dachler, B. R. Baliga, and C. A. Schriesheim (eds.) *Emerging Leadership Vistas*, (Lexington, Mass.: Lexington Books, 1988), pp. 29–49.

59. R. H. G. Field, "Leadership Defined: web Images Reveal the Differences Between Leadership and Management," Paper presented at the Administrative Sciences Association of Canada Annual Conference, Organizational Behaviour Division, Winnipeg, Manitoba May 2002; J. Kotter, *A Force for Change* (Cambridge, MA: Harvard Business School Press, 1990); W. Bennis and B. Nanus, *Leaders: The Strategies for Taking Charge* (New York: Harper & Row, 1985), p. 21; A. Zaleznik, "Managers and Leaders: Are They Different?" *Harvard Business Review*, 55(5) (1977), pp. 67–78.

60. C. P. Egri and S. Herman, "Leadership in the North American Environmental Sector: Values, Leadership Styles, and Contexts of Environmental Leaders and Their Organizations," *Academy of Management Journal*, 43 (August 2000), pp. 571–604.

61. For discussion on the tendency to slide from transformational to transactional leadership, see: W. Bennis, *An Invented Life: Reflections on Leadership and Change*, (Reading, MA.: Addison-Wesley, 1993).

62. J. A. Conger and R. N. Kanungo, "Toward a Behavioral Theory of Charismatic Leadership in Organizational Settings," *Academy of Management Review*, 12 (1987), pp. 637–47; R. J. House, "A 1976 Theory of Charismatic Leadership," in J. G. Hunt and L. L. Larson (eds.) *Leadership: The Cutting Edge*, (Carbondale, IL.: Southern Illinois University Press, 1977), pp. 189–207.

63. Y. A. Nur, "Charisma and Managerial Leadership: The Gift that Never Was," *Business Horizons*, 41 (July 1998), pp. 19–26; J. E. Barbuto, Jr., "Taking the Charisma Out Of Transformational Leadership," *Journal of Social Behavior & Personality*, 12 (September 1997), pp. 689–97.

64. L. Sooklal, "The Leader as a Broker of Dreams," *Organizational Studies*, (1989), pp. 833–55.

65. J. R. Sparks and J. A. Schenk, "Explaining the Effects of Transformational Leadership: An Investigation of the Effects of Higher-Order Motives in Multilevel Marketing Organizations," *Journal of Organizational Behavior*, 22 (2001), pp. 849–69; I. M. Levin, "Vision Revisited," *Journal of Applied Behavioral Science*, 36 (March 2000), pp. 91–107; J. M. Stewart, "Future State Visioning—A Powerful Leadership Process," *Long Range Planning*, 26 (December 1993), pp. 89–98; Bennis and Nanus, *Leaders*, pp. 27–33, 89.

66. T. J. Peters, "Symbols, Patterns, and Settings: An Optimistic Case for Getting Things Done," *Organizational Dynamics* 7 (Autumn 1978), pp. 2–23.

67. I. R. Baum, E. A. Locke, and S. A. Kirkpatrick, "A Longitudinal Study of the Relation of Vision and Vision Communication to Venture Growth in Entrepreneurial Firms," *Journal of Applied Psychology*, 83 (1998), pp. 43–54; S. A. Kirkpatrick and E. A. Locke, "Direct and Indirect Effects of Three Core Charismatic Leadership Components on Performance and Attitudes," *Journal of Applied Psychology*, 81 (1996), pp. 36–51.

68. "Canadian CEOs Give Themselves Top Marks for Leadership!" *Canada NewsWire*, September 9, 1999.

69. G. T. Fairhurst and R. A. Sarr, *The Art of Framing: Managing the Language of Leadership* (San Francisco, CA: Jossey-Bass, 1996); J. A. Conger, "Inspiring Others: The Language of Leadership," *Academy of Management Executive*, 5 (February 1991), pp. 31–45.

70. R. S. Johnson, "Home Depot Renovates," *Fortune*, November 23, 1998, pp. 200–206.

71. Fairhurst and Sarr, *The Art of Framing*, Chapter 5; J. Pfeffer, "Management as Symbolic Action: The Creation and Maintenance of Organizational Paradigms," *Research in Organizational Behavior*, 3 (1981), pp. 1–52.

72. L. Black, "Hamburger Diplomacy," *Report on Business Magazine*, 5 (August 1988), pp. 30–6; S. Franklin. *The Heroes: A Saga of Canadian Inspiration* (Toronto: McClelland and Stewart, 1967), p. 53.

73. McGill and Slocum, Jr., "A Little Leadership, Please?"; N. H. Snyder and M. Graves, "Leadership and Vision," *Business Horizons*, 37 (January 1994), pp. 1–7; D. E. Berlew, "Leadership and Organizational Excitement," in D. A. Kolb, I. M. Rubin, and J. M. McIntyre (eds.), *Organizational Psychology: A Book of Readings*, (Englewood Cliffs, NJ: Prentice Hall, 1974).

74. M. F. R. Kets de Vries "Charisma in Action: The Transformational Abilities of Virgin's Richard Branson and ABB's Percy Barnevik," *Organizational Dynamics*, 26 (Winter 1998), pp. 6–21; M. F. R. Kets de Vries, "Creative Leadership: Jazzing Up Business," *Chief Executive*, March 1997, pp. 64–66; F. Basile, "Hotshots in Business Impart their Wisdom," *Indianapolis Business Journal*, July 21, 1997, p. A40.

75. M. Proulx, "Suncor Boss One Cool CEO," *Edmonton Sun*, March 13, 2000, p. 42; S. Ewart, "Unique Suncor Boasts Unique CEO," *Calgary Herald*, September 11, 1999, p. 1; C. Cattaneo, "The Man who Saved Suncor," *National Post*, September 11, 1999, p. D1; G. Gordon, "An Interview with this Year's EXCEL Honoree Rick George," *Communication World*, 15 (August 1998), pp. 36–40.

76. E. M. Whitener, S. E. Brodt, M. A. Korsgaard, and J. M. Werner, "Managers As Initiators Of Trust: An Exchange Relationship Framework For Understanding Managerial Trustworthy Behavior," *Academy of Management Review*, 23 (July 1998), pp. 513–30; Bennis and Nanus, *Leaders*, pp. 43–55; Kouzes and Posner, *Credibility: How Leaders Gain and Lose It, Why People Demand It*.

77. J. J. Sosik, S. S. Kahai, and B. J. Avolio, "Transformational Leadership And Dimensions Of Creativity: Motivating Idea Generation In Computer-Mediated Groups," *Creativity Research Journal*, 11 (1998), pp. 111–21; P. Bycio, R. D. Hackett, and J. S. Allen, "Further Assessments of Bass's (1985) Conceptualization of Transactional and Transformational Leadership," *Journal of Applied Psychology*, 80 (1995), pp. 468–78; W. L. Koh, R. M. Steers, and J. R. Terborg, "The Effects of Transformational Leadership on Teacher Attitudes and Student Performance in Singapore," *Journal of Organizational Behavior*, 16 (1995), pp. 319–33; Howell and Avolio, "Transformational Leadership, Transactional

Leadership, Locus of Control, and Support for Innovation."

78. J. Barling, T. Weber, and E. K. Kelloway, "Effects of Transformational Leadership Training on Attitudinal and Financial Outcomes: A Field Experiment," *Journal of Applied Psychology*, 81 (1996), pp. 827–32.

79. A. Bryman, "Leadership in Organizations," in S. R. Clegg, C. Hardy, and W. R. Nord (eds.) *Handbook of Organization Studies*, (Thousand Oaks, CA: Sage, 1996), pp. 276–92.

80. Egri and Herman, "Leadership in the North American Environmental Sector"; B. S. Pawar and K. K. Eastman, "The Nature and Implications of Contextual Influences on Transformational Leadership: A Conceptual Examination," *Academy of Management Review*, 22 (1997), pp. 80–109.

81. K. Boehnke, A. C. DiStefano, J. J. DiStefano, and N. Bontis "Leadership for Extraordinary Performance," *Business Quarterly*, 61 (Summer 1997), pp. 56–63.

82. For a review of this research, see: House and Aditya, "The Social Scientific Study Of Leadership: Quo Vadis?"

83. R. J. Hall and R. G. Lord, "Multilevel Information Processing Explanations of Followers' Leadership Perceptions," *Leadership Quarterly*, 6 (1995), pp. 265–87; R. Ayman, "Leadership Perception: The Role of Gender and Culture," in M. M. Chemers and R. Ayman (eds.) *Leadership Theory and Research: Perspectives and Directions*, (San Diego, CA: Academic Press, 1993), pp. 137–66; J. R. Meindl, "On Leadership: An Alternative to the Conventional Wisdom," *Research in Organizational Behavior*, 12 (1990), pp. 159–203.

84. G. R. Salancik and J. R. Meindl, "Corporate Attributions as Strategic Illusions of Management Control," *Administrative Science Quarterly*, 29 (1984), pp. 238–54; J. M. Tolliver, "Leadership and Attribution of Cause: A Modification and Extension of Current Theory," *Proceedings of the Annual ASAC Conference, Organizational Behavior Division*, 4, pt. 5 (1983), pp. 182–91.

85. L. M. Ah Chong and D. C. Thomas, "Leadership Perceptions in Cross-Cultural Context: Pakeha and Pacific Islanders in New Zealand," *Leadership Quarterly*, 8 (1997), 275–93; J. L. Nye and D. R. Forsyth, " The Effects of Prototype-Based Biases on Leadership Appraisals: A Test of Leadership Categorization Theory," *Small Group Research*, 22 (1991), pp. 360–79; S. F. Cronshaw and R. G. Lord, "Effects of Categorization, Attribution, and Encoding Processes on Leadership Perceptions," *Journal of Applied Psychology*, 72 (1987), pp. 97–106.

86. Meindl, "On Leadership: An Alternative to the Conventional Wisdom," p. 163.

87. J. Pfeffer, "The Ambiguity of Leadership," *Academy of Management Review*, 2 (1977), pp. 102–12; Yukl, *Leadership in Organizations*, pp. 265–67.

88. Cronshaw and Lord, "Effects of Categorization, Attribution, and Encoding Processes on Leadership Perceptions," pp. 104–5.

89. Six of the Project GLOBE clusters are described in a special issue of the *Journal of World Business*, 37 (2000). For an overview of Project GLOBE, see: House, Javidan, Hanges, and Dorfman, "Understanding Cultures and Implicit Leadership Theories Across the Globe: An Introduction to Project GLOBE"; House, Javidan, and Dorfman, "Project GLOBE: An Introduction."

90. J. C. Jesiuno, "Latin Europe Cluster: From South to North," *Journal of World Business*, 37 (2002), p. 88. Another GLOBE study of Iranian managers also reported that charismatic visionary stands out as a primary leadership dimension. See: A. Dastmalchian, M. Javidan, and K. Alam, "Effective Leadership and Culture in Iran: An Empirical Study," *Applied Psychology: An International Review*, 50 (2001), pp. 532–58.

91. E. Szabo et al., "The Europe Cluster: Where Employees Have a Voice," *Journal of World Business*, 37 (2002), pp. 55–68; F. C. Brodbeck et al., "Cultural Variation of Leadership Prototypes Across 22 European Countries," *Journal of Occupational and Organizational Psychology*, 73 (2000), pp. 1–29; D. N. Den Hartog et al., "Culture Specific and Cross-Cultural Generalizable Implicit Leadership Theories: Are Attributes of Charismatic/Transformational Leadership Universally Endorsed?" *Leadership Quarterly*, 10 (1999), pp. 219–56. The Mexican study is reported in: C. E. Nicholls, H. W. Lane, and M. B. Brechu, "Taking Self-Managed Teams to Mexico," *Academy of Management Executive*, 13 (August 1999), pp. 15–25.

92. The study was conducted by the Conference Board of Canada and was reported in L. Elliott, "Women Switch Jobs to Climb the Power Ladder," *Toronto Star*, June 15, 2000, p. NE1.

93. N. Wood, "Venus Rules," *Incentive*, 172 (February 1998), pp. 22–27; S. H. Appelbaum and B. T. Shapiro, "Why Can't Men Lead Like Women?" *Leadership and Organization Development Journal*, 14 (1993), pp. 28–34; J. B. Rosener, "Ways Women Lead," *Harvard Business Review*, 68 (November-December 1990), pp. 119–25.

94. G. N. Powell, "One More Time: Do Female and Male Managers Differ?" *Academy of Management Executive*, 4 (August 1990), pp. 68–75; G. H. Dobbins and S. J. Platts, "Sex Differences in Leadership: How Real Are They?" *Academy of Management Review*, 11 (1986), pp. 118–27. In contrast with these studies, one review cites an unpublished study reporting that women demonstrate more people-oriented leadership and are rated higher than men on their leadership. See M-T. Claes, "Women, Men and Management Styles," *International Labour Review*, 138 (1999), pp. 431–46.

95. A. H. Eagly and B. T. Johnson, "Gender and Leadership Style: A Meta-Analysis," *Psychological Bulletin*, 108 (1990), pp. 233–56.

96. J. Eckberg, "When it's Time to Get Tough—it's Tough," *Cincinnati Enquirer*, August 28, 2000, p. B18; A. H. Eagly, S. J. Karau, and M. G. Makhijani, "Gender and the Effectiveness of Leaders: A Meta-Analysis," *Psychological Bulletin*, 117 (1995), pp. 125–45; M. E. Heilman and C. J. Block, "Sex Stereotypes: Do They Influence Perceptions of Managers?" *Journal of Social Behavior & Personality*, 10 (1995), pp. 237–52; R. L. Kent and S. E. Moss, "Effects of Sex and Gender Role on Leader Emergence," *Academy of Management Journal*, 37 (1994), pp. 1335–46; A. H. Eagly, M. G. Makhijani, and B. G. Klonsky, "Gender and the Evaluation of Leaders: A Meta-Analysis," *Psychological Bulletin*, 111 (1992), pp. 3–22.

97. M. Sappenfield, "Women, it Seems, are Better Bosses," *Christian Science Monitor*, January 16, 2001. R. Sharpe, "As Leaders, Women Rule," *Business Week*, November 20, 2000, C. D'Nan Bass, "Women May Outdo Men As Sales Managers, Study Says," *Chicago Tribune*, January 26, 2000.

CHAPTER FIFTEEN

1. A. Fraser, "Chief of Flying Tribe Clips his Wings," *The Australian*, July 29, 2002, p. 31; E. Johnston, "Elf Boys," *Boss Magazine*, June 8, 2001, p. 26; S.K. Witcher, "Flight Center Founder Prides Company On Being Deliberately Unconventional," *Wall Street Journal*, December 11, 2000, p. C15; J. Palmer, "Flight Center has an Unusual Team Culture," *Business Day* (South Africa), April 20, 2000, p. 28; M. Massey, "Travel Agency Succeeds By Going Tribal," *Business Review Weekly*, March 22, 1999, p. 69.

2. S. Ranson, R. Hinings, and R. Greenwood, "The Structuring of Organizational Structure," *Administrative Science Quarterly*, 25 (1980), pp. 1–14.

3. J-E. Johanson, "Intraorganizational Influence," *Management Communication Quarterly*, 13 (February 2000), pp. 393–435.

4. "Ford Motor Company Announces Consumer-Focused Organization for the 21st Century," *Auto Channel* (online), October 18, 1999.

5. H. Mintzberg, *The Structuring of Organizations* (Englewood Cliffs, NJ: Prentice Hall, 1979), pp. 2–3.

6. H. Fayol, *General and Industrial Management*, trans. C. Storrs (London: Pitman, 1949); E. E. Lawler III, *Motivation in Work Organizations* (Monterey, Calif.: Brooks/Cole, 1973), Chapter 7; and M. A. Campion, "Ability Requirement Implications of Job Design: An Interdisciplinary Perspective," *Personnel Psychology*, 42 (1989), pp. 1–24.

7. A. N. Maira, "Connecting Across Boundaries: The Fluid-Network Organization," *Prism*, First Quarter 1998, pp. 23–26; D. A. Nadler and M. L. Tushman, *Competing by Design: The Power of Organizational Architecture*, (N.Y.: Oxford University Press, 1997), Chapter 6; Mintzberg, *The Structuring of Organizations*, pp. 2–8.

8. C. Downs, P. Clampitt, and A. L. Pfeiffer, "Communication and Organizational Outcomes," In G. Goldhaber & G. Barnett (eds.) *Handbook of Organizational Communication*, (Norwood, N.J.: Ablex, 1988), pp. 171–211; H. C. Jain, "Supervisory Communication and Performance in Urban Hospitals," *Journal of Communication*, 23 (1973), pp. 103–17.

9. V. L. Shalin, and G. V. Prabhu, "A Cognitive Perspective on Manual Assembly." *Ergonomics*, 39 (1996), pp. 108–27; I. Nonaka and H. Takeuchi, *The Knowledge-Creating Company* (New York: Oxford University Press, 1995).

10. A. L. Patti, J. P. Gilbert, and S. Hartman, "Physical Co-location and the Success of New Product Development Projects," *Engineering Management Journal*, 9 (September 1997), pp. 31–37; M. L. Swink, J. C. Sandvig, and V. A. Mabert, "Customizing Concurrent Engineering Processes: Five Case Studies," *Journal of Product Innovation Management*, 13 (1996), pp. 229–44; W. I. Zangwill, *Lightning Strategies for Innovation: How the World's Best Firms Create New Products* (New York: Lexington, 1993).

11. For a recent discussion of the role of brand manager at Procter & Gamble, see C. Peale, "Branded for Success," *Cincinnati Enquirer*, May 20, 2001, p. A1. Details about how to design integrator roles in organizational structures are presented in: J. R. Galbraith, *Designing Organizations* (San Francisco: Jossey-Bass, 2002), pp. 66–72.

12. Fayol's work is summarized in J. B. Miner, *Theories of Organizational Structure and Process* (Chicago: Dryden, 1982), pp. 358–66.

13. J. A. Conger, *Winning 'em Over* (New York: Simon & Shuster, 1998), Appendix A.

14. Y-M Hsieh, A. Tien-Hsieh, "Enhancement of Service Quality with Job Standardisation," *Service Industries Journal*, 21 (July 2001), pp. 147–166.

15. J. H. Sheridan, "Lessons from the Best," *Industry Week*, February 20, 1995, pp. 13–22.

16. J.P. Starr, "Reintroducing Alcoa to Economic Reality," In W. E. Halal (ed.)

The Infinite Resource (San Francisco: Jossey-Bass, 1998), pp. 57–67.

17. C. Sittenfeld, "The Factory Powered by People" *National Post*, July 10, 1999, p. D11. This point is also discussed in: J. Pfeffer, "Seven Practices of Successful Organizations," *California Management Review*, 40 (1998), pp. 96–124.

18. D. D. Van Fleet and A. G. Bedeian, "A History of the Span of Management," *Academy of Management Review*, 2 (1977), pp. 356–72; Mintzberg, *The Structuring of Organizations*, Chapter 8; D. Robey, *Designing Organizations*, 3rd ed. (Homewood, Ill.: Irwin, 1991), pp. 255–59.

19. B. Simon, "Bank Leads By Example In Transformation," *Business Day* (South Africa), July 30, 1998, p. 17.

20. S. Ellis, "A New Role for the Post Office: An Investigation into Issues Behind Strategic Change at Royal Mail," *Total Quality Management*, 9 (May 1998), pp. 223–34; R. H. Kluge, "An Incentive Compensation Plan with an Eye on Quality," *Quality Progress*, 29 (December 1996), pp. 65–68.

21. T. Peters, *Thriving on Chaos* (New York: Knopf, 1987), p. 359.

22. L. A. Bossidy, "Reality-based leadership," *Executive Speeches*, 13 (August–September 1998), pp. 10–15.

23. Q.N. Huy, "In Praise of Middle Managers," *Harvard Business Review*, 79 (September 2001), pp. 72–79; L. Donaldson and F. G. Hilmer, "Management Redeemed: The Case Against Fads that Harm Management," *Organizational Dynamics*, 26 (Spring 1998), pp. 6–20.

24. "Taking Care of the People," *Canadian Healthcare Manager*, 6 (April–May 1999), pp. 5–9.

25. Mintzberg, *The Structuring of Organizations*, p. 136.

26. The number of layers at Microsoft is inferred from an example in Jebb, "Don't Call Me Sir." (F. Jebb, "Don't Call Me Sir," *Management Today*, August 1998, pp. 44–47.)

27. P. Brabeck, "The Business Case Against Revolution: An Interview with Nestle's Peter Brabeck," *Harvard Business Review*, 79 (February 2001), p. 112.

28. Mintzberg, *The Structuring of Organizations*, Chapter 5.

29. B. Victor and A. C. Boynton, *Invented Here* (Boston: Harvard Business School Press, 1998), Chapter 2; M. Hamstra, "McD Speeds Up Drive-Thru With Beefed Up Operations," *Nation's Restaurant News*, April 6, 1998, p. 3; G. Morgan, *Creative Organization Theory: A Resourcebook* (Newburg Park, CA: Sage, 1989), pp. 271–73; K. Deveny, "Bag Those Fries, Squirt that Ketchup, Fry that Fish," *Business Week*, October 13, 1986, p. 86.

30. T. Burns and G. Stalker, *The Management of Innovation* (London: Tavistock, 1961).

31. A. Lam "Tacit Knowledge, Organizational Learning and Societal Institutions: An Integrated Framework," *Organization Studies*, 21 (May 2000), pp. 487–513.

32. Mintzberg, *The Structuring of Organizations*, p. 106.

33. Mintzberg, *The Structuring of Organizations*, Chapter 17.

34. Galbraith, *Designing Organizations*, pp. 23–25; Robey, *Designing Organizations*, pp. 186–89.

35. E. E. Lawler, III, *Rewarding Excellence: Pay Strategies for the New Economy* (San Francisco: Jossey-Bass, 2000), pp. 31–34.

36. M. Hamstra, "McD's To Decentralize US Management Team," *Nation's Restaurant News*, June 2, 1997, p. 1

37. "Microsoft Splits Into Five Groups in Reorganization," *Reuters*, March 29, 1999; "Microsoft Plans Realignment To Focus On Microsoft Plans Realignment To Focus On Customers," *Reuters*, February 8, 1999.

38. M. Goold and A. Campbell, "Do You Have a Well-Designed Organization?" *Harvard Business Review*, 80 (March 2002), pp. 117–24.

39. "Nortel plans 3,500 more Job Cuts," *Canadian Press*, May 29, 2002; "A World of Networks: Building the Foundation for the Future," *Telesis*, October 1995; "Nortel Splits Operating Roles," *Globe and Mail*, December 23, 1993, p. B3; and L. Surtees, "Power Shifts at Northern Telecom," *Globe and Mail*, February 14, 1991, pp. B1, B2.

40. T.H. Davenport, J.G. Harris, and A.K. Kohli, "How Do They Know their Customers So Well?" *Sloan Management Review*, 42 (Winter 2001), pp.

63–73. Also see: J. R. Galbraith, "Organizing to Deliver Solutions," *Organizational Dynamics*, 31 (2002), pp. 194–207; Lawler, *Rewarding Excellence*, Chapter 1.

41. "Axa Executive Says Global Insurers Must Pool Local Expertise," *Best's Insurance News*, May 1, 2001. The evolution of organizational structures in global organizations is further discussed in J. R. Galbraith, "Structuring Global Organizations," In S. A. Mohrman, J. R. Galbraith, E. E. Lawler III, and Associates (Eds.) *Tomorrow's Organization* (San Francisco: Jossey-Bass, 1998), pp. 103–29.

42. Robey, *Designing Organizations*, pp. 191–97; A. G. Bedeian and R. F. Zammuto, *Organizations: Theory and Design* (Hinsdale, Ill.: Dryden, 1991), pp. 162–68.

43. "Tearing Down Silos to Build a Corporate-wide Communication Plan," *PR News*, July 10, 2000.

44. R. Waters, "SAP America Faces Up to Challenge of Change," *Financial Times*, June 13, 2001.

45. J. Belanger, C. Berggren, T. Bjorkman and C. Kohler (eds.): *Being Local Worldwide. ABB and the Challenge of Global Management* (Ithaca, NY: Cornell University Press, 1999); M. F. R. Kets de Vries, "Charisma in Action: The Transformational Abilities of Virgin's Richard Branson and ABB's Percy Barnevik," *Organizational Dynamics*, 26 (Winter 1998), pp. 6–21; D. A. Nadler and M. L. Tushman, *Competing by Design* (New York: Oxford University Press, 1997), Chapter 6.

46. R. C. Ford and W. A. Randolph, "Cross-Functional Structures: A Review and Integration of Matrix Organization and Project Management," *Journal of Management*, 18 (1992), pp. 267–94.

47. H. F. Kolodny, "Managing in a Matrix," *Business Horizons*, March-April 1981, pp. 17–24; S. M. Davis and P. R. Lawrence, *Matrix* (Reading, Mass.: Addison-Wesley, 1977).

48. K. Knight, "Matrix Organization: A Review," *Journal of Management Studies*," May 1976, pp. 111–30.

49. C. Herkströter, "Royal Dutch/Shell: Rewriting the Contracts," In G. W. Dauphinais and C. Price (Eds.) *Straight From the CEO* (New York: Simon &

Schuster, 1998), pp. 86–93; G. Calabrese "Communication and Co-operation in Product Development: A Case Study of a European Car Producer," *R & D Management*, 27 (July 1997), pp. 239–52; J. L. Brown and N. M. Agnew, "The Balance of Power in a Matrix Structure," *Business Horizons*, November-December 1982, pp. 51–54.

50. C. Campbell-Hunt et al, *World Famous in New Zealand* (Auckland: University of Auckland Press, 2001), p. 89.

51. J. R. Galbraith, *Competing with Flexible Lateral Organizations*. (Boston, MA: Addison-Wesley, 1994).

52. K. Dorrell, "The Right Stuff," *Plant*, December 16, 1996, pp. 18–19; D. Jones, "Robo-Shop," *Report on Business Magazine*, March 1994, pp. 54–62; L. Gutri, "Pratt & Whitney Employees Don't Want to Be Managed: Teams Demand Leadership," *Canadian HR Reporter*, May 2, 1988, p. 8; J. Todd, "Firm Fashions Workplace for High-Tech Era," *Montreal Gazette*, December 12, 1987, p. B4.

53. R. Bettis and M. Hitt, "The New Competitive Landscape," *Strategic Management Journal*, 16 (1995), pp. 7–19; J. R. Galbraith, E. E. Lawler III, & Associates, *Organizing for the Future: The New Logic for Managing Complex Organizations* (San Francisco, CA: Jossey-Bass, 1993).

54. P. C. Ensign, "Interdependence, Coordination, and Structure in Complex Organizations: Implications for Organization Design," *Mid-Atlantic Journal of Business*, 34 (March 1998), pp. 5–22.

55. L. Y. Chan and B. E. Lynn, "Operating in Turbulent Times: How Ontario's Hospitals are Meeting the Current Funding Crisis," *Health Care Management Review*, 23 (June 1998), pp. 7–18; M. M. Fanning, "A Circular Organization Chart Promotes A Hospital-Wide Focus On Teams," *Hospital & Health Services Administration*, 42 (June 1997), pp. 243–54.

56. R. Cross, "Looking Before You Leap: Assessing the Jump to Teams in Knowledge-based Work," *Business Horizons*, 43, (September, 2000), pp. 29–36; W. F. Joyce, V. E. McGee, J. W Slocum Jr., "Designing Lateral Organizations: An Analysis Of The Benefits, Costs, And Enablers Of Nonhierarchi-

cal Organizational Forms," *Decision Sciences*, 28 (Winter 1997), pp. 1–25.

57. R. Hacki And J. Lighton, "The Future Of The Networked Company," *Business Review Weekly*, August 30, 2001, p. 58; A. M. Porter, "The Virtual Corporation: Where is It?," *Purchasing*, March 23, 2000, pp. 40–48; J. A. Byrne "The Corporation Of The Future," *Business Week*, August 31, 1998, pp. 102–04.

58. J.R. Galbraith, "Designing the Networked Organization," In *Tomorrow's Organization*, pp. 102; C. Baldwin and K. Clark, "Managing in an Age of Modularity," *Harvard Business Review*, 75 (September–October 1997), pp. 84–93; R. E. Miles and C. C. Snow, "The New Network Firm: A Spherical Structure Built on a Human Investment Philosophy," *Organizational Dynamics*, 23 (4) (1995), pp. 5–18; W. Powell, "Neither Market nor Hierarchy: Network Forms of Organization." *Research in Organizational Behavior*, 12 (1990), pp. 295–336.

59. R. Hacki and J. Lighton, "The Future of the Networked Company," *McKinsey Quarterly*, 2001 (3), pp. 26–39; J. Hagel, III and M. Singer, "Unbundling the Corporation," *McKinsey Quarterly*, 2000 (3), pp. 148–61; T. W. Malone and R. J. Laubacher, "The Dawn of the E-lance Economy," *Harvard Business Review*, 76 (September–October 1998), pp. 144–52.

60. G. Ip, "Outsourcing Becoming a Way of Life for Firms," *Globe and Mail*, October 2, 1996, p. B8.

61. J. Vardy, "Mitel Outsources Manufacturing to New Company," *National Post*, September 6, 2001; J. Hagel, III and M. Singer, "Unbundling the Corporation," *Harvard Business Review*, 77 (March-April 1999), pp. 133–41. For a discussion of core competencies, see G. Hamel and C. K. Prahalad, *Competing For the Future* (Boston: Harvard Business School Press, 1994), Chapter 10.

62. M. A. Schilling and H. K. Steensma, "The Use of Modular Organizational Forms: An Industry-Level Analysis," *Academy of Management Journal*, 44 (December 2001), pp. 1149–68.

63. L. Fried, *Managing Information Technology in Turbulent Times*, (New York: John Wiley and Sons, 1995); W. H. Davidow and M. S. Malone, *The Virtual Corporation* (New York: HarperBusiness, 1992).

64. C. Taylor, "Agency Teams Balancing in an Ever-Changing Media World," *Media Week*, June 1, 2001, p. 20.

65. G. Morgan, *Imagin-I-Zation: New Mindsets for Seeing, Organizing and Managing* (Thousand Oaks, CA: Sage, 1997); G. Morgan, *Images of Organization*, 2nd Ed. (Newbury Park: Sage, 1996).

66. C. Meyer and S. Davis, *Blur: The Speed of Change in the Connected Economy*, (Reading, MA: Addison-Wesley, 1998); P. M. J. Christie and R. Levary, "Virtual Corporations: Recipe for Success," *Industrial Management*, 40 (July 1998), pp. 7–11; H. Chesbrough and D. J. Teece, "When is Virtual Virtuous? Organizing for Innovation," *Harvard Business Review*, January-February 1996, pp. 65–73.

67. Mintzberg, *The Structuring of Organizations*, Chapter 13; and D. S. Pugh and C. R. Hinings (eds.), *Organizational Structure: Extensions and Replications* (Farnborough, England: Lexington Books, 1976).

68. T. A. Stewart, *Intellectual Capital: The New Wealth of Organizations*, (New York: Doubleday/Currency, 1997), Chapter 10.

69. Robey, *Designing Organizations*, p. 102.

70. C. Perrow, "A Framework for the Comparative Analysis of Organizations," *American Sociological Review*, 32 (1967), pp. 194–208.

71. Mintzberg, *The Structuring of Organizations*, Chapter 15.

72. Burns and Stalker, *The Management of Innovation*; P. R. Lawrence and J. W. Lorsch, *Organization and Environment* (Homewood, Ill.: Irwin, 1967); and D. Miller and P. H. Friesen, *Organizations: A Quantum View* (Englewood Cliffs, N.J.: Prentice Hall, 1984), pp. 197–98.

73. Mintzberg, *The Structuring of Organizations*, p. 282.

74. R. H. Kilmann, *Beyond the Quick Fix* (San Francisco: Jossey-Bass, 1984), p. 38.

75. J. Child, "Organizational Structure, Environment, and Performance: The Role of Strategic Choice," *Sociology*, 6 (1972), pp. 2–22.

76. A. D. Chandler, *Strategy and Structure* (Cambridge, Mass.: MIT Press, 1962).

77. M. E. Porter, *Competitive Strategy* (New York: The Free Press, 1980).

78. D. Miller, "Configurations of Strategy and Structure," *Strategic Management Journal*, 7 (1986), pp. 233–50.

CHAPTER SIXTEEN

1. T. Wanless, "Let's Hear it for Workers!" *Vancouver Province*, June 13, 2002; D. Brown, "Good Ideas Going Wrong," *Canadian HR Reporter*, May 6, 2002, p. 2; D. Mowat, "The VanCity Difference—A Case for the Triple Bottom Line Approach to Business," *Corporate Environmental Strategy*, 9 (February 2002) pp. 24–29; D. Grigg and J. Newman, "Corporate Values Can Help Leaders, Workers," *Vancouver Sun*, November 24, 2001, p. E2.

2. T. O. Davenport, "The Integration Challenge; Managing Corporate Mergers," *Management Review*, 87 (January 1998), pp. 25–28; E. H. Schein, "What Is Culture?" in P. J. Frost, L. F. Moore, M. R. Louis, C. C. Lundberg, and J. Martin (eds.) *Reframing Organizational Culture* (Beverly Hills, CA: Sage, 1991), pp. 243–53; A. Williams, P. Dobson, and M. Walters, *Changing Culture: New Organizational Approaches* (London, England: Institute of Personnel Management, 1989).

3. A. Sagie and D. Elizur, "Work Values: A Theoretical Overview and a Model of Their Effects," *Journal of Organizational Behavior*, 17 (1996), pp. 503–14; W. H. Schmidt and B. Z. Posner, *Managerial Values in Perspective* (New York: American Management Association, 1983).

4. M. Brady, "Wellness Program Paying Off in the Poutine Capital," *National Post*, June 12, 2000, p. C19; C. Tremblay, "MDS Nordion 'Happiest, Healthiest Workplace'," *Ottawa Citizen*, November 15, 1999; "Healthy Workplace Award Reflects a 'Win-Win-Win' Culture," *Canadian Newswire*, October 29, 1999; R. Andrew, "Years of Living Dangerously," *CA Magazine*, March 1999, pp. 26–30. The Telus example is described in: "Efficiency Top Priority for Telus, Says CEO," *Victoria Times Colonist*, July 12, 2002.

5. B. M. Meglino and E. C. Ravlin, "Individual Values in Organizations: Concepts, Controversies, and Research," *Journal of Management*, 24 (May 1998), pp. 351–89; C. Argyris and D. A. Schön, *Organizational Learning: A Theory of Action Perspective* (Reading, MA: Addison-Wesley, 1978).

6. Human Resource Development Canada, "Northwood Technologies," Work-Life Balance in Canadian Workplaces. Found in October 2002 at http://labour.hrdc-drhc.gc.ca/work-life/northwood-technologies-en.cfm

7. J. Jamieson, "This Pair Prospers while Others Slump," *Vancouver Province*, March 25, 2001, p. A46; P. Brethour, "Software Grunt Follows Unsexy Growth Path," *Globe and Mail*, April 22, 1998, p. B25.

8. M. Cooke, "Humiliation as Motivator?" *Meetings & Conventions*, 36 (July 2001), p. 26; G. Groeller, "Eat Or Be Eaten Ethic Boosts Bottom Line," *Orlando Sentinel*, April 30, 2001, p. 16.

9. S. Scott; B. Faught and J. Guise, "Shock of the New," *National Post Business Magazine*, August 1, 2002, pp. 44ff; K. Crowley, "RIM Ready to Rev up Production," *Kitchener-Waterloo Record*, August 9, 2000; G. Crone, "You Know a Company is Doing Well when Barenaked Ladies Come to Entertain," *National Post*, January 19, 2000, p. C4; S. Chilton, "High-Flying RIM Reaches for the Stars," *Kitchener-Waterloo Record*, May 22, 1999, p. E1.

10. S. Sackmann, "Culture and Subcultures: An Analysis of Organizational Knowledge," *Administrative Science Quarterly*, 37 (1992), pp. 140–161; J. Martin and C. Siehl, "Organizational Culture and Counterculture: An Uneasy Symbiosis," *Organizational Dynamics*, Autumn 1983, pp. 52–64; J. S. Ott, *The Organizational Culture Perspective* (Pacific Grove, CA: Brooks/Cole, 1989), pp. 45–47; T. E. Deal and A. A. Kennedy, *Corporate Cultures* (Reading, Mass.: Addison-Wesley, 1982), pp. 138–39.

11. A. Boisnier, and J. Chatman, "The Role of Subcultures in Agile Organizations," In R. Petersen & E. Mannix (Eds.), *Leading and Managing People in Dynamic Organizations*. (Mahwah, NJ: Lawrence Erlbaum Associates, in press); A. Sinclair, "Approaches to Or-

ganizational Culture and Ethics," *Journal of Business Ethics*, 12 (1993), pp. 63–73.

12. M. O. Jones, *Studying Organizational Symbolism: What, How, Why?* (Thousand Oaks, CA: Sage, 1996); Ott, *The Organizational Culture Perspective*, Chapter 2; J. S. Pederson and J. S. Sorensen, *Organizational Cultures in Theory and Practice* (Aldershot, England: Gower, 1989), pp. 27–29.

13. E. H. Schein, *The Corporate Culture Survival Guide* (San Francisco: Jossey-Bass, 1999), Chapter 4; A. Furnham and B. Gunter, "Corporate Culture: Definition, Diagnosis, and Change," *International Review of Industrial and Organizational Psychology*, 8 (1993), pp. 233–61; E. H. Schein, "Organizational Culture," *American Psychologist*, February 1990, pp. 109–19; Ott, *The Organizational Culture Perspective*, Chapter 2; W. J. Duncan, "Organizational Culture: 'Getting a Fix' on an Elusive Concept," *Academy of Management Executive*, 3 (1989), pp. 229–36.

14. J. C. Meyer, "Tell Me A Story: Eliciting Organizational Values from Narratives," *Communication Quarterly*, 43 (1995), pp. 210–24.

15. A. Gordon, "Perks and Stock Options are Great, But It's Attitude that Makes the Difference," *Globe and Mail*, January 28, 2000.

16. This story is cited in K. Foss, "Isadore Sharp," *Foodservice and Hospitality*, December 1989, pp. 20–30; J. DeMont, "Sharp's Luxury Empire," *Maclean's*, June 5, 1989, pp. 30–33. Also see: S. Kemp and L. Dwyer, "An Examination of Organizational Culture—The Regent Hotel, Sydney," *International Journal of Hospitality Management*, 20 (March 2001), pp. 77–93.

17. J. Z. DeLorean, *On a Clear Day You Can See General Motors* (Grosse Pointe, MI: Wright Enterprises, 1979).

18. R. Zemke, "Storytelling: Back to a Basic," *Training*, 27 (March 1990), pp. 44–50; A. L. Wilkins, "Organizational Stories as Symbols Which Control the Organization," in L. R. Pondy, P. J. Frost, G. Morgan, and T. C. Dandridge (eds.) *Organizational Symbolism*, (Greenwich, CT: JAI Press, 1984), pp. 81–92; J. Martin and M. E. Powers, "Truth or Corporate Propaganda: The Value of a Good War Story," in Pondy

et al. (eds.) *Organizational Symbolism*, pp. 93–107.

19. J. Martin et. al., "The Uniqueness Paradox in Organizational Stories," *Administrative Science Quarterly* 28 (1983), pp. 438–53.

20. P. S. DeLisi, "A Modern-Day Tragedy: The Digital Equipment Story," *Journal of Management Inquiry*, 7 (June 1998), pp. 118–30. Digital's famous shouting matches are also described in E. Schein, "How to Set the Stage for a Change in Organizational Culture," In P. Senge et al, *The Dance of Change*, (N. Y.: Currency Doubleday, 1999), pp. 334–44.

21. J. M. Beyer and H. M. Trice, "How an Organization's Rites Reveal Its Culture," *Organizational Dynamics*, 15(4) (1987), pp. 5–24; L. Smirchich, "Organizations as Shared Meanings," in Pondy et al (eds.) *Organizational Symbolism*, pp. 55–65.

22. D. Roth, "My Job at the Container Store," *Fortune*, January 10, 2000, pp. 74–78.

23. L. A. Krefting and P. J. Frost, "Untangling Webs, Surfing Waves, and Wildcatting," in P. J. Frost, L. F. Moore, M. R. Louis, C. C. Lundberg, and J. Martin (eds.) *Organizational Culture*, (Beverly Hills, CA: Sage, 1985), pp. 155–68.

24. R. E. Quinn and N. T. Snyder, "Advance Change Theory: Culture Change at Whirlpool Corporation," In J. A. Conger, G. M. Spreitzer, and E. E. Lawler III, *The Leader's Change Handbook* (San Francisco: Jossey-Bass, 1999), pp. 162–93.

25. "Design Scales New Heights on Eco Values," *Toronto Star*, April 8, 2002. Also see: "Co-op's Stores and Products Shaped to Reflect an Alternative Approach to Business," *Canada Newswire*, September 25, 2002; K. MacQueen, "The Anti-Retailer: Vancouver's Mountain Equipment Co-op Succeeds in Spite of Itself," *Maclean's*, April 29, 2002, p. 30; L. Hendry, "Friend of the Earth," *Winnipeg Free Press*, March 16, 2002, p. A16.

26. J. M. Kouzes and B. Z. Posner, *The Leadership Challenge* (San Francisco: Jossey-Bass, 1995), pp. 230–31.

27. B. Bergman, J. DeMont, J. Intini, K. Macklem, and K. MacQueen, "Can-

ada's Top 100 Employers," *Maclean's*, October 28, 2002, pp. 26–34.

28. C. Siehl and J. Martin, "Organizational Culture: A Key to Financial Performance?" in *Organizational Climate and Culture*, ed. B. Schneider (San Francisco, CA: Jossey-Bass, 1990), pp. 241–81; J. B. Barney, "Organizational Culture: Can It Be a Source of Sustained Competitive Advantage?" *Academy of Management Review*, 11 (1986), pp. 656–65; V. Sathe, *Culture and Related Corporate Realities* (Homewood, Ill.: Irwin, 1985), Chapter 2; Deal and Kennedy, *Corporate Cultures*, Chapter 1. Information about Viant, Inc. comes from L. Daniel, "Within the Viant Experiment," *WebTechniques*, April 2000 (www.webtechniques.com).

29. J. A. Chatman and S. E. Cha, "Leading by Leveraging Culture," In Subir Chowdhury (Ed), *Next Generation Business Series: Leadership*, (Financial Times-Prentice Hall Publishers, forthcoming, 2003); J. C. Helms Mills and A. J. Mills, "Rules, Sensemaking, Formative Contexts, and Discourse in the Gendering of Organizational Culture," In N. Ashkanasy, C. Wilderom, & M. Peterson (Eds.), *International Handbook of Organizational Climate and Culture*. (Thousand Oaks, CA.: Sage, 2000), pp. 55–70; C. A. O'Reilly and J. A. Chatman, "Culture as Social Control: Corporations, Cults, and Commitment," *Research in Organizational Behavior*, 18 (1996), pp. 157–200. For a discussion of organizational culture as social control at The Regent Sydney, see: S. Kemp and L. Dwyer, "An Examination of Organizational Culture—The Regent Hotel, Sydney," *International Journal of Hospitality Management*, 20 (March 2001), pp. 77–93.

30. B. Ashforth and F. Mael, "Social Identity Theory and the Organization," *Academy of Management Review*, 14 (1989), pp. 20–39.

31. S. G. Harris, "Organizational Culture and Individual Sensemaking: A Schema-based Perspective," *Organization Science*, 5 (1994), pp. 309–21; M. R. Louis, "Surprise and Sensemaking: What Newcomers Experience in Entering Unfamiliar Organizational Settings," *Administrative Science Quarterly*, 25 (1980), pp. 226–51.

32. G. S. Saffold, III, "Culture Traits, Strength, and Organizational Performance: Moving Beyond 'Strong' Culture," *Academy of Management Review*, 13 (1988), pp. 546–58; Williams et al., *Changing Culture*, pp. 24–27.

33. J. P. Kotter and J. L. Heskett, *Corporate Culture and Performance*, (New York: Free Press, 1992); G. G. Gordon and N. DiTomasco, "Predicting Corporate Performance from Organizational Culture," *Journal of Management Studies*, 29 (1992), pp. 783–98; D. R. Denison, *Corporate Culture and Organizational Effectiveness* (New York: Wiley, 1990).

34. C. Fishman, "Why Can't Lego Click?" *Fast Company*, 50 (September 2001), p. 144.

35. E. H. Schein, "On Dialogue, Culture, and Organizational Learning," *Organization Dynamics*, Autumn 1993, pp. 40–51.

36. J. Kotter, "Cultures and Coalitions," *Executive Excellence*, 15 (March 1998), pp. 14–15; Kotter and Heskett, *Corporate Culture and Performance*.

37. The features of adaptive cultures are described in W. F. Joyce, *MegaChange: How Today's Leading Companies Have Transformed Their Workforces* (N.Y.: Free Press, 1999), pp. 44–47.

38. M. Acharya, "A Matter of Business Ethics," *Kitchener-Waterloo Record*, March 23, 1999, p. C2. For conceptual discussion on organizational culture and ethics, see: S. Peck and J. Larson, "Making Change: Some Major Corporations are Making Sustainability their Business," *Alternatives*, 27 (Spring 2001), pp. 17–20; S. J. Carroll and M. J. Gannon. *Ethical Dimensions of International Management*. (Thousand Oaks, CA: Sage Publications, 1997), Chapter 5; A. Sinclair, "Approaches to Organizational Culture and Ethics," *Journal of Business Ethics*, 12 (1993), pp. 63–73.

39. I. Aaltio-Marjosola and A. J. Mills, [Eds.], *Gender, Identity and the Culture of Organizations*. (London: Routledge, 2002); Helms Mills and Mills, "Rules, Sensemaking, Formative Contexts, and Discourse in the Gendering of Organizational Culture"; Also see: Aaltio-Marjosola, I., Mills, A. J., and Helms Mills, J. [Eds.] Special Issue on "Exploring

Gendered Organizational Cultures" in *Culture and Organization*, 8 (2) (2002).

40. C. Fox, "Mergers and Desires II," *Business Review Weekly*, May 11, 2001.

41. D. B. Marron, "Is This Marriage Made in Heaven?" *Chief Executive*, May 2001, pp. 50–52; P. Troiano "Post-Merger Challenges," *Management Review*, 88 (January 1999), p. 6. For discussion of corporate culture issues in mergers, see: M. L. Marks, "Mixed Signals," *Across the Board*, May 2000, pp. 21–26; M. L. Marks, "Adding Cultural Fit to Your Diligence Checklist," *Mergers & Acquisitions*, December 1999; E. H. Schein, *The Corporate Culture Survival Guide* (San Francisco: Jossey-Bass, 1999), Chapter 8; A. F. Buono and J. L. Bowditch, *The Human Side of Mergers and Acquisitions* (San Francisco, Calif.: Jossey-Bass, 1989), Chapter 6.

42. M. Lamey, "Sun Sets for Godfrey," *Montreal Gazette*, June 15, 2000; "The Newspaper Wars," *Canoe* (Online) March 2, 1999. For a discussion of how mergers suffer from incompatible corporate cultures, see: M. L. Marks, "Adding Cultural Fit to Your Diligence Checklist," *Mergers & Acquisitions*, 34, (December 1999), pp. 14–20.

43. E. Krell, "Merging Corporate Cultures," *Training*, 38 (May 2001), pp. 68–78; J.K. Stewart, "Imperfect Partners," *Chicago Tribune*, March 18, 2001, p. 1.

44. M. L. Marks, "Adding Cultural Fit to Your Diligence Checklist," *Mergers & Acquisitions*, December 1999; S. Greengard, "Due Diligence: The Devil in the Details," *Workforce*, October 1999, p. 68; E. H. Schein, *The Corporate Culture Survival Guide*, (San Francisco: Jossey-Bass, 1999). A corporate culture audit is also recommended for joint ventures. For details, see: K. J. Fedor and W. B. Werther, Jr., "The Fourth Dimension: Creating Culturally Responsive International Alliances," *Organizational Dynamics*, 25 (Autumn 1996), pp. 39–53.

45. D. Kramer-Kawakami, "Merging Cultures: The Challenges of Convergence," *LIMRA's MarketFacts*, 19 (September-October 2000), p. 24.

46. M. L. Marks, "Mixed Signals," *Across the Board*, May 2000, pp. 21–26; M. L. Marks, "Adding Cultural Fit to

Your Diligence Checklist," *Mergers & Acquisitions*, December 1999; S. Greengard, "Due Diligence: The Devil in the Details," *Workforce*, October 1999, p. 68; J. MacFarland, "An Unusual Team, on Paper," *Globe and Mail*, February 19, 1997, pp. B1, B11; G. MacDonald, "What Happens After the Deal is Done," *Globe and Mail*, February 20, 1997, p. B14.

47. D. Buckner, "Nortel versus Cisco," *Venture, CBC TV*, January 4, 2000; R. N. Ashkenas, L. J. DeMonaco, and S. C. Francis "Making The Deal Real: How GE Capital Integrates Acquisitions," *Harvard Business Review*, 76 (January–February 1998), pp. 165–76.

48. K. W. Smith, "A Brand-New Culture for the Merged Firm," *Mergers and Acquisitions*, 35 (June 2000), pp. 45–50; A. R. Malekazedeh and A. Nahavandi, "Making Mergers Work by Managing Cultures," *Journal of Business Strategy*, May/June 1990, pp. 55–57.

49. A. Levy, "Mergers Spread Despite Failures," *Plain Dealer*, August 9, 1998, p. H1.

50. S. Feschuk, "Lean, Mean Anderson Trims Home Oil's Fat," *Globe and Mail*, October 17, 1995, p. B8.

51. J. P. Kotter, "Leading Change: The Eight Steps of Transformation," In J. A. Conger, G. M. Spreitzer, and E. E. Lawler III, *The Leader's Change Handbook* (San Francisco: Jossey-Bass, 1999), pp. 87–99.

52. R. House, M. Javidan, P. Hanges, and P. Dorfman, "Understanding Cultures and Implicit Leadership Theories Across the Globe: An Introduction to Project GLOBE," *Journal of World Business*, 37 (2002), pp. 3–10; R. House, M. Javidan, and P. Dorfman, "Project GLOBE: An Introduction," *Applied Psychology: An International Review*, 50 (2001), pp. 489–505; E. H. Schein, "The Role of the Founder in Creating Organizational Culture," *Organizational Dynamics*, 12(1) (Summer 1983), pp. 13–28.

53. E. H. Schein, *Organizational Culture and Leadership* (San Francisco, Calif.: Jossey-Bass, 1985), Chapter 10; T. J. Peters, "Symbols, Patterns, and Settings: An Optimistic Case for Getting Things Done," *Organizational Dynamics*, 7(2) (Autumn 1978), pp. 2–23.

54. A. Effinger, "With Charm, Poise And Attitude Fiorina Rousting Hewlett-Packard," *Seattle-Post intelligencer*, January 3, 2000, p. E1.

55. J. Kerr and J. W. Slocum, Jr., "Managing Corporate Culture Through Reward Systems," *Academy of Management Executive*, 1 (May 1987), pp. 99–107; Williams et al., *Changing Cultures*, pp. 120–24; K. R. Thompson and F. Luthans, "Organizational Culture: A Behavioral Perspective," in *Organizational Climate and Culture*, ed. Schneider pp. 319–44.

56. B. Broadway, "Good for the Soul—and for the Bottom Line," *Washington Post*, August 19, 2001, p. A1; N. Hoogeveen, "Reinventing industry," *Business Record*, April 10, 2001, p. 22; M. Haskell, "It's Incredibly Important that Businesses Wake Up Now and Get it Straight," *Maine Times*, October 12, 2000, p. 3.

57. W. G. Ouchi and A. M. Jaeger, "Type Z Organization: Stability in the Midst of Mobility," *Academy of Management Review*, 3 (1978), pp. 305–14; K. McNeil and J. D. Thompson, "The Regeneration of Social Organizations," *American Sociological Review*, 36 (1971), pp. 624–37.

58. M. De Pree, *Leadership Is an Art* (East Lansing, Mich.: Michigan State University Press, 1987).

59. C. Daniels, "Does This Man Need a Shrink?" *Fortune*, February 5, 2001, pp. 205–08.

60. Chatman and Cha, "Leading by Leveraging Culture"; A. E. M. Van Vianen, "Person-Organization Fit: The Match Between Newcomers' And Recruiters' Preferences For Organizational Cultures," *Personnel Psychology*, 53 (Spring 2000), pp. 113–49; C. A. O'Reilly III, J. Chatman, and D. F. Caldwell, "People and Organizational Culture: A Profile Comparison Approach to Assessing Person–Organization Fit," *Academy of Management Journal*, 34 (1991), pp. 487–516.

61. "Corporate Culture Rivals Company Benefits in Importance to Job Applicants," News Release, Robert Half International, May 1, 1996.

62. P. Tam, "Frugal Founder Rewards Employees," *Ottawa Citizen*, November 21, 1999.

CHAPTER SEVENTEEN

1. M. Evans, "Telus Chief Juggles Growth Strategy, Fiscal Responsibility," *National Post*, November 14, 2002, p. FP1; M. Evans, "Rapid Revamp Lifts Telus Shares," *National Post*, November 5, 2002, p. FP1; M. Mark, "Strike Looms In West As Telus Staff Votes," *Calgary Sun*, November 3, 2002, p. 4; H. Enchin, "Onerous Provisions in B.C. Contract with Union," *Vancouver Sun*, October 31, 2002, p. C8; M. Anderson, "Case Study: Telus Corp." *National Post Business Magazine*, September 1, 2002, pp. 31ff; H. Enchin, "Corporate Strategy is Sound, Entwistle Says," *Vancouver Sun*, July 22, 2002, p. D1; "Efficiency Top Priority for Telus, says CEO," *Victoria Times Colonist*, July 11, 2002; P. Arab, "Telus Union Criticized," *Hamilton Spectator*, July 6, 2002, p. B3; G. Bellett, "New-Age Telus has a Story to Tell," *Vancouver Sun*, May 2, 2002; "Telus Plans to Tighten Belt," *Victoria Times Colonist*, May 2, 2002, p. C9.

2. K. Lewin, *Field Theory in Social Science* (New York: Harper & Row, 1951).

3. M. Moravec, O. J. Johannessen, and T. A. Hjelmas, "The Well-Managed SMT," *Management Review*, 87 (June 1998), pp. 56–58; M. Moravec, O.J. Johannessen, and T. A. Hjelmas, "Thumbs Up for Self-Managed Teams," *Management Review*, July 17, 1997, p. 42.

4. C. O. Longenecker, D. J. Dwyer, and T. C. Stansfield, "Barriers and Gateways to Workforce Productivity," *Industrial Management*, 40 (March–April 1998), pp. 21–28. Several sources discuss resistance to change, including: D. A. Nadler, *Champions of Change* (San Francisco, CA: Jossey-Bass, 1998), Chapter 5; P. Strebel, "Why Do Employees Resist Change?" *Harvard Business Review*, May–June 1996, pp. 86–92; R. Maurer, *Beyond the Wall of Resistance: Unconventional Strategies to Build Support for Change* (Austin, TX: Bard Books, 1996); C. Hardy, *Strategies for Retrenchment and Turnaround: The Politics of Survival* (Berlin: Walter de Gruyter, 1990), Chapter 13.

5. F. Vogelstein and P. Sloan, "Corporate Dowagers go for a Makeover," *U.S. News & World Report*, November 6, 2000.

6. M. Riley, "High-revving Nasser Undone by a Blind Spot," *Sydney Morning Herald*, November 3, 2001; J. McCracken, "Nasser Out; Ford In," *Detroit Free Press*, October 30, 2001; M. Truby, "Can Ford Chief Ride out Storm?" *Detroit News*, June 24, 2001; M. Truby, "Ford Revolution Spawns Turmoil," *Detroit News*, April 29, 2001.

7. E. B. Dent and S. G. Goldberg, "Challenging 'Resistance to Change'," *Journal of Applied Behavioral Science*, 35 (March 1999), pp. 25–41.

8. D. A. Nadler, "The Effective Management of Organizational Change," in *Handbook of Organizational Behavior*, ed. J. W. Lorsch (Englewood Cliffs, N.J.: Prentice Hall, 1987), pp. 358–69; and D. Katz and R. L. Kahn, *The Social Psychology of Organizations*, 2nd ed. (New York: Wiley, 1978).

9. "Making Change Work for You—Not Against You," *Agency Sales Magazine*, 28 (June 1998), pp. 24–27.

10. M. E. McGill and J. W. Slocum, Jr., "Unlearn the Organization," *Organizational Dynamics*, 22 (2) (1993), pp. 67–79.

11. R. Katz, "Time and Work: Toward an Integrative Perspective," *Research in Organizational Behavior*, 2 (1980), pp. 81–127.

12. D. Nicolini, and M. B. Meznar, "The Social Construction of Organizational Learning: Conceptual and Practical Issues in the Field," *Human Relations*, 48 (1995), pp. 727–46.

13. D. Miller, "What Happens after Success: The Perils of Excellence," *Journal of Management Studies*, 31 (1994), pp. 325–58.

14. H. Trinca, "Her Way," *Boss Magazine*, October 9, 2000.

15. R. Mitchell, "Feeding the Flames," *Business 2.0*, May 1, 2001.

16. J. P. Kotter and D. S. Cohen, *The Heart of Change* (Boston, Harvard Business School Press, 2002), pp. 15–36; T. G. Cummings, "The Role and Limits of Change Leadership," In J. A. Conger, G. M. Spreitzer, and E. E. Lawler III, *The Leader's Change Handbook* (San Francisco: Jossey-Bass, 1999), pp. 301–20.

17. J. P. Donlon, et al., "In Search of the New Change Leader," *Chief Executive* (U.S.), November, 1997, pp. 64–75.

18. W.J. Holstein, "Dump the Cookware," *Business 2.0*, May, 2001; S.N. Mehta, "Can Corning Find Its Optic Nerve?" *Fortune*, March 19, 2001, pp.148–50.

19. L. D. Goodstein and H. R. Butz, "Customer Value: The Linchpin Of Organizational Change," *Organizational Dynamics*, 27 (June 1998), pp. 21–35.

20. A. Gore, "Joel Kocher: Power COO Says It's Time to Evolve," *MacUser*, April 1997.

21. J. P. Kotter and L. A. Schlesinger, "Choosing Strategies for Change," *Harvard Business Review*, March–April 1979, pp. 106–14.

22. Kotter and Cohen, *The Heart of Change*, pp. 83–98.

23. T. White, "Supporting Change: How Communicators at Scotiabank Turned Ideas into Action," *Communication World*, 19 (April 2002), pp. 22–24.

24. K. H. Hammonds, "Grassroots Leadership—Ford Motor Company," *Fast Company*, April 2000, p. 138; S. Wetlaufer, "Driving Change: An Interview with Ford Motor Company's Jacques Nasser," *Harvard Business Review*, 77 (March–April 1999), pp. 76–88.

25. D. Tarrant, "Boss Aha!" *Australian Financial Review*, December 29, 2000, p. 24. For discussion of employee involvement in change management, see: J. P. Walsh and S-F. Tseng, "The Effects Of Job Characteristics On Active Effort At Work," *Work & Occupations*, 25 (February 1998), pp. 74–96; K. T. Dirks, L. L. Cummings, and J. L. Pierce, "Psychological Ownership in Organizations: Conditions Under Which Individuals Promote and Resist Change," *Research in Organizational Change and Development*, 9 (1996), pp. 1–23.

26. M. Evans, T. Hamilton, L. Surtees and S. Tuck, "The Road to a Billion," *Globe and Mail*, January 6, 2000; R. Dyck and N. Halpern, "Team-based Organizations Redesign at Celestica," *Journal for Quality & Participation*, 22 (September–October 1999), pp. 36–40; "Celestica Nurtures Strong Corporate Culture Within," *Northern Colorado Business Report*, July 16, 1999, p. B5; K. Damsell, "Celestica Escapes from its

Cage," *National Post*, September 1, 1998, p. 9.

27. M. Weisbord and S. Janoff, *Future Search: An Action Guide to Finding Common Ground in Organizations And Communities*. (San Francisco: Berrett-Koehler, 2000); B. B. Bunker and B. T. Alban, *Large Group Interventions : Engaging the Whole System for Rapid Change* (San Francisco, CA: Jossey-Bass, 1996); M. Emery and R. E. Purser, *The Search Conference: A Powerful Method for Planning Organizational Change and Community Action* (San Francisco, CA: Jossey-Bass, 1996). For a description of the origins of search conferences, see: M. R. Weisbord, "Inventing the Search Conference: Bristol Siddeley Aircraft Engines, 1960," In M. R. Weisbord (ed.) *Discovering Common Ground* (San Francisco: Berret-Koehler, 1992), pp. 19–33.

28. J. Pratt, "Naturalists Deserve More Credit," *St. John's Telegram*, June 22, 2002, p. B3; R. E. Purser and S. Cabana, *The Self-Managing Organization* (New York: Free Press, 1998), Chapter 7; T. McCallum, "Vision 2001: Staying Ahead of the Competition," *Human Resource Professional*, November 1996, pp. 25–26.

29. For criticism of a recent search conference, for lacking innovative or realistic ideas, see: R. MacFarlane, "Thin Gruel," *Montreal Gazette*, April 1, 2002, p. B3

30. P. H. Mirvis and M. L. Marks, *Managing the Merger* (Englewood Cliffs, NJ: Prentice Hall, 1992).

31. R. Greenwood and C. R. Hinings, "Understanding Radical Organizational Change: Bringing Together the Old and the New Institutionalism," *Academy of Management Review*, 21 (1996), pp. 1022–54.

32. J. Lublin, "Curing Sick Companies Better Done Fast," *Globe and Mail*, July 25, 1995, p. B18.

33. F. Shalom, "Dorel's Profit Soars," *Montreal Gazette*, May 31, 2002.

34. Nicolini and Meznar, "The Social Construction of Organizational Learning."

35. Kotter and Cohen, *The Heart of Change*, pp.161–77.

36. E. E. Lawler, III, "Pay can be a Change Agent," *Compensation & Bene-*

fits Management, 16 (Summer 2000), pp. 23–26; R. H. Miles, "Leading Corporate Transformation: Are You Up to the Task?" In J. A. Conger, G. M. Spreitzer, and E. E. Lawler III, *The Leader's Change Handbook* (San Francisco: Jossey-Bass, 1999), pp. 221–67; L. D. Goodstein and H. R. Butz, "Customer Value: The Linchpin Of Organizational Change," *Organizational Dynamics*, 27 (Summer 1998), pp. 21–34.

37. C.L. Bernick, "When Your Culture Needs a Makeover," *Harvard Business Review*, 79 (June 2001), pp. 53–61.

38. D. A. Nadler, "Implementing Organizational Changes," In D. A. Nadler, M. L. Tushman, and N. G. Hatvany, (Eds.) *Managing Organizations: Readings and Cases* (Boston: Little, Brown, and Company, 1982), pp. 440–59.

39. B. McDermott and G. Sexton, "Sowing the Seeds of Corporate Innovation," *Journal for Quality and Participation*, 21 (November–December 1998), pp. 18–23.

40. "CHC Completes Final Step in Rival's Takeover," *St. John's Telegram*, October 29, 1999; CHC Helicopter Corporation, *Annual Report 1999*; C. Flanagan, "Birdman of Newfoundland," *Canadian Business*, August 27, 1999, p. 55.

41. J. P. Kotter, "Leading Change: The Eight Steps to Transformation," In J. A. Conger, G. M. Spreitzer, and E. E. Lawler III, *The Leader's Change Handbook* (San Francisco: Jossey-Bass, 1999), pp. 221–67; J. P. Kotter, "Leading Change: Why Transformation Efforts Fail," *Harvard Business Review*, March–April 1995, pp. 59–67.

42. M. Beer, R. A. Eisenstat, and B. Spector, *The Critical Path to Corporate Renewal* (Boston, Mass.: Harvard Business School Press, 1990).

43. R. E. Walton, *Innovating to Compete: Lessons for Diffusing and Managing Change in the Workplace* (San Francisco: Jossey-Bass, 1987); Beer et al., *The Critical Path to Corporate Renewal*, Chapter 5; and R. E. Walton, "Successful Strategies for Diffusing Work Innovations," *Journal of Contemporary Business*, Spring 1977, pp. 1–22.

44. D. Coghlan, "Putting 'Research' back into OD and Action Research: A Call to OD Practitioners," *Organization Development Journal*, 20 (Spring 2002),

pp. 62–65; P. Reason and H. Bradbury, *Handbook of Action Research*. (London: Sage, 2001); D. Avison, F. Lau, M. Myers, and P. A. Nielsen, "Action Research," *Communications of the ACM*, 42 (January 1999), pp. 94ff.

45. Action research is closely associated with organization development (OD). However, this chapter does not specifically discuss OD because of doubts about its distinction from change management. For example, see: N. A. M Worren, K. Ruddle, and K. Moore, "From Organizational Development to Change Management: The Emergence of a New Profession," *Journal of Applied Behavioral Science*, 35 (September 1999), pp. 273–286.

46. L. Dickens and K. Watkins, "Action Research: Rethinking Lewin," *Management Learning*, 30 (June 1999), pp. 127–40; J. B. Cunningham, *Action Research and Organization Development* (Westport, Conn.: Praeger, 1993). For a discussion of early applications of action research, see: R. Sommer, "Action Research: From Mental Hospital Reform in Saskatchewan to Community Building in California," *Canadian Psychology*, 40 (February 1999), pp. 47–55.

47. M. Beer and E. Walton, "Developing the Competitive Organization: Interventions and Strategies," *American Psychologist*, 45 (February 1990), pp. 154–61.

48. For a case study of poor diagnosis, see M. Popper, "The Glorious Failure," *Journal of Applied Behavioral Science*, 33 (March 1997), pp. 27–45.

49. K. E. Weick and R. E. Quinn, "Organizational Change and Development," *Annual Review of Psychology*, 1999, pp. 361–86; D. A. Nadler, "Organizational Frame Bending: Types of Change in the Complex Organization," in R. H. Kilmann, T. J. Covin, and Associates (eds.) *Corporate Transformation: Revitalizing Organizations* for a *Competitive World*, (San Francisco: Jossey-Bass, 1988), pp. 66–83.

50. J. M. Watkins and B. J. Mohr, *Appreciative Inquiry: Change at the Speed of Imagination* (San Francisco: Jossey-Bass, 2001); G. Johnson and W. Leavitt, "Building on Success: Transforming Organizations Through an Appreciative Inquiry," *Public Personnel Management*, 30 (March 2001), pp. 129–36;

D. Whitney and D. L. Cooperrider, "The Appreciative Inquiry Summit: Overview and Applications," *Employment Relations Today*, 25 (Summer 1998), pp. 17–28.

51. A. Trosten-Bloom, "Case Study: Hunter Douglas Window Fashions Division," In J. M. Watkins and B. J. Mohr, *Appreciative Inquiry: Change at the Speed of Imagination* (San Francisco: Jossey-Bass, 2001), pp. 176–80. For more details about the Hunter Douglas appreciative inquiry intervention, see: D. Whitely and A. Trosten-Bloom, *Positive Change @ Work: the Appreciative Inquiry Approach to Whole System Change* (Euclid, OH: Lakeshore Communications, 2002).

52. The history of this and other aspects of appreciative inquiry are outlined in J. M. Watkins and B. J. Mohr, *Appreciative Inquiry*, pp. 15–21. For other descriptions of the appreciative inquiry model, see: D. Whitney and C. Schau, "Appreciative Inquiry: An Innovative Process For Organization Change," *Employment Relations Today*, 25 (Spring 1998), pp. 11–21; F. J. Barrett and D. L. Cooperrider, "Generative Metaphor Intervention: A New Approach for Working with Systems Divided by Conflict and Caught in Defensive Perception," *Journal of Applied Behavioral Science*, 26 (1990), pp. 219–39.

53. G. R. Bushe and G. Coetzer, "Appreciative Inquiry as a Team-Development Intervention: A Controlled Experiment," *Journal of Applied Behavioral Science*, 31 (1995), pp. 13–30; L. Levine, "Listening with Spirit and the Art of Team Dialogue," *Journal of Organizational Change Management*, 7 (1994), pp. 61–73.

54. A. Vido, "Chrysler and Minivans: Are we There Yet?" *CMA Magazine*, November 1993, pp. 11–16.

55. M. Schiller, "Case Study: AVON Mexico," In J.M. Watkins and B.J. Mohr, *Appreciative Inquiry: Change at the Speed of Imagination* (San Francisco: Jossey-Bass, 2001), pp. 123–26.

56. G. R. Bushe, "Five Theories of Change Embedded in Appreciative Inquiry," Paper presented at the 18th Annual World Congress of Organization Development, Dublin, Ireland, July 14–18, 1998.

57. E. M. Van Aken, D. J. Monetta, and D. S. Sink, "Affinity Groups: The Missing Link in Employee Involvement," *Organization Dynamics*, 22 (Spring 1994), pp. 38–54; and G. R. Bushe and A. B. Shani, *Parallel Learning Structures* (Reading, Mass.: Addison-Wesley, 1991).

58. M. Evans, T. Hamilton, L. Surtees and S. Tuck, "The Road to a Billion," *Globe and Mail*, January 6, 2000; R. Dyck and N. Halpern, "Team-based Organizations Redesign at Celestica," *Journal for Quality & Participation*, 22 (September–October 1999), pp. 36–40; "Celestica Nurtures Strong Corporate Culture Within," *Northern Colorado Business Report*, July 16, 1999, p. B5; K. Damsell, "Celestica Escapes from its Cage," *National Post*, September 1, 1998, p. 9.

59. C-M. Lau, "A Culture-Based Perspective of Organization Development Implementation," *Research in Organizational Change and Development*, 9 (1996), pp. 49–79.

60. R. J. Marshak, "Lewin Meets Confucius: A Review of the OD Model of Change," *Journal of Applied Behavioral Science*, 29 (1993), pp. 395–415; T. C. Head and P. F. Sorenson, "Cultural Values and Organizational Development: A Seven-Country Study," *Leadership and Organization Development Journal*, 14 (1993), pp. 3–7; J. M. Putti, "Organization Development Scene in Asia: The Case of Singapore," *Group and Organization Studies*, 14 (1989), pp. 262–70; A. M. Jaeger, "Organization Development and National Culture: Where's the Fit?" *Academy of Management Review*, 11 (1986), pp. 178–90.

61. For an excellent discussion of conflict management and Asian values, see several articles in K. Leung and D. Tjosvold (Eds.) *Conflict Management in the Asia Pacific: Assumptions and Approaches in Diverse Cultures* (Singapore: John Wiley & Sons (Asia), 1998).

62. C. M. D. Deaner, "A Model of Organization Development Ethics," *Public Administration Quarterly*, 17 (1994), pp. 435–46; and M. McKendall, "The Tyranny of Change: Organizational Development Revisited," *Journal of Business Ethics*, 12 (February 1993), pp. 93–104.

63. G. A. Walter, "Organization Development and Individual Rights," *Journal of Applied Behavioral Science*, 20 (1984), pp. 423–39.

64. "Perils of Public Sector Work: A Case Study," *Consultants News*, April 1996, p. 5; S. Parker, Jr. "SaskTel Dials the Wrong Number," *Western Report*, February 26, 1996, pp. 14–17.

65. Burke, *Organization Development*, pp. 149–51; Beer, *Organization Change and Development*, pp. 223–24.

APPENDIX A

1. Kerlinger, *Foundations of Behavioral Research* (New York: Holt, Rinehart, & Winston, 1964), p. 11.

2. J. B. Miner, *Theories of Organizational Behaviour* (Hinsdale, Ill.: Dryden, 1980), pp. 7–9.

3. Ibid. pp. 6–7.

4. J. Mason, *Qualitative Researching* (London: Sage, 1996).

5. A. Strauss and J. Corbin (Eds.). *Grounded Theory in Practice*. (London: Sage Publications, 1997); B. G. Glaser and A. Strauss. *The Discovery of Grounded Theory: Strategies for Qualitative Research*. (Chicago, IL: Aldine Publishing Co, 1967).

6. Kerlinger, *Foundations of Behavioral Research*, p. 13.

7. A. Strauss and J. Corbin (Eds.). *Grounded Theory in Practice*. (London: Sage Publications, 1997); B. G. Glaser and A. Strauss. *The Discovery of Grounded Theory: Strategies for Qualitative Research*. (Chicago, IL: Aldine Publishing Co, 1967).

8. W. A. Hall and P. Callery, "Enhancing the Rigor of Grounded Theory: Incorporating Reflexivity and Relationality," *Qualitative Health Research*, 11 (March 2001), pp. 257–72.

9. P. Lazarsfeld, *Survey Design and Analysis* (New York: The Free Press, 1955).

10. This example is cited in D. W. Organ and T. S. Bateman, *Organizational Behaviour*, 4th ed. (Homewood, Ill.: Irwin, 1991), p. 42.

11. Ibid. p. 45

12. R. I. Sutton and A. Hargadon, "Brainstorming Groups in Context: Effectiveness in a Product Design Firm," *Administrative Science Quarterly*, 41 (1996), pp. 685–718.

URL INDEX

"What do zebras have to do with organizational behaviour?"

Zebras and organizational behaviour?

Doesn't organizational behaviour apply only to people and their interactions within companies?

Well, yes. And no.

Organizational behaviour is a natural sociological and biological rhythm to which most living creatures adhere: fish, birds, zebras — not just people sitting behind desks.

Like human beings, no two zebras are exactly alike. Each one is unique, both in appearance and behaviour. In order to thrive, each must be able to work as a part of the group, striving toward common goals of survival and success. How well the group functions depends entirely on how well the individuals within it are able to do this.

For many of us, working in the world of business will likely involve being a part of a group or large company. Understanding how the organization functions, and what our role is within it, will be key to our success.

Zebras? They figured that one out a long time ago.